THE ROUGH GUIDE TO

Tuscany & Umbria

written and researched by

Tim Jepson, Jonathan Buckley & Mark Ellingham

with additional contributions by

Jeffrey Kennedy

ROUGH
GUIDES

roughguides.com

Contents

Introduction to
Tuscany & Umbria

Tuscany and Umbria harbour the classic landscapes of Italy, familiar from a thousand Renaissance paintings, with their backdrop of medieval hill-towns, rows of cypresses, vineyards and olive groves, and artfully sited villas and farmhouses. It's a stereotype that has long held an irresistible attraction for northern Europeans. Shelley referred to Tuscany as a "paradise of exiles", and ever since his time the English, in particular, have seen the region as an ideal refuge from a sun-starved and overcrowded homeland.

The expatriate's perspective may be distorted, but the central provinces – especially in Tuscany – are indeed the essence of Italy in many ways. The national language evolved from Tuscan dialect, a supremacy ensured by Dante, who wrote the *Divine Comedy* in the vernacular of his birthplace, Florence. Other great Tuscan writers of the period – Petrarch and Boccaccio – reinforced its status, and in the nineteenth century Manzoni came here to purge his vocabulary of any impurities while working on *The Betrothed*, the most famous of all Italian novels. But what makes this area pivotal to the culture not just of Italy but of all Europe is, of course, the **Renaissance**, that extraordinarily creative era that takes its name from another Tuscan, Giorgio Vasari, who wrote in the sixteenth century of the "rebirth" of the arts with the humanism of Giotto and his successors.

Nowadays Tuscany and Umbria are among the wealthiest regions of the modern Italian state, a prosperity founded partly on agriculture and tourism, but largely on their industrial centres, which are especially conspicuous in the Arno valley. Nonetheless, both Tuscany and Umbria are predominantly **rural**, with great tracts of land still looking much as they did half a millennium ago. Just as the hill-towns mould themselves to the summits, the terraces of vines follow the lower contours of the hills and open fields spread across the broader valleys, forming a distinctive balance between the natural and human world.

ABOVE MONTERIGGIONI **RIGHT** CYPRESSES

Where to go

Florence was the most active centre of the Renaissance: every eminent artistic figure from Giotto onwards is represented here in an unrivalled gathering of churches, galleries and museums. But although Florence tends to take the limelight today, the longstanding rivalries between the towns of Tuscany and Umbria ensured that pictures and palaces were sponsored by everyone who could afford them. Exquisite Renaissance works adorn almost every place of any size, from the coast to the Apennine slopes of eastern Umbria, while the largest towns can boast artistic projects every bit as ambitious as those to be seen in Florence – the stunning fresco cycles in Arezzo (Piero della Francesca), Orvieto (Luca Signorelli), Siena (Pinturicchio), San Gimignano (Benozzo Gozzoli), Montefalco (Gozzoli again), Perugia (Perugino) and Prato (Fra' Filippo Lippi) are just a selection of the region's riches.

And of course the art of the Renaissance did not spring out of thin air: both Tuscany and Umbria can boast a cultural lineage that stretches back unbroken to the time of Charlemagne and beyond. **Lucca** has some of the most handsome Romanesque buildings in Europe, and **Pisa** – whose Campo dei Miracoli, with its Leaning Tower, is one of Europe's most brilliant monumental ensembles – is another city whose heyday came in the Middle Ages. **Siena**'s red-brick medieval cityscape makes a refreshing contrast with the darker tones of Florence, while a tour through Umbria can seem like a procession of

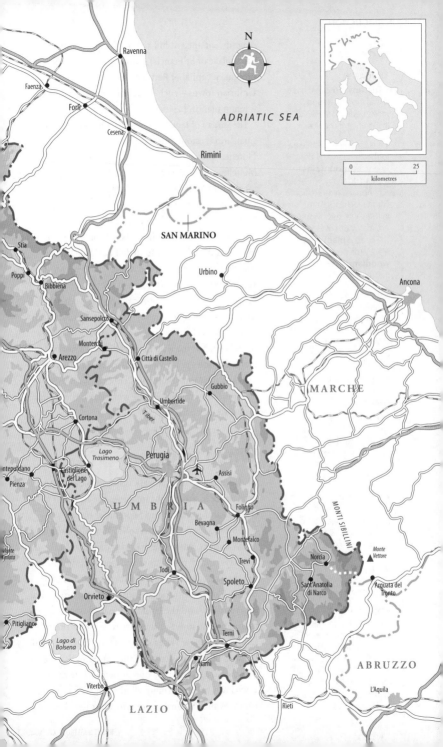

N

ADRIATIC SEA

Ravenna

Faenza

Forlì

Cesena

Rimini

0   25
kilometres

SAN MARINO

Urbino

Ancona

Stia

Poppi

Bibbiena

Sansepolcro

Monterchi

Città di Castello

Arezzo

Gubbio

MARCHE

Cortona

Umbertide

T. Iber

Lago
Trasimeno

Perugia

Assisi

Intepulciano

Castiglione
del Lago

Pienza

U   M   B   R   I   A

Folingo

Bevagna

MONTI SIBILLINI

Montefalco

Monte
Vettore

Monte
Amiata

Todi

Trevi

Spoleto

Norcia

Sant'Anatolia
di Narco

Arquata del
Tronto

Orvieto

Pitigliano

Lago di
Bolsena

Terni

ABRUZZO

Narni

L'Aquila

Viterbo

LAZIO

Rieti

FACT FILE

TUSCANY

• **Tuscany** (Toscana) has a population of around 3.5 million, with some 400,000 in Florence, its capital.

• It is bordered by the **sea** to the west, and by the Apennine **mountains** to the east; in the north lie the Alpi Apuane (where Monte Prado reaches 2054m), while in the south rises Monte Amiata. South of Livorno lies the coastal **plain** of the Maremma. Tuscany has more **woodland** than any other Italian region.

• Tourism is a major contributor to the region's **economy**, as are agriculture (especially beef, wine and olive oil) and textile production, which is concentrated in the Arno valley and Prato.

UMBRIA

• **Umbria** is the only landlocked region of the Italian peninsula. Of its 900,000 **population**, 150,000 live in Perugia, the capital.

• The **terrain** is gentler than Tuscany, but the Apennines run along the eastern border where, in the Sibillini mountains, Monte Vettore reaches 2476m just over the border in Marche. Some thirty percent of Umbria is woodland.

• Perugia manufactures food and clothing, and factories dot the Vale of Spoleto, but the major **industries** (steel, chemicals, textiles, paper and food) are in the south, around Terni. Traditional **crafts** are also significant, especially pottery.

magnificent ancient hill-towns. The attractions of **Assisi** (birthplace of St Francis), **Spoleto** and the busy provincial capital of **Perugia** are well known, but other Umbrian towns – such as **Gubbio**, **Bevagna** and **Todi** – retain plentiful evidence of their ancient past, too.

The variety of **landscape** within this comparatively small area is astounding. A short distance from central Florence spread the thickly wooded uplands of the **Mugello** and the **Casentino**, while Lucca is a springboard for the **Alpi Apuane**, whose mountain quarries have supplied Europe's masons with white marble for centuries. Along the Tuscan shoreline, the resorts are interspersed by some of Italy's best-kept wildlife reserves, including the fabulous **Monti dell'Uccellina**, the last stretch of virgin coast in the whole country. Out in the **Tuscan archipelago**, the island of **Giglio** is relatively unspoilt by the sort of tourist development that has infiltrated – though certainly not ruined – nearby **Elba**.

Landlocked Umbria may not be as varied as its neighbour, but the wild heights of the **Valnerina**, the **Piano Grande**'s prairie-like expanse and the savage peaks of the **Monti Sibillini** all contrast with the tranquil, soft-contoured hills with which the region is most often associated.

When to go

Midsummer in central Italy is not as pleasant an experience as you might imagine: the heat can be stifling, and from May to September most accommodation is booked solid. If at all possible, avoid **August**, when the majority of Italians take their holidays: many restaurants and hotels close, and the beaches are jammed solid. It's best to visit shortly **before Easter** or in the **late autumn** – the towns are quieter then, and the countryside is blossoming or taking on the tones of the harvest season. The Umbrian climate varies slightly from Tuscany's, chiefly because of its distance from the sea; temperatures in summer are fractionally higher here, while the hill-top towns can be surprisingly windy and cool at other times. **Winter** is often quite rainy, but the absence of

SAINTS

Florence has St Peter Martyr and the more obscure St Giovanni Gualberto; Siena has St Catherine, joint patron of Italy, and St Bernardino, patron saint of advertising…but Tuscany's roll-call of the holy is meagre compared to that of its neighbour, the so-called *terra dei santi* ("land of the saints"). Umbria's towns and villages are littered with shrines to holy men and women, the greatest of them being the church dedicated to St Francis in Assisi, which stands a short distance from the resting-place of his devout companion, St Clare. The founder of western monasticism, St Benedict, hailed from Norcia, not far from the hometown of St Rita, patron saint of the impossible. And just outside Terni, there's a pilgrimage site dedicated to St Valentine, thought to have been born there. The one Umbrian saint who could be said to rival the fame of Francis, Valentine differs from him in one crucial respect: in all likelihood, he didn't exist.

crowds makes this a good option for the cities on the major art trails. Bear in mind, however, that high-altitude roads are impassable in midwinter, and in places such as the Sibillini the snow might not melt until March or even April.

It's always worth checking when each town has its **festivals** or pilgrimages (see p.32). Accommodation is tricky during these mini-peak seasons, but some of the festivities – such as Siena's famous **Palio** and Gubbio's semi-pagan **Corsa dei Ceri** – are enjoyable enough to merit planning a trip around. Costumed **jousts** and other martial displays are a feature of several town calendars, notable examples being the jousts in Pistoia and Arezzo and the twice-yearly **crossbow competitions** between Gubbio and Sansepolcro. **Holy days** and **saints' days** bring in the crowds in equal numbers, with Assisi leading the way as the most venerated site.

Among the innumerable **arts festivals**, the highest profiles are achieved by the contemporary arts extravaganza in Spoleto, the Umbria Jazz festival in Perugia and the

REGIONAL WINES

Wine in Tuscany and Umbria was made more or less the same way for centuries – in small quantities, by small producers, and using old-fashioned techniques and two robust and workaday grape varieties (Sangiovese and Trebbiano). Much – apart from the ubiquitous Chianti – was made for local consumption, and quality was variable, to put it mildly.

Then came **Denominazione d'Origine Controllata** (**DOC**), a state-inspired, countrywide system aimed at bringing order to Italy's many thousands of wines. For a while it worked, and quality improved. Then, like most Italian bureaucratic initiatives, it ran into trouble: virtually every wine of note had a DOC listing, and the label ceased to mean very much at all. Enter (in 1980) **DOCG**, where the quality of far fewer wines (Brunello di Montalcino, Vino Nobile di Montepulciano and Chianti in Tuscany, and Sagrantino in Umbria) was *garantita* – guaranteed.

Both systems, however, impose strict production controls, and in the last twenty years or so, many younger, more experimental producers have disdained both classifications. Instead, they have introduced modern, New World production methods and "foreign" grape varieties, especially the Cabernets and Pinot Noirs of France. The result has been the so-called "**Super Tuscans**", often sublime (and hugely expensive) wines, many from the Bolgheri region in the Maremma, and usually marketed under the most humble classification of all, Vino da Tavola – table wine.

Maggio Musicale in more conservative Florence – but as with the more folkloric events, even the smallest towns have their cultural season. Finally, there's scarcely a hamlet in Tuscany or Umbria that doesn't have a **food** or **wine** festival, the region seeming to find an excuse to celebrate almost everything that breathes or grows. Often lasting for just a day, these events place less stress on the hotels, though it might be a good idea to book a room if you're dropping by.

PIENZA

Author picks

Over the last two decades, our authors have explored every cranny of Tuscany and Umbria while researching this book. Here's their selection of unforgettable places that don't feature on every tourist itinerary.

Walking country The unexpectedly wild mountain landscapes of the Alpi Apuane (p.198), Monti Sibillini (p.498) and Monte Cucco (p.431) offer great hiking along marked trails.

Undiscovered hill-towns You're spoilt for choice, but after the obvious lure of Siena, Assisi and San Gimignano, don't miss Barga (p.203), Monteriggioni (p.296), Pienza (p.341), Montepulciano (p.346), Cortona (p.386) and Trevi (p.467).

Scenic drives Take the Chiantigiana (p.151) from Florence to Siena to admire Chianti; the road from Lucca to Aulla to see the Garfagnana (p.202); and a loop from Montalcino (p.331) to Montepulciano (p.346) via Sant'Antimo, Bagno Vignoni and Pienza for the best of southern

Tuscany. In Umbria, head east from Spoleto to Norcia (p.491) via Scheggino and Gavelli (p.486), and then drive across the Piano Grande to Castelluccio (p.496).

Open-air art In addition to its museums, galleries and art-filled churches, Tuscany has some fascinating collections of site-specific sculpture: make time for the Fattoria Le Celle (see p.168), the Chianti Sculpture Park (see p.155) and the wacky Giardino dei Tarrocchi (see p.253).

No-cost pampering Tuscany has some of the swankiest spa towns in all of Italy, but at Bagno Vignoni (p.339) and Saturnia (p.360) you can soak in an outdoor sulphur pool without paying a cent.

It's not all about the artists Tuscany has produced many great scientists, but they tend to fall off the tourist radar – redress the balance in Florence at the Museo Galileo (p.76) and the eye-popping waxworks of La Specola (p.114).

Our author recommendations don't end here. We've flagged up our favourite places – a perfectly sited hotel, an atmospheric café, a special restaurant – throughout the guide, highlighted with the ★ symbol.

18

things not to miss

It's not possible to see everything that Tuscany and Umbria have to offer in one trip – what follows is just a selection of the regions' highlights: great places to visit, outstanding buildings, spectacular scenery and unforgettable events. All entries have a page reference to take you straight into the guide, where you can find out more. Coloured numbers refer to chapters in the Guide section.

1

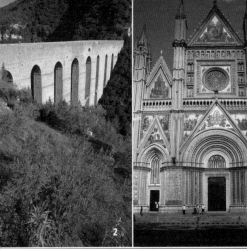

1 PIANO GRANDE
Page 496

The Piano Grande, an extraordinary upland plain above Norcia, is the most striking feature of the Sibillini mountains.

2 SPOLETO
Page 472

The astounding Ponte delle Torri spans the gorge on the edge of Spoleto's medieval centre.

3 ORVIETO
Page 522

Umbria's most striking hill-town crowns a dramatic volcanic outcrop, and is dominated by one of Italy's great cathedrals.

4 SAN GIMIGNANO
Page 302

San Gimignano's amazing skyline is dominated by its fifteen medieval towers.

5 CAMPO DEI MIRACOLI, PISA
Page 213

The Campo is a breathtaking array of buildings: the Leaning Tower, the cathedral, the magnificent baptistery and the beautiful cemetery known as the Camposanto.

15

16

17

18

Itineraries

You could spend a fortnight in Florence and still not see everything – but if time is tight, make a priority of the places listed below. For a sample of the varied Tuscan terrain, follow our suggested loop – it's a long drive, but endlessly rewarding. In Umbria, the central coronet of hill-towns is easily visited in a day's drive, though almost any of the places en route make good places to stop, too. Siena, too, could be seen in a day, but it's a town that rewards more relaxed sightseeing.

A WEEKEND IN FLORENCE

DAY ONE

The Uffizi Start the day with one of the world's greatest art collections. See p.64

Duomo and Baptistery Round off the morning at the cathedral, clambering to the top of the dome if there's time. See p.46

Museo dell'Opera del Duomo The so-called Doors of Paradise are a highpoint of this superb museum. See p.57

Santa Croce After an hour or two in the mighty Santa Croce, go for drinks and dinner in the Sant'Ambrogio district. See p.102

DAY TWO

Bargello The city's major sculpture museum, featuring Donatello, Michelangelo and lots more. See p.74

San Lorenzo The Medici bankrolled this church, and hired Michelangelo to design a couple of wonderful additions. See p.87

Santa Maria Novella The interior here is replete with magnificent frescoes. See p.82

Palazzo Pitti Palazzo Pitti houses yet another extraordinary array of art, and has the city's biggest garden. See p.110

San Miniato. Walk up the hill to this beautiful Romanesque building, then wander down into Oltrarno for the evening. See p.119

A WEEKEND IN SIENA

DAY ONE

The Campo Siena's great main square is where you'll find the Museo Civico and the vertiginous Torre del Mangia. See p.263

The Duomo Sumptuous on the outside and overflowing with colour and artworks within, including sculpture by Michelangelo and paintings by Pintoricchio. See p.272

Santa Maria della Scala Siena's vast former hospital contains an extraordinary wealth of art. See p.275

Sant'Agostino Explore the quieter streets south of the Duomo, or browse the shops on Via di Città. See p.286

DAY TWO

Pinacoteca Nazionale Siena's principal art gallery gives a thorough account of the city's art over several centuries. See p.284

Museo dell'Opera del Duomo Duccio's majestic Maestà is the main draw, but don't overlook the many other works, nor the superb views from the upper terrace. See p.280.

San Francesco Devote the rest of the day to exploring the quiet streets around the church of San Francesco to the north (**see p.289**) and Santa Maria dei Servi to the east (**see p.283**).

A GREAT TUSCAN DRIVE

❶ **Chianti** You could start in Siena or anywhere else on the southern edge of Chianti, an area whose vineyards, hills and winding roads comprise a classic Italian landscape. See p.148

❷ **Vallombrosa** Cross the Arno River and drive up through the thickly wooded slopes around Vallombrosa. See p.371

❸ **Poppi** In the heart of the lush Casentino, Poppi is the obvious place to stop for lunch. See p.383.

❹ **The Valdichiana** Head south, via Arezzo and Cortona, to traverse the agricultural plain of the Valdichiana. See p.386

❺ **Pienza** This small hilltop-town commands wonderful views over the Val d'Orcia and Monte Amiata. West of here, the road to San Quirico d'Orcia is an unforgettable experience. See p.341

❻ **Bagno Vignoni** Siena is a short drive north of San Quirico, but if time allows, take a short detour to see the sulphurous pools of Bagno Vignoni. See p.339.

A DRIVE THROUGH THE HEART OF UMBRIA

❶ **Assisi** Start in the town of St Francis and head over Monte Subasio to Spello, via the Eremo delle Carceri and Collepino, for superb views and the chance to jump out for a stroll on the high, open slopes. See p.434

❷ **Spello** Stop in Spello for an hour or so, and be sure to see Pinturicchio's frescoes in the church of Santa Maria Maggiore. See p.453

❸ **Montefalco** Take back roads from Spello stopping in Bevagna to admire its sleepy main square. In Montefalco leave an hour for the art in San Francesco and the town's other churches. See p.462

❹ **Trevi** Drop down to the Valle di Spoleto and drive south before climbing to lofty Trevi, the least-visited of Umbria's small central hill-towns. Finish the day in Spoleto. See p.467

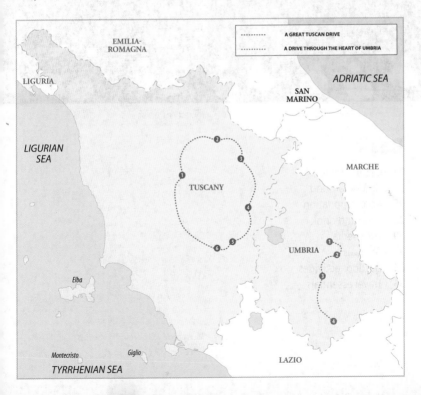

BRUNELLO WINES

Basics

Getting there

The main airports serving Tuscany and Umbria are at Pisa, Rome and Bologna, though the smaller ones at Florence and Perugia can also be useful. From the UK and Ireland, competitive prices for charter, no-frills or scheduled flights with major carriers outweigh the inconvenience of the long rail journey. Flights from Canada, North America and Australasia mostly come into Rome (or, less conveniently, Milan), with one airline flying to Pisa from the US. From down under, you may find it cheaper to fly to London and get a budget onward flight from there.

You'll get the best prices during the November-to-March low season (excluding Christmas and New Year). It's generally more expensive to fly at weekends; prices quoted below assume midweek travel.

Flights from the UK and Ireland

The biggest **budget airlines** serving Pisa from the UK are Ryanair, flying from London Stansted, Bournemouth, East Midlands, Liverpool, Edinburgh and Glasgow, and easyJet, flying from Gatwick, Luton and Bristol. In the summer, Jet2 flies from Manchester, Leeds, Newcastle and Bradford, and Thomson fly from Gatwick, Coventry, Leeds and Manchester. If you book well in advance you can sometimes find **fares** for as little as £25 return for off-peak flights, though these rock-bottom prices tend to apply only to early-morning or late-evening services. For more reasonable flight times, prices are £100–150 return in summer, as long as you make your reservation well in advance: book less than two weeks before departure, and you'll pay as much as for a seat on a full-service airline.

Of the **full-service airlines** in the UK, British Airways serves **Pisa** several times daily out of London Gatwick and Manchester, and Alitalia flies via Milan or Rome. A return flight with Alitalia or BA from London to Pisa in low season can cost around £100, with prices from £150 to £300 in high season. Keep your eyes open for special offers, which have become more numerous in the wake of competition from the no-frills outfits. Meridiana is currently the only airline with non-stop flights from Gatwick to **Florence Perétola**; their tickets tend to be considerably more expensive than flights to Pisa, as do Air France and CityJet flights to Perétola from London City airport.

BA also operates regular flights to **Bologna** Marconi from London Gatwick. This is generally a cheaper option than flying to Pisa, and you can often find seats when the Pisa flights are sold out. Bologna airport is a shuttle-bus ride from Bologna train station, from where Florence is an hour's train ride away. (Forlì airport, the point of arrival for Ryanair flights to Bologna, is a good deal more distant.)

For Umbria, flying into **Rome** is simplest, with an onward journey by road or rail of around two hours to Perugia or Spoleto (it's three hours to Florence). **Fiumicino**, the common name for Rome's Leonardo da Vinci airport, is about 30km west of the city centre, from where a half-hourly train takes thirty minutes to reach Stazione Termini, Rome's principal station. Many charter flights and no-frills airlines use Rome's smaller **Ciampino** airport, southeast of the city, from where regular coaches make the forty-minute trip to Termini. The tiny airport at **Perugia** has Ryanair flights from Stansted and easy travel links to the city and the region. The east-coast port of **Ancona** is another possibility, with a shuttle bus from the airport to the main train station for onward travel into Umbria.

From Dublin, Aer Lingus has two flights a week to Bologna (Marconi) and daily services to Rome Fiumicino; Alitalia also has regular flights (via Paris) to Bologna and Rome. In high season Ryanair flies from Dublin to Pisa daily; otherwise you could pick up a Ryanair flight from Dublin or Shannon to Stansted and catch a Pisa plane from there.

There are no direct flights from Northern Ireland; **from Belfast**, the cheapest option is to buy a ticket to London and an onward flight to Pisa.

Flights from the US and Canada

The only **direct service** between North America and Tuscany (and thus northern Umbria) is offered by Delta, which flies from New York JFK to Pisa five times a week. Otherwise, there are plenty of flights **from the US and Canada** to Rome or Milan Malpensa, from where you can pick up an onward train to Pisa or Florence. Alitalia and Delta have daily flights to Milan from New York, Miami, Chicago and Boston, and to Rome from New York. Other options to Rome include American Airlines from Chicago, and Alitalia and Air Canada from Toronto (usually with a connection in Europe en route). Many European carriers also fly from major US and Canadian cities (via their capitals) to Rome, Milan and Pisa. The cheapest return **fares** to Rome from New York in low season are around $700, rising to $1400 during the summer.

A BETTER KIND OF TRAVEL

At Rough Guides we are passionately committed to travel. We feel that travelling is the best way to understand the world we live in and the people we share it with – plus tourism has brought a great deal of benefit to developing economies around the world over the last few decades. But the growth in tourism has also damaged some places irreparably, and climate change is exacerbated by most forms of transport, especially flying. All Rough Guides' trips are carbon-offset, and every year we donate money to a variety of charities devoted to combating the effects of climate change.

Flights from Australia and New Zealand

Plenty of airlines fly **from Australia or New Zealand** to Rome and Milan via Asian hubs. Round-trip **fares** from Sydney with the major airlines (Alitalia, Qantas, Japan, Singapore or Malaysian) start at around A$1600 in low season, rising to upwards of A$3000 in high season. From New Zealand you can expect to pay from around NZ$2500 in low season to NZ$3500 in high season.

Trains

The choice of rail routes and fares is hugely complex, but the most direct **route** is to take the Eurostar from London to Paris, then pick up the "Palatino" overnight service from Paris to Florence, via Milan (Ⓦ artesia.eu), or take the high-speed TGV from Paris to Milan, and change there for Florence; total journey time is 14–18 hours, and with some online research you can put together a one-way **ticket** for a little over £100 in low season, though peak prices can go as high as £250. Discounts for under-26s are sometimes available and advance booking is essential. If you're planning to include Italy as part of a longer European trip you could invest in a **rail pass** – the Rail Europe website is a useful source of information.

RAIL CONTACTS

European Rail Ⓦ europeanrail.com. Independent specialist in European rail travel.

Eurostar Ⓦ eurostar.com.

InterRail Ⓦ interrail.net.

Rail Europe Ⓦ raileurope.co.uk. Information on international train travel, including tickets and passes.

The Man in Seat 61 Ⓦ seat61.com. An excellent site, packed with useful tips.

Trainseurope Ⓦ trainseurope.co.uk. Another good agency for European rail tickets.

Airlines, agents and operators

AIRLINES

Air Canada Ⓦ aircanada.com
Air France Ⓦ airfrance.co.uk
Alitalia Ⓦ alitalia.com
American Airlines Ⓦ aa.com
British Airways Ⓦ ba.com
Delta Ⓦ delta.com
easyJet Ⓦ easyjet.com
Jet2 Ⓦ jet2.com
Meridiana Ⓦ meridiana.it
Ryanair Ⓦ ryanair.com
Thomsonfly Ⓦ thomsonfly.com

AGENTS AND OPERATORS

Abercrombie & Kent UK Ⓦ abercrombiekent.co.uk, US Ⓦ abercrombiekent.com. Deluxe village-to-village hiking and biking tours, as well as rail journeys.

ATG-Oxford UK Ⓦ atg-oxford.co.uk. Excellent and long-established specialist in group or flexible self-guided walking and cycling holidays, with luggage transported between hotels.

CIT Australia Ⓦ cittravel.com.au. Italian specialists, with packages to Florence and elsewhere.

Citalia UK Ⓦ citalia.com. Long-established company offering city-break packages in three- and four-star hotels.

Flight Centre Australia Ⓦ flightcentre.com.au, NZ Ⓦ flightcentre.co.nz. Specializes in discount airfares and holiday packages.

Italiatours UK Ⓦ italiatours.co.uk, US Ⓦ italiatours.com. Package deals, city breaks and specialist Italian-cuisine tours. Also offers tailor-made itineraries and can book local events and tours.

North South Travel UK Ⓦ northsouthtravel.co.uk. Friendly, competitive travel agency, offering discounted fares worldwide. Profits are used to support projects in the developing world, especially the promotion of sustainable tourism.

STA Travel UK Ⓦ statravel.co.uk, US Ⓦ statravel.com, Australia Ⓦ statravel.com.au, NZ Ⓦ statravel.co.nz. Worldwide specialists in low-cost flights and tours for students and under-26s, though other customers welcome. Also offers student IDs, travel insurance, car rental, rail passes and more.

Getting around

Use of a car is a major advantage if you want to travel extensively around Tuscany and Umbria. You can still get to all the major places by public transport, but away from main routes services can be slow and sporadic. In general, trains are more convenient for longer journeys, buses for local routes.

By car

Travelling **by car** in Italy is relatively painless. The roads are generally good, the motorway (autostrada) network comprehensive and Italian drivers rather less erratic than their reputation suggests. The major autostrada are **toll-roads**, on which you take a ticket as you join and pay as you exit. **Speed limits** are 50kph in built-up areas, 90kph on minor roads outside built-up areas, 110kph on main roads (dual carriageways), and 130kph on nearly all autostradas (a few stretches have a 150kph limit). Note that in wet weather, an 80kph limit applies on minor roads, 90kph on main roads and 110kph on autostradas. If you **break down**, dial ❶116 at the nearest phone and tell the operator (who will sometimes speak English) where you are, the type of car and your number plate; the Automobile Club d'Italia (ACI) will send someone out to fix your car – at a price, so you might consider getting cover with a motoring organization in your home country before you leave.

Car rental is pricey, with a small Fiat costing as much as €300 per week with unlimited mileage. There are plenty of companies at the airports and in the major cities, but it works out cheapest to book before leaving.

Bringing **your own vehicle**, you need a valid full driving licence (with paper counterpart if you have a photocard licence) and an international driving permit if you are a non-EU licence-holder. It's compulsory to carry your car documents and passport while you're driving: you may be required to present them if stopped by the police – not an uncommon occurrence.

By train

The **train** service offered by Italian State Railways (Trenitalia, but still often referred to as Ferrovie dello Stato, or **FS**; ⓦ trenitalia.com) between major towns and cities is relatively inexpensive, reasonably comprehensive and fairly efficient. For extensive train travel in Tuscany and Umbria, however, bear in mind that although cities such as Florence and Pisa have centrally located stations, in many towns the station is a bus ride away, even at heavily visited places such as Siena and Montepulciano. To add insult to injury, you'll often find the vagaries of timetables and routings forcing you to change trains in otherwise dull little towns such as Teróntola or Orte. In addition, some places (Gubbio, the Chianti district and much of southern Tuscany and eastern Umbria) are inaccessible by train.

There are various categories of train, the quickest of which are the **Eurocity** services (EC), which connect major cities across Europe. **Eurostar Italia** (ES) runs between major cities and is faster and more efficient than **Intercity** (IC) trains. You need to reserve for all these services, and pay a supplement of about thirty percent of the ordinary fare. There are no supplements for the other types of train: **Espresso** (EX), which stop at major towns; **Regionale Veloce** (RV), similar to the Espresso, but with more stops; and **Regionale** (Reg), the slowest services, often stopping at every station on the line.

At train stations, separate **timetables** are used for departures (*partenze* – usually yellow) and arrivals (*arrivi* – usually white). Pay attention to the timetable **notes**, which specify the dates between which some services run (*"si effetua dal ... al ..."*), or whether a service is seasonal (*periodico*). The term *giornaliero* means the service runs daily, *feriali* from Monday to Saturday, *festivi* on Sundays and holidays only.

In addition to the routes operated by FS, there are a number of **privately run lines**, often using separate stations, though charging similar fares; where a private line uses an FS station (such as at Arezzo or Terni), there may often be a separate ticket counter.

Tickets and fares

Fares are calculated by the kilometre: a return fare (*andata e ritorno*) is exactly twice that of a single (*andata*). A ticket (*biglietto*) can be bought from a station ticket office (*biglietteria*), online at ⓦ trenitalia .com, from ticket machines at the station, some travel agents and sometimes from station news

---

TICKET MACHINES

All stations have small yellow machines at the end of the platforms or in ticket halls in which you must **stamp your ticket** before boarding the train. If you don't validate your ticket, you become liable for an on-the-spot fine.

kiosks or bars (for short trips). All tickets must be **validated** just before travel: once validated, tickets for journeys up to 200km are valid for six hours, over 200km for 24 hours. Children aged 4–12 pay half price; under-4s travel free.

Train services in Tuscany and Umbria

Florence is the centre of the Tuscan rail network. Two lines run westwards from the city, one of them passing through **Prato**, **Pistoia**, **Montecatini** and **Lucca** on its way to the coast at **Viareggio**, the other going through **Empoli** and **Pisa** before reaching the sea at **Livorno**. From Lucca, a pictur-esque line runs through the Garfagnana to **Aulla**, providing access to the Lunigiana region and connections to La Spezia and Milan. To the east, a line rises through the **Mugello** district and then loops out of Tuscany towards Faenza, roughly parallel to the route through the mountains to Bologna.

South of Florence, mainline trains follow the River Arno to **Arezzo**, then south past **Cortona** to **Chiusi**, **Orvieto** and Rome. From Arezzo, a private line branches up into the Casentino region. Just beyond Cortona, **Teróntola** marks the junction for the branch line east to **Perugia**, the fulcrum of Umbria's network; a couple of trains a day run directly from Florence to Perugia and on to **Foligno** and **Spoleto**. Trains also run from Florence to **Siena** – often with a change at Empoli – although the direct bus journey is quicker and easier. From Siena, train routes continue southeast to Chiusi, and southwest to **Grosseto**.

Mainline trains from Rome to Genoa run along – or just inland from – the Tuscan coast, on a route linking **Orbetello**, Grosseto, Livorno, Pisa, Viareggio and the resorts of the Versilia coast, principally Massa and **Carrara**. At **Cecina**, near Livorno, there's a spur inland to within a few kilometres of **Volterra**, where the line abruptly ends.

All Umbria's major towns, with the exception of Gubbio, are easily accessible by train. In the west, the **Rome–Florence** route is the main artery, with branch-line connections throughout the region. Most of the high-speed services between the two cities stop at no Umbrian stations other than **Orvieto**; you'll probably have to change onto a slower train in order to reach the junction towns of Orte (for Narni and Spoleto), Chiusi (for Siena) or Teróntola (for Perugia and Assisi).

From **Orte**, just over the Lazio border in the south, trains run through the heart of Umbria via **Narni**, **Terni** (terminus of the FCU line), **Spoleto**, **Foligno** and **Gualdo Tadino** on their way to Ancona on the coast. From Teróntola, on the Rome–Florence line, trains head east along the northern shore of Lago Trasimeno to **Perugia**, and on to **Assisi** and **Spello**, meeting the Rome–Ancona route at Foligno. Perugia lies midway along the **Ferrovia Centrale Umbra** (FCU), a private railway that fills some crucial gaps left by the state network, linking the city with **Terni** and **Todi** in the south, and **Città di Castello** and **Sansepolcro** in the north. Services are frequent, though buses often replace trains over certain sections.

By bus

There are dozens of different **bus companies**, all of which are under joint public and private ownership. Some of the companies operate solely on local routes, others run nationwide between major cities; almost everywhere has some kind of bus service, but schedules can be sketchy, and are drastically reduced – sometimes non-existent – on Sundays. Bear in mind also that in rural areas schedules are often designed with the working and/or school day in mind, meaning a frighteningly early start if you want to catch the sole bus out of town and perhaps no buses at all during school holidays.

In larger towns, the **bus terminal** (*autostazione*), where you can buy tickets and pick up timetables, is usually very close to the train station; in smaller towns and villages, most buses pull in at the central piazza, which may have a newsstand selling bus tickets (if not, you can buy tickets on the bus).

City buses are always cheap, usually about €1 per ticket, valid either for a single journey or for any number of journeys within a set period (typically 60–90min). You must always buy a ticket before getting on the bus, from local *tabacchi* or the kiosks at bus terminals and stops; and you must validate them on board. In most cities there are regular ticket checks, with hefty spot-fines for offenders.

By bike or motorbike

Cycling is seen as a sport rather than a way of getting around in Italy: on a Sunday you'll see plenty of people out for a spin on their Campag-nolo-equipped machines, but you'll not come across many luggage-laden tourers. Only in major towns will you find a shop stocking spares for non-racing bikes. It's possible to rent bikes in major towns, but **mopeds** and **scooters** are easier to find: expect to pay €60–70 a day. Crash helmets are compulsory.

Accommodation

Accommodation is a major cost in Tuscany and Umbria, where prices of hotels tend to rise annually, as there's huge demand. There are few really inexpensive hotels, at least in the major Tuscan centres, and only a scattering of hostels.

Most tourist offices carry full **lists of hotels** and other accommodation such as B&B and agriturismo options, and some can help you find a room at short notice. In high season it is essential to **book rooms in advance**; for Florence and Siena, this is advisable at any time of year. The same applies during religious holidays (notably Easter) in towns such as Assisi, and anywhere where a festival is taking place.

Hotels

Hotels in Italy are known by a variety of names. Most are simply tagged **hotel** or **albergo**; others may be called a **locanda**, a name traditionally associated with the cheapest sort of inn, but now sometimes self-consciously applied to smart hotels. A **pensione** was also traditionally a cheap place to stay, though the name now lacks any official status: anywhere still describing itself as a *pensione* is probably a one-star hotel.

All hotels in Italy are **star-rated** from one to five; prices are officially registered for each room and must be posted at the hotel reception and in individual rooms (usually on the back of the door). A star rating can give a good idea of the facilities to expect – a two-star hotel, for example, will always have rooms with a private bathroom – but the system is based on an often eccentric set of criteria relating to facilities rather than to comfort, character or location. A three-star, for example, must have a phone in every room: if it hasn't, it remains a two-star, no matter how magnificent the rest of the hotel.

One-star hotels in tourist towns in high season tend to start at about €50 for a double room without private bath; **two-star** hotels cost upwards of €80 for an en-suite double; **three-star** places are rarely cheaper than €100. **Four-star** hotels are a marked step up: everything has more polish, and in rural four-stars you'll probably get a swimming pool; €150–200 is the typical range here (though some are much pricier), while for a deluxe **five-star** (rare outside the major centres) expect to pay upwards of €250 a night. Prices in Florence and Siena, and to a lesser extent Perugia, Assisi and Orvieto, are higher than anywhere else in the region: you can pay around €100 for an en-suite one-star room in peak season, while €500 per night is far from rare in the five-stars.

In the more popular cities, especially Florence, it's not unusual for hotels to impose a **minimum stay** of three nights in summer.

Self-catering

High hotel prices in much of Tuscany and Umbria make **self-catering** an attractive proposition. Travelling with a group, or even just in a pair, it's worth considering renting a **villa** or **farmhouse** for a week or two. These are not too expensive if you can split costs, are of a consistently high standard, and often enjoy marvellous locations.

PROPERTY RENTAL COMPANIES

Bridgewater's Ⓦ bridgewater-travel.co.uk. A company with over 25 years' experience of apartments in Florence and Siena, and of agriturismo and villas across Tuscany and Umbria.

Cottages to Castles Ⓦ cottagestocastles.com. Numerous Tuscan and Umbrian cottages, villas and apartments.

Cuendet Ⓦ www.italianlife.co.uk. Database of hundreds of properties across both regions.

CV Travel Ⓦ cvtravel.co.uk. A long-established, high-end company with a reputation for securing the most sumptuous properties in Tuscany and Umbria.

Holiday Rentals Ⓦ holiday-rentals.co.uk. This site puts you directly in touch with the owners of scores of Tuscan and Umbrian properties.

IST Italian Breaks Ⓦ www.italianbreaks.com. A good range of villas and apartments.

To Tuscany Ⓦ to-tuscany.com. Offers a large number of properties, in all price ranges.

Traditional Tuscany Ⓦ traditionaltuscany.co.uk. B&B in Florentine palaces and on working farms and vineyards, plus a selection of villas and converted farms.

ACCOMMODATION PRICES

Throughout this book, we've given high-season prices for **hotel** and **B&B** accommodation. For **hostels**, we've also given rates for dorm beds, while **campsites** have prices for adult campers and for pitches.

AGRITURISMO

An increasingly popular accommodation option is **agriturismo**, a scheme whereby farmers rent out converted barns and farm buildings. Usually these comprise a self-contained flat or building, though a few places just rent rooms on a bed-and-breakfast basis. This market has boomed in recent years, and while some rooms are still annexed to working farms or vineyards, many are smart, self-contained rural vacation properties. Attractions may include home-grown food, swimming pools and a range of activities, from walking and riding to archery and mountain biking. Many agriturismi have a **minimum-stay requirement** of one week in busy periods.

Tourist offices keep lists of local properties, or you can search one of the growing number of agriturismo websites – there are hundreds of properties at ⓦagriturismo.com, ⓦagriturismo .net, ⓦagriitalia.it and ⓦagriturist.it.

Bed & breakfast and residenze

There are hundreds of **B&B** places in Tuscany and Umbria, with the greatest concentration in the main tourist towns. Prices at the lower end of the scale are comparable to one-star hotels, but there's also a large number of upscale B&Bs – known as **residenze**, or **residenze d'epoca** when they occupy an old building – in castles, palaces and large private homes. Tourist offices and local websites often carry lists of B&Bs, and ⓦbed-and -breakfast.it is another useful resource. In addition to registered B&Bs you'll also find "**rooms for rent**" (*affittacamere*) advertised in some towns. These differ from B&Bs in that breakfast is not always offered, and they are not subject to the same regulations as official B&Bs; nearly all *affittacamere* are in the one-star price range.

Hostels and student accommodation

Most hostels belong to the **Hostelling International (HI)** network (ⓦhihostels.com), and strictly speaking you need to be an HI member to stay at them. Many, however, allow you to join on the spot, or simply charge a small supplement. Whether or not you're an HI member, you'll need to **book ahead** in the summer months. The most efficient way to book at main city hostels is using HI's own online booking system; for more out-of-the-way locations, contact the hostel direct.

Religious organizations

Religious organizations all over Tuscany and Umbria offer cheap accommodation in lodgings annexed to **convents** or **monasteries**, or in pilgrim hostels. Most have rooms with and without bathroom; a few have dorm rooms with bunks. Some accept women only, others will take only families or single travellers of either sex. Most have a curfew, but few, contrary to expectations, pay much heed to your coming and going. Virtually none offer meals.

Camping

There are surprisingly few **campsites** in rural Tuscany and Umbria, but camping is popular along the coast, where the sites are mostly on the upmarket side. Prices in high season tend to start from around €7–10 per person, plus €5–15 per pitch. If you're camping extensively, it's worth checking Italy's informative camping website, ⓦcamping.it, for details of sites and booking facilities.

Food and drink

The traditional dishes of Tuscany are Italy's most influential cuisine: the ingredients and culinary techniques of the region have made their mark not just on the menus of the rest of Italy but also abroad. Umbrian cooking may not be accorded quite the same degree of reverence, but its produce is of equally high quality, with its truffles and ham being especially prized. And wine has always been central to the area's economy and way of life, familiar names such as Chianti and Orvieto representing just a portion of the enormous output from Tuscan and Umbrian vineyards.

Breakfast and snacks

Many Italians start their day in a bar, their **breakfast** (*prima colazione*) consisting of a coffee and *cornetto* or brioche – a croissant, either filled with jam, custard or chocolate, or unfilled (*un cornetto semplice*).

Sandwiches (*panini*) can be quite substantial, and sandwich bars (*paninoteche*) can be found in many larger towns; grocers' shops (*alimentari*) will often make sandwiches to order. Bars may offer *tramezzini*, ready-made sliced white bread with mixed fillings.

There are a number of options for **takeaway food**. It's possible to find slices of pizza (*pizza al taglio* or *pizza rustica*) pretty much everywhere. You can get pasta and other plain hot meals in a **tavola calda**, a sort of snack bar that's at its best in the morning when everything is fresh. The speciality in a **rosticceria** is usually spit-roasted chicken, alongside fast food such as pizza slices, chips and burgers.

All across Italy, **pizza** comes thin and flat, not deep-pan. The best are cooked in the traditional way, in wood-fired ovens (*forno a legna*): they arrive blasted and bubbling on the surface, and with a distinctive charcoal taste. **Pizzerias** range from stand-up counters selling slices *al taglio* to fully fledged sit-down restaurants.

Other sources of snacks are **markets**, some of which sell take-away food, including *focacce* (oven-baked pastries topped with cheese or tomato or filled with spinach, fried offal or meat) and *arancini* or *supplì*, which are deep-fried balls of rice filled with meat (*rosso*) or butter and cheese (*bianco*).

Restaurants

Traditionally, Tuscan and Umbrian **restaurant** meals (lunch is *pranzo*, dinner is *cena*) are long affairs, starting with an antipasto, followed by a risotto or a pasta *primo*, leading on to a fish or meat *secondo*, cheese, and finished with fresh fruit and coffee. Modern minimalism has made inroads into the more expensive restaurants, but the staple fare at the majority of places is exactly what it might have been a century ago. **Vegetarians** will generally manage fine: there are plenty of meat-free pasta, pizza and salad options to choose from. Beware vegetable soups, however: they may be made with meat stock.

Restaurants are most commonly called either **trattorie** or **ristoranti**. Traditionally, a trattoria is a cheaper and more basic purveyor of home-style cooking (*cucina casalinga*), while a ristorante is more upmarket, with aproned waiters and table-cloths. These days, however, there's a fine line between the two, as it's become chic for an expensive restaurant to call itself a trattoria. It's in the rural areas that you're most likely to come across an old-style trattoria, the sort of place where there's no written menu and no bottled wine (it comes straight from the vats of the local farm). A ristorante will always have a written menu and a reasonable choice of wines, though even in smart places it's standard to choose the ordinary house wine.

Osterie used to be old-fashioned places specializing in home cooking, though recently the osteria tag more often signifies a youngish ownership and clientele, and adventurous foods. Other types of restaurant include **spaghetterie** and **birrerie**, bar-restaurants that serve basic pasta dishes, or beer and snacks.

The menu and the bill

The cheapest – though not the most rewarding way – to eat in city restaurants is to opt for a set-price **menù turistico**. This will usually give you a first course (pasta or soup), main course, dessert, half a litre of water and a quarter litre of wine per person.

Working your way through an Italian menu is pretty straightforward. The **antipasto** (literally "before the meal") generally consists of cold cuts of meat, seafood and cold vegetable dishes. The next course, is typically soup, risotto or pasta. This is followed by **il secondo** – the meat or fish course, usually served alone, except for perhaps a wedge of lemon or tomato. Watch out when ordering fish or Florence's famous *bistecca alla fiorentina*, which will usually be served by weight. Anything marked S.Q. or hg means you are paying by weight: hg stands for a hectogram (*etto* in Italian) – 100g, or around 4oz. Vegetables (**contorni**) and salads (**insalata**) are ordered and served separately.

For afters, you nearly always get a choice of fresh fruit (*frutta*) and desserts (**dolci**) – often ice cream or home-made flans (*torte*). At the end of the meal, ask for the bill/check (**il conto**). Almost everywhere you'll pay a **cover charge** (*pane e coperto* or just *coperto*), on top of your food, usually of €1–2 per head. As well as the *coperto*, **service** (*servizio*) will

There's a detailed **menu reader** of Italian terms on p.568.

often be added, generally about ten percent; if it isn't, you should **tip** about the same amount.

Tuscan cuisine

The most important ingredient of Tuscan cooking is **olive oil**, which comes into almost every dish – as a dressing for salads, a medium for frying, or simply drizzled over vegetables and into soups and stews just before serving. Olive-picking begins around November, before the olives are fully ripe; the oil produced from the first pressing is termed *extra vergine*, the purest and most alkaline, with less than one-percent acidity. The quality of the oil declines with subsequent pressings.

The biggest influences on Tuscan cooking are the simple rustic dishes of **Florence**, the most famous of which is *bistecca alla fiorentina*, a thick T-bone steak grilled over charcoal, usually served rare. You'll find a lot of "**hunters' dishes**" (*cacciatore*), most commonly *cinghiale* (wild boar) and *pollo* (chicken). The Florentines are also fond of the unpretentious *arista*, roast pork loin stuffed with rosemary and garlic, and of *pollo alla diavola*, a flattened chicken marinated with olive oil and lemon juice or white wine, then dressed with herbs before grilling.

Each major Tuscan town has its culinary specialities, a vestige of the days when the region was divided into city states. **Pisa**'s treats include black cabbage soup, new-born eels (*cieche*) fried with garlic and sage, and *torta coi bischeri*, a cake filled with rice, candied fruit, chocolate, raisins and pine nuts, and flavoured with nutmeg and liqueur. Many of the specialities of **Siena** date back to the medieval period, including *salsicce secche* (dried sausages) and *panforte di Siena*, a celebrated spicy cake of nuts and candied fruit. **Arezzo** has *acquacotta*, a soup of fried onion, tomato and bread, mixed with egg and cheese.

Everywhere in the province, **soups** are central to the cuisine, the most famous being *ribollita*, a thick vegetable concoction traditionally including leftover beans (hence "reboiled"). *Pappa al pomodoro* is a popular broth with bread, tomatoes and basil cooked to a sustaining stodge. White cannellini **beans** are the favourite vegetables, boiled with rosemary and doused with olive oil, or cooked with tomatoes (*all'uccelletto*). Also typically Tuscan is **spinach**, which is served as a side vegetable, in combination with omelettes, poached eggs or fish, mixed with ricotta to make *gnocchi*, or as a filling for *crespoline* (pancakes). Spinach and green beans are often eaten cold, usually with a squeeze of lemon.

Wild chestnuts are another staple: there's a long tradition of specialities based on dried chestnuts and chestnut flour, such as the delicious *castagnaccio* (chestnut cake), made with pine nuts, raisins and rosemary. Sheep's milk pecorino is the most widespread Tuscan **cheese**, but the most famous is the oval *marzolino* from the Chianti region, which is often grated over meat dishes.

Dessert menus will often include *cantuccini*, hard biscuits which are dipped in a glass of Vinsanto, or *zuccotto*, a brandy-soaked sponge cake filled with cream mixed with chocolate powder, almonds and hazelnuts – like tiramisù elsewhere in Italy.

Umbrian cuisine

Umbria's cooking also relies heavily on rustic staples – pastas and roast meats – and tends to be simple. Umbria is, however, the only region in Italy apart from Piemonte to offer **truffles** in any abundance (see box, p.497). Traditionally the white truffle is the most highly prized on account of its aroma, but locals swear by the Umbrian grey-white (*bianchetto*) variety and the black truffle that's most common to the area around Spoleto and Norcia. You're most likely to come across them with *tagliolini* (a superfine thread of pasta that enables you to taste the truffle), as a modest sprinkling over a dish of tagliatelle or meat, or on *crostini* – at a price that prohibits overindulgence.

Meat, and in particular **pork**, is the staple of the Umbrian main course, usually grilled or roasted. The region's small, free-range black pigs are famous, and have lately been joined by wild boar (*cinghiale*) – apparently emigrés from Tuscany, now reproducing at a prodigious rate. **Norcia** is the heart of pig country, with a superb selection of all things porcine, though other towns boast their own specialities. **Città di Castello** produces a *salame* made with spices and fennel seed; **Cascia** and **Preci** are known for their *mortadella*; **Foligno** has a distinctive dry *salame*; and **Gualdo Tadino** does a special sausage, the *soppressata*. Also look out for the extraordinary fruit-and-nut-flavoured *salame mezzafegato*. Endemic to the region is *porchetta*, roast suckling pig stuffed with herbs and spices and eaten sliced in crusty white rolls. It's an Umbrian concoction that has spread through most of central Italy, available as a snack from markets and roadside stalls. Other specialities are the lentils of **Castelluccio**, the beans of **Trasimeno**, the peas from **Bettona** and the celery and *cardoons* from around **Trevi**. Umbrian **olive**

oil, though not as hyped as the Tuscan oils, has a high reputation, especially that from around Trevi and Spoleto.

Game may crop up on some menus, most often as pigeon, pheasant or guinea fowl. Despite Umbria's lack of a coast, some restaurants make the effort to bring in fresh **fish**, and there's a reasonable selection available close to lakes and mountain rivers. **Cheeses** follow the usual variations, with the only genuine one-offs to be found in the mountains around Norcia and Gubbio.

Perugino **chocolate** is outstanding, but it's available throughout Italy. One genuine novelty are the white **figs** of Amelia, mixed in a tooth-rotting combination of almonds and chocolate.

Drinking

Drinking is essentially an accompaniment to food: there's little emphasis on drinking for its own sake. Locals sitting around in bars or cafés – whatever their age – will spend hours chatting over a single drink.

Outside the big towns, most bars are functional, brightly lit places, with a chrome counter, a Gaggia coffee machine and a picture of the local football team on the wall. There are no set licensing hours and children are always allowed in. In some more rural places it's difficult to find a bar open much after 9pm. It's nearly always cheapest to drink **standing** at the counter (there's often nowhere to sit anyway), in which case you often pay first at the cash desk (*cassa*), present your receipt (*scontrino*) to the barperson and give your order; sometimes you simply order your drink and pay as you leave. There's always a list of prices (*listino prezzi*) behind the bar. If there's waiter service, you can **sit** where you like, though bear in mind that to do this means your drink will cost perhaps twice as much, especially if you sit outside on the terrace. These different prices for the same drinks are shown on the price list as bar, *tavola* and *terrazza*.

Coffee, tea and soft drinks

One of the most distinctive smells in an Italian street is that of fresh **coffee** wafting out of a bar. The basic choice is either small and black (espresso, or just *caffè*), or white and frothy (cappuccino). If you want a longer espresso ask for a *caffè lungo* or americano; a double espresso is *una doppia*, while a short, extra-strong espresso is a *ristretto*. A coffee topped with un-frothed milk is a *caffè latte*; with a drop of milk it's *caffè macchiato*;

with a shot of alcohol it's *caffè corretto*. Many places also now sell decaffeinated coffee (ask for the brand-name Hag, even when it isn't). In summer you might want to have your coffee cold (*caffè freddo*); for a real treat, ask for *caffè granita*, cold coffee with crushed ice, usually topped with cream. Hot **tea** (*tè caldo*) comes with lemon (*con limone*) as standard, unless you ask for milk (*con latte*); in summer you can drink it cold (*tè freddo*). **Milk** itself is drunk hot as often as cold, or you can get it with a dash of coffee (*latte macchiato*) and sometimes as a milkshake (*frappè*).

There are numerous **soft drinks** (*analcoliche*). A **spremuta** is a fruit juice, usually orange (…*d'arancia*), lemon (…*di limone*) or grapefruit (…*di pompelmo*), fresh-squeezed at the bar, with optional added sugar. A *succo di frutta* is a bottled fruit juice, widely drunk at breakfast.

Tap water (*acqua normale* or *acqua dal rubinetto*) is quite drinkable, and free in bars. **Mineral water** (*acqua minerale*) is a more common choice, either still (*senza gas*, *liscia*, *non gassata* or *naturale*) or sparkling (*con gas*, *gassata* or *frizzante*).

Beer and spirits

Beer (*birra*) is nearly always a lager-type brew that comes in bottles or on tap (*alla spina*) – standard measures are a third of a litre (*piccola*) and two-thirds of a litre (*media*). Commonest and cheapest are the Italian brands Peroni, Moretti and Dreher, all of which are very drinkable; to order these, either state the brand name or ask for *birra nazionale* – otherwise you may be given a more expensive imported beer. You may also come across darker beers (*birra scura* or *birra rossa*), which have a sweeter, maltier taste and resemble stout or bitter.

All the usual **spirits** are on sale and known mostly by their generic names. There are also Italian brands of the main varieties: the best local brandies are Stock and Vecchia Romagna. A shot of these costs about €2, much more for imported stuff or in smart city bars. The home-grown Italian firewater is **grappa**, made from the leftovers of the winemaking process (skins, stalks and the like) and drunk as a *digestivo* after a meal. The best Tuscan varieties are from Montalcino (Brunello) and Montepulciano.

You'll also find **fortified wines** like Martini, Cinzano and Campari. For the real thing, order *un Campari bitter*; ask for a "Campari-soda" and you'll get a ready-mixed version from a little bottle. The luridly orange, non-alcoholic Crodino is also a popular *aperitivo*. You might also try Cynar, an artichoke-based sherry-type liquid often drunk as an aperitif.

There's a daunting selection of **liqueurs**. **Amaro** is a bitter herbal after-dinner drink; the top brands, in rising order of bitterness, are Montenegro, Ramazotti, Averna and Fernet-Branca. Strega is another drink you'll see in every bar – the yellow stuff in elongated bottles: it's as sweet as it looks. Also popular, though considered slightly naff in Italy, is *limoncello*, a bitter-sweet lemon spirit.

Wine

Tuscany is the heartland of Italian wine production, with sales of Chianti accounting for much of the country's wine exports, and the towns of Montalcino and Montepulciano producing two of the very finest Italian vintages. Tuscan wines are predominantly based on the local Sangiovese grape, the foundation of heavyweights such as Chianti, Brunello di Montalcino and Vino Nobile di Montepulciano. Traditionally, the best Tuscan wines are reds, but new techniques have boosted the quality of many whites.

Umbria, by contrast, is low-key, except for the white Orvieto (a wine developed by the Etruscans). It has only a handful of DOC regions, many producing cheap, serviceable wine that rarely finds its way outside the immediate area. Most are made from similar grapes and in similar ways to the workaday reds of Tuscany; however, innovation is producing ever more interesting high-quality vintages, and there's a trove of little-known wines that repay searching out.

Wine is **inexpensive**: in some bars you can get a glass of good local produce for as little as €0.50, and table wine in restaurants rarely costs more than €6 a bottle. Expect to pay from around €10 for a major-name bottle in a restaurant, less than half that from a shop or supermarket.

The media

Newspapers form an essential accompaniment to Italian bar culture: particularly in small towns, folk are drawn to a bar for a read as much as for a drink. Television also plays a central role in Italian life: many households have the TV switched on from morning to night, regardless of the poor quality of Italy's numerous local and national channels.

A WINE CHECKLIST

TUSCAN WINES

Bianco di Pitigliano Delicate dry white from southern Tuscany.
Bianco Vergine della Valdichiana Soft dry white from south of Arezzo.
Brunello di Montalcino Full-bodied red from south of Siena; one of Italy's finest wines.
Carmignano A dry red produced west of Florence; this area also produces **Vin Ruspo**, a fresh rosé.
Chianti Italy's most famous red – see p.152.
Colline Lucchesi A soft and lively DOC red from the hills east of Lucca.
Galestro A light, dry summer white.
Grattamacco Produced southeast of Livorno, this non-DOC wine comes as a fruity white and a full, dry red.
Montecarlo A full and dry white – one of Tuscany's finest – from east of Lucca.
Montecucco DOC red from Cinigiano and Civitella Paganico near Grosseto.
Monteregio di Massa Maríttima Another newish DOC red from the Alta Maremma region.
Morellino di Scansano A fairly dry, robust, up-and-coming DOC red, made southeast of Grosseto.
Pomino DOC from near Rúfina; an excellent red, plus white and Vinsanto.
Rosso di Montalcino A full-bodied DOC, aged less than the great Brunello di Montalcino. One of the great Italian reds. See p.336.
Rosso di Montepulciano Excellent-value red table wine.
Sammarco Big Cabernet wine from the Chianti region.
Sassicaia Full ruby wine from near Livorno made from Cabernet Sauvignon grapes; best left a few years.
Solaia Another Cabernet Sauvignon from the Antinori estate.
Spumante Sparkling wines are a relatively new departure in Tuscany, but vineyards all over the

Newspapers

Tuscany's major **newspaper** is the Florence-based *La Nazione* – technically a national paper, but its sales are concentrated in the central provinces of Italy. It produces local editions, with supplements, including informative entertainments listings, for virtually every major Tuscan town. In Umbria, the leading local paper is the *Corriere dell'Umbria*, with detailed regional and small-town coverage. Of the other nationals, the centre-left *La Repubblica* and right-slanted *Corriere della Sera* are the two most widely read. *L'Unità*, which has evolved from the newspaper of the former Italian communist party, has experienced hard times, even in the party's Tuscan and Umbrian strongholds: circulation now is around fifty thousand The most avidly read papers are the pink *Gazzetta dello Sport* and *Corriere dello Sport*; essential reading for the serious Italian sports fan, they devote as much attention to players' ankle problems as most papers would give to the resignation of a government. News **magazines** are also widely read in Italy, from *L'Espresso* and *Panorama* to the lighter offerings of *Gente* and *Oggi*.

TV and radio

Italy's three main national **TV** channels are RAI 1, 2 and 3. Silvio Berlusconi's Mediaset runs three additional nationwide channels: Canale 5, Rete 4 and Italia 1. Although all six are blatantly pro-Berlusconi, the degree of sycophancy displayed on the TG4 news has reached such ludicrous heights (newscaster Emilio Fede is variously overcome by tears of joy or despair, depending on the fortunes of Berlusconi) that many Italians now tune in solely for a giggle. Although the stories of Italian TV's stripping housewives are overplayed, the output is generally unchallenging (and sexist) across the board, with the accent on quiz shows, soaps and plenty of American imports. The RAI channels carry less advertising and try to mix the dross with documentaries and news coverage. Numerous local channels concentrate on sport and shopping.

The situation in **radio** is even more anarchic, with FM so crowded that you continually pick up new stations whether you want to or not. There are some good small-scale stations if you search hard enough, but on the whole the RAI stations are the most professional.

province are now using the *champenoise* or *charmat* method to produce quality vintages.
Tavernelle California-style red from western Chianti.
Tignanello Traditional Sangiovese Chianti, again from Antinori.
Vernaccia di San Gimignano Subtle dry white DOC from the hills of San Gimignano.
Vin santo Aromatic wine, made from semi-dried grapes and sealed in casks for at least three years. Produced all over Tuscany (and Umbria too), it ranges from dry to sweet, and is often served at dessert.
Vino Nobile di Montepulciano A full, classy red DOC from around Montepulciano, south of Siena.

UMBRIAN WINES
Cabernet Sauvignon di Miralduolo Purplish dry red from Torgiano.
Cervaro della Sala A new white wine, aged in French oak.
Chardonnay di Miralduolo Flowery, dry white from Torgiano, also aged in wood.
Colli Altotiberini A new Tiber valley DOC, best drunk young.
Colli Amerini Another new DOC, best known for its reds.
Colli Perugini Umbria's newest DOC – red, white and rosé.
Colli del Trasimeno Huge area producing reds and whites of ever-rising standard.
Decugnano dei Barbi Rosso Fruity red from near Lago di Corbara.
Montefalco A soft, dry red – Montefalco Rosso – and the more robust Sagrantino di Montefalco, plus Sagrantino Passito, a superb red dessert wine. See also p.464.
Orvieto Umbria's most famous DOC wine, a dry, light white, or a lightly sweet dessert wine (*abboccato*).
San Giorgio A bold, full-bodied red, made in Torgiano.
Solleone Dry, sherry-like aperitif.
Torgiano DOC region southeast of Perugia, producing both red and white wines; look out for the dry, fruity white Torre di Giano, the wood-aged white Torre di Giano Riserva, and the opulent Rubesco Riserva, one of Italy's finest reds.

Festivals

Both Tuscany and Umbria have a plethora of local festivals, with saints' days being the most common excuse for some kind of binge. Many cities, towns and villages have their home-produced saint, whose mortal remains or image are paraded through the streets amid much noise and spectacle. There are plenty of other occasions for a festa – either to commemorate a local miracle or historic event, or to show off the local products or artistic talent.

Many festivals happen at Easter, in May or September, or around Ferragosto (Aug 15); dates are detailed below. For **national holidays**, see p.38; for further information on the major festivals, see individual chapters.

Tickets for some cultural festivals – such as the Maggio Musicale in Florence or Spoleto's Festival dei Due Mondi – can be difficult to obtain. If you have no luck with a festival's box office, it may be worth trying **Liaisons Abroad** (Ⓦ liaisonsabroad .com), an agency for tickets to major Italian opera and musical events, timed museum tickets, Siena's Palio, Serie A football matches and more.

Food, wine and arts festivals

Food- and **wine**-inspired festivals are more low-key affairs than the religious and traditional events, but no less enjoyable for that. They generally celebrate the edible speciality of the region to the accompaniment of dancing, music from a local band and fireworks at the end of the evening. At Easter and through the summer and autumn there are literally hundreds of such events, most of them catering to locals rather than tourists; for details, ask at tourist offices or check the local newspapers (where you'll find them listed as **sagre**). The ancient inter-town rivalries across Tuscany and Umbria – encapsulated neatly by the term *campanilismo*, implying that the only things that matter are those that take place within the sound of your village's church bells – find a positive expression in the willingness of local councils to put money into promoting their own **arts festivals**. For the size of the towns involved, the events are often almost ludicrously rich, celebrating the work of a native composer or artist by inviting major international names to perform or direct. Many festivals are given added enjoyment by their location: in summer, open-air performances are often staged in ancient amphitheatres, churches or town squares.

Religious and traditional festivals

Many of the local **religious processions** have strong pagan roots, marking important dates on the calendar subsequently adopted and sanctified by the Church. **Good Friday** is also a popular time for processions, with images of Christ on the cross paraded through towns accompanied by white-robed, hooded figures singing penitential hymns. The separate motivations to make some money, have a good time and pay your spiritual dues all merge in the celebrations for a town's **saint's day**, where it's not unusual to find a communist mayor and local bishop officiating side by side.

In recent years there's been a revival of **carnival** (*carnevale*), the last fling before Lent, although anarchic fun has generally been replaced by elegant, self-conscious affairs, with costumes and handmade masks – at their most extravagant in **Viareggio**. Carnival usually lasts for the five days before Ash Wednesday; because it's connected with Easter the dates change from year to year.

A festival calendar

JANUARY

Foligno (Jan 24) Festa di San Feliciano; traditional fair.
Trevi (Jan 27) Festa di Sant'Emiliano; torchlit procession.

FEBRUARY

Norcia (3–4 days in Feb) Truffle and sausage festival.
Spello (Feb 5) Olive and bruschetta festival.
Viareggio and **San Gimignano** (early/mid-Feb) Carnevale.
Terni (Feb 14) St Valentine's Day fair.

MARCH

Norcia (March 20–24) Crossbow competition.
Assisi Holy Week celebrations – one of the world's biggest concentrations of nuns, monks and fanatics.
Grassina (near Florence), **Gubbio** and **Bevagna** Good Friday processions.
Florence (Easter Sun) Scioppio del Carro; fireworks in Piazza del Duomo.
San Miniato (first Sun after Easter) National kite-flying championships.

APRIL

Montecatini Terme (April 16) Fettunta festival; oil and garlic speciality.
Lucca (April–June) Sacred music festival.
Florence (April–June) Maggio Musicale festival.

MAY

Terni (May 1) Canta Maggio; parade of illuminated floats.

Assisi (a week from the first Tues in May) Calendimaggio; a huge festival, celebrating St Francis's more worldly early years.

Gubbio (May 15) Corsa dei Ceri; candle race.

Foligno (May 15) Giostro della Quintana; medieval joust.

Massa Maríttima (first Sun after May 19) Balestro del Girifalco; crossbow competition.

Cascia (May 21 & 22) Celebrazioni Ritiane; thousands of devotees – mainly women – attend the torchlight procession in honour of St Rita.

Gubbio (last Sun) Crossbow matches against team from Sansepolcro.

JUNE

Orvieto and **Spello** (early June) Corpus Domini procession.

Pisa (June 16 & 17) Luminaria torchlit celebration; precedes Regatta di San Ranieri boat race.

Spoleto (June & July) Festival dei Due Mondi; internationally renowned month-long event; classical concerts, film, ballet, street theatre and performance art, staged in the ancient walled town.

Pisa (third Sun) Gioco del Ponte.

Florence (week beginning June 24) Festa di San Giovanni; fireworks and the Calcio Storico football game.

Fiesole (mid-June to Aug) Estate Fiesolana; music, cinema, ballet and theatre.

San Gimignano (late June to Oct) Summer festival of music and film.

Bevagna (last week) Mercato delle Gaite; medieval craft fair.

Piediluco (end June) Sagra del Pesce.

JULY

Siena (July 2) Palio horse races, preceded by trial races on June 29 & 30 and July 1.

Torre del Lago (July & Aug) Puccini festival.

Perugia (July & Aug) Umbria Jazz; major jazz event.

Fivizzano (second Sun) Archery contest.

Siena (mid-July) Settimana Musicale.

Gubbio (mid-July to mid-Aug) Spettacoli Classici; classical plays staged in the town's Roman amphitheatre.

Barga (second half July) Opera and theatre festival.

Lucca (third Sun) Festa di San Paolino; torchlit parade and crossbow contest.

Pistoia (July 25) Giostro dell'Orso; jousting.

Le Ghiaie (last week July) Wine festival on Elba.

AUGUST

Cortona (first week) Festival del Sole; arts festival with an emphasis on classical music.

Massa Maríttima (second Sun) Second leg of the crossbow competition.

Montepulciano (second Sun) Food and wine festival.

Città della Pieve (mid-Aug) Festa della Fontana; flooding of the town fountain with wine.

Lucca (Aug 14) Luminaria di Santa Croce; torchlit procession.

Montepulciano (Aug 14–16) Il Bruscello; folkloric song festival.

Cortona (Aug 15) Festa della Bistecca; excessive consumption of local beef.

Florence (Aug 15) Festa del Grillo; fair in the Cascine park.

Orvieto (Aug 15) Festa della Palombella; horse race.

Porto Santo Stefano (Aug 15) Palio Marinaro; parade and rowing race.

Siena (Aug 16) Palio horse races, preceded by trial races on Aug 14 & 15.

Livorno (Aug 17) Palio Marinaro; boat races.

Città di Castello (mid-Aug to early Sept) Chamber music festival.

Arezzo (last two weeks) International choral festival.

Città di Castello (last week) Festival delle Nazioni di Musica da Camera; highly respected festival of chamber music.

Montepulciano (last Sun) Bravio delle Botti; barrel race through town.

SEPTEMBER

Todi (ten days in Sept) Arts festival.

Arezzo (first Sun) Giostro del Saraceno; jousting.

Cerreto Guidi (first Sun) Renaissance procession.

Florence (Sept 7) Festa delle Rificolone; torchlit procession.

Prato (Sept 8) Festa degli Omaggi; costumed procession.

Sansepolcro (second Sun) Crossbow matches against Gubbio.

Greve (second Sun) Chianti Classico wine festival.

Foligno (second weekend) Torneo della Quintana; jousting by six hundred medieval knights.

Lucca (Sept 14) Festa di Santa Croce/Settembre Lucchese; procession of sacred image and cultural events.

Perugia (last week) Sagra Musicale Umbra; classical music festival, one of the region's most prestigious cultural events.

OCTOBER

Trevi (Oct 1) Palio dei Terzieri; cart race.

Assisi (Oct 3–4) Festa di San Francesco; Umbria's biggest religious festival, drawing religious leaders and pilgrims from all over Italy.

Piediluco (mid-Oct) Wine and chestnut fair.

Umbertide (mid-Oct) Sagra della Castagna; chestnut fair.

NOVEMBER

Perugia (Nov 1–5) Festa dei Ognissanti; All Saints Fair.

DECEMBER

Siena (Dec 13) Festa di Santa Lucia; pottery fair.

Prato (Dec 25 & 26) Display of Holy Girdle.

Outdoor activities

In the popular imagination, much of the landscape of Tuscany and Umbria is a pastoral patchwork of low hills, vineyards and wooded valleys, but the reality is rather different. The variety of landscape is extraordinary, from the clay hills of the Sienese crete and brooding uplands around Volterra to the high peaks of the Alpi Apuane and the pristine maritime landscapes of the Maremma, and this diverse terrain offers a wide range of outdoor activities. Some, such as hiking, are potentially outstanding, despite a relative lack of marked paths and good maps in many areas – though parts of Umbria, southern Tuscany and the Alpi Apuane are well covered. Cycling and riding are also first-rate, and there are good opportunities for climbing, caving, sailing and diving.

Walking

Tuscany and Umbria offer a plethora of **walking** opportunities. The gentle pastoral landscapes of both regions are perfect for easygoing strolls, while the high-mountain terrains of areas such as the Alpi Apuane in Tuscany and Monte Cucco and the Monti Sibillini in Umbria provide the chance for longer and more challenging hikes. Spring is by far the best time for hiking, with glorious wildflowers and verdant countryside from mid-April in the lowlands and late May to early June in the mountains. Temperatures are equally kind in September – midsummer is too hot for comfortable

hiking – and the weather a touch more reliable, with less chance of rain than in spring, but the landscapes can be sun-scorched.

However, hiking in this part of Italy is still in its infancy. You'll find very few marked **trails** or recognized footpaths, and even fewer **maps** of sufficient detail to let you navigate with confidence. Certain areas do have marked trails, generally the work of local enthusiasts or the **Club Alpino Italiano** (CAI; Ⓦ cai.it). Most towns have a CAI office, but these are typically open only for a few hours each week: you're better off visiting a local tourist office for details of local trails. Such paths exist in the Alpi Apuane, Orecchiella, Monte Cucco and parts of the Monti Sibillini, as well as in other areas with an active local CAI branch, such as the Val d'Orcia south of Montalcino, parts of Elba, the Casentino, areas around Spoleto and on Monte Subasio above Assisi. Shorter trails can be found in protected parks such as the Monti dell'Uccellina in the Maremma. All CAI paths are indicated by **red and white markers**, but are often not of sufficient quality to let you follow a route confidently or safely without a map. This is especially true in the mountains.

Other activities

Unlike walking, **cycling** is extremely popular among Italians, and on Sunday mornings in particular you'll find a lot of enthusiasts on the road – albeit on expensive racing machines rather than tourers or off-roaders. It's as well to remember that much of Tuscany and Umbria is hilly and that summer temperatures, especially in the afternoon, are high. Also bear in mind that many minor country roads are gravel-surfaced *strade bianche*.

Many companies offer **horseriding** holidays,

FLORA AND FAUNA

For **wild flowers** the prime times are late April and May (later in the mountains), and the best areas in Tuscany are the **Orecchiella** and **Alpi Apuane**, at the meeting point of Alpine and Mediterranean vegetation zones. In Umbria, the **Martani** hills, **Monte Subasio** and the **Piano Grande** are blanketed in orchids, fritillaries and countless other flowers in May and June. In olive groves and on hillsides you'll see masses of poppies, primroses, violets, grape hyacinth, cyclamen, irises, cistus and many more species. Specially adapted marine species can be found in the reserves of the Maremma.

Cypresses and **umbrella pines** are the defining trees of the Tuscan countryside, while oak forests blanket many of the interior hills, in Chianti in particular. Elsewhere there are large tracts of virgin oak, beech and pine forest, especially in the Casentino. On the higher hills, notably in the Sibillini, there are clumps of high **beech forest**, the predominant tree of the Apennines and of limestone in general. **Sweet chestnut** dominates in the Orecchiella and Alpi Apuane, rolling unbroken across mile after mile of the lower hills. Coastal areas, especially in the **Monti dell'Uccellina**, have preserved the classic profiles of Mediterranean *macchia*: dwarf trees

usually in Chianti or the Maremma, but virtually every rural town and village has at least one stable (*un maneggio* or *club ippico*) where you can take a horse out by the hour, the day or longer. Tourist offices have information on these, and on agriturismi, many of which also offer riding.

Climbing is possible in the Alpi Apuane, where the limestone and marble offer some of the best rock on the Italian peninsula. CAI publish books on climbs in the region, available from larger bookshops in Lucca, Pisa or Florence, and you can pick up local information from CAI offices or the park office in Castelnuovo di Garfagnana (see p.204). In Umbria, there are climbs on Le Lecce and Fossa Secca around Monte Cucco, while the crags around Ferentillo have become one of Italy's leading free-climbing centres. The karst formations of much of the region offers Italy's best **caving**, especially around Monte Cucco (see p.431), which has some of the world's deepest cave systems and at least twenty pots open to speleologists (some for experts only). There are almost equally good opportunities in the Alpi Apuane, including the Grotta del Vento (see p.204), which is also accessible to non-specialists.

Italy's best **hang- and para-gliding** is also found on and around Monte Cucco, notably the Val di Ranco, and in the Sibillini above the Piano Grande, where the thermals and steep and treeless slopes provide ideal conditions.

Sailing and **windsurfing** are common up and down the Tuscan coast, where all the larger resorts have rental outlets for sailboards, catamarans and the like. You can also rent scuba **diving** and **snorkelling** equipment, or take guided day or night dives, especially around the key diving destinations of Monte Argentario, Elba and smaller islands such as Giannutri.

Travel essentials

Costs

Delicious picnic **meals** can be put together for under €5, and a pizza or plate of pasta in a cheap pizzeria or trattoria should come to €6–10. However, in most restaurants in the major tourist centres you'll be lucky to get away with paying €35 a head for a three-course meal with house wine. **Public transport** is good value: the train journey from Florence to Siena (100km), for example, costs around €12 for a second-class return. **Accommodation** in major centres, though, is expensive (see p.25).

Overall, an average minimum **daily budget** for a couple staying in one-star hotels and eating one modest-priced meal out a day would be in the region of €90 per person. Single hotel rooms are disproportionately expensive, so if you're travelling alone you can expect this figure to increase by about 25 percent – though not, of course, if staying in a hostel.

Youth/student ID cards soon pay for themselves in savings, principally on entertainment and admission to larger museums and attractions. Full-time students are eligible for the International Student ID Card (**ISIC**); anybody aged 26 or less qualifies for the **International Youth Travel Card**; and teachers qualify for the **International Teacher Card** – all of which carry the same benefits. Check Ⓦisiccard.com for details. **Discounts** for under-18s and over-65s are also usually available for major attractions and state museums.

(usually oak), and a scrub of laurel, broom, lentisk, heather and fragrant plants. Coastal areas offer the richest **bird habitats**, especially the reserves set aside to protect them: Lago di Burano, Laguna di Orbetello and the Monti dell'Uccellina. These closely connected areas draw numerous migrant species, many of them rare. Inland, you can see hoopoes, doves, woodpeckers and run-of-the-mill wrens, thrushes and starlings. Mountain areas boast a few hawks and buzzards, and even golden eagles.

Of the larger mammals in the area, the **wild boar** is best known, found through much of Tuscany and now spreading into Umbria. **Porcupines**, though also elusive, are common, and you often find quills on country walks. **Roe deer** have been reintroduced into the reserves at Bólgheri and the Monti dell'Uccellina; elsewhere they've been hunted to extinction.

Wolves drift into the Valnerina from their heartlands in the Abruzzo mountains to the south. There are at least 150 to 200 specimens in Italy, all protected – in theory. Elsewhere, you may see **smaller mammals** – hares, rabbits, foxes and weasels – though these too have been much depleted by hunting. Wilder upland areas are home to a few **wild cats**. **Snakes**, and the viper in particular, are common, particularly around abandoned farmland.

Crime and personal safety

In Florence, the only trouble you've much chance of encountering is from **scippatori** ("snatchers"), often kids, who operate in crowded streets or markets, train stations and packed tourist sights. As well as handbags, *scippatori* grab wallets, tear off any visible jewellery and, if they're really adroit, unstrap watches. You can **minimize the risk** by being discreet: wear money in a belt or pouch; don't put anything down on café or restaurant tables; don't flash anything of value; keep a firm hand on your camera; and carry shoulder bags slung across your body. Never leave anything valuable in your car and park in car parks or well-lit, well-used streets.

Italy's reputation for **sexual harassment** of women is based largely on experiences in the south of the country. However, even in the "civilized" north, travelling on your own, or with another woman, you can expect to attract some unwelcome attention. Indifference is the most effective policy.

In Italy there are several different branches of the **police**, ostensibly to prevent any single branch seizing power. You're not likely to have much contact with the Guardia di Finanza, who investigate smuggling, tax evasion and other finance-related felonies. Drivers may well come up against the **Polizia Urbana**, or town police, who are mainly concerned with traffic and parking offences, and also the **Polizia Stradale**, who patrol autostradas.

The **Carabinieri** – the ones Italians are most rude about – are dressed in military-style uniforms and white shoulder belts (they're part of the army), and deal with general crime, public order and drugs control. The **Polizia Statale**, the other general crime-fighting branch, enjoy a fierce rivalry with the Carabinieri, and are the ones to whom you should **report a theft** at their base, the **Questura** (police station). They'll issue you with a *denuncia*, a form which you'll need for any insurance claims after you get home.

EMERGENCY PHONE NUMBERS

Police (Carabinieri) ☎ 112
Any emergency service (Soccorso Pubblico di Emergenza) ☎ 113
Fire service (Vigili del Fuoco) ☎ 115
Roadside assistance (Soccorso Stradale) ☎ 116

Electricity

The supply is 220V, though anything requiring 240V will work. Most **plugs** are two round pins: UK equipment will need an adaptor, US equipment a 220-to-110 transformer as well.

Entry requirements

All EU citizens can enter Italy, and stay as long as they like, on production of a valid passport. Citizens of the United States, Canada, Australia and New Zealand need only a valid passport, but are limited to stays of ninety days. All other nationals should consult the relevant embassies about visa requirements. Legally, you're required to **register with the police** within three days of entering Italy; if you're staying at a hotel this will be done for you. Some policemen are punctilious about registration, though others would be astonished by any attempt to register yourself at the local station while on holiday.

ITALIAN EMBASSIES AND CONSULATES ABROAD

Australia Embassy: 12 Grey St, Deakin, Canberra, ACT 2600
☎ 02 6273 3333, ⊕ www.ambcanberra.esteri.it. Consulates in Melbourne ☎ 03 9867 5744 and Sydney ☎ 02 9392 7900.
Canada Embassy: 275 Slater St, Ottawa, ON K1P 5H9 ☎ 613 232 2401, ⊕ www.ambottawa.esteri.it. Consulates in Montréal ☎ 514 849 8351 and Toronto ☎ 416 977 1566.
Ireland Embassy: 63–65 Northumberland Rd, Dublin 4 ☎ 01 660 1744, ⊕ www.ambdublino.esteri.it.
New Zealand Embassy: 34–38 Grant Rd, PO Box 463, Thorndon, Wellington ☎ 04 473 5339, ⊕ www.ambwellington.esteri.it.
UK Embassy: 14 Three King's Yard, London W1Y 2EH ☎ 020 7312 2200, ⊕ www.amblondra.esteri.it. Consulates in Edinburgh ☎ 0131 226 3695 and Manchester ☎ 0161 236 9024.
US Embassy: 3000 Whitehaven St NW, Washington DC 20008 ☎ 202 612 4400, ⊕ www.ambwashingtondc.esteri.it. Consulates in Chicago ☎ 312 467 1550, New York ☎ 212 737 9100 and San Francisco ☎ 415 292 9210.

EMBASSIES AND CONSULATES IN ITALY

Australia Embassy: Via Alessandria 215, 00198 Rome ☎ 06 852 721, ⊕ australian-embassy.it.
Canada Embassy: Via Zara 30, 00198 Roma ☎ 06 85444 2911, ⊕ www.canada.it.
Ireland Embassy: Piazza di Campitelli 3, 00186 Roma ☎ 06 697 9121, ⊕ www.ambasciata-irlanda.it.
New Zealand Embassy: Via Clitunno 44, 00198 Roma ☎ 06 853 7501, ⊕ nzembassy.com/italy.
UK Embassy: Via XX Settembre 80a, 00187 Roma ☎ 06 4220 0001, ⊕ ukinitaly.fco.gov.uk. Consulate in Florence: Lungarno Corsini 2 ☎ 055 284 133.

US Embassy: Via V Veneto 119/a, 00187 Rome ☎ 06 46 741, ⓦ usembassy.it. Consulate in Florence: Lungarno Vespucci 38 ☎ 055 266 951, ⓦ florence.usconsulate.gov.

Gay and lesbian travellers

Attitudes to **gay men and women** in Tuscany and Umbria are on the whole tolerant, and Florence has a particularly thriving gay scene, but public displays of affection that extend much beyond hand-holding might raise a few eyebrows, especially outside the bigger towns. The age of consent in Italy is 18.

Health

If you're arriving in Italy from elsewhere in Europe, North America or Australasia, you don't need any jabs. **EU citizens** are entitled to emergency medical care under the same terms as the residents of the country. As proof of entitlement, British citizens will need a **European Health Insurance Card (EHIC)**, which is free of charge and valid for five years – application forms are issued at UK post offices, or you can apply online at ⓦ www.dh.gov.uk. Note, however, that the EHIC won't cover the full cost of major treatment (or dental treatment), and high medical charges make travel insurance essential. You normally have to pay the full cost of emergency treatment upfront, and claim it back when you get home (minus an excess); make sure you hang onto full doctors' reports, signed prescription details and all receipts to back up your claim.

In an **emergency**, call ☎ 113 and ask for *ospedale* or *ambulanza*, or go to the Pronto Soccorso (Casualty/A&E) section of the nearest hospital. Major train stations and airports often have first-aid facilities.

Italian pharmacists (farmacie) are well qualified to give advice on **minor ailments** and to dispense prescriptions. There's generally one open all night in the bigger towns and cities – they work on a rota system, and the address of the one currently open is posted on any farmacia door. If you require a **doctor** (*médico*), ask for help in the first instance at your hotel or the local tourist office. Alternatively look in the Yellow Pages (*Pagine Gialle*): larger towns will have English-speaking doctors. Follow a similar procedure if you have dental problems.

Mosquitoes (*zanzare*) can be a nuisance between June and September; most supermarkets and pharmacies sell sprays, mosquito coils and after-bite cream.

Insurance

Even though EU health care privileges apply in Italy, you'd do well to take out an **insurance policy** before travelling to cover against theft, loss, illness or injury. Before paying for a new policy, however, check whether you're already covered: some all-risks home insurance policies may cover your possessions when overseas, and many private medical schemes include cover when abroad.

If your existing policies don't cover you, contact a specialist **travel insurance** company, or consider Rough Guides' own travel insurance deal (see box below). A typical travel policy usually provides health cover, plus cover for the loss of baggage, tickets and – up to a certain limit – cash or cheques, as well as cancellation or curtailment of your journey. Most exclude so-called dangerous sports unless an extra premium is paid. For medical coverage, ascertain whether benefits will be paid as the treatment proceeds or only after you return home, and whether there is a 24-hour medical emergency number. When securing baggage cover, make sure that the per-article limit will cover your most valuable possession. If you need to make a claim, you should keep receipts for medicines and medical treatment, and in the event you have anything stolen, you must obtain an official statement from the police.

Internet

Internet cafés are widespread in the larger towns; they are often to be found near the train station. It's increasingly common for hotels and even hostels to provide internet access, usually for free (three-, four- and five-star hotels are obliged to offer wi-fi, but are allowed to charge); in the more sizeable towns, you'll also come across cafés and bars offering free wi-fi.

Mail

Opening hours of main **post offices** are usually Monday to Saturday 8.30am–7.30pm, although smaller offices tend to close at 1pm. You can also buy **stamps** (*francobolli*) in *tabacchi*, and in some gift shops. The Italian postal system is one of the slowest in Europe so if your letter is urgent make sure you send it *posta prioritaria*, which has varying rates according to weight and destination.

Maps

The **maps** in this guide should be fine for most purposes, and nearly all tourist offices hand out free maps as well. More detailed maps are produced by a multitude of companies, notably Italy's leading street-plan publisher LAC (Litografia Artistica Cartografica), and the TCI (Touring Club Italiano). The Rough Guide Map: Florence and Siena is printed on waterproof, crease-resistant paper, as is Rough Guides' 1:200,000 Tuscany map, which has all the information you'll need for driving around the area. Otherwise, the widely available TCI 1:200,000 maps (separate sheets for Tuscany and Umbria) are excellent.

Money

The Italian currency is the **euro** (€), which is composed of 100 cents. You'll usually get the best rate of exchange (*cambio*) from a **bank**. Banking hours vary slightly, but generally are Monday to Friday 8.30am to 1.30pm and 3pm to 4.30pm, with some major branches staying open continuously 8.30am to 4.30pm and opening for a couple of hours on Saturday morning. American Express and Travelex offices are open longer hours and in the larger towns you'll find an **exchange bureau** at the train station that stays open late. As a rule, though, the kiosks offer pretty bad rates.

Although it's a good idea to have some cash when you first arrive, **credit and debit cards** can be used either in an ATM (*bancomat*) or over the counter. MasterCard, Visa and American Express are accepted in most larger city stores, hotels and restaurants, but cash still reigns supreme in much of Italy, so check first before embarking on a big meal out. ATMs are found in even small towns, and most accept all major cards. Remember that all cash advances on a credit card are treated as loans, with interest accruing daily from the date of withdrawal.

Opening hours and public holidays

Most **shops** are open Monday to Saturday from 8/9am until around 1pm, and again from about 3pm until 7/8pm, though in Florence and other main centres, it's become increasingly common for shops to stay open continuously from around 10am to 7.30pm (with slightly shorter hours on Sun). Opening hours for **museums**, **galleries** and **churches** vary and tend to change annually, but only by half an hour or so; we've detailed the current hours throughout the Guide. **Restaurants** typically open for lunch at about 12.30pm and close at 3pm, opening again for dinner at 7/7.30pm. Most are closed at least one day a week.

Everything, except some bars and restaurants, closes on Italy's official **national holidays**, which are: January 1, January 6 (Epiphany), Easter Monday, April 25 (Liberation Day), May 1 (Labour Day), June 2 (Day of the Republic), August 15 (*Ferragosto*; Assumption), November 1 (*Ognissanti*; All Saints), December 8 (Immaculate Conception), December 25, December 26.

Phones

Public phone tariffs are among the most expensive in Europe. For national calls, the

---

CALLING HOME FROM ABROAD

Note that the initial zero is omitted from the area code when dialing the UK, Ireland, Australia and New Zealand from abroad.

Australia international access code + 61
New Zealand international access code + 64
Republic of Ireland international access code + 353
UK international access code + 44
US and Canada international access code + 1

TEMPERATURES AND RAINFALL

The table below shows average maximum and minimum daytime **temperatures**, and average monthly **rainfall**.

	Jan	Feb	Mar	Apr	May	Jun	Jul	Aug	Sep	Oct	Nov	Dec
Florence												
Max °C/°F	9/48	11/52	15/59	20/68	23/73	28/82	31/88	31/88	27/81	20/68	14/57	10/50
Min °C/°F	1/34	2/36	4/39	7/45	11/52	14/57	17/63	16/61	14/57	10/50	5/41	2/36
Rainfall (mm)	73	69	80	78	73	55	40	76	78	88	111	91
Spoleto												
Max °C/°F	8/47	11/51	13/56	17/62	22/71	26/78	29/85	29/84	26/78	19/67	13/56	9/48
Min °C/°F	0/32	1/34	3/37	5/41	9/48	12/54	14/58	15/59	13/55	8/47	4/39	1/34
Rainfall (mm)	58	69	61	71	73	71	46	61	69	77	94	71

off-peak period runs Monday to Friday 6.30pm to 8am, then Saturday 1pm until Monday 8am. Area codes are an integral part of the number and must always be dialled, regardless of where you're calling from. **Phone cards** for use in public phones can be bought from many *tabacchi* or stores displaying a Telecom Italian sticker. The **international phone code** for Italy is 39. International **directory enquiries** is on ☏176; an English-speaking operator is on ☏170. Numbers beginning ☏800 are free.

To use your **mobile phone**, check with your provider whether it will work in Italy and what the charges will be. Technology in Italy is GSM. Unless you have a triband phone, it's unlikely that a mobile bought for use in North America will work in Italy.

Time

Italy is on **Central European Time** (CET): one hour ahead of London, six hours ahead of New York and eight hours behind Sydney.

Tourist information

Before you leave home, you might want to contact the **Italian State Tourist Office** (ENIT) for maps and accommodation listings – though you can usually pick up far fuller information from tourist offices in Italy. Details of every town's tourist offices are given in the Guide.

TUSCANY AND UMBRIA WEBSITES

ⓦ **enit.it** Italian State Tourist Board.

ⓦ **museionline.it** Links to museums and exhibition sites.

ⓦ **terraditoscana.com** Well-designed, informative site covering every aspect of Tuscany from walking and sleeping to wild flowers and local cuisine.

ⓦ **www.turismo.toscana.it** Official website of the Tuscan tourist board.

ⓦ **regioneumbria.eu** Official website of the Umbria tourist board.

Travellers with disabilities

As part of the **European Turismo per Tutti** (Tourism for All) project, Italian museum, transport and accommodation facilities for the disabled have improved remarkably in recent years. However, stairs and steps continue to present the most obvious difficulties, while other problems can arise from cars being parked thoughtlessly, and from the sheer distances of car parks from old-town centres. Public transport is becoming more attuned to the needs of travellers with disabilities, but bus services are still more of a challenge than trains. Another thing to bear in mind – especially in Florence – is that budget hotels often occupy the upper floors of town houses, and may not have lifts; always check before booking.

Travelling with children

Children are adored in Italy and will be made a fuss of in the street, and welcomed and catered for in bars and restaurants. The only hazards in summer are the heat and sun. The rhythms of the summer climate tend to modify the way you approach the day, and you'll soon find it quite natural to use siesta-time to recover flagging energy, and to carry on past normal bedtimes at night. In high summer, it's not unusual to see Italian children out at midnight, and not looking much the worse for it. You can buy **baby** equipment – nappies, creams and foods – in pharmacies.

See the website ⓦ www.travelforkids.com for more information on child-friendly sights and activities in Italy.

Florence

THE FLORENCE SKYLINE AND PONTE VECCHIO

1

Florence

Since the early nineteenth century, when Stendhal staggered around its streets in a stupor of aesthetic delight, Florence (Firenze) has been celebrated as the pinnacle of Italian culture, and for most modern visitors the first impressions tend to confirm the myth. The stupendous dome of the cathedral is visible the moment you step out of the train station, and when you reach Piazza del Duomo the close-up view is even more breathtaking, with the multicoloured duomo rising behind the marble-clad bapistry. Nearby, beyond the Piazza della Signoria and the immense Palazzo Vecchio, the water is spanned by the shop-laden medieval Ponte Vecchio, with the magnificent San Miniato al Monte glistening on the hill behind. It's an astounding spectacle.

It has to be said, however, that intensive exploration of the city is not always a stress-free business. The wonders of Florence are known to the whole world, which means that in high season the sheer number of tourists at the major sights is overwhelming – the Uffizi, for instance, is all but impossible to get into unless you've prebooked your tickets. And yet, such is the wealth of monuments and artistic treasures here, it's impossible not to find the experience an enriching one.

Tuscany was the powerhouse of what has come to be known as the Renaissance, and Florence – the region's dominant political and cultural centre – is the continent's supreme monument to European civilization's major evolutionary shift into modernity. The development of this new sensibility can be plotted stage by stage in the vast picture collection of the **Uffizi**, and charted in the sculpture of the **Bargello**, the **Museo dell'Opera del Duomo** and the guild church of **Orsanmichele**. Equally revelatory are the fabulously decorated chapels of **Santa Croce** and **Santa Maria Novella**, forerunners of such astonishing creations as Masaccio's frescoes at **Santa Maria del Carmine**, Fra' Angelico's serene paintings at **San Marco** and Andrea del Sarto's work at **Santissima Annunziata**, to name just a few. During the fifteenth century, the likes of Brunelleschi and Alberti began to transform the cityscape of Florence, raising buildings that were to provide generations of architects with examples from which to take a lead, and still adorn the fabric of the city today. The Renaissance emphasis on harmony and rational design is expressed with unrivalled eloquence in Brunelleschi's interiors of **San Lorenzo**, **Santo Spirito** and the **Cappella dei Pazzi**, and in Alberti's work at Santa Maria Novella

THE DUOMO

Highlights

❶ The Duomo Climb Brunelleschi's dome, the city's signature building. **See p.46**

❷ The Uffizi The world's greatest collection of Italian Renaissance paintings. **See p.64**

❸ The Bargello Magnificent sculpture and applied arts collection. **See p.74**

❹ Santa Maria Novella Amazing frescoes by Masaccio, Ghirlandaio, Uccello and others. See p.82

❺ San Lorenzo Crowds flock to see *David* at the Accademia, but the Michelangelos at San Lorenzo are just as remarkable. **See p.87**

❻ San Marco Showcase for the devotional art of Fra' Angelico. **See p.94**

❼ Santa Croce Giotto's frescoes and Brunelleschi's superb Pazzi chapel. **See p.102**

❽ Palazzo Pitti Another top-flight art gallery, and Florence's finest garden. **See p.110**

❾ Cappella Brancacci Epoch-defining art in the church of Santa Maria del Carmine. See p.116

❿ Vinai Stop for a snack at one of Florence's last remaining stand-up wine bars. **See p.130**

HIGHLIGHTS ARE MARKED ON THE MAP ON P.44

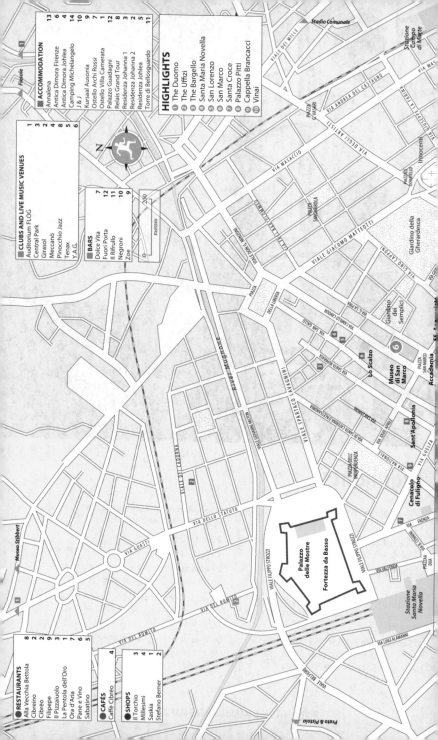

FLORENCE

1

FLORENTINE ADDRESSES

Note that there is a double **address** system in Florence, one for businesses and one for all other properties – that, at least, is the theory behind it, though in fact the distinction is far from rigorous. Business addresses are followed by the letter **r** (for *rosso*) and are marked on the building with a red number on a white plate, sometimes with an r after the numeral. The two series are independent of each other, which means that no. 5 may be followed by no. 18r, for example, while no. 120 might be a long way from no. 120r. Properties are numbered according to their relation to the river: if the street is parallel to the Arno, numbers start from the east; if the street is perpendicular to the river, the numbering starts from the end nearer the water.

and the Palazzo Rucellai. The bizarre architecture of San Lorenzo's **Sagrestia Nuova** and the marble statuary of the **Accademia** – home of the *David* – display the full genius of **Michelangelo**, the dominant creative figure of sixteenth-century Italy. Every quarter of Florence can boast a church or collection worth an extended call, and the enormous **Palazzo Pitti** constitutes a museum district on its own: half a dozen museums are gathered here, one of them an art gallery that any city would envy.

So there are sights enough to fill a month, but to enjoy a visit fully it's best to ration yourself to a couple each day, and spend the rest of your time strolling and involving yourself in the life of the city. Though Florence might seem a little sedate on the surface, its university – and the presence of large numbers of language and art schools – guarantees a fair range of term-time diversions and **nightlife**. The city has some excellent **restaurants** and **café-bars** amid the tourist joints, and there's certainly no shortage of special events – from the high-art festivities of the **Maggio Musicale** to the licensed bedlam of the **Calcio Storico**, a series of costumed football matches held in June.

The centre of the city

Piazza del Duomo – location of the **Duomo**, the **Baptistery**, the **Campanile** and the great sculpture collection of the **Museo dell'Opera del Duomo** – is one of the two nuclei of the city, and the focal point of its religious life. The other nucleus, **Piazza della Signoria** – the site of the mighty **Palazzo Vecchio** and forecourt to the **Uffizi** – has always been the centre of its secular existence, as the stage for major civic events and the home of the city's bureaucrats. After work hundreds of Florentines take their evening passeggiata along the shop-lined pedestrianized avenue of **Via dei Calzaiuoli**, which connects the two great squares, passing the extraordinary church of **Orsanmichele**. The nearby **Badìa Fiorentina** is the most important of several buildings in a district that has strong associations with Florence's – indeed Italy's – foremost poet, Dante Alighieri, and stands opposite the forbidding bulk of the **Bargello**, where you'll find another superb assemblage of sculpture, plus excellent collections of enamels, ivories, glassware, silverware and other *objets d'art*. And as a corrective to the notion that Florence's contribution to European civilization has been limited to the arts, you might call in at the fascinating **Museo Galileo**, which is tucked away at the back of the Uffizi.

The Duomo

Piazza del Duomo • Mon–Wed & Fri 10am–5pm, Thurs 10am–4.30pm (May & Oct closes 4pm, July–Sept closes 5pm), Sat 10am–4.45pm, Sun 1.30–4.45pm • Free • ⊕ www.operaduomo.firenze.it

Some time in the seventh century the seat of the Bishop of Florence was transferred from San Lorenzo to Santa Reparata, a sixth-century church which stood on the site of the present-day **Duomo**, or **Santa Maria del Fiore**. Later generations modified this older church until 1294, when Florence's rulers were stung into action by the magnificence

FLORENCE'S MUSEUMS: TICKETS AND INFORMATION

All of Florence's state-run museums belong to an association called **Firenze Musei**, which sets aside a daily quota of tickets that can be **reserved in advance**. The Uffizi, the Accademia and the Bargello belong to this group, as do the Palazzo Pitti museums (including the Bóboli gardens), the Medici chapels, the archeological museum and the San Marco museum. The best source of **online information** for all of these museums is ⓦ uffizi.firenze.it. For Florence's civic museums – of which the main ones are the Museo Bardini, Museo di Santa Maria Novella, Palazzo Vecchio and the Cappella Brancacci – the website is ⓦ museicivicifiorentini.it.

You can **reserve tickets** for state-run museums (booking fee of €4 for Uffizi and Accademia, €3 for the rest) by phoning ☎ 055 294 883 (Mon–Fri 8.30am–6.30pm, Sat 8.30am–12.30pm), online at ⓦ firenzemusei.it and ⓦ uffizi.firenze.it, at the Firenze Musei booth at Orsanmichele (Mon–Sat 10am–5.30pm), and at the museums themselves, in the case of the Uffizi and Pitti. If you book by phone, an English-speaking operator will allocate you a ticket for a specific hour, to be collected at the museum at a specific time, shortly before entry. That's the theory, but in reality the line tends to be engaged for long periods at a stretch. Generally, the under-publicized Orsanmichele booth – which is set into the wall of the church on the Via Calzaiuoli side – is the easiest option. Prebooking is very strongly recommended at any time of year for the Uffizi (see p.66 for more) and the Accademia, whose allocation of reservable tickets is often sold out many days ahead.

The **Firenze Card**, costing €50, is valid for 72 hours from the first time you use it, and gives access to more than thirty museums in greater Florence (including all the big ones), plus unlimited use of public transport. It also enables you to bypass the queues, as the major museums have separate gates for card holders. You do, though, have to pack a hell of a lot into each day to make it worth the investment. The card can be bought at the Via Cavour and Piazza Stazione tourist offices, from the Uffizi, Bargello, Palazzo Pitti, Museo Bardini and Museo di Santa Maria Novella, and at ⓦ firenzecard.it.

Admission to all state-run museums is free for EU citizens under 18 and over 65; 18–25s get a fifty percent discount, as do teachers. Nearly all of Florence's major museums are routinely **closed on Monday**. In the majority of cases, museum ticket offices close thirty minutes before the museum itself. At the Palazzo Vecchio and Museo Stibbert, however, it's one hour before, while at the Uffizi, Bargello, Museo dell'Opera del Duomo, the dome of the Duomo, the Campanile and Pitti museums it's 45 minutes.

of newly commissioned cathedrals in Pisa and Siena. Their own cathedral, they lamented, was "crudely built and too small for such a city".

A suitably immodest plan to remedy this shortcoming was ordered from Arnolfo di Cambio, who drafted a scheme to create the largest church in the Roman Catholic world and "surpass anything of its kind produced by the Greeks and Romans in the times of their greatest power". Progress on the project faltered after Arnolfo's death in 1302, but by 1380 Francesco Talenti and a string of mostly jobbing architects had brought the nave to completion. By 1418 the tribunes (apses) and the dome's supporting drum were also completed. Only the dome itself – no small matter – remained unfinished (see p.53).

The exterior

Parts of the Duomo's exterior date back to Arnolfo's era, but most of the overblown and pernickety main **facade** is a nineteenth-century simulacrum of a Gothic front. The original facade, which was never finished, was pulled down in 1587 on the orders of Ferdinand I. A competition to produce a new front proved unsuccessful, and for three centuries the cathedral remained faceless. After Florence became capital of the newly unified Italy in 1865, however, no fewer than 92 plans were submitted. The winning entry, by Emilio de Fabris, was completed in 1887. To its credit, the new frontage at least retained the original colour scheme and materials, with marble quarried from three different sources: white from Carrara, red from the Maremma and green from Prato.

The cathedral's south (right) side is the oldest part of the exterior – both its side portals deserve a glance – but the most attractive adornment is the **Porta della Mandorla**

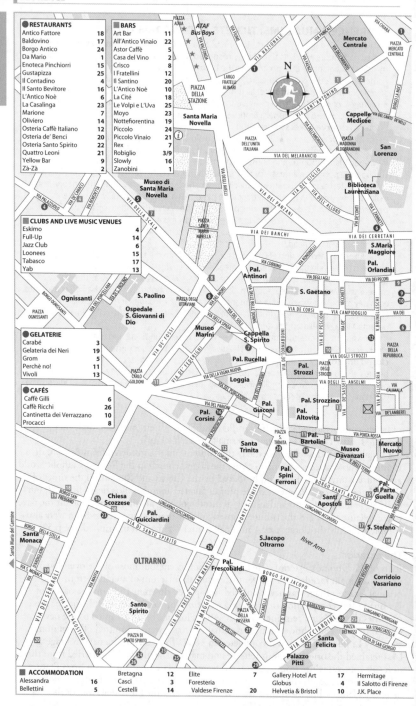

1

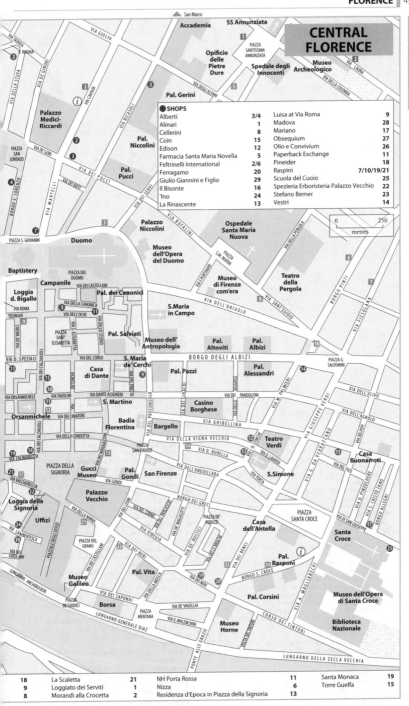

San Marco

CENTRAL FLORENCE

● **SHOPS**

Alberti	3/4	Luisa at Via Roma	9
Alinari	1	Madova	28
Cellerini	8	Mariano	17
Coin	15	Obsequium	27
Edison	12	Olio e Convivium	26
Farmacia Santa Maria Novella	5	Paperback Exchange	11
Feltrinelli International	2/6	Pineider	18
Ferragamo	20	Raspini	7/10/19/21
Giulio Giannini e Figlio	29	Scuola del Cuoio	25
Il Bisonte	16	Spezieria Erboristeria Palazzo Vecchio	22
'Ino	24	Stefano Bemer	23
La Rinascente	13	Vestri	14

0 — 250 metres

18	La Scaletta	21	NH Porta Rossa	11	Santa Monaca	19
9	Loggiato dei Serviti	1	Nizza	6	Torre Guelfa	15
8	Morandi alla Crocetta	2	Residenza d'Epoca in Piazza della Signoria	13		

1

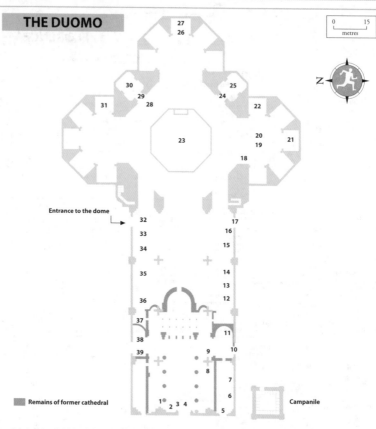

THE DUOMO

0 _____ 15
metres

N

Entrance to the dome

Remains of former cathedral

Campanile

1 Stained glass: St Stephen (left), Assumption (centre) and St Lawrence (right), Lorenzo Ghiberti
2 Tomb of Antonio d'Orso, bishop of Florence (1323), Tino da Camaino
3 Mosaic: Coronation of the Virgin (1300), attributed to Gaddo Gaddi
4 Clock (1443) – decoration, Paolo Uccello
5 Stained glass: St Lawrence and Angels, Lorenzo Ghiberti
6 Tondo: Bust of Brunelleschi (1447), Andrea Cavalcanti
7 Bust: Giotto at Work (1490), Benedetto da Maiano
8 Gothic water stoup (1380), attributed to Urbano da Cortona
9 Entrance and steps to Santa Reparata
10 Porta del Campanile
11 Painting: St Bartholomew Enthroned (1408), Rossello di Jacopo Franchi
12 Painted sepulchral monument: Fra Luigi Marsili (1439), Bicci di Lorenzo
13 Statue: Isaiah (1427), Bernardo Ciuffagni
14 Painted sepulchral monument: Archbishop Pietro Corsino of Florence (1422), Bicci di Lorenzo
15 Stained glass: Six Saints (1395), Agnolo Gaddi
16 Bust: Marsilio Ficino (1521), philosopher friend of Cosimo de' Medici, holding a copy of Plato's works
17 Porta dei Canonici: sculpture (1395–99), Lorenzo d'Ambrogio
18 Eight statues of the Apostles (1547–72) against the pillars of the octagon
19 Tribune: each tribune has five chapels; each chapel has two levels of stained glass, most by Lorenzo Ghiberti
20 Frescoes below windows of west and east tribunes: Saints (1440), attributed to Bicci di Lorenzo
21 Altar, attributed to Michelozzo

22 Fresco fragment: Madonna del Popolo (13th century), attributed to Giotto
23 Dome fresco cycle: The Last Judgement (1572–79), Giorgio Vasari and Federico Zuccari
24 Enamelled terracotta (above door): Ascension (1450), Luca della Robbia
25 Sagrestia Vecchia (Old Sacristy)
26 Bronze reliquary (1432–42) of St Zenobius (below altar), Lorenzo Ghiberti
27 Candle-holders: Two Angels (1450), Luca della Robbia
28 Enamelled terracotta: Resurrection (1444), Luca della Robbia
29 Bronze doors (1446–67), Luca della Robbia and Michelozzo
30 Sagrestia Nuova (New Sacristy): intarsia (1436–45), Benedetto and Giuliano da Maiano
31 Former site of Michelangelo's Pietà, currently in the Museo dell'Opera
32 Porta della Mandorla: sculpture, Nanni di Banco and Donatello
33 Painting: Dante with the Divine Comedy (1465), Domenico di Michelino
34 Fresco: SS Cosmas and Damian (1429), Bicci di Lorenzo; two windows by Agnolo Gaddi
35 Statue (in recess) designed for old cathedral facade: King David (1434), Bernardo Ciuffagni
36 Equestrian portrait: Sir John Hawkwood (1436), Paolo Uccello
37 Equestrian portrait: Niccolò da Tolentino (1456), Andrea del Castagno
38 Bust: Antonio Squarcialupi (former cathedral organist, 1490), Benedetto da Maiano
39 The Prophet Joshua (1415), Nanni di Bartolo; the head is by Donatello

(number 32 on our plan), on the other side. This takes its name from the almond-shaped frame (or *mandorla*) that contains the grime-streaked relief of the *Assumption of the Virgin* (1414–21), sculpted by Nanni di Banco; the lunette features a mosaic of the Annunciation (1491) to a design by Ghirlandaio. The two heads in profile either side of the gable may be early works by Donatello.

The interior

The Duomo's **interior** is the converse of the exterior – a vast, uncluttered enclosure of bare masonry. The fourth-largest church in Europe, it once held a congregation of ten thousand to hear Savonarola (see p.95) deliver one of his inflammatory sermons, and the ambience is still more that of a public assembly hall than a devotional building. Its apparently barren walls, however, hold a far greater accumulation of treasures than at first appears.

The frescoes

The most conspicuous decorations are a pair of memorials to *condottieri* (mercenary commanders). Paolo Uccello's monument to **Sir John Hawkwood** (36), created in 1436, is often cited as the epitome of Florentine mean-spiritedness; according to local folklore – unsupported by any evidence – the mercenary captain of Florence's army was promised a proper equestrian statue as his memorial, then was posthumously fobbed off with this *trompe l'oeil* version. Perhaps the slight was deserved. Before being employed by Florence, Hawkwood and his White Company had marauded their way through Tuscany, holding entire cities to ransom under threat of ransack. Look back at the entrance wall and you'll see another Uccello contribution to the interior – a **clock** (4) adorned with the four Evangelists. It uses the old *hora italica*, common in Italy until the eighteenth century, when the 24th hour of the day ended at sunset.

Andrea del Castagno's monument to **Niccolò da Tolentino** (37), created twenty years later than the Hawkwood fresco, is clearly derived from it, but has an aggressive edge that's typical of this artist. Just beyond the horsemen, Domenico di Michelino's 1465 work *Dante Explaining the Divine Comedy* (33) gives Brunelleschi's dome – then only nearing completion – a place scarcely less prominent than the mountain of Purgatory.

Judged by size, the major work of art in the Duomo is the 1572–79 fresco of **The Last Judgement** (23), which fills much of the interior of the dome. Even at the time of its execution, however, a substantial body of opinion thought Vasari and Zuccari's combined effort did nothing but deface Brunelleschi's masterpiece.

The sacristies

Barriers usually prevent you from getting close to the high altar, so you might not be able to look into the **Sagrestia Nuova** (30), where the lavish panelling is inlaid with beautiful intarsia work (1436–45) by Benedetto and Giuliano Maiano. The relief of the *Resurrection* (1442) above the entrance is by Luca della Robbia, his first important commission in the enamelled terracotta for which he became famous. The stunning **sacristy door** (29) created in conjunction with Michelozzo (1445–69) was his only work in bronze. It was in this sacristy that Lorenzo de' Medici took refuge in 1478 after his brother Giuliano had been mortally stabbed on the altar steps by the Pazzi conspirators (see p.52): small portraits on the handles commemorate the brothers.

Across the way, della Robbia's *Ascension* (1450) can be seen above the door of the **Sagrestia Vecchia** (25); it was once accompanied by Donatello's sublime *cantoria*, or choir-loft, now in the Museo dell'Opera del Duomo. Luca della Robbia's equally mesmeric *cantoria*, in the same museum, occupied a matching position above the Sagrestia Nuova.

Santa Reparata

Mon–Wed & Fri 10am–5pm, Sat 10am–4.45pm • €3

In the 1960s, remnants of the Duomo's predecessor, **Santa Reparata** (9), were uncovered underneath the west end of the nave, where a flight of steps leads down into

1

the excavation, a complicated jigsaw of Roman, Paleochristian and Romanesque remains, plus fragments of mosaic and fourteenth-century frescoes: to make sense of it all, you'll have to keep referring to the colour-coded model in the farthest recess of the crypt. In 1972, further digging revealed **Brunelleschi's tomb**, a marble slab so simple that it had lain forgotten under the south aisle. The tombstone's present position is hardly any more glorious (it can be seen, for free, through a grille to the left at the foot of the steps), but the architect does at least have the honour of being one of the very few Florentines to be buried in the Duomo itself.

THE PAZZI CONSPIRACY

The **Pazzi Conspiracy**, perhaps the most compelling of all Florence's murkier acts of treachery, had its roots in the 1472 election of **Sixtus IV**, a pope who distributed money and favours with a largesse remarkable even by papal standards. Six of his nephews were made cardinals, one of them, the uncouth **Girolamo Riario**, coming in for particularly preferential treatment. Sixtus's plan was that Riario should take over the town of Imola as a base for papal expansion, and accordingly he approached Lorenzo de' Medici for the necessary loan. Aware that Imola was too close to Milan and Bologna to be allowed to fall into papal hands, Lorenzo rebuffed the pope, despite the importance of the Vatican account with the Medici bank, and the family's role as agents for the papacy's alum mines in Tuscany (alum was vital to the dyeing industry, and therefore essential to Florence's textile trade). Enraged by the snub, and by Lorenzo's refusal to recognize **Francesco Salviati** as archbishop of Pisa (Sixtus had ignored an agreement by which appointments within the Florentine domain could only be made by mutual agreement), Sixtus turned to the Pazzi, the Medici's leading Florentine rivals as bankers in Rome.

Three co-conspirators met in Rome in the early months of 1477: Riario, now in possession of Imola but eager for greater spoils; Salviati, incandescent at Lorenzo's veto; and **Francesco de' Pazzi**, head of the Pazzis' Rome operation. Military muscle was to be provided by a mercenary called **Montesecco**, who proved wary of the whole enterprise: "Beware of what you do," he counselled, "Florence is a big affair." In the end he made his cooperation conditional on papal blessing, a benediction that was readily obtained. "I do not wish the death of anyone on any account," said Sixtus, "since it does not accord with our office to consent to such a thing" – yet he knew full well Lorenzo's death was essential if the plot was to succeed. "Go, and do what you wish," he added, "provided there be no killing." **Jacopo de' Pazzi**, the Pazzis' wizened godfather, was also won over by Sixtus's disingenuous support, despite being on good terms with the Medici – indeed, one of his nephews was married to Lorenzo's sister.

After numerous false starts, it was decided to **murder** Lorenzo and his brother Giuliano whilst they attended Mass in the cathedral. The date set was Sunday, April 26, 1478. Montesecco, however, now refused "to add sacrilege to murder", so Lorenzo's murder was delegated to two embittered priests, Maffei and Bagnone, whereas Giuliano was to be dispatched by Francesco de' Pazzi and **Bernardo Baroncelli**, a violent Pazzi sidekick deeply in debt to the family. Salviati, meanwhile, accompanied by an armed troop, was to seize control of the Palazzo della Signoria.

It all went horribly wrong. Giuliano was killed in a crazed frenzy, his skull shattered and his body rent with nineteen stab wounds, but Lorenzo managed to escape, fleeing wounded to the Duomo's new sacristy, where he and his supporters barricaded themselves behind its heavy bronze doors. Across the city, Salviati was separated from his troops and soon arrested.

Apprised of the plot, a furious mob dispensed **summary justice** to several of the conspirators: Salviati's troops were massacred to a man, whilst Salviati and Francesco de' Pazzi were hanged from a window of the Palazzo della Signoria. Maffei and Bagnone, the bungling priests, were castrated and hanged. Baroncelli escaped to Constantinople but was extradited and executed; Montesecco was tortured, then given a soldier's execution in the Bargello. Jacopo's end was the most sordid. Having escaped Florence, he was recaptured, tortured, stripped naked and hanged alongside the decomposing Salviati. He was then buried in Santa Croce, but exhumed by a mob, who blamed heavy rains on his evil spirit. His corpse was dragged through the streets and finally propped up outside the Pazzi palace, where his head was used as a door knocker. Eventually the putrefying body was thrown in the Arno, fished out, flogged and hanged again, and finally cast back into the river.

1

BRUNELLESCHI'S DOME

Since Arnolfo di Cambio's model of the Duomo collapsed some time in the fourteenth century, nobody has been sure quite how he intended to crown his achievement. In 1367 Neri di Fioraventi proposed the construction of a magnificent **cupola** that was to span nearly 43m (broader than the dome of Rome's Pantheon, which had remained the world's largest for 1300 years) and rise higher than the vaulting of any Gothic cathedral.

There was just one problem: nobody had worked out how to build the thing. Medieval arches were usually built on wooden "centring", a network of timbers that held the stone in place until the mortar was set. In the case of the Duomo, the weight of the stone would have been too great for the timber, and the space to be spanned was too great for the measuring cords that would be needed to guide the masons. A committee of the masons' guild was set up to solve the dilemma, and after years of bickering the project was thrown open to competition. A goldsmith and clockmaker called **Filippo Brunelleschi** presented the winning scheme, defeating Ghiberti in the process – revenge of sorts for Ghiberti's triumph seventeen years earlier in the competition to design the Baptistery doors. Doom-mongers, Ghiberti among them, criticized Brunelleschi at every turn, eventually forcing the authorities to employ both rivals. An exasperated Brunelleschi feigned illness and resigned. Ghiberti, left to his own devices, found himself baffled, and in 1423 Brunelleschi was invited to become the dome's sole "inventor and chief director".

The key to Brunelleschi's success lay in the construction of the dome as two masonry shells, each built as a stack of ever-diminishing rings: secured with hidden stone beams and enormous iron chains, these concentric circles formed a lattice that was filled with lightweight bricks laid in a herringbone pattern that prevented the higher sections from falling inward. The dome's completion was marked by the **consecration** of the cathedral on March 25, 1436 – Annunciation Day, and the Florentine New Year – in a ceremony conducted by the pope. Even then, the topmost piece, the lantern, remained unfinished, with many people convinced the dome could support no further weight. But once again Brunelleschi won the day, beginning work on the dome's final stage in 1446, a few months before his death. The whole thing was finally completed in the late 1460s, when the cross and gilded ball, both cast by Verrocchio, were hoisted into place.

It remains the largest masonry dome in the world. Only the gallery around the base remains incomplete – abandoned with just one face finished after Michelangelo compared it to "cages for crickets". This criticism aside, Michelangelo was awestruck: gazing on the cupola he is supposed to have said: *Come te non voglio, meglio di te non posso* ("Similar to you I will not, better than you I cannot").

The dome

Mon–Fri 8.30am–7pm, Sat 8.30am–5.40pm • €8

Climbing the dome is an amazing experience, but you should be prepared for a long queue at the entrance (on the north flank of the nave), and for the 463 lung-busting steps. Claustrophobics should also note that the climb involves some very confined spaces.

After an initial ascent, you emerge onto a narrow gallery that runs around the interior of the dome, with a dizzying view down onto the maze-patterned pavement of the nave. It's also the best vantage point from which to inspect the seven **stained-glass roundels**, designed by Uccello, Ghiberti, Castagno and Donatello, below Vasari's *Last Judgement* fresco. Beyond the gallery, you enter the confines of the **dome** itself. As you clamber up between the inner and outer shells, you can observe many ingenious features of Brunelleschi's construction: the ribs and arches, the herringbone brickwork, the wooden struts that support the outer shell – even the hooks and holes left for future generations of repairers. From the base of the white marble lantern that crowns the dome, the views across the city are breathtaking.

The Campanile

Piazza del Duomo • Daily 8.30am–7.30pm • €6 • ⊕ www.operaduomo.firenze.it

The **Campanile** was begun in 1334 by Giotto during his period as official city architect and *capo maestro* (head of works) of the Duomo. By the time of his death three years

1

later, the base – the first of five levels – had been completed. Andrea Pisano, fresh from creating the Baptistery's south doors, continued construction of the second storey (1337–42), probably in accordance with Giotto's plans. Work was rounded off by Francesco Talenti, who rectified deficiencies in Giotto's original calculations in the process: the base's original walls teetered on the brink of collapse until he doubled their thickness. When completed, the bell tower reached 84.7m, well over the limit set by the city in 1324 for civic towers.

The tower's decorative **sculptures and reliefs** (they are copies, the originals being in the Museo dell'Opera del Duomo) are intended to illustrate humanity's progress from original sin to a state of divine grace, a progress facilitated by manual labour, the arts and the sacraments, and guided by the influence of the planets and the cardinal and theological virtues. Thus the first storey is studded with two rows of bas-reliefs: the lower register (some designed by Giotto, but all executed by Pisano and pupils) illustrates the Creation and Arts and Industries, while in the diamond-shaped panels of the upper register are allegories of the Seven Planets, Seven Sacraments and Seven Virtues. A century or so later Luca della Robbia added the Five Liberal Arts (Grammar, Philosophy, Music, Arithmetic and Astrology) on the north face. Further works in the second-storey niches by Pisano were eventually replaced by Donatello and Nanni di Bartolo's figures of the Prophets, Sibyls, Patriarchs and Kings (1415–36).

The **parapet** at the top of the tower is a less lofty but in many ways more satisfying viewpoint than the cathedral dome, if only because the view takes in the Duomo itself. Be warned, though, that there are 414 steps to the summit – and no lift.

The Baptistery

Piazza del Duomo • Mon–Sat 12.15–7pm, Sun & first Sat of month 8.30am–2pm • €4 • ⊕ www.operaduomo.firenze.it

Generally thought to date from the sixth or seventh century, the **Baptistery** is Florence's oldest building – it was first documented in 897, when it was recorded as the city's cathedral before Santa Reparata. The Florentines were always conscious of their **Roman** ancestry, and for centuries believed that the Baptistery was converted from a Roman temple built to celebrate the defeat of Fiesole and the city's foundation. This belief was bolstered by the interior's ancient granite columns, probably taken from the city's Capitol (other columns from this site found their way to San Miniato). Further proof was apparently provided by traces of an ancient pavement mosaic, now thought to belong to a Roman bakery. But if the building itself is not Roman, its exterior marble cladding – applied between about 1060 and 1130 – is clearly classical in inspiration, while its most famous embellishments, the gilded **bronze doors**, mark the emergence of a more scholarly, self-conscious interest in the art of the ancient world.

The south doors

Responsibility for the Baptistery's improvement and upkeep lay with the Arte di Calimala, the most powerful of Florence's guilds, who initiated the building's eleventh-century revamp before, in the 1320s, turning their attention to the exterior, in particular to the question of a suitably majestic entrance. In this they were stung into action by arch-rival Pisa, whose cathedral was not only famous for its bronze portals, but whose craftsmen had recently completed some celebrated bronze doors for the cathedral at Monreale in Sicily.

The arrival of Andrea Pisano in Florence in 1330 offered the chance of similar glories. Within three months the Pisan sculptor had created wax models for what would become the Baptistery's **south doors**. (They were originally placed in the east portal, but were displaced by Ghiberti's "Gates of Paradise".) It took another eight years to cast the doors in bronze. Twenty of the 28 panels form a narrative on the life of St John the

1

Baptist, patron saint of Florence and the Baptistery's dedicatee; the lowest eight reliefs depict Humility and the Cardinal and Theological Virtues. The figures above the portal – the Baptist, Salome and executioner – are copies of late sixteenth-century additions; the originals are in the Museo dell'Opera del Duomo.

The north doors

Some sixty years of financial and political turmoil, and the ravages of the Black Death, prevented further work on the Baptistery's other entrances until 1401, when a competition was held to design a new set of doors, each of the six main entrants being asked to create a panel showing the Sacrifice of Isaac.

The judges were equally impressed by the work of two young goldsmiths, Brunelleschi and **Lorenzo Ghiberti** (both winning entries are displayed in the Bargello). Unable to choose, the judges suggested that the two work in tandem. Brunelleschi replied that if he couldn't do the job alone he wasn't interested – whereupon the contract was handed to Ghiberti, leaving his rival to stomp off to study architecture in Rome. Ghiberti, barely 20 years old, was to devote much of the next 25 years to this one project, albeit in the company of distinguished assistants such as Masolino, Donatello and Paolo Uccello. His fame rests almost entirely on the extraordinary result.

His **north doors** (1403–24) show a new naturalism and classicized sense of composition, copying Pisano's 28-panel arrangement while transcending its Gothic approach: the upper twenty panels depict scenes from the New Testament, while the eight lower panels describe the Four Evangelists and Four Doctors of the Church.

The east doors

The north doors, while extraordinary, are as nothing to the sublime **east doors** (1425–52), ordered from Ghiberti as soon as the first set was finished. The artist would spend some 27 years on the new project. These doors have long been known as the "Gates of Paradise", supposedly because Michelangelo once remarked that they deserved to be the portals of heaven. However, it's more likely that the name came about because the space between a cathedral and its baptistery was called the *Paradiso*, as the sacrament of baptism put its recipient on the threshold of paradise.

Unprecedented in the subtlety of their casting, the **Old Testament scenes** – the Creation, the Ten Commandments, the Sacrifice of Isaac and so on – are a primer of early Renaissance art, using rigorous perspective, gesture and sophisticated groupings to intensify the drama of each scene. Ghiberti's power of compression and detail is such that several narratives are often woven into a single scene. The sculptor has also included an understandably self-satisfied self-portrait in the frame of the left-hand door: his is the fourth head from the top of the right-hand band – the bald chap with the smirk. The gorgeous golden doors now in place are reproductions; the original panels are exhibited in the Museo dell'Opera del Duomo.

The pair of pitted **marble columns** to the side of the east doors were presented by the city of Pisa in the twelfth century. Another marble column, just north of the Baptistery, is decorated with bronze branches and leaves to commemorate a miracle of January 429 AD, brought about by the body of St Zenobius, Florence's first bishop; as the corpse was being carried from San Lorenzo into Santa Reparata it brushed against a barren elm here, which thereupon sprang into leaf.

The interior

The Baptistery **interior** is stunning, with its black-and-white marble cladding and miscellany of ancient columns below a blazing **mosaic ceiling**. Mosaics were not a Florentine speciality, but in the thirteenth century they were the predominant decorative medium. Encouraged by the interest surrounding the restoration of mosaics then taking place in the early Christian basilicas of Rome and Ravenna, the city was keen to match its rivals, principally Venice.

The earliest mosaics (1225) lie above the square apse, and depict the Virgin and John the Baptist. Above them, a wheel of prophets encircles the Lamb of God. The main vault is dominated by a vast figure of Christ in Judgement, flanked by depictions of Paradise and Hell. Just to the left of the monstrous, man-eating Lucifer, the poet Virgil (in a white cloak) can be seen leading Dante (in black) through the Inferno. These figures were a later insertion, added after the poet's death. The other five sections of the octagonal ceiling depict Biblical scenes, beginning above the north doors with the Creation, and proceeding through the stories of Joseph and John the Baptist towards the Crucifixion and Resurrection, seen above the south doors.

The interior's semi-abstract **mosaic pavement** also dates from the thirteenth century. The empty octagon at its centre marks the spot once occupied by the huge font in which every child born in the city during the previous twelve months would be baptized on March 25 (New Year's Day in the old Florentine calendar).

To the right of the altar lies the **tomb of Baldassare Cossa**, the schismatic Pope John XXIII, who was deposed in 1415 and died in Florence in 1419. At the time of his death he was a guest of his financial adviser and close friend, Giovanni di Bicci de' Medici, the man who established the Medici at the political forefront of Florence. It was through Pope John that Giovanni became chief banker to the Papal Curia, a deal that laid the foundations of the Medici fortune: for years over half the Medici's profits would come from just two Rome-based banks. The monument, draped by an illusionistic marble canopy, is the work of Donatello and his pupil Michelozzo.

Museo dell'Opera del Duomo

Piazza del Duomo 9 • Mon–Sat 9am–7.30pm, Sun 9am–1.40pm • €6 • ⓦ www.operaduomo.firenze.it

In 1296 a body called the Opera del Duomo, literally the "Work of the Duomo", was created to oversee the maintenance of the Duomo. In the early fifteenth century it took occupation of a building opposite the east end of the cathedral, which now also houses the **Museo dell'Opera del Duomo**, a repository of the most precious and fragile works of art from the Duomo, Baptistery and Campanile, second only to the Bargello as an overview of the sculpture of Florence.

The ground floor

Beyond the ticket office, rooms devoted to sculpture from the Baptistery (mostly works by Tino da Camaino) and the Duomo's lateral doors precede the museum's **courtyard**: it was here that much of Michelangelo's *David* was sculpted. Now glazed over, the courtyard is home to Ghiberti's panels from the "Doors of Paradise", sharing the space with the graceful *Baptism of Christ* (1502–25), by Andrea Sansovino and assistants.

The largest room on this floor is a large hall devoted to the original sculptures of the cathedral's west front, foremost among which are works by the cathedral's first architect, **Arnolfo di Cambio** (and his workshop), including an eerily glass-eyed *Madonna and Child*; all were rescued from Arnolfo's quarter-finished cathedral facade, which was pulled down in 1587. Equally striking are the sculptor's *St Reparata*, one of Florence's patron saints, and the ramrod-straight statue of *Boniface VIII*, whose corruption earned him a place in Dante's *Inferno*, which was partly written during

---

MUSEO DI FIRENZE COM'ERA

The **Museo di Firenze com'era** ("Museum of Florence as it used to be"), which charted the city's evolution from Roman times to the present, until recently occupied a building at Via dell'Oriuolo 24. It was a fascinating array of pictures and models, but very few people visited, so the decision has been taken to convert the collection into the core of a new **City Museum** that's being planned for the Palazzo Vecchio. No date has yet been set for the opening of this new museum.

1

Boniface's pontificate. Along the entrance wall are four seated figures of the Evangelists, also wrenched from the facade: Nanni di Banco's *St Luke* and **Donatello**'s *St John* are particularly fine.

The room off the far end of the hall features a sequence of **marble reliefs** (1547–72) by Bacio Bandinelli and Giovanni Bandini, part of an unfinished sequence of three hundred panels proposed for the choir of the cathedral. The adjoining modern **octagonal chapel** features an assembly of reliquaries which contain, among other saintly remains, the jaw of Saint Jerome and an index finger of John the Baptist. It's easy to miss the room off to the right of the **Lapidarium** (a collection of modest works in stone), which contains items removed from the cathedral's Porta della Mandorla, including a lovely terracotta *Creation of Eve* (1410) attributed to Donatello.

The upper floor

Upstairs on the mezzanine level stands **Michelangelo**'s anguished **Pietà** (1550–53), moved from the cathedral in 1981 while restoration of the dome was in progress, but probably fated to stay here. This is one of the sculptor's last works, carved when he was almost 80, and was intended for his own tomb; Vasari records that the face of Nicodemus is a self-portrait. Dissatisfied with the quality of the marble, Michelangelo mutilated the group by hammering off the left leg and arm of Christ; his pupil Tiberio Calcagni restored the arm, then finished off the figure of Mary Magdalene, turning her into a whey-faced supporting player.

The Cantorie and the Campanile statues

Although he's represented on the lower floor, it's upstairs that **Donatello**, the greatest of Michelangelo's precursors, really comes to the fore. The first room at the top of the stairs features his magnificent **Cantoria**, or choir-loft (1433–39), with its playground of boisterous putti. Facing it is another splendid *cantoria* (1431–38), the first-known major commission of the young Luca della Robbia (the originals are underneath, with casts replacing them in the *cantoria* itself); the earnest musicians embody the text from Psalm 150 which is inscribed on the frame: "Praise him with the sound of the trumpet; praise him with the psaltery and harp." Both lofts were dismantled and removed from their position above the cathedral's sacristies in 1688 on the occasion of the ill-fated marriage of Violante Beatrice of Bavaria to Ferdinand de' Medici. The ceremony gave the cathedral authorities the excuse to decorate the cathedral in a more fitting "modern" style, and the ensuing clearout left the *cantorie* languishing in dusty storage for some two centuries.

Around the room are arrayed the life-size figures that Donatello carved for the Campanile, perhaps the most powerful of which is the prophet Habbakuk, the intensity of whose gaze is said to have prompted the sculptor to seize it and yell "Speak, speak!" Donatello was apparently also responsible for the bald-headed statue's nickname, *Lo Zuccone* (the Pumpkin). Keeping company with Donatello's work are four Prophets (1348–50) and two Sybils (1342–48) attributed to Andrea Pisano, and *The Sacrifice of Isaac* (1421), a collaboration between Nanni di Bartolo and Donatello.

The Magdalene room

Donatello's later style is exemplified by the gaunt wooden figure of **Mary Magdalene** (1453–55), which confronts you on entering the room off the *cantorie* room. The *Magdalene* came from the Baptistery, as did the silver altar-front at the far end of the room, a dazzling summary of the life of St John the Baptist. Begun in 1366, the piece was completed in 1480, the culmination of a century of labour by, among others, Michelozzo (responsible for the central figure of *John the Baptist*), Verrocchio (the *Decapitation* to the right) and Antonio del Pollaiuolo (the *Birth of Jesus* on the left side), who was the chief creator of the silver cross atop the altar. Ranged around the walls are more reliquaries, fabrics, copes and other religious vestments, including 27 sublimely worked **needlework panels** that were produced between 1466 and 1487 by French, Flemish and Florentine artists, to designs by Pollaiuolo. Not surprisingly, they portray scenes from the life of the Baptist.

The Campanile bas-reliefs
In the room on the other side of the *cantorie* room you'll find the **bas-reliefs** that once adorned the Campanile. Though darkened with age, their allegorical panels remain both striking and intelligible, depicting the spiritual refinement of humanity through labour, the arts and, ultimately, the virtues and sacraments. The display reproduces the reliefs' original arrangement, the key panels being the hexagonal reliefs of the lower tier, all of which – save for the last five, by Luca della Robbia (1437–39) – were the work of Andrea Pisano and his son Nino (c.1348–50), probably to designs by Giotto.

The rest of the museum
A corridor at the end of Room II leads past a mock-up of Brunelleschi's building site, complete with broken bricks, wooden scaffolding and some of the tools that were used to build the dome, many invented specifically for the purpose by Brunelleschi, whose **death mask** is also here. The sequence of rooms beyond displays various proposals for

---

THE FLORENTINE REPUBLIC

Dante compared Florence's constant political struggles to a sick man forever shifting his position in bed, and indeed its medieval history often appears a catalogue of incessant civic unrest. Yet between 1293 and 1534 – bar the odd ruction – the city maintained a **republican** constitution that was embodied in well-defined institutions. The nucleus of this structure was formed by the city's merchants and guilds, who covertly controlled Florence as early as the twelfth century and formalized their influence during the so-called **Primo Popolo** (1248–59), a quasi-democratic regime whose ten-year rule, claimed Dante, was the only period of civic peace in Florence's history. During the **Secondo Popolo** (1284), the leading guilds, the *Arti Maggiori*, introduced the **Ordinamenti della Giustizia** (1293), a written constitution that entrenched mercantile power still further and was to be the basis of Florence's government for the next 250 years.

The rulers of this much-vaunted republic were drawn exclusively from the ranks of guild members over the age of 30, and were chosen in a public ceremony held every two months, the short tenure designed to prevent individuals or cliques assuming too much power. At this ceremony, the names of selected members were placed in eight leather bags (*borse*) kept in the sacristy of Santa Croce; the ones picked from the bags duly became the **Priori** (or *Signori*), forming a government called the **Signoria**, usually comprising nine men, most of them from the *Arti Maggiori*.

Headed by the **Gonfaloniere** (literally the "Standard-Bearer"), the *Signoria* consulted two elected councils or **Collegi** – the **Dodici Buonomini** (Twelve Citizens) and **Sedici Gonfalonieri** (Sixteen Standard-Bearers) – as well as committees introduced to deal with specific crises. Permanent officials included the Chancellor (a post once held by Machiavelli) and the **Podestà**, a chief magistrate brought in from a neighbouring city as an independent arbitrator, and housed in the Bargello. In times of extreme crisis, such as the Pazzi Conspiracy, all male citizens over the age of 14 were summoned to a **Parlamento** in Piazza della Signoria by the tolling of the Palazzo Vecchio's bell, known as the *Vacca* (Cow), after its deep, bovine tone. The *Parlamento* was then asked to approve a **Balìa**, a committee delegated to deal with the situation as it saw fit.

All this looked good on paper but in practice it was far from democratic. The lowliest workers, the **Popolo Minuto**, were excluded, as were the **Grandi**, or nobles. And despite the *Signoria*'s apparently random selection process, political cliques had few problems ensuring that only the names of likely supporters found their way into the *borse*. If a rogue candidate slipped through the net, or things went awry, then a *Parlamento* could be summoned, a *Balìa* formed, and the offending person replaced by a pliable candidate. It was by such means that the mercantile dynasties of Florence – the Peruzzi, the Albizzi, the Strozzi, and of course the Medici – retained their power even when not technically in office.

completing the balcony of the drum below the cupola and the Duomo's west front, including models created by Michelangelo, Giuliano da Maiano, Giambologna, Antonio da Sangallo and Andrea Sansovino. The wooden model of the **cathedral lantern** is presumed to have been made by Brunelleschi as part of his winning proposal for the design of the lantern in 1436. The final room shows plans submitted to the three competitions held in the 1860s, when Florence was briefly capital of Italy and the question of the facade standing "ignominious in faded stucco", as George Eliot put it, once more became pressing.

The Museo del Bigallo

Piazza San Giovanni 1 • Wed–Mon 9.30am–5.30pm • €5 • ⓦ bigallo.net

The **Loggia del Bigallo**, which stands on the south side of the Baptistery, was built in the 1350s for the Compagnia della Misericordia, a charitable organization founded by St Peter Martyr in 1244, to give aid to the sick and to bury the dead. (The Misericordia's current HQ is just across the road, with its ambulances parked outside.) By the time the loggia was built, the Misericordia was also functioning as an orphanage – the building was commissioned as a place to display abandoned babies, in the hope that they might be recognized before being given to foster parents. For most of the fifteenth century the Misericordia operated in conjunction with another orphanage, the Compagnia del Bigallo (from the village in which it began), hence the loggia's name. Nowadays it houses the three-room **Museo del Bigallo**, which contains a tiny collection of religious paintings commissioned by the two companies. As you might expect, the Madonna and Child is a dominant theme, and St Peter Martyr is present as well, but the two highlights are a remnant of a fresco painted on the outside of the loggia in 1386, showing the transfer of infants to their adoptive parents, and the *Madonna of the Misericordia*, painted by a follower of Bernardo Daddi in 1342, which features the oldest known panorama of Florence.

Piazza della Repubblica

A minute's stroll south of the Bigallo you'll find the vacant expanse of **Piazza della Repubblica**. Impressive solely for its size, this square was planned in the late 1860s, when it was decided to demolish the central marketplace (Mercato Vecchio) and the tenements of the Jewish quarter in order to give Florence a public space befitting the capital of the recently formed Italian nation. The clearance had not even begun when, in 1870, the capital was transferred to Rome, and it wasn't until 1885 that the Mercato Vecchio and its disease-ridden slums were finally swept away. On the west side a vast **arch** bears the triumphant inscription: "The ancient city centre restored to new life from the squalor of centuries." The freestanding **column** is the solitary trace of the piazza's history: once surrounded by stalls, it used to be topped by Donatello's statue of *Abundance*, and a bell that was rung to signal the start and close of trading.

Nowadays, Piazza della Repubblica is best known for the three large and expensive **cafés** that stand on the perimeter: the *Gilli*, the most attractive of the trio, founded way back in 1733 (albeit on a different site – it moved here in 1910); the *Giubbe Rosse*, once the intellectuals' café of choice (the Futurist manifesto was launched here in 1909); and the *Paszkowski*, which began business as a beer hall in the 1840s and now bears the suffix "Caffè Concerto", betokening the smarmy music with which it beguiles the piazza most evenings.

Piazza della Signoria

Piazza della Signoria took on a public role in 1307, when a small area was laid out to provide a suitable setting for the Palazzo Vecchio, then known as the Palazzo dei Priori.

1

All efforts to enlarge it over the next hundred years were hampered by work on the palace and Loggia della Signoria. Contemporary accounts talk of decades when the area was little more than a rubble-filled building site, but by 1385 it was completely paved, and wheeled traffic was banned from the area (as it still is). Further restructuring occurred during Cosimo I's reordering of the Uffizi around 1560, and more alterations followed in 1871, when the medieval Loggia dei Pisani was demolished, opening up much of the square's present-day westward sweep.

The piazza's statues

Florence's political volatility is encapsulated by the piazza's array of **statues**. From left to right, the line-up starts with Giambologna's equestrian statue of **Cosimo I** (1587–94): an echo of the famous Marcus Aurelius statue in Rome, it was designed to draw parallels between the power of Florence (and thus Cosimo) and the glory of imperial Rome. Next comes Ammannati's fatuous **Neptune Fountain** (1565–75), a tribute to Cosimo's prowess as a naval commander; Neptune, a lumpen lout of a figure, provoked Michelangelo to coin the rhyming put-down *Ammannato, Ammannato, che bel marmo hai rovinato* ("…what a fine piece of marble you've ruined").

After a copy of Donatello's **Marzocco** (1418–20), the original of which is in the Bargello, comes a copy of the same sculptor's **Judith and Holofernes** (1456–60), which freezes the action at the moment Judith's arm begins its scything stroke – a dramatic conception that no other sculptor of the period would have attempted. Commissioned by Cosimo de' Medici, this statue doubled as a fountain in the Palazzo Medici but was removed to the Piazza della Signoria after the expulsion of the family in 1495, to be displayed as an emblem of vanquished tyranny; a new inscription on the base reinforced the message for those too obtuse to get it. The original is in the Palazzo Vecchio.

Michelangelo's **David**, at first intended for the Duomo, was also installed here as a declaration of civic solidarity by the Florentine Republic; the original is now in the Accademia. Conceived as a partner piece to the *David*, Bandinelli's **Hercules and Cacus** (1534) was designed as a personal emblem of Cosimo I and a symbol of Florentine fortitude. It's a sobering thought that the marble might well have ended up as something more inspiring. In the late 1520s, when the Florentines were once again busy tearing the Medici emblem from every building on which it had been stuck, Michelangelo offered to carve a figure of Samson to celebrate the Republic's latest victory over tyranny; other demands on the artist's time put paid to this project, and the stone passed to Bandinelli, who duly vented his mediocrity on it. Benvenuto Cellini described the musclebound Hercules as "a sackful of melons".

Loggia della Signoria

The square's grace note, the **Loggia della Signoria**, was completed in 1382 and served as a dais for city dignitaries, a forum for meeting foreign emissaries and a platform for the swearing-in of public officials. Its alternative name, the Loggia dei Lanzi, comes from Cosimo I's bodyguard of Swiss lancers, who were garrisoned nearby.

In the corner nearest the Palazzo Vecchio stands a figure that has become one of the iconic images of the Renaissance, Benvenuto Cellini's **Perseus** (1545), which was made for Cosimo I to symbolize the triumph of firm Grand Ducal rule. The base is a copy of the original, which is now in the Bargello.

Equally attention-seeking is Giambologna's last work, **The Rape of the Sabine** (1583), the epitome of the Mannerist obsession with spiralling forms. The sculptor intended the piece as a study of old age, male strength and female beauty: the present name was coined later. The figures along the back wall are Roman works, while of the three central statues only one – Giambologna's **Hercules Slaying the Centaur** (1599) – deserves its place. The seven figures in the spandrels between the arches above depict the Virtues (1384–89), all carved to designs by Agnolo Gaddi save the head of *Faith*, which was replaced by Donatello when the original crashed to the ground.

1

Gucci Museo

Piazza della Signoria 10 • Daily 10am–8pm • €6

The fourteenth-century Palazzo della Mercanzia now houses the **Gucci Museo**, which opened in late 2011 to mark the ninetieth anniversary of Florence's most famous fashion house. As you'd expect, there are some fabulous clothes here (though the museum underplays the crucial part that Texan designer Tom Ford played in resurrecting the company in the 1990s), plus a plethora of ridiculous examples of brand extension, such as Gucci monogrammed golf clubs and scuba flippers. Contemporary art from the vast collection of François-Henri Pinault, boss of the company that owns Gucci, is also on show; there's a bookshop, café and gift shop, too, in case you want to drop a couple of hundred euros for a Gucci belt.

Palazzo Vecchio

Piazza della Signoria • April Mon–Wed & Sun 9am–midnight, Thurs 9am–2pm; rest of the year daily 9am–7pm • €6 •
Ⓦ museicivicifiorentini.it

Probably designed by Arnolfo di Cambio, the **Palazzo Vecchio**, Florence's fortress-like town hall, was begun as the Palazzo dei Priori in the last year of the thirteenth century, to provide premises for the *Priori* of the ruling *Signoria*. Later changes in the Florentine constitution entailed alterations to the layout of the palace, the most radical coming in 1540, when Cosimo I moved his retinue here from the Palazzo Medici and grafted a huge extension onto the rear. The Medici remained in residence for only nine years before moving to the Palazzo Pitti; the "old" (*vecchio*) palace, which they left to their son, Francesco, then acquired its present name. Between 1865 and 1870, during Florence's brief tenure as capital of a newly united Italy, the palace housed the country's parliament and foreign ministry.

The courtyard

Work on the palace's beautiful inner **courtyard** was begun by Michelozzo in 1453, but the decoration was largely added by Vasari, court architect from 1555 until his death in 1574, on the occasion of Francesco de' Medici's marriage to Johanna of Austria in 1565. The bride's origin explains the otherwise puzzling presence of cities belonging to the Habsburg Empire amid the wall's painted townscapes. Vasari also designed the central fountain, though the winsome putto and dolphin (1476) at its crown are the

---

PERCORSI SEGRETI

The Palazzo Vecchio's various so-called **Percorsi Segreti** ("Secret Passageways") allow access – on guided tours only, of up to twelve people at a time – to parts of the building that are normally off limits. Visually most impressive is the trip up through the palace and into the **Attic of the Salone del Cinquecento**. From the vantage point of a balcony high above the hall, the guide describes the complex way in which Vasari created such a huge space within the medieval structure, and explains the allegorical meaning of the paintings. You are then led up into the vast attic itself, where two sets of trusses support the roof above and the ceiling below.

Less spectacular, but still worth it for the guide's commentary, is the route that takes you up the secret **Stairway of the Duke of Athens**. The doorway was knocked through the exterior wall of the Palazzo in 1342 as an emergency escape route for the duke; he never in fact used the staircase, because his fall from grace came rather sooner than he had imagined. Another Percorso allows you inside the **Studiolo di Francesco I**, then through one of the hidden doors and up a secret little staircase to the *studiolino* or **Tesoretto** (6), Cosimo's tiny private study, which was built ten years before the *studiolo*.

Tickets cost €8 (including admission to the Palazzo Vecchio); tours take place every day between 10am and 5pm in Italian, French and/or English, and last 75–90 minutes. There's usually at least one English-language party for each Percorso every day. Places must be reserved, either at the office next to the Palazzo Vecchio ticket desk or by phone, on ☎ 055 276 8224.

work of Verrocchio (these are copies; the originals are upstairs). Vasari was also let loose on the **monumental staircase**, which leads to the first floor, though visitors are usually directed to take a different route upstairs.

The Salone dei Cinquecento

Vasari was given full rein in the huge **Salone dei Cinquecento** at the top of the stairs. It was originally built in 1495 as the meeting hall for the Consiglio Maggiore (Great Council), the ruling assembly of the penultimate republic. The chamber might have had one of Italy's most remarkable decorative schemes: Leonardo da Vinci and Michelangelo were employed to paint frescoes on opposite sides of the room, but Leonardo's work, *The Battle of Anghiari*, was abandoned after his experimental technique went wrong, while Michelangelo's *The Battle of Cascina* had got no further than a fragmentary cartoon when he was summoned to Rome by Pope Julius II in 1506. Instead, the hall received six drearily bombastic murals (1563–65) – painted either by Vasari or under his direction – illustrating Florentine military triumphs over Pisa (1496–1509) and Siena (1554–55). It has generally been assumed that Vasari obliterated whatever remained of Leonardo's fresco before beginning his work, but the discovery of a cavity behind *The Battle of Marciano* has raised the possibility that Vasari instead constructed a false wall for his fresco, to preserve his great predecessor's painting. Investigations are proceeding.

The **ceiling**'s 39 panels, again by Vasari, are focused on the *Apotheosis of Cosimo I*, a scene surrounded by the crests of the city's guilds and further paeans to the prowess of Florence and the Medici. Of the **sculptures**, the highlight is Michelangelo's *Victory*, almost opposite the entrance door. Carved for the tomb of Pope Julius II, the statue was donated to the Medici by the artist's nephew, then installed here by Vasari in 1565 to celebrate Cosimo's defeat of the Sienese ten years earlier. Directly opposite, on the entrance wall, is the original plaster model of a companion piece for the *Victory*, Giambologna's **Virtue Overcoming Vice**, another artistic metaphor for Florentine military might – this time Florence's victory over Pisa. The remaining statues, by sixteenth-century artist Vincenzo de' Rossi, portray the **Labours of Hercules** and are yet another example of Florentine heroic propaganda: Hercules is one of Florence's many civic symbols.

The Studiolo, Quartiere di Leone X and Sala dei Dugento

From the Salone del Cinquecento, a roped-off door allows a glimpse of the strangest room in the building, the **Studiolo di Francesco I** (5). Designed by Vasari and decorated by no fewer than thirty Mannerist artists (1570–74), this windowless cell was created as a retreat for the introverted son of Cosimo and Eleanor. Each of the miniature bronzes and nearly all the paintings reflect Francesco's interest in the sciences and alchemy: the entrance wall pictures illustrate the theme of Earth, while the others, reading clockwise, signify Water, Air and Fire. The outstanding paintings are the two that don't fit the scheme: Bronzino's portraits of the occupant's parents, facing each other across the room. The oval paintings on the panels at the base hinted at the presence of Francesco's most treasured knick-knacks, which were once concealed in the compartments behind; the wooden structure is a nineteenth-century re-creation, though the paintings are original.

Much of the rest of this floor is still used by council officials, though if the seven rooms of the **Quartiere di Leone X** and **Sala dei Dugento** are open (they rarely are), don't miss the opportunity. The latter, in particular, is outstanding: Benedetto and Giuliano da Maiano, excellent sculptors both, were responsible for the design (1472–77) and for the fine wooden ceiling; the tapestries (1546–53) were created to designs by Bronzino, Pontormo and others.

The Quartiere degli Elementi

Steps lead from the Salone to the **second floor**, passing an intriguing fresco (1558) showing Piazza della Signoria during the celebrations for the feast of St John the

1

Baptist. Turn left at the top of the stairs and you enter the **Quartiere degli Elementi**, one of the floor's three distinct suites of rooms. All five salons here are slavishly devoted to a different member of the Medici clan. Persevere, though, if only to enjoy the city **views** from the Terrazza di Saturno and Verrocchio's original *Putto and Dolphin* statue on the Terrazzo di Giunone.

The Quartiere di Eleonora di Toledo

Return to the stairs, head straight on and you cross a gallery with views down into the Salone. Immediately afterwards come the **Quartiere di Eleonora di Toledo**, the private apartments of Cosimo I's wife, where the star turn is the tiny and exquisite **Cappella di Eleonora**, vividly decorated by Bronzino in the 1540s. The wall paintings show scenes from the life of Moses, episodes probably intended to draw parallels with the life of Cosimo. In the *Annunciation* that flanks the *Deposition* on the back wall, Bronzino is said to have used Cosimo and Eleonora's eldest daughter as the model for the Virgin.

The Sala dell'Udienza and Sala dei Gigli

Those who find all this Mannerist stuff unhealthily airless can take refuge in the more summery rooms which follow. The **Sala dell'Udienza**, originally the audience chamber of the Republic, boasts a stunning gilt-coffered ceiling by Giuliano da Maiano. The Mannerists reassert themselves, however, with a vast fresco sequence (1545–48) by Cecchino Salviati, this artist's most accomplished work.

Giuliano was also responsible, with his brother Benedetto, for the intarsia work on the doors and the lovely doorway that leads into the **Sala dei Gigli**, a room that takes its name from the lilies (*gigli*) that adorn most of its surfaces – the lily is the emblem of Saint Zenobius and of the Virgin, both patron saints of Florence. The room has another splendid ceiling by the Maiano brothers, and a wall frescoed by Domenico Ghirlandaio with Sts Zenobius, Stephen and Lawrence (1481–85) and lunettes portraying *Six Heroes of Ancient Rome*. The undoubted highlight here, however, is Donatello's original **Judith and Holofernes** (1455–60), removed from Piazza della Signoria.

The rest of the palazzo

Two small rooms are attached to the Sala dei Gigli: the **Cancelleria**, once Machiavelli's office and now containing a bust and portrait of the oft-maligned political thinker, and the lovely **Sala delle Carte**, formerly the *Guardaroba* (Wardrobe), the repository of Cosimo's state finery. It's decorated with 57 maps painted in 1563 by the court astronomer Fra' Ignazio Danti, depicting what was then the entire known world. The final section of the museum, just before the exit – devoted to second-rate pictures once owned by the American collector Charles Loeser – seems something of an afterthought, and is often closed.

The Uffizi

Piazzale degli Uffizi • ⓦ www.uffizi.firenze.it

The **Galleria degli Uffizi** is quite simply the finest picture gallery in Italy: so many masterpieces are collected here that you can only skate over the surface in a single visit. The gallery is housed in what were once government offices (*uffizi*) built by Vasari for Cosimo I in 1560. After Vasari's death, work on the elongated U-shaped building was continued by Buontalenti, who was asked by Francesco I to glaze the upper storey so that it could house his art collection. Each of the succeeding Medici added to the family's trove of art treasures. The accumulated collection was preserved for public inspection by the last member of the family, Anna Maria Luisa, whose will specified that it should be left to the people of Florence and never be

PIAZZA DEGLI UFFIZI >

1

VISITING THE UFFIZI

The Uffizi is open **Tuesday to Sunday from 8.15am to 6.50pm**; in high summer and at festive periods it sometimes stays open until 10pm. After the Vatican this is the busiest museum in the country, so during peak season you've almost no chance of getting in without paying the €4 surcharge for booking a ticket **in advance**. For next-day tickets, there's a reservations desk that opens at 8.15am at Door 2 (which is also where you queue if you haven't prepaid), and has an allocation of just two hundred. For reservations further in advance, go to Door 3, call the Firenze Musei line on ☏ 055 294 883, reserve through the Firenze Musei website, or call at the Orsanmichele ticket office (see p.47). Even if you have bought an advance ticket, get there at least twenty minutes before your allotted time, because the queue at Door 1, for prepaid admission, is often enormous and slow-moving.

Full-price **tickets** cost €6.50 but EU citizens aged 18–25 pay half price and entry is free to under-18s and over-65s; there are, however, frequent special exhibitions, during which the price is raised. In 2004 it was announced that over the next few years the Uffizi would be doubling the number of rooms open to the public, in order to show some eight hundred works usually kept in storage. Construction of new first-floor exhibition spaces is well underway, which means that some pictures may not be on show where they appear in the following account. It's also rare for the whole Uffizi to be open; a board by the entrance sometimes tells you which sections are closed.

allowed to leave the city. In the nineteenth century a large proportion of the statuary was transferred to the Bargello, while most of the antiquities went to the Museo Archeologico, leaving the Uffizi as essentially a gallery of paintings supplemented with some classical sculptures.

Pre-Renaissance: Duccio to Gentile da Fabriano

You can take a lift up to the galleries, but if you take the staircase instead, you'll pass the entrance to the Uffizi's prints and drawings section. The bulk of this vast collection is reserved for scholarly scrutiny but samples are often on public show.

Three altarpieces of the *Maestà* (Madonna Enthroned) dominate **Room 2**: the *Madonna Rucellai*, *Maestà di Santa Trìnita* and *Madonna d'Ognissanti*, by **Duccio**, **Cimabue** and **Giotto** respectively. These great works, which dwarf everything around them, show the softening of the Byzantine style into a more tactile form of representation. Painters from fourteenth-century Siena fill **Room 3**, with several pieces by Ambrogio and Pietro Lorenzetti and **Simone Martini**'s glorious *Annunciation*, the Virgin cowering from the angel amid a field of pure gold. Also in this room is Giottino's *San Remigio Pietà* (c.1360), notable both for its emotional intensity and for the alluring portrait of one of the donors – an elegant young woman, dressed in what was then the height of fashion.

Beyond a room of Giotto-esque artists such as **Orcagna** and **Bernardo Daddi** comes a display of paintings that mark the summit of the precious style known as International Gothic. **Lorenzo Monaco** is represented by an *Adoration of the Magi* and his greatest masterpiece, *The Coronation of the Virgin* (1415). Equally arresting is the *Adoration of the Magi* (1423) by **Gentile da Fabriano**, a picture spangled with gold so thick in places that the crowns of the kings, for instance, are like low-relief jewellery. It's crammed with so much detail that there's no real distinction between what's crucial and what's peripheral, with as much attention lavished on incidentals such as a snarling leopard as on the supposed protagonists.

Fra' Angelico to Filippino Lippi

Room 7 reveals the sheer diversity of early Renaissance painting. **Fra' Angelico**'s gorgeous *Coronation of the Virgin* takes place against a Gothic-like field of gold, but there's a very un-Gothic sensibility at work in its individualized depiction of the attendant throng. **Paolo Uccello**'s *The Battle of San Romano* once hung in Lorenzo il

1

Magnifico's bedchamber, in company with its two companion pieces now in the Louvre and London's National Gallery. Warfare is the ostensible subject, but this is just as much a compendium of perspectival effects – a toppling knight, the foreshortened legs of a kicking horse, a thicket of lances. The Madonna and Child in **Masolino**'s *Madonna and Child with St Anne* are thought to have been added by his pupil Masaccio, to whom the nearby tiny *Madonna and Child* is also attributed. The *Madonna and Child with Sts Francis, John the Baptist, Zenobius and Lucy* is one of only twelve extant paintings by **Domenico Veneziano**, who spent much of his life in Venice but died destitute in Florence.

Veneziano's greatest pupil, **Piero della Francesca**, is represented in **Room 8** by the paired portraits of *Federico da Montefeltro* and *Battista Sforza*, the duke and duchess of Urbino. These panels were painted two years after Battista's death; in the background of her portrait is the town of Gubbio, where she died giving birth to her ninth child and only son, Guidobaldo. A lot of space in Room 8 is given over to **Filippo Lippi**, whose *Madonna and Child with Two Angels* supplies one of the gallery's most popular faces: the model was Lucrezia Buti, a convent novice who became his mistress. Lucrezia puts in an another appearance in Lippi's crowded *Coronation of the Virgin*, where she's the young woman gazing out in the right foreground; Filippo himself, hand on chin, makes eye contact on the left side of the picture. Their liaison produced a son, the aptly named **Filippino** ("Little Philip") **Lippi**, whose *Madonna degli Otto* – one of several works by him here – is typical of the more melancholic cast of the younger Lippi's art.

The Pollaiuolo brothers

Lippi's great pupil, Botticelli, steals some of the thunder in **Room 9** – *Fortitude*, one of the series of cardinal and theological virtues, is a very early work by him. The rest of the series is by **Piero del Pollaiuolo**, who collaborated with his brother **Antonio** on the superb altarpiece of *Sts Vincent, James and Eustace*, which was made for the church of San Miniato (where a copy is now on display). Antonio – who was a fine sculptor and goldsmith, whereas his brother concentrated on painting – also created the two sinewy images of Hercules, which show evidence of the brothers' assiduous study of human anatomy. This room usually contains the *Portrait of Young Man in a Red Hat*, sometimes referred to as a self-portrait by Filippino Lippi, but believed by some to be an eighteenth-century fraud.

Botticelli

It's in the merged **rooms 10–14** that the greatest of **Botticelli**'s creations are gathered. A century ago most people walked past his pictures without breaking stride; nowadays – despite their elusiveness – the *Primavera* and the *Birth of Venus* stop all visitors in their tracks.

La Primavera and The Birth of Venus

The identities of the characters in the **Primavera** are not contentious: on the right Zephyrus, god of the west wind, chases the nymph Cloris, who is then transfigured into Flora, the pregnant goddess of spring; Venus stands in the centre, to the side of the three Graces, who are targeted by Cupid; on the left Mercury wards off the clouds of winter. What this all means, however, has occupied scholars for decades. Some see it as an allegory of the four seasons, but the consensus seems to be that it shows the triumph of Venus, with the Graces as the physical embodiment of her beauty and Flora the symbol of her fruitfulness – an interpretation supported by the fact that the picture was placed outside the wedding suite of Lorenzo di Pierfrancesco de' Medici.

The **Birth of Venus** probably takes as its source the myth that the goddess emerged from the sea after it had been impregnated by the castration of Uranus, an allegory for the

1

creation of beauty through the mingling of the spirit (Uranus) and the physical world. The supporting players are the nymph, Cloris, and Zephyrus, god of the west wind. Zephyrus blows the risen Venus to the shore where the goddess is clothed by Hora, daughter and attendant of Aurora, goddess of dawn. A third allegory hangs close by: *Pallas and the Centaur*, perhaps symbolizing the ambivalent triumph of reason over instinct.

The devotional paintings

Botticelli's devotional paintings are generally less perplexing. *The Adoration of the Magi* is traditionally thought to contain a gallery of Medici portraits: Cosimo il Vecchio as the first king, his sons Giovanni and Piero as the other two kings, Lorenzo il Magnifico on the far left, and his brother Giuliano as the black-haired young man in profile on the right. Only the identification of Cosimo is reasonably certain, along with that of Botticelli himself, on the right in the yellow robe. In later life, influenced by Savonarola's teaching, Botticelli confined himself to devotional pictures and moral fables, and his style became increasingly severe and didactic. The transformation is clear when comparing the easy grace of the *Madonna of the Magnificat* and the *Madonna of the Pomegranate* with the more angular and agitated *Calumny*. Even the *Annunciation* (1489), painted just as Savonarola's preaching began to grip Florence, reveals a new intensity in the expression of the angel and in the twisting body of the Virgin, whose posture embodies her ambivalent reaction to the message.

Not quite every masterpiece in this room is by Botticelli. Set away from the walls is the *Adoration of the Shepherds* by his Flemish contemporary **Hugo van der Goes**. Brought to Florence in 1483 by Tommaso Portinari, the Medici agent in Bruges, it provided the city's artists with their first large-scale demonstration of the realism of northern European oil painting, and had a great influence on the way the medium was exploited here.

Leonardo to Perugino

Works in **Room 15** trace the formative years of **Leonardo da Vinci**, whose distinctive touch appears first in the *Baptism of Christ* by his master Verrocchio. Vasari claimed that only the wistful angel in profile was by the 18-year-old apprentice, and the misty landscape in the background, but recent X-rays have revealed that Leonardo also worked on the figure of Christ. A similar terrain of soft-focus mountains and water occupies the far distance in Leonardo's slightly later *Annunciation*, in which a diffused light falls on a scene where everything is observed with a scientist's precision. In restless contrast to the aristocratic poise of the *Annunciation*, the sketch of *The Adoration of the Magi* – abandoned when Leonardo left Florence for Milan in early 1482 – presents the infant Christ as the eye of a vortex of figures, all drawn into his presence by a force as irresistible as a whirlpool.

Most of the rest of the room is given over to Raphael's teacher, **Perugino**, who is represented by a typically placid and contemplative *Madonna and Child with Saints* (1493), and *Pietà* (1494–95). It also contains an *Incarnation* – a rare depiction of the mystery of Christ's conception – by **Piero di Cosimo**, of whom more later.

The Tribuna

Room 18, the octagonal **Tribuna**, now houses the most important of the Medici's collection of **classical sculptures**, chief among which is the *Medici Venus*, a first-century BC copy of the Praxitelean *Aphrodite of Cnidos*. Around the walls are hung some fascinating portraits by **Bronzino**: Cosimo de' Medici, Eleonora di Toledo, Bartolomeo Panciatichi and his wife Lucrezia Panciatichi, all painted as figures of porcelain, placed in a bloodless, sunless world. More vital is Andrea del Sarto's flirtatious *Ritratto d'Ignota* (Portrait of a Young Woman), and there's a deceptive naturalism to Vasari's portrait of Lorenzo il Magnifico and Pontormo's of Cosimo il Vecchio, both painted long after the death of their subjects.

Signorelli to Mantegna

Signorelli and **Perugino** – with some photo-sharp portraits – are the principal artists in **Room 19**, and after them comes a room largely devoted to **Cranach** and **Dürer**. Each has an *Adam and Eve* here, with Dürer taking the opportunity to show off his proficiency as a painter of wildlife. Dürer's power as a portraitist is displayed in the *Portrait of the Artist's Father*, his earliest authenticated painting, and Cranach has a couple of pictures of Luther on display, one of them a double with his wife. Here you'll also find a bizarre *Perseus Freeing Andromeda* by **Piero di Cosimo**, the wild man of the Florentine Renaissance. Shunning civilized company, Piero did everything he could to bring his life close to a state of uncompromised nature, living in a house that was never cleaned, in the midst of a garden he refused to tend, and eating nothing but hard-boiled eggs. Where his contemporaries might seek inspiration in Plato, he would spend hours staring at the sky, at peeling walls, at the pavement – at anything where abstract patterns might conjure scenes in his imagination.

A taste of the Uffizi's remarkable collection of Venetian painting follows, with an impenetrable *Sacred Allegory* by **Giovanni Bellini**, and three works attributed to **Giorgione**. A clutch of northern European paintings includes some superb portraits by **Holbein** (notably *Sir Richard Southwell* and a self-portrait) and **Hans Memling**. In the following room – called the **Correggio** room, after the trio of pictures by the artist on show here – there's a triptych by **Mantegna** which is not in fact a real triptych, but rather a trio of exquisite small paintings shackled together. To the side of them are two other pictures by Mantegna – a swarthy portrait of Carlo de' Medici and the *Madonna delle Cave*, which takes its name from the minuscule quarries (cave) in the background.

Michelangelo to Raphael

Beyond the statues in the short corridor overlooking the Arno, the main attraction in **Room 25** is **Michelangelo**'s *Doni Tondo*, the only easel painting he came close to completing. (Regarding sculpture as the noblest of the visual arts, Michelangelo dismissed all non-fresco painting as a demeaning chore.) Nobody has yet explained the precise significance of every aspect of this picture, but plausible explanations for parts of it have been put forward. The five naked figures behind the Holy Family seem to be standing in a half-moon-shaped cistern or font, which would relate to the infant Baptist to the right, who – in the words of St Paul – prefigures the coming of Christ just as the new moon is "a shadow of things to come". In the same epistle, Paul goes on to commend the virtues of mercy, kindness, humility, modesty and patience, which are perhaps what the five youths represent. **Albertinelli**'s *Visitation* tends to get upstaged by Michelangelo, but it's a lustrous and extraordinarily touching picture.

Room 26 contains **Andrea del Sarto**'s sultry *Madonna of the Harpies* and a number of compositions by **Raphael**, including his self-portrait, the lovely *Madonna of the Goldfinch* and *Pope Leo X with Cardinals Giulio de' Medici and Luigi de' Rossi* – as shifty a group of ecclesiastics as was ever gathered in one frame.

The Mannerists, Titian and his contemporaries

The Michelangelo tondo's contorted gestures and virulent colours were greatly influential on the Mannerist painters of the sixteenth century, as can be gauged from *Moses Defending the Daughters of Jethro* by **Rosso Fiorentino**, one of the seminal figures of the movement, whose works (or possibly copies of them, in some cases) hang in **Room 27**, along with major works by Bronzino and his adoptive father, Pontormo.

Room 28 is almost entirely given over to another of the titanic figures of sixteenth-century art, **Titian**, with nine paintings on show. His *Flora* and *A Knight of Malta* are stunning, but most eyes tend to swivel towards the *Urbino Venus*, the most provocative of all Renaissance nudes, described by Mark Twain as "the foulest, the vilest, the obscenest picture the world possesses". **Sebastiano del Piombo**'s *Death of Adonis* was reduced to little more than postage-stamp tatters by the Mafia bomb

1

which in 1993 destroyed part of the Uffizi and killed five people; the restoration is little short of miraculous.

A brief diversion through the painters of the sixteenth-century Emilian school follows, centred on **Parmigianino**, whose *Madonna of the Long Neck* is one of the pivotal Mannerist creations. Parmigianino was a febrile and introverted character who abandoned painting for alchemy towards the end of his short life, and many of his works are marked by a sort of febrile refinement, none more so than this one.

Rooms 31 to 34 feature a miscellany of sixteenth-century artists (look out for the El Greco) and some top-class works from Venice and the Veneto, including **Moroni**'s *Portrait of Count Pietro Secco Suardi*, **Paolo Veronese**'s *Annunciation* and *Holy Family with St Barbara*, a gathering of fine pieces by **Lorenzo Lotto** and a female nude by **Bernardino Licino** that's unusual in seeming to have no mythological pretext – the subject is not Venus, but simply a naked woman.

The seventeenth and eighteenth centuries

The Uffizi's collection of seventeenth-century art features strong work from **Van Dyck** and **Rubens**, whose *Portrait of Isabella Brandt* is perhaps his finest painting here. The most overwhelming, however, are the huge *Henry IV at the Battle of Ivry* and *The Triumphal Entry of Henry IV into Paris* – Henry's marriage to Marie de' Medici is the connection with Florence. This pair are displayed in the majestic Niobe Room, which takes its name from the sculptures of *Niobe and her Daughters*, Roman copies of Greek originals, which were unearthed in a vineyard in Rome in 1583.

In this section of the gallery you'll also see some superb portraits by **Rembrandt**. His sorrow-laden *Self-Portrait as an Old Man*, painted five years or so before his death, makes a poignant contrast with the self-confident self-portrait of thirty years earlier. Although there are some good pieces from **Giambattista Tiepolo**, portraits again command the attention in the adjacent room of eighteenth-century paintings, notably a brace by **Goya** and **Chardin**'s demure children.

The rooms downstairs are used for temporary exhibitions and as a showcase for Italian art of the seventeenth century. Dramatic images from Salvator Rosa, Luca Giordano and Artemisia Gentileschi make quite an impression, but the presiding genius is **Caravaggio**, with his virtuosic *Medusa* (the severed head is painted on a shield), the smug little *Bacchus*, and the *Sacrifice of Isaac*. Works by lesser (but still impressive) talents show the huge influence of Caravaggio's high-contrast and high-impact art.

Orsanmichele

Via dei Calzaiuoli • Daily 10am–5pm

Looming like a fortress over Via dei Calzaiuoli, the foursquare **Orsanmichele** is the oddest church in Florence – a unique hybrid of the sacred and secular, it resembles no other church in the city, and it's not even immediately apparent which of its walls is the front. It's a major monument in itself, and its exterior was once the most impressive outdoor sculpture gallery in the city. Nowadays all of the pieces outside are replicas (most of the originals are on display in the attached museum), but copies or not, this church is one of the city's great sights.

The first building here was a small oratory secreted in the orchard or vegetable garden (*orto*) of a Benedictine monastery. A larger church stood on the site from the ninth century: San Michele ad Hortum, later San Michele in Orte – hence the compacted form of Orsanmichele. Even after the church was replaced by a **grain market** in the thirteenth century, the place retained its religious associations. In 1300, the chronicler Giovanni Villani claimed "the lame walked and the possessed were liberated" after visiting a miraculous image of the Virgin painted on one of the market pillars. After a fire in 1304, the building was eventually replaced by a **loggia** designed by Francesco Talenti to serve as a trade hall for the Arti Maggiori, the Great Guilds which governed the city. Between 1367 and 1380 the loggia was walled in, after which the site was again dedicated almost exclusively to religious functions, while leaving two upper storeys for use as emergency grain stores.

As far back as 1339, plans had been made to adorn each pillar of the building with a patron statue, each assigned to a different guild. In the event, only one statue was produced in sixty years – a St Stephen commissioned by the Arte della Lana. In 1408, weary of the delay, the city elders set a ten-year deadline, warning that the niches would be allocated to rival guilds if commissions remained unfulfilled. The delay was to posterity's benefit, for the resultant statues spanned the emergent years of the Renaissance.

The exterior

Beginning on the far left of Orsanmichele's Via dei Calzaiuoli flank, the first tabernacle is occupied by Ghiberti's **John the Baptist**, the earliest life-size bronze statue of the Renaissance. It was made for the Calimala, the guild of wholesale cloth importers. The adjacent niche is occupied by *The Incredulity of St Thomas* by Verrocchio, which replaced an earlier gilded statue by Donatello, *St Louis of Toulouse*, now in the Museo dell'Opera del Duomo; Giambologna's *St Luke* similarly replaced an earlier statue by Lamberti now in the Bargello.

Round the corner there's *St Peter*, usually attributed to Bernardo Ciuffagni, though some scholars have argued for the authorship of Brunelleschi or Donatello. He's followed by two works from Nanni di Banco: *St Philip* and his masterpiece, the so-called **Quattro Coronati**. The original Quattro Coronati were four anonymous Romans who were martyred by Diocletian; known as the Four Crowned Ones because the crown was a badge of martyrdom, they somehow became conflated with a group of Christian stonemasons, executed by Diocletian for refusing to carve a pagan idol – the latter group (who were actually five in number), became the patron saints of the masons' guild, sponsors of this niche. Donatello's *St George* occupies the next niche – the original is in the Bargello, as is the original accompanying bas-relief of *St George and the Dragon*.

On the church's west side stand *St Matthew* and *St Stephen*, both by Ghiberti, and *St Eligius* by Nanni di Banco; the *St Matthew*, posed and clad like a Roman orator, makes a telling comparison with the same artist's *St John*, cast just ten years before but still semi-Gothic in its sharp-edged drapery and arching lines. Earlier than both is Donatello's **St Mark**, made in 1411 when the artist was 25; the work is often considered one of the first statues of the Renaissance, for the naturalism of St Mark's stance and the intensity of his gaze. Pietro Lamberti's *St James* precedes the benign **Madonna della Rosa**, probably by Simone Talenti; the weakest of the sculptures, Baccio da Montelupo's *John the Evangelist*, brings up the rear.

The interior

Orsanmichele's interior centrepiece is a pavilion-sized glass and marble **tabernacle** by Orcagna, the only significant sculptural work by the artist. Decorated with lapis lazuli,

1

stained glass and gold, it frames a Madonna painted in 1347 by Bernardo Daddi as a replacement for the miraculous image of the Virgin, which was destroyed by the 1304 fire. The brotherhood that administered Orsanmichele paid for the tabernacle from thanksgiving donations in the aftermath of the Black Death; so many people attributed their survival to the Madonna's intervention that the money received in 1348 alone was greater than the annual tax income of the city coffers. Other paintings can be seen on the pillars: devotional images of the guilds' patron saints, they can be regarded as the low-cost ancestors of the Orsanmichele statues.

Museo di Orsanmichele
Daily 10am–5pm • Free

The original lines of the bricked-up loggia are still clear, and the vaulted halls of the upper granaries also survive. The lower of these halls now houses the **Museo di Orsanmichele**, entered via the footbridge from the Palazzo dell'Arte della Lana, the building opposite the church entrance. Having been restored, nearly all of the exterior statues are on show here – the main exception is the most famous of all, Donatello's *St George*, which belongs to the Bargello. From time to time exhibitions are held here, in which case an entrance fee is charged.

Badìa Fiorentina

Via del Proconsolo • Tourist visits permitted Mon 3–6pm

The **Badìa Fiorentina** is one of the most impressive churches in the centre of the city, and is also a place of special significance for admirers of **Dante**: this was the parish church of Beatrice Portinari, for whom he conceived a lifelong love when he observed her during Mass here. It was also here that Boccaccio delivered his celebrated lectures on Dante's epic. Nowadays the church belongs to the Fraternity of Jerusalem, a French monastic order founded in the 1970s.

Founded in 978 by Willa, widow of the Margrave of Tuscany, in honour of her husband, the Badìa was one of the focal buildings in medieval Florence: the city's sick were treated in a hospital founded here in 1031, while the main bell marked the divisions of the working day. The hospital also owed much to Willa's son, Ugo, who further endowed his mother's foundation after a vision of the hellish torments which awaited him by "reason of his worldly life, unless he should repent". The 1280s saw the church overhauled, probably under the direction of Arnolfo di Cambio, architect of the Duomo and Palazzo Vecchio. Later Baroque additions smothered much of the old church, though the narrow **campanile** escaped unharmed. Completed around 1330, it remains a prominent feature of the Florentine skyline.

The interior and the cloister

As you enter from Via Dante Alighieri, on the left hangs **Filippino Lippi**'s superb *Apparition of the Virgin to St Bernard*; set back to the right is the church's second highlight, the **tomb monument** to Ugo, sculpted by Mino da Fiesole between 1469 and 1481. Mino was also responsible for the nearby tomb of Bernardo Giugni and an altar frontal of the *Madonna and Child with Sts Leonard and Lawrence*. Giugni was a lawyer and diplomat, hence the figures of Justice and Faith accompanying his effigy.

A staircase leads from the choir to the upper storey of the **Chiostro degli Aranci** (Cloister of the Oranges), named after the fruit trees that used to be grown here. Two of its flanks are graced with a fresco cycle (1436–39) on the life of St Benedict, thought to be the work of Giovanni di Consalvo, a Portuguese contemporary of Fra' Angelico. A later panel – showing the saint throwing himself into bushes to resist temptation – is by the young Bronzino (1526–28). The cloister itself is the work of Bernardo Rossellino, one of the leading lights of early Renaissance architecture.

The "Dante district"

After visiting the Badìa, you might want to explore the city's knot of buildings with **Dante** associations – some of them admittedly spurious – that are clustered in the grid of narrow streets behind the Badìa, between Piazza del Duomo and Piazza della Signoria.

Casa di Dante

Via Santa Margherita 1 • April–Sept daily 10am–6pm; Oct–March Tues–Sun 10am–5pm • €4 • ⓦ museocasadidante.it

Somewhat fraudulently marketed as Dante's house, the **Casa di Dante** is actually a

---

DANTE ALIGHIERI

Dante signed himself "Dante Alighieri, a Florentine by birth but not by character", a bitter allusion to the city he served as a politician but which later cast him into exile and was to inspire some of the most vitriolic passages in his great epic poem, *La Divina Commedia* (*The Divine Comedy*).

The poet was born in 1265 into a minor and impoverished noble family. He was educated at Bologna and later at Padua, where he studied philosophy and astronomy. The defining moment in his life came in 1274 when he met the 8-year-old **Beatrice Portinari**. Dante – just 9 at the time of the meeting – later described his feelings following the encounter: "Love ruled my soul," he wrote, "and began to hold such sway over me … that it was necessary for me to do completely all his pleasure. He commanded me often that I should endeavour to see this so youthful angel, and I saw in her such noble and praiseworthy deportment that truly of her might be said these words of the poet Homer – *She appeared to be born not of mortal man but of God*."

Unhappily, Beatrice's family had decided their daughter was to marry someone else – Simone de' Bardi. The ceremony took place when she was 17; seven years later she was dead. Dante, for his part, had been promised – aged 12 – to Gemma Donati. The wedding took place in 1295, when the poet was 30.

His romantic hopes dashed, Dante settled down to a military and political career. In 1289 he fought for Florence against Arezzo and helped in a campaign against Pisa. Later he joined the Apothecaries' Guild, serving on a variety of minor civic committees. In June of 1300 he sought to settle the widening breach between the **Black** (anti-imperial) and **White** (more conciliatory) factions of Florence's ruling Guelph party, a dispute that had its roots in money: the Whites contained leading bankers to the imperial powers (the Cerchi, Mozzi, Davanzati and Frescobaldi), while the Blacks counted the Pazzi, Bardi and Donati amongst their number, all prominent papal bankers. Pope Boniface, not surprisingly, sided with the Blacks, who eventually emerged triumphant. Dante's White sympathies sealed his fate. In 1302, following trumped-up charges of corruption, he was sentenced with other Whites to two years' exile. While many of the deportees subsequently returned, Dante rejected his city of "self-made men and fast-got gain". He wandered instead between Forlì, Verona, Padua, Luni and Venice, writing much of *The Divine Comedy* as he went, before finally settling in Ravenna, where he died in 1321.

Running to more than fourteen thousand lines, **La Commedia** (the *Divina* was added after Dante's death) is an extraordinarily rich allegory, recounting the poet's journey through Inferno (Hell), Purgatorio (Purgatory), and Paradiso (Paradise), accompanied initially by the Roman poet Virgil (Dante was fully aware that his work would bear comparison with the greats) and then by Beatrice. Each of these three realms of the dead is depicted in 33 *canti* (a "prologue" to the Inferno brings the total up to one hundred), composed in a verse scheme called **terza rima**, in which lines of eleven syllables follow the rhyme scheme *aba, bcb, cdc, ded*, etc. This may seem an inflexible framework, but Dante employs it to achieve an amazing variety of tone, encompassing everything from the desperate abuse of the damned, through the complex theological argumentation of Purgatorio to the exalted lyricism of his vision of heaven. And the range of subject matter is astonishing too: *The Divine Comedy* is both a metaphysical epic in which the entire late medieval view of the cosmos is encapsulated, and an incisive critique of the society in which Dante lived – a critique in which he doesn't flinch from naming names. Equally remarkable is the fact that Dante wrote his poem in the Tuscan dialect, at a time when Latin was regarded as the only language suitable for subjects of such seriousness. Before *La Commedia*, Tuscan was the language of the street; afterwards, it began to be seen as the language of all Italian people, from peasants to philosophers.

1

medieval pastiche dating from 1910. The museum upstairs is a homage to the poet rather than a shrine: it contains nothing directly related to his life, and in all likelihood Dante was born not on the house's site but somewhere in the street that bears his name. Numerous editions of *La Divina Commedia* are on show – including a poster printed with the whole text in minuscule type – along with copies of Botticelli's illustrations to the poem and a variety of context-setting displays.

Santa Margherita de' Cerchi
Via Santa Margherita • Mon–Sat 10am–noon & 3–5pm, Sun 10am–noon

As contentious as the Casa di Dante's claims is the story that Dante married Gemma Donati in the ancient little church of **Santa Margherita de' Cerchi**. Documented as early as 1032, the building does, however, contain several tombs belonging to the Portinari, Beatrice's family; the porch also features the Donati family crest, as this was also their local parish church.

San Martino del Vescovo
Piazza San Martino • Mon–Thurs & Sat 10am–noon & 3–5pm, Fri 10am–noon

The tiny **San Martino del Vescovo** was built on the site of a tenth-century oratory that served as the Alighieri's parish church. Rebuilt in 1479, it became the headquarters of the Compagnia di Buonomini, a charitable body dedicated to aiding impoverished better-class citizens for whom begging was too demeaning a prospect. The Buonomini commissioned from Ghirlandaio's workshop a sequence of frescoes showing various altruistic acts and scenes from the life of St Martin, and the result is as absorbing a record of daily life in Renaissance Florence as the Ghirlandaio frescoes in Santa Maria Novella.

The Torre della Castagna

Opposite San Martino soars the thirteenth-century **Torre della Castagna**, meeting place of the city's *Priori* before they decamped to the Palazzo Vecchio. This is one of the most striking remnants of Florence's medieval townscape, when over 150 such towers rose between the river and the Duomo, many of them over two hundred feet high.

Museo Nazionale del Bargello
Via del Proconsolo 4 • Tues–Sat 8.15am–1.50pm, plus second & fourth Sun of month and first, third & fifth Mon of month, same hours • €4, longer hours and higher charge for special exhibitions • ⓦ www.uffizi.firenze.it

The Renaissance sculpture collection of the **Museo Nazionale del Bargello** is the richest in Italy, but a vast amount of space is also devoted to the decorative arts: carpets, enamels, ivories, glassware, tapestries, silverware and other *objets d'art* of the highest quality. Although they receive scant attention from most visitors, it would be easy to spend as much time on the dozen or more rooms filled with these treasures as the four rooms devoted to sculpture.

The Bargello's home, the daunting Palazzo del Bargello, was built in 1255 immediately after the overthrow of the aristocratic regime. The first of the city's public palaces, it soon became the seat of the *Podestà*, the city's chief magistrate, and the site of the main law court. Numerous malefactors were tortured, tried, sentenced and executed here, the elegant courtyard having been the site of the city's gallows and block. The building acquired its present name after 1574, when the Medici abolished the post of *Podestà*, the building becoming home to the chief of police – the *Bargello*. Torture and capital punishment were banned in 1786 (the first such abolition in Europe), though the building remained a prison until 1859.

The ground floor: Michelangelo and his successors

You've no time to catch your breath in the Bargello: the first room to the right of the ticket office is crammed with treasures, chief of which are the work of **Michelangelo**, in whose shadow every Florentine sculptor laboured from the sixteenth century onwards. The tipsy, soft-bellied figure of *Bacchus* (1496–97) was his first major sculpture, carved at the age of 22, a year or so before his great *Pietà* in Rome. Michelangelo's style soon evolved into something less ostentatiously virtuosic, as is shown by the tender *Tondo Pitti* (1503–05), while the rugged expressivity of his late manner is exemplified by the square-jawed *Bust of Brutus* (c.1540), the artist's sole work of this kind. A powerful portrait sketch in stone, it's a coded celebration of anti-Medicean republicanism, carved soon after the murder of the nightmarish Duke Alessandro de' Medici.

Works by Michelangelo's followers and contemporaries are ranged in the immediate vicinity. **Benvenuto Cellini**'s huge *Bust of Cosimo I* (1545–47), his first work in bronze, was a sort of technical trial for the casting of the *Perseus*, his most famous work. Alongside the two preparatory models for the *Perseus* in wax and bronze are displayed the original marble base and four statuettes that comprise the statue's pedestal; Perseus himself still stands in his intended spot, in the Loggia della Signoria.

Close by, **Giambologna**'s voluptuous *Virtue Overcoming Vice* or *Florence Defeating Pisa* (1575) – a disingenuous pretext for a female nude if ever there were one – takes up a lot of space, but is eclipsed by his best-known creation, the wonderful *Mercury* (1564), a nimble figure with no bad angles. Comic relief is provided by the reliably inept Bandinelli, whose *Adam and Eve* look like a grandee and his wife taking an *au naturel* stroll through their country estate. The powerfully erotic *Leda and the Swan* by **Ammannati** (1540–50) was inspired by a painting of the subject by Michelangelo that was later destroyed.

The courtyard

Part two of the ground floor's collection lies across the Gothic **courtyard**, which is plastered with the coats of arms of the *Podestà*. Against the far wall stand six allegorical figures by Ammannati from the fountain of the Palazzo Pitti courtyard. Of the two rooms across the yard, the one to the left features largely fourteenth-century works, notably pieces by Arnolfo di Cambio and Tino da Camaino; temporary exhibitions are often held in the room to the right.

The first floor

At the top of Giuliano da Sangallo's **staircase** (1502), the first-floor loggia has been turned into a menagerie for Giambologna's bronze animals and birds, imported from the Medici villa at Castello, just outside Florence. From here you step into the **Salone del Consiglio Generale**, the museum's second key room. Here again the number of masterpieces is breathtaking, though this time the presiding genius is **Donatello**, the fountainhead of Renaissance sculpture.

Vestiges of the sinuous Gothic manner are evident in the drapery of Donatello's marble *David* (1408), but there's nothing antiquated in the **St George** (1416), carved for the tabernacle of the armourers' guild at Orsanmichele and installed in a replica of its original niche at the far end of the room. Whereas St George had previously been little more than a symbol of valour, this alert, tensed figure represents not the act of heroism but the volition behind it.

Also here is the sexually ambivalent bronze **David** (1430–40), the first freestanding nude figure created since classical times. A decade later the sculptor produced the strange prancing figure known as Amor-Atys, which was mistaken for a genuine statue from classical antiquity – the highest compliment the artist could have wished for. Donatello was just as comfortable with portraiture as with Christian or pagan imagery, as his breathtakingly vivid terracotta *Bust of Niccolò da Uzzano* demonstrates; it may be the earliest Renaissance portrait bust. When the occasion demanded, Donatello could also produce a straightforwardly monumental piece like the nearby *Marzocco* (1418–20), Florence's heraldic lion.

Donatello's master, **Ghiberti**, is represented by his relief of *Abraham's Sacrifice*, his winning entry in the competition to design the Baptistery doors in 1401, easily missed

1

on the right-hand wall; the treatment of the theme submitted by Brunelleschi, is hung alongside. Set around the walls of the room, **Luca della Robbia**'s simple, sweet-natured humanism is embodied in a sequence of glazed terracotta Madonnas.

The applied art collection

The rest of this floor is occupied by a superb collection of European and Islamic applied art, with dazzling specimens of work in enamel, glass, silver, majolica and ivory: among the ivory pieces from Byzantium and medieval France you'll find combs, boxes, chess pieces and devotional panels featuring scores of figures crammed into a space the size of a paperback. Room 9, the **Cappella di Santa Maria Maddalena**, is decorated with frescoes discovered in 1841 when the room was converted from a prison cell; long attributed to Giotto, they're now thought to be by followers.

The second floor

Sculpture resumes upstairs, with a room largely devoted to the della Robbia family, a prelude to the **Sala dei Bronzetti**, Italy's best assembly of small Renaissance bronzes. Giambologna's spiralling designs predominate, a testament to his popularity in late sixteenth-century Florence: look out for the Hercules series, showing the hero variously wrestling and clubbing his opponents into submission. An interesting contrast is provided by **Antonio del Pollaiuolo**'s earlier and more violent *Hercules and Antaeus* (c.1478), which stands on a pillar nearby. Like Leonardo, Pollaiuolo unravelled the complexities of human musculature by dissecting corpses.

   Also on this floor there's another roomful of della Robbias and a splendid display of bronze medals, featuring specimens from the great pioneer of this form of portable art, Pisanello. Lastly, there's a room devoted mainly to **Renaissance portrait busts**, where the centrepiece is Verrocchio's *David*, clearly influenced by the Donatello figure downstairs. Around the walls you'll find Mino da Fiesole's busts of Giovanni de' Medici and Piero il Gottoso (the sons of Cosimo de' Medici), Antonio del Pollaiuolo's *Young Cavalier* (which is probably another Medici portrait), and a bust labelled *Ritratto d'Ignoto* (Portrait of an Unknown Man) – beside Verrocchio's *Madonna and Child* – which may in fact depict Macchiavelli. Other outstanding pieces include Francesco Laurana's *Battista Sforza* (an interesting comparison with the Piero della Francesca portrait in the Uffizi), the *Woman Holding Flowers* by Verrocchio, and the fraught marble relief in which Verrocchio portrays the death of Francesca Tornabuoni-Pitti, from whose tomb this panel was taken.

Museo Galileo

Piazza dei Giudici 1 • Mon & Wed–Sun 9.30am–6pm, Tues 9.30am–1pm • €8 • ⓦ museogalileo.it

Long after Florence had declined from its artistic apogee, the intellectual reputation of the city was maintained by its scientists, many of them directly encouraged by the ruling Medici-Lorraine dynasty. Two of the latter, Grand Duke Ferdinando II and his brother Leopoldo, both of whom studied with Galileo, founded a scientific academy called the Accademia del Cimento (Academy of Experiment) in 1657 – its motto was "Try and try again." The instruments made and acquired by this academy are the core of the city's science museum, recently rebranded as the **Museo Galileo**.

The first floor

Some of Galileo's original instruments are on show on the first floor, such as the lens with which he discovered the four moons of Jupiter, which he tactfully named the Medicean planets. (An enormous lodestone given by Galileo to Ferdinando II is on display by the ticket desk.) On this floor you'll also find the museum's holy relics – bones from two of Galileo's fingers, plus a tooth. Other cases are filled with beautiful Arab astrolabes, calculating machines, early telescopes and some delicate and ornate thermometers. The most imposing single exhibit on this floor is a massive armillary sphere made in 1593 for Ferdinando I to provide a visual proof of the supposed veracity of the earth-centred Ptolemaic system.

The second floor
On the floor above there are all kinds of exquisitely manufactured **scientific and mechanical equipment**, several of which were built to demonstrate the fundamental laws of physics. Dozens of clocks and timepieces are on show too, along with some spectacular electrical machines, and a huge lens made for Cosimo III, with which Faraday and Davy managed to ignite a diamond by focusing the rays of the sun. At the end there's a **medical section** full of alarming surgical instruments and anatomical wax models for teaching obstetrics, plus the contents of a medieval pharmacy, displaying such unlikely cure-alls as Sangue del Drago (Dragon's Blood) and Confetti di Seme Santo (Confections of Blessed Semen).

West of the centre

Despite the urban improvement schemes of the nineteenth century and the bombings and shellings of World War II, several of the streets immediately west of Piazza della Signoria retain their medieval character: an amble through Via Porta Rossa, Via delle Terme and Borgo Santi Apostoli will give you some idea of the feel of Florence in the Middle Ages, when every big house was an urban fortress. Best of these medieval redoubts is the **Palazzo Davanzati**, whose interior looks little different from the way it did six hundred years ago. Nearby, the fine church of **Santa Trìnita** is home to an outstanding fresco cycle by Domenico Ghirlandaio, while beyond the glitzy **Via de' Tornabuoni** – Florence's prime shopping street – you'll find a marvellous chapel designed by Alberti and a museum devoted to the work of Marino Marini. The exquisite ancient church of **Santi Apostoli** shouldn't be overlooked, and neither should **Ognissanti**. And if all this art is beginning to take its toll, you could take a break in the tree-lined avenues of the **Cascine** park, right on the western edge of the city centre.

Mercato Nuovo
Piazza di Mercato Nuovo • Mid-Feb to mid-Nov daily 9am–7pm; mid-Nov to mid-Feb Tues–Sat 9am–5pm

One block west of the southern end of Via dei Calzaiuoli lies the **Mercato Nuovo**, or Mercato del Porcellino, where there's been a market since the eleventh century, though the present loggia dates from the sixteenth. A small group is invariably gathered round the bronze boar known as *Il Porcellino*: you're supposed to earn yourself some good luck by getting a coin to fall from the animal's mouth through the grille below his head. This superstition has a social function, as the coins go to an organization that runs homes for abandoned children. The boar is a copy of a copy made by Pietro Tacca of a Hellenistic sculpture that's now in the Uffizi; Tacca's original copy is now in the Bardini museum.

Museo Davanzati
Via Porta Rossa 13 • Tues–Sun 8.15am–1.50pm, plus second & fourth Mon of month, same hours • €2 • Visitors have unrestricted access to the first floor; visits to the second and third floors are at 10am, 11am & noon, and must be booked in advance in person or by phone • ☎ 055 238 8610

Perhaps the most imposing exterior in this district is the thirteenth-century Palazzo di Parte Guelfa, which was financed from the confiscated property of the Ghibelline faction, but for more of an immersion in the world of medieval Florence you should visit the fourteenth-century **Palazzo Davanzati**, nowadays maintained as the **Museo Davanzati**. In the nineteenth century the palazzo was divided into flats, but at the beginning of the twentieth it was restored to something very close to the appearance it had in the 1580s,

1

when a loggia replaced the battlements on the roof, and the Davanzati stuck their coat of arms on the front. Apart from those emendations, the place now looks much as it did when first inhabited. Virtually every room is furnished and decorated in predominantly medieval style, using genuine artefacts gathered from a variety of sources.

The interior

The owners of this house were well prepared for the adversities of urban living, as can be seen in the siege-resistant doors, the huge storerooms for the hoarding of provisions and the private water supply. The courtyard's **well** was something of a luxury at a time when much of Florence was still dependent on public fountains: a complex series of ropes and pulleys allowed it to serve the entire house. Similarly, the palace's **toilets** were state-of-the art affairs by the standards of 1330.

The Sala Grande and Sala dei Pappagalli

An ancient staircase – the only one of its kind to survive in the city – leads to the **first floor** and the Sala Grande or **Sala Madornale**. This room, used for family gatherings, underlines the dual nature of the house: furnished in the best style of the day, it also has four wood-covered hatches in the floor to allow bombardment of a besieging enemy. Merchants' houses in the fourteenth century would typically have had elaborately painted walls in the main rooms, and the Palazzo Davanzati preserves some fine examples of such decor, especially in the dining room or **Sala dei Pappagalli**, where the imitation wall hangings of the lower walls are patterned with a parrot (*pappagallo*) motif, while the upper walls depict a garden terrace.

The Sala Piccola

Before the development of systems of credit, wealth had to be sunk into tangible assets such as the tapestries, ceramics, sculpture and lacework that alleviate the austerity of many of these rooms; any surplus cash would have been locked away in a strongbox like the extraordinary example in the **Sala Piccola**, whose locking mechanism looks like the innards of a primitive clock. There's also a fine collection of *cassoni*, the painted chests in which the wife's dowry would be stored.

The Sala dei Pavoni

Plushest of the rooms is the first-floor bedroom, or **Sala dei Pavoni** – complete with en-suite bathroom. It takes its name from the beautiful frescoed frieze of trees, peacocks (*pavoni*) and other exotic birds: the coats of arms woven into the decoration are the crests of families related to the Davizzi. The rare Sicilian linen bed cover is decorated with scenes from the story of Tristan.

The kitchen

The arrangements of the rooms on the upper two floors, together with their beautiful array of furniture and decoration, mirror that of the first floor. For all the splendour of the lower rooms, the spot where the palace's occupants would have been likeliest to linger is the third-floor **kitchen**. Located on the uppermost floor to minimize damage if a fire broke out, it would have been the warmest room in the house. A fascinating array of utensils are on show here: the *girapolenta* (polenta-stirrer) is extraordinary. The leaded glass would have been considered a marvel at a time when many windows were covered only with turpentine-soaked rags stretched across frames to repel rainwater.

Santi Apostoli

Piazza del Limbo • Mon–Sat 10am–noon & 4–5.30pm, Sun 4–5.30pm

Between Via Porta Rossa and the Arno, on Piazza del Limbo (the former burial ground of unbaptized children), stands the church of **Santi Apostoli**. A replica of an ancient inscription on the facade records the legend that it was founded by Charlemagne – it's not quite that old, but it certainly predates the end of the first millennium. Probably rebuilt in the middle of that century, Santi Apostoli bears a close resemblance to the city's other Romanesque basilica, San Miniato al Monte, though side chapels were added to it in the fifteenth and sixteenth centuries. Despite these alterations, and the addition of paintings during the Counter-Reformation, Santi Apostoli still has an austere beauty quite unlike any other church in the city centre, with its expanses of bare stone wall and columns of green Prato marble. According to Vasari, it was this "small and most beautiful" building that Brunelleschi employed as his primary model for the churches of San Lorenzo and Santo Spirito.

The chief treasures of Santi Apostoli are some stone fragments from the Holy Sepulchre in Jerusalem, supposedly presented by Godfrey de Bouillon to Pazzino de' Pazzi as reward for his crusading zeal. On Holy Saturday sparks struck from these stones are used to light the flame that ignites the "dove" that in turn sets off the fireworks in front of the Duomo (see p.134). The brazier in which the holy fire is borne to the cathedral is kept in the first chapel on the left.

Piazza and Ponte Santa Trìnita

West of Palazzo Davanzati, Via Porta Rossa runs into **Piazza Santa Trìnita** – not really a square, more a widening of Via de' Tornabuoni. The centrepiece of the piazza is the Colonna della Giustizia (Column of Justice), raised by Cosimo I in 1565 on the spot where, in August 1537, he had heard of the defeat of the anti-Medici faction at Montemurlo.

Santa Trìnita church

Piazza Santa Trìnita • Mon–Sat 8am–noon & 4–6pm, Sun 4–6pm

The antiquity of the church of **Santa Trìnita** is manifest in the Latinate pronunciation of its name: modern Italian stresses the last, not the first syllable. The church was founded in 1092 by a Florentine nobleman called **Giovanni Gualberto**, scenes from whose life are illustrated in the frescoes in the alcove at the top of the left aisle. One Good Friday, so the story goes, Gualberto set off intent on avenging the murder of his brother. On finding the murderer he decided to spare his life and proceeded to San Miniato, where a crucifix is said to have bowed its head to honour his act of mercy. Giovanni went on to become a Benedictine monk and found the reforming Vallombrosan order; notwithstanding the mayhem created on Florence's streets by his militant supporters, he was eventually canonized.

The church was rebuilt between about 1300 and 1330, before work was interrupted by the Black Death. Further rebuilding took place between 1365 and 1405, while the facade – by Buontalenti – was added in 1594. Piecemeal additions over the years have lent the church a pleasantly hybrid air: the largely Gothic interior contrasts with the Mannerist facade, itself at odds with the Romanesque front wall of the interior.

The Cappella Cialli-Sernigi has a damaged Mystic Marriage of St Catherine (1389) by Spinello Aretino, and the neighbouring Cappella Bartolini-Salimbeni is decorated with frescoes of episodes from the Life of the Virgin by Lorenzo Monaco (1420–25), who also painted its Annunciation altarpiece. The next chapel, the Cappella Ardinghelli, features Giovanni Toscani's frescoed Pietà (1424–25), but the church's highlight is the Cappella Sassetti, at the head of the right aisle.

The Capella Sassetti

The Cappella Sassetti's frescoes of scenes from the Life of St Francis were painted by Domenico Ghirlandaio (1483–86) and commissioned by Francesco Sassetti, a friend of Lorenzo il Magnifico. The intention, in part, was to eclipse the chapel in Santa Maria

1

Novella that was sponsored by Sassetti's rival, Giovanni Tornabuoni, which was also painted by Ghirlandaio. St Francis, floating in the sky, is shown bringing a child back to life in Piazza Santa Trìnita, with the church in the background. (Opposite the church you can see the child plummeting to his temporary death.) Above this scene, *St Francis Receiving the Rule* sets the action in Piazza della Signoria and features (right foreground) a portrait of Sassetti between his son, Federigo, and Lorenzo il Magnifico (Sassetti was general manager of the Medici bank). On the steps below them are the humanist Poliziano and three of his pupils, Lorenzo's sons; the blond boy, at the back of the line, is Giovanni, the future Pope Leo X.

Ghirlandaio has depicted himself in the lower scene, with his hand on his hip, and is also present in the chapel's altarpiece, the *Adoration of the Shepherds* (1485) – he's the shepherd pointing to the Child and, by way of self-identification, to the garland (*ghirlanda*). The figures of the donors – Sassetti and his wife, Nera Corsi – kneel to either side; they are buried in Giuliano da Sangallo's black tombs under the side arches.

The rest of the church

Displayed in the neighbouring **Cappella Doni** is the miraculous crucifix, formerly in San Miniato, which is said to have bowed to Gualberto. The last of the church's major works, a powerful composition by Luca della Robbia – the **tomb of Benozzo Federighi**, bishop of Fiesole – occupies the left wall of the **Cappella Scali**; created for the church of San Pancrazio, it was transported here in 1896. The fine wooden **statue of Mary Magdalene**, which owes much to Donatello's *Magdalene* in the Museo dell'Opera del Duomo, was begun by Desiderio da Settignano and probably completed by Benedetto da Maiano.

The bridge

Construction of the sleek **Ponte Santa Trìnita** was begun in 1567 on Cosimo de' Medici's orders, ten years after its predecessor had been demolished in a flood – and a decade after Siena had finally become part of Florentine territory, a subjugation which the bridge was intended to commemorate. What makes this the classiest bridge in Florence is the graceful low curve of its arches; ostensibly the design was conjured up by Ammannati, one of the Medici's favourite artists, but the curve so closely resembles the arc of Michelangelo's Medici tombs that it's likely the credit belongs to him.

In 1944 the Nazis blew the bridge to smithereens and seven years later it was decided to **rebuild** it using as much of the original material as could be dredged from the Arno. To ensure maximum authenticity, all the new stone that was needed was quarried from the Bóboli gardens, where the stone for Ammannati's bridge had been cut. Twelve years after the war, the reconstructed bridge was opened, lacking only the head from the statue of *Spring*, which had not been found despite the incentive of a hefty reward. In 1961 the missing head was at last fished from the riverbed; having lain in state for a few days on a scarlet cushion in the Palazzo Vecchio, it was returned to its home.

Palazzo Strozzi

Piazza degli Strozzi • W palazzostrozzi.org

In recent years **Via de' Tornabuoni** and nearby Piazza Strozzi have come to be monopolized by high-end designer stores – Versace, Ferragamo, Prada, Pucci, Gucci and Armani all have outlets here, to the dismay of those who lament the erosion of Florentine identity by the ever-burgeoning megabrands. But conspicuous wealth is nothing new on Via de' Tornabuoni: looming above everything is the vast **Palazzo Strozzi**, the most intimidating of all Florentine Renaissance palaces, with windows as big as gateways and embossed with lumps of stone the size of boulders. It was begun by the banker Filippo Strozzi, a figure so powerful that he was once described as "the first man of Italy", and whose family provided the ringleaders of the anti-Medici faction in Florence. He bought and demolished a dozen town houses to make space for Giuliano da Sangallo's palazzo, the construction of which lasted from 1489 to 1536. Now administered by the Fondazione Palazzo Strozzi, the building has become a venue for outstanding art exhibitions; it has a nice café too.

Palazzo Rucellai and the Loggia dei Rucellai

Some of Florence's other plutocrats made an impression with a touch more subtlety than the Strozzi. In the 1440s Giovanni Rucellai, one of the richest businessmen in the city (and an esteemed scholar too), decided to commission a new house from Leon Battista Alberti. The resultant **Palazzo Rucellai**, Via della Vigna Nuova 18, was the first palace in Florence to follow the rules of classical architecture; its tiers of pilasters, incised into smooth blocks of stone, evoke the exterior wall of the Colosseum.

In contrast to the feud between the Medici and the Strozzi, the Rucellai were on the closest terms with the city's de facto royal family: the **Loggia dei Rucellai** across the street (now a shop) was in all likelihood built for the wedding of Giovanni's son to the granddaughter of Cosimo il Vecchio, and the frieze on the Palazzo Rucellai features the heraldic devices of the two families, the Medici emblem alongside the Rucellai sail.

Museo Marino Marini

Piazza San Pancrazio • Mon & Wed–Sat 10am–5pm • €4 • ⓦ museomarinomarini.it

Round the corner from Palazzo Rucellai stands the ex-church of San Pancrazio, deconsecrated by Napoleon, then successively the offices of the state lottery, the magistrates' court, a tobacco factory and an arsenal. It is now the swish **Museo Marino Marini**, which holds some two hundred works left to the city in Marini's will. Variations on the sculptor's trademark horse-and-rider theme make up much of the show.

Cappella di Santo Sepolcro

Via della Spada • Open for mass Oct–June Sat 5.30pm

Once part of the church but now entirely separate from the museum, the **Cappella Rucellai**, which was redesigned by Alberti, houses the **Cappella di Santo Sepolcro**, the most exquisite of his creations. Designed as the funerary monument to Giovanni Rucellai, it takes the form of a diminutive reconstruction of Jerusalem's Church of the Holy Sepulchre. Volunteers occasionally keep the chapel open for a few hours each week, but the only time you're guaranteed to be able to take a look is just before Saturday mass.

Ognissanti

Borgo Ognissanti • **Church** Mon–Sat 7.30am–12.30pm & 4–8pm, Sun 9am–1pm & 4–8pm • **Refectory** Mon, Tues & Sat 9am–noon • Free

In medieval times one of the main areas of cloth production – the mainstay of the Florentine economy – was in the western part of the city. **San Salvatore in Ognissanti**, the main church of this quarter, stands on a piazza that might be taken as a symbol of the state of the present-day Florentine economy, dominated as it is by the de luxe *Grand* and *Excelsior* hotels.

The church was founded in 1256 by the Umiliati, a Benedictine order from Lombardy whose speciality was the weaving of woollen cloth. In 1561 the Franciscans took over the church, the new tenure being marked by a Baroque overhaul which spared only the medieval campanile.

The interior and the refectory

The young face squeezed between the Madonna and the dark-cloaked man in **Ghirlandaio**'s *Madonna della Misericordia* (1473) – on the second altar on the right – is

1

said to be that of Amerigo Vespucci, an agent for the Medici in Seville, whose two voyages in 1499 and 1501 would lend his name to a continent. The altar was paid for by the Vespucci, a family of silk merchants from the surrounding district, which is why other members of the clan appear beneath the Madonna's protective cloak. Among them is Simonetta Vespucci (at the Virgin's left hand), the mistress of Giuliano de' Medici and reputedly the most beautiful woman of her age – the face of Botticelli's Venus, in his *Birth of Venus*, is said to be hers. The idea may not be so far-fetched, for Botticelli also lived locally, and his family was on good terms with the Vespucci.

Botticelli is buried in the church, beneath a round tomb slab in the south transept, and his painting of *St Augustine's Vision of St Jerome* (1480) hangs on the same side of the church as the Madonna. Facing it is Ghirlandaio's more earthbound *St Jerome*, also painted in 1480, which is when he painted the *Last Supper* in the **refectory** (reached through the cloister entered to the left of the church). And don't miss the dazzling Crucifix that hangs in the left transept of Ognissanti: in 2010 it emerged from a seven-year restoration, and in the course of the cleaning it was established by infrared and X-ray analysis that it's almost certainly by **Giotto**.

The Cascine

Florence's public park, the **Cascine**, begins close to the Ponte della Vittoria and dwindles away 3km downstream, at the confluence of the Arno and the Mugnone. Once the Medici dairy farm (*cascina*), then a hunting reserve, this narrow strip of green mutated into a high-society venue in the eighteenth century: if there was nothing happening at the opera, all of Florence's *beau monde* turned out to promenade under the trees of the Cascine. A fountain in the park bears a dedication to Shelley, who was inspired to write his *Ode to the West Wind* while strolling here on a blustery day in 1819.

Thousands of people come out here on Tuesday mornings for the colossal market beyond the former train station (which now houses an arts centre, the Stazione Leopolda), and on any day of the week the Cascine swarms with joggers, cyclists and rollerbladers. Parents bring their kids out here too, to play on the grass – a rare commodity in Florence. However, the Cascine also has a reputation as a haunt for the city's drug addicts, and it's emphatically not a place for a nocturnal stroll.

The Santa Maria Novella district

Scurrying from the train station in search of a room, or fretting in the queues for a rail ticket, most people barely give a glance to **Santa Maria Novella train station**, but this is a building that deserves as much attention as many of the city's conventional monuments. Its principal architect, Giovanni Michelucci, was one of the leading figures of the Modernist movement, which was marginalized in Mussolini's Italy, where pompous Neoclassicism was the preferred mode. Accordingly, there was some astonishment when, in 1933, Michelucci and his colleagues won the open competition to design the main station for one of the country's showpiece cities. It's a piece of impeccably rational planning, so perfectly thought-out that it was adequate for the city's needs until the start of this century, when approval was given for the construction of a terminal for the high-speed Milan–Florence–Rome–Naples rail line, 2km to the north; designed by Foster Associates, the new station is due to open in 2015.

Santa Maria Novella

Piazza Santa Maria Novella • Mon–Thurs 9am–5.30pm, Fri 11am–5.30pm, Sat 9am–5pm, Sun noon–5pm • €3.50

Santa Maria Novella – focal point of the recently refurbished piazza of the same name – stands on the site of the more humble Santa Maria delle Vigne, which in 1221 was handed to the Dominicans, who set about altering the place to enable preachers to address their sermons to as large a congregation as possible. By 1360 the interior was finished, but only the Romanesque lower part of the **facade** had been completed. This state of affairs lasted until 1456, when Giovanni Rucellai paid for Alberti to design an elegantly classicized upper storey that would blend with the older section while improving the facade's proportions. The sponsor's name is picked out across the facade in Roman capitals (iohanes·oricellarivs…), while the Rucellai family emblem, the billowing sail of Fortune, runs as a motif through the central frieze. One other external feature is worth noting: the route into the church takes you through the cemetery, which – uniquely – is ringed by an arcade of *avelli*, the collective burial vaults of upper-class families.

The nave

Entwined around the second nave pillar on the left is a **pulpit** designed by Brunelleschi (marked 5 on our plan), notorious as the spot from which the Dominicans first denounced Galileo for espousing the Copernican theory of the heavens. The carving was completed by Buggiano, Brunelleschi's adopted son, who may have advised Masaccio on the architectural details present in the background of his extraordinary 1427 fresco of the **Trinity** (6) which is painted on the wall nearby. This was one of the earliest

SANTA MARIA NOVELLA

0   25
metres

PIAZZA DELLA STAZIONE

VIA DEGLI AVELLI

Refectory

Entrance to Church
PIAZZA SANTA MARIA NOVELLA
Entrance to Museum

1 Annunciation, anon. 14th-century Florentine painter
2 Nativity (lunette above door), attrib. Botticelli
3 Annunciation (1602), Santi di Tito
4 Tomb of Beata Villana delle Botti (d. 1361), a Dominican nun, by Bernardo Rossellini (1451) and Desiderio da Settignano
5 Pulpit (1443), Brunelleschi
6 Trinity (1427), Masaccio
7 Crucifix, Giotto (c. 1288–90)
8 Tomb of the Patriarch of Constantinople (d.1440)
9 Cappella Rucellai (1303–52): Madonna and Child (1348), Mino da Fiesole; tombplate of Leonardo Dati (1425–6), Ghiberti
10 Cappella Bardi: 14th-century frescoes
11 Cappella di Filippo Strozzi: frescoes (1489–1502), Filippino Lippi; tomb of Filippo Strozzi (1491–5), Benedetto da Maiano
12 Chancel: fresco cycle (1485–90), Domenico Ghirlandaio
13 Cappella Gondi: crucifix (1410–14), attrib. Brunelleschi
14 Cappella Strozzi: frescoes (1350–7), Narno di Cione; altarpiece (1357), Orcagna
15 Chiostro Verde
16 The Flood (1425–30), Paolo Uccello
17 Cappellone degli Spagnoli
18 Chiostrino dei Morti
19 Chiostro Grande

works in which the rules of perspective and classical proportion were rigorously employed, and Florentines queued to view the illusion on its unveiling, stunned by a painting which appeared to create three-dimensional space on a solid wall. Amazingly, the picture was concealed behind an altar in 1570 and rediscovered only in 1861.

Giotto's crucifix (7), a radically naturalistic and probably very early work (c.1288–90), hangs in what is thought to be its intended position, poised dramatically over the centre of the nave. Hitherto, it had been hidden away in the sacristy, veiled by a layer of dirt so thick that many scholars refused to recognize it as the work of the master; the attribution is still disputed by some.

Cappella di Filippo Strozzi

In 1486 the chapel to the right of the chancel (11) was bought by Filippo **Strozzi**, a wealthy banker, who then commissioned Filippino Lippi to paint a fresco cycle on the life of his namesake, St Philip the Apostle, a saint rarely portrayed in Italian art. The

1

paintings, a departure from anything seen in Florence at the time, were much interrupted and were completed in 1502, well after Strozzi's death. Before starting the project Filippino spent some time in Rome, and the work he carried out on his return displays an archeologist's obsession with ancient Roman culture. The right wall depicts Philip's *Crucifixion* and his *Miracle before the Temple of Mars*. In the latter, the Apostle uses the cross to banish a dragon which had been an object of pagan worship in a Temple of Mars. The enraged temple priests then capture and crucify the saint. The figures swooning from the dragon's stench are almost overwhelmed by an architectural fantasy derived from Rome's recently excavated Golden House of Nero. Look carefully in the top right-hand corner and you'll see a minuscule Christ, about the same size as one of the vases behind the figure of Mars.

The left wall depicts *The Raising of Drusiana* and the *Attempted Martyrdom of St John*: the latter scene alludes to the persecutions of the emperor Domitian, during which John was dipped in boiling oil in an attempt to kill him – but the Apostle emerged miraculously rejuvenated by the experience. The vaults portray Adam, Noah, Jacob and Abraham and, like the chapel's stained glass and impressive *trompe l'oeil* decoration, were also the work of Lippi. Behind the altar of this chapel is **Strozzi's tomb** (1491–95), beautifully carved by Benedetto da Maiano.

The chancel (Cappella Tornabuoni)

Ostensibly depicting scenes from the life of the Virgin and episodes from the life of St John the Baptist, **Domenico Ghirlandaio**'s pictures around the **chancel** (12) were commissioned by **Giovanni Tornabuoni**, a banker and uncle of Lorenzo de' Medici, and are liberally sprinkled with portraits of the Tornabuoni clan. Such self-glorification made the frescoes the object of special ire after they were completed, drawing the vitriol of Savonarola during his hellfire sermons. No other frescoes in the city are so self-conscious a celebration of Florence at its zenith – indeed, one of the frescoes on the right-hand wall includes a prominent Latin inscription (on an arch to the right) which reads: "The year 1490, when the most beautiful city renowned for abundance, victories, arts and noble buildings profoundly enjoyed salubrity and peace."

Ghirlandaio himself features in the scene in which Joachim, the Virgin's father, is chased from the temple because he has been unable to have children – the painter is the figure in the right-hand group with hand on hip. In the neighbouring fresco, the young woman in the white and gold dress leading the group of women is Ludovica, Tornabuoni's only daughter, who died in childbirth aged 15. Across the chancel, on the right wall, the **Visitation** features Giovanna degli Albizi, Tornabuoni's daughter-in-law, who also died in childbirth – she's the first of the trio of women to the right of the Virgin. The **Birth of St John the**

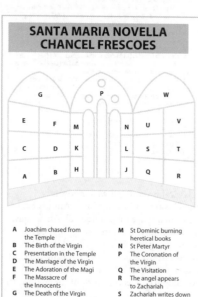

SANTA MARIA NOVELLA CHANCEL FRESCOES

A	Joachim chased from the Temple	M	St Dominic burning heretical books
B	The Birth of the Virgin	N	St Peter Martyr
C	Presentation in the Temple	P	The Coronation of the Virgin
D	The Marriage of the Virgin		
E	The Adoration of the Magi	Q	The Visitation
F	The Massacre of the Innocents	R	The angel appears to Zachariah
G	The Death of the Virgin and Assumption	S	Zachariah writes down the name of his son
H	Giovanni Tornabuoni (donor) at prayer	T	The birth of St John the Baptist
J	Francesca Pitti, wife of Giovanni Tornabuoni	U	The baptism of Christ
K	The Annunciation	V	St John the Baptist preaching
L	St John in the Wilderness	W	The Feast of Herod

Baptist features Tornabuoni's sister, Lucrezia, better known as the mother of Lorenzo de' Medici: she's the woman in front of the servant carrying the fruit on her head.

Cappella Gondi and Cappella Strozzi

The next chapel beyond the chancel is the **Cappella Gondi** (13), which houses Brunelleschi's crucifix, supposedly carved as a riposte to the uncouthness of Donatello's cross in Santa Croce. Legend claims that Donatello was so struck on seeing his rival's work that he dropped a basket of eggs.

Even more startling, however, is the great fresco cycle in the **Cappella Strozzi** (14), which is raised above the level of the rest of the church at the end of the north transept. Its frescoes (1350–57) were commissioned as an expiation of the sin of usury by Tommaso Strozzi, an ancestor of Filippo Strozzi, and are the masterpiece of Nardo di Cione, brother of the better-known Orcagna (Andrea di Cione), with whom Nardo collaborated to design the chapel's stained glass. The central fresco depicts the *Last Judgement*, with Dante featured as one of the saved (in white, third from the left, second row from the top); so, too, are Tommaso Strozzi and his wife, shown being led by St Michael into paradise. The theme of judgement is continued in the bleached fresco of Dante's *Inferno* on the right wall, faced by a thronged *Paradiso* on the left.

Orcagna alone painted the chapel's magnificent high altarpiece, *Christ Presenting the Keys to St Peter and the Book of Wisdom to Thomas Aquinas* (1357). A propaganda exercise on behalf of the Dominicans, the picture shows Christ bestowing favour on both St Peter and St Thomas Aquinas, the latter a figure second only to St Dominic in the order's hierarchy.

Museo di Santa Maria Novella

Piazza Santa Maria Novella • Mon–Thurs & Sat 9am–5pm, Sun 9am–2pm • €2.70 • ⓦ museicivicifiorentini.it

Further remarkable paintings are to be found in the Romanesque conventual buildings to the left of the church of Santa Maria Novella, home to the **Museo di Santa Maria Novella**. The first set of cloisters, the **Chiostro Verde**, dating from 1332 to 1350, features damaged but nonetheless remarkable frescoes of *Stories from Genesis* (1425–30) executed by Paolo Uccello and his workshop. The cloister takes its name from the green *terra verde* base pigment they used, which now gives the paintings a spectral undertone.

The windswept image of **The Flood**, the best-preserved of the frescoes, is rendered almost unintelligible by the telescoping perspective and the double appearance of the ark (before and after the flood), whose flanks form a receding corridor in the centre of the picture: on the left, the ark is rising on the deluge, on the right it has come to rest as the waters subside. In the foreground, two men fight each other in their desperation to stay alive; the chequered lifebelt that one of these men is wearing around his neck is a favourite Uccello device for demonstrating a mastery of perspective – it's a *mazzocchio*, a 72-faceted wicker ring round which a turbaned headdress was wrapped. Another man grabs the ankles of the visionary figure in the foreground – presumably Noah, though he is a much younger Noah than the hirsute patriarch leaning out of the ark on the right to receive the dove's olive branch. In the right foreground there's a preview of the universal devastation, with tiny corpses laid out on the deck, and a crow gobbling an eyeball from one of the drowned.

Cappellone degli Spagnoli

The **Cappellone degli Spagnoli** (Spanish Chapel), which was the chapterhouse of the immensely rich convent of Santa Maria and for a time was the headquarters of the Inquisition, received its present name after Eleonora di Toledo, wife of Cosimo I, reserved it for the use of her Spanish entourage. Presumably she derived much inspiration from its majestic fresco cycle (1367–69) by Andrea di Firenze, an

1

extended depiction of the triumph of the Catholic Church that was described by Ruskin as "the most noble piece of pictorial philosophy in Italy".

The frescoes

Virtually every patch of the walls is covered with frescoes, whose theme is the role of the Dominicans in the battle against heresy and in the salvation of Christian souls. The **left wall** as you enter depicts *The Triumph of Divine Wisdom*, a triumph exemplified by Thomas Aquinas, who is portrayed enthroned below the Virgin and Apostles amidst the winged Virtues and the "wise men" of the Old and New Testaments.

The more spectacular **right wall** depicts *The Triumph of the Church*, or more specifically, the "Mission, Work and Triumph of the Dominican Order". At the bottom is Florence's cathedral, imagined one hundred years before the structure was completed. Before it stand the pope and Holy Roman Emperor, society's ultimate spiritual and temporal rulers. In front of them stand ranks of figures representing religious orders, among which the Dominicans are naturally pre-eminent. Note St Dominic, the order's founder, unleashing the "hounds of the lord", or Domini Canes, a pun on the Dominicans' name.

Among the group of pilgrims (just below the Duomo) are several **portraits**, real or imagined: Cimabue (standing in a large brown cloak); Giotto (beside him in profile, wearing a green cloak); Boccaccio (further right, in purple, holding a closed book); Petrarch (above, with a cloak and white ermine hood); and Dante (alongside Petrarch in profile, with a white cap). Above and to the right are scenes of young people dancing, playing music and engaging in other pleasures of the sort that the Dominicans so heartily condemned.

Those able to resist such abominations are shown being marshalled by a nearby friar, who hears their confession before dispatching them towards St Peter and the Gate of Paradise. Once through the gate, the blessed are shown in adoration of God and the angels with the Virgin in their midst. Foremost among those confessing is Buonamico Guidalotti (shown kneeling), who paid for the chapel in honour of his wife, who died during the 1348 plague. The far wall shows scenes connected with the Crucifixion, while the near (entrance) wall, which is excluded from the frescoes' unified theme, contains episodes from the life of St Peter Martyr, one of the Dominicans' leading lights.

Chiostrino dei Morti and Chiostro Grande

The contemporaneous decoration of the **Chiostrino dei Morti**, the oldest part of the complex, has not aged so robustly; it was closed for restoration at the time of writing. The **Chiostro Grande**, to the west, is also out of bounds, because it's owned by the *carabinieri*. The **museum** adjoining the Chiostro Grande is notable chiefly for some peculiarly glamorous fourteenth- and fifteenth-century reliquary busts, containing remnants of St Ursula and Mary Magdalene, among others.

Museo Nazionale Alinari Fotografia

Piazza Santa Maria Novella 14ar • Mon, Tues & Thurs–Sun 10am–6.30pm • €9 • ⓦ mnaf.it

Back at the start of the thirteenth century the colonnaded building that faces Santa Maria Novella across the piazza was the hospital of San Paolo, a refuge for the sick and the destitute, and also the base for the Dominicans before they moved to Santa Maria Novella. At the beginning of the fifteenth century the administration of the hospital passed to the Arte dei Giudici e Notari (the guild of judges and notaries), and it was they who enlarged the building, probably to a design by Michelozzo, whose loggia – the **Loggia di San Paolo** – is a close imitation of Brunelleschi's Spedale degli Innocenti (see p.99). In the 1490s Andrea della Robbia added the terracotta medallions and lunettes, further emphasizing the similarity between the two buildings. One of the lunettes depicts the momentous meeting of St Francis (who founded a Franciscan convent next door) and his fellow monastic reformer St Dominic, an event that's generally believed to have happened in Rome in 1217, but is said by local folklore to have occurred a little sooner, on this very spot.

In the 1780s the hospital was suppressed and the building became a school for impoverished girls and unmarried young women, which it remained until World War II, when it was used by the Fascists as a prison. After the war it reopened as a state school, and now, having been handsomely restored, it's home to the **Museo Nazionale Alinari Fotografia**. Part of the museum is set aside for one-off photography exhibitions, but most of the space is given over to changing displays drawn from Alinari's archive of more than four million pictures, covering everything from 1840s daguerreotypes to the work of present-day photographers. The technology of the art is featured too, with a variety of cameras on show, plus stereoscopes and camera obscuras.

North of the centre

A few blocks east of the train station and the Duomo lies the San Lorenzo district, the city's main market area, with scores of stalls encircling a vast food hall. The racks of T-shirts, leather jackets and belts almost engulf the church of **San Lorenzo**, a building of major importance that's attached to another of the city's great draws, the **Cappelle Medicee** (Medici Chapels). While various eminent Medici are buried in the main part of San Lorenzo, dozens of lesser lights are interred in these chapels, with two of them being celebrated by some of **Michelangelo**'s finest sculpture. The Medici also account for the area's other major sight, the **Palazzo Medici-Riccardi**, with its exquisite fresco-covered chapel, while the most celebrated of all Michelangelo's works in stone – the *David* – can be admired in the nearby galleries of the **Accademia**. The devotional art of Fra' Angelico fills the nearby **Museo di San Marco**, which in turn is but a stroll away from **Piazza Santissima Annunziata**, one of Florence's most photogenic squares.

San Lorenzo

Piazza San Lorenzo • Daily 10am–5.30pm; March–Oct closes Sun 1.30pm • €3.50

Founded in 393, **San Lorenzo** has a claim to be the oldest church in Florence. For some three hundred years it was the city's cathedral, before renouncing its title to Santa Reparata, the precursor of the Duomo. By 1060 a sizeable church had been constructed here, a building which in time became the Medici's parish church.

The Medici were in a particularly generous mood in 1419, when a committee of eight parishioners headed by Giovanni di Bicci de' Medici, founder of the family's fortune, offered to finance a new San Lorenzo. **Brunelleschi** was commissioned to begin the project, starting work on the Sagrestia Vecchia (Old Sacristy) before being given the go-ahead two years later to rebuild the entire church. Construction lapsed over the next twenty years, hampered by financial problems, political upheavals and Brunelleschi's simultaneous work on the cathedral dome. Giovanni's son, Cosimo de' Medici, eventually gave the work fresh impetus with a grant of 40,000 *fiorini* (florins) – at a time when 150 florins would support a Florentine family for a year. Cosimo's largesse saved the day, but was still not sufficient to provide the church with a facade. No less a figure than Michelangelo laboured to remedy the omission, one of many to devote time to a scheme to provide a suitable frontage. None of the efforts was to any avail: to this day the exterior's bare brick has never been clad.

The nave

When you step inside the church, what strikes you first is the cool rationality of Brunelleschi's design: San Lorenzo was the earlier of Brunelleschi's great Florentine churches (the other is Santo Spirito) but already displays his mastery of Classical

1

SAN LORENZO

PIAZZA MADONNA DEGLI ALDOBRANDINI

CANTO DE' NELLI

PIAZZA SAN LORENZO

1 Marriage of the Virgin (1523), Rosso Fiorentino
2 Bronze pulpits (1455–66), Donatello
3 Pala del Sacramento (1458–61), Desiderio da Settignano
4 Sarcophagus, fresco and crucifix (1470), Antonio da Pollaiuolo
5 Tomb of Cosimo de' Medici (Cosimo il Vecchio)
6 Tomb of Giovanni and Piero de' Medici (Cosimo's sons)
7 Tomb of Giovanni and Piccarda de' Medici (Cosimo's parents)
8 Funerary memorial to Donatello
9 Annunciation (1440), Filippo Lippi
10 Martyrdom of St Lawrence (1565–9), Bronzino
11 Stairs to Ricetto and Biblioteca
A Entrance to the Cappelle Medicee
B Cappella dei Principi
C Sagrestia Nuova
D Sagrestia Vecchia
E Ricetto (vestibule), Michelangelo
F Biblioteca Medicea-Laurenziana

decorative motifs and mathematically planned proportions.

The first work of art to catch your attention, in the second chapel on the right, is Rosso Fiorentino's **Marriage of the Virgin** (marked 1 on our plan) with its uniquely golden-haired and youthful Joseph. There's another arresting painting at the top of the left aisle – Bronzino's enormous fresco of *The Martyrdom of St Lawrence* (10) – but it seems a shallow piece of work alongside the nearby bronze pulpits by **Donatello** (2). Clad with reliefs depicting scenes preceding and following the Crucifixion, these are the artist's last works (begun c.1460), and were completed by his pupils as increasing paralysis limited their master's ability to model in wax. Jagged and discomforting, charged with more energy than the space can contain, these panels are more like brutal sketches in bronze than conventional reliefs. Donatello is buried in the nave of the church, next to his patron, Cosimo de' Medici, and commemorated by a **memorial** (8) on the right wall of the chapel in the north transept, close to Filippo Lippi's 1440 altarpiece of the Annunciation (9).

In the centre of the church, the **tomb of Cosimo de' Medici** (5) bears the inscription "Pater Patriae" (Father of the Fatherland) – a title once borne by Roman emperors.

Sagrestia Vecchia

Four more leading Medici members lie buried in the **Sagrestia Vecchia** or Old Sacristy, one of Brunelleschi's earliest projects (1421–26), and the only one completed in his lifetime. It was commissioned by Giovanni Bicci de' Medici as a private chapel, and on his death he and his wife Piccarda were buried beneath the massive marble slab at the centre of the chapel. Another tomb lies immediately to the left as you enter: the last resting place of Giovanni's grandsons, Giovanni and Piero de' Medici, it was commissioned from Verrocchio in 1472 by Lorenzo de' Medici. To the modern eye the tomb looks plain, but a Florentine of the day would have been well aware that it was made from three of the most precious materials of antiquity – marble, porphyry and bronze.

Donatello's sculptures and doors

More arresting than either of the tombs, however, is the chapel's ornamentation. Here Brunelleschi's genius was complemented by the decorative acumen of Donatello, who worked in the sacristy between 1434 and 1443: he was responsible for both the cherub-filled frieze and the eight tondos above it, depicting the four Evangelists and a quartet of scenes from the life of St John the Evangelist. Two large **reliefs**, also probably by Donatello, adorn the space above the two doors on the end wall: one shows Sts Lawrence and Stephen, twin protectors of Florence, the other Sts Cosmas and Damian. These last two were the patron saints of doctors (*medici*) and thus of the Medici, who were probably descended from doctors or apothecaries. By happy coincidence, Cosimo de' Medici, the church's chief patron, was born on the saints' feast day (27 Sept), so they are often seen in paintings or buildings commissioned or connected with him.

Donatello was also responsible for the two **bronze doors**, with their combative martyrs to the left, and the *Apostles and Fathers of the Church* to the right. The chapel beyond the left door has a beautiful little marble lavabo, probably by Verrocchio: many of its fantastic creatures have Medici connections – the falcon and lamb, for example, are the symbols of Piero de' Medici, who commissioned the work.

The fresco

The **stellar fresco** above the recessed altar inevitably draws your eye. Opinion differs as to whether the painted stars represent the state of the heavens on July 16, 1416, the birthday of Piero de' Medici, or on July 6, 1439, the date on which the union of the Eastern and Western churches was celebrated at the Council of Florence.

Biblioteca Medicea-Laurenziana

Piazza San Lorenzo • Mon, Fri & Sat 8.30am–2pm, Tues–Thurs 8am–5pm • €3 • ⓦ www.bml.firenze.sbn.it

A gateway to the left of the church facade leads through a cloister and through a doorway up to the **Biblioteca Medicea-Laurenziana**. Wishing to create a suitably grandiose home for the precious manuscripts assembled by Cosimo and Lorenzo de' Medici, Pope Clement VII – Lorenzo's nephew – asked Michelangelo to design a new Medici library in 1524. Michelangelo's **Ricetto** (1559–71), or vestibule, is a revolutionary showpiece of Mannerist architecture, delighting in paradoxical display: brackets that support nothing, columns that sink into the walls rather than stand out from them, and a flight of steps so large that it almost fills the room, spilling down like a solidified lava flow.

From this eccentric space, you're sometimes allowed into the tranquil **reading room**; here, too, almost everything is the work of Michelangelo, even the inlaid desks. Exhibitions in the connecting rooms draw on the 15,000-piece Medici collection, which includes manuscripts as diverse as a fifth-century copy of Virgil – the collection's oldest item – and a treatise on architecture by Leonardo.

Cappelle Medicee

Piazza Madonna degli Aldobrandini 6 • Tues–Sat 8.15am–5.50pm, plus first, third & fifth Sun of month and second & fourth Mon of month, same hours • €6 • ⓦ www.uffizi.firenze.it

Michelangelo's most celebrated contribution to the San Lorenzo complex forms part of the **Cappelle Medicee**, entered from Piazza Madonna degli Aldobrandini, at the back of the church. Hardly any of the Medici, however humble, suffered the indignity of a modest grave. Some might have expected more, though, than the low-vaulted **crypt** of the Cappelle Medicee, home to the brass-railed tombs of many of the family's lesser lights. Most were placed here in 1791 by Ferdinand III with what appears to have been scant regard for his ancestors: one contemporary recorded how the duke had the corpses thrown together, "caring scarcely to distinguish one from the other".

Cappella dei Principi

After filing through the crypt, you climb into the larger of the chapels, the **Cappella dei Principi** (Chapel of the Princes), an oppressive marble-plated hall built as a mausoleum

1

for Cosimo I and the grand dukes who succeeded him. The extent of Medici conceit was underlined by the chapel's intended centrepiece – the Holy Sepulchre of Christ, a prize that had to be forfeited when the pasha refused to sell it and an expedition sent to Jerusalem to steal it returned empty-handed. Dismissed by Byron as a "fine frippery in great slabs of various expensive stones, to commemorate rotten and forgotten carcasses", this was the most expensive building project ever financed by the Medici, and the family were still paying for it in 1743 when the last of the line, Anna Maria Luisa, joined her forebears in the basement. Restoration has been in progress since a section of cornice fell off in 1999, revealing major structural faults.

Sagrestia Nuova

Begun in 1520, the **Sagrestia Nuova** was designed by Michelangelo as a tribute to, and reinvention of, Brunelleschi's Sagrestia Vecchia. Architectural experts go into raptures over the sophistication of the architecture, notably the empty niches above the doors, which play complex games with the vocabulary of classical architecture, but the lay person will be drawn to the three fabulous **Medici tombs** (1520–34), two wholly and one partly by Michelangelo. The sculptor was awarded the commissions by Pope Leo X – a Medici – and the pope's cousin, Cardinal Giulio de' Medici, later Pope Clement VII.

The tombs

As you enter, the tomb on the left belongs to **Lorenzo, duke of Urbino**, the grandson of Lorenzo the Magnificent. Michelangelo depicts him as a man of thought, and his sarcophagus bears figures of *Dawn* and *Dusk*, the times of day whose ambiguities appeal to the contemplative mind. Opposite stands the tomb of Lorenzo de' Medici's youngest son, **Giuliano, duke of Nemours**; as a man of action, his character is symbolized by the clear antithesis of *Day* and *Night*. A contemporary recorded that the sculptor gave his subjects "a greatness, a proportion, a dignity … which seemed to him would have brought them more praise, saying that a thousand years hence no one would be able to know that they were otherwise." The protagonists were very much otherwise: Giuliano was in reality an easygoing but somewhat feckless individual, while Lorenzo combined ineffectuality with unbearable arrogance. Both died – young and not greatly lamented – of tuberculosis, combined in Lorenzo's case with syphilis.

The two principal effigies were intended to face the equally grand tombs of Lorenzo de' Medici and his brother Giuliano, two Medici who had genuine claims to fame. The only part of the project completed by Michelangelo is the **Madonna and Child**, the last image of the Madonna he ever sculpted. The figures to either side are Cosmas and Damian, which were completed to Michelangelo's original design. Michelangelo planned these tombs to include allegorical figures of Heaven and Earth and statues of river gods representing the Tiber and Arno, and sketches relating to this scheme are visible behind the altar (visitors are allowed to see them, under supervision, every 30min). The chapel was never completed as Michelangelo intended: in 1534, four years after the Medici had returned to Florence in the wretched form of Alessandro, Michelangelo decamped to Rome, where he stayed for the rest of his life.

Palazzo Medici-Riccardi

Via Cavour 1 • Thurs–Tues 9am–7pm • €7 • ⓦ palazzo-medici.it

On the edge of Piazza San Lorenzo stands the **Palazzo Medici-Riccardi**, built for Cosimo de' Medici by Michelozzo between 1444 and 1462, supposedly after Cosimo had rejected a design by Brunelleschi on political grounds, saying "envy is a plant one should never water". With its heavily rusticated exterior, this palace was the prototype for several major Florentine buildings, most notably the Palazzo Pitti and Palazzo Strozzi, and it remained the family home and Medici business headquarters until Cosimo I moved to the Palazzo Vecchio in 1540. After 1659 the palace was greatly altered by its new owners, the Riccardi, and it now houses the offices of the provincial government. The chief attraction for tourists is the cycle of Gozzoli **frescoes** in the tiny upstairs chapel, which a maximum of fifteen people may view at any one time.

The Gozzoli frescoes
Painted around 1460, Benozzo Gozzoli's sequence ostensibly shows *The Journey of the Magi*, but probably portrays the pageant of the Compagnia dei Magi, the most patrician of the city's religious confraternities, whose annual procession took place at Epiphany. Several of the Medici, inevitably, were prominent members, including Piero de' Medici (Piero il Gottoso), who may have commissioned the pictures. It's known that several of the Medici household are featured in the procession, but putting names to these prettified faces is a problem. The man leading the cavalcade on a white horse is almost certainly Piero, while the figure behind him, in the black cloak, is probably his father, Cosimo il Vecchio. Piero's older son, the future Lorenzo il Magnifico, 11 years old when the fresco was painted, is probably the gold-clad young king in the foreground, riding the grey horse, while his brother, Giuliano, is probably the one preceded by the black bowman, to the left of Cosimo il Vecchio. The artist himself is in the crowd at the rear of the procession, his red beret signed with the words "Opus Benotii" in gold. Finally, the bearded characters among the throng might be portraits of the retinue of the Byzantine emperor John Paleologus III, who had attended the Council of Florence twenty years before the fresco was painted.

The first floor
Another set of stairs leads from the passageway beside the courtyard up to the **first floor**, where a display case in the lobby of the main gallery contains a *Madonna and Child* by **Filippo Lippi**, one of Cosimo de' Medici's more troublesome protégés. Cosimo set up a workshop for him in the Medici palace, from which the artist often absented himself to go chasing women. On one occasion Cosimo actually locked Filippo in the studio, but he escaped down a rope of bed sheets; having cajoled him into returning, Cosimo declared that he would in future manage the painter with "affection and kindness", a policy that seems to have worked more successfully.

The ceiling of the grandiloquent **gallery** glows with Luca Giordano's fresco of *The Apotheosis of the Medici* (1683), from which one can only deduce that Giordano had no sense of shame. Accompanying Cosimo III on his flight into the ether is his son, Gian Gastone (d.1737), the last male Medici, who grew to be a man so dissolute and inert that he could rarely summon the energy to get out of bed in the morning.

Mercato Centrale
Via dell'Ariento • Mon–Sat 7am–2pm

The **Mercato Centrale** was designed by Giuseppe Mengoni, architect of Milan's famous Galleria, and is Europe's largest covered food hall. Opened in 1874, it received a major overhaul a century later, reopening in 1980 with a new first floor. Butchers, *alimentari*, tripe-sellers, greengrocers, pasta stalls – they're all gathered under the one roof, and charging prices lower than you'll readily find elsewhere in the city. Get there close to the end of the working day and you'll find some good reductions.

Each day from 8am to 7pm (except Sun) the streets around the Mercato Centrale are thronged with **stalls** selling clothing and leather goods. Most of the stuff is of doubtful quality, but this is the busiest of Florence's daily street markets, and an immersion in the haggling mass of customers can be fun.

1

Cenacolo di Fuligno

Via Faenza 42 • Tues, Thurs & Sat 9am–noon • Donation requested

One of Florence's many *cenacoli* (Last Suppers), the **Cenacolo di Fuligno**, is to be found a short distance from the market in the former Franciscan convent of Sant'Onofrio. Discovered under layers of whitewash and grime in 1840, it was once thought to be by Raphael, then reassigned to Raphael's mentor Perugino. Latest research indicates that it was painted by a member of Perugino's workshop but designed by the master in the 1490s – the orderliness and wistful tranquillity of the scene is typical of Perugino's style, and the Apostles' poses are drawn from a repertoire of gestures which the artist frequently deployed.

Fortezza da Basso

Piazza Adua 1

North of Via Faenza, the **Fortezza da Basso** was built to intimidate the people of Florence by the vile Alessandro de' Medici, who ordained himself Duke of Florence after a ten-month siege by the army of Charles V and Pope Clement VII (probably Alessandro's father) had forcibly restored the Medici. Michelangelo, the greatest Florentine architect of the day, had played a major role in the defence of the city during the siege; the job of designing the fortress fell to the more pliant Antonio da Sangallo.

Within a few years the cruelties of Alessandro had become intolerable; a petition to Charles V spoke of the Fortezza da Basso as "a prison and a slaughterhouse for the unhappy citizens". Charles's response to Alessandro's atrocities was to marry his daughter to the tyrant. In the end, another Medici came to the rescue: in 1537 the distantly related **Lorenzaccio de' Medici** stabbed Alessandro to death as he waited for an amorous assignation in Lorenzaccio's house. The reasons for the murder have never been clear, but it seems that Lorenzaccio's mental health was little better than Alessandro's: in his earlier years he and Alessandro had regularly launched lecherous sorties on the city's convents, and he had been expelled from Rome after lopping the heads off statues on the Arch of Constantine. The assassination, however, had favourable consequences for the city: as Alessandro died heirless, the council proposed that the leadership of the Florentine republic should be offered to **Cosimo de' Medici**, the great-grandson of Lorenzo il Magnifico. Subsequent Medici dukes had no need of a citizen-proof fort, and the Fortezza da Basso fell into dereliction after use as a gaol and barracks.

Since 1978 the vast modern pavilions in the centre of the complex have been used for trade fairs and events such as the Pitti Moda fashion shows (Jan & July) and the Biennale of contemporary art, held in December in odd-numbered years. Major artworks are restored at the **Opificio delle Pietre Dure** (see opposite) laboratory within the fort.

The Accademia

Via Ricasoli 66 • Tues–Sun 8.15am–6.50pm • €6.50 • ⓦ www.uffizi.firenze.it

Florence's first academy of drawing, the Accademia del Disegno, was founded in 1563 by Bronzino, Ammannati and Vasari. Initially based in Santissima Annunziata, it moved in 1764 to Via Ricasoli, and soon afterwards was transformed into a general arts academy, the Accademia di Belle Arti. Twenty years later the Grand Duke Pietro Leopoldo I founded the nearby **Galleria dell'Accademia**, filling its rooms with paintings for the edification of the students, a collection later augmented with pieces from suppressed religious foundations and other sources. Since 1873, it has been the home of Michelangelo's *David*, hence the perpetual queues.

The **picture galleries** which flank the main sculpture hall are generally unexciting, with copious examples of the work of "Unknown Florentine" and "Follower of…". The pieces likeliest to make an impact are Pontormo's *Venus and Cupid* (1532), painted to a cartoon by Michelangelo; a *Madonna of the Sea* (1470) attributed to Botticelli; and the painted fifteenth-century Adimari Chest, showing a Florentine wedding ceremony in the Piazza del Duomo. A cluster of rooms near the exit house gilded religious works from the thirteenth and fourteenth centuries, including an altarpiece of the Pentecost by Orcagna (c.1365).

The David

Commissioned by the Opera del Duomo in 1501, the **David** was conceived to invoke parallels with Florence's freedom from outside domination, and its recent liberation from Savonarola and the Medici. It's an incomparable show of technical bravura, all the more impressive given the difficulties posed by the marble from which it was carved. The four-metre block of stone – thin, shallow and riddled with cracks – had been quarried from Carrara forty years earlier. Several artists had already attempted to work with it, notably Agostino di Duccio, Andrea Sansovino and Leonardo da Vinci, but Michelangelo succeeded where others had failed, completing the work in 1504 when he was still just 29.

Thoroughly cleaned in recent years, the *David* occupies a specially built alcove, protected by a glass barrier that was built in 1991, after one of its toes was cracked by a hammer-wielding vandal. With its massive head and gangling arms, the *David* is an ungainly figure, but its proportions would not have appeared so graceless in the setting for which it was first conceived: when they gave Michelangelo his commission, the Opera del Duomo had in mind a statue that would be placed high on the Duomo's facade. Perhaps because the finished *David* was even larger than had been envisaged, it was decided that it should be placed instead at ground level, in Piazza della Signoria. Four days and a team of forty men were required to move the statue from the workshop to the Piazza; another three weeks were needed to raise it onto its plinth. During the move the statue required protection day and night to prevent it being stoned by Medici supporters who were all too aware of its symbolism. Damage was done a few years later, in 1527, when the Medici were again expelled from the city: a bench, flung from a window of the Palazzo Vecchio by anti-Medici rioters, smashed the left arm, but the pieces were gathered up and reassembled. The statue remained exposed to the elements in its outdoor setting until it was sent to the Accademia, by which time it had lost its gilded hair and the gilded band across its chest.

The Slaves and St Matthew

Michelangelo once described the process of carving as being the liberation of the form from within the stone, a notion that seems to be embodied by the remarkable unfinished **Slaves** (or *Prisoners*). His procedure, clearly demonstrated here, was to cut the figure as if it were a deep relief, and then to free the three-dimensional figure; often his assistants would perform the initial operation, working from the master's pencil marks, so it's possible that Michelangelo's own chisel never actually touched these stones.

Probably carved in the late 1520s, the statues were intended for the tomb of Julius II, perhaps to symbolize the liberal arts left "enslaved" by Julius's demise. The tomb underwent innumerable permutations before its eventual abandonment, however, and in 1564 the artist's nephew gave the carvings to the Medici, who installed them in the grotto of the Bóboli garden. Four of the original six statues came to the Accademia in 1909; two others found their way to the Louvre.

Close by is another unfinished work, *St Matthew* (1505–6), started soon after completion of the *David* as a commission from the Opera del Duomo; they requested a full series of the Apostles from Michelangelo, but this is the only one he ever began. It languished half-forgotten in the cathedral vaults until 1831.

Museo dell'Opificio delle Pietre Dure

Via degli Alfani 78 • Mon–Sat 8.15am–2pm • €4 • ⓦ opificiodellepietredure.it

The **Museo dell'Opificio delle Pietre Dure**, which occupies a corner of the Accademia

1

building, was founded in 1588 to train craftsmen in the distinctively Florentine art of creating pictures or patterns with polished, inlaid semi-precious stones. The museum clearly elucidates the highly skilled processes involved in the creation of *pietre dure* work, and has some remarkable examples of the genre. If you want to see some more spectacular specimens, you should visit the Cappelle Medicee or the Palazzo Pitti's Museo degli Argenti. While several local workshops still maintain the traditions of this specialized art form, the Opificio itself has evolved into one of the world's leading centres for the restoration of stonework and paintings.

Museo di San Marco

Piazza San Marco • Tues–Fri 8.15am–1.50pm, Sat & Sun 8.15am–4.50pm, plus first, third & fifth Mon of month 8.15am–1.50pm • €4 • Ⓦ www.uffizi.firenze.it

A whole side of Piazza San Marco is taken up by the church of San Marco and its Dominican convent, now the home of the **Museo di San Marco**. The Dominicans acquired the site in 1436, after being forced to move from their former home in Fiesole, and the complex promptly became the recipient of Cosimo de' Medici's most lavish patronage: in the 1430s he financed Michelozzo's enlargement of the conventual buildings, and went on to establish a vast library here. Ironically, the convent became the centre of resistance to the Medici later in the century: Girolamo **Savonarola**, leader of the government of Florence after the expulsion of the Medici in 1494, was the prior of San Marco. In 1537 Duke Cosimo expelled the Dominicans once more, reminding them that it was another Cosimo who had established the building's magnificence in the first place.

As Michelozzo was altering and expanding San Marco, the convent's walls were being decorated by one of its friars and a future prior, **Fra' Angelico**. Born to a wealthy landowner in Vicchio di Mugello, probably in the mid-1390s, he entered the Dominican monastery of Fiesole at around the age of 20, and was then known as Fra' Giovanni da Fiesole. Already recognized as an accomplished artist, he came to San Marco in 1436 and was encouraged by the theologian Antonino Pierozzi, the convent's first prior, who later became archbishop of Florence. By the time Fra' Giovanni succeeded Pierozzi as prior, the pictures he had created here and for numerous churches in central Italy (including the Vatican) had earned him the title "the angelic painter". In 1982 he was beatified (a halfway house to sainthood), thus formalizing the name by which he had long been known, Beato Angelico, or the Blessed Angelico.

The ground floor

Immediately beyond the **entrance** lies the **Chiostro di Sant'Antonino**, designed by Michelozzo and dominated by a vast cedar of Lebanon. Most of the cloister's faded frescoes are sixteenth-century depictions of episodes from the life of Antonino Pierozzi, Fra' Angelico's mentor, who was canonized as St Antonine in 1523. Fra' Angelico himself painted the frescoes in its four corners, of which the most striking is the lunette of *St Dominic at the Foot of the Cross*.

Ospizio dei Pellegrini

Twenty or so paintings by the artist are gathered in the **Ospizio dei Pellegrini**, or Pilgrims' Hospice, which lies between the cloister and the piazza. Many of the works – including several of Angelico's most famous – were brought here from churches and galleries around Florence; all display the artist's brilliant colouring and spatial clarity, and an air of imperturbable piety. On the right wall as you enter is a *Deposition* (1432–35); commissioned by the Strozzi family for the church of Santa Trìnita, the painting was begun by Lorenzo Monaco, who died after completing the upper trio of triangular pinnacles, and continued by Fra' Angelico. At the opposite end of the room hangs the *Madonna dei Linaiuoli*, Angelico's first major public painting (1433), commissioned by the *Linaiuoli* or flax-workers' guild, for their headquarters. Halfway down the room, on the inner wall, the so-called *Pala di San Marco* (1440), though badly damaged by the passage of time and a disastrous restoration, demonstrates Fra' Angelico's familiarity with the latest developments in artistic theory: its figures are

1

SAVONAROLA

Girolamo **Savonarola** was born in 1452, the son of the physician to the Ferrara court. An abstemious, melancholic and pious young man, he absconded to a Dominican monastery in Bologna at the age of 23, informing his father by letter that he was "unable to endure the evil conduct of the heedless people of Italy".

Within a few years, the Dominicans had dispatched him to preach all over northern Italy. Though physically unattractive – he was frail, with a beak of a nose and a blubbery mouth – Savonarola had an intensity of manner and of message that drew a committed following when he came to the monastery of **San Marco** in 1489. By 1491, his sermons had become so popular that he was asked to deliver his Lent address in the Duomo. Proclaiming that God was speaking through him, he berated the city for its decadence, for its paintings that made the Virgin "look like a whore", and for the tyranny of its Medici-led government. Following the death of Lorenzo il Magnifico, the rhetoric became apocalyptic. "Wait no longer, for there may be no more time for repentance," he told another Duomo congregation, summoning images of plagues, invasions and destruction.

When Charles VIII of France marched into Italy in September 1494 to press his claim to the throne of Naples, Savonarola presented him as the instrument of God's vengeance. Violating Piero de' Medici's declaration of Tuscan neutrality, the French army massacred the garrison at Fivizzano, and Florence prepared for an onslaught, as Savonarola declaimed, "The Sword has descended; the scourge has fallen." Piero capitulated to Charles, and within days the Medici had fled. Hailed by Savonarola as "the Minister of God, the Minister of Justice", Charles and his vast army passed peacefully through Florence on their way to Rome.

The political vacuum in Florence was filled by the declaration of a **republican constitution**, but Savonarola was now in effect the ruler of the city. Continual decrees were issued from San Marco: profane carnivals were to be outlawed, fasting was to be observed more frequently, children were to act as the agents of the righteous, informing the authorities whenever their parents transgressed the Eternal Law. Irreligious books and paintings, expensive clothes, cosmetics, board games, trivialities and luxuries of all types were destroyed, a ritual purging that reached a crescendo with a colossal "**Bonfire of the Vanities**" on the Piazza della Signoria.

Meanwhile, Charles VIII was installed in Naples and a formidable alliance was being assembled to overthrow him: the papacy, Milan, Venice, Ferdinand of Aragon and the emperor Maximilian. In July 1495 the army of this Holy League confronted the French and was badly defeated. Charles's army continued northwards back to France, and Savonarola was summoned to the Vatican to explain why he had been unable to join the campaign against the intruder. He declined to attend, claiming that it was not God's will that he should make the journey, and thus set off a chain of exchanges that ended with his **excommunication** in June 1497. Defying Pope Alexander's order, Savonarola celebrated Mass in the Duomo on Christmas Day, which prompted a final threat from Rome: send Savonarola to the Vatican or imprison him in Florence, otherwise the whole city would join him in excommunication.

The people of Florence began to desert him. The region's crops had failed, plague had broken out again, and the city was at war with Pisa. The Franciscans of Florence, sceptical of the Dominican monk's claim to divine approval, now issued a terrible challenge. One of their community and one of Savonarola's would walk through an avenue of fire in the Piazza della Signoria: if the Dominican died, Savonarola would be banished; if the Franciscan died, Savonarola's main critic, Fra' Francesco da Puglia, would be expelled.

A thunderstorm prevented the trial from taking place, but the mood in the city had turned irrevocably. The following day, Palm Sunday 1498, a siege of the monastery of San Marco ended with Savonarola's **arrest**. Accused of heresy, he was tortured to the point of death, then **burned at the stake** in front of the Palazzo Vecchio, with two of his supporters. When the flames had finally been extinguished, the ashes were thrown into the river, to prevent anyone from gathering them as relics.

1

arranged in lines that taper towards a central vanishing point, in accordance with the principles laid out in Alberti's *Della Pittura* (On Painting), published just two years before the picture was executed. The work was commissioned by the Medici, hence the presence of the family's patron saints Cosmas and Damian, who can be seen at work as doctors in the small panel immediately to the right.

Sala del Lavabo, refectory and adjoining rooms

Back in the cloister, a doorway in its top right-hand corner opens into the **Sala del Lavabo**, where the monks washed before eating. Its entrance wall has a *Crucifixion with Saints* by Angelico, and its right wall two panels with a pair of saints, also by Angelico. The left wall contains a damaged lunette fresco of the *Madonna and Child* by Paolo Uccello, plus part of a predella by the same artist.

The adjoining **Refettorio Grande** (Large Refectory) is dominated by a fresco of the Crucifixion by the sixteenth-century painter Giovanni Sogliani. Of more artistic interest are the rooms devoted to paintings by **Fra' Bartolomeo** and **Alesso Baldovinetti**. Note in particular Fra' Bartolomeo's intense portrait of Savonarola, and his unfinished *Pala della Signoria* (1512), originally destined for the Salone dei Cinquecento in the Palazzo Vecchio.

Sala Capitolare, Refettorio Piccolo and Foresteria

Further round the cloister lies the **Sala Capitolare**, or Chapter House, which now houses a large conventual bell, the **Piagnone**, which was rung to summon help on Savonarola's arrest on the eve of April 8, 1498: it became a symbol of anti-Medici sentiment ever after. One wall is covered by a magnificent fresco of the **Crucifixion**, painted by Fra' Angelico and assistants in 1441.

At the rear of this room, entered via a passageway alongside the Chapter House, lies the **Refettorio Piccolo**, or Small Refectory, with a lustrous *Last Supper* (1480) by Ghirlandaio. This forms an anteroom to the **Foresteria**, home to the convent's guest rooms, which is cluttered with architectural bits and pieces salvaged during nineteenth-century urban improvement schemes.

The first floor

Stairs off the cloister by the entrance to the Foresteria lead up to the first floor, where almost immediately you're confronted with one of the most sublime paintings in Italy. For the drama of its setting and the lucidity of its composition, nothing in San Marco matches Angelico's **Annunciation**. The pallid, submissive Virgin is one of the most touching images in Renaissance art, and the courteous angel, with his scintillating wings, is as convincing a heavenly messenger as any ever painted. An inscription on this fresco reminds the passing monks to say a Hail Mary as they venerate the image.

The cells

Angelico and his assistants also painted the pictures in each of the 44 **dormitory cells** on this floor, into which the brothers would withdraw for solitary contemplation and sleep. Almost all of the outer cells of the corridor on the left have works by Angelico himself, and the marvellous **Madonna delle Ombre** (*Madonna of the Shadows*), on the wall facing these cells, is probably also by him. Several of the scenes include one or both of a pair of monastic onlookers, serving as intermediaries between the occupant of the cell and the personages in the pictures: the one with the star above his head is St Dominic; the one with the split skull is St Peter Martyr, who was stabbed to death, supposedly by heretics.

At the end of the far corridor is a knot of rooms once occupied by Savonarola. These now contain various relics, including what is supposed to be a piece of wood from his funeral pyre, which is depicted in a couple of paintings here. If you turn right at the main *Annunciation* and continue to the end of the corridor you'll come to the cells that were the personal domain of Cosimo de' Medici. The fresco of the *Adoration of the Magi* (possibly by Angelico's star pupil, Benozzo Gozzoli) may have been suggested by Cosimo himself, who liked to think of himself as a latter-day wise man and gift-giving king.

Michelozzo's Library

On the way to these VIP cells you'll pass the entrance to **Michelozzo's Library**, built in 1441–44 to a design that exudes an atmosphere of calm study, though – as the plaque by the doorway tells you – it was here that Savonarola was finally cornered and arrested in 1498. Cosimo's agents roamed as far as the Near East garnering precious manuscripts and books; in turn, Cosimo handed all the religious items over to the monastery, stipulating that they should be accessible to all, making it Europe's first public library. At the far end, a door leads through to the **Sala Greca** (usually open for guided visits on the hour), which was added to house a growing collection of manuscripts of ancient Greek texts.

San Marco church

Piazza San Marco • Mon–Sat 9.30am–noon & 4–5.30pm

Much altered since Michelozzo's intervention, the church of **San Marco** is worth a quick call for two works on the second and third altars on the right: a *Madonna and Saints* painted in 1509 by Fra' Bartolomeo, and an eighth-century mosaic of *The Madonna in Prayer* (surrounded by later additions), brought here from Constantinople. The latter had to be cut in half in transit, and you can still see the break across the Virgin's midriff. The preserved body of St Antonine lies in the left transept in a chapel designed by Giambologna, and the great Renaissance humanists Pico della Mirandola and Poliziano are entombed in the left wall of the nave, above the statue of Savonarola.

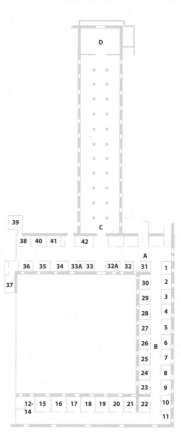

MUSEO DI SAN MARCO FIRST FLOOR

A Annunciation
B Madonna delle Ombre
C Library
D Sala Greca
1 Noli Me Tangere
2 The Body of Christ
3 Annunciation
4 Crucifixion
5 Nativity
6 Transfiguration
7 Mockery of Christ
8 The Marys at the Sepulchre
9 Coronation of the Virgin
10 Presentation in the Temple
11 Madonna and Child with Saints
12–14 Savonarola's cells
22 Crucifixion with the Virgin
23 Crucifixion with the Virgin and St Dominic
24 Baptism of Christ
25 Crucifixion with the Virgin, Magdalen and St Dominic
26 Pietà with St Dominic or St Thomas
27 Christ at the Column with the Virgin and St Dominic
28 Christ Carrying the Cross
29 Crucifixion with the Virgin and St Dominic
30 Crucifixion with the Virgin and St Dominic
31 Christ in Limbo
32 Sermon on the Mount
33 Arrest of Christ
34 Agony in the Garden
35 Institution of the Eucharist
36 Crucifixion
37 Crucifixion
38 Adoration of the Magi
39 Crucifixion with SS. Cosmas and Damian
40 Crucifixion
41 Crucifixion
42 Crucifixion with SS. Mark, Dominic, Mary and Martha

Cenacolo di Sant'Apollonia

Via XXVII Aprile 1 • Tues–Sun 8.15am–1.50pm, plus second & fourth Sun of month and first, third & fifth Mon of month, same hours • Free

Most of the the former Benedictine convent of **Sant'Apollonia** has been turned into apartments, but one entire wall of the former refectory houses Andrea del Castagno's *Last Supper*, one of the earliest uses of rigorous perspective in Renaissance art. Blood-red is the dominant tone, and the most commanding figure is the diabolic, black-bearded Judas, who sits on the near side of the table. Painted around 1450 (which makes it the first of the city's Renaissance *cenacoli*), the fresco was plastered over by the nuns before being uncovered in the middle of the nineteenth century. Above the illusionistic recess in which the supper takes place are the faded remains of a *Resurrection, Crucifixion and Deposition* by Castagno, who also painted the lunettes of the *Crucifixion* and *Pietà* on the adjacent walls.

Chiostro dello Scalzo

Via Cavour 69 • Mon, Thurs & Sat 8.15am–1.50pm • Free

To the north of San Marco is **Lo Scalzo**, the home of the Brotherhood of St John, whose vows of poverty entailed walking around barefoot (*scalzo*). The order was suppressed in 1785 and their monastery sold off, except for the **cloister**. This was the training ground for Andrea del Sarto, an artist venerated in the nineteenth century as a painter with no imperfections, but now regarded with rather less enthusiasm on account of this very smoothness. His monochrome paintings of the Cardinal Virtues and scenes from the life of the Baptist occupied him off and on for a decade from 1511, beginning with the *Baptism*, finishing with the *Birth of St John*. A couple of the sixteen scenes – *John in the Wilderness* and *John meeting Christ* – were executed by his pupil Franciabigio in 1518, when del Sarto was away in Paris.

Giardino dei Semplici

Via La Pira • Summer Mon, Tues & Thurs–Sun 10am–7pm; winter Mon, Sat & Sun 10am–5pm • €6

The **Giardino dei Semplici** or **Orto Botanico,** northeast of San Marco, was set up in 1545 for Cosimo I as a medicinal garden, following the examples of Padua and Pisa. Covering five acres, most of which are taken up by the original flowerbeds and avenues, it's the nearest equivalent to the Bóboli gardens on the north side of the city, but the entrance charge is excessive. The **university museums** that adjoin the Giardino dei Semplici – the Museo Botanico, the Museo di Mineralogia e Litologia and the Museo di Geologia e Paleontologia – are of specialist interest, and the first of the trio is open only to scholars.

MUSEO STIBBERT

About 1500m north of San Marco, at Via Stibbert 26 (bus #4 from the station), is the loopiest of Florence's museums, the **Museo Stibbert** (Mon–Wed 10am–2pm, Fri–Sun 10am–6pm; compulsory guided tour €6; Ⓦ museostibbert.it). This rambling mansion was the home of the half-Scottish, half-Italian Frederick Stibbert, who in his twenties made a name for himself in Garibaldi's army. Later he inherited a fourteenth-century house from his mother, then bought the neighbouring mansion and joined the two together, thus creating a place big enough to accommodate the fruits of his compulsive collecting. The 64 rooms contain over fifty thousand items, ranging from snuff boxes to paintings by Carlo Crivelli and a possible Botticelli.

Militaria were Frederick's chief enthusiasm, and the Stibbert **armour** collection is one of the world's best. It includes Roman, Etruscan and Japanese examples, as well as a fifteenth-century *condottiere*'s outfit and the armour worn by the great Medici commander Giovanni delle Bande Nere, retrieved from his grave in San Lorenzo in 1857. The big production number comes in the great hall, between the two houses, where a platoon of mannequins is clad in full sixteenth-century gear. Also on show is the regalia in which Napoleon was crowned king of Italy.

Piazza Santissima Annunziata

1

Nineteenth-century urban renewal schemes spoiled many of the squares of central Florence, which makes the pedestrianized **Piazza Santissima Annunziata**, with its distinctive arcades, all the more attractive a public space. It has a special importance for the city, too. Until the end of the eighteenth century the Florentine year used to begin on March 25, the Festival of the Annunciation – hence the Florentine predilection for paintings of the Annunciation, and the prestige of the Annunziata church, which has long been the place for big weddings. The festival is still marked by a huge fair in the piazza and the streets leading off it; later in the year, on the first weekend in September, the square is used for Tuscany's largest crafts fair.

Brunelleschi began the piazza in the 1420s, with additions made later by Ammannati and Antonio da Sangallo. The equestrian **statue** of Grand Duke Ferdinand I (1608) at its centre was Giambologna's final work, and was cast by his pupil Pietro Tacca from cannons captured at the Battle of Lepanto. Tacca was also the creator of the grotesque **fountains** (1629), on each of which a pair of aquatic monkeys spit water at two whiskered sea slugs.

The Spedale degli Innocenti

The eastern flank of Piazza Santissima Annunziata is occupied by the **Spedale degli Innocenti**. Commissioned in 1419 by the Arte della Seta, the silk-weavers' guild, it opened in 1445 as the first foundlings' hospital in Europe, and is still an orphanage today. It was largely designed by Brunelleschi, and his nine-arched loggia was one of Europe's earliest examples of the new classically influenced style. (The mirror-image building opposite was designed a century later, by Antonio da Sangallo and Baccio d'Agnolo, as accommodation for the Servite friars who staffed the orphanage.)

Andrea della Robbia's blue-backed ceramic tondi (1487) of well-swaddled babies advertise the building's function, but their gaiety belies the misery associated with it. Slavery was part of the Florentine economy as late as the fifteenth century (it's probable that Leonardo da Vinci's mother was a slave), and many of the infants given over to the care of the Spedale were born to domestic slaves. From 1660 children could be abandoned anonymously in the *rota*, a small revolving door whose bricked-up remains are still visible at the extreme left of the facade; it remained in use until 1875.

Museo degli Innocenti

Daily 10am–7pm • €4 • ⓦ istitutodeglinnocenti.it

The Spedale degli Innocenti centres on two beautiful cloisters, Brunelleschi's central **Chiostro degli Uomini** (Men's Cloister) and the narrow, graceful **Chiostro delle Donne** (Women's Cloister) to the right. Stairs from the former lead up to the **Museo degli Innocenti**, a miscellany of Florentine Renaissance art that includes one of Luca della Robbia's most beguiling Madonnas and an *Adoration of the Magi* (1488) by Domenico Ghirlandaio. The latter, commissioned as the altarpiece of the building's church, features a background depicting the *Massacre of the Innocents*. The parallel of the slaughter of Bethlehem's first-born with the orphanage's foundlings, or *innocenti*, was deliberately made.

Santissima Annunziata

Piazza Santissima Annunziata • Daily 7am–12.30pm & 4–6.30pm

Santissima Annunziata is the mother church of the Servites, or Servi di Maria (Servants of Mary), a religious order founded by Filippo Benizzi and six Florentine aristocrats in 1234. From humble beginnings, the order blossomed after 1252, when a painting of the Virgin begun by one of the monks, and abandoned because of his inability to create a truly beautiful image, was supposedly completed by an angel while he slept. So many people came to venerate the image that by 1444 a new church, financed by the Medici, was commissioned from Michelozzo (who happened to be the brother of the Servites'

1

head prior). The project, completed by Leon Battista Alberti in 1481, involved laying out the present-day Via dei Servi, designed to link Santissima Annunziata and the cathedral, thus uniting the city's two most important churches dedicated to the Madonna.

Chiostrino dei Voti

As the number of pilgrims to the church increased, so it became a custom to leave wax votive offerings (*voti*) in honour of its miraculous Madonna. Eventually these became so numerous that in 1447 a special atrium, the **Chiostrino dei Voti**, was built onto the church. In time this came to house some six hundred wax figures, some of them life-sized depictions of the donor – there was even a wax horse in attendance. The collection was one of the city's great tourist attractions until 1786, when the whole lot was melted down to make candles.

More lasting alterations to the cloister's appearance, in the shape of a major **fresco cycle**, were made in the 1510s, following the canonization of Filippo Benizzi, the Servites' founding father. Three leading artists of the day, Andrea del Sarto, Jacopo Pontormo and Rosso Fiorentino, were involved, together with some lesser painters. A few of the panels are in a poor state – all were removed from the walls and restored after the 1966 flood – but their overall effect is superb. There are two sequences here, one depicting scenes from the life of the Virgin, the other portraying scenes from the life of St Filippo Benizzi. If you start to the right of the entrance to the cloister, the sequence works backwards from the Virgin's death, beginning with an **Assumption** by Rosso Fiorentino, painted when he was aged around 19. Alongside is Pontormo's beautiful **Visitation**, one of the cloister's two masterpieces, the other being Andrea del Sarto's **Birth of the Virgin**.

The interior

Inside, Santissima Annunziata makes a startling first impression, thanks to all the gilt and stucco that was applied in the seventeenth and eighteenth centuries. The ornate **tabernacle** (1448–61), immediately on your left as you enter, was designed by Michelozzo to house the miraculous image of the Madonna. Michelozzo's patron, Piero di Cosimo de' Medici, made sure that nobody remained unaware of the money he sank into the shrine: an inscription reads *Costò fior. 4 mila el marmo solo* ("The marble alone cost 4000 florins"). The painting encased in the marble has been repainted many times.

To the tabernacle's right lies a chapel (1453–63) originally created as an oratory for the Medici, adorned with five panels of inlaid stone depicting the Virgin's principal symbols (sun, moon, star, lily and rose) and a small picture of the *Redeemer* (1515) by Andrea del Sarto. The **Cappella Feroni**, next door, features a fresco by Andrea del Castagno of *Christ and St Julian* (1455–56), while the adjacent chapel contains a more striking fresco by the same artist, the *Holy Trinity and St Jerome* (1454). Both frescoes were painted over after Vasari spread the rumour that Castagno had poisoned his erstwhile friend, Domenico Veneziano, motivated by envy of the other's skill with oil paint. Castagno was saddled with this crime until the nineteenth century, when an archivist discovered that the alleged murderer in fact predeceased his victim by four years.

Separated from the nave by a triumphal arch is the unusual **tribune**, begun by Michelozzo but completed to designs by Alberti; you get into it along a corridor from the north transept. The chapel at the farthest point was altered by Giambologna into a monument to himself, complete with bronze reliefs and a crucifix by the sculptor. The chapel to its left contains a sizeable *Resurrection* (1550) by Bronzino.

The Chiostro dei Morti

The spacious **Chiostro dei Morti** is worth visiting for Andrea del Sarto's intimate *Madonna del Sacco* (1525), over the door that connects with the north transept (you may also be able to enter the cloister from the street); depicting the *Rest during the Flight into Egypt*, the picture takes its name from the sack on which St Joseph is leaning.

Museo Archeologico

Via della Colonna 36 • Tues–Fri 8.30am–7pm, Sat & Sun 8.30am–2pm • €4 • ⓦ firenzemusei.it/archeologico

The **Museo Archeologico** houses the finest collection of its kind in northern Italy, but struggles to draw visitors for whom the Renaissance is the beginning and the end of Florence's appeal. And to tell the truth, it's not the most alluring museum in the city: it suffered terrible damage in the flood of 1966, and renovation work is still going on. Nonetheless, the new ground-floor galleries are a good space for one-off exhibitions, and the main collection is slowly being put into better order.

The Etruscan and Egyptian collections

Its great strength is its **Etruscan** collection, much of it bequeathed, inevitably, by the Medici. Most of the finds are on the first floor, where there's a large array of funerary figures and two outstanding bronze sculptures. The first of these, the *Arringatore* (Orator), is the only known large Etruscan bronze from the Hellenistic period; made some time around 100 BC, it was discovered near Lago Trasimeno in 1566 and promptly sold to Cosimo I. Nearby is the *Chimera*, a triple-headed monster made in the fourth century BC. Showing the beast wounded in its fight with Bellerophon (it might have been part of a group that included a figure of the hero), the *Chimera* was unearthed on the outskirts of Florence in 1553.

Numerous dowdy cabinets are stuffed with unlabelled Etruscan figurines, and much of the **Egyptian collection** – the third largest such collection in Italy, after the Vatican's and the Egyptian museum in Turin – is displayed in a similarly uninspiring manner, though some of the rooms were handsomely decorated in mock-Egyptian style in the late nineteenth century. The single most remarkable object amid the assembly of papyri, statuettes and mummy cases is a Hittite chariot made of bone and wood, dating from the fourteenth century BC.

The Greek and Roman collections

There are more Etruscan pieces on the top floor (sometimes open only to guided tours), but here the primary focus is on the **Greek and Roman collections**. The star piece in the huge hoard of Greek vases is the large *François Vase*, a sixth-century BC *krater* discovered in an Etruscan tomb near Chiusi in 1844. Another attention-grabbing item is the life-size bronze torso known as the *Torso di Livorno*, either a fifth-century BC Greek original or a Roman copy. There's some debate also about the large horse's head that's on show in the same room. This fragment of a full-size statue is probably an early Hellenistic bronze from around 100 BC, but again it may be a Roman copy; what's known for certain is that it was once in the garden of the Palazzo Medici, where it was studied by Donatello and Verrocchio. Also on this floor you'll see two beautiful sixth-century BC Greek *kouroi*, dubbed *Apollo* and *Apollino*, and the bronze statue of a young man known as the *Idilono di Pésaro* – yet again its origins are disputed, but it's generally thought to be a Roman replica of a Greek figure dating from around 100 BC.

East of the centre

The focal point of the eastern side of central Florence is **Piazza Santa Croce**, one of Florence's largest squares and traditionally one of its chief arenas for ceremonies and festivities – the insane Gioco di Calcio Storico (see p.134) is held here every year. The Santa Croce district was one of Florence's more densely populated areas before November 4, 1966, when the Arno burst its banks, with catastrophic consequences for this low-lying zone, which was then packed with tenements and workshops. Many residents moved out permanently in the following years, but now the more traditional businesses that survived the flood have been joined by a growing number of new and often extremely good bars and restaurants, a transformation that's particularly

FLORENCE'S FLOODS

The calamity of the November 1966 flood had plenty of precedents. Great areas of the city were destroyed by a flood in **1178**, a disaster exacerbated by plague and famine. In **1269** the Carraia and Trìnita bridges were carried away on a torrent that turned most of Florence into a lake, and a flood in **1333** was preceded by a four-day storm of such violence that all the city's bells were tolled to drive away the evil spirits thought to be responsible. Cosimo I instituted an urban beautification scheme after a deluge put parts of the city under nearly twenty feet of muddy water in **1557**; on that occasion the Trìnita bridge was hit so suddenly that everyone on it was drowned, except for two children who were left stranded on a pillar in midstream for two days.

It had rained continuously for forty days prior to **November 4, 1966**, with nearly half a metre of rain falling in the preceding two days. When the water pressure in an upstream reservoir threatened to break the dam, it was decided to open the sluices. The only people to be warned about the rapidly rising level of the river were the jewellers of the Ponte Vecchio, whose private nightwatchman phoned them in the small hours of the morning with news that the bridge was starting to shake. When the banks of the Arno finally broke, a flash flood dumped around 500,000 tonnes of water and mud on the streets, moving with such speed that people were drowned in the underpass of Santa Maria Novella train station. In all, 35 Florentines were killed, 6000 shops put out of business, more than 10,000 homes made uninhabitable, some 15,000 cars wrecked, and thousands of works of art damaged, many of them ruined by heating oil flushed out of basements.

Within hours an impromptu army of rescue workers had been formed to haul pictures out of slime-filled churches and gather fragments of paint in plastic bags. Donations came in from all over the world, but the task was so immense that the restoration of many pieces is still unaccomplished. Some rooms in the archeological museum, for example, have remained closed since the flood, and many possessions of the National Library are still in the laboratories. Two labs – one for paintings and one for stonework – are operating full time in Florence, developing restoration techniques that are taken up by galleries all over the world. Today, throughout the city, you can see small marble plaques with a red line showing the level the floodwaters reached on that dreadful day in 1966.

noticeable around the **Sant'Ambrogio** market. In addition to the great Franciscan church of **Santa Croce** and its museum, the other main cultural attractions in this part of the city are the **Museo Horne**, a modest but pleasing collection of art treasures, and the **Casa Buonarroti**, a modest homage to Michelangelo.

Santa Croce

Piazza Santa Croce • Mon–Sat 9.30am–5.30pm, Sun 1–5.30pm • €5 • ⓦ santacroceopera.it

Santa Croce is the Franciscans' principal church in Florence – a rival to the Dominicans' Santa Maria Novella – and is often said to have been founded by St Francis himself. In truth it was probably begun seventy or so years after Francis's death, in 1294, possibly by the architect of the Duomo, Arnolfo di Cambio. It replaced a smaller church on the site, a building that had become too small for the vast congregations gathering to hear the Franciscans' homilies on poverty, chastity and obedience in what was then one of the city's poorest areas. Ironically, it was Florence's richest families who funded the construction of Santa Croce, to atone for the usury on which their fortunes were based. Plutocrats such as the Bardi, Peruzzi and Baroncelli sponsored the extraordinary **fresco cycles** that were lavished on the chapels over the years, particularly during the fourteenth century, when artists of the stature of Giotto and the Gaddi family worked here. In further contradiction of the Franciscan ideal of humility, Santa Croce has long served as the national pantheon: the walls and nave floor are lined with the **monuments** to more than 270 illustrious Tuscans, including Michelangelo, Galileo, Machiavelli, Alberti, Dante and the great physicist Enrico Fermi (though the last two are not buried here). The **facade** is a neo-Gothic sham which dates from 1863. The church had languished for centuries without a suitable frontage, a situation remedied when someone claimed to have discovered long-lost plans for the "original" facade; in truth the scheme was no more than a giant-sized pastiche of Orcagna's tabernacle in Orsanmichele. The vast interior is infinitely more satisfying.

The south aisle

Exploration of Santa Croce is best begun with a walk down the **south aisle**. Against the first pillar stands the tomb of Francesco Nori, one of the victims of the Pazzi Conspiracy,

SANTA CROCE

Primo Chiostro

1	Madonna del Latte (1478), Antonio Rossellino
2	Tomb of Michelangelo (1570), Giorgio Vasari
3	Cenotaph to Dante (1829), Stefano Ricci
4	Pulpit (1472–6), Benedetto da Maiano
5	Monument to Vittorio Alfieri (1810), Antonio Canova
6	Tomb of Niccolò Machiavelli (1787), Innocenzo Spinazzi
7	Annunciation (1435), Donatello
8	Tomb of Leonardo Bruni (1446–7), Bernardo Rossellino
9	Tomb of Giacchino Rossini (1900), Giuseppe Cassioli
10	Cappella Castellani: frescoes (1385), Agnolo Gaddi
11	Cappella Baroncelli: frescoes (1332–8), Taddeo Gaddi
12	Cappella Medici (1434), designed by Michelozzo
13	Madonna and Child altarpiece (1480), Andrea della Robbia
14	Church shop
15	Sacristy
16	Cappella Rinuccini: frescoes (1365), Giovanni da Milano
17	Cappella Velluti: altarpiece, Giovanni di Biondo
18	Cappella Peruzzi: Lives of St John the Evangelist and St John the Baptist (1326–30), Giotto
19	Cappella Bardi: Life of St Francis (1315–20), Giotto
20	Chancel: Frescoes and stained glass (1380), Agnolo Gaddi
21	Cappella Pulci-Beradi: Martyrdom of SS Lorenzo and Stefano (1330) frescoes, Bernardo Daddi
22	Cappella Bardi di Vernio: Scenes from the Life of San Silvestro (1340) frescoes, Maso di Banco
23	Cappella Bardi: wooden crucifix (1412), Donatello
24	Monument to Leon Battista Alberti (d. 1472), Lorenzo Bartolini (early 19th-century)
25	Tomb of Carlo Marsuppini (1453), Desiderio da Settignano
26	Pietà (1560), Agnolo Bronzino
27	Tomb of Lorenzo Ghiberti and his son Vittorio (pavement slab)
28	Tomb of Galileo (1737), Giulio Foggini
29	Cappella dei Pazzi
30	Refectory and museum
31	Inner Cloister

1

THE COUNCIL OF FLORENCE

Of all the events that have happened at Santa Croce, none was more momentous than the **Council of Florence**, held in 1439 in an attempt to reconcile the differences between the Roman and Eastern churches. Attended by the pope, the Byzantine emperor and the Patriarch of Constantinople, the council arrived at a compromise that lasted only until the Byzantine delegation returned home. Its more enduring effect was that it brought scores of classical scholars to the city, some of whom stayed on to give an important impetus to the Florentine Renaissance.

---

surmounted by Antonio Rossellino's lovely relief of the *Madonna del Latte* (marked 1 on our plan). Nearby is Vasari's **tomb of Michelangelo** (2); the sculptor's body was brought back from Rome to Florence in July 1574, ten years after his death, and his tomb is said to have been positioned close to the church's entrance at his own request, so that when the graves fly open on the Day of Judgement, the first thing to catch his eye will be Brunelleschi's cathedral dome. The bland nineteenth-century **monument to Dante** (3) is a cenotaph rather than a tomb, as the exiled poet is buried in Ravenna, where he died in 1321. Against the third pillar there's a marvellous **pulpit** by Benedetto da Maiano (4), adorned with niche statuettes of the virtues and scenes from the life of St Francis.

Canova's **monument to Alfieri** (5) was funded by the poet-dramatist's mistress, the Countess of Albany, erstwhile wife of Charles Edward Stuart (aka Bonnie Prince Charlie); she also modelled for the main figure, personifying Italy bereaved by Alfieri's death. The nearby **tomb of Machiavelli** (6), carved 260 years after his death, is unexceptional save for its famous inscription: *Tanto nomini nullum par elogium* ("No praise can be high enough for so great a name"). The side-door at the end of the aisle is flanked by Donatello's gilded stone relief of the *Annunciation*.

Beyond the door is Bernardo Rossellino's much-imitated **tomb of Leonardo Bruni** (8), chancellor of the Republic, scholar and author of the first history of the city – his effigy is holding a copy. Bruni, who died in 1444, was the first man of any great eminence to be buried in the church, which is a little surprising given his predominantly humanist rather than Christian beliefs. The tomb, one of the most influential of the Renaissance, makes the point: for the first time the human figure dominates, with the Madonna and Child banished to a peripheral position high in the lunette.

Cappella Castellani

The **Cappella Castellani** (10), at the end of the south aisle, is strikingly, if patchily, covered in frescoes by Agnolo Gaddi and his pupils. To the right are depicted the stories of St John the Baptist and St Nicholas of Bari: the latter, the patron saint of children (he's the St Nicholas of Santa Claus fame), is shown saving three girls from prostitution and reviving three murdered boys. The left wall features episodes from the lives of St John and St Antony Abbot; the latter gave away his wealth, making him a favourite of the Franciscans. Also note the chapel's fine tabernacle, the work of Mino da Fiesole, and its funerary monuments, including that of the Countess of Albany.

Cappella Baroncelli

The adjoining **Cappella Baroncelli** (11) was decorated by Agnolo's father, Taddeo, a long-time assistant to Giotto. Taddeo's cycle, largely devoted to the life of the Virgin, features one of the first night scenes in Western painting, the *Annunciation to the Shepherds*, in which the angel appears amid a blaze of light that's believed to be a representation of Halley's Comet. The main altar painting, the *Coronation of the Virgin*, may also be by Taddeo, though some attribute it to his master.

The Cappella Medici and Cappella Rinuccini

The corridor to the right ends at the **Cappella Medici** (12), usually open only for those taking Mass. It's notable for the large terracotta altarpiece by Andrea della Robbia (13) and a nineteenth-century forged Donatello; the chapel, like the corridor, was designed by Michelozzo, the Medici's pet architect.

Finely carved wooden doors lead off the corridor into the beautifully panelled **sacristy** (15), where the highlight is a marvellous *Crucifixion* by Taddeo. The tiny **Cappella Rinuccini** (16), separated from the sacristy by a grille, is impressively covered with frescoes on the life of the Virgin (on the left) and St Mary Magdalene (on the right): the artist responsible, Giovanni da Milano, was one of Giotto's most accomplished followers.

Cappella Peruzzi and Cappella Bardi: Giotto's frescoes

Both the **Cappella Peruzzi** (18) and the **Cappella Bardi** (19) – the two chapels on the right of the chancel – are entirely covered with frescoes by Giotto, with some assistance in the latter. Their deterioration was partly caused by Giotto's having painted some of the pictures onto dry plaster, rather than the wet plaster employed in true fresco technique, but the vandalism of later generations was far more destructive. In the eighteenth century they were covered in whitewash, then they were heavily retouched in the nineteenth; restoration in the 1950s returned them to as close to their original state as was possible.

Scenes from the lives of St John the Evangelist and St John the Baptist cover the Peruzzi chapel, while a better-preserved cycle of the life of St Francis fills the Bardi. Despite the areas of paint destroyed when a tomb was attached to the wall, the *Funeral of St Francis* is still a composition of extraordinary impact, the grief-stricken mourners suggesting an affinity with the lamentation over the body of Christ – one of them even probes the wound in Francis's side, echoing the gesture of Doubting Thomas. The *Ordeal by Fire*, showing Francis about to demonstrate his faith to the sultan by walking through fire, shows Giotto's mastery of understated drama, with the sultan's entourage skulking off to the left in anticipation of the monk's triumph. On the wall above the chapel's entrance arch is the most powerful scene of all, *St Francis Receiving the Stigmata*, in which the power of Christ's apparition seems to force the chosen one to his knees.

The chancel

Agnolo Gaddi was responsible for the design of the **stained glass** in the lancet windows round the high altar, and for all the chancel **frescoes** (20), which depict the legend of the True Cross – a complicated tale tracing the wood of the Cross from its origins as the Tree of Paradise (see p.374). The vast polyptych on the high altar is a composite of panels by several artists.

Cappella Bardi di Vernio and Cappella Bardi

The **Cappella Bardi di Vernio** (22) was painted by Maso di Banco, perhaps the most inventive of Giotto's followers. Following tradition, the frescoes, showing scenes from the life of St Sylvester, portray the saint baptizing Emperor Constantine, notwithstanding the fact that Sylvester died some time before the emperor's baptism. The second **Cappella Bardi** (23) houses a wooden crucifix by Donatello, supposedly criticized by Brunelleschi as resembling a "peasant on the Cross". According to Vasari, Brunelleschi created his own crucifix for Santa Maria Novella to show Donatello how it should be done.

The north aisle

As you walk back towards the entrance along the north aisle, the first pillar you pass features a ghastly nineteenth-century **monument to Leon Battista Alberti** (24), the Renaissance architect and artistic theorist whose writings did much to influence Rossellino in his carving of the Bruni tomb across the nave. The Bruni tomb in turn influenced the outstanding **tomb of Carlo Marsuppini** (25) by Desiderio da Settignano. Marsuppini's lack of Christian qualifications for so prominent a church burial is even more striking than Bruni's: he's said to have died without taking confession or

1

communion. The tomb inscription opens with the words, "Stay and see the marbles which enshrine a great sage, one for whose mind there was not world enough."

A Pietà by the young Bronzino (26), briefly disturbs the parade of tombs that follows. A surprisingly modest pavement slab marks the **tomb of Lorenzo Ghiberti** – the artist responsible for the Baptistery's marvellous doors – and his son Vittorio (27). The **tomb of Galileo** (28) is more ostentatious, though it was some ninety years after his death in 1642 that the "heretic" scientist was deemed worthy of a Christian burial in Florence's pantheon.

Cappella dei Pazzi

The door in the south aisle leads through into the Primo Chiostro (First Cloister), site of Brunelleschi's glorious **Cappella dei Pazzi** (29), the epitome of the learned, harmonious spirit of early Renaissance architecture. It was commissioned in 1429 as a chapter house for Santa Croce, by Andrea de' Pazzi, a member of a banking dynasty that played a prominent role in the Pazzi Conspiracy (see p.52). It remained unfinished at the time of the plot, however, and it seems none of the family was ever buried here. Dogged by financial problems, the construction of the chapel was completed only in the 1470s, some thirty years after the architect's death.

Geometrically perfect without being pedantic, the chapel is exemplary in its proportion and in the way its decorative detail harmonizes with the design. The polychrome lining of the portico's shallow cupola is by Luca della Robbia, as is the garland of fruit which surrounds the Pazzi family crest. The frieze of angels' heads is by Desiderio da Settignano, though Luca was responsible for the tondo of *St Andrew* (1461) over the door. The portico itself may be the work of Giuliano da Maiano, while the majestic wooden doors (1472) are the product of a collaboration between the Maiano brothers, Giuliano and Benedetto. Inside, the twelve blue and white tondi of the *Apostles* are by Luca della Robbia, while the four vividly coloured tondi of the *Evangelists* in the upper roundels were produced in the della Robbia workshop, possibly to designs by Donatello and Brunelleschi.

Museo dell'Opera di Santa Croce

The **Museo dell'Opera di Santa Croce** (30), which flanks the first cloister, houses a sizeable miscellany of works of art, the best of which are gathered in the ex-refectory. Foremost of these is Cimabue's famous *Crucifixion*, very badly damaged in 1966 and now the emblem of the havoc caused by the flood. Other highlights include a detached fresco of the *Last Supper* (1333), which is considered to be the finest work by Taddeo Gaddi (end wall) and is the earliest surviving example of the many Last Suppers (*cenacoli*) dotted around the city. Also compelling are Donatello's enormous gilded *St Louis of Toulouse* (1424), made for Orsanmichele, and Bronzino's *Descent of Christ into Limbo*. Fragments of Orcagna's frescoes of *The Triumph of Death* and *Hell* (on the side walls), and Domenico Veneziano's *Sts John and Francis*, were all salvaged from Santa Croce after Vasari had carried out his supposed improvements. Elsewhere in the museum you'll find more frescoes rescued from the church, plus some excellent della Robbia ceramics.

A series of rooms sparsely filled with various damaged fragments leads you towards the spacious **Inner Cloister** (31), another late project by Brunelleschi. Completed in 1453, after the architect's death, it is the most peaceful spot in the centre of Florence, its atmosphere enhanced by the slow rhythm of the narrow, widely spaced columns.

Museo Horne

Via dei Benci 6 • Mon–Sat 9am–1pm • €6 • ⓦ museohorne.it

On the south side of Santa Croce, down by the river, stands one of Florence's more recondite museums, the **Museo della Fondazione Horne**. Its collection was left to the state by the English art historian Herbert Percy Horne (1864–1916), who was instrumental in rescuing Botticelli from neglect with a pioneering biography in 1908. The half-a-dozen or so rooms of paintings, sculptures, pottery, furniture and other domestic objects contain no real masterpieces, but are diverting enough if you've already done the major collections.

The pride of Horne's collection was its drawings, which are now salted away in the Uffizi, though a small display is maintained in the room on the right of the **ground floor**. On the **first floor**, the highlight of Room 1 is a tiny and badly damaged panel by Masaccio, showing *Scenes from the Life of St Julian*; nearby there's an unfinished and age-darkened *Deposition* by Gozzoli, his last documented work. The next room contains the collection's big draw, Giotto's *St Stephen* (a fragment from a polyptych), which was probably painted at around the time that Giotto was at work in Santa Croce. Room 3 has a tondo of the *Holy Family* by Beccafumi, who is also attributed with a *Drunkenness of Noah* on the **second floor**, where you'll find minor works by Filippo and Filippino Lippi. One of the main exhibits on this storey is a piece of little artistic merit but great historical interest: a copy of part of Leonardo's *Battle of Anghiari*, once frescoed on a wall of the Palazzo Vecchio.

Casa Buonarroti

Via Ghibellina 70 • Mon & Wed–Sun 10am–5pm • €6.50 • ⓦ casabuonarroti.it

The enticing name of the **Casa Buonarroti** is somewhat misleading. Michelangelo Buonarroti certainly owned three houses on this site, and probably lived in them intermittently between 1516 and 1525, but on his death they passed to his nephew, Leonardo, whose son converted them into a single palazzo, leaving little trace of the earlier houses (though he built a gallery dedicated to his great-uncle). Michelangelo's last descendant, Cosimo, left the building to the city after he died in 1858. Today the house contains a smart if low-key museum, but among the jumble of works only a handful are by Michelangelo: most were created in homage to the great man.

The two main treasures are to be found in the room on the left at the top of the stairs. The **Madonna della Scala** (c.1490–92) is Michelangelo's earliest known work, a delicate relief carved when he was no older than 16. The similarly unfinished *Battle of the Centaurs* was created shortly afterwards, when the boy was living in the Medici household. In the adjacent room you'll find the artist's wooden model (1517) for the facade of San Lorenzo. Close by is the largest of all the sculptural models on display, the torso of a **River God** (1524), a work intended for the Medici chapel in San Lorenzo. Other rooms contain small and fragmentary pieces, possibly by the master, possibly copies.

Mercato delle Pulci

Piazza dei Ciompi • Mon–Sat 9am–7pm, plus last Sun of month same hours

Much of the stuff on sale at the **Mercato delle Pulci** or Flea Market is overpriced junk, though you can find a few interesting items at modest cost – old postcards, posters and so on. Vasari's Loggia del Pesce (1567) gives the square a touch of style; built for the fishmongers of the Mercato Vecchio in what is now Piazza della Repubblica, it was dismantled when that square was laid out, and rebuilt here in 1951.

Mercato di Sant'Ambrogio

Piazza Ghiberti • Mon–Sat 7am–2pm

Out of the orbit of most tourists, the **Mercato di Sant'Ambrogio** is a smaller, tattier but equally enjoyable version of the San Lorenzo food hall. The *tavola calda* (snacks and meals stall) here is one of Florence's lunchtime bargains, and – as at San Lorenzo – the stalls bring their prices down in the last hour of trading.

1

Sant'Ambrogio

Piazza di Sant'Ambrogio • Daily 8am–12.30pm & 4–7pm

Sant'Ambrogio is one of Florence's oldest churches, having been documented in 988, though rebuilding over the centuries means that it is now somewhat bland in appearance. Inside, the most compelling feature is the Cappella del Miracolo, the chapel to the left of the high altar, and its tabernacle (1481–83) by Mino da Fiesole, an accomplished sculptor whose name crops up time and again across Tuscany. This was one of Mino's last works – he died in 1484 – making it fitting that he should be buried close by, in a pavement tomb at the chapel entrance. (Another great artist, Verrocchio, who died in 1488, is buried in the fourth chapel.) The narrative **fresco** (1486) alongside Mino's tabernacle alludes to the miracle that gave the Cappella del Miracolo its name. Painted by Cosimo Rosselli, it describes the discovery of a chalice full of blood in 1230; the Florentines believed this chalice saved them from, among other things, the effects of a plague outbreak in 1340. The painting is full of portraits of Rosselli's contemporaries, making it another of Florence's vivid pieces of Renaissance social reportage: Rosselli himself is the figure in the black beret at the extreme left of the picture.

The Synagogue

Via Farini 4 • April–Sept Sun–Thurs 10am–6pm, Fri 10am–2pm; Oct–March Sun–Thurs 10am–3pm, Fri 10am–2pm • €5

The enormous domed building rising to the north of Sant'Ambrogio church is the **Synagogue**; the ghetto established in this district by Cosimo I was not demolished until the mid-nineteenth century, which is when the present Moorish-style synagogue was built. It contains a museum that charts the history of Florence's Jewish population.

Santa Maria Maddalena dei Pazzi

Borgo Pinti • **Church** Mon–Sat 8am–12.30pm & 4–7pm, Sun 8am–12.30pm • **Perugino fresco** Tues & Thurs 2.30–5.30pm

West of the synagogue stands the convent of **Santa Maria Maddalena dei Pazzi**, named after a Carmelite nun – a member of the clan who murdered Giuliano de' Medici (see p.52) – who was famed for her healing powers and religious ecstasies: when possessed by the spirit she would spew words at such a rate that a team of eight novices was needed to transcribe her inspired dictation. Such fervent piety was much honoured in Counter-Reformation Florence, and a cult grew up around her immediately after her death in 1607; canonization followed in 1669.

Founded in the thirteenth century, the church is fronted by a lovely courtyard designed by Giuliano da Sangallo. Inside, paintings celebrating St Maria – including a pair by Luca Giordano – adorn the marble-clad chancel. In contrast to all this Baroque fervour, the convent's chapterhouse – entered from Via della Colonna – is decorated with a radiant **Perugino** fresco of the *Crucifixion*. As always with Perugino, there is nothing troubling here, the Crucifixion being depicted not as an agonizing death but rather as the necessary prelude to the Resurrection.

San Salvi

Via San Salvi 16 • Tues–Sun 8.15am–1.50pm • Free • Bus #10 from the train station, or #6 from Piazza San Marco

Twenty minutes' walk beyond Piazza Beccaria, east of Sant'Ambrogio, is the ex-convent of **San Salvi**, which was reopened in 1982 after the restoration of its most precious possession, the glorious *Last Supper* by Andrea del Sarto. As a prelude to this picture, there's a gallery of big but otherwise unremarkable Renaissance altarpieces, a gathering of pictures by various del Sarto acolytes, and some beautiful reliefs from the tomb of Giovanni Gualberto, founder of the Vallombrosan order to whom this monastery belonged. The tomb was smashed up by Charles V's troops in 1530 but they refused to damage the *Last Supper*, which is still in the refectory for which it was painted, accompanied by three del Sarto frescoes brought here from other churches in Florence.

Stadio Artemio Franchi

Viale Manfredo Fanti • Bus #17 from the train station • ⓦ en.violachannel.tv

The **Stadio Artemio Franchi** (or **Stadio Comunale**) at **Campo di Marte** is the home to Fiorentina football club, known as the **Viola** after the violet hue of their shirts. The stadium was designed by Pier Luigi Nervi in 1930, as a consequence of two decisions: to create a new football club for Florence and to stage the 1934 World Cup in Italy.

This was the first major sports venue to exploit the shape-making potential of reinforced concrete, and its spiral ramps, cantilevered roof and slim central tower still make most other arenas look dreary. From the spectator's point of view it's far from perfect (visibility from some parts of the ground is frankly awful), but the architectural importance of Nervi's work meant that when Florence was chosen as one of the hosts for the 1990 World Cup there could be no question of simply building a replacement, nor of radically altering the existing one: most of the extra space in the all-seater stadium was created by lowering the pitch a couple of metres below its previous level, in order to insert more seats. Though the Viola play in Serie A, the top flight of Italian football, **tickets** cost from as little as €10; they can be bought at the ground itself, or three or four days in advance from various outlets around the city – the chief of which are Box Office (see p.132) and the kiosk in Via Anselmi, off the west side of Piazza della Repubblica.

Oltrarno

Florentines refer to the parts of the city to the north of the river as *Arno di quà* ("over here"), while the other side, hemmed in by a ridge of hills that rises a short distance from the river, is *Arno di là* ("over there"). More formally, the latter is known as **Oltrarno** – literally "beyond the Arno" – a terminology that has its roots in medieval times, when the district was not as accessible as the numerous bridges now make it. Traditionally an artisans' quarter, Oltrarno is still home to plenty of small workshops (particularly furniture restorers and leather-workers), and Via Maggio remains the focus of Florence's thriving antiques trade. The ambience is less tourist-centred here than in the area immediately across the water, though the bars and restaurants around **Piazza Santo Spirito** and **Piazza del Carmine** attract their share of outsiders. Which is not to say that Oltrarno doesn't have major sights – **Palazzo Pitti**, **Santa Maria del Carmine**, **San Miniato** and **Santo Spirito** are all essential visits.

Ponte Vecchio

The direct route from the city centre to the heart of Oltrarno crosses the Arno at the river's narrowest point via the **Ponte Vecchio**, the last in a series of bridges that stretches back to Etruscan and Roman times. Until 1218 the crossing here was the city's only bridge, though the version you see today dates from 1345, built to replace a wooden bridge that had been swept away by floods – its name (Old Bridge) was coined to distinguish it from the Ponte alla Carraia, the bridge that was raised in 1218. Much later in its history the Ponte Vecchio was the only bridge not mined by the Nazis in 1944 as they retreated before the advancing American Fifth Army. Much of the rest of Florence, including medieval quarters at each end of the bridge, was not so lucky: the Nazis reneged on a promise to spare the city, blowing up scores of old buildings to hamper the Allied advance.

The Ponte Vecchio has always been loaded with **shops**. Their earliest occupants were butchers and fishmongers, attracted to the site by the proximity of the river, which provided a convenient dumping ground for their waste. They were later joined by tanners, who used the river to soak their hides before treating them with horses' urine. The current plethora of jewellers dates back to 1593, when Ferdinando I evicted the butchers' stalls and other practitioners of what he called "vile arts", replacing them with jewellers and **goldsmiths** – taking the opportunity to double the rents. Florence had long revered the art of the goldsmith, and several of its major artists were skilled in the craft: Ghiberti, Donatello and Cellini, for example. The third of this trio is celebrated by a bust in the centre of the bridge.

Santa Felìcita

Piazza Santa Felicita • Mon–Sat 9.30am–noon & 3.30–5.30pm

Santa Felìcita might be the oldest church in Florence, having possibly been founded in the second century by Greek or Syrian merchants, pioneers of Christianity in the city. It's known for certain that a church existed on the site by the fifth century, by which time it had been dedicated to St Felicity, an early Roman martyr who is often shown in Renaissance paintings with her seven sons, each of whom was executed in front of her for refusing to renounce his faith (the saint herself was either beheaded or thrown into boiling oil). New churches were built on the site in the eleventh and fourteenth centuries, while in 1565 Vasari added an elaborate portico to accommodate the *corridoio* linking the Uffizi and Palazzo Pitti; a window from the corridor looks directly into the church. All but the facade was extensively remodelled in the 1730s.

Cappella Capponi

The interior demands a visit for the amazing **Pontormo** paintings in the **Cappella Capponi**, which lies to the right of the door, surrounded by obstructive railings. Under the cupola are four tondi of the *Evangelists* (painted with help from his adoptive son, Bronzino), while on opposite sides of the window on the right wall are the Virgin and the angel of Pontormo's delightfully simple *Annunciation* – the arrangement alludes to the Incarnation as the means by which the Light came into the world. The chapel's focal point is Pontormo's *Deposition* (1525–28), a startling masterwork of Florentine Mannerism. Nothing in this picture is conventional: the people bearing Christ's body are androgynous quasi-angelic creatures; billows of gorgeously coloured drapery almost engulf the scene; many of the figures seem to be standing in midair rather than on solid ground; and there's no sign of the cross, the crucified thieves, the soldiers or any of the other scene-setting devices usual in paintings of this subject – the only contextual detail is a solitary cloud. The bearded brown-cloaked figure on the right (Nicodemus) is believed to be a self-portrait.

Palazzo Pitti

Piazza Pitti • ⓦ www.uffizi.firenze.it

The largest palace in Florence, the **Palazzo Pitti** was commissioned by banker and merchant Luca Pitti to outdo his rivals, the Medici. Work started around 1457, possibly using a design by Brunelleschi which had been rejected by Cosimo de' Medici for being too grand. No sooner was the palace completed, however, than the Pitti's fortunes began to decline, and by 1549 they were forced to sell out to the Medici. Palazzo Pitti subsequently became the Medici's base in Florence, growing in bulk until the seventeenth century, when it achieved its present gargantuan dimensions. During Florence's brief tenure as the Italian capital between 1865 and 1870, it housed the Italian royal family.

Today the Palazzo Pitti and the pavilions of the Giardino di Bóboli contain several museums, of which the foremost is the **Galleria Palatina**, a painting collection second in importance only to the Uffizi. One of the eight, the **Museo delle Carrozze** (Carriage

Museum) has been closed for years and will almost certainly remain so for the foreseeable future; two of the others – the Galleria del Costume and Museo delle Porcellane, which are open the same hours as the Museo degli Argenti and are visitable on the same ticket – are unlikely to thrill anyone without a specialist interest.

The Galleria Palatina and Appartamenti Reali

Tues–Sun 8.15am–6.50pm • €8.50, includes admission to Galleria d'Arte Moderna • ⓦ www.uffizi.firenze.it

Many of the paintings gathered by the Medici in the seventeenth century are now arranged in the **Galleria Palatina**, a suite of almost thirty rooms on the first floor of one wing of the palace. The pictures are not arranged in the sort of didactic order observed by most galleries, but are instead hung as they would have been in the days of their acquisition, three deep in places, with the aim of making each room pleasurably varied.

The current itinerary first takes you through a suite containing mostly less famous works, though some individual paintings are well worth seeking out, notably: **Fra' Bartolomeo**'s *Deposition*; a tondo of the *Madonna and Child with Scenes from the Life of St Anne* (1452) by **Filippo Lippi**; his son Filippino's *Death of Lucrezia*; a *Sleeping Cupid* (1608) by **Caravaggio**; and **Cristofano Allori**'s sexy *Judith and Holofernes*, for which Allori, his mother and his mistress provided the models.

The del Sarto and Raphael collections

In the second and more captivating part of the gallery, **Andrea del Sarto** is represented in strength, his seventeen works including a beautifully grave *Annunciation*. Even more remarkable is the Pitti's collection of paintings by his great contemporary, **Raphael**. When Raphael settled in Florence in 1505, he was besieged with commissions, and in the next three years he painted scores of pictures for such people as Angelo Doni, the man who commissioned Michelangelo's *Doni Tondo* (now in the Uffizi). Raphael's portraits of Doni and his wife, Maddalena (1506–7), display an unhesitating facility and perfect poise, and a similar sense of absolute certainty illuminates Raphael's *Madonna della Seggiola* (1515), or Madonna of the Chair, which for centuries was Italy's most popular image of the Virgin: nineteenth-century copyists had to join a five-year waiting list to paint it. According to Vasari, the model for the famous *Donna Velata* (Veiled Woman), in the Sala di Giove, was the painter's mistress, a Roman baker's daughter known to posterity as La Fornarina.

The Titian collection

The assembly of paintings by the Venetian artist **Titian** (fourteen in all) includes a number of his most trenchant portraits. The libidinous and scurrilous Pietro Aretino – journalist, critic, poet and one of Titian's closest friends – was so thrilled by his 1545 portrait that he gave it to Cosimo I; Titian painted him on several other occasions, sometimes using him as the model for Pontius Pilate. Also here are likenesses of Philip II of Spain and the young Cardinal Ippolito de' Medici (1532), and the so-called *Portrait of an Englishman* (1540), who scrutinizes the viewer with unflinching sea-grey eyes. Nearby is the same artist's sensuous and much-copied *Mary Magdalene* (1531), the first of a series on this theme produced for the Duke of Urbino. In the same room, look out for Rosso Fiorentino's *Madonna Enthroned with Saints* (1522), and the gallery's outstanding sculpture, Canova's *Venus Italica*, commissioned by Napoleon as a replacement for the *Venus de' Medici*, which he had whisked off to Paris.

The Appartamenti Reali

Much of the rest of the Pitti's first floor comprises the **Appartamenti Reali**, the Pitti's state rooms. They were renovated by the dukes of Lorraine in the eighteenth century, and then by Vittorio Emanuele when Florence became the country's capital, so the rooms display three distinct decorative phases. You pass into the apartments directly from the Palatina, and after Raphael and Titian it can be difficult to sustain a great deal of enthusiasm for such ducal elegance, notwithstanding the sumptuousness of the furnishings.

Galleria d'Arte Moderna

Tues–Sun 8.15am–6.50pm • €8.50, includes admission to Galleria Palatina & Appartamenti Reali • Ⓦ www.uffizi.firenze.it

On the floor above the Palatina is the **Galleria d'Arte Moderna**, a chronological survey of primarily Tuscan art from the mid-eighteenth century to 1945. Most rewarding are the products of the Macchiaioli, the Italian division of the Impressionist movement; most startling, however, are the sculptures, featuring amazing kitsch such as Antonio Ciseri's *Pregnant Nun*.

Museo degli Argenti

Daily: March 8.15am–5.30pm; April, May, Sept & Oct 8.15am–6.30pm; June–Aug 8.15am–7.30pm; Nov–Feb 8.15am–4.30pm; closed first & last Mon of each month • €7 joint ticket with Museo delle Porcellane, Galleria del Costume & Giardino di Bóboli • Ⓦ www.uffizi.firenze.it

The **Museo degli Argenti**, entered from the main palace courtyard, is a museum not just of silverware but of luxury artefacts in general. The lavishly frescoed reception rooms themselves fall into this category: the first hall, the Sala di Giovanni da San Giovanni, shows Lorenzo de' Medici giving refuge to the Muses; the other three ceremonial rooms have *trompe l'oeil* paintings by seventeenth-century Bolognese artists. As for the exhibits, the least ambivalent response is likely to be aroused by Lorenzo iL Magnifico trove of antique vases, all of them marked with their owner's name. With many of the pieces, though, you might well be torn between admiring the skills of the craftsman and deploring the ends to which those skills were employed; by the time you reach the end of the jewellery show on the first floor, you'll have lost all capacity to be surprised or revolted by seashell figurines, cups made from ostrich eggs, rock-crystal vases, impossibly complicated ivory carvings (including a long-haired dog), portraits in stone inlay and the like. Exhibitions are sometimes held here, which can affect the ticket price and opening hours.

Giardino di Bóboli

Daily: March 8.15am–5.30pm; April, May, Sept & Oct 8.15am–6.30pm; June–Aug 8.15am–7.30pm; Nov–Feb 8.15am–4.30pm; closed first & last Mon of month • €7 joint ticket with Museo degli Argenti, Galleria del Costume & Museo delle Porcellane, also valid for Giardino Bardini, which can be entered from the upper part of the Bóboli • Ⓦ www.uffizi.firenze.it

The garden of Palazzo Pitti, the **Giardino di Bóboli**, takes its name from the Bóboli family, erstwhile owners of much of this area, which was once a quarry; the bedrock here is one of the sources of the yellow sandstone, known as *pietra forte* (strong stone), that gives much of Florence its dominant hue. Shaped into a rough, boulder-like texture, this stone was also used to "rusticate" the Palazzo Pitti's great facade. When the Medici acquired the house in 1549 they set to work transforming their back yard into an 111-acre garden, its every statue, view and grotto designed to enhance nature by the judicious application of art.

Work continued into the early seventeenth century, by which stage this steep hillside had been turned into a maze of statue-strewn avenues and well-trimmed vegetation. Opened to the public in 1766, it is the only extensive area of accessible greenery in the centre of the city, and can be one of the most pleasant spots for a midday picnic or coffee. It's no place to seek solitude, however: each year it gets some five million visitors, more than at any other Italian garden. If the queues at the main entrance are too daunting, walk three hundred metres along Via Romana, where you'll find another, invariably quieter, entrance.

The amphitheatre

Aligned with the central block of the palazzo, the garden's **amphitheatre** was redesigned in the early seventeenth century as an arena for Medici entertainments, having earlier

1

been laid out by Ammannati as a garden in the shape of a Roman circus. For the wedding of Cosimo III and Princess Marguerite-Louise, cousin of Louis XIV, twenty thousand guests were packed onto the stone benches to watch a production that began with the appearance of a gigantic effigy of Atlas with the globe on his back; the show got under way when the planet split apart, releasing a cascade of earth that transformed the giant into the Atlas mountain. Such frivolities did little to reconcile Marguerite-Louise to either Florence or her husband, and after several years of miserable marriage she returned to Paris, where she professed to care about little "as long as I never have to set eyes on the grand duke again".

The Grotta del Buontalenti

Of all the garden's embellishments, the most celebrated is the **Grotta del Buontalenti** (1583–88), to the left of the entrance, beyond Giambologna's statue of Cosimo I's favourite dwarf astride a giant tortoise. Embedded in the grotto's faked stalactites and encrustations are replicas of Michelangelo's *Slaves* – the originals were lodged here until 1908. Lurking in the deepest recesses of the cave (which is usually opened on the hour) is Giambologna's *Venus Emerging from her Bath*, leered at by imps.

The Isolotto

Another spectacular set piece is the fountain island called the **Isolotto**, which is the focal point of the far end of the garden; from within the Bóboli the most dramatic approach is along the central cypress avenue known as the **Viottolone**, many of whose statues are Roman originals. These lower parts of the garden are its most pleasant – and least visited – sections. You come upon them quickly if you enter the Bóboli by the little-used Porta Romana entrance.

Casa Guidi

Piazza San Felice 8 • April–Nov Mon, Wed & Fri 3–6pm • Free, but donations welcome

The former home of Robert Browning and Elizabeth Barrett Browning, the **Casa Guidi** is something of a shrine to Elizabeth, who wrote much of her most popular verse here (including, naturally enough, *Casa Guidi Windows*) and who died here. Virtually all of Casa Guidi's furniture went under the hammer at Sotheby's in 1913, and there's just a piano and an oil painting left, but two of the three rooms still manage to conjure up something of the Brownings' spirit.

La Specola

Via Romana 17 • Tues–Sun: summer 10.30am–5.30pm; winter 9.30am–4.30pm • €6 • ⓦ msn.unifi.it/CMpro-l-s-11.html

Taking its name from the telescope (*specola*) on its roof, **La Specola** is a tripartite zoology collection. One section, comprising the country's largest collection of skeletons, is open to the public only on Saturday mornings. Of the other parts, the first is conventional enough, with ranks of shells, insects and crustaceans, followed by a veritable ark of animals stuffed, pickled and desiccated, including a hippo that used to reside in the Bóboli garden. The last section, however, is one of the most amazing museums in Florence.

The Cere Anatomiche

The **Cere Anatomiche** (Anatomical Waxworks) are a startling spectacle: wax arms, legs and internal organs cover the walls, arrayed around satin beds on which wax cadavers recline in progressive stages of deconstruction, each muscle fibre and nerve cluster moulded and dyed with amazing precision. Most of the six hundred models – and nearly all of the full-body mannequins – were made between 1775 and 1791 by one Clemente Susini and his team of assistants, and were intended as teaching aids, in an age when medical ethics and refrigeration techniques were not what they are today.

In a separate room towards the end, after the obstetrics display and a few zoological models, you'll find the grisliest section of La Specola, a trio of tableaux that were moulded in the late seventeenth century by **Gaetano Zumbo**, a cleric from Sicily who was one of the pioneers of the art of anatomical waxworks. Whereas Susini's masterpieces were created to educate, these were made to horrify, and to horrify one man in particular: the hypochondriacal Cosimo III, a Jesuit-indoctrinated bigot who regarded all genuine scientific enquiry with suspicion. Enclosed in tasteful display cabinets, they depict Florence during the plague, with rats teasing the intestines from rotting corpses, and the pink bodies of the freshly dead heaped on the suppurating semi-decomposed. A fourth tableau, illustrating the horrors of syphilis, was damaged in the 1966 flood, and now consists of a loose gathering of the deceased and diseased. In the centre of the room is displayed a dissected waxwork head, built on the foundation of a real skull; it's as fastidious as any of Susini's creations, but Zumbo couldn't resist giving the skin a tint of putrefaction, before applying a dribble of blood to the mouth and nose.

Santo Spirito

Piazza di Santo Spirito • Mon, Tues & Thurs–Sat 10am–12.30pm & 4–5.30pm, Sun 4–5.30pm

Designed in 1434 as a replacement for a thirteenth-century church, **Santo Spirito** was one of Brunelleschi's last projects, a swansong later described by Bernini as "the most beautiful church in the world". It's so perfectly proportioned that nothing could seem more artless, yet the plan is extremely sophisticated: a Latin cross with a continuous chain of 38 chapels round the outside and a line of 35 columns running without a break round the nave, transepts and chancel. The exterior wall was originally designed to follow the curves of the chapels' walls, creating a flowing, corrugated effect. As built, however, the exterior is a plain, straight wall, and even the main facade remained incomplete, covered today by blank plaster. Inside the church, only a Baroque baldachin – about as nicely integrated as a jukebox in a Greek temple – disrupts the harmony.

The interior

A fire in 1471 destroyed most of Santo Spirito's medieval works, including famed frescoes by Cimabue and the Gaddi family, but as a result, the altar paintings in the many chapels comprise an unusually unified collection of religious works, most having been commissioned in the aftermath of the fire. Most prolific among the artists is the so-called **Maestro di Santo Spirito**, but the best paintings are in the transepts: in the south transept is **Filippino Lippi's** *Nerli Altarpiece*, an age-darkened Madonna and Child with saints; across the church, in the north transept, there's an unusual *St Monica and Augustinian Nuns* (1460–70) – probably by Verrocchio or Francesco Botticini, it's virtually a study in monochrome, with black-clad nuns flocking round their black-clad paragon.

A door in the north aisle leads through to Giuliano da Sangallo's stunning vestibule and **sacristy** (1489–93), the latter designed in imitation of Brunelleschi's Pazzi chapel. The meticulous proportions and soft grey-and-white tones create an atmosphere of extraordinary calm that is disrupted only by the exuberantly botanical carvings of the capitals, some of which were designed by Sansovino. Hanging above the altar is a delicate wooden crucifix, attributed to **Michelangelo**. It's known that the young Michelangelo was commissioned by the monks of Santo Spirito to make a crucifix for the church in the early 1490s, and several scholars believe that this sculpture – discovered in Santo Spirito in 1963 – is the work in question; others, though, think it was made half a century later by one Taddeo Curradi.

Cenacolo di Santo Spirito

Piazza di Santo Spirito 29 • Sat 10.30am–1.30pm • €2.20

The 1471 fire destroyed all of the monastery except its refectory (entered to the left of the main church), which is now the home of the **Cenacolo di Santo Spirito**. This one-room collection comprises an assortment of carvings, many of them Romanesque, and a huge fresco of *The Crucifixion* (1365) by Orcagna and his workshop.

Santa Maria del Carmine

Piazza del Carmine

On the outside, **Santa del Carmine** is a drab box of shabby brick; inside – in the frescoes of the **Cappella Brancacci** – it provides one of Italy's supreme artistic experiences. The Brancacci chapel is barricaded off from the rest of the Carmine (usually visitable only through the chapel), and visits are **restricted** to a maximum of thirty people at a time, for just fifteen minutes. The time limit is strictly enforced in high season, but tends to become more flexible as the crowds ebb away. At the time of writing, **tickets** could be obtained only by reserving in advance on ☎055 276 8224; this system is so cumbersome, however, that it surely will be replaced, eventually, by something less visitor-repellent.

The Cappella Brancacci

Mon & Wed–Sat 10am–5pm, Sun 1–5pm • €4 • ⓦ museicivicifiorentini.it

The **Cappella Brancacci** frescoes were commissioned in 1424 by Felice Brancacci, a silk merchant and leading patrician figure, and the paintings were begun in the same year

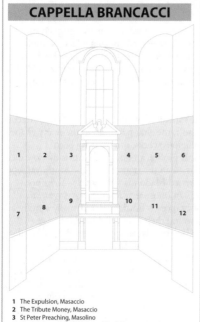

CAPPELLA BRANCACCI

1. The Expulsion, Masaccio
2. The Tribute Money, Masaccio
3. St Peter Preaching, Masolino
4. The Baptism of the Neophytes, Masaccio
5. The Healing of the Cripple and the Raising of Tabitha, Masolino–Masaccio
6. The Temptation, Masolino
7. St Paul Visits St Peter in Prison, Filippino Lippi
8. The Raising of the Son of Theophilus and St Peter Enthroned, Masaccio–Lippi
9. St Peter Healing the Sick with his Shadow, Masaccio
10. The Distribution of Alms and the Death of Ananias, Masaccio
11. The Disputation, Filippino Lippi
12. St Peter Freed from Prison, Filippino Lippi

by **Masolino** (1383–1447), fresh from working as an assistant to Lorenzo Ghiberti on the Baptistery doors. Alongside Masolino was his pupil, Tommaso di Ser Giovanni di Mone Cassai – known ever since as **Masaccio**, a nickname meaning "Mad Tom". Although the overall design of the cycle was probably Masolino's, the radicalism of these paintings – their unprecedented representation of the texture and drama of the real world – is attributable to Masaccio, who was left to work alone here in 1426, when Masolino was recalled to Budapest, where he was official painter to the Hungarian court. In 1428, after another spell in Florence, Masolino was called away to Rome, and Masaccio again continued to work here on his own, until – for reasons unknown – he too departed for Rome. Neither would return to the chapel. Masaccio died the same year, aged just 27, but, in the words of Vasari, "all the most celebrated sculptors and painters since Masaccio's day have become excellent and illustrious by studying their art in this chapel." (Michelangelo used to come here to make drawings of Masaccio's scenes, and had his nose broken on the chapel steps by a young sculptor whom he enraged with his condescension.) Some fifty years later the paintings were completed by **Filippino Lippi**, whose copying skills were such that his work was only recognized as distinct from that of his predecessors in 1838.

The Masaccio frescoes

The small scene on the left of the entrance arch (marked 1 in our plan) is the quintessence of Masaccio's art. Plenty of artists had depicted the **Expulsion of Adam and Eve** before, but none had captured the desolation of the sinners so graphically: Adam presses his hands to his face in bottomless despair, Eve raises her head and screams. The monumentalism of these stark naked figures – whose modesty was preserved by strategically placed sprigs of foliage prior to the restoration – reveals the influence of Donatello, who may have been involved in the planning of the chapel. In contrast to the emotional charge and sculptural presence of Masaccio's couple, Masolino's almost dainty **Adam and Eve** (6), on the opposite arch, pose as if to have their portraits painted.

St Peter is chief protagonist of all the remaining scenes. It's possible that the cycle was intended as propaganda on behalf of the embattled papacy, which had only recently resolved the long and bitter Great Schism, during which one pope held court in Rome and another in Avignon. By celebrating the primacy of St Peter, the rock upon whom the Church is built, the frescoes by implication extol the apostolic succession from which the pope derives his authority.

Three scenes by Masaccio are especially compelling. First off is the **Tribute Money** (2), the Renaissance's first monumental fresco. The narrative is complex, with no fewer than three separate events portrayed within a single frame. The central episode shows Christ outside the gates of Capernaum being asked to pay a tribute owing to the city. To the left, St Peter fetches coins from the mouth of a fish in order to pay the tribute, Christ in the central panel having pointed to where the money will be found. The third scene, to the right, depicts Peter handing over the money to the tax official. Masaccio's second great panel is **St Peter Healing the Sick with his Shadow** (9), in which the shadow of the stern and self-possessed saint (followed by St John) cures the infirm as it passes over them, a miracle invested with the aura of a solemn ceremonial. The third panel is the **Distribution of Alms and Death of Ananias** (10), in which St Peter instructs the people to give up their possessions to the poor. One individual, Ananias, retains some of his wealth with the knowledge of his wife, Sapphira. Rebuked by Peter, Ananias dies on the spot, closely followed by a similarly castigated Sapphira.

The Masaccio/Lippi frescoes

Filippino Lippi's work included the completion of Masaccio's **Raising of Theophilus's Son and St Peter Enthroned** (8), which depicts St Peter raising the son of Theophilus, the Prefect of Antioch (apparently after he'd been dead for fourteen years). The people of Antioch, suitably impressed by the miracle, build a throne from which St Peter can preach, shown as a separate episode to the right. The three figures to the right of the throne are thought to be portraits of Masaccio, Alberti and Brunelleschi, who made a trip to Rome together. Masaccio originally painted himself touching Peter's robe, a reference to the enthroned statue of Peter in Rome, which pilgrims touch for good luck. Lippi considered the contact of the artist and saint to be improper and painted out the arm; at the moment, his fastidious over-painting has been allowed to remain, but you can clearly see where the arm used to be. Lippi left another portrait in the combined scene of **Sts Peter and Paul in Disputation with Simon Magus before Nero** (11) and the **Crucifixion of St Peter**: the central figure looking out from the painting in the trio right of the crucifixion is Botticelli, the painter's teacher, while Filippino himself can be seen at the far right.

1

Forte di Belvedere

Via di San Leonardo 1 • Daily 10am-5pm • Free

The fortress that overlooks the back of Palazzo Pitti, the **Forte di Belvedere**, is sometimes accessible from the Bóboli gardens, but the usual approach is from the **Costa di San Giorgio**, which rises from behind Santa Felìcita. The fort was built by Buontalenti on the orders of Ferdinando I between 1590 and 1595, ostensibly to protect the city, but in fact to intimidate the grand duke's subjects. The urban panorama from here is superb, and ambitious exhibitions are often held in and around the shed-like palace in the centre of the fortress, as are occasional summer evening film screenings. The city's Museo delle Arme (Arms and Armour Museum) is due to open here, at some unspecified point in the future. East from the Belvedere stretches the best-preserved section of Florence's fortified **walls**, paralleled by Via di Belvedere.

Giardino Bardini

Entrance at Costa di San Giorgio 2 or Via de' Bardi 1r • Daily: March 8.15am–5.30pm; April, May, Sept & Oct 8.15am–6.30pm; June–Aug 8.15am–7.30pm; Nov–Feb 8.15am–4.30pm; closed first & last Mon of every month • €7 joint ticket with Museo degli Argenti, Galleria del Costume, Museo delle Porcellane & Giardino di Bóboli • ⓦ bardinipeyron.it

The **Giardino Bardini** occupies the slope that was formerly the olive grove of the **Palazzo dei Mozzi**, a colossal house built in the late thirteenth century by the Mozzi family, at that time one of the richest families in Florence. (The palazzo houses a collection of seven hundred paintings donated to the city in 1937 by Fortunata Carobbi Corsi; there's a plan to put them on public show.)

After Stefano Bardini (see below) bought the property in 1913, he set about creating a semi-formal garden which has now been restored to the appearance he gave it, with a neo-Baroque staircase and terraces dividing the fruit-growing section from the miniature woodland of the "*bosco inglese*". At the summit of the garden, reached by a lovely long pergola of wisteria and hortensia, a colonnaded belvedere gives a splendid view of the city.

Villa Bardini

Costa di San Giorgio 2 • Tues–Sun 10am–7pm • €6 • ⓦ bardinipeyron.it

At the top of the Giardino Bardini stands the **Villa Bardini**, which was built in the seventeenth century as the Villa Manadora and extended by Stefano Bardini. Having been thoroughly restored, the villa is used as an exhibition space and also houses a museum dedicated to **Pietro Annigoni** (1910–88), a vehemently anti-Modernist painter who was best known for his portraits of luminaries such as Pope John XXIII, the Shah of Iran and Queen Elizabeth II. Fashionistas may enjoy the villa's collection of **clothes** created by Roberto Capucci (born 1930). Dubbed the "Givenchy of Rome" by his admirers, Capucci made his name with frocks that seemed intent on upstaging their wearer – one of his most celebrated creations was a nine-layered dress that became famous when worn by a model in Cadillac ads in the 1950s.

Museo Stefano Bardini

Piazza de' Mozzi 1 • Sat–Mon 11am–5pm • €5 • ⓦ museicivicifiorentini.it

The **Museo Stefano Bardini**, which stands at the end of the handsome Via de' Bardi, houses the collection of **Stefano Bardini** (1836–1922), once the most important art dealer in Italy, whose tireless activity – at a time when Renaissance art was relatively cheap and unfashionable – laid the cornerstone of many important European and American museums. Determined that no visitor to his native city should remain unaware of his success, he bought the former monastery of San Gregorio alla Pace, which at the time was doing service as a hat factory, and converted it into a vast house for himself and his collection. Sculpture, paintings, ceramics, armour, furniture, picture frames, carpets, wooden ceilings, tombstones – Bardini bought it all, and he bequeathed the whole lot to the city. Reopened in 2011 after a protracted restoration, the museum now looks much as it did when Bardini died, though a few pieces – notably Pietro Tacca's bronze boar and Giambologna's so-called Diavolino (Little Devil) – were added after his death.

The Bardini is more like a colossal showroom than a modern museum, with miscellaneous *objets d'art* strewn all about the place, sometimes arranged thematically, but often following their owner's personal logic. Many of the items are unlabelled too: on the **ground floor**, for example, Tino da Camaino's *Charity* is one of the very few pieces to be individually identified. The most interesting items are **upstairs**, where you'll find two reliefs of the *Madonna and Child* that may be by Donatello (in a room that's stacked with similar reliefs), a beautiful terracotta *Virgin Annunciate* from fifteenth-century Siena, and some fine drawings by Giambattista Tiepolo and his son Lorenzo. Most of the paintings are unremarkable, but there are exceptions, notably Guercino's *Atlas*, Michele Giambono's *St John the Evangelist*, and a *St Michael* by Antonio del Pollaiuolo. The main staircase is hung with gorgeous carpets, the largest of which was damaged by Hitler's spurs when it was laid out to welcome the Führer at Santa Maria Novella station.

San Niccolò sopr'Arno

Via San Niccolò • Daily 8.30–10am & 5.30–7pm

San Niccolò sopr'Arno, which was founded in the eleventh century and rebuilt in the fourteenth, took the full brunt of the 1966 flood. The subsequent rebuilding uncovered several frescoes behind the side altars, but the most appealing painting in the church is in the sacristy: known as *The Madonna of the Girdle*, it is generally attributed to Baldovinetti.

The city gates and Piazzale Michelangelo

In medieval times, San Niccolò sopr'Arno was close to the edge of the city, and two of Florence's fourteenth-century gates still stand in the vicinity: the diminutive **Porta San Miniato**, set into a portion of the walls within sight of the church, and the huge **Porta San Niccolò**, overlooking the Arno, five minutes' stroll east. From either gate you can begin the climb up to San Miniato: the path from Porta San Niccolò weaves up through **Piazzale Michelangelo**, with its replica *David* and bumper-to-bumper tour coaches; the more direct path from Porta San Miniato offers a choice between the steep Via del Monte alle Croci or the stepped Via di San Salvatore al Monte, both of which emerge a short distance uphill from Piazzale Michelangelo and downhill from San Miniato.

San Miniato al Monte

Via del Monte alle Croci • Daily 8am–12.30pm & 3–5.30pm

One of the finest Romanesque structures in Tuscany, **San Miniato al Monte** is also the oldest surviving church building in Florence after the Baptistery. Its brilliant multicoloured facade lures hordes of visitors up the hill from Oltrarno, and the church and its magnificent interior and works of art more than fulfil the promise of its distant appearance.

The church's dedicatee, **St Minias**, was Florence's first home-grown martyr. Possibly a Greek merchant or the son of an Armenian king, he made a pilgrimage to Rome and then, around 250, back in Florence, became caught up in the anti-Christian persecutions of the Emperor Decius. Legend has it that after martyrdom by

1

decapitation – close to the site of Piazza della Signoria – the saintly corpse was seen to carry his severed head over the river and up the hill to this spot, an area where he'd previously lived as a hermit: a shrine was subsequently erected on the slope. The hill, known as **Mons Fiorentinus**, was already the site of several pagan temples and a secret oratory dedicated to Peter the Apostle. A chapel to Miniato is documented on the site in the eighth century, though construction of the present building began in 1013. Initially run as a Benedictine foundation, the building passed to the Cluniacs until 1373, and then to the **Olivetans**, a Benedictine offshoot, who reside here to this day, and sell their famous liquors, honeys and tisanes from the shop next to the church.

The exterior

San Miniato's gorgeous marble **facade** alludes to the Baptistery in its geometrical patterning, and, like its model, the church was often mistaken for a structure of classical provenance during the later Middle Ages. The lower part of the facade is possibly eleventh century, while the upper levels date from the twelfth century onwards, and were financed in part by the Arte di Calimala (cloth merchants' guild), the body responsible for the church's upkeep from 1288: their trademark, an eagle clutching a bale of cloth, perches on the roof. The mosaic of Christ between the Virgin and St Minias dates from 1260. The original **bell tower** collapsed in 1499 and was replaced in the 1520s by the present campanile, still unfinished. During the 1530 siege of Florence it was used as an artillery post, thus attracting the attention of enemy gunners. Michelangelo, then advising on the city's defences, had it wrapped in woollen mattresses to protect it from cannonballs.

The interior

With its choir raised on a platform above the large crypt, the sublime **interior** of San Miniato has changed little since the mid-eleventh century, and the later additions and decorations in no way spoil its serenity. The columns' capitals are Roman and Byzantine, removed from older buildings, while the intricately patterned **pavement** is dated 1207; some claim the zodiac and animal motifs were inspired by Sicilian fabrics, others that they are of Byzantine origin, introduced into Italy through trade and the Crusades.

The Cappella del Crocefisso

The lovely tabernacle, or **Cappella del Crocefisso**, which dominates the middle of the nave, was designed in 1448 by Michelozzo, and is one of the few works commissioned by Piero de' Medici during his brief tenure as head of the Medici dynasty. The marble medallion to the rear and other parts of the work are adorned with Piero's motto (*Semper*) and several Medici symbols – the eagle holding three feathers and a diamond ring, the latter a symbol of durability and toughness. The chapel originally housed the miraculous crucifix associated with St Giovanni Gualberto (see p.79), which was moved to Santa Trìnita in 1671. Today it contains painted **panels** by Agnolo Gaddi depicting the *Annunciation*, *Stories of the Passion* and *Sts Giovanni Gualberto and Miniato* (1394–96). Maso di Bartolomeo crafted the twin eagles (1449), symbols of the Calimala, to stress that while Piero was the work's sponsor, the guild was responsible for overseeing all stages of its construction. The terracotta in the barrel vault is by Luca della Robbia.

The crypt

Steps each side of the Cappella lead down to the **crypt**, the oldest part of the church, where the original high altar still contains the bones of St Minias. The vaults, supported by 36 wonderfully mismatched pillars, contain gilt-backed frescoes (1341) of the saints, martyrs, prophets, virgins and Evangelists by Taddeo Gaddi.

1

The choir, presbytery and sacristy

Back in the main body of the church, steps beside the Cappella del Crocefisso lead to the raised **choir** and **presbytery**, where there's a magnificent Romanesque **pulpit** and screen dating from 1207. The odd totem-like figures supporting the lectern may represent three of the four Evangelists or, possibly, humanity placed in a middle state between the animal world (the lion) and the divine (the eagle). The great **mosaic** in the apse was created in 1297, probably by the same artist who created the facade mosaic, as their subjects are identical – Christ Pantocrator enthroned between the Virgin and St Minias. Off the presbytery lies the **sacristy**, whose walls are almost completely covered in a superlative fresco cycle devoted to the life of St Benedict by Spinello Aretino (1387).

The Cappella del Cardinale del Portogallo

The **Cappella del Cardinale del Portogallo**, off the left-hand side of the nave, is one of the masterpieces of Renaissance chapel design and a marvellous example of artistic collaboration. Completed in 1473, it was built as a memorial to Cardinal James of Lusitania, who died in Florence in 1459, aged just 25. Aside from that of Minias himself, this is – remarkably – the church's only tomb.

The basic design was the work of Antonio di Manetto (or Manetti), a pupil and biographer of Brunelleschi, who borrowed heavily from his master's work in San Lorenzo's Sagrestia Vecchia. The **tomb** itself was carved by Antonio and Bernardo Rossellino; their elder brother Giovanni oversaw the chapel's construction after Manetto's death. Antonio Rossellino's tondo of the Madonna and Child keeps watch over the deceased. The chapel's architectural and sculptural work was augmented in 1466 by the frescoes and **paintings**: an *Annunciation* (to the left) and the *Evangelists* and *Doctors of the Church* by Alesso Baldovinetti (lunettes and beside the arches). Antonio and Piero del Pollaiuolo produced the **altarpiece** depicting the cardinal's patron saint, St James, with Sts Vincent and Eustace: the present picture is a copy, the original being in the Uffizi. The ceiling's tiled decoration and four glazed terracotta medallions were provided by Luca della Robbia. All the decorative details were carefully designed to complement one another and create a unified artistic whole. Thus Rossellino's tondo of the *Madonna and Child*, for example, echoes the round windows of the walls; the colours in Baldovinetti's *Annunciation* echo the tones of the surrounding porphyry and serpentine inlays; and the curtain held aside by angels on the cardinal's tomb is repeated in a similar curtain half-shielding the altar.

ARRIVAL AND DEPARTURE   **FLORENCE**

Unless you're driving into the city, your point of arrival will be **Santa Maria Novella** station, just a few minutes' walk from the heart of the historic centre: rail and bus connections from the three airports that serve the city all terminate at the station, as do international trains and buses from all over Tuscany and Umbria.

BY PLANE

PISA – GALILEO GALILEI

The most popular airport for Florence is Pisa's Galileo Galilei (☎ 050 849 300, ⓦ pisa-airport.com), 95km west of Florence. For details of connections to Florence, see p.220.

PERÈTOLA

A small number of international air services use Perètola (or Amerigo Vespucci) airport (☎ 055 306 1300, ⓦ aeroporto .firenze.it), 5km northwest of the city centre. There's a tiny arrivals hall with an exchange machine, car rental desks and a tourist office (daily 8.30am–8.30pm; ☎ 055 315 874). Volainbus (ⓦ ataf.net) provides half-hourly shuttles into the

city from immediately outside the arrivals area. The first bus into the city is at 6am (last 11.30pm), the first out to the airport at 5.30am (last 11pm). Tickets (€5) can be bought on board or from machines at the airport, and the journey takes thirty minutes.

BOLOGNA – MARCONI

Bologna's Marconi airport (ⓦ bologna-airport.it) – about the same distance from Florence as Pisa – is an alternative gateway. Aerobus shuttles depart every twenty minutes (7.30am–11.45pm) from outside Terminal A to Bologna's main train station (about 25min), from where regular trains run to Florence in about an hour. Note, however, that

1

Ryanair services to "Bologna" in fact fly to **Forlì airport**, which is more than 60km southeast of Bologna, and very inconvenient for Florence.

BY TRAIN

Florence is the hub of the Tuscan rail system, and nearly all trains arrive at the main Santa Maria Novella station ("Firenze SMN" on timetables), a few blocks west of the Duomo. There are left-luggage facilities and a 24hr pharmacy. A few trains – mostly in the small hours of the morning – use Stazione Campo di Marte, over in the east of the city, from where there are regular buses into the centre. Destinations Arezzo (hourly; 1hr); Empoli (every 30min; 35min); Lucca (every 30min; 1–2hr); Pisa central (every 30min; 60–80min); Pistoia (every 20–30min; 40–55min); Prato (every 20–30min; 20–30min); Siena (via hourly connection at Empoli; 1hr 20min).

BY BUS

The main operator is SITA, which has a terminal right opposite the train station at Via Santa Caterina da Siena; all the other companies are based on the eastern side of the station.
Destinations
CAP (Largo Fratelli Alinari 9 ☎ 055 214 637, 🖳 capautolinee .it): Borgo San Lorenzo, Impruneta, Montepiano, Prato and Pistoia.
CLAP (Piazza Stazione ☎ 055 283 734, 🖳 clapspa.it): Lucca and Lucca province.
COPIT (Piazza Stazione ☎ 055 215 451, 🖳 copitspa.it): Castelfiorentino and Certaldo.

Lazzi (Piazza Stazione ☎ 166 845 010, 🖳 lazzi.it): Cerreto Guidi, Empoli, Forte dei Marmi, Incisa Valdarno, Livorno, Lucca, Marina di Carrara, Marina di Massa, Montecatini Terme, Montevarchi, Pisa, Pistoia, Pontassieve, Prato, Torre del Lago and Viareggio.
SITA (Via Santa Caterina da Siena 15; Tuscany routes ☎ 055 483 651, national routes ☎ 055 214 721; 🖳 sitabus.it): Barberino di Mugello (17 daily; 40min); Bibbiena (8 daily, 2hr 15min); Castellina in Chianti (1 daily; 1hr 35min); Certaldo (4 daily; 1hr 40min); Gaiole (2 daily Mon–Fri; 2hr); Greve (around 30 daily; 1hr 5min); Poggibonsi (10 daily; 1hr 20min); Pontassieve (12 daily; 50min); Poppi (9 daily; 2hr 5min); Radda in Chianti (1 daily Mon–Sat; 1hr 40min); San Casciano (14 daily; 40min); Siena (12 express services daily; 1hr 15min; also 9 stopping services); Volterra (6 daily; 2hr 25min).

BY CAR

Car parks Only residents are allowed to park in the centre, so you have to leave your car in one of the main car parks, unless you're staying at a hotel with reserved spaces. North of the Arno, the car parks nearest the centre are underneath the train station, just off Piazza della Libertà, and at Piazza Annigoni, near Santa Croce; south of the river the best option is Piazza della Calza, at the southwest tip of the Bóboli gardens.
Free parking The best place is Piazzale Michelangelo, which is about twenty minutes' walk from Piazza della Signoria, or a short ride on bus #12 or #13. Watch out for a scam in which bogus car-park attendants direct you into a parking space, implying there's a charge: there isn't.

GETTING AROUND

ON FOOT

Most of the major sights are within a few minutes' walk of the Duomo, and the increasing pedestrianization of the historic core makes walking a pleasure. You can get right across the city centre from Santa Maria Novella to Santa Croce in about half an hour, without rushing.

BY BUS

Pending completion of the Tramvia, the frequent ATAF buses are the best option for crossing town in a hurry or visiting the peripheral sights. Most routes that are useful to tourists stop by the station, notably #7 (for Fiesole) and #12/13: #13 goes clockwise through Piazzale Michelangelo, San Miniato and Porta Romana (all on the south side of the river), while #12 goes anticlockwise round the same route.
Tickets are valid for unlimited usage within ninety minutes (€1.20), 24hr (€5), 72hr (€12) or seven days (€18). A Biglietto Multiplo gives four tickets for €4.50; better value is the ATAF electronic card ticket called the Carta Agile, which comes in two versions – the €10 one is equivalent to ten tickets, the €20 to 21. Each Carta Agile

can be used by more than one passenger at a time, and is valid for one year. Tickets are available from the main ATAF information office to the east of Santa Maria Novella train station (daily 7am–8pm), from shops and stalls displaying the ATAF sign and from automatic machines all over Florence. Once you're on board, you must validate your ticket by stamping it in the machine; there's a hefty on-the-spot fine if you don't.

BY BIKE, SCOOTER OR MOPED

Limitations on car traffic have made cycling in Florence considerably less hazardous than it used to be. For bike rental go to Florence by Bike, Via San Zanobi 120–122r (☎ 055 488 992, 🖳 florencebybike.it). If a scooter or moped is more your style, visit Alinari, Via Zanobi 38r (☎ 055 280 500, 🖳 alinarirental.com).

TAXIS

You can't flag down a taxi in the street – you have to phone for one (☎ 055 4242, ☎ 055 4798, ☎ 055 4499 or ☎ 055 4390) or go to a taxi rank; key locations include the train

1

THE TRAMVIA

In an attempt to solve central Florence's perpetual congestion, the authorities are building a controversial tram network called **Tramvia**, despite objections that the city-centre streets are too narrow to accommodate tramlines. The system is intended to consist of three lines: one connecting Santa Maria Novella with Scandicci, to the southwest; the second running from Perètola to Piazza della Libertà, via the station and Duomo; and the last going from Careggi, to the north of the city centre, to Santa Maria Novella, possibly with an extension to Bagno a Ripoli in the southeast. At the time of writing, just one line – T1, a commuter service between Santa Maria Novella and the suburb of Scandicci – is in operation. Various major problems are still to be solved, such as how to run a line past the Duomo without disfiguring this unique urban landscape with a web of overhead cables. It seems a fair bet that it'll be some time before the Tramvia is fully operational.

station, Piazza della Repubblica, Piazza del Duomo, Piazza Santa Maria Novella, Piazza San Marco, Piazza Santa Croce and Piazza Santa Trinita. If you order a cab by phone, you'll be given the car's code name – usually a town, city or country – and its number, both of which are emblazoned on the vehicle. All rides are metered; at the start of the journey the meter should be set at €3.20, €5.10 if it's a Sunday or public holiday, or €6.40 between 10pm and 6am. Supplements are payable for journeys outside the city limits (to Fiesole, for example), for each piece of luggage placed in the boot (€1), and for phoning for a cab (€1.90). The charge per kilometre is €1.

INFORMATION

Tourist offices The main office at Via Cavour 1r (Mon–Sat 8.30am–6.30pm, Sun 8.30am–1.30pm; ☎ 055 290 832 or 055 290 833, ⓦ firenzeturismo.it) also handles information on the whole of Florence province. There are also offices at Borgo Santa Croce 29, just off Piazza Santa Croce (March–Oct Mon–Sat 9am–7pm, Sun 9am–2pm; Nov–Feb Mon–Sat 9am–5pm, Sun 9am–2pm; ☎ 055 234 0444); and Piazza della Stazione 4, opposite the train station (Mon–

Sat 8.30am–7pm, Sun 8.30am–2pm; ☎ 055 212 245).
Tourist information One of the best sources of information on events is *Firenze Spettacolo* (ⓦ firenzespettacolo.it; €1.80), a monthly, partly bilingual listings magazine available from bookshops and larger newsstands. *The Florentine* (ⓦ theflorentine.net) is a useful bi-weekly English-language paper, available free at the tourist office, most bookshops and various other spots.

ACCOMMODATION

Demand for **accommodation** in Florence is almost limitless, which means that prices are high and some hoteliers less than scrupulous. There's rarely a let-up in the tourist invasion: "low season" is officially the period from mid-November to mid-March (except for Christmas and New Year), plus the weeks from mid-July to the end of August, but anytime between March and October you should book your room well in advance. The tourist office at the station can find you a hotel (for a fee), but you'd be ill-advised to roll into town without having somewhere already sorted out. If none of our recommended places has a room, search the listings on the official tourism website ⓦ firenzeturismo.it. Never respond to the touts who hang around the train station: their hotels are likely to be expensive, or remote, or unlicensed private houses.

HOTELS AND RESIDENZE

Hotel **prices** in Florence are higher than anywhere else in Tuscany, but many places reduce their rates considerably in low season – and with the recession, online discounts have become commonplace, even in summer. To be classified as a hotel in Florence, a building has to have at least seven bedrooms. Places with fewer rooms operate as **affittacamere** ("rooms for rent") or **residenze** – though, confusingly, a *residenza d'epoca* (a *residenza* in a historic building) might have as many as a dozen rooms. Several *residenze*, and most *residenze d'epoca*, are small hotels in all but name, offering some of the most atmospheric accommodation in Florence. Many *affittacamere* and *residenze* are on the upper floors of large buildings, and can be reached only by stairs.

CITY CENTRE

Alessandra Borgo Santi Apostoli 17 ☎ 055 283 438, ⓦ www.hotelalessandra.com; map pp.48–49. One of the best and friendliest of the central two-stars, with 27 rooms (most with bathroom) occupying a sixteenth-century palazzo and furnished in a mixture of antique and modern styles. **€110–170**
Bretagna Lungarno Corsini 6 ☎ 055 289 618, ⓦ hotelbretagna.net; map pp.48–49. This three-star riverfront hotel has a superb location and rococo-style breakfast and living rooms. Six of the rooms overlook the Arno, and most of the rest are en suite and a/c. **€100–150**
★ **Cestelli** Borgo SS Apostoli 25 ☎ 055 214 213, ⓦ hotelcestelli.com; map pp.48–49. Spotlessly

1

maintained by its young owners, this eight-roomed one-star occupies part of a house that once belonged to a minor Medici, whose bust adorns the facade. The rooms are a good size, and most are en suite. **€70–100**

Elite Via della Scala 12 ☎055 215 395, ⓦhotelelitefirenze.com; map pp.48–49. A basic, clean and inexpensive ten-room two-star run by a very pleasant management. Most rooms have private bathrooms; ask for a room at the back, as they're somewhat quieter. **€55–70**

Gallery Hotel Art Vicolo dell'Oro 5 ☎055 27 263, ⓦlungarnohotels.com; map pp.48–49. In a small, quiet square a few paces from the Ponte Vecchio, this immensely stylish four-star is unlike any other hotel in central Florence. It has a sleek, minimalist and hyper-modern look – lots of dark wood and neutral colours – and tasteful contemporary art displayed in the reception and all 74 rooms. There's a small but smart bar, a sushi restaurant and an attractive lounge with art-filled bookshelves and comfortable sofas. **€300–400**

★ **Helvetia & Bristol** Via dei Pescioni 2 ☎055 26 651, ⓦroyaldemeure.com; map pp.48–49. In business since 1894 and favoured by such luminaries as Pirandello, Stravinsky and Gary Cooper, this is undoubtedly Florence's finest small five-star hotel. The public spaces and 67 bedrooms and suites (each unique) are faultlessly designed and fitted, mixing antique furnishings and modern facilities – such as jacuzzis in many bathrooms – to create a style that evokes the *belle époque* without being twee. If you're going to treat yourself, this is a leading contender. **€250–400**

Hermitage Vicolo Marzio 1/Piazza del Pesce ☎055 287 216, ⓦhermitagehotel.com; map pp.48–49. Prebooking is recommended year-round to secure one of the 28 rooms in this three-star hotel right next to the Ponte Vecchio, with unbeatable views from some rooms as well as from the flower-filled roof garden. The service is friendly, and rooms are cosy, decorated with the odd antique flourish; bathrooms are small but nicely done. **€125–200**

Il Salotto di Firenze Via Roma 6 ☎055 218 347, ⓦilsalottodifirenze.it; map pp.48–49. This *residenza* has six well-appointed rooms, with three overlooking Piazza del Duomo. Perhaps not a good choice if you're a light sleeper, but the standard of accommodation is high, prices low and the location unbeatable. **€80–130**

J.K. Place Piazza Santa Maria Novella 7 ☎055 264 5181, ⓦjkplace.com; map pp.48–49. One of the most appealing of Florence's designer hotels occupies a fine eighteenth-century building on Piazza Santa Maria Novella. The twenty rooms of this elegant town house have been designed by Michele Bönan in retro-modernist hybrid style, and have DVD players and flat-screen TVs. **€350–500**

★ **NH Porta Rossa** Via Porta Rossa 19 ☎055 271 0911, ⓦnhportarossa.hotelinfirenze.com; map pp.48–49. Florence's most venerable four-star hotel, the 72-room *Porta Rossa* has been in business since the beginning of the nineteenth century and has hosted,

among others, Byron and Stendhal. Recently reopened after a long renovation, it retains something of its old ambience whilst the rooms have been fitted out in crisp but luxuriously modern style, with red and white the dominant tones. Doubles **€200–300**

Nizza Via del Giglio 5 ☎055 239 6897, ⓦhotelnizza .com; map pp.48–49. A smart eighteen-room family-run two star, with helpful staff and very central location. All rooms are en suite, and are better furnished and decorated than many in this category. **€60–100**

Residenza d'Epoca in Piazza della Signoria Via dei Magazzini 2 ☎055 239 9546, ⓦinpiazzadellasignoria .com; map pp.48–49. This luxurious *residenza d'epoca* has ten spacious bedrooms, several of them giving a view of the piazza. The style is antique, but tastefully restrained, and the management is very friendly. **€220–280**

Torre Guelfa Borgo SS Apostoli 8 ☎055 239 6338, ⓦhoteltorreguelfa.com; map pp.48–49. Twenty tastefully furnished rooms are crammed into the third floor of this ancient tower, the tallest private building in the city; there are marvellous views from the small roof garden. There are also six cheaper doubles on the first floor (no TV and more noise from the road). Though slightly shabby in places, this is a characterful hotel, and very popular. **€100–200**

NORTH OF THE CENTRE

Antica Dimora Firenze Via San Gallo 72 ☎055 462 7296, ⓦjohanna.it; map pp.44–45. This plush *residenza*, run by the owners of the neighbouring *Antica Dimora Johlea* and *Residenza Johlea*, has six very comfortable double rooms , some with four-poster beds. **€90–160**

Antica Dimora Johlea Via San Gallo 80 ☎055 461 185, ⓦjohanna.it; map pp.44–45. Slightly pricier and a little more luxurious than the *Antica Dimora Firenze*, this lovely *residenza* also has a nice roof terrace, giving a roofline view of the Duomo and the hills beyond. **€100–170**

Bellettini Via dei Conti 7 ☎055 213 561, ⓦwww .hotelbellettini.com; map pp.48–49. The warm welcome of owner Signora Gina counts for much in this simple 27-room two-star; so, too, do her copious breakfasts. Most of the rooms have private bathrooms (those without are much cheaper); all have TVs and a/c. **€60–120**

★ **Casci** Via Cavour 13 ☎055 211 686, ⓦhotelcasci .com; map pp.48–49. It would be hard to find a better two-star in central Florence than this 26-room hotel, which occupies part of a building in which Rossini once lived. Only two (sound-proofed) rooms face the busy street; the rest are very quiet, and all are clean and neat. The welcome is warm and the owners are unfailingly helpful. The big buffet breakfast under the frescoed ceiling of the reception area is a plus, as is free internet. **€80–150**

Globus Via Sant'Antonino 24 ☎055 211 062, ⓦhotelglobus.com; map pp.48–49. The *Globus* has a refreshingly different style from most of Florence's three-stars – wenge wood furniture and natural tones predominate, rather than antiques and chintz. **€75–150**

Kursaal Ausonia Via Nazionale 24 ☎055 496 324, ⓦkursonia.com; map pp.44–45. Welcoming, recently refurbished three-star near the station, with accommodation ranging from spacious "superior" doubles, in faux-antique style, to rather more bland and functional "standard" rooms. **€70–120**

★ **Loggiato dei Serviti** Piazza Santissima Annunziata 3 ☎055 289 592, ⓦloggiatodeiservitihotel.it; map pp.48–49. Elegant three-star in one of Florence's most celebrated squares. Its 38 rooms have been incorporated into a structure designed in the sixteenth century in imitation of the Brunelleschi hospital across the square, to accommodate the Servite priests who worked there. The plainness of some rooms reflects something of the building's history, but all are decorated with fine fabrics and antiques, and look out either onto the piazza or peaceful gardens to the rear: top-floor rooms have glimpses of the Duomo. The five rooms in the nearby annexe, at Via dei Servi 49, are similarly styled, but the building doesn't have the same charisma. **€90–180**

Morandi alla Crocetta Via Laura 50 ☎055 234 4747, ⓦhotelmorandi.it; map pp.48–49. An intimate three-star gem, whose small size and friendly welcome ensure a home-from-home atmosphere. Rooms are tastefully decorated with antiques and old prints, and vivid carpets laid on parquet floors. Two rooms have balconies opening onto a modest garden; another – with fresco fragments and medieval nooks and crannies – was converted from the site's former convent chapel. **€110–150**

Relais Grand Tour Via Santa Reparata 21 ☎055 283 955, ⓦflorencegrandtour.com; map pp.44–45. The very hospitable owners have done a great job in turning two floors of this old palazzo, adjoining an eighteenth-century private theatre, into a superb guesthouse, with three large bedrooms on the second floor and three suites on the floor above. Each room is unique – one is replete with Neapolitan majolica tiles, another has a gold-leaf wooden ceiling and a third – formerly a dressing-room – is loaded with mirrors ("suitable for a couple", as the website has it). Usually two-night minimum stay. **€100–130**

Residenza Johanna I Via Bonifacio Lupi 14 ☎055 481 896, ⓦjohanna.it; map pp.44–45. The longest-established of the *Johanna/Johlea* family of *residenze*, this genteel place is hidden away in an unmarked apartment building in a quiet, leafy corner of the city, a 5min walk north of San Marco. Rooms are cosy and well kept, and the management are as friendly and helpful as you could hope for. **€70–140**

Residenza Johanna II Via Cinque Giornate 12 ☎055 473 377, ⓦjohanna.it; map pp.44–45. The location of this *residenza* – to the north of the Fortezza da Basso – is less convenient than that of its siblings, but the accommodation is of the same high standard, as is the hospitality. **€70–120**

Residenza Johlea Via San Gallo 76 ☎055 463 3292, ⓦjohanna.it; map pp.44–45. Another venture from the owners of *Residenza Johanna*, offering the same low-cost, high-comfort package. **€70–140**

SANT'AMBROGIO DISTRICT

J & J Via di Mezzo 20 ☎055 263 121, ⓦjandj .hotelinfirenze.com; map pp.44–45. The bland exterior of this former fifteenth-century convent conceals a romantic nineteen-room four-star hotel. Some rooms are vast split-level affairs, but all have charm and are furnished with modern fittings and a few antiques. Common areas are decked with flowers, and retain frescoes and vaulted ceilings from the original building. In summer breakfast is served in the convent's lovely old cloister. **€135–235**

OLTRARNO

Annalena Via Romana 34 ☎055 222 402, ⓦhotelannalena.it; map pp.44–45. A short way beyond Palazzo Pitti (and right by an entrance to the Bóboli gardens), this bargain-priced twenty-room three-star occupies a building once owned by the Medici. The best rooms open onto a gallery with garden views, and a sprinkling of antiques lend a hint of old-world charm. **€80–120**

La Scaletta Via Guicciardini 13 ☎055 283 028, ⓦlascaletta.com; map pp.48–49. Some of the rooms in this tidy and recently refurbished sixteen-room two-star give views across to the Bóboli gardens; those on the Via Guicciardini side are double-glazed against the traffic. Drinks are served on the rooftop terraces, where you look across the Bóboli in one direction and the city in the other. All rooms are en suite and nicely decorated in creamy tones. **€100–130**

Palazzo Guadagni Piazza Santo Spirito 9 ☎055 265 8376, ⓦpalazzoguadagni.com; map pp.44–45. A well-presented three-star with huge double rooms overlooking the piazza, some with fantastic frescoed ceilings. The rooftop loggia bar gives spectacular views. **€100–150**

★ **Torre di Bellosguardo** Via Roti Michelozzi 2 ☎055 229 8145, ⓦtorrebellosguardo.com; map pp.44–45. It's not central – it's perched on a hill about 2km from the heart of Oltrarno – but the four-star *Bellosguardo* is one of the most beautiful hotels in the city. Dating back to the thirteenth century, and once home to Galileo, it's girdled by magnificent gardens (with a pool), and each of its sixteen rooms (each uniquely and exquisitely furnished) is palatial. **€280–400**

HOSTELS

Foresteria Valdese Firenze – Istituto Gould Via dei Serragli 49 ☎055 212 576, ⓦistitutogould.it; map pp.48–49. Run by the Waldensian church, this hostel-cum-evangelical college occupies part of a

1

seventeenth-century palazzo between Santo Spirito and the Carmine. The 99 beds (in 39 rooms) are extremely popular, so book in advance, especially during the academic year. Street-front rooms can be noisy (rear rooms cost a little more), but the old courtyard, terracotta floors and stone staircases provide atmosphere throughout. Check-in Mon–Fri 8.45am–1pm & 3–7.30pm, Sat 9am–1.30pm & 2.30–6pm; reception closed Sun. No curfew. Dorm bed €22, single room €45

Ostello Archi Rossi Via Faenza 94r ☎ 055 290 804, ⊚ hostelarchirossi.com; map pp.44–45. A 5min walk from the train station, this privately owned 147-bed guesthouse/hostel is spotlessly clean and has a pleasant garden and terrace. Dorm sizes vary, and not all have internal bathrooms; all prices include breakfast and internet access. Disabled access rooms available. Dorm beds €22–29, single rooms €40–90

Ostello Villa Camerata Viale Augusto Righi 2–4 ☎ 055 601 451, ⊚ ostellofirenze.it; map pp.44–45. Tucked away in a beautiful park northeast of the city, 5km from Santa Maria Novella station, this campsite and HI hostel is one of Europe's most attractive, set in a sixteenth-century house with frescoed ceilings, fronted by lemon trees. Doors open at 2pm; if you'll arrive later,

call ahead to make sure there's space (bookings by email or fax only). There are 322 dorm beds; breakfast and sheets are included, but there are no kitchen facilities. Films in English are shown every night. Midnight curfew. Bus #17b from the train station takes about 30min. Dorm beds from €18

Santa Monaca Via Santa Monaca 6 ☎ 055 268 338, ⊚ ostello.it; map pp.48–49. This privately owned hostel in Oltrarno, close to the Carmine, has 115 beds in rooms sleeping between two and twenty. Kitchen facilities (no utensils), washing machines and a useful noticeboard with information on lifts and onward travel. Check-in 6am–2am; bedrooms have to be vacated between 10am and 2pm. Curfew 2am. It's a 15min walk from the station, or take bus #11, #36 or #37. Dorm beds €16–25

CAMPSITES

Camping Michelangelo Viale Michelangelo 80 ☎ 055 681 1977, ⊚ ecvacanze.it; map pp.44–45. A 240-pitch site that's always crowded, owing to its superb hillside location in an olive grove overlooking the city centre. Kitchen facilities and a well-stocked, if expensive, nearby shop. Take #13 bus from the station. Adults €9.50, plus pitches from €11.50

EATING

As you'd expect in a major tourist city, Florence has plenty of **restaurants**, but – unsurprisingly – a large number of them are aimed squarely at the outsiders, so standards are often patchy. Some locals will swear there's scarcely a single genuine Tuscan restaurant left in the Tuscan capital, and certainly there are some dire establishments in the environs of Piazza della Signoria and Piazza del Duomo. But the situation is nowhere near as bad as some would have it – in fact it's been improving in recent years, with the appearance of several stylish and good-value restaurants. Bear in mind also that simple meals are served in many Florentine bars and cafés.

CITY CENTRE

Antico Fattore Via Lambertesca 1–3r ☎ 055 288 975, ⊚ anticofattore.it; map pp.48–49. Simple Tuscan dishes dominate the menu here, and the soups are particularly good. This is the nearest thing you'll find to a genuine trattoria near the Uffizi (mains €10–14). Tues–Sun noon–2.45pm & 7–10.30pm; closed Aug.

★ **Oliviero** Via delle Terme 51r ☎ 055 240 618, ⊚ ristorante-oliviero.it; map pp.48–49. *Oliviero* has a welcoming and old-fashioned feel – something like an Italian

restaurant of the 1960s – and the menu, though predominantly Tuscan, includes dishes from other regions of Italy. Fresh fish, when available, features strongly – something of a rarity in Florence. Expect to pay upwards of €50, without wine – reasonable for cooking of this calibre. Mon–Sat 7–11pm; closed Aug.

Yellow Bar Via del Proconsolo 39r ☎ 055 211 766; map pp.48–49. This place looks like a fast-food joint, but the queues of Florentines waiting for a table give you a clue that first impressions are misleading. Inside, the convivial

---

FLORENTINE CUISINE

In Italian gastronomic circles, **Florentine cuisine** is accorded as much reverence as Florentine art, a reverence encapsulated in the myth that French eating habits acquired their sophistication in the wake of Catherine de' Medici's marriage to the future Henry II of France. In fact, Florentine food has always been characterized by modest raw materials and simple technique: steak (*bistecca*), tripe (*trippa*) and liver (*fegato*) are typical ingredients, while grilling (*alla fiorentina*) is a favoured method of preparation. In addition, white beans (*fagioli*) will feature on most menus, either on their own, garnished with liberal quantities of local olive oil, or as the basis of such dishes as *ribollita*.

1

SNACKS AND FOOD SHOPS

If you want to put together a picnic, obvious places to shop are the **Mercato Centrale** by San Lorenzo church (see p.91) and the **Mercato Sant'Ambrogio** over by Santa Croce (see p.107). Every district has its **alimentari**, which in addition to selling the choicest Tuscan produce will often make sandwiches to order. For the choicest local produce, you can't beat these four: 'Ino, very close to the Uffizi at Via de' Georgofili 3–7r; Mariano, near Santa Maria Novella at Via del Parione 19r; the Olio e Convivium café-bar-restaurant-shop, at Via Santo Spirito 4, in Oltrarno; and Il Santino (see p.130). Nearly all wine bars sell bottles to take away, or you could go to a specialist shop such as Millesimi, at Borgo Tegolaio 35r, or Obsequium, at Borgo San Jacopo 17 – both in Oltrarno. Chocoholics should check out Vestri, at Borgo degli Albizi 11r, which offers deliciously thick chocolate to drink and a mouthwatering array of chocolate products, including ice cream.

For a hearty sit-down lunchtime snack, the Mercato Centrale and Mercato Sant'Ambrogio each has an excellent **tavola calda**, serving meatballs, pasta, stews, soups and sandwiches. If you really want to go native, you could join the throng around the tripe stall in Piazza dei Cimatori, between the Duomo and Piazza della Signoria (Mon–Fri 8.30am–8.30pm; closed four weeks July/Aug). Its speciality is the local delicacy called lampredotto: hot tripe served in a bun with a spicy sauce. The stall also sells wine, so you can wash the taste away should you realize you've made a horrible mistake. There's a similar operation parked outside the Cibrèo restaurant in Via de' Macci (Mon–Sat 7.15am–3pm).

---

atmosphere in the large dining room is matched by superlative pan-Italian food (including excellent pizzas) in large portions at very reasonable prices. Meats are especially good, and the quality and presentation remain high despite the bustle and quick turnover. You can often get a table in the mildly less appealing rooms downstairs when the main dining room is busy. Mon & Wed–Sun noon–3pm & 7pm–midnight, Tues noon–3pm.

WEST OF THE CENTRE

★ **Il Contadino** Via Palazzuolo 69–71r ⓦ trattoriailcontadino.com; map pp.48–49. Small, popular place with a simple black-and-white interior and fascinating large photos of old Florence on the walls. Fast and friendly service, shared tables (no booking) and very cheap but good food. Three-course lunch and dinner menu costs a mere €13. Mon–Fri noon–9.30pm.

Marione Via della Spada 27r ⓣ 055 214 756. Simple, good-value Tuscan cooking, at prices that are a pleasant surprise for this location, a stone's throw from Via Tornabuoni. Mains from just €7. Daily 12.30–2.30pm & 7.30–10.30pm; closed first two weeks of Aug.

NORTH OF THE CENTRE

★ **Da Mario** Via Rosina 2r ⓣ 055 218 550, ⓦ trattoria -mario.com; map pp.48–49. Located close to the Mercato Centrale, Da Mario has probably been packed out every lunchtime since the Colsi family started running the place in 1953. For earthy Florentine cooking at very low prices, there's nowhere better; it's just a pity it isn't open in the evenings. Note that they don't take reservations. Mon–Sat noon–3.30pm; closed Aug.

Zà-Zà Piazza del Mercato Centrale 26r ⓣ 055 210 756,

ⓦ trattoriazaza.it; map pp.48–49. In business for more than thirty years, Zà-Zà is one of the best of several trattorie close to the Mercato Centrale. The interior is dark, stone-walled and brick-arched, with a handful of tables – though in summer there's plenty more space on the outside terraces. There's usually a set menu for around €15, with a choice of three or four pastas and mains; otherwise you'll pay around €30 per head. Booking is virtually obligatory in summer. Daily noon–3pm & 7pm–1am; closed Aug.

EAST OF THE CENTRE

★ **Baldovino** Via San Giuseppe 22r ⓣ 055 241 773, ⓦ baldovino.com; map pp.48–49. This superb place, run by an imaginative Scottish couple, is renowned for its pizzas (made in a wood-fired oven), but the main menu, which changes monthly, is full of good Tuscan and Italian dishes, with most mains at €12–17. Portions are very generous. The adjacent café-bar – Baldobar – is good for a quick snack. Tues–Sun 11.30am–3pm & 7pm–1am.

Cibrèo Via de' Macci 118r ⓣ 055 234 1100, ⓦ edizioniteatrodelsalecibreofirenze.it; map pp.44–45. Fabio Picchi's restaurant is the first Florentine port-of-call for many foodies, its creative take on Tuscan classics having achieved fame well beyond the city. Some think it's been resting on its laurels for too long, but many still rate it very highly indeed. You'll need to book days in advance for a table in the main part of the restaurant, but next door there's a small, somewhat spartan and sometimes overly busy trattoria (Cibreino) where the food is virtually the same (though the menu is smaller), no bookings are taken and the prices are much lower: around €15 for mains, as opposed to €35 in the restaurant. Both open Tues–Sat 1–2.30pm & 7–11.15pm; closed Aug.

1

Enoteca Pinchiorri Via Ghibellina 87 ☎ 055 242 777, ⊕ enotecapinchiorri.com; map pp.48–49. This is the only Tuscan restaurant to have been given three Michelin stars, and no one seriously disputes the *Pinchiorri*'s claim to be Florence's best restaurant. However, formality of the place is not to everyone's taste, and the prices are delirious: most main courses are €90, while the set menus are €200 per person for six courses, and €275 for ten, wine excluded. The wine list has no equal in Italy, with some 150,000 bottles lying in the cellars; bottles start at about €60. Tues & Wed 7.30–10pm, Thurs–Sat 12.30–2pm & 7.30–10pm; closed Aug & Dec 15–27.

★ **Il Pizzaiuolo** Via de' Macci 113r ☎ 055 241 171, ⊕ ilpizzaiuolo.it; map pp.44–45. The Neapolitan pizzas here are the best in the city. Other dishes and wines also have a Neapolitan touch, as does the atmosphere, which is friendly and high-spirited. Booking's a good idea in the evening. Mon–Sat 12.30–3pm & 7.30pm–midnight; closed Aug.

L'Antico Noè Volta di San Piero 6r ☎ 055 234 0838, ⊕ lanticonoe.com; map pp.48–49. Situated next door to the *vinaio* of the same name, this tiny trattoria has a somewhat insalubrious setting (the Volta di San Piero is the one place in central Florence where you're guaranteed to see a drunk or two), but the food is fine and the prices low – mains from around €10. Mon–Sat noon–3pm & 7–11pm.

La Pentola dell'Oro Via di Mezzo 24r ☎ 055 241 821, ⊕ lapentoladelloro.it; map pp.44–45. Giuseppe Alessi's restaurant has one of the more imaginative menus in Florence, mingling the innovative with the profoundly traditional (some recipes date back to the sixteenth century). The main basement restaurant isn't the cosiest of dining rooms, but the quality is difficult to match for the price. Expect to pay upwards of €40, or a little less in the more informal ground-floor section, which focuses on traditional rather than aristocratic cuisine. Mon–Sat noon–3.30pm & 9pm–midnight.

★ **Ora d'Aria** Via Ghibellina 3c/r ☎ 055 200 1699, ⊕ oradariaristorante.com; map pp.44–45. This stylish venture offers a high-quality mix of the traditional and the innovative, with an unusual emphasis on fish and seafood dishes, while the cool, pale and spacious dining room is one of the most relaxing in the city. The tasting menus (from €60) are very good value; à la carte main courses are around €32. Mon 7.30–11pm, Tues–Sat noon–3pm & 7.30–11.30pm.

Osteria Caffè Italiano Via Isola delle Stinche 11–13r ☎ 055 289 368, ⊕ caffeitaliano.it; map pp.48–49. The cuisine at this smart café-restaurant is typically Tuscan (lots of beef, veal and wild boar) and first-rate; expect to pay upwards of €40 per head. Tues–Sun 10am–1am.

Osteria de' Benci Via de' Benci 13r ☎ 055 234 4923, ⊕ osteriadeibenci.it; map pp.48–49. A modern, busy and friendly *osteria*, with a pretty interior and outdoor tables that attract a lot of customers in summer. The moderately priced menu offers well-prepared standards: pasta dishes (more than a dozen varieties) and grilled meat are the strong points. Restaurant Mon–Sat 1–2.45pm & 7.30–10.45pm; café-bar 8am–midnight.

OLTRARNO

Alla Vecchia Bettola Viale Lodovico Ariosto 32–34r ☎ 055 224 158, ⊕ allavecchiabettola.com; map pp.44–45. Located on a major traffic intersection a couple of minutes' walk from the Carmine, this place – with its long marble-topped tables – has something of the atmosphere of an old-style drinking den, which is what it once was; nowadays it boasts a good repertoire of Tuscan meat dishes, with mains from €10 and an excellent choice of wines by the glass, too. Mon–Sat noon–2.30pm & 7.30–10.30pm.

Borgo Antico Piazza di Santo Spirito 6r ☎ 055 210 437, ⊕ borgoanticofirenze.com; map pp.48–49. In summer the outside tables here are invariably packed, and the majority of the clientele are usually foreigners. But *Borgo Antico* is not one of Florence's cynical tourist-traps: the food (pizza plus Tuscan standards) is generally good, prices are fair and the servings are generous to a fault. (The *Osteria Santo Spirito*, at 16r, is run by the same people, and serves hearty Tuscan dishes.) Daily noon–midnight.

Filipepe Via San Niccolò 39r ☎ 055 200 1397, ⊕ filipepe .com; map pp.44–45. An imaginative place, with a menu that's markedly different from most of the competition – it markets itself as a "Mediterranean restaurant", and offers delicious food drawn from a variety of Italian regional cuisines. The wine list is similarly wide-ranging, and the decor offbeat and attractive. Most main courses are in the €14–20 range. Daily 7.30–11pm; closed two weeks in Aug.

Gustapizza Via Maggio 46r; map pp.48–49. The wood-fired Neapolitan pizzas served here are the best in Oltrarno – and pizzas are all they do, which is always a good thing. No reservations, and the dining room is not large, so be prepared to queue. Tues–Sun 11.30am–3pm & 7–11pm.

Il Santo Bevitore Via Santo Spirito 64–66r ☎ 055 211 264, ⊕ ilsantobevitore.com; map pp.48–49. The Holy Drinker is an airy "gastronomic *enoteca*" with a small and enticing menu (around €35 for a meal without drinks) to complement its excellent wine list. It's one of the most popular restaurants in Oltrarno, so not the place for a quiet romantic evening. Daily 12.30–2.30pm & 7.30–11.30pm; closed three weeks in Aug.

★ **La Casalinga** Via del Michelozzo 9r ☎ 055 218 624, ⊕ trattorialacasalinga.it; map pp.48–49. Located in a sidestreet off Piazza di Santa Spirito, this long-established family-run trattoria serves up some of the best low-cost Tuscan dishes in town (€10 for a *secondo*). No frills – paper tablecloths, so-so house wine by the carafe and brisk service

– but most nights it's filled with regulars and a good few outsiders. By 8pm there's invariably a queue. Mon–Sat noon–2.30pm & 7–10pm; closed three weeks in Aug.

Pane e Vino Piazza di Cestello 3r ☎055 247 6956, ⓦ ristorantepaneevino.it; map pp.44–45. *Pane e Vino* began life as a bar, so it's no surprise that the wine list is excellent and well priced, with bottles from around €15. The ambience is stylish yet relaxed and the menu small and consistently excellent (*secondi* €15–20), featuring two very enticing set menus. Small TV screens in the dining area show the chefs beavering away in the kitchen, producing some of the best food in town – the ravioli with asparagus in a lemon cream melts in your mouth. Mon–Sat 7.30pm–midnight; closed two weeks in Aug.

Quattro Leoni Via dei Vellutini 1r ☎055 218 562, ⓦ4leoni.com; map pp.48–49. One of the most pleasant places to eat in Florence: inside, there are three medieval rooms with splashy modern paintings hung on the rough stone walls; outside, the tables are shaded by vast canvas umbrellas in a corner of the tiny Piazza della Passera. Some say the quality of the food and service has declined slightly with the rising popularity, but it's never less than a cut above the average. Expect to pay around €40 a head. Daily 12.30–2.30pm & 7.30–11pm; closed Wed lunch.

Sabatino Via Pisani 2r ☎055 225 955; map pp.44–45. Situated right by Porta San Frediano, this old-fashioned, long-established family osteria is absolutely authentic, very good and ridiculously inexpensive by Florentine standards. Mon–Fri noon–2.30pm & 7.15–10pm; closed Aug.

CAFÉS AND GELATERIE

As elsewhere in Italy, the distinction between Florentine bars and **cafés** can be tricky to the point of impossibility, as almost every café serves alcohol and almost every bar serves coffee. That said, there are some cafés in which the emphasis is on coffee, cakes and ice cream – they are the ones listed here, along with the charmingly eccentric *Procacci*. Devotees of Italian **ice cream** will find that Florence offers plenty of opportunities to indulge: the city has several superb *gelaterie*, and many would claim that *Vivoli* is one of the top purveyors in the country.

CITY CENTRE

Caffè Gilli Piazza della Repubblica 36–39r ☎055 213 896; map pp.48–49. Founded in 1733, this most appealing of this square's expensive cafés moved to its present site in 1910. The lavish *belle époque* interior is a sight in itself (though there are rumours of an imminent modernization), but most people choose to sit on the big outdoor terrace. On a cold afternoon try the famous hot chocolate – it comes in five blended flavours: almond, orange, coffee, *gianduia* (hazelnut) and cocoa. Daily 8am–midnight.

Gelateria dei Neri Via dei Neri 20–22r; map pp.48–49. Small place in contention for the best ice cream in town, close to the Uffizi but away from the crowds. The range of flavours is fantastic – fig and walnut, Mexican chocolate (very spicy), rice – and they also have some non-dairy ice cream. Daily 11am–midnight.

Grom Via del Campanile; map pp.48–49. Founded in Turin in 2003, *Grom* is a retro-styled but very slick operation, concocting fabulous *gelati* from top-quality ingredients gathered from all over Italy. The house speciality is Crema di Grom, made from organic eggs, soft *meliga* biscuits and Ecuadorian chocolate. Daily: April–Oct 10.30am–midnight, Nov–March 10.30am–11pm.

Perchè No! Via de' Tavolini 19r; map pp.48–49. Superb *gelateria*, in business since the 1930s; go for the classic *crema*, the chocolate or the gorgeous pistachio. Mon & Wed–Sun 11am–11pm, Tues noon–8pm; closed Nov.

Procacci Via de' Tornabuoni 64r ☎055 211 656; map pp.48–49. This famous café doesn't serve coffee, just wine and cold drinks. Its reputation comes from the delicious (and minuscule) *tartufati*, or truffle-butter rolls – from Oct to Dec, when truffles are in season, the wood-lined interior here is a swooningly aromatic spot. Mon–Sat 10.30am–8pm; closed Aug.

Robiglio Via Tosinghi 11r ☎055 215 013; map pp.48–49. Renowned for its pastries and chocolates, *Robiglio* also makes good ice cream and specializes in a hot chocolate drink that's so thick it's barely a liquid. There are four other branches, the most central of which – and the original one, founded in 1928 – is at Via dei Servi 112r, near Santissima Annunziata. Mon–Sat 8am–8pm.

NORTH OF THE CENTRE

Carabé Via Ricasoli 60r; map pp.48–49. Wonderful Sicilian ice cream made with Sicilian ingredients as only they know how. Also serves a variety of cakes. Daily: May–Oct 9am–1am; Nov–April 9am–8pm; closed mid-Dec to mid-Jan.

EAST OF THE CENTRE

Caffè Cibrèo Via Andrea del Verrocchio 5r ☎055 234 5853; map pp.44–45. Possibly the prettiest café in Florence, *Caffè Cibrèo* opened in 1989, but the wood-panelled interior gives it the look of a place that's at least two hundred years older. Cakes and desserts are great, and the light meals bear the culinary stamp of the *Cibrèo* restaurant kitchens opposite. Tues–Sat 8am–1am.

Vivoli Via Isola delle Stinche 7r; map pp.48–49. Operating from deceptively unprepossessing premises in a sidestreet close to Santa Croce, this café has long been rated one of the best ice-cream-makers in Florence. Tues–Sun: summer 7.30am–midnight; winter 7.30am–9pm; closed two weeks in Aug.

1

OLTRARNO

Caffè Ricchi Piazza di Santo Spirito 9r ☎055 215 864; map pp.48–49. Best of the cafés on Piazza Santo Spirito, with a good selection of cakes, ice cream and sandwiches. Mon–Sat: summer 7am–1am; winter 7am–10pm; closed two weeks in Feb & two weeks in Aug.

DRINKING

As you'd expect in a city that lies close to some of the best vineyards in the country, Florence has plenty of bars dedicated to the **wines** of Chianti and other Tuscan producers. At one end of the scale there's the endangered species known as the **vinaio**, which consists of little more than a few shelves of workaday wines plus a counter of snacks. At the opposite pole there's the **enoteca**, which is a wine-bar-cum-restaurant; all *enoteche* have vast wine menus, but in some cases the kitchen has come to play so large a role that the place is now more a restaurant than a bar, which is why you'll find some *enoteche* listed in our restaurant section. Wine bars tend to see most of their customers at lunchtime and in the early evening. Other **bars**, however, are busiest at night, when the distinction between bars and clubs can be hard to draw: many of Florence's hotter bars try to keep the punters on the premises by serving free snacks with the *aperitivi* (usually about 7–9pm) before the music kicks in – either live or (more often) supplied by a DJ.

WINE BARS

CITY CENTRE

Cantinetta dei Verrazzano Via dei Tavolini 18–20r ☎055 268 590; map pp.48–49. Owned by Castello dei Verrazzano, a major Chianti vineyard, this wood-panelled place near Orsanmichele is part-bar, part-café, part-bakery, making its own excellent pizza, *focaccia* and cakes. A perfect spot for a light lunch or an early evening drink. July & Aug Mon–Sat 8am–4pm; Sept–June Mon–Sat 8am–9pm.

★ **Casa del Vino** Via dell'Ariento 16r ☎055 215 609; map pp.48–49. Located a few yards south of the Mercato Centrale, the *Casa del Vino* is particularly busy in the middle of the day, when market traders pitch up for a drink, a quick bite and a chat with owner Gianni Migliorini. Mon–Fri 9.30am–5.30pm, Sat 10am–3.30pm; closed Aug.

Zanobini Via Sant'Antonino 47r ☎055 239 6850; map pp.48–49. Like the nearby *Casa del Vino*, this is an authentic and long-established place, but here the emphasis is much more on the wine: few bars in Florence have a better selection. Mon–Sat 8am–2pm & 3.30–8pm.

OLTRARNO

Fuori Porta Via del Monte alle Croci 10r ☎055 234 2483; map pp.44–45. If you're climbing up to San Miniato you could take a breather at this superb and justly famous *enoteca-osteria*. There are over four hundred wines by the bottle, and an ever-changing selection by the glass, as well as grappas and malt whiskies. Cheese and cold meats are available, as well as pasta dishes and salads. There's a summertime terrace and large dining area, but it's still wise to book if you're coming here to eat. Mon–Sat 12.30–3.30pm & 7pm–12.30am; closed two weeks mid-Aug.

Il Santino Via Santo Spirito 60r ☎055 230 2820; map pp.48–49. This small gastronomic *alimentari*-cum-wine bar is an offshoot of the neighbouring Santo Bevitore, and is proving just as successful. The wines on offer are top-quality, as are the snacks. Daily 10.30am–11pm.

★ **Le Volpi e L'Uva** Piazza dei Rossi 1r ☎055 239 8132; map pp.48–49. This discreet, friendly little *enoteca* does good business by concentrating on the wines of small producers, and providing tasty cold meats and snacks to help them down (the selection of cheeses is tremendous). At any

VINAI

The *vinaio* was once a real Florentine institution. Customers at these tiny seat-less places would typically linger for no more than a couple of minutes – long enough to down a tumbler of wine and exchange a few words with the proprietor. The number of *vinai* has declined markedly in recent years; the following are the notable survivors.

All'Antico Vinaio Via dei Neri 65r; map pp.48–49. Though recently revamped, this place – located between the Uffizi and Santa Croce – preserves much of the rough-and-ready atmosphere that's made it one of Florence's most popular wine bars for the last hundred years. Also serves coffee, rolls and pasta. Mon–Sat 8am–10pm; closed three weeks late July/early Aug.

I Fratellini Via dei Cimatori 38r; map pp.48–49. This minuscule, dirt-cheap bar is clinging on in the vicinity of the high-rent Via dei Calzaiuoli. Serves decent panini and local wines. Mid-June to Aug Mon–Fri 8am–5pm; Sept to mid-June daily 8am–8pm.

L'Antico Noè Volta di San Piero 6r; map pp.48–49. A long-established stand-up wine bar, tucked into an uninviting little alley to the north of Santa Croce. Mon–Sat noon–3pm & 7pm–midnight.

Piccolo Vinaio Piazza del Grano 10; map pp.48–49. Little more than a window in a wall at the back of the Uffizi, serving snacks, and wine in tiny glasses called *rasini*. Daily 10am–11pm; closed Jan & Feb.

one time you can choose from at least two dozen different wines by the glass. Mon–Sat 11am–9pm.

BARS

CITY CENTRE

Art Bar Via del Moro 4r ☎ 055 287 661; map pp.48–49. A fine little bar near Piazza di Carlo Goldoni. The interior looks like an antique shop, while the club-like atmosphere attracts a studenty crowd. Especially busy at happy hour (6.30–9pm), when the low-priced cocktails are in heavy demand. Daily 7pm–midnight; closed three weeks in Aug.

Astor Caffè Piazza del Duomo 20r ☎ 055 284 305; map pp.48–49. From its modest streetfront opposite the northeast corner of the Duomo you wouldn't guess that this was the hottest spot on the piazza, but inside you'll find a glitzy and spacious three-storey setup. Food is served in the upstairs bar and grill, the basement has DJs playing anything from hip-hop to Brazilian music most nights, and in the ground-floor bar you sip cocktails with the city's gilded youth. Mon–S--at 10am–3am, Sun 5pm–3am.

Slowly Via Porta Rossa 63r ☎ 055 264 5354; map pp.48–49. This extremely trendy bar, with its neat little banquettes and candle lanterns, tends to attract a showy, beautifully dressed young crowd, who while away the hours chatting over pricey cocktails and bar snacks (the *aperitivo* buffet is one of the best in Florence). The atmosphere is pretty laidback, even when the DJ gets to work. Mon–Sat 7pm–2am.

EAST OF THE CENTRE

Moyo Via de' Benci 23r ☎ 055 247 9738; map pp48–49. A young crowd flocks to this bar every evening – the food's pretty good (come for the early evening *aperitivo* buffet) and the free wi-fi access is a plus, but it's the buzz that really brings them in. With *Osteria de' Benci* just down the road, this is one of the city's sparkiest corners. Mon–Thurs & Sun 8am–2am, Fri & Sat 8am–3am.

★ **Rex** Via Fiesolana 25r ☎ 055 248 0331; map pp.48–49. One of the city's big night-time fixtures, a friendly bar-club with a varied and loyal clientele. Vast curving lights droop over the central bar, which is studded with turquoise stone and broken mirror mosaics. The cocktails and DJs are good, and the snacks excellent – the *aperitivi* session is 7–9.30pm. Daily 5pm–3am; closed June–Aug.

OLTRARNO

Dolce Vita Piazza del Carmine 6r ☎ 055 284 595; map pp.44–45. This smart, pricey and extremely popular bar-club has been going for more than 25 years and has stayed ahead of the game through constant updating. Install yourself on one of the aluminium bar stools and preen with Florence's beautiful young things. Live music (often Latin or jazz) Wed & Thurs 7.30–9.30pm; *aperitivo* buffet 7.30–9.30pm, then the DJ gets to work. Tues–Sun 5pm–2am.

Il Rifrullo Via San Niccolò 53–57r ☎ 055 234 2621; map pp.44–45. Lying to the east of the Ponte Vecchio–Pitti Palace route, this place attracts fewer tourists than many Oltrarno café-bars. Delicious snacks with the early-evening *aperitivi* (when the music gets turned up), as well as more substantial (and quite pricey) dishes in the restaurant section, and the Sunday brunch is always packed out. There's a pleasant garden terrace, too. Daily 8am–2am; closed two weeks in Aug.

La Cité Borgo San Frediano 20r ☎ 055 210 387; map pp.48–49. With its huge windows, mezzanine balcony and shelves of books (to buy or just to browse), this café-bar-bookshop has an arty quasi-Parisian ambience. An area is set aside for live performances (usually music), and food-tastings are regular occurrences too. Sun & Mon 3.30pm–midnight, Tues–Sat 10.30am–midnight.

Negroni Via dei Renai 17r ☎ 055 243 647; map pp.44–45. Set back from the Arno, on the south side of the Piazza Demidoff, *Negroni* has been a fixture on the Florentine scene for years. It takes its name from the drink (gin+vermouth+Campari) created on this spot for Count Camillo Negroni way back at the start of the last century, and cocktails are still a major attraction, along with the early-evening aperitivo buffet and the music – there's a DJ most nights. Mon–Fri 8pm–2am, Sat & Sun 7pm–2am; closed two weeks in Aug.

Nottefiorentina Borgo San Frediano 17r ☎ 055 538 5469; map pp.48–49. Styled like a gutted factory, this bar is the HQ of local station Radio Nottefiorentina, and an info point for city nightlife. Happy hour daily from 7–10pm, and live music or DJ set Tues–Sat: DJs start at 8.30pm, live bands at 10pm. Daily 8am–1am.

Zoe Via dei Renai 13r ☎ 055 243 111; map pp.44–45. Perennially popular for summer evening drinks, but also attracts lots of young Florentines right through the day: 8am–noon is breakfast time, lunch is noon–3pm, then it's "Aperitif" from 6–10pm, when the "American Bar" theme takes over (the Crimson Zoe cocktail is notorious). It also does good snacks and simple meals, there's a DJ in the back room, and it's something of an art venue too. Mon–Thurs 8am–1.30am, Fri & Sat 8am–2am, Sun 6pm–1am.

CLUBS AND LIVE MUSIC

Florence has a decent **club scene**, though most Florentines frequent clubs to see and be seen rather than dance or drink. Foreigners are a different matter, and one or two places have a slightly more sweaty and familiar atmosphere as a result. For information on clubs and concerts, keep an eye out for posters and flyers, check the listings in the monthly *Firenze Spettacolo*,

1

GAY AND LESBIAN FLORENCE

Florenzer was, during the seventeenth century at least, German slang for gay, and the city remains, for the most part, tolerant towards gay and lesbian visitors. Florence's main gay and lesbian venues are listed below. For lesbian contacts, check the noticeboard at the women's bookshop Libreria delle Donne, Via Fiesolana 2b (Mon 3.30–7.30pm, Tues–Sat 9.30am–1pm & 3.30–7.30pm).

Crisco Via Sant'Egidio 43r ☎ 055 248 0580, ⓦ criscoclub.it; map pp.48–49. The city's leading gay bar, a short distance east of the Duomo. The ambience can be a bit heavy for some tastes. Mon, Wed, Thurs & Sun 11pm–3am, Fri & Sat 10pm–6am.

Piccolo Borgo Santa Croce 23r ☎ 055 200 1057; map pp.48–49. This café-bar has a chilled-out atmosphere, and attracts a mixed gay and lesbian crowd. Daily 8pm–2.30am.

Tabasco Piazza Santa Cecilia 3r ☎ 055 213 000; map pp.48–49. Hidden in a tiny square very near Piazza della Signoria, *Tabasco* has been going for nearly forty years and remains Florence's key bar-club. Tues–Sun 10pm–6am.

Y.A.G. Via de' Macci 8r ☎ 055 246 9022, ⓦ yagbar .com; map pp.44–45. This stylish and spacious bar-club near Santa Croce (it occupies a deconsecrated church) draws a mixed gay and lesbian crowd. Daily 8pm–3am.

call in at at Box Office, near the Sant' Ambrogio market at Via Delle Vecchie Carcere 1 (Mon–Fri 9.30am–7pm, Sat 9.30am–2pm; ⓦ boxofficetoscana.it) – it sells tickets for most events. Online, a great info source is ⓦ nottefiorentina.it.

CLUBS

Faced with a low income from the bar, most clubs charge a fairly stiff admission – €15–25 for the bigger and better-known places – though this often includes a drink. In addition to the places listed below, plenty of **temporary clubs** spring into existence in the summer months, often as open-air venues on the edge of town, in spots such as Piazza della Libertà and the Cascine.

Central Park Via Fosso Macinante 2, Parco delle Cascine ☎ 055 353 505, ⓦ centralfirenze.it; map pp.44–45. One of the city's biggest and most commercial clubs, with three dance floors and DJs who know what they're doing. First drink is included in the admission – around €20–25. Summer Tues–Sat 11.30pm–4.30am; winter Fri & Sat same hours.

Full-Up Via della Vigna Vecchia 25r ☎ 055 293 006, ⓦ fullupclub.com; map pp.48–49. Situated close to the Bargello, this club has been going so long it's become something of an institution. Best nights are usually Thurs (hip-hop) and Fri (house). *Aperitivi* from 10.30pm each night; the music begins an hour later. Admission free. Mon–Sat 10.30pm–4am; closed June–Sept.

Girasol Via del Romito 1g/r ☎ 055 474 948, ⓦ girasol .it; map pp.44–45. Located on a minor road due north of the Fortezza da Basso, the hugely popular Girasol is a restaurant-pizzeria-cocktail bar, with a dance floor that's kept moving by DJs who play the best of Latin sounds, from Brazilian bossa nova to Cuban son. It occasionally has good live acts too. Tues–Sun 8pm–2am.

Meccanò Viale degli Olmi 1/Piazzale delle Cascine ☎ 055 331 371; map pp.44–45. People flock here from across half of Tuscany. The place is labyrinthine, with a trio of lounge and bar areas, and a huge and invariably packed dancefloor playing mostly house. In summer, when the action spills outdoors, you can cool off in the gardens bordering the Cascine. The €15–20 admission includes a drink. Summer Tues–Sat 11.30pm–4am; winter Thurs–Sat same hours; closed Nov & two weeks in Aug.

Tenax Via Pratese 46 ☎ 055 632 958, ⓦ tenax.org; map pp.44–45. Florence's biggest club, pulling in the odd jet-setting DJ. Given its location in the northwest of town, near the airport (there's usually a shuttle bus from the train station – otherwise, take a taxi), you'll escape the hordes of *internazionalisti* in the more central clubs. With two large floors, it's a major venue for concerts as well. Admission €20–25. Thurs–Sat 10.30pm–4am; closed mid-May to mid-Sept.

Yab Via Sassetti 5r ☎ 055 215 160, ⓦ yab.it; map pp.48–49. This long-established basement club (full name: *You Are Beautiful*) has been popular for years, and is known throughout the country for Monday's Yabsmoove – Italy's longest-running hip-hop night. It doesn't have the most up-to-the-minute playlist in the world, but still offers probably the most relaxed and reliable night's clubbing in central Florence. You're given a card and pay on leaving if you've spent less than €15 at the bar. Mon, Tues & Thurs–Sat 9pm–4am; closed June–Sept.

LIVE MUSIC

Florence's live music scene isn't the hottest in Italy, but there's a smattering of venues for small-time local outfits. Bigger names play at the Viper Theatre, a couple of kilometres west of the Cascine on Via Pistoiese (ⓦ viperclub .eu), at Palasport Mandela Forum on Viale Pasquale Paoli

(📟 mandelaforum.it), and at the Saschall-Teatro di Firenze, a couple of kilometres east of the city centre on Via Fabrizio de André (📟 saschall.it). The biggest use the Artemio Franchi football stadium.

Auditorium FLOG Via Michele Mercati 24b 📞 055 490 437, 📟 flog.it; map pp.44–45. One of the city's best-known mid-sized venues, and a perennial student favourite – with a suitably downbeat look and feel – for all forms of live music events (and DJs), but particularly local indie bands. It's usually packed, despite a position way out in the northern suburbs; to get there take bus #4, #8, #14, #20 or #28.

Eskimo Via dei Canacci 12r 📞 055 715 794; map pp.48–49. A small, well-established club close to Santa Maria Novella with nightly live music. Its long-standing status as the prime lefty student bar is reflected in the music, which tends to be Italian solo singers or trios. The atmosphere is welcoming and you may catch the odd theatre and other cultural event. Members only, but you can get annual membership on the door, for around €7. Tues–Sun 9pm–3am; closed June–Sept.

Jazz Club Via Nuova de' Caccini 3 📞 055 247 9700, 📟 jazzclubfirenze.com; map pp.48–49. This small jazz venue has been a fixture for years. The €9 "membership" fee gets you down into the medieval brick-vaulted basement, where the atmosphere's informal and there's live music most nights; Mon usually sees a jam session. Cocktails are good, and you can also snack on bar nibbles and *focaccia*. Tues–Sat 9pm–2am; closed July & Aug.

Loonees Via Porta Rossa 15 📞 055 212 249; map pp.48–49. Set up by a former biker from Birmingham, this sweltering subterranean bar is a favourite with the city's students. The music is loud right through the night, and live from Wed to Sat. Free entry. Mon–Sat 9pm–3am.

Pinocchio Jazz Viale Giannotti 13 📞 055 680 362, 📟 pinocchiojazz.it; map pp.44–45. Italian jazzers rule the roost here, but excellent guest artists are often imported too, particularly for the club's low-key festival, which runs from Jan to March. Buses #8, #23, #31, #32 and #80 go close. Closed Sun.

CULTURAL EVENTS AND FESTIVALS

The **Maggio Musicale**, Italy's oldest and most prestigious music festival, is the most conspicuous sign of the health of the city's classical music scene, though it should be said that the fare tends towards the conservative. In addition to this and the festival in Fiesole (see p.143), the **Amici della Musica** host a season of chamber concerts with top-name international performers from September to April, mostly in the Teatro della Pergola, and the **Orchestra da Camera Fiorentina** (Florence Chamber Orchestra; 📟 orcafi.it) plays concerts from March to October, often in Orsanmichele. The Lutheran church on Lungarno Torrigiani regularly holds free chamber music and organ recitals.

CONCERT VENUES

Teatro del Maggio Musicale Fiorentino Corso Italia 16 📞 055 213 535, 📟 maggiofiorentino.com. Florence's main municipal theatre, out to the west of Santa Maria Novella, hosts many of the city's major classical music, dance and theatre events. It has its own orchestra, chorus and dance company, attracting top-name international guest performers. The main season for dance and opera runs from Oct to Dec, with classical music concerts taking over from Jan until the start of the Maggio Musicale festival. Chamber music and other small-scale events are held in the theatre's Teatro Piccolo.

Teatro Goldoni Via Santa Maria 15 📞 055 210 804.

This exquisite little eighteenth-century theatre, near the Palazzo Pitti, is used for chamber music, opera and dance productions.

Teatro della Pergola Via della Pergola 18 📞 055 226 4353, 📟 teatrodellapergola.com. The beautiful little Pergola was built in 1656 and is Italy's oldest surviving theatre. From Oct to April it plays host to chamber concerts, small-scale operas and some of the best-known Italian theatre companies.

Teatro Verdi Via Ghibellina 99–101 📞 055 212 320, 📟 teatroverdionline.it. Home to the Orchestra della Toscana, which performs once or twice a month between November and May.

CINEMA

In Italy the vast majority of English-language films are dubbed, but **Odeon Original Sound**, Piazza Strozzi 2 (📞 055 214 068; closed Aug), screens films in their original language (*versione originale*) once a week, generally on Monday, for most

LE MURATE

In 2011 the former prison of **Le Murate** (📟 lemurate.comune.fi.it), at Piazza della Madonna della Neve in the Sant'Ambrogio district, was reopened as a cultural centre, with two large halls and several smaller spaces. Various arts organisations already have moved into the centre, and it's intended that Le Murate will become Florence's main showcase for contemporary music, video events and other performances. It's open daily from noon to midnight.

1

FLORENCE'S FESTIVALS

SCOPPIO DEL CARRO

The first major festival of the year is Easter Sunday's Scoppio del Carro (Explosion of the Cart), when a cartload of fireworks is hauled by six white oxen from the Porta a Prato to the Duomo; there, during midday Mass, the pile is ignited by a "dove" that whizzes down a wire from the high altar. The origins of this incendiary descent of the Holy Spirit lie with Pazzino de' Pazzi, leader of the Florentine contingent on the First Crusade. On returning home he was entrusted with the care of the flame of Holy Saturday, an honorary office which he turned into something more festive by transporting the flame round the city on a ceremonial wagon. His descendants continued to manage the festival until the Pazzi conspiracy of 1478, after which the city authorities have taken care of business.

FESTA DEL GRILLO

On the first Sunday after Ascension Day (forty days after Easter), the "Festival of the Cricket" is held in the Cascine park. In amongst the market stalls and the picnickers you'll find people selling tiny mechanical crickets – live crickets were sold until recently, a vestige of a ritual that may hark back to the days when farmers had to scour their land for locusts.

MAGGIO MUSICALE FIORENTINO

The highlight of Florence's cultural calendar and one of Europe's leading festivals of opera and classical music, a rich mix of opera and concert; confusingly, it isn't restricted to May (Maggio), but lasts for a couple of months from late April or early May. Information and tickets can be obtained from the Teatro del Maggio Musicale Fiorentino (see p.133). ⓦmaggiofiorentino.com

ST JOHN'S DAY AND THE CALCIO STORICO

The saint's day of John the Baptist, Florence's patron, is June 24 – the occasion for a massive fireworks display on Piazzale Michelangelo, and for the final of the Calcio Storico on Piazza Santa Croce. Played in sixteenth-century costume to commemorate a game played at Santa Croce during the siege of 1530, this uniquely Florentine mayhem is a three-match series, with two games in early June preceding the bedlam of June 24. Each of the four historic quarters fields a team of 27 players, with Santa Croce in green, San Giovanni in red, Santa Maria Novella in blue and Santo Spirito in grossly impractical white. The prize for the winning side is a calf, which gets roasted in a street party after the tournament and shared among the four teams and the inhabitants of the winning quarter. The Calcio Storico has been undergoing something of a crisis since the 2006 event, when the semi-final between Santa Croce and Santo Spirito became so violent that the game was stopped. The 2007 event was then cancelled, and revisions to the rules are now being introduced – under the traditional "rules", virtually any method of tackling short of outright murder was permitted.

FESTA DELLE RIFICOLONE

The "Festival of the Lanterns" takes place on the Virgin's birthday, September 7, with a procession of children to Piazza Santissima Annunziata, where a small fair is held. Each child carries a coloured paper lantern with a candle inside it – a throwback to the days when people from the surrounding countryside would troop by lantern light into the city for the Feast of the Virgin. The procession is followed by a parade of floats and street parties.

---

of the year, plus Tuesday and Thursday in summer. This is the only cinema still in operation in the centre of Florence, apart from the Fulgor, near Ognissanti in Via Maso Finiguerra, which rarely has *versione originale* screenings. In summer there are often **open-air screens** at the Forte Belvedere and a few other spots – check *Firenze Spettacolo* for the latest screenings. In July and August there's also the **Premio Fiesole ai Maestri del Cinema**, in which the films of a single director are screened in Fiesole's Roman theatre.

SHOPPING

Florence is known as a producer of **luxury items**, notably gold jewellery and top-quality leather goods. The whole Ponte Vecchio is crammed with goldsmiths, but the city's premier shopping thoroughfare is **Via de' Tornabuoni**, where you'll find not only an array of expensive jewellery and shoe shops but also the showrooms of Italy's top fashion designers: Prada, Gucci, Armani and Dolce & Gabbana are all here, as well as the country's main outlets for the top three Florentine fashion houses – Pucci, Roberto Cavalli and Ferragamo. For cheap and cheerful stuff there's the plethora of street stalls around the San Lorenzo market, while if you want everything under one roof, there's also a handful of **department stores**. Marbled paper is another Florentine speciality, and, as you'd expect in this arty city, Florence is also one of the best places in the country to pick up **books** on Italian art, architecture and culture. For **food** shops, see the box on p.127.

BOOKS AND MAPS

Edison Piazza della Repubblica 27r ☎ 055 213 110; map pp.48–49. This US-style operation is arranged on four floors, with English-language books at the top; the stock is impressive, as are the opening hours. Mon–Sat 9am–midnight, Sun 10am–midnight.

Feltrinelli International Via Cavour 12–20r ☎ 055 219 524; map pp.48–49. Bright and well staffed, this has a good selection of English and other foreign-language books, plus newspapers, videos, posters, cards and magazines. There's another big branch in the city centre at Via de' Cerretani 30r. Mon–Sat 9am–7.30pm.

Paperback Exchange Via delle Oche 4r ☎ 055 293 460; map pp.48–49. Located just a few metres south of the Duomo, this shop always has a good stock of English and American books, with the emphasis on Italian-related titles and secondhand stuff; also exchanges secondhand books and has informative and friendly staff. Mon–Fri 9am–7.30pm, Sat 10am–7.30pm.

CLOTHING

Luisa at Via Roma Via Roma 19–21r ☎ 055 217 826, ⓦ luisaviaroma.com; map pp.48–49. A long-standing fixture at this address, with a host of different labels every season. Mon–Sat 10am–7.30pm, Sun 11am–7pm.

Raspini Via Por Santa Maria 70r & Via Roma 25–29r ☎ 055 215 796, ⓦ raspini.com; map pp.48–49. Florence's biggest multi-label clothes shop, with a good stock of diffusion lines. These are the two main branches; the "vintage" outlets at Via de' Martelli 5–7r and Via Calimaruzza 17r sell the previous season's stock at reduced prices. Sun & Mon 2.30–7.30pm.

DEPARTMENT STORES

Coin Via dei Calzaiuoli 56r ☎ 055 280 531, ⓦ coin.it; map pp.48–49. Central, clothes-dominated chain store. Quality is generally high, though styles are conservative except for one or two youth-oriented franchises on the ground floor. Also a good place for linen and other household goods. Mon–Sat 10am–8pm, Sun 11am–8pm.

FASHION FACTORY OUTLETS

Armani, Prada, Florence-based Gucci and all the other big Italian names have a massive presence on Via Tornabuoni, but if you want to get hold of top-label clothing without breaking the bank, you'll need to take a trip into Florence's hinterland. Tuscany is the powerhouse of the country's textile industry, and the Arno valley is the home of many of the factories that manufacture clothes for the top labels. Several retail outlets within easy reach of Florence sell each season's leftovers at discounts as high as sixty percent. The best are below; ask at the tourist office for a full list.

Barberino Designer Outlet Via Meucci, Barberino di Mugello ☎ 055 842 161, ⓦ www .mcarthurglen.it/barberino. The biggest range, including Cavalli, D&G, Ferré, Missoni and Prada, plus discounted high-street gear from labels such as Diesel, Benetton and Furla. SITA bus from Via Santa Caterina da Siena or shuttle bus from outside Santa Maria Novella station (2 daily). Mon 2–8pm (Jan, June–Sept & Dec), Tues–Fri 10am–8pm, Sat & Sun 10am–9pm.

Dolce & Gabbana Via Pian dell'Isola 49, Località Santa Maria Maddalena ☎ 055 833 1300. This two-storey shed, a few kilometres north of Incisa Val d'Arno, is packed with clothes, accessories and household items from Dolce & Gabbana. Train to Rignano sull'Arno-Reggello, then taxi. Daily 10am–7.30pm.

The Mall Via Europa 8, Leccio Regello ☎ 055 865 7775, ⓦ themall.it. Outlets for Balenciaga, Bottega Veneta, Cavalli, Pucci, Fendi, Armani, Marni, Salvatore Ferragamo, Sergio Rossi and Valentino, among others. Gucci is the dominant presence, with a huge range of bags, shoes and sunglasses. SITA bus from Via Santa Caterina da Siena or shuttle bus from outside Santa Maria Novella station (2 daily). Daily 10am–7pm.

Space Levanella, Montevarchi ☎ 055 91 901. On a small industrial estate in the Levanella district (on the SS69), this outlet is stacked with Prada clothes, as well as a good selection from the Miu Miu diffusion label. Train to Montevarchi, then taxi. Sun–Fri 10.30am–8pm, Sat 9.30am–8pm.

1

MARKETS

Cascine The biggest of all Florence's markets happens on Tuesday morning (8am–1pm) at the Cascine park (bus #1, #9, #12 or #17c), where hundreds of stallholders set up an alfresco budget-class department store. Clothes (some secondhand) and shoes are the best bargains.

San Lorenzo An open-air warehouse of cheap clothing in Piazza di San Lorenzo, this is as well organized as a shopping mall: huge waterproof awnings ensure that the weather can't stop the trading, and some of the stallholders even accept credit cards. Leather jackets and bags are something of a speciality here. Daily 8am–7pm.

Mercato Centrale Europe's largest indoor food hall – see p.91

Mercato Nuovo The main emporium for straw hats, plastic *Davids* and the like – see p.77

Mercato delle Pulci A flea market stacked with antiques and bric-a-brac, pitched in Piazza dei Ciompi (Mon–Sat 9am–7pm). More serious antique dealers swell the ranks on the last Sunday of each month (same hours). On the second Sunday of each month there's a smaller flea market on Piazza Santo Spirito, from 8am to 6pm.

Mercato di Sant'Ambrogio Big food market near Santa Croce – see p.107

La Rinascente Piazza della Repubblica 1 ☎055 219 113, ⓦwww.rinascente.it; map pp.48–49. Like Coin, La Rinascente is part of a countrywide chain, though it's perhaps a touch more upmarket than its nearby rival. Sells clothing, linen, cosmetics, household goods and other staples. Mon–Sat 10am–9pm, Sun 10.30am–8pm.

MUSIC

Alberti Via de' Pucci 16r & Borgo San Lorenzo 49r ☎055 284 346; map pp.48–49. Founded in 1873, this is the city's leading supplier of DVDs and CDs. The Borgo San Lorenzo store is good for opera, classical and jazz, while the Via de' Pucci shop (a couple of blocks east) concentrates on contemporary music (dance, rock, etc). Mon 3.30–7.30pm, Tues–Sat 9am–7.30pm.

PAPER AND STATIONERY

★ **Giulio Giannini e Figlio** Piazza Pitti 36r ☎055 212 621, ⓦgiuliogiannini.it; map pp.48–49. Established in 1856, this paper-making and book-binding firm has been honoured with exhibitions dedicated to its work. Once the only place in Florence to make its own marbled papers, it now offers a wide variety of diaries, address books and so forth as well. Mon–Sat 10am–7.30pm, Sun 10.30am–6.30pm.

Il Torchio Via de' Bardi 17 ☎055 234 2862, ⓦlegatoriailtorchio.com; map pp.44–45. Now owned by young Sicilian-Canadian Erin Ciulla, Il Torchio produces marbled paper, desk accessories, diaries, albums and other items in paper and leather. Mon–Fri 9.30am–1.30pm & 2.30–7pm, Sat 9.30am–1pm.

Pineider Piazza della Signoria 13r ☎055 284 655, ⓦpineider.com; map pp.48–49. Pineider produces briefcases, pens, picture frames and other accessories for home and office, but their reputation rests on their colour coordinated calling cards, handmade papers and envelopes – as used by Stendhal, Byron and Shelley, to name just a few past customers. Daily 10am–7pm.

PERFUME AND TOILETRIES

★ **Farmacia Santa Maria Novella** Via della Scala 16 ☎055 216 276, ⓦwww.smnovella.it; map pp.48–49. Occupying the pharmacy of the Santa Maria Novella monastery, this sixteenth-century shop was founded by Dominican monks as an outlet for their herbal potions, ointments and remedies. Many of these are still in production, together with face creams, shampoos, and more esoteric concoctions. The shop's as famous for its wonderful aromatic interior as for its products, which are sold worldwide. Mon–Sat 9.30am–7.30pm, Sun 10.30am–6.30pm; closed Sun in Feb & Nov.

Spezieria Erboristeria Palazzo Vecchio Via Vaccherreccia 9r ☎055 239 6055; map pp.48–49. A celebrated old shop, selling its own natural remedies and a range of unique perfumes, such as Acqua di Caterina de' Medici. July & Aug Mon–Fri 9am–7.30pm, Sat 9am–5pm; Sept–June Mon–Sat 9.30am–7.30pm, first & last Sun of month 1.30–7pm.

PRINTS AND PHOTOS

★ **Alinari** Largo Alinari 15 ☎055 23 951, ⓦalinari .com; map pp.48–49. Founded in 1852, this is the world's oldest photographic business. They sell books, calendars, posters and cards, and will print any image you choose from their huge catalogue, the largest archive of old photographs in Italy. Mon–Fri 9am–1pm & 2–6pm; closed two weeks in mid-Aug.

SHOES AND ACCESSORIES

Cellerini Via del Sole 37r ☎055 282 533, ⓦwww .cellerini.it; map pp.48–49. Bags, bags and more bags. Everything is made on the premises under the supervision of the firm's founders, the city's premier exponents of the craft; bags don't come more elegant or durable. Summer Mon–Fri 9am–1pm & 3–7pm, Sat 9am–1pm; winter Mon 3–7pm, Tues–Sat 9am–1pm & 3–7pm.

Ferragamo Via de' Tornabuoni 14r ☎ 055 292 123, ⓦ salvatoreferragamo.it; map pp.48–49. Established by Salvatore Ferragamo, once the most famous shoemaker in the world, Ferragamo now produces ready-to-wear outfits, but the company's reputation still rests on its beautiful shoes. The shop, occupying virtually the entire ground floor of a colossal palazzo on Piazza Santa Trìnita, is unbelievably grandiose, and even has a shoe museum. Mon–Sat 10am–7.30pm.

Il Bisonte Via del Parione 31–33r ☎ 055 215 722, ⓦ ilbisonte.com; map pp.48–49. Beautiful and robust bags, briefcases and accessories, many of them made from *vacchetta*, a soft cowhide which ages very nicely. Mon–Sat 9.30am–7pm.

★ **Madova** Via Guicciardini 1r ☎ 055 239 6526, ⓦ madova.com; map pp.48–49. The last word in gloves – every colour, every size, every style, lined with lambswool, silk, cashmere or nothing. Prices range from around €40 to €200. Mon–Sat 9.30am–7.30pm.

Saskia Via di Santa Lucia 22–24r ☎ 055 293 291; map pp.44–45. Trained in Hamburg and Florence, Vivian Saskia Wittmer produces exquisite made-to-measure shoes in classic designs. Her workshop, located near Ognissanti, specializes in men's footwear, but makes a few designs for women too. Mon–Sat 9am–1pm & 3.30–7.30pm.

Scuola del Cuoio Via San Giuseppe 5r ☎ 055 244 533, ⓦ www.scuoladelcuoio.com; map pp.48–49. This academy for leather-workers at the back of Santa Croce church sells bags, jackets, belts and other accessories at prices that compare very favourably with the shops. You won't find any startlingly original designs, but the quality is very high and the staff knowledgeable and helpful. Mon–Sat 9.30am–6pm, Sun 10am–6pm.

Stefano Bemer Via Camaldoli 10r ☎ 055 222 558, ⓦ bemers.it; map pp.44–45. Stefano Bemer is perhaps the most famous shoemaker in Italy, and his bespoke footwear (produced in a small workshop at Borgo San Frediano 143r) is in the "if you have to ask, you can't afford them" league. He does, however, produce around forty styles of prêt-à-porter shoes, sold at the Via Camaldoli branch – still expensive, but they'll last forever. Mon–Fri 9am–1pm & 3–7.30pm, Sat 9am–1pm.

DIRECTORY

Banks and exchange Florence's main bank branches are on or around Piazza della Repubblica.

Consulates The UK consulate for northern Italy is at Via San Paolo 7, Milan ☎ 02 723 001; the US has a consulate in Florence, at Lungarno Amerigo Vespucci 38 ☎ 055 266 951.

Doctors The Tourist Medical Service is a private service used to dealing with foreigners; they have doctors on call 24hrs a day on ☎ 055 475 411 (ⓦ medicalservice.firenze. it), or you can visit their clinic at Via Lorenzo il Magnifico 59 (Mon–Fri 11am–noon & 5–6pm, Sat 11am–noon). Note that you'll need insurance cover to recoup the cost of a consultation, which will be at least €50. Florence's central hospital is on Piazza Santa Maria Nuova.

Internet access Internet Train (ⓦ internettrain.it) has branches at Via de Benci 36r, Via Porta Rossa 38r and Vial dell'Oriuolo 40r – they're open Mon–Sat 10am–midnight, Sun 3–11pm. The tourist office has a full list of current internet points.

Lost property Lost property handed into the city or railway police ends up at Via Circondaria 17b (Mon–Sat 9am–noon; ☎ 055 367 943; bus #23 to Viale Corsica). There's also a lost property office at Santa Maria Novella station, on platform 16 next to left luggage.

Pharmacies The Farmacia Comunale, on the train station concourse, is open 24hr, as are All'Insegna del Moro, Piazza San Giovanni 20r, on the north side of the Baptistery, and Farmacia Molteni, Via dei Calzaiuoli 7r.

Police To report a theft or other crime, go to the Carabinieri at Borgo Ognissanti 48 (open 24hr), or the city police, at Via Pietrapiana 50r (Mon–Fri 8.30am–7.30pm, Sat closes 1.30pm) – you're likelier to find an English speaker at the latter.

Post office The main central post office is near Piazza della Repubblica at Via Pellicceria 3 (Mon–Sat 8.15am–7pm).

Around Florence

MONTECATINI TERME

Around Florence

Having paid their respects to the sights of Florence, most people doing a Tuscan tour set off for another of the big-league towns, such as Siena or Pisa, leapfrogging the city's immediate surroundings. Yet there's a lot to be gained by lingering a few days in this area, either using Florence as a base, or staying at a couple of the smaller places within the city's orbit.

2

Inside the boundaries of Greater Florence, city buses run to the village of **Fiesole** – once Florence's keenest rival – and to many of the **Medici villas**, countryside retreats now all but engulfed by the suburbs. Further afield but readily accessible by train, **Prato** and **Pistoia** each make fine day-trips, with their medieval buildings and Florentine-inspired Renaissance art.

West of Florence, an industrialized stretch of the Arno valley leads to **Empoli**, the point of access for a number of upland attractions: **Vinci** (Leonardo da Vinci's village), the imperial settlement of **San Miniato** and the hill-towns of **Castelfiorentino** and **Certaldo**. To the north and south of Florence lie two rural regions that require independent transport for proper investigation: the **Mugello**, the wooded and agricultural area around the upper valley of the Sieve River; and **Chianti**, one of Italy's premier wine regions.

GETTING AROUND

The places covered in this chapter lie on or very near several of the principal routes through Tuscany, three of which radiate from Florence: to Pisa (via Empoli); to Lucca (via Prato and Pistoia); and to Siena (via Chianti). The first two can be done by train or bus, the third by bus. The fourth route – from Empoli to Siena via Castelfiorentino and Certaldo – is also possible by train or bus. Bus and train services from Florence are covered in Chapter One (see p.122).

Fiesole

The hill-town of **FIESOLE**, which spreads over a cluster of hills above the Mugnone and Arno valleys some 8km northeast of Florence, is conventionally described as a pleasant retreat from the crowds and heat of summertime Florence. Unfortunately, its tranquillity has been so well advertised that in high season it's now hardly less busy than Florence itself. That said, Fiesole offers a grandstand view of the city, retains something of the feel of a country village, and bears many traces of its history – which is actually lengthier than that of Florence. First settled in the Bronze Age, later by the Etruscans, and then absorbed by the Romans, it rivalled its neighbour until the early twelfth century, when the Florentines overran the town. From that time Fiesole became a satellite, favoured as a semi-rural second home for wealthier citizens such as the ubiquitous Medici.

TEATRO ROMANO, FIESOLE

Highlights

❶ **Fiesole** Escape Florence's crowds by taking a quick trip up the hill to Fiesole, a town with a pedigree that goes all the way back to the Etruscans. **See p.140**

❷ **Medici villas** Visit the country houses of Florence's pre-eminent family. **See p.145**

❸ **Greve in Chianti** Situated in the midst of the famous vineyards and rolling hills, Greve is one of the busiest – and most attractive – towns in Chianti. **See p.151**

❹ **Prato** Tuscany's second city deserves much more attention than most tourists give it: a handsome medieval centre lurks within the palisade of factories. **See p.159**

❺ **Pistoia** Prato's neighbour is well worth a day's investigation for some remarkable architecture and sculptures. **See p.164**

❻ **San Vivaldo** This "Jerusalem in Tuscany" is one of the region's most beguiling treasures. **See p.174**

❼ **Certaldo** Tiny and perfectly preserved, Certaldo is the quintessential hill-town, giving a grandstand view of the terrain that encompasses it. **See p.175**

HIGHLIGHTS ARE MARKED ON THE MAP ON P.142

The Duomo

Piazza Mino da Fiesole • Daily: summer 7.30am–noon & 3–6pm; winter 7.30am–noon & 3–5pm

When the Florentines wrecked Fiesole in 1125, the only major building spared was the **Duomo di San Romolo**. Subsequently, nineteenth-century restorers managed to ruin the exterior, which is now notable only for its lofty campanile. The most interesting part of the bare interior is the raised choir: the altarpiece is a polyptych, painted in the 1440s by Bicci di Lorenzo, and the Cappella Salutati, to the right, contains two fine pieces carved around the same time by Mino da Fiesole – an altar frontal of the *Madonna and Saints* and the tomb of Bishop Salutati. Fiesole's patron saint, St Romulus, is buried underneath the choir in the ancient crypt.

Museo Bandini

Via Dupré 1• March & Oct daily 10am–6pm; April–Sept daily 10am–7pm; Nov–Feb Wed–Mon 10am–2pm • Joint one-day ticket covering all Fiesole's museums €10 • ⓦ museidifiesole.it

AROUND FLORENCE

EMILIA-ROMAGNA

MUGELLO

CHIANTI

HIGHLIGHTS
1. Fiesole
2. Medici villas
3. Greve in Chianti
4. Prato
5. Pistoia
6. San Vivaldo
7. Certaldo

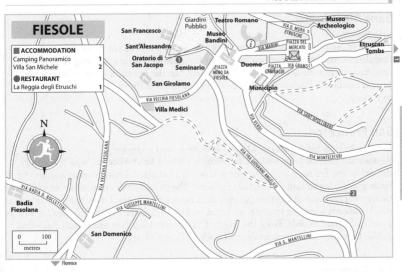

The **Museo Bandini** possesses a collection of glazed terracotta in the style of the della Robbias, the odd piece of Byzantine ivory work and a few thirteenth- and fourteenth-century Tuscan pictures, including pieces by Bernardo Daddi, Lorenzo Monaco and Taddeo Gaddi.

Teatro Romano and the Museo Archeologico

Via Portigiani 1 • March & Oct daily 10am–6pm; April–Sept daily 10am–7pm; Nov–Feb Wed–Mon 10am–2pm • Joint one-day ticket covering all Fiesole's museums €10 • Ⓦ museidifiesole.it

Across the road from the museum, the 3000-seat **Teatro Romano** was built in the first century BC and excavated towards the end of the nineteenth century. It's in such good repair that it's used for performances during the Estate Fiesolana festival, though parts of the site are sometimes closed for excavation work. Most of the exhibits in the site's small **Museo Archeologico** were excavated in this area, and encompass pieces from the Bronze Age to Roman occupation; the well-presented Etruscan section is the highlight.

Oratorio di San Jacopo

Via San Francesco • Summer Sat & Sun 10am–7pm; winter closes 5pm • Joint one-day ticket covering all Fiesole's museums €10

The steep Via San Francesco runs past the **Oratorio di San Jacopo**, a little chapel containing a fifteenth-century fresco of *The Coronation of the Virgin* and some fine examples of ecclesiastical goldsmithing. A little further up, a terrace offers a knockout view of Florence.

ESTATE FIESOLANA

Slightly less exclusive than Florence's Maggio Musicale, Fiesole's **Estate Fiesolana** (Ⓦ estatefiesolana.it) is an annual cultural festival which usually takes place from mid-June to late August or early September The programme concentrates on chamber music, orchestral music and jazz, but film and theatre are also featured, and most events are held in the Teatro Romano.

Sant'Alessandro

Via San Francesco

The rarely open church of **Sant'Alessandro**, at the top of Via San Francesco, was founded in the sixth century on the site of Etruscan and Roman temples; repairs have rendered the outside a whitewashed nonentity, but the beautiful *marmorino cipollino* (onion marble) columns of the basilical interior make it the most atmospheric building in Fiesole.

2

San Francesco

Via San Francesco • Daily: April–Sept 9am–noon & 3–7pm; Oct–March 9am–noon & 3–6pm • Free

Restoration has not improved the fourteenth-century **San Francesco**, which occupies the site of the Etruscan acropolis: the interior is a twentieth-century neo-Gothic renovation, but the tiny cloisters are genuine. The church itself contains an *Immaculate Conception* by Piero di Cosimo (second altar on the right), and below the church is a small **museum** featuring material gathered mainly by missions to the Far East, as well as a piece of Etruscan wall. From the front of San Francesco a gate opens into a wooded public park, the most pleasant descent back to Piazza Mino.

San Domenico

Church Daily: summer 7.30am–12.30pm & 4.30–6.30pm; winter 8.30am–noon & 4–5pm

The most enjoyable excursion from Fiesole is a wander down the narrow Via Vecchia Fiesolana, which passes the **Villa Medici** built for Cosimo il Vecchio by Michelozzo – on its way to the hamlet of **SAN DOMENICO**. Fra' Angelico was once prior of the Dominican monastery at this village, and the **church** retains a *Madonna and Angels* by him, in the first chapel on the left; the chapterhouse also has a Fra' Angelico fresco of *The Crucifixion*.

Badìa Fiesolana

Mon–Fri 9am–5.30pm, Sat 9am–12.30pm

Five minutes' walk northwest from San Domenico stands the **Badìa Fiesolana**, Fiesole's cathedral from the ninth century to the eleventh. Cosimo il Vecchio had the church altered in the 1460s, a project which kept the magnificent Romanesque facade intact while transforming the interior into a superb Renaissance building.

ARRIVAL AND INFORMATION   FIESOLE

By bus Fiesole is an easy hop from central Florence: bus #7 makes the half-hour journey from Santa Maria Novella train station to Fiesole's central Piazza Mino da Fiesole three times an hour.

Tourist office Via Portigiani 3/5, next to the entrance to the archeological site (March–Oct Mon–Sat 9.30am–6.30pm, Sun 10am–1pm & 2–6pm; Nov–Feb Mon–Sat 9am–5pm, Sun 10am–4pm; ☎055 598 720, ⓦ www.comune.fiesole.fi.it).

ACCOMMODATION AND EATING

Camping Panoramico Via Peramonda 1 ☎055 559 069, ⓦ florencecamping.com. A 120-pitch three-star site with a bar, restaurant, pool and supermarket. Open mid-March to Dec. Adults from €9, tents €6

La Reggia degli Etruschi Via San Francesco 18 ☎055 59 385. As you'd expect, Fiesole has plenty of restaurants to cater for the day-trippers, but none is better than this place – the food is fine (mains €15–20), and the views from its dining rooms and terraces are tremendous. Mon & Wed–

Sun lunch & dinner.

Villa San Michele Via Doccia 4 ☎055 567 8200, ⓦ villasanmichele.com. This fabulous and fabulously expensive place is one of Tuscany's most sybaritic hotels. Occupying a former monastery that was designed in part by Michelangelo, it's surrounded by gorgeous parkland, offering terrific views, and has a great restaurant. Good online deals available. Restaurant April to mid-Nov 1–2.30pm & 7.30–10pm. €900

The Medici villas

Many of the finest country houses of the Florentine hinterland were, predictably enough, built for the **Medici**. The earliest of these were primarily intended as fortified refuges to which the family could withdraw when the political temperature in the city became a little too hot, but in time, as the family grew more secure, the houses became somewhere to show off the humanistic culture of the Medici. In the sixteenth and seventeenth centuries, with the Medici established as unchallenged rulers of Florence, the villas became more ostentatious, as if to express the might of the dynasty through their sheer luxuriousness. The land they were built on later became a valuable asset: when Florence's importance as a manufacturing centre was diminished, the Medici were able to divert some resources into agriculture.

2

Not every Medici villa is described in this section, just the ones that are easily accessible on a day-trip from Florence and whose interior or grounds are open to the public. The villas at Trebbio, Cafaggiolo and Cerreto Guidi are described later in this chapter.

Villa Medicea La Petraia

Daily: June–Aug 8.15am–7.30pm; April, May & Sept 8.15am–6.30pm; March & Oct 8.15am–5.30pm; Nov–Feb 8.15am–4.30pm; closed second & third Mon of month • Free • Bus #28 from Florence's Santa Maria Novella station

The **Villa La Petraia**– which stands about 8km northwest of central Florence – was adapted from a medieval castle in the 1570s and 1580s by Buontalenti, working to a commission from the future Grand Duke Ferdinando I. Only the watchtower of the fortress was retained, to serve as a high-rise belvedere above the simple two-storey house. The **interior** was altered in turn by Vittorio Emanuele II, who glassed over the innercourtyard to convert it into a ballroom. Its walls are covered by a seventeenth-century fresco cycle glorifying the Medici and the Knights of St Stephen, a pseudo-chivalric order founded by Cosimo I to rid the Tuscan coast of pirates. The suffocating style of the House of Savoy tends to prevail in the villa's apartments, though this is offset by the occasional sixteenth-century tapestry or painting. There is also Giambologna's bronze statue of *Venus*, transplanted from the fountain on the upper terrace of the garden.

Laid out in geometrical order, in half-hearted imitation of the Castello estate, the garden isn't much to get excited about, but the **park** behind the villa to the east is glorious, with its ancient cypress trees.

Villa Medicea di Castello

Gardens Daily: June–Aug 8.15am–7.30pm; April, May & Sept 8.15am–6.30pm; March & Oct 8.15am–5.30pm; Nov–Feb 8.15am–4.30pm; closed second & third Mon of month • Free

The **Villa di Castello** – which you reach from La Petraia by following Via della Petraia past Villa Bel Riposo (where *Pinocchio* was written), then turning right into Via di Castello – was acquired in 1477 by Lorenzo and Giovanni de' Medici, second cousins of Lorenzo il Magnifico, and the principal patrons of Botticelli; the *Birth of Venus* and the *Primavera* both used to hang here. Wrecked after the expulsion of the Medici, it was rebuilt for Cosimo I, and is now the headquarters of the Accademia della Crusca, the society charged since 1585 with maintaining the purity of the Italian language.

The Accademia doesn't allow visitors into the house, but that's no great hardship, as its Pontormo and Bronzino frescoes perished a long time back, and the villa's fame rests entirely on its **gardens**, which were laid out by Tribolo for Cosimo I and continued by Buontalenti, who also redesigned the house. Delighted by their labyrinths, sculptures, fountains and myriad water tricks, Montaigne judged Castello's gardens to be the best in Europe. Of the surviving eccentricities, the outstanding set pieces are Ammannati's colossal figure of *January*, the triple-bowled fountain topped by the same sculptor's *Hercules and Antaeus*, and the Grotto degli Animali by Giambologna and his pupils – a man-made cave with a menagerie of plaster birds and animals. (The bronze originals of many of these are on show in the Bargello in Florence.)

Villa Medicea di Poggio a Caiano

Daily: June–Aug 8.15am–7.30pm; April, May & Sept 8.15am–6.30pm; March & Oct 8.15am–5.30pm; Nov–Feb 8.15am–4.30pm; closed second & third Mon of month • Free • ☎ 055 877 012 • COPIT bus from Florence (every 30min; 30min)

For the most complete picture of what life was like in the Medici villas during the family's heyday, make the trip to the **Villa Medicea di Poggio a Caiano**, 18km northwest of Florence on the crest of the main road through the village of **POGGIO A CAIANO**. Lorenzo il Magnifico bought a farmhouse on this site in 1480 and commissioned Giuliano da Sangallo to rebuild it as a classical rural palace – the only architectural project instigated by Lorenzo that has survived, and the first Italian house to be built specifically as a place of country leisure. Raised on a kind of arcaded podium, it is the most elegant of the Medici villas and its impact is enhanced by later additions: the entrance *loggia*, for instance, was commissioned by Lorenzo's son Giovanni, the future Pope Leo X, and the curving double stairway was added in the eighteenth century. The house was often used to accommodate guests of state before their ceremonial entrance into Florence: Charles V stayed here, and it was at Poggio a Caiano that Eleanor of Toledo was introduced to her future husband, Cosimo I.

But Poggio a Caiano is associated above all with the story of **Bianca Cappello** and her husband, Francesco I. Born into an upper-class Venetian family, she fled her native city with a young man, whom she quickly dumped to become Francesco's mistress. Banned from the city by Francesco's first wife, she remained an outcast even after she had become his second, being blacklisted by many of Florence's elite. In October 1587 both she and her husband died here on the same day – perhaps poisoned, perhaps victims of a virulent virus.

The interior

You enter the villa through the basement, where the plush **games room** and private **theatre** hint at the splendour to come. Upstairs, the focal point is the double-height **salone** which Sangallo created out of the courtyard between the two main blocks, and which Vasari pronounced the most beautiful room in the world. Its sixteenth-century frescoes include del Sarto's *Caesar Receiving Egyptian Tribute* (the giraffe shown in the background was a gift to Lorenzo from the Sultan of Egypt), Franciabigio's *Triumph of Cicero* (a reference to Cosimo il Vecchio's return from exile) and, best of the lot, Pontormo's gorgeous *Vertumnus and Pomona*, the perfect evocation of a sweltering afternoon.

The entire top floor is given over to the **Museo della Natura Morte**, showcasing the collection of two hundred still-life paintings amassed by the Medici in the seventeenth and eighteenth centuries. A lot of wall space is taken up with the extraordinarily precise horticultural paintings of Bartolomeo Bimbi, commissioned by Cosimo III for the Villa Topaia, which was surrounded by a botanical garden. Visitor numbers to the museum are strictly limited. To be sure of getting in, call ahead, though it's usually possible to book a place at the front desk.

> **SAN MICHELE**
>
> Some 5km west of Poggio a Caiano in the village of Carmignano, the church of **San Michele** (daily: May–Sept 7.30am–6pm; Oct–April 7.30am–5pm; CAP bus from Poggio) contains one of Pontormo's most celebrated paintings, *The Visitation*. Created in the early 1530s, it's a typically imaginative interpretation of a common theme: attended by two stunned-looking handmaidens, Mary and Elizabeth seem to be clutching each other in a sort of anxious dance.

The gardens

In Lorenzo's time the grounds of Poggio a Caiano were far more extensive than they are today, and included a farm and a hunting estate; in the eighteenth century the **gardens** were converted into an English-style landscape, now containing some magnificent old trees.

Villa di Artimino

Museum Feb–Oct Mon, Tues & Thurs–Sat 9.30am–12.30pm, Sun 10am–noon • €4 • CAP bus from Poggio

The **Villa di Artimino** is known as La Ferdinanda after Grand Duke Ferdinando I, for whom Buontalenti designed the house as a hunting lodge, and unlike most of the Medici villas it's still in a rural setting, with superb views towards Florence in one direction and along the Arno in the other. A white rectangular block with details picked out in grey *pietra serena*, the house has the appearance of a rather dandified fortress, and its most distinctive external feature has earned it the nickname "the villa of the hundred chimneys". The villa is now a hotel-cum-conference centre; in the basement, however, there's a newly refurbished **museum** of Etruscan finds from the tombs at nearby Comeana.

Parco Demidoff

April–Sept Thurs–Sun 10am–8pm; March & Oct Sun 10am–6pm • €3 • Bus #25 from Florence

Nothing remains of Francesco I's favourite villa at **Pratolino**, 12km north of Florence, except for its huge park – and even this is but a shadow of its former self. The mechanical toys, trick fountains and other practical jokes that Buontalenti installed here were the most ingenious ever seen, and required so much maintenance that there was a house in the grounds just for the court plumbers. The only surviving pieces are a couple of fountains, a little temple by Buontalenti and Giambologna's immense *Appennino*, a shaggy man-mountain. Nonetheless, the park – known as the **Parco Demidoff**, after the nineteenth-century owners of the estate – is still one of the most pleasant green spaces within easy reach of Florence.

Chianti

Chianti, the territory of vineyards and hill-towns that stretches between Florence and Siena, can seem like a place where every aspect of life is in perfect balance: the undulating landscape is harmoniously varied; the climate for most of the year is balmy; and on top of all this there's the **wine**, the one Italian vintage that's familiar to just about everyone. The British, and others from similarly ill-favoured zones, long ago took note of Chianti's charms, and tourism has overtaken wine to become the region's most important cash crop. The influx of second-homers has pushed property prices beyond the reach of the local population and altered the tone of certain parts irreparably, even though foreign residents still account for only five percent of Chianti's 45,000 inhabitants. There is, nonetheless, much to enjoy in Chianti – quiet

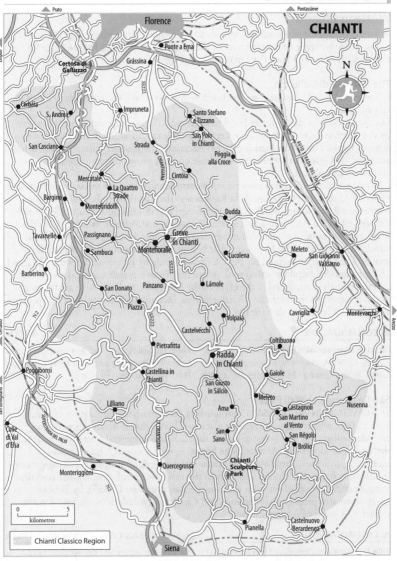

back roads, hundreds of acres of woodland, medieval villages and hamlets, and of course the vineyards.

GETTING AROUND

Buses from Florence and Siena connect with the main Chianti towns, but your own transport allows you to roam the quieter recesses and to visit any of the area's wine producers: every village mentioned below has tastings on offer within a few hundred metres of the main street.

CHIANTI

There's basically a choice of two main roads to follow through Chianti: the old Florence-to-Siena road (N2) along the western edge of the region, or the so-called Chiantigiana road (SS222), through the Chianti heartland.

Western Chianti

A stretch of *superstrada* connects Florence to Siena along the western edge of Chianti, but to get some sense of the character of the land it's better to opt for the older **N2** road, which takes in a few of the major Chianti sights en route.

The Certosa di Galluzzo

Summer Tues–Sat 9–11am & 3–5pm, Sun 3–5pm; winter Tues–Sat 9–11am & 3–4pm, Sun 3–4pm • Free, but donation expected • Bus #37 from Florence

On the city side of the Autostrada del Sole, beyond Poggio Imperiale, the N2 sweeps by the Carthusian monastery of the **Certosa di Galluzzo**, founded in the fourteenth century by the Florentine banker Niccolò Acciaioli. The Certosa (charterhouse) is now occupied by Cistercian monks, one of whose number shows visitors round the enormous complex.

Its main architectural attraction is the **Chiostro Grande**, with its *tondi* of prophets and saints by Andrea and Giovanni della Robbia and their workshop. Beyond, the tour reaches the **Palazzo degli Studi**, now a picture gallery, though built as a study centre by the well-educated Acciaioli, who counted Boccaccio and Petrarch among his friends. The Certosa was once so rich that it owned over five hundred works of art, most of which were carried off by Napoleon. The best of those that remain are the five lunette scenes of the *Passion*, painted for the Chiostro Grande by Pontormo between 1522 and 1525; he and his pupil Bronzino took refuge here from a plague outbreak in the city.

In the **church** itself, down in the crypt of the lay brothers' choir, there are the tombs of the monastery's founder and his descendants, including a beautiful slab that is now attributed to Francesco da Sangallo.

ACCOMMODATION BOTTAI

Camping Internazionale Firenze Via San Cristofano 2 ☏ 055 237 4704, ⓦ www.florencecamping.com. In nearby Bottai, *Camping Internazionale Firenze* has four-berth bungalows as well as pitches, plus a pool, kitchen facilities, a play area and internet access. Open March–Oct. Adults from €9, tents €6

San Casciano in Val di Pesa

SAN CASCIANO IN VAL DI PESA, 17km south of Florence, has a population of a little over 15,000, which makes it the only place in Chianti that is much more than an extended village. It's also home to one of the slickest commercial operations in Tuscany, the six-hundred-year-old **Antinori wine house**, as well as one of Chianti's most interesting churches, **Santa Maria del Prato**, which stands by the one surviving gateway in the town walls. The church was built in the early fourteenth century and contains some beautiful works of art from the same period, notably a Crucifix by Simone Martini, an altarpiece of the Madonna and Child by Ugolino di Nerio, and a pulpit carved by a pupil of Andrea Pisano.

ACCOMMODATION SAN CASCIANO IN VAL DI PESA

Villa Il Poggiale Via Empolese 69 ☏ 055 828 311, ⓦ villailpoggiale.it. The best place to stay in the vicinity is the spectacular *Villa Il Poggiale*, set amid a cypress grove about 3km west of San Casciano, rebuilt in the sixteenth century and discreetly decorated in the style of the early nineteenth century. It's a beautiful and spacious building, with a restaurant, outdoor pool and sauna. €200

Bargino to Barberino

Back on the N2, south of San Casciano you pass the **Castello di Bibbione** – home of the Buondelmonte family, who triggered the Guelph versus Ghibelline battles – before coming into **BARGINO**, from where it's a short diversion east to the impressively fortified village of **Montefiridolfi**, whose castle once belonged to the sons of Ridolfo Buondelmonte (*figli di Ridolfo*). South of Bargino lies **BARBERINO VAL D'ELSA**; a few well signposted kilometres southwest of the village stands a beautiful Romanesque church, the **Pieve di Sant'Appiano**, parts of which date back to the tenth century. Due south, on the main road, is the major town of Poggibonsi (see p.302), hub for buses to San Gimignano and Siena.

ACCOMMODATION

BARGINO TO BARBERINO

Camping Semifonte Via Ugo Foscolo 4 ☎055 807 5454, ⓦsemifonte.it. Located on the outskirts of Barberino, this is a modest sixty-pitch campsite with a pool. Open Easter to late Oct. Adults from €8, tents €5

Ostello del Chianti Via Roma 137 ☎055 805 0265, ⓦostellodelchianti.it. Situated in Tavarnelle Val di Pesa, between Bargino and Barberino, this modern 82-bed HI hostel is a rather brisk place, but the location is good – and it's

one of only two hostels in all of Chianti. By public transport, it's most easily reached by train to Poggibonsi from Empoli, then SITA bus. Open March 15–Oct 31. Dorm beds €15

Toscana Colliverdi Via Marcialla 34 ☎0571 669 334, ⓦcamping.it/toscana/colliverdi. This excellent two-star rural campsite is right on the edge of the Chianti hills, 4km northwest of Tavarnelle. Open mid-March to mid-Oct. Adults from €7, tents €8

The Chianti heartland

There's no better way to experience the village life of Chianti than to drive along the **Chiantigiana** road (**SS222**), which cuts right across the hills from Florence to Siena, connecting with a tangle of minor roads that traverse the most unspoilt parts of the region.

Santa Caterina d'Antella

As you leave Florence on the SS22, a short detour just before the *autostrada* brings you to the village of **PONTE A EMA**. One kilometre beyond, at Rimezzano, the church of **Santa Caterina d'Antella** has a fine cycle of scenes from the life of St Catherine of Siena, painted by Spinello Aretino in 1387.

Impruneta

Another rewarding detour, this time just south of the *autostrada*, presents itself at **Grássina**. Take a right turn here and, after 9km of winding road, you arrive at **IMPRUNETA**, which has long been a centre of the **terracotta** industry. The handsome **Collegiata** here, restored after heavy bomb damage in 1944, was founded in the eleventh century to house a miraculous icon of the Madonna and Child dug up in a nearby field and said to have been painted – as these things often are – by St Luke. It's housed in one of a pair of matching chapels by Michelozzo, the second of which contains an alleged fragment of the True Cross; both have lovely enamelled terracotta decoration by Luca della Robbia.

Santo Stefano a Tizzano and Strada in Chianti

Go east rather than west at Grássina and you'll come to **Santo Stefano a Tizzano**, with its Romanesque church and contemporaneous Castello di Tizzano, a producer of good wines but best known for its olive oil. About 2km further is **San Polo in Chianti**, where a major iris festival, the Festa del Giaggiolo, held in mid-May, celebrates the crop of Florence's floral emblem. From San Polo a minor road reconnects with the Chiantigiana near **Strada in Chianti**. The turn-off southeast from Strada to Dudda is overlooked by the mighty Castello di Mugnana, which once protected this stretch of road down into the Arno valley and is now the headquarters of a massive wine estate.

Greve in Chianti

GREVE IN CHIANTI, 10km south from Strada, is the venue for Chianti's biggest **wine fair** (the Rassegna del Chianti Classico, usually held during the first week in Sept), and it's a town with wine for sale on every street: two of the best outlets are the Enoteca del Gallo Nero, Piazzetta Santa Croce 8, and Le Cantine di Greve in Chianti, at Galleria delle Cantine 2, which claims to have the biggest selection of Chianti Classico wines in the whole region.

2

CHIANTI WINES

Chianti became the world's first officially defined wine-producing area in 1716, the year Cosimo III drew the boundaries within which vineyards could use the region's name on their product. Modern Chianti dates from the 1860s when Bettino Ricasoli, the second prime minister of unified Italy, established the classic formula for the wine at his estate at Brolio, based on **Sangiovese** – central Italy's predominant red grape. White *Malvasia bianca* grapes were another component of Ricasoli's recipe, but since 1995 Chianti growers have been allowed to produce wines with no white grapes in the mix.

Given the wide area over which Chianti is produced, it can never be a consistent wine, but the overall quality is nowadays far higher than it used to be, and the kitschy straw-covered bottle known as a *fiasco* is no longer used by serious producers, whose number has burgeoned since Chianti became a **Denominazione d'Origine Controllata e Garantita (DOCG)** in 1984. The area's total output is now about one hundred million litres per annum, making it Italy's highest-volume DOCG by far.

The wine-growing area is split into eight classified **regions**, of which the most highly regarded are Chianti Classico and Chianti Rúfina. Many Chiantis are fine when young, though the better wines take at least four years to mature; the best recent vintages are 2004 and 2006, but one to avoid is 2002 – this was the worst Chianti summer in living memory, with torrential rain that rotted the vines all over the region.

THE CHIANTI DISTRICTS

Chianti Classico The original delineated district (see map, p.149), accounting for a third of the Chianti produced. In 1924 Chianti Classico took as its trademark the black cock (*Gallo Nero*) that was once the heraldic symbol of the baronial alliance called the Lega di Chianti.

Chianti Colli Aretini From the hills on the east side of the Arno valley, to the north of Arezzo. Tends to be lighter than Classico and is best drunk young.

Chianti Colli Fiorentini From the area immediately south and east of Florence, and along the Arno and Pesa valleys. Good quaffing wine and staple *rosso* of many a restaurant in Florence.

Chianti Colli Senesi The largest Chianti zone, split into three distinct districts: around Montalcino, around Montepulciano and south of the Classico region east of San Gimignano. Variable quality, with the name of the producer all-important.

Chianti Colline Pisane The lightest Chianti comes from this region, southeast of Pisa, around Casciana Terme.

Chianti Montalbano From the hills west of Florence and south of Pistoia, these wines are usually soft and scented.

Chianti Montespertoli Created in 2002, this is the newest and smallest of the Chianti districts; it adjoins the western side of the Colli Fiorentini.

Chianti Rúfina The lower Sieve valley, northeast of Florence, produces some of the most refined and longest-living Chiantis.

Though razed in 1325 by Castruccio Castracani (the ruler of Lucca), by the fifteenth century Greve had re-established itself as a thriving mercantile town, focused on the funnel-shaped **Piazza Matteotti**, where a Saturday-morning market is still held today. Its irregular arcades are explained by the fact that various merchants paid for the construction of their own stretches of colonnade. The statue in the centre is of Giovanni da Verrazzano, the first European to see what became Manhattan; he was born in the nearby Castello di Verrazzano.

Museo d'Arte Sacra di San Francesco

Via San Francesco 4 • April–Sept Thurs & Fri 10am–1pm, Sat & Sun 4–8pm; Oct–March Thurs & Fri 10am–1pm, Sat & Sun 3.30–6.30pm • €3

Other than the piazza, Greve has just one feature that might be classified as a sight: the **Museo d'Arte Sacra di San Francesco**, a minor museum where the chief exhibit is a painted terracotta *Lamentation*, created in the 1530s, and thus one of the last examples of a genre that originated with Luca della Robbia more than a century earlier.

INFORMATION   **GREVE IN CHIANTI**

Tourist office Via delle Capanne 11 (Mon–Fri 10.30am–2pm & 3–6pm ☎ 055 854 5243).

ACCOMMODATION AND EATING

★ **Da Verrazzano** 28 Piazza Matteotti ☎ 055 853 189, ⓦ albergoverrazzano.it. A plain but characterful three-star hotel which also has a good restaurant, with full meals at around €40; in summer you can eat on the terrace overlooking the piazza. Tues–Sat lunch & dinner, plus Sun lunch; closed mid-Jan to mid-Feb. **€110**

Montefioralle and Badìa a Passignano

Five minutes' drive from Greve, west up a steep zigzagging road, lies the picture-perfect hamlet of **MONTEFIORALLE**, which began life as a fortified monastery in the tenth century. Today it has a population of just one hundred, and comprises a single elliptical street that encompasses a few tower houses and a pair of Romanesque churches. It has a pair of superb restaurants too (see below).

Continuing west from Montefioralle, the road passes the vestiges of the castle of Montefili, whose owners were benefactors of the **Badìa a Passignano**, situated a few kilometres on, towards the N2. A monastery was founded here towards the end of the ninth century, then in 1049 was re-dedicated to the Vallombrosan order, whose founder, St Giovanni Gualberto, died here in 1073 and is buried in the abbey church of San Michele. It became one of the wealthiest religious houses in Tuscany, but is now occupied by just a handful of Vallombrosan monks, who on Sunday afternoons (usually 3pm) allow visitors to explore the site. A painting by Alessandro Allori and a bust of Giovanni Gualberto are on display, but the highlight is the refectory fresco of the *Last Supper*, painted in 1476 by Davide and Domenico Ghirlandaio.

ACCOMMODATION, EATING AND DRINKING   **MONTEFIORALLE**

La Castellana Via di Montefioralle ☎ 055 853 134. Located about 500m outside Montefioralle, on the narrow road from Greve, this is a perfect Tuscan trattoria: homely, small and genuine, serving delicious food at honest prices. Tues–Sun lunch & dinner.

Taverna del Guerrino Via di Montefioralle ☎ 055 853 106. Another simple, inexpensive and excellent family-run trattoria, located in the core of the village, with gorgeous views from its terrace. Summer dinner daily, plus Thurs–Sun lunch; winter Thurs–Sun lunch & dinner; closed Jan–Feb & Nov.

Villa Bordoni Via San Cresci 31–32, Mezzuola ☎ 055 884 0004, ⓦ villabordoni.com. A kilometre west of Montefioralle, you'll find one of the best hotels in Chianti – a magnificent country house that was rescued from dereliction by the owners of the *Baldovino* restaurant in Florence. Each of the ten bedrooms and suites is uniquely and beautifully furnished, and the restaurant is good as well; a pool and open-air fitness pavilion complete the package. **€250**

Panzano

About 8km south of Greve along the Chiantigiana, the town of **PANZANO** overlooks a circle of hills known as the Conca d'Oro (Golden Valley) because of their sun-trap properties; the resultant wines can be sampled at the Enoteca del Chianti Classico, Via Giovanni da Verrazzano 8. Signposted down a branch road, the Romanesque **Pieve di San Leolino**, 1km south of the village, is one of the oldest churches in Chianti, and traces its origins to the first Christian settlers.

Panzano is best known, however, as the home of the **Antica Macelleria Cecchini**, the most famous butcher's shop in the country, though it compares to ordinary butcher's shops in the same way a Ferrari relates to a Fiat – it even has a room for wine tastings, art shows and concerts. In existence at Via XX Luglio 11r for 250 years, it's run by Dario Cecchini, a charismatic and eloquent champion of Tuscan carnivorous cuisine and Chianti traditions in general who has opened a cluster of terrific meat-centric **restaurants** around the shop. Most of the meat is from local producers, but quality, to quote Cecchini himself, knows no boundaries – for the very best steak, he often has to go to Catalonian farmers.

2

Dario+ Via XX Luglio 11r. Located above the Antica Macelleria Cecchini, and otherwise known as MacDario, this is the big man's fast-food place, selling what are of course the best burgers in Italy – €10, including water. No reservations.. Mon–Sat noon–3pm.

Officina della Bistecca ☎ 055 852 176. The speciality at this Dario Cecchini operation is steak – €50 gets you a huge slab of prime beef (*Bistecca alla Fiorentina, Costata Panzanese*), plus wine, coffee and grappa. Reservations advised. Sittings Tues, Fri & Sat 8pm, Sun 1pm.

★ **Solociccia** ☎ 055 852 727. Dario Cecchini's superb *Solociccia* ("Only Meat"), opposite his shop, was his first restaurant. There is never a menu: you pay €30 per person and you get what you're given; the price excludes wine, which you're encouraged to bring along. Reservations compulsory. Sittings Thurs–Sun 7pm & 9pm, Sun 1pm.

Villa Sangiovese Piazza Bucciarelli ☎ 055 852 461, ⓦ villasangiovese.it. A very nice three-star hotel in the heart of the village, with an excellent restaurant, with garden tables in summer. Mon, Tues & Thurs–Sun lunch & dinner. **€120–175**

Castellina in Chianti

The summit of the next main hill, 15km south, is occupied by well-heeled **CASTELLINA IN CHIANTI**, which formerly stood on the front line of the continual wars between Florence and Siena. The walls, fortress and the covered walkway known as the **Via delle Volte** – a kind of gallery looking east from underneath the town (it was originally open, but houses were later built over it) – all bear testimony to an embattled past.

Traces of a more distant era can be seen at the **Ipogeo Etrusco di Montecalvario** (daylight hours; free), a complex of subterranean sixth-century BC Etruscan burial chambers, carved into the summit of a small hill that's five minutes' walk north of the village.

The area's distant history is illuminated in the **Museo Archeologico del Chianti Senese** (Mon, Tues & Thurs–Sun 10am–1pm & 3.30–6.30pm; €3), which also gives you access to the town's tower, but neither the Etruscans nor Castellina's one sizeable church – the neo-Romanesque San Salvatore, which is notable only for a single fifteenth-century fresco and the mummified remains of the obscure St Fausto – are what brings in the tourists. Wine is of course Castellina's primary attraction, as is evident from the power-station bulk of the **wine cooperative** on the main road; the local vintages (and olive oil) can be sampled at several places in town.

Tourist office The office at Via Ferruccio 40 (daily 9am–1pm & 2.30–6.30pm; ☎ 0577 741 392, ⓦ comune

.castellina.si.it) is one of the most helpful in Chianti.

ACCOMMODATION AND EATING

La Torre Piazza del Comune 15, ☎ 0577 740 236. Situated right in the centre of the town, this plain and well-priced trattoria is a rarity for upmarket Chianti – and is by far the best place to eat in Castellina. Mon–Thurs, Sat & Sun lunch & dinner.

★ **Palazzo Squarcialupi** Via Ferruccio 22 ☎ 0577 741

186, ⓦ palazzosquarcialupi.com. Pick of the hotels is the three-star *Palazzo Squarcialupi*, which occupies the upper floors of a vast fifteenth-century *palazzo*. The rooms are large and well-furnished, and there's a sauna in the basement and a pool in the garden, which commands a wonderful view. **€105–160**

Radda in Chianti and around

The best of Chianti lies east of Castellina and the Chiantigiana, in the less domesticated terrain of the **Monti del Chianti** – the stronghold of the Lega di Chianti, whose power bases were Castellina itself and the two principal settlements of this craggy region, Radda and Gaiole. The nearer of these, the ancient Etruscan-founded town of **RADDA IN CHIANTI**, became the league's capital in 1384, and the imprint of the period is still strong here – though perhaps not quite as strong as the imprint of middle-class tourism, which has almost smothered the town's identity. The minuscule *centro storico* is focused on Piazza Ferrucci, where the frescoed and shield-studded Palazzo Comunale faces a church raised on a high platform.

INFORMATION RADDA IN CHIANTI

Tourist office Radda's tourist office is hidden in the corner of the tiny Piazza del Castello behind the church (Mon–Sat 10am–1pm & 3.15–7pm, Sun 10.30am–12.30pm; ☎ 0577 738 494, ⓦ comune.radda-in-chianti.si.it)

ACCOMMODATION, EATING AND DRINKING

Palazzo Leopoldo Via Roma 33 ☎0577 735 603, ⓦ palazzoleopoldo.it. This place was founded as a pilgrims' hostel, then converted into a magnificent town house prior to becoming an extremely elegant four-star hotel, with a good restaurant, plus gym, sauna and pool. **€110–230**

Relais Vignale Via Pianigiani 9, hotel ☎ 0577 738 012, restaurant ☎0577 738 094, ⓦvignale.it. The elegant *Relais Vignale* occupies a nicely converted seventeenth-century manor house on the edge of the village; it has a pool in the garden, a wine bar in the cellars, and a good if slightly pricey restaurant – but this is a pricey little town. Restaurant lunch & dinner daily March–Nov. **€240**

Volpaia

About 7km north of Radda lies the unspoilt village of **Volpaia**, which from the tenth to the sixteenth century was an important military lookout over the valley of the Pesa. The medieval donjon still stands, but the most interesting structure is the deconsecrated **Commenda di Sant'Eufrosino**, designed by Michelozzo, and now used as a *cantina* and exhibition space by the Castello di Volpaia wine estate (ⓦvolpaia.it).

Ama

Some 7km south of Radda is **Ama**, once a fortification on the southern edge of Florentine territory. Round the village are ranged the vineyards of one of Chianti's first-rank wine estates, **Castello di Ama**, which offers tastings throughout the year, except in August.

Chianti Sculpture Park

Daily 10am–sunset • €7.50 • ⓦ chiantisculpturepark.it

About 9km south of Ama, on the north side of Pievasciata (on the minor road parallel to the N408), you'll come across the **Chianti Sculpture Park**, an intriguing initiative where artists from a great range of cultures (India, Zimbabwe, Colombia and Japan are all represented) have been commissioned to create site-specific open-air work.

Badìa a Coltibuono

On a hill 6km east of Radda stands the **Badìa a Coltibuono**. This Vallombrosan abbey was founded on the site of an eighth-century hermitage, and its church of San Lorenzo, built in 1050, is one of Tuscany's finest Romanesque buildings. The monastic complex is now owned by one of the biggest wine estates in the region, whose vintages are served at the famous Badìa a Coltibuono **restaurant**. The Badìa is also celebrated for its lavish residential cookery courses, detailed on its website, and since 2005 – when it began marketing itself as Italy's first "wine resort" – has also been offering **accommodation**.

ACCOMMODATION AND EATING BADÌA A COLTIBUONO

Badìa a Coltibuono ☎ 0577 74 481 (rooms), ☎0577 749 031 (restaurant), ⓦcoltibuono.com. Eight of the Badìa's monastic cells have been beautifully converted into guest bedrooms, and there are three apartments here as well, with a three-night minimum stay. The restaurant, adjoining the abbey, has a superb *menu degustazione* that costs in the region of €50, wine included. Restaurant March–Oct daily noon–3pm & 7–9.30pm. Rooms **€160–190**, apartments **€570**

Gaiole and around

Modern times have caught up with the third of the Lega di Chianti triad, **GAIOLE**, 5km south of Coltibuono. Now a brisk market town, it has a **wine cooperative** at Via Mulinaccio 10 which offers splendid tasting opportunities, as does the Enoteca

Montagnani, Via Bandinelli 13–17. The most impressive sights in the immediate area are the ruins of the **Castello di Vertine**, occupying the heights 3km west of the village, and the fortified village of **Barbischio**, up a winding little road to the east. Devotees of military ruins could follow the signposted Strada dei Castelli from Gaiole, an itinerary of half a dozen fortresses between Spaltena (1km) and Vistarenni (6km).

Castello di Meleto

Guided tours: Mon–Sat at 11.30am, 3pm & 4.30pm, Sun 11.30am, 4.30pm & 5pm • Tours from €10 • ⓦ castellomeleto.it

A couple of kilometres south of Gaiole, the towers of the **Castello di Meleto** peer from behind a screen of cypresses over the road leading to Castagnoli. Meleto was founded by the monks of Coltibuono, but by 1269 it was in the hands of the Ricasoli family, who built its massive fortifications in the fifteenth century. Various **guided tours** are on offer, at various prices; the highlights are the delicate eighteenth-century theatre and the visit to the *cantina*, where you can sample the Meleto estate's olive oil, wine or food (the price of the tour varies according to which option you choose). It's possible to stay at Meleto, too – details of its rooms and plush apartments can be found on the website.

Castello di Brolio

Guided tours: March 27–Oct 30 daily 3pm, plus Mon, Wed & Fri–Sun 10.30am and Mon & Fri 5pm • Gardens and chapel €5, or gardens, chapel & museum €8 • ⓦ ricasoli.it

The birthplace of Chianti wine is the **Castello di Brolio**, overlooking the tiny village of **Brolio**. The building passed to the Ricasoli family as far back as the twelfth century, and was the object of frequent tussles between the Florentines and the Sienese. Demolished by the Sienese army, it was rebuilt in the sixteenth century, then converted in the nineteenth century into a colossal mock-medieval country residence by the vinicultural pioneer **Baron Bettino Ricasoli**, who allegedly moved here in order to keep his attractive young wife away from her admirers in Florence. The Ricasoli still own the castle, so most of the building is out of bounds, but you can visit the **gardens**, the **chapel** and the family **museum**, in which armaments feature heavily. **Wines** from Brolio estate can be bought at the huge *enoteca* (Mon–Fri 9am–7.30pm, Sat & Sun 11am–7pm) at the entrance to the castle, or sampled as an accompaniment to a meal in the *Osteria del Castello* (see below).

ACCOMMODATION AND EATING
BROLIO

Borgo Argenina San Marcellino Monti ☏ 0577 747 117, ⓦ borgoargenina.com. Situated 5km west of Brolio, this rustic B&B in a beautifully renovated tenth-century hamlet is the ideal Chianti bolt-hole. Elena Nappa, who undertook the entire restoration, is the perfect host, and the rooms are immaculate. Accommodation ranges from a double room to a villa that sleeps four. From **€170**

Osteria del Castello Madonna a Brolio ☏ 0577 747 277, ⓦ ricasoli.it/osteria. As you'd expect, the wine list at the Brolio restaurant is impressive, and the kitchen is excellent too – many of the ingredients are produced in the Brolio gardens, in which the outdoor seating is set. Expect to pay upward of €40 per person. Mon–Wed & Fri–Sun lunch & dinner.

The Mugello

The **MUGELLO**, the lush region on the Tuscan side of the Apennine ridge that separates the province from Emilia-Romagna, is rather like a low-key Chianti: a benign, mild, humanized sort of landscape, with far fewer tourists than Chianti, though it's a favourite weekend hangout for Florentines. Its celebrated olive groves and vineyards are concentrated in the central Mugello basin, formed by the Sieve and its tributary valleys; elsewhere the vegetation is principally oak, pine and chestnut forest, interspersed with small resorts whose customers tend to be short-stay vacationers from the city. The fringes of the eastern part of the Mugello lie inside the Parco Nazionale delle Foreste Casentinesi – see p.382.

Vicchio

The N67 trails the valley through a moderately industrialized area up to Rúfina, then on through **Dicomano**, where it veers off towards Forlì (in Emilia-Romagna), passing through the Alpe di San Benedetto. Hugging the course of the Sieve beyond Dicomano, the N551 runs on through **VICCHIO**, the birthplace of Fra' Angelico. Unsurprisingly, the village makes the most of the Angelico connection, but the **Museo di Arte Sacra e Religiosità Popolare Beato Angelico** (Sat & Sun 10am–1pm & 3–7pm; €4) doesn't contain anything by the man himself – the collection consists chiefly of minor paintings gathered from abandoned Mugello churches.

2

GETTING AROUND   THE MUGELLO

By car As with Chianti, you'll need your own transport to see anything much. Three main roads run from Florence: the Via Bologna (N65), which passes Pratolino on its way to the Passo della Futa; the N302 direct to Borgo San Lorenzo; and the N67/551, which winds up to Borgo San Lorenzo along the Sieve.

By public transport There's a choice between the Sieve valley train line to Borgo San Lorenzo (nearly all of these Faenza-bound trains depart from Campo di Marte station rather than Santa Maria Novella), or SITA and CAP buses along the same route; buses run from Borgo San Lorenzo to the western and northern parts of the Mugello.

ACCOMMODATION   CAMPESTRI

Villa Campestri 6km south of Vicchio at Via di Campestri 19–22 ☎ 055 849 0107, ⓦ villacampestri.it. Perhaps the best place in the whole of the Mugello is the parkland-girdled, four-star *Villa Campestri*, which is very good value, has a fine restaurant and is home to Italy's first *oleoteca*, where hotel guests can sample and learn about the region's finest olive oils. **€110–150**

Vespignano

Five kilometres west of Vicchio is another exalted birthplace, **Vespignano**, where **Giotto** was born in around 1266. His career started, so the story goes, when Cimabue happened to pass by the spot where the boy was tending his father's flock; Giotto was drawing a picture of one of the sheep on a stone, and Cimabue was so astonished by the shepherd's proficiency that he immediately took him on as an apprentice. The bridge where the crucial encounter is said to have occurred is a few hundred metres out of Vespignano and is well signposted. The farmhouse in which Giotto was born, the **Casa di Giotto** (Sat & Sun 10am–1pm & 3–7pm; free), is 1km off to the north; as with the homes of Leonardo and Michelangelo, this has value only as a pilgrimage site.

Borgo San Lorenzo

With a population of 15,000 or so, **BORGO SAN LORENZO** is the giant of the Mugello towns, with industrial plots and tracts of new housing spreading further with each year – improved rail connections with Florence have given an added boost to the town in recent years. Substantially rebuilt after a massive earthquake in 1919, it has just one major building, the **Pieve di San Lorenzo**, an eleventh-century foundation that was renovated in the sixteenth century but still retains its Romanesque tower. This isn't the most photographed sight in town, though – that honour goes to the statue of *Fido* in Piazza Dante. Fido's owner was killed in a bombing raid on San Lorenzo in 1943, but for the next fourteen years, every day, the faithful hound continued to go to the bus stop at which his master used to arrive from work.

INFORMATION   BORGO SAN LORENZO

Tourist office The Borgo San Lorenzo tourist office, in the Villa Pecori Giraldi, Via P. Togliatti (Tues–Sun 10am–1pm & 3.30–6.30pm ☎ 055 845 6230), is the main office for the whole of the Mugello.

San Piero a Sieve

The N551 continues up the Sieve from Borgo San Lorenzo to **SAN PIERO A SIEVE**, where it crosses the N65 coming up from Florence. San Piero's Romanesque church, spoiled by an eighteenth-century facade, houses a beautiful terracotta font, possibly by Luca della Robbia; its other main monument is the Medici fortress overlooking the town, built by Buontalenti in 1571. Other than that, San Piero is fairly nondescript, but the Mugello landscape is at its best here, with farmland foregrounding the slopes of tree-crested conical hills.

The Medici villas

The Medici were originally from Mugello, and the environs of San Piero contain two rough-hewn villas which encapsulate something of the flavour of the period when the family secured its political ascendancy.

Trebbio

Near Novoli, an unsurfaced road runs west from the Via Bologna to the Medici castle of **Trebbio**, whose fortified tower peeps over a cordon of cypresses from the top of its hill. This fourteenth-century castle was converted into a country abode by Michelozzo in 1461 and became a particular favourite with Giovanni delle Bande Nere and his branch of the Medici clan: it was from here that Giovanni's son, Cosimo, rode down to Florence to assume power after the assassination of Alessandro de' Medici. Parts of the estate have now been converted into holiday apartments, while the produce of the Trebbio vineyards and olive groves can be sampled and bought at the castle's shop.

Cafaggiolo

Guided tours: mid-April to mid-Oct Wed & Fri 2.30–6.30pm, Sat & Sun 10am–12.30pm & 2.30–6.30pm; rest of the year Sat & Sun 10am–12.30pm & 2.30–6.30pm • €5 • ⓦ castellodicafaggiolo.it

A short distance north, on the Via Bologna, lies the villa of **Cafaggiolo**, which like Trebbio was a fortress converted for less bellicose use by Michelozzo. When Cosimo il Vecchio set about consolidating the family fortune through land acquisition, one of his first ventures was to buy this estate, which comprised the castle and tracts of land for hunting and agriculture. It was at Cafaggiolo that Cosimo's immediate descendants Lorenzo il Magnifico and his brother grew up, and Lorenzo's own children – Piero, Giovanni (Pope Leo X) and Giuliano – were taught here by such luminaries as Ficino, Poliziano and Pico della Mirandola. In those days the house would have had a more robust appearance than it does now: alterations in the nineteenth century did away with the surrounding walls, the moat, the drawbridge and one of its towers. The interior (now home to a cooking school) can be seen only on guided tours, but contains little of Medicean interest.

North of Cafaggiolo, the gradient of the road gets pretty savage as it begins the climb to Passo della Futa, from whose 900-metre vantage all of the Mugello's valleys and ridges are visible.

Bosco ai Frati

Daily 9am–noon

The secluded monastery of **Bosco ai Frati**, reached by taking a left turn off the N503 immediately north of San Piero (it's a rough 4km track), traces its roots back to a community of Greek monks who arrived here in the seventh century. In the early eleventh century the settlement was abandoned, but two centuries later St Francis established his order here. One of the earliest Franciscan saints, Bonaventure, was the prior at Bosco ai Frati. A man of exemplary modesty, he refused to put on the cardinal's attire brought to him by a papal delegation until he'd finished washing up his brothers' pots and pans; the tree where the outfit was hung is still there. Cosimo il Vecchio sank a lot of money into this monastery, hiring Michelozzo to redesign the complex in the plainest early Renaissance style; the tiny museum attached to Michelozzo's porticoed **church** holds the most remarkable work of art in the Mugello: a pain-racked *Crucifix*, probably carved by Donatello for the Medici, and certainly donated to the monastery by them.

Scarperia and Firenzuola

North of the turning for Bosco ai Frati, the N503 continues to **SCARPERIA**, a centre for the cutlery industry. Sitting on a platform of rock above a valley 5km from San Piero, it's essentially a one-street town, laid out by the Florentines after they turned it into their chief military base in the region in 1306. The **Palazzo dei Vicari**, built along the lines of Florence's Palazzo Vecchio, was constructed that year. If there are crowds around the town, they'll be on their way to the **motor-racing track** on the eastern outskirts; built in the 1970s, it's best known as Italy's grand prix motorbike circuit.

The N503 becomes a thrilling switchback north of Scarperia, swooping through the region known as Mugello's "Little Switzerland" to the hill resort of **Firenzuola**, which was rebuilt after a fierce battle in 1944 and has few blandishments.

Prato

Taking its name from the meadow (*prato*) where the ancient settlement's great market used to be held, **PRATO** has long been a commercial success and is now – with a population of around 190,000 – the second-largest city in Tuscany, after Florence. It's been Italy's chief textile centre since the early Middle Ages, and even though recession and competition from China have had a big impact on Prato's factories, as has Chinese immigration, there are still hundreds of local companies involved in the production and marketing of fabrics.

A close Florentine connection goes back to 1350, when Prato was besieged by its neighbour, which was becoming alarmed at the economic threat of Prato's cloth mills. The year after, Florence bought the titles to the town from its Neapolitan rulers, thus sealing their union. Thereafter, political events in the capital were mirrored here, a relationship that was to cost Prato dearly after Savonarola's example led the Pratese to join him in rejecting the Medici. Under the direction of Leo X, the imperial army

PRATO'S CHINESE REVOLUTION

Between 2000 and 2010 the number of Italian-owned textile businesses in Prato fell by 50 percent to a little below 3000. Yet the volume of clothing produced by the city increased in the same period, because there are now more than 3000 **Chinese-owned garment workshops** here, which have transformed Prato's economic profile: once associated primarily with high-end fabrics, it's now a high-volume producer of inexpensive clothing, often made from cheap material imported from China and India. The Chinese influx began in the late 1980s; today, with 12,000 legal Chinese immigrants and perhaps more than 30,000 illegals concentrated in the western quarter of the city (Via Pistoiese is the focal point), Prato has the second-largest Chinese community in Italy after Milan, and the clothing industry is its lifeblood. Chinese-run businesses have brought a lot of money into Prato, but a great deal of **resentment** has been generated too, some of it simply xenophobic, some fuelled by a conviction that the Chinese entrepreneurs are feeding too little of their profits into the local economy: the Bank of Italy has estimated that around one million euros flow from Prato to China every day. Police raids on Chinese factories have become a common occurrence, and it's indicative of the city's mood that in 2009 Prato elected its first right-wing mayor since World War II, after a campaign that played heavily on fears of the "Chinese invasion".

2

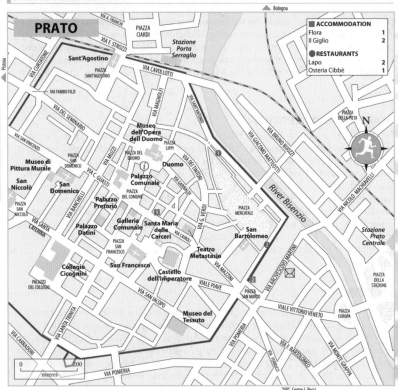

sacked Prato in 1512 as a warning to the rebellious Florentines: two days of slaughter and pillage ensued, in which thousands died.

Thereafter Florence asserted its power over Prato by imposing quotas on its neighbour's factories. Today the balance has shifted somewhat: while Prato manufactures things, Florence struggles to find alternatives to a service-based economy. It might not feature on a list of the most attractive places in the region, but its long-time wealth has left a fair legacy of buildings and art, including a wonderful fresco cycle by **Filippo Lippi** in the **Duomo**.

The historic centre is enclosed within a hexagon of grey stone walls, and is focused on two main squares, **Piazza del Duomo** and **Piazza del Comune**; if you arrive at the Porta al Serraglio station, you're just a short, straight walk from the former; the approach from Prato Centrale station takes you to Piazza San Marco, where the traffic swirls around a large Henry Moore sculpture; a short distance from here, at the end of the broad Viale Piave, stands Prato's signature building, the Castello dell'Imperatore.

The Duomo

Mon–Sat 7.30am–7pm, Sun 7.30am–noon & 3–7pm

The wide and lively Piazza del Duomo forms an effective space for the Pisan-Romanesque facade of the **Duomo**, distinguished by another Andrea della Robbia terracotta over the portal and by Donatello's and Michelozzo's beautiful **Pulpit of the Sacred Girdle**. This unique addition, wedged into the edge of the church, was constructed for the ceremonial display of the girdle of the Madonna, a garment allegedly dropped into the hands of the ever-incredulous apostle Thomas at her Assumption. The girdle (or *Sacro Cingolo*) supposedly came into the possession of a crusader from Prato, who brought it back to his home town in 1141. Replicas have replaced the Donatello reliefs of gambolling children, the originals now being housed in the cathedral museum. The girdle itself is displayed here five times a year: on Easter Sunday, May 1, August 15, September 8 and Christmas Day.

The story is detailed in the chapel immediately to the left of the main entrance, in Agnolo Gaddi's fresco cycle of *The Life of the Virgin and the Legend of the Holy Girdle* (1392–95) – though it's all but invisible behind the grating, as is the Madonna and Child carved by Giovanni Pisano in 1317. The *Sacro Cingolo* is kept in a crystal container on the high altar. Close by, in the left aisle, is another fine piece of stonework, a chalice-shaped pulpit by Antonio Rossellino and Mino da Fiesole.

Filippo Lippi's frescoes

Mon–Sat 10am–5pm, Sun 3–5pm • €3

Filippo Lippi's frescoes, around the high altar, were completed over a period of fourteen years (1452–66) and depict the lives of John the Baptist and St Stephen. These are marvellously sensuous paintings in which even the Baptist's wilderness looks quite enticing, and Lippi's characteristic tenderness is much in evidence too, notably in the scene depicting John taking his leave of his parents. There's a scandalous story to the creation of these pictures: during the period of their creation, Lippi – himself a friar – became so besotted with a young nun named Lucrezia Buti that he abducted her as she was preparing to attend the ceremony of the girdle. Later to become the mother of Filippino Lippi, Lucrezia is said to have been the model for the dancing Salome. Her lover is also believed to have depicted himself among the superb gallery of portraits around the body of St Stephen: it's most likely that he's the third mourner from the right.

Your ticket also gives you access to the scenes from the lives of the Virgin and St Stephen in the chapel to the right of the high altar. Some believe that these were begun by Paolo Uccello in 1435, a year before he was called away to Florence to paint the Hawkwood monument in the Duomo, having finished just the vault and the lunettes of *The Birth of the Virgin*, *The Birth of St Stephen* and *The Stoning of St Stephen*; the lower part of the chapel was painted by Andrea di Giusto.

Museo dell'Opera del Duomo

Piazza del Duomo • Mon, Thurs & Fri 9am–1pm & 2.30–6.30pm, Wed 9am–1pm, Sat 10am–1pm & 2.30–6.30pm, Sun 10am–1pm • €5, or joint ticket with Castello and Museo di Pittura Murale €8

Housed alongside the Duomo, around the cloister of the bishop's palace, the **Museo dell'Opera del Duomo** contains the Donatello panels from the great pulpit; they are badly cracked and stained but their sculpted putti make a sprightly contrast with the lumbering little lads on Maso di Bartolomeo's tiny silver Reliquary for the Sacred Girdle, the museum's other main treasure. Also on show is Filippino Lippi's plucky *St Lucy*, unperturbed by the gigantic sword lodged in her neck, and the magnificent painting that Filippo Lippi produced to demonstrate his suitability for the fresco commission, *The Death of Jerome*. A doorway on the far side of the cloister opens into the Duomo's frescoed crypt; beside the altar is the head of one of the city's main wells, which – as the inscription records – was choked with corpses by the invaders of 1512.

Museo di Pittura Murale

Piazza San Domenico 8 • Summer Mon, Thurs & Fri 9am–1pm & 2.30–6.30pm, Wed 9am–1pm, Sat 10am–1pm & 2.30–6.30pm, Sun 10am–1pm; winter Wed–Mon 9am–1pm, plus Fri & Sat 3–6pm • €5, or joint ticket with Museo dell'Opera del Duomo and Castello €8

Occupying the ex-monastery adjoining the church of San Domenico, the **Museo di Pittura Murale** houses one of the town's star attractions – Filippo Lippi's *Madonna del*

Ceppo. The painting contains portraits of the five men who financed the picture; Datini coughed up more than the other four, so he's the one depicted large-scale. Among the other Lippi pieces on show is a tender *Nativity with Sts George and Vincent Ferrer*: the Madonna and Christ were probably modelled on Lucrezia and Filippino. There are works by Filippino here as well, plus – among a variety of fourteenth-century altarpieces – a predella by Bernardo Daddi narrating the story of the Girdle of the Madonna. The rest of the display features a hotchpotch of minor frescoes, culled mostly from churches in and around Prato.

2

Piazza del Comune

Prato's most celebrated citizen is Francesco di Marco Datini (c.1335–1410) the subject of Iris Origo's classic book, *The Merchant of Prato*. He became one of Europe's richest men through his dealings in the cloth trade, and played a crucial role in the rationalization of accounting methods: on his death, his offices were found to contain tens of thousands of scrupulously kept ledgers, all inscribed "To God and profit". He's commemorated with a statue and bronze reliefs at the centre of the trim little **Piazza del Comune**, and inevitably crops up again amongst portraits of local worthies in the **Quadreria Palazzo Comunale** (free by appointment – call ☎0574 616 220). Across from the *palazzo* sits the huge medieval **Palazzo Pretorio**, whose museum, the **Museo Civico**, has been undergoing restoration for many years; in the meantime, its contents have been transferred to the Museo di Pittura Murale.

Palazzo Datini

Via Ser Lapo Mazzei 43 • Mon–Fri 9am–12.30pm & 3–6pm, Sat 9am–12.30pm • Free

Datini's house, **Palazzo Datini**, is behind the Palazzo Pretorio. Built in the 1390s, this is now home to the city archives and the Ceppo, a charity established by Datini himself. The barely legible fresco sketches on the facade – heavily retouched in 1910 – show scenes from his life; the ground floor of the interior is also frescoed, mostly with fleur-de-lys ceilings and engagingly cack-handed hunting scenes, though there's a more than competent *St Christopher* at the foot of the stairs, by Niccolò di Pietro Gerini.

Castello dell'Imperatore

Piazza Santa Maria delle Carceri • Wed–Mon: April–Sept 9am–1pm & 4–7pm; Oct–March 9am–1pm • €2.50, or joint ticket with Museo dell'Opera del Duomo & Museo di Pittura Murale €8

The **Castello dell'Imperatore** was built in the 1230s for Emperor Frederick II as a base for his representative in the city and as a way-station for imperial progresses between Germany and his domains in southern Italy and Sicily. The exterior view is its most impressive aspect: the castle has been heavily restored and empty except for the rooms used for temporary exhibitions, but you can wander around the ramparts.

Santa Maria delle Carceri

Piazza Santa Maria delle Carceri • Daily 7am–noon & 4–7pm

Prato's major Renaissance monument, Giuliano da Sangallo's church of **Santa Maria delle Carceri**, lies in the shadow of the castle. A demonstration of the correctness of the Brunelleschian style, it was built in 1485 to honour a miraculous talking image of the Virgin that was painted on the walls of the gaol here – hence the name "Mary of the Prisons". The interior – lightened by Andrea della Robbia's ceramic frieze and *tondi* of the Evangelists – is designed so that on the exact anniversary of the moment at which the Virgin spoke (3.18pm on July 15) a beam of light shines through the top of the cupola and strikes the centre of the altar.

THE TEATRO METASTASIO AND CENTRO PECCI

Prato can boast one of Italy's most famous theatres and one of its most innovative centres for the visual arts. The magnificent **Teatro Metastasio**, at Via Cairoli 59 (☎0574 608 501, ⊛metastasio.net), began life in 1830 as a privately owned venture; now owned by the city, it's become a top-flight venue for concerts (both classical and jazz) and theatre productions. Art exhibitions and other cultural events are organized year-round by the **Centro per l'Arte Contemporanea L. Pecci** (Mon & Wed–Sun 10am–7pm; ⊛www.centropecci.it), 2km southeast of the centre in Viale della Repubblica (reached by bus from Viale Pieve). It has a good collection of postwar art, featuring such names as LeWitt, Pistoletto and Kounellis, and its one-off shows are usually exciting.

2

San Francesco

Piazza San Francesco • Daily 8am–noon & 4–7pm

The thirteenth-century church of **San Francesco**, which presents its back to the castle, has a couple of fine monuments inside: on the left wall of the single aisle you'll find Bernardo Rossellino's worn-down tomb of Gemignano Inghirami, and set into the floor near the high altar is the slab of Francesco di Marco Datini. Off the cloister, the Cappella Migliatori has lovely frescoes of *The Lives of St Anthony Abbot and St Matthew* and *The Crucifixion*, painted in the 1390s by Niccolò di Pietro Gerini.

Museo del Tessuto

Via San Iacopo • Mon & Wed–Fri 9.30am–2.30pm, Sat 10am–6pm, Sun 4–7pm • €6, free on Sun • ⊛museodeltessuto.it

The former Campolmi factory, a huge nineteenth-century textile mill that's tucked against the city walls to the south of the castle, has been converted into an impressive home for the **Museo del Tessuto**. Tracing the city's literal rise from rags to riches, the museum also displays a collection of more than five thousand fabrics from all over the world, ranging right back to the third century. It's a venue for one-off exhibitions on textile- and fashion-related themes, too.

ARRIVAL AND DEPARTURE   PRATO

By train Prato has two train stations: Porta al Serraglio (which is very close to Piazza del Duomo) and Prato Centrale (fifteen minutes' walk south of the centre). Destinations Florence (every 20–30min; 20–30min); Lucca (hourly; 1hr); Montecatini (hourly; 30min); Pistoia (every 20–30min; 15min); Viareggio (hourly; 1hr 30min).

By bus The main bus station is at Prato Centrale. Destinations Florence, Lucca, Montecatini, Pisa, Pistoia and Viareggio (Lazzi); Florence and Siena (CAP).

INFORMATION

Tourist office The office at Palazzo Vestri, Piazza del Duomo (Mon–Sat 9am–1pm & 3–6pm, Sun 10am–1pm; ☎0574 24 112, ⊛pratoturismo.it) dispenses information on the whole Prato province.

ACCOMMODATION

Flora Via Cairoli 31 ☎0574 33 521, ⊛hotelflora.info. The 31-room *Flora* occupies a handsome nineteenth-century *palazzo* very close to the Piazza del Comune. It may not be a contender for any shortlist of hip Tuscan hotels, but this well-run three-star is the pick of central Prato's accommodation. €75–150

Il Giglio Piazza San Marco 14 ☎0574 37 049, ⊛www.albergoilgiglio.it. This little two-star, tucked against the city walls, has been offering simple and functional rooms for forty years now, and the styling hasn't changed greatly in the interim. All rooms are en suite and a/c, however, and the prices are low. €60

EATING AND DRINKING

While you're in Prato, you might want to sample the local speciality, the *biscotto di Prato*, a very hard yellow biscuit made a touch less resistant by dipping in wine or coffee. The best outlet for these and other pastries is Antonio Mattei, which has been in existence at Via Ricasoli 22 (near Piazza San Francesco) since 1858.

Lapo Piazza Mercatale 141 ☎ 0574 23 745. Like Cibbè, at the opposite end of the huge market square, this is an inexpensive and friendly trattoria, catering predominantly for locals. Mon–Sat lunch & dinner.

★ **Osteria Cibbè** Piazza Mercatale 49 ☎ 0574 60 759. There are several **restaurants** on or near Piazza Mercatale, and this is the best of them – the pasta dishes are especially good, and the wine list is excellent. Mon–Sat 12.30–2.30pm & 7.30–11pm.

Pistoia

The provincial capital of **PISTOIA** – known throughout Tuscany for the acres of garden nurseries on the slopes around – is visited by few tourists, but at its heart there's a well-preserved medieval town that's well worth a look for its splendid Romanesque churches, three of which are adorned with magnificent examples of early Tuscan sculpture. The liveliest time to visit is July, for the **Luglio Pistoiese**, a month-long programme of concerts and events (including the Pistoia Blues music festival), and culminating in the Giostra dell'Orso, Pistoia's answer to the shenanigans of Siena's Palio (see p.167).

If you've arrived by public transport, you'll approach the centre from the south side; the sights of Pistoia begin about a hundred metres inside the city walls, at the junction of two of the widest avenues, Corso Gramsci and Corso Fedi.

Museo Marino Marini

Corso Fedi 30 · Mon–Sat: April–Sept 10am–6pm; Oct–March 10am–5pm; €3.50 or joint ticket · ⓦ www.fondazionemarinomarini.it

The **Museo Marino Marini** shows a wide selection of work – sculptures, drawings, paintings – by Pistoia's most famous modern son. Marini found an early influence in the realism of Etruscan sarcophagi, expressed in the sculptures of horses and riders that he produced throughout his life; in the 1940s he diversified into portraiture – subjects here include Thomas Mann, Henry Miller and Marc Chagall.

Cappella del Tau

Corso Fedi · Mon–Sat 8.15am–1.30pm · Free

Next door to the Museo Marini, the **Cappella del Tau**, or Sant'Antonio Abate, preserves a chaos of mainly fourteenth-century frescoes depicting the Creation (in the vault), the life of St Anthony Abbot and the story of the sacred girdle (see p.160).

PISTOIA, THE MURDEROUS CITY

The city's **Roman** forerunner, Pistoria, was where Catiline and his fellow conspirators against the republic were finally run to ground; the town went on to earn itself a reputation as a lair of malcontents. Pistoia was a Ghibelline city until its conquest by the Guelph city of Florence in 1254, and local folklore has it that Pistoia is where, soon afterwards, the Guelphs were riven into the Black and White factions. Supposedly, one Pistoiese child injured another while playing with a sword; the miscreant's father sent him to apologize, whereupon the father of the injured party chopped the offender's hand off, telling him, "Iron, not words, is the remedy for sword wounds." The city promptly polarized into the Neri and the Bianchi camps (taking the names from ancestors of the two parties), and by some osmotic process these battle names were taken up in Florence. Such was Pistoia's reputation for mayhem, Dante found it entirely appropriate that this should have been the home of the thuggish Vanni Fucci, whose exploits included stealing the silver from the cathedral; he's encountered in the *Inferno*, enmeshed in a knot of snakes and cursing God. For centuries the mythology of murderous Pistoia endured, and Michelangelo spoke for many when he referred to the Pistoiese as the "enemies of heaven". It's fitting that, according to one school of thought, the word **pistol** should be derived from this violent town; meaning "from Pistoia", a *pistole* was originally a dagger, but the name was transferred to the first firearms made here in the sixteenth century.

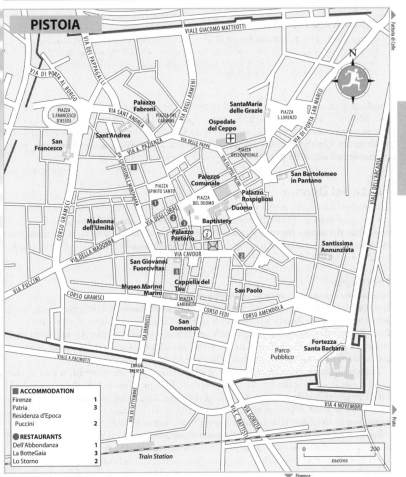

San Domenico

Piazza San Domenico •Daily 7.30am–noon & 4.30–6pm, Sun closes 8pm

The thirteenth-century church of **San Domenico** was rebuilt in the 1970s after terrible wartime damage. Scraps of medieval frescoes remain inside, but the most arresting feature is the Rossellino brothers' tomb of the teacher Filippo Lazzari, on the right near the door. In the cloister there are remnants of a fresco of *The Journey of the Magi* by Benozzo Gozzoli, who died of the plague in Pistoia and is buried here.

San Giovanni Fuorcivitas

Via Cavour • Daily 7.30am–noon & 5–7pm

Now the main shopping street of the city's inner core, the pedestrianized Via Cavour was once the settlement's outer limit – as the name of the majestic **San Giovanni Fuorcivitas** (Saint John Outside the Walls) proclaims. The church was founded in the eighth century, but rebuilt between the twelfth and fourteenth centuries, when it received the dazzling green-and-white flank that serves as its **facade**: the pattern of its

PISTOIA MUSEUM TICKETS

Entry to each of Pistoia's **museums** is €3.50, except for Palazzo Fabroni, which costs €5. A €6 ticket gets you into any two museums, excluding the Fabroni, or for €7 you can get into any two including the Fabroni. Also available are a €9 ticket for all the museums other than the Fabroni, and €12 ticket for the whole lot.

2

bands of contrasting marble is echoed in the oratory across the alleyway (now a bar). The **interior** is remarkable chiefly for the pulpit carved in 1270 by a pupil of Nicola Pisano, whose son, Giovanni, executed the cardinal and theological virtues on the holy water stoup. On the opposite side of the church is a life-size terracotta *Visitation*, probably by Luca della Robbia.

Piazza del Duomo

The medieval complex of the vast **Piazza del Duomo** – best reached from Via Cavour via the busy market square, Piazza della Sala – is a superb and slightly eccentric ensemble: the ornate baptistery lurks in one corner and the Duomo faces it, turning its flank to the open space and leaving the huge campanile and monolithic civic buildings to take the limelight.

The Duomo

Piazza del Duomo • Daily 8am–12.30pm & 3.30–7pm • Free, Cappella di San Jacopo €2

If you've come from Pisa or Lucca, the style of Pistoia's **Duomo**, the Cattedrale di San Zeno, will be immediately familiar, with its tiered arcades and distinctive Pisan-Romanesque decoration of striped black and white marble. Set into this soberly refined front is a tunnel-vault portico of bright terracotta tiles by Andrea della Robbia, creator also of the *Madonna and Child* above the door.

The **interior** has an outstanding array of sculptural pieces, one of which is part of the entrance wall – a font designed by Benedetto da Maiano, showing incidents from the life of the Baptist. Close by, on the wall of the right aisle, is the monument to Dante's friend, the diplomat, teacher and poet Cino da Pistoia; it is said that Boccaccio is one of the pupils to whom he's shown lecturing in the bottom panel.

Just beyond this monument is the **Cappella di San Jacopo**, which boasts one of the richest pieces of silverwork to be seen in Italy, the **Altarpiece of St James**. Weighing almost a ton and populated with 628 figures, it was begun in 1287 and completed in the fifteenth century, when Brunelleschi cast the two half-figures of prophets on the left-hand side.

In the chapel to the left of the high altar you'll find Antonio Rossellino's bust of Bishop Donato de' Medici, and the so-called *Madonna di Piazza*, begun by Verrocchio and finished by Lorenzo di Credi; Verrocchio, with his workshop, was also responsible for the tomb of Cardinal Forteguerri, in the left aisle by the door.

The Campanile

Piazza del Duomo • Guided tours usually Sat & Sun 11am, noon, 4pm and 5pm • €6

The Duomo's **Campanile** was originally a Lombard watchtower, then was spruced up with Romanesque arcades in the twelfth century and a Gothic turret in the sixteenth; the swallowtail crenellations near the summit give away the town's old Ghibelline loyalties.

The Baptistery and Palazzo del Podestà

Piazza del Duomo • **Baptistery** Tues–Sun 10am–6pm • Free

The dapper Gothic **Baptistery** was designed by Giovanni Pisano and completed in the mid-fourteenth century by Cellino di Nese, creator of the Duomo's monument to Cino da Pistoia. Art shows sometimes fill the space around the font. Though the neighbouring **Palazzo del Podestà** (or Palazzo Pretorio) is closed to the public, you can

THE GIOSTRA DELL'ORSO

The origins of the **Giostra dell'Orso** are recorded in a chronicle of 1300: on March 10 of that year, a dozen knights fought a ceremonial battle against a bear dressed in the town's coat of arms. The form of this joust changed many times over the following centuries but some version of it was fought every year until 1666, when it seems to have been abandoned. In 1947 it was revived in more humane form and now takes place on July 25, feast of the city's patron, St James. It forms the centrepiece of the festival season known as the **Luglio Pistoiese** (Pistoia July).

The fun begins with a procession of around three hundred standard-bearers, trumpeters, knights, halberdiers and assorted costumed extras from the Porta Lucchese to the Piazza del Duomo. These characters represent the villages around Pistoia, the city's crafts and trades and the four districts of the historic centre. Each of these four districts is represented in the joust by three knights, their regalia bearing the heraldic emblems of the Lion, the Stag, the Griffon and the Dragon. Having led the procession into the arena laid out on the piazza, the knights are separated into pairs, who then ride against each other around the track, scoring points by hitting the two stylized "bears" set on bales on opposite sides of the circuit. Points are awarded according to which parts of the target are hit with the lance, and at the end of the day two prizes are awarded – to the highest-scoring district and the highest-scoring knight.

The *giostra* is always a sell-out; to be sure of **tickets**, contact the tourist office at least a month in advance (☎0573 21 622; ⓦgiostradellorso.it).

take a look at the courtyard, which is adorned with the coats of arms of Pistoia's magistrates, whose home this was.

Museo di San Zeno

Piazza del Duomo • Guided tours Tues, Thurs & Fri at 10am, 11.30am & 3.30pm; must be booked via the tourist office • €3

Alongside the Duomo, the partly clad Palazzo dei Vescovi is now home of the small **Museo di San Zeno**, where the chief exhibits are Ghiberti's reliquary of St James and a fourteenth-century reliquary of St Zeno. The basement has a modest archeological collection, with relics from Roman Pistoria.

The Museo Civico

Piazza del Duomo • Thurs–Sun 10am–6pm • €3.50, or joint ticket

On the far side of the square, the flaking pale limestone facade of the **Palazzo Comunale** bears a small basalt head that may be a portrait of the Moorish king of Mallorca whom the Pistoiese defeated in the twelfth century; local folklore prefers to interpret it as the image of a man who betrayed the city to the army of Castruccio Castracani in 1315, which is about the time the head was mounted here. The *palazzo* contains the **Museo Civico**, where the customary welter of run-of-the-mill medieval and Renaissance pieces is counterweighted by an impressive showing of Baroque hyperactivity – including a couple of gruesome battle scenes by Ciccio Napoletano. Attached to the museum is a display devoted to Pistoia-born architect **Giovanni Michelucci**, featuring models and photographs of his major buildings, and some nine hundred of his drawings.

Palazzo Rospigliosi

Ripa del Sale • Tues–Sat 10am–1pm & 3–6pm • €3.50, or joint ticket

The Palazzo Rospigliosi houses the combined **Museo Diocesano**, **Museo Rospigliosi** and **Museo del Ricamo**, where much of the space is occupied by chalices, censers, crosses, miscellaneous ecclesiastical accoutrements, mediocre paintings and various pieces of furniture, many of them bequeathed by Pope Clement IX, another illustrious Pistoian, who occupied the papal throne from 1667 to 1669. The last museum of the trio is a two-room showcase for some remarkably elaborate embroidery, a skill for which Pistoia's artisans were long renowned.

Abbazia di San Bartolomeo in Pantano

Piazza San Bartolomeo • Daily 8am–noon & 4–6pm

The **Abbazia di San Bartolomeo in Pantano** (St Bartholomew in the Swamp) is named after the marshy ground on which it was raised in the eighth century. The semi-complete facade is as appealing as any of the city's more polished fronts, and inside there's the earliest of Pistoia's trio of remarkable thirteenth-century pulpits. Executed in 1250 by Guido da Como, and reconstructed from its dismantled parts, it's less sophisticated than the other two, comprising a rectangular box whose principal scenes are filled with figures arrayed in ranks like a crowd in a stadium.

2

Ospedale del Ceppo

Piazza Giovanni XXIII

The most photographed feature of the Pistoia townscape is not a church but a hospital in a square at the end of Via Pacini – the **Ospedale del Ceppo**, which takes its name from the hollowed-out tree stump (*ceppo*) in which alms were traditionally collected. Established in the thirteenth century (which makes it one of the world's oldest functioning hospitals), it was embellished in the fifteenth with a portico like the one Brunelleschi designed for the Innocenti in Florence. Emblazoned along its length is the feature that makes it famous: Giovanni della Robbia's painted terracotta frieze of the *Theological Virtues* and the *Seven Works of Mercy*. Completed in the early sixteenth century, it is a startlingly colourful Renaissance panoply of social types and costumes.

Pistoia Sotterranea

Guided tours daily 10.30am–12.30pm & 2–5pm • €9

To the left of the Ospedale, a doorway gives access to **Pistoia Sotterranea**, a 650-metre system of medieval underground vaults that were created when a branch of the Brana river was diverted beneath the city, where it drove the Ceppo's olive oil mill and other machines. The tour also takes you into the Ceppo's museum of surgical instruments and its tiny anatomy theatre.

Palazzo Fabroni

Via Sant'Andrea 18 • Variable opening hours • €5, or joint ticket

The vast **Palazzo Fabroni** is Pistoia's chief venue for one-off art exhibitions, and also houses a permanent collection of modern art, which is based on work from the Museo Civico's collection and augmented with pieces bought from or donated by various Italian artists; it's a moderately engaging assembly, but the special events are generally of greater interest.

FATTORIA DI CELLE

Established in 1982, some 4km east of Pistoia at Santomato, the **Fattoria di Celle** is known chiefly for the large-scale outdoor pieces of its **sculpture park**. Artists from all over the world have contributed to its development, devising a variety of responses to its woodlands and grassy slopes, and to the wider cultural environment of Tuscany. Most of the installations date from the inaugural year, but new pieces are being commissioned all the time, maintaining the Fattoria di Celle's status as one of the most vital art centres in the country.

The centre is open for **guided tours** (May–Sept Mon–Fri; free), but visitors must first make an appointment (most easily done through the website, ⓦ goricoll.it); the tour lasts three to four hours, so, as the website says "the tour is advisable only for people who are true lovers of contemporary art and are not put off by challenging walks".

Sant'Andrea

Via Sant'Andrea • Daily 8.30am–5.30pm

The twelfth-century church of **Sant'Andrea** – which probably stands on the site of Pistoia's first cathedral – has a typically Pisan facade with a pair of Romanesque lions and a panel of *The Journey of the Magi* stuck onto it. The corridor-slim aisle contains the third and greatest of the pulpits: carved in 1297 by Giovanni Pisano, it is based on his father's design for the Pisa baptistery pulpit and only marginally less elaborate than his own slightly later work in Pisa cathedral. It shows scenes from the life of Christ and the Last Judgement, the figures carved in such deep relief that they are almost freestanding. Giovanni was the first to appreciate the glory of his achievement; Nicola Pisano had boasted of being the greatest living sculptor, and Giovanni's inscription brags that he has now surpassed his father. The church also has two other pieces by Giovanni – the wooden Crucifixes mounted on each side wall.

San Francesco al Prato

Piazza di San Francesco d'Assisi • Daily 7.30am–noon & 4–6.30pm

The plain Franciscan church of **San Francesco al Prato** has tattered fourteenth-century frescoes in the nave, and some healthier specimens in the chapels at the east end, where there's a fine *Triumph of Augustine* in the chapel to the left of the high altar. To the side of the church, a memorial has been built to Aldo Moro, the Italian prime minister killed by the Red Brigades on May 9, 1978, and to the five men killed when Moro was kidnapped on March 16; the bronze plaques are imprinted with newspaper headlines from the day Moro's body was found.

ARRIVAL AND DEPARTURE

PISTOIA

By train The train station is a couple of minutes' walk south of the historic centre, at the end of Viale XX Settembre.
Destinations Florence (every 20–30min; 40–55min); Lucca (hourly; 45min); Montecatini (hourly; 15min);

Viareggio (hourly; 1hr 15min).
By bus Buses stop in front of the train station
Destinations Florence, Lucca, Montecatini, Pisa, Prato & Viareggio (Lazzi); Empoli, Montecatini, Poggio a Caiano & Vinci (COPIT).

INFORMATION

Tourist office The office at Piazza del Duomo 4 (Mon–Sat 9am–1pm & 3–6pm, Sun 10am–1pm & 3–6pm; ☎ 0573

21 622, ⓦ www.comune.pistoia.it) is the chief outlet for information on the whole of the province.

ACCOMMODATION

Firenze Via Curtatone e Montanara 42 ☎ 0573 231 141, ⓦ hotel-firenze.it. The twenty-room *Firenze* is Pistoia's only two-star, and it offers good value for money – all bedrooms have a/c and en-suite bathroom, and are brightly turned out. **€60–90**
Patria Via Crispi 6–8 ☎ 0573 358 800, ⓦ patriahotel .com. Recently renovated and restyled, the 27-room four-star

Patria is now the best hotel in central Pistoia. **€110–180**
Residenza d'Epoca Puccini, Vicolo Malconsiglio 4 ☎ 0573 26 707, ⓦ puccini.tv. The rooms in this central eleven-room *residenza* are bright, large and spotlessly maintained; eighteenth- and nineteenth-century frescoes adorn many of them, but the furnishings are modern, and quite austere. **€120**

EATING AND DRINKING

★ **Dell'Abbondanza** Via Dell'Abbondanza 10 ☎ 0573 368 037. A superb and homely trattoria, with main courses around €15. The menu is classic Tuscan, and features quite a few offal-based dishes. Mon, Tues & Fri–Sun lunch & dinner; Thurs dinner only.
La BotteGaia Via del Lastrone 4 ☎ 0573 365 602. A good-value and always busy *osteria* (around €30 a head),

very close to Piazza della Sala, with an enticing *menù degustazione*, main courses from €10 and a terrific wine list. Tues–Sat lunch & dinner, Sun dinner only.
Lo Storno Via del Lastrone 8 ☎ 0573 26 193. This welcoming and busy *osteria* serves robust local dishes at prices similar to the neighbouring *BotteGaia*. Mon–Sat lunch & dinner.

2

The Valdinievole

Known as the **Valdinievole** (Valley of Mists), the area to the west of Pistoia is a region of subterranean streams and springs that harbours one of Italy's main concentrations of **spa towns**. As with German spas, these resorts as a rule don't have the same aura of social exclusivity as they do in Britain, but the two big centres of the Valdinievole, **Montecatini Terme** and **Monsummano Terme**, are nonetheless unlikely to tempt you to linger overnight, though you might want to stop for a couple of hours just to sample the peculiar *belle époque* ambience – or even to sample a spa treatment. As long as you're not passing through some time between November and Easter, that is, because in winter these places are comatose. Florence-to-Viareggio trains stop at Montecatini, but Monsummano has no station.

Montecatini Terme

No spa in Italy has a glossier reputation than **MONTECATINI TERME**, as can be gauged from the fact that the likes of Gucci and Gianfranco Ferre have outlets here – and it was in Montecatini that Fellini filmed the spa scenes in *8 1/2*. A leafy grid of indistinguishable apartment blocks and villas, where it seems to be eternally siesta time, surround the central **Parco delle Terme**, in which each of the nine sulphate springs is encased in its own building. Fronting the piazza at the edge of the park is the pompous **Terme Leopoldine**, a shrine to the healing properties of mud baths. North of this is the **Tettuccio**, discovered in the fourteenth century but not exploited to the full until Grand Duke Leopoldo I gave it the works in the eighteenth; inside, Art Nouveau paintings and ceramics create a suitably sybaritic environment. Across the way, the Palladian home of the **Regina** spring seems to promise more astringent regimes, while at the back of the park, the mock-medieval **Torretta** embodies the straightforwardly escapist element of all spa resorts. All these spas are open from May to October; there's one establishment, the Neo-Renaissance-Modernist **Excelsior**, that's open all year. For information on the spas, visit ⓦtermemontecatini.it.

Across the road from the Regina spa you'll find the **Accademia d'Arte** (Tues–Sun 2.30–6.30pm; free), a mishmash of gifts from illustrious guests such as Verdi, who composed much of *Otello* while staying in Montecatini, working at the piano that's kept here. A few minutes' walk away, a **funicular** rises to Montecatini Alto; if you drive, it's a 5km haul. The original Montecatini settlement here offers excellent views, especially of Monsummano, and in summer the tiny Piazza Giusti becomes a pleasant outdoor extension of its cafés and pizzerias. A couple of kilometres below Montecatini, the stalactite-heavy **Grotta Maona** (April to mid-Oct daily 9am–noon & 3–6pm; €5) is the only cave in Italy that contains two separate springs.

Monsummano Terme

Montecatini's sister spa, **MONSUMMANO TERME**, a few kilometres southeast, has its own speciality: the steam cave. The family of the poet Giuseppe Giusti – who was born here in 1809 – set the business in motion when they discovered a flooded cave filled with mineral-saturated steam. Divided into chambers tagged Inferno, Purgatorio and Paradiso, the **Grotta Giusti** (ⓦgrottagiustispa.com), on the eastern outskirts, is still the town's big draw – half luxury hotel, half medical centre, it charges from around €40 for a session of sweltering and massage. Competition is provided by the artificial **Grotta Parlanti** to the north. More information on both spas can be found at ⓦcomune .monsummano-terme.pt.it. The old town of **Monsummano Alto**, 3km from the centre up a steep and narrow road, is now little more than a twelfth-century church and a very ruined castle; the panorama is spectacular, though.

Empoli and around

The **N67**, tracking the Arno west of Florence, is as dispiriting as the road that follows the river to the east. Busy and slow, it's strung with drab towns, industrial sites, megastores and warehouses, and the main town on this route, **Empoli**, doesn't have a great deal to detain you. To the north of Empoli, the most popular attraction is to be found in **Vinci**, birthplace of Leonardo, while to the south lie three low-key hill-towns, **San Miniato**, **Castelfiorentino** and **Certaldo**.

2

Empoli

The manufacturing town of **EMPOLI**, purveyor of glass and raincoats to the nation, is a major junction of road and rail routes between Florence, Pisa, the coast and Siena, and thus might well be a place you'll find yourself passing through. If you have time for a quick look around, head for the central **Piazza Farinata degli Uberti**, named after the commander of the Ghibelline army of Siena which defeated the Florentine Guelphs at Montaperti in 1260; he's revered for his advocacy at the "parliament of Empoli", when he dissuaded his followers from wrecking Florence. The green and white **Collegiata**, on the square, might have been founded as far back as the fifth century; its lower portion is the most westerly example of Florentine Romanesque architecture, the top a nineteenth-century imitation, reconstructed after bomb damage in World War II.

Museo Collegiata and Santo Stefano

Piazzetta della Propositura • Tues–Sun 9am–noon & 4–7pm • €3

The highlights of the **Museo Collegiata** are a couple of triptychs by Lorenzo Monaco, a small *Maestà* attributed to Filippo Lippi, a superb Masolino *Pietà*, sculptures by Bernardo Rossellino and Mino da Fiesole, and Lorenzo di Bicci's *St Nicholas of Tolentino Saving Empoli from the Plague*, featuring a view of the town in the 1440s. The museum also possesses an item relating to one of Tuscany's stranger Easter rituals, a winged mechanical donkey that used to be propelled from the Collegiata tower down to Piazza Farinata degli Uberti, where it would ignite a pile of fireworks. Nowadays a papier-mache beast performs the role.

The museum ticket gives you access to the adjacent church of **Santo Stefano**, where you can see the remnants of frescoes by Masolino and a marble *Annunciation* by Bernardo Rossellino.

Pontorme

If you're keen on Pontormo's paintings, you might want to drive out to the suburb of **Pontorme**, on the road to Florence. This was the birthplace of the artist baptized as Jacopo Carrucci, and the parish church of San Michele (Mon–Sat 8am–noon) retains a couple of fine pictures by him, a *St John the Evangelist* and a *St Michael*.

ARRIVAL AND DEPARTURE	EMPOLI
By train The train station is a short distance south of the town centre.	30min; 25min); Poggibonsi (hourly; 40min); Siena (hourly; 1hr).
Destinations Castelfiorentino (hourly; 20min); Certaldo (hourly; 30min); Florence (every 30min; 25min); Pisa (every	**By bus** Buses stop in front of the train station. Destinations Cerreto Guidi and Vinci (COPIT); Castelfiorentino and Certaldo (SITA).

Cerreto Guidi

Daily 9am–7pm, closed second & third Mon of month • Free • COPIT bus from Empoli

From the time of Cosimo I to the end of the dynasty, the Medici administered their estates in this northern part of Tuscany from the villa at **CERRETO GUIDI**, 8km

2

northwest of Empoli. Having converted this former castle into something more domestic, and commissioned Buontalenti to build the huge approach ramps that remain the villa's most distinctive feature, the clan set about making it the focus of rural life in the Empoli district: they instituted a weekly fair here, with compulsory attendance for the local peasants. The villa is a plain box and the church that Cosimo built next door is similarly austere – though there's a good view from the top of the ramps. The Cerreto Guidi hunting museum might please bloodsport enthusiasts, but most visitors will prefer the **gallery** of Medici portraits. One section is entitled "Unhappy marriages among the descendants of Cosimo I" and includes a likeness of Cosimo's daughter Isabella, murdered here by her husband in 1576 for her infidelity; the Medici hitmen caught up with her alleged lover in Paris the following year.

Vinci

Sitting amid rolling vineyards and olive groves on the southern slopes of Monte Albano, 11km north of Empoli, **VINCI** draws the coach parties for its association with **Leonardo da Vinci**, who in April 1452 was born in the nearby hamlet of Archiano and baptized in Vinci's church of Santa Croce. By bus, Vinci can be reached most easily from Empoli – there are about fifteen buses daily (Mon–Sat) and the journey takes half an hour.

Museo Leonardiano

Via Rossi & Castello dei Conti Guidi • Daily: March–Oct 9.30am–7pm; Nov–Feb 9.30am–6pm • €6 • ⓦ museoleonardiano.it

Vinci itself is a torpid place but preserves a mighty thirteenth-century castle, the **Castello dei Conti Guidi**, which houses the main part of the **Museo Leonardiano** – the ticket office is in the smaller part of the museum, the Palazzina Uzielli, in Via Rossi. Opened on the five-hundredth anniversary of Leonardo's birth, the museum is dedicated to Leonardo the inventor and engineer rather than Leonardo the artist, with a large display of models – tanks, water cannon, flying machines, looms and gear mechanisms – reconstructed from his notebook drawings, which are reproduced alongside the relevant contraptions. Avoid visiting on a Sunday, when it can feel as if half the population of Tuscany has turned up.

Leonardo's birthplace

Daily: March–Oct 9.30am–7pm; Nov–Feb 9.30am–6pm • Free

Leonardo's **birthplace** is in **ANCHIANO**, a pleasant 3km walk north into the hills. The house was owned by his father, a Florentine clerk called Ser Piero; Leonardo's mother is generally believed to have been either a *contadina* (peasant girl) or an Arab slave, but the only things known for certain are that her name was Caterina and she didn't marry his father, possibly because Ser Piero was already betrothed. Within eight months of his son's birth Ser Piero had married the sixteen-year-old daughter of a Florentine notary, and soon afterwards Caterina married a man who went by the name of Accattabriga, who may have been a soldier. (Meaning something like "trouble-maker", Accattabriga was a common nickname among mercenaries.) Placard-size captions and a couple of reproduction drawings are pretty well all there is to see inside the house.

San Miniato

The strategic hill-top site of **SAN MINIATO**, more or less equidistant between Pisa and Florence, has been exploited since the era of Augustus, when the Roman settlement of Quarto was founded here. A Lombard town succeeded it, and at the end of the tenth century Otto I made this an outpost of the Holy Roman Empire. A later emperor, Frederick II, gave the town its landmark fortress, and the imperial connection led to the nickname San Miniato dei Tedeschi ("of the Germans"). Today it's a brisk little agricultural town, renowned throughout Italy for the quality of the white truffles that grow in the surrounding soil.

Piazza del Popolo and Piazza della Reppublica

Beyond the town gate, a right turn leads to **Piazza del Popolo**, where a plan of the town is displayed outside the tourist office. At the top end of the square is the much rebuilt church of **San Domenico**, which contains the fine tomb of a Florentine doctor named Giovanni Chellini. Carved by one Pagno di Lapo Portigiani, it's modelled on the tomb of Leonardo Bruni in Florence's Santa Croce. From here Via Conti rises to the **Piazza della Repubblica**, which is jazzed up by seventeenth-century *sgraffiti* on the long facade of the seminary.

Prato del Duomo

Opposite the seminary, a flight of steps rises to the **Prato del Duomo**, where a tower of the imperial fortress now houses a hotel. Next door, the **Palazzo dei Vicari dell'Imperatore** is a relic of the time when San Miniato was the seat of the vicars of the Holy Roman Empire: Countess Matilda of Tuscia (see p.538), daughter of one of these vicars, was born here.

The red-brick **Duomo**, dedicated to St Genesius, the patron saint of actors, is hacked-about Romanesque, with an interior of Baroque gilding and marbling. Next door, the tiny **Museo Diocesano** (Thurs–Sun: April–Oct 10am–6pm, Nov–March 10am–5pm; €2.50) has a *Crucifixion* by Filippo Lippi and a terracotta bust of Christ by Verrocchio.

The Rocca

Daily: April–Sept 11am–6pm, Oct–March 11am–5pm • €2.50

It's a short walk up from the Prato del Duomo to the tower of the **Rocca**, which was rebuilt by Frederick II and restored after damage in World War II; the main point of the climb is the panorama of the surrounding countryside. Dante's *Inferno* perpetuates the memory of Pier della Vigna, Frederick's treasurer, who was imprisoned and blinded here, a fate that drove him to suicide by jumping from the tower – as the inscription at its foot records.

San Francesco

Piazza San Francesco

Below the tower, on the opposite side from the Duomo, stands the church of **San Francesco**, occupying the site where the Lombards dedicated the chapel to St Miniatus that gave the town its name. The church was altered by the Franciscans, who were given the property after Francis himself had visited the town, and traces of their Romanesque building can just about be discerned through the later Gothic.

ARRIVAL AND DEPARTURE   SAN MINIATO

By train The train station is in the modern lower town, San Miniato Basso, 4km below San Miniato Alto, the old quarter. A minibus connects the two, depositing you just below the walls in Piazzale Dante Alighieri, which is also the place to park.

ACCOMMODATION AND EATING

Miravalle ☎0571 418 075, ⊕albergomiravalle.com. The tower of the Prato del Duomo is now occupied by the three-star *Miravalle* hotel, San Miniato's best place to stay, with a good restaurant and marvellous views. Restaurant daily noon–2.30pm & 7.30–10.30pm. **€130**

Castelfiorentino

A fief of the bishops of Florence from the twelfth century onwards, **CASTELFIORENTINO** remained in the city's orbit through most of its uneventful history. Today it's a fairly large urban centre, with light industry and block housing spreading from the modern, lower quarter of town, across the River Elsa.

The Museo Benozzo Gozzoli

Via Testaferrata • June to mid-Sept Mon, Tues, Sat & Sun 10am–noon & 4–7pm, Thurs 4–7pm, Fri 10am–2pm; rest of year Tues & Thurs 4–7pm, Sat & Sun 10am–noon & 4–7pm • €3, joint ticket with Santa Verdiana museum €4

Located in the lower town, less than a hundred metres from the train station, the **Museo Benozzo Gozzoli** was built to house two sets of **Gozzoli** frescoes that have been detached from local sanctuary chapels. The earlier of the pair, painted for the tabernacle of Madonna della Tosse in 1484, is centred on a *trompe l'oeil* altarpiece which is flanked by scenes of the death and assumption of the Virgin. The name means "Our Lady of the Cough" – the tabernacle was visited by parents anxious to cure their children of whooping cough, which was a common and often fatal illness. More fragmentary but no less interesting are the flood-damaged frescoes and sinopie from the Tabernacle of the Visitation, dating from 1490. These again depict episodes from the life of the Virgin, and of her parents, Joachim (Gioacchino) and Anne.

Santa Verdiana

Via Cesare Battisti • **Church** Daily 8am–noon & 5–6pm • **Museum** Sat 4–7pm, Sun 10am–noon & 4–7pm • €3

A couple of minutes' stroll to the south, a small park gives onto the Baroque church of **Santa Verdiana** dedicated to the town's patron saint, who died here in 1242, having spent the last 34 years of her life in a cell adjoining the church that formerly stood on this spot. Several of the church's humdrum paintings depict St Verdiana, as you'd expect. She's often shown with a couple of serpents because, according to legend, she bore without complaint the attacks of two snakes that infiltrated her cell – she even preached to them, as St Francis had preached to the birds. Adjacent, there's a museum displaying paintings from churches in the town and region, including works by Duccio, Taddeo Gaddi and Gozzoli.

San Francesco

Piazza San Francesco • Fri 5–6pm

Many of the panels in the Santa Verdiana museum came from nearby **San Francesco**, which has fragmentary fourteenth-century frescoes of his life; the church claims foundation by St Francis himself, who is said to have admitted Verdiana into the Franciscan Order in 1211.

The upper town

To reach the **Castello** – the old, upper town – head up the steps at the corner of the lower town's main square, Piazza Gramsci, by the Teatro del Popolo. This brings you to Via dei Tilli, which runs into **Piazza del Popolo**, which is flanked by the Collegiata of San Lorenzo – built on Lombard foundations – and the nineteenth-century Municipio. The stepped street above the piazza leads to the summit of the town, marked by the Romanesque **Pieve di Santi Ippolito e Biagio** (closed for restoration). A plaque in the facade records that it was here, in 1197, that the Tuscan League was formed by Florence, Volterra, Lucca, San Miniato and Siena, to defend the cities against "any emperor, king, or prince" – Castelfiorentino's only real episode in the limelight.

San Vivaldo

If you have your own transport and feel like a rambling cross-country drive to San Gimignano, follow the road west of Castelfiorentino, through the minor spa of Gambassi Terme (which has the lovely Romanesque **Pieve a Chianni** on its outskirts) and the quiet little hill-town of Montaione, to the village of **SAN VIVALDO**. Some time around 1300, a hermit by the name of Vivaldo Stricchi – later S Vivaldo – withdrew to a wooded hill here, where he is said to have made himself a cell inside a chestnut tree. After his death a Franciscan monastery developed on the site, and in the early sixteenth century the monks transformed the surrounding slopes into the **Sacro Monte**, an array of 25 chapels, each corresponding to a sacred site in or around Jerusalem.

Sacro Monte

April–Oct Mon–Sat 3–7pm, Sun 10am–7pm; Nov–March daily 10am–5pm • €3.50

The **Sacro Monte** – a "Jerusalem in Tuscany" – was intended to provide the faithful with an approximation of the experience of a pilgrimage to the Holy Land, and the project was backed by the highest of authorities – Pope Leo X granted indulgences to anyone who came here. Clustered below the monastery, the eighteen surviving chapels contain remarkably dramatic terracotta tableaux, depicting events from the Annunciation to Pentecost.

Certaldo

Even without its Boccaccio connection, **CERTALDO** would justify a visit. A tiny but striking hill-town of red-brick towers, battlements and mansions, it's visible for miles along the Elsa valley, and itself has views out to San Gimignano. For a spell in the twelfth century, its rulers, the Alberti dukes of Prato, controlled a domain stretching north to the Arno, but subsequent domination by Florence and incursions by Siena led to its assuming a more modest role. Nowadays its lower town, built along the N429, is a prosperous place, making its money from wine and agriculture, as well as glass, brick and pasta factories. In late July or early August the town holds the atmospheric **Mercantia festival**, which features various street-theatre events, many of them in medieval or Renaissance costume, and all illuminated by torches and candles. There's also a **cultural festival** in September, the first Sunday of which is the feast of Beata Giulia della Rena, when emigrants from the town traditionally return for a reunion.

Casa del Boccaccio

Via Boccaccio 18 • April–Oct daily 9.30am–1.30pm & 2.30–7pm; Nov–March Tues–Sun 9.30am–1.30pm & 2.30–4.30pm • €4 joint ticket with Palazzo Vicariale, or €6 joint ticket with Palazzo Vicariale and Museo d'Arte Sacra • ⓦ casaboccaccio.it

Certaldo's upper town is little more than a single street, predictably dubbed **Via Boccaccio**, which stretches from the western side (where the funicular arrives from

---

BOCCACCIO

Giovanni Boccaccio was born, according to the account he gave his friend Petrarch, in Paris, probably in 1313. The son of a banker from Certaldo, he returned to Tuscany fairly early in his childhood. As a youth he rejected the banking career planned by his family, instead going to study in Naples, where he fell in love with Fiammetta, an illegitimate princess and the inspiration for numerous of his sonnets. He returned to Florence reluctantly, after the collapse of his father's business, and there – as well as in Milan and Avignon, where he served as a diplomat – he wrote his major works, including the **Decameron**. Completed in 1353, the *Decameron* is set during the Black Death, which had recently devastated much of Tuscany, and is narrated by ten characters, each of whom tells ten stories during the two weeks they spend taking refuge from the epidemic in a villa in Fiesole; the vast majority of Boccaccio's one hundred tales were borrowed from existing sources, and the *Decameron* has in turn been quarried by innumerable writers, including such disparate figures as Luther, Molière and Keats.

Aged around 50, Boccaccio met a monk who so impressed him that he decided to reject his worldly excesses of old and retire to Certaldo. The rest of the years here were spent producing learned volumes on geography, mythology and the vanity of human affairs, and writing lectures on Dante. He died on December 21, 1375.

2

Certaldo Basso) to the archetypally Tuscan town hall, or Palazzo Vicariale. Halfway along the street stands the **Casa del Boccaccio**, where you buy your tickets for all Certaldo's museums. This building may well have been the house in which the poet spent the last twelve years of his life – in very modest circumstances, despite a considerable reputation – but some scholars think that the towered house specified in Boccaccio's will was not this one. Not only is the attribution uncertain, but the house contains nothing of any great antiquity, other than a case of medieval shoes. Instead, you get photos of portraits of the writer, illustrations of scenes from the *Decameron* and various editions of his masterpiece, in the original and in translation.

Santi Michele e Jacopo

Via Boccaccio • **Church** Daily 9am–1pm & 2.30–7pm • **Museum** Daily: April–Oct 9.30am–1.30pm & 2.30–7pm; Nov–March Tues–Sun 9.30am–1.30pm & 2.30–4.30pm • €3, or €6 joint ticket with Palazzo Vicariale and Casa del Boccaccio

Boccaccio is buried in the church that he attended, **Santi Michele e Jacopo**. A simple marble diamond on the floor of the nave marks his grave, above a mock-medieval funerary slab, which replaces the tomb that was destroyed in 1783: the burghers of Certaldo – having concluded, as the author did, that the *Decameron* was an ungodly work – ripped up the tombstone and scattered his ashes. Byron, who came to pay his respects a few years later, was scandalized:

… even his tomb
Uptorn must bear the hyena bigot's wrong;
No more amidst the meaner dead find room.

Byron's verses had an effect, prompting the Marquise Carlotta Lenzoni dei Medici to buy and restore the alleged Boccaccio house and arrange the **monument** on the left-hand wall of the church, which comprises a sixteenth-century bust and a slab bearing the lines the poet wrote as his own epitaph. The church also contains the tomb of the Blessed Giulia della Rena, who spent thirty years in a walled-up cell beside the sacristy, and at whose death in 1367 all the bells of Certaldo are said to have spontaneously begun to ring. (The same story is told of the death of Castelfiorentino's Santa Verdiana.) The small **Museo d'Arte Sacra**, off the church's cloister, is a typical small-town collection of humdrum paintings and ecclesiastical applied art.

Palazzo Vicariale

April–Oct daily 9.30am–1.30pm & 2.30–7pm; Nov–March Tues–Sun 9.30am–1.30pm & 2.30–4.30pm • €4 or €6 joint ticket with Museo d'Arte Sacra and Casa del Boccaccio

The **Palazzo Vicariale** (or Pretorio) is blazoned with coats of arms that attest to its use as the governor's residence, after the demise of its original owners, the Alberti. Inside, the arcaded courtyard displays further coats of arms and a fragmentary array of frescoes, many either painted or repainted at the end of the fifteenth century. To the right as you enter, the room in which the law court convened is dominated by a fresco of Doubting Thomas, attributed to Gozzoli. Cells for minor felons adjoin this room; serious offenders were dispatched to the dungeons at the rear of the courtyard. Upstairs are the more spacious chambers of the governor and his staff, again with the odd faded fresco.

Back downstairs, a door from the magistrates' hall opens onto a walled garden from which you enter the deconsecrated church of **San Tommaso e Prospero**, which contains a miscellany of frescoes and sinopie, the most notable being the *Deposition* that forms the focus of Gozzoli's Tabernacle of the Condemned, which was moved here from the local chapel for which it was created.

ARRIVAL AND INFORMATION   CERTALDO

By train and bus Buses and trains deposit you close to the central Piazza Boccaccio in the lower town; to get to the

upper town you can either walk up the steep Vicolo Signorini or take the funicular (daily: summer 7am–midnight; winter

7am–10pm; every 15min).
By car You're not allowed to drive into Certaldo Alto unless you're staying overnight up there.
Tourist office Casa del Boccaccio, Via Boccaccio 18 (daily:

April–Oct 9.30am–1.30pm & 2.30–7pm; Nov–March Tues–Sun 9.30am–1.30pm & 2.30–4.30pm; ☎0571 656 721, ⓦwww.comune.certaldo.fi.it).

ACCOMMODATION, EATING AND DRINKING

Il Castello Via della Rena 6 ☎0571 668 250, ⓦalbergoilcastello.it. The three-star *Il Castello* occupies an appealingly dowdy old mansion at the western end of Via Boccaccio; it has a splendid garden overlooking the lower town, and offers basic Tuscan food in its restaurant. Restaurant Mon & Wed–Sun lunch & dinner. €100

La Saletta Via Roma 3, ☎0571 668 188. This offshoot of the Niccolini family's excellent and long-established Dolci Follie pasticceria – which it adjoins – is the best restaurant in the lower town. The menu is small but changes constantly according to what's in season, the

wine list is outstanding and the dining room is very cosy. Mon & Wed–Sun 12.30–3pm & 7.30–10pm.

Osteria del Vicario Via Rivellino 3 ☎0571 668 228, ⓦosteriadelvicario.it. The bedrooms of the *Osteria del Vicario*, by the Palazzo Vicariale, are a little plusher than at *Il Castello*, but they're also considerably smaller, and only four are in the same thirteenth-century monastic building as the restaurant; others are in less charismatic nearby buildings. The restaurant is also more expensive (around €45 per person) and rather more refined than the *Castello*. Restaurant Mon, Tues & Thurs–Sun lunch & dinner. €100

Lucca and northern Tuscany

ALPI APUANE

Lucca and northern Tuscany

NORTHERN TUSCANY is one of the province's least-known regions. The one
city here on the sightseeing trail is Lucca – though even here, tourism is very
much a secondary consideration. Very few non-Italians holiday on its
resort-lined coast, the so-called Riviera della Versilia, and fewer still penetrate
inland to the mountains of the Alpi Apuane or the remote hills and valleys of
the Garfagnana and Lunigiana.

Contained within vast, park-lined walls, **Lucca** is an urbane, affluent place, with as
rewarding an ensemble of Romanesque churches as any you'll find in Italy. For a quick
break by the sea, the sands of the **Riviera della Versilia** are pleasant enough, and easily
reached from Lucca. Though there is often little to distinguish the resorts, where the
beaches are usually staked out by private operators, the town of **Viareggio** has its
moments – especially during February's carnival, when it mounts Italy's most amazing
procession of floats, and in high summer, when it's a popular place for a day out by the
sea. And from this coast it's a simple matter to explore the jagged peaks of the **Alpi
Apuane**, which run parallel to the sea for some 40km. The mountains are best known
for the **marble quarries** around **Carrara**, but head beyond these and you'll find yourself
amid steep forested valleys, threaded by a network of clearly marked **footpaths** and
longer trails.

Equally easy to visit from Lucca is the **Garfagnana**, a lovely rural enclave that
focuses on the **Serchio valley** and is flanked by the eastern slopes of the Apuane on
one side and the more rounded mountains of the **Orecchiella** on the other. Plenty of
trails strike off into these upland regions, each of which is protected by a regional
nature reserve. **Castelnuovo di Garfagnana** is the only town of any size, a good base
for excursions to the hills or a visit to nearby **Barga**, the one outstanding medieval
centre. North of the Serchio is one of the most marginalized areas of Tuscany, the
Lunigiana, a wild and unspoilt region of rocky, forested landscape peppered with
castles and tiny hamlets.

Lucca

LUCCA is the most graceful of Tuscany's provincial capitals; set inside a ring of
Renaissance walls fronted by gardens and huge bastions, it's quiet without being dull.
The city absorbs its tourists with ease, with a peaceful, self-contained historic centre
where it's delightful to wander at random: this is one of the few places in Tuscany
where many locals ride bikes, and as a result much of the old centre is refreshingly
traffic-free. The city is reputed to have once had seventy **churches**, and even today you
can hardly walk for five minutes without coming upon a small piazza and a fine,
marble-fronted church **facade**. Most were built obliquely to the grid of streets, so you
rarely confront a church head on, but rather as a sudden apparition as you enter a
square. Endowed with excellent **museums**, including one commemorating **Puccini's**
birthplace, the city evokes elegance and a cultured way of life.

LUCCA

Highlights

❶ Duomo di San Martino Chock full of artistic treasures, Lucca's cathedral is a stunning example of the region's marvellous Romanesque architecture. **See p.186**

❷ Lucca's walls Walk or cycle the fortifications that still completely encircle the old city. **See p.191**

❸ Villa Reale The best of several villas and gardens set in the hills around Lucca. **See p.193**

❹ Carnevale Viareggio's extravagant parade is famous throughout Italy. **See p.196**

❺ Walking in the Alpi Apuane There's a range of inspiring walks in the dramatic mountains

that rise just behind the Riviera della Versilia. **See p.199**

❻ Carrara This historic town is the fascinating centre of Tuscany's marble mining region. **See p.192**

❼ Barga This delightful Garfagnana village has a dramatically situated historic centre, a fine cathedral and a rich cultural and gastronomic heritage. **See p.203**

❽ The Orecchiella This verdant patchwork of valleys and mountains in the northeastern Garfagnana offers excellent hiking. **See p.205**

HIGHLIGHTS ARE MARKED ON THE MAP ON P.182

Lucca's proximity to Pisa makes it an excellent first or last Tuscan stop if you're flying in or out of **Pisa airport**. It's also an easy **day-trip** from Florence (the train takes around an duomo), though it's also well worth at least an overnight stay.

Brief history

Founded by the **Etruscans**, Lucca lies at the heart of one of Italy's richest agricultural regions, praised by Henry James as "half-smothered in oil and wine and corn and all the fruits of the earth". The city has prospered since the **Romans**, whose gridiron orthodoxy is still obvious in the layout of the streets. Under the **Lombards** it was the capital of Tuscia (Tuscany), though its heyday was between the eleventh and fourteenth centuries, when banking and the silk trade brought wealth and, for a time, political power. In a brief flurry of military activity Lucca lost its independence to Pisa in 1314, but regained it under the command of a remarkable adventurer, **Castruccio Castracani**, who went on to forge an empire covering much of western Tuscany. Pisa and Pistoia both fell to the Lucchesi, and but for Castracani's untimely death from malaria, Florence might have followed. In subsequent centuries the city remained largely independent – if fairly inconsequential – until passing to **Napoleon** (and rule by his sister, Elisa Baciocchi), the Bourbons and, just short of Italian Unification, to the Grand Duchy of Tuscany.

LUCCA & NORTHERN TUSCANY

HIGHLIGHTS
1. Duomo di San Martino
2. Lucca's walls
3. Villa Reale
4. Carnevale
5. Walking in the Alpi Apuane
6. Carrara
7. Barga
8. The Orecchiella

ORIENTATION

Confined within its walls, Lucca is an easy place to get your bearings. The main square is ostensibly **Piazza Napoleone**, a huge expanse carved out by the Bourbons to house their administration. A block east of here the **Via Fillungo** – the "long thread" – heads north through the heart of the medieval city, cutting through Lucca's luxury shopping district.

You're most likely to gravitate to **Piazza San Michele**, home to the eponymous church, the apotheosis of the Pisan-Romanesque style. From here, you might want to potter around the streets to the west, or push immediately on to the **Duomo**, another Romanesque gem, with one of Italy's most sublime funerary sculptures. Further east, the Fosso ("ditch") cuts off the quarter around **San Francesco**, while to the north is **Piazza Anfiteatro**, built over the old Roman arena, and **San Frediano**, the third of the city's trio of outstanding churches. A trip to Lucca is not complete without strolling part of the panoramic and tree-lined promenade atop the **walls**, accessed from almost any part of the city.

Today, the city is reckoned among the wealthiest in Tuscany, a prosperity gained largely through **silk** that was produced here by scores of small family businesses, and through the region's high-quality **olive oil** and other produce. There is, too, a tradition of decorum, traceable to eighteenth- and nineteenth-century court life. In fact, up until the turn of the twentieth century, smart Italian families sent their daughters to Lucca to pick up the gracious manners presumed to prevail here.

San Michele in Foro

Piazza San Michele • Daily: summer 7.40am–noon & 3–6pm; winter 9am–noon & 3pm–5pm; closed during services • Free

Head to the historical heart of Lucca and you come to the site of the Roman forum, now the square surrounding the church of **San Michele in Foro**, which has one of Tuscany's most exquisite facades. The church is first mentioned in 795, but most of the present structure dates from between 1070 and the middle of the twelfth century (you can see the date 1143 marked on a pillar on the left side of the main portal's triumphal arch). The building is unfinished, however, money having been diverted to the **facade**, begun in the thirteenth century; funds ran out before the body of the church could be raised to the standard of the facade. The effect is wonderful, the upper loggias and the windows fronting air, like the figure of the archangel at their summit. Its Pisan-inspired intricacy is a triumph of eccentricity, mirrored in many of Lucca's churches. Each of its myriad columns is different – some twisted, others sculpted or candy-striped. The impressive twelfth-century **campanile** is the city's tallest.

ON THE PUCCINI TRAIL

Nearly every corner of Lucca has a connection with the great composer Giacomo Puccini, and lovers of his music make regular pilgrimages to all the significant sites of both his life and his renowned operas. Very close to San Michele, where Puccini's father and grandfather both played the organ, is the **Casa di Puccini**, Corte San Lorenzo 9 (Mon & Wed–Sun April–Oct 10am–6pm; Nov–March 11am–5pm; €7; ☎0583 469 225, ⊛puccini.it), the composer's birthplace and family home. It now houses a school of music and a small museum containing the Steinway on which he wrote *Turandot*, as well as scores, photographs and even his overcoat.

Just round the corner from the Puccini house, in Piazza della Citadella, there's a life-size bronze statue of the composer, and a short way west is the church of **San Paolino**, where Puccini cut his musical teeth as organist. You can hear Puccini's work performed during the Puccini e la sua Lucca **music festival** (⊛puccinielasualucca.com), which sees daily concerts from mid-March to mid-November in churches and historic venues all over town.

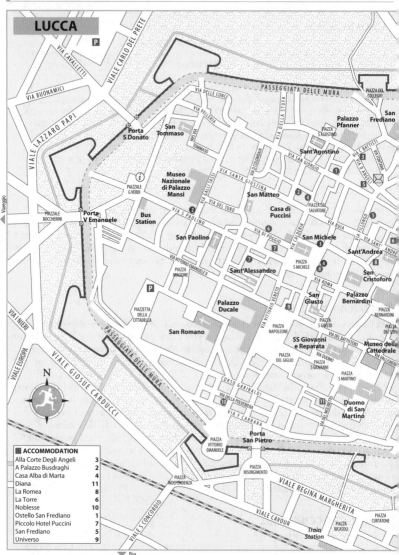

LUCCA

ACCOMMODATION

Alla Corte Degli Angeli	3
A Palazzo Busdraghi	2
Casa Alba di Marta	4
Diana	11
La Romea	8
La Torre	6
Noblesse	10
Ostello San Frediano	1
Piccolo Hotel Puccini	7
San Frediano	5
Universo	9

The interior

It would be hard to match the facade's bravura architectural display, and the **interior** barely tries. On the rear wall is a statue of the *Madonna and Child* by local sculptor Matteo Civitali, previously on the facade. Italians flock for spiritual regeneration to the second altar on the left, the so-called Rifugio dei Peccatori (Refuge of Sinners). On the opposite altar is a modest terracotta *Madonna and Child* by **Andrea della Robbia**; the best work of art is a beautifully framed painting of *Sts Jerome, Sebastian, Roch and Helena* by **Filippino Lippi**, at the end of the right-hand nave. Look out also for the organ, marvellously painted with intricate fleurs-de-lys.

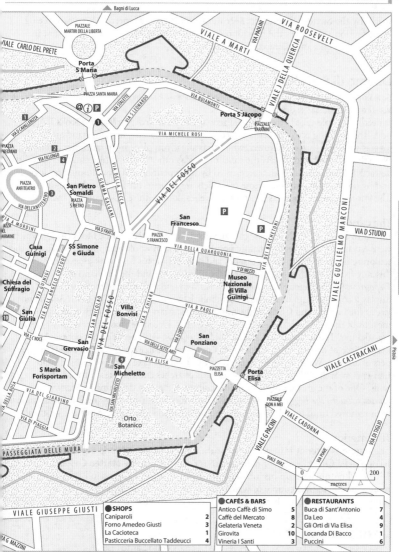

Museo Nazionale di Palazzo Mansi

Via Galli Tassi 43 • Tues–Sat 8.30am–7.30pm, Sun 8.30am–1.30pm • €4, or joint ticket with Museo Guinigi €6.50

The **Museo Nazionale di Palazzo Mansi** is set in a seventeenth-century building boasting some magnificently over-the-top Rococo decor; from a vast, frescoed music salon, you pass through three drawing rooms hung with seventeenth-century Flemish **tapestries** to a spectacularly gilded bridal suite. Rooms 11–14 in the far wing house the **Pinacoteca Nazionale**, an eclectic grouping of pictures whose real highlights are a **Pontormo** portrait, possibly of Alessandro de' Medici (see p.92 for the dirt on this sensitive youth); **Bronzino**'s portrait of Cosimo I; two male portraits by **Tintoretto**; and works by the Sienese Mannerists **Beccafumi** and Rutilio Manetti. Also worth seeing is the section that traces the development of Lucca's important **textile** industry, in particular its silks and damasks.

Duomo di San Martino

Piazza San Martino • Mid-March to Oct Mon–Fri 9.30am–5.45pm, Sat 9.30am–6.45pm, Sun 9–10.45am & noon–5pm; rest of year Mon–Fri closes 4.45pm, Sun 6pm • Free

It needs a double-take before you realize why the **Duomo di San Martino** looks slightly odd. The building is fronted by a severely asymmetric facade, its right-hand arch and loggias squeezed by the belltower, which was already in place from an earlier building. Nonetheless, the building sets the tone for Lucca's other Romanesque churches, and little detracts from its overall grandeur, created by the repetition of tiny columns and loggias and by the stunning **atrium**, whose bas-reliefs are some of the finest sculptures in the city. The **interior** houses the city's most revered relic, along with several painting masterpieces.

The carvings

It's worth looking closely at these carvings, some dated as early as the fifth century, which were executed by a variety of mainly Lombard artists, most of them unknown. Part of the sculpture is attributed to **Nicola Pisano**, and may well be his first work after arriving in Tuscany from Apulia. His are probably the offerings around the left-hand door: the *Deposition* (in the lunette), *Annunciation*, *Nativity* and *Adoration of the Magi*. Other panels display a compendium of subjects: a symbolic labyrinth, a Tree of Life (with Adam and Eve at the bottom and Christ at the top), dragons, bears, a bestiary of grotesques and the months of the year with their associated activities – December has a particularly graphic pig-sticking. The panels of the *Life of St Martin* (1204–10), between the doors, are the masterpiece of the architect, **Guidetto da Como**, responsible for the upper facade's three tiers of arcades. Walk along the flanks of the building to take in the ornate apse and transepts, as well as the extraordinary patterns of arches and marbles in the bricked-up side walls. One of the greatest of the exterior sculptures, a group depicting *St Martin on Horseback with the Beggar* by an unknown early fourteenth-century Lombard sculptor, has been removed from inside the church, and stands at the rear right against the west wall.

The interior

The Duomo's **interior** is best known for the sacristy's **Tomb of Ilaria del Carretto** by Jacopo della Quercia and for the numerous contributions by **Matteo Civitali** (1435–1501), who only gave up his job as a barber to become a sculptor in his mid-30s. He's represented here by a couple of water stoups near the entrance, the pulpits and several tombs and altars – notably the tomb of Pietro da Noceto, secretary to Pope Niccolò V

THE VOLTO SANTO

A cedarwood Crucifix with bulging eyes, the Duomo's **Volto Santo** ("Holy Face") is said to be a true effigy of Christ carved by Nicodemus, an eyewitness to the Crucifixion, but is probably a thirteenth-century copy of an eleventh-century copy of an eighth-century original. Legend has it that the *Volto Santo* came to Lucca of its own volition in 782, first journeying by boat from the Holy Land, and then brought by oxen guided by divine will – a story similar to the ecclesiastical sham of St James's bones at Santiago di Compostela in Spain. As at Santiago, the icon brought considerable power to the local church: it may be no coincidence that it appeared during the bishopric of Anselmo di Baggio, who was later elevated to the papacy. The effigy attracted pilgrims from all over Europe and inspired devotion in all who heard of it: King William Rufus of England used to swear by it ("Per sanctum vultum de Lucca!"), London merchants kept a copy of it and in France a certain St Vaudeluc was conjured into existence from a corruption of *saint vault de Lucques*, the French name for the icon.

(right wall of the south transept); the tomb of Domenico Bertini, to the left of the preceding tomb on the transept's adjoining wall; and the altar of San Regolo, on the chancel wall immediately right of the apse. Civitali's most famous work is the **Tempietto**, the gilt and marble octagon halfway down the church. Some fanatically intense acts of devotion are performed in front of it, directed at the **Volto Santo**, Lucca's most famous relic.

Other pictorial highlights of the cathedral include a *Madonna and Child* in the enclosed chapel to the left of the high altar in the north transept, painted in 1509 by **Fra' Bartolommeo**. In the main part of the Duomo, the first chapel on the left has a *Presentation of the Virgin* by **Alessandro Allori** (1598), and the third altar on the right a *Last Supper* (1592) by **Tintoretto**.

The sacristy

Mid-March to Oct Mon–Fri 9.30am–5.45pm, Sat 9.30am–6.45pm, Sun 9.30am–10.45pm; Nov to mid-March Mon–Fri 9.30am–4.45pm, Sat 9.30am–6.45pm, Sun noon to 6pm • €2, or €6 with Museo della Cattedrale and church of Santi Giovanni

Entered midway down the south nave, the sacristy houses one of the Duomo's most famous works, the **Tomb of Ilaria del Carretto** (1407–10). Considered the masterpiece of Sienese sculptor **Jacopo della Quercia**, it consists of a dais and the sculpted body of Ilaria, second wife of Paolo Guinigi, one of Lucca's medieval big shots. In a touching, almost sentimental gesture, the artist has carved the family dog at Ilaria's feet, a symbol of fidelity. Also within the sacristy is a superb *Madonna Enthroned with Saints* by Domenico Ghirlandaio.

3

Museo della Cattedrale

Piazza Antelminelli • Mid-March to Oct daily 10am–6pm; Nov to mid-March Mon–Fri 10am–2pm, Sat & Sun 10am–5pm • €4, or €6 with the cathedral sacristy and Santi Giovanni

Occupying a converted twelfth-century building across from the cathedral is the **Museo della Cattedrale**, whose four floors are home to a collection of ecclesiastical and other ephemera interspersed with the occasional artistic gem. Room I has a collection of illustrated miniatures, while Room II on the floor above houses a reliquary from Limoges decorated with stories from the life of St Thomas à Becket; an ivory diptych from Constantinople dated 506; and – one of the highlights – the *Croce dei Pisani*, an ornate crucifix probably commissioned by Paolo Guinigi after 1408. Room VII contains sculpture from the cathedral, most notably a large statue of St John the Evangelist by **Jacopo della Quercia**.

Santi Giovanni e Reparata

Piazza San Giovanni • Mid-March to Oct daily 10am–6pm; Nov to mid-March Mon–Fri 10am–2pm, Sat & Sun 10am–5pm • €2.50, or €6 with cathedral sacristy and Museo della Cattedrale

The large basilica of **Santi Giovanni e Reparata** was Lucca's cathedral until 715. Rebuilt many times, it preserves a lion-flanked carved Romanesque portal, saved during restructuring of the facade in 1589. Inside, excavations have uncovered a tangle of architectural remains, embracing a wide range of much earlier buildings on the site. Earliest fragments include first-century Roman villa **mosaics** (columns in the present nave are mostly Roman in origin), parts of the original fourth-century church pavement, an eighth-century baptistery with fine 1393 ceiling, and traces of a ninth-century Carolingian church and crypt of San Pantaleone.

San Frediano

Piazza San Frediano • Mon–Sat 8.30am–noon & 3–5.30pm, Sun 9–11.30am & 3–5.30pm, closed during services • Free

The church of **San Frediano** is Pisan-Romanesque, built between 1112 and 1147 on the site of a sixth-century basilica of San Vincenzo but orientated back to front (west-facing), probably because the old entrance would have been blocked by the new set of medieval city walls nearby. In place of the characteristic multiple loggias of Lucca's other great churches, San Frediano's **facade** is topped by a spectacular thirteenth-century mosaic of *The Ascension* with the apostles lined up below. The **interior** lives up to the facade's promise – a delicately lit, hall-like basilica, with subtly varied columns and capitals and some fine treasures.

The Fonte Lustrale

Immediately facing the door is one of the highlights of the interior, the **Fonte Lustrale**. This huge twelfth-century baptismal font was the work of three different craftsmen. The first, an unknown Lombard, carved the stories of Moses on the outer slabs of the basin, including a superb *Crossing of the Red Sea*, with the Egyptian soldiers depicted as medieval knights. The second, one Maestro Roberto, added the Good Shepherd and six prophets on the other two basin slabs, their enframing arches showing a clear Byzantine influence. To the third sculptor, an unknown Tuscan, is owed the decoration of the Apostles and the Months on the cup above the basin and the beautiful fantasy masks from which the water is disgorged. Set behind the font is an *Annunciation* attributed to **Matteo della Robbia**, festooned with trailing garlands of ceramic fruit.

The Cappella Fatinelli

A figure of St Bartholomew by **Andrea della Robbia** is to be found lower down to the left, close to the left-hand of the two chapels behind the font, the Cappella Fatinelli. This houses the "incorrupt" body of **St Zita** (died 1278), a thirteenth-century Lucchese maidservant who achieved sainthood from a fortuitous white lie: she used to give bread from her household to the poor and when challenged one day by her boss as to the contents of her apron, replied "only roses and flowers" – into which the bread was duly transformed. The saint is commemorated on April 27 by a **flower market** outside the church of San Frediano, where she reposes, and by the Lucchesi freeing her of her finery and bringing her out to touch.

The Cappella di Sant'Agostino

The best **frescoes** in the city adorn the **Cappella di Sant'Agostino**: Amico Aspertini's *The Arrival of the Volto Santo* and *The Baptism of St Augustine* on the left wall, and *The Miracle of St Frediano* on the right, the last depicting the River Serchio in flood being diverted by the saint's crib. Dating from the early sixteenth century, the murals are painted in a style that is much influenced by the realism of Flemish and German painters. The large fresco of the *Madonna and Child* on the right of the entrance door is also by Aspertini, while the nearby statue *Virgin Annunciate* is by **Matteo Civitali**.

The rest of the church

The top of the church holds the wonderful twelfth-century **Cosmati marble pavement** of the presbytery, while on the left are fragments of the original **tomb of San Frediano**, an Irish monk who is said to have brought Christianity to Lucca in the sixth century.

Moving back down the left (north) nave from the high altar, the first chapel, the **Cappella Trenta**, contains a superb carved altarpiece with niche statues of the Madonna, Child and Saints by Jacopo della Quercia; the worn pavement tombs of the chapel's donors, Lorenzo Trenat and his wife, are also by della Quercia.

Palazzo Pfanner

Via degli Asili 33 • April–Oct Mon, Tues & Thurs–Sun 10am–6pm • Garden or palace €3, joint ticket €4.50 • ⓦ palazzopfanner.it

Just west of San Frediano is the **Palazzo Pfanner**, whose gorgeous rear loggia, fountains

and gardens dotted with eighteenth-century statues, also visible from the city walls, provide a gracious foretaste of the villas and gardens outside of the city.

Piazza Anfiteatro

East of San Frediano is the remarkable **Piazza Anfiteatro**, aerial shots of which feature in just about all of Lucca's tourist literature. A ramshackle circuit of medieval buildings, it incorporates elements of the Roman amphitheatre that once stood here. Much of the original stone was carted off in the twelfth century to build the city's churches, while parts of the old structure were used as a medieval prison and salt warehouse, but arches and columns can still be seen embedded in some of the houses, particularly on the north side of the outer walls. Medieval slums used to occupy the centre of the arena, but these were cleared in 1830 on the orders of the Bourbon ruler, Marie Louise.

Torre Guinigi

Via Sant'Andrea • Daily: March 9am–5pm; April 9.30am–9pm; May & Oct 10am–6pm; June–Sept 9am–midnight; Nov–Feb 9.30am–5pm • €3.50

The battlemented **Torre Guinigi**, south of Piazza Anfiteatro, is the strangest sight in Lucca's cityscape. Attached to the fifteenth-century **Casa Guinigi**, town house of Lucca's leading family, it's surmounted by an ancient holm oak whose roots have grown into the room below. You can climb the 44-metre tower for a close-up of the tree and easily the best view over the city. The adjacent fortress, which has some wonderful austere medieval details, fronts a startling number of streets.

Museo Nazionale di Villa Guinigi

Via della Quarquonia • Tues–Sat 8.30am–7.30pm, Sun 8.30am–1.30pm • €4 • Combined ticket with Palazzo Mansi €6.50 • W luccamuseinazionali.it

Due east of the Torre is the much-restored Villa Guinigi, built to supplement the family's medieval town house. It's now home to Lucca's major museum, the **Museo Nazionale di Villa Guinigi**, an extremely varied collection of painting, sculpture, furniture and applied arts. The lower floor is mainly sculpture and archeological finds, with numerous Romanesque pieces and works by **Jacopo della Quercia** and **Matteo Civitali**. Upstairs, the gallery moves on to paintings, with lots of big sixteenth-century canvases, and more impressive works by early Lucchese and Sienese masters, as well as fine Renaissance offerings from artists such as **Fra' Bartolommeo.**

Orto Botanico

Via del Fosso • Daily: Mid-March to April & mid-Sept to Nov 10am–5pm; May–June 10am–6pm; July to mid-Sept 10am–7pm; rest of the year open by reservation • €3 • ☎ 0583 583 086, ✉ ortobotanico@lunet.it

The most attractive part of Lucca's eastern quarter is the **Orto Botanico** at the southern end of Via del Fosso, an extensive patch of green laid out in 1820 that neatly complements the ramparts. The rarer exhibits include medicinal plants, a sequoia, gingko tree, camphor tree and a cedar of Lebanon planted at the garden's opening.

ARRIVAL AND DEPARTURE   LUCCA

By train The train station is on Piazza Ricasoli, a short way outside the walls to the south.

Destinations Aulla (10 daily; 2hr); Bagni di Lucca (10 daily; 30min); Barga (10 daily; 40min); Castelnuovo di Garfagnana (10 daily; 1hr); Florence (hourly; 1–2hr); Montecatini (hourly; 25min); Pisa (hourly; 30min); Pisa airport (4 daily; 45min); Pistoia (hourly; 40min); Prato (hourly; 1hr); Viareggio (hourly; 20min).

By bus The bus station is just inside the western stretch of the walls, in Piazzale Giuseppe Verdi. CLAP (☎ 0583 5411, W clapspa.it & W www.vaibus.com) and Lazzi (☎ 0583 587 897, W www.lazzi.it) run an extensive network all

AROUND LUCCA'S WALLS

Climbing up at any of Lucca's bastions, some of which are signposted, you can follow the 4km circuit of the **city walls**, either by bike or on foot. The mid-afternoon shutdown is perhaps the best time to walk their broad promenade, which is lined with plane, lime, ilex and chestnut trees. Bikes can be rented from a cluster of outlets around the tourist office in Piazza Santa Maria.

Construction of the walls started around 1500, prompted by the need to replace medieval ramparts rendered inadequate by advances in weapon technology. By 1650 the work was completed, with eleven bastions to fortify walls that were 30m wide at the base, 12m high and surrounded by moats 35m across. There were originally just three gates. Perhaps the best feature, from the present-day perspective, was the destruction of all trees and buildings within a couple of hundred metres of the walls, creating a green belt of lawns that has shielded the old town from the ugliness that's sprouted on the outside.

Ironically, having produced a perfect set of walls, Lucca was never called on to defend them. The only siege was against the floodwaters of the River Serchio in 1812, when the gates were sealed against the deluge that had flooded the countryside. Napoleon's sister and city governor, Elisa Baciocchi, one of the last people allowed in, had to be winched over the ramparts by crane. Marie Louise of Bourbon, her successor, had the walls transformed to their present garden aspect, arranging them, as the local tourist handout puts it, "with unparalleled good taste and moderation".

3

around the region.

Destinations Bagni di Lucca, via Borgo a Mozzano (8 daily; 55min); Barga (11 daily; 1hr 15min); Castelnuovo di Garfagnana (8 daily; 1hr 30min); Florence (every hour; 1hr 15min); La Spezia (2 daily; 2hr 50min); Marina di Carrara (8 daily; 1hr 40min); Massa (5 daily; 1hr 50min); Pisa (hourly; 50min); Torre del Lago (6 daily; 30min); Viareggio (at least hourly; 45min).

INFORMATION

Provincial Tourist Office Piazza Santa Maria 35 (April–Oct daily 9am–7pm; Nov–March Mon–Sat 9am–12.30pm & 3–6.30pm; ☎ 0583 919 931, ⓦ luccaturismo.it).

City Tourist Office Piazzale Verdi (Daily: April–Sept 9am–7pm; Nov–March 9am–5pm; ☎ 0583 583 150, ⓦ luccaitinera.it).

GETTING AROUND

Bike rental Cicli Bizzarri, Piazza Santa Maria 32 ☎ 0583 496 682, ⓦ ciclibizzarri.net; €12.50/day) or Biciclette Poli (Piazza Santa Maria 42 ☎ 0583 493 787, ⓦ biciclettepoli.

com; €15/day).

Taxis ☎ 0583 333 434 or ☎ 0583 955 200.

ACCOMMODATION

Though Lucca isn't a major stop on the tourist trail, its limited **accommodation** always seems in demand: it's wise to book ahead at any time of year. There are very few hotels within the city walls so you might consider the more central private **rooms** or **B&Bs**, or the **hostel**.

HOTELS

★ **Alla Corte Degli Angeli** Via degli Angeli 23 ☎ 0583 469 204, ⓦ allacortedegliangeli.com. Bright, airy, friendly and tasteful, this boutique hotel offers ten romantic rooms with exposed wood beams and period furniture and fittings. Amenities include a/c, wi-fi and even a sound station for your iPod. Excellent breakfast included. **€200**

A Palazzo Busdraghi Via Fillungo 170 ☎ 0583 950 856, ⓦ apalazzobusdraghi.it. With only seven rooms, this small boutique hotel has charm – furnishings are a bit shabby-chic – as well as amenities such as a/c and wi-fi. One room boasts a wardrobe once owned by Puccini himself. Breakfast included. **€200**

Diana Via del Molinetto 11 ☎ 0583 492 202, ⓦ albergodiana.com. This small hotel is divided into the original building, a little dated and with fewer amenities, and the newer property just 40m away, where rooms costs about 25 percent more. Some rooms have a/c; wi-fi in the lobby costs €4.50/hour. Parking nearby at €5 per day. No breakfast. **€65**

★ **La Romea** Vicolo delle Ventaglie 2 ☎ 0583 464 175, ⓦ laromea.com. For a warm welcome choose this tiny hotel in a fourteenth-century building, run by a young couple who see personally to the sumptuous breakfast (included in the rates). The four varied rooms and en suite have a/c and internet. **€135**

3

Noblesse Via Sant'Anastasio 23 ☎0583 440 275, ⓦhotelnoblesse.it. Eight rooms and five suites over three floors in a plushly converted eighteenth-century *palazzo*, with period antiques, Persian rugs and a warm, intimate atmosphere. Buffet breakfast included, and there's a restaurant on site. Parking €30/day. Steep discounts available booking online. €400

★ **Piccolo Hotel Puccini** Via di Poggio 9 ☎0583 55 421, ⓦhotelpuccini.com. This handsome little hotel has been winning repeat clients for years. Rooms are simple, trim and well-appointed, with no a/c but very effective ceiling fans. Private parking for an extra €15; breakfast is €3.50. €95

Universo Piazza del Giglio 1 ☎0583 954 854, ⓦuniversolucca.com. Lucca's grand old hotel evokes the glory of another era, with sixty somewhat faded but still genteel rooms. The staff try very hard to please, and each room has a/c and wi-fi; ask for one with a view of the piazza. Airport transfer service available. Buffet breakfast included. €200

RESIDENZE

Casa Alba di Marta Via Fillungo 142 ☎0583 495 361, ⓦcasa-alba.com. Five clean, pleasant rooms (doubles and singles) with private bathroom in a third-floor apartment, most on the quiet inner courtyard. Rooms are simple and clean and have a/c and wi-fi. There's self-service coffee and a fridge for guests' use. Home-made continental breakfast included. €85

La Torre Via del Carmine 11 ☎0583 957 044, ⓦroomslatorre.com. Five homely, individually decorated doubles with or without bathroom; the same family have self-catering apartments, too. Large, farm-fresh breakfast included, and free wi-fi. Courtesy parking and free pick-up. €80

San Frediano Via degli Angeli ☎0583 469 630, ⓦsanfrediano.com. The six rooms here, including singles, doubles and triples with a choice of private and shared bathrooms, have wi-fi, some a/c, others ceiling fans, and some have original wood-beam ceilings and parquet floors, but can get noisy. Parking nearby. Continental breakfast included. €100

HOSTEL

Ostello San Frediano Via della Cavallerizza 12 ☎0583 469 957, ⓦostellolucca.it. This HI hostel occupies a handsome old monastery with a garden. Cleanliness is patchy, it can be noisy and service can be indifferent, but it's inexpensive. Wi-fi in the lobby, breakfast €3, lunch or dinner €11. Midnight curfew. Dorm beds from €19, doubles €60

EATING AND DRINKING

As a gastronomic centre, Lucca has some high-quality **restaurants**. Local specialities include *zuppa di farro*, a thick soup of an ancient variety of spelt, which is grown in the Garfagnana; roast mountain goat (*capretto*) and puddings based on chestnut flour, such as *castagnaccio*. **Bars** and **cafés** are plentiful.

RESTAURANTS

★ **Buca di Sant'Antonio** Via della Cervia 3 ☎0583 55 881, ⓦbucadisantantonio.it. Lucca's finest restaurant has been around for over two hundred years and still retains its old-world charm. Excellent service, and a menu featuring *zuppa di farro*, top-quality meat (such as rabbit in an olive sauce) or fish (try the cubed swordfish), delicious house pasta and desserts. From €40 a head, depending on wine. Booking essential. Tues–Sat 12.30–3pm & 7.30–11pm, Sun 12.30–3pm.

★ **Da Leo** Via Tegrimi 1 ☎0583 492 236, ⓦtrattoriadaleo.it. This fun-loving, family-run, old-fashioned trattoria is very popular. Try the local *garmugia*, a hearty soup of asparagus, artichokes, peas, beans and sausage, just €6; or stewed guinea fowl with balsamic vinegar at €9.50. Terrace seating. Mon–Sat 12.30–3pm & 7.30–11pm, Sun 12.30–3pm.

★ **Gli Orti di Via Elisa** Via Elisa 17 ☎0583 491 241, ⓦristorantegliorti.it. This popular and classy bistro-style pizzeria/trattoria has wonderful risottos, kid-meat kebabs a speciality, and some vegetarian dishes, such as the ubiquitous *zuppa di farro* with pumpkin. About €30 per person. Mon–Sat 12.30–2.30pm & 7.30–10.30pm; closed Wed eve.

Locanda Di Bacco Via San Giorgio 36 ☎0583 493 136. An excellent restaurant with a lovely wood-panelled interior and quality cuisine. Specialities include salt cod with pureed chickpeas, but don't overlook the porcini mushroom salad; there's a vegan menu, too. About €45 per person, depending on wine. Terrace seating available. Mon, Tues & Thurs–Sun 12.30–3pm & 7.30–11pm.

Puccini Corte San Lorenzo 1 ☎0583 316 676, ⓦristorantepuccini.it. A top-of-the-line restaurant with a gracious interior – dedicated, of course, to mementoes of the maestro and his music – elegant service and an imaginative menu, mainly featuring fresh fish and seafood. Shrimp-stuffed squid au gratin goes for €13, most main courses for about €7. Mon & Thurs–Sun 12.30–2.30pm & 7.30–10pm, Wed 7.30–10pm.

CAFÉS AND BARS

★ **Antico Caffè di Simo** Via Fillungo 58 ☎0583 496 234. Lucca's famous century-old café has its original Art Nouveau-style furnishings and delicious cakes and pastries, as well as a few simple hot dishes for €6–8. Tues–Sun 7am–9pm.

Caffè del Mercato Piazza San Michele 17 ☎0583 494 127, ⊛ilbarino.it. The most alluring of the bars around the main piazza, particularly as the church keeps it nice and shady throughout lunch. Lots of nice plates of cold cuts, hot dishes and, of course, sweets and coffees. Mon–Sat 8am–10pm.

★ **Gelateria Veneta** Via Vittorio Veneto 74 ☎0583 467 037, ⊛gelateriaveneta.net. This *gelateria* has been serving some of Lucca's best ice cream since 1927 and is open conveniently late, till 11pm. Chocolates, fruit *gelati* and sorbets, plus frozen yoghurt, all from €2 a serving. Daily 10am–1am; closed Nov–Feb.

Girovita Piazza Antelminelli 2 ☎0583 469 412. With tables on the quiet piazza opposite the cathedral, this trendy hangout is the place to come for a lengthy afternoon coffee or an *aperitivo*, and then into the night. Happy hour buffet Thurs–Sun 7–11pm. Tues–Fri noon–midnight; Sat & Sun noon–1am.

Vineria I Santi Via dell'Anfiteatro 29a ☎0583 496 124, ⊛vineriaisanti.it. With nice tables on a small piazza, this wine bar is a great place to sample the Tuscan reds on the extensive wine list. It also serves inventive, well-prepared dishes, such as goose-liver paté with marmalade, various *carpaccios* and salads; a full meal will run to about €45/person, wine included. Mon, Tues & Thurs–Sun 1–4pm & 8pm–midnight.

SHOPPING

Caniparoli Via San Paolino 96 ☎0583 53 456. Don't miss this wonderful chocolate shop, chock full of chocolate slabs sold by weight, plus cakes and cookies, including mouthwatering *bruti ma buoni*, famously chewy meringue-hazelnut creations. Tues–Sat 8.20am–12.20pm & 3.40–7.40pm.

Forno Amedeo Giusti Via Santa Lucia 18–20 ☎0583 496 285. Look for the Art Nouveau entrance to find sixty types of bread, rolls or delicious *focaccia* (freshly baked every two hours). Mon–Fri 7am–1pm & 4.30–7.45pm, Sat & Sun 7am–1pm; closed Wed in winter.

La Cacioteca Via Fillungo 242 ☎0583 496 346. Head to this traditional deli for a wide variety of cheeses – cow, sheep, goat, buffalo – from all around the region, with a focus on *caciotte* cheese. Mon–Sat 7.30am–1.30pm & 3.30–8pm.

Pasticceria Buccellato Taddeucci Piazza San Michele 34 ☎0583 494 933, ⊛www.taddeucci.com. Justly renowned for its signature ring-shaped cakes (the aniseed and raisin *buccellato* is the traditional favourite), and its original 1881 wood-panelled and mosaic-tiled interior. Look for the red and white rings above the entrance. Mon–Wed & Fri–Sun 8am–1pm & 3–8pm.

DIRECTORY

Banks and exchange Change facilities at the train station (daily 6am–9pm) plus many banks and numerous ATMs throughout the town.

Hospital Campo di Marte, Via dell'Ospedale ☎0583 9701.

Market A vast antiques market takes place on the third weekend of the month in and around Piazza San Martino.

Police Questura, Viale Cavour 38 ☎0583 4551.

Post office Via Vallisneri 2 (Mon–Fri 8.15am–7pm, Sat 8.30am–12.30pm).

East of Lucca

As with the hinterlands of Florence, Lucca's surroundings are dotted with outstanding **villas**, built by wealthy merchants as retreats from the rigours of city life, or simply as an indulgence on the part of aristocratic landowners. Some of these started life as simple country houses, others had grandiose ambitions from the word go; most have been repeatedly altered since their construction. Many involved the leading architects of their day, either in the construction of the villas themselves, or in the design of the magnificent **gardens** that accompanied them. Three of the villas – **Villa Reale**, **Villa Mansi** and **Villa Torrigiani** (also known as the Villa di Camigliano) – lie within a ten-kilometre radius of Lucca to the northeast; they can all be reached in an hour or so by bike. Slightly further afield is the **Villa Garzoni** at Collodi, which competes for attention with its allied **Parco di Pinocchio**, which you'll see advertised on roadside hoardings all over Tuscany.

Villa Reale

Guided tours March–Nov Tues–Sun hourly 10am–1pm & 2–6pm; Dec–Feb by appointment only • €7 • ☎0583 30 108, ⊛parcovillareale .it • Access via the SS445 from Lucca to Barga, turning off to Marlia after 8km; a less direct but better signed route is the SS435 for Montecatini Terme, taking a left turn after 7km

---

THE FRENCH CONNECTION

Villa Reale's life as a country house started with the destruction of a fortress on this site in the fourteenth century, its first gardens being laid out a century later. The present Neoclassical look dates from 1806, when Napoleon's sister, **Elisa Baciocchi**, compelled the Orsetti family to sell up. Having ousted the owners, she and her personal architect, Morel, set about a radical remoulding of the villa and garden, completely refurbishing the interior and planning an English park complete with huge monumental lake. Some of the garden's most important earlier fixtures were respected, though Napoleon's downfall and Elisa's subsequent eviction undoubtedly saved other older components from destruction. Sadly, the vigour of court life at the Villa Reale also vanished with Elisa. The violinist **Paganini** had been employed as resident composer; he was later known to claim his playing had caused his patroness to swoon with ecstasy.

By general consent, the **Villa Reale** at Marlia is the most beautiful of the villas close to Lucca. Only the **garden** is open to the public, and only on guided tours. Its most striking aspect is the sweeping lawn that runs from the house down to the lake, a feature of the original layout that was enlarged under the Baciocchi regime. To its left, set deep in the woods, is the **Grotto of Pan**, an elaborate two-storey hideaway with mosaic floor, much trailing greenery and a ceiling of stone plants and flowers. To one side of the lawn, an avenue of ilex trees leads to the heart of the original garden, centred on a trio of **garden rooms**, which become progressively more confined. The first has a collection of lemon trees and a pool on which swans drift; the second features a high-spouting **fountain**; the third is a tiny and intimate "green theatre", its orchestra pit and seats all made of box and yew hedges, and edged with a variety of exotic flora.

Villa Mansi

May–Oct Tues–Sun 9.30am–noon & 3.30–8pm; Nov–April Tues–Sun 10am–12.30pm & 2.30–5pm • €6.50 • ☎ 0583 920 234

Perhaps the least interesting of the villa quartet is the **Villa Mansi**, 5km east of Marlia at Segromigno. Originally a plain sixteenth-century country house, it was enlarged in 1635 by Muzio Oddi and expanded many times in subsequent centuries. The harmonious late Renaissance facade remains, much adorned with statuary and flanked by two pavilions joining the three-arched portico, but the **garden** has suffered more brutal treatment. The few early sections that remain intact are the best: the French-inspired eastern part, with its star-shaped avenues and irregular arrangement of fountains and basins; and the western part, laid out between 1725 and 1732 by the Sicilian architect **Filippo Juvarra** – the man who refashioned Turin. At the beginning of the nineteenth century much of Juvarra's geometric work was replaced by haphazard borrowings from English garden design. Innovations by the present owners have continued the garden's dubious development.

Villa Torrigiani

Daily: March–May & Oct to first week of Nov 10am–1pm & 3–5pm • June, July & Sept 10am–1pm & 3–6.30pm • Garden €7, garden and villa €10 • ☎ 0583 928 041, ⓦ villeepalazzilucchesi.it • From Lucca, take the SS435 for Montecatini Terme, fork left at Borgonuovo (11km), and follow signs from Camigliano

At **Camigliano**, 2km from the Villa Mansi, the **Villa Torrigiani** (or Villa di Camigliano) was built for the Buonvisi family in the sixteenth century, and transformed almost entirely by Alfonso Torrigiani in the eighteenth century to conform with the prevailing taste for villas and gardens in the English manner. A magnificent avenue of cypresses leads to the villa's stately Baroque facade, adorned with a similar surfeit of statuary to the Villa Mansi's; Oddi was probably the architect here, too. The **interior** has been slightly diminished by a spate of burglaries, but there's still a wealth of furniture and some odd points of passing interest. The extravagantly decorated central hall and the elliptical staircase are outstanding, both products of the eighteenth-century modifications.

The gardens

Villa Torrigiani's **gardens**, and larger park alongside, are complex and beautiful affairs, noted above all for their **giochi d'acqua** (water games). Intended to drench unsuspecting visitors with hidden sprays and fountains activated by the owner, or by the pressure of footsteps on levered flagstones, these tricks were especially popular with Mannerist gardeners, but in fact were first used in Roman times.

The devices here, initiated by the fun-loving Marquis Niccolò Santini – Lucca's ambassador to the court of Louis XIV – are among the finest examples still functioning. They're all contained in the sunken **Garden of Flora** to the east of the villa – all that has survived the garden's eighteenth-century Anglicization. The Marquis would first herd his guests into the garden from an upper terrace, whereupon they would find their path blocked by a wall of spray. Attempting to retreat back down the beautiful pebble-mosaic path, they would discover that this too was now awash with water. Seeking sanctuary on the roof of the Temple of Flora, a small cupola-topped grotto, they would blunder into the biggest soaking of all, as water gushed from the domed roof, from the four statues set in the walls (representing the four winds) and, as if this weren't enough, shot up from the floor as well.

In 1985, frosts damaged some of the underground piping, but the gardeners occasionally provide impromptu demonstrations of the temple's aquatic surprises.

Collodi

When, in 1881, Carlo Lorenzini published the first instalment of the children's book that was to make him famous, he used the penname Carlo Collodi, in honour of his mother's birthplace, a small town 15km east of Lucca. And so, whereas other Tuscan towns are devoted to a patron saint, **COLLODI** has dedicated itself to a living puppet with an erectile nose – **Pinocchio**. To English-speakers reared on the Disney version, it's difficult to appreciate the reverence accorded Pinocchio in his homeland, where the tale's moral simplicity and exemplary Tuscan prose ensures it a massive following. It's indicative of *Pinocchio*'s standing that an Italian national newspaper poll once shortlisted the book as a contender for the title of "Greatest Novel of All Time", and that actor-director Roberto Benigni lavished so much attention on his 2002 film version that it ended up being the most expensive film ever made in Italy.

Villa Garzoni

Daily: March–Oct 9am–sunset; Nov–Feb Sun & public holidays 10am–sunset • €13, or combined ticket with Parco di Pinocchio €20

The vast **Villa Garzoni** evolved from a castle that stood here in the days before Lucca surrendered this region to Florence. The house (closed to visitors) took on its present form in the second half of the seventeenth century, but it was towards the end of the following century that it acquired the magnificent formal **garden** that makes this one of Italy's finest villas.

Access is usually through a gate on the main road, but the garden was designed to be entered through the wood adjoining the villa, so that the visitor would emerge from the wilderness into this precisely orchestrated landscape. Maximizing the theatrical possibilities of the steep slope, it deploys the full resources of the Baroque garden: circular fountains, topiary animals, patterns of flowers and coloured stones, a water staircase, a zigzagging cascade of steps and terraces, and terracotta figures in every corner. There's also a **butterfly house**, home to a huge variety of tropical species, and the grounds provide a venue for concerts and other cultural events in summer. A café serves local fare.

Parco di Pinocchio

Daily March–Oct 8.30am–sunset • €11, combined ticket with Villa Garzoni €20 • 🌐 pinocchio.it

Created in the 1950s, the **Parco di Pinocchio** honours the famous book with some two dozen sculptural works by Italian artists, most by Pietro Consaga, but also with pieces by Emilio Greco and Venturino Venturi. All the figures and imaginative structures are laid out to evoke Pinocchio's adventures, set on a winding pathway amidst dense greenery. The monsters and mazes are fun without any background knowledge, but you'll need to have read the book in order to get the most from the park – and to field questions should you be visiting with infatuated children.

Other attractions include a puppetry workshop, puppet shows and other performances. Pinocchio's importance to the nation can be gauged from the fact that Michelucci – architect of Florence's train station and several prestigious churches – was commissioned to design the restaurant and museum near the park entrance.

3 The Riviera della Versilia

The northern coast of Tuscany is known, somewhat hyperbolically, as the **Riviera della Versilia**. The beach resorts that run unbroken around **Viareggio** offer Italian beach culture in all its glory. Much of the sand is leased to the virtually indistinguishable *stabilimenti*, who in turn charge admission to their strips and rent out chairs and umbrellas; there are free public beaches (*spiaggia pubblica*), however, at regular intervals. For a swim and some sun in cheerfully crowded conditions, this coast is not as bad as it's usually painted: there are beach cafés and restaurants, the water may be cleaner elsewhere but it's not filthy, and the sand is immaculately groomed. Bus and train links to all points are excellent, especially in the summer, when you can move up and down the coast with more ease than anywhere else in Tuscany. Just 3km south of Viareggio, **Torre del Lago** is a major point of pilgrimage for lovers of Puccini's creations.

Viareggio

The best town on the coast, **VIAREGGIO** is also one of Tuscany's biggest seaside resorts, graced with an air of elegance lent mainly by the long avenue of palms that runs the length of its seafront promenade. A modest collection of Art Nouveau-style frontages – designed by the father of Italian Art Nouveau, Galileo Chini – adds to the sense of refinement, though for the most part the buildings are old-style seaside hotels. In the early part of last century, the town's reputation for exclusivity was well deserved; these days all that's left is the high prices. The excellent **beaches** are all private, charging €20 and upwards for admission – except for the free stretch between Viareggio and Torre del Lago – and in summer the few hotels that aren't full usually hold out for *pensione completa*. You may prefer to join the majority and cram into the train for a day-trip: this is what many Florentines do – in summer, special early-morning trains from the city are packed with raucous *ragazzi*.

VIAREGGIO CARNEVALE

The only time **Viareggio** hits national headlines is during its **Carnevale** (Feb/March), one of the liveliest in Italy. For four weeks, there's a Sunday parade of colossal floats, or *carri*, bearing lavishly designed papier-mâché models of politicians and celebrities. The "Cittadella del Carnevale" to the north of Viareggio has been designed as a home for the vast hangars in which the artists construct their imaginative creations, often politically or socially satirical, and also boasts a theatre and multimedia museum, which you can visit all year round; contact the Fondazione Carnevale, Piazza Mazzini 22 (☎ 0584 580 755, 🌐 viareggio.ilcarnevale.com) for further details.

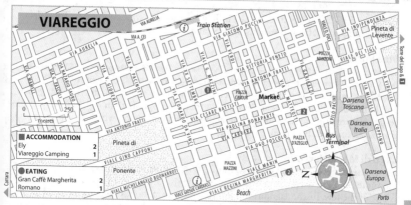

3

Viareggio's main focus is its promenade, the **Passeggiata Margherita** along Viale Regina Margherita, the broad thoroughfare that runs along the seafront for 3km. Most of the Art Nouveau fronts are crowded together around the town's best-known spot, the *Gran Caffè Margherita*, close to the start of the passeggiata near the marina. Across the marina and distinct from the town, the **Viale dei Tigli** is a beautiful avenue of lime trees that stretches 6km south, giving access to various beaches and most of the town's campsites.

ARRIVAL AND INFORMATION

By train Viareggio's train station is ten-minutes' walk back from the seafront.

Destinations Carrara (hourly; 25min); Florence (hourly; 1hr 40min); Lucca (hourly; 20min); Pisa (hourly; 20min); Torre del Lago (hourly; 5min).

By bus Buses stop near the centre at Piazza d'Azeglio and Piazza Mazzini. Vaibus (☎0584 30 996, ⓦwww.vaibus .com) have an office in Piazza d'Azeglio for tickets and

information.

Destinations Florence (hourly; 1hr 30min); Marina di Massa (hourly; 50min); Torre del Lago (every 30min; 15min).

Tourist office Viale Carducci 10 (Mon–Sat 9am–2pm & 3–7pm, Sun 9am–2pm, plus 3–7.30pm in July & Aug; ☎0584 962 233, ⓦaptversilia.it).

ACCOMMODATION AND EATING

Gran Caffè Margherita Viale Margherita 30 ☎0584 581 143, ⓦristorantemargherita.info.This historic spot is an exotic Italian Art Nouveau temple to seaside living, dating from 1928. The menu focuses on fish, but also has regional vegetable and meat dishes. A full meal for two can run to €80, but it's also good just for a coffee. Touristy but worth enduring the off-hand service for the promenade spectacle. Daily 8am–1am.

Romano Via Mazzini 120 ☎0584 31 382, ⓦromanoristorante.it. For sublime fish and seafood, make for this elegant Michelin-starred spot. From the incredibly refined antipasti to amazing seafood pastas and main

courses, everything is perfect, including the chic setting, and there are some 1400 wines to choose from. About €80 per person, depending on wine. Tues–Sat 1–4pm & 8–11pm; closed Jan, & Tues lunch in July & Aug.

Viareggio Camping Via Comparini 1 ☎0584 391 012, ⓦcampingviareggio.it. Just 1.5km from the town centre, and surrounded by pine forest, this makes a convenient choice. There's a café and mini-market on site, as well as a pool (extra charge), wi-fi, and four-person bungalows. Open April–Sept. Adult campers €10, plus €13 per pitch, bungalows from €100

Torre del Lago

The journey south from Viareggio along Viale dei Tigli is worth it just for the lime trees; whether you press on to the hamlet of **TORRE DEL LAGO** depends on how much you value Puccini, who spent the later part of his life in a villa on the edge of **Lago di Massaciuccoli**. The master's works are performed during the **Festival Pucciniano**

(☎0584 359 322, ⓦpuccinifestival.it) in July and August, with concerts in Torre del Lago's outdoor theatre and various other venues.

Villa Puccini

Guided tours every 40min: Jan, Nov & Dec 10am–12.40pm & 2.30–5.10pm; Feb & March 10am–12.40pm & 2.30–5.50pm; April–Oct Tues–Sun 10am–12.40pm & 3–6.20pm; last entrance 40min before closing • €7 • ☎0584 341 445, ⓦgiacomopuccini.it

It's easy to miss the **Villa Puccini**, set back from the shore and surrounded by bars, trees and high iron railings. Visits are in guided groups of no more than eighteen people; the rooms feature original furnishings, mementos and the piano on which Puccini composed many of his operas.

Lago di Massaciuccoli

Reservations for boat trips ☎0584 342 069 • Price depends on group size • Optional meal served on board at extra cost

No more than 2m deep, yet covering an area the size of Pisa, the **Lago di Massaciuccoli** is one of the few Tuscan lagoons not lost to land reclamation. Once it supported virtually all Italy's species of aquatic bird, but many have been wiped out by pollution and hunters; Puccini himself came here to practise "my second favourite instrument, my rifle".

The lake now forms part of the **Parco Regionale di Migliarino-San Rossore** (ⓦparks.it), and is a protected bird sanctuary; as a result there are some 80 breeding and another 65 occasional species on the lake, which you can observe on hour-long **boat trips** that circuit from Piazzale Belvedere. International regattas are also held here through the summer.

ARRIVAL AND DEPARTURE   TORRE DEL LAGO

By train and bus Half-hourly buses #2 and #4 from Viareggio's Piazza d'Azeglio drop off in the centre of Torre del Lago. Trains leave hourly for Viareggio (5min) from Torre del Lago's train station on Via Dante Alighieri, in the south of town about 1km west of the lake.

ACCOMMODATION AND EATING

Bosco Verde Camping Viale Kennedy 5 ☎0584 359 343, ⓦboscoverde.com. Set in pinewood parklands, this extensive campground is an easy stroll from the beach. As well as a café and restaurant, there's also a pool, wi-fi and double rooms. Open April–Sept. Adult campers €9.50, plus pitches €9.50, doubles €40

Butterfly Belvedere Puccini 24 ☎0584 341 024, ⓦalbergobutterfly.it. This clean, unpretentious hotel is right on the lake, with a porch and a terrace facing the water. The simple rooms, some with balconies with panoramic views, have a/c. There's free parking, and wi-fi at extra charge. Breakfast €10 per person, and a popular restaurant on site. €115

Turandot Viale Kennedy 27 ☎0584 341 025, ⓦhotelturandot.com. Fine little hotel, located amidst greenery and just steps from the sea and a nice beach. The simple rooms have a/c and are rather handsomely decorated; the sun roof-terrace is a plus. Breakfast is included, and there's a good restaurant/bar. €130

The Alpi Apuane

Tuscany's Versilia coast is dominated by the mountains of the **Alpi Apuane**, a forty-kilometre spread of genuinely Alpine spectacle. Now a protected Parco Regionale, they are crisscrossed by well-marked footpaths and offer huge rewards for the walker and naturalist. Aside from busy, modern Massa, the main town here is **Carrara**, known above all else as the marble capital of Italy, characterized by huge blocks of stone littering the roadsides, fine white dust everywhere and mine-scarred rockfaces.

Thanks to their position and height, the Alpi Apuane comprise a perfect combination of different ecological habitats, from tundra through Alpine meadow to Mediterranean grassland. At this meeting point of Alpine and Mediterranean vegetation zones, the ecosystems here constitute one of the finest floral zones in the country: two-thirds of Italy's known flower species grow here, and in late spring the upland meadows are

WALKS FROM VAGLI DI SOTTO

VAGLI DI SOTTO (Ⓦingarfagnana.it) is the starting point for a couple of excellent **walks** onto the highest ridges of the Alpi Apuane, for which the Multigraphic map is invaluable. The first path follows the road southwest up the Tambura valley, east to CAI #144, which takes you to the top of **Monte Sumbra** (1764m), and then in a wide circle via the Tassetora valley back to Vagli di Sotto – a fantastic and varied day's walk (16km).

The second path, CAI #177, climbs to the Passo della Focolaccia (1650m), a meeting point of several other trails. The pass offers excellent views to the Apuane's highest point, **Monte Pisanino** (1947m), just to the north, and gives access to a superb ridge (trail #179) that takes you to the top of **Monte Grondilice** (1805m). From the summit you can carry on to Carrara, or north (on the GT) to the *Rifugio Serenaia*, the starting point for many Alpi Apuane trails.

Rifugio Serenaia Ⓣ349 142 4641, Ⓦrifugialpiapuane.it. Some 4km southwest of Minucciano, this refuge is the starting point for many Alpi Apuane trails, and is accessible by road from the Serchio valley to the north, via Piazza al Serchio and Gramolazzo. There are dorms, four-person private rooms and camping pitches. Open daily 18 June–18 Sept; weekends only May & Oct. Adult campers €3.50, pitches €5, dorm bed with breakfast €25

3

carpeted with wildflowers. In the autumn, there's also a wide variety of fungi, but the most noticeable plantlife are the immense **forests** of chestnut and beech which cover virtually all the lower slopes. These shelter some of the mountains' three hundred species of **birds**, including the golden eagle, kestrels, buzzards and sparrowhawks. The reserves here abound in often spectacular **mammals**, too, such as wolves and red deer, and you may see marmots – rare in the Apennines – on the higher, sunnier slopes.

EXPLORING THE APUANE

If you want to do more than admire the jagged knife-edge ridge of the mountains from afar, you can **walk** the numerous marked trails starting from roadheads deep in the mountains; the biggest concentration of these tracks is amongst the peaks centred on **Pania della Croce** (1859m) and **Monte Forato** (1223m).

Information The park visitor centre for the Parco Regionale is at Piazza delle Erbe 1, Castelnuovo Garfagnana (daily June–Sept 9.30am–1pm & 3–7pm; April & May 9.30am–1pm & 3.30–6.30pm; Oct–Mar 9.30am–1pm & 3.30–5.30pm; Ⓣ0583 644 242, Ⓦparcapuane.toscana.it). During the summer, the office organizes walks with professional guides, starting at €110 for about three hours; book in advance.

Maps The detailed Multigraphic 1:25,000 map (available locally) marks all the main walking trails and refuges.

Carrara

You can't get away from marble in **CARRARA**, a town whose very name is said to derive from *kar*, the Indo-European word for stone. Once you leave behind the sprawling factories around the station, however, the town itself is a surprisingly attractive place. Set in the hills above the factories, central Carrara has a rural feel, with peeling pastel stucco on its houses, elegant sidestreets lined with rows of green shutters, and a couple of piazzas and a **Duomo** that would do credit to any Tuscan town. By contrast, the town's "resort", **Marina di Carrara**, is grim – more a container port than a beach. If you want the sea, it's best to drive inland to Massa, and then drop down to the coast there.

Brief history

Carrara feels like a self-sufficient town, and its people have always had a reputation as a breed apart – something they preserved even under the long-term domination of the **Malaspina** nobles, the local big shots during the Middle Ages. Before their rule, the town had developed as a trading centre poised between Tuscany, the mountains and the Ligurian coast. **Roman** exploitation of marble made trade with the nearby colony of

Luni, over the Ligurian border, particularly brisk; something of its scale can be seen in the **ruins** of the colony excavated there.

Piazza Alberica

Carrara's **old town** centres on **Piazza Alberica**, a gracious square whose beauty owes much to the hills which come down on two sides, and to the elegant colours and tone more often associated with Liguria than Tuscany. Stray blocks of marble sit at its centre, a legacy of the biennial Scolpire all'Aperto, a festival in which sculptors from around the world are invited to the town, given a block of marble, and left to work in the middle of the square. If you're here between late July and early October, you may get to watch them chipping away. The piazza's fountain, known locally as **Il Gigante** (The Giant), is an incomplete work by the lacklustre Florentine Bandinelli. Also in the square is the house where **Michelangelo** put up while checking out his marble supplies; nearby in Via Santa Maria are **Petrarch**'s digs, Casa Repetti.

The Duomo

Piazza del Duomo

A short walk brings you to the eleventh-century **Duomo**, rather squashed into its

CARRARA MARBLE QUARRIES

Ever-present on the Versilia coast, whether as blocks awaiting shipment or as huge snow-like scars on the mountains, **marble** has been the lifeblood of the region for over two thousand years. Marble is a metamorphic form of limestone, hardened by colossal heat and pressure. Though it takes many forms, **Carrara stone** is usually white-grey and is prized for its flawless lustre. The many other types you'll see are mostly blocks that have been imported – from as far away as Russia – to be worked by the highly rated local factories.

The **Romans** were the first to extract this stone commercially, driving pegs of fig-wood into natural faults and then soaking them until the swollen wood split the stone. In time they used scored lines and iron chisels to produce uniform blocks. Practices remained little changed until the Renaissance, when **Michelangelo** began to visit the area. His wet nurse was from this part of Tuscany, and he claimed he became a sculptor by ingesting the marble dust in her milk; he also claimed to have introduced the art of quarrying to Carrara, a process he considered as important as sculpting itself. The *David* is sculpted from Carrara marble, and local folklore is full of Michelangelo's pilgrimages to distant corners of the mountains in search of perfect stone.

Any short trip into the interior brings you across the huge scars of the marble **quarries**, some of the most startling sights in Tuscany. A particularly accessible site is at **Colonnata** (taking its name from a column of Roman slaves brought in to work the mines), 8km from Carrara and served in summer by eight daily CAT buses from Carrara's main bus terminus at Via Don Minzoni. Don't go all the way to Colonnata village, but get off at the *Visita Cave* signs by the mine; if you're driving, follow the yellow *Cava di Marmo* signs from the town up the twisting road. You'll see a huge, blindingly white marble basin, its floor and sides perfectly squared by the enormous wire saws used to cut the blocks that litter the surroundings. There are even bigger quarries farther south, notably at **Monte Corchia**.

3

piazza, but graced with a huge tower and a lovely facade built to the inevitable Pisan-Romanesque pattern. Only the intricate rose window, a superb fourteenth-century addition, departs from the style. The interior has a severe simplicity but contains some beautiful works – a fifteenth-century **pulpit** and five appealing statues by the fourteenth-century sculptor Bergamini.

Museo Civico di Marmo

Via XX Settembre • Mon–Sat: May–Sept 9.30am–1pm & 3.30–6pm; Oct–April 9am–12.30pm & 2.30–5pm • €4.50 • Buses from Via Don Minzoni

Some 2km southwest of town on the Marina di Carrara road is the **Museo Civico di Marmo**. Run as a promotional and educational exercise by the local Chamber of Commerce, it's an impressive display that looks at the history and production of the stone – lots of photographs, examples of different types of marble, and a room devoted to rather dubious examples of marble art.

ARRIVAL AND INFORMATION

CARRARA

By train Carrara's train station is close to the sea and has a regular bus service to the old town.
Destinations Pisa (every half hour; 45min); Viareggio (hourly; 25min).
By bus Buses from La Spezia and Florence arrive in Piazza Menconi in Marina di Carrara; services from more local

towns use the terminal at Via Don Minzoni.
Destinations Colonnata (9 daily; 30min); Lucca (8 daily; 1hr 40min).
Tourist office Via XX Settembre 46 (Mon–Sat: June–Aug 8.30am–5.30pm; Sept–May 9am–4pm ☎ 0585 844 136.

ACCOMMODATION

★ **Carrara** Via Petacchi 21 ☎ 0585 857 616, ⓦ hotelcarrara.it. This spotless and friendly hotel is really rather stylish, with gardens and antiques to set it off, and all the amenities: wi-fi, free parking, a/c, balconies.

Excellent buffet breakfast included. **€105**
Michelangelo Corso Carlo Rosselli 3 ☎ 0585 777 161, ⓦ michelangelocarrara.it. Very comfortable hotel, with vast bedrooms all decorated with works by local

contemporary artists. Carrara marble bathrooms, parquet floors, a/c, wi-fi, a terrace bar with panoramic views, plus other amenities, and a full buffet breakfast included. Substantial discounts available booking online. €200

3

EATING

★ **Locanda Apuana** Via Comunale 1, Colonnata ☎ 0585 768 017, ⓦ locandaapuana.com. This cosy, atmospheric restaurant is an excellent option, with most dishes at €6–8. One of their great pasta specialities is chestnut tagliatelle with gorgonzola, and, of course, Colonnata is the place to try the famous *lardo*, made here since Roman times. Sublime home-made desserts €5. Tues–Sat 12.30–3.30pm & 7.30–10.30pm.

'L Purtunzin Ninan Via Bartolini 3 ☎ 0585 74 741. An elegant little restaurant with some 400 wines. Their superb house speciality is seafood ravioli with baby squid, and the *frittura di pesce*, a rustic fried fish dish, is also excellent. A full meal runs about €50 per person, not including wine. Tues–Sun 12.30–3.30pm & 7.30–11pm.

Osteria Merope Via Ulivi 2 ☎ 0585 776 961, ⓦ osteriamerope.it. Named for the owner's grandmother, whose recipes are the menus high points, this elegant spot offers the full range of regional dishes, with an emphasis on fish. Home-made pasta dishes average about €12, main courses €15. Tues–Sun 12.30–3.45pm & 7.30–10.45pm, open daily in Jul & Aug.

The Garfagnana

The **Garfagnana** is the general name for the area encompassing the Serchio valley north of Lucca, one of Tuscany's least-explored yet most spectacular corners. The paucity of visitors is accounted for by the lack of any great sights – medieval **Barga** and the spa town of **Bagni di Lucca** are the only historic towns – but there are rewards aplenty for anyone with an interest in hiking or fine scenery. Much of the Garfagnana is protected as a regional **nature reserve**, whose excellent on-the-ground organization has mapped and signposted a good range of walks. The best of these are on the east of the Serchio valley, up in the mountainous **Orecchiella** range. The Serchio's western flanks comprise the equally spectacular mountains of the Alpi Apuane, best reached from the coastal side.

GETTING AROUND

By train If you don't have your own transport, the best way to see the Garfagnana is the train line which runs the entire length of the Serchio valley, past Barga and the region's rather lacklustre hub, Castelnuovo di Garfagnana – the handiest place to stay as a base for exploring. The line then cuts through the head of the valley to Aulla, centre of the Lunigiana, from where you can drop down by train to

La Spezia (in Liguria), and complete a loop back to Lucca, via Massa and Viareggio. Since Bagni di Lucca's train station is about 4km out of town, it's best to travel there by bus from Lucca.

By bus Buses from Lucca run up and down the valley with stops in Barga, Castelnuovo di Garfagnana and elsewhere.

Bagni di Lucca

Though it had been a spa for centuries, the river village of **Bagni di Lucca**, 25km north of Lucca, hit the social big time only in the early nineteenth century, when the patronage of **Elisa Baciocchi**, Napoleon's sister (see p.194), brought in Europe's fashionable elite. Elisa established one of Europe's first official **casinos** – roulette was invented here – and the town was graced by the presence of such luminaries as Byron, Shelley and Browning. Today, Bagni di Lucca retains its charm, though the atmosphere is relatively subdued.

INFORMATION

Tourist Office Via Casinò Municipale, 2km west along the river road from Bagni di Lucca in Ponte a Serraglio (mid-March to mid-Sept Mon–Sat 9.30am–2.30pm

& 3.30–6.30pm, Sun 9.30am–12.30pm; mid-Sep to mid-March Mon & Wed–Sat 9.30am–12.30pm ☎ 0583 805 745, ⓦ bagnidiluccaonline.it).

EATING

Circolo Dei Forestieri Piazza Jean Varraud 10 ☎ 0583 86 038, ⓦ circolodeiforesti.it. A good option for fine dining, serving exquisite cuisine such as *taglioni* with crab in a beautiful setting, with an elegant columned dining room and a scenic terrace. Set menus start at €40. Tues–Sun 12.30–3.45pm & 7.30–11pm.

Barga

The ancient hill-town of **BARGA** marks the start of the Garfagnana's best scenery, dominated by hills and incredibly lush vegetation. A couple of tempting minor roads lead into the wild country of the Orecchiella, offering stunning **views** over steep wooded slopes and across to the jagged profiles of the Alpi Apuane. The steep old village is quiet, pretty and charming, with a particularly impressive **Duomo**, a flourishing cultural life in the form of two small but high-quality summer **music festivals**, Barga Jazz and Opera Barga and, oddly, strong Scottish ties – many of Scotland's Italian immigrants came from the village and surrounding area.

Barga has a long tradition of independence and a strong economic base founded on silk and, later, wool: felt hats became a speciality in the nineteenth century. It grew up originally around a Lombard castle, and was besieged by Lucca and Pisa before falling to Florence, under whose influence it remained until 1859. Where it differed from other Lucchesi strongholds was in its rule by elected council, a system it retained even under the Florentines.

The Duomo

Piazza del Duomo 1

Barga's **Duomo**, San Cristofano, stands at the village's highest point, fronted by a terrace that provides a huge panorama of rooftops, mountains and villa-spotted hills. It was founded in the ninth century and expanded over the next four hundred years, with remedial work in 1920 after a severe earthquake. Built in a honey-blonde stone known as *alberese di Barga*, the **facade**, probably adapted from part of the earliest church, is decorated in a shallow pattern of Lombard Romanesque-influenced reliefs and tiny arches, a delicate contrast to the **campanile**, which seems to have erupted from the tiled roof. Left of the door is a wonderful little relief of an obviously convivial feast, sculpted in 1200; on the architrave is an equally rustic harvest scene and twin lions.

The interior

Inside, the **naves** are beautifully divided by low walls of inlaid marble and overlooked by a superlative and idiosyncratic **pulpit** which, prior to the pulpits of Nicola and Giovanni Pisano in Pisa, Siena and elsewhere, was widely considered one of the finest such creations. Probably created by the thirteenth-century sculptor Guido Bigarelli da Como (or a pupil), it consists of a huge rectangular stand, lavishly carved with scenes from the Scriptures and supported by four red marble pillars, the front pair propped up by another pair of lions: one, with an inane smirk, surmounts a dragon (a symbol of evil), while the other stands on a man (a symbol of heresy) who is simultaneously stroking and stabbing the animal. The rear left pillar is supported by a grotesque dwarf, snub-nosed symbol of the pagan world. The church's other unmissable artefact is a tenth- or twelfth-century **statue** of St Christopher, looking rather like a huge wooden puppet; continuing the building's eccentric streak, the saint carries a child on one shoulder and a club the size of a small tree on the other. Around the church, you'll spot a cluster of della Robbia glazed terracottas in the right chapel, **frescoes** on several pillars, a carved choir screen and two Giottesque **Crucifixes** – the overpoweringly framed example above the altar is particularly good.

3

3

By train It's a long haul uphill from the Barga-Gallicano train station up to Barga, a distance of 3.5km.
Destinations Castel Nuovo di Garfagnana (8 daily; 45min); Lucca (10 daily; 40min).

By bus Coming from Lucca it's easier to use the bus. All services arrive at the Porta Reale, alongside the big car park where the road stops outside the walls.
Destinations Bagni di Lucca (4 daily; 40min); Castelnuovo di Garfagnana (8 daily; 30min); Lucca (8 daily; 1hr 15min).

Tourist Office Via di Mezzo 45 (Mon–Fri 8am–2pm, Sat & Sun 10am–noon & 2.30–5pm; ☎ 0583 724 743, ⓦ barganews.com).

ACCOMMODATION, EATING AND DRINKING

★ **Alpino** Via Pascoli 41 ☎ 0583 723 336, ⓦ bargaholiday.com. This handsome hotel, about 300m down from the historic centre, has been run by the same family since the late eighteenth century. It's operated like a home, with you as the family guest, and the restaurant features all the freshest local cuisine. Free wi-fi, a/c and breakfast is included. Closed Nov. **€65**

Caffè Capretz Piazza Salvo Salvi 1 ☎ 0583 723 001. For drinks and snacks, or even a full meal, this friendly, historic spot, set in a splendid medieval loggia perched halfway up to the Duomo, provides great views and decent local cooking. Pasta dishes go for about €7, mains around €13. Tues–Sun 12.30–3.30pm & 7.30–10.30pm; closed part of Nov.

★ **L'Altana** Via di Mezzo 1 ☎ 0583 723 192. About 300m southwest of the Duomo, L'Altana offers amazingly good food: everything is home-made and gourmet quality, accompanied by expert service and a colourful setting. Don't miss the fresh pasta with parmesan and truffle shavings. As little as €40 for two, depending on wine. Be sure to book. Mon, Tues & Thurs–Sun 12.30–3pm & 7.30–10pm; closed part of Feb.

Grotta del Vento

April–Nov daily 1hr tours hourly 10am–noon & 2–6pm; 2hr tours 11am, 3pm, 4pm & 5pm; 3hr tours 10am & 2pm; rest of the year 1hr tours Mon–Sat same hours, plus 1, 2 & 3hr tours Sun and public holidays, same hours • Tours €9, €14 or €20 respectively • ☎ 0583 722 024, ⓦ grottadelvento.com

From Gallicano, across the river from Barga-Gallicano train station, you can drive west for 9km, following the bottom of the Turrite valley, to what is rated as Tuscany's best cave, the rather commercialized **Grotta del Vento** in **Fornovo Lasso**. Three different tours are available through the caverns and lakes of this bizarre subterranean landscape.

Castelnuovo di Garfagnana

Garfagnana's main town, **CASTELNUOVO DI GARFAGNANA**, is a disappointment, despite its mountain-ringed location. A rather featureless sprawl, it has a daytime market bustle to its centre but virtually no life after 5pm, balmy summer evenings excepted. However, Castelnuovo is the obvious base if you intend to explore the Orecchiella and eastern Alpi Apuane. Some of the mountain roads that radiate east and west offer astounding views for drivers, and the villages around are highly attractive. For serious hiking, it's also worth stopping in order to pick up maps and information at the Park Visitor Centre (see opposite).

The only thing to see is the fourteenth-century **Rocca**, built by the Este dukes of Ferrara and best known for its former commander, the poet **Ariosto**, author of the romantic epic *Orlando Furioso*. By all accounts he didn't much enjoy his tour of duty in the 1520s, and mournful evocations of the area's landscape were to colour much of his later poetry. The rest of the town was badly damaged by bombing in World War II, though a lovely **terracotta** of *St Joseph and the Angels*, attributed to Verrocchio or the della Robbia family, survives on the Duomo's north wall.

By bus The main bus stop is in Piazza Umberto.

Destinations Barga (8 daily; 45min); Lucca (9 daily; 1hr 30min).

INFORMATION

Park visitor centre Piazza delle Erbe 1, just beyond the arch of Piazza Umberto I, the town's main square (daily: June–Sept 9am–1pm & 3–7pm; Oct–May 9am–1pm & 3.30–5.30pm; ☎0583 644 242, ⓦparcapuane.toscana.it or ⓦparks.it). Information on trekking and tourism in the Garfagnana, and a booking service for hotels, agriturismi and rifugi.

Tourist office Via Cavalieri di Vittorio Veneto (summer Mon–Sat 9.30am–1pm & 3.30–7pm, Sun 9.30am–1pm & 3.30–6pm; winter Mon–Sat 10am–1pm & 3.30–6.30pm, Sun 10am–12.30pm; ☎0583 641 007, ⓦcastelnuovogarfagnana.org).

Club Alpino For information on climbing and all other mountain activities, contact Club Alpino, below the car park at Via Vittorio Emanuele 3 (☎0583 65 577, ⓦgarfagnanacai.it).

EATING

2 Mulino Via Vittorio Emanuele 12 ☎0583 62 192. This friendly, century-old delicatessen offers panini, prosciutto, cheese and olives, as well as a great range of wines by the bottle or glass. Simple meals at about €25 per person, are also available; don't miss the *castagnaccio* for dessert. Tues–Sun 7.30am–8pm.

The Orecchiella

Though higher than the spectacular Alpi Apuane, the **Orecchiella** mountains are generally tamer – but no less beautiful: rounded and thickly wooded, with steep lateral valleys and gentle grassy slopes above the treeline. The one monument of note is the monastery at **San Pellegrino**, now home to a museum of rural Garfagnana life. If you have transport – and whether you intend to hike or not –it's well worth following some of the minor roads into the mountains for a glimpse of one of the prettiest and least known of Tuscany's scenic enclaves.

Orecchiella Nature Museum and Visitor Centre

June–Sept daily 9am–7pm; Nov–Easter Sun 9am–7pm; rest of the year by appointment • €2 • ☎0583 619 098, ⓦingarfagnana.it

It's worth heading 7km northwest Castelnuovo di Garfagnana through the wild countryside to visit the excellent chalet-style **Orecchiella Nature Museum and Visitor Centre** at San Romano in Garfagnana. It has a restaurant, bar, phones, wildlife museums, a lake with nicely situated picnic spots, and a fine botanical garden.

ACCOMMODATION AND EATING   COLLEMANDINA

Rifugio Isera Villa Collemandina ☎0583 660 203, ⓦrifugioisera.it. Some 4km southeast of San Roman in Garfagnana, this refuge offers a camping area and clean, fairly comfortable dorms, with heating in winter; booking

---

HIKING IN THE ORECCHIELLA

If you're going in for serious **hiking** in the Orecchiella, you should pick up one of the widely available Multigraphic 1:25,000 maps, which show all marked trails in the area. There are three marked circular walks pioneered by *Airone*, the Italian natural history magazine, which don't involve too much planning; staff at the park centre near Corfino can help you make sense of the routes, and there's a board-plan at the centre. **Walk 1** (5hr) takes in the summit of the craggy limestone Cima Pania (1602m) and the nature reserve of the Pania di Corfino, the most important of the three special reserves in the park and a noted area for nesting birds of prey, including peregrine falcons. **Walk 2** (4hr) passes through oak and beech forest and a stretch of grassy meadow. **Walk 3** needs two days, with a choice of overnight stops: *Rifugio C. Battisti* (ⓦrifugiobattisti.it) or *Rifugio La Bargetana* (ⓦrifugiobargetana.it).

For a real challenge, there's also a long-distance marked path known as **Garfagnana Trekking**, which starts and finishes at Castelnuovo and is designed to take about ten days. As well as taking in the best of the Orecchiella, five stages of this walk lead you through the Alpi Apuane. For details, ask at the park visitor centre in Castelnuovo. An even more ambitious long-distance route, the linear **Grande Escursione Appenninica (GEA)**, runs through the Orecchiella on its 24-stage trail from Sansepolcro across the roof of Tuscany to the Passo dei due Santi above La Spezia. Contact the Club Alpino for details (ⓦcai.it).

is a must, as is your own sleeping bag, though disposable ones are on sale for €5. There's a bar-restaurant on site.

Open April–Oct. Dorm beds €18

San Pellegrino in Alpe

From Castelnuovo, the drive 16km up a minor road northeast to **SAN PELLEGRINO IN ALPE** (1524m) offers stunning views over the steep valleys and ridges of the Orecchiella. The adjacent hamlet to San Pellegrino has a bar, a couple of places to stay and eat, and shops where you can buy local honey, oil, mushrooms, grappa and sweet chestnut flour, once the area's staple diet.

Museo della Campagna

Via del Voltone 14 • April & May Tues–Sun 9am–12pm & 2–5pm; June–Sept Tues–Sun 9.30am–1pm & 2.30–7pm; Oct–March Tues–Sat 9am–1pm, Sun 9am–12pm & 2–5pm • €2.50 • ☎ 0583 649 072

San Pellegrino's magnificently sited stone monastery is partly given over to an excellent **Museo della Campagna**. This unusually fascinating display centres on the Garfagnana's peasant life and traditions, its four floors and fourteen rooms exploring every aspect of country life, including looms, presses and hand tools.

Il Casone Casone di Profecchia ☎0583 649 028, ⓦhotelilcasone.it. This all-purpose hotel, restaurant and ski resort is perched at 1300m in a great location about 6km from the pass. The rustic rooms feature terracotta floors and knotty-pine furniture, and facilities include a tennis court. Breakfast included. **€70**

Lunardi Passo delle Radici ☎0583 649 071, ⓦalbergolunardi.com. This isolated chalet-style hotel-restaurant and ski resort stands on the Foce delle Radici pass at the top of the SP72 road. Rooms are basic, and some have shared baths. Breakfast is extra. **€55**

The Lunigiana

Few people make it to Tuscany's northernmost tip, the **Lunigiana**. A land of rocky, forested landscape, with just two sizeable towns – Aula and the more interesting **Pontrémoli** – this is one of the most insular regions in Tuscany. Its isolation was ensured over centuries by its mountainous approaches, only breached in the nineteenth century by the carving out of a rail tunnel and twisting mountain road at Piazza al Serchio.

The Lunigiana's name derives from the **Luni**, an ancient tribe who proved a tough nut for the Romans to crack and were equally impervious for some centuries to Christianity. Later, numerous would-be rulers built castles to exact tolls from anyone passing through the valley – hence the tourist board's name for the area, "Land of the Hundred Castles". Many of these castles are now in private hands and many others were left in ruins after World War II, but the region still repays a visit for its scenery and self-contained atmosphere.

Pontrémoli

PONTRÉMOLI is the Lunigiana's biggest centre and the northernmost town in Tuscany. Parts of it are still evocatively medieval, especially the area rambling north of the **Torre del Campanone**. Now the Duomo's campanile, the tower originally formed part of a fortress built by Lucca's Castruccio Castracani in 1322 to keep the town's warring factions apart: hence its nickname, *Cacciaguerra* – "chaser-away-of-war". The Duomo itself is a typically Baroque affair.

Museo delle Statue-Stele Lunigianesi

Daily: May–Sept 9am–12.30pm & 3–6pm; Oct–April 9am–12.30pm & 2.30–5.30pm • €4 • ☎ 0187 831 439, ⓦ statuestele.org

The town's most captivating attraction is the collection of twenty or so prehistoric **stele** housed in the **Museo delle Statue-Stele Lunigianesi**, whose home is the Castello del Piagnaro, a bleak fourteenth-century castle. These highly stylized statues fall into three groups. The oldest date from 3000–2000 BC, and are crude rectangular blocks with just a "U" for a face, and only the suggestion of arms and trunk. The second group (2000–800 BC) have more angular heads and more detail; the last pieces (700–200 BC) are more sophisticated still, and usually have a weapon in each hand. Most stele were funerary headstones, but here it's thought they represented a pagan communion between heaven (the head), earth (the arms and their weapons) and the underworld (the buried bottom third). Those with heads missing perhaps suffered at the hands of Christians intent on doing away with idolatry.

ARRIVAL AND INFORMATION   PONTRÉMOLI

By train The train station is 1km southeast of the centre, across the river.

Destinations Carrara (10 daily; 1hr); La Spezia (10 daily; 50min); Parma (hourly; 1hr 20min); Viareggio (10 daily; 1hr 10min–1hr 40min).

Tourist office Piazza Repubblica 6 (irregular hours, weekdays only; ☎ 0187 833 309); on weekends local info is available from the town hall, on the same piazza (☎ 0187 460 111).

ACCOMMODATION, EATING AND DRINKING

Antica Pasticceria degli Svizzeri Piazza Repubblica 21–22 ☎ 0187 830 160. For drinks, *gelato* and wonderful cakes (the *torrone* nougat and *spongata* nut cake are legendary), head for this old-fashioned spot on the main square. The wonderful Liberty setting is all mirrors, wood, brass and marble. Tues–Sun 8.30am–12.30pm & 4.30–7.30pm; Sun 8.30am–1pm.

★ **Caveau del Teatro** Via del Teatro 4 ☎ 0187 833 328, ⓦ caveaudelteatro.it. With a charming Art Nouveau-style dining area, this restaurant creates tempting gourmet dishes, such as *carpaccio* of swordfish with raspberry

vinegar (€9) or antipasto *misto* for €12. Home-made pastas average about €10, mains about €14. They also have eight elegant, antique-filled rooms, each named after a renowned Italian composer. Breakfast included. Restaurant open Mon, Tues & Thurs–Sun 12.30–3.30pm & 7.30–10.30pm. €90

Napoleon Piazza Italia 2/bis ☎ 0187 830 544, ⓦ hotelnapoleon.net. This modern hotel has handsome rooms with marble floors and warm wood accents. They offer free parking, and the concierge can help you plan the many activities in the area. Breakfast €5 extra. €80

3

Pisa, the central coast and Elba

CAMPO DEI MIRACOLI, PISA

Pisa, the central coast and Elba

Flying into Tuscany you'll most likely arrive at Pisa, a city which – thanks to its leaning tower – is known, at least in name, to almost every visitor to Italy. Like Lucca, a little way to the north, Pisa bears the architectural stamp of the Middle Ages, the tower being just one element of its Campo dei Miracoli, or Field of Miracles, Italy's most refined ensemble of medieval architecture. Because it's seen by most outsiders on a whistle-stop trip, finding accommodation is usually less troublesome than in Tuscany's more overtly enticing towns. It's also a lively place: since before the time of Galileo, Pisa has had one of Italy's major universities, and student life remains an important aspect of the city's strong sense of identity.

The chief city of the central Tuscan coast, the port of Livorno, offers ferry connections and excellent seafood, but very little else. To the south, the Costa degli Etruschi, or Etruscan Riviera, is one of the least attractive areas of Tuscany, with its dingy resorts and drab hinterland of low hills and reclaimed swampland. However, it's not all bad: there are pockets of unspoilt sand around Baratti, and some beautiful areas of pine woodland (*pineta*) have been preserved at an important nature reserve at Bólgheri.

Close to Baratti, at the southern tip of the flatlands, Piombino provides the main point of embarkation for the biggest island of the Tuscan archipelago, Elba. Though peak-season crowds fill every hotel room on the island, Elba can be a seductive place in spring or early autumn, when it almost rivals the charm of outlying Capraia, a spot still remarkably little touched by tourism.

Pisa

In the world at large, PISA is known for just one thing – the Leaning Tower. It is indeed a freakishly beautiful building, a sight whose impact no amount of prior knowledge can blunt. Yet it's just a single component of the amazing Campo dei Miracoli, where the Duomo, Baptistery and Camposanto complete an unrivalled quartet of medieval masterpieces. These, and a dozen or so churches and *palazzi* scattered about the town, belong to Pisa's golden age, from the eleventh to the thirteenth centuries when the city, then still a port, was one of the great powers of the Mediterranean.

The city's political zenith came in the second half of the eleventh century with a series of victories over the Saracens, whom the Pisans drove out from Corsica, Sardinia and the Balearic islands, and harassed even in Sicily. Decline set in early, however, with defeat at sea by the Genoese in 1284 followed by the silting up of the harbour. From 1406 the city was governed by Florence, whose Medici rulers re-established the University of Pisa, one of the intellectual forcing houses of the Renaissance; Galileo, Pisa's most famous native, was a teacher there. Subsequent

ELBA

Highlights

❶ The Leaning Tower, Pisa Saved from collapse in the nick of time, Italy's signature building is now safe for the next few centuries at least. **See p.213**

❷ The Duomo, Pisa The vast cathedral of Pisa is one of the finest Romanesque structures in all of Italy – and the pulpit is an extraordinary creation. **See p.213**

❸ The Baptistery, Pisa Italy's largest baptistery is famed for its distinctive form, its sculptures and its amazing acoustics. **See p.215**

❹ The Camposanto, Pisa The tranquil, grassy cloister of Pisa's ancient cemetery was badly damaged in Word War II, but some beautiful frescoes and impressive tombs have survived. **See p.216**

❺ Elba For a dose of sunbathing and a splash in the sea, head for the beaches of Elba. **See p.225**

❻ Capraia And if the crowds of Elba are too much, you can always take refuge here. **See p.233**

HIGHLIGHTS ARE MARKED ON THE MAP ON P.212

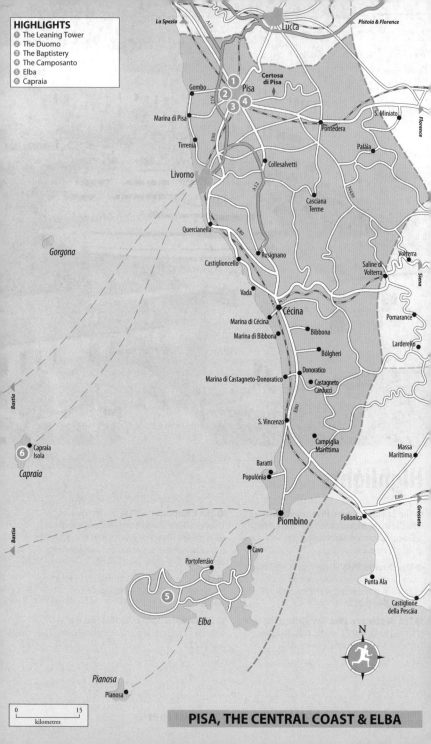

HIGHLIGHTS
1. The Leaning Tower
2. The Duomo
3. The Baptistery
4. The Camposanto
5. Elba
6. Capraia

La Spezia
A12
Lucca
Pistoia & Florence

Gombo
① Pisa
② ③ ④
Certosa di Pisa

S. Miniato

Marina di Pisa
E80
Pontedera
Florence

Tirrenia
Paláia

Livorno
Collesalvetti
A12

Casciana Terme
N439

Quercianella
E80

Gorgona
Castiglioncello
Rosignano
Saline di Volterra
Volterra

Vada
Siena

Cécina
Pomarance

Marina di Cécina
Bibbona
Larderello

Marina di Bibbona
Bólgheri

Marina di Castagneto-Donoratico
Donoratico
Castagneto Carducci

S. Vincenzo
E80

Campiglia Maríttima
Massa Maríttima

Bastia
⑥ Capraia Isola
Baratti
Populónia

Capraia

Follónica
Grosseto

Piombino
E80

Bastia
Cavo

Portoferráio
Punta Ala

⑤
Castiglione della Pescáia

Elba

N

Pianosa
Pianosa

0 ———— 15
kilometres

PISA, THE CENTRAL COAST & ELBA

centuries saw the city fade into provinciality – its state when the Shelleys and Byron took *palazzi* here, forging what Shelley termed their "paradise of exiles". Modern Pisa has been revitalized by its airport and industrial suburbs and, of course, by revenue from mass tourism.

The Campo dei Miracoli

The name of the **Campo dei Miracoli** (Field of Miracles) comes from the notoriously over-excitable Gabriele D'Annunzio, but the label is no mere bombast – the ecclesiastical centre of Pisa is a stunning spectacle. Nowhere else in Italy are the key religious buildings – the cathedral, baptistery and bell tower – so perfectly in harmony. And the mere existence of such enormous structures on this spot is remarkable in itself, because beneath the pavements and the turf lies a soggy mix of sand and silt, whose instability accounts for the angle of the Leaning Tower and the lesser tilt of its companions: take a close look at the Baptistery and you'll see that it's inclined some way off the vertical, while the facade of the Duomo is a few degrees out of true as well.

The Leaning Tower

Daily: Jan & Dec 10am–4.30pm; Feb & Nov 9.30am–5pm; March 9am–5.30pm; April, May & Sept 8.30am–8pm; June–Aug 8.30am–10.30pm; Oct 9am–7pm; • Tours in English three times daily April–Sept • €15 • For booking details see box (p.215)

The **Leaning Tower**, or Torre Pendente, has always been a leaning tower. Begun in 1173, it started to subside when it had reached just three of its eight storeys, but it tilted in the opposite direction to its present one. Odd-shaped stones were inserted to correct this deficiency, whereupon the tower lurched the other way. Over the next 180 years a succession of architects continued to extend the thing upwards, each one endeavouring to compensate for the angle, the end result being that the main part of the tower is slightly bent. Around 1350, Tommaso di Andrea da Pontedera completed the magnificent stack of marble and granite arcades by crowning it with a bellchamber, set closer to the perpendicular than the storeys below it, so that it looks like a hat set at a rakish angle.

By 1990 the tower was leaning 4.5m from the upright and nearing its limits, and so it was shut to the public. Steel bands were wrapped round the lowest section to prevent the base from buckling under the weight of the 15,000 tonnes of marble above, and more than 900 tonnes of lead ingots were attached to the base to counterbalance the force of the titling stonework. In 1998, when it was clear that the weights had stabilized the structure, the project entered its second phase, with a delicate drilling operation to remove water and silt from beneath the tower's northern foundations. The resulting subsidence corrected the building's southwards tilt by ten percent, bringing it back to the angle by which it was tilting in the first half of the nineteenth century; to ensure that it stayed that way for the foreseeable future, the foundations were strengthened and steel reinforcement bars were inserted into the walls of the tower. In November 2001 the tower was reopened.

The **ascent** leads you to the bell chamber up a dark and narrow spiral staircase of 294 steps, at a disorientating five-degree angle. It's not for the claustrophobic or acrophobic.

The Duomo

Daily: March 10am–6pm; April–Sept 10am–8pm; Oct 10am–7pm; Nov–Feb 10am–12.45pm & 2–5pm • No admittance to tourists before 1pm on Sun • Free Nov–Feb, otherwise €2 or combined ticket (see box, p.215)

The **Duomo** was begun a century before its campanile, in 1064. With its four levels

For an elevated view of the Campo, you could take a stroll on the small portion of the **city walls** that borders the northwest corner (March–Oct 10am–1pm & 3–6pm; €4).

of variegated colonnades and its subtle interplay of dark grey marble and white stone, it's the archetype of the Pisan-Romanesque style, a model often imitated but never surpassed. **Inside**, the impact of the crisp black-and-white marble of the long arcades – recalling Moorish architecture – is slightly diminished by the incongruous gilded ceiling, the fresco in the squashed circle of the dome, and the massive air vents that have been bunged through the upper arches. Much of the interior was redecorated, and some of the chapels remodelled, after a huge fire in 1595.

PISA

TICKETS FOR THE CAMPO DEI MIRACOLI MONUMENTS

There are two **ticket offices** for the **Campo dei Miracoli** sights: on the north side of the Leaning Tower and inside the Museo delle Sinopie. **Tickets** for the Leaning Tower can be bought only from the first of these; tickets for the Campo dei Miracoli's other five museums and monuments – the Duomo, Baptistery, Museo dell'Opera, Camposanto and Museo delle Sinopie – can be bought from either. Admission to the Duomo costs €2 (free Nov 1 to March 1); single admission to the other sights costs €5. Admission to any two sights is €6, to any four is €8, and to all five is €10; these **combined tickets** are valid for the day of issue only.

There's a separate ticket (€15) for the **Leaning Tower**; groups of thirty are allowed in for half an hour, and you should expect a long wait in high season. For an extra €2 you can **pre-book your visit** online at ⓦ www.opapisa.it, as long as you're making your reservation between 45 and fifteen days in advance. Children under the age of 8 are not allowed into the tower.

The Cimabue mosaic and the pulpit

The Duomo's huge bronze doors were made after the 1595 blaze, in Giambologna's workshop, but the magnificent apse **mosaic** of *Christ in Majesty* survived the conflagration. It was completed by Cimabue in 1302, the year in which **Giovanni Pisano** began to sculpt the cathedral's extraordinary **pulpit**. This was packed away after the fire, sixteenth-century Pisans evidently no longer concurring with its Latin inscription, which celebrates Giovanni as "superior to all other sculptors…incapable of creating clumsy and ungraceful figures". Only in 1926 was it rediscovered and reassembled. The last of the great series of pulpits created in Tuscany by Giovanni and his father Nicola (the others are in Siena and Pistoia), it is a work of amazing virtuosity, the whole surface animated with figures almost wholly freed from the block. Its narrative density rewards close attention: much of the story of the Passion, from Judas's betrayal to the scourging of Christ, for instance, is condensed into a single panel.

The tomb of Henry VII

In the right transept is the mummified body of Pisa's patron saint, **Ranieri**, and (set into the east wall) the tomb of the Holy Roman Emperor **Henry VII**, who died in 1313 (aged just 38) near Siena – probably from malaria, though some said from eating a poisoned wafer at Mass. After laying Siena to waste, the pro-imperial Pisans bore the body of their hero back home, where Tino da Camaino carved this fine image. The Pisans weren't the only ones to revere the young emperor – Dante saw "alto Arrigo" as a man who could unite Italy within a new Christian empire, and in the *Divine Comedy* accorded him a throne of honour in heaven (hence the quotation from Dante below the sarcophagus). The tomb was originally in the centre of the transept, but was later broken up; only in 1921 were the effigy and sarcophagus placed in their current position, with other pieces of the tomb being transferred to the Museo dell'Opera del Duomo.

The Baptistery

Daily: March 9am–6pm; April–Sept 8am–8pm; Oct 9am–7pm; Nov–Feb 10am–5pm • €5, or combined ticket (see box above)

The **Baptistery** was begun in the mid-twelfth century by a certain Deotisalvi ("God save you"), who left his name on the column to the left of the door. Lack of money – caused mainly by Genoa's incursions into the Pisan trade network – prevented its completion until the second half of the thirteenth century, when the Gothic top storeys and attendant flourishes were applied by Nicola and Giovanni Pisano, who rounded off the job with a glorious gallery of statues – the originals of which are now in the Museo dell'Opera del Duomo.

This is the largest baptistery in Italy, and the plainness of the vast interior is immediately striking, with its unadorned arcades and bare dome. The acoustics are astonishing too, as is often demonstrated by the custodian. At the centre is a mosaic-inlaid **font** by Guido da Como (1246), overlooked by Nicola Pisano's splendid **pulpit**, which was sculpted in 1260 and was the sculptor's first major commission. Though the architectural details recall the stonework of French Gothic churches, the pulpit clearly shows the influence of classical models: the seated Virgin in the *Adoration of the Magi* is derived from a Roman image, while the nude figure of Daniel (underneath the *Adoration*) is Hercules under an alias.

The Camposanto

Daily: March 9am–6pm; April–Sept 8am–8pm; Oct 9am–7pm; Nov–Feb 10am–5pm • €5, or combined ticket (see box, p.215)

The screen of sepulchral white marble running along the north edge of the Campo dei Miracoli is the perimeter wall of what has been called the most beautiful cemetery in the world, the **Camposanto**. According to Pisan legend, at the end of the twelfth century the city's archbishop brought back from the Crusades a cargo of soil from Golgotha, in order that eminent Pisans might be buried in holy earth. The building enclosing this sanctified site was completed almost a century later.

The cloister

The Camposanto takes the form of an enormous **cloister**, which since the fourteenth century has housed a large array of Roman sarcophagi, some of which were reused for local dignitaries. Later tombs constitute a virtual encyclopedia of commemorative styles, ranging from pavement slabs that record the occupant's name, dates and nothing else, to extravagances such as the monument surmounted by a woman identified as "The Inconsolable". However, when Ruskin described the Camposanto as one of the three most precious buildings in Italy (with the Sistine Chapel and the Scuola di San Rocco in Venice), it was not its tombs but its **frescoes** that he was praising. Paintings once covered more than two thousand square metres of cloister wall, but bombs dropped by Allied planes on July 27, 1944 set the roofing on fire and drenched the frescoes in a river of molten lead, and masterpieces by Taddeo Gaddi, Spinello Aretino, **Benozzo Gozzoli** and others were all but destroyed.

The Triumph of Death

The most important surviving frescoes are a remarkable cycle that's been removed to a room opposite the entrance, beyond a photographic display of the Camposanto before the bombing. Some experts attribute this work to an artist called **Buonamico Buffalmacco**, though others assign it to an anonymous *Maestro del Trionfo della Morte*, the "Master of the Triumph of Death". There's also some dispute about the date: the frescoes are labelled as having been created in 1336–41, but many argue that they were painted after the Black Death of 1348, a pestilence which hit Tuscany so badly that it was known throughout Europe as the Florentine Plague. The most famous episode of the *Triumph* shows a trio of aristocratic huntsmen stopped in their tracks by a trio of coffins, the contents of which are so putrescent that one of the riders has to pinch his nose. Over to the right, squadrons of angels and demons bear away the souls of the dead, whose final resting place is determined in the terrifying *Last Judgement* and *Inferno* at the far end of the room.

The Museo dell'Opera del Duomo

Daily: March 9am–6pm; April–Sept 8am–8pm; Oct 9am–7pm; Nov–Feb 10am–5pm • €5, or combined ticket (see box, p.215)

A vast array of statuary from the Duomo and Baptistery, plus ecclesiastical finery, paintings and other miscellaneous pieces are displayed in the **Museo dell'Opera del Duomo**, at the southeast corner of the Campo. If you have time for just one museum in Pisa, make it this one.

The first masterpieces you encounter are the extraordinary **bronze doors** made for the Duomo by **Bonanno Pisano**, the first architect of the Leaning Tower, in 1180. (Replicas are now in place at the **Portale di San Ranieri**, opposite the tower.) The panel showing

The *Massacre of the Innocents* exemplifies Bonanno's powerfully schematic style, employing the smallest possible cast – Herod, one mother, one soldier and three babies. In the next room, exhibits dating from the period of the Duomo's construction illustrate the various influences at work in Pisan culture of the time. There's stonework from a Roman basilica, adapted for use in the cathedral, and items showing how Islamic culture filtered into the city's art, notably in the marble inlays from the Duomo facade. The most striking work, however, is from Burgundy, source of the strange painted wooden Crucifix, a gigantic figure with a tiny head and mantis-thin arms.

The sculpture rooms

Sculptures by the various Pisanos are the high points of the museum, even if Nicola and Giovanni's figures from the Baptistery are too eroded to give much more than an approximate idea of their power. Room 7, which is given over to works by **Giovanni Pisano**, contains the most affecting statue in Pisa, the **Madonna del Colloquio**, so called because of the intensity of the gazes exchanged by the Madonna and Child. Giovanni's great contemporary, **Tino da Camaino**, monopolizes the next room, where fragments from the tomb of Emperor Henry VII are assembled.

Nino Pisano – no relation to Nicola and Giovanni – is the subject of room 9, where his marble monuments to archbishops Giovanni Scherlatti and Francesco Moricotti show the increasing suavity of Pisan sculpture in the late fourteenth century. Giovanni Pisano returns in the **treasury**, his ivory *Madonna and Child* showing a remarkable ingenuity in the way it exploits the natural curve of the tusk from which it was carved. The other priceless object here is the Pisan Cross, which was carried by the Pisan contingent on the First Crusade.

The upper floor

Upstairs, large altarpiece paintings take up a lot of room, none of them as impressive as the museum's remarkable examples of intarsia, the art of inlaid wood. The strangest objects on view are the two ancient parchment rolls known as **Exultets**, from the opening word of the chant on the eve of Holy Saturday. It was during this service that the cantor would unfurl these scrolls from the pulpit, so that the congregation could follow his words through the pictures painted on them. Beyond a small collection of **Roman and Etruscan** pieces, where a thin-lipped bust of Julius Caesar commands attention, the museum closes with a sequence of engravings by **Carlo Lasinio**, whose efforts were instrumental in rescuing the Camposanto from ruin at the beginning of the nineteenth century.

The Museo delle Sinopie

Daily: March 9am–6pm; April–Sept 8am–8pm; Oct 9am–7pm; Nov–Feb 10am–5pm • €5, or combined ticket (see box, p.215)

After the catastrophic damage wreaked on the Camposanto by the bombers, the building's restorers removed its sinopie (monochrome sketches for the frescoes) to the **Museo delle Sinopie**. These great plates of plaster are now hung from the walls of the high-tech museum, where gantries and galleries give you the chance to inspect the painters' preliminary ideas at close range. It's a rather scholastic enterprise, though.

The rest of the city

Within a short radius of the Campo dei Miracoli, Pisa takes on a quite different character, because very few tourists choose to explore the squares and streets of the city centre. While it's true that nothing in Pisa comes close to having the impact of the Campo, a tour of its lesser churches and other monuments could easily fill a day. Make time to cross over to the area south of the Arno; popularly known as the *mezzogiorno* (the name used in Italy to refer to the under-developed south of the country), this part of the city has two exquisite churches and Pisa's most lively exhibition centre.

Piazza dei Cavalieri

The **Piazza dei Cavalieri**, the obvious next stop after the Campo, was perhaps the site of the Roman forum, and became the main civic square of medieval Pisa, before being remodelled by Vasari for the Knights of St Stephen. This order was established by Cosimo I, ostensibly for crusading, though they amounted to little more than a gang of licensed pirates, given state sanction to plunder Turkish shipping. Their palace, the graffiti-covered **Palazzo dei Cavalieri** (now a school), is fronted by a statue of Cosimo and adjoins the order's church of **Santo Stefano**, which is hung with banners captured from the Turks. On the other side of the square is the **Palazzo dell'Orologio**, with its archway and clock tower. Remodelled in the Renaissance, this tower was where the military leader Ugolino della Gherardesca was starved to death in 1288, along with his sons and grandsons, as punishment for his alleged duplicity with the Genoese enemy – a grisly episode described in Dante's *Inferno* and Shelley's *Tower of Famine*.

Santa Caterina

Piazza Santa Caterina • Mon–Sat 8am–12.30pm & 4–7pm, Sun 8am–12.30pm

Northeast from Piazza dei Cavalieri, across the wide Piazza dei Martiri della Libertà, stands the Dominican church of **Santa Caterina**, whose Romanesque lower facade dates from the year of its foundation, 1251. Inside, there's an *Annunciation* and a tomb by Nicola Pisano, and a fourteenth-century painting of the *Triumph of Thomas Aquinas*, the ideological figurehead of the Dominicans.

San Francesco

Piazza San Francesco • Mon–Sat 8am–12.30pm & 4–6.30pm, Sun 8am–12.30pm

To the south of Santa Caterina, the plain-faced thirteenth-century church of **San Francesco** contains some well-preserved frescoes by Taddeo Gaddi above the high altar, and a Crucifixion by Spinello Aretino in the second chapel to the right of the altar, but its masterpieces – by Giotto and Cimabue – were carted off to the Louvre by Napoleon. Count Ugolino and his offspring are buried here, too.

Borgo Stretto

South of Piazza dei Cavalieri, Via Dini swings into the arcaded **Borgo Stretto**, Pisa's main shopping street. On the west side of Borgo Stretto you'll find Pisa's **market** area (Mon–Fri mornings & Sat all day), with fruit, vegetable, fish, meat and clothing stalls filling Piazza Vettovaglie, Piazza San Omobono and the neighbouring lanes; the university's main building is beyond the market, on the south side of the lively **Piazza Dante**. On the east flank of Borgo Stretto you'll see the Romanesque-Gothic facade of **San Michele in Borgo**, built on the site of the Roman temple to Mars. The Borgo meets the river at the traffic-knotted Piazza Garibaldi and **Ponte di Mezzo**, the city's central bridge.

Museo Nazionale di San Matteo

Piazza San Matteo 1 • Tues–Sat 8.30am–7pm, Sun 9am–1.30pm • €5, or €8 with Palazzo Reale

A left turn along the *lungarno* takes you past the **Palazzo Toscanelli** (once Byron's residence house, now the city archives) to the **Museo Nazionale di San Matteo**, where most of the major works of art from Pisa's churches are now gathered.

MARKET DAYS

On the second Sunday and the preceding Saturday of each month the north and south banks of the river are linked by a big street **market**, with stalls selling jewellery, candles and the like filling the lower reaches of Borgo Stretto, and furniture and general bric-a-brac around the south bank's **Logge di Banchi**. Formerly the city's silk and wool market, this vast loggia (which often has exhibitions in its upper storey) stands at the top of the main shopping street of the *mezzogiorno*, the pedestrianized and increasingly upmarket Corso Italia.

PISA'S FESTIVALS

Pisa's biggest traditional event is the **Gioco del Ponte**, held on the last Sunday of June, when twelve teams from the north and south banks of the city stage a series of "push-of-war" battles, shoving a seven-tonne carriage over the Ponte di Mezzo. First recorded in 1568, the contest and attendant parades are still held in Renaissance costume. Other celebrations – concerts, regattas, art events – are held throughout June (the **Giugno Pisano**), a month during which the city has a distinctly festive feel. Most spectacular of the ancillary shows is the **Luminara di San Ranieri** (June 16), when buildings along both riverbanks are lit by 70,000 candles in honour of Pisa's patron saint. At 6.30pm the following evening, the various quarters of the city compete in the **Palio di San Ranieri**, a boat race along the Arno.

Fourteenth-century religious paintings make up most of the collection, with a Simone Martini polyptych and work by Antonio Veneziano outstanding in the early sections. Later on, there's a stash of Middle Eastern ceramics pilfered by Pisan adventurers, a panel of *St Paul* by Masaccio, Gozzoli's *Crucifixion* and Donatello's reliquary bust of the introspective *St Rossore*. Also housed in the museum are the antique armour and wooden shields used in the annual *Gioco del Ponte* pageant (see box above).

Museo Nazionale di Palazzo Reale

Lungarno Pacinotti 46 • Mon & Wed–Fri 9am–2.30pm, Sat 9am–1.30pm • €5, or €8 with San Matteo museum

Fronting the river to the west of the Ponte di Mezzo is the **Museo Nazionale di Palazzo Reale**, displaying artefacts that once belonged to the Medici, Lorraine and Savoy rulers of the city, who successively occupied the house. Lavish sixteenth-century Flemish tapestries share space with antique weaponry, ivory miniatures, porcelain and a largely undistinguished picture collection; the best-known painting, a version of Bronzino's portrait of Eleanora di Toledo, is displayed alongside a dress that belonged to her.

San Nicola

Via Santa Maria • Mon–Sat 8am–12.30pm & 4–7pm, Sun 8am–12.30pm

Behind the Palazzo Reale rises Pisa's second leaning tower, the thirteenth-century campanile of **San Nicola**; according to Vasari, the tower was designed by Nicola Pisano. Inside the church, the Crucifix in the chapel to the left of the high altar is attributed to Giovanni Pisano, while Nino Pisano is credited with the wooden *Madonna and Child* in the fourth chapel on the north side. On the opposite side of the church, the first chapel has a beautiful *Madonna and Child* by Francesco Traini.

Orto Botanico

Via Luca Ghini 5 • Mon–Fri 8.30am–5pm, Sat 8.30am–1pm • €2.50

North of San Nicola lies the university's **Orto Botanico**. Founded in 1543, in a different part of the city, this can claim to be the oldest botanical garden in Europe; it moved to this three-hectare site in 1591. A serene oasis of ponds, herb gardens and exotic trees, it has one of Italy's first iron-framed hothouses and one distinctly odd building – the seashell-encrusted botany institute, built in the year the gardens opened here.

Arsenale Mediceo

Lungarno Ranieri Simonelli

West along the river from the Palazzo Reale lies the **Arsenale Mediceo**. Built by Cosimo I, it is now being converted into the Museo della Navigazione, primarily to house the sixteen Roman ships which have been excavated since 1998 from the silt at nearby San Rossore, which was a port for the Roman colony at Pisa. Almost perfectly preserved in mud for two millennia, the cargo-laden fleet includes what experts believe could be the oldest Roman warship ever found. No date has been finalised for the opening of the museum; progress reports on the restoration of the ships can be found at ⓦcantierenavipisa.it.

4

Palazzo Blu

Lungarno Gambacorti 9 • Tues–Fri 10am–6pm, Sat & Sun 10am–7pm • Free, except during special exhibitions • ⓦ palazzoblu.org

West of the Ponte di Mezzo, the somewhat monotonous line of *palazzi* – mirroring those on the north bank – is enlivened by the brightly hued **Palazzo Blu**, which opened as a cultural centre in 2009. It holds a permanent collection of regional art from the fourteenth to the twentieth centuries, as well as big-name exhibitions on the ground floor.

Santa Maria della Spina

Lungarno Gambacorti • March–Oct Tues–Fri 10am–1.30pm & 2.30–6pm, Sat & Sun 10am–7pm; Nov–Feb Tues–Sun 10am–2pm, except second Sun of month 10am–1pm & 2.30–5pm • €1.50

The dainty little oratory of **Santa Maria della Spina** – the finest flourish of Pisan-Gothic – was founded in 1230 but rebuilt in the 1320s by a merchant who had acquired a thorn (*spina*) from Christ's crown. Originally built closer to the water, it was moved here for fear of floods in 1871. The single-naved interior has lost most of its furnishings, but contains a trio of statues by Andrea and Nino Pisano.

San Paolo a Ripa d'Arno

Lungarno Sonnino • Daily 9.30am–noon & 4–6.30pm

The most striking feature of **San Paolo a Ripa d'Arno** – which probably occupies the site of Pisa's very first cathedral – is the Romanesque arcaded facade, built in imitation of the present cathedral in the twelfth century; the interior, badly damaged in World War II, has a handsome Roman sarcophagus and a finely carved capital (second on left). Go round the back of the church to see the freestanding octagonal **Cappella di Sant'Agata**, which was also built in the twelfth century.

ARRIVAL AND DEPARTURE   PISA

BY PLANE

Galileo Galilei airport (ⓘ 050 849 300, ⓦ pisa-airport .com) lies about 3km south of the city centre.

TRANSPORT FROM THE AIRPORT

By car The drive to Florence is straightforward (an airport slip road takes you directly onto the motorway), but the road into Pisa is so confusing that, without directions from the car-rental desk, you may well end up getting lost.

By train Trains from the airport to Florence's Santa Maria Novella station cost €5.80; there are only eight direct services daily (taking 1hr, most of them stopping only at Pisa Centrale), but every 30min a shuttle runs from the airport to Pisa Centrale (5min), where you can change to one of the regular services to Florence. Train tickets can be bought from the office at the opposite end of the concourse from the station; at the time of going to press, this office was levying a surcharge of €1 on each ticket. The first train from the airport to Pisa Centrale is at 6.50am, and the last departs at 9pm; the last train from Pisa Centrale to Florence is at 10pm, with services resuming at around 6.40am.

By bus Terravision buses to Florence are scheduled to synchronize with budget airline flights and leave from in front of the terminal; they take 1hr 10min to reach Florence's Santa Maria Novella station, and tickets (€10 single) are sold at the stand right in front of you as you come out into the airport concourse.

BY TRAIN

Pisa Centrale station is about 1km south of the River Arno; the Campo dei Miracoli is about a 30min walk north, or a 5min ride on bus #1, which leaves from outside the station.

Destinations Empoli (every 30min; 35min; change for Volterra and Siena); Florence (every 30min; 1hr–1hr 20min); Lucca (hourly; 20min); Pisa Airport (every 30min; 5min).

BY BUS

Piazza Sant'Antonio The main bus terminus in front of the train station.

Destinations Florence (hourly via Lucca and Montecatini; 2hr 30min; quicker service departs from airport – see above); Livorno (hourly; 40min); Lucca (hourly; 50min); Viareggio (hourly; 50min).

INFORMATION

Tourist office The main office is at Piazza Vittorio Emanuele 13, near the train station (Mon–Fri 9am–7pm, Sat 9am–1.30pm; ⓘ 050 42 291, ⓦ pisaunicaterra.it); there's also an info desk inside the Museo dell'Opera del Duomo (daily: March 9am–6pm; April–Sept 8am–8pm, Oct 9am–7pm; Nov–Feb 10am–5pm; no phone).

ACCOMMODATION

Most people cover Pisa as a day-trip, or stay just one night, so **accommodation** is usually not hard to find. In summer, however, it's still best to reserve in advance, especially during the June festival.

Di Stefano Via Sant'Apollonia 35 ☎050 553 559, ⊛hoteldistefano.it. This tidy three-star, located in a quiet street just off Piazza dei Cavalieri, occupies two buildings – the better rooms are in a restored eleventh-century tower, and cost around €180 in high season. Other rooms are considerably less expensive. €80–180

Galileo Via Santa Maria 12 ☎050 40 621, ✉info .hotelgalileo@gmail.it. Nine big – and in some cases very nicely decorated – one-star rooms, with and without private bathrooms; not the quietest hotel in town, but central and good value. €60

★ **Novecento** Via Roma 37 ☎050 500 323, ⊛hotelnovecento.pisa.it. This newish three-star *residenza d'epoca* occupies a handsome old town house, but the rooms are immaculately modern in style. The rates are very reasonable (you can pay twice as much for similar accommodation closer to the Campo), the location convenient, and it has a pleasant garden as well. €150

Rinascente Via del Castelletto 28 ☎050 580 460, ⊛rinascentehotel.com. This very popular one-star occupies an old *palazzo* hidden away a short distance south of Piazza dei Cavalieri – follow the signs from Via San Frediano. Shared or private bathrooms. €60

★ **Royal Victoria** Lungarno Pacinotti 12 ☎050 940 111, ⊛royalvictoria.it. Run by the same family since its foundation in 1837, this old-fashioned and appealingly frayed three-star is the most characterful of central Pisa's hotels – and the best value. The public rooms, with their musty engravings and antique furniture, are redolent of the place's history, but if you're deterred by wobbly door-handles and patched-up ceiling frescoes, it's not the place for you. €80–145

HOSTEL

Walking Street Corso Italia 58 ☎393 064 8737, ⊛walkingstreethostel.com. Opened in 2010, this private hostel is by far the best in Pisa – it has an excellent location (on the main drag on the south side of the river), friendly staff, clean little dorms, a pool table, free internet access and a kitchen for guests' use. Space is limited, with twenty beds in six rooms, so book ahead. Dorm beds €22

EATING AND DRINKING

Pisa's proximity to the coast means that seafood is the staple of its **restaurant** menus, with *baccalà alla pisana* (dried cod in tomato sauce) and *pesce spada* (swordfish) featuring prominently. Avoid the temptation to eat or drink at one of the plethora of places in the vicinity of the Campo dei Miracoli – it's in the backstreets that you'll find the best places.

RESTAURANTS

Funiculì Via Luigi Bianchi 33 ☎050 551 062. This homely little place serves probably the best pizzas in Pisa, and though it's only a few minutes' stroll from the Campo dei Miracoli its clientele are overwhelmingly local. Tues–Sun 8–11pm.

Il Campano Via Domenico Cavalca 19 ☎050 580 585. Home-made pasta and *gnocchi*, and local seafood, are the draw at this first-rate trattoria – though they also do meaty Tuscan classics, including a 1kg Fiorentina steak (to share, of course). This may also be the only Pisan restaurant with ostrich on the menu. Good selection of wines, too. Mon, Tues & Fri–Sun 12.30–3pm & 7.30–10.30pm, Thurs 7.30–10.30pm.

La Clessidra Via del Castelletto 26–30 ☎050 540 160. Tucked away in an alley not far from San Frediano, *La Clessidra* offers a small but elegant menu of classic Tuscan dishes, with two tasting menus (one fish, one meat) at €35 for four courses; à la carte, mains are mostly around €12. Mon–Sat 7.30pm–midnight.

La Ghiotteria Vicolo delle Donzelle 9–11 ☎348 406 4725. The ideal place for a quick but satisfying meal, *La Ghiotteria* is tiny, rowdy and very cheap, and serves hearty plates of pasta and simple fish and meat dishes. A meal will set you back little more than €10, including house wine. Daily noon–4pm & 7pm–midnight; closed Wed in winter.

★ **La Sosta dei Cavalieri** Via San Frediano 3 ☎050 991 2410. This is the smaller, cosier and slightly more refined sibling of the *Osteria dei Cavalieri*, over the road. Mains average around €20 on a menu that concentrates on classic Pisan meat and fish dishes. Mon–Sat 12.30–2.30pm & 7.45–10.30pm.

★ **Osteria dei Cavalieri** Via San Frediano 16 ☎050 580 858. The *Osteria dei Cavalieri* has built a solid reputation over the years for its straightforward local food and very reasonable prices; reservations recommended in high season. Mon–Sat 12.30–2.30pm & 7.45–10.30pm.

San Omobono Piazza San Omobono 6 ☎050 540 847. This basic city-centre trattoria serves authentic Pisan home cooking, featuring dishes such as *brachette alla renaiaola* – pasta in a puree of greens and smoked fish. Mon–Fri 7.30–10pm, Sat 12.30–2pm & 7.30–10pm; closed two weeks in Aug.

CAFÉS AND GELATERIE

Bottega del Gelato Piazza Garibaldi 11 ☎050 575 467. In business for more than a quarter of a century, this

4

ever-popular *gelateria* has a great range of flavours – the *Tuttobosco* (forest fruits) is gorgeous. Daily noon–1am; closed Wed in winter.

★ **De' Coltelli** Lungarno Pacinotti 23 ☎ 345 481 1903. The de' Coltelli family are credited with having devised the recipe for ice cream back in the seventeenth century, and the shop that bears their name is one of Italy's top-rank *gelaterie*, with a penchant for adventurous concoctions – anyone for seafood ice cream? Mon–Thurs & Sun noon–11pm, Fri & Sat noon–midnight; closed Jan.

Pasticceria Salza Borgo Stretto 46 ☎ 050 580 144. The best-known café-pasticceria in Pisa; it has a restaurant section at the back, but the food isn't as good as you'll find elsewhere. Tues–Sun 8am–8.30pm.

BARS

Bazeel Piazza Garibaldi 15 ☎ 340 288 1113. This bar has been one of Pisa's favourite hangouts for some time – the interior is cool and spacious, but when the weather's good the punters prefer the outside tables. DJs on Fri & Sat, live music Thurs & Sun. Daily 5pm–2am.

Mani'omio Piazza Sant'Omobono 11 ☎ 050 319 5517. This suave and good-looking new bar does serve food, but essentially the cocktails and the after-hours buzz are what it's all about. Frequently has music, too. Mon–Thurs & Sun 7pm–1am, Fri–Sat 7pm–2am.

Around Pisa

Immediately to the east of Pisa, the one compelling detour is to the **Certosa di Pisa**, a marvellous Baroque charterhouse. This stretch of the Arno valley, however, is unremittingly industrialized: **Pontedera** is of interest as the home of Piaggio, manufacturer of the ubiquitous Vespa scooter, but that's just about all you need to know. On the routes south towards Volterra and Siena, across the Pisan hills, only the spa town of **Casciana Terme** and the thirteenth-century Romanesque church at **Paláia** warrant a call. West of Pisa, **Marina di Pisa** and **Tirrenia** are the city's local resorts. Neither is very inspiring, but the area just inland has the **Parco Regionale di San Rossore** and the ancient church of **San Piero a Grado**.

The Certosa di Pisa

Certosa di Pisa Guided tours hourly: Tues–Sat 9am–6.30pm, Sun 9am–12.30pm • €4 • **Natural history collection** July to mid-Sept Tues–Fri 10am–7pm, Sat & Sun 10am–8pm; mid-Sept to June Mon–Sat 9am–6pm, Sun 10am–7pm • €7 • CPT bus #120 or 160 from Pisa.

Of the thirty Carthusian monasteries left intact in Italy, none makes a more diverting excursion than the vast fourteenth-century **Certosa di Pisa**, set at the foot of the forested Monte Pisano near the village of **Calci**, 10km east of Pisa.

The size of the Certosa is startling. From the frescoed central **church**, the tour passes through eleven other **chapels** in which Sunday Mass was apparently conducted simultaneously. Looking as fresh as the day they were decorated (they have not been restored), these are strangely sybaritic interiors – all powder blue, baby pink, pale violet and pallid green, with stucco details and *trompe l'oeil* pillars and balustrades. Floors are covered with tiles that are only paint-deep, and there's a rectangular chapel tricked out to look like an oval room with a dome.

This ballroom decor contrasts with the austerity of the **cloister** and its cells. Each monk had a suite of three rooms – a bedroom, a study and a workroom. Attached to every suite is a self-contained garden, walled so that the monks could maintain their soul-redeeming isolation. Their meals were served through hatches, positioned to minimize the possibility of coming face to face – except on Sundays, when conversation was permitted and all the monks ate together.

From the cloister the tour progresses to the **refectory**, where frescoes of seminal moments in the history of the monastery are interspersed with images of the months and their associated crops as a reminder of the order's self-sufficiency. Nearby are the luxuriously appointed **guest rooms**, where high-born VIPs – various Medici among them – would stay for a bout of not-too-rigorous scourging of the spirit. Their private cloister features yet more *trompe l'oeil*, its windows "opening" onto the dining room and monks' cloister. At the end of the tour, look for an inscription above the gate; directed at any monks leaving on a mission into the outside world, it reads "Egredere sed non omnius" (Leave, but not entirely).

Parts of the Certosa complex are owned by the University of Pisa, who have installed their **natural history museum** here; it's a vast assemblage of skeletons, fossils and rocks, but non-specialists might not find the €7 ticket is a good investment.

San Piero a Grado

Daily 9am–6pm

Some 6km southwest of Pisa, on the road to Marina di Pisa, is the monastic complex of **San Piero a Grado**, allegedly founded by St Peter himself, on his way to Rome and martyrdom. The site is now in ruins except for the glorious eleventh-century basilica, a double-apsed church built from lustrous local yellow sandstone. St Peter's story is detailed in a sequence of pale fourteenth-century frescoes inside the basilica, at one end of which a section of a fourth-century oratory has been excavated, the most ancient Christian site in this part of Tuscany.

Parco Regionale di San Rossore

Park visitor centre Tenuta di San Rossore, Cascine Vecchie • Sat & Sun: summer 8am–7.30pm, winter 8am–5.30pm • ☏ 050 533 755, ⓦ parcosanrossore.it

The **Parco Regionale di San Rossore**, which spreads over the coastal hinterland between Viareggio and Livorno, encloses some 230 square kilometres of unspoiled dunes, marshland, peat bogs and dense pine woods, which support substantial populations of deer, goat and wild boar. (Until World War II the woodlands were also home to a herd of dromedaries, descendants of animals placed here by Grand Duke Ferdinando II in the 1620s.) Much of the park can be explored freely, and the main **visitor centre** at Cascine Vecchie, 6km from Pisa, offers excellent **guided tours** as well as bike rental.

At the centre of the park's coastline lies the village of **Gombo**, scene of the cremation of Shelley, who drowned here in 1822 and was reduced to ashes in the presence of his friends Lord Byron and Edward Trelawny. **Marina di Pisa**, to the south of Gombo, is an unenticing resort; **Tirrenia**, 5km south, is a better bet, with finer sand that's separated from the road by pines and parkland; both can be reached easily by bus from Pisa.

Livorno and around

As Tuscany's third-largest city (after Florence and Prato) and Italy's second-biggest port (after Genoa), **LIVORNO** should really have more going for it than it does. Unfortunately, its docks invited blanket bombing in World War II, and the rebuilt commercial centre is not pretty. There are a few diversions in town however, but just south of Livorno are the beaches of the so-called **Costa degli Etruschi**.

The **Porto Mediceo** – the canal-enclosed area in which the Piazza Grande stands – is Livorno's most picturesque corner, and still conforms to the pentagonal plan devised for the Medici by Buontalenti in 1557. The focal point of the piazza is the **Duomo**, a postwar reconstruction of interest mainly for its doorway by Inigo Jones, whose subsequent plan for London's Covent Garden was a direct copy of the square. From here Via Grande leads down to the sea, where Sangallo's **Fortezza Vecchia** guards the bustling harbour and its tributary canals, about 100m north of central Livorno's only artwork of note, the **Quattro Mori** statue (1623) by the Carraran sculptor Pietro Tacca. To the east of the Duomo, on Via Buontalenti, the ochre **Mercato Centrale** stands at the heart of a boisterous street market.

Museo Civico Giovanni Fattori

Via San Jacopo in Acquaviva 65 • Tues–Sun 10am–1pm & 4–7pm • €4 • Bus #1

The **Museo Civico Giovanni Fattori**, 1km south of the centre in the beautiful Villa Mimbelli, is devoted to Fattori and the late nineteenth-century **Macchiaioli movement**, Italy's equally refined yet homelier precursor Impressionism, alongside works by Post-Macchiaioli and Divisionisti painters.

The Fortezza Nuova

About 1km northeast of the Fortezza Vecchia lies the Venezia district, where crumbling old tenement buildings overlook the bulky **Fortezza Nuova**, a moated, semi-derelict fortress ringed by quiet canals. At the end of July and beginning of August the area comes alive with the **Effetto Venezia**, a lively street festival (ⓦ effettovenezia.com) featuring international dance performances, live music, acrobats, fire jugglers, puppetry, fireworks and, of course, food.

ARRIVAL AND DEPARTURE   LIVORNO

Dozens of **ferries** sail from Livorno daily to **Corsica**, **Sardinia**, **Sicily** and the **Tuscan islands**. If you're taking a car to Sardinia, note that most companies offer discount deals if you cross to Corsica and drive the 180km to the southern tip of the island – and often the subsequent ferry to Sardinia is free.

BY TRAIN

Livorno train station is 2km east of the centre; buses #1 and #2 run from here to Piazza Grande.

Destinations Campiglia Maríttima (every 30min; 1hr); Castagneto Carducci (for Populonia, every 30min; 45min); Castiglioncello (every 30min; 25min); Florence (12 daily; 1hr 30min); Quercianella (every 30min; 15min); Rome (hourly; 3–4hr).

BY BUS

Most long-distance buses also stop in Piazza Grande, although buses from Florence, Pisa and Lucca use Piazza Manin, a short distance south.

Destinations Castiglioncello (every 30min; 35min); Piombino (for Elba, 2 daily; 1hr 30min); Pisa (hourly; 40min).

BY FERRY

Nearly all ferries to Corsica and Sardinia leave from alongside the Stazione Maríttima, west of the centre behind the Fortezza Vecchia, although some (and boats to Sicily) depart from Varco Galvani, a long way west of town. Ferries to Capraia leave from the central Porto Mediceo. Check with the tourist office and the companies themselves for times and prices, and reserve well ahead in summer.

FERRY COMPANIES

Corsica Ferries/Sardinia Ferries Stazione Maríttima, Calata Carrara ☎ 199 400 500 or ☎ 0586 881 380, ⓦ corsicaferries.it. To Bastia (Corsica) and Golfo Aranci (Sardinia).

Grandi Navi Veloci (Grimaldi) Varco Galvani, Calata Tripoli, Porto Nuovo ☎ 06 4208 3567, ⓦ grimaldi-ferries.it. To Palermo (Sicily).

Moby Lines Stazione Maríttima, Calata Carrara ☎ 0586 899 950, ⓦ mobylines.it. To Bastia (Corsica), Porto Vecchio (Corsica), Olbia (Sardinia) and Barcelona.

Toremar Porto Mediceo ☎ 0586 896 113, ⓦ toremar.it. To Gorgona and Capraia.

INFORMATION

Tourist office The local and regional offices are at Piazza del Municipio 1 & 4 (Mon–Fri 9am–1pm & 3–5pm, Sat 9am–1pm; local ☎ 0586 820 111, ⓦ www.comune.livorno .it; regional ☎ 0586 257 111, ⓦ provincia.livorno.it).

ACCOMMODATION AND EATING

Cavour Via Adua 10 ☎ 0565 899 604, ⓦ hotelcavour -livorno.it. A rather nondescript but friendly old hotel, with a dozen or so simple rooms, all large and scrupulously maintained, with ceiling fans. Wi-fi is available, but no breakfast, though there is a coffee machine. **€60**

Vecchia Livorno Scali delle Cantine 34 ☎ 0565 884 048, ⓦ vecchialivornoristorante.it. This excellent restaurant serves up fresh fish meals for around €35 per person. The fish-based *frittura* is a speciality, as well as typical Livorno dishes such as *caciucco* (spicy seafood stew) and *triglie* (mullet). Booking advisable. Mon–Sat 12.30–3pm & 7.30–10.30pm.

POPULONIA AND THE GOLFO DI BARATTI

Some 50km to the south of Livorno, perched on a high, rocky headland 5km off the coast road, **Populonia** was once a centre of Etruscan and Roman iron production. Now it's a tiny place looking down on the broad, half-moon bay of the **Golfo di Baratti**, with some of the best beaches for miles around. The enterprising inhabitants have opened a small private **museum** of Etruscan odds and ends at Via San Giovanni di Sotto 8 (April, May & Oct Tues–Fri 9am–1pm, Sat & Sun 10am–1pm & 3–7pm; June & Sept Tues–Sun 10am–1pm & 3–7pm; July & Aug Tues–Thurs & Sat–Sun 10am–1pm & 4–8pm, Fri 10am–1pm & 4–11pm; Nov–Feb Sat & Sun 10am–5pm; March Sat & Sun 10am–1pm & 3–7pm; €6).

In the bay below, once Populonia's port, there's a cluster of houses glorified with the name of **Baratti**, a colourful base for fishing boats, whose Etruscan roots are celebrated in an eighty-hectare **archeological park** (same hours as museum; €9–12 depending on number of sites visited; ☎ 0565 225 445, ⓦ parchivaldicornia.it), where you could spend a whole day exploring the various zones or taking a guided tour of the ancient mines.

The Costa degli Etruschi

There's little to distinguish the resorts that cling to the road south from Livorno along the so-called **Costa degli Etruschi** (Etruscan Coast; ⓦ costadeglietruschi.it), though there are a few pleasant **beaches** to explore, as well as **Etruscan remains** in and around the ancient site of **Populonia** (see box above). About 13km south of Livorno, **Quercianella** is a relatively small resort with a pebbly beach. **Castiglioncello**, 8km farther south, is the biggest of the resorts, sprawling over several bays; some with sand, most with pebbles) and all crammed with boats and beach huts. The best beach here is the fee-charging **Quercetano**, while **Vada**, 7km farther on, has a featureless modern centre but is preferable to Castiglioncello due to its good town beach and long, flat stretch of sand and pines to the south.

All the main towns along this coast are served by several trains daily from Livorno.

ACCOMMODATION AND EATING   COSTA DEGLI ETRUSCHI

Alba Via Baratti 57, Baratti ☎ 0565 29 521. This ten-room hotel is the nicest on Baratti's seafront and has a pleasant garden and a restaurant. Breakfast and parking included. **€67**

Da Ugo Via Pari 3a Castagneto Carducci ☎ 0565 763 746. On the main SS1 midway between Castiglioncello amd Populonia, this family-run restaurant has great views and focuses on Tuscan country specialities, such as wild boar and pigeon, served either roasted or with egg pasta, and there's fresh fish, too, at €70 per kilo. A full meal for two should average about €90, wine and dessert included. Tues–Sun 12.30–3.30pm & 7.30–11pm; closed part of Nov.

Paradiso Verde Piazza del Forte 1, Marina di Bibbona ☎ 0565 600 022, ⓦ hotelparadisoverde.it. Located about 40km south of Livorno and set midst greenery just steps from the Blue Flag beach, this large, modern resort hotel has forty rooms, all with a/c, plus private free parking, a swimming pool, a restaurant and a bar. Half- or full-board only, drinks not included. Doubles including half-board **€132**

Tripesce Camping Via Cavallaggeri 88, Vada ☎ 0586 788 017, ⓦ campingtripesce.it. The private white-sand beach here is wonderful, and watersports opportunities abound, including windsurfing, canoeing and snorkelling. Facilities include a bar and a restaurant, a market, a secure car-park, and the sites are shady. Open April to mid-Oct. Adults **€8**, plus pitch **€18**

Elba

Nearly 30km long and 20km across, **ELBA** is the third-largest Italian island (after Sicily and Sardinia), yet until thirty years ago it was known only for its mineral resources and as Napoleon's place of exile. Now, however, it's suffering the fate of many a Mediterranean idyll, devoured by tourism in the summer and all but deserted in the long off-season. If you come here in August, when an estimated one million visitors flood onto Elba, you'll have trouble finding a room or even space to camp. To get the most out of the island, visit in spring or late summer.

Elba has been inhabited since about 3000 BC owing to its **mineral** wealth. The Greeks named it **Aethalia** ("Sparks") after its many forges, and Roman swords were made of Elban iron. The last iron ore mine closed in 1984, but it's still a geologist's dream, with an estimated thousand different minerals, from andalusite to zircon.

The island's enduring appeal comes from its exceptionally clear water, fine white-sand beaches and a mountainous interior suited to easy summer strolls. Development is spread over a series of fairly restrained resorts, and the towns and villages retain their distinct characters. **Portoferraio** is very much the capital and centre of the road and transport network; **Marina di Campo**, on the south coast, has the best beach. The least visited and loveliest part of the island centres on **Monte Capanne** (1018m) and the western coast from Marciana to Fetovaia. **Poggio** and the central interior villages are sheltered by lush woods and give access to hikes in the hills. In the island's eastern segment – the old mining district – **Porto Azzurro**, and the more pleasant **Capoliveri**, give access to a string of smaller but much-visited villages.

ARRIVAL AND DEPARTURE ELBA

The main port of departure to Elba is **Piombino**, 75km south of Livorno – not a great place to stay, since it was flattened in World War II, and these days it makes its living from a giant steelworks. If you're arriving by **train**, you'll probably have to change at Campiglia Maríttima station, from where connecting trains run through the town to Piombino Maríttima (hourly; 30min) and Populonia (2 daily; 15min).

By ferry Most people head to Elba's Portoferraio, to where Toremar, Blu Navy and Moby ferries run every day of the year, the first around 5.50am and the last around 10.30pm (earlier and later in high summer; summer every 30min; winter every 2hr; journey time 1hr). There are ticket outlets for all ferry companies in Piombino; tickets cost about €70 one-way for a car and driver, including port taxes, €15 for additional passengers and foot passengers, tax included. If you're looking to cut costs, get Toremar's cheaper ferry (about €50; foot passengers €8) to Rio Marina on the island's east coast.

Note that you should book your return ticket from Elba as far in advance as possible in summer. Contact details for ferry companies are given on p.224.

By hydrofoil and fast ferry From Piombino, Toremar hydrofoils (*aliscafo*) head to Rio Marina (summer 2–3 daily), Porto Azzurro (summer 1 daily), Cavo (summer 5 daily; winter 3 daily; 20min) and Portoferraio (summer 4 daily). Toremar's additional rapid ferry, or *linea veloce*, serves Portoferraio (summer 2 daily; 40min) and Rio Marina (summer 3 daily; 30min). Fares for hydrofoils and fast ferries are about €20 per person, including tax.

GETTING AROUND

By bus Buses run to just about everywhere on the island (limited service after 8pm); the key services from Portoferraio are to Procchio, Marina di Campo and Porto Azzurro; other routes are more sporadic.

By boat Boats are much used to reach out-of-the-way beaches and they're well advertised at all the ports; in high season, expect to pay €70–100 per day, excluding fuel.

By bike, scooter and car Renting a bike or scooter is a good way of exploring the island, but car rental is less advisable: roads to the beaches and around the major resorts can get nastily congested in high season, while winter bookings can be hard to come by.

TUSCANY'S ISLANDS

The seven Tuscan islands – Elba, Capraia, Gorgona, Montecristo, Pianosa, Giglio and Giannutri (private) – together comprise the largest protected marine park in Europe, the **Parco Nazionale Arcipelago Toscano** (islepark.it). **Capraia** was once a prison island, a function still performed by **Gorgona**, the tiny island to the north. The jail on nearby Pianosa is now closed and although access is limited, an occasional ferry shuttles day-trippers from Elba. The rocky islet of **Montecristo** – poking 645m above the waves south of Elba – is accessible only to research scientists. Reached from Porto Santo Stefano further south, **Giglio** is a popular holiday destination (see p.253).

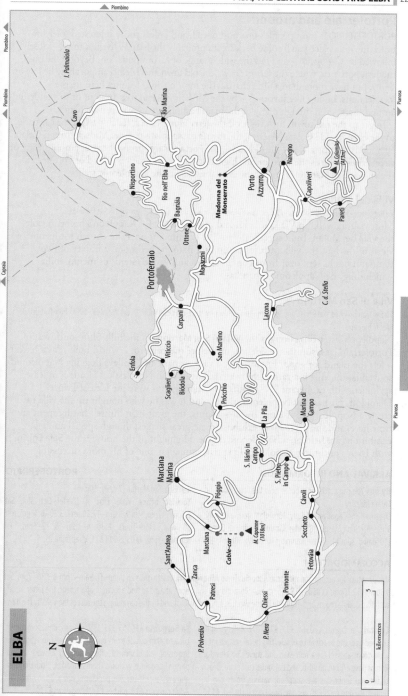

ELBA

4

Portoferraio and around

PORTOFERRAIO is most people's first port of call, and unless you're interested solely in beach life it's a place you'll come back to: it's probably the island's liveliest town – closely followed by Capoliveri – and has the widest range of accommodation. Beyond the busy modern port area, where the ferries arrive, the **old town** and Medicean **port** may be low on sights, but have more than a little charm. The most obvious features here are the **fortifications**, built – like Livorno's – by the Medici; you can pass an hour or so wandering around them, even though many of the main bastions are now in private hands.

To get to the old town, turn right off the ferry along Calata Italia, past all the car parks, to the harbourside Calata Mazzini, the town's **passeggiata** parade. Midway round Calata Mazzini is the entrance to the old town, the **Porta a Mare**, from where an amphitheatre of streets rises towards the walls on the high cliffs. A few kilometres inland of Portoferraio, the villa at **San Martino** is one of the crucial sights on the Napoleonic trail.

Villa dei Mulini

Via Napoleone • Mon & Wed–Sat 9am–7pm, Sun 9am–1pm • €3, or joint three-day ticket with Villa di San Martino €5

Most visitors walk up Via Garibaldi and make straight for **Napoleon**'s home in exile, the **Villa dei Mulini**. Built specifically for the ex-emperor on a site chosen for its fine views of the bay, the villa features a stunning Baroque bedroom, a library of two thousand books sent over from Fontainebleau and various items of memorabilia – including the Napoleonic Elban flag.

Villa di San Martino

Via San Martino • Wed–Sat 9am–7pm, Sun 9am–1pm • €3, or joint three-day ticket with Villa dei Mulini €5 • Bus #1 from Portoferraio goes to the gates

Napoleon's sister Elisa bought the **Villa di San Martino**, in the hills 5km southwest of Portoferraio, as a summer residence just before the emperor – who'd built it as a retreat – left the island for good. Engulfed by a vast car park and trolleys flogging Napoleonic souvenirs, the villa is a rather chilly affair, but its drab Neoclassical facade is at least sprinkled with exuberant "N" motifs. The monograms were the idea of Prince Demidoff, husband of Napoleon's niece – and it was he who bought up the villa to create a Napoleonic museum. By all accounts, the great man himself hardly spent any time here, and the permanent exhibits are no great shakes, though special annual exhibitions are held on a Napoleonic theme. Highlight of the house is the **Sala Egizio**, with friezes outlining Napoleon's Egyptian campaign, one of his more successful.

ARRIVAL AND INFORMATION
PORTOFERRAIO

By bus You can catch most buses near the ferry docks, at Calata Mazzini.

Destinations Capoliveri (7 daily; 30min); Marciana (8 daily; 1hr); Marciana Marina (8 daily; 35min); Marina di Campo (10 daily; 30min); Porto Azzurro (10 daily; 30min); Rio nell'Elba/Rio Marina (7 daily; 50min).

Tourist office Viale Elba 4 (Easter–Oct Mon–Sat 8.30am–7pm, Sun 9.30am–12.30pm & 3.30–6.30pm; rest of year Mon–Thurs 8.30am–1pm & 2–5pm, Fri 8.30am–1pm; ☎ 0565 914 671, ⓦ aptelba.it).

ACCOMMODATION

If you're stuck for accommodation, the **Associazione Albergatori**, Calata Italia 26 (Mon–Fri 9am–1pm & 3.30–7pm, Sat 9.30am–12.30pm; ☎ 0565 915 555, ⓦ elbapromotion.it) will phone around to find a room or apartment, the latter mostly with two double rooms and available by the week in July and August and by the day during the rest of the year by the day.

Crystal Via Cairoli ☎ 0565 917 971, ⓦ hotelcrystal.it. Located near the beach at Le Ghiaie, this hotel-restaurant is a bit down-at-heel for a four-star, and there's no elevator. Rooms have a/c but no wi-fi, and balconies cost extra. Beach chairs and umbrellas are supplied; various boats can be rented. Parking costs €10 per day. Breakfast included. **€150**

La Sorgente ☎ 0565 917 139, ⓦ campinglasorgente.it. Located 4km out of town on the road west to Viticcio, this beachside establishment offers camping as well as four-person bungalows with a/c. There's a market, picnicking areas and a restaurant-bar with panoramic views. Open April–Oct. Adult campers **€14**, pitches **€14**, bungalows **€130**

L'Ape Elbana Salita Cosimo de' Medici 9 ☎0565 914 245, ⓦape-elbana.it. With an ideal central position just off the main piazza, this mustard-yellow hotel-restaurant is the island's oldest and handy to everything. Rooms (and bathrooms especially) are very basic: the best are the generally more spacious options overlooking the piazza. Breakfast included. Free private parking just in front. €110

Massimo Calata Italia 23 ☎0565 914 766, ⓦelbahotelmassimo.it. Accommodation here is certainly nothing special, and this modern hotel-restaurant is right at the port, so it can get noisy, but it's handy for the beaches and the old town. The simple, rather worn rooms all have balconies and a/c, and there's a lift. Breakfast included. €130

EATING AND DRINKING

Enoteca della Fortezza Via Scoscesa ☎335 839 3722. Deep in the labyrinthine Rocca, with views of the port from the battlements – at the gate, tell them you're going to the *enoteca*. Plates of cheese, snacks and desserts go for about €6, while glasses of the good local wines start at just €2. Tues–Sun 11am–3pm & 6pm–midnight.

Il Castanacciaio Via del Mercato Vecchio ☎0565 915 845. This deeply authentic place is a Portoferraio institution. There's a host of wood-fired pizzas to choose from, but don't overlook their local specialities, the *torta di ceci*, a kind of *focaccia* made with chickpea flour, and the

catagnaccio, something similar but sweet and made with chestnut flour. Mains €6–8 per dish. Tues–Sun noon–midnight.

La Carretta Magazzini 92 ☎0565 933 223. This excellent fish restaurant is run by a very friendly family who always make you feel at home. The cuisine is simple, but the fish is very fresh, and the seafood ravioli is perhaps the best on the island – there's often home-made cheesecake for dessert, too. €35–40 per person, depending on wine. May–Oct daily 7pm–midnight; Nov–April Fri–Sun 7–11pm.

Eastern Elba

Eastern Elba is a distinct geographical area, comprising two tongues of land, each dominated by mountain ridges. The main centres are the mildly diverting **Porto Azzurro** and **Capoliveri**; **Rio Marina**, a port of call for Toremar ferries, isn't one of Elba's more appealing towns, though it does have one of the island's better restaurants. Away from the towns you'll find comparatively quiet hamlets, some with good **beaches**, although much of the southern isthmus – Monte Calamita (Magnet) – was the heart of the mining industry, and is still owned by the quarrying companies.

4

NAPOLEON AND ELBA

Elba is indissolubly linked with **Napoleon**, even though he was exiled here for little more than nine months – from May 4, 1814 to February 26, 1815. According to island tradition, after renouncing the thrones of France and Italy by the Treaty of Fontainebleau, Napoleon chose Elba as his place of exile for the "gentleness of its climates and its inhabitants". In fact, he had no choice: the allies packed him off here, sweetening the pill by ordaining that Elba would be "a separate principality for his lifetime, held by him in complete sovereignty". The dethroned emperor spent the journey south doodling a new flag for his pocket-sized domain: a red diagonal on a white background – echoing the Medici banner – plus the bees of his own imperial emblem.

After a confusing episode in which his ship was shelled from Portoferraio, Napoleon came ashore to a rousing welcome, and soon set about reorganizing the island's **economy** and **infrastructure**. Some of this work might have been motivated by altruism or an inability to forgo politics, but much of what he achieved was for his own ends. The iron ore mines were revamped to supplement his income, his promised salary from Louis XVII having never materialized; the public works were to occupy and pay for the five-hundred-strong Napoleonic Guard that stuck by him. Portoferraio was given drains because the stench offended the imperial nostrils.

Some of the longer-term planning, however, undoubtedly paid dividends to the islanders: education and the legal system were overhauled, roads were built, agriculture was modernized, land was cleared, defences were repaired. These multifarious schemes suggested that Napoleon had resigned himself to his life sentence, but intrigue, rumour and unrest in France persuaded him to have another go. The day after Sir Neil Campbell, his British keeper, left for Livorno, he returned to France and the "Hundred Days" that were to culminate in his defeat at Waterloo.

Porto Azzurro

The resort of **PORTO AZZURRO** was heavily fortified by Philip III of Spain in 1603 as protection against continual raids by the French and the Austrians; today his fortress is the island's prison but you can walk around the walls and admire the inmates' artwork at a small craft shop. The town's small, pretty old quarter, closed to traffic, centres on **Via d'Alarcon**, a bustle of bars, shops and restaurants, with traditional open-front shops and balconied houses in the cobbled area near Piazza Matteotti.

The best place to swim is from the rocks east of the harbour. **Boat trips** (around €20 for 3hr) run south along the coast in summer.

Capoliveri

CAPOLIVERI, 3.5km south of Porto Azzurro, is the best of the towns in eastern Elba, a prosperous centre whose close-knit streets have made few concessions to tourism. Occupying a naturally fortified spot, it's amongst the oldest settlements on the island: in Roman times its name was Caput Liberi. Its hinterland remains undeveloped, as the mining companies have not yet sold their disused plots to the hoteliers – though consequently much of the area is out of bounds.

There's nothing specific to see, but **old streets** such as Via Roma, Via Cavour and Vicolo Lungo are pleasant to roam, and there are numerous half-hidden bars in the alleyways, as well as a sprawl of outside tables in the central piazza. The town is at its busiest on Thursdays, when locals and tourists flood in for the weekly street market; it is also very lively in the evenings, with a reputation for being the place to go for a night out.

4

INFORMATION
EASTERN ELBA

Tourist office Via Palestro, Capoliveri (June to mid-Sept Mon–Sat 10am–1pm & 5–8pm; ☎0565 967 029, ⓦaptelba.it).

ACCOMMODATION

LACONA

Il Lacona Camping ☎0565 964 161, ⓦcamping -lacona.it. Set in pine woods on the eastern arm of the Golfo di Lacona, just 100m from a pebble beach and 400m from a sandy beach with dunes and good areas for snorkelling. The grounds are well shaded, and facilities include a market, café, pool and internet, and there are bungalows (rentable by the week only) as well as tent pitches. Open April–Oct. Adult campers €14.50, pitches €11.50

Stella Mare Camping ☎0565 964 007, ⓦstellamare .it. This attractive campsite is out along the headland, built on terraces sloping down to the beach amidst plenty of greenery. There's a bar and a restaurant, wi-fi and two-person chalets as well as camping pitches. Free bike rental and windsurfing lessons, too. Open April–Oct. Adult campers €14.50, pitches €11.50, chalet €125

PORTO AZZURO

Belmare Banchina IV Novembre 25 ☎0565 95 012, ⓦelba-hotelbelmare.it. Right on the waterfront, this modern hotel has simple rooms with balconies and an Astroturf sun terrace with sea or mountain views. Seaview rooms, which have a/c, cost extra. Free private parking, and buffet breakfast included. €110

★ **Villa Italia** Viale Italia 41 ☎0565 95 119, ⓦvillaitaliahotel.it. Just 100m from the beach, this

---

THE BEST OF THE EASTERN BEACHES

Along with the lively towns, there are some good beaches and swimming areas spread all around the eastern shores. Following the twisting coast road around the bay east and then north you'll come to the tiny twin hamlets of **Nisporto** and **Nisportino**, marking the beginning of the least developed beaches and coastline on Elba's north shore.

On the southern isthmus, beyond Porto Azzurro, **Naregno** is a small resort with a good, big beach capped by the Forcardo fortress. Working clockwise around the coast and west of Porto Azzurro, **Lacona** is one of the island's main camping centres, and its flat foreshore is crowded with bars and clubs designed to cater to the beach crowd once the sun's gone down. The central part of the beach is the least developed stretch, and the water remains shallow for some distance out to sea, making it especially good for children.

family-run hotel with a small garden has twelve pleasant, newly redone rooms, some with balcony. Breakfast is included, and parking available nearby. Surcharge for a/c is €5 per day. **€93**

NAREGNO
Franks ☎ 0565 968 144, ⓦ frankshotel.com. This modern 53-room hotel-restaurant, occupying several buildings, has a lot of pluses, though some of the facilities need freshening up. Rooms are spacious, some with balconies, plus there are garden areas. The beach is a 10min walk away, and chairs and umbrellas are generally provided. Their restaurant is excellent, with terraces and live music in the evening. Doubles including half-board **€150**

NISPORTO
Sole e Mare Camping ☎ 0565 934 907, ⓦ soleemare .it. This campsite is just about the only accommodation in Nisporto, 20m from the sea and fully shaded by a variety of trees. Eating options include a pizzeria, a restaurant and a market, and four-person bungalows are available. Adults **€15**, pitches **€15**

EATING

CAPOLIVIERI
Il Chiasso Vicolo Sauro 9 ☎ 0565 968 709. Seafood is the speciality at this charming, somewhat off-the-beaten-path restaurant, a favourite with locals. Try the black *fettuccine* with red shrimp – but all the fish is scrupulously fresh. A full meal runs at €50–60 per person. June–Sept daily noon–4pm & 6pm–midnight; May & Oct Mon & Wed–Sun 6pm–midnight; closed Nov–Easter.

RIO MARINA
★ **Da Oreste la Strega** Piazza Vittorio Emanuele ☎ 0565 962 211. Very good fish restaurant and pizzeria. The *gnocchi* with octopus is memorable, as is the seafood ravioli, and there's a pleasant terrace seating. Wonderful home-made *mascarpone* for dessert. About €40 per person, depending on wine. Daily noon–4pm & 7–11pm; closed Tues Nov–Easter.

Western Elba

Western Elba's road system allows for a circular tour of the area, but many people make immediately for specific targets – usually **Marina di Campo**, with its huge beach and many hotels. Upmarket alternatives are offered by the north-coast resorts of **Procchio** and **Marciana Marina**, while backpackers favour the relatively less commercialized area around the Capo d'Énfola.

Fewer visitors venture inland to **Marciana**, one of Elba's most attractive villages, or explore the long sweep of the **western coast**, whose hamlets and beaches are amongst the island's most tranquil. Though the western zone tends to be rockier than the east, it's better for **walking**, the highlights being **Monte Capanne** and its surrounding ridges.

Capo d'Énfola and around

For a spread of beach and a choice of campsites near Portoferraio, follow the scenic road below Monte Poppe to the headland at **Capo d'Énfola**, where the land narrows to a 75-metre-wide isthmus with beaches on both sides. The road ends at a small car park where you can get down to either strip of pebbly beach. You can also continue on to **VITICCIO**, another spot with a dead-end road, parking area and sand-and-shingle beach. From Viticcio, a footpath runs 2km round the coast to Scaglieri and Biodola, otherwise reached by a side road from the main highway out of Portoferraio. **BIODOLA** consists simply of a road, two big hotels and a superb **beach**, which inevitably gets a summer blitz of visitors. **SCAGLIERI** is similar but a touch livelier and more picturesque, fronted by a shop, two bars and a sprinkling of places to stay and eat.

Procchio to Poggio

PROCCHIO suffers from being at a junction of main roads, the greenery of its surroundings offset by an incessant stream of summer traffic. With its shops and bars it's not a place to get away from it all, but the sea is good and the white **beach** excellent; access to much of the sand is free and it's large enough not to seem overcrowded.

About 4km on from Procchio is charming **MARCIANA MARINA**, its pebble beach overlooked by a Pisan watchtower. Some 5km inland from Marciana Marina, **POGGIO** is

4

renowned for its **Fonte di Napoleone** mineral water and a tight medieval centre whose decorated doorways and patchwork of cheerful gardens make it an attractive place to stay.

Marciana

It's a few steep kilometres up the mountain road from Poggio to the high and isolated village of **MARCIANA**, the oldest settlement on Elba, which is perfectly placed between great beaches (Promonte and Sant'Andrea) and a modern centre for supplies (Procchio); it's also well-placed for exploring the mountainous interior around Monte Capanne. Marciana's **old quarter** is a delight, too, its narrow alleys, arches, belvederes and stone stairs festooned with flowers and climbing plants. There's virtually no traffic or commercial development, and with the skeletal outline of its old fortifications it feels very distinct from the rest of the island's towns.

Sant'Andrea and south to Seccheto

The dispersed village of **SANT'ANDREA**, 6km west of Marciana, just off the coast road, is one of Elba's more fashionable retreats, with villas and hotels creeping further into the wooded hinterland each year. It's popular with divers, drawn here by what is reputedly some of the clearest water around Elba.

Immediately south is the hamlet of **PATRESI**, rated as having the island's finest seas and still fairly unspoilt into the bargain. Cliffs drop to the sea, as they do all round this section of coast, with plenty of rock pillars and stacks for underwater enthusiasts.

Further on, **SECCHETO** is good for a swim from the rocks at the western end of town, or for tanning on the largely nudist stretch beyond, known as **le piscine**, where the water forms deep pools in the hollows of a Roman granite mine.

Marina di Campo

Set in one of the island's few areas of plain, **MARINA DI CAMPO** was the first and is now the largest resort on Elba. The huge white **beach** is what makes the place popular: the water's clean, and there's space if you walk to the east end or out to the rockier west. There's also all the tourist frippery and **nightlife** you'd expect in any major seaside centre.

ACCOMMODATION   WESTERN ELBA

CAPO D'ÉNFOLA AND AROUND

Casa Rosa Via Biodola 1, Biodola ☎ 0565 969 931, ⓦ elbasolare.it. Extensive resort located right in the centre of Biodola's fine white-sand beach and surrounded by the greenery of the national park, with a pool, tennis court and basic, clean rooms with a/c. Meals created from their own farm produce are served on the restaurant's terrace. Breakfast included. Open March 15–Oct 20. **€160**

Danila Spiaggia di Scaglieri ☎ 0565 969 915, ⓦ hoteldanila.it. This hotel-restaurant is set amidst beautiful gardens, which makes up for the generally small rooms and rather outdated furnishings. Larger rooms with views cost more. Buffet breakfast included on the restaurant terrace; half-board required in high season. April to mid-Oct. Doubles with half-board **€160**

Enfola Camping Enfola ☎ 0565 939 001, ⓦ campingenfola.it. A shady garden campsite set in the perfect place for all sorts of watersports, especially skin and scuba-diving. Amenities include laundry facilities and a playground, and there's a bar, a café, a pizzeria and a restaurant. April to mid-Oct. Adult campers **€15**, pitches **€18.50**, bungalows **€95**

Paradiso Viticcio ☎ 0565 939 034, ⓦ elbaturistica.it. Family-run and very friendly, this hotel-restaurant isn't luxurious but is pleasant. The pool is good, the restaurant often excellent – €15 for a set menu – and the staff are always ready to help. Pluses include wi-fi and free guided hikes. Buffet breakfast included. Three-night minimum stay. **€160**

PROCCHIO

Monna Lisa Via Fontalleccio 10, Proccio ☎ 0565 907 519, ⓦ hotelmonnalisa.it. Just 100m from the sandy beach, this is a modest hotel surrounded by trees and gardens. Somerooms are rather small, whereas some have balconies and are priced accordingly. The restaurant serves good local cuisine as well as light salad lunches, and breakfast is included in the rates. Mid-May to mid-Sept. **€130**

SANT'ANDREA

★ **La Cernia** ☎ 0565 908 210, ⓦ hotelcernia.it. Right on the beach, this pleasant hotel-restaurant is set amidst tropical vegetation, and has its own pool. Each room is uniquely furnished, with the emphasis on freshness and calm. Breakfast included. Open April–Sept. **€150**

MONTE CAPANNE

If you don't want to walk up Monte Capanne, there's a popular **cable car** (June–Sept 10am–12.15pm & 2.30–6.30pm; Oct–May 10am–12.15pm & 2.30–5.30pm; €10 one-way, €15 return) 1km south of Marciana which takes you to the top; most people choose to walk down either back to Marciana or to Poggio, though if you're trekking with your gear you could drop down to the coast via one of the numerous **marked trails**.

MARINA DI CAMPO

★ **Piccolo Versilia** Via del Acquedotto ☎0565 976 123, ⓦpiccolohotelversilia.it. This small, homely resort gets top marks for comfort, friendliness and location, with great views of the sea. Although on the small side, the rooms are well-appointed and comfortable, all with a/c. The restaurant serves Elban specialities and has both indoor and gazebo seating. Breakfast included. **€120**

EATING

POGGIO

Publius Piazza Castagneto 11 Poggio ☎0565 99 208. Poggio can rightly claim one of the island's leading restaurants, with a charming setting inside, a panoramic terrace and classic Elban cooking, including cacciucco (the local fish stew or soup), chestnut gnocchi with duck ragout, or wild boar with mushrooms. Very professional and friendly service. Full meal €40–50 per person, depending on wine. April to mid-June & mid-Sept to Nov Tues–Sun noon–3.30pm & 7–11pm; mid-June to mid-Sept Mon 7–11pm, Tues–Sun noon–3.30pm & 7–11pm; closed Dec–March.

MARCIANA

★ **Osteria del Noce** Via della Madonna 14 ☎0565 901 284. This excellent restaurant has magnificent views. The menu focuses on fresh fish, with one speciality being grilled triglie (mullet), but don't overlook home-made pastas and scrumptious desserts. Expect to pay €65–85 for two, depending on wine. Book ahead for terrace seating. Daily 1–4pm & 7–10.30pm; closed Oct–mid-March.

MARINA DI CAMPO

Il Cacciucco Piazza Cavour 10 ☎0565 976 489, ⓦilcacciucco.com. For fish, come to this popular spot, where everything is fresh and well turned-out. Their signature fish stew needs to be ordered in advance and costs €28; pasta dishes include seafood spaghetti (€14) and risotto with shellfish (€15). Catch-of-the-day sold by weight. Home-made desserts average €7. A full meal for two will come at least €60, depending on wine. Easter–Oct daily noon–3pm & 8–10.30pm; closed Mon Nov–March.

Capraia

The island of **CAPRAIA**, 30km northwest of Elba, is unspoilt, with just a couple of hotels and one road that links the small port to the old town on the hill. Its former use as a penal colony ensured that the rough, wild terrain remained largely untouched, and now – despite considerable pressure from potential hoteliers – the local council have held back on commercial development, instead promoting the island's status as a **national park** to protect the natural heritage. This makes it difficult to visit, and the two hotels and single campsite come close to saturation point in summer: it's best to come slightly out of season.

ARRIVAL AND DEPARTURE
CAPRAIA

Ferries Toremar (see p.224) run daily ferries from Livorno to Capraia's port throughout the year, and twice-daily services in summer on Thurs and Fri.

Capraia Isola

It's a gentle walk of about 1km from the tiny harbour to the town of **CAPRAIA ISOLA**, the only inhabited part of the island except the port (there's a regular bus in summer). The island's long periods of desolation, mainly because of pirate raids, have done little for its monuments. Capraia Isola's Baroque church and Franciscan monastery of **Sant'Antonio** is still in use, and the big castle, the **Fortezza di San Giorgio**, is privately owned; plans to transform it into luxury apartments have faltered so far.

CAPRAIA'S FAUNA AND FLORA

Capraia's isolation has favoured the development of various indigenous animal and vegetable species, several of them similar to species otherwise confined to Corsica and Sardinia. These include subspecies of buzzard, sparrow, large finch and La Marmora's warbler amongst the **birds**, and campion, toadflax and blue button amongst the **plants**. Birds are the main natural interest, with numerous itinerant visitors and forty resident species including peregrines, shearwaters and up to a hundred pairs of the rare Corsican gull. You can also sight the majestically horned mufflon mountain **goats**, which were introduced to the island when it was a hunting preserve.

INFORMATION AND TOURS

CAPRAIA ISOLA

Tourist information You can get information on wildlife, walking, accommodation and boat trips from the tourist office on the harbourfront, at Via Assunzione 42 (April–Sept daily 10am–6pm; ☎ 0586 905 138) and from the adjoining Cooperativa Parco (same hours; ☎ 0586 905 071, ⓦ isoladicapraia.it).

Boat trips Both the Cooperativa Parco and Agenzia Della Rosa, Via Assunzione 22 (☎ 0586 905 266, ⓦ capraiavacanze

.it) run boat trips round the entire island, usually twice daily in season. You'll see many boats for rent in Capraia Isola, but light craft are not advisable here as the shoreline areas are turbulent and rocky. The authorities are also very strict about how close private craft can come to preserves and where people can fish; the oblivious are liable to be fined.

Scuba diving Capraia Diving Club, Via Assunzione 100 (☎ 0586 905 137, ⓦ capraiadiving.it).

ACCOMMODATION AND EATING

As well as the **hotels** listed here (which may insist on half board during high season), there are numerous private **rooms** and **apartments**; the tourist office will call round for you, or you can just wander through town and look for the signs. There's also a campsite. In terms of **eating**, there are several restaurants, pizzerias and snack bars.

Da Beppone Via Assunzione 78 ☎ 0586 905 001, ⓦ dabeppone.it. This very modest family-run hotel-restaurant, just a few steps up from the sea, has a dining room with picture windows looking out on the port scene and a menu of fresh fish creations (full meals €35). The twelve small rooms have port views and share a communal terrace. Breakfast included. Restaurant open noon–3pm & 8–10.30pm; closed Jan & Feb. €95

★ **La Garitta** Via Genova 14–16 ☎ 0586 905 230. Up near the castle, this is one of the island's best restaurants. Run as a sailing enthusiasts' bar during the day, it's a rustic,

informal place, dedicated to simple, perfectly fresh seafood. The seafood lasagne is extraordinary, as is the grilled calamari. Expect to pay €40–50 for a full meal, exclusive of wine. Easter–Oct daily 1–3.30pm & 8–11pm.

Le Sughere Camping ☎ 0586 905 066, ⓦ campeggiolesughere.it. The island's only campsite is in a woodsy, rustic setting about 200m behind the village's tiny church. There's a market, a pizzeria and a *tavola calda*, as well as pitches and self-catering four-person bungalows, available by the week only. May–Sept. Adult campers €13, pitches €9.50

The interior and the beaches

The scrubby, almost treeless island has a knobbly spine of 400m hills, with the eastern slope shallow and riven with gullies and gulches, and the western coast featuring cliffs rising almost sheer from the sea. **Hiking** tracks crisscross the whole island, and from Capraia Isola you can strike off straight into the wild, uninhabited interior. There are four distinct and fairly obvious **hikes** from the town: to the **Torre dello Zenobito**, a Genoese watchtower on the island's southernmost tip; to **Il Piano** and the Pisan church of **Santo Stefano**, using the rough road south of the town; to the **lighthouse** on the west coast, farther down the same track as the Il Piano walk; and to the **Laghetto**, a tarn in the hills. Bear in mind that there are no services at all outside of Capraia Isola, so be sure to bring food and water with you, and be prepared for rough terrain. Winter storms in 1998 stripped the island's only real beach, the **Cala della Mortola**, of all its sand. However, there are plenty of rocky coves and the water is clean and clear everywhere.

The Maremma

BUTTERI (P.241)

5

The Maremma

The Maremma was long Tuscany's forgotten corner, its coastal plains, marshes, forest-covered hills and wild, empty upland interior having been a place of exile and fear for much of the last five hundred years: unknown, unvisited and virtually uninhabited. Malaria was always the problem, combined with bandits in the interior and pirate attacks on the coast, but with these afflictions finally eradicated, the province's fortunes have improved considerably.

While it lacks truly dazzling towns such as Siena or Arezzo, the Maremma's hill-town **Massa Maríttima** holds its own – although **Grosseto**, the provincial capital, is little more than a transport hub. Elsewhere inland, much of the high, rolling hill country remains untouched and all but unvisited; yet take any of the minor country lanes off the main road from Grosseto to Siena road and you'll encounter countryside as good as any in Tuscany. Efforts have been made to preserve the region's natural treasures, especially in and around the regional park of **Monti dell'Uccellina** and the mountainous island of **Giglio**, which offers hikes, beaches, marinas, towers and a castle. There are many seaside resorts, too, including **Castiglione della Pescaia**, **Porto Santo Stefano** and **Porto Ercole**.

Brief history

The province was the northern heartland of the **Etruscans**, whose drainage and irrigation canals turned it into an area of huge agricultural potential. Their good work, however, was largely lost under the Romans, who abandoned much of the land and left it to revert to **marsh**: "Only the wild beasts that hate the cultivated fields make their lairs in the Tuscan Maremma", wrote Dante. For years, virtually the only inhabitants were migrant charcoal burners and shepherds (who in summer abandoned the pestilential lowlands for the hill-villages of Amiata), and the famous *butteri* (see box, p.241), **cowboys** who even today tend the local oxen and horses. Modern attempts to revive the Maremma were started in 1828 by Grand Duke Leopoldo of Tuscany, who instigated new drainage schemes to combat malaria, but real progress only began under Mussolini; the malarial mosquito was finally banished in 1950. Since then, efforts have been made to preserve the province's unspoiled ecosystems by creating extensive nature reserves.

GETTING AROUND

By train The coast is served by the main Rome–Pisa rail line. To cut across country, there's a rail link from Grosseto to Siena **By bus** A few buses run inland from Grosseto, Orbetello and Massa Maríttima.

By car The old Roman road, the Via Aurelia (now SS1), cuts through the area.

Massa Maríttima

Once the second city of the Sienese Republic and still graced with some of Siena's civic style, **MASSA MARÍTTIMA** is the best-preserved hill-town of the Maremma. Named "Massa" by the Romans – their word for a large country estate – it gained its maritime suffix in the Middle Ages, when it became the pre-eminent town of this coastal area.

The Butteri p.241
Roccatederighi p.243
Fauna and flora in the Uccellina p.249
Walks from Porto Ercole p.251
St Mamiliano's arm p.254

MASSA MARÍTTIMA

Highlights

❶ **Massa Maríttima** This classic Tuscan hill-town has a glorious Romanesque cathedral and provides the perfect setting for scenic rambles. **See p.238**

❷ **Roccatederighi** Tightly clustered round a rock pinnacle, this minuscule stone hamlet affords extraordinary views. **See p.243**

❸ **Castiglione della Pescaia** With a marina and medieval castle, plus beaches and nature reserves nearby, this ancient, picturesque village is a lovely spot to spend a few nights. **See p.245**

❹ **Monti dell'Uccellina** Italy's most pristine stretch of coastal scenery, with a varied and

beautiful terrain of marshes, hills, cliffs and beaches. **See p.246**

❺ **Monte Argentario** A spectacular headland with several fashionable coastal resorts. **See p.250**

❻ **Giardino dei Tarocchi** A whimsical sculpture garden with Gaudí-esque representations of mythic Tarot figures. **See p.253**

❼ **Giglio** This little jewel of an island boasts citadels, stone villages and panoramic mountain hikes, as well as beaches and watersports. **See p.253**

HIGHLIGHTS ARE MARKED ON THE MAP ON P.240

The sea has since receded and is now 20km distant across a silt-filled plain, scarcely visible from the town's position. The historic centre of town is divided into the older lower town, **Città Vecchia**, and the somewhat less old upper town, **Città Nuova**.

Massa, like Volterra to the north, has long been a **mining** town, its silver, copper and other mineral reserves generating wealth since Neolithic times, a story told in the town's **Museo della Miniera**. Regrettably for Massa, its mineral riches attracted the rival attentions of Pisa and Siena, the latter finally absorbing the town in 1335. Those

HIGHLIGHTS
1. Massa Maríttima
2. Roccatederighi
3. Castiglione della Pescaia
4. Monti dell'Uccellina
5. Monte Argentario
6. Giardino dei Tarocchi
7. Giglio

THE MAREMMA

0   10
kilometres

THE BUTTERI

The **butteri**, the Maremmani cowboys, have for centuries taken care of the province's half-feral horses and celebrated white cattle, a special breed imported from Asia for their resilience to the rigours of the Maremma climate and terrain. For most of the year, the *butteri* ride with the herds on the Maremma's grasslands, the key event of the year being the *merca* in April, when the one-year-old calves and foals are rounded up, counted, roped and branded – an electrifying, rough-and-tumble spectacle.

You stand most chance of seeing the *butteri* in action on the Ombrone River estuary, particularly on the road to Marina di Alberese, although from time to time they put on shows during local festivals and special events. Such performances are nothing new: in 1911 Buffalo Bill brought a travelling troupe of cowboys to Rome, where they were trounced by the *butteri* in a series of events in the Piazza del Popolo. Today the best known of their tourist shows is the August **rodeo** in Alberese, and they also prove their skills in perhaps the most demanding equestrian arena in the world – as riders in the Siena Palio.

hundred years of glory, however, funded the building of its monuments – notably the exquisite **Duomo**. Subsequent visitations of plague and malaria, together with a downturn in mining activity, left Massa a virtual ghost town by 1737, its population reduced to just 537. Like other Maremma towns, its recovery began only with the reopening of mines and the draining of coastal marshes in the 1830s.

Città Vecchia

The lower part of town, the mainly Romanesque **Città Vecchia**, is focused on the medieval splendour of Piazza Garibaldi. The square is a small, eccentric, exquisite example of Tuscan town planning, with the thirteenth-century **Duomo** set on broad steps at a dramatically oblique angle to the square, and it's also the site of the civic **museum**.

The Duomo

Daily 8am–noon & 3–7pm

The **Duomo** is essentially Pisan Romanesque, with a few later additions blending harmoniously with the blind arches and tiny columns (most notably the extraordinary Gothic **campanile**, added in about 1400). The cathedral's dedication is to **St Cerbone**, the Bishop of Populonia in the sixth century. Like St Francis, St Cerbone had a legendary way with animals. Although perhaps most famous for persuading a flock of geese to follow him when he was summoned to Rome on heresy charges, he is usually depicted with a bear licking his feet, a reference to the beast he tamed when Totila the Hun threw him into a pit full of wild animals. Bas-reliefs in the architrave of the main door show scenes from his life.

The interior

Inside, the bare stone walls set off some superb carvings and works of art. The most admired carvings are the thirteenth-century ones by Giraldo da Como, on the huge **baptistery** and also the quadrangular **font**. Almost as arresting are the fifteenth-century **tabernacle** (under the marble canopy of the baptistery), and some eleventh-century Romanesque carvings close to the entrance featuring powerful and primitive grinning faces, that are in dramatic contrast with the severe, polished Roman sarcophagus to their right. Over the altar is a large Giovanni Pisano **altarpiece**, and behind it the *Arca di San Cerbone*, an arch of **bas-reliefs** depicting the life of the saint, carved by Gori di Gregorio in 1324. Take a look, too, at the *Madonna delle Grazie* at the end of the left transept, a damaged but gorgeous Sienese work attributed to Duccio or Simone Martini. Finally, the fine little crypt has a single fresco featuring St Cerbone and St Bernardino.

5

Museo Archeologico e Pinacoteca

Piazza Garibaldi • Tues–Sun: April–Oct 10am–12.30pm & 3.30–7pm; Nov–March 10am–12.30pm & 3.30–5pm • €3

The smaller of the two palaces on Piazza Garibaldi, the Palazzo del Podestà, contains the **Museo Archeologico e Pinacoteca**, where the chief exhibit is one of the finest altarpieces in Tuscany, a *Maestà* painted in 1335 by **Ambrogio Lorenzetti**. Vivid pink, green and tangerine illuminate the figures of Faith, Hope and Charity below the Madonna, while Cerbone and his devoted geese lurk in the right-hand corner. The museum otherwise houses only a handful of minor paintings and some local archeological finds.

Museo della Miniera

Via Corridoni • April–Sept Tues–Sun 10am–12.45am & 3.30–5.45pm; winter 10am–noon & 3–4.30pm • Entry by €5 guided tour only • ☎ 0566 902 289

Inevitably, given its mining heritage, Massa has a **Museo della Miniera** (mining museum), set in an old travertine marble quarry that served as an air-raid shelter during World War II. The claustrophobically authentic mock-up mine has 700m of tunnels, with recreations of mining methods, life in the mines and displays of tools and equipment, and there's also an exhibit centred on the *Codice Mineraio*, Europe's first charter for the protection of miners, produced in Massa in 1310.

Città Nuova

The upper **Città Nuova**, "new" town, is generally Gothic in appearance and was built largely as a residential centre. An immensely steep and picturesque lane, **Via Moncini**, connects the old town with the new, passing through an archway, **Porta alle Silici**, while side alleys along the way reveal gardens and good views. Via Moncini terminates at

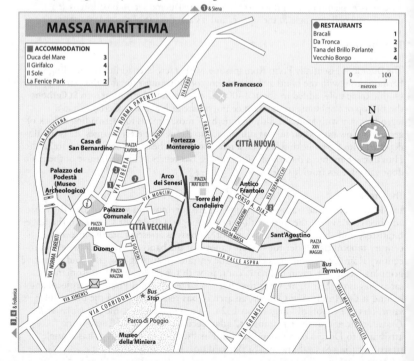

5

Piazza Matteotti, with its fourteenth-century tower, **Torre del Candeliere**, rendered dramatic by its adjoining arch, which resembles a flying buttress.

ARRIVAL AND DEPARTURE

MASSA MARÍTTIMA

By train The nearest train station is Massa–Follonica, 19km west of Massa on the main Pisa–Rome line; hourly buses connect the station with the town.

By bus Buses from Siena, Grosseto and Larderello, as well as shuttles from the train station, stop on Via Corridoni

close to Piazza Garibaldi: get off when you see the campanile of the Duomo.

Destinations Grosseto (1 daily; 1hr 20min); Larderello (for Volterra; 4 daily); Piombino (2 daily; 25min); Siena (2 daily; 1hr 40min).

INFORMATION

Tourist office Via Todini 3 (Mon–Sat 9.30am–12.30pm & 3–6pm, plus April–Sept Sun 10am–1pm & June–Sept Sun 4–7pm; ☎ 0566 902 756, ⓦ massamarittima.info).

ACCOMMODATION

Duca del Mare Piazza Dante Alighieri 1–2 ☎ 0566 902 284, ⓦ www.ducadelmare.it. This modern hotel is a steep walk down from the centre. All rooms are non-smoking and have balconies, a/c, wi-fi (€1 per hr) and modern, quietly plush decor. There's an outdoor pool and garden, plus a restaurant with breakfast room and outside dining in summer. **€85**

Il Girifalco Via Massetana Nord 25 ☎ 0566 902 177, ⓦ ilgirifalco.com. This traditional, family-run hotel has clean rooms, best of which with fine balcony views. There's a children's play area, a pool and plenty of open space. Ample buffet breakfast included. Free parking and wi-fi.

Easter to mid-Oct. **€85**

Il Sole Via della Libertà 43 ☎ 0566 901 971, ⓦ ilsolehotel.it. Handsome hotel set in a very picturesque converted *palazzo*. Rooms – all with a/c, some with views – are quiet and a bit on the austere side. There's a lift up from the free parking lot. Breakfast included. **€95**

★ **La Fenice Park** Corso Diaz 63 ☎ 0566 903 941, ⓦ lafeniceparkhotel.it. This elegant hotel has spacious rooms and really luxurious suites, all with sumptuous marble bathrooms and some with their own spas and lots of extras. There's an immaculate garden and outdoor pool. Buffet breakfast included. Open mid-Feb to Dec. **€160**

EATING AND DRINKING

Bracali Via di Perolla 2, Località Perolla ☎ 0566 902 318, ⓦ mondobracali.it. Sophisticated Michelin-starred foodie paradise, 6km southeast of town. The chef, Francesco Bracali, is judged by many to be Italy's best; depending on the season, mains might include such creations as pigeon with carrots and chocolate or cream and mushroom risotto. Antipasti and pastas are €35. Mains €50. Wed & Thurs 7.30–11pm, Fri–Sun 1–4pm & 7.30–11pm.

Da Tronca Vicolo Porte 5 ☎ 0566 901 991. This traditional osteria offers good local cooking in an atmospheric setting with stone walls and a vaulted ceiling. The speciality is *tortelli maremma* (spinach and ricotta ravioli with ragù), and the house red is memorable. About €30 per person. Arrive early. Mon, Tues & Thurs–Sun 7.30–10.30pm.

★ **Tana del Brillo Parlante** Vicolo del Ciambellano 4 ☎ 0566 901 274, ⓦ massamarittima.info/tanabrillo. Look for the sign with Jiminy Cricket. If you want to try wild boar or something with truffles, this rustic osteria is the place, but save room for the fantastic home-made desserts. Seating is very limited, so book ahead. About €30 per person. Mon, Tues & Thurs–Sun 1–3.30pm & 7.30–10.30pm; winter hours vary.

Vecchio Borgo Via Parenti 12 ☎ 0566 903 950, ⓦ massamarittima.info/vecchioborgo. Excellent value, and with a very charming medieval setting; try the home-made barley soup, juicy game grills or pasta with *porcini*, made in the local tradition. About €35 per person. Tues–Sat 7.30–11pm; closed mid-Feb to mid-March.

ROCCATEDERIGHI

Situated 15km east of Massa, **Roccatederighi** is difficult to fit into any logical itinerary, but with your own transport it's well worth the twenty-minute drive. Perched on a needle of rock – gird yourself for the haul up some impossibly steep alleys – the village has been literally carved from the living rock, and its upper reaches offer some of the finest panoramic views in all of the Maremma.

Grosseto

Travelling by train, the chances are that you'll pass the provincial capital, **GROSSETO**, with no more than a glance, but by bus or car you'll encounter the heart of its largely unappealing centre. Located about 40km southeast of Massa, ringed by a factory-ridden plain and composed mainly of characterless condominiums, this commercial metropolis was raised from the ruins of heavy bombing and now serves principally as a functional and administrative centre. Timetabling often leaves about an hour or so between train connections – which is about all the time you might need for the **old centre**, contained within a largely intact hexagon of walls commissioned by Cosimo I, after the Florentines wrested control of the city from Siena. Each Thursday (8am–1.30pm), a huge weekly **market** on Piazza Esperanto, Piazza de Maria and Via Ximenes, selling everything from traditional cheeses to clothes, draws people from all over the province.

To get to the old centre, walk straight out from the train station to join Via Roma, and turn right.

Piazza Dante

The best of what survives in old Grosseto is on **Piazza Dante**, where a quirky statue shows Leopoldo II protecting Mother Maremma and crushing the serpent malaria underfoot. The **Duomo** was started in 1294, and, though pleasant enough, there's virtually nothing left to suggest antiquity: the white and pink marble facade is a product of the nineteenth century, while the interior has suffered repeated and ill-advised modifications.

Museo Archeologico

Piazza Baccarini • March & April Tues–Sun 9am–1pm & 4–6pm; May–Oct Tues–Sun 10am–1pm & 5–8pm; Nov–Feb Tues–Fri 9am–1pm, Sat & Sun 9am–1pm & 4–6pm • Free

The best works from the Duomo have been transferred to the **Museo Archeologico**. The upper-floor **Pinacoteca** has a handful of good Sienese paintings, notably Sassetta's *Madonna of the Cherries*, and a *Madonna and Child* attributed to Simone Martini. Most of the archeological finds are from the nearby Etruscan settlements at Vetulonia and Rusellae (modern Roselle), neatly arranged and well labelled.

San Francesco to the walls

The town's only other significant work is an early Crucifix by **Duccio** in the church of **San Francesco**, just north of the museum. The cloisters are distinguished by a sixteenth-century cistern, the *Pozzo della Bufala* (commemorating a legendary buffalo that, attempting to escape the butcher, fell in and died). From San Francesco you can take a walk round the **walls** (40min). Apart from one, which retains some fortifications, public gardens fill the spaces in the corner turrets.

ARRIVAL AND DEPARTURE	GROSSETTO
By bus and train The train and bus stations are on Piazza Marconi, 1km northwest of the old centre. Most trains on the main Rome–Pisa line stop here.	Rome (hourly; 1hr 30min–2hr 30min); Siena (8 daily; 1hr 20min).
Train destinations Capalbio (hourly; 35min); Follónica (hourly; 35min; change for Massa Maríttima); Florence (8 daily via Siena; 3–4hr); Orbetello (hourly; 30min);	Bus destinations Castiglione della Pescaia (6–11 daily; 20–45min); Florence (8 daily; 2hr 30min); Massa Maríttima (2 daily; 1hr 15min); Orbetello (3 daily; 1hr); Roccatederighi (2 daily; 1hr 10min); Siena (10 daily; 1hr 35min).

INFORMATION

Tourist office Via Monterosa 206, about 2km north of the old centre and 1km northeast of the train station (Mon–Sat 9am–1pm, plus 4.30–6.30pm April–Oct; ☎ 0564 462 611, ⊛ turismoinmaremma.it).

ACCOMMODATION AND EATING

Buca di San Lorenzo da Claudio Via Manetti 1 ☎ 0564 25 142. This popular spots occupies arched medieval rooms under the Medicean ramparts. The setting is rustic, but the cuisine, with emphasis on the freshest fish and seafood, is gourmet, the service excellent. Never mind the menu, the waiter announces the day's offerings. About €45 per person. Tues–Sat 1–3.30pm & 7.30–10pm; closed two weeks in Jan & July.

Nuova Grosseto Piazza Marconi 26 ☎ 0564 414 105, ⊛ hotelnuovagrosseto.com. Located just across from the train station, this hotel is modern, clean and well appointed. The rather plain rooms are soundproofed, with parquet or carpeted floors, and have a/c and free wi-fi. Breakfast included. **€90**

Vineria da Romolo Via Vinzaglio 3 ☎ 0564 27 551, ⊛ vineriadaromolo.it. The old centre's most *simpatico* wine bar-cum-osteria, with a full menu that includes substantial *bruschette*, home-made local pastas, rustic soups and every sort of grilled steak or chop – wonderful cheeses and cured meats, too. About €25 per person. Wed–Sun 1.30–4pm & 7pm–midnight.

Castiglione della Pescaia and around

The best small resort along the coastline hereabouts is easygoing **CASTIGLIONE DELLA PESCAIA**, some 20km west of Grosetto. Set among low, wooded hills, the town still affects the air of a fishing village, and of all the Maremma resorts, this is where you're most likely to have a good time. The bars are fun, the beach is decent, and the walled **old town** on the hill – believed to have been an Etruscan port – is a charming spot to wander, offering great views from the castle. The harbourfront fish **market**, in the morning and late afternoon, is worth checking out if you're self-catering.

ARRIVAL AND INFORMATION

By bus The main bus stop is on Via Ponte Giorgini, at the canal marina.
Destination Grosseto (6–11 daily, 20–45min).

CASTIGLIONE DELLA PESCAIA

Tourist office Piazza Garibaldi 6 (Mon–Fri 9am–1pm & 2–6pm, Sat 9am–5pm; ☎ 0564 933 678, ⊛ castiglione dellapescaia.it).

ACCOMMODATION AND EATING

★ **Approdo** Via Ponte Giorgini 29 ☎ 0564 933 466, ⊛ hotellapprodo.com. This crisply contemporary hotel is located right on the marina. Rooms have a/c and many have balconies with sea views. They also have their own restaurant, specializing in local cheeses, mushrooms, Florentine steak and chestnut dishes (about €30 per person). There's a roof terrace for buffet breakfast (included) and free wi-fi in the reception area. **€70**

Aurora Via Fratelli Bandiera 19 ☎ 0564 933 718, ⊛ www.aurora-albergo.it. This modern pink-painted hotel, recently restored and with its own restaurant, is just 100m from the beach. There's a roof terrace with views of both the sea and the old town, and rooms are simple, soundproofed and clean, all with a/c and balconies. Half-board required. Open mid-March to Oct. Doubles with half board **€142**

Etruria Camping on the road towards Grosseto ☎ 0564 933 483, ⊛ campeggioetruria.net. Just under 1km south of town, set amidst a forest of umbrella pine and with direct access to a broad sandy beach. It offers all the facilities of a small town, including a restaurant with Maremmani dishes; and there's beach volleyball and a park for kids. Open May–Sept. Adults **€11.50**, plus pitch **€10.50**

Miramare Via Vittorio Veneto 35 ☎ 0564 933 524, ⊛ hotelmiramare.info. This modern hotel, on its own beach, overlooks the sea and the old town. All rooms are spacious, with balconies and a/c, and the decor is tastefully neutral in tone. The buffet breakfast is included, and they have their own restaurant. **€108**

Romolo Corso Libertà 10 ☎ 0564 933 533, ⊛ daromolo.com. Traditional and airy, with red-checked tablecloths, this central restaurant serves mostly fish, but some Maremmani game specialities, too. The wine list is extensive, with four hundred reds and rosés, and many more whites and sparkling choices. About €30 per person. June–Sept daily 1.30–3.30pm & 7–11pm; rest of the year Wed–Sun same hours; closed for part of Nov & Dec.

Votapentole Via IV Novembre 15 ☎ 0564 934 763. A tiny, rather chic fish restaurant, with room for just eighteen diners (fourteen more outside in fine weather).

5

Their speciality, prawns with tortelli, is a real palate pleaser; try the tasting menu for a full range of original creations. About €40 per person. Tues–Sun 1.30–3.30pm & 7–10pm.

Diaccia Botrona nature reserve

The road immediately south of Castiglione della Pescaia runs through a beautiful forest of umbrella pines (*pineta*), a small section of which is administered as the **Diaccia Botrona nature reserve** by the World Wide Fund for Nature. Most of the woodland – about twelve square kilometres in all – is accessible on foot: you can leave your car on the roadside and walk down to the superb beaches via one of the many tracks through the trees.

Museo Multimediale della Casa Rossa Xiemenes
Tues–Sun 4–10pm • €5

About 2km east of Castiglione, at the entrance to the reserve, is the **Museo Multimediale della Casa Rossa Xiemenes**. Built in 1765, this "Red House" has been restored and converted into a high-tech observation point over the reserve, which is one of the most important wetland areas in Italy. Visitors can observe the local wldlife via three strategically positioned webcams without disturbing the ecosystem.

Monti dell'Uccellina

The hills and coastline of the **MONTI DELL'UCCELLINA** are protected as the **Parco Naturale Regionale della Maremma**, an area claimed to be the last virgin coastal landscape on the Italian peninsula. The "Mountains of the Little Bird" take their name from the number of birds that use these hills as a landing strip between Europe and North Africa.

The heart of the park is a hump of hills that rises suddenly from the plain, about 12km south of Grosseto. A breathtaking piece of countryside that combines cliffs, coastal marsh, *macchia*, forest-covered hills, pristine beaches and some of the most beautiful stands of **umbrella pines** in the country, it is a microcosm of all that's best in the Maremma – devoid of the commercialization and half-finished houses that have destroyed much of the Italian littoral. Kept remote for centuries by malaria and impassable swamp, it's now preserved through the determination of its owners to keep this terrain sacrosanct. The result is an area that rewards the casual walker, birdwatcher, botanist or anyone simply in search of a stretch of unspoilt sand.

Once off the bus from Alberese at Pratini, most people rush headlong along the Strada degli Olivi for the **beach**, an idyllic curving bay backed by cliffs and wooded hills; the obvious stretch is to the left, though you can trudge the beach for miles to the right, round the huge *pineta* towards the mouth of the Ombrone, Tuscany's second-longest river.

ESSENTIALS   **PARCO NATURALE REGIONALE DELLA MAREMMA**

Getting there There is no public road access into the park: drivers park near the reserve headquarters in the main square at Alberese. Hourly buses (#15, #16 & #17) run there from Grosseto station, and there's one morning train to Alberese station, 4km from the village.

Information The park headquarters and visitors' centre, at Via del Bersagliere 7–9 in Alberese (daily: mid-March to mid-Sept 8.30am–7pm, rest of the year 8.30am–1.30pm; ☎0564 407 098, ⊛parks.it), has details of walks – both

guided and self-guided – and can book a 3hr night walking tour. The centre can also provide information on renting bikes and canoes.

Park practicalities Admission to the park (daily: July to Sept 7.30am–dusk; Oct–June 9am–dusk; €6) secures you a basic map and a place on an hourly bus, which runs 10km into the hills, drops you at the trailhead Pratini (really just a field) and leaves you to your own devices. It's about a 20min stroll from Pratini to the beach. Energetic types

FROM TOP MAREMMA COUNTRYSIDE; CASTIGLIONE DELLA PESCAIA (P.245) >

might walk all the way from Alberese; if you want to see the wildlife at dusk (the best time) you'll have to walk back anyway, as the last bus back from Pratini departs at 5.30pm in summer, earlier in winter. You can buy bus tickets for the return journey from Alberese to Grosseto at *Bar Il Parco*, just behind the visitors' centre.

Walks in the Uccellina

There are a number of **marked trails** that crisscross each other within the park, plus several shorter routes, if you're just looking for a quick stroll.

Trail A1

The best of the marked routes is the circular **Trail A1** (*San Rabano*; 6km; 5hr; guided walks in summer at 8am), which starts from Pratini. The track climbs quickly to the Uccellina's main ridge (417m), with **views** to the coast and to Monte Amiata in the interior, reaching the abbey of San Rabano after about ninety minutes. Built in the eleventh century and abandoned five hundred years later, the church is now an ivy-covered ruin, with stone carvings littering the grass. The path then drops right, returning below the ridge to the Strada degli Olivi through evergreen woods.

Trail A2

Trail A2 (*Le Torri*; 5km; 3hr; guided walks in summer at 9am & 4pm; tours in English every Fri 4.30pm) starts nearer the beach and connects some of the medieval watchtowers built by the Spanish, who, with the Sienese, were the only people to brave the area, using it as a source of cork and charcoal. Taking in several coastal habitats, it offers an extraordinary view over the **umbrella pines** on the sand bar and dunes below. These are the park's crowning glory and one of the most memorable natural sights in Tuscany – a vast canopy of emerald green that stretches almost as far as the eye can see. It's well worth dropping down from the tower to explore the woods, where you could roam for hours, restricted only by the areas of marsh at their fringes. Many of these pines were planted (the domestic variety to be harvested for their pine nuts, the maritime ones to consolidate the dunes on the estuary).

Trail A3

The level **Trail A3** (*Le Grotte*; 8km; 4hr) takes in a long stretch of the woods and the canals that divide the park; although it's one of the less rewarding walks, it is quite remote and offers good chances to see **wildlife**. It starts near no. 2 and its ultimate destination is a group of caves, one of which (La Grotta della Fabbrica) has yielded some of the oldest human remains found in Italy.

Trail A4

Trail A4 (*Cala di Forno*; 12km; 6hr) is the longest, most varied, and least used of the trails, taking in hill, coast and cliff scenery, and reaching the large Cala di Forno headland that dominates the bay to the south. The return takes you along the **dunes** and a superb stretch of beach at Portovecchio.

Talamone

At the southern tip of the Uccellina, just outside the park's confines, **TALAMONE** is a fishing village and discreet summer resort. Save for a yacht-filled marina, most of its old charm remains intact. The Sienese – who never had a proper outlet to the sea – once planned to turn its hole-in-the-wall harbour into a port to rival Pisa's, but clogging weed doomed the project to failure (in the *Inferno*, Dante used this as a metaphor for pointless enterprise). The town's greatest moment came in 1860, when Garibaldi and the Thousand stopped here for three days on their way to Sicily. Talamone's sixteenth-century Spanish castle is closed to the public.

5

FAUNA AND FLORA IN THE UCCELLINA

You'd have to be unlucky not to see any interesting wildlife in the protected environment of the Uccellina. An extraordinary range of species thrive here, in what is effectively a compendium of Mediterranean coastal habitats – wooded hills, olive groves, pastures, marshland, *pineta*, *macchia*, dunes, retro-dunal areas, estuary and mudflats.

The Ombrone estuary is the key target of serious **birdwatchers** during the spring and autumn migratory cycles, when an assortment of waders, ducks, herons and egrets can be seen. Rarities like ospreys, bee-eaters, flamingos and even falcons and short-toed eagles can be spotted in the rockier hinterland, and you're almost guaranteed the sight of herons wheeling away from the canals, perhaps with hoopoes, shrikes, kingfishers, and the rare, brightly coloured black-winged stilt.

Other species are most likely to be encountered towards dusk, with **roe-deer** prevalent in the hills. The famous **wild boar** is an often audible inhabitant of the scrub and pine forest; an indigenous Maremma breed, it's a smaller specimen than other Italian boar, most of which are descended from bulky, Eastern European stock. The crested **porcupine**, introduced by the Romans, is also fairly common (Italy is the only place it's found outside Africa), as are badgers and foxes; it is hoped that the increasingly rare **otter** will flourish here too. In the cultivated land to the north and on the flat fringes of the estuary you'll see the semi-wild **horses** for which the Maremma is famous. Tracking down **flora** is more a job for the specialist, though the pines and cork oaks are unmissable, as are the huge banks of rosemary bushes, purple with flowers in the late summer. The dwarf pine, Italy's only indigenous pine, has its northernmost natural limit in the park, and numerous floral rarities pepper the park's dunes, *macchia* and marshes, including a tiny local orchid.

ACCOMMODATION

TALAMONE

★ **Baia di Talamone** Via della Marina 23 ☎0564 887 310, ⓦhbt.it. This very friendly hotel offers rooms and self-catering studios, both spacious and some with balconies. The decor is light and vaguely tropical, with rattan furniture and exotic touches, while the terrace breakfast/bar is just steps away from the marina. Free parking nearby; breakfast included. Open March–Oct. €115

Talamone Camping ☎0564 887 026 ⓦtalamone campingvillage.com. Located 1km south of Talamone, this huge campsite has it all: its own beach, a large pool and sport facilities, wooded campsites and a restaurant, plus bungalows that sleep four. Open April–Sept. Adults €13, plus pitches €13

Telamonio Piazza Garibaldi 4 ☎0564 887 008, ⓦhoteliltelamonio.com. Out on the peninsula near the beach, the castle and the old wall, this hotel has a sun terrace with panoramic views. Rooms are smallish, but some have balconies. Breakfast included. Free parking up the hill. €120

EATING

Buca Via Porta Piazza Garibaldi 1–3 ☎0564 887 067. This popular trattoria/osteria has great outdoor seating, and reservations are a must in high season. Their speciality is seafood, including a wonderful *orrechiette ai moscardini* (octopus). Try the *misto* for the full antipasto experience. About €35 per person. Tues–Sun 1–4pm & 7–11pm.

Flavia Piazza IV Novembre ☎0564 887 091, ⓦristoranteflavia.com. This excellent fish restaurant has cosy, elegant indoor or garden seating. From succulent *insalata di mare* for antipasto to seafood pasta or a mixed fish grill, the quality is always reliable. About €50 per person for a full meal. Mon & Wed–Sun 1.30–3.30pm & 7.30–10.30pm; closed mid-Jan to mid-Feb.

The Argentario and around

In the southwest corner of Tuscany, some 35km south of Grosseto and just before the Lazio border, the beautiful and unspoilt **Argentario** is home to the mountainous peninsula of **Monte Argentario** as well as a cluster of coastal resort towns, from unpretentious **Orbetello** to the stylish **Porto Santo Stefano** and **Porto Ercole**. Just to the south, **Ansedonia** boasts one of Tuscany's few ancient Roman sites, while inland, **Capalbio** rates as one of the area's loveliest villages. Nearby is the **Giardino dei Tarocchi**, a small park of fantastical sculptures that's become a major attraction.

5

Orbetello

ORBETELLO is principally distinguished by its strange location on a narrow isthmus in the middle of the **Laguna di Orbetello**. The ancient settlement here occupied a peninsula sticking out into the lagoon; the Romans built a causeway to link the town to Monte Argentario, forming a third spit of land and dividing the lagoon in two.

Little in Ortebello excites real attention today, but it has become something of a resort, thanks to its position as gateway to the dramatic rocky outcrop of Monte Argentario, bottlenecked on summer weekends with cars full of tourists en route to the Argentario's premier resorts. Still, Orbetello is a pleasant place, graced with palm trees and a main street – **Corso Italia** – thronged each evening with a particularly vigorous passeggiata and a lively street market on Saturdays. The pastel-coloured **fortifications** left by the Spanish after they wrested control of the town from the papacy in 1559, establishing a military *Presidio* with Orbetello as its capital, are the town's most conspicuous feature and a fine example of military architecture. Nearby, the **Duomo** on Piazza della Repubblica appears promising with its lovely Gothic façade, only to disappoint with a grim Baroque interior. The town's last claim to fame was as the headquarters of Mussolini's seaplane squadrons; the surviving aircraft hangar is one of Tuscany's more bizarre architectural attractions.

ARRIVAL AND DEPARTURE

ORBETELLO

By train The train station is 4km east at Orbetello Scalo, on the mainland edge of the lagoon, a prominent stop for trains on the Rome–Pisa line. There are connections for Siena, and slow trains to smaller stations to the north and south.

By bus Connecting buses run from Orbetello Scalo train station to the bus terminal just off Piazza della Repubblica,. Destinations Capalbio (3 daily; 45min); Grosseto (3 daily; 1hr); Porto Ercole (14 daily; 20min); Porto Santo Stefano (6 daily; 15min).

INFORMATION

Tourist office Piazza della Repubblica 3 (April–Sept daily 9am–1pm & 4–8pm; Oct–March Mon–Fri 9am–1pm & 3–7pm, Sat & Sun 9am–1pm; ☏0564 860 447, ⓦturismoinmaremma.it).

ACCOMMODATION AND EATING

Nocchino Via Furio Lenzi 64 ☏0564 860 329. Old-fashioned spot just off Piazza della Repubblica, offering a cosy, homely dining experience and outdoor seating in season. If you don't see it on the menu, ask for the *gnochetti* with porcini and shrimp. About €30 per person. March–Oct Mon & Wed–Sun 1–3.45pm & 7.30–10.45pm; Nov–April closed Mon–Thurs.

★ **Pescatori** Via Leopardi 9 ☏0564 860 611. Something akin to a *sagra* (village food festival), this restaurant run by the fishermen's cooperative is in a charming setting just outside the ramparts. Arrive early, then pay, take a ticket, place your order and wait. The fish is extraordinarily fresh and perfectly done. Set menu €35 per person. Mon–Fri 7–10pm, Sat & Sun 1–3.30pm & 7–10pm.

Piccolo Parigi Corso Italia 169 ☏0564 867 233, ⓦalbergopiccoloparigi.it. Simple, old-fashioned and unpretentious, this modest, family-run hotel is centrally located and right near the water on both sides. Rooms are available both with and without private bath. Breakfast included. **€75**

Monte Argentario

The high, rocky terrain of **Monte Argentario** is as close to wilderness as southern Tuscany comes. The interior is mountainous, reaching 635m at its highest point, **Il Telegrafo**, and the coast is sectioned dramatically into headlands, bays and shingle beaches. Away from the villas of rich Romans, much of the area is still uninhabited scrub and verdant woodland, badly prone to forest fires but superb walking country. The main centres of **Porto Santo Stefano** and **Porto Ercole** once had a reputation for exclusivity, but these days they're too well known to pander solely to the top end of the market. With your own transport you could follow the touted *gita panoramica* (scenic drive) around half the mountain.

5

Porto Santo Stefano

PORTO SANTO STEFANO, in the north, is the more developed of the Argentario resorts, and also the more fashionable – which in Italy is a lot worse than just being popular. Something of the charm that first brought people here still shines through, however, despite the hotels and villas that have all but obliterated the original village. A few fishing boats still cluster in the town's smaller harbour, having relinquished the main port to the marina and its mega-yachts. You'll probably stay only as long as it takes to get a **ferry** to the island of Giglio.

INFORMATION

Tourist office Piazzale Sant'Andrea 1, at the eastern end of the port (April–Oct daily 9am–1pm & 4–8pm; Nov–March Mon–Fri 9am–1pm & 2–6.30pm, Sat 9am–1pm & 2–7pm; ☎ 0564 814 208, ⊛ comunemonteargentario.it).

ACCOMMODATION AND EATING

Alfiero Via Cuniberti 12 ☎ 0564 814 067, ⊛ hotelalfiero.com. Very central, just steps away from the ferry dock, this small hotel has spartan but spacious rooms, all with free wi-fi and some with balconies and good views. Breakfast is included, served in the tiny entrance foyer. **€90**

Gigetto Via del Molo 9 ☎ 0564 814 495. If you don't want to throw money around, this portside pizzeria is a great option. Their house speciality is topped with prosciutto, sausage and mushrooms, and loads of bubbly cheese. Look for the striped awning. About €20 per person. Daily noon–midnight.

Veliero Via Panoramica 149151 ☎ 0564 812 226. A steep hike above the port for a fairly steep price, but the fresh grilled fish and stunning views are unbeatable. The house speciality is courgettes stuffed with shrimp. Expect at least €50 per person, depending on wine. April–Oct Tues–Sun 1.30–4pm & 7.30–11pm.

Porto Ercole

On the southeast side of Monte Argentario, **PORTO ERCOLE** is more intimate than Santo Stefano, with an attractive old quarter and a fishing-village atmosphere. Though founded by the Romans, its chief historical monuments are Spanish **fortresses**, two facing each other on opposing sides of the harbour and a third one above the new town. At the entrance to the old town, a plaque on the stone gate commemorates the notoriously brawl-prone painter **Caravaggio**, who stopped off in Porto Ercole in 1610 on his way to Rome to receive a pardon for killing a man in a sword fight four years earlier. He's said to have keeled over from sunstroke on a beach nearby; taken to a local tavern, he soon died of a fever, and was buried in the parish church of Sant'Erasmo.

INFORMATION

Tourist office Piazza Roma (April–Dec: Mon, Tues, Thurs, Fri & Sat 10am–1pm & 4pm–sunset; Dec–March Mon, Tues & Thurs–Sat 10am–1pm & 3.30pm–sunset; ☎ 0564 811 970, ⊛ comunemonteargentario.it).

ACCOMMODATION

★ **Don Pedro** Via Panoramico 7 ☎ 0564 833 914, ⊛ hoteldonpedro.it. Located at the top of the town and enjoying a commanding view of the port, this hotel offers private balconies and a rooftop terrace, plus a private beach

WALKS FROM PORTO ERCOLE

There are a couple of good **walks** from the village, the most obvious being along the **Tombolo di Feniglia**, which has one of Italy's most beautiful *pinete*, a long sandy dune covered in parasol pines, and roe deer in its small nature reserve. The road along it is off-limits for cars, though you can walk its whole course, dropping down to the lagoon side for great views, or to the other side for a fine beach.

The other walk is to the top of **Il Telegrafo**, accessible either by road and track from the ridge that runs up from the lighthouse to the south, or on a rough road that leaves the port to the north and then runs west under the main ridge. The way is fairly open, and superb views make the haul worthwhile.

5

and their own restaurant. Rooms are elegantly appointed and all have a/c, though bathrooms tend to be a bit small. Handy parking options. Breakfast included. Open Easter to Oct. €130

Feniglia Camping ☎ 0564 831 090, ⓦ campingfeniglia .it. This campsite is 2km north of Porto Ercole, right on the beach and backed by a green hillside. There's a supermarket, café and barbecue facilities, and they offer knotty pine bungalows (sleeping two to six; weekly rentals only) as well as shady campsites. Adults €12, plus pitch €9

Pellicano Località Sbarcatello ☎ 0546 858 111, ⓦ pellicanohotel.com. Some 4.5km southwest of Porto Ercole, this is one of Italy's premier resorts, complete with pool, spa, tennis courts and a Michelin two-star restaurant. Simply palatial, with every luxury you could ever dream of. Open April–Oct. €630

EATING AND DRINKING

Gambero Rosso Lungomare Andrea Doria 70 ☎ 0564 832 650. This waterfront establishment serves excellent fish and seafood, such as *papardelle alle cozze* (mussels) and grilled catch of the day; the seafood risotto goes for €14. For dessert, the lemon sorbet with vodka strikes the right, light note. Mid-Feb to mid-Nov Mon, Tues & Thurs–Sun 1–4pm & 7.30–11pm.

Nobili Santi Via dell'Ospizio 8–10 ☎ 0564 833 105. Central and modern, this excellent restaurant is famous for fish, and the antipasti and fish ravioli are wonderful too. A meal will run about €45 per person, depending on wine. July to mid-Sept Tues–Sun 7.30–10.30pm; mid-Sept to June Thurs–Sun 12.30–3.30pm & 7.30–10.30pm; closed Nov.

Ansedonia

ANSEDONIA crouches under a rocky crag at the end of the Tombolo di Feniglia sand spit. Peppered with holiday villas, it has a long **beach** and, on the hilltop above the modern town, the remains of **Cosa**, founded by the Romans in 273 BC as a frontier post against the Etruscans.

Cosa

Site Daily: May–Sept 9am–7pm, Oct–April 9am–1pm · Free · **Museo Archeologico** Same hours · €2

Cosa was one of the Roman's most important commercial centres in the area, until its population – according to the historian Rutilius – was driven out by an army of mice. Most of the old *municipium* was devastated by the Visigoths in the fourth century, and what survived was sacked by the Sienese in 1330. Recent excavations have exposed enough of the Roman colony to suggest some idea of its former layout. You'll find a ring of **walls** 8m high in places, the remains of a defensive cordon of eighteen towers; there's also the outline of the gridiron street plan, a forum (with basilica and senate discernible nearby), two temples and some mosaics and wall paintings. It's worth climbing to the top of the hill, not only to see the remains of the **acropolis**, but also for fine views across to Monte Argentario. Halfway up the hill is a small **Museo Archeologico**, housing some of the site's finds.

To get there, take Via del Rosmarino up to where it intersects with Via delle Ginestre, from where a path goes on up to the site.

Capalbio

Stranded in empty country just 10km northeast of Ansedonia, the hill-village of **CAPALBIO** is virtually unknown to outsiders, though not to Rome's cultural and political elite, many of whom have homes in the locality. Most are attracted by the almost perfectly medieval interior, which at night is a deathly quiet maze of streets straight out of the Middle Ages. Daytime views are superb, across the fertile plains to the sea.

ARRIVAL AND DEPARTURE
CAPALBIO

By train A handful of trains to and from Grosseto stop at Chiarone Scalo station, on the coast about 10km south of town.

ACCOMMODATION AND EATING

Capalbio Camping Via Graticciaia ☎0564 890 101, Ⓦilcampeggiodicapalbio.it. Due south of Capalbio, at the end of the road to the dunes, with its own beach bar, restaurant, tennis courts, mini-market and shady pitches, plus sport options, a kids' play area and two- or four-person caravans. Mid-April to Sept. Adults **€14**, plus pitch **€14**, caravan **€100**

Torre da Carla Via Vittorio Emmanuele 33 ☎0564 896 070. A picturesque setting in the heart of the old town, all stone and flowers, this trattoria offers classic Tuscan cooking. Try the home-made *fettuccine* with wild boar sauce, and ask for some truffle shavings on top. Fish dishes, too. About €35 per person for a full meal. Easter to Sept Mon–Wed & Fri–Sun 1–3.30pm & 7.30–10pm; Oct–Easter Sat & Sun same hours.

Valle del Buttero Via Silone 21 ☎0564 896 097, Ⓦwww.valledelbuttero.it. Located about 200m east of the historic centre, and comprising several buildings with attractive rooms, plus a gym, billiards, extensive gardens and a pool. Breakfast €9 extra. Self-catering apartments also available. **€100**

Giardino dei Tarocchi

April to mid-Oct daily 2.30–7.30pm • €10.50 • Ⓦ nikidesaintphalle.com

Located 5km southeast of Capalbio, and clearly visible from the Via Aurelia, is one of Italy's oddest collections of modern art, **Il Giardino dei Tarocchi** (Tarot Garden), a sculpture garden of prodigious works by Niki de Saint Phalle, who died in 2002 and is most famous for the *Fontaine Stravinsky*, created with her husband Jean Tinguely outside the Pompidou Centre in Paris.

The brightly coloured opus inhabits land donated by friends and took the artist almost seventeen years to complete (1979–1996). The result is a truly staggering sight – an unpredictable dose of Gaudí mixed with arcane symbolism and a dash of Miró: sheer fun that children love and adults marvel at. Each piece represents one of the Tarot's 22 major arcana, with plants and fountains forming an integral part of the prolific spectacle.

Giglio

The largest of the Tuscan **islands** after Elba, **GIGLIO**, 18km west of Monte Argentario, is visited by an ever-increasing number of foreign tourists and is so popular with holidaying Romans that in high season you may find that there's standing-room only on the ferries. Yet it's well worth making the effort to stay on this fabulous island. Thankfully, since most visitors are day-trippers, the rush is fairly short-lived, and few explore the tracks across the unspoilt interior, a mix of barren rock and reforested upland. Part of the Parco Nazionale Arcipelago Toscano, the island is rich in **fauna** such as peregrine falcons, mouflon, kestrels and buzzards, and in **wild flowers** too: this is the only place outside North Africa to shelter wild mustard, and the sole spot in Tuscany to support the yellow flowers of artemisia.

Brief history

The island derives its name not from *giglio* (lily), but from the Roman colony Aegilium, in its day a resort for the rich and famous, a function it continued to fulfil throughout most of the Middle Ages. In the thirteenth century it was acquired by Pisa and later by the Medici family. Granite quarries kept the economy buoyant, and Giglio stone was used to construct many medieval churches. Over the last fifty years, the town has become a haven for low-key outdoor activities.

Giglio Porto and the beaches

Small, rock-girdled **GIGLIO PORTO** has no particular sights, but the view from the ferry is wonderful as the town draws closer, its pale-coloured houses offset by a backdrop of

5

terraced vineyards and framed between two lighthouses. The narrow harbourfront is crammed with a mix of touristy restaurants and boat mechanics, but behind the **Torre del Saraceno**, built by Ferdinand I in 1596, you'll find a tranquil, barely visited little inlet, with the wall of a Roman eel farm visible below the waterline.

As much of the land around rises sheer from the sea, Giglio's **beaches** are modest: you'll find one to the north of the port at Punta Aranella, a couple to the south at Cala delle Canelle and Cala delle Caldane, and the best one at Giglio Campese.

Giglio Castello and around

GIGLIO CASTELLO, up 6km of hairpins from the port and perched almost at the island's highest point – the peak of Poggio della Pagana is 496m – was for a long time the island's only settlement and the sole spot safe from pirate attack. Surprisingly well preserved, its maze of arches and medieval alleyways is still surrounded by thick walls. Buses stop near a vine-covered patio bar in the large **Piazza Gloriosa**, also the entrance to the granite fortress and medieval quarter. The **castle** was begun by the Pisans and completed by the Grand Duchy of Tuscany; rough paths around the walls enable you to clamber over the rocks for superb views over the island and ruins far below. For a look at St Mamiliano's miraculous arm, check out the Baroque **church**.

To explore Giglio's interior, follow a minor road that winds from Castello 9km south all along the spine of the ridge to **Punta del Capel Rosso**, the southernmost tip of the island – a wild and lonely bike ride or three-hour hike. Walking from Castello down to either Campese or Porto takes less than an hour.

Giglio Campese

At the western end of the island road is the resort of **GIGLIO CAMPESE**. It has the island's best **beach**, a fine stretch of sand overlooked by an eighteenth-century Medici tower and curving for 2km from a huge phallic rockstack (Faraglione) that the tourist brochures are too modest to photograph. Around the base of the old tower is a modern, turreted apartment complex with a couple of restaurants, tennis courts and all manner of **watersports** facilities – including dive shops with lessons and gear to rent.

ARRIVAL AND INFORMATION
GIGLIO

By ferry The embarkation point for Giglio is Porto Santo Stefano (see p.251), which is served by regular buses direct from the train station at Orbetello Scalo and also from Orbetello town. Both Toremar (☎ 0564 810 803, ⊚ toremar. it) and Maregiglio (☎ 0564 812 920, ⊚ maregiglio.it) operate ferries to Giglio Porto (summer almost hourly,

winter 3–5 daily; 1hr; €20–24 return). It's usually no problem to buy your ticket from a quayside kiosk and board immediately.

Tourist office Via Provinciale 9, Giglio Porto (daily 9am–1pm & 3–7pm; ☎ 0564 809 400, ⊚ isoladelgiglio.it).

GETTING AROUND

By bus From the Giglio Porto ferry dock, there's an excellent bus service to the island's two other main villages, Giglio Castello and Giglio Campese.

Bikes and mopeds You can rent bikes and mopeds in Giglio Porto and Castello; ask at the tourist office.

By car You should leave your car on the mainland; it's

ST MAMILIANO'S ARM

As recently as the eighteenth century, coastal raids by Saracen pirates were still a problem in Giglio, despite the miraculous defensive power of the right arm of **St Mamiliano**, a relic hacked from a sixth-century Sicilian bishop exiled on the island of Montecristo. The limb proved effective when waved at Tunisian pirates in 1799, but less so on other occasions – notably much earlier, in the twelfth century, when Barbarossa killed or carried off into slavery most of the island's population.

expensive (about €40 one-way) to take it onto the island at any time of year, and in high season private vehicles are forbidden. If leaving your car on the mainland, it's best to use one of the many trustworthy parking companies on the Porto Santo Stefano waterfront (roughly €10 per day); parking on the street is both unsafe and lays you open to hefty fines.

ACCOMMODATION AND EATING

GIGLIO PORTO

★ **Demo's** Via Thaon de Revel 45 ☎0564 809 235, ⓦhoteldemos.com. This modern hotel is right on a small beach backed with palms. The elegant rooms are bright and spacious rooms, and most have sea views, as do the restaurant and bar. Breakfast included. €210

Paloma Via Umberto I 48 ☎0564 809 233. This fish restaurant is generally the best choice in town. The catch of the day prepared according to the chef's inspiration – ignore the menu and let the waiter guide you; or try the spaghetti with seafood and cuttlefish ink, and for dessert apple and cinnamon *sfogliate*. Expect to pay about €45 per person. Daily 12.30–3.30pm & 7.30–10.30pm; Sept–June closed Mon.

Pardini's Hermitage Cala degli Alberi ☎0564 809 034, ⓦhermit.it. This small and incredibly quiet and private three-star on the sea – 3km south of Giglio Porto but accessible only by boat or on foot – makes a perfect getaway, as the name suggests. Extremely cosy and well appointed, it has just thirteen rooms, so book ahead; half or full-board only. Open April–Sept. Doubles with half board €320

Ruggero Via del Saraceno 86 ☎0564 809 121, ✉daruggero@tin.it. This simple, modern hotel stands just a few steps from the harbour and ferry dock, but is set apart in a side street so that you're away from the noise. All ten rooms have private bath, a/c and balconies with sea or mountain views. Breakfast included. €80

GIGLIO CASTELLO

Airone Via Contrada Santa Maria ☎0564 806 074, ⓦcamerealgiglio.vze.com. Simple, homely rooms in various buildings in the old town, all with private bath, many with good views to the sea. No breakfast. The owners also have self-catering apartments. €60

Da Maria Via della Casa Matta 12 ☎0564 806 062 This large, family-run restaurant does typical island cookery, both fish and meat dishes; the pasta with crab is memorable. Expect to pay about €45 per person, depending very much on the wine you select. Mon, Tues & Thurs–Sun 1–3.45pm & 7–10.45pm; closed Jan–Feb.

GIGLIO CAMPESE

Baia del Sole Camping Località Sparavieri ☎0564 804 036, ⓦcampingbaiadelsole.net. Composed of shaded terraces descending to the sea, this campsite is just 500m northeast of Campese. Facilities include a restaurant and a mini-market, and wi-fi is available, as are basic two-person bungalows without kitchen or private bathroom. Open May to Oct. Adult campers €10.20, plus pitches €14, bungalow €46

Campese Via della Torre 18 ☎0564 804 003, ⓦhotelcampese.com. This Mediterranean-style villa complex has been family-run for over half a century; all rooms have a/c and balconies. It's situated directly on a private beach, and has its own restaurant; breakfast is included. Open Easter–Sept. €160

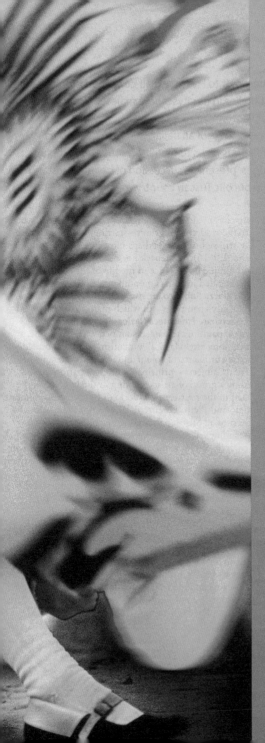

Siena

PALIO SBANDIERATA (P. 265)

Siena

Siena is the perfect counterpoint to Florence. Self-contained behind its medieval walls, its attraction lies in its cityscape, a majestic Gothic whole that could be enjoyed without venturing into a single museum. In its great piazza, Il Campo, it has the loveliest of all Italian public squares; in its zebra-striped Duomo, a religious focus to match; and the city's whole construction, on three ridges, presents a succession of beautiful vistas over medieval cityscapes to the bucolic Tuscan countryside on all sides.

Siena is also a place of immediate charm: airy, easy-going and pedestrianized – where Florence is cramped, busy and traffic-ridden – and can be startlingly free of visitors away from the few centres of day-trip sightseeing. Perhaps most important of all, the city is host to the **Palio** (July 2 and Aug 16), a bareback horse race around the Campo of immense sheer excitement and unique importance to the life of the community.

The contrasts with Florence are extended in Siena's monumental and artistic highlights. The city's Duomo and **Palazzo Pubblico** are two of the purest examples of Italian Gothic, and the finest of the city's paintings – of which many are collected in the Palazzo's **Museo Civico** and the separate **Pinacoteca Nazionale** – are in the same tradition. Other outstanding Sienese paintings remained stamped with Byzantine, Romanesque and Gothic influences long after classical humanism had transformed Florence. It is a style characterized by brilliance of colour and decorative detail and an almost exclusive devotion to religious subjects – principally the city's patroness, the Virgin. Its traditions were shaped by a group of artists working in the last half of the thirteenth century and the first half of the fourteenth: Duccio di Buoninsegna, Simone Martini and the brothers Ambrogio and Pietro Lorenzetti. The first of these was responsible for arguably the greatest of all Siena's paintings, a magnificent *Maestà*, housed in another of Siena's outstanding galleries, the **Museo dell'Opera del Duomo**. Another supreme work, the fresco cycle of Domenico di Bartolo, an artist working on the cusp of the Renaissance, fills part of **Santa Maria della Scala**, a former hospital that's now one of its premier exhibition spaces.

As a provincial capital, Siena has good **transport links** with some of the finest sights and countryside of Tuscany. The city makes a good base for much of the territory covered in the following two chapters, while to the north, the wine heartland of Chianti extends to Florence (78km).

Brief history
Though myth attributes its origins to Senius and Acius, sons of Remus (hence the she-wolf emblem of the city), Siena was an Etruscan and then Roman colony. Over the course of the next millennium it became an independent **republic**, and in the thirteenth century was one of the major cities of Europe. It was almost the size of Paris, controlled most of southern Tuscany and its flourishing wool industry, dominated the

THE CAMPO, SIENA

Highlights

❶ The Campo Soak up the atmosphere and superb architecture in Siena's vast, scallop-shaped piazza, one of the greatest medieval squares in Europe. **See p.263**

❷ Museo Civico Majestic and important frescoes by Simone Martini, Ambrogio Lorenzetti and many others adorn the medieval salons of the Campo's vast Palazzo Pubblico. See p.267

❸ The Palio Run over three frenetic laps of the Campo, Siena's historic, chaotic horse race is a vital component of the city's social and cultural life. **See p.264**

❹ The Duomo The dazzling, art-filled cathedral features sculptures by Michelangelo, a superb fresco cycle by Pinturicchio in the Libreria Piccolomini, and an astounding pulpit by Nicola Pisano. **See p.272**

❺ Santa Maria della Scala Once the city hospital, now a remarkable medieval monument, with frescoed halls and chapels. See p.275

❻ Museo dell'Opera del Duomo A treasure-chest of religious art that also provides access to super viewpoint, atop the walls of the Duomo's abandoned new nave. **See p.280**

HIGHLIGHTS ARE MARKED ON THE MAP ON PP.260–261

CENTRAL SIENA

0 _____ 100
metres

Fortezza di S. Barbara & 2

DRAGO

Stadio
Comunale

PIAZZA
ANTONIO
GRAMSCI

Porta Camollia & Train Station

VIALE DELLO STADIO

VIALE DEI MILLE

VIALE CURTATONE

PIAZZA
G. MATTEOTTI

PIAZZA
MADRE TERESA
DI CALCUTTA

San
Domenico

VIA DEL PARADISO

Oratorio
delle
Suore

Oratorio
Santa Maria
delle Nevi

San Pellegrino
alla Sapienza

VIA DELLA SAPIENZA

Casa e Santuario
di Santa Caterina

Biblioteca
Comunale

Palazzo
Tantucci

Palazzo
Salimbeni

PIAZZA
SALIMBENI

Palazzo
Spannocchi

San
Donato

PIAZZA DELL'
ABBADIA

San
a

San
Cristof

VIA DI PANTANETO

OCA

Fonte Branda

VIA S. CATERINA

VIA DELLA GALLUZZA

VIA DI FONTEBRANDA

Palazzo
Tolomei

PIAZZA
INDIPENDENZA

Loggia di
Mercanzia

PIAZZA
TOLOMEI

VIA ESTERNA DI FONTEBRANDA

SELVA

Palazzo
Arcivescovile

Baptistery

PIAZZA S.
GIOVANNI

Fonte Gaia

PIAZZA
CAMP

Torre del
Mangia

Pa
Pu

San
Sebastiano

SS
Annunziata

Duomo

PIAZZA
S. ELVA

Museo dell'Opera
del Duomo

Prefettura

Police

PIAZZA
DEL DUOMO

Santa Maria
della Scala

Palazzo
Chigi-Saracini

Palazzo
delle Papesse

AQUILA

VIA DEL CAPITANO

VIA DI CITTA

PIAZZA DI
POSTIERLA

Chiesa delle
Clarisse

Porta Laterina

VIA PAOLO MASCAGNI

PIAZZA
DELLE
DUE PORTE

PIAZZA DEL
CONTE

Pinacoteca
Nazionale

TARTUCA

Or
d
Giu

PANTERA

San
Pietro

San
Quirico

Sant'Ansano

PIAN DEI MANTELLINI

TARTUCA

VIA DI CASTELVECCHIO

CASATO DI SOPRA

VIA S. AGATA

Sant'
Agostino

ON

PRATO SANT'
AGOSTINO

Orto Botanico

San Niccolò
al Carmine

Porta San Marco

Porta Tufi

Con
Tol

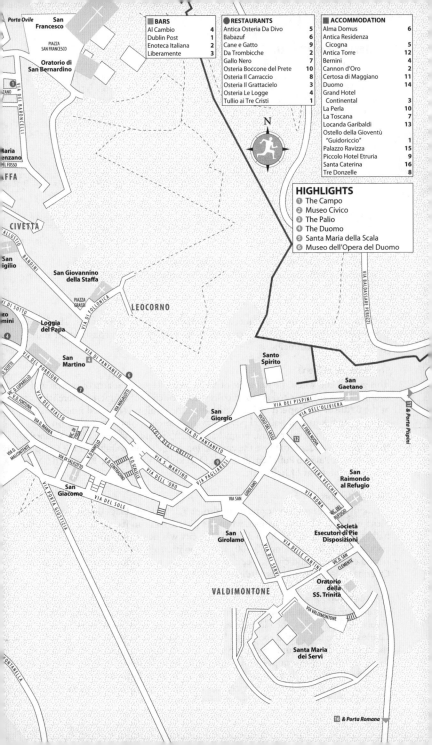

SIENA'S CONTRADE

Within the fabric of the medieval city, Siena preserves its ancient division into wards, or **contrade**. These are integral to the competition of the Palio and sustain a unique neighbourhood identity, clearly visible as you wander around the streets. Each of the seventeen *contrade* has its own church, social centre and museum, as well as a flag and heraldic **animal motif**, after which most of them take their names. The animals – giraffe, snail, goose, porcupine and others – can be seen all around the city on plaques and are represented in a series of modern fountains near the *contrada* churches or headquarters, in each of the city's three *terzi*.

Allegiance to one's *contrada* – conferred by birth – remains a strong element of social life. After a conventional church baptism, anyone born in a ward division is baptized for a second time in their *contrada* fountain. Subsequently, the *contrada* plays a central role in activities: for kids in the flag-twirling and drumming for the Palio and local *contrada* festivals, for adults in the social clubs – a mix of bar and dining club – and in the attendance of a herald at marriages and funerals. *Contrade* also dispense social assistance to needy members. The respect accorded to the institution of *contrade* has a significant effect on the city's social cohesion. Certainly, for a city of its size, Siena has remarkably low levels of crime and drug usage.

Each *contrada* also has its own **annual celebration**, accompanied by parades and feasts. And at almost any time of year, you'll see groups practising flag-waving and drum-rolling in the streets.

trade routes from France to Rome, and maintained Italy's richest banks. The city also developed a highly sophisticated civic life, with its own written constitution and a quasi-democratic council.

The Republic of Siena

This golden era, when the Republic of Siena controlled a great area of central and southern Tuscany, reached an apotheosis with the defeat of a superior Florentine army at the **Battle of Montaperti** in 1260. Although the result was reversed nine years later, shifting the fulcrum of political power towards Florence, Siena embarked on an unrivalled urban development. From 1287 to 1355, under the rule of the **Council of Nine**, the city underwrote first the completion of the **Duomo** and then the **Campo**, with its exuberant **Palazzo Pubblico**; and with Duccio, Martini and the Lorenzettis, Siena was at the forefront of Italian art.

Siena in decline

Prosperity and innovation came to an abrupt halt with the **Black Death**, which reached Siena in May 1348. By October, when the disease had run its course, the population had dropped from 100,000 to 30,000. The city was never fully to recover (the population today is around 60,000) and its politics, always factional, moved into a period of intrigue and chaos, a period redeemed by two nationally renowned saints, **Caterina** (1347–80) and **Bernardino** (1380–1444).

Florentine control

As the sixteenth century opened, Siena was embroiled in ever-expanding intrigues involving the Borgias, the Florentines, the papacy, the French and the empire of **Charles V**. The last proved too big to handle as imperial troops laid siege (1554–55) to the city and the surrounding countryside. The effects proved more terrible than the Black Death, with the population plummeting from 40,000 to 8000. Two years after the siege, Philip II, Charles's successor, gave up Siena to **Cosimo I**, Florence's Medici overlord, in payment for war services, the city subsequently becoming part of Cosimo's Grand Duchy of Tuscany. This was the death knell.

ORIENTATION

The centre of Siena is its great square, the **Campo**, built at the intersection of a Y-shaped configuration of hills and the convergence of the city's principal roads, the **Banchi di Sopra**, **Banchi di Sotto** and **Via di Città**. Each of these roads leads out across a ridge, straddled by one of the city's three medieval districts, or *terzi* (literally "thirds"): the **Terzo di Città** to the southwest, the **Terzo di San Martino** to the southeast, and the **Terzo di Camollia** to the north.

This central core – almost entirely medieval in plan and appearance – is initially disorientating, though with the Campo as a point of reference you won't go far wrong. Movement is also made easier by the fact that the city centre is pedestrianized. Everywhere of use or interest in the city is within easy walking distance, with the exception of the *Guidoriccio* hostel.

Modern Siena

Siena's swift decline from republican capital to market town explains its astonishing state of medieval preservation. The city also managed to escape damage in World War II (unlike nearby Poggibonsi and other Tuscan towns); Siena was taken, unopposed, by the French Expeditionary Force on July 3, 1944. Since the war, however, Siena has again become prosperous, partly due to **tourism**, partly to the resurgence of the **Monte dei Paschi di Siena**. This bank, founded in Siena in 1472, is one of the major players in Italian finance and in its home base is one of the city's largest employers.

The Campo

The Campo is the centre of Siena in every sense: the main streets lead into it, the Palio takes place around its perimeter, and in the evenings it is the natural place to meet, for visitors and residents alike. Four hundred years ago, Montaigne described it as the most beautiful square in the world – an assessment that still seems pretty fair.

With its amphitheatre curve, the Campo appears an almost organic piece of city planning. In fact, when the Council of Nine began buying up land in 1293, they were adopting the only possible site – the old marketplace, which lay at the convergence of the city quarters but was a part of none (the old Roman forum probably also occupied the site). To build on it, it was necessary to construct an enormous buttress beneath the lower half of the square, where the Palazzo Pubblico was to be raised. The piazza itself was completed in 1349, when the council laid its nine segments of paving to commemorate their highly civic rule and pay homage to the Virgin, the folds of whose cloak it was intended to symbolize.

SIENA MUSEUM ADMISSION

Siena has several passes that offer reduced-price entry to some of the main sights. The **cathedral authorities** have an "**OPA SI Pass**" which gives single entry to the Duomo, Museo dell'Opera, the Baptistery and San Bernardino for €10 (valid three days). The **civic museum authorities** have their own two-day pass (the "**Cumulativo Musei Comunali**"), which gives entry to the Museo Civico (but *not* the Torre del Mangia) and Santa Maria della Scala, for €11. A joint ticket covering the Museo Civico and Torre del Mangia costs €13, and is available from the ticket office of the former in the courtyard of the Palazzo Pubblico.

The seven-day "Art Itinerary" pass – the **SIA Inverno**, or **Itinerario d'Arte Inverno** (Winter Art Itinerary; available Nov to mid-March) covers entry to the Museo dell'Opera, the Baptistery, Museo Civico and Santa Maria della Scala for €14; the seven-day **SIA Estate**, or **Itinerario d'Arte Estate** (Summer Art Itinerary; available mid-March to Oct) is valid for all these, plus the Oratorio San Bernardino and the church of Sant'Agostino, and costs €17. The SIA passes and Cumulativo Musei Comunali can be bought online at ⓦ www.comune.siena.it (click on "Biglietteria"). Note that the Pinacoteca Nazionale is not included on any of the passes.

6

THE SIENA PALIO

The **Siena Palio** is the most exciting and spectacular festival event in Italy, a twice-yearly bareback horse race around the Campo, supported by days of preparation, pageantry and intrigue. It has been held since at least the thirteenth century, in honour – like almost everything in Siena – of the Virgin, and it remains a living tradition, felt and performed with an intensity that comes as a shock in these days of cosily preserved folklore.

Except at times of war, the Palio has virtually always taken place. In 1798, for example, when the city was in chaos after an earthquake, the July Palio was cancelled but the August race took place. The following year, however, the Palio was again cancelled, due to political unrest: Sienese counter-revolutionaries took the opportunity to rise against the French-held fortress and sacked the ghetto area of the city. In 1919, when half of Italy was in the throes of strikes and rioting, Siena's factions of the left and right agreed to defer such politics until after the Palio.

Originally the Palio followed a circuit through the town, but since the sixteenth century it has consisted of three laps of the **Campo**, around a track covered with sand and padded with mattresses in an attempt to minimize injury to horses and riders. Despite all probabilities no jockey has ever been killed.

Even before the race, fortune plays the pre-eminent part: as there is only room for ten riders, each year the *contrade* have to draw lots to take part. The participants also draw lots both for the horses and for starting positions in the race itself – the jockeys are paid "mercenaries", and employed according to an unreliable and shifting combination of loyalties reinforced by large cash payments and bonuses, and sometimes the threat of violence if they are treacherous. The result of all this is that in any one year perhaps three or four *contrade* have a serious chance of victory; for those disadvantaged by poor horses or riders, and the seven *contrade* who aren't even taking part, the race becomes a vehicle for schemes, plots and general mayhem. Each *contrada* has its traditional rival, and ensuring that one's rival loses is as important as winning for oneself. The only **rule of the race** is that the jockeys cannot interfere with the others' reins; everything else is accepted and practised. The jockeys are professional outsiders, traditionally

the **butteri**, or cowboys, of the Maremma area, who during the Palio live in fear of the threats of rival *contrade* and under the suspicions of their own. They may be bribed to throw the race, or to whip a rival or his horse; *contrade* have been known to drug horses, and even to mount an ambush on a jockey making his way to the race. And it's the horse that wins – it doesn't matter if the jockey has been thrown en route to victory.

THE RACE

There are two annual Palios, held on **July 2** (formerly the Feast of the Visitation) and **August 16** (the day after the Feast of the Assumption), each of which is preceded by all manner of trial races, processions and the presentation and blessing of the horses

At around 5pm on the day of the race the town hall bell begins to ring and the *corteo storico*, a pageant of horses, riders and medieval-costumed officials, processes through the city to the Campo. The *corteo* includes **comparse** – symbolic groups of equerries, ensigns, pages and drummers – from each of the *contrade*, who perform various **sbandierata** (flag-twirling) and athletic feats in the square. They are preceded by officials of the *comune* of Siena and representatives from all the ancient towns and villages of the Sienese Republic, led by the standard-bearer of Montalcino, which offered refuge to the last republicans.

The **race itself** begins at 7.45pm in July, 7pm in August, lasts for little more than ninety seconds and there's no PA system to tell you what's going on. At the start (in the northwest corner of the Campo) all the horses except one are penned between two ropes; the free one charges the group from behind, when his rivals least expect it, and the race is on. It's a hectic, violent and bizarre spectacle, and the jockeys don't even stop at the finishing line, but gallop at top speed out of the Campo, followed by the frenzied mass of supporters. Losers can be in danger of assault, especially if there are rumours of the race being "fixed" flying about.

The **palio** – a silk banner – is subsequently presented to the winning *contrada*, who then make their way to the church of **Provenzano** (in July) or the **Duomo** (in Aug) to give thanks. The younger *contrada* members spend the rest of the night and much of the subsequent week celebrating their victory, even handing out celebratory sonnets. In the evening all members of the *contrada* hold a jubilant street banquet.

6

From the start, the stage-like Campo was a focus of city life. As well as its continuing role as the city's marketplace – for livestock as well as produce – it was the scene of executions, bullfights, communal boxing matches, and, of course, the Palio. St Bernardino preached here, too, holding before him the monogram of Christ's name in Greek ("IHS"), which he urged the nobles to adopt in place of their own vainglorious coats of arms. A few did so (the monogram is to be seen on various *palazzi*), and it was adopted by the council on the facade of the **Palazzo Pubblico**, alongside the city's she-wolf symbol, a reference to Siena's legendary foundation by the sons of Remus.

Fonte Gaia

At the highest point of the Campo is the Renaissance **Fonte Gaia** ("Gay Fountain"), designed and carved by Jacopo della Quercia in the early fifteenth century. Its panels are poor, nineteenth-century reproductions – some of the original is in Santa Maria della Scala – but they give an idea of what was considered one of the city's masterpieces. Its conception – the Virgin at the centre, flanked by the Virtues – was a conscious emulation of the Lorenzetti frescoes on *Good and Bad Government* in the Palazzo Pubblico. The fountain's name comes from festivities celebrating its inauguration in 1419, the climax of a long process that began in the 1340s, when masons managed to channel water into the square.

The Palazzo Pubblico

The **Palazzo Pubblico**, bristling with crenellations and glorious medieval detail, occupies virtually the entire south side of the Campo, flanked by its giant bell tower, the **Torre del Mangia**. Built largely in the first decade of the fourteenth century, the palace's lower level of arcading is characteristic of Sienese Gothic, as are the columns separating the windows. The council was so pleased with this aspect of the design that they ordered its emulation on all other buildings on the square.

The other main exterior feature of the Palazzo Pubblico is the **Cappella di Piazza**, a stone loggia set at the base of the tower, which the council vowed to build at the end of the Black Death in 1348. Funds were slow to materialize, however, and by 1376, when the chief mason at the cathedral turned his hand to its design, new Florentine ideas were already making their influence felt. The final stage of construction, a century later, when the chapel was heightened and a canopy added, was wholly Renaissance in concept.

The Museo Civico

Daily: mid-March to Oct 10am–7pm; Nov & Feb to mid-March 10am–6pm • €8 or €7.50 if booked online; for details of passes and joint tickets see p.263 • ⓦ www.comune.siena.it

In the days of the *comune*, the lower floors of the Palazzo Pubblico housed the city accounts, and the upper storeys, as today, the council. Nowadays, its principal rooms have been converted into the **Museo Civico**, entered through the courtyard to the right of the Cappella di Piazza.

The museum starts on the first floor of the *palazzo* with the **Sala del Risorgimento** (1878–90), painted with scenes commemorating Vittorio Emanuele, first king of Italy. These depict various battle campaigns, the king's coronation and his earlier meeting with Garibaldi and his army on the road to Capua.

Sala di Balia

The first room of real interest is the **Sala di Balia** (or Sala dei Priori), frescoed by Spinello Aretino and his son, Parri, in 1407 with episodes from the life of Siena-born Pope Alexander III – in particular his conflict with Frederick Barbarossa, the German Holy Roman Emperor. The story is a complex one. The pope and emperor came into dispute following Barbarossa's destruction of Milan in 1162, an event that caused the formation of a Lombard League of Italian states, supported by the Vatican and the Venetians. Barbarossa entered Rome in 1166, whereupon the pope fled to Venice (where he is depicted, disguised as a monk, but recognized by a French pilgrim). The scenes include a superbly realized naval conflict – in which the Venetians are shown capturing the emperor's son and the Germans desperately trying to rescue him – and the pope's eventual reconciliation with Barbarossa, in a procession led by the doge of Venice.

Anticamera del Concistoro

Beyond is the **Anticamera del Concistoro** (or Sala dei Cardinali). A detached fresco, *Three Saints and Donor*, attributed to Ambrogio Lorenzetti, graces the wall by the

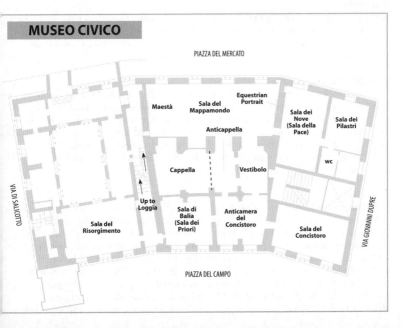

6

entrance door, probably once part of a much larger work depicting the *Madonna and Child*: in such pictures the donor would have been shown kneeling at the feet of the Madonna. In the centre of the left wall is a beautiful *Madonna and Child* attributed to Matteo di Giovanni, whose Madonna has the unquiet look typical of this painter: his propensity for the unsettling found expression in several grisly depictions of the *Massacre of the Innocents*, one of which is on display in the Sala dei Pilastri (see p.270).

Sala del Concistoro

The next room is the **Sala del Concistoro**, entered via an ornate marble doorway (1448) by Bernardo Rossellino, the sculptor and architect responsible for redesigning much of the southern Tuscan town of Pienza for Pope Pius II. Mannerist star Domenico Beccafumi superbly frescoed the room's vault between 1529 and 1535. The panels are either allegories or describe events from Greek and Roman history, but (like virtually every painting in the *palazzo*) deliberately evoke parallels with the civic virtues or historical achievements of Siena itself.

Vestibolo

Doors from the Anticamera behind you lead into the **Vestibolo**, which contains a damaged fresco of the *Madonna and Child* (1340) by Ambrogio Lorenzetti and a gilded bronze of the *She-Wolf Suckling Romulus and Remus* (1429), an allusion to the city's mythical foundation by Senius, son of Remus.

Anticappella

Left off the Vestibolo is the more interesting **Anticappella**, decorated between 1407 and 1414 by Taddeo di Bartolo, the last major exponent of Siena's conservative Gothic style, with a vast *St Christopher* and frescoes – like those in the Sala del Concistoro – whose Greek and Roman themes reflect Siena's own civic concerns.

Cappella

Taddeo also frescoed the **Cappella** alongside with episodes from the *Life of the Virgin* (1407–08), work overshadowed by Sodoma's altarpiece, the vast wrought-iron screen (1435–45) – attributed to Jacopo della Quercia – and the exceptional set of inlaid choir stalls (1415–28).

Sala del Mappamondo

All these works are little more than a warm-up for the **Sala del Mappamondo**, one of the great set pieces of Italian art. Taking its name from its now scarcely visible ceiling fresco of a map of the cosmos, executed by Ambrogio Lorenzetti, the room was used for several centuries as the city's law court and contains one of the greatest of all Italian frescoes, **Simone Martini**'s fabulous and recently restored *Maestà*, a painting of almost translucent colour, which was the *comune*'s first major commission for the palace.

The Maestà

The **Maestà**'s political dimension is apparent in the depiction of the Christ Child holding a parchment inscribed with the city's motto of justice, and the inscription of two stanzas from Dante on the steps below the throne, warning that the Virgin will not intercede for those who betray her or oppress the poor. It is one of Martini's earliest known works, painted in 1315 at the age of 30; before this extraordinary debut not a thing is known of him. The richly decorative style is archetypal Sienese Gothic and its arrangement makes a fascinating comparison with the *Maestà* by Duccio (with whom Martini perhaps trained) in the Museo dell'Opera del Duomo. Martini's great innovation was the use of a canopy and a frieze of medallions which frame and organize the figures – a sense of space and hint of perspective that suggest a knowledge of Giotto's work. Martini was to experiment further in this direction, in his great cycle of the *Life of St Martin* in Assisi, painted a couple of years later.

The Equestrian Portrait of Guidoriccio da Fogliano

The fresco on the opposite wall, the marvellous **Equestrian Portrait of Guidoriccio da Fogliano** was, until recently, also credited to Martini. Depicting the knight setting forth from his battle camp to besiege a walled hill-town (thought to be Montemassi, a village southwest of Siena near Roccastrada), it would, if it were by Martini, be accounted one of the earliest Italian portrait paintings. Art historians, however, have long puzzled over the apparently anachronistic castles: according to some, they are of a much later architectural style than the painting's supposed date of 1328. The work would also seem to be part-painted over a fresco to the right by Lippo Vanni, which is dated 1364. In the mid-1980s the waters were further muddied when, during restoration, another apparently anachronistic fresco was found – the painting now beneath the equestrian portrait showing two men in front of a castle, believed to be the one at Arcidosso in southern Tuscany; it has been variously attributed to Martini, Duccio, Pietro Lorenzetti and Memmi di Filippuccio.

The coffered figures to the right and left of the uncovered fresco beneath the equestrian portrait are a pair of saints by Sodoma dating from 1529. The other large frescoes in the room also depict Sienese military victories. Don't miss the figures on the pilasters below the latter, which from left to right are Sodoma's *Blessed Tolomei* (1533), founder of the abbey at Monte Oliveto Maggiore; *St Bernardino* (1450) by Sano di Pietro; and *St Catherine of Siena* (1461) by Vecchietta.

Sala dei Nove (Sala della Pace)

The Palazzo Pubblico's most important and interesting frescoes adorn the **Sala dei Nove** (or **Sala della Pace**) next door; these are Ambrogio Lorenzetti's **Allegories of Good and Bad Government**, commissioned in 1338 to remind the councillors of the effects of their duties, and widely considered one of Europe's most important surviving cycles of secular paintings. The walled city they depict is clearly Siena, along with its countryside and domains, and the paintings are full of details of medieval life: agriculture, craftwork, trade and building, even hawking and dancing. They form the first-known panorama in Western art and show an innovative approach to the human figure – the beautiful, reclining Peace (Pax) in the *Good Government* hierarchy is based on a Roman sarcophagus still on display in the Palazzo Pubblico. Ironically, within a decade of the frescoes' completion, Siena was engulfed by the Black Death – in which Lorenzetti and his family were among the victims – and the city was under tyrannical government.

Good Government

The moral theme of the frescoes is expressed in a complex iconography of allegorical virtues and figures. **Good Government**, painted on the more brightly lit walls and better preserved, is dominated by a throned figure representing the *comune* (he is dressed in Siena's colours), flanked by the Virtues (Peace – from which the room takes its name – is the nonchalantly reclining figure in white) and with Faith, Hope and Charity buzzing about his head. To the left, on a throne, Justice (with Wisdom in the air above) dispenses rewards and punishments, while below her throne Concordia advises the republic's councillors on their duties. All hold ropes, symbol of agreement.

Bad Government

Bad Government is ruled by the figure of Fear (or the Devil), whose scroll reads: "Because he looks for his own good in the world, he places justice beneath tyranny. So nobody walks this road without Fear: robbery thrives inside and outside the city gates." Fear is surrounded by figures symbolizing the Vices.

Sala dei Pilastri

The room adjoining the Sala della Pace, the **Sala dei Pilastri** (or delle Colonne), displays panel paintings from the thirteenth to the fifteenth centuries, whose conservatism and strict formulaic composition points up the scale of Lorenzetti's achievement. Notable among them is one of the earliest Sienese masterpieces, Guido da Siena's gripping *Maestà* (1221-60), for which Duccio repainted the Virgin's face; a fascinating picture of *St Bernardino Preaching in the Campo* by Neroccio di Bartolomeo (note how the men and women in the crowd are separated by a white cloth); and a graphically violent *Massacre of the Innocents* removed from Sant'Agostino, painted by Matteo di Giovanni – one of four he completed in the city. The stained-glass figure of St Michael in one of the windows is attributed to Ambrogio Lorenzetti.

The loggia

Backtracking through the museum, it is worth climbing the stairs between the Sala del Risorgimento and Sala di Balia to the rear **loggia**, where you can enjoy a view over the Piazza del Mercato. It is here you realize how abruptly the town ends: buildings rise to the right and left for a few hundred metres along the ridges of the Terzo di San Martino and Terzo di Città, but in the centre the land drops away to a rural valley.

The Torre del Mangia

Daily: mid-March to Oct 10am–7pm; rest of year 10am–4pm • €8, or €13 with the Museo Civico

Within the Palazzo Pubblico's courtyard, opposite the entrance to the Museo Civico, is separate access to the 87-metre **Torre del Mangia**. Climb it and you have fabulous, vertigo-inducing views across the town and countryside. Built between 1338 and 1348 – the cresting was designed by Lippo Memmi – the tower takes its name from its first watchman, a spendthrift (*mangiaguadagni*) named Giovanni di Balduccio, who is commemorated by a statue in the courtyard. It was the last great project of the *comune* before the Black Death and exercised a highly civic function: its bell was rung to order the opening of the city gates at dawn, the break for lunch, the end of work at sunset and the closing of the city gates three hours later.

Piazza del Duomo

Siena's mighty **Duomo** is the focus of an ensemble of art and architecture arrayed around the **Piazza del Duomo**. The southwest side of the square is occupied by the medieval complex of **Santa Maria della Scala**, Siena's former hospital and now a museum and arts complex that displays some staggering medieval frescoes as well as the modest but well-presented **Museo Archeologico**. The other sides of the square continue the history of Sienese power, with the Palazzo dei Vescovi (Archbishop's Palace), the Palazzo del Magnifico, built in 1508, and the Palazzo Granducale, erected later the same century for the Medici. More interesting than any of these, though, is the **Museo dell'Opera del Duomo**, home to Siena's single greatest work of art – Duccio's *Maestà* – and a range of other significant sculptures and paintings.

Antico Panpepato
Prodotto da forno
a base di frutta candita e mandorle e spezie
Ingredienti: zucchero, mandorle, farina, scorze d'arancia candite,
melone candito, nocciole, miele, zucchero caramello, sciroppo di
glucosio, spezie, cacao in polvere 22/24%, noce di muscato.
€. 23,50 al Kg

The Duomo

March to mid-June Mon–Sat 10.30am–7.30pm, Sun 1.30–7.30pm; mid-June to mid-Oct Mon–Sat 10.30am–8pm, Sun 1.30–6pm; Nov–Feb Mon–Sat 10.30am–6.30pm, Sun 1.30–5.30pm • €3, or €6 during the summer uncovering of the marble pavement; for details of passes and combined tickets, see p. 263 • ⓦ operaduomo.siena.it

Few buildings reveal so much of a city's history and aspirations as Siena's **Duomo**. Completed to virtually its present size around 1215, the church was subjected to constant plans for expansion throughout the city's years of medieval prosperity. A project at the beginning of the fourteenth century attempted to double its extent by building a baptistery on the slope below and using this as a foundation for a rebuilt nave, but the work ground to a halt as the walls gaped under the pressure. Then a new scheme aimed to re-orientate the cathedral instead, using the existing nave as a transept and building a **new nave** out towards the Campo. Again cracks appeared, and then in 1348 came the Black Death. With the population halved and funds suddenly cut off, the plan was abandoned once and for all. The part-built extension still stands at the north end of the square, a vast structure that would have created the largest church in Italy outside Rome.

The facade

Despite all the abandoned plans, the Duomo is still a delight. Its style is an amazing conglomeration of Romanesque and Gothic, delineated by bands of black and white marble, an idea adapted from Pisa and Lucca – though here with much bolder and more extravagant effect. The lower part of the **facade** was designed by the Pisan sculptor Giovanni Pisano, who from 1284 to 1296 created, with his workshop, much of its statuary – the philosophers, patriarchs and prophets, now removed to the Museo dell'Opera and replaced by copies.

  In the next century the **Campanile** was added, as was the Gothic **rose window** above the doors. Thereafter work came to a halt, with the **mosaics** designed for the gables having to wait until the nineteenth century, when money was found to employ Venetian artists. Immediately above the central door, note St Bernardino's bronze monogram of Christ's name.

The pavement

The facade's use of black and white decoration is echoed by the Duomo's great marble **pavement**, or floor, which begins with geometric patterns and a few scenes outside the church and takes off into a startling sequence of 56 figurative panels within. These were completed between 1349 and 1547, with virtually every artist who worked in the city trying his hand on a design. The earliest employed a simple *sgraffito* technique, which involved chiselling holes and lines in the marble and then filling them with pitch; later tableaux are considerably more ambitious, worked in multicoloured marble. Unfortunately, the whole effect can only be seen for about a month in August (dates vary); the rest of the year, most of the panels are protected by boarding

The panels

The subjects chosen for the **panels** are a strange mix, incorporating biblical themes, secular commemorations and allegories. The most ordered part of the scheme are the ten Sibyls – mythic prophetesses who foretold the coming of Christ – on either side of the main aisle. Fashioned towards the end of the fifteenth century, when Sienese painters were still imprinting gold around their conventional Madonnas, they are totally Renaissance in spirit. Between them, in the central nave, are the much earlier *She-Wolf Suckling Romulus and Remus* (marked A on our plan), and the *Wheel of Fortune* (E), along with Pinturicchio's *Allegory of the Hill of Wisdom* (D), a rocky island of serpents with a nude posed between a boat and the land. Moving down the nave, the central hexagon is dominated by Domenico Beccafumi's *Stories from the Life of Elijah* (F–I). Beccafumi worked intermittently on the pavement from 1518 to 1547, also

SIENA: THE DUOMO

0   25
metres

Baptistery

Sacristy

Pecci Tomb

Pulpit

PIAZZA DEL DUOMO

Santa Maria della Scala

DUOMO PAVEMENT

A She-Wolf Suckling Romulus and Remus
B Sibyl (1483). Benvenuto di Giovanni.
C Sibyl (1483). Matteo di Giovanni.
D Allegory of The Hill of Wisdom (1505). Pinturicchio.
E Wheel of Fortune (restored in nineteenth century). Attributed to Domenico dei Cori.
F Akab is mortally wounded. Domenico Beccafumi.
G The pact between Akab and Elijah. Domenico Beccafumi.
H The Sacrifice of Elijah. Domenico Beccafumi.
I Death of the Prophets. Domenico Beccafumi.
J Sacrifice of the Priests. Domenico Beccafumi.
K Massacre of the Innocents (1482). Matteo di Giovanni.
L Judith and Holofernes (restored 1790). Francesco di Giorgio Martini.
M Moses Striking Water from the Rock (1524). Domenico Beccafumi.
N Adoration of the Golden Calf (1531). Domenico Beccafumi.
O The Sacrifice of Isaac (1547). Domenico Beccafumi.

SIENA DUOMO

1 Altare Piccolomini (1491). Andrea Bregno. Sculptures by Michelangelo.
2 Libreria Piccolomini. Frescoes on the life of Pope Pius II (1505–07) by Pinturicchio.
3 Flagpole from the Battle of Montaperti.
4 Cappella di San Giovanni Battista. Frescoes (1501–04) by Pinturicchio; bronze by Donatello of St John the Baptist (1457).
5 Pulpit. Nicola Pisano and assistants (1268).
6 Tomb of Bishop Pecci of Grosseto (1426–7). Donatello.
7 Tomb of Cardinal Riccardo Petroni (1314–18). Tino da Camaino.
8 Bronze candleholders (1548–50). Domenico Beccafumi.
9 Bronze candleholders (1497–99). Francesco di Giorgio Martini.
10 High altar (1532). Baldassare Peruzzi.
11 Ciborio (1467–72). Vecchietta.
12 Stained glass (1288). To a design by Duccio.
13 Cappella del Sacramento. Bas-reliefs (1425) by Domenico dei Cori.
14 Cappella Chigi (1659–62). To a design by Gian Lorenzo Bernini.
15 Tomb of Tommaso Piccolomini (1484–5). Neroccio di Bartolomeo Landi. Below: bas-reliefs of Episodes from the Life of the Virgin (1451) by Urbano da Cortona.

designing the vast friezes of *Moses Striking Water from a Rock* (M) and *The Sacrifice of Isaac* (O). To the left of the hexagon is a *Massacre of the Innocents* (K), the chosen subject of Matteo di Giovanni.

The pulpit

The rest of the cathedral interior is equally arresting, with its zebra-stripe bands of marble, and the line of popes' heads set above the pillars. The greatest individual artistic treasure is the **pulpit** (marked 5 on our plan), completed by Nicola Pisano in

1268, soon after his pulpit for the Baptistery at Pisa, with help from his son Giovanni and Arnolfo di Cambio. The design of the panels duplicates those in Pisa, though they are executed with much greater detail and high relief. The carving's distance from the Byzantine world is perhaps best displayed by the statuette of the *Madonna*, whose breast is visible beneath the cloak for the first time in Italy, and by the *Last Judgement*, with its mastery of the human figure and organization of space.

The sculptures

Almost all the sculpture is of an exceptional standard. Near the pulpit in the north transept are Tino di Camaino's *Tomb of Cardinal Petroni* (1314–18), a prototype for Italian tomb architecture over the next century, and, in front, **Donatello**'s bronze pavement *Tomb of Bishop Pecci* (1426). Superb candelabra-carrying angels by Beccafumi flank the Renaissance high altar. In the **Piccolomini Altarpiece** (1) the young **Michelangelo** also makes an appearance. He was commissioned to carve a series of fifteen statues here, but after completing saints Peter, Paul, Pius and Gregory in the lower niches he left for a more tempting contract in Florence – the *David*.

The chapels

There are further Renaissance sculptural highlights in the two circular transept chapels. The **Cappella di San Giovanni Battista** (4) focuses on a bronze statue of the *Baptist* by Donatello, cast in 1457, a couple of years after his expressionist *Mary Magdalene* in Florence, whom the Baptist's stretched and emaciated face recalls. The frescoes in this chapel, with their delightful landscape detailing, are by Pinturicchio.

The **Cappella Chigi** (14) or Cappella del Voto, was the last major addition to the Duomo, built at the behest of the Sienese Pope Alexander VII in 1659. It was designed by Bernini as a new setting for the *Madonna del Voto*, a thirteenth-century painting that commemorated the Sienese dedication of their city to the Virgin on the eve of the Battle of Montaperti. The style of the chapel is Roman Baroque, most notably seen in the four niche statues, two of which are by Bernini – wild, semi-clad figures of Mary Magdalene and St Jerome. Outside the chapel, the walls are covered in a mass of devotional objects – silver limbs and hearts, *contrada* scarves, even the odd Palio costume and crash helmet.

Libreria Piccolomini

Midway along the nave, Pinturicchio's brilliantly coloured fresco of the *Coronation of Pius II* marks the entrance to the **Libreria Piccolomini** (2), well worth a visit for the beautiful fresco cycle within. The frescoes and library were commissioned from Pinturicchio, an eminent Umbrian painter who worked in the Sistine Chapel, among other places, by Francesco Piccolomini (who for ten days was Pope Pius III) to house the books of his uncle, Aeneas Sylvius Piccolomini (Pius II). Pius, born at nearby Pienza in 1405, was the archetypal Renaissance man, writing poetry and the *Commentaries*, a deeply humanist work in which he enthuses over landscape, antiquity and architecture and describes the languages, customs and industries encountered on his travels.

Pinturicchio's frescoes

Pinturicchio's frescoes, painted with an equal love of nature and classical decor as well as a keen sense of drama, commemorate the gamut of Pius's career. The cycle begins to the right of the window, with Aeneas's secular career as a diplomat: attending the Council of Basle as secretary to an Italian bishop (panel 1); presenting himself as an envoy to James II of Scotland (panel 2); being crowned poet laureate by the Holy Roman Emperor, Frederick III (panel 3); and then representing Frederick on a visit to Pope Eugenius IV (panel 4). Aeneas subsequently returned to Italy and took orders, becoming first Bishop of Trieste and then of Siena, in which role he is depicted presiding over the meeting of Frederick III and his bride-to-be, Eleonora of Portugal, outside the city's Porta Camollia (panel 5).

In 1456 Aeneas was made a cardinal (panel 6) and just two years later was elected pope (panel 7), taking the title **Pius II**. In political terms, his eight-year rule was not a great papacy, despite his undoubted humanism and diplomatic skill, with much of the time wasted in crushing the barons of Romagna and the Marche. The crusade he called in 1456 at Mantua (panel 8) to regain Constantinople from the Turks – who took the city in 1453 – came to nothing, and the last picture of the series (panel 10) shows his death at Ancona, where he had gone to encourage the troops. It was said that his death was brought on by grief for the failure to get the crusade off the ground, or possibly by poisoning by the troops, eager to terminate their pledge. Between these two panels is the event for which Siena most remembers him – the canonization of St Catherine.

The choirbooks and Three Graces

The library is now used to display the cathedral's **choirbooks**, illuminated by Sano di Pietro and other Sienese Gothics. At the centre of the room is a Roman statue of the **Three Graces**, supposedly copied from a lost Greek work by Praxiteles. It was bought by the Piccolomini nephew and was used as a model by Pinturicchio and Raphael.

The Baptistery

Piazza San Giovanni • Daily: March to mid-June & mid-Sept to Oct 9.30am–7pm; mid-June to mid-Sept 9.30am–8pm; rest of year 10am–5pm • €3, or €10 with joint ticket (see p.263) • ⓦ operduomo.siena.it

The cathedral **Baptistery** contains one of the city's great Renaissance works – a hexagonal font with scenes illustrating the Baptist's life. It's unusual in being placed beneath the main body of the church: to reach it, turn left out of the Duomo, follow the walls left and then take the flight of steps leading down behind the cathedral.

The font

The cathedral chapter responsible for the **font** (1417–30) must have had a good sense of what was happening in Florence at the time, for they managed to commission panels by **Ghiberti** (*Baptism of Christ* and *John in Prison*) and **Donatello** (*Herod's Feast*), as well as by the local sculptor **Jacopo della Quercia** (*The Angel Announcing the Baptist's Birth*). Jacopo also executed the marble tabernacle above, and the summit statue of *John the Baptist* and five niche statues of the Prophets. Of the main panels, Donatello's scene, in particular, is a superb piece of drama, with Herod and his cronies recoiling at the appearance of the Baptist's head. Donatello was also responsible for two of the corner angels (*Faith* and *Hope*) and (with Giovanni di Turino) for the miniature angels on the tabernacle above.

The walls

The lavishly frescoed **walls** almost overshadow the font, their nineteenth-century overpainting having been removed. With your back to the entrance, the best include (on the left arched vault lunette) a fresco of scenes from the life of St Anthony (1460) by Benvenuto di Giovanni, a pupil of Vecchietta; scenes from the life of Christ by Vecchietta himself (inside left wall of the central stepped chapel); and the same artist's *Prophets*, *Sibyls* and *Articles of the Creed* (the main vaults), the last a repeat of a theme he would use in Santa Maria della Scala.

Santa Maria della Scala

Piazza del Duomo • Daily: mid-March to mid-Oct 10am–6.30pm; rest of year 10.30am–4.30pm • €6, €5.50 when booked online at ⓦ www.comune.siena.it, or joint ticket (see p.263) • ⓦ santamariadellascala.com

6

A HISTORY OF SANTA MARIA DELLA SCALA

According to legend, the hospital of Santa Maria della Scala was founded by **Beato Sorore**, a ninth-century cobbler-turned-monk who worked among orphans. Sorore was almost certainly mythical, his name a corruption of *suore*, or nuns, who for centuries tended the sick as a part of their vocation. The hospital was probably founded by the cathedral's canons, the first written record of its existence appearing in 1090. Its development was prompted by the proximity of the **Via Francigena**, a vital trade and pilgrimage route between Rome and northern Europe, which in the early Middle Ages replaced the deteriorating Roman consular roads used previously. Its route passed below Siena's walls, giving rise to the growth of numerous rest-places (*ospedali*) where travellers and pilgrims could seek shelter and succour. Some forty of these grew up in Sienese territory alone, the most important of which was Santa Maria della Scala. Initially pilgrims were the main concern: hospital work, in the modern sense, came later: "hospitality rather than hospitalization" was the credo.

The foundation was one of the first European examples of the **Xenodochium**, literally an "abode", a hospital that not only looked after the sick but could also be used as a refuge and food kitchen for an entire town in times of famine and plague. This role made it a vital part of the city's social fabric. In time it passed from the cathedral canons into the hands of hospital friars, and in 1404, after an intense dispute, into the care of the *comune*, who appointed its rectors and governing body. Alms and bequests over the centuries kept it richly endowed.

Some of the donated funds were diverted to artistic and architectural commissions: as early as 1252, Siena's bishop gave permission for Santa Maria's abbot to build a **church**, the precursor of the present Santissima Annunziata. In 1335 the hospital commissioned Simone Martini and Pietro and Ambrogio Lorenzetti, the city's three leading painters, to fresco the building's facade (works since lost to the elements). In 1359 it paid an exorbitant sum to acquire from Constantinople a nail used during the Passion, a piece of the True Cross, and a part of the Virgin's girdle, along with a miscellany of **saints' relics**. In 1378 it financed the setting of a stone bench along the length of the hospital's exterior, its original purpose being to provide the hospital's dignitaries with somewhere to sit during the city's interminable religious and civic ceremonies – and still much used today as a shady spot from which to view the facade of the Duomo.

Santa Maria della Scala served as the city's hospital for over eight hundred years. Its closure in 1995 aroused mixed feelings, for the functioning building gave a sense of purpose to the cathedral square, which isn't matched by its use as Siena's principal cultural space. The last few years have seen the restoration of the church of **Santissima Annunziata**; the **Cappella del Sacro Chiodo**, with its highly acclaimed fresco cycle by Vecchietta; a beautiful Beccafumi fresco in the **Cappella del Manto**; the **Oratorio di Santa Caterina della Notte**, a finely decorated subterranean chapel; and Jacopo della Quercia's original marble panels from the Fonte Gaia in the **Fienile**. Best of all, in the **Sala del Pellegrinaio**, is a vast secular fresco cycle by Domenico di Bartolo, a work third only to the frescoes in the Duomo and Palazzo Pubblico in Siena's artistic pantheon. Siena's **Museo Archeologico** also finds a home in the complex.

Sala del Pellegrinaio

The highlight of the complex, the **Sala del Pellegrinaio**, is a majestic long hall typical of the "longitudinal" architectural elements introduced into Italy by French Cistercians travelling the Via Francigena, its walls completely covered in a fresco cycle of episodes from the history of Santa Maria della Scala by Domenico di Bartolo and Vecchietta. Incredibly, this astounding space was used as a hospital ward until relatively recently.

The ward was built around 1380 and the **frescoes** begun in 1440, their aim being to not only record scenes from the hospital's history, but also to promote the notion of charity towards the sick and – in particular – the orphaned, whose care had been a large part of the hospital's early function. Their almost entirely **secular** content was extraordinary at the time they were painted, still some years short of the period when Renaissance ideas would allow for other than religious narratives. It's well worth taking the trouble to study the eight major panels in detail – each is full of insights into the Sienese daily life of the time – along with the two paintings on the end wall by the window. The cycle starts at the left end of the left wall and moves clockwise.

The first panel

The **first panel**, *The Dream of the Mother of Beato Sorore*, is by Vecchietta. It depicts in part a dream in which the mother of Sorore, the hospital's mythical founder, foresees her son's destiny. Her vision focuses on the abandoned children of the hospital, the *gettatelli* (from *gettare*, to throw away), who are shown ascending to Paradise and the arms of the Madonna. Sorore is shown twice: on the right with upraised hand receiving the first *gettatello*, and kneeling at the foot of the child-filled ladder.

This **ladder** (*scala*) is probably the reason for Santa Maria della Scala's name. Another version of the story suggests that a three-runged ladder, a symbol of the Trinity, was found during the hospital's construction – although the more likely explanation is that the hospital was simply built opposite the steps, or *scala*, of the Duomo. Whatever the origins, a three-runged ladder surmounted by a cross is the symbol on the museum's literature and displays.

The second panel

The **second panel**, *The Building of the Hospital*, depicts a mounted bishop of Siena at the head of a procession passing the hospital, which is in the process of being built, and almost running down a stonemason in the process. Note the buildings, a strange mixture of Gothic and Renaissance that bear little relation to anything in Siena, and the rector of the hospital, portrayed behind the ladder on the right doffing his hat to the visiting dignitaries.

The third and fourth panels

The **third panel**, the weakest of the cycle, is by Priamo della Quercia, brother of the more famous Jacopo, and shows the *Investiture of the Hospital Rector by the Blessed Agostino Novello*, the latter traditionally, but erroneously, credited as being the author of the hospital's first statute.

The **fourth panel** shows one of Santa Maria's defining moments, when in 1193 Pope Celestine III gave the hospital the right to elect its own rector, thus transferring power from the religious to lay authorities. For the rest, the fresco is an excuse to portray day-to-day life in Siena – note, for example, the preponderance of oriental merchants.

The end wall

The paintings on either side of the **end wall** are late sixteenth-century works, but illustrate two fascinating aspects of the hospital's work. The vast number of orphans taken in meant that an equally large number of wet nurses, or *baliatici*, were needed to feed the infants. At one time their numbers were such that feeding took place in the huge hall alongside the Sala. The pictures here show the nurses in action, and the payment for their services: in grain (on the left wall) and hard cash (on the right).

The fifth panel

On the long right wall, the **fifth panel**, the most famous in the cycle, shows *The Tending of the Sick*, a picture crammed with incident, notably the close scrutiny being given to a urine sample by two doctors on the left, the youth with a leg wound being washed, and the rather ominous scene on the right of a monk taking confession from a patient prior to surgery.

The sixth panel

The **sixth panel** shows *The Distribution of Charity*, one of the hospital's main tasks, an event that takes place in the old hospital church (now replaced by Santissima Annunziata), with the central door of the Duomo just visible in the background. Bread is distributed to beggars, pilgrims and children (one of whom passes it on to his mother); at the centre an orphan puts on clothes that it has been given. In one strange vignette a child is shown trying to express milk from its mother's breast. On the left, meanwhile, the hospital's rector is shown doffing his hat, possibly to Sigismondo.

The seventh panel

The **seventh panel** illustrates further work of the hospital, underlining the vital part it played in maintaining the social fabric of the city. It shows the reception, education and marriage of one of the female orphans, who were provided with a small grant designed to enable them to marry, stay on in the hospital or join a convent. Also included are details that suggest how the hospital not only took in children, but committed itself to caring for them over a long period. Thus the wet nurses are shown in action on the table to the left, along with scenes to suggest weaning, education and play.

The eighth panel

The final **eighth panel**, which details the feeding of the poor and the elderly, is less engaging than the rest, partly because of the awkwardly sited window, reputedly built by a nineteenth-century superintendent so that he could survey the sick from his upper-floor office without the bother of having to go down into the ward.

Santissima Annunziata

At the heart of the complex is the church of **Santissima Annunziata**, remodelled in the fifteenth century and disappointingly bland, but worth a look for the high altar's marvellous bronze statue of the *Risen Christ* by Vecchietta, its features so gaunt the veins show through the skin. Vecchietta clearly understood and absorbed the new approach of Donatello, and several art historians consider this the finest Renaissance sculpture in the city. Before the church's remodelling, frescoes by Vecchietta had entirely covered its walls, a loss as tantalizing as the missing Martini and Lorenzetti frescoes on the hospital's exterior.

The Cappella del Manto

Close to the Sala is the **Cappella del Manto**, which contains an arresting and beautifully restored fresco of *St Anne and St Joachim* (1512), the earliest major work in Siena by the Mannerist Domenico Beccafumi. The protagonists depicted are the parents of the Virgin, whose story – popular in Tuscan painting – is told in the apocryphal gospels, biblical adjuncts reintroduced to the medieval world in the *Golden Legend* by Jacopo da Voragine. Having failed to conceive during twenty years of marriage, each is told by an angel to meet at Jerusalem's Golden Gate. Here they kiss (the scene depicted in the fresco), a moment which symbolizes the Immaculate Conception of their daughter.

The Cappella del Sacro Chiodo

Some idea of what was lost in the remodelling of Santissima Annunziata can be grasped in Vecchietta's fresco cycle (1446–49) in the **Cappella del Sacro Chiodo**, so named because it once housed the nail (*chiodo*) from the Passion and other holy relics. Some art critics pay these frescoes more attention than the Bartolo cycle in the Sala del Pellegrinaio, but for the casual viewer they are less easy to interpret, principally because the subject matter – an illustration of the *Articles of the Creed* – requires some theological knowledge. Each lunette illustrates one or more articles, the figure of one of the Apostles to the right holding the text of the article in question, the scenes below or to the left depicting an episode from the Old Testament which embodies the article's meaning.

The frescoes are extremely unusual, partly in that they illustrate a written text – something that remained rare until much later in the Renaissance – and partly in that they revolve around the figure of Christ (depicted twice in the main vaults). The latter was a strange choice in a city dedicated to the Madonna, where virtually every work of note either eulogizes Siena itself or includes Christ only as an adjunct to the Virgin. It's thought that the choice was suggested by the "nail from the Cross" contained in the chapel, a relic with obvious relevance to the story of Christ.

Madonna della Misericordia

Domenico di Bartolo's **high altarpiece**, the *Madonna della Misericordia* (1444), is more intelligible than much of the cycle, and shows the Madonna casting a protective cloak over several of Siena's inhabitants. This theme, a common one in Sienese and other central Italian works, derives from a vision of the Madonna experienced by a ninth-century Cistercian monk. At first painters depicted only members of the religious orders beneath the protective cloak, monks to one side, nuns to the other. At the beginning of the twelfth century members of religious confraternities were allowed protection, and a few decades later the privilege was extended to all inhabitants of a town or city. Men and women usually remained segregated, however, which makes this version – in which they're mixed – unusual.

The fresco once graced the Cappella del Manto, the Virgin's cloak (*manto*) having given the chapel its name. It was detached and fixed here in 1610, its side parts torn away to fit the dimensions of the new altar; in 1969, however, the discarded fragments were found and reattached.

The Fienile

Stairs lead down to the **Fienile**, the hospital's old hayloft, now housing Jacopo della Quercia's original marble panels from the Fonte Gaia (1409–19), transferred here from the Palazzo Pubblico. With their serious state of erosion it was hard to appreciate that Vasari rated Jacopo della Quercia on a par with Donatello and Ghiberti, with whom he competed for the commission of Florence's Baptistery doors. Michelangelo, too, was an admirer, struck perhaps by the physicality evident in the *Expulsion of Adam and Eve*.

Oratorio di Santa Caterina della Notte

Adjacent to the Fienile, the **Oratorio di Santa Caterina della Notte** belonged to one of a number of the medieval confraternities that maintained oratories in the basement vaults of the hospital. It's a dark and strangely spooky place, despite the wealth of decoration; you can easily imagine St Catherine passing nocturnal vigils down here. Even if you prove immune to the atmosphere, it's worth coming down here for Taddeo di Bartolo's sumptuous triptych of the *Madonna and Child with Sts Andrew and John the Baptist* (1400).

Compagnia della Madonna sotto le Volte

Stairs lead down again to the lavishly decorated **Compagnia della Madonna sotto le Volte**, the oratory and meeting-room of the Società di Esecutori di Pie Diposizioni, the oldest of the lay confraternities, where you'll find a wooden crucifix said to be the one that inspired St Bernardino to become a monk.

Museo Archeologico

The **Museo Archeologico** houses private collections from the late nineteenth century and plenty of local finds from excavation work in and around Siena, Chianti, the upper Val d'Elsa and Etruscan Murlo.

The Museo dell'Opera del Duomo

Daily: March to mid-June & mid-Sept to Oct 9.30am–7pm; mid-June to mid-Sept 9.30am–8pm; rest of year 10am–5pm • €6, or €10 with joint ticket (see p.263) • ⓦ operaduomo.siena.it

Tucked into a corner of the proposed – and abandoned – new nave of the Duomo is the impressive **Museo dell'Opera del Duomo**, which offers the bonus of fine views over Siena.

Galleria delle Statue

On the ground floor, in the **Galleria delle Statue**, the statuary by Giovanni Pisano (1250–1314) seems a little bizarre when displayed at eye level: the huge, elongated, twisting figures are obviously adjusted to take account of the original viewing position, which was ranged across the Duomo's facade. They are totally Gothic in conception, and for all their subject matter – philosophers from antiquity are represented alongside Old Testament prophets and other characters – show little of his father Nicola's experiment with classical forms on the cathedral pulpit. In marked contrast is Donatello's ochre-coloured *Madonna and Child*, a delicate piece at the near end of the room (removed from the door of the Duomo's south transept), alongside a bas-relief by Jacopo della Quercia of *St Anthony Abbot and Cardinal Antonio Casini*.

Sala di Duccio

Upstairs is the **Sala di Duccio**, curtained and carefully lit to display the artist's vast and justly celebrated **Maestà**. Originally painted on both sides, it depicts the *Madonna and Child Enthroned* (or *Maestà*) and the *Story of the Passion*. The four saints in the front rank of the main painting, the *Maestà*, are Siena's patron saints at the time – Ansano, Savino, Crescenzio and Vittore – while the ten smaller figures at the rear of the massed ranks represent ten of the Apostles. (Peter and Paul are in the second rank, accompanied by John the Baptist and other saints.)

The Maestà

On its completion in 1311 the **Maestà** was, as far as scholars can ascertain, the most expensive painting ever commissioned, and had occupied Duccio for almost four years. It was taken in a ceremonial procession from Duccio's studio around the Campo and then to a special Mass in the Duomo; everything in the city was closed and virtually the entire population attended. It then remained on the Duomo's high altar until 1505. This is one of the superlative works of Sienese art – its iconic, Byzantine spirituality accentuated by Duccio's flowing composition and a new attention to narrative detail in the panels of the predella and the reverse of the altarpiece, both now displayed to its side.

The *Maestà* – the Virgin as Queen of Heaven surrounded by her "court" of saints – was a Sienese invention, designed as a "sacrifice" to the Virgin, the city's patron (the consecration took place in 1260), a quality emphasized by the lavish use of gold. Duccio's rendering of the theme was essentially the prototype for the next three centuries of Sienese painters.

This quality is best observed in the narrative panels, most of which were gathered here following the altarpiece's dismemberment in 1771 and its removal to the museum in 1887. Only a handful of panels are missing and will not be released by their owners to the city: two are in Washington, three in London's National Gallery and three in the Frick and Rockefeller collections in New York.

The rest of the room

Also in the room is a *Madonna di Crevole*, an early work by Duccio, and Pietro Lorenzetti's triptych of the *Nativity of the Virgin*, the latter remarkable for breaking with the tradition of triptych painting by running a single scene across two of the painting's three panels. The gilded statues in the room off to the right of the *Madonna and Child with Four Saints* are attributed to Jacopo della Quercia, as is the separate statue of *St John the Baptist*.

Sala di Tesoro

For the art that followed Duccio, and some that preceded him, you need to make your way upstairs again. Here you enter the **Sala di Tesoro**, featuring amid its reliquaries the head of St Galgano and a startling *Christ on the Cross* (1280), an important early work in wood by Giovanni Pisano in which Christ is shown on a Y-shaped tree growing out of the skull of Adam. The latter symbolizes the Tree of Life, or Tree of Knowledge, which grew from a sprig planted in the dead Adam's mouth and would – in the apocryphal story – eventually yield the wood used to crucify Christ (Piero della Francesca tells this story in Arezzo's fresco cycle depicting the *Story of the True Cross*; see p.374).

Sala della Madonna dagli Occhi Grossi

Beyond the Sala di Tesoro you reach the **Sala della Madonna dagli Occhi Grossi**. The work that gives its name to this room is the cathedral's original, pre-Duccio altarpiece – a stark, haunting Byzantine icon (literally the "Madonna of the Big Eyes") in the centre of the room. It occupies a special place in Sienese history, for it was before this painting that Siena's entire population came to pray before their famous victory over the Florentines at Montaperti in 1260. It was also a promise made in front of the painting prior to the battle that saw Siena dedicated to the Madonna in the aftermath of victory.

Around it are grouped a fine array of **panels**, including works by Simone Martini, Pietro Lorenzetti and Sano di Pietro. Note the panels flanking Sano's *Madonna and Child*: one shows St Bernardino preaching in the Campo and Piazza San Francesco, the latter now home to the saint's oratory (see p.289); the other shows St Apollonia, patron saint of dentists, martyred in Alexandria in the fourth century for refusing to make sacrifices to pagan gods.

Panorama dal Facciatone

Don't miss the tiny entrance to the so-called **Panorama dal Facciatone**: this leads to steep spiral stairs that climb out of the building, up within the walls of the abandoned nave. The sensational view from the top over the city and surrounding hills is definitely worth the two-stage climb, but beware that the topmost walkway – teetering along the very summit of the abandoned nave walls – is narrow and scarily exposed.

Terzo di San Martino

Banchi di Sotto, the main thoroughfare through the **Terzo di San Martino**, leads southeast from the Campo past the imposing Renaissance buildings of the **Palazzo Piccolomini, San Martino** and the **Loggia del Papa** towards the medieval Servite order's huge monastic base, **Santa Maria dei Servi**. Students outnumber visitors in this university-dominated area that ends at the south gate of the city, **Porta Romana**, but there is plenty of scope for aimless wandering through the quiet backstreets off Via Pantaneto.

Loggia di Mercanzia

Banchi di Sotto

Marking the start of Banchi di Sotto is the **Loggia di Mercanzia** (or Loggia dei Mercanti), designed as a tribune house for merchants to conduct business. The structure was the result of extraordinary architectural indecision by the city authorities, the chronicles recording that "on one day they build in a certain way and on the following destroy and rebuild in a different manner." It was completed in 1421 in accordingly hesitant style, with Gothic niches for the saints carved by Vecchietta and Antonio Federighi, two of the city's leading Renaissance sculptors.

Palazzo Piccolomini

Banchi di Sotto 52

Southeast of the loggia, you pass the more committed Renaissance buildings of the **Palazzo Piccolomini** and the linked **Loggia del Papa**, commissioned in the 1460s by Pope Pius II, the Pienza-born Aeneas Sylvius Piccolomini. Pius was the city's great Renaissance patron and an indefatigable builder. The loggia was built in 1462 by Federighi. The palace was designed by Bernardo Rossellino, architect of Piccolomini's famous "new town" of Pienza (see p.341); note the half-moon symbols, Pius's coat of arms, across much of the facade.

Archivio di Stato

Guided visits Mon–Sat 9.30am, 10.30am & 11.30am • Free • ⓦ archiviostato.si.it/assi

The Palazzo Piccolomini now houses the **Archivio di Stato**, the city's archives, an unmissable if little-known detour. You're taken through corridors of archives – great bundles of vellum and leather-bound documents for each of the towns and villages in Siena's domain, each one labelled in ancient medieval script with the year in question: 1351, 1352, 1353 – a quite overwhelming amount of information for any potential historian, and most of it still unread. If you're lucky you'll also be able to pop out onto the palace's terrace, which offers a rarely seen view of the Campo.

Museo delle Tavolette di Biccherna

Part of the Arhivio, and included in the tour, the **Museo delle Tavolette di Biccherna** contains the city's account books, tax records (the *Gabelle*) and manuscripts dating back to the earliest days of Siena's recorded history. The chief exhibits, though, are the *Tavolette*, fascinating painted wooden panels designed as covers for civic records and accounts: what makes them more interesting still is the fact that the *comune* commissioned some of the leading painters of the day to execute the beautifully detailed vignettes. Among those employed were Sano di Pietro and Ambrogio Lorenzetti, who painted the 1344 *Gabella* with a version of his *Good Government* fresco in the Palazzo Pubblico. The paintings began with religious themes, but soon moved towards secular images of city life, providing a record of six centuries of Sienese history.

The city is depicted frequently in the background, protected by the Virgin and mushrooming with towers. Early panels include several pictures of the *camerlingo* (a duty always filled by a Cistercian monk from San Galgano) doing the audits. Later ones move into specific events: victories over the Florentines; Pius's coronation as pope (1458); entrusting the city keys to the Virgin in the Duomo (1483); the demolition of the Spanish fortress (1552); the fall of Montalcino, the Sienese Republic's last stand (1559), and the entry into Siena of Cosimo I (1560); war with the Turks (1570); and subsequent Medicean events.

San Martino

Via del Porrione • Mon–Sat 7.30am–12.20pm & 4–7pm, Sun 4–7pm

From the Palazzo Piccolomini, Via di Pantaneto, Via del Porrione or Via di Salicotto take you quickly away from the bustle around the Campo towards the Porta Romana. Before setting off, however, Mannerist fans should spend a couple of minutes in the church of **San Martino**, founded in the eighth century or earlier, but now a pale

Baroque shadow of its former self. The third altar on the left (north) wall features an outstanding *Nativity* (1522–24) by Domenico Beccafumi, a work painted at the same time as the artist was working on the Duomo's pavement, and one which encapsulates his passion for bizarre structures and peculiar light effects. The Virgin's strange gesture, in which she covers the infant Jesus with a veil, prefigures the Crucifixion, at which she also covers Christ's naked body.

Santa Maria dei Servi

Via dei Servi/Piazza Manzoni • Daily 8.30am–6.30pm • Free

Via di Salicotto or Via San Martino brings you southeast into the Valdimontone *contrada*, dominated by the massive brick church and campanile of **Santa Maria dei Servi**, the Servites' monastic base. The church, which is well worth the walk, is set in a quiet piazza, approached by a row of cypresses and shaded by a couple of spreading trees – good for a midday picnic or siesta. It also offers tremendous views across the city.

The interior

The Renaissance-remodelled **interior** is remarkable for a variety of fine paintings. The first, above the first main altar on the right (south) wall, is the so-called *Madonna di Bordone* (1261) by **Coppo di Marcovaldo**, a Florentine artist captured by the Sienese at the Battle of Montaperti and forced to paint this picture as part of his ransom for release. The next altar to the left features the *Nativity of the Virgin* (1625) by Rutilio Manetti, Siena's leading follower of Caravaggio.

Two altars down, in the last altar of the left aisle, is Matteo di Giovanni's *Massacre of the Innocents* (1491), one of two versions of this episode in the church, and one of four in the city by the infanticide-obsessed Matteo. The popularity of this subject in the late fifteenth century may have been due to the much-publicized massacre of Christian children by the Saracens at Otranto in 1480.

Around the high altar

Violence also characterizes Pietro Lorenzetti's much earlier version of the *Massacre*, which is found on the right wall of the second chapel to the right of the **high altar**. (Note Herod watching the carnage from a balcony on the left.) The serene *Madonna and Child* to the right is by Segna di Bonaventura, nephew of the great Duccio. Lorenzetti is further represented by damaged frescoes of the *Banquet of Herod* and the *Death of John the Baptist*, located on the right wall of the second chapel to the left of the high altar. A fine *Adoration of the Shepherds* (1404) by one of Lorenzetti's followers, Taddeo di Bartolo, hangs in the same chapel.

Porta Romana

From Santa Maria dei Servi, you're just 100m from the **Porta Romana**, the massively bastioned south gate of the city. Its outer arch has a fragmentary fresco of the *Coronation of the Virgin*, begun by Taddeo di Bartolo and completed by Sano di Pietro. If you leave the city here, and turn left along Via Girolamo Gigli, you could follow the walls north to the **Porta Pispini**, another impressive example of defensive architecture and again flanked by a fresco of the Virgin, this time a Renaissance effort by Sodoma.

Società Esecutori di Pie Disposizioni

Via Roma 71 • Open on request: ring the bell Mon–Fri 9am–1pm • Free

Just inside the Porta Romana, the sacristy alongside the little church of Santuccio houses the premises of the **Società Esecutori di Pie Disposizioni** (the Society of

284 SIENA TERZO DI CITTÀ

Benevolent Works, formerly the Society of Flagellants). This medieval order, suppressed in the eighteenth century, and later refounded along more secular lines, maintains a small collection of artworks, including a triptych of the *Crucifixion, Flagellation and Burial of Christ* attributed to Duccio, and a semicircular tablet, with wonderful Renaissance landscape, of *St Catherine of Siena Leading the Pope Back to Rome*.

6 Terzo di Città

Via di Città, one of Siena's key streets, cuts across the top of the Campo through the city's oldest quarter, the **Terzo di Città**, the area around the cathedral. The street and its continuation, Via di San Pietro, are fronted by some of Siena's finest private *palazzi*, including the Buonsignori, home to the **Pinacoteca Nazionale**, Siena's main picture gallery. The district is also worth exploring for its own sake, with a variety of options taking you in loops past churches such as **Sant'Agostino** and some of the city's tucked-away corners.

Palazzo Chigi-Saracini

Via di Città 89 · Guided tours of art collection usually Fri & Sat 11am, noon, 3pm & 4pm; months vary; call for current times · ☎ 0577 290 948, ⓦ chigiana.it

Just southwest of the Campo is the **Palazzo Chigi-Saracini**, a Gothic beauty with a curved facade and back courtyard. Although the palace is closed to the public, it houses the **Accademia Chigiana**, which sponsors music programmes throughout the year and maintains a small art collection, including exceptional works by Sassetta, Botticelli and Donatello. It was from this palace that the Sienese victory over the Florentines at Montaperti was announced, the town herald having watched the battle from the tower.

Pinacoteca Nazionale

Via San Pietro 29 · Tues–Sat 8.15am–7.15pm, Sun & Mon 9am–1pm · €4 · ⓦ pinacotecanazionale.siena.it

Set in the fourteenth-century Palazzo Buonsignori, the superb collection of the **Pinacoteca Nazionale** is a roll of honour of Sienese Gothic painting, and if your interest has been spurred by the works by Martini in the Palazzo Pubblico or Duccio in the cathedral museum, a visit here is the obvious next step. The collection offers an unrivalled chance to assess the development of art in the city from the twelfth century through to late Renaissance Mannerism.

Room 1

The main rooms are arranged in chronological order, starting on the second floor. **Room 1** begins with the earliest known Sienese work, an altar frontal dated 1215 of *Christ Flanked by Angels*, with side panels depicting the *Discovery of the True Cross*. The figures are clearly Romanesque; the gold background – intricately patterned – was to be a standard motif of Sienese art over the next two centuries.

Room 2

The first identified Sienese painter, Guido da Siena, covers the same subject in **room 2**, though the influences on his work – dated around 1280 – are distinctively Byzantine rather than Romanesque, incorporating studded jewels amid the gold. In some of his narrative panels – *Christ Entering Jerusalem, The Life of St Peter* and *St Clare Repelling a Saracen Attack* – his hand seems rather freer, though the colouring is limited to a few delicate shades.

Rooms 3 and 4

Duccio di Buoninsegna (1260–1319), the dominant figure in early Sienese art, is represented along with his school in **rooms 3 and 4**. Bernard Berenson considered Duccio the last great painter of antiquity, in contrast to Giotto, the first of the moderns. A rather more Gothic and expressive character is suggested by Ugolino di Nerio's *Crucifixion* and *Madonna* in room 4.

Sienese art over the next century has its departures from Duccio – Lorenzetti's mastery of landscape and life in the *Good and Bad Government* in the Palazzo Pubblico, for example – but the patrons responsible for commissioning works generally wanted more of the same: decorative paintings, whose gold backgrounds made their subjects stand out in the gloom of medieval chapels. As well as specifying the required materials and composition, the Sienese patrons – bankers, guilds, religious orders – would often nominate a particular painting as the model for the style they wanted.

6

Room 5

Even within the conventions required by patrons, however, there were painters whose invention and finesse set them apart. One such was Simone Martini. Though his innovations – the attention to framing and the introduction of a political dimension – are perhaps best seen in the Palazzo Pubblico, there are several great works on show here, mainly in **room 5**, housing one of his masterpieces, the *Blessed Agostino Novello and Four of his Miracles*.

Rooms 7 and 8

Perhaps more rewarding, however, are the works by the Lorenzetti brothers, Pietro and Ambrogio, in **rooms 7 and 8**. Pietro's include a marvellous *Risen Christ*, which could almost hold company with Masaccio, and the *Carmine Altarpiece*, whose predella has five skilful narrative scenes of the founding of the Carmelite order. Attributed to Ambrogio, or, more likely, to Sassetta, are two tiny panels in room 12, *City by the Sea* and *Castles by a Lake*, which the art historian Enzo Carli claims are the first ever "pure landscapes", without any religious purpose. They were probably painted on a door, one above the other.

Rooms 9 to 11

Moving through the fourteenth century, in **rooms 9 to 11** you come to the major Sienese artists Bartolo di Fredi (1353–1410) and his pupil Taddeo di Bartolo (1362–1422). Bartolo is best known for the New Testament frescoes in San Gimignano, whose mastery of narrative is reflected in his *Adoration of the Magi*. Taddeo, painter of the chapel in the Palazzo Pubblico, has archaic elements – notably the huge areas of gold around a sketch of landscape – but makes strides in portraiture and renders one of the first pieces of dynamic action in the museum in his *Stoning of Sts Cosmas and Damian*. These advances are taken a stage further in Sassetta's *St Anthony Beaten by Devils*, where Siena seems at last to be entering the mainstream of European Gothic art, and taking note of Florentine perspective.

Rooms 12 to 18

The influence of the patrons, however, is still prevalent in the mass of stereotyped images – gold again very much to the fore – by Giovanni di Paolo (1403–82), which fill most of **rooms 12 and 13**, and the exquisite Madonnas by Sano di Pietro (1406–81) and Matteo di Giovanni (1435–95) in **rooms 14 to 18**. It is astonishing to think that their Florentine contemporaries included Uccello and Leonardo. Subsequent rooms include some sublime works by Beccafumi, Antonio Bazzi (better known as Sodoma) and Bernardino Mei, the last an increasingly studied and admired seventeenth-century artist.

The third floor

The **third floor** of the museum – not always open – presents the self-contained **Collezione Spannocchi**, a miscellany of Italian, German and Flemish works, including a Dürer, a fine Lorenzo Lotto *Nativity*, Paris Bordone's perfect Renaissance *Annunciation*, and Sofonisba Anguissola's *Bernardo Campi Painting Sofonisba's Portrait* – the only painting in the museum by a woman.

6 Sant'Agostino and around

South of the Pinacoteca is the church of **Sant'Agostino**, open some years, closed others, where – if you are lucky – you can admire a *Crucifixion* (1506) by Perugino (second altar of the south aisle), an *Adoration of the Magi* (1518) by Sodoma and a lunette fresco of the *Madonna and Child with Saints* by Ambrogio Lorenzetti (both in the Cappella Piccolomini), and two monochrome lunette medallions by Luca Signorelli (Cappella Bichi, south transept). The church **piazza** is a pleasant space. Along with the Campo, this square was the site of violent medieval football matches which the Palio eventually displaced from the festival calendar.

Via della Cerchia

An interesting walk from Sant'Agostino is to loop along the **Via della Cerchia**, a route that takes you to the Carmelite convent and church of **San Niccolò al Carmine** (or Santa Maria del Carmine). The church, a Renaissance rebuilding, contains a sensational *St Michael* by Domenico Beccafumi (midway down the south wall), painted following the monks' rejection of his more intense Mannerist version of the subject in the Pinacoteca (deemed to contain too many nudes for comfort). A hermaphrodite St Michael is shown at the centre of the crowded painting, looked down on by God, who has ordered the saint to earth to dispatch the Devil; the latter's extraordinary face can be seen at the base of the picture. To the painting's left is a fragment of an *Annunciation* attributed to Ambrogio Lorenzetti.

Via del Fosso di Sant'Ansano

If you follow the **Via del Fosso di Sant'Ansano**, north of Piazza delle Due Porte, you find yourself on a country lane, above terraced vineyards and allotments, before emerging at the Selva (wood) *contrada*'s square and **museum**, and the church of **San Sebastiano**. Climb up the stepped Vicolo di San Girolamo from here and you come out at the Duomo.

ST CATHERINE OF SIENA

Born Caterina Benincasa, the daughter of a dyer, on March 25, 1347 – Annunciation Day – **St Catherine** had her first visions aged 5 and took the veil at age 8 (16 in some versions), against strong family opposition. She spent three years in silent contemplation, before experiencing a mystical "Night Obscure". Thereafter she went out into the turbulent, post-Black Death city, devoting herself to the poor and sick, and finally turning her hand to **politics**. She prevented Siena and Pisa joining Florence in rising against Pope Urban V (then absent in Avignon), and proceeded to bring him back to Rome. It was a fulfillment of the ultimate Dominican ideal – a union of the practical and mystical life. Catherine returned to Siena to a life of contemplation, visions and stigmata, retaining a political role in her attempts to reconcile the later schism between the popes and anti-popes. After her death in Rome in 1380, she was canonized by Pius II (as depicted in the cathedral) in 1460. She joined St Francis as a patron saint of Italy in 1939 and was declared co-patron of Europe by John Paul II in 1999.

Terzo di Camollia

The northern **Terzo di Camollia** is flanked, to west and east, by the churches of the most important medieval orders, the **Dominicans** and **Franciscans**, vast brick piles which rear above the city's outer ridges. Each has an important association with Siena's major saints, the former with **Catherine**, the latter with **Bernardino**.

The central part of the Camollia takes in the main thoroughfare of **Banchi di Sopra**, the base of the **Monte dei Paschi** – long the city's financial power. North from here, you move into a quiet residential quarter, all the more pleasant for its lack of specific sights or visitors. To the west, interestingly detached from the old city, is the **Fortezza di Santa Barbara**.

6

San Domenico

Piazza Madre Teresa di Calcutta • Daily: March–Oct 7am–1pm & 3–6.30pm; Nov–Feb 9am–6pm • Free • ⓦ basilicacateriniana.com

The Dominicans founded their monastery in the city in 1125. Its church, **San Domenico**, begun in 1226, is a vast, largely Gothic building, typical of the austerity of this militaristic order. The Catherine association is immediately asserted. On the right of the entrance is a kind of raised chapel, the **Cappella delle Volte**, with a contemporary portrait of her by her friend and disciple Andrea Vanni, who according to tradition captured her likeness from life during one of her ecstasies in 1414; below are steps and a niche, where she received the stigmata, took on the Dominican habit and performed several of her miracles. The saint's own chapel, the **Cappella di Santa Caterina** (1488), is located midway down the right (south) side of the church. Its entrance arch has images of saints Luke and Jerome by Sodoma, and the marble tabernacle on the high altar (1466) encloses a reliquary containing Catherine's head (other parts of her body lie dotted across Italy).

The frescoes

The church's highlights – **frescoes** by Sodoma (1526) – occupy the walls to the left and right of the chapel's altar and, respectively, depict her swooning and in ecstasy. Just to the left of the chapel, above the steps to the crypt, is a detached fresco of the *Madonna and Child, John the Baptist and Knight* by Pietro Lorenzetti.

Other notable paintings are found in some of the other chapels, especially the first to the right of the high altar, which contains a Matteo di Giovanni triptych of the *Madonna and Child with Sts Jerome and John the Baptist* and fragments of detached frescoes by Lippo Memmi and Andrea Vanni. The high altar boasts a fine marble tabernacle and two sculpted angels (1465) by the sculptor and architect Benedetto da Maiano, best known for the Palazzo Strozzi in Florence. The second chapel to the left of the high altar houses *St Barbara, Angels and Sts Catherine and Mary Magdalene* surmounted by an *Epiphany*, considered the masterpiece of Matteo di Giovanni, though its effect is undermined by the odd eighteenth-century frescoes around it. The more appealing *Madonna and Child with Saints* (1483) opposite is by the Florentine-influenced Benvenuto di Giovanni.

Casa e Santuario di Santa Caterina

Costa di Sant'Antonio • Daily 9am–12.30pm & 3–6pm • Free

The family home of St Catherine (see box opposite), the **Casa e Santuario di Santa Caterina**, where she lived as a Dominican tertiary – of the order but not resident – is just south of San Domenico, down the hill on Via Santa Caterina. The building has been much adapted, with a Renaissance loggia and a series of oratories – one on the site of her cell, while the paintings here are mostly unexceptional Baroque canvases.

Piazza Salimbeni

Between the two monastic churches lies the heart of business Siena, the **Piazza Salimbeni**, whose three interlocking *palazzi* have formed, since the fifteenth century, the head office of the **Monte dei Paschi di Siena**. Banking was at the heart of medieval Sienese wealth, the town capitalizing on its position on the Via Francigena, the "French road" between Rome and northwest Europe, and the main road between Rome and Florence and Bologna. Sienese banking families go back to the twelfth century and by the end of the thirteenth they were trading widely in France, Germany, Flanders, England and along the Danube, where they maintained networks of corresponding dealers.

Activity declined after the Black Death, but in the fifteenth century the Republic set up the Monte dei Paschi di Siena as a lending and charitable institution, to combat the abuses of usury. It consolidated its role under Medici rule and slowly moved into more strictly banking activities. In the twentieth century it merged with other Tuscan and Umbrian banks to become one of Italy's key financial institutions.

The **Spannocchi**, on the right, was the first great Renaissance palace built in Siena (1473) and the prototype for the Palazzo Strozzi in Florence, while the **Salimbeni**, in the centre, was a last flourish of the Gothic. The last (and less arresting) **Tantucci** palace dates from the end of the sixteenth century. The statue (1882) in the piazza depicts Sallustio Bandini (1677–1760), an eminent Sienese-born economist and philosopher.

To Porta Camollia

North of the Piazza Salimbeni, Banchi di Sopra becomes **Via dei Montanini** and then **Via di Camollia**, which run through the less monumental parts of the Terzo di Camollia, good for regular shopping and local bars and restaurants.

Two churches are worth a brief look on this street, though both are only rarely open. **Santa Maria delle Nevi** contains a famous altarpiece – *Our Lady of the Snows* (1477) – by Matteo di Giovanni, while **San Bartolomeo** fronts one of the nicest *contrada* squares in the city, home of the Istrice (porcupine). At the end of Via di Camollia is the Renaissance **Porta Camollia**, inscribed on its outer arch "Siena opens her heart to you wider than this gate." It was here that a vastly superior Florentine force was put to flight in 1526, following the traditional Sienese appeal to the Virgin.

A short distance east of Via dei Montanini – reached by a circuitous network of alleys – is another of the city's fountains, the **Fonte Nuova**. A further, highly picturesque fountain, the **Fonte Ovile**, is to be seen outside the Porta Ovile, a hundred metres or so beyond. Both were built at the end of the twelfth century. Near the Fonte Nuova, in Via Vallerozzi, is the church of **San Rocco**, home of the Lupa (she-wolf) *contrada*.

Fortezza di Santa Barbara

Free access

To the west of Via dei Montanini, behind the church of Santo Stefano, the gardens of **La Lizza** – taken over on Wednesdays by the town's large market – lead to the walls of the **Fortezza di Santa Barbara** (also directly accessible from San Domenico on Via dei Mille). The fortress was built by Charles V after the siege of 1554–55, but subsequently torn down by the people, and had to be rebuilt by Cosimo I, who then moved his troops into the garrison. Its Medicean walls resemble the walls of Lucca, designed by the same architect. Occasional summer concerts are held within the fort, which is also home to the *Enoteca Italiana* (see p.293).

San Francesco and around

Piazza San Francesco • Daily 7.30am–noon & 4–5.30pm • Free

St Bernardino, born in the year of Catherine's death, began his preaching life at the chill monastic church of **San Francesco**, on the east side of the city. A huge, hall-like structure, like that of San Domenico, it was heavily restored after damage by fire in 1655 and subsequent use as a barracks. Its remaining **artworks** include fragmentary frescoes by Pietro and Ambrogio Lorenzetti: a *Crucifixion* (1331) by Pietro in the first chapel to the left of the high altar and two collaborative frescoes in the third chapel to the left of the high altar (the latter depicting *St Louis of Toulouse becoming a Franciscan* and the graphic *Martyrdom of Six Franciscans at Ceuta in Morocco*). There is also a glittering polyptych by Lippo Vanni of the *Madonna and Child with Four Saints* (1370) in the sacristy (entered from the right of the south transept). It's also worth hunting down the detached fresco right of the entrance door, its choir of angels part of a *Coronation of the Virgin* (1447) by Sassetta that once decorated the city's original Porta Romana. It was completed by Sano di Pietro, a pupil of Sassetta, after the master contracted a fatal chill while working outdoors on the fresco.

6

Tomba dei Tolomei

If you walk past the side door of San Francesco, you'll find the fourteenth-century **Tomba dei Tolomei**, the best of the church's many funerary monuments. It houses various scions of the Tolomei, one of Siena's grandest medieval families. The clan provided numerous of the city's bankers, as well as some of its leading churchmen, among them Bernardo Tolomei, founder of the abbey at Monte Oliveto Maggiore (see p.328). Also reputedly buried here (beneath a nearby pavement slab) is Pia de' Tolomei, first wife of Baldo Tolomei, who came to live in Siena after his marriage to his second wife. Pia died, consumed with jealousy, in a castle in the Maremma, prompting Dante's famous reference to her in the *Purgatorio*: *Siena me fé, disfecemi Maremma* ("Siena made me, the Maremma unmade me").

Oratorio di San Bernardino

Piazza San Francesco • Mid-March to Oct Mon–Sat 10.30am–1.30pm & 3–5.30pm • €3, or joint ticket (see p.263)

In the piazza to the right of San Francesco as you face the church, adjoining the cloisters, is the **Oratorio di San Bernardino**. The best artworks here are in the beautifully wood-panelled upper chapel: fourteen large **frescoes** by Sodoma, Beccafumi and Girolamo del Pacchia on the *Life of the Virgin*, painted between 1496 and 1518 when the former pair were Siena's leading painters. In the lower chapel are seventeenth-century scenes of the saint's life, which was taken up by incessant travel throughout Italy, preaching against usury, denouncing the political strife between the Italian city states and urging his audience to look for inspiration to the monogram of Christ. Sermons in the Campo, it is said, frequently went on for the best part of a day. Bernardino's actual political influence was fairly marginal but he was canonized within six years of his death in 1444, and remains one of the most famous of all Italian preachers. His dictum on rhetoric – "make it clear, short and to the point" – was rewarded in the 1980s with his adoption as the patron saint of advertising.

ARRIVAL AND DEPARTURE   SIENA

BY TRAIN

Arrival Siena's train station is at Piazza Fratelli Rosselli, in the valley 2km northeast of town, and has a train information office, exchange facilities, basic tourist information and a counter selling city bus tickets. To get into town, take just about any city bus – #3, #9 to Tozzi; #7, #17, #77 to Garibaldi/Sale; #8 or #10 to Gramsci. Tickets are €1, or €2 if bought on board. All drop off at points on or near Piazza Matteotti or Piazza Gramsci on the northern edge of the centre.

Trains from Florence Trains run at least hourly from Florence direct to Siena (fastest journey 1hr 28min; €6.40), but some services involve changing at Empoli (1hr 46min). Destinations Asciano (12 daily; 35min); Buonconvento

(10 daily; 22–32min); Chiusi (12 daily; 1hr 35min); Empoli (hourly; 50min–1hr 20min; change for Pisa and Florence); Grosseto (8 daily; 1hr 17–35min).

BY BUS

Arrival Most intercity buses arrive in the city centre on Viale Federico Tozzi, the road running alongside Piazza Antonio Gramsci, or at La Lizza nearby, but note that some stop near the church of San Domenico or terminate at the train station. Ticket offices beneath Piazza Antonio Gramsci have information on all routes. The bus company serving Siena and its hinterland is TRA-IN (☎0577 204 111, ⓦtrainspa.it and ⓦsienamobilita.it).

Buses to Siena From Florence, hourly or more frequent TRA-IN buses for Siena depart from the bus station on Via di Caterina da Siena, just west of the main train station; take a Corse Rapide or Rapido (about 1hr 15min; €7.80 in advance, €10 on board), as some buses (misleadingly called Corse Dirette or Diretta) are much slower and run via Colle di Val d'Elsa and Poggibonsi. Both services arrive at La Lizza-Piazza Antonio Gramsci.

Destinations Arezzo (8 daily; 1hr 30min); Asciano (3 daily; 1hr); Buonconvento (7 daily; 50min); Castellina in Chianti (7 daily; 35min); Castiglione della Pescaia (2 daily in summer; 1hr 55min); Chianciano (2 daily; 1hr 40min); Colle di Val d'Elsa (hourly; 30min); Florence (hourly; 1hr 15min); Gaiole in Chianti (5 daily; 50min); Grosseto (hourly; 1hr 25min); Montalcino (7 daily; 1hr 15min); Montepulciano (5 daily; 1hr 25min); Monticiano (4 daily; 1hr 5min); Monteriggioni (hourly; 25min); Pienza (6 daily; 1hr 15min); Pisa Airport (1 daily; 1hr 50min); Poggibonsi (hourly; 45min); Radda in Chianti (5 daily; 55min); San Gimignano (10 daily; 1hr 15min); Sinalunga (2 daily; 50min).

BY CAR

Florence and Siena are linked by a fast four-lane highway that starts from the Firenze Certosa junction on the A1 autostrada, 6km south of Florence; from central Florence, head through the Oltrarno to the Porta Romana and follow "Certosa" signs.

Parking Finding a space can be a problem. Garages (ⓦsienaparcheggi.com) are clearly signposted, secure and affordable, but the two biggest are misleadingly named: "Parcheggio Il Campo" is a long way from the Campo, just inside the Porta Tufi, and "Parcheggio Il Duomo" is just within Porta San Marco, nowhere near the Duomo. Street-parking outside the city walls can be expensive and hard to find. Follow signs to the *centro* and try to find a space at one of the following: around Piazza Antonio Gramsci; the large triangle of La Lizza (except market day, Wed 8am–2pm); opposite San Domenico in the car park alongside the stadium; off Viale Manzoni, which loops around the northeast wall of the city; or around the Porta Romana. Viale Manzoni has free parking; at the others a machine or an attendant issues tickets, usually by the hour: rates are reasonable. If you know you'll be driving in, arrange parking with your hotel in advance. You can drive through the old town alleys only in order to load or unload luggage.

BY TAXI

There are taxi ranks by the train station and on Piazza Matteotti, or taxis can be called between 7am and 9pm (☎0577 49 222). Note, however, that in Siena it's virtually impossible to book taxis in advance and you should allow plenty of time for cabs to reach you through the city's labyrinthine one-way system.

INFORMATION AND TOURS

Tourist office Piazza del Campo 56 (Mon–Sat 9am–7pm; ☎0577 280 551, ⓦterresiena.it).

Guided walks Booked through Siena Hotels Promotion,

Piazza Madre Teresa di Calcutta 5 (☎0577 288 084, ⓦhotelsiena.com).

ACCOMMODATION

Securing a **hotel room** in Siena for any time between Easter and October requires booking six months in advance. If you arrive without a booking, and the places listed below are full, make your way to the Siena Hotels Promotion booth (Mon–Sat 9am–7pm; winter closes 6pm; ☎0577 288 084, ⓦhotelsiena.com), opposite the church of San Domenico at Piazza Madre Teresa di Calcutta, where staff can book rooms in any of the city's hotels for free. The city's second specialist agency, Vacanze Senesi, is in the tourist office at Piazza del Campo 56 (Mon–Fri 9am–7pm; ☎0577 45 900, ⓦofferte.bookingsiena.it).

HOTELS

Alma Domus Via Camporegio 37 ☎0577 44 177, ⓦhotelalmadomus.it. An old pilgrim hotel behind San Domenico, with en-suite doubles, triples and quads. Curfew 1am. **€75**

★ **Antica Residenza Cicogna** Via dei Termini 67 ☎0577 285 613, ⓦanticaresidenzacicogna.it. A little-known B&B in a perfect (if tucked-away) location. The

owner is charming, and there are five en-suite rooms, all frescoed, delightfully appointed and well restored – "Liberty" and "Leoni" are especially recommended. Breakfast is taken in an extraordinary high-ceilinged room with colossal beams. Wi-fi available. **€85–100**

Antica Torre Via Fieravecchia 7 ☎0577 222 255, ⓦanticatorresiena.it. By far the nicest and most intimate of Siena's three-star places: just eight smallish rooms squeezed into an old medieval tower. Top rooms have views. **€100**

Bernini Via della Sapienza 15 ☎0577 289 047, ⓦalbergobernini.com. Nine inexpensive but rather poky one-star rooms, most en suite. **€65**, en-suite **€85**

Cannon d'Oro Via Montanini 28 ☎0577 44 321, ⓦcannondoro.com. A stylish 30-room two-star hotel tucked down an alleyway. Friendly and well maintained, this is the best choice among the central mid-price hotels. **€60–105**

★ **Certosa di Maggiano** Via Certosa 82 ☎0577 288 180, ⓦcertosadimaggiano.com. This former monastery in the countryside 1km southeast of Siena offers luxurious comfort in its few tasteful rooms, and its library cloister and tranquil terrace make an alluring retreat. From **€370**

Duomo Via Stalloreggi 34 ☎0577 289 088, ⓦhotelduomo.it. Rooms are reliable but unexceptional – apart from those with views of the Duomo – but this is nonetheless the best located of the city's three-star hotels. **€105–150**

★ **Grand Hotel Continental** Via Banchi di Sopra 85 ☎0577 56 011, ⓦroyaldemeure.com. For years Siena had no luxury five-star hotel – until the hugely expensive restoration of this former palace. The frescoed public spaces are astounding, and there's a large covered courtyard. The best rooms are also exceptional – vast, entirely frescoed, and with stunning views of the Duomo. Other rooms are superbly appointed, but mostly lack the period details you'll see on the website. Discounts online or via tour-operator deals. **€570**

La Perla Via delle Terme 25 ☎0577 47 144, ⓦhotellaperlasiena.com. Regular one-star with thirteen en-suite rooms, in a very central location, two blocks north of the Campo. **€75**

La Toscana Via Cecco Angiolieri 12 ☎0577 46 097, ⓦalbergolatoscanasiena.com. Big, well-priced three-star in an atmospheric and central location, on an alley behind Piazza Tolomei. Rooms with and without bathrooms

– unusual in this category. **€40–83**

Locanda Garibaldi Via Giovanni Dupré 18 ☎0577 284 204, ⓔlocanda.garibaldi@virgilio.it. A good, no-nonsense seven-room two-star (with four shared bathrooms), situated above one of the city's better low-cost restaurants, just south of the Campo. **€75**

★ **Palazzo Ravizza** Pian dei Mantellini 34 ☎0577 280 462, ⓦpalazzoravizza.it. This elegant three-star, located in a pleasant area near San Niccolò al Carmine, has been run by the same family since the 1920s, and has been renovated in a way that has freshened the place without sacrificing its charm. Rooms are tastefully furnished with antiques, and paved with terracotta or parquet, with ceiling frescoes in several of them. The little garden at the back is a lovely place for afternoon tea. **€170**

Piccolo Hotel Etruria Via Donzelle 3 ☎0577 288 088, ⓦhoteletruria.com. A very neat two-star, and deservedly popular: advance booking for high season is a must to secure one of its thirteen rooms. **€80–110**

Santa Caterina Via Piccolomini 7 ☎0577 221 105, ⓦhscsiena.it. A 22-room three-star, with a/c and parking, and a 10min walk from the Campo. Pleasant garden and rooms and public areas adorned with fine old prints. **€85–195**

Tre Donzelle Via Donzelle 5 ☎0577 280 358, ⓦtredonzelle.com. A one-star option right in the heart of town, just off Banchi di Sotto. Decent, clean rooms, some with private bath, but all 27 are often booked solid. **€60**

HOSTELS

Ostello della Gioventù "Guidoriccio" Via Fiorentina 89, Lo Stellino ☎0577 52 212, ⓦostellosiena.it. Rather sterile and uninspiring hostel with 111 beds, 4km northwest of the centre. Take bus #15 from Piazza Antonio Gramsci, or, if you're coming from Florence, ask to be let off at "Lo Stellino", just after the Siena city sign. Has a restaurant (meals €10) and a bar. Curfew 11.30pm. Dorm beds **€20**

EATING

Siena's **restaurants** once had a poor reputation, but things have improved in recent years, with a range of imaginative new osterie and a general hike in standards. The only place you need surrender gastronomic ideals is in the Campo, where

SIENESE SPECIALITIES

You should eat well in Siena, especially if you have a sweet tooth. The city shares many basic Tuscan dishes with the rest of the region, but has **specialities** of its own, notably *pici* (noodle-like pasta with toasted breadcrumbs), *salsicce secche* (dried sausages), *finocchiona* (minced pork flavoured with fennel), *capolocci* (spiced loin of pork), *pappa col pomodoro* (bread and tomato soup), *tortino di carciofi* (artichoke omelette) and *fagioli all'uccelletto* (bean and sausage stew). The city is especially famous for its **cakes** and **biscuits**, including the ubiquitous *panforte*, a dense and delicious wedge of nuts, fruit and honey that originated with pilgrimage journeys, as well as *cavallucci* (aniseed, nut and spice biscuits), *copate* (nougat wafers) and *ricciarelli* (rich almond biscuits).

6

SIENA'S FESTIVALS

The most prestigious classical music festival – often featuring a major opera – is July and August's **Estate Musicale Chigiana** (☎0577 22 091, ⓦchigiana.it), organized by the Monte dei Paschi and Accademia Chigiana, who also sponsor impressive concerts throughout the year. Other cultural events include **Siena Jazz** (ⓦsienajazz.it), which features concerts in venues around the city and the local area in late July and August; and the modest but increasingly popular **Terre di Siena International Film Festival** (☎0577 222 999, ⓦterradisienafilmfestival.it) in late summer. Information on these and more minor events can be found at ⓦterresiena.it.

an (expensive) pizza is the safest bet. For cheaper meals, you'll generally do best walking out a little from the centre, west towards San Niccolò al Carmine, or north towards Porta Camollia.

RESTAURANTS

Antica Osteria Da Divo Via Franciosa 25-29 ☎0577 286 054, ⓦosteriadadivo.it. A close second behind *Osteria Le Logge* for ambience, thanks to its extraordinary subterranean cellar dining rooms. Upstairs is pretty, too, and the food is well above average, with starters at €8–12, pastas at €10 and mains at €20–24. Mon & Wed–Sun noon–2.30 & 7–10.30pm.

Babazuf Via Pantaneto 85–87 ☎0577 222 482, ⓦosteriababazuf.com. Recently opened, and very slightly off the beaten track, so not yet overrun with visitors. It's welcoming and informal, with a single calm, contemporary dining room, low prices and a limited menu of classic Tuscan dishes with the occasional twist. Tues–Sun noon–4pm & 7pm–midnight.

Cane e Gatto Via Pagliaresi 6 ☎0577 222 482. Don't be put off by the un-Sienese Art Nouveau-style decor: this friendly restaurant serves superb Tuscan *cucina nuova*, featuring seven courses on its *menù degustazione*, or tasting menu (around €75, with a selection of wines included). Mon–Wed & Fri–Sun 7–10.30pm.

Da Trombicche Via delle Terme 66 ☎0577 288 089, ⓦtrombicche.it. A tiny, youthful, no-nonsense trattoria with a limited menu of glorified snacks – soup, cheese, salami and meat stews – accompanied by rough wine served straight from the barrel. Mon–Sat 10am–3pm & 5.30–10pm.

Gallo Nero Via del Porrione ☎0577 284 356, ⓦgallonero.it. A quirky, vaulted place, offering a straightforward Tuscan menu (reckon on €18 for three courses) and another (for a few euros more) based on medieval Tuscan recipes that might include dishes such as sweet and sour duck with cheese ravioli, or chicken in sweet wine with fruit. Also offers a good selection of gluten-free pastas and other dishes. Daily noon–3.30pm & 7pm–midnight; may close Mon or Tues Nov–Feb.

Osteria Boccone del Prete Via di San Pietro 17 ☎0577 280 388. One of Siena's newer restaurants, near the Pinacoteca Nazionale, serving delicious *crostini*, salads and pasta dishes in a stylish setting. Mon–Sat noon–3pm & 7–11pm.

Osteria Il Carroccio Via del Casato di Sotto 32 ☎0577 41 165. Just 50m from the Campo, this small osteria has few tables but serves up fine, inexpensive Tuscan food in a welcoming, informal atmosphere. Menus change weekly. Mon, Tues & Thurs–Sun 12.30–2.30pm & 7.30–10pm.

Osteria Il Grattacielo Via Pontani 8 ☎334 631 1458. A very local place serving wine and snacks, this minuscule café-osteria – ironically named "The Skyscraper" – makes a popular lunch stop for its marinated anchovies, Tuscan beans and salami. Mon & Sun noon–3.30pm, Tues–Sat 8am–3.30pm & 7–10pm.

Osteria Le Logge Via del Porrione 33 ☎0577 48 013, ⓦosterialelogge.it. The best-looking restaurant in central Siena, occupying a fine old cabinet-lined *farmacia* off the Campo, by the Loggia del Papa (but avoid the far less attractive upstairs room). Good pasta and some unusual *secondi*, but the quality of food – once exceptional – is these days merely above average. Mon–Sat 12.15–3.30pm & 7.15–11pm.

★ **Ullio ai Tre Cristi** Vicolo Provenzano 1 ☎0577 280 608. A Sienese institution since 1830, this is the traditional neighbourhood restaurant of the Giraffa *contrada* – though its prices these days are those of a top-end establishment. A good, if smart and expensive place for a romantic meal or treat, serving an ambitious, predominantly fish and seafood menu. Terrace tables in summer. Mon–Sat 12.20–2.30pm & 7.30–10.30pm.

DRINKING, NIGHTLIFE AND ENTERTAINMENT

Siena feels distinctly provincial after Florence. The main action of an evening is the passeggiata from Piazza Matteotti along Banchi di Sopra to the Campo – and there's not much in the way of nightlife to follow, though the presence of the university ensures a bit of life in the **bars**, with pleasant neighbourhood spots in most *contrade* and plenty of modern establishments scattered around the city for quick refreshment. City centre nightlife, however, is virtually non-existent.

BARS AND CAFÉS

Dublin Post Piazza Antonio Gramsci 20–21 ☎0577 289 089, ⓦdublinpost.it. You'll find cold lager in all bars and cafés, but for Guinness or ales, and a (faux) pub interior, head to the *Dublin Post*, uninspiringly situated on a modern piazza. Mon–Sat noon–2am, Sun 6pm–midnight.

Enoteca Italiana Fortezza di Santa Barbara, Piazza Libertà del Porrione 33 ☎0577 288 811, ⓦenoteca-italiana.it. Italy's largest national wine collection. Its cellar stocks every single Italian wine (almost a thousand of them), and there's a bar where you can order a glass of any of the cheaper wines, or buy any bottle. Mon noon–8pm, Tues–Sat noon–1am.

Liberamente Piazza del Campo 27 ☎0577 274 733, ⓦliberamenteosteria.it. Of the terrace cafés ringing the Campo, the small and long-established *Liberamente* at the corner of Casato dei Barbieri has more charm and intimacy than most. Plenty of wines by the glass (with free antipasti) plus a light menu of cold cuts, soups and pasta. Daily 11am–1pm.

CLUBS

Al Cambio Via di Pantaneto 48 ☎339 817 7044, ⓦalcambio.net. Club life is fairly limited in Siena, but for a glimpse of the smart Sienese on the dance floor try this dark, moody place with conventional dance music and a steep entrance fee.

DIRECTORY

Lost property Comando Polizia Municipale, Palazzo "Ex Bagni", Via Federico Tozzi 3 (Mon & Fri 11am–1.30pm, plus Tues & Thurs 3–5pm; ☎0577 292 588).

Market A huge weekly general market sprawls over La Lizza (Wed 8am–2pm).

Police The *Questura* is at Via del Castoro 6 ☎0577 201 111.

Post office Piazza Matteotti 37 (Mon–Wed 8.15am–7pm, Sat 8.15am–1.30pm; ☎0577 214 295, ⓦposteitaliane.it).

The Sienese hill-towns

SAN GIMIGNANO

The Sienese hill-towns

Just as Siena provides a perfect antidote to Florence, so the HILL-TOWNS around the old capital of the Sienese Republic provide an intimate counterpoint to the larger towns that crowd the Tuscan capital. Most of Siena's satellites are more appealing than their Florentine equivalents, and benefit from surroundings that exemplify the timeless pastoral quality for which the region is renowned.

San Gimignano is the best-known, thanks mainly to its famous towers, a vision of medieval perfection that is badly compromised in summer by the huge numbers of day-trippers. That said, the fresco-lined Collegiata, a clutch of minor churches and one of Tuscany's best civic museums are unmissable attractions, and make the town well worth an overnight stay.

Monteriggioni, a relatively unspoiled medieval village, is another must-see and can easily be incorporated into a visit to **Colle di Val d'Elsa**, another centuries-old enclave, but one with unlovely outskirts. You should also try to see **Volterra**; slightly cut off from the other Sienese hill-towns, it's a dramatically situated, brooding town whose Etruscan origins are never far from the surface. Known primarily for its archeological museum, and more recently as a setting in the Twilight novels, it also has a fascinating art gallery and a captivating cathedral square.

West to Casole d'Elsa

Heading west from Siena, most people have San Gimignano in their sights. The best route to follow is the N2 as far as the turreted fortress-hamlet of **Monteriggioni**, then west to **Colle di Val d'Elsa**, whose striking medieval upper town extends along a narrow ridge. From Colle, a scenic minor road runs via Bibbiano to San Gimignano.

GETTING AROUND

By bus On public transport, you can stop at Colle before catching another bus to the semi-industrial town of Poggibonsi and a connection from there to San Gimignano; for Monteriggioni, catch a bus to the turning up to the village (and hail another one on from there to Colle or back to Siena). Some buses from Siena to San Gimignano involve a Poggibonsi connection, though there are direct services. Note that the route north from Poggibonsi to Empoli – via Certaldo and Castelfiorentino – is covered from p.174 onwards.

Monteriggioni

The perfectly preserved walls of **MONTERIGGIONI** declare their presence for miles ahead from the N2 and the Siena–Florence link road. The citadel, begun by the Sienese in 1213, was a strategic target for any troops marching on Siena from the north and is immortalized in Dante's *Inferno*, in which he compares the fourteen towers – added during reconstruction in 1260 after the Sienese victory at Montaperti – to giants in an abyss. The verse greets you on the wall of the gate as you enter the village, which consists of a couple of dozen houses, the odd restaurant and bar and several overpriced tourist outlets. A small **museum** devoted to the walls can be found in the tourist office

VOLTERRA

Highlights

❶ **Monteriggioni** Dante alluded to the towers of this fortified citadel, and they still lord it over the countryside today, part of a village whose appearance and unspoiled surroundings can barely have changed in five hundred years. **See p.296**

❷ **San Gimignano** Italy's best-known village is famous for its towers as well as its excellent provincial art gallery, the art-filled Sant'Agostino church and the stunning, comprehensively frescoed Collegiata. **See p.302**

❸ **Colle di Val d'Elsa** Slightly off the beaten track but long celebrated for its glassware, this intimate and relatively unvisited town holds a medley of tiny but appealing churches and museums. **See p.298**

❹ **Volterra** One of the settings for Stephanie Meyer's Twilight novels, this moody and idiosyncratic town, high in the lonely hills east of Siena, has its roots in the Etruscan era, and is celebrated for its alabaster workshops and an exceptional museum. **See p.313**

HIGHLIGHTS ARE MARKED ON THE MAP ON P.298

(daily: April–Oct 9.30am–1.30pm & 2–7.30pm; Nov–March 10am–1.30pm & 2–4pm; €3 or €3.50 with special access to part of the walls). The houses give way to gardens as they near the ramparts, and an athlete could probably run the main street, from south to north gates, in about ten seconds. All of which, of course, accounts for the charm of the place, though like San Gimignano, it's severely compromised in summer by day-trippers.

ARRIVAL AND INFORMATION | MONTERIGGIONI

By train and bus The train station is 3km north at Castellina Scalo. Buses 130A or 130R (hourly; 25min) run to Monteriggioni from Siena.

Tourist office Roma 23 (Daily: April–Oct 9.30am–1.30pm & 2–7.30pm; Nov–March 10am–1.30pm & 2–4pm; ☎ 0577 304 834, ⓦ monteriggioniturismo.it).

ACCOMMODATION, EATING AND DRINKING

Il Pozzo Piazza Roma 20 ☎ 0577 304 127, ⓦ ilpozzo .net. Of the town's two moderately priced restaurants, *Il Pozzo*, in a fine old stone building in the main square, is marginally the better, and has a small but pretty pergola for summer dining. Tues–Sat 12.30–2.30pm & 7.30–10.30pm, Sun 12.30–3pm.

La Casalta Via Matteotti 22 ☎ 0577 301 002, ⓦ ristorantecasalta.it. Some 4km west of town in the hamlet of Strove, this ten-room, three-star hotel is

worth the trip just for the excellent and moderately priced restaurant. Restaurant Thurs–Tues 12.30–2.30pm & 7.15–10.30pm; closed early Jan to early Feb; hotel closed early Jan to late March & ten days in Nov. €85

Monteriggioni Via I Maggio 4 ☎ 0577 305 009, ⓦ hotelmonteriggioni.net. A classy and very pleasant four-star hotel, whose twelve rooms are quickly snapped up, despite the steep prices. €230

Colle di Val d'Elsa

COLLE DI VAL D'ELSA is relatively unexplored, perhaps thanks to the sprawl of light industry and housing in its lower town, **Colle Bassa**. The walled upper town of **Colle Alta**, however, is a beauty, stretching along a ridge with its one long street lined with medieval *palazzi*.

Of pre-Roman foundation, the town occupies a noted place in the annals of Florentine and Sienese rivalry, for it was at the **Battle of Colle** in 1269 that the Florentines avenged their defeat by the Sienese at Montaperti nine years earlier. In 1333 the town voluntarily put itself under the protection of Florence; the ensuing period of relative peace enabled it to develop its wool and paper industries, both of

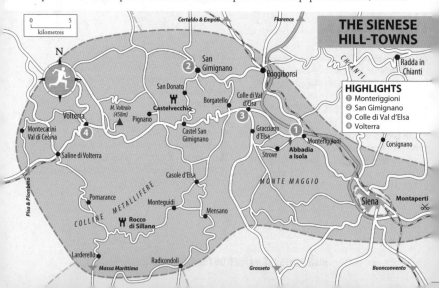

THE SIENESE HILL-TOWNS

HIGHLIGHTS
① Monteriggioni
② San Gimignano
③ Colle di Val d'Elsa
④ Volterra

which made use of the abundant supplies of local water, channelled through the area in a series of canals. Glass and paper are still local specialities.

Colle Bassa

Colle Bassa's main square, and site of the town's busy Friday market, **Piazza Arnolfo** is named after Arnolfo di Cambio, the architect of the Duomo and Palazzo Vecchio in Florence, who was born here around 1232. A block north is the town's major piece of modern architecture, the regional headquarters of the Monte dei Paschi bank – not a captivating building.

Museo del Cristallo

Via dei Fossi 8a • Easter–Oct Tues–Sun 10am–noon & 4–7.30pm; Nov–Easter Tues–Fri 3–7pm, Sat & Sun 10am–noon & 3–7pm • €3 • ⓦ cristallo.org

Just south of the piazza, the **Museo del Cristallo** was built on the site of an eighteenth-century glass furnace. It outlines the transition from Colle's traditional glass-making industry from pre-industrial pieces to 1820, the year of the first furnace, and from 1820 to the beginning of crystal production in 1963; today, Colle produces 95 percent of Italy's crystal, and 15 percent of the world's.

Sant'Agostino

Piazza Sant'Agostino, cnr Via della Pieve in Piano • Usually Mon–Sat 8am–noon & 4–7.30pm, Sun 4–7.30pm

The thirteenth-century church of **Sant'Agostino** was largely rebuilt by Antonio da Sangallo the Elder in 1521, three years after embarking on his masterpiece, the church of San Biagio in Montepulciano (see p.352). The second altar on the right contains a glorious *Madonna and Child with Saints* by Taddeo di Bartolo, probably a surviving panel of a triptych. The eye-catching marble tabernacle in the north aisle, the *Madonna del Piano*, is attributed to Baccio da Montelupo (1469–1535).

Colle Alta

From Piazza Arnolfo, it's a steep ten-minute climb to **Colle Alta**: follow Via San Sebastiano and then the brick-paved *costa*, which brings you out at the eastern tip of the town. If you drive or take a bus up, you're directed around a circuitous route to the west end of the ridge, via the Porta Nuova.

Via del Castello

At the top of the *costa*, you've little choice but to follow **Via del Castello**, the centre of a three-street grid, past a scattering of tower houses; Arnolfo di Cambio was born at no. 63, in the so-called Torre di Arnolfo. A little further down is the Romanesque church of **Santa Maria in Canonica**, built in the twelfth or thirteenth century, but thought to have older origins. Its interior is notable for a stupendous late fourteenth-century tabernacle of the *Madonna and Child with Saints* by Pier Francesco Fiorentino; the frame, almost as impressive as the painting, is original.

The Duomo

Piazza del Duomo • Usually Mon–Sat 7am–12.30pm & 4–7.30pm, Sun 4–7.30pm

Midway along Via del Castello is the **Duomo**, whose Romanesque origins have been all but obliterated by later remodelling (1603–1815). The **interior** features a marble pulpit (1465) by Giuliano da Maiano, who used four pillars and capitals from a much older work to frame his bas-reliefs. His brother Benedetto was responsible for the font (1468), the two having worked together during the same period in San Gimignano. The fourth chapel on the right has a famous *Nativity* (1635), the masterpiece of Rutilio Manetti, the leading Sienese follower of Caravaggio.

In the depths of the right transept stands the **Cappella del Santo Chiodo**, commissioned by Pienza's Piccolomini pope, Pius II, to house a nail (*chiodo*) from the

Cross, the relic providing the inspiration for the beautiful tabernacle attributed to Mino da Fiesole. The nearby bronze lectern, palm branch and eagle are by Pietro Tacca, a pupil of Giambologna, whose eccentric work will be familiar if you've seen his fountains in Florence's Piazza Santissima Annunziata. Tacca also probably cast the impressive bronze Crucifix above the high altar, the work having been designed by Giambologna.

Museo Archeologico

Piazza del Duomo 42 • May–Sept Tues–Sun 10.30am–12.30pm & 4.30–7.30pm; Oct–April Tues–Fri 3.30–5.30pm, Sat & Sun 10.30am–12.30pm & 3–6pm • €3 • ⓦ museocolle.it

Located in the Palazzo Pretorio (1335), the **Museo Archeologico "Ranuccio Bianchi Bandinelli"** is only of passing interest, save for the finds from the local *Tomba dei Calisna Sepu*, one of Tuscany's most important Etruscan tombs: its treasures are scattered in museums as far afield as Berlin.

Museo Civico e Diocesano d'Arte Sacra

Via del Castello 33 • Tues–Sun 11.30am–5pm, but hours vary • €3

Just out of the piazza, the attractive **Museo Civico e Diocesano d'Arte Sacra** housed in the Palazzo dei Priori, the old bishops' palace, retains frescoes of hunting scenes by Bartolo di Fredi, as well as a fair collection of Sienese paintings gathered from local churches. The most interesting canvas is a *Maestà* from Abbadia Isola, once attributed to Duccio, but now given to the anonymous Maestro di Badia a Isola.

Palazzo Campana

Via del Castello

About 100m beyond Piazza del Duomo, the **Palazzo Campana** is a Mannerist tour de force built in 1539 by Baccio d'Agnolo, the architect responsible for the rather less amenable Palazzo Bartolini in Florence. From here, a bridge connects the town's medieval core to its fifteenth- and sixteenth-century expansions.

San Francesco

Via San Francesco • Usually Mon–Sat 7am–noon & 4.30–7.30pm, Sun 4.30–7.30pm

Close to the northwest edge of the old town (follow Via Campana and then Via Dietro le Mura west from Piazza del Duomo) stands an imposing Franciscan monastery, whose church, **San Francesco**, claims a high altarpiece (occasionally removed) of the *Madonna and Child with Four Saints* (1479) by Sano di Pietro, a painting that's more than worth the walk (ring the bell of the seminary if the church is shut). The scenes in the predella illustrate episodes from the lives of the saints depicted in the main painting (Benedict, Cyrinus, Donatus and Justina). The second panel from the left shows Cyrinus, a Croatian saint, preaching to the crowd that has come to watch his martyrdom: he's shown miraculously floating on the stone that had been tied round his neck in an attempt to drown him. Donatus, patron saint of Arezzo (his birthplace), was martyred in the fourth century, and is remembered primarily for frightening off a dragon which had been poisoning local wells: Sano shows him with his mule, bravely marching to meet the dragon emerging from its cave. The right-hand scene shows the third-century Justina, a royal princess, patron of Padua but much venerated in Pisa, being martyred on the orders of her father.

ARRIVAL AND DEPARTURE   COLLE DI VAL D'ELSA

By train The nearest station is Poggibonsi, with very regular trains from Florence, Siena and Empoli; from here you will need to take a taxi or the 130 or 1300 TRA-IN bus (ⓦ trainspa.it) into Colle di Val d'Elsa.

By bus Inter-town buses run to Colle Bassa's Piazza Arnolfo. Destinations Casole d'Elsa (4 daily; 20min); Florence (hourly; 1hr); Monteriggioni (hourly; 15min); Poggibonsi (hourly; 15min); Siena (hourly; 30min); Volterra (3–5 daily; 45min).

INFORMATION

Tourist office Via Francesco Campana 43, Colle Alta (April–Oct Mon–Sat 10am–1pm & 2.30–7pm, Sun 10am–1pm & 3–6pm; Nov–Jan & March Mon–Sat 10am–1pm & 2.30–5pm; ☎ 0577 922 791, ⓦ www .comune.colle-di-val-d-elsa.si.it).

ACCOMMODATION

Arnolfo Via Francesco Campana 53, Colle Alta ☎ 0577 922 020, ⓦ arnolfobb.it. Colle Alta's principal hotel closed in 2010, but the owners have opened a pretty B&B in a medieval *palazzo* close by, with a total of ten spacious and newly updated rooms across three apartments. **€70–€100**

Hotel Villa Belvedere ☎ 0577 920 966, ⓦ villabelvedere.com. Some 2km east of town, on the road to the Colle di Val d'Elsa Sud junction of the Florence-Siena Raccordo road, the *Hotel Villa Belvedere* occupies an eighteenth-century villa, with fifteen rooms, fine grounds, tennis courts and a pool. **€120**

La Vecchia Cartiera Via Oberdan 5–9, Colle Bassa ☎ 0577 921 107, ⓦ lavecchiacartiera.it. A decent three-star option, but its location is not as good as the *Arnolfo*. Rooms are clean, functional and plain, but there is a gargantuan swimming pool. **€70**

EATING AND DRINKING

Arnolfo Via XX Settembre 50–52a, Colle Bassa ☎ 0577 920 549, ⓦ arnolfo.com. The two-Michelin-starred *Arnolfo* offers sophisticated food a long way from the no-nonsense rustic cooking of most Tuscan trattorias – but at a considerable price (starters around €40–45, mains €45–50). Mon & Thurs–Sun 12.30–2.30pm & 7.30–10pm; closed Jan 22 to Feb 27 & and July 29 to Aug 12.

L'Officina della Cucina Popolare Via Gracco del Secco 86 ☎ 0577 921 796, ⓦ cucina-popolare.com. Charming, young and cosmopolitan owners and cooks (from Denmark, Tuscany and Piemonte) offer great Tuscan staples at fair prices (allow around €25 for a full meal) in a small restaurant close to the medieval entrance to Colle Alta. May–Oct daily 12.30–2.30pm & 7.30–10.30pm; Nov–April Mon–Fri 7.30–10.30pm, Sat & Sun 12.30–2.30pm & 7.30-10.30pm.

Molino il Moro Via della Ruota 2, Colle Bassa ☎ 0577 920 862, ⓦ molinoilmoro.it. This large and beautifully converted twelfth-century mill (the millstream passes under the main dining room) offers good, moderately priced local food and wine. Tues 7–10pm, Wed–Sun 12.30–2.30pm & 7–10pm.

Casole d'Elsa

The roads south of Colle di Val d'Elsa lead into the **Colline Metallífere**, dotted with geothermal energy plants (the largest are out towards Larderello) and their snaking pipelines. Other sights are few, though the countryside, as ever, is liberally sprinkled with Romanesque churches, beautiful farmhouses and artfully placed cypresses. One very pretty rural route leads through **CASOLE D'ELSA**, a village that looks inviting from a distance but yields relatively little of interest. Buses also pass this way from Colle. Council offices now occupy Casole's fortress, the village's most imposing sight.

Museo Civico e della Collegiata

Piazza del Duomo 2 • Easter to mid-Oct Tues–Sun 10am–1pm & 4–7pm; rest of the year Sat & Sun 10am–1pm & 4–6pm • €3

An Etruscan tomb discovered nearby, reputedly one of the richest ever found, contributed some of the treasures in the attractively presented **Museo Civico e della Collegiata**, which also has rooms devoted to painting and the decorative arts. Highlights of the latter rooms are a *Maestà* by a follower of Duccio, several works by Alessandro Casolani, a sixteenth-century artist, and a bust of Bishop Tommaso Andrei, a local cleric who died in 1303, by Gano di Fazio.

The Collegiata

Piazza del Duomo • Easter to mid-Oct Tues–Sun 10am–1pm & 4–7pm; rest of the year Sat & Sun 10am–1pm & 4–6pm; sometimes closed Sun morning

The museum stands alongside the fifteenth-century Gothic **Collegiata** church (restored after war bomb damage), which holds an important *Madonna and Child* and *Massacre* *of the Innocents* by Andrea di Niccolò, and a *Madonna and Child* attributed to Segna di Buonaventura.

INFORMATION

CASOLE D'ELSA

Tourist office Piazza della Libertà 1 (Easter to mid-Oct Tues–Sun 10am–1pm & 4–7pm; rest of the year Sat & Sun 10am–1pm & 4–6pm; ☎0577 948 705, ⓦ casole.it).

ACCOMMODATION

Relais La Suvera ☎0577 960 300, ⓦlasuvera.it. This stunning and sumptuous five-star hotel in the nearby hamlet of Pievescola was originally a Sienese castle, and was converted into a villa by Baldassare Peruzzi during the Renaissance. With its loggia, extensive grounds, stepped terraces, antique furniture, priceless works of art, ritzy suites and beautiful rooms, it's an outstanding but eye-wateringly expensive period piece. **€410**

Poggibonsi

POGGIBONSI, 8km east of San Gimignano, has little more than its transport links and its politics to recommend it. A serious industrial town, conspicuously ugly alongside its Tuscan neighbours, it is home to what is reputed to be Italy's reddest council. Prior to World War II, it might have looked more like Colle, but bombing left little trace of its past other than the **Castello della Magione**, a little Romanesque complex, possibly with Templar origins, consisting of a chapel and pilgrim hospice. The unfinished Medici fort at the top of the town isn't worth the slog, although the superb **hotel** up here is (see below).

ARRIVAL AND DEPARTURE

POGGIBONSI

By train Poggibonsi station is 200m east of the town centre, off Via Trento, and is on the line between Empoli, for connections to Florence (hourly; 1hr 15min), and Siena (hourly; 25min).
By bus Buses stop by the railway station at other points along the main Via Trento-Via Senese road through the heart of the town.
Destinations Colle di Val d'Elsa (hourly; 15min); Florence (hourly; 50min); San Gimignano (every 30min; 25min); Siena (hourly; 45min).

ACCOMMODATION

Villa San Lucchese Località San Lucchese 5 ☎0577 937 119, ⓦ villasanlucchese.com. A lovely four-star villa hotel with pool and tennis courts in a rural setting that seems a world away from the tatty town below. **€135**

San Gimignano

SAN GIMIGNANO – "delle Belle Torri" – and its stunning skyline of towers, built in aristocratic rivalry by feuding nobles in the twelfth and thirteenth centuries, evoke the appearance of medieval Tuscany more than any other sight. The town's image as a "Medieval Manhattan" has long caught visitors' imaginations, helped by its convenience as a day-trip from Florence or Siena, 27km away to the southeast.

San Gimignano is all it's cracked up to be: quietly monumental, well preserved, enticingly rural and with a fine array of frescoes. However, from Easter until October, it has little life of its own – and a lot of day-trippers, who don't always respect the place: antisocial behaviour and litter can be a problem. If you want to get any feel for the town, beyond the art or quaintness, you need to come well out of season. If you can't, then aim to spend the night here: in the evenings San Gimignano takes on a very different pace and atmosphere and the town deserves at least a day, both for the frescoes in the churches and museums, and for the surrounding countryside – some of the loveliest in Tuscany.

Getting around is easy, as the town is not much more than a village, centred on two interlocking main squares, **Piazza della Cisterna** and **Piazza del Duomo**: you could walk from one end to the other in fifteen minutes, or around the walls in an hour.

Brief history

San Gimignano was probably founded by the **Etruscans** and later inhabited by the **Romans**. It reputedly took its name in 450 from St Gimignano, a bishop of Modena, whose intervention supposedly saved the settlement from Attila the Hun. During the tenth century a castle was built on the site, a stronghold that was soon surrounded by houses, and which, by the twelfth century, had become a free *comune*. A second (surviving) set of walls was added in the middle of the thirteenth century, about the time of the first **towers**.

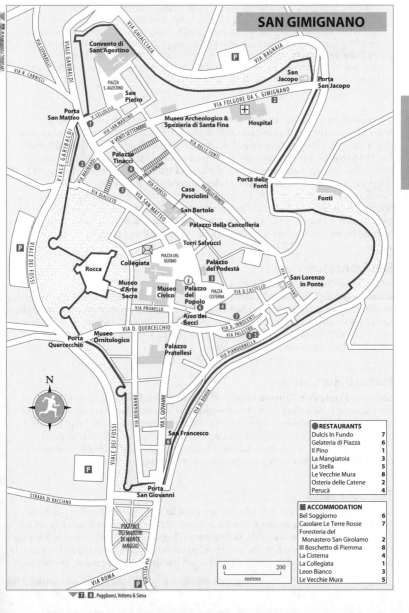

SAN GIMIGNANO

RESTAURANTS

Dulcis In Fundo	7
Gelateria di Piazza	6
Il Pino	1
La Mangiatoia	3
La Stella	5
Le Vecchie Mura	8
Osteria delle Catene	2
Perucà	4

ACCOMMODATION

Bel Soggiorno	6
Casolare Le Terre Rosse	7
Foresteria del Monastero San Girolamo	2
Ill Boschetto di Piemma	8
La Cisterna	4
La Collegiata	1
Leon Bianco	3
Le Vecchie Mura	5

7, 8, Poggibonsi, Volterra & Siena

7

SAN GIMIGNANO'S TOWERS

The Palazzo del Popolo's **Torre Grossa** was completed in 1311, some time after a 1255 ordinance in which the *comune* decided that the town's tower-building frenzy had run its course. The **Torre della Rognosa** of the Palazzo del Podestà, which survives, was set as the maximum height (54m) for any subsequent private tower, the idea being that none should exceed the towers of the civic authorities. The Salvucci clan responded by building two towers in Via San Matteo, the **Torri Salvucci**, each shorter than the maximum, but arranged so close together as to make it clear that their combined height would be higher than anything conjured up by the *comune*.

To the left (northwest) of Piazza della Cisterna, beside an arch leading through to the Piazza del Duomo, are the twin Ardinghelli towers and palace; another of the Salvucci rivals rears up close by. The tower on the square's northeast flank, topping the Palazzo Cortesi, is known as the **Torre del Diavolo**, so named, according to legend, because its owner returned after a long journey convinced that it had grown taller, the only explanation for the phenomenon, he alleged, being that a DIY-inclined devil had been busy during his absence.

San Gimignano's population of 15,000 (twice the present number) prospered as a result of agriculture and a position close to the Via Francigena, the ancient trade and pilgrimage route between Rome and northern Europe. Two families, the **Ardinghelli** and the **Salvucci**, mostly controlled the town and inter-family feuds often caused havoc. The vendettas ended only after the Black Death in 1348, which devastated both the population and – as the pilgrim trade collapsed –the economy.

Subjection to Florence in 1353 broke the power of the nobles, leaving San Gimignano unaffected by the struggles between aristocracy and local councils that racked other Tuscan towns. The **tower houses**, when real control lay elsewhere, posed little threat and so were not torn down; today, fifteen (of an original 72) survive.

San Francesco

Via San Giovanni 69 • Daily 9.30am–7.30pm • ⓦ tollena.it

On the right of palazzo-lined Via San Giovanni, about a hundred metres up from the town's main southern gate, Porta San Giovanni (1262), **San Francesco** is a Pisan-style Romanesque church converted to a shop selling local Vernaccia white wine and other products. Walk through to the lovely garden at the rear, where you can enjoy an incomparable view across the Tuscan hills.

Piazza della Cisterna

You enter **Piazza della Cisterna** through the **Arco dei Becci**, part of the original fortifications built before the town expanded and acquired its second set of thirteenth-century walls. The square is flanked by a cluster of towers and *palazzi*, and is named after the cistern (1273) – still functioning – at its centre. The well was extended in 1346 on the orders of the then *Podestà*, Guccio de' Malvoli, whose coat of arms adorns one of the faces: note the rope-cut grooves, witness to centuries of use.

The Collegiata

Piazza del Duomo • April–Oct Mon–Fri 9.30am–7.10pm, Sat 10am–5.10pm, Sun 12.30–5.10pm; Feb, March & Nov 1–15 Mon–Sat 10am–4.40pm, Sun 12.30–4.30pm; Jan & Nov 16–30 religious services only • €3.50, or combined ticket with Museo d'Arte Sacra €5.50

The first church on the site of the **Collegiata** was begun in the tenth century. Work on the present building began in the early twelfth century, with alterations by Giuliano da Maiano in 1466. The plain facade (1239) could hardly provide a greater contrast with

FROM TOP MONTERIGGIO (P.296); COLLEGIATA FRESCOES, SAN GIMIGNANO (P.306); GELATERIA DI PIAZZA, SAN GIMIGNANO (P.313) >

the **interior**, whose frescoes fill just about every available space, their brilliant colours offset by Pisan-Romanesque arcades of black and white marble.

The principal fresco cycles

Three fresco cycles fill the right and left walls of the church, plus two short walls that protrude from the facade's inside wall. Beginning on this rear wall you'll find a fresco of *St Sebastian* (1465) by Benozzo Gozzoli, painted five or six years after the artist's fresco cycle in the Palazzo Medici-Riccardi in Florence. Sebastian was often invoked during plague epidemics – one had struck San Gimignano in 1464, which was the reason for Gozzoli's commission – thanks largely to his powers of recovery: he survived an assault with arrows – though remains the patron saint of archers – and was eventually martyred by being pummelled to death.

The Archangel Gabriel and the Madonna Annunciate

Either side of Sebastian, on pedestals, are two **statues** of the *Archangel Gabriel* and the *Madonna Annunciate*, carved by the Sienese sculptor Jacopo della Quercia in 1421 and given their garish painted finish five years later. In front of each statue are pillars painted with frescoes by Gozzoli of the *Annunciation* and saints Anthony, Augustine and Bernardino. These pillars anchor the side walls containing the first of the church's fresco cycles, Taddeo di Bartolo's *Last Judgement* (1410), with *Paradiso* depicted to the right, *Inferno* to the left. The latter offers a no-holds-barred illustration of the Seven Deadly Sins, including Bosch-like fantasies on lust and gluttony.

The Old Testament scenes

The other cycles in the main part of the church depict scenes from the Old Testament (two tiers on the left wall) and the New Testament (two tiers on the right); in the lunettes above, scenes of the Creation above the Old Testament episodes are paralleled across the church by episodes from the Nativity. Somewhat surprisingly, the **Old Testament** and **Creation** scenes (26 in all), whose vision seems entirely medieval, were painted later, between 1356 and 1367.

Created by Bartolo di Fredi, they reflect the influence of Lorenzetti's *Good and Bad Government* in Siena in their delight in narrative detail: *Abraham and Lot leading their flock towards Canaan*, for example, is a Tuscan farming scene. They are also quirkily naturalistic – there are few odder frescoes than that of the *Drunkenness of Noah*, exposing a prominent penis in his stupor: Noah is traditionally considered to have been the first to promote agriculture and viticulture, and – more to the point – the first to have abused the products of the vine.

The cycle (which is read left to right, top to bottom) follows the story of the *Flood* with those of *Abraham and Lot* (their trip to Canaan), *Joseph* (his dream; being let down the well; having his brothers arrested and being recognized by them), *Moses* (changing a stick into a serpent before the Pharaoh; the Red Sea; Mount Sinai) and *Job* (temptation; the devil killing his herds and destroying his house; thanking God; and being consoled by friends).

ST FINA

St Fina, the subject of the frescoes and the frieze of the Cappella di Santa Fina, was born in San Gimignano in 1238 and struck by an incurable disease at the age of 10. She gave herself immediately to God, repented her sins (the worst seems to have been accepting an orange from a boy), and insisted on spending the agonized five years until her death lying on a plank on the floor (the idea being that she would be brought closer to Christ through increased suffering). As a result of her position, and her complete paralysis during her final days, she was tormented, among other things, by mice, which she was unable to scare away. The board, on her death, was found covered in flowers.

The New Testament scenes

The authorship of the **New Testament** scenes (begun 1333) is disputed, attributed now to Lippo Memmi, collaborator and brother-in-law of Simone Martini, or to a member of Memmi's workshop. Traditionally, the attribution is to Barna di Siena, another follower of Martini, who is supposed to have died in a fall from the scaffolding while at work here in the 1350s.

The scenes of Christ's life and the Passion mark a departure from Martini's style, with their interest in emotional expression. In *The Kiss of Judas* the focus of the eyes is startlingly immediate, as is the absorption of all the figures in the action – St Peter thrusting into the foreground with his assault on the Roman soldier, while the other disciples gather their cloaks and flee. One of the most dramatic scenes is the *Resurrection of Lazarus*, in which a dumbstruck crowd witnesses the removal of a door to reveal the living Lazarus in the winding bandages of burial.

The chapels

Many of the cathedral's chapels were remodelled between 1468 and 1475 as part of Giuliano da Maiano's renovation of the church. The **Cappella di San Gimignano**, to the left of the high altar, features an altar by Giuliano's brother, Benedetto da Maiano, partly constructed from fragments of an earlier work, though both brothers reserved their best work for the **Cappella di Santa Fina**, a Renaissance masterpiece located at the top of the right (south) aisle. Giuliano designed the chapel (1468–75), while Benedetto designed its altar, marble shrine and bas-reliefs (1475), though the most eye-catching part of the ensemble, dedicated to San Gimignano's patron saint, is a pair of frescoes in opposing lunettes by Domenico Ghirlandaio (1475).

The St Fina frescoes

Both the mice and flowers that feature in the story of Fina's life appear in the fresco of the right lunette, which depicts the *Announcement of Death*, the time of Fina's demise having been vouchsafed to her by St Gregory in a vision (notice the flower-covered board and the mouse in the semi-darkness to the rear of the composition).

The fresco in the opposite (left) lunette, the *Funeral of St Fina* shows the saint on her deathbed with the towers of San Gimignano in the background. Also depicted are three miracles associated with Fina: the restoration of a blind choirboy's sight; the curing of her nurse's paralysed hand; and the ringing of San Gimignano's bells by angels on the saint's death.

Ghirlandaio left a self-portrait (in the figure behind the bishop saying Mass), as well as portraits (in the figures to either side) of Davide, his brother, and Sebastiano Mainardi, his brother-in-law. Both probably assisted with the frescoes. The fresco's composition, with the dead saint surrounded by onlookers, owes much to Benozzo Gozzoli's almost identical scene painted ten years earlier in Sant'Agostino (see p.310), which in turn was influenced by Giotto's *Funeral of St Francis* in Santa Croce in Florence.

Accessed by a loggia in the same courtyard as the entrance to the Collegiata is the **Baptistery**, frescoed with an *Annunciation* by Ghirlandaio and Sebastiano Mainardi (1482).

Museo d'Arte Sacra

Piazza Pecori 1 • April–Oct Mon–Fri 9.30am–7.10pm, Sat 10am–5.10pm, Sun 12.30–5.10pm; Feb, March & Nov 1–15 Mon–Sat 10am–4.40pm, Sun 12.30–4.30pm; Jan & Nov 16–30 religious services only • €3, or combined ticket with Collegiata €5.50

The **Museo d'Arte Sacra** is housed in the old Rectors' Palace off to the left of the courtyard in Piazza Pecori. Its highlights include a *Madonna and Child* by Bartolo di Fredi, a superb wooden Crucifix, probably eleventh century, several glorious illuminated choir books, and a marble bust of *Onofrio di Pietro* (1493) by Benedetto da Maiano, a work commissioned by San Gimignano's *comune* to honour Di Pietro, a local scholar.

Museo Civico

Piazza del Duomo • Daily March–Oct 9.30am–7.20pm; Nov–Feb 10am–5.30pm • €5, or €7.50 combined ticket with Museo Archeologico, Spezieria di Santa Fina and Galleria d'Arte Moderna

The Palazzo del Popolo was begun in 1270, probably to a plan by Arnolfo di Cambio, born in nearby Colle di Val d'Elsa. Most of the building is devoted to the **Museo Civico** (or Pinacoteca), home to an outstanding miscellany of paintings, and to the **Torre Grossa**, the only one of San Gimignano's towers you can climb.

You first enter a courtyard, built in 1323 during extension work on the palace. Its well (1360) incorporates fragments removed from local Etruscan tombs, while the stone crests around the walls represent the coats of arms of medieval magistrates. A **loggia** opens on the right, from which justice and public decrees were proclaimed, hence the subject matter of its three frescoes, all of which make an allusion to justice: the left wall features an allegory (1513) by Sodoma depicting a throned magistrate flanked by the figures of Dishonesty, Prudence and Truth; in front is a *Madonna and Child* by Taddeo di Bartolo (the artist responsible for the Collegiata's *Last Judgement*) in which the Madonna is flanked by saints Gimignano and Gregory – the Child meanwhile holds a biblical inscription recommending sagacity in the administration of justice; the right wall features a *chiaroscuro* by Sodoma depicting St Ivo, a Breton lawyer whose pro bono legal work among the poor, widowed and orphaned saw him canonized in 1366 and made patron saint of lawyers, jurists and magistrates.

Sala del Consiglio

The first of the museum's rooms and the *palazzo*'s public chambers, frescoed with hunting and tournament scenes, is known as the **Sala del Consiglio**, or Sala di Dante – the poet visited as Florence's ambassador to the town in 1300. Most of the paintings displayed are fourteenth-century works, Sienese in origin or inspiration, and executed in the years before San Gimignano passed under Florentine influence.

The highlight is Lippo Memmi's *Maestà* (1317), his finest work, closely modelled on Simone Martini's painting on an identical theme, completed two years previously, in Siena's Palazzo Pubblico. San Gimignano's *Podestà* at the time, Mino de' Tolomei, is shown kneeling at the Madonna's feet, looked down on by a multitude of saints arranged in distinct rows. Benozzo Gozzoli added the two saints at the extreme right and left in 1466. The fresco on the end wall shows San Gimignano's population swearing allegiance to Charles of Anjou.

Smaller rooms on this floor are often given over to temporary exhibitions, usually easily ignored in favour of the main **Pinacoteca**, or art gallery, on the next floor.

The Pinacoteca

The **finest pictures** here are in the large salon on the right at the top of the stairs. On the wall on the right as you enter is a superb painted *Crucifix* (1260–65) by Coppo di Marcovaldo, a Florentine artist – believed to have been the teacher of Cimabue – captured by the Sienese at the Battle of Montaperti in 1260. This work, one of the masterpieces of early Tuscan painting, was probably painted while the artist was in "captivity". The similar – but eight-metre high – *Christ* on Florence's baptistery ceiling is attributed to Marcovaldo. Panels next to each of Christ's hands depict the Madonna and St John, and the three Marys. Six scenes from the Passion flank Christ's body.

Other outstanding pictures in the room include two early tondi of the *Annunciation* (1482–83) by Filippino Lippi, with the Madonna portrayed separately in one, the Archangel Gabriel in the other. Between them is Pinturicchio's *Madonna Enthroned with Sts Gregory and Benedict* (1512), one of the last works and masterpieces of this Umbrian artist. Equally arresting are two contrasting paintings of the *Madonna and Child with Saints* by Benozzo Gozzoli, both painted in 1466. The more interesting of the two shows the Madonna with John the Baptist, Mary Magdalene, St Augustine and St Martha, the last (the sister of Lazarus) being particularly venerated in Tuscany, as she is the patron saint of builders and – more significantly – of cooks.

Taddeo di Bartolo's triptych

In the larger of the two rooms to the right, look for the **triptych** by Taddeo di Bartolo depicting *Scenes from the Life of St Gimignano* (1393). It was painted when Taddeo was working on the *Last Judgement* frescoes in the Collegiata, where the painting was originally installed above the high altar. The large central panel, which shows the saint with San Gimignano on his lap, is flanked on each side with vignettes from his life.

The most extraordinary is one of the four scenes on the right, in which the saint is disturbed while praying by what is described as a "*bisogno*" or need – in other words, a desperate call of nature. In answering the call he finds himself met by the Devil, whom he causes to vanish by making the sign of the Cross. The other panels on the right, which describe the saint's exorcism of the Byzantine emperor's daughter, show Gimignano being borne to Constantinople, his calming of a storm during the voyage and the eventual exorcism of the princess. The three main panels on the left depict St Severus officiating at Gimignano's burial; saving San Gimignano from Attila the Hun (the saint is seen remonstrating with Attila); and preventing a downpour of rain soaking his followers in a leaky church.

Also of interest are *Scenes from the Life of St Bartholomew* (1401) by Lorenzo di Niccolò, whose panels include the attempt to martyr the saint by flaying him alive (top right) – the operation is shown in graphic detail – and his subsequent beheading, in which bloody strips of skin hanging from the saint's body hamper the work of the exasperated executioners.

The reliquary tabernacle

The same artist was responsible for the double-sided **reliquary tabernacle** showing *St Fina and St Gregory* and *Eight Scenes from the Life of St Fina* (1402), San Gimignano's patron saint. Fina is shown holding San Gimignano in one hand, and a bunch of violets – a symbol of humility – in the other. The scenes on one face show the mother of St Fina looking after her daughter (with a relative desperately trying to beat off hordes of mice) and the Devil casting Fina's mother down some stairs (to no ill effect); and the funeral procession during which Fina's nurse, Beldia, miraculously recovered the use of her paralyzed hand. The panels on the other face show Fina extinguishing a fire; saving a boat in a storm; saving a builder falling from a building; and exorcising a man possessed by the Devil.

The wedding frescoes

Perhaps the gallery's most enjoyable paintings are the **frescoes of wedding scenes** in a small room off the stairs (straight ahead on exiting the main salon). Unique in their subject matter, they show a tournament where the wife rides on her husband's back, followed by the lovers taking a shared bath and climbing into bed: the man, remarkably, manages to retain the same red hat through all three operations. Some commentators, however, have seen the pictures in a less jolly light, describing them as allegorical scenes designed to warn men of the wiles of women. They were completed in the 1320s by Memmo di Filippuccio, the father of Lippo Memmi, who since 1303 had been working as a more or less official painter for the *comune*.

The Rocca and around

Just behind Piazza del Duomo, a lane leads to the **Rocca**, the old fortress, with its one surviving tower. It was built in 1353, to Florentine orders but at local expense, "in order to remove every cause of evil thinking from the inhabitants". A couple of centuries later, its purpose presumably fulfilled, it was dismantled by Cosimo I. Nowadays its perimeter encloses a public garden with figs, olives and a well. From the ramparts, there are superb views over the countryside.

San Lorenzo in Ponte to San Jacopo

The Romanesque **San Lorenzo in Ponte** (1240), on Via di Castello, boasts an interior almost completely covered with frescoes (1413) by the little-known but accomplished Florentine Cenni di Francesco. The dramatic fragments include a *Last Judgement* on the left wall and (in the presbytery) the figures of the *Apostles, Christ and the Virgin with Angels*, and *Scenes from the Life of St Benedict*. Cenni was also responsible for the frescoes in the adjoining oratory, notably the entrance wall's *St Lawrence and Saints* and *Madonna and Child with Angels*, in which the Madonna's head – an earlier work – has been attributed to Simone Martini.

At the end of Via di Castello a rural lane winds down to the walls, a public well – the **Fonti** – and open countryside. The little Pisan-Romanesque church here, **San Jacopo**, has a painting of St James by Pier Francesco Fiorentino.

Convento di Sant'Agostino

Daily: April–Oct 7am–noon & 3–7pm; Nov–March 7am–noon & 3–6pm

Via San Matteo leads north from Piazza del Duomo, with quiet alleyways branching off to the walls. Passing a couple of mighty tower houses, the street ends at the **Porta San Matteo**, just inside which is the **Convento di Sant'Agostino**, a large, hall-like thirteenth-century structure with several fine paintings, an impressive Renaissance altar, and an outstanding fresco cycle by Benozzo Gozzoli on the *Life of St Augustine*.

Cappella di San Bartolo

On the rear wall, on the left as you enter by the church's side door, is the **Cappella di San Bartolo**. Framed by a draped marble curtain, it houses the remains of St Bartolo (1228–1300), another of San Gimignano's patron saints. Born near Pisa, he became a lay Franciscan, but at 52 contracted leprosy and was forced to retire to a leper colony, where he died twenty years later. According to legend, while he was in the colony several of his toes came off in the hands of a nun who was washing his feet. Mortified, he took the loose toes and miraculously reattached them to his foot.

This is one of three miracles depicted in the predella reliefs on the magnificent **altar** by Benedetto da Maiano (1495). The three figures above are the *Theological Virtues*, while the frescoes to the left, by Sebastiano Mainardi, depict saints Lucy, Nicholas of Bari and Gimignano; the last holds the town of San Gimignano in his arms.

On the right (south) wall are several striking **frescoes**, among them a *Madonna and Child with Eight Saints* (1494) by Pier Francesco Fiorentino and a figure of *Christ with the Symbols of the Passion* by Bartolo di Fredi (author of the Collegiata's Old Testament cycle), who was also responsible for the frescoes on the *Life of the Virgin* (1356) on the side walls of the chapel to the right of the high altar. The chapel's striking altarpiece, the *Nativity of the Virgin* (1523), is by Vincenzo Tamengi (1492–1530), an otherwise little-known local artist.

The Life of St Augustine

All paintings in the church, however, pale beside those on the walls around the high altar, a seventeen-panel cycle on the **Life of St Augustine** (1463–67) by Benozzo

Gozzoli, pictures which provide a superb record of life in Renaissance Italy, particularly the city life of Florence, which forms a backdrop to many of the scenes.

Read from low down on the left, the first panels depict the saint – who was born in 354 in what is now Tunisia – being taken to school by his parents and flogged by his teacher, studying grammar at Carthage university and crossing the sea to Italy. The next recount his academic career: teaching philosophy and rhetoric in Rome and Milan – Gozzoli depicts the journey between the cities as a marvellously rich procession – and being received by the Emperor Theodosius. Then come the turning points in his life, when he listens to the preaching of St Ambrose, and then, while reading St Paul's Epistle to the Romans, hears a child's voice extolling him "*Tolle, lege*" (take and read). After this, Augustine was baptized, returned to Tunisia to form a monastic community, was subsequently made bishop of Hippo and went on to become one of the fathers of the early Christian Church. Gozzoli depicts just a few crucial scenes: Augustine meeting the child whose voice he had heard; the death of his mother, St Monica; blessing the people, as bishop; confuting a heretic; having a vision of St Jerome in Paradise; and his death, a scene which almost exactly prefigures Ghirlandaio's depiction of the death of St Fina in the Collegiata.

Given the richness of the cycle, it's remarkable that the high altar's *Coronation of the Virgin* (1483) manages to hold its own. It's by Piero del Pollaiuolo, brother and collaborator of the more famous Antonio.

The sacristy and cloister
Moving back down the left (north) wall you come to a door leading to the **sacristy** and Renaissance **cloister** and another fresco by Sebastiano Mainardi of *San Gimignano Blessing Three Dignitaries* (1487). The effigy above is of *Fra' Domenico Strambi*, the patron who commissioned the Gozzoli frescoes and Pollaiuolo altarpiece. The marble reliefs (1318) beyond, showing four half-figures of bishops, are believed to be part of the original shrine to St Bartolo, and are attributed to Tino da Camaino. The fresco fragment beyond, a *Madonna* by Lippo Memmi, is overshadowed by a large fresco of *St Sebastian*, painted by Gozzoli in 1464, the year in which plague ravaged San Gimignano.

Museo Archeologico and Spezieria dello Spedale di Santa Fina
Via Folgore da San Gimignano 11 • April–Dec daily 11am–5.30pm • €3.50, or €7.50 combined ticket with Museo Civico

Just south of Sant'Agostino is the former convent of Santa Chiara, home to the **Museo Archeologico**, which boasts a large collection of local finds and details the history of the area from the Etruscans to the eighteenth century. In the same complex is a reproduction of the **Spezieria dello Spedale di Santa Fina**, one of Tuscany's oldest pharmacies, exhibiting all sorts of exotic herbal remedies and other sixteenth-century medicinal concoctions. Upstairs is the **Galleria d'Arte Moderna e Contemporanea**, showing work by nineteenth- and twentieth-century Tuscan artists and temporary exhibits.

ARRIVAL AND DEPARTURE   **SAN GIMIGNANO**

By train and bus Most people visit San Gimignano as a day-trip. You can take a bus from Siena (10 daily; 1hr 15min), or a train or bus to Poggibonsi ((10 daily; 25min), and then one of the roughly hourly buses from the station for the 20min journey to San Gimignano. There's also a bus service from Colle Val d'Elsa.
Buses stop either at Piazzale dei Martiri di Monte Maggio, just outside Porta San Giovanni, the south gate, or by the

northern gate, Porta San Matteo. You can buy bus tickets and pick up timetables at the tourist office.
By car Cars are banned from the centre. The simplest option for a short stay is the car parks on the road that runs around the wall. Free parking is possible on the outskirts of town, close to Piazzale dei Martiri di Monte Maggio, but this is only worthwhile if you need a space for several days.

SAN GIMIGNANO FESTIVAL

San Gimignano's first summer arts **festival** was held at the end of the 1920s, and except for a break during World War II has run just about every year since in July and August. It features a series of classical concerts (usually with local performers), plus theatre and open-air films and regular early evening wine tastings, the last courtesy of the town's local producers.

Its once quiet provincial air is increasingly compromised by outsiders, particularly at the highlights of the event – the outdoor opera performances in Piazza del Duomo. The atmosphere remains cheerfully informal, however, with the steps of the Collegiata set aside as terracing for the town's kids. These days the festival goes under the name of the "San Gimignano Estate".

Festival tickets and further details are available from the tourist office; you can also get more information from their website, **ⓦ** sangimignano.com.

INFORMATION

7

Tourist office Piazza del Duomo (daily April–Oct   ☎ 0577 940 008, **ⓦ** sangimignano.com).
9am–1pm & 3–7pm; Nov–March 9am–1pm & 3–6pm;

ACCOMMODATION

Crucial to enjoying the town is a room inside the walls – which from Easter to October means booking ahead or arriving early in the day. The town's main **hotels** are all expensive three-stars, but **private rooms** offer a budget alternative, with doubles from around €70; most have shared bathrooms. It's also possible to rent **apartments** by the day, but be sure to book. The tourist office website (**ⓦ** sangimignano.com) has details of rooms and apartments.

Bel Soggiorno Via San Giovanni 91 ☎ 0577 940 375, **ⓦ** pescille.it/belsoggiorno. Similar to the *Leon Bianco* in quality, price and facilities, though you may need to take full board in summer. The 22 rooms are smallish but beautifully done, with a choice of town or countryside views, and there's a good restaurant. €110

★ **Casolare Le Terre Rosse** Località San Donato ☎ 0577 9021, **ⓦ** hotelterrerosse.com. This three-star hotel has 42 rooms in a classic Tuscan country house in a lovely rural setting, 4km to the southwest on the road to Castel San Gimignano. A great choice out of town, and the big pool is a summer draw. Open March–Oct. €109

Foresteria del Monastero San Girolamo Via Folgore da San Gimignano ☎ 0577 940 573, **ⓦ** monaster osangirolamo.it. Nine very popular, basic, quiet rooms for two to five people in a convent run by Benedictine nuns just behind Porta San Jacopo. You can use kitchen facilities for a small additional fee; breakfast is €3. Children are half price. Doubles €54

La Cisterna Piazza della Cisterna 24 ☎ 0577 940 328, **ⓦ** hotelcisterna.it. Established in 1919, this elegant hotel is built into a medieval ensemble at the base of some of the piazza's fourteenth-century towers. It's worth paying more for a room with either a (potentially noisy) piazza outlook, or a (more restful) countryside view; others have a bland courtyard view. €140

La Collegiata Località Strada 27 ☎ 0577 943 201, **ⓦ** lacollegiata.it. Sixteenth-century Franciscan convent 2km north of town off the Certaldo road, converted into one of Tuscany's breed of super-expensive hotels, for very special occasions. It's set in lovely grounds, with a pretty pool area, and each of the twenty rooms is sumptuously and individually furnished. €300

Leon Bianco Piazza della Cisterna 13 ☎ 0577 941 294, **ⓦ** leonbianco.com. Tasteful three-star hotel with seventeen a/c rooms, occupying a fourteenth-century mansion in the main square. The better rooms, which have medieval features such as vaulted ceilings, look out over the square or the Val d'Elsa. The roof terrace for breakfast, drinks or lounging is a bonus. €138

Le Vecchie Mura Via Piandornella 15 ☎ 0577 940 270, **ⓦ** vecchiemura.it. A couple of double rooms above a restaurant, but more appealing than it sounds, with welcoming owners and superb views. €60

CAMPSITES

Il Boschetto di Piemma Santa Lucia ☎ 0577 940 352, **ⓦ** boschettodipiemma.it. The nearest campsite to the town, 3km downhill from Piazzale Martiri di Monte Maggio, off the Volterra road, with a bar, restaurant and pool. Adults €10, small tent €7

EATING AND DRINKING

San Gimignano isn't noted for its **food** – there are too many visitors and too few locals to ensure high standards. However, the tables set out in summer on the car-less streets and squares and the local wines still make for a beguiling evening.

Dulcis In Fundo Via degli Innocenti 21 ☎ 0577 941 919, ⓦ ristorantedulcisinfundo.it. An airy, family-run restaurant just a touch off the main visitor trail, with ingredients sourced from the family's farm or other small local producers; try the *polpettine di maiale* (pork meatballs). Reckon on around €25 for three courses, without wine. Mon, Tues & Thurs–Sun 12.20–2.30pm & 7–10.30pm.

Gelateria di Piazza Piazza della Cisterna 4 ☎ 0577 942 244, ⓦ gelateriadipiazza.com. As an after-meal treat, drop in on this award-winning *gelateria*, whose patron, Sergio Dondoli, is renowned for his unusual (and trademarked) flavours such as Champelmo (pink grapefruit and sparkling wine) and Crema di Santa Fina (cream with saffron and pine nuts). Daily 9am–11pm; closed Dec–Feb.

Il Pino Via Cellolese 6, cnr Via San Matteo ☎ 0577 940 415, ⓦ ristoranteilpino.it. One of the town's older restaurants, founded in 1929, with a calm, if rather chintzy interior. Specializes in antipasti and dishes sprinkled with truffle. Full meals start at €30. Mon–Wed & Fri–Sun 12.30–2.30pm & 7.30–10.30pm.

La Mangiatoia Via Mainardi 2 ☎ 0577 941 528. Popular restaurant with good Tuscan staples (pasta €8–10, mains €12–14), including some gluten-free pasta options, and a garden open in the summer. Mon & Wed–Sun 12.30–3pm & 7.15–10.30pm.

La Stella Via San Matteo 75 ☎ 0577 940 289, ⓦ lastellaristorante.com. Attractive restaurant with stone arches and medieval walls that serves produce from its own farm – the food, though, is uneven, so stick to basics. It's often full of visitors, but is still good value, with pasta dishes around €10. Mon, Tues & Thurs–Sun 12.30–2.30pm & 7.30–10.30pm.

Le Vecchie Mura Via Piandornella 15 ☎ 0577 940 270, ⓦ vecchiemura.it. Housed in an old vaulted stable built into the town walls, and with a contemporary decorative edge; follow the sign off Via San Giovanni. Good atmosphere and reasonable value, with starters at €5–10, pasta €9–10 and mains around €13, and a pretty terrace with panoramic views. Be sure to book. Mon & Wed–Sun 12.30–2.30pm & 7.30–10.30pm.

Osteria delle Catene Via Mainardi 18 ☎ 0577 941 966, ⓦ osteriadellecatene.it. A reliable place for straightforward Tuscan food. With over a hundred choices, the wine list is good, too. Pastas cost €8–9, mains €13–14.50. Mon, Tues & Thurs–Sun 12.30–2.30pm & 7.30–10.30pm.

Perucà Via dei Capassi 16 ☎ 0577 943 136, ⓦ peruca .eu. A superb medieval setting in what was once a *cantina* in one of the town's oldest palaces, with a wonderful low, vaulted space. Robust Tuscan food, with lots of truffle and mushroom options, and decent prices – pastas around €8 and mains from €10. April–Oct Mon 7.30–10.30pm, Tues–Sun 12.20–2.30pm & 7.30–12.30pm; rest of the year Tues–Sun 12.20–2.30pm & 7.30–12.30pm.

Volterra

Built on a high plateau enclosed by volcanic hills, lofty **VOLTERRA** has a bleak, isolated appearance – a surprise after the pastoral prettiness of the surrounding countryside. D.H. Lawrence wrote, accurately, that "it gets all the wind and sees all the world…a sort of inland island, still curiously isolated and grim." However, its small, walled medieval heart does merit a stop, with its cobbled and austere streets, dark stone *palazzi* and walled gateways. There are great views from the windswept heights, enjoyable walking and one of the country's most important Etruscan museums. The

VOLTERRA'S HISTORY

Volterra lies at the heart of a mining region that yields **alabaster** (every other shop sells artefacts) and other minerals. The mines – and the easily defended site – made it one of the largest **Etruscan** settlements, Velathri. During the Dark Ages it became an important Lombard centre, and even sheltered the Lombard kings for a time. In the Middle Ages, however, the mines proved Volterra's downfall as the **Florentines** began to cast a covetous eye over their wealth. Florence took control from 1360, and in 1472 – anxious to secure the town's alum deposits, vital for Florence's dyeing industry – crushed all pretensions to independence with a terrible siege and pillage by Lorenzo de' Medici and the Duke of Urbino, one of the three principal crimes Lorenzo confessed to Savonarola on his deathbed.

Subsequently, Volterra was a Florentine fief, sliding into provincial obscurity. Physically, the town also began to subside, its walls and houses slipping away to the west over the **Balze** (cliffs). Today, Volterra occupies less than a third of its ancient extent.

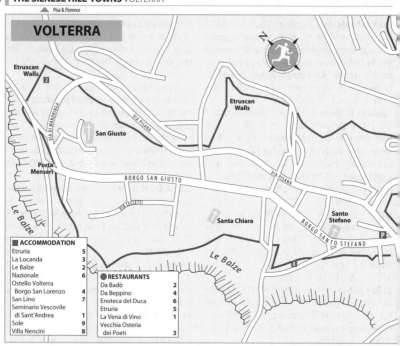

town has recently received a boost in the shape of visitors attracted by its appearance in Stephanie Meyer's **Twilight** books. If this appeals, the tourist office has details of themed walks and guided tours.

Piazza dei Priori is the town's heart, enclosed by an almost totally medieval group of buildings. The battlemented town hall, or **Palazzo dei Priori**, is the eyecatcher, surmounted by the Torre del Porcellino (Piglet's Tower), named after the much-worn carved boar on a bracket to the right of the top window, but the square is also close to the town's cathedral and other key period buildings. From here it's a short walk to the **Pinacoteca**, the standout picture gallery, and about five minutes from the **Museo Etrusco Guarnacci**, home to the pick of the region's Etruscan heritage. Before (or after) seeing the museum, it makes sense to take time out in the **Parco Archeologico**, an attractive park and garden. A longer walk west – allow around fifteen minutes – is required to see the Balze, Volterra's celebrated eroded cliffs.

Palazzo dei Priori

Piazza dei Priori • Sala del Consiglio e della Giunta mid-March to Oct daily 10.30am–5.30pm; Nov to mid-March Sat, Sun & public hols 10am–5pm • €1.50

Built between 1208 and 1257, and said to be the oldest such palace in Italy, the **Palazzo dei Priori** may have served as the model for Florence's Palazzo Vecchio – though the influences are largely reversed on its facade, which is studded with Florentine medallions. It's worth paying the admission for the spectacular views from the top of the tower. In the main building, you can take a look at the upper-floor **Sala del Consiglio e della Giunta**, used as the town's council chamber since 1257. Its end wall is frescoed with a huge *Annunciation* (1383) attributed to Jacopo di Cione.

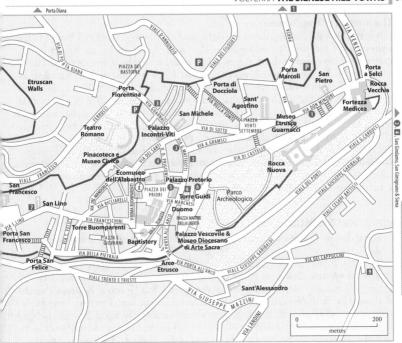

Museo Diocesano di Arte Sacra

Via Roma 13 • Daily: mid-March to Oct 9am–1pm & 3–6pm; Nov to mid-March 9am–1pm • Joint ticket with Pinacoteca e Museo Civico and Museo Etrusco €10

Formerly the town's granary, the **Palazzo Vescovile** (or Bishop's Palace) houses the rich little **Museo Diocesano di Arte Sacra**. Displays in the first room include an Andrea della Robbia bust of *St Linus*, a Volterran who was St Peter's successor as pope. There's also a silver reliquary bust of *St Ottaviano* by Andrea del Pollaiuolo; a fifteenth-century painted wooden tabernacle by Bartolomeo della Gatta, better known for his work around Arezzo and Cortona; and a clutch of Sienese altarpieces by Neri di Bici, Taddeo di Bartolo and Segna di Bonaventura. The second room has a gilded Crucifix by Giambologna, though the real highlights reside in room 3, which features Rosso Fiorentino's *Madonna di Villamagna* (1521) and the *Madonna di Ulignano* (1545) by the leading local artist Daniele da Volterra.

The Duomo and Baptistery

Piazza del Duomo • Mon–Sat 8am–12.30pm & 3–6pm, Sun 3–6pm

The **Duomo**, or Basilica di Santa Maria Assunta (consecrated in 1120), and **Baptistery** (second half of the thirteenth century) are essentially Pisan-Romanesque in style, clad in bands of black-and-white marble. Behind the Baptistery, della Robbia plaques of swaddled babies signal a building that was once a foundlings' hospital. On the Baptistery's exterior, note the main portal, whose rounded arch contains the carved heads of Christ, the Madonna and the Apostles (1283). Inside are a water stoup fashioned from an old Etruscan funerary monument and a fine baptismal font (1502) by Andrea Sansovino.

The interior of the Duomo

Inside the Duomo, moving down the **right** (**south**) **aisle**, you come to a chapel in the right transept with an outstanding Pisan *Deposition* (1228), its life-size figures disarmingly repainted in their original bright colours. On the right side of the choir lies the Cappella di Sant'Ottaviano, which contains the body of the eponymous saint, a sixth-century hermit whose relics saved Volterra from a plague in 1522 – he is one of the town's patron saints. The high altar, a nineteenth-century travesty, is surmounted by an exquisite tabernacle (1471) by Mino da Fiesole, who also carved the two kneeling angels flanking the high altar. In the **left** (**north**) aisle the highlights are two fifteenth-century terracotta figures in the oratory near the entrance: they depict the *Nativity* and *Adoration of the Magi*, the former graced with a painted background by Benozzo Gozzoli. Further down is a thirteenth-century Pisan pulpit, assembled in 1584 from a variety of earlier fragments. On the altar alongside is a beautiful *Annunciation* (1497), generally attributed to Fra' Bartolommeo.

Pinacoteca e Museo Civico

Via dei Sarti 1 • Daily: mid-March to Oct 9am–7pm; Nov to mid-March 8.30am–1.45pm • Joint ticket with Museo d'Arte Sacra and Museo Etrusco €10

Paintings and sculpture gathered from Volterra's churches are displayed at the **Pinacoteca e Museo Civico**, set in the Palazzo Minucci-Solaini. The collections are arranged chronologically, starting with **statuary** from San Giusto al Bostro, a church swallowed by the Balze, the crumbling escarpment on the town's western margins.

The **paintings** begin with largely Sienese works, notably Taddeo di Bartolo's polyptych of the *Madonna and Child with Saints* (1411) and the same artist's *Madonna della Rosa*, part of a dismembered polyptych, and a panel of *Sts Nicola da Tolentino and Peter*. Major Renaissance paintings include a *Christ in Glory* (1492) with a marvellous imaginary landscape by Ghirlandaio, and a *Madonna and Saints* (1491) and *Annunciation* by Luca Signorelli, one of the artist's masterpieces.

The museum's best work is **Rosso Fiorentino**'s extraordinary *Descent from the Cross*, painted for the church of San Francesco in 1521. This is one of the masterpieces of Mannerism, its figures, without any central focus, creating an agitated, circular tension from sharp lines and blocks of discordant colour.

Ecomuseo dell'Alabastro

Via dei Sarti 1 • Mid-March to Oct daily 11am–5pm; Nov to mid-March Sat, Sun & public hols except Dec 25 & Jan 1 9am–1.30pm • €3.50

The Palazzo Minucci-Solaini's Torre Minucci holds the **Ecomuseo dell'Alabastro**, devoted to the local alabaster industry. The museum has details of driving itineraries taking in points of interest connected with the industry. There are also displays chronicling the industry's development, as well as contemporary and historic objects in alabaster.

Palazzo Incontri-Viti

Via dei Sarti 41 • April–Oct daily 10am–1pm & 2.30–6.30pm; Nov–March by appointment only via the tourist office • €4

The **Palazzo Incontri-Viti** is a private residence built in about 1500; its forty-metre street frontage is attributed to Bartolomeo Ammannati. A variety of its beautifully frescoed and luxuriously furnished rooms are open to the public.

Parco Archeologico and the Rocco Nuova

South of Piazza dei Priori, Via Marchesi leads to a lush area of grass, trees and shade known as the **Parco Archeologico** (mid-March to Oct daily 10.30am–5.30pm; Nov to nid-March Sat, Sun & public hols except Dec 25 & Jan 1 10am–4pm). There's not much archeology – just parts of the Etruscan Acropoli off Via di Castello and a Roman theatre – but it's a beautiful part of town.

Overlooking the Parco Archeologico to the east is the **Rocca Nuova**, built by the Medici after their sacking of the town; with its rounded bastions and central tower, it's one of the great examples of Italian military architecture.

Arco Etrusco

South of Via Marchesi, Via Porta all'Arco runs downhill to the **Arco Etrusco**, a third-century Etruscan gateway built in Cyclopean blocks of stone, with Roman and medieval surrounds; the three blackened and eroded lumps on its outer face are probably images of Etruscan gods. The gate was narrowly saved from destruction in World War II during the course of a ten-day battle between the partisans (Volterra was a stronghold) and the Nazis. A memorial commemorates the partisan losses.

7

Via di Porta Diana

The **Via di Porta Diana**, straight ahead from the Piorta Fiorentina, makes for a pleasant walk, leading past the cemetery to remains of the Etruscan Porta Diana. Out beyond here tracks lead through farmland that was once a vast **Etruscan necropolis**; wandering through, you'll spot various unmarked, underground tombs.

Museo Etrusco Guarnacci

Via Don Monzoni 15 • Daily: mid-March to Oct 9am–7pm; Nov to mid-March 8.30am–1.45pm • Joint ticket with Museo Diocesano di Arte Sacra and Pinacoteca e Museo Civico €10

Volterra's Etruscan legacy is represented most importantly at the **Museo Etrusco Guarnacci**. One of Italy's major archeological museums, it's full of local finds, including some six hundred **funerary urns**. Made of alabaster, tufa and terracotta, the urns date from the fourth to first centuries BC – earlier tombs were lost as the cliffs fell away. On their sides, bas-reliefs depict domestic events (often boar hunting) or Greek myths (usually a trip to the underworld); on the lid are a bust of the subject and symbolic flowers – one for a young person, two for middle-aged, three for elderly.

Most of the best are arranged on the top floor and date from the "golden age" of the third and second centuries BC, notably the **Urna degli Sposi**, a disturbing portrait scene of a supposed husband and wife – all piercing eyes and dreadful looks. The star piece, among a number of small bronze sculptures, is the exceptional **Ombra della Sera** ("Evening Shadow"), an elongated nude. The farmer who unearthed it used it as a poker for years.

To the Balze

En route to the Balze – Volterra's famous eroded cliffs – you'll pass the church of **San Francesco**, at the western end of Via San Lino, whose adjoining Cappella della Croce di Giorno, built in 1315, contains fascinating narrative frescoes (1410) of the *Legend of the True Cross* by Cenni di Francesco, an accomplished but little-known local artist. Rosso Fiorentino's famous *Descent from the Cross*, now in the Pinacoteca e Museo Civico, once stood above the high altar. From the nearby **Porta San Francesco**, follow Borgo Santo Stefano and its continuation, Borgo San Giusto, past the Baroque church and former abbey of **San Giusto**, its dilapidated but striking facade framed by an avenue of cypress trees.

At the **Balze** themselves, almost 2km west of Piazza dei Priori, you gain a real sense of the extent of Etruscan Volterra, whose old town walls drop into the chasms. Gashes in the slopes and the natural erosion are made more dramatic by alabaster mines, ancient and modern. Below are buried great tracts of the Etruscan and Roman city, and landslips continue – as evidenced by the locked and ruined eleventh-century Badia monastery ebbing away over the precipice.

ARRIVAL AND DEPARTURE VOLTERRA

By train The nearest train station is 9km west at Saline di Volterra, from where CPT #790 buses (ⓦwww.cpt.pisa.it) shuttle into town (20min). Trains run between Saline and Cecina (8 daily; 35min) for connections to Pisa and Rome.
By bus Buses arrive on the south side of the town at Piazza Martiri della Libertà.

Destinations Colle di Val d'Elsa (3–4 daily; 45min); Pisa (daily; 1hr 10min); Saline di Volterra (5–8 daily; 20min).
By car It's best to park outside the north circuit of th walls, by the Porta San Francesco or Porta Fiorentina. If yo can find a spot, the signed, underground "Dogana" parkin is convenient for the Duomo.

INFORMATION

Tourist office Piazza dei Priori 20 (daily: April–Oct 9am–1pm & 2–7pm; Nov–March 10am–1pm & 2–6pm;

ⓣ0588 87 257, ⓦwww.volterratur.it).

ACCOMMODATION

Etruria Via Matteotti 32 ⓣ0588 87 377, ⓦalbergoetruria .it. Best value of the hotels proper – and located on Volterra's main street – this restored eighteenth-century building has 21 comfortable rooms and a private garden. **€99**
La Locanda Via Guarnacci 24–28 ⓣ0588 81 547, ⓦhotel-lalocanda.com. The *San Lino* had its own way for years among Volterra's top hotels, but the four-star *La Locanda*, smartly converted from a former nunnery, is now first choice, enjoying a slightly more central position. **€105**
Nazionale Via dei Marchesi 11 ⓣ0588 86 284, ⓦhotelnazionale-volterra.it. In the heart of town, this three-star hotel is the inn D.H. Lawrence stayed at when researching *Etruscan Places* – the medieval *palazzo* was transformed into a hotel in 1860. It's now much modernized, with 36 mostly tiny en-suite rooms. **€88**
Ostello Volterra Borgo San Lazzero, Via del Teatro 4, Località San Girolamo ⓣ0588 86 613 Nov–Feb, ⓣ0588 80 050 rest of the year, ⓦostellovolterra.it. Volterra's superb hostel occupies a wonderful and recently restored former monastery dating from 1445, with a choice of dorm beds or private rooms (some en suite) for between one and six people. It is in a peaceful setting 750m northeast of the Fortezza's old town gate; walk east from the gate down Viale G. Carducci into Borgo San Lazzero and turn left up Via del Teatro past the hospital. Dorm beds **€18**, doubles **€69**
San Lino Via San Lino 26 ⓣ0588 85 250,

ⓦhotelsanlino.com. It's somewhat overtaken by *Lo Locanda*, but this four-star place, created in 1982 from a former nunnery (and revamped in 1994), is still a decent bet, with 43 dated but trim, clean rooms created in the nuns' former cells, and the bonus of a nice outdoor pool. **€90**
Seminario Vescovile di Sant'Andrea Viale Vittorio Veneto 2 ⓣ0588 86 028, ⓔsemvescovile @diocesivolterra.it. This former seminary is situated in the northeast outskirts of town – to reach it follow the road out of Porta Marcoli. There are beautiful views from the old cells, now let as private singles or doubles with or without private bathrooms. Doubles **€28–€40**
Sole Via dei Cappuccini 10/a ⓣ0588 84 000, ⓦhotelsolevolterra.com. A modern three-star in a quiet location outside the town walls, near the church of Sant'Alessandro. All ten rooms are en suite. **€70**
Villa Nencini Borgo Santo Stefano 55 ⓣ0588 86 386, ⓦwww.villanencini.it. Attractive three-star hotel in a seventeenth-century building on the town's northwest edge, with a pool and garden. **€88**

CAMPSITE

Le Balze Via Mandringa ⓣ0588 87 880. This well-equipped campsite 1km west of the centre has a pool and tennis courts; riding can also be arranged. Open April– Sept. Adults **€9**, small tents **€8**

EATING AND DRINKING

⭐ **Da Badò** Borgo San Lazzero 9 ⓣ0588 86 477, ⓦtrattoriadabado.com. Excellent local trattoria on the SS68 Florence–Siena road, run by two amiable locals (with the mother of one in the kitchen). Serves delicious *crostini* and Volterran game staples such as *pappardelle alla lepre*. Mon, Tues & Thurs–Sun 12.15–2.30pm & 7.15–

10.30pm; closed for part of July and Sept.
Da Beppino Via delle Prigioni 13–21 ⓣ0588 86 051. Reliable, long-established and family-run restaurant in the heart of the old town, with lots of space and some outdoor tables. Serves home-made pasta, pizzas and plenty of hunting dishes, with an emphasis on truffles and

mushrooms. Mon–Wed & Fri–Sun 12.20–2.30pm & 7.30–10.30pm; closed mid-Nov to mid-Dec.

Enoteca del Duca Via di Castello 2, cnr Via dei Marchesi ☎ 0588 81 510, ⍟ enoteca-delduca -ristorante.it. On the edge of the old centre, this small restaurant (with an impressive *cantina*) has surprisingly fair prices and decent Tuscan food with a creative twist; the garden is a major plus in summer. July–Sept daily 12.30–2.30pm & 7.30–10.30pm; rest of the year Mon & Wed–Sun 12.30–2.30pm & 7.30–10.30pm; closed late Jan & mid-Nov.

Etruria Piazza dei Priori 6 ☎ 0588 86 064. Best of the more expensive places, located in an old *palazzo* on the main square, with period furniture and frescoes. Despite its fancy dishes based around truffles or porcini and its a la carte prices, it has inexpensive tourist menus, too, offering Tuscan staples such as *crostini* and *pappadelle* with meat

sauces, though the quality of the food can be uneven. Mon, Tues & Thurs–Sun 12.30–2.30pm & 7.15–10.30pm.

La Vena di Vino Via Don Minzoni 30 ☎ 0588 81 491, ⍟ lavenadivino.com. Offbeat and often lively osteria and wine bar (its ceiling is festooned with a collection of bras and bikini tops) that offers snacks, cold cuts, hearty soups (at €6), pastas and light meals wide selection of wines. There are also three light set menus, including a vegetarian option at €13. Mon & Wed–Sun 11am–1am.

★ **Vecchia Osteria dei Poeti** Via Giacomo Matteotti 55–57 ☎ 0588 86 029. One of the most popular and welcoming restaurants in town – and they don't stint on portions. A central location, with one dining room and a rustic appearance that retains many features of the original medieval building. Around €30 for a full meal, without wine. Mon–Wed & Thurs–Sun 11.30am–3pm & 6–9pm; closed mid-Jan to mid-Feb.

7

Southern Tuscany

FOR SALE, PIENZA

Southern Tuscany

The region south of Siena is Tuscany at its best: a pastoral picture of hills, trees and cultivation that encompasses the Crete Senese, the vineyards of Montepulciano and Montalcino, the Monte Amiata uplands and a landscape of sulphurous springs and castle-topped volcanic outcrops. The *crete*, especially, is fabulous: a sparsely populated region of pale clay hillsides, dotted with sheep, cypresses and the odd monumental-looking farmhouse.

The towns on the whole live up to this environment. **Montepulciano** is the most elegant and makes a superb base, with its independent hill-town life, acclaimed Vino Nobile wine and backdrop of Renaissance buildings. **Montalcino**, too, has appealing wines (its Brunello is among Tuscany's finest) and classic hill-town looks, while **Pienza** is a unique Renaissance monument, a town created by the great humanist pope, Pius II. In the south of the region, the urban highlights are **Pitigliano**, isolated on an extraordinary crag, and nearby the medieval town of **Sovana**.

Monasteries are also a major attraction, and feature some of the greatest houses of the medieval Italian orders: Cistercian **San Galgano** and **Abbadia San Salvatore**, Benedictine **Monte Oliveto Maggiore** and **Sant'Antimo**, and Vallombrosan **Torri**. All are tremendous buildings, encompassing the best Romanesque and Gothic church architecture in Tuscany.

Almost as memorable are the extraordinary **sulphur springs** that erupt from the rocks, or are channelled into geothermal energy, punctuating the landscape with pillars of steam. Several of the springs have long formed the nucleus of spas: the most interesting is **Bagno Vignoni**, still with its Medicean basin in the village square. Here, and at **Bagni di Petriolo**, **Bagni San Filippo** and – most spectacularly – **Saturnia**, you can immerse yourself in open-air rock pools below warm cascades.

San Galgano and the western crete

The route past the abbeys of **Santi Trinità e Mustiola** and **San Galgano**, the sulphur spring of **Bagni di Petriolo** and the villages of the western *crete* makes a good trip from Siena. It could be done in a day, or with a night's stop at Buonconvento, Montalcino or one of the Murlo villages. If you're dependent on public transport, content yourself with San Galgano, just off the N73 Siena–Massa Maríttima road; in a day, you could return to Siena, continue to Massa Maríttima, or stop nearby.

Monastero dei Santi Trinità e Mustiola

Driving south from Siena, follow the N223 road as far as the junction for Brenna, Stigliano and Torri. Taking this minor road, you find yourself in the **Rosia valley**, a belt of farmland marred by a chemical factory, and overlooked by a series of cream-stone

SANT'ANTIMO

Highlights

❶ Monte Oliveto Maggiore A mighty monastery set amid wonderful upland countryside and centred on one of Tuscany's largest Renaissance fresco cycles. **See p.328**

❷ Montalcino This perfect pocket hill-town produces some of Tuscany's finest wines, and boasts a superb museum and a bristling fortress with sweeping views. **See p.331**

❸ Sant'Antimo Italy's most austerely beautiful Romanesque abbey dates back over 1200 years and sits at the heart of idyllic pastoral countryside. **See p.336**

❹ Bagno Vignoni A tiny and atmospheric village, with a wonderful natural hot spring and

Medici-era pool rather than a central piazza. See p.339

❺ Pienza One of the region's most picturesque villages, with exceptional views and a tiny 15th-century central core that Pope Pius II intended to be Italy's first model Renaissance town. **See p.341**

❻ Montepulciano Tuscany's highest hill-town is a beguiling medley of tiny streets, redoubtable palaces and far-reaching views. See p.346

❼ Pitigliano A dramatically situated cliff-top village in the deep south of the region with a rich Etruscan and Jewish heritage. **See p.361**

HIGHLIGHTS ARE MARKED ON THE MAP ON P.324

villages, all pastoral beauties, set along the wooded ridge to the south. The **Monastero dei Santi Trinità e Mustiola** is at **TORRI**, the last of the villages, just 2km east of the Siena–Grosseto road. The monastery, founded in the eleventh century, was an important power base for the Vallombrosan order, until difficulties with the papacy led to its suppression by Pius II in 1464. It retains its Romanesque church and a magnificent three-tiered cloister, executed in panels of black and white marble. The capitals of the lower tier, in particular, are outstanding; their style and subject matter (fantastic animals and Old Testament stories) recalling the French-influenced work at

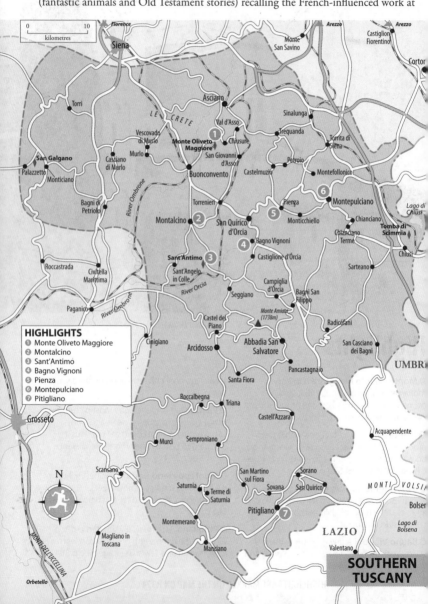

HIGHLIGHTS
1 Monte Oliveto Maggiore
2 Montalcino
3 Sant'Antimo
4 Bagno Vignoni
5 Pienza
6 Montepulciano
7 Pitigliano

SOUTHERN TUSCANY

Sant'Antimo (see p.336). Abandoned in the sixteenth century, the complex was bought privately in 1966 and opening times are erratic – ask at the Siena tourist office for the latest update.

Abbazia di San Galgano

The **Abbazia di San Galgano** is among the greatest Gothic buildings in Italy. It is certainly the most romantic – roofless, with grass for a nave, patches of fresco amid the vegetation, and panoramas of the sky, clouds and hills through a rose window.

In the twelfth and thirteenth centuries, this was one of the **Cistercians**' two largest foundations in Italy, and the leading monastic power in Tuscany. Its abbots ruled over disputes between the cities, and at Siena its monks supervised the building of the Duomo and held posts as *casalinghi* (accountants) for the *comune*. The monks were a mix of Italians and French, and through them the ideas of Gothic building were imported to Italy, along with sophisticated schemes for land drainage and agriculture.

The abbey

Daily: March–Sept 9am–8pm; Oct–April 9am–6pm • €2 • ⓦ sangalgano.org

The Cistercian order built the **church** and abbey between 1218 and 1288, at which time the complex must have looked like a small town, with its numerous workshops, dormitories and guest quarters. However, at the end of the century, during the wars between the Tuscan cities, the English *condottiere* Sir John Hawkwood and his mercenaries sacked the abbey, and by 1397 the abbot was San Galgano's sole occupant. During the fifteenth century it was repopulated for a while, until the papacy handed its income to a particularly profligate cardinal; the monks left and the building gradually decayed.

Cappella di Monte Siepi

St Galgano's hermitage was transformed into the circular **Cappella di Monte Siepi** – the building on the hill above the main abbey – between 1182 and 1185, with the **sword in the stone** forming the centrepiece. The chapel was designed as a mausoleum, but Galgano's body has been lost, though his head is preserved in the Siena cathedral museum. In the fourteenth century a Gothic second chapel was added to the original Romanesque chapel, and in the 1700s a rectory was attached, the three forming a rustic, farmhouse-like group. It is well worth the climb up the hill, as much for the views as for the chapels themselves. The interior of the rotunda is interesting for its strange striped dome, while the side chapel has patches of frescoes by Ambrogio Lorenzetti, including a just-about-discernible image of Galgano offering the rock-embedded sword to St Michael.

INFORMATION

SAN GALGANO

Tourist office There's a tourist office to one side of the abbey, in the old vaulted scriptorium (March–Sept Mon–Fri 10am–1pm & 3–6pm; Sat & Sun 10am–1pm & 2.30–6.30pm; Oct–April Mon–Fri 10am–1pm & 3–6pm; Sat & Sun 10am–1pm & 2.30–6pm; ☎ 0577 756 738).

ST GALGANO GUIDOTTI

The monastery commemorates **St Galgano Guidotti**, a noble from the nearby village of Chiusdino, who spent his youth in the usual saintly apprenticeship of dissipation and battles. Upon having a vision of St Michael, he renounced the life of a knight and embarked on a career as a hermit. His conviction was fortified by a kind of reversed sword-in-the-stone miracle when, during a visit from his family and fellow knights (who tried to persuade him to return to the world), he ran his sword into a rock beside his hut: it stuck fast, forming a crucifix. In 1181, at the age of 33, Galgano died, and within four years had been canonized.

8

ACCOMMODATION AND EATING

Albergo Il Palazzetto ☎ 0577 751 160, ⓦ sangalgano .org/albergopalazzetto/home.htm. Simple but spacious and clean rooms in a modern building in the village of Palazzetto, 4km south of the abbey on the Massa road; the hotel also has a good, inexpensive restaurant/pizzeria. Restaurant Mon & Thurs–Sun 12.20–2.30pm & 7.15–10.30pm. €65

Bagni di Petriolo

From San Galgano, you can cut to the N223 Siena–Grosseto road by means of a minor road that leaves the N73 at the walled village of Monticiano. The road east of Monticiano is attractive if unremarkable, twisting through wooded hills before emerging on the N223 20km south of Siena.

South from here, the N223 follows the River Merse before rearing into the hills by way of various viaducts. To reach the spa of **BAGNI DI PETRIOLO** you need to turn right after about 4km, then follow this road for 9km to a bridge beside the River Farma and a rough enclosure of huge medieval walls. Just below the bridge on the left, the spa's **sulphur springs** continue to flow freely into little rock pools before mixing with the river. If you're going for a soak, leave your clothes well away from the sulphur, and wash off afterwards with a dip in the river.

The Murlo villages

With transport, you can follow a paved track off the Petriolo road, through the hills to **CASCIANO DI MURLO**. Scarcely more than a hamlet, Casciano is a fine place to break your journey, or base yourself for a few days. East of Casciano, a high and beautiful road leads into the *crete*, with hills punctuated by the occasional lake and farmhouse on the approach to **VESCOVADO DI MURLO**, a largely modern village. A couple of kilometres south of Vescovado is **MURLO** – a tiny medieval *borgo* whose ring of houses forms defensive walls, enclosing the town hall and church.

Antiquarium di Poggio Civitate

Piazza della Cattedrale • April, May & June–Sept Tues–Sun 10am–1pm & 3–7pm; July & Aug Daily 10am–7pm; March & Oct Tues–Sun 10am–1pm & 3–5pm; Nov–Feb Tues–Fri 10am–1pm, Sat & Sun 10am–1pm & 3–6pm • €3.50 • ⓦ www.comune.murlo.si.it or ⓦ prolocomurlo.com

Murlo's Etruscan past is commemorated in the local museum, the **Antiquarium di Poggio Civitate**, housed in the Castello di Murlo. Exhibits include sphinx statues, a large terracotta tomb frieze depicting hunting scenes and some odd bowls, decorated with warriors holding women whose legs form the handles.

ACCOMMODATION   **THE MURLO VILLAGES**

Albergo di Murlo Via Martiri di Rigosecco 1–3, Vescovado ☎ 0577 814 033, ⓦ albergodimurlo.com. A convenient but bland, modern three-star hotel with spotless, if distinctly uncosy rooms; the swimming pool is a bonus, however. €75

Borgo Antico Via di Lucignano 45 ☎ 0577 374 688, ⓦ hotelborgoantico.com. This 24-room three-star in the medieval hamlet of Lucignano d'Arbia, 9km northeast of Vescovado, has the most characterful rooms in the area. €90

Le Soline Casafranci ☎ 0577 817 410, ⓦ lesoline.it. large, year-round campsite close to Casciano di Murlo, with a pretty semi-wooded setting and the bonus of a large pool with views over the hills. Adults €8, small tents €5

Palazzina Strada Provinciale di Murlo ☎ 334 817 0333, ⓦ lapalazzina.com. An eighteenth-century farmhouse, in a rural setting between Casciano and Vescovado, that has been converted into seven apartments, with shared swimming pool. Daily €90, weekly from €450

Monte Oliveto and the central crete

The heartland of the *crete* is the area southeast of Siena, around the superb Benedictine monastery of **Monte Oliveto Maggiore**. The region embraces some classic Tuscan countryside, studded with lonely cypresses on sun-baked clay hills. The abbey is reached easily enough by car via **Asciano** or **Buonconvento**, 9km distant to the north and west, respectively.

Buonconvento

BUONCONVENTO is the obvious base if you are visiting Monte Oliveto Maggiore and travelling on south. The small town looks industrial as you approach, but once through the suburbs you come upon a perfect, walled medieval village; in its day, this was one of Siena's key outer defences.

Museo d'Arte Sacra della Val d'Arbia

Via Soccini 18 • Mid-March to mid-Oct Tues–Sun 10am–1pm & 3–7pm; mid-Oct to mid-March Sat & Sun 10am–1pm & 2.30–6pm • €3.50 • ⓦ museoartesacra.it

Buonconvento's old centre is characteristically Sienese, with its brick bastions, town hall and works of art, most of which have been removed from local churches to the excellent **Museo d'Arte Sacra della Val d'Arbia**. Pride of place here goes to a small *Madonna and Child with Angels* by Matteo di Giovanni; other notable works include a *Madonna and Child* attributed to Duccio; a *Madonna and Saints* (1470–82) and *Coronation of the Virgin* by Sano di Pietro; a lovely four-panelled *Annunciation* (1397) by Andrea di Bartolo; and the curious *Madonna del Latte* by Luca di Tommè showing a breast-feeding *Madonna*. The *Annunciation* (1490–1500) by Benvenuto di Giovanni is a Florentine-influenced work that strikes an anomalous note among the surrounding Sienese treasures.

Museo della Mezzadria

Via Tinaia del Taja • Tues, Thurs, Sat & Sun 10am–1pm & 3–6pm; Wed & Fri 10am–1pm • €3.50 • ⓦ museomezzadria.it

The **Museo della Mezzadria** has varied and fascinating displays devoted to the region's rural and social history. It occupies a superb brick-vaulted space, a late medieval granary built in and around part of the town's old walls. Numerous original objects and artefacts document an almost-vanished agrarian world, and one in which most Tuscan families would have lived virtually unchanged for generations until about fifty years ago. The second floor contains part of a reconstructed *casa colonica*, the classic rural Tuscan farmhouse, offering a vivid glimpse into the life and living conditions of Tuscan peasant farmers.

8

ARRIVAL AND INFORMATION · BUONCONVENTO

By train Buonconvento's station is a short walk from the old centre, on the southeast edge of town.
Destinations Grosseto (10 daily; 1hr) and Siena (10 daily; 30min).

By bus Coming from Siena and the north, buses stop after crossing the bridge, just beyond Via dei Macelli; there's also a stop just past the railway station.

Destinations Abbadia San Salvatore (5 daily; 1hr 10min); Montalcino (9 daily; 20min); Montepulciano (7 daily; 1hr); Pienza (7 daily; 35min); Siena (6 daily; 40min); Torrenieri (6 daily; 25min).

Tourist office Piazzale Garibaldi 1 (April–Sept Tues–Sun 10am–1pm & 3–6pm; Oct–March Tues–Fri 10am–1pm, Sat & Sun 10am–1pm & 3–6pm; ☏ 0577 807 181).

ACCOMMODATION AND EATING

Da Mario Via Soccini 61 ☏ 0577 806 157, ⓦ www ristorantemario.it. A perfect family-run trattoria of the old school, with an unfussy, beamed dining room (plus outside tables in good weather) and straightforward Tuscan cooking; reckon on €25 or less for a filling meal. Mon–Fri & Sun 12.30–2.30pm & 7.30–10.30pm.

Ghibellino Via Dante Alighieri 1 ☏ 0577 809 112, ⓦ www.hotelghibellino.it. A decent, well-presented three-star with 23 spacious, modern rooms that are comfortable if rather sparsely decorated and furnished. **€86**
Pieve a Salti Pieve a Salti ☏ 0577 807 244, ⓦ www .pieveasalti.it. Up in the hills, just 4km east of town (signed from Buonconvento), this agriturismo is comfortable and welcoming, and the swimming pool has views over what seems like half of southern Tuscany. You can rent rooms for the night, or simple self-contained

apartments (prices vary) in the rustic houses dotted across the estate. Meals are available in the cosy central house. Doubles from €104
Roma Via Soccini 14 ☎ 0577 806 021, ☎ 0577 807 284. A

simple but recently renovated two-star with an inexpensive restaurant next door, much patronized by locals, the represents a perfect piece of old-fashioned 1950s Italian. Restaurant daily noon–2pm & 7–9pm. €60

Abbazia di Monte Oliveto Maggiore

Daily: summer 9.15am–noon & 3.15–6pm; winter 9.15am–noon & 3.15–5pm• Free • ⓦ monteolivetomaggiore.it

The **Abbazia di Monte Oliveto Maggiore**, 26km southeast of Siena, is sited in one of the most beautiful tracts of Sienese countryside. Approaching from Buonconvento, you climb through forests of pine, oak and cypress, and then into the olive groves that enclose the monastery. From the east, coming through Asciano or San Giovanni d'Asso, the road passes through the wildest section of the *crete*. It all appears much as it would have to Pope Pius II, who in 1459 praised the woods and gardens the monks had created from the hills, and the way the russet-coloured brick buildings merged with their setting. Also preserved here is one of the most absorbing Renaissance fresco cycles that you'll find anywhere, a *Life of St Benedict* by Sodoma and Luca Signorelli.

Brief history

Monte Oliveto Maggiore was founded around 1300 by Giovanni Tolomei, a Sienese noble, who renounced all worldly goods after being struck blind and experiencing visions of the Virgin. Adopting the name Bernardo, he came with two companions to the *crete* and lived the life of a hermit. The trio soon drew a following, and within six years the pope recognized them as an order – the **Olivetans**, or White Benedictines.

Attempting to recapture the simplicity of the original Benedictine rule, these first Olivetans were a remarkable group, going out in pairs during the Black Death to nurse the sick and minister to the dying in the Sienese towns. After months of perilous work Bernardo died in 1348, as did many of the brothers.

The remaining monks rebuilt the order, and over the following two centuries Monte Oliveto was transformed into one of Italy's most powerful monasteries. It only fell from influence with the nineteenth-century suppression of the Italian orders, and after the last war, the Italian government allowed Olivetan monks to repopulate it. They have largely **restored** the buildings and gardens, which they continue to maintain as a monument, supplementing their income with a shop and a workshop restoring ancient books.

The abbey

From the **gateway**, surmounted by a square watchtower and niches containing della Robbia terracottas, an avenue of cypresses leads to the abbey. Off to the right, signs direct you along a walk to the **Blessed Bernardo's grotto** – a chapel built on the site where Tolomei settled as a hermit.

The **abbey** complex is huge, though much remains off limits to visitors. The entrance leads to the **Chiostro Grande**, covered by frescoes of the *Life of St Benedict*, the man traditionally regarded as the founder of Christian monasticism. The cycle was begun by **Luca Signorelli**, a painter from Cortona who trained under Piero della Francesca before working for the papacy on the Sistine Chapel. He worked at Monte Oliveto in 1497, completing nine panels (in the middle of the series) before abandoning the work for a more stimulating commission at Orvieto Cathedral. Like much of his work elsewhere, the scenes show a passionate interest in human anatomy, with figures positioned to show off their muscularity to maximum effect.

Sodoma's frescoes

A few years after Signorelli's departure, Antonio Bazzi (known as **Il Sodoma**), took over painting the remaining 27 scenes between 1505 and 1508. Sodoma was from Milan and familiar with Leonardo's work, which he often emulated. How he took his nickname is unclear: Vasari suggests it was apt since "he was always surrounded by young men, in whose company he took great pleasure", though letters by Sodoma himself speak of three wives and thirty children. Whatever, the artist was a colourful figure, keeping an extraordinary menagerie of pets: "Badgers, apes, cat-a-mountains, dwarf asses, horses and barbs to run races, magpies, dwarf chickens, tortoises, Indian doves…".

Sodoma brought a sizeable contingent of these pets to Monte Oliveto, including a raven that imitated his voice, and they make odd appearances throughout his colourful, sensual frescoes – a badger is depicted at his feet in a self-portrait in the third panel. There's a notable eroticism, too, in many of the secular figures: the young men coming to join Benedict as monks, and the "evil women", seen tempting the monks in a panel towards the end of the series – these were originally nudes, before protests from the abbot.

The **cycle** begins on the east wall, on the right of the door into the church. St Benedict, who was born in Norcia in 480, is shown in the early panels leaving home to study in Rome, before withdrawing to the life of a hermit, where he experiences various tribulations and temptations before agreeing to become abbot to a group of disciples. He was an indefatigable builder of monasteries, and the next panels focus on this activity: the foundation of the twelve houses, which formed the basis of the Benedictine order, as well as depictions of various miracles to help in their construction.

The mid-sequence of the **Life of St Benedict** cycle depicts various attempts by an evil priest, Florentius, to disrupt the saint's work: he tries first to poison Benedict and then sends in the temptresses, before God steps in and flattens his house (the first of Signorelli's panels). The following eight scenes painted by Signorelli depict aspects of monastic life, and Benedict's trial by – and reception of – Totila, king of the Goths, before Sodoma takes over again, with the saint foretelling the destruction of Monte Cassino, the chief Benedictine house, by the Lombards. More scenes of monastic life follow, including the burial of a monk whom the earth would not accept, another monk's attempted escape (Benedict intercepts him with a serpent) and the release of a peasant persecuted by a Goth.

The rest of the monastery

Everything else in the monastery is inevitably overshadowed by the frescoes. The main **church** – entered off the Chiostro Grande – was given a Baroque remodelling in the eighteenth century and some superb stained glass in the twentieth. Its main treasures are the **choir stalls**, inlaid by Giovanni di Verona and others, from 1500 to 1520, with architectural, landscape and domestic scenes (including a nod to Sodoma's pets with a depiction of a cat in a window).

Back in the cloister, stairs lead up, past a Sodoma fresco of the Virgin, to the **library**, a fine Renaissance arcade lavished with carvings by Giovanni and associates. Sadly, it usually has had to be viewed from the door since the theft of sixteen codices in 1975. Also on view is the **refectory**, a vast room frescoed with allegorical and Old Testament figures, which gives some idea of Monte Oliveto's heyday.

Asciano

ASCIANO, 9km north of Monte Oliveto, lies on a tiny branch rail line between Siena and Grosseto that takes you through marvellous *crete* countryside. The road approach, the N438 from Siena, is still more scenic, with scarcely a hamlet amid the hills. Of Etruscan foundation, Asciano is first mentioned in records in 715. In 1169 it passed to Siena, which promptly ordered the destruction of the town's fortress, though the town remains partially walled. Its most famous son is Domenico di Bartolo (1400–45), the painter responsible for the fresco cycle in Siena's Santa Maria della Scala.

Museo Civico Archeologico e d'Arte Sacra

Palazzo Corboli, Corso Matteotti 120 • March–Oct Tues–Sun 10.30am–1pm & 3–6.30pm; Nov–Feb Fri–Sun 10.30am–1pm & 3–5.30pm • €4.50

Like the museum in Buonconvento, the **Museo Civico Archeologico e d'Arte Sacra** contains an unexpected wealth of Sienese paintings and an Etruscan collection. It has a dozen or so works by major Sienese painters, including Ambrogio Lorenzetti, Sano di Pietro, Taddeo di Bartolo and Matteo di Giovanni.

ARRIVAL AND INFORMATION

By train Asciano's station is just under a kilometre east of the old centre, off the road to Rapolano Terme.
Destinations Siena (hourly; 30min) and Sinalunga (hourly; 50min).

Tourist office Via delle Fonti (April–Oct Tues, Fri & Sat 10.30am–1pm & 3–6pm; Wed, Thurs & Sun 10am–1pm; rest of the year Sat & Sun 10am–1pm; ☎ 0577 718 811).

ACCOMMODATION, EATING AND DRINKING

Il Bersagliere Via Roma 39–41 ☎ 0577 718 715, ⓦ hotellapace.net. A reasonably priced hotel with rooms that are spick and span, but which don't look as if they, or their fittings, have been upgraded since the place opened in 1989. The slightly grander three-star sister hotel, *La Pace* is about 30m away. **€59–88**

La Pievina La Pievina ☎ 0577 718 368, ⓦ www .osterialapievina.com. The best restaurant in the vicinity is the moderately priced *La Pievina*, 5.5km north along the Siena road at the hamlet of the same name. Wed–Sun 12.20–2.30pm & 7.30–10.30pm.

8

San Giovanni d'Asso

SAN GIOVANNI D'ASSO is a quiet, rustic place, whose medieval past is hinted at by the presence of half a dozen churches. Romanesque San Pietro, an eleventh-century gem, is the most interesting, and there's an imposing, if extremely blunt thirteenth-century **castle**. Only ever a Sienese fiefdom, the fortress was inhabited at various times by the Buonsignori, whose Sienese palace now houses the city's Pinacoteca, and by the Salimbeni, whose dynastic seat in the city is now the headquarters of the Monte dei Paschi bank. Later it became a granary, and in time was given to Siena's Santa Maria della Scala.

Museo del Tartufo

Piazza Gramsci 1 • Hours change monthly, for updates check online or call ☎ 0577 803 268 • €3 • ⓦ museodeltartufo.it

San Giovanni is in truffle country, and has a museum devoted to the tuber (the first in Italy), the **Museo del Tartufo**, housed in part of the castle. As well as insights into truffles, the museum also offers the chance to admire some of the castle's austere but, in parts, prettily frescoed chambers.

Trequanda

East from San Giovanni, a fine road meanders towards Sinalunga. The attraction here is primarily the landscape – classic Tuscan miniatures – though the road is marked out by a series of hill-top villages, most of them endowed with a castle and a smattering of medieval churches. **TREQUANDA**, a slightly larger village with a couple of restaurants and bars, also preserves a good section of its castle. In the central square, the simple Romanesque parish church of **Sts Pietro e Andrea**, fronted by a brown-and-white chequered stone facade, has a fresco by Sodoma of the *Transfiguration*, and a high altarpiece of the *Madonna and Saints* by Giovanni di Paolo. The inlaid wooden urn contains the body of Bonizella Piccolomini (1235–1300), a beatific who never reached the heights of more illustrious family descendants such as Aeneas Piccolomini (Pope Pius II).

Sinalunga

East of Trequanda you reach **SINALUNGA**, a modern centre with rail connections to Siena, Arezzo and Chiusi. It has one notable painting – an *Annunciation* by Benvenuto di Giovanni – in the church of **San Francesco**, sited beside the Franciscan convent at the top of an avenue of cypresses.

Montalcino

MONTALCINO, 37km south of Siena, is a classic Tuscan hill-town, approached through bucolic swathes of vineyards and pretty pastoral countryside: views to all

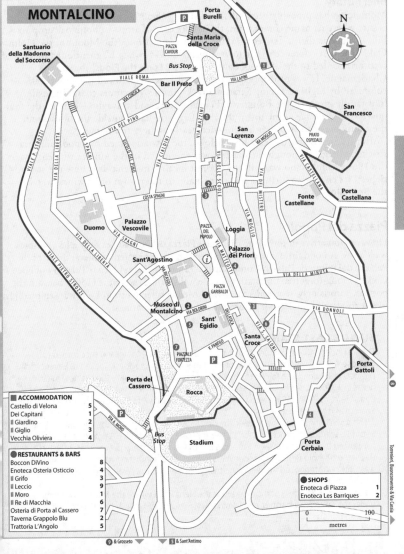

MONTALCINO

N

Santuario della Madonna del Soccorso

Porta Burelli

PIAZZA CAVOUR

Santa Maria della Croce

VIALE ROMA

Bus Stop

Bar Il Prato

VIA LAPINI

VIA CONSICA

VIA DEL PINO

VICOLO DEL PINO

VIA SPAGNI

VIA CIALDINI

VIA MAZZINI

San Lorenzo

VIA MIGLIO

San Francesco

PRATO OSPEDALE

VIA CASTELLANA

COSTA SPAGNI

VIA DELLE SCUOLE

VIA DEL MISTERO

Fonte Castellane

Porta Castellana

VIALE DELLA LIBERTA

Duomo

Palazzo Vescovile

VIA SPAGNI

PIAZZA DEL POPOLO

Loggia

VIA MATTEOTTI

VIA MIGLIO

VIALE PIETRO STROZZI

VIALE F. STROZZI

VIA DELLA LIBERTA

Sant'Agostino

VIA RICASOLI

Palazzo dei Priori

VIA DELLA MINUTA

PIAZZA GARIBALDI

Museo di Montalcino

VIA BOLDRINI

Sant' Egidio

VIA DI LUCA

VIA DONNOLI

VIA S. SALONI

PIAZZALE FORTEZZA

Santa Croce

V. PANFILO

Porta Gattoli

Porta del Cassero

Rocca

VIA MORO

Porta Cerbaia

Bus Stop

Stadium

0   100
metres

Tornieri, Buonconvento & Via Cassia

9 & Grosseto   5 & Sant'Antimo

■ ACCOMMODATION

Castello di Velona	5
Dei Capitani	1
Il Giardino	2
Il Giglio	3
Vecchia Oliviera	4

● RESTAURANTS & BARS

Boccon DiVino	8
Enoteca Osteria Osticcio	4
Il Grifo	3
Il Leccio	9
Il Moro	1
Il Re di Macchia	6
Osteria di Porta al Cassero	7
Taverna Grappolo Blu	2
Trattoria L'Angolo	5

● SHOPS

| Enoteca di Piazza | 1 |
| Enoteca Les Barriques | 2 |

8

sides are stupendous. Perched 567m above sea level, it's set within a full circuit of walls, and watched over by a castle of almost fairytale perfection. A quiet, immediately likeable place, affluent in an unshowy way, it has scarcely changed in appearance since the sixteenth century. It looks wonderful from below, its walls barely sullied by any modern building; once up in the town, you find yourself on a road that rings the walls, and the rolling hills, vineyards, orchards, olive groves and ancient oaks look equally lovely in turn. Montalcino makes an excellent base for much of southern Tuscany, lying within easy striking distance of the abbeys of Monte Oliveto and Sant'Antimo, and close to the towns of Pienza, 20km east, and Montepulciano, 11km further.

Brief history

Montalcino has probably been inhabited since **Paleolithic** or **Etruscan** times. No one is sure where its name comes from, though its coat of arms – a holm oak atop six hills – suggests that it derives from the Latin *Mons Ilcinus* (the Mount of the Holm Oak). The first reference to the town appears in 814, when it's mentioned in a list of territories ceded to the abbey of Sant'Antimo by **Louis the Pious**, the son of Charlemagne. It was probably only permanently settled around the year 1000, colonized by fugitives fleeing Saracen attacks on the Maremma coast. The exiles' four family groups – the Borghetto, Pianello, Ruca and Travaglio – defined the four quarters or *contrade* of the town: the rival flags still hang outside the houses and they compete against each other in twice-yearly archery tournaments.

After its Sienese heyday (see box, below), the town declined to a poor, malaria-stricken village. Although the malaria was eradicated in the nineteenth century, in the 1960s Montalcino was still the poorest locality in Siena. It is now the second-richest, its change in fortunes due principally to the revival of its wines, notably the **Brunello**.

Piazza del Popolo

However you arrive in town, the triangular **Piazza del Popolo** lies only a few minutes' walk away. An odd little square, it is set beneath the elongated medieval tower of the **Palazzo dei Priori**, or Palazzo Comunale (1292), modelled on Siena's Palazzo Pubblico. Crests of long-forgotten dignitaries dot the walls, while the statue (1564) beneath the portico, surprisingly, represents the reviled Medici ruler, Cosimo I – it was sculpted just five years after Montalcino had surrendered to the Florentines.

> ### SIENA'S LAST STAND
>
> Though independent for much of its early medieval history, Montalcino succumbed to **Sienese** rule in 1260 after the Battle of Montaperti, having previously looked to Florence for protection. Having been forced to change sides, the town eventually took its new rulers to heart. In 1526 it took just two days for its citizens to fight off a besieging army dispatched by Pope Clement VII. In 1553, over a period of four months, it withstood the attack of a combined Spanish and Medici army.
>
> The town's finest hour, however, came in 1555, when on April 21 the venerable Sienese Republic was forced, once and for all, to capitulate to the Medici. A group of Sienese exiles, supported by the French, then formed a last bastion of Sienese power in Montalcino, flying the flag of the old Republic for four years in the face of almost constant attack. Surrender was only countenanced following the treaty of Cateau Cambrésis (1559) between France and Spain.
>
> This heroic interlude is acknowledged at the Siena Palio, where the Montalcino contingent, under their medieval **banner** proclaiming "The Republic of Siena in Montalcino", still takes place of honour.

The Rocca

April to last Sun in Oct daily 9am–8pm; Nov–March Tues–Sun 10am–6pm • Courtyard free, ramparts €4, or joint ticket with Museo di Montalcino €6

Following Via Matteotti, or the parallel Via Ricasoli, and curving up to the right, you emerge at the south end of town by the **Rocca**, or Fortezza. This was begun in 1361 on the orders of the Sienese, but by the end of the fifteenth century the advent of artillery had left the castle all but redundant – not that this discouraged those who defended it during the 1526, 1553 and 1555 sieges. The ramparts were added by Cosimo I in 1571, together with the large Medici crest (a shield with six balls), whose present peripheral position – tucked away at the back above the road junction – is surely no accident.

The view from the **ramparts** is said to have inspired Leonardo's drawing of a bird's-eye view of the earth; the Val d'Órcia is easily made out and on a clear day you can even see Siena.

Museo di Montalcino e Raccolta Archeologica Mediovale e Moderna

Via Ricasoli 31 • Tues–Sun 10am–1pm & 2–5.50pm • €4.50, or joint ticket with the Rocca ramparts €6

The excellent **Museo di Montalcino e Raccolta Archeologica Mediovale e Moderna** is set in the former seminary of Sant'Agostino. Like many galleries in the region, the quality of the paintings is out of all proportion to the size of the town. The collection begins with a superb *Crucifixion* dating from the end of the twelfth century – one of the oldest pieces of Sienese art in existence. An anonymous work, it was originally hung in the abbey at Sant'Antimo. A more mannered *Madonna and Child with Two Angels* comes soon after, a lovely anonymous late-thirteenth-century work. Bartolo di Fredi has two works on show: an oddly narrow *Deposition* and a more conventional *Coronation of the Virgin*. There's also a *Madonna and Child* by Bartolo's collaborator, Luca di Tommè.

Madonna dell'Umiltà

One of the gallery's most interesting works is the *Madonna dell Umiltà* (Madonna of Humility) by Sano di Pietro, a comparatively rare subject, in which the Virgin is shown sitting or kneeling on a simple cushion rather than poised on a throne or chair. Its appearance dates from the beginning of the fourteenth century, and coincided with the ideas promulgated by the more radical wing of the Franciscan order, which advocated a return to the more rigorous and humble outlook of the first Franciscans.

Girolamo di Benvenuto

Two paintings by Girolamo di Benvenuto (1470–1524) also merit a close look: an *Adoration of the Shepherds* (with ugly shepherd and fractious Child) and the more spectacular and unusual *Madonna della Cintola*. The latter concerns the Apostle Thomas, who according to legend cast doubt on the Assumption into Heaven of the Virgin (hence "doubting Thomas"). To assuage his worries he opened her tomb, which he found covered in flowers – beautifully depicted in this painting. Casting his eyes upwards, he then saw the Virgin, who removed her belt, or girdle (*cintola*), and let it fall into the hands of the kneeling Thomas. The subject was particularly popular in Tuscany – Agnolo Gaddi, for example, devoted an entire fresco cycle to the theme in Prato, which claims to have the girdle in question (see p.161).

Sculptures and the decorative arts

Among the gallery's **sculptures** and miscellaneous **decorative arts**, make a special point of looking for the pair of illuminated twelfth-century Bibles and the rare polychrome wooden statue *St Peter*, one of the few documented works of the sculptor Francesco di Valdambrino: it was commissioned in 1425 and given by Pius III to the town's Confraternity of St Peter. You'll also notice an almost comical *Annunciation*, an early fifteenth-century Umbro-Sienese work, in which the puppet-like Gabriel and the Virgin sport impossibly rosy cheeks and beautifully mannered hairstyles.

Sant'Agostino

Walking a few paces up Via Ricasoli from the museum brings you to the church of **Sant'Agostino**, a severe Gothic-Romanesque affair begun in 1360. The barn-like single nave is dotted with patches of fresco, the most extensive of which – and with a wide variety of themes – cover the arched presbytery, and are probably the work of Bartolo di Fredi. The most interesting pictures, however, are two anonymous panels of *Scenes from the Passion*. One, on the left wall, also shows St Anthony Abbot sharing bread with a curiously attired St Augustine; the second, to the right of the side entrance, is an extraordinary and almost surreal collection of disembodied heads and symbols.

The Duomo and Santuario della Madonna del Soccorso

Via Spagni

An eleventh-century Romanesque church, the **Duomo**, or San Salvatore, was horrendously remodelled in Neoclassical style between 1818 and 1832; its interior is unarresting, save for an impressive little pyramid of reliefs in the baptistery chapel salvaged from the original church.

Via Spagni continues to emerge in front of the distinctive Renaissance **Santuario della Madonna del Soccorso**, a seventeenth-century sanctuary built over an ancient chapel; its chief appeal is the sensational view from the adjoining park.

Santa Maria della Croce

Piazza Cavour

Viale Roma heads to **Santa Maria della Croce**, a hospital founded in the thirteenth century, more recently appropriated by the local council. Just inside the main entrance is the former pharmacy, still covered in a pretty little array of original frescoes.

San Francesco and around

Facing the Porta Castellana is a medieval washhouse, the **Fonte Castellane**, and beyond it on Prato Ospedale is the deconsecrated church of **San Francesco**, graced with pleasant cloisters, della Robbia school terracottas and an annexe that was once a medieval hospital.

SANT'ANGELO IN COLLE

There are plenty of easy day- and half-day trips from Montalcino, with one of the best being the tiny walled village of **SANT'ANGELO IN COLLE**, set on a low hill 9km southwest of the town (it can also be reached on a beautiful but partly gravel-surfaced road from Sant'Antimo). The Sienese used it as a military base against Montalcino in the mid-thirteenth century and as part of their frontier thereafter. It has some interesting frescoes inside the Romanesque church, **San Michele**, on the piazza (check out the lovely views from behind the church) and a couple of bar-restaurants.

ARRIVAL AND DEPARTURE

By train For rail connections to and from Siena or Grosseto, head to Buonconvento, Torrenieri or to Sant'Angelo. Most trains are slow, stopping services, but buried in the timetable are a couple of fast through trains daily to Florence (via Siena) and Grosseto (for connections to Rome and Pisa).

By bus Buses will stop just below the Rocca, but terminate in Piazza Cavour at the northern end of Via Mazzini, the main street: either point is convenient for Piazza del Popolo. TRA-IN buses (☎ 0577 204 111, ⍵ trainspa.it) run hourly from Piazza Cavour and Viale P. Strozzi to

MONTALCINO

Buonconvento (30min) and Siena (1hr 10min) via Torrenieri (20min). At Torrenieri you can pick up one of six daily buses to San Quírico, Pienza and Montepulciano. There are also four Bargagli buses (⍵ bargagliautolinee.it) daily from Montalcino to Sant'Angelo Scalo and one during the school term to Abbadia San Salvatore and Piancastagnaio via San Quírico and Castiglione d'Orcia. There's also a daily SIRA bus (⍵ italybus.it) to and from Rome.

By car If you're driving, aim to park in the large car park below the Rocca (take the second turning on the right at the mini-roundabout below the Rocca).

INFORMATION

Tourist office Costa del Municipio 8, just up from Piazza del Popolo (Tues–Sun 10am–1pm & 2–5.40pm;

☎ 0577 849 331, ⍵ prolocomontalcino.it).

ACCOMMODATION

Accommodation in town is limited and it's wise to book at almost any time of year, though if you have transport you could try one or two tempting places in the countryside nearby. The tourist office has lists of private rooms and agriturismi in and around town.

★ **Castello di Velona** Località Castello di Velona, Castelnuovo dell'Abate ☎ 0577 835 553, ⍵ castello divelona.it. Until 2001 this twelfth-century "castle" 10km south of Montalcino was little more than a pile of rubble: it's now a superb twenty-room five-star hotel, set in lovely open countryside on its own hill and ringed by cypresses. Expensive, but there are often web deals. Closed Nov–March. **€345**

Dei Capitani Via Lapini 6 ☎ 0577 847 227, ⍵ deicapitani.it. A good, slick three-star choice, with the bonus of a small swimming pool. The 29 rooms vary, however: some are smallish and have no view; others look out over marvellous countryside; ask to see a selection. Closed Dec–Jan. **€150**

Il Giardino Piazza Cavour 4 ☎ & 📠 0577 848 257. The

cheapest hotel option in town is cheap for a reason – its ten two-star rooms are pretty sparse, and those facing onto the piazza are likely to be a little noisy. **€70**

Il Giglio Via Soccorso Saloni 5 ☎ 0577 848 167, ⍵ gigliohotel.com. A long-established hotel in a central, sixteenth-century town house that offers pleasant, clean rooms, some with terraces. **€128**

Vecchia Oliviera Via Landi 1, Porta Cerbaia ☎ 0577 846 028, ⍵ vecchiaoliviera.com. Like *Dei Capitani*, this is a relatively new three-star hotel, but more expensive and not quite as central as its rival. However, its patio has excellent views, and the eleven fine rooms form part of a well-restored former olive mill close to Porta Cerbaia and the walls. Rooms, however, can suffer from noise from the road nearby. **€120–190**

EATING AND DRINKING

Montalcino is blessed with decent **restaurants**, but even some of the best places have off nights and uneven service in the face of huge numbers of visitors. In summer it's worth booking a table at just about any of the places below. Sampling and buying local **wines** is easily done in numerous shops and café-bars around town.

Boccon DiVino Via Traversi dei Monti 201, Località Colombaio Tozzi ☎ 0577 848 233, ⍵ boccon divinomontalcino.it. A kilometre east of town on the Torrenieri road, this is a great wine bar and restaurant with superb views and a lovely summer terrace. It's housed in an old rural property, and the dining rooms have a rustic air. Food, though, is quite refined – and expensive: reckon on €40 or so for a full meal. Mon & Wed–Sun 12.15–2.30pm & 7.30–10.30pm; closed part of Nov & Dec.

Enoteca di Piazza Piazza Garibaldi 2–4 ☎ 0577 849 194, ⍵ enotecadipiazza.com. Wines from over 150 local

producers. In addition to the classic Brunello and the more briefly barrel-aged Rosso di Montalcino table wine, it's worth trying some of the white Moscadelletto di Montalcino, a dessert wine. Daily 9am–8pm.

Enoteca Les Barriques Via Boldrini 19 ☎ 0577 846 046, ⍵ lesbarriques.com. Over 800 Tuscan wines, including the major Brunello and Rosso di Montalcino labels. Mon & Wed–Sun 9.30am–noon & 1–7.30pm; closed for a month from late Jan.

Enoteca Osteria Osticcio Via Matteotti 23 ☎ 0577 848 271, ⍵ osticcio.it. Among the smarter of Montalcino's many

8

VINEYARDS AROUND MONTALCINO

Brunello is one of Italy's premier wines, and it's worth visiting one of the **vineyards around Montalcino**. While some are detailed below, information on visits to the other estate can be availed at the winegrower's headquarters at Piazza Cavour 8 (☎ 0577 848 246, ✆ consorziobrunello dimontalcino.it); appointments can also be made via the Consorzio's (English-version) website.

Castello Banfi ☎ 0577 877 505, restaurant ☎ 0577 877 524, ✆ castellobanfi.com. The Castello Banfi is 18km southwest of Montalcino, just outside the village of Sant'Angelo Scalo. With a third of its 3000 hectares devoted to vineyards, it is Montalcino's largest and most modern producer; you can call or email to arrange tastings and estate visits. The on-site *Enoteca & Balsameria* is a shop and wine bar offering bread, cheeses and salami plus local food and other artisan products, while the large and medieval but slightly soulless *La Taverna* restaurant serves good-quality local cuisine, with a la carte options and a choice of three tasting menus (booking essential; from around €35 for a three-course meal). Enoteca daily 10am–7.30pm (closes 6pm Nov–

Feb), restaurant Tues–Sat 7.30–10pm.

Fattoria dei Barbi Località Podernovi ☎ 0577 841 111, restaurant ☎ 0577 841 200, ✆ fattoriadeibarbi .it. The Fattoria dei Barbi lies 7km southeast of Montalcino, signposted left just after the hamlet of La Croce on the Sant'Antimo road. Its cantina offers free tastings and a superb stock of vintages, and there's a fine restaurant, the *Taverna dei Barbi*, with outdoor summer dining and local recipes at moderate prices – lots of *porcini, pici, papardelle* and delicious grilled pork, the *brasato al Brunello*. Cantina Mon–Fri 10am–1pm & 2.30–6pm, Sat & Sun 2.30–6pm; open until 7pm in summer; restaurant daily 12.30–2.30pm & 7.30–10pm.

wine bars, but worth paying a little over the odds for your glass of Brunello and light meal (pastas cost from €9) simply to enjoy the spectacular views over the Tuscan countryside. Mon–Sat noon–2.30pm & 7.30–10.30pm.

Il Grifo Via Mazzini 18 ☎ 0577 847 070, ✆ ilgrifo.com. Attentive service and a pleasant – if plain and slightly cramped – beamed interior, with lovely views from the rear. The menu offers a choice between mid-priced, basic Tuscan pastas and other dishes or large, well-made pizzas. Tues–Sun 12.30–2.30pm & 7.30–10.30pm.

Il Leccio Via Costa Castellare 1, Sant'Angelo in Colle ☎ 0577 844 175, ✆ illeccio.net. Fine food at decent prices, welcoming service and a romantic medieval setting (plus tables on the square in summer) have put this place on the map. There are signs that it can't quite cope with its new-found popularity, but on a quiet day it retains its charm. Mon, Tues & Thurs–Sun 12.30–2.30pm & 7.30–10pm.

Il Moro Via Mazzini 44 ☎ 0577 849 384. Don't expect frills or fancy cooking in this usually reliable and no-nonsense modern trattoria offering low-budget meals. Mon–Wed & Fri–Sun 12.30–2.30pm & 7.30–10.30pm.

Il Re di Macchia Via Soccorso Saloni 21 ☎ 0577 846

116. Montalcino's swankiest restaurant. While the food is usually excellent, its sometimes pretentious *cucina nuova* leanings may not be to all tastes. Mon–Wed & Fri–Sun 12.30–2.30pm & 7.30–10.30pm.

Osteria di Porta al Cassero Via della Libertà 9 ☎ 0577 847 196. A long-established family-run osteria of the old school, nicely situated in part of the Rocca's former stables. A simple setting, with old marble tables and period photographs on the walls, and robust peasant Tuscan food on the plates: the *polpette di carne e patate* (meatballs) are excellent. Around €20 a head for a main meal. Thurs–Sun noon–2.30pm & 7–9.30pm; closed part of Nov & Jan.

Taverna Grappolo Blu Via Scale di Moglio 1 ☎ 0577 847 150. Located in a little alley off Via Mazzini. The old stone-walled interior is cool and appealing, the service amenable and the sometimes unusual pastas are excellent. Daily 12.15–2.30pm & 7.30–10.30pm.

Trattoria L'Angolo Via Ricasoli 9 ☎ 0577 848 017. Informal and vaguely trendy little bar-trattoria just down from the Rocca, serving snack lunches and local pasta dishes. Around €20, but service and food can be uneven. Mon & Wed–Sun 12.30–2.30pm & 7.30–10.30pm.

Abbazia di Sant'Antimo

Mon–Sat 10.15am–12.30pm & 3–6.30pm, Sun 9.15–10.45am & 3–5pm • Free • ✆ antimo.it

It's a moot point which of Tuscany's many abbeys is the most beautiful, has the most fascinating history, or boasts the loveliest setting, but many would put the **Abbazia di Sant'Antimo** near the top of their list. It's a glorious, isolated Benedictine monastery that stands comparison with the nearby foundations of San Galgano, Monte Oliveto and San Salvatore.

Located a short distance from the hamlet of Castelnuovo dell'Abate, 10km south of Montalcino, and splendidly isolated in a timeless landscape of fields, olive groves and wooded hills, the abbey stood empty for some five hundred years, and is today maintained by a small group of French monks – a Cistercian offshoot known as the Premonstratensians.

Brief history

Tradition ascribes the foundation of the abbey to **Charlemagne**, who, while returning with his army from Rome in 781, halted in the nearby Starcia valley. Here he prayed to God, asking for relief from the disease which was crippling his troops, and offering to found a church if his prayers were answered. An angel appeared, showing the emperor a herb which he was instructed to give to his men with wine. The cure worked as promised, and Charlemagne duly founded Sant'Antimo.

If this story sounds too good to be true, it is known that the abbey existed in 814, when Charlemagne's son, **Louis the Pious**, enriched it with vast tracts of land and privileges in a charter dated December 29 of that year. Other scholars suggest it may have been founded on the site of a Roman villa, or possibly by the last of the area's Lombards in about 760, the date of the foundation of the Abbadia di San Salvatore (see p.355). In fact **St Antimo** (feast day May 11) was probably a bishop martyred in Rome during the persecutions of Diocletian and Maximian (AD 304–5). Certainly it's known that in 781, the year of the abbey's supposed foundation, Charlemagne gave St Antimo's relics, along with those of St Sebastian, to Pope Hadrian I.

The pre-Romanesque abbey

8

Whatever Sant'Antimo's origins, the **pre-Romanesque** style of parts of the primitive church, together with documentary evidence, confirm a late eighth- or early ninth-century foundation. Over the two centuries that followed, the abbey's importance grew, thanks in part to its location close to the intersection of several of central Italy's most important medieval **trade and pilgrimage routes**. Oldest of these was a former Etruscan road linking Chiusi with Rusellae on the coast, a route that passed directly in front of the abbey (traces of the sunken lane can still be seen). This was crossed by the old Roman consular road, Via Clodia, again right in front of the abbey. The most important of the ancient roads, however, was the **Via Francigena**, which for centuries was the most important pilgrimage route between Rome and northern Europe.

The abbey's rise and fall

Sant'Antimo's heyday dates from 1118, when an enormous **bequest** allowed work to begin on the main body of the present church and a complex of monastic buildings (now largely lost). The grant's deed – a document many hundreds of words long – was engraved in the steps of the altar, where it survives to this day. With new funds, the abbey authorities had access to expertise and ideas from elsewhere in Europe, and looked for inspiration to the great Benedictine mother house at Cluny, in Burgundy, and to **French architects**, whose plans for the new church appear to have been based on the abbey church of Vignory (begun in 1050) in the Haute-Marne.

Over the years funds began to run low – hence the unfinished facade – as religious bequests increasingly found their way to new orders such as the Camaldolese and Cistercians. By 1293 it retained only a fifth of its original possessions, which had once made it the second richest abbey in Tuscany. **Financial problems** were soon followed by moral and spiritual decline.

The abbey soldiered on under the auspices of the bishops of Siena and the newly created diocese of Montalcino, but after 1492 – when Montalcino's bishops opted to live instead in the town – it was largely **abandoned**, its buildings ransacked for stone for use in Castelnuovo and Montalcino. What remained was bought by the state in 1867.

The church

The monks' quarters aside, little remains of the plundered monastic buildings. The twelfth-century **church**, however, is in excellent repair and is one of the most outstanding examples of Italian Romanesque.

The **facade** was the last part of the church to be built, and so suffered most from the shortfall of funds. The traces of arches in the stones, and the pilasters with attached columns, suggest that a portico once provided a grander entrance: the lions that supported the portico, and symbolized the power of Satan waiting to devour the faithful, are now inside the abbey.

Recent studies suggest the portal on the church of Santa Maria in nearby San Quírico d'Órcia was one of two intended for Sant'Antimo, and was perhaps given away in the light of its subsequent decline. The surviving **portal** contains a twelfth-century lintel plus capitals, frieze and recessed, fluted arch all lifted directly from French (Languedoc) models. Around the corner, on the left (north) wall, the little filled-in doorway and lintels survive from the earlier ninth-century church.

The high altar

The French flavour becomes more marked in the lovely **interior**, whose basilican plan – with an ambulatory, and radiating chapels – is unique in Tuscany, and found elsewhere in Italy in only a handful of churches. Its presence allowed pilgrims to walk around the apse and pray before the martyrium, the spot under the high altar that contained the relics of the saint. The **high altar** features a polychrome statue of the crucified Christ, an outstanding Romanesque work dating from the end of the twelfth century. Note the inscription on the altar steps (see above).

The capitals

The **capitals** on the pillars of the ambulatory display some exquisite carving, a feature for which the abbey is particularly celebrated. Many are carved in lustrous alabaster, a stone that features elsewhere in the building, lending a beautifully subtle tone to the walls and sculpture. Here the carving is more Lombard than French, leading to the theory that two separate workshops – one from France (the Auvergne) and one from Lombardy (Pavia) may have worked alongside one another. Equally plausible is the idea that many of the capitals derive from the earlier Carolingian church, built before the French-inspired church of 1118.

The abbey's finest capital sits atop the second column on the right of the nave. It depicts *Daniel in the Lions' Den*, the protagonist – arms raised in prayer – a study of calm while his fellow prisoners are crushed and eaten by rampant beasts. It is the work of the **Master of Cabestany**, a sculptor of French or Spanish origin whose distinctive hand has been identified in abbeys across France, Catalonia and Italy – he seems always to have worked for the Benedictines. By way of comparison, study the capital on the second column on the left, which depicts a shepherd and sheep in a far more mundane style.

The rest of the church

The rest of the church is often closed to visitors. Areas affected include the **sacristy**, which occupies part of the ninth-century Carolingian church, entered (when open) from a door in the right aisle. It features an array of primitive black-and-white frescoes with such details as a rat looking up attentively at St Benedict, and a pair of copulating pigs. Note the stoup with Pius's Piccolomini crest at each corner. Further frescoes are to be found in some of the rooms built around the **women's gallery**, fitted out in the fifteenth century by the bishops of Montalcino: it's approached from the nave by a circular stairway, though here, too, access is often restricted.

The Val d'Órcia

The **Val d'Órcia** stretches from San Quírico d'Órcia down towards the border with Lazio and the lake of Bolsena. A gorgeous stretch of country, it is marked at intervals by fortresses built from the eighth century on, when the road through the valley, the **Via Francigena**, was a vital corridor north from Rome.

The first major attraction is the remarkable Medicean sulphur baths of **Bagno Vignoni**. With transport you might strike south from here to the region's medieval power base, the monastery of San Salvatore (see p.355), being sure to detour to the superbly situated **Radicofani**.

San Quírico d'Órcia

A rambling, part-walled village, **SAN QUÍRICO D'ÓRCIA** is a quiet and appealing place. An odd mix of modern and medieval, it's overlooked by the precarious ruins of a seventeenth-century palazzo, whose Baroque exterior frescoes are fading before your eyes. Its name comes from San Quírico a Osenna, an ancient church on the Via Francigena, though of the eponymous saint little is known except that he was martyred, probably in the fourth century. Hospitals and hospices sprang up here to accommodate pilgrims in the early Middle Ages, as they did in Siena and other settlements along the Via Francigena.

The Collegiata

Via delle Carbonaie 1 • Mon–Sat 8am–noon & 4–7pm

The main reason for stopping in the town is to look around the exceptionally pretty Romanesque **Collegiata**, with its three portals sculpted with lions and other beasts; the south door may be the work of Giovanni Pisano (or his school), while the main portal is rightly considered the finest piece of Lombard work in the region. The church was built in the twelfth century, probably on the ruins of a still older church. Inside is a delicate triptych of the *Virgin and Saints* by Sano di Pietro in the north transept, as well as a marvellous set of nine Renaissance choir stalls, whose figures and *trompe l'oeil* may have been executed to designs by Luca Signorelli. The stalls originally formed part of a larger nineteen-stall set in the Cappella del Battistero in Siena cathedral.

8

ARRIVAL AND INFORMATION

By bus TRA-IN inter-town buses drop on the Via Cassia on the east side of the village.
Destinations Montepulciano (7 daily; 30min); Pienza (7 daily; 10min); Siena (5 daily; 1hr 10min); Torrenieri (7 daily; 15min).

Tourist office Piazza Chigi 2, within the Comune building (Mon–Fri 10am–1pm & 3–6pm, Sat 10am–1pm; ☎ 0577 897 211, ⓦ www.comunesanquirico.it).

ACCOMMODATION

Castello Ripa d'Órcia Ripa d'Órcia ☎ 0577 897 376, ⓦ castelloripadorcia.com. This stunning hotel, about 5km southwest of San Quírico at the end of a minor but perfectly passable gravelled road, is an isolated and peaceful place to stay. It's located in an ancient castle that's visible for miles around; the views are sensational, and there are lovely strolls and marked trails down to the Órcia valley and Sant'Antimo from right outside the walls. Two-night minimum stay. Open late March to Oct. **€125–145**

Bagno Vignoni

Six kilometres south of San Quírico, tiny **BAGNO VIGNONI** is known for its central square, one of Tuscany's most memorable sights, occupied by an arcaded Renaissance *piscine* built by the Medici, who took the sulphur cure here. The hot springs still bubble away in the bath, though they are out of bounds for bathing. You can, however, walk in the sulphur pools at the foot of the hillside below the village.

INFORMATION

Tourist office Strada di Bagni Vignoni (Fri–Sat 10am–6pm; ☎ 0577 888 975).

ACCOMMODATION AND EATING

Antica Osteria del Leone Via dei Mulini 3 ☎ 0577 887 300. The best place to eat in town: moderately priced Tuscan cooking with a twist, and several vegetarian options on the menu, too. Tues–Sun 12.15–2.30pm & 7.30–10pm.

Le Terme Piazza delle Sorgenti 13 ☎ 0577 887 150, ⓦ albergoleterme.it. The chief attraction of the village's most central hotel is that it overlooks the *piscine;*

family-run, 36 pretty and bright rooms, and with a superb modern spa in the garden to the rear. **€85–117**

Locanda La Loggiata Piazzetta del Moretto 30 ☎ 0577 888 925, ⓦ albergoleterme.it. Charming B&B in an old, village-centre house nicely converted by two women, with delightful and romantic rooms – don't be put off by their rather fey names (Dream, Air, Fire…). **€130–180**

Castiglione d'Órcia

Some 3km south of Bagno Vignoni, **CASTIGLIONE D'ÓRCIA** is a fine-looking place with a trio of medieval churches, dominated by the **Rocca d'Órcia** (summer 10am–1pm & 3–6pm; winter Sat & Sun 10am–1pm & 2.30–6.30pm; €2) on its northern edge, visible almost the whole way from San Quírico: from the eleventh to the fourteenth centuries this dramatic pile of a castle belonged, like almost every castle along this stretch of the Via Francigena, to the **Aldobrandeschi** family.

Radicófani

Fourteen kilometres south of Castiglione d'Órcia, a road veers east off the N2 into the hills to the majestically situated **Rocca** of **RADICÓFANI** (783m), which vies with the Rocca d'Órcia for the title of most imposing fortress in southern Tuscany. Clamped to a basalt outcrop, it commands the strategic heights between the Paglia and Órcia valleys; views from the walls are stunning. Hours vary from year to year: for the latest details contact the tourist office.

Below the castle, which was devastated by an explosion in the eighteenth century, is a handsome little village, with an old Capuchin convent, a cluster of churches and the **Palazzo La Posta** – the "Great Duke's Inn", where centuries of grand tourists – including Montaigne and Charles Dickens – put up on their way to Rome.

San Pietro

Via del Teatro 1 • Irregular hours

The best of the churches, the Romanesque **San Pietro**, features several good glazed terracotta works from the school of Andrea della Robbia, together with a polychrome wooden *Madonna* (second pillar on the left) by Francesco di Valdambrino. A rare sculptor, Valdambrino (1375–1435) often collaborated with the great Sienese sculptor Jacopo della Quercia, having worked with him on the panels for the Fonte Gaia, now displayed in Siena's Palazzo Pubblico. He is best known for his *St Peter* in Montalcino (see p.334).

INFORMATION

Tourist office Via Renato Magi 57 (summer only, irregular hours; ☎ 0578 55 684)

ACCOMMODATION

La Torre Via Giacomo Matteotti 7 ☎ 0578 55 943, ⓦ ristorantealbergolatorre.com. Radicófani's setting makes the village an impressive place in which to stay, but

the only option is this modest but well-run two-star hotel in the same family for three generations, on the eastern edge of the old centre. **€78**

Pienza

PIENZA, 20km east of Montalcino, is a tiny Renaissance creation, conceived as a Utopian "New Town" by **Pope Pius II**, Aeneas Sylvius Piccolomini (see p.274). The site Pius chose was the village of Corsignano where he was born in 1405, the first of eighteen children of a noble family exiled from Siena in 1385 (the village, at least in part, formed part of the Piccolominis' traditional feudal domain). Archeological evidence suggests it was inhabited as early as the Bronze Age, and in Roman times it was a hill-top fort of some renown. Today there's little to see beyond Pius's central Renaissance piazza – the pope's death marked the end of his beloved project – though few places in Tuscany have as much immediate charm. There are also some extraordinary **views** from the walls, a scattering of good **bars and restaurants**, and a range of **accommodation** – from rooms to an historic hotel – if you want to stay.

Brief history

The **construction** of Pienza began in 1459, less than a year after Pius's election to the papacy. It's thought that the new pope wished to avenge himself on Siena – which had unjustly exiled his family – by building a city that would be both Siena's antithesis and its superior. It's also claimed Pius couldn't live with the shame of having come from a village as humble as Corsignano. His architect on the project was **Bernardo Rossellino**, who worked on all the major buildings here under the guidance of Leon Battista Alberti, the great theorist of Renaissance art, building and town planning.

Rossellino's commission was to build a cathedral, papal palace and town hall, but Pius instructed the various cardinals who followed his court to build their own residences, too, turning the project into nothing less than a Vatican in miniature. Astonishingly, the cathedral, the papal and bishop's palaces, and the core of the town were completed in just three years. Limited though it was, it constituted the first "Ideal City" of the Renaissance to become a reality.

After consecration of the cathedral, Pius issued a papal bull rechristening the "city" Pienza, in his own honour, and stipulating that no detail of the cathedral or palaces should be changed. The wish was fulfilled rather more easily than he could have expected, for he died within two years, and of his successors only Pius III, his nephew, paid Pienza any regard. The city, intended to spread across the hill, never grew beyond a block to either side of the main Corso, and its population remained scarcely that of a village.

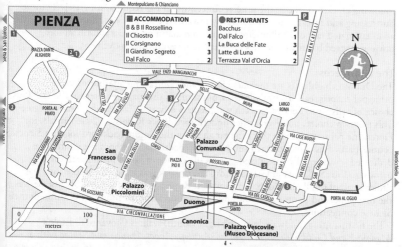

■ ACCOMMODATION		● RESTAURANTS	
B & B Il Rossellino	5	Bacchus	5
Il Chiostro	4	Dal Falco	1
Il Corsignano	1	La Buca delle Fate	3
Il Giardino Segreto	3	Latte di Luna	4
Dal Falco	2	Terrazza Val d'Orcia	2

Piazza Pio II

The juxtaposition of civic and religious buildings that enclose the **Piazza Pio II** was deliberate, and aimed to underline the balance between Church and town through architectural harmony. Apart from the Palazzo Comunale, based on the medieval Palazzo Vecchio in Florence, the ensemble is entirely Renaissance in conception. If it all seems cramped, it's partly because Rossellino wished to retain the existing east–west axis of Corsignano's main street, and partly because of Pius's insistence that his palace loggia should command a view and that the Duomo should be flooded with light, meaning that the piazza's two key buildings had to be orientated towards the valley to the rear. For the Duomo, in particular, this was to have near-disastrous structural consequences.

The piazza's small well, the **Pozzo dei Cani**, sets the tone, its twin columns and classical frieze a perfect miniature of Renaissance ambitions.

The Duomo

Piazza Pio II • Mon–Sat 8am–12.30pm & 4–7.30, Sun 4–7.30pm • Free

The **Duomo**, or Santa Maria Assunta, has one of the earliest Renaissance **facades** in Tuscany, its three-tiered veneer of Istrian marble surmounted by a vast garland of fruit enclosing Pius's papal coat of arms. The **campanile**, rocked by an earthquake in 1545, was virtually rebuilt in 1570.

On Pius's orders, the **interior** took inspiration from Franciscan Gothic churches and the German *Hallenkirchen*, or hall-churches, which he had seen on his pre-papal travels as a member of the Curia. Hall-churches were distinguished, as here, by naves and aisles of equal height. The tall **windows** were also a papal whim, designed to produce a *domus vitrea* (hall of glass), whose flood of light was intended to symbolize the age's humanist enlightenment. Pius's *Commentaries* also talk of the strangely elongated **capitals** of the nave's columns as *felici errori*, or "happy errors". Legend claims the pope found the church's earlier columns too short and insisted that Rossellino find some way of lengthening them. In fact, Rossellino deliberately introduced the capitals, partly to accentuate the nave's soaring Gothic effect, and partly to evoke parallels with similar capitals in Siena's Loggia di Mercanzia and the Duomo, Loggia dei Lanzi and church of San Lorenzo in Florence.

To satisfy Pius's whims, and to fit the cramped site, Rossellino had to build on sandstone with a substratum of clay. Before completion a crack appeared, and following an earthquake in the nineteenth century it has required progressively more buttressing and ties. The nave dips crazily towards the back of the church – still shifting at an estimated rate of a millimetre a year – and alarming cracks are still all too obvious, tagged by small glass ties designed to reveal further movement.

The altarpieces

The Duomo's highlights are the outstanding and contrasting **altarpieces** in the principal chapels, each commissioned from some of the major painters of the age. Pius's choice of artists was deliberate: each was Sienese, as was he (at least by family origin). This partisan choice, however, rather undermined Pius's Renaissance credentials, for Florentine painters were by this time far ahead of their more backward-looking Sienese counterparts. His choice of each subject – the Madonna, to whom the church was dedicated – was equally considered, as was the choice of saints included in each painting. Thus St Sabina in Giovanni di Paolo's work was featured because Pius was titular head of the Basilica di Santa Sabina in Rome; St Peter appeared because he was the first pope; and saints Catherine and Bernardino achieved prominence through their Sienese connections.

The first painting, midway down the right (south) wall, is Giovanni di Paolo's *Madonna and Child with Sts Bernardino, Anthony Abbot, Francis and Sabina* with a

Pietà above – note the Piccolomini arms at the bottom left and right of the frame. The first apse chapel features Matteo di Giovanni's *Madonna and Child with Sts Catherine of Alexandria, Matthew, Bartholomew and Lucy* with the *Flagellation* above: here, too, there's a nod to Pius in the shape of more coats of arms.

The reliquary and font

The next apse contains a travertine tabernacle attributed to Rossellino, behind whose little central door is a **reliquary** containing bones alleged to be from the head of St Andrew, Pienza's patron saint. Another work by Rossellino, a vast **font**, can be seen in the crypt, along with Romanesque fragments recovered from Santa Maria, the former church near the site. The central apse – normally containing the high altar – is empty, Pius having stipulated that nothing should block the light coming from the central windows. Instead he commissioned the choir (1462), the tell-tale papal shield again appearing at the top of the central bishop's throne.

The fourth chapel

The **fourth chapel** houses a triptych of the *Assumption with Sts Agatha, Callistus, Pius I and Catherine of Siena* by **Vecchietta**, born in nearby Castiglione dell'Órcia: it's considered one of his masterpieces and is by far the finest of the church's altarpieces. The fifth chapel features Sano di Pietro's *Madonna and Child with Sts Philip, James, Anne and Mary Magdalene*.

Pius, realizing his Sienese painters lagged behind Florentine thinking, made specific requests in an attempt to bring a little Renaissance flavour to what were essentially Gothic works. Thus Sano was asked to replace the niches traditionally used in the predella (panels in the lower part of altarpieces) with a more classical frame of small pillars. The "V" arrangement of the saints around the Virgin was also new – at least in the works of Sano. Vecchietta similarly staked a claim for modernity by enclosing his *Assumption* triptych – very much a Gothic conceit – in a fixed frame that effectively made the painting a single, rather than hinged, tripartite work. Similar efforts towards a more Renaissance effect are found in the last painting, Matteo di Giovanni's *Madonna and Child with Sts Nicholas, Martin, Augustine and Jerome*, midway down the north wall. The saints here, for example, are set on different levels – compare the same artist's painting across the nave (where they are on one level) – while the Virgin's upper throne is decorated with heads whose classical inspiration is unmistakable.

Palazzo Piccolomini

Piazza Pio II

Pius's residence, the **Palazzo Piccolomini**, was modelled on Alberti's Palazzo Rucellai in Florence, and built by Rossellino over the demolished remains of the Piccolomini's former feudal holding in the village. All three main facades are identical, novelty being provided by the imaginative addition of a triple-tiered loggia at the back, making it the first Italian building to be designed specifically to afford views over a swathe of countryside.

For these views, you can walk into the superb courtyard and through (on the left) to the original "hanging garden" behind; it has remained unchanged over the centuries and is the perfect embodiment of the Renaissance concept that gardens form an intermediary between nature and architecture. The triple-tiered loggia, with its three orders of classical columns (Ionic, Doric and Corinthian), owes a clear debt to the great imperial buildings of ancient Rome.

The papal apartments

Tues–Sun: mid–March to mid–Oct 10am–6.30pm; rest of the year 10am–4.30pm, but closed Jan 7–Feb 14 and last 2 weeks of Nov; open Mon on public holidays • €7 • ⊕ palazzopiccolominipienza.it

For a glimpse of the splendour envisaged for Pius you need to climb the steps in the courtyard to the first-floor **papal apartments**, occupied until 1962 by the Piccolomini family. Guided tours conduct you to Pius II's dining room, library and music room, each filled with furniture, books, carpets and manuscripts. The highlights, though, are the papal bedroom – complete with a gloriously vulgar canopied bed – and the cavernous Sala d'Armi, filled with rows of fearsome pikes and other weapons.

Palazzo Vescovile

Piazza Pio II

The **Palazzo Vescovile**, or Palazzo Borgia, began as a single-storey Gothic palace, but was given to Roderigo Borgia by Pius on condition that he demolish it and rebuild in a more modern manner. Borgia, then a cardinal, would later become the infamous **Pope Alexander VI** and father four children, among them the notorious **Lucrezia** and **Cesare Borgia**. Showing the astuteness (if not the meanness) that would characterize his papacy, Borgia refrained from knocking down the palace, but saved money by altering a few superficial details and adding an extra storey. Thus on the ground floor – clearly of different vintage – you can still see the outlines of the old Gothic windows, bricked in to form tiny square windows more in keeping with Renaissance ideas. Still more visible are the holes that pockmark the upper part of the building, the legacy of a mortar bombardment during **World War II** that also knocked chunks out of the cathedral's apse. The highest marks have an even earlier vintage, having been inflicted by the artillery of Charles V and the Medici during their assault on the Sienese Republic between 1552 and 1559. How much time Borgia spent in the palace is uncertain – though the Borgia arms are clearly visible on the shield on the corner of the building. In any event, it appears he made a gift of the building in 1468, when it became the Palazzo Vescovile, or Bishop's Palace. It now houses the Museo Diocesano.

Museo Diocesano

Corso Rossellino 30 • Mid-March to Oct Mon & Wed–Sun 10am–1pm & 3–7pm; Nov to mid-March Sat & Sun 10am–1pm & 3–6pm • €4.10

Like many small southern Tuscan museums, the **Museo Diocesano** deserves more attention than it receives. Its star attraction is a superb thirteenth- or fourteenth-century *piviale*, or **cope**, an English work (signed *Opus Anglicanum*) of fantastically embroidered silk embellished with scenes from the life of the Virgin and St Catherine of Alexandria, together with various saints and apostles (originally the cope would also have been studded with pearls and precious stones). Tradition claims it was given to Pius by Thomas Paleologus, prince of the Peloponnese and brother of the Byzantine emperor. However, it's more likely to derive from a papal wardrobe dating from the papacy's sojourn in Avignon, where it appears in an inventory dated 1369.

The museum also contains superb tapestries, crosiers, miniatures, illuminated manuscripts, choir books with miniatures by Sano di Pietro and others – produced for Orvieto cathedral but bought by Pius – and several top-notch **paintings**.

The paintings

Look out in particular for the *Madonna dell Umiltà and Sts Elizabeth of Hungary and John the Baptist*, an anonymous work (by the "Maestro dell'Osservanza"), so-called because its Madonna is shown seated on a simple oriental carpet rather than the more usual ornate throne. Also outstanding are a famous *Madonna della Misericordia* (c.1364) by Bartolo di Fredi, his first signed and dated work; among the figures sheltered by the vermilion-robed Madonna are the Emperor Charles IV (in red cloak and crown on the right), who visited Siena in 1355 en route for Rome, together with the pope (alongside) and Charles's queen (to the left, crowned, in pink). It seems likely Siena's Council of Twelve, then in thrall to the emperor, commissioned the work to commemorate the visit.

More eye-catching still is a magnificent 48-panel painting whose tiny anonymous miniatures depict scenes from the life of Christ. It was one of only a handful of surviving "portable" paintings once used by mendicant monks as a preaching aid during their perambulations around the countryside. The picture was brought here from the castle of Spedaletto in the Val d'Órcia, together with a painting often regarded as the first Renaissance Sienese painting: Vecchietta's seminal polyptych of the *Madonna and Child with Sts Blaise, Florian, John the Baptist and Nicholas* (1462). The lunette, clearly Florentine in flavour, depicts the *Annunciation*, whose receding classical columns and three naves of equal height deliberately recall the design of the Duomo. The predella, by contrast, depicts three scenes with a more Sienese touch: the *Crucifixion*, with Siena's bare-hilled *crete* as background; the *Miracles of St Nicholas*; and the *Martyrdom of St Blaise* (for more on Blaise, see p.352).

San Francesco and the town walls

Corso Rossellino

San Francesco (Mon–Sat 9.30am–7pm, Sun 4–7pm; free) is one of two churches to survive from the original Corsignano, and the only significant medieval building remaining in Pienza. Its walls were once entirely covered in fourteenth-century frescoes, only a few of which (scenes from the life of St Francis) survive. More remains of the large Crucifix on the right, a fourteenth-century work by a follower of Duccio, and the arresting *Madonna della Misericordia* on the left, attributed to Luca Signorelli.

Be certain to take the alley to the left of the church – or those to either side of the Duomo – to gain access to Pienza's **walls**, rebuilt after being razed by the armies of the Medici and Charles V of Spain in 1559. You can see why Pius wanted his loggia, for the views from the walls are some of the finest from any town in Tuscany. Head east along the walls and you come to a lovely series of little **lanes** leading back into the village, each with impossibly twee names – such as Via dell'Amore (street of love) and Via del Bacio (street of the kiss): the names were altered from more warlike ones in the nineteenth century so as to be more in keeping with the village's Renaissance idea of itself. In the other direction a more rural lane runs out of Piazza Dante along a level ridge past public gardens.

Pieve di Corsignano

Not to be missed is the ten-minute downhill walk from Piazza Dante (signed off the south side) to the **Pieve di Corsignano** (or San Vito), the village's original parish church, and the place where Pius was baptized. It probably dates from the tenth century, and is one of the best Romanesque churches for miles around. The cylindrical tower – used to shelter the townspeople during bandit raids – is highly unusual, as are the carvings above the main and side doors. You can get the key from the farmhouse just behind the church – leave a small tip.

ARRIVAL AND INFORMATION   PIENZA

By bus Buses drop off just outside the walls in Piazza Dante. Destinations TRA-IN services to Buonconvento (7 daily; 35min); Montepulciano (7 daily; 20min); San Quírico (7 daily; 10min); Siena (5 daily; 1hr 30min); Torrenieri (7 daily; 25min).

Tourist office Corso Rossellino 30, within the Museo Diocesano (Mid-March to Oct Mon & Wed–Sun 10am–1pm & 3–7pm; Nov to mid-March Sat & Sun 10am–1pm & 3–6pm; ☎ 0578 749 305, ⓦ comunepienza.it).

ACCOMMODATION

B&B Il Rossellino Corso Rossellino 97 ☎ 0578 748 322, ⓦ soggiornoapienza.it. Two charming and spacious rooms, each with private bathroom, at the quieter eastern end of the Corso. **€60**

Il Chiostro di Pienza Corso Rossellino 26 ☎ 0578 748 400, ⓦ www.relaisilchiostrodipienza.com. If you're doing Tuscany in style, or fancy a treat, the obvious choice is this four-star, though it often has large groups staying. The

---

MONTICCHIELLO AND THE TEATRO POVERO

Monticchiello, 4km east of Pienza, is a walled village with a leaning watchtower, lovely views of Pienza and a great **church** which houses numerous fourteenth-century Sienese frescoes – look out for the gargantuan *St Christopher* – and a *Madonna* by Pietro Lorenzetti.

During the last week of July and the first week of August, the village puts on a now-renowned **Teatro Povero** (☎0578 755 118, ⓦteatropovero.it) featuring a play written and performed by the villagers to evoke the local folk and farming traditions – a kind of Tuscan *Archers*. It's a pleasantly informal occasion, enjoyed equally for the food at the taverna set up for the duration of the festival. A large **exhibition** (free guided tours on the hour Tues–Sun 10am–6pm) in a former granary at Piazza Nuova 1 displays props, stage sets and audiovisual displays connected with the play and its history.

---

only in-town hotel (as opposed to private rooms), it's a stylish conversion – complete with frescoes, vaults and other medieval trappings – which has been infiltrated into the old cloister and buildings of a Franciscan monastery. Good online deals. **€300**

Il Corsignano Via della Madonnina 11 ☎0578 748 501, ⓦhotelcorsignano.it. It's a shame to stay outside the walls, but you may have no choice during busy times; the *Corsignano* is a modern, recently upgraded and very pleasant four-star about 150m west of the piazza on the left. Rooms at the back have little terraces and something

of a view. **€130**

★ **Il Giardino Segreto** Via Condotti 13 ☎0578 748 539, ⓦcretedisiena.it. The "Secret Garden" is just that: a pretty garden hidden behind high walls a few moments from the Corso, and at your disposal if you stay in one of the five plain but peaceful rooms here (plus two more in an annexe). **€60–115**

Ristorante Dal Falco Piazza Dante 8 ☎0578 748 551, ⓦristorantedalfalco.it. Six simple rooms, each with bathroom, but as they're some of the cheapest in town, each is quickly snapped up. **€60**

EATING AND DRINKING

Pienza is centre of a region producing **pecorino** sheep's cheese, and has gone overboard on food shops, especially on the main Corso Rossellino. There are also several **restaurants** where standards generally remain high, despite the many visitors.

Bacchus Corso Rossellino 70 ☎0578 749 080, ⓦbacchusosteria.com. Though small and easily missed, *Bacchus* is ideal for light meals and a quick lunch: the home-made *pici* are excellent, especially with the saffron sauce, a house speciality. A couple of courses should come in at under €20. Mon–Wed & Fri–Sun 12.15–2.30pm & 7–10pm.

Dal Falco Piazza Dante 8 ☎0578 748 551, ⓦristorantedalfalco.it. A simple trattoria outside the walls which offers superb *gnocchi* and a filling *pecorino alla griglia* (hot cheese wrapped in prosciutto), at around €25 for a full meal. Mon–Thurs & Sat–Sun 12.30–2.30pm & 7.30–10pm; closed ten days in late Nov.

La Buca delle Fate Corso Rossellino 38a ☎0578 748 272, ⓦlabucadellefatepienza.com. Reasonably good value, with full meals around €30, and housed in part of the fifteenth-century palace of the Gonzagas, with rather austere dining rooms but thoroughly Tuscan country food.

Tues–Sun 12.30–2.30pm & 7.15–10.30pm; closed part of Jan & June.

Latte di Luna Via San Carlo 2–4 ☎0578 748 606. Excellent, friendly and moderately priced, blessed with a small, pretty terrace for outdoor eating and an ancient well incorporated into the old interior. Classic Tuscan food, including home-made *pici*, wild boar in winter and orange or hazelnut *semifreddo* for pudding. Mon & Wed–Sun 12.15–2.30pm & 7.15–10pm; closed part of Nov & Feb.

★ **Terrazza Val d'Orcia** Viale Santa Caterina 1–3 ☎0578 749 924, ⓦterrazzavaldorcia.com. On a summer's day, when tables are laid outside, there can be few restaurants in Italy, never mind Tuscany, with the sort of views that spread out below this long-established place (Igor Stravinsky praised the panorama when he visited in 1961). The food doesn't disappoint, either, with a short and fairly priced menu of *pici*, *ribollita* and other Tuscan classics. Daily noon–2.30pm & 7.30–10pm; closed Nov.

Montepulciano

One of the highest of the Tuscan hill-towns, **MONTEPULCIANO** (665m) is built along a narrow ridge, with a long main street and alleys that drop away to the walls. It's a stunningly good-looking town, full of vistas, odd squares and corners, and endowed with dozens of Renaissance *palazzi* and churches, which embody the state of architecture fifty years after Bernardo Rossellino's pioneering work at Pienza. Largely forgotten in subsequent centuries, the town now makes most of its money from its famed **Vino Nobile**. Along with Montalcino or Pienza, it makes a good base for much of southern Tuscany.

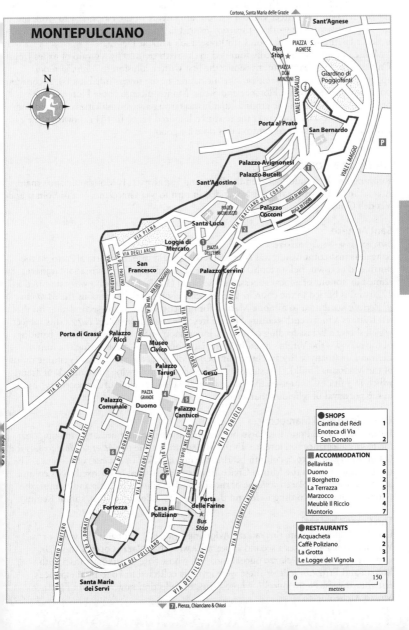

MONTEPULCIANO

8

SHOPS

| Cantina del Redi | 1 |
| Enoteca di Via San Donato | 2 |

ACCOMMODATION

Bellavista	3
Duomo	6
Il Borghetto	2
La Terrazza	5
Marzocco	1
Meublè Il Riccio	4
Montorio	7

RESTAURANTS

Acquacheta	4
Caffè Poliziano	2
La Grotta	3
Le Logge del Vignola	1

0   150
metres

Brief history

Montepulciano's unusually consistent array of Renaissance *palazzi* and churches is a reflection of its remarkable development after 1511, when, following intermittent alliance with Siena, the town finally threw in its lot with Florence. In that year the Florentines sent **Antonio da Sangallo the Elder** to rebuild the town's gates and walls, which he did so impressively that the council took him on to work on the town hall and a series of churches. The local nobles, meanwhile, hired him, his nephew and later the Modena-born architect **Vignola** – a founding figure of the Baroque – to work on their own *palazzi*. The work of this trio, assured in both its conception and execution, makes a fascinating comparison with Rossellino's work at Pienza.

Montepulciano was reputedly founded in the sixth century by a group of **exiles** from Chiusi fleeing the barbarian invasions, the first written allusion to *Mon Politianus* appearing in 715 (hence *poliziani*, the nickname for the town's inhabitants). A constant point of dispute between Florence and Siena, Montepulciano chose Florence as its protector in 1202 – on the grounds that it was farther away. Both cities captured and lost the town several times over the next two hundred years. In 1511, however, the Florentines again assumed control, this time for good.

Along the Corso

Running north to south between the Prato and Farine gates is Montepulciano's main street, the **Corso**, whose name is appended in turn to Via Gracciano, Via di Voltaia and Via dell'Opio.

8

Sant'Agnese

Piazza Sant'Agnese • Irregular hours • Free

Sangallo's first commission was Montepulciano's main gate, the **Porta al Prato**, at the north end of town. Before embarking on the climb up the Corso, visit **Sant'Agnese**, named in honour of a local abbess, Agnese Segni (1268–1317), who was canonized in 1726 and is buried in the church. The first chapel on the right contains the *Madonna di Zoccoli*, attributed to Simone Martini (or his school), while the second altar on the left features a fourteenth-century Sienese fresco of the *Madonna del Latte*. This subject, which shows a breast-feeding Madonna, is common in Sienese (and Tuscan) painting of the period – the Virgin's milk, in Christian iconography, symbolizing the font of Eternal Life (many a Tuscan church in the Middle Ages claimed to have genuine drops of the Madonna's milk). The subject vanished entirely following the Council of Trent, which in a fit of Counter–Reformationary zeal banned any use of "unnecessary" nudity in the portrayal of religious characters.

The Colonna del Marzocco

Inside the Porta al Prato the **Corso** begins, with the *palazzi* immediately making clear the town's allegiance to Florence. In the first square, beside the *Albergo Marzocco*, is the **Colonna del Marzocco**, a column bearing the heraldic lion (*marzocco*) of Florence. The original lion, now in the Museo Civico (this is an 1856 copy), was fixed to its column in 1511, when it replaced a statue of the she-wolf suckling Romulus and Remus, the symbol of Siena (according to legend the city was founded by Senius, son of Remus).

The Corso's palazzi

Lion heads also decorate the **Palazzo Avignonesi** (no. 91), probably the work of Vignola. Sangallo makes a second appearance with the **Palazzo Cocconi** (no. 70), virtually opposite the **Palazzo Bucelli** (no. 73), whose base is strikingly inset with Roman and Etruscan reliefs. These were lovingly collected in 1648 by the palace's erstwhile owner, Pietro Bucelli, whose Etruscan collection now resides in Florence's Museo Archeologico.

Sant'Agostino

South of the *palazzi* is the eye-catching church of **Sant'Agostino**, designed around 1427 by an earlier Medici protégé, Michelozzo – who also carved the terracotta relief of the *Madonna and Child* above the door; within are a *Crucifixion* on the third altar on the left wall by Lorenzo di Credi and an equally good *St Bernardino* by Giovanni di Paolo on the right wall. Pride of place goes to a polychrome Crucifix on the high altar attributed to Donatello.

The tower house and around

Across the street from Sant'Agostino, a medieval **tower house**, a rare survival in Montepulciano, is surmounted by a *commedia dell'arte* figure of a clown, the **Pulcinella**, which strikes the hours on the town clock. About a hundred metres farther along you reach the Renaissance **Loggia di Mercato** and a fork in the road: turn right here if you want to make straight for the Piazza Grande (see below). The Corso continues to the left past further *palazzi*, including the **Palazzo Cervini**, attributed to Sangallo and begun for the doomed Marcellus II before he became pope.

Gesù and around

South of the Palazzo Cervini, you pass the church of **Gesù**, remodelled in Baroque style by Andrea Pozzo (as are many other churches in the town and region), before the road turns a corner and rambles outside the town walls. Just prior to the turn – at no. 5 – is the **Casa di Poliziano**, birthplace of the Renaissance humanist and poet Angelo Ambrogini (1454–94), or Poliziano, who translated many of the Greek classics under the patronage of Lorenzo de' Medici, as well as teaching the Medici children.

8

Santa Maria dei Servi and the Fortezza

Via di Poliziano loops outside the town walls to the Gothic-fronted **Santa Maria dei Servi**, with another Baroque interior by Pozzo. Inside is the much-venerated *Madonna della Santoreggia*, a fifteenth-century fresco (second altar on the left). The only other attention-grabbing work is a *Madonna and Child*, oddly inserted into a larger painting (third altar on the right) by a follower of Duccio.

Via di Poliziano then re-enters town by the old **Fortezza**, now partly occupied by houses, and becomes Via di San Donato as it loops back to the Piazza Grande.

Santa Lucia and around

A block to the north of the Loggia di Mercato, a beautiful little piazza fronts the church of **Santa Lucia**, built in 1633, which has a fabulous, if damaged, *Madonna* by Luca Signorelli in a chapel on the right, though the church is rarely open. South of here, Via del Poggiolo runs down to the church of **San Francesco**: note the ruined pulpit to the side of the facade, from which St Bernardino of Siena is supposed to have preached.

The Museo Civico

Via Ricci • April–July & Sept–Oct Tues–Sun 10am–1pm & 3–7pm; Aug Tues–Sun 10am–7pm; Sept–March Sat & Sun 10am–1pm & 3–6pm • €5

The Sienese Gothic Palazzo Neri-Orselli is home to the **Museo Civico**, an extensive collection of small-town Gothic and Renaissance works. Here you'll find the original Florentine *marzocco* lion removed from the Corso, and a series of glazed terracottas by Andrea della Robbia. The most important panel is a *St Francis*, painted by the saint's near-contemporary, Margaritone da Arezzo; the most enjoyable is Jacopo de Mino's lush *Coronation of the Virgin*.

The Piazza Grande

The **Piazza Grande**, Montepulciano's theatrical flourish of a main square, is built on the highest point of the ridge, providing the obvious site for the town's Duomo. Its most distinctive building, however, is the **Palazzo Comunale**, a thirteenth-century Gothic palace to which Michelozzo added a tower and rustication in imitation of the Palazzo Vecchio in Florence. The tower offers views that, on the clearest days, stretch to Siena, 65km northwest; it's usually open in summer (daily 10am–6pm; €1.60), but hours vary.

Sangallo designed two of the square's *palazzi*. The **Palazzo Nobili-Tarugi**, by the lion and griffon fountain, is a highly innovative building, with a public loggia cut through one corner. More tangible pleasures await at the **Palazzo Cantucci**, one of many buildings scattered about the town that serve as *cantine* for the **wine trade**, offering *degustazione* and sale of the Vino Nobile. The lower part is by Sangallo, the upper by Baldassare Peruzzi, who was Siena's leading sixteenth-century architect.

The Duomo

Piazza Grande · Daily 9am–1pm & 3.30–7pm · Free

Sangallo and his contemporaries never got around to building a facade for the **Duomo**, whose plain brick pales against the neighbouring *palazzi*. Begun in 1680 by Ippolito Scalzi, the building was raised over an earlier church, of which the ugly fourteenth-century campanile is virtually the only reminder. The **interior** boasts an elegant Renaissance design, and contains several outstanding works of art.

The tomb of Bartolomeo Aragazzi

The first notable artworks are the fragments of the **tomb of Bartolomeo Aragazzi** (1427–36) by the multi-talented Michelozzo, which was dismembered in the nineteenth century. Aragazzi was born in Montepulciano, and achieved prominence as the secretary to Pope Martin V (pontiff from 1417 to 1431), the first pope to occupy the Holy See in Rome after the Grand Schism (1378–1417) divided the papacy between Rome and Avignon. He is often described as the first "Renaissance" pope, his election coinciding with the competition to design the baptistery doors in Florence.

Martin was assisted in his adopted role by Aragazzi, who scoured French and German monasteries for manuscripts and oversaw the publication of classical texts by Vitruvius and others. Bas-reliefs from the tomb can now be seen at the base of the first two columns on either side of the nave (right and left), and the effigy of Aragazzi himself is mounted on the rear (west) wall to the right of the door. At the other end of the church, two of the tomb's **statues** surmount the high altar – which is also garlanded by *putti* and festoons from the tomb: two sculpted angels from the piece can be found even farther away, in London's British Museum.

The Assumption

Aragazzi also commissioned a painting that would be a highlight of this or any other church: **Taddeo di Bartolo's** iridescent high altarpiece of the *Assumption*, the supreme rendition of a subject that was a favourite among Siena's leading artists. The date of the painting's commission (1401) is noteworthy, for it came at a time when Montepulciano – which oscillated between Florentine and Sienese domination – found itself free of Florentine rule for a brief period (1390–1404); Aragazzi's choice of a Sienese artist, and a subject dear to the Sienese, is thus revealed as an act of political as well as artistic significance.

The main panels of the triptych, its predella and its gilt-turreted upper panels are crammed with detail and incident. Note, in particular, the apostles gathered around the Virgin's tomb in the main painting: Doubting Thomas is shown receiving the Madonna's girdle (see p.161), while a grief-stricken St John views her flower-decked sepulchre. Behind the latter to the right is the Apostle Thaddeus, Taddeo's namesake; the face is

> **SAN BIAGIO**
>
> **San Biagio** (St Blaise in English) was an Armenian doctor who became a bishop before being called by God to abandon his worldly affairs in favour of a contemplative life in the mountains. There he lived in a cave, surrounded by wild animals that brought him food and drink, and in return were healed by him when they became sick; he's often depicted, St Francis-like, talking to the birds. He was eventually imprisoned on a charge of practising magic, and tortured by having his body scraped with a sharp-pronged instrument used to card wool. Paintings of him always show him holding such an instrument. Thus he became the patron saint of carders and textile workers, which is why he appears so frequently in Florentine and Tuscan paintings, the textile industry having been the bedrock of the region's medieval prosperity. In a more domestic vein, he is also invoked by Italians against sore throats, having once saved a child who'd had a fish bone stuck in her throat.

probably a self-portrait, an extremely unusual feature in a painting executed on the cusp of the Renaissance, when such self-advertisement would later become quite common.

The rest of the church

Though best known as a painter, Vecchietta is represented by an excellent piece of sculpture: the marble **ciborium** in the chapel to the right of the high altar. On the left (north) wall of the church, opposite the pillar of the third nave, is a poetic *Madonna del Pilastro* (Madonna of the Pillar) by Sano di Pietro. At the bottom of the north aisle, close to the main remnants of Aragazzi's tomb, the first chapel – the **Baptistery** – contains a wealth of eye-catching big-name art: the font and its six bas-reliefs (1340) are by Giovanni d'Agostino; the riot of glazed terracotta on the wall, the so-called **Altare dei Gigli** (Altar of the Lilies), is by Andrea della Robbia – it frames a relief of the *Madonna and Child* attributed to Benedetto da Maiano; and the niche statues of St Peter and John the Baptist are attributed to Mino da Camaino.

San Biagio

Via di San Biagio • Daily 9am–12.30pm & 3–6/7pm • Free

Antonio da Sangallo's greatest commission came in 1518, when he was invited by the town's Ricci nobles to design the pilgrimage church of **San Biagio** on the hillside below the town. The model for this was his brother Giuliano's design for the facade of San Lorenzo in Florence, which was never built. The Montepulciano project was more ambitious – the only bigger church project of its time was St Peter's in Rome – and occupied Antonio until his death in 1534. He lived to see its inauguration, however (in 1529), the ceremony performed by the Medici pope Clement VII. To reach the church, follow Via di San Biagio southwest from the Porta di Grassi; it's about fifteen minutes' walk.

The church, built over an earlier chapel to San Biagio, or St Blaise (see box, p.352), is one of the most harmonious Renaissance creations in Italy, constructed inside and out from soft, honey-coloured travertine. A deeply intellectualized building, its major architectural novelty was the use of freestanding towers (only one was completed, in 1545) to flank the facade (note the tower's three orders of Classical columns – Doric, Ionic and Corinthian). Within, it is spoilt a little by extraneous decoration – a Baroque *trompe l'oeil* covers the barrel vault – but is equally harmonious. It also has superb acoustics. Nearby, scarcely less perfect a building, is the **Canonica** (rectory), endowed by Sangallo with a graceful portico and double-tiered loggia.

ARRIVAL AND DEPARTURE	**MONTEPULCIANO**

By train Montepulciano's station is on the Siena–Chiusi line, with hourly trains from Siena (1hr), but you'll need a bus for the 10km trip into town. Regular buses also link with more frequent mainline trains at Chiusi, not much farther away. These buses stop first at the Porta di Farine (climb the steps above the bus stop to get into town), and then Porta al Prato, the main "bus station".

By bus LFI buses (☏ 0578 31 174, ⓦ www.lfi.it) run more or less every half-hour to Chianciano Terme (25min), Chiusi (50min) and Chiusi station; there's also one Siena (1hr 25min) and one to three Florence (2hr) services daily. To the west, TRA-IN has seven buses daily on the circuit through Pienza (20min), San Quírico d'Órcia (40min), Torrenieri (50min; change for Montalcino) and Buonconvento (1hr),

with between three and five daily continuing to Siena (90min). All buses leave from outside Porta al Prato and Porta di Farine.

By car If you're driving, follow the road around below the east circuit of walls and look for a parking space; don't be tempted by the area around the Porta al Prato or you'll be ticketed. Up around the Fortezza is also a good place to start looking.

INFORMATION

Tourist office Piazza Don Minzoni 1 (April–Oct Mon–Sat 9.30am–12.30pm & 3–7/8pm, Sun 9.30am–12.30pm; Nov–March Mon–Sat 9.30am–12.30pm & 3–6pm, Sun 9.30am–12.30pm; ☏ 0578 757 341, ⓦ prolocomonte pulciano.it).

ACCOMMODATION

Accommodation is sparse, and it's well worth booking ahead. If the places below are full, contact the tourist office for private rooms or agriturismo options, or visit the local hoteliers' website, ⓦ montepulcianohotels.it. Unless you have transport, don't settle for a room or hotel at the outlying station area (Montepulciano–Stazione/ Acquaviva), or at Sant'Albino/Terme di Montepulciano (5km southeast).

★ **Bellavista Gabriella Massoni** Via Ricci 25 ☏ 0578 716 341, ⓦ cretedisiena.com/Camerebellavista. Six well-situated private rooms, five with private bath. Four have stupendous views, some have terraces, and all have beams and other fine period touches. No one lives on site, so you must ring first, and the owner will drive up to let you in: there's a public phone in the doorway downstairs. **€70–90**

Duomo Via San Donato 14 ☏ 0578 757 473, ⓦ albergoduomomontepulciano.it. A friendly welcome, thirteen spacious and comfortable rooms, three-star facilities and a nice setting off the Piazza Grande make this the town's best upmarket hotel. **€90–110**

Il Borghetto Via Borgo Buio 7 ☏ 0578 757 535, ⓦ ilborghetto.it. Montepulciano's grandest three-star hotel, in a very tastefully refurbished old house off Via

Gracciano nel Corso. Just eleven rooms, so be sure to book. **€105**

La Terrazza Via Piè al Sasso 16 ☏ 0578 757 440, ⓦ laterrazzadimontepulciano.it. Pleasant two-star hotel in an ancient house near the Duomo. Many parts of the building have wonderful beamed ceilings and period features, and there's the bonus of a small garden and a terrace with a view over the Corso. **€90**

Marzocco Piazza Giralomo Savonarola 18 ☏ 0578 757 262, ⓦ albergoilmarzocco.it. This elegant nineteenth-century inn with a full-size billiard table is the smartest hotel in town. Very courteous owners, but loses out to the *Duomo* in terms of location. **€90**

Meublè Il Riccio Ivana Migliorucci, Via Talosa 21 ☏ 0578 757 713, ⓦ ilriccio.net. Five well-kept private double rooms, each with private bathroom, TV and phone, off Piazza Grande. **€100**

Montorio Strada per Pienza 2 ☏ 0578 717 442, ⓦ montorio.com. Historic country house just outside Montepulciano on the Pienza road, with a lovely garden and terraces covered with cypresses and olive trees. There are five apartments for two or four people, each with kitchen and furnished with antiques. **€130**

EATING AND DRINKING

Acquacheta Via del Teatro 2 ☏ 0578 717 086, ⓦ acquacheta.eu. A small, bustling, rustic-looking osteria that offers hearty, Tuscan food, including plenty of meat, sausage and salami options. Prices are incredibly fair: pastas come in at €4–8, mains €6.50–9. Wed–Sun 12.30–3pm & 7.30–10.30pm.

Caffè Poliziano Via di Voltaia nel Corso 27–29 ☏ 0578 758 615, ⓦ caffepoliziano.it. An often over-busy 1868 tearoom restored to a classic Art Nouveau design; it serves pastries and pots of tea, while its adjoining restaurant, *Il Grifin d'Oro*, serves somewhat pricey meals (at around €25), such as *pici* (fat spaghetti) with wild boar *ragù*, and offers great views from a small terrace. Daily 7am–midnight.

La Grotta Via di San Biagio 15 ☏ 0578 757 607, ⓦ lagrottamontepulciano.it. Opposite San Biagio church, about 1km outside the city walls, the elegant and brick-vaulted *La Grotta* serves pricey, classic Tuscan cuisine in a sixteenth-century building with its own pretty garden. Mon, Tues & Thurs–Sun 12.30–2.30pm & 7.30–10.30pm; closed part of Jan & Feb.

Le Logge del Vignola Via delle Erbe 6 ☏ 0578 717 290, ⓦ leloggedelvignola.com. *Le Logge* has made a name for itself, but while the "creative" Tuscan dishes (such as pork with grapefruit purée) usually come off, they are not for purists, and with mains at around €20, you need to keep an eye on prices, too. Mon & Wed–Sun 12.30–2.30pm & 7.30–10.30pm; closed part of Dec & Jan.

8

VINO NOBILE

Vino Nobile di Montepulciano has been acclaimed since medieval times and today boasts a top-rated DOCG mark – something the townspeople have not been shy in exploiting. Montepulciano's streets are filled with wine shops selling gift sets, and local vineyards often offer **tastings** in the town (generally free, but usually requiring advance notice). Every restaurant can provide a range of vintages, the very cheapest of which will still set you back at least €20. The tourist office can organize a wine-tasting ramble for you, and has a complete list of the town's **wine outlets**, while the Strada del Vino Nobile, Piazza Grande 7 (❶0578 717 484, ⓦstradavinonobile.it), has information on local wine and wine tours, including driving routes around vineyards and producers. Some of the many places to check out include the venerable Contucci, Via San Donato 15 (❶0578 757 006, ⓦcontucci.it) and the Cantina Del Redi, Via di Collazi 5 (❶0578 716 092, ⓦcantinadelredi.com).

East to Chiusi

If you have transport, the minor road that runs south just before Montepulciano's own little spa at Sant'Albino makes an enjoyable way to get to **Chiusi**. It follows a fine, scarcely populated stretch of the Val d'Órcia down through the estates of Castelluccio and La Foce – the latter the home for many years of the American writer Iris Origo, author of the classic *The Merchant of Prato*. It was at La Foce that she hid partisans and Allied troops during the German occupation of Italy after Mussolini's fall in 1943, events recorded in her autobiography *War in Val d Órcia*.

Otherwise, you could go via **CHIANCIANO TERME**, midway between Montepulciano and Chiusi. It's one of Tuscany's major **spas** (ⓦtermechianciano.it), as evidenced by the presence of some two hundred hotels and clinic-like spa buildings.

Chiusi

CHIUSI, 14km southeast of Montepulciano, is useful mostly as a transport hub. As a target in its own right, it's only really worth a special detour for Etruscan enthusiasts: the town – known to the Etruscans as Camars – has a reasonable archeological museum and around half a dozen ancient tombs on its periphery, out towards Lago di Chiusi.

Museo Archeologico Nazionale

Via Porsenna • Daily 9am–8pm • €4

The **Museo Archeologico Nazionale** ought to be good, for the region is littered with tombs. Several exhibits, however, have been spirited away to Florence and Rome and what remains is a modest collection: numerous sarcophagi, a few terracottas and the odd treasure – notably the *Gualandi Urn*. The ticket is also valid for entry, by arrangement with the museum, to two **tombs**, the Leone and Pellegrina, 3km from town on the road to Lago di Chiusi.

The Duomo

Piazza del Duomo • Mon–Sat 8am–noon & 4–7pm • Free

At the Romanesque **Duomo** nearby there is further evidence of Chiusi's ancient past. The building itself consists almost entirely of Etruscan and Roman blocks (the interior is a mass of what appears at first sight to be mosaic work, but is in reality mock-Byzantine paintwork, created in 1915).

Museo della Cattedrale and the Labirinto di Porsenna

Via Caccialupa 9 • **Museo** June to mid-Oct & Dec 24–Jan 6 daily 9.45am–12.45pm & 4–6.30pm; mid-Oct to Dec 24 9.45am–12.45pm; Jan 7–March Tues, Thurs & Sat 9.45am–12.45pm; rest of year Mon–Sat 9.45am–12.45pm, Sun 9.45am–12.45pm & 4–6pm • €2 • **Labirinto** same hours, guided tours at 10.10am, 10.50am, 11.30am, 12.10pm, 4.10pm, 4.50pm, 5.30pm & 6.10pm • €3, or combined ticket with Museo della Cattedrale €4

The **Museo della Cattedrale** has a fine little collection of sculpture, paintings and archeological artefacts and gives access to the **Labirinto di Porsenna**, where guided tours take you through the atmospheric tunnels of the Etruscan water-catchment system below the piazza to a huge Roman cistern, and then up inside the twelfth-century campanile.

Museo Civico

Via Seconda Ciminia 1 • Guided tours April–Oct Tues–Sun 10.15am, 11.30am, 12.45pm, 3.15pm, 4.30pm & 5.45pm; Nov–March Thurs & Fri at 10.10am, 11.10am & 12.10pm, Sat & Sun 10.10am, 11.10am, 12.10pm, 3.10pm, 4.10pm & 5.10pm • €3

Still more of the ancient underground city can be seen at the **Museo Civico**, off the north side of Piazza XX Settembre. Atmospheric guided tours lead through 140m of Etruscan tunnel and aqueduct to a lake now some 28m below street level.

ARRIVAL AND INFORMATION

CHIUSI

By train Chiusi–Chianciano Terme railway station is 2.7km southeast of the old centre just off the road to Città della Pieve. Destinations Asciano (10 daily; 50min); Florence (hourly; 1hr 5min–1hr 40min); Montepulciano (hourly; 15min); Siena (hourly; 1hr 30min); Sinalunga (hourly; 25min).

By bus Buses stop in the old centre near the junction of Via Garibaldi and Via delle Torre, around 300m southwest of Piazza del Duomo.
Destinations Chianciano (14 daily; 30min); Montepulciano (14 daily; 45min).

Tourist office Via Porsenna 79 (April–Aug Mon–Sat 9am–1pm & 3–6pm, Sun 9am–1pm; Sept same hours except Sun 10am–1pm; Oct daily 10am–2pm; rest of the year daily 9.30am–12.30pm; ☏0578 227 667, ✆prolocochiusi.it).

ACCOMMODATION AND EATING

Ristorante Zaira Via Arunte 12 ☏0578 20 260, ✆zaira.it. This restaurant has been in business since 1910, and serves Tuscan staples plus some "Etruscan dishes" – boar, pigeon and the like – at moderate prices. It also has access to an extraordinary Etruscan grotto (be sure to ask for a visit), home to an excellent wine cellar. Tues–Sun 12.30–2.30pm & 7.30–10pm.

Villa il Patriarca Querce al Pino ☏0578 274 407, ✆ilpatriarca.it. An extremely good out-of-town four-star hotel, some 4km from Chiusi. The beautifully restored country villa is set in fine grounds (with a pool), and has a superb, if expensive and rather grand restaurant, *I Salotti*, that is renowned in its own right. Restaurant Tues–Sun 12.30–2.30pm & 7.30–10pm. **€139**

Monte Amiata and around

At 1738m, **MONTE AMIATA** is the highest point in southern Tuscany, a broad-based mountain whose hazy outline forms the backdrop to many a town and landscape in the region. A circle of towns rings its lower slopes – some historical spots, others more modern. None, with one exception, are worth a trip for their own sake, but the effect of the villages together – plus pretty streets, old castles and plenty of bucolic countryside – makes this a good area to tour by car or bike for a day or so. It's also delightful walking country, refreshingly cool in summer and with skiing in winter.

The main centre and transport hub is **Abbadia San Salvatore**, worth a visit for its great abbey, whether you intend to venture onto the mountain or not. If you have transport, the ring of towns around Monte Amiata is worth a little exploration. None has outstanding features but all claim a rural setting and more or less medieval centres – usually built around an Aldobrandeschi castle.

Abbadia San Salvatore

There's been a settlement on the site of **ABBADIA SAN SALVATORE** since prehistoric times, though its real significance dates from the eighth century when its great abbey became the controlling centre of the Via Francigena. Its importance only waned with the rise of the Aldobrandeschi in the eleventh century. Thereafter it was contested by Orvieto and Siena, but in 1559 – along with most of southern Tuscany – fell within the orbit of the Medici's Grand Duchy of Tuscany.

Today the town is an initially disorientating modern sprawl that hides a perfect and largely self-contained **medieval quarter**. The abbey itself is actually in the modern part of the town.

The abbey

Piazzale Michelangelo, off Via Cavour • Mon–Sat 7.30am–5pm, Sun 10.30am–5pm, depending on services • Free

Church tradition dates the **Abbadia San Salvatore** to 743, making it one of the oldest abbeys in Tuscany, and ascribes its foundation to King Rachis, a Lombard king who is supposed to have converted to Christianity while contemplating a Crucifix now affixed to the abbey's south wall. The actual story of the abbey's birth is slightly different. For a start, the Crucifix element is anachronistic, as the work dates from the twelfth century, some four hundred years after Rachis' death. Rachis himself, however, was involved in the foundation, though it appears his withdrawal into monastic isolation was forced on him, principally by leading Lombard nobles who opposed his ever-increasing leanings towards Rome. Forced to abdicate, the king symbolically awarded his crown to the pope and was succeeded by his brother, Astolfo.

The present Romanesque **church**, built in Amiata's distinctive brown trachite, was consecrated in 1036, a rebuilding programme having been instigated a year before when the abbey was at the height of its wealth and power. The present crypt dates from this period, though other parts of the building were altered during the brief tenure of the Camaldolese and later the Cistercians, who took over the abbey from the Benedictines in 1228. Among the Cistercian additions was the triform window in the **facade**, though critics are unable to agree on the age of the two distinctive towers (one clearly unfinished), features found in very few other churches in Italy.

The interior

The narrow frontage, squeezed between the towers, prepares you for a thin and immensely long **interior**, whose Latin-cross plan is generally considered the first of any Romanesque church in Tuscany. The single-naved basilica culminates in a raised chancel, framed by a series of broad and beautifully decorated arches. Little survives in the way of art, much having been removed to Florence when the abbey was owned by the Medici – a period when it remained monkless for 157 years. The best of what remains is the wooden **Crucifix** involved in the Rachis legend (at the beginning of the right-hand wall), though it's a disquietingly modern-looking piece, and easily passed by. Many of the paintings are by the Nasini clan, a three-generation dynasty of painters born in nearby Castel del Piano. The south transept features **frescoes** on the *Legend of King Rachis* by Giuseppe Nasini (1657–1736), the north transept panels on the *Life of the Virgin*; none is terribly accomplished, but they have a faintly ridiculous charm all the same.

The crypt

The **crypt**, by contrast, is outstanding: one of the most monumental in Tuscany, it is an astounding space of bare, crude stone supported by 35 strange, fluted columns. Atop each pillar is a superbly carved lintel, whose motifs and figures show a Lombard and in some cases Byzantine hand, the latter – distinguished by a more rectangular approach – typical of northern Italian work of the period. Note, too, how each pillar is worked in a wide variety of styles.

Parco Museo Minerario

Piazzale Renato Rossaro 6 • Daily 9am–1.30pm & 3.30–8.30pm • €6 • ⓦ museominerario.it

The superb **Parco Museo Minerario** is located in part of what was once one of the world's most important mercury mines, the metal having been extracted locally since the end of the nineteenth century. It offers numerous examples of industrial archeology, with old machines and the fittings, fixtures and tools used in the mines, as well as lots of archive photographs and other documentary material.

By buses Buses stop on Via Gorizia, around 250m south of the Abbadia, and several other points on the edge of the compact old centre.
Destinations Arcidosso (10 daily; 45min); Buonconvento (5 daily; 1hr 10min); Chiusi (4–5 daily; 1hr 25min);

Grosseto (5 daily; 2hr 15min); Santa Fiora (10 daily; 30min); Siena (2–3 daily; 2hr).
Information Monte Amiata has an excellent official website, ⓦ amiataturismo.it, that covers the entire region and its many villages.

The Monte Amiata summit and slopes

The summit of **Monte Amiata** is accessible by road and in summer is packed with vehicle-delivered parties. In July and August it has a thrice-daily bus from Abbadia San Salvatore. A number of the tatty bars at the summit rent out mountain bikes to explore the lower slopes.

At the car park is what amounts to an alpine hamlet, with bars, a handful of hotels and a short ski run – all in the shadow of a peculiar Eiffel Tower structure adapted in the form of a cross, erected in 1946 by Pope Pius XII. Alongside are a crop of radio masts, and huts selling some of the trashiest trinkets conceivable. None of this detracts from the **views**, which stretch southeast to Bolsena and west to the sea, with the nearer towns neatly delineated in a circle below. The best viewpoint is from the so-called *Madonna delle Scout*, a statue littered with the pendants of innumerable scout troops.

Hotel Contessa Prato della Contessa ☎ 0564 959 000, ⓦ hotelcontessa.it. In a similarly pretty setting as the *Macinaie*, the modern, three-star *Contessa* is at an altitude of 1500m, and on the summit approach road, is 2km closer to the actual summit than *Le Macinaie*. It has outdoor activities and themed hiking, skiing and other weekend offers. **€80**

Le Macinaie ☎ 0564 959 001, ⓦ lemacinaie.com. This hotel in Prato Macinaie (1385m), a tree-enclosed patch of meadow and the site of one of Amiata's ski lifts, is the best place to stay on the mountain,. It's not far from the summit, but distant enough to be unspoilt and detached from the commercialism. **€90**

Piancastagnaio

Five kilometres south of Abbadia San Salvatore, **PIANCASTAGNAIO**, at 772m, spreads across the slopes of a mountain plateau, capped by one of the area's most impressive fortresses, a fourteenth-century Aldobrandeschi number. It has a maze of pretty streets, plus a fine Romanesque church – the twelfth-century Santa Maria Assunta. On the road outside the village, left of the main gate, the church of **Santa Maria delle Grazie** has a recently uncovered fifteenth-century fresco cycle by Nanni di Pietro. Another

AMIATA WALKING: THE ANELLO DELLA MONTAGNA

Away from the summit, the woods and pathways of Monte Amiata's **lower slopes** make up one of the region's most beautiful natural enclaves, blanketed by huge forests of beech and chestnut that provide refuge for deer and wild boar. The mountain's extravagant greenery, so at odds with much of the surrounding countryside, derives from its volcanic origins, eruptions having formed ridges of trachite, which is fertile when broken down and also porous, allowing surface water to filter away. When the water hits the impervious volcanic rock below, it flows out in a series of **springs**, a striking feature of Amiata, whose slopes frequently echo to the sound of running water.

The combination of Amiata's lush vegetation and crisp mountain air makes it superb **walking** territory. Detailed Multigraphic and other maps have made hiking in the region a fairly straightforward undertaking, and considerable effort has gone into marking the **Anello della Montagna**, a path which circles the mountain between about 900m and 1300m. With a car you can join the path from virtually any of the roads that climb from the surrounding towns; large boards mark the departure points.

recently discovered cycle resides in **San Bartolomeo**, a humble Franciscan church on the Abbadia road restructured in the eighteenth century. The pictures, which depict the *Life of the Virgin*, are in the chapterhouse, off the cloister.

Santa Fiora

SANTA FIORA's craggy position drew an admiring observation from Dante as to its impregnability; its castle – of which only a tower remains – provided the feudal seat of one of the major branches of the **Aldobrandeschi**. This clan, which ruled much of southern Tuscany and the Maremma from the ninth century, had its roots in a Lombard dynasty from Lucca – the family name is an Italian corruption of "Hildebrand", testament to the family's northern German origins. In 1274 the clan divided into two main branches, one of which was installed in Santa Fiora, ruling Monte Amiata and the northern Maremma, the other in nearby Sovana, from where they controlled the coast and the southern Maremma. Santa Fiora then passed through the family's female line, and was eventually ceded by marriage to the Sforza Cesarini family, whose **palazzo**, built from the old fortress, lies alongside the Aldobrandeschi **tower**, now a clock tower overlooking a picturesque little square.

Pieve di Santa Fiora e Lucilla

The **Pieve di Santa Fiora e Lucilla**, reached on Via Carolina from the square, has its walls, altar and pulpit adorned with a wide variety of top-notch terracottas (1480–90) by Andrea della Robbia and his workshop. The beautiful church, incidentally, was named after two local saints whose relics, brought here in the eleventh century, reside in the nearby priest's house.

Parco della Peschiera

Daily 9am in summer until sunset; winter hours vary • €1

The road northwest from Santa Fiora's old centre leads to the oratory of **Madonna delle Nevi** – the della Robbia figures above the entrance are the local saints Fiora and Lucilla – and then to the village's nicest feature, the **Peschiera**, a spring-fed lake and eighteenth-century garden surrounded by woodland and gurgling brooks. The road beyond passes evidence of Amiata's industrial side, tall chimneys signalling the thermal power plants and mercury mines that once kept the area's economic head above water.

Castel del Piano

CASTEL DEL PIANO is the main commercial town in this area, and though it looks appealing from a distance it doesn't really live up to the promise, though the **old centre** warrants a quick wander, with its covered market, Palazzo Pretorio and Romanesque San Leonardo.

Seggiano

SEGGIANO is an old Etruscan centre, today distinguished principally by its Renaissance church of the **Madonna della Carità**, set in an olive grove just outside the village. The town's inhabitants built it as a votive offering in 1603 as thanks for deliverance from famine. They wouldn't be too impressed to see what's become of their labour of love, for the church has managed to have every one of its altarpieces stolen: grim modern paintings have taken their place. Better-educated thieves might have made for the nicely situated **Oratorio di San Rocco**, also on the village's outskirts, whose *Madonna Enthroned* (1493) by Girolamo di Domenico is by far the best of the paintings in the immediate vicinity.

South to Saturnia and Manciano

Around 14km from Arcidosso, **Triana** stands on the junction of the roads west to Grosseto and south to **Saturnia** and Pitigliano. A perfect little fortified hamlet, it commands huge views from its castle. A rewarding detour west takes you to the lonely village of **Roccalbegna**. Otherwise follow the pretty minor roads south to **Manciano**, the main centre in this largely unpopulated region.

Roccalbegna

ROCCALBEGNA is one of the finest villages in southern Tuscany: aerial pictures of its perfect medieval streets decorate many local tourist offices, but barely hint at the rugged grandeur of its position, perched 522m up the slopes of Monte Labbro above the Albegna valley.

Santi Apostoli Pietro e Paolo

Off Via Roma • Irregular hours

The Romanesque church of **Santi Apostoli Pietro e Paolo** is notable for its medieval interior and patches of fresco, but the highlight is a tremendous triptych of the *Madonna and Child with Sts Peter and Paul* (1340) by Ambrogio Lorenzetti. It's astonishing to find a painting here, in the middle of nowhere, by one of Siena's finest – the artist was responsible for the frescoes of *Good and Bad Government* in Siena's Palazzo Pubblico. In a touching detail, Lorenzetti has painted the Madonna affectionately clasping the Child's foot. Note too, the cherries held in the Infant's hands, symbols of Heaven, eternal life and the rewards of a righteous life.

Oratorio del Crocifisso

Via del Crocifisso • June–Sept 10am–noon & 5–7pm; at other times open by appointment only • ☎ 0564 989 032

Steps up from Santi Apostoli Pietro e Paolo lead to the small **Oratorio del Crocifisso**, now a museum. Its high altar contains a fourteenth-century painted Crucifix (1360) by Luca di Tommè, whose presence in Roccalbegna is no accident – Lorenzetti was his main influence.

The Rocca

The **Rocca** of the town's name is obvious from afar, poised on a crag that rises almost to a pyramid above the village. Like so many in the region, it formed a defensive retreat for the Aldobrandeschi, overlords of the Maremma for several centuries. A superb walk to the top starts from Piazza IV Novembre at the far end of the village. The views over the wild and rocky countryside are tremendous, though outdone by the famed vista over the village's grid of streets. The local saying *se il sasso scrocca, addio la Rocca* ("If the rock crumbles, it's goodbye to the village") seems incontrovertible from this point.

Semproniano to Rocchette

Moving south toward Saturnia, there are a couple of minor places of note. After 10km you reach **SEMPRONIANO**, a crumbling half-forgotten village centred on another Aldobrandeschi castle. Its Romanesque church, Sts Vincenzo e Anastasio, has a painting of a dragon supposedly slain nearby; by contrast, neighbouring Romanesque Santa Croce has a noted wooden medieval Crucifix. On a minor road 5km to the east is the virtually abandoned hamlet of **ROCCHETTE**, sited below a castle on a spur overlooking the Albegna valley. If you make the detour you'll find one of the prettiest places for miles, along with some cracking views.

8

Saturnia

Word is spreading about the sulphurous hot springs at **SATURNIA**, 25km south of Triana, as the almost year-round convoys of battered Volkswagen campers and crowds of noisy Italians testify. Nonetheless, they're not that easy to find. If all you want is a dip you should initially ignore the hill-town and follow the road south towards Montemerano. A large **spa complex** (ⓦtermedisaturnia.it) – with fierce admission charges, a vast pool and a five-star hotel – is signposted to the left, and about 200m on (as the road takes a sharp curve) a dirt track heads off straight, usually signalled by a cluster of cars and vans.

The cascatelle

A two-minute walk from the spa brings you to the **cascatelle**, sulphur streams and springs which burst from the ground, forming natural rock-pool jacuzzis of warm water, in which you can lie around for hours submerged up to your neck. The bubbling main pool is a bizarre sight, the water an intense turquoise, and all the more surreal if the weather is overcast and the steam rising overhead. Entrance is unrestricted and free, and even on cold days there are invariably a few people ready to indulge. The heavy pedestrian traffic means there's a bit of litter, but apart from an inexpensive bar/pizzeria there's surprisingly little commercialism.

ARRIVAL AND DEPARTURE   SATURNIA

By bus There are three daily buses along the road between Semproniano and Manciano: be sure to get out at the springs (Le Terme) and not at Saturnia village.

ACCOMMODATION AND EATING

Bacco e Cerere Via Mazzini 4 ☎0564 601 805. The service is friendly, the atmosphere intimate (there's room for just thirty diners) and the food – puddings especially – worth every cent of the €35 it'll cost to do the job properly. There's also a less formal bar downstairs for snacks, light meals and wine by the glass. Restaurant daily noon–3pm & 7.30–10pm; bar daily 8.30am–9.30pm (closes 8.30pm Nov–March); both closed Mon Nov–March.

Villa Clodia Via Italia 43 ☎0564 601 212 ⓦhotelvillaclodia.com. A delightful three-star period villa, tucked away in one of the village's nicer quarters, with pretty rooms and public areas (including a lovely salon with huge fire) and a pool. **€100**

Montemerano

Midway between Saturnia and Manciano lies **MONTEMERANO**, a medieval hill-village (with modern component below) cannily fortified on two levels, its balconies and interlocked alleys decked with a more-than-usual abundance of geraniums and other hanging greenery. For the time being, it remains a pretty and all-but-undocumented little gem.

San Giorgio

Piazza della Chiesa • Irregular hours

Once you've pottered around the streets – which will take only a few minutes – head for **San Giorgio**, a prettily frescoed little church full of artistic treasures. The first, on the right (south) wall, is a wooden bas-relief of the *Assumption* (1455–65) by Vecchietta, a painter who also successfully turned his hand to sculpture. Beyond it, by the door, is a faded fresco of *St Orsola*. Ahead, at the bottom of the arch beside the high altar, is the winsome and wonderfully titled *Madonna della Gattaiola* ("of the Cat-flap"), painted around 1450 by an anonymous follower of Sassetta known as the "Master of Montemerano". Originally one half of an *Annunciation* (note the Virgin's Bible, a feature of such paintings), the picture probably formed part of an organ or double-doored tabernacle; the archangel Gabriel would have occupied the second panel. It was then used as the door to a granary, probably the point at which it received the hole in the bottom right of the Virgin's cloak which led

:o its nickname. All this is simply a light-hearted prelude to the church's real highlights, namely a polychrome wooden statue of *St Peter* (1455–60), another work by Vecchietta (left of the high altar steps), and a glorious fifteenth-century polyptych by Sano di Pietro of the *Madonna and Child with Sts Peter, George, Lawrence and Anthony of Padua*.

ACCOMMODATION AND EATING — MONTEMERANO

Da Caino Via della Chiesa 4 ☎ 0564 602 817, ⓦ dacaino it. The coveted Michelin rosettes (*Da Caino* has two) are not the recommendation in Tuscany they might be elsewhere, but here they reflect absolutely first-class cooking. There are just 22 covers, so booking is essential, and you're looking at around €100 or more per head if you're going to stretch the chef. Tues 7.30–10pm, Thurs– Sun 12.30–2.30pm & 7.30–10pm; closed late Jan to late Feb & two weeks in July.

Oliveto Via Enrico Fermi 20 ☎ 0564 602 849, ⓦ www .loliveto.it. Located on the outskirts near the turn-off for Saturnia, the large three-star *Oliveto* is a bland, if reliable, modern choice. €48

Osteria Passaparola Vicolo delle Mura 21 ☎ 0564 602 835. For less than a third of the price of *Da Caino*, you can also eat at the moderately priced *Osteria Passaparola*, a small and pleasingly simple family-run place that offers classic Tuscan food with odd surprises that might include truffles, wild boar in season and rabbit with orange. Mon– Wed & Fri–Sun 12.30–2.30pm & 7.30–10pm; closed part of Feb & July.

Villa Acquaviva 2km north of Montemerano ☎ 0564 602 890, ⓦ relaisvillaacquaviva.com. The pastorally situated *Villa Acquaviva* is a definite first-choice treat, with rooms in two attractively converted buildings, surrounded by the hotel's own wine estate, plus large pool, tennis courts and a fine restaurant. €180

Pitigliano

PITIGLIANO, the largest town in Tuscany's deep south, is best approached along the road from Manciano, to the west, from where it soars above on a spectacular outcrop of tufa, with medieval buildings perched above the valley floor, its quarters linked by the arches of an immense aqueduct. **Etruscan tombs** – some converted to storage cellars for wine – honeycomb the cliffs, a feature repeated all over the surrounding area. The town has a slightly grim, occasionally sinister sort of grandeur, the result partly of its mighty fortress, which divides the upper town from the more modern lower suburb, but on a sunny day Pitigliano is one of the great little Tuscan towns.

Brief history

Neolithic remains suggest a settlement on the site from earliest times, though it first rose to prominence as an Etruscan and later Roman town. In the early Middle Ages

PITIGLIANO'S JEWISH HERITAGE

Pitigliano was once home to a thriving **Jewish community**, established during the sixteenth century under the protection of the Orsini. In 1622, however, the Medici confined the town's Jews to a **ghetto**, where they remained until 1735, when legislation introduced by the last Medici ruler, Gian Gastone, lifted the proscription against Jewish commercial activity and led to the expansion of Jewish businesses on present-day Via Zuccarelli.

Before long Pitigliano was being referred to as "Little Jerusalem", and boasted a Jewish university that attracted students from around Europe. By the time of Italian Unification, around 400 of Pitigliano's 2200 residents were Jewish, but in the last decades of the nineteenth century many emigrated to Palestine, a process which accelerated after World War II – though the great majority of Pitigliano's Jews survived the Nazi occupation. Today, though, in what was formerly one of the centres of Jewish learning in southern Europe, only a handful of Jewish residents remain.

However, still surviving are an exquisite tiny **synagogue** and a modest museum of Jewish culture just off Via Zuccarelli (both Mon–Fri & Sun: May–Oct 10am–12.30pm & 4–7pm; Nov–April 10am–12.30pm & 3–6pm, closed Jewish public holidays; €3), the former beautifully restored after having fallen into disrepair in the late 1950s.

the town belonged to the ubiquitous **Aldobrandeschi**, who ruled it from nearby Sovana, then one of the clan's two principal southern Tuscan power bases.
In 1293 it passed to the counts of **Orsini**, a Roman family who produced three popes and countless cardinals, bishops and minor papal dignitaries. Its ultimate fate (in 1608), like much of the region, was to become a part of the Grand Duchy of Tuscany.

Piazza Petruccioli and the fortress

The major entry point to the medieval town is **Piazza Petruccioli** – host to a small belvedere that looks along the houses and cliffs on the town's southern edge. Immediately through the gate is the high-walled and rather claustrophobic Piazza Garibaldi, and beyond it the massive **aqueduct** (1543) and **fortress**, completed in the sixteenth century under Giuliano da Sangallo, along with a complex string of fortifications.

Museo Civico Archeologico della Civiltà Etrusca

April–mid-June Mon, Thurs & Fri 10am–5pm, Sat & Sun 10am–6pm; mid- to end-June Mon & Wed–Fri 10am–5pm, Sat & Sun 10am–6pm; July Mon–Fri 10am–5pm, Sat & Sun 10am–6pm; Aug daily 10am–7pm; Oct Mon & Thurs–Sun 10am–5pm • €2.50

Within the fortress is the mostly private Renaissance **Palazzo Orsini**, begun in the thirteenth century and extended by Niccolò Orsini two centuries later. It is home to the five-room **Museo Civico Archeologico della Civiltà Etrusca**, which houses an interesting collection of vases, jewellery and trinkets unearthed in the nearby Etruscan site of Poggio Buco.

Museo della Civiltà Giubonnai

Hours vary; contact the tourist office

The **Museo della Civiltà Giubonnai** is located in cellars beneath the fortress, which were discovered by accident during a clean-up. Some of the labyrinth had remained unseen and untouched for three hundred years; other parts had been filled with rubble during Sangallo's work on the foundations. The growing collection of exhibits centres on folk, domestic and agricultural ephemera of the Maremma.

Piazza della Repubblica

The fortress backs onto **Piazza della Repubblica**, the town's elongated and beautiful main square, its symmetry accentuated by a pair of fountains and immaculately pollarded ilex trees. Wander over to the balcony for a panorama taking in the river, trees, waterfalls and the faint outline of Monte Amiata away to the north.

Santa Maria

Via Zuccarelli • Irregular hours

The main door to the Renaissance church of **Santa Maria** is flanked by the arms of the Orsini family. To the left of the door under the tower, note the twelfth-century bas-relief depicting a human figure and two winged dragons. Inside are a few patches o fresco, less interesting than the building's peculiar trapezoidal plan.

The Duomo

Piazza Gregorio VII • Mon–Sat 8am–noon & 4–7pm

The town's present Baroque **Duomo**, with its giant campanile, is a surviving portion of a much earlier Romanesque church on the site. The western end of the square features a prominent travertine pillar (1490) with a text praising the Orsini.

ARRIVAL AND INFORMATION

By bus Buses arrive and depart from Piazza Petruccioli. **Destinations** Albinia (6 daily; 1hr); Grosseto via Manciano (3 daily; 1hr 40min); Orbetello (5 daily; 1hr 25min); San Quírico (4 daily; 15min); Semproniano (1 daily; 45min); Sorano (5 daily; 10min); Sovana (3 daily; 10min).

Tourist office Piazza Garibaldi 12 (April–Oct Tues–Sun 10.20am–1pm & 3–7pm; Nov–March 10.20am–1pm & 2–6pm; ☎0564 617 111, ☜turismoinmaremma.it or ☜tuttomanciano.com).

ACCOMMODATION AND EATING

Albergo Guastini Piazza Petruccioli ☎0564 616 065, ☜albergoguastini.it. Close to the heart of the old town, and run by the same family since 1905, with 27 unfussy and well-kept rooms, some with beams and other period features. €66
Hosteria dei Ceccottino Piazza San Gregorio VII 64 ☎0564 614 273, ☜ceccottino.com. An inexpensive wooden-beamed restaurant close to the cathedral, with a few tables outside for summer dining. Some dishes have their origins in the traditional Jewish cuisine of the nearby former ghetto. Reckon on €30 for a meal. Mon–Wed & Fri–Sun 12.30–2.30pm & 7.30–10pm; closed mid-Jan to mid-March.

★**Osteria Il Tufo** Allegro Vicolo della Costituzione 1 ☎0564 616 192. An intimate, mid-priced osteria – a meal comes in at around €35 – at the heart of town, not far from the synagogue and partly contained, as the name suggests, in a space carved from the local stone. Good wine list. Wed 7.30–10.30pm (plus 12.30–2.30pm in Aug), Mon & Thurs–Sun 12.30–2.30pm & 7.30–10.30pm ; closed Jan.
Valle Orientina Località Valle Orientina ☎0564 616 611, ☜valleorientina.it. An out-of-town hotel in a rural setting 3km from Pitigliano. It's pleasantly rustic and family run, and has a swimming pool, tennis courts, natural mineral spa and offers the opportunity to rent bikes or horses. €90

Sovana

8

Fine Etruscan tombs, attractive old streets and pristine Romanesque architecture would place **SOVANA** firmly on the tour circuit, if only it were closer to Siena or Florence. As it is, you can often explore this breathtaking medieval centre in virtual solitude – save at weekends, when it can become busy.

The town dates to at least the seventh century BC, when the Etruscans took up residence. It fell to the Romans in the third century BC, later becoming a Lombard fiefdom. The principal monuments, though, derive from Sovana's time as the capital of the **Aldobrandeschi**, a noble clan whose domain extended over much of southern Tuscany and northern Lazio; they were said to have a castle for every day of the year. Their golden age came with the birth in Sovana in 1020 of a scion, Hildebrand, who in 1073 was to become Pope Gregory VII, a great reformer who also kept a favourable eye on family business. Decline set in during the fourteenth century, when Sovana's low-lying position made it vulnerable both to malaria and Sienese attacks, and its population and power drifted to nearby Pitigliano. Siena took control of the town in 1410, ceding power to the Grand Duchy of Tuscany in 1557.

Via di Mezzo

Sovana's main street, **Via di Mezzo**, is almost the sum of the place, a broad expanse of fishbone-patterned brick paving, laid in 1580 by Ferdinand I de' Medici and restored to impressive effect. Guarding its start are the ruins of the Aldobrandeschi castle, built in the eleventh century on Etruscan foundations: it fell into greater disrepair with each of its subsequent owners – the Sienese, Orsini and Medici, who tried to repopulate the place in the seventeenth century by importing 58 families from Albania.

Santa Maria

At its end, Via di Mezzo swells slightly to form the **Piazza del Pretorio**, a perfect medieval ensemble dominated on the left by **Santa Maria**, one of the most beautiful churches in southern Tuscany. Built in the thirteenth century to a Romanesque-Gothic plan, it has a simple stone interior dominated by an exquisite **ciborium**, a unique piece of pre-Romanesque paleo-Christian sculpture from the eighth or ninth century. Such canopies disappeared from churches in about the thirteenth century, confirming the work's far earlier provenance. Superbly preserved early frescoes around the walls set the seal on a marvellous building.

Palazzo Pretorio

Piazza del Pretorio • Museum and gallery Tues–Sat 10am–1pm & 4–7pm • €3

The thirteenth-century **Palazzo Pretorio** is home to a small **museum** and **gallery** which traces the area's history through local Etruscan tombs and discoveries. The reconstructions of **tombs** are well worth seeing if you intend to explore the necropolis (see box, below). The nine stone banners here are those of the town's Sienese and Medici governors, while the little pillar to the right of the main door was used to pin up public declarations.

The Duomo

Via del Duomo • April–Oct 9am–1pm & 3–8pm; Nov–March 10am–1pm & 3–6pm • Free

From the Piazza del Pretorio, a back lane leads through gardens and olive groves to the huge **Duomo**, or Cattedrale di Sts Pietro e Paolo, whose exterior wall and superb portal bear some of the finest Lombard-Romanesque **carvings** in Tuscany. The church's nucleus went up in the eighth century (the date of many of the carvings) or possibly earlier – it's known the town was a centre of a diocese in the sixth century – and was augmented in the tenth with the addition of an apse and crypt.

The bare, triple-naved **interior** features some twelfth-century carved capitals; the finest is that on the second pillar in the left aisle, a work which suggests the hand of Lombard masons. There are also traces of fresco, a fine Gothic font and a wonderful **crypt**, divided into five tiny naves by ancient columns. The urn in the main church contains the remains of St Mamiliano, a sixth-century saint who evangelized much of the region.

Beyond the Duomo you can walk down to an old town **gateway** and traces of Etruscan wall, or turn back to Piazza del Pretorio along the village's modest residential street.

ACCOMMODATION AND EATING SOVANA

Hotel Scilla Via Rodolfo Silviero 1–3 ☎ 0564 616 531, ⓦ albergoscilla.com. Just off the piazza, the eight-room

Scilla has eight bright, airy rooms recently upgraded from one to three stars, and some pretty common areas – the

---

ETRUSCAN TOMBS NEAR SOVANA

All round Sovana, but especially on the road to Saturnia, **Etruscan tombs** riddle the countryside, many approached by original "sunken" Etruscan roads. Why these roads should be sunken still puzzles scholars: some believe the purpose was defensive, in that they would enable people to move unseen from town to town; others posit that they were used for moving livestock, and were cut below ground level to prevent the animals from straying.

The larger graves are well marked off the road. The necropolis as a whole, of which the marked tombs form a tiny part, extends for miles and rates in archeological (if not tourist) terms with the graves at Tarquinia and Cerveteri. Most of the tombs date from the seventh century BC and just about every type of Etruscan grave is present, including *colombari*, small niches cut into the rock to take cinerary urns. What the tombs lack in paintings they often make up for with elaborate carvings.

The key tombs are the **Tomba Ildebranda** (daily: March–Oct 9.30am–dusk; Nov–Feb 10am–dusk; €7 combined ticket with Fortezza Orsini in Sorano, and Vitozza caves near San Quírico), considered the best single tomb in Tuscany, and the **Tomba della Sirena** (same hours and ticket). After the tunnel on the road to Saturnia, however, you'll spot more tombs, most of which can be visited, including the Poggio Pesca and the Pola, a couple of minutes' uphill scramble from the road.

vast stone fireplace in the main salon is a wonderful feature. The *Dei Merli* restaurant offers Maremman cuisine and a beautiful setting, with a pergola draped in flowers and greenery. Reckon on around €35 for three courses. Restaurant Mon & Wed–Sun 12.30–2.30pm & 7.30–10pm; open daily in Aug. **€75–120**

★ **Sovana Hotel & Resort** Via del Duomo 66 ☎ 0564 617 126, ⊛ hotelsovana.com. This recently opened four-star is a superb place to stay, close to the Duomo, and with just eighteen beautiful rooms in three categories, all with period features and some with views over the surrounding countryside. From **€120**

★ **Taverna Etrusca** Piazza del Pretorio 16 ☎ 0564 616 531, ⊛ tavernaetrusca.com. A first-rate restaurant, with a beautifully elegant interior scattered with covetable antique furniture, and fine food at around €35 for three courses. Mon, Tues & Thurs–Sun 12.30–2.30pm & 7.15–10pm (open daily in Aug); closed for part of Jan.

Sorano and around

SORANO, 9km northeast of Pitigliano, is less obviously pretty than Sovana, but has seen much of its medieval heart restored in recent years and, like nearby **San Quírico**, is close to more Etruscan tombs. All the approaches to the town are extraordinary: from the south the route is lined with caves and tombs cut into the hillside; from the west, the road is cut into walls of tufa. The village itself is full of intriguing medieval corners, but has little in the way of specific sights.

Fortezza Orsini

Daily: March–Oct 9.30am–dusk; Nov–Feb 10am–dusk • €7 combined ticket with Tomba Ildebranda in Sovana and Vitozza caves near San Quírico

An old castle dominates the centre of Sorano, now converted into a fine three-star **hotel**, the *Della Fortezza*. The other fortress as you enter the town is the **Fortezza Orsini**, a blunt and perfectly preserved piece of Renaissance military engineering. Built over an old Aldobrandeschi fort in 1552, it was often besieged but never captured.

INFORMATION

Tourist office Piazza Busati (April–Oct daily 10am–1pm & 3–8pm; Nov–March Fri–Sun 10am–1pm & 3–6.30pm; ☎ 0564 633 099, ⊛ turismoinmaremma.it or ⊛ tutto manciano.com).

SORANO

ACCOMMODATION

Della Fortezza Piazza Cairoli ☎ 0564 632 010, ⊛ hoteldellafortezza.com. The fifteen rooms here are wood-beamed and simply but elegantly furnished with antiques, and the views over the town and countryside are superb. **€120**

San Quírico

From Sorano there are constant views over the wooded gorge of the River Lente, whose rushing waters echo through the streets. Down on the valley floor, tantalizing ancient tracks crisscross the countryside, linking clearly visible rock tombs, Roman wells and old watermill workings. Some 5km east is the hamlet of **SAN QUÍRICO**, to the north of which you can explore the **Rupestre di Vitozza** (daily: March–Oct 9.30am–dusk; Nov–Feb 10am–dusk; €7 combined ticket with with Tomba Ildebranda in Sovana and Fortezza Orsini in Sorano), a series of two hundred tombs, grottoes and paleo-Christian remains, and the remnants of Vitozza, San Quírico's medieval antecedent.

ACCOMMODATION AND EATING

SAN QUÍRICO

Agnelli Piazza della Republica 9 ☎ 0564 619 015, ⊛ lavecchiafonte.com. The fifteen rooms here are better and more spacious than the bland modern exterior suggests, though hardly compelling and really only worth an overnight stop if you can't make Sovana or Pitigliano, but the restaurant has a decent atmosphere on busy nights. In addition to inexpensive pizzas, it serves surprisingly good fish and seafood bought in fresh daily. Prices are keen (around €25), making it popular with locals. Restaurant Tues–Sun 12.30–3pm & 7.30–10pm. **€80**

Arezzo Province

ANTIQUES MARKET, AREZZO

9

Arezzo Province

Upstream from Florence, the Arno valley – the VALDARNO – is quite an industrialized district, with warehouses and factories enclosing many of the small towns strung along the train line. Some of the villages up on the valley sides retain a medieval square or a cluster of attractive buildings, but there's no very compelling stop before you reach the provincial capital of the upper Arno region, AREZZO, one hour's train ride from Florence. This solidly bourgeois city has its share of architectural delights – including one of the most photogenic squares in central Italy – though most visitors to Arezzo are there to see just one thing: the fresco cycle by PIERO DELLA FRANCESCA in the church of San Francesco. Italians flock here in even greater numbers for antiques, traded each month on the Piazza Grande in quantities scarcely matched anywhere else in the country.

For art lovers, there are two essential calls in the vicinity of Arezzo. The first is the modest hill-town of **Monterchi**, where della Francesca painted one of the most powerful images of the Renaissance, the pregnant *Madonna del Parto*. Two other magnificent works by the same artist are to be seen in his birthplace, **Sansepolcro**, almost on the Umbrian border to the east.

Art is far from being this province's sole attraction, however. In the **Casentino**, to the north of Arezzo, small hill-towns such as **Poppi** stand above a terrain of rich farmland that's cradled by thickly wooded upland. The secluded peaks of the Casentino also harbour two of Italy's most influential monasteries, **Camáldoli** and the Franciscan sanctuary of **La Verna**, Tuscany's busiest pilgrimage site. The ancient woodlands cradling these sanctuaries have been protected within the new **Parco Nazionale delle Foreste Casentinesi**, an area that extends across the surprisingly high, wild and forested border country of northern Tuscany into Emilia-Romagna.

To the south of Arezzo stretches the agricultural plain of the **Valdichiana**, where the ancient hill-town of **Cortona** is the major attraction, its steep streets forming a distinctive urban landscape and giving an unforgettable view over Lago Trasimeno and the Valdichiana. It's also home to a pair of fine museums, one of which features major paintings by Fra' Angelico and locally born Luca Signorelli.

GETTING AROUND AREZZO PROVINCE

Trains on the Florence–Rome rail line run up the Arno valley, through Arezzo and on down the Valdichiana: for Cortona the nearest station on this line is Camucia, though more services stop at the slightly more distant Teróntola. For the Casentino, there's the LFI private rail line from Arezzo. Note that the private FCU railway from Sansepolcro to Perugia by way of Città di Castello gives you another way into Umbria.

Arezzo and Cortona are the centres of overlapping **bus** networks, which between them cover most of Arezzo province. That said, a car is essential if you want to get to some of the region's wilder reaches.

CORTONA

Highlights

❶ Arezzo The capital of the province is a well-off place, thanks mainly to its antiques dealers and goldsmiths, and to the tourists who come here for Piero della Francesca's sublime fresco cycle. **See p.372**

❷ Monterchi This minuscule village, between Arezzo and Sansepolcro, is home to another Piero masterpiece, the *Madonna del Parto*. **See p.379**

❸ Sansepolcro This small walled town is another essential stop on the Piero trail, as its museum is home to several paintings by him, including the magnificent *Resurrection*. **See p.380**

❹ The Casentino The forested slopes of the Casentino national park, to the north of Arezzo, offer some fine walks. **See p.381**

❺ La Verna St Francis's mountaintop retreat, which is still a thriving Franciscan monastery, commands wonderful views of the Apennines. **See p.382**

❻ Cortona The ancient and lofty hill-town of Cortona attracts busloads of tourists nowadays, but its steep little streets have not yet lost their charm. **See p.386**

HIGHLIGHTS ARE MARKED ON THE MAP ON P.370

9

From Florence to Arezzo

If you're travelling by public transport from Florence to Arezzo there's no choice of route, as buses and trains all follow the **Valdarno**. By car, the obvious choice is between the two major roads that run roughly parallel to the river: the Autostrada del Sole and the SS69. If you want to see the few sights of the Valdarno, go for the latter, but be warned that the tarmac is clogged with lorries rumbling in and out of the industrial estates that pepper this part of the region. There is a third alternative, in the shape of the road that skirts the upland region known as the **Pratomagno**.

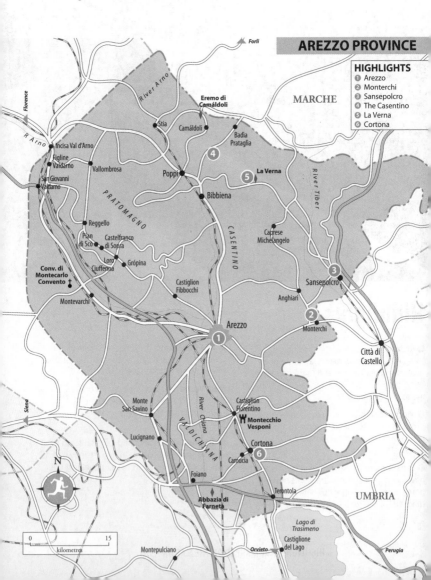

AREZZO PROVINCE

HIGHLIGHTS
❶ Arezzo
❷ Monterchi
❸ Sansepolcro
❹ The Casentino
❺ La Verna
❻ Cortona

The Valdarno route

River, rail line and autostrada come together at the bottleneck known as Incisa Val d'Arno, 25km out of central Florence. Petrarch grew up here and some vestiges of the old town are preserved – but insufficient to make the place appealing. **Figline Valdarno**, 5km south, was the birthplace of another eminent Tuscan, Marsilio Ficino, court scholar-philosopher to Lorenzo il Magnifico. The old quarter around Piazza Ficino has a few handsome buildings and one interesting interior – the frescoed Collegiata di Santa Maria, which contains a fourteenth-century *Madonna* by the so-called Maestro di Figline.

San Giovanni Valdarno

SAN GIOVANNI VALDARNO, midway between Florence and Arezzo, is the most heavily industrialized but also the most rewarding town in the valley. Its arcaded Palazzo Comunale is a design by Arnolfo di Cambio, architect of Florence's Palazzo Vecchio and Duomo, who in the thirteenth century was put in charge of fortifying this Florentine town against the citizens of Arezzo.

At the back of the *palazzo*, next to the church of Santa Maria della Grazia, the **Museo della Basilica di Santa Maria della Grazia** (summer Mon–Sat 10am–1pm & 2.30–6.30pm, Sun 2.30–6.30pm; winter opens 1hr later in afternoons; €3.50) is worth a visit for Fra' Angelico's *Annunciation,* painted for the Convento di Montecarlo. Also on show is work by Lo Scheggia, younger brother of the much more famous Masaccio, whose birthplace, at Corso Italia 83, is now the **Museo Casa Masaccio**, which is used as an exhibition space.

Montevarchi

In the Pliocene era the Valdarno was a vast lake, its shores patrolled by troops of prehistoric elephants. Fossils of these colossal beasts are the pride of **MONTEVARCHI**, where they are installed in the **Museo Paleontologico** (Tues–Sat 9am–noon & 4–6pm, Sun 10am–noon; €3); around 1500 other exhibits keep them company. In the centre of town in Via Isidoro del Lungo, the sacristy of the Collegiata di San Lorenzo has been converted into a small **Museo di Arte Sacra** (Thurs 10am–noon, Sat & Sun 10am–noon & 4–6pm; €3), where the main exhibit is a gorgeous little chapel covered in ceramics by Andrea della Robbia.

The Pratomagno

The **Pratomagno** route, along the wooded east bank of the Arno, is a fairly testing drive, with a gear-change required every couple of hundred metres, but the views across to Chianti are gorgeous, and there's the odd Romanesque church along the way, one of them boasting a superb painting by Masaccio.

Vallombrosa

The most famous spot in the Pratomagno is **VALLOMBROSA**, whose abbey is the mother foundation of the Vallombrosan order, established in 1038 by the Florentine Giovanni Gualberto (see p.79). After Giovanni was canonized in 1193 this abbey became extremely influential, and by the fifteenth century it was administering wide tracts of Tuscan territory. Much rebuilt since, it now resembles a fortified villa and impresses mainly by its location, pillowed against the fir-covered hills. Part of the complex is still occupied by Vallombrosan monks, and part by a forestry school; none of it is open to the public.

Pieve di San Pietro a Cascia

Beyond Saltino the terrain opens out, with terraces bordering the road as it snakes down to characterless **REGGELLO**. A kilometre to the south, the Romanesque **Pieve di**

9

San Pietro a Cascia is worth a stop for the **Museo Masaccio d'Arte Sacra** (Tues & Thurs 3–7pm, Sat & Sun 10am–noon & 3–7pm; €3; ⓦmuseomasaccio.it). Opened to mark the six hundredth anniversary of the birth of Masaccio, who was born in nearby San Giovanni Valdarno, this tiny museum houses the earliest known work by the artist, the *San Giovenale Triptych*, which was painted in 1422. A ground-floor room is devoted to background information on the triptych, while the other rooms are given over to miscellaneous documents, furnishings and minor artworks.

Pian di Scò to Loro Ciuffenna

More Romanesque architecture appears at **Pian di Scò**, 10km on, where there's an eleventh-century *pieve*. **Castelfranco di Sopra**, 2km farther, was yet another town fortified by Arnolfo di Cambio, but the street plan and one gate are virtually the only traces of his handiwork; its most attractive feature is the thirteenth-century *badìa* on the main road. Another 10km brings you to **Loro Ciuffenna**, where ranks of new apartments form an unflattering prelude to a small medieval quarter down by the Ciuffenna River; a Romanesque tower and bridge form the core. The bridge – the Ponte Vecchio – is one of the seven that gave the old Pratomagno pilgrimage route its name, the Setteponti.

Grópina to Castiglion Fibocchi

The most interesting building in this part of the Arno valley comes a couple of kilometres on, in the hamlet of **Grópina**. Here the ancient church of **San Pietro** (daily 10am–noon & 3–5pm) has some of the finest Romanesque carving in Tuscany, dating from the early thirteenth century. The capitals depict knights, fighting animals and various standard motifs, while the pulpit is adorned with knotted columns and rows of alarmed-looking figures with upraised arms.

The last place of any interest before Arezzo is **Castiglion Fibocchi**, whose central patch – now enclosed by light industry – has changed little in appearance since the Middle Ages, though no monument in particular stands out.

Arezzo

Maecenas, the wealthy patron of Horace and Virgil, was born in **AREZZO** and it's still a place with the moneyed touch, thanks in large part to its many jewellers and goldsmiths. Topping up the coffers are the proceeds of Arezzo's antiques industry: shops in the vicinity of the Piazza Grande are filled with museum-quality furniture, and every month the **Fiera Antiquaria** turns the piazza into a vast showroom. Though Arezzo is nowadays making more of an effort to market itself to visitors, this is still very much a self-sufficient city.

Occupying a site that controls the major passes of the central Apennines, Arezzo was one of the most important settlements of the Etruscan federation. It maintained its pre-eminence under Roman rule, and was a prosperous independent republic in the Middle Ages until, in 1289, its Ghibelline allegiances brought about a catastrophic

ORIENTATION

There are two distinct parts to Arezzo: the **older quarter**, at the top of the hill, and the businesslike **lower town**. From the train station forecourt, go straight ahead for Via Guido Monaco, the traffic axis between the upper and lower town. The parallel **Corso Italia**, now pedestrianized, is the route to walk up the hill. Off to the left of the Corso, on Via Cavour, not far from its summit, stands the building everyone comes to Arezzo to see: the basilica of **San Francesco**.

Virtually all the principal sights of Arezzo are in the upper part of the town, none of them more than a short stroll from San Francesco. At the bottom of the hill there are just two significant things to see: the archeological museum and the church of Santa Maria delle Grazie.

● BARS, CAFÉS &
   GELATERIE
Bacco e Arianna   2
Fiaschetteria de' Redi   5
Il Gelato   6

● RESTAURANTS
Antica Osteria L'Agania   4
Il Saraceno   3
Miseria e Nobiltà   1

■ ACCOMMODATION
Antiche Mura   2
Foresteria San Pier Piccolo   3
Graziella Patio Hotel   4
Ostello Villa Severi   1
Vogue Hotel   5

Santa Maria delle Grazie

clash with the Guelph Florentines at Campaldino (see p.384). Arezzo temporarily recovered from this reversal under the leadership of **Bishop Guido Tarlati**, whose bellicosity eventually earned him excommunication. However, subjugation came about in 1384, when Florence paid the ransom demanded of Arezzo by the conquering army of Louis d'Anjou. When the French departed, the city's paymaster was left in power.

Even as a mortgaged political power, Arezzo continued to be a major cultural force. Already renowned as the birthplace of the man known as Guido d'Arezzo or Guido Monaco (c.991–1050), who is widely regarded as the inventor of modern musical notation, Arezzo was brought further prestige by Petrarch (1304–74), and then by the writer Pietro Aretino (1492–1556) and the artist-architect-biographer Giorgio Vasari (1511–74). Yet it was an outsider who gave Arezzo its greatest monument – **Piero della Francesca**, whose frescoes for the church of San Francesco belong in the same company as Masaccio's cycle in Florence and Michelangelo's in Rome.

MUSEUM ADMISSION IN AREZZO

A €12 ticket gives you a **single admission** to each of the following monuments and museums: Museo Archeologico, Museo d'Arte Medievale e Moderna, the Casa di Giorgio Vasari and the della Francesca frescoes in San Francesco. The ticket can be bought at any of these four locations.

9

THE LEGEND OF THE TRUE CROSS

9	10	11	b	1	a
7	6	3	a	2	b
8	12	4		5	

1a. Adam announces his death and implores Seth, his son, to seek the oil of mercy from the Angel of Eden.

1b. Instead the Angel gives Seth a sprig from the Tree of Knowledge, which is planted in the dead Adam's mouth.

2a. Solomon orders a bridge to be built from a beam fashioned from the tree that grew from Adam's grave. The Queen of Sheba, visiting Solomon, kneels in prayer before the bridge, sensing the holiness of the wood.

2b. The Queen of Sheba foresees that the beam will later be used to crucify a man, and that the death will bring disgrace to the Jews; she tells Solomon of her prophecy.

3. Solomon orders the beam to be buried.

4. The Emperor Constantine has a vision of the Cross, hearing a voice that declares: Under this sign shall you be victorious.

5. Constantine defeats the rival emperor Maxentius, and then is baptized. The figure of Constantine — the first emperor to rule Byzantium — may be a portrait of John Paleologus, the penultimate Byzantine emperor, who had been in Florence in 1439 to attend the Council of Florence.

6. The Levite Judas, under torture, reveals to the servants of St Helena — mother of Constantine — the burial place of the three crosses from Golgotha.

7. The crosses are excavated; the true Cross is recognized when it brings about a man's resurrection. Arezzo — serving as Jerusalem — is shown in the background.

8. The Persian king Chosroes, who had stolen the Cross, is defeated by the Emperor Heraclius. On the right he kneels awaiting execution; behind him is visible the throne into which he had incorporated the Cross.

9. Heraclius returns the Cross to Jerusalem.

10. Isaiah.

11. Jeremiah.

12. The Annunciation.

San Francesco

Piazza San Francesco

Built in the 1320s, the church of **San Francesco** earned its renown in the early 1450s, when the Bacci family commissioned **Piero della Francesca** to continue the decoration of the choir. The project had been started by Bicci di Lorenzo, who had painted only the *Evangelists* (in the vault) and part of the *Last Judgement* (on the arch outside the chapel) before he died. For the wall paintings, Piero's patrons nominated a subject with rather fewer dramatic possibilities, but which suited the personality of the artist perfectly.

The frescoes

The theme chosen for the frescoes was **The Legend of the True Cross**, a story in which the physical material of the Cross forms the link in the cycle of redemption that begins with humanity's original sin. The literary source for the cycle, the *Golden Legend* by Jacopo de Voragine, is a convoluted story, and the way the episodes are arranged adds to the opacity, as Piero preferred to organize the scenes according to the precepts of symmetry rather than in chronological order: thus the two battle scenes face each other across the chapel, rather than coming where the story dictates. Smaller-scale symmetries are present in every part of the work: for example, the retinue of the Queen of Sheba appears twice, in mirror-image arrangement, and the face of the queen is exactly the same as the face of the Empress Helena. This orderliness, combined with the pale light and the statuesque quality of the figures, create an atmosphere of contemplative rationality that's unique to Piero.

Damp has badly damaged areas of the chapel and some bits have peeled away, partly as a result of Piero's notoriously slow method of working (the frescoes occupied most of his time from 1452 to 1466), but most of the rest has emerged in magnificent condition after a decade's restoration work. Our plan is a basic guide to the events depicted. The images of the *Annunciation* and two prophets on the window wall (Isaiah – painted by one of Piero's assistants – to the left; Jeremiah to the right) have nothing to do with the legend, but relate to the theme of the redemptive significance of the Cross, a point underlined by the cruciform plan of the *Annunciation*, which in turn echoes the plan of the *Vision of Constantine* on the other side of the window, where the tent pole and the rim of the tent form a cross.

Pieve di Santa Maria

Corso Italia • Daily: summer 8am–1pm & 3–7pm; winter 8am–noon & 3–6pm

At the top of the Corso stands one of the finest Romanesque structures in Tuscany, the twelfth-century **Pieve di Santa Maria**. Its arcaded facade belongs to a type associated more with Pisa and western Tuscany, and is doubly unusual in presenting its front to a fairly narrow street rather than to the town's main square. Dating from the 1210s, the lively carvings of the months over the portal are the most notable adornment of the exterior. The campanile, known locally as "the tower of the hundred holes", was added in the fourteenth century. The oldest section of the chalky grey **interior** is the raised sanctuary, where the altarpiece is Pietro Lorenzetti's *Madonna and Saints* polyptych, painted in 1320. The unfamiliar saint on the far left, accompanying Matthew, John the Baptist and John the Evangelist, is St Donatus, the second bishop of Arezzo, who was martyred in 304. His relics are in the crypt, encased in a beautiful gold-and-silver bust made in 1346 by local goldsmiths.

Casa-Museo Ivan Bruschi

Corso Italia 14 • Tues–Sun: summer 10am–6pm; winter 10am–1pm & 2–6pm • €5 • ☻ www.fondazionebruschi.it

Opposite the Pieve, occupying the fourteenth-century Palazzo del Capitano del Popolo, the **Casa-Museo Ivan Bruschi** commemorates the man who started Arezzo's antiques fair. Bruschi's collection of sculptures, armour, books and miscellaneous *objets d'art* are nicely displayed in a simulated jumble, but it's a museum to leave until you've seen the rest of the city's sights.

Piazza Grande

The steeply sloping **Piazza Grande**, on the other side of the Pieve, is generally a peaceful spot, but comes alive for the *Fiera Antiquaria* and – more raucously – for September's Giostra del Saracino. A diverting assortment of buildings encloses the space, with the balconied apartments on the east side facing the apse of the Pieve, the Baroque Palazzo dei Tribunali and the **Palazzetto della Fraternità dei Laici**. The upper level of the Palazzetto is adorned by a relief of the *Madonna della Misericordia* and niche statues, all carved by Bernardo Rossellino in 1434; below, there's a lunette fresco of the *Pietà* by Spinello Aretino, dating from the 1370s, while the beautiful loggia and cornice across the top of the *palazzo* date from 1460. The piazza's northern edge is formed by the arcades of the **Loggia di Vasari**, occupied by shops that in some instances still retain their original sixteenth-century stone counters.

The Duomo

Piazza del Duomo • Daily 6.30am–12.30pm & 3–6.30pm

At the summit of the town rises the large and unfussy **Duomo**: begun in 1278, it was virtually finished by the start of the sixteenth century, but the campanile dates from 1859 and the facade from 1914. The **stained-glass windows**, a rarity in Italy, were

AREZZO'S FESTIVALS

Arezzo's premier folkloric event is the **Giostra del Saracino**, which was first recorded in 1535 and is nowadays held in the Piazza Grande on the first Sunday in September. The day starts off with various costumed parades; at 5pm the action switches to the jousting arena in the piazza, with a procession of some three hundred participants leading the way. Each quarter of the city is represented by a pair of knights on horseback, who do battle with a wooden effigy of a Saracen king. In one hand it holds a shield marked with point scores, a bit like a dartboard; in the other it has a cat-o'-three-tails which swings round when the shield is hit, necessitating nifty evasive action from the rider. A golden lance is awarded to the highest-scoring rider. In the days immediately preceding the joust you'll see rehearsals taking place, and in recent years the event has become so popular that a reduced version of the show is now held on the penultimate Saturday of June; check at the tourist office for information.

The musical tradition that began with Guido d'Arezzo is kept alive chiefly through the international choral competition that bears his name: the **Concorso Polifonico Guido d'Arezzo**, held in the last week of August.

The **Fiera Antiquaria** takes over the Piazza Grande on the first Sunday of each month and the preceding Saturday. The most expensive stuff is laid out by the Vasari loggia, with cheaper pieces lower down the square and in the side streets.

made around 1520 by Guillaume de Marcillat, an Arezzo-based Frenchman who also contributed some frescoes to San Francesco; they let in so little light that his other contributions to the interior – the paintings on the first three bays of the nave – are almost invisible. Off the left aisle, separated from the nave by a huge screen, the Cappella della Madonna del Conforto has terracottas by the della Robbia family, but the best of the building's artworks lie further down the aisle. Just beyond the organ is the **tomb of Bishop Guido Tarlati** (died 1327), head of the *comune* of Arezzo during its resurgence in the early fourteenth century; the monument, plated with marble reliefs showing scenes from the militaristic bishop's career, was possibly designed by Giotto. The small fresco nestled against the right side of the tomb is **Piero della Francesca**'s *Magdalene*, his only work in Arezzo outside San Francesco.

Museo Diocesano and around

As the opening hours suggest, the **Museo Diocesano** (Thurs–Sat 10am–noon; €2.50), alongside the Duomo, isn't expecting many visitors, and it's hard to imagine that this small collection of ecclesiastical paraphernalia will make anyone's day, but the **Passeggio del Prato**, which extends from the east end of the Duomo to the **Fortezza Medicea**, is a good place to take a picnic. Cosimo I's fortress here was demolished in the eighteenth century, leaving only the ramparts.

San Domenico

Piazza San Domenico • Daily 8am–7pm

A short distance north of the Duomo, the church of **San Domenico** was constructed mostly in the late thirteenth century but with a Gothic campanile. Inside there are tatters of fifteenth- and sixteenth-century frescoes on the walls, while above the high altar hangs a dolorous Crucifix by Cimabue (1260), painted when the artist would have been about 20.

Casa di Giorgio Vasari

Via XX Settembre 55 • Mon & Wed–Sat 9am–7pm, Sun 9am–1pm • €2, or €12 combined ticket (see p.373)

The **Casa di Giorgio Vasari** was designed by the eponymous biographer-architect-artist who was born in Arezzo in 1511, was taught to paint by his distant relative Luca Signorelli, and went on to become general artistic supremo to Cosimo I. His major contribution to Western culture is his *Lives of the Most Excellent Italian Architects, Painters and Sculptors*, a primary source for all histories of the Renaissance. The industrious Vasari frescoed much of his house with portraits and mythological characters, a decorative scheme that makes this one of the brashest domestic interiors in Tuscany. Portraits include his wife as the muse of conjugal love (in the Chamber of Apollo) and Michelangelo and Andrea del Sarto (in the Chamber of Fame). Work by other minor artists are strewn all over the place.

Museo d'Arte Medievale e Moderna

Via San Lorentino 8 • Tues–Sun 8.30am–7.30pm • €4, or €12 combined ticket (see p.373)

The fifteenth-century Palazzo Bruni-Ciocchi houses the **Museo d'Arte Medievale e Moderna**, containing a collection of paintings by local artists and majolica pieces from the thirteenth to the eighteenth centuries, generously spread over three floors. Highlights are the first floor's medieval and Renaissance paintings by the likes of Spinello Aretino, Luca Signorelli and Bartolomeo della Gatta, and the five rooms filled with ceramics from Deruta, Gubbio, Faenza and other major Italian centres of production.

Badìa di Santi Flora e Lucilla

Piazza della Badia • Mon–Sat 8am–noon & 4–7pm, Sun 7am–12.30pm

If you follow Via Cavour from the Museo d'Arte, a huge Baroque tower soon signals the presence of the hulking **Badìa di Santi Flora e Lucilla**. The interior was extensively remodelled by Vasari, who also contributed the monstrous main altarpiece, designed as a monument to his family.

Museo Archeologico

Via Margaritone • Daily 8.30am–7.30pm • €4, or €12 combined ticket (see p.373)

The **Museo Archeologico** occupies part of an abandoned Olivetan monastery that was built into a wall of the town's Roman amphitheatre, to the east of the train station. The remains of the amphitheatre (entrance free) amount to little more than the base of the perimeter wall. More impressive are the museum's marvellously coloured coralline **vases**; produced here in the first century BC, they show why Arezzo's glassblowers were renowned throughout the Roman world.

Santa Maria delle Grazie

Viale Mecenate • Daily 8am–7pm

Ten minutes' walk south of the train station, you'll come upon Arezzo's most exquisite church, **Santa Maria delle Grazie**. In the sixth century BC the Etruscans held fertility rites here, beside a spring in the midst of the woods that covered this area. At the instigation of St Bernardino the site was purged of its pagan associations by the plugging of the spring and the construction of the church, which still has a Carmelite convent attached. Fronted by a tiny pine-ringed meadow that's flanked by a pair of arcades, the church is entered through a delicate portico built by Benedetto da Maiano in the 1470s. The church is essentially a single room, containing little more than a few seats and an altarpiece by Parri Spinello, painted on the instructions of St Bernardino; the beautiful marble and terracotta altar that encases it was created by Andrea della Robbia.

ARRIVAL AND DEPARTURE

AREZZO

By train Sitting on the main line between Florence and Rome, Arezzo is a major hub for train services. From the train station, it's an easy walk up to the Upper town.

Destinations Assisi (12 daily; 1hr 35min); Bibbiena (hourly; 50min); Camucia-Cortona (hourly; 20min); Florence (hourly; 1hr); Orvieto (7 daily; 1hr 20min); Perugia (every 2hr; 1hr

15min); Poppi (Mon–Sat hourly, Sun 5 services; 1hr).

By bus Buses into Arezzo all terminate by the train station. Destinations Città di Castello (at least 12 daily; 1hr 30min); Cortona (hourly; 1hr); Sansepolcro (17 daily, some via Monterchi, most via Anghiari; 1hr); Siena

(5 daily Mon–Fri; 1hr 30min).

By car There are car parks by the train station and the archeological museum, but you'll more easily find spaces in the car park outside the northern stretch of the city walls (near San Domenico), or in the streets to the south of the rail line.

INFORMATION

Tourist office Palazzo Comunale, Piazza della Libertà 1 (Mon–Fri 10am–1pm & 2–7pm, Sat & Sun 10am–7pm; ☎ 0575 401 945, ⊚ apt.arezzo.it). There's also a 24-hour touch-screen info booth in front of the train station, on Piazza della Repubblica.

ACCOMMODATION

If you're planning on staying in Arezzo, book **accommodation** as early as possible: there aren't many nice hotels in the city, and demand is very high on the first weekend of every month, because of the antiques fair; in addition it's booked solid at the end of August and beginning of September, when the Concorso Polifonico Guido d'Arezzo and the Giostra del Saracino festivals follow in quick succession. At the time of going to press, the city's youth hostel, the *Ostello Villa Severi* (some way east of the centre at Via Francesco Redi 13), was closed for rebuilding; check the tourist office website for the latest information.

Antiche Mura Piaggia di Murello 35 ☎ 0575 20 410, ⊚ antichemura.info. This six-room B&B has an excellent location at the top of the town, just a short walk from the Duomo; wood-beamed ceilings and stone floors give it an appealingly rustic feel. Breakfast is taken in a nearby bar. **€75**

Foresteria San Pier Piccolo Via Bicchieraia 32 ☎ 0575 370 474, ⊚ www.foresteriasanpierpiccolo.it. Offering some of the nicest budget accommodation in central Arezzo, *La Foresteria* comprises a dozen unfussy and well-decorated rooms in the former convent of the church of San Pier Piccolo. **€75**

★ **Graziella Patio Hotel** Via Cavour 23 ☎ 0575 401 962, ⊚ hotelpatio.it. Geared to business travellers, most of central Arezzo's hotels are rather cheerless places, but this small and welcoming four-star, almost next door to San Francesco, is an exception. The rooms are colourful and cosy, and their decor is inspired, apparently, by the work of Bruce Chatwin, hence their names – Utz, Oxiana, Cobra Verde and so on. **€170**

★ **Vogue Hotel** Via Guido Monaco 54 ☎ 0575 24 361, ⊚ voguehotel.it. This four-star hotel has 26 rooms, each uniquely styled, but all with a sleek, modern look that makes a refreshing change from the antique-clogged interiors favoured by many of Arezzo's hotels. **€170–220**

EATING AND DRINKING

★ **Antica Osteria L'Agania** Via Mazzini 10 ☎ 0575 25 381. A very good and informal trattoria with a welcoming atmosphere and excellent local dishes (special emphasis on truffles and mushrooms in season), at around €35 per head. The adjoining *Antica Vineria d'Agania* serves soups, salads and other simple meals, and has a nice selection of wines. Tues–Sun noon–3.30pm & 6.30–11pm.

Bacco e Arianna Via Cesalpino 10 ☎ 0575 299 598. A terrific little *enoteca*, very close to San Francesco, with good inexpensive food – an ideal place for a quick lunch. Mon & Thurs–Sun 11am–3pm & 7–11pm, Wed 7–11pm.

Fiaschetteria de' Redi Via de' Redi 10 ☎ 0575 355 012. Busy little osteria with a superb range of vintages and decent simple meals. Summer daily 11.30am–3pm & 7pm–midnight; closed Mon in winter.

Il Gelato Via de' Cenci 24. The best ice creams in town; try the *nocciola* (hazelnut) or pistachio. Summer 11am–midnight; winter 11am–8pm; closed Wed.

Il Saraceno Via Mazzini 6 ☎ 0575 27 644. Family-run trattoria, founded in 1946, with a well-stocked wine cellar and menus of traditional Aretine specialities (notably duck) at around €35 per head; good wood-oven pizzas too. Mon, Tues & Thurs–Sun noon–3.30pm & 7–11pm; closed 2 weeks in Jan.

Miseria e Nobiltà Piaggia di San Bartolomeo 2 ☎ 0575 21 245. With its enticing pan-Italian menu and medieval vaulted dining room, this very stylish (but not expensive) restaurant is one of the best and busiest in town. Tues 6pm–12.30am, Wed–Sun 12.30–2.30pm & 6pm–12.30am.

The Piero trail: from Arezzo to Sansepolcro

Arezzo is the springboard for one of Tuscany's most rewarding art itineraries: the **Piero della Francesca trail**, which extends east of the city to **Monterchi** and **Sansepolcro** (the artist's birthplace), and continues via Perugia, where you'll find a stunning Piero altarpiece in the main art gallery. (The trail then reaches beyond the region covered in this guide, going through Urbino and on to Rimini.)

GETTING AROUND

By bus There's no train link between Arezzo and Sansepolcro, but the SITA bus company runs nearly twenty services a day between the two towns. Most of these buses continue to Città di Castello for train connections to Perugia, and five stop at Monterchi at convenient times for a visit.

Monterchi

The farming village of **MONTERCHI** is 25km east of Arezzo, and for the last few kilometres of the journey the roadsides bear signs for the **Madonna del Parto** – surely the only painting in Tuscany to be signposted as if it were a town. The fresco was painted for a cemetery chapel on the outskirts of Monterchi, and remained hidden under plaster for centuries before its rediscovery in 1889 – by which time the *St Lucy* and the *Pietà* that Piero also painted here had both been lost.

The Madonna del Parto

Via della Reglia • Daily: April–Oct 9am–1pm & 2–7pm; Nov–March 9am–1pm & 2–6pm • €3.50

In 1993, the *Madonna* fresco was moved from the chapel to an ex-primary school on Via della Reglia, to undergo major restoration, and it remains there as the focal point of a permanent **exhibition** recounting the technical details of the fresco's restoration, and that of the San Francesco cycle in Arezzo. The picture is still an object of veneration, and the museum is sometimes cleared when local pregnant women come to pray to the Virgin; pregnant tourists are also admitted free. Images of the expectant Mary, exemplifying the mystery of the Incarnation, began to appear in Tuscan art some time in the 1330s – the earliest major example was the *Madonna del Parto* painted for the church of San Francesco di Paola in Florence by Taddeo Gaddi, around 1335. Piero della Francesca's tender and solemn masterpiece, created around 1467, was one of the last additions to the genre.

Anghiari

Most buses from Arezzo to Sansepolcro call at **ANGHIARI**, an agricultural and textile-producing hill-town set amid fields of sunflowers and tobacco, with a lucrative side-line in furniture restoration – the town has a renowned training centre for specialists in the craft, and hosts an antiques fair on the third Sunday of each month, as well as a huge annual crafts market in late April. Anghiari's diminutive historic centre commands a fine view across the upper Tiber towards Sansepolcro.

It was on this ground, on June 29, 1440, that the Florentine army defeated the Milanese troops of Filippo Maria Visconti, an engagement that became the subject of the most famous lost artwork of the Renaissance: Leonardo da Vinci's fresco in Florence's Palazzo Vecchio. There's a small **exhibition** relating to the battle in the Palazzo del Marzocco on Piazza Mameli (daily 9am–7pm; €2).

Museo Statale

Piazza Mameli • Tues–Sat 8.30am–7pm, Sun 9am–1pm • €2

The imposing Palazzo Taglieschi is home to the **Museo Statale**, a well-displayed collection of mostly unexceptional artworks and domestic items, but with one outstanding piece: a painted wooden *Madonna* by Jacopo della Quercia. The Child that was once perched on her knee has been displayed separately since the sculpture was restored, as the restorers believe it may not have been carved at the same time.

9

Caprese Michelangelo

Michelangelo, Leonardo's competitor in the decoration of the Palazzo Vecchio, was born 17km north of Anghiari in the place that now carries the name **CAPRESE MICHELANGELO**; it was just plain Caprese before being renamed in honour of the prodigious son of the town's chief magistrate and his wife. The ancient village is perched high on a cliff overlooking the car park, bus stop (with regular services from Anghiari) and a hotel-restaurant.

The castle and Michelangelo's supposed birthplace, the Casa del Podestà, have been converted into an undernourishing **Museo Michelangiolesco** (daily: summer 9.30am–6.30pm; winter 9.30am–4.30pm; €4), which contains little more than a few pieces of Renaissance furniture and some plaster casts of the great man's work.

Sansepolcro

SANSEPOLCRO is an unassuming small town that makes its way in the world as a manufacturer of lace and, more lucratively, pasta. Tourism adds a bit of cash to the town's coffers as well, because thousands of people come here each year to see **Piero della Francesca**'s paintings, though most of them leave a couple of hours later. In truth, there isn't much more to see than these pictures, but Sansepolcro is a relaxing and good-looking place, and has a couple of fine restaurants too. It also has a lively festival on the second Sunday in September, the **Palio della Balestra** festival. The return leg of the crossbow competition against the archers of Gubbio, it's preceded by some very flashy flag-hurling, whose practitioners are clad in costumes inspired by Piero's paintings.

The Museo Civico

Via Niccolò Aggiunti 65 • Daily: June 15–Sept 15 9.30am–1pm & 2.30–7pm; rest of year closes 6pm • €6 • ⓦ museocivicosansepolcro.it

The **Museo Civico** houses a sizeable collection of pictures, including work by Pontormo, Signorelli and Santi di Tito, but there's only one focus of attention here, and that's Piero della Francesca. A couple of minor della Francescas are hung in the vicinity of the **Madonna della Misericordia**, his earliest known painting and the epitome of his graceful solemnity. It was created in the 1440s, soon after he had been made a member of Sansepolcro's governing council, a position he was to hold for the rest of his life. Tiny panels surround the central image of the compassionate and powerful Madonna, who protects her worshippers with a cape as solid as a wall. The hooded man at her feet is wearing the uniform of the charity called the Compagnia della Misericordia, della Francesca's patrons; the sinister garb still worn by members of the modern Misericordia when bearing a body to a funeral.

The **Resurrection**, in the next room, was painted for the adjoining town hall, probably in the early 1450s, and moved here in the sixteenth century. Aldous Huxley once dubbed this "the greatest painting in the world", a piece of hyperbole that may well have saved it from obliteration. In 1944 the British Eighth Army was ordered to bombard Sansepolcro, but an officer recalled Huxley's article and delayed the attack in the hope that the Germans would withdraw – which they did. Much of the picture's

---

PIERO IN SANSEPOLCRO

Born here at some time around 1420, **Piero della Francesca** spent much of his life in the backwater of what was then the village of Borgo San Sepolcro; a three-year sojourn in Florence was probably his longest continuous absence, though patrons in Ferrara, Rome and Urbino also called upon his services. He returned to Sansepolcro permanently in the 1470s, having abandoned painting as his eyesight failed. Most of his last twenty years were devoted to working on his treatises *On Perspective in Painting* and *On the Five Regular Bodies*, in which he propounded the geometrical rules that he deemed essential to an accurate representation of the world, and extolled the human form as the exemplar of perfect proportion.

power comes from its emphasis on the Resurrection as a physical event: muscular and implacable, Christ steps onto the edge of the tomb – banner in hand – as if it were the rampart of a conquered city. The strange landscape in the background – with leafless trees on one side and reborn foliage on the other – was the starting point for Kenneth Clark's description, which pinpoints a pre-Christian strand to the painting's significance: "This country god, who rises in the grey light while humanity is asleep, has been worshipped ever since man first knew that the seed is not dead in the winter earth, but will force its way upwards through an iron crust."

Aboca Museum

Via Niccolò Aggiunti 75 • Daily: April–Sept 10am–1pm & 3–7pm; Oct–March 10am–1pm & 2.30–6pm • €8 • ⓦ abocamuseum.it

Sansepolcro's newest museum, the **Aboca Museum**, is a few doors down from the Museo Civico. Spread over two storeys of an imposing mansion, this is Italy's only museum dedicated to the history of herbal medicine, and it's extremely well done, with rooms full of nicely displayed old equipment, ceramics and books; there's even a reconstructed seventeenth-century laboratory.

The Duomo

Via Matteotti • Daily 7.30am–noon & 3.30–6.30pm

The main feature of the Romanesque-Gothic **Duomo**'s plain facade is a rose window that's glazed with thin panels of alabaster, as are the other windows, giving the interior a pleasantly warm gloom. Inside, the chapel to the left of the chancel houses a mighty tenth-century Crucifix known as the *Volto Santo*. (The crown and gown with which this Crucifix is dressed for November's Feast of the Redeemer are usually on show in the Museo Civico.) Nearby, on the wall of the left aisle, hangs an *Ascension* by Perugino.

San Lorenzo

Via Santa Croce • Daily 9am–1pm & 3–7pm; shorter hours in winter

One other church merits a look – **San Lorenzo**. The main altarpiece is a *Deposition* by the Mannerist painter Rosso Fiorentino, painted within half a century of della Francesca's last works but seeming to belong to another world.

INFORMATION   SANSEPOLCRO

Tourist office Piazza Garibaldi (daily: April–Oct 9.30am–noon & 2–7pm; Nov–March 10am–noon & 2–6pm;   ☏ 0575 730 231, ⓦ www.comune.sansepolcro.ar.it).

ACCOMMODATION, EATING AND DRINKING

Da Ventura Via Niccolò Aggiunti 30 ☏ 0575 742 560, ⓦ albergodaventura.it. The family-run *Da Ventura* is another fine place to eat – you'll pay around €35 per person. It also has inexpensive accommodation upstairs, but the rooms aren't as nice as at *La Locanda del Giglio*. Restaurant open lunch & dinner Tues–Sat, lunch only on Sun. **€70**

⭐ **La Locanda del Giglio** Via Pacioli 60 ☏ 0575 742

033 ⓦ ristorantefiorentino.it. This B&B is the best place to stay in Sansepolcro, with four simply furnished en-suite rooms, right in the heart of the town. In the same building there's an excellent and well-priced restaurant, the *Fiorentino*, run by the same people. (The adjoining *Fiorentino* hotel is an entirely separate operation.) Restaurant lunch & dinner Mon, Tues & Thurs–Sun. **€85**

North of Arezzo: the Casentino

North of Arezzo, beyond the factories, lies the lush upper valley of the Arno, an agricultural area known as the **Casentino**, whose unshowy little towns see few tourists, even though a large part of the area has now been designated a national park. From **Bibbiena** to **Pratovecchio** the valley is a broad green dish, ruffled by low hills and bracketed by the peaks of the Pratomagno on one side and on the other by the ridge between the Arno and the Tiber. Thick woodlands of oak, beech and pine covers

9

PARCO NAZIONALE DELLE FORESTE CASENTINESI

The **Parco Nazionale delle Foreste Casentinesi** (W parks.it/parco.nazionale.for.casentinesi), encompassing a vast area that spans Tuscany and Emilia-Romagna, has been created to conserve the region's terrain and wildlife, as well as the historic monuments of La Verna and Camáldoli. The tourist office in Arezzo is a good place to start if you want to plan a trip, but the park **headquarters** is in Pratovecchio, at Via G. Brocchi 7 (Mon–Thurs 8am–1pm & 3–5pm, Fri 8am–1pm; ☎ 0575 50 301). The forests are crisscrossed by dozens of paths and tracks, most of them marked on the SELCA 1:25,000 map *Carta Escursionistica-Parco Nazionale delle Foreste Casentinesi, Monte Falterona, Campigna*, which is available from the park centres and local bookshops.

---

much of the upper slopes, the remnant of the forest that used to coat much of the Casentino, and supplied the shipyards of Pisa, Livorno and Genoa, as well as the building sites of Tuscany.

Florence did not always have territorial rights in this region. From the eleventh century the northern part of the Casentino was ruled by the **Guidi** dynasty of **Poppi**, who kept control from a string of castles – their ruins still litter the hills. In the Middle Ages Arezzo, landlord of the southern Casentino, brawled constantly with Florence for possession of this lucrative valley. After Florence bested the Aretines at the battle of Campaldino, the traditionally Ghibelline Guidi counts recognized the authority of the Guelph victors, and were in return allowed to maintain their power base here; within a century or so, however, the Florentines had ousted them. The seclusion of the higher ground fostered a strong monastic tradition as well, and the communities at **Camáldoli** and at **La Verna** continue to be important centres for their respective orders.

GETTING AROUND

By train and bus Without your own wheels, the best target for a day-trip from Arezzo is Poppi; it's connected to the city by bus and by the private LFI train line which shares the state FS station in Arezzo. There are fourteen trains daily (five on Sun, when services may be replaced by a bus): journey time is 55min.

By car Visiting the monasteries of La Verna and Camáldoli requires a car, unless you want to stay overnight; buses run from Bibbiena to Badia Prataglia, Camáldoli and Chiusi della Verna (the nearest stop to the monastery of La Verna), but they are too infrequent to make a round trip feasible in a day.

Bibbiena

The chief commercial town of the Casentino is **BIBBIENA**, a place swathed in light industrial developments. In the moderately attractive inner quarter, the main sight is the church of **San Lorenzo**, a fifteenth-century building that contains a fair quantity of terracotta from the della Robbia workshops. At the top end of town, close to Piazza Tarlati – its name a sign of its links with Arezzo (see p.373) – the oddly shaped church of **Santi Ippolito e Donato** has a fine altarpiece by Bicci di Lorenzo. Once you've seen these, there's no reason to hang around.

La Verna

Sanctuary daily 6am–8.30pm

In 1213 a pious member of the Guidi clan, Count Orlando, donated to **St Francis** and his closest followers a plot of land at **LA VERNA**, 23km east of Bibbiena. It was here, on September 14, 1224, that Francis received the stigmata from a vision of the crucified Christ, a badge of sanctity never previously bestowed.

Francis's mountain-top sanctuary rapidly grew into a monastic village, whose ten chapels are connected by a network of corridors, cloisters, dormitories and pathways. Nowadays tens of thousands of pilgrims come here annually, some of them staying in he guesthouse adjoining the monks' quarters, most coming to pay an hour's homage at he site of the miracle, or merely out of curiosity. Unlike at the basilica at Assisi, however, sightseers rarely obscure the purpose of the place.

Relics of the saint – his walking stick, belt, drinking glass – are displayed in the fifteenth-century **basilica**, where there's a glorious *Ascension* by Andrea della Robbia, whose other masterpieces are the focal points of the Chiesa delle Stimmate (built on he spot where Francis received the stigmata) and the Cappella di Santa Maria degli Angeli. A walkway painted with modern scenes of the story of St Francis leads to the Chiesa delle Stimmate; halfway along, a small door opens into a gash in the crag, where Francis used to sleep on a bed of stone. (According to Franciscan orthodoxy, the rocks at La Verna split apart at the moment of Christ's death.) The route also passes the cell n which St Anthony of Padua stayed in 1230. The Sasso Spicco, reached by a flight of steps near the corridor, was Francis's preferred place of meditation. A path through the forest above the sanctuary leads to the summit of **La Penna** (1283m), from where there's a panorama of the Casentino meadows in one direction and the serrations of the Apennines in the other. The drive from La Verna to Sansepolcro is a fabulous descent into the upper Tiber valley; the valley itself, however, is a mess of industry and quarries.

Poppi

POPPI, 6km north of Bibbiena and plainly visible from there, amounts to not much more than a couple of tiny squares and a narrow arcaded main street, but it is lent a monumental aspect by the Casentino's chief landmark, the **Castello dei Conti Guidi**.

Castello dei Conti Guidi

Piazza della Repubblica • March 15–June 30, Sept & Oct daily 10am–6pm; July & Aug daily 10am–7pm; rest of year Thurs–Sun 10am–5pm • €5

Built for the Guidi lords in the 1270s, the **Castello dei Conti Guidi** is based closely on Florence's Palazzo Vecchio, and it's likely that Arnolfo di Cambio was one of the architects here as well. The deep courtyard, with its wooden landings and beautiful staircases, is the most attractive piece of secular architecture in the Casentino; the stone figure at the head of the stairs is a portrait of Count Simone di Battifolle, for whom the castle was built, and whose ghost is said to haunt the place. In the **cellars** there's a display on warfare and fortifications in the era of the Guidi, featuring a teeming model of the battle of Campaldino, with a dismembered knight under the floorboards for added impact; under the stairs you'll find the castle dungeon.

Upstairs, a fine old library has changing displays of books and manuscripts, and the top-floor chapel is frescoed with scenes from the life of the Virgin, John the Baptist and John the Evangelist, painted in the 1330s by Taddeo Gaddi. You get a fine view from the windows on this storey, but the best vantage point is the summit of the **tower**, a 104-step ascent.

The oratory and the Badìa di San Fedele

At the upper end of Via Cavour, the main street of Poppi, stands the domed **Oratorio del Madonna contro il Morbo**, raised in the sixteenth century to give thanks to Mary for – as the name tells you – delivering the town from plague. At its lower end, the street climaxes at the magnificent twelfth-century **Badìa di San Fedele** (daily 10am–noon & 3–7pm), which contains an array of paintings by some obscure sixteenth-century artists, and the splendid reliquary bust of St Torello, a Vallombrosan monk who was born in Poppi in 1202 and spent the last six decades of his life immured in a cell in this church.

ACCOMMODATION, EATING AND DRINKING · POPPI

★ **Casentino** Piazza della Repubblica 6 ☎ 0575 529 090, ⓦ albergocasentino.it. Located in the shadow of the castle, the plain, homely and inexpensive three-star Casentino has a nice courtyard garden, a bar and a very popular restaurant. Restaurant open for lunch & dinner Mon, Tues & Thurs–Sun. **€70**

9

> ## THE BATTLE OF CAMPALDINO
> A short distance north of Poppi, marked by a column where the road divides, is the site of the **Battle of Campaldino**, where on June 11, 1289 the Florentine Guelphs defeated the Arezzo Ghibellines to establish Florence's pre-eminence in the power struggles of Tuscany. Warfare in Italy during this era was chiefly conducted by relatively small companies of hired troops, who would typically hold a town to ransom and then depart with their cash, maybe after a bit of skirmishing. Pitched battles on the scale of Campaldino were a rarity: some 22,000 men fought here, and nearly 2000 of them were killed. One who survived was Dante, then 24 years old.

San Lorenzo Piazza Bordoni 2–5 ☎ 0575 520 176, ⓦ poppi-sanlorenzo.com. Poppi's other hotel, the ten-room *San Lorenzo*, is likewise right by the castle. It's equipped with a sauna and health centre in the cellar, and the rooms are furnished with contemporary cast-iron furniture; some of them give good views over the valley. **€85**

Camáldoli

One of the best bases for the national park is **CAMÁLDOLI**, just over 15km northeast of Poppi, where in 1012 San Romualdo (St Rumbold) founded an especially ascetic order of the Benedictines. Notwithstanding the severity of its order, this sylvan retreat became a favourite with non-monastic penitents, so much so that a second site was opened to accommodate visitors and to administer the woodlands that Romualdo had been granted. This lower complex has been much rebuilt and the only point of interest is its sixteenth-century pharmacy, which sells herbal products.

On summer weekends lots of people come out here for strolls through the forest up to the **Eremo** (daily: summer 9am–noon & 3–6pm; winter 9am–noon & 3–5pm), the heart of the monastery, which is around 3km away. These days both men and women can visit, but no one is allowed near the living quarters, except to take a peek at Romualdo's cell.

Pratovecchio

PRATOVECCHIO, the birthplace of Paolo Uccello, retains some attractive old arcaded streets, but the major attractions are outside the town, on a narrow little lane to the west of the main road. The **Pieve di Romena**, though patched up a few times since its foundation in the twelfth century, is a wonderfully preserved Romanesque church, with splendid capitals and a beehive-shaped sacristy. An inscription on the first column to the right identifies the sculptor as the parish priest, Albericus; on the second pillar on the left another states that the work was completed during a famine in 1152.

Castello di Romena

June, Sept & Oct Thurs–Sun 10am–1pm & 2–6pm; July & Aug daily 10am–6pm • €4

Close to the Pieve are the impressive ruins of the oldest and mightiest castle in the Casentino, the **Castello di Romena**, which was built at the end of the tenth century and taken over by the Guidi counts in the twelfth. Dante was a guest here, and in the *Inferno* he mentions one of its former tenants, Adamo da Brescia, whose counterfeit coins wreaked such havoc with the local economy that the enraged Florentines roasted him alive. There's a small archeological collection and armoury at the castle – with a shop at which you can buy a souvenir fake florin.

Stia

The LFI rail line finishes 2km on at **STIA**, the nearest town to the source of the Arno, which rises to the north on Monte Falterona. The hills around Stia are dotted with natural springs, and in the town's park – the Parco del Palagio Fiorentino – a spa

9

complex has been built around the Fonte di Calcedonia, a long-established source that nowadays provides one of Italy's best-known mineral waters. The porticoed Piazza Tanucci is the heart (and summit) of the medieval town, where the steep roofs give the place an alpine feel. Stia's chief monument, the Romanesque **Santa Maria Assunta**, houses a *Madonna* by Andrea della Robbia and a triptych by Bicci di Lorenzo.

South of Arezzo: the Valdichiana

Travelling south from Arezzo you enter the **Valdichiana** (the valley of the Chiana River), prosperous agricultural country that nurtures the Chianina breed of cattle, source of the best Florentine *bistecca* – though the Chianina is much rarer than it used to be, and much *bistecca* now comes from Spanish herds. As with the Maremma, this former swampland was first drained by the Etruscans, whose work was allowed to unravel in medieval times, when the encroaching marshes drove the farmers of the region back up to the hill-towns. Only in the nineteenth century, with the reclamation schemes of the Lorraine dukes of Tuscany, did the Valdichiana become fertile again. It's an underwhelming landscape, but its flatness does mean that the towns on its flanks – of which **Cortona** is the most inspiring – have very long sight-lines.

GETTING AROUND

By train Frequent trains from Florence and Arezzo run down the valley, most of them stopping at Camucia or Teróntola (some stop at both), the access points for Cortona.

By bus Buses from Arezzo serve the intervening villages while services from Cortona cover routes across the Valdichiana.

Cortona

From the valley floor, a five-kilometre road winds up through terraces of vines and olives to the hill-town of **CORTONA**, whose heights survey a vast domain, encompassing the entire Valdichiana, with Lago Trasimeno visible over the low hills to the south. Via Nazionale is the only horizontal road in the *centro storico*, and the steep streets are more or less untouched by modern building: limitations of space have confined almost all later development to the lower suburb of Camucia, which is where the approach road begins. In recent years Cortona's tourist traffic has increased markedly, in the wake of Frances Mayes' *Under the Tuscan Sun* and *Bella Tuscany*, books that continue to entice coachloads of her (mainly American) readers to the place where Mayes realized the expat dream of the good life in the land of life-affirming Latins. The first week of August sees the town filled to capacity by audiences for the **Festival del Sole**, an arts event (mainly classical music) that was founded in 2003, partly at Mayes' instigation, and which has quickly become one of Italy's biggest.

Folklore has it that Cortona was founded by Dardanus, later to establish the city of Troy. Whatever its precise origins, there was already a sizeable settlement here when the **Etruscans** took over in the eighth century BC. About four hundred years later it passed to the **Romans** and remained a significant Roman centre until its destruction by the Goths. By the eleventh century it had become a free *comune*, constantly at loggerheads with Perugia and Arezzo; in 1258 the **Aretines** destroyed Cortona, but the town soon revived under the patronage of Siena. It changed hands yet again at the start of the fifteenth century, when it was appropriated by the Kingdom of Naples and then sold off to the **Florentines**, who never let go.

MAEC

Piazza Signorelli 9 • April–Oct daily 10am–7pm; Nov–March Tues–Sun 10am–5pm • €8, or combined ticket with Museo Diocesano €10 • Ⓦ www.cortonamaec.org

Piazza della Repubblica, where the staircase of the Palazzo Comunale gives the *ragazzi*

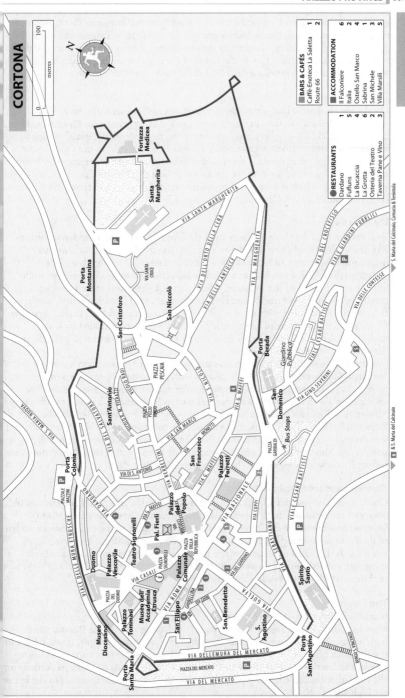

CORTONA

N

0 metres 100

Fortezza
Medicea

Santa
Margherita

VIA SANTA MARGHERITA

Porta
Montanina

San Cristoforo

VIA SANTA
CROCE

San Niccolò

VIA DELL'ORTO DELLA CERA

VIA DELLE SANTUCCE

VIA S. MARGHERITA

VIA S. MARGHERITA

PIAZZA
PESCAIA

VIA TICCIO

VIA G. MAFFEI

Porta
Berada

Giardino
Pubblico

VIALE GIARDINI PUBBLICI

Sant'Antonio

VIA DI S. ANTONIO

VIA DELL'OSPEDALE

VIA DI PIETRO

VIA BERRETTINI

VIA SAN MARCO

San
Domenico

VIA GINO SEVERINI

VIALE CESARE BATTISTI

VIALE DELLE CONTESSE

Porta
Colonia

PIAZZALE
MAZZINI

VIA MONTETTI

PIAZZA
POZZO

San Francesco

VIA G. MAFFEI

Palazzo
Ferretti

PIAZZA
GARIBALDI

Bus Stops

VIALE DEL CROCIFISSO

VIA DELLE MURA NUOVE

VIA S. MARIA NUOVA

Duomo

Palazzo
Vescovile

Teatro Signorelli

Pal. Fierli

VIA G. MAFFEI

Palazzo
del Popolo

VIA NAZIONALE

VIA COPPI

VIA S. SEBASTIANO

VIALE CESARE BATTISTI

VIALE DELLE MURA ETRUSCHE

Museo
Diocesano

Palazzo
Tommasi

PIAZZA
DEL
DUOMO

Museo dell'
Accademia
Etrusca

San Filippo

Palazzo
Comunale

PIAZZA
SIGNORELLI

VIA CASALI

PIAZZA
DELLA
REPUBBLICA

VIA ROMA

VIA GHIBELLINA

VIA GUELFA

VIA DEL GESÙ

VIA DEL GARDINO

San Benedetto

S. Agostino

Spirito
Santo

Porta
Santa Maria

Porta
Sant'Agostino

VIA DELLE MURA DEL MERCATO

PIAZZA DEL MERCATO

VIA DEL MERCATO

BORGO S. VINCENZO

▶ & S. Maria del Calcinaio

▶ S. Maria del Calcinaio, Camucia & Terontola

● RESTAURANTS	
Dardano	1
Fufluns	5
La Bucaccia	4
La Grotta	6
Osteria del Teatro	2
Taverna Pane e Vino	3

■ BARS & CAFÉS	
Caffe-Enoteca La Saletta	1
Route 66	2

■ ACCOMMODATION	
Il Falconiere	6
Italia	2
Ostello San Marco	4
Sabrina	1
San Michele	3
Villa Marsili	5

9

grandstand from which to appraise the world as it goes by, flows into **Piazza Signorelli**, which is named after the artist Luca Signorelli, Cortona's most famous son – as is the decorously peeling nineteenth-century theatre-cinema. Across the road from the theatre stands the hulking Palazzo Casali, the home of the town's main big museum, the **Museo dell'Accademia Etrusca e della Città di Cortona** – or **MAEC**, for short.

The ground floor

On the lowest floor, which charts the development of Cortona from the earliest recorded settlements to Roman times, some spectacular specimens of **Etruscan** gold, turquoise and crystal jewellery catch the eye in the first rooms, along with armour, weaponry and miscellaneous grave goods excavated from tombs in the valley below Cortona. Special prominence is given to the *Tabula Cortonensis*, a fragmentary bronze plaque inscribed with a legal text in the Etruscan language. Beyond that, you're into the **Roman** section, which is dominated by finds – mainly mosaics and terracotta – from a large villa 5km south of Cortona.

The main floor

Founded in 1727 by three brothers from the Venuti family, the **Accademia Etrusca** was one of the world's first academies devoted to archeology, and such was its prestige that Voltaire and Montesquieu were both enrolled as members. The Accademia is still in existence, and its huge collection of antiquities and art works fills the upper floors of the museum, where there's a good deal more Etruscan material on show, most notably an Etruscan bronze lamp from the fourth century BC, which is honoured with a room all to itself. Etruscan and later bronze figurines fill an avenue of cabinets in the middle of the main hall, surrounded by some undistinguished pictures, though there's work by Pietro da Cortona, Signorelli and Pinturicchio amongst the dross.

Another large room is centred on an extraordinary piece of porcelain known as the **Tempio di Ginori**; made in 1737, it's covered with portraits of 76 members of the Medici clan. The bronze medals from which the porcelain images were derived are displayed in a wall case, along with portrait medals by Pisanello, a pioneer of this genre. Also on this floor you'll find a clutch of pictures by the Venetian artist Giambattista Piazzetta, a stack of Roman inscriptions from the collection of the Venuti brothers and – at the end – one of the most alluring items in the whole museum: a painting, on slate, of the Muse Polimnia. Long believed to date from the first or second century, the picture is now widely thought to be an eighteenth-century fake.

The library and the Severini collection

On the top floor you can admire a small array of Egyptian antiquities and the vast old **library** of the Academy. Back downstairs, on a mezzanine level, the painter **Gino Severini**, another native of Cortona, gets a room to himself at the end. Once an acolyte of the Futurist firebrand Filippo Marinetti, Severini was nothing if not versatile, as you'll see in this small collection, where jagged quasi-Cubist prints hang alongside some very conventional portraits, including his best-known image, *Maternity* – the sort of thing that Marinetti would have consigned to the flames.

The Duomo

Piazza del Duomo • Daily 8.30am–12.30pm & 3–6.30pm

Via Casali links Piazza Signorelli with Piazza del Duomo, where the **Duomo** stands hard up against the town walls. Raised on the ruins of a pagan temple, it was rebuilt in the sixteenth century, but retains elements of its Romanesque precursor in its flaking facade; the interior is rather chilly and grey, but there's a Pietro da Cortona *Nativity* on the third altar on the left, and a possible Andrea del Sarto (an *Assumption*) to the left of the high altar.

Museo Diocesano

Piazza del Duomo • April–Oct daily 10am–7pm; Nov–March Tues–Sun 10am–5pm • €5, or combined ticket with MAEC €10

The church that used to face the Duomo now forms part of the **Museo Diocesano**, a tiny but high-quality collection of Renaissance art plus a fine Roman sarcophagus, carved with fighting centaurs. Predictably Luca Signorelli features strongly, though only two works – *Lamentation* (1502) and *The Communion of the Apostles* (1512) – are unequivocally his: seven others are attributed to him and his school. Paintings from Sassetta, Bartolomeo della Gatta and Pietro Lorenzetti are also on show, but none measures up to Fra' Angelico, represented by a *Madonna, Child and Saints* and an exquisite *Annunciation*, painted when he was based at Cortona's monastery of San Domenico.

San Francesco

Via Berrettini • Daily 9am–6.45pm

To get the full taste of Cortona take Via Santucci from Piazza della Repubblica and then clamber along Via Berrettini, at the lower end of which stands the crusty and ancient church of **San Francesco** – designed by St Francis's disciple Brother Elias, this was the first Franciscan church to be built outside Assisi after Francis' death. Recently reopened after being *in restauro* for many years, it houses a Byzantine ivory reliquary that is said to contain a piece of the True Cross – it's on the high altar, behind which Brother Elias is buried. To the left of the altar are displayed various items that are reputed to have belonged to St Francis, while on the third altar on the left of the nave hangs an *Annunciation* by the man the street is named after, Pietro Berrettini, otherwise known as Pietro da Cortona. (He was born at no. 33, further up the hill.) This is Pietro's last work, and was left unfinished; the best of his art is in Rome, where he and Bernini were two of the most influential figures in the creation of Roman Baroque.

San Niccolò

Via San Niccolò • Fri 3.30–6.30pm, Sat & Sun 11am–1pm & 3.30–6.30pm • €1 minimum donation expected

A further work by Signorelli is to be found in the church of **San Niccolò**, a frail little building with a delicate portico and a fine wooden ceiling that's sagging with age. Signorelli's high altarpiece is a standard which he painted on both sides: a characteristically angular *Entombment* on the front and a *Madonna and Saints* on the back.

Santa Margherita

Piazza Santa Margherita • Daily: summer 8am–noon & 3–7pm; winter 9am–noon & 3–6pm

Built to honour the town's patron saint, **St Margaret of Cortona**, the neo-Romanesque church of **Santa Margherita** was begun in 1297, the year of her death, but was remodelled so extensively in the nineteenth century that the rose window is the only original part that remains. The daughter of a local farmer, Margaret seems to have been a spectacularly beautiful young woman who led a wild life before becoming the servant and lover of a lord whose castle was near Montepulciano. When she was 27 years old he was murdered, and soon afterwards Margaret underwent a drastic conversion: she took vows as a Franciscan nun and devoted herself to helping the poor and sick of Cortona, for whom she founded a hospital close to the site of the church.

Her tomb (1362), with marble angels lifting the lid of her sarcophagus, is mounted on the wall to the left of the chancel; it's unoccupied, as her mummified body lies in a glass coffin at the high altar. The main altarpiece, Signorelli's *Lamentation*, has been removed to the Museo Diocesano, but in the chapel to the right of the chancel you can see a thirteenth-century Crucifix that is said to have spoken to Margaret on a number of occasions, when it was hanging in San Francesco.

The Fortezza Medicea

The **Fortezza Medicea (or Fortezza del Girifalco)**, at the summit of the town, is sometimes used as an exhibition space in summer, and the area in front of it is good

9

ground for a picnic, offering superb views over ruined Etruscan and Roman walls towards Trasimeno. You could descend to Piazza Garibaldi by the stepped Via Crucis, where the Stations of the Cross are represented by mosaics by Severini.

San Domenico

Largo Beato Angelico • Daily 3–6pm

The last church to check out in central Cortona is **San Domenico**, a few metres to the east of Piazza Garibaldi. Completed in 1438, it has a fine high altarpiece by Lorenzo di Niccolò Gerini (*Coronation of the Virgin*), yet another Signorelli (*Madonna and Child with Saints*) and a dilapidated fresco by Fra' Angelico in the lunette above the main door

Santa Maria del Calcinaio

Località Il Calcinaio • Summer Mon–Sat 4–7pm & Sun 10am–12.30pm; winter Mon–Sat 3–5pm & Sun 10am–12.30pm

Below Piazza Garibaldi, the middle distance is occupied by the perfectly proportioned – though severely eroded – Renaissance church of **Santa Maria del Calcinaio**. The masterpiece of Giorgio di Martini, it was begun in 1484 to enshrine a miraculous image of Mary that a lime-burner (*calcinaio*) had unearthed at the tannery here (lime was used in the tanning process). Another Tuscan church of this vintage – Santa Maria delle Carceri in Prato – was founded for similar reasons, but the sheer number of pilgrims who flocked to Cortona necessitated the construction of a rather more capacious build. Inside, the miraculous Madonna is still displayed on the high altar.

The Tanella di Pitagora

Just past Santa Maria, signs direct you farther down the hill to the **Tanella di Pitagora** – a well-preserved Etruscan chamber tomb that's fancifully identified with the Greek mathematician Pythagoras. In fact it was constructed for a wealthy family by the name of Cuso, who are cited in the *Tabula Cortonensis*.

ARRIVAL AND DEPARTURE
CORTONA

By train Trains from Arezzo call at Camucia-Cortona station, from where a shuttle (roughly every 30min) takes ten minutes to run up to the old town; buy tickets at the station bar. Florence–Rome trains stop at Teróntola, 10km south, which is also served by a shuttle roughly every hour (25min to Cortona's Piazza Garibaldi);

Teróntola is the station to get off at if you are approaching from Umbria.
By bus There are hourly LFI buses between Cortona and Arezzo, taking 50min.
By car The centre is closed to all but essential traffic, but there are several free car parks on the periphery.

INFORMATION

Tourist office Palazzo Casali, Piazza Signorelli 9 (May 16–Sept 30 Mon–Sat 9am–1pm & 3–6pm, Sun 9am–1pm; rest of year Mon–Fri 9am–1pm & 3–6pm, Sat 9am–1pm ☎ 0575 637 223, ⓦ cortonaweb.net).

ACCOMMODATION

Il Falconiere San Martino a Bocena ☎ 0575 612 679, ⓦ ilfalconiere.com. Located 3km away on the SS71 towards Arezzo, this intimate four-star has nineteen rooms, all of them beautifully presented (some frescoed), and two pools: one in the luscious garden, the other in the hotel's spa. The Michelin-starred restaurant is terrific and expensive, and residential cookery courses are offered too. Doubles from **€300**

Italia Via Ghibellina 5 ☎ 0575 630 254, ⓦ hotelitaliacortona.com. An inexpensive three-star, occupying a renovated fifteenth-century house very near Piazza della Repubblica, with 26 rooms and a breakfast terrace with panoramic views. **€90–120**

Ostello San Marco Via G. Maffei 57 ☎ 0575 601 765, ⓦ cortonahostel.com. Clean and spacious eighty-bed HI hostel in an old monastery in the heart of town, with fantastic views from the dormitories. Open mid-March to mid-Oct; reception daily 7–10am & 3.30pm–midnight. Dorm beds **€16.50**; doubles and family rooms **€21** per person

Sabrina Via Roma 37 ☎ 0575 630 397, ⓦ cortonastoric .com. With just eight rooms, Cortona's other three-star is considerably smaller than the *Italia*, and somewhat cheaper as well. The breakfasts are excellent and it has a nice family atmosphere. **€85**

San Michele Via Guelfa 15 ☎ 0575 604 348, ⓦ hotelsanmichele.net. The most luxurious in-town hoice, this handsome 43-room four-star has been converted from a rambling medieval town house. The rooms are a generous size, even if the decor is rather routine. Huge online discounts. **€90–300**

★ **Villa Marsili** Via Cesare Battisti 13 ☎ 0575 605 252, ⓦ villamarsili.net. This capacious four-star – occupying an eighteenth-century villa – looks unexceptional from the outside, but the rooms are nicely furnished with antiques, and command a great view of the valley. The website often has large reductions, even in summer. **€150–200**

EATING AND DRINKING

For a town of its size, Cortona has an abundance of good restaurants and bars. Nearly all the places to eat and drink are within a short distance of Piazza della Repubblica.

RESTAURANTS

★ **Dardano** Via Dardano 24 ☎ 0575 601 944. An excellent, unpretentious, inexpensive and very popular trattoria – it's full to bursting most nights. Mon & Wed–Sun noon–2.45pm & 7–10pm.

Fufluns Via Ghibellina 3 ☎ 0575 604 140. If a pizza is all you need, this spacious and bustling place is the first choice. Mon & Wed–Sun noon–2.30pm & 7.15–10.30pm.

La Bucaccia Via Ghibellina 17 ☎ 0575 606 039. Husband and wife team Romano and Agostina are at the helm of this refined restaurant, with an atmospheric Etruscan-themed stone-walled dining room and impressive wine cellar. You can eat very well for €40. Daily noon–4pm & 7–11.30pm; closed Mon in winter.

La Grotta Piazzetta Baldelli 3 ☎ 0575 630 271. Much like *Dardano*, *La Grotta* is a straight-down-the-line trattoria, albeit with a slightly higher percentage of tourists among the clientele. Mon & Wed–Sun noon–2pm & 7.30–11pm.

★ **Osteria del Teatro** Via Maffei 5 ☎ 0575 630 556. Occupying the entire lower floor of a rambling old mansion, this is a good-naturedly busy (sometimes frantic) place, featuring delicious home-made pastas on a meat-heavy menu; portions are generous and prices more than fair – the bill should be around €35 per person, without wine. Mon, Tues & Thurs–Sun 12.30–2.30pm & 7.30–10pm.

Taverna Pane e Vino Piazza Signorelli 27 ☎ 0575 631 010. A good choice if you're after a quick lunch or a light evening meal: the menu offers various types of bruschetta, a wide selection of salamis and cheeses, plus a few more substantial dishes – and the wine list runs to some 900 different vintages. Tues–Fri & Sun 12.30–3pm & 7.30–10.30pm, Sat 12.30–3pm & 7.30–11.30pm.

BARS AND CAFÉS

Caffè-Enoteca La Saletta Via Nazionale 26–28 ☎ 0575 603 366. A glossy café-cum-wine shop, which also does simple meals. Daily 7.30am–2am; closed Wed Nov–April.

Route 66 Via Nazionale 78 ☎ 0575 627 27. This self-styled "Disco Dance Café" attracts the youngest crowd in town – the soundtrack is usually loud, and there are regular DJ nights. It does food too, but it's not the nosh that makes it popular. Tues–Sun 11am–2am.

Castiglion Fiorentino

Looming high above the road and railway 12km north of Cortona are the walls and massive tower of **CASTIGLION FIORENTINO** – known as Castiglion Aretino until Arezzo became a Florentine possession in 1384. The fortified old town is so far above the train station that it makes more sense to visit by bus; the half-hourly bus from Arezzo to Cortona bowls through here thirty minutes into its one-hour journey, stopping right outside the walls in Piazza Matteotti.

The upper town

From Piazza Matteotti the Corso Italia rises to the elegant Piazza del Municipio, the navel of the *centro storico*. Up the hill behind the Municipio, the modest **Pinacoteca Comunale** (April–Oct Tues–Sun 10am–12.30pm & 4–6.30pm; Nov–March Sat &

MONTECCHIO VESPONI

Some 4km south of Castiglion Fiorentino, the eleventh-century castle of **Montecchio Vesponi** jabs up from the horizon. Commanding a great sweep of the valley, this property was acquired in 1384 by the fearsome *condottiere* Sir John Hawkwood (he of the fresco in Florence's Duomo), and is the only one of his numerous ill-gotten residences to survive intact. It's still in private hands.

9

Sun 10am–12.30pm & 3.30–6pm; €3, or €5 with archeological museum) has works by Taddeo Gaddi and two fine paintings by Bartolomeo della Gatta. Inside the neighbouring library you'll find the equally modest **archeological museum** (same hours; €3, or €5 with Pinacoteca), where the chief exhibit is a reconstructed fragment of an Etruscan temple; the entrance ticket also covers the excavations of the Etruscan walls underneath the summit of the hill. From the summit of the hill rises the **Torre del Cassero** (May–Sept Sat & Sun 10am–1pm & 4–7pm; €1.50), Castiglion Fiorentino's landmark tower, built to the orders of Arezzo's pugnacious Bishop Tarlati.

The lower town

Opposite the Palazzo Comunale, a handsome **loggia** – supposedly designed by Vasari – forms a picture-frame for the hills to the east. Look to the right through the loggia and you'll see the town's major church, the **Collegiata**, which has a *Holy Family* by Lorenzo di Credi to the right of the high altar. The remnant of the adjoining **Pieve di San Giuliano** has been converted into a museum of sacred art (Sat & Sun 10am–noon & 3.30–6.30pm; €3), a typical small-town miscellany of paintings, sculptures and applied art, in which the most interesting item is a thirteenth-century wooden figure called the Madonna di Petrognano.

The Abbazia di Farneta

Daily 9am–1pm & 2–4pm

About 10km southwest of Cortona, in the middle of the valley, stands the ancient Benedictine **Abbazia di Farneta**. Built largely with stone plundered from a nearby Roman temple, this beautifully plain building first appeared in local records in 1014, but may have been founded as far back as the eighth century, by the Lombards. It had fallen into utter disrepair by 1937, when a remarkable priest by the name of Monsignor Sante Felici arrived here. Over the course of the next sixty years he almost single-handedly stripped the abbey of the accretions that had defaced the Romanesque structure, and excavated the ancient **crypt**, an operation that yielded numerous archeological and paleontological discoveries. The most spectacular of Monsignor Felici's fossils are on show in Florence's museum of paleontology, while the church's main artefacts have gone to Cortona's MAEC.

ACCOMMODATION FARNETA

Relais Villa Petrischio Via Del Petrischio, Farneta ☎ 0575 610 316, 🌐 villapetrischio.it. Sitting amid cypresses and pines on a hill that commands a wide sweep of the Valdichiana, this four-star country hotel has a pool, a good restaurant, and very comfortable, spacious antique-furnished rooms and suites. Doubles from **€160**

Foiano dell Chiana

FOIANO DELLA CHIANA, 4km west of the Abbazia di Farneta, sometimes bills itself as "La Città di Carnevale", because it was here, in the 1860s, that allegorical floats were first produced for carnival parades, thereby inaugurating a form of folk art that nowadays is best represented by the Viareggio carnival. Other than at carnival, Foiano is a workaday small town, though the weathered brick fortifications of the old centre are quite impressive, and devotees of della Robbia ceramics might want to take a look at the family's work in the churches of **San Michele Arcangelo**, **Santa Maria della Fraternità** and the **Collegiata**, the last of which also houses the final painting by Luca Signorelli.

Lucignano

It may not have any great sights, but the village of **LUCIGNANO** – located midway between Arezzo and Siena, on the opposite side of the Valdichiana from Cortona – is a trim and perfectly preserved little place, which makes a restful stop for a night or two. Laid out in a pattern of concentric ellipses, the streets within the town walls encircle the medieval Palazzo Comunale and the **Collegiata**, an unexceptional church that's given a touch of panache by the double semicircular staircase leading to its door. Adjacent to the Palazzo Comunale, the church of **San Francesco** has some thirteenth- and fourteenth-century frescoes, and there's a crumbly Medici fortress on the hill to the north, but Lucignano's main draw is inside the tiny museum, which occupies the ground floor of the Palazzo Comunale.

Museo Comunale

Piazza del Tribunale 22 • April–Oct Mon & Wed–Fri 10am–1pm & 2–6pm, Sat & Sun closes 7pm Nov–March Mon 10am–1pm, Wed–Fri 10am–1pm & 2–5pm, Sat & Sun 10am–1pm & 2–6pm; • €5

The **Museo Comunale** contains a couple of minor paintings by Signorelli or his workshop, and the most arresting artefact on this side of the Valdichiana, an amazing fourteenth-century gilded silver reliquary known as the *Albero di Lucignano* or *Albero d'Oro*, for its tree-like shape. Made in Arezzo between 1350 and 1470, it stands 2.5m high and its branches are adorned with coral, rock crystal and enamels.

ACCOMMODATION, EATING AND DRINKING   LUCIGNANO

Il Cassero Via Circonvallazione 61 ☎0575 836 260, ⌨ ilcassero-tuscany.com. The best place to stay in Lucignano is this six-apartment *residenza d'epoca* adjoining the village's tower; the proprietors are extremely welcoming, and guests have the use of a pool in the countryside close to the village. The owners also rent out a large apartment within the town. **€100**

★ **Il Goccino** Via Matteotti 88–90 ☎0575 836 707. Tiny though it is, Lucignano has several decent places to eat, and two that are exceptionally good. *Il Goccino*, slightly the less expensive of the pair, has a lovely terrace at the

back, which overlooks the Valdichiana; the wine list is very impressive too. Tues–Sun noon–2.30pm & 6.30–10.30pm.

★ **La Rocca** Piazza Ser Vanni 1 ☎0575 836 775. Lucignano's best-known restaurant was founded back in 1903, and has recently moved to spacious premises adjoining the town's eastern gate, the Porta San Giovanni. Like *Il Goccino*, *La Rocca* prides itself on its top-quality local ingredients and vast selection of wines. Open lunch & dinner Mon & Wed–Sun; closed Jan.

Monte San Savino

Once a contentious border post between the territories of Florence, Siena and Arezzo, **MONTE SAN SAVINO** is not one of Tuscany's most charismatic hill-towns, though it retains an unspectacular mix of medieval and Renaissance buildings. Should you want to explore, there are regular trains from Arezzo to the station in the lower town, from where there's a bus shuttle; buses from Cortona also periodically cross the valley.

The town was the birthplace of **Andrea Sansovino**, mentor of Jacopo Sansovino, a crucial figure in Venice's artistic history, who took his teacher's surname. Terracotta was one of Andrea's preferred media – Monte San Savino remains a major producer of majolica – and some of his best ceramic altarpieces are in the church of **Santa Chiara**, which stands in Piazza Gamurrini. Virtually next to the church, the fourteenth-century Sienese castle known as the **Cassero** (Sat & Sun 9am–noon & 3–6pm; €1.60) has a modest **Museo Civico** that's largely given over to ceramics; it also houses a small tourist office and holds occasional exhibitions.

Continuing down the narrow main street from Piazza Gamurrini you'll pass the **Loggia dei Mercanti**, a collaboration between Sansovino and Antonio da Sangallo the Elder – architect of the Palazzo Comunale opposite. Beyond the Palazzo Pretorio lies the small central square, Piazza di Monte, on both of whose churches Sansovino left a mark: he designed the now crumbling portal of **San Giovanni**, and added the cloister to the fourteenth-century **Sant'Agostino**, which contains some fifteenth-century frescoes and an altarpiece by Vasari.

Perugia and northern Umbria

CASTIGLIONE DEL LAGO

Perugia and northern Umbria

10

Perugia makes for a distinctly uncharacteristic introduction to Umbria. The home of Buitoni pasta and Perugino chocolate, its historic core is hidden within a ring of industrialized suburbs, and its big-city feel makes it wholly different from its bucolic hill-town neighbours. If you've come to Umbria for the rural experience, you may be tempted to bypass Perugia altogether. But its medieval heart demands at least a day's exploration: the Palazzo dei Priori is justifiably hyped as one of Italy's greatest public palaces, while the Galleria Nazionale dell'Umbria boasts the region's best collection of Umbrian art. And if actually staying here doesn't appeal, Perugia's highlights can be taken in on day-trips from Assisi, Montefalco or other nearby towns.

To the west of Perugia is **Lago Trasimeno**, Italy's fourth largest lake, an intermittently pretty body of water, fringed by low hills and farming country. **Castiglione del Lago** is the most appealing of several small towns on its shores, thanks to a handful of small beaches, an attractive waterfront and historic centre, and a decent choice of hotels and restaurants. Brasher **Passignano** is the main camping and after-hours resort. North of Perugia is a pretty pastoral region centred on the upper reaches of the **Tiber valley**. Road and rail routes follow the river's course, useful mainly for onward forays into Tuscany and the Marche – in particular to Sansepolcro or Urbino for the paintings of Piero della Francesca. Unheralded **Città di Castello** is a worthwhile port of call, with an appealing historic centre and an **art gallery** that contains the region's only painting by Raphael, an artist apprenticed to Perugino, Umbria's pre-eminent Renaissance painter.

East of the Tiber, minor roads climb through swathes of attractively barren country to **Gubbio**, one of Italy's medieval gems and – given Assisi's increasing commercialism – the region's least spoiled hill-town. Much in the town merits comparison with Siena, not least its overbearing civic palace, the **Palazzo dei Consoli**, a magnificent piece of medieval bluster. Churches and galleries abound, and the honeycomb of old streets is riddled with local colour. Moving further east, you come up against the foothills of the Apennines, with the mountains behind – **Monte Cucco** in particular – providing the area's best scenery as well as opportunities for some straightforward hiking.

ARRIVAL AND GETTING AROUND

By train and bus Perugia is one of the key transport hubs for the region, with direct national trains to and from all major cities. The private FCU train line serves certain towns, while a fast highway (toll-free superstrada) connects Perugia to the A1 toll-road, the Autostrada del Sole, with quick links to Orvieto, Siena, Florence, Rome and beyond. Buses run to most major centres and many minor ones.

PALAZZO DEI CONSOLI

Highlights

❶ **Corso Vannucci, Perugia** Umbria's best passeggiata, with some wonderful people-watching. **See p.399**

❷ **Collegio del Cambio, Perugia** A medieval chamber decorated with outstanding frescoes by Perugino. **See p.402**

❸ **Galleria Nazionale dell'Umbria, Perugia** The finest collection of the region's medieval and Renaissance art. **See p.403**

❹ **Isola Maggiore** Lago Trasimeno's island makes for a pleasant wander amidst greenery and medieval remains. **See p.418**

❺ **Città di Castello** The Pinacoteca Comunale and Museo Diocesano here hold paintings by Raphael, Signorelli, Rosso Fiorentino and others. **See p.419**

❻ **Palazzo dei Consoli, Gubbio** A majestic medieval palace, with sweeping views from its belvedere. **See p.425**

❼ **Monte Ingino funicular** A dizzying six-minute ride over woods and crags into the mountains above Gubbio. **See p.430**

❽ **Parco Regionale del Monte Cucco** Wonderful mountain scenery with some great hiking and spelunking opportunities. **See p.431**

HIGHLIGHTS ARE MARKED ON THE MAP ON P.398

Perugia

PERUGIA is a place of some style – at least in its old centre – and a city proud of its big-league attractions, its chocolate, its university for foreigners and its football team. In terms of sights, Perugia's interest is essentially medieval, despite its considerable Etruscan heritage. In addition to the **Palazzo dei Priori**, home to the **Galleria Nazionale** and the Perugino-painted **Collegio del Cambio**, there is the **Duomo** and a full quota of memorable churches. A drink on the **Corso Vannucci**, Perugia's central street, reveals a buzz you won't find elsewhere in the region, a sense of dynamism embodied by the cosmopolitan **Università Italiana per Stranieri**, created by Mussolini to improve the image of Italy abroad; now privately run, it's the country's largest language school. This same dynamism remains evident in Perugia's above-average number of film screenings, concerts and miscellaneous cultural events, and is highlighted further at July's **Umbria Jazz** (ⓦumbriajazz.com), Italy's foremost jazz festival, whose stars have included Miles Davis, Stan Getz and Wynton Marsalis. Also hugely popular is the **Eurochocolate festival** (ⓦeurochocolate.com) in October, when Perugians flee the city in the face of the crowds of outsiders who come for this vast fair, in which hundreds of booths offer chocolate in every conceivable form.

Brief history

Perugia's command of the Tiber and its major routes has made it the region's main player throughout a long history – albeit not quite as long as early chroniclers made

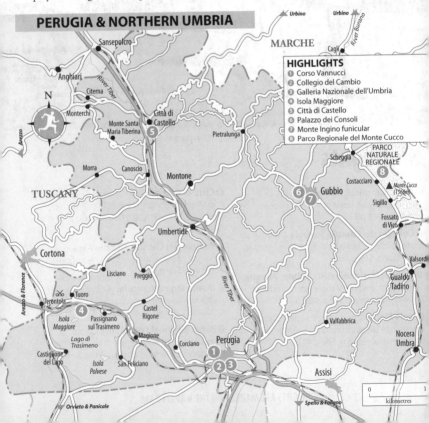

PERUGIA & NORTHERN UMBRIA

HIGHLIGHTS
1. Corso Vannucci
2. Collegio del Cambio
3. Galleria Nazionale dell'Umbria
4. Isola Maggiore
5. Città di Castello
6. Palazzo dei Consoli
7. Monte Ingino funicular
8. Parco Regionale del Monte Cucco

ORIENTATION

The old city centre revolves around **Corso Vannucci**, one of Italy's great people-watching streets, its broad expanse packed from dawn to the early hours with shoppers, students and style-makers. Named after the city's most celebrated artist, Pietro Vannucci, better known simply as Perugino, the street has several of the city's key sights. It's capped at its northern end by the **Piazza IV Novembre** – home to the **Fontana Maggiore**, the **Palazzo dei Priori** and the **Duomo** – and in the south by **Piazza Italia**, jumping-off point for the southern quarters. The twisting medieval alleys off the Corso are initially disorientating, but by dividing the area into western, northern and southern sections you soon get to grips with the layout.

West of the Corso, Via dei Priori curves downhill through a slice of the old city, culminating in the **Oratorio di San Bernardino**, one of Perugia's prime pieces of sculpture. East of the Corso, there are a couple of diversions – not least an impressive Etruscan well and Raphael fresco – in the fine medieval quarter beyond **Piazza Danti**. Both routes meet up at **Piazza Fortebraccio**, access point for the city's northern quarters, which hold few sights as such, but make a pleasant place for a stroll. Perugia's other highlights are grouped along Corso Cavour in the southern quarters: **San Domenico**, Umbria's largest church, housing the region's archeological museum, and the tenth-century basilica of **San Pietro**.

You can **walk** everywhere, although you'll cover a fair bit of ground in the course of a day's sightseeing – particularly if you take in sights at the extreme northern and southern ends of town. You should also be prepared for **steep climbs** between Perugia's many levels: there are some lifts and escalators, but they help out only occasionally.

10

out when they claimed to have traced its foundation to Noah. The easternmost of the twelve key cities of the **Etruscan** federation, Perusia, as it was called, was conquered by **Rome** in 309 BC, later taking the wrong side in the civil war that followed the death of Julius Caesar. Allying itself with Mark Antony, it suffered a debilitating siege at the hands of his opponent Octavius, later the emperor Augustus. It might have survived the ordeal but for the actions of Gaius Cestius, one of the city's less stout defenders, who set fire to his own house in a panic-stricken funk. The ensuing conflagration destroyed the city, and Augustus rebuilt it as Augusta Perusia.

The city's passage through the Dark Ages is obscure, though legend claims it was besieged by Totila in 547 and saved from destruction by its bishop, St Ercolano (Herculanus). By 592 it had been absorbed into the **Lombard** Duchy of Spoleto, later emerging as a papal vassal and finally, around 1140, as an independent *comune*.

Medieval Perugia

By all accounts, **medieval Perugia** was a hellish place to be. "The town had the most warlike people of Italy," wrote the historian Sismondi, "who always preferred Mars to the Muse." Male citizens played a game – for pleasure – in which two teams, wearing beaked helmets and clothes stuffed with deer hair, stoned each other mercilessly until the majority on one side was dead or wounded. Children were encouraged to join in to promote "application and aggression". In 1265 Perugia was also the birthplace of the **Flagellants**, who within ten years had half of Europe whipping themselves into a frenzy before the movement was declared heretical. In addition to some hearty scourging, they took to the streets on moonlit nights, wailing, singing dirges and clattering human bones together – all as expiation for the sins of the world.

Using its economic muscle and numerous short-lived alliances, the city built up a huge power base, peaking with its **conquest of Siena** in 1358. Around this time the *Priori* (members of the ten leading guilds), noble families and papal agents began vying for control, plunging Perugia into a period when, according to one chronicler, "perfect pandemonium reigned in and about the city". Individual *condottieri* rose briefly from the chaos, the key figures being Biondo Micheletti – stabbed to death in 1398, after five years in power – and the oddly named Braccio Fortebraccio (Arm Strongarm), whose eight years of rule brought short-lived stability. The Oddi nobility ran the town until 1488, when the colourful but demented **Baglioni** took over. Their story is the stuff of a vampire soap opera: complicated vendettas, incestuous marriages, hearts torn from bodies and eaten, and any number of people murdered on their wedding nights. After one episode was settled with a hundred murders, the bloodied cathedral had to be washed down with wine and reconsecrated. One Baglioni, Malatesta IV, assigned the defence of Florence in 1530, famously sold his services to the enemy, earning the title "world's greatest traitor".

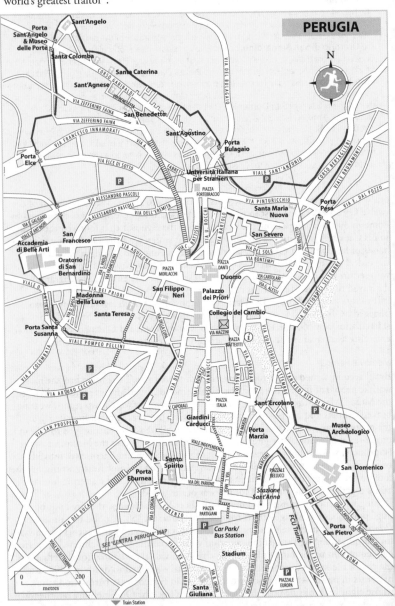

PERUGIA'S MUSEUM PASS

The **Perugia Città Museo** is a museum pass offering a choice of time and price bands for entry into a maximum of twelve sites: Cappella di San Severo, Galleria Nazionale dell'Umbria, Museo Archeologico dell'Umbria, Museo Capitolare della Cattedrale di San Lorenzo, Museo delle Porte e Mura Urbiche, Collegio di Cambio, Collegio della Mercanzia, Palazzo Baldeschi al Corso, Pozzo Etrusco, Ipogeo dei Volumni, Centro Servizi Museali della Rocca Paolina and Palazzo della Penna.

There are **two passes** available from all participating sights, as well as from select hotels or the Palazzo della Penna, Via Podiani 11 (☎075 577 2834 or 800 961 993; ⊛perugiacittamuseo .it): **A** (€10; one adult plus one child under 18, valid for a choice of five sights over 48hrs from first use; and **U** (€6; for university students with ID, valid for five sites from one month from first use).

The following "**Membership**" cards are sold only at the Galleria Nazionale dell'Umbria and Palazzo della Penna: **C1** (€20; valid for one person, covering all sights for a year from first use); and **C2** (€35; valid for a family of four, covering all sights for a year from first use).

10

Papal Perugia and liberation

When the last Baglioni, the wimpish Ridolpho, bungled an assassination of the papal legate, it was a cue for the papacy to step in again. **Pope Paul III**, one of the more powerful and peculiar pontiffs, razed the Baglioni palaces in 1538, then entered the city demanding that all its nuns line up and kiss his feet. Thus refreshed, he built the Rocca Paolina, a huge fortress that guaranteed church supremacy for three centuries.

During the nineteenth-century unification of Italy, Perugia's liberation from the papacy was particularly violent, with numerous citizens massacred by Swiss Guards sent to bolster Church control. By contrast, a later liberation, from the Nazis in 1944 – courtesy of the British Eighth Army – was considerably less bloodthirsty.

The Fontana Maggiore

Piazza IV Novembre

The **Fontana Maggiore** has quite a pedigree: it was designed in 1277 by Fra' Bevignate, the Silvestrine monk who had a hand in shaping Orvieto's cathedral, and sculpted by the father-and-son team of Nicola and Giovanni **Pisano**, possibly with help from **Arnolfo di Cambio**. It was installed to receive the water from the town's new aqueduct, a 5km affair designed by a leading hydraulic engineer of the age, the Venetian Boninsegna. However, as the chronicler Bonazzi observed, "beasts, barrels and unwashed pots and unclean hands were forbidden the use of the water, and indeed it was guarded with such jealous care that it seemed as though the people of Perugia had built their fountain for the sake of beauty only".

The **sculptures** and **bas-reliefs** on the two polygonal basins were part of a carefully conceived decorative scheme designed to illustrate the city's glory and achievements. By some canny calculation none of them line up directly, encouraging you to walk around the fountain chasing a point of repose that never comes. The lower basin has 25 double reliefs, twelve showing the *Labours of the Months*, together with the appropriate sign of the zodiac – December's pig-sticking is particularly graphic. The remaining reliefs include a lion and griffon, Perugia's medieval symbols; four double panels depicting the Liberal Arts; scenes from the Old Testament (note the relief of the large lion and smaller lion being beaten, an allegory expounding the virtues of punishment); and reliefs portraying Roman scenes and two of Aesop's fables. Most of the 24 upper basin statues are by Giovanni Pisano and depict a wide range of characters, among them saints, Old Testament heroes and a variety of allegorical figures representing Victory, Theology and the like. Giovanni also completed the three figures in the basin, believed to represent the three Cardinal Virtues – Faith, Hope and Charity.

The Palazzo dei Priori

Corso Vannucci 19

The northern end of the Corso is dominated by the gaunt bulk of the **Palazzo dei Priori**, with its majestic Gothic doorway, rows of trefoil windows (from which convicted criminals were thrown to their deaths) and businesslike Guelph crenellations. Often cited as Italy's most impressive civic palace (it's certainly one of the largest), it was begun in 1293 by two local architects and completed in 1443, its impressive effect deriving as much from its sheer bulk as the harmonious beauty created by the buildings around it. Four separate sights are hidden within its precincts: the **Sala dei Notari**, **Sala del Collegio della Mercanzia**, **Collegio del Cambio** and – the star turn – the **Galleria Nazionale dell'Umbria**. All are worthwhile, but orientation within the *palazzo* can be a little confusing; it's easiest to tackle them in the order given below.

10

Sala dei Notari

Corso Vannucci 19 • Daily 9am–1pm & 3–7pm; Oct–May closed Mon • Free

The **Sala dei Notari**, the medieval lawyers' meeting hall, is entered via the fan-shaped steps opposite the Duomo. It's an obvious point of reference, its doorway topped by copies of a bronze Guelph lion and Perugian griffon (the originals are in the Galleria Nazionale). Once thought to be Roman, the figures were probably made in 1274 or 1281, making them among the first pieces of large-scale casting in medieval Italy. Latest research, however, suggests the body of the griffon, at least, may be Etruscan, the wings having been added during the thirteenth-century casting. The chains below, according to tradition, were snatched from the gate and gallows of Siena during a raid in 1358. The triple-arched **loggia** is thought to be a remnant of San Severo, a church demolished to make way for the palace in the thirteenth century.

The Sala is one of the oldest parts of the *palazzo*, dating from the late 1290s – about the same time as the civic palaces in Florence and Siena were being raised. It's a tremendous space, overarched by superb vaulting. Before the lawyers got their hands on it, it was used as a meeting place for the townspeople in times of crisis and decision. Its celebrated **frescoes**, however, were substantially repainted in the nineteenth century, the net result being little more than flashes of colour, fancy flags and swirls. They represent the arms of various *podestà*, or magistrates of the city, from 1297 to 1424, infinitely duller than the hard-to-see thirteenth-century frescoes of scenes from Aesop's Fables and the Old Testament that adorn the upper arches.

Sala del Collegio della Mercanzia

Corso Vannucci 15 • March–Oct & Dec 20–Jan 6 Tues–Sat 9am–1pm & 2.30–5.30pm, Sun 9am–1pm; rest of year Tues, Thurs & Fri 8am–2pm, Wed & Sat 8am–5pm, Sun 9am–1pm, though winter openings variable • €1.50, or joint ticket with Collegio di Cambio €5.50

The **Sala del Collegio della Mercanzia** is hidden behind an inconspicuous door further down the Corso side of the *palazzo* (right of the main portal). Since 1390 it has been the seat of the merchants' guild – the city's most important, and a body that survives as a charitable institution to this day. At first glance it amounts to little, but at close quarters the room reveals intricately inlaid wooden panelling, breathtaking fifteenth-century work that is considered some of Italy's finest.

The Collegio del Cambio

Corso Vannucci 25 • Mon–Sat 9am–12.30pm & 2.30–5.30pm, Sun 9am–12.30pm • €5.50, includes Collegio della Mercanzia

The **Collegio del Cambio** was the hall of the town's moneychangers, a guild (founded in 1259) that survives as a charitable body to this day. **Frescoes** by **Perugino** cover its walls; these are not only considered his masterpieces, but also reckoned one of the best-preserved Renaissance schemes in the country. The bankers' guild awarded him the commission in 1496, about the same time as Perugino was approached to fresco part of the Duomo in Orvieto, an undertaking eventually executed by Luca Signorelli. The city's bankers were determined to have paintings commensurate with their own sense of self-importance, and to this end probably paid Perugino – then at the peak of his powers – more than was on offer in Orvieto. This most likely explains the painter's mysterious disappearance from that city after just five desultory days of work in the cathedral.

Having paid their money, the bankers were determined to impose upon the painter their **theme** of choice; Francesco Maturanzio, a leading humanist theorist, was brought in as consultant, and proposed a fusion of Classical and Christian culture, painting Christian icons alongside figures of Greco-Roman myth. Though not an unusual Renaissance conceit, the vigour and uncompromising way in which the themes are yoked together created a distinctly curious juxtaposition. The thesis intended to suggest that there was unity in variety, and that human perfection, expressed by Classical art, was obtainable through Christ's example.

10

The frescoes

Whatever the metaphysical intent, the frescoes certainly succeed aesthetically, unified by Perugino's melancholy, idealized, soft-focus figures and mellow landscapes. The paintings cover virtually all the walls and ceiling vaults of the single room, part of which – probably the prophets and sibyls on the right-hand wall (behind the ticket desk) – was allegedly painted by Perugino's pupil **Raphael**, then only about 13 years old. Up on the door-side wall there's a famous but unremarkable self-portrait of the master, looking on with sour-faced disapproval – ironically, the only element disturbing the frescoes' beautiful evenness of tone.

The ceiling vaults illustrate the main gods of the Classical world: Apollo on his chariot at the centre; Saturn, Jupiter and Mars above the Corso wall; Mercury, Venus and Diana towards the window. Right of the window are portraits of famous Greeks and Romans, real and mythical, with the allegorical figures of Prudence and Justice joined by Cato (symbol of Wisdom), and with Socrates and Trajan, among others, below. The end wall, farthest from the entrance, introduces the Christian strand, with a *Nativity* and the *Transfiguration*. The right-hand wall shows God amongst the angels, with sibyls to the right and men to the left: Isaac, Moses, Daniel (possibly a portrait of Raphael), David, Jeremiah and Solomon. The lovely little chapel to the rear, the **Cappella di San Giovanni Battista**, is smothered in a frescoed *Life of John the Baptist* (1513–18) by Giovanni di Paolo – like Raphael, a former pupil of Perugino.

The Galleria Nazionale dell'Umbria

Corso Vannucci 19 • Tues–Sun 8.30am–7.30pm • €6.50 • Ⓦ www.gallerianazionaleumbria.it

The **Galleria Nazionale dell'Umbria**, on the fourth floor of the palace complex, is the region's main repository of Umbrian art. Its entrance is through the opulent doorway on the Corso; having pushed past harassed Perugians on their way to do battle with council bureaucracy, you might well find the small lift isn't working, in which case you have to clamber up the stairs, a route once taken by nobles on horseback.

The gallery is certainly one of central Italy's best and traces the entire chronology of the Umbrian art canon, from its Byzantine-influenced roots, its parallel development with the Sienese in the thirteenth and fourteenth centuries, through to its late fifteenth-century golden age when Perugia became the main focus of endeavour. The region's premier painters, **Perugino** and **Pinturicchio**, are predictably well covered, as are their imitators, alongside artists who worked in a late-Renaissance vein and fall outside the confines of the Umbrian school.

Be certain to follow the gallery's prescribed **itinerary**: after passing through the *rotonda*, make for room 2 straight ahead and left. Free guides in several languages are usually available just beyond the ticket office. Note that some paintings may be moved: the gallery seems to be in a constant state of flux. Sometimes in summer there is a special **late opening** (mid-June to mid-Sept until 11pm).

10

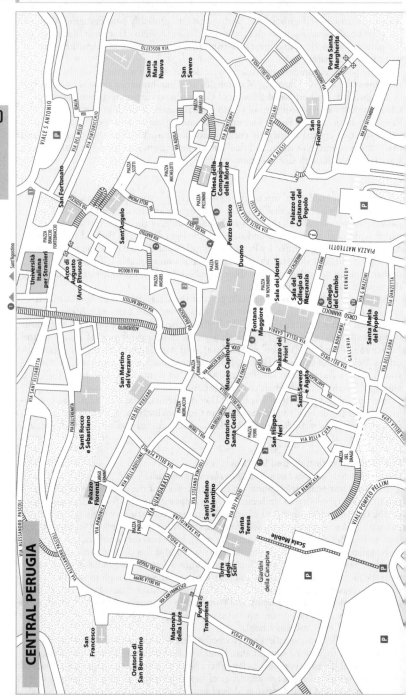

CENTRAL PERUGIA

Santa Maria Nuova

San Severo

Porta Santa Margherita

San Fiorenzo

Chiesa della Compagnia della Morte

Palazzo del Capitano del Popolo

Pozzo Etrusco

San Fortunato

Sant'Angelo

Arco di Augusto (Arco Etrusco)

Università Italiana per Stranieri

Duomo

PIAZZA MATTEOTTI

Sala dei Notari

Sala del Collegio di Mercanzia

Collegio del Cambio

Santa Maria del Popolo

Fontana Maggiore

Palazzo dei Priori

Museo Capitolare

San Martino del Verzaro

Santi Rocco e Sebastiano

Oratorio di Santa Cecilia

San Severo e Agata

San Filippo Neri

Palazzo Florenzi

Santi Stefano e Valentino

Santa Teresa

Torre degli Sciri

San Francesco

Oratorio di San Bernardino

Madonna della Luce

Porta Trasimena

Giardini della Canapina

Scala Mobile

10

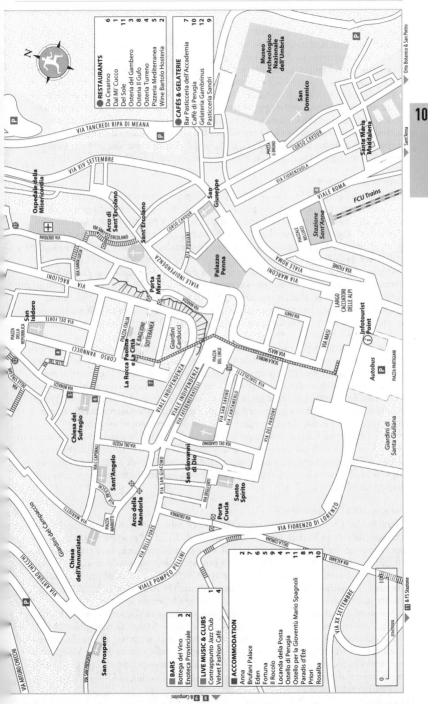

● RESTAURANTS
Da Cesarino 6
Del Mi' Cucco 1
Del Sole 11
Osteria del Gambero 3
Osteria Il Gufo 8
Osteria Turreno 4
Pizzeria Mediterranea 5
Wine Bartolo Hosteria 2

● CAFÉS & GELATERIE
Bar Pasticceria dell'Accademia 7
Caffè di Perugia 10
Gelateria Gambrinus 12
Pasticceria Sandri 9

■ BARS
Bottega del Vino 3
Enoteca Provinciale 2

■ LIVE MUSIC & CLUBS
Contrappunto Jazz Club 1
Velvet Fashion Café 4

■ ACCOMMODATION
Anna 2
Brufani Palace 7
Eden 6
Fortuna 5
Il Rocolo 9
Locanda della Posta 4
Ostello di Perugia 1
Ostello per la Gioventù Mario Spagnoli 11
Paradis d'Eté 8
Priori 3
Rosalba 10

Early Sienese schools

Some of the gallery's finest moments have nothing to do with indigenous painters. This is particularly true of early rooms, where the **Sienese** largely hold sway. Amongst a welter of anonymous works, the first highlight is a large *Crucifixion* by the so-called Maestro di San Francesco, one of the gallery's earliest pieces, and painted by the anonymous hand believed to be responsible for some of the superlative frescoes in the nave of the Lower Church in Assisi's Basilica di San Francesco. Also look out for an outstanding *Madonna and Angels* by **Duccio** (1304–08), its static beauty the obvious model for many of the Umbrian works that follow. Other named Sienese masters include Bartolomeo da Siena, Domenico di Bartolo and Taddeo di Bartolo, the last responsible here for three altarpieces, including a *Pentecost* that displays a radical approach to composition, at odds with the more conservative Umbrians to come.

Early Umbrian schools

In acknowledging the increasing influence of Tuscan painters on Umbrians as the fifteenth century progressed, the gallery almost allows a pair of paintings by outsiders to steal the show. One is an astounding triptych by **Fra' Angelico**, the *Madonna and Child with Angels and Saints*. Radiant with the painter's gorgeous swathes of blue, it was painted in 1437 for Perugia's church of San Domenico. The other is more extraordinary still: **Piero della Francesca**'s sensational polyptych of the *Madonna and Child and Sts Anthony of Padua and John the Baptist with Sts Francis and Elizabeth of Hungary*, executed for Perugia's Sant'Antonio convent church around 1460, about the time of his Arezzo cycle. It's full of eccentric compositional nuances, particularly in the small *Annunciation* hinged to the top of the main painting, in which a mannered succession of arches around the Virgin recedes into a blank wall. The predella depicts miracles performed by the saints in the main painting.

Dozens of anonymous early fifteenth-century Umbrian works follow, amounting in many cases to no more than a surfeit of the religious iconography that fills Umbrian paintings, without the redeeming dulcet qualities of the Sienese. The better of the Umbrians are Matteo da Gualdo and **Niccolò Alunno**, the latter represented by a *gonfalone*, or painted banner, a genre later to become the special preserve of Perugian painters. Alunno's banner hangs next to a similar work by **Benedetto Bonfigli**, an important mid-period Umbrian painter, who is also represented by a superb *Annunciation and St Luca*; more significantly, he decorated the *palazzo*'s chapel between 1454 and 1480 with surviving fragmentary episodes from the life of Ercolano and Louis of Toulouse, Perugia's patron saints. The frescoes provide a detailed picture of aspects of fifteenth-century Perugia – walls, towers and monuments – that have now largely vanished.

Perugino and the Renaissance

Heralded by a bevy of Perugian contemporaries – talked of by his contemporaries in the same breath as Michelangelo and Leonardo da Vinci – **Perugino** marks the apotheosis of the Umbrian school. About a dozen sublime works here encapsulate his immense output. The loveliest painting is probably the *Madonna della Consolazione* (1496–98), a work whose imagery and bravura technique underline just how much Raphael, Perugino's pupil, would take from his master. Almost equally fine are two earlier pieces painted around 1475, a *Pietà* and an *Adoration of the Magi*.

The second-ranked Umbrian, and Perugino's occasional collaborator, **Pinturicchio**, is not so well represented, save for the gargantuan *Pala di Santa Maria dei Fossi* (1495), widely considered one of the masterpieces of the Umbrian canon. This aside, however, there is little to compare with the artist's frescoes of Spello's Santa Maria Maggiore or the works in Siena's Libreria Piccolomini. Other rooms contain perfectly good works by followers of Perugino, all fluent interpreters of his merging of Umbrian and Florentine traditions.

The Duomo

Piazza IV Novembre • Mon–Sat 7am–12.45pm & 4–7.45pm, Sun 7am–1pm & 4–7pm • Free

Piazza IV Novembre is backed by the plain-faced **Duomo**, or Cattedrale di San Lorenzo. There's been a church on this site for a thousand years, but the cornerstone for the present building was laid in 1345, though the Black Death (1348) almost immediately interrupted subsequent construction. Most of the building was completed late in the following century and even then the facade, which is in the lovely pink stone of most local towns, was left unfinished. Taking a pragmatic approach to the problem, the Perugians stole the marble facing intended for Arezzo's cathedral, though a subsequent hammering from Arezzo brought about its shame-faced return.

To the left of the portal on the building's southern flank is a bronze statue (1555) of Pope Julius III by Vincenzo Danti, and to the right an unfinished **pulpit** built for the roving St Bernardino of Siena, who was something of a hit with the Perugians. It was here that he preached a Bonfire of the Vanities, urging women to burn their wigs and everyone else to give up books, fine clothes and general good times. To the left are remains of the Loggia Fortebraccio (1423), taken from the house of one of the city's medieval rulers.

The interior

The Baroque **interior** is imposing enough, though short on artworks. Its pride and joy is the Virgin's "wedding ring", a novel relic, housed in the Cappella del Santo Anello (first chapel on the left). An unwieldy piece of agate, said to change colour according to the character of the person wearing it, the ring was stolen by the Perugians from Chiusi in 1473 and encased in a series of fifteen boxes, fitted like Russian dolls; it's brought out for public edification once a year on July 30. Embedded in the wall nearby are fragments of an altar by **Agostino di Duccio** (1473); next to them is a lovely painting by Berto di Giovanni showing 1520s Perugia in the background.

In the right aisle, the first chapel (closed by an iron screen) contains a widely admired *Deposition* painted in 1569 by Barocci, apparently under the influence of poison administered by a jealous rival. More toxin-related mementos are contained in the transepts, where urns hold the ashes of Pope Martin IV, who died in the city after eating too many eels, and Urban IV, who was reputedly poisoned with *acquetta*, an imaginative little brew made by rubbing arsenic into pork fat and distilling the resultant ooze. The most conspicuous piece of art is the *Madonna delle Grazie* attributed to Giannicola di Paolo, on the third pillar of the right nave. Easily recognized by its tinselly votive offerings, it's supposed to have miraculous powers, and mothers still bring their newly baptized children to kneel before it.

The Museo Capitolare della Cattedrale di San Lorenzo

Tues–Sun 10am–1pm & 2.30–5.30pm • €3.50

Through the cathedral sacristy (or if it's closed, through a courtyard to the left of the entrance) are the cloisters and **Museo Capitolare**, or Museo dell'Opera del Duomo, inaugurated in 1923 on the four hundredth anniversary of Perugino's death. It's a rich treasury scattered through 26 rooms with some fine examples of the miniatures for which medieval Perugia was renowned, as well as a *Madonna and Saints* (1484) by **Luca Signorelli**, and works by Umbrian and Sienese masters. Despite the listed opening hours, note that you often have to ring the bell at the cathedral chapterhouse for entry.

West of the Corso: Via dei Priori to San Francesco

The steeply sloping **Via dei Priori**, if you're to believe the medieval chroniclers, was a conduit for almost constantly flowing rivers of blood from those killed in the vendettas and intrigues for which Perugia was famous. The side streets, too, have associations with Perugia's gory past, notably **Via della Gabbia**, the first street down on the right, where there once hung a large iron cage used to imprison thieves and wayward clergymen. You can still make out long spikes on some of the lower walls of the street, used for the heads of executed criminals.

San Filippo Neri and the Torre degli Sciri

Via dei Priori

San Filippo Neri, on the right-hand side of Via dei Priori, is a Baroque church worth a look for its high altarpiece, a painting of the *Immaculate Conception* (1662) by **Pietro da Cortona**, a local star who would go on to make his name in Rome and Florence. Further down still is the unmissable 46-metre **Torre degli Sciri**, one of the few medieval towers (they reputedly numbered seven hundred) to have survived.

Madonna della Luce and the Porta Trasimena

Via dei Priori

Near the end of Via dei Priori comes **Madonna della Luce** (1513–19), dominated by a vault frescoed by G.B. Caporali and an altarpiece by Tiberio d'Assisi, both accomplished followers of Perugino. The tiny chapel takes its name ("Madonna of the Light") from an incident in 1513, when a young barber swore so profusely on losing at cards that a Madonna in a wayside shrine closed her eyes in horror, and kept them closed for four days. The miracle inspired celebrations, processions and the building of this new church. Immediately to the left, the **Porta Trasimena**, or Arco di San Luca, has been one of the principal entrances to the city since Etruscan times.

Oratorio di San Bernardino

Piazza San Francesco • Daily 9am–1pm & 3.30–6pm; winter closes 5.30pm • Free

Bearing right beyond the Madonna della Luce brings you to a welcoming patch of grass, often frequented by students from the art school next door, and conveniently placed for admiring Agostino di Duccio's colourful **Oratorio di San Bernardino**. Its richly embellished facade is far and away the best piece of sculpture in the city, an odd but appealing mix of bas-reliefs and coloured marble, commissioned in 1457 by the city's magistrates in gratitude to St Bernardino for trying to bring peace to Perugia. The detail of the carving warrants a close look, especially the lower frieze depicting the Bonfire of the Vanities – a pile of Perugian wigs, books and hosiery elicited by the saint's preaching. The church interior contains the tomb of Fra' Angelo, who ordered the oratory's construction, and a high altar fashioned from a fourth-century Christian sarcophagus.

San Francesco

Piazza San Francesco

Alongside the Oratorio di San Bernardino is what's left of **San Francesco**, Bernardino's lodging in the city, and in its time Perugia's most sumptuous church. Started just four years after Francis's death in 1226, it's been laid low by earthquakes and landslips, though the curiously jumbled facade is still just about standing and the interior is often used as a concert hall. From San Francesco, Via Alessandro Pascoli leads east to Piazza Fortebraccio.

East of the Corso

Piazza Danti, the pleasant little square behind the Duomo, is the scene of a weekend flower and terracotta **market** and site of a third-century BC **Pozzo Etrusco**, well worth the few minutes it takes to see. The church of San Severo is the main draw here, though Santa Maria is also worth a look.

The Pozzo Etrusco

Piazza Danti 18 • April & Aug daily 10am–1.30pm & 2.30–6pm; May–July, Sept & Oct Tues–Sun 10am–1.30pm & 2.30–6.30pm; rest of year Tues–Sun 11am–1.30pm & 2.30–5pm • €2.50, includes admission to San Severo & Museo delle Mura e delle Porte Urbiche

Little in the dim, ancient alley that drops to the entrance of the **Pozzo Etrusco**, or Etruscan well, hints at the scale of the structure, a massive affair that dramatically illustrates the engineering and technical skills of its Etruscan builders. Its 430,000-litre capacity was sufficient to supply the entire city – water still gathers here from moisture-bearing strata – and was at least 35m deep: the precise depth is impossible to ascertain because of debris at the bottom of the shaft.

San Severo

Piazza Raffaello 13 • April & Aug daily 10am–1.30pm & 2.30–6pm; May–July, Sept & Oct Tues–Sun 10am–1.30pm & 2.30–6.30pm; rest of year Tues–Sun 11am–1.30pm & 2.30–5pm • €2.50, includes admission to Pozzo Etrusco & Museo delle Mura e delle Porte Urbiche

10

Close by the Pozzo Etrusco, the church of **San Severo** is the chief sight of this district. Legend claims it was built on the site of a pagan temple to the sun – the spot is east-facing and the town's highest point – which gave its name to the Porta Sole district of the Etruscan city. There would once have been five such districts, spreading down from the temple to five corresponding gates in the outer wall.

Most of the church is a Baroque rehash, grafted onto a building that dates from 1007, though one chapel was spared – a survivor that contains one of **Raphael**'s first complete works, a *Holy Trinity and Saints* (1505–8 and 1521), probably painted shortly before (or just after) he settled in Florence in 1505. The fresco, as often in paintings of the Trinity, is on three levels, though the upper level – God the Father – is missing. Notice the figure of Christ, whose nudity echoes the nudity of the heroes of Classical art, and which shows the young Raphael's assimilation of new Renaissance notions. The painter was summoned to Rome to work in the Vatican and never completed the picture.

In a poignant piece of artistic irony, the lower panels, depicting *Six Saints*, were painted in 1521 by Perugino, then in his dotage, a year after the death of his erstwhile pupil. Perugino's work shows him at his most stilted, an artist who found a winning formula from which he never moved on, even in old age: Raphael's debt to his master is obvious, but even as a fledgling talent in this fresco he demonstrates his more dynamic approach, not least in the arrangement of his figures: where Perugino's saints stand in a line, face on, Raphael's figures are arranged facing out or sideways, creating a more dramatic compositional effect.

Santa Maria Nuova

Via Pinturicchio 87

From San Severo, it's easy to continue to Piazza Fortebraccio by way of **Santa Maria Nuova**, a sprawling and much knocked-about church restored more or less to its original Gothic appearance (to reach it, return to Via Bontempi and turn left downhill). Its main point of interest is the *gonfalone* (banner) in the second chapel on the right; created in 1472 by Bonfigli, it features a view of Perugia under attack from divine thunderbolts.

The northern quarters

The **northern quarters** of the *centro storico* start at **Piazza** Braccio Fortebraccio, ten-minutes' walk downhill from Piazza IV Novembre, and a similar distance from San Francesco and Santa Maria Nuova. The area encompasses Perugia's oldest street, the 2500-year-old **Via Ulisse Rocchi**, the modern university buildings and the famous raised walkway of **Via del Acquedotto**. The latter is the best way to see this part of the city – the views are great and there's no traffic.

Piazza Fortebraccio

Unlovely **Piazza Fortebraccio** is dominated by the **Arco di Augusto**, or Arco Etrusco, a massive gateway whose lowest section represents one of the few remaining monuments to Etruscan Perugia. It dates from the second century BC, when it was the main entrance to the city. The upper arch and bulwarks were added by the Romans when they recaptured the city in 40 BC; under the arch you can still see the letters spelling out its new name, Augusta Perusia – the first part immodestly large, the latter considerably smaller. The top-storey loggia is a sixteenth-century addition. On the western side of the square, housed in the Palazzo Gallenga, is the **Università Italiana per Stranieri**, founded in 1925 and now a favourite of foreigners studying Italian art, language and culture.

Sant'Angelo

Corso Garibaldi • Tues–Sun 9.30am–noon & 3.30pm–dusk

At the end of Corso Garibaldi, tucked into the northern corner of the walls, is the circular **Sant'Angelo**, founded in the fifth century as a temple to St Michael the Archangel. One of the oldest churches in Umbria – Spoleto's San Salvatore just pips it for antiquity – it was probably built on the site of a Roman temple, its two rings of pillars deriving from an earlier building (there was once a third set, removed to build the church of San Pietro; see p.412). Further evidence of a pagan predecessor lurks in the high altar, which is cobbled together from Roman fragments. The church is beautifully plain, its Baroque additions having been stripped away. The setting, too, is delightful, a grassy and tranquil retreat, the shade of the walls and cypresses providing a favourite siesta spot.

Museo delle Porte delle Mura Urbiche

Corso Garibaldi • April & Aug daily 10am–1pm & 2.30–6pm; May–July, Sept & Oct Tues–Sun 10am–1.30pm & 2.30–6pm; Nov–March Tues–Sun11am–1.30pm & 2.30–5pm • €2.50, includes admission to Pozzo Etrusco & San Severo

Housed in the fourteenth-century **Porta Sant'Angelo**, the largest of Perugia's medieval gateways, the small **Museo delle Porte e delle Mura Urbiche** details the history of the city's walls, gateways and other fortifications, but its real draw is the superb view from the top of the gate's tower.

The southern quarters

Perugia's other highlights are conveniently clustered along **Corso Cavour** in the southern side of town, the busy main road out of town towards Assisi, which you can reach by walking down from **Piazza Italia** across Via Baglioni and the stepped alley off Via Oberdan under the Arco di Sant'Ercolano.

En route, you'll pass the strange octagonal church of **Sant'Ercolano** (now a war memorial), raised between 1297 and 1326 on the spot where the head of Perugia's first bishop miraculously reattached itself after it had been removed by the Goths.

Via Baglioni Sotteranea

A little southwest of Sant'Ercolano is the **Porta Marzia** (daily 8am–7pm), a superb Etruscan archway above an entrance to **Via Baglioni Sotteranea**, part of an extraordinary complex of submerged medieval streets that can also be accessed from the escalators on the southwest side of Piazza Italia and from Piazza Partigiani. The streets' houses, built over Etruscan ruins, now form part of the foundations for Piazza Italia above, and were once part of the **Rocca Paolina**, the colossal sixteenth-century papal fortress.

La Rocca Paolina e La Città

May–July, Sept & Oct Tues–Sun 10.30am–1.30pm & 2.30–6pm; April & Aug daily 10am–1.30pm & 2.30–6pm; Nov–March Tues–Sun 11am–1.30pm & 2.30–5pm • €1

The Rocca Paolina is home to the **La Rocca Paolina e La Città**, a modest exhibition divided into four chronological groups that document the fortress's history via maps, engravings and paintings. Designed by **Sangallo**, the Rocca was a gargantuan affair, the remains of which can best be seen coming up on the escalators from Piazza Partigiani (or down from the west side of Piazza Italia). Taking in ten churches and four hundred houses, the Rocca was connected by tunnels to strategic points throughout the city. It was pulled down at Unification, using dynamite and bare hands, by what appears to have been every man, woman and child in the city – and even then the process took thirty years. Trollope, watching the demolition, wrote that "few buildings have been laden with a heavier amount of long-accumulated hatred".

San Domenico
Corso Cavour

The unmissable landmark on Corso Cavour is **San Domenico**, which, at 122m in length, is Umbria's biggest church. Its unfinished exterior has an attractively melancholy air, with pigeons nesting and grass growing on the pinkish marble, but the interior (begun in 1305) collapsed in the sixteenth century to be replaced by a vast, cold Baroque conversion (1632).

Nevertheless, it's full of hints of past beauties. In the fourth chapel on the right, the Cappella della Madonna del Voto, is a superb **carved arch** by **Agostino di Duccio** (1459), a fragment of the original church spoilt only by nineteenth-century frescoes and a doll-like Madonna. On the right wall of the first chapel to the right of the high altar is the **tomb of Benedict XI**, another pope who died in Perugia – this time from eating poisoned figs – after ruling for just eight months in 1304. He left to posterity one of the greatest Gothic carvings of its kind in Italy, an elegant and well-preserved piece by one of the period's leading sculptors – **Giovanni Pisano**, **Lorenzo Maitani** or **Arnolfo di Cambio**; nobody knows which, although it's modelled on the tomb of Cardinal de Braye in Orvieto, one of Arnolfo's most influential works.

In the next chapel to the right are extensive patches of fresco, another good choir, and – a welcome splash of colour – some impressive stained-glass windows (1411), the largest in Italy after those of Milan's cathedral. Also worth hunting out is the *gonfalone* (painted banner) by **Giannicola di Paolo** in the third chapel in the south transept. It was painted as a votive offering after the plague of 1494 and shows Christ above with the people of Perugia and a view of the city below flanked by saints Dominic and Catherine of Siena. The right wall of the left-most chapel in the north transept has an interesting **fresco of St Sebastian** in which, for once, the saint is not depicted riddled with arrows: the painting instead shows the archers preparing to fire.

It is possible to view **Le Soffitte di San Domenico**, the church's imposing vaults and lofts, which contain works by Giovanni **Pisano** and Carlo Maderno. Guided visits (Sat & Sun only) are by prior appointment on ☎075 573 1635.

The Museo Archeologico Nazionale dell'Umbria
Piazza Giordano Bruno 10 • Mon 2.30–7.30pm, Tues–Sun 8.30am–7.30pm • €4; the ticket office is on the first floor of the cloister

The cloisters of San Domenico church hold the **Museo Archeologico Nazionale dell'Umbria**. Before being hammered by Augustus, Perugia was a big shot in the twelve-strong Etruscan federation of cities, which is why the city has one of Italy's most extensive **Etruscan collections**. There's far more here than the usual run of Etruscan urns and funerary monuments. Particularly compelling are the **Carri Etruschi di Castel San Marino**, some quite exquisite sixth-century BC bronze chariots; a witty collection of eye-opening artefacts devoted to fashion and beauty in the Etruscan era; and a series of bronze helmets and shields. Most important for Etruscan scholarship is the **Cippo Perugino**, discovered in 1822, a travertine stele carved on both sides with the longest inscription so far found in the Etruscan language.

Also, be sure to check out the bewildering **Bellucci Collection**, a hoard of charms and amulets used through the ages: everything from the obvious – lucky horseshoes – to stranger and often more sinister charms such as snakeskins, dried animals, feathers and odd scraps of wool. The exhibits span several thousand years and form a unique and oddly poignant picture of fears and superstitious hopes across the millennia.

San Pietro

Borgo Venti Giugno 74

Further south, through the double-arched Porta San Pietro (1147), is the tenth-century basilica of **San Pietro**, the city's first cathedral and still the most beautiful and idiosyncratic of its churches. Advertised by a rocket-shaped bell tower visible for miles around (rebuilt in 1463), it's tangled up in a group of buildings belonging to the university's agricultural department; the entrance is through a doorway in the far left-hand corner of the first courtyard off the road.

10

The interior

The **interior** comes as a shock. Few churches, even in Italy, are so sumptuously decorated, every inch of space being covered in gilt, paint or marble. The effect is appealing, and in the candlelit gloom the church actually feels like a sacred place. That so much of the Romanesque building survives is due to events at Unification, when the church's Benedictine monks sided with the townspeople in their revolt against papal control. Loyalty to the cause of liberation was not forgotten, and when the religious houses were broken up a year later, San Pietro was allowed to keep its patrimony.

The interior's finest single component is the extraordinary **choir** (1526), which has been called the greatest in Italy. All the woodwork here is superb: look out also for the intricately gilded side-pulpits. As for the **paintings**, there's a *Pietà* by **Perugino** between the first and second altars on the left, three works by **Vasari** in the Cappella del Sacramento, and a much-praised depiction of *Christ on the Mount* by Guido **Reni** (located on the left wall of the Cappella Ranieri); the eleven eye-catching frescoes around the upper walls are by a disciple of Veronese. The baffling fresco on the rear wall is a genealogical tree of the Benedictines, collecting together the most eminent members of the order. The best pictures of all are five saints by Perugino and a possible Raphael, gathered in the **sacristy**; ask the sacristan to let you in.

ARRIVAL AND DEPARTURE   **PERUGIA**

BY PLANE

Aeroporto Regionale Umbro Sant'Egido (☎075 592 141, ⍵www.airport.umbria.it), 12km east of the centre, is served by Alitalia or Ryanair flights. Bus shuttles (€3.50) from the airport to Piazza Italia and the train station generally coordinate with flights. A taxi should cost about €30.

BY TRAIN

Fontivegge station The main train station, at Piazza Vittorio Veneto, is 3km southwest of the *centro storico*: it's too far to walk from here, as it's all uphill on busy roads, but the new MiniMetro runs to the centre in 15min. Services depart every two minutes (7am–9pm), and tickets (€1) are available from machines. Hold on to your ticket, as you need it to exit the system. Buses from outside the station run to Piazza Italia or Piazza Matteotti in 10min. Tickets (for unlimited journeys in 1hr 10min) are available from the station newsagent or a booth on the left of the forecourt as you exit the station; paying on board costs €1.50, and you must have the right change.

Stazione Sant'Anna Trains on the private FCU rail line (☎075 575 401, ⍵fcu.it) come into the more central Stazione Sant'Anna, Piazzale Bellucci 14–16, in the southern part of town near the Piazza dei Partigiani bus

terminal. To reach the centre, cross the main road outside the terminal for the ramp leading to the *scala mobile* (escalator) to Piazza Italia.

Destinations FS trains: Assisi (hourly; 25min); Florence (6 daily; 1hr 30min–2hr 10min); Foligno (connections to Rome, Spoleto, Fossato di Vico, Terni, Narni and Orte; hourly; 40min); Gubbio (7 daily; 1hr 30min); Orvieto (10 daily; 1hr 15min); Passignano (hourly; 30min); Rome (4–5 direct; 2hr 15min–3hr); Spello (hourly; 30min); Todi (hourly; 50min).

BY BUS

Bus terminal Buses arrive at the Piazza dei Partigiani terminal in the southern part of town. To reach the centre, cross the main road outside the terminal for the ramp leading to the *scala mobile* (escalator) to Piazza Italia.

Bus enquiries ASP ☎075 573 1707 or ☎075 751 145, ⍵apmperugia.it; SIT ☎0743 212 211; ATC ☎0744 402 900; Sulga ☎800 099 661, ⍵sulga.it.

Destinations Assisi (3–9 daily; 35–50min); Castiglione del Lago (Mon–Sat 6–10 daily; 1hr); Deruta (4 daily; 15–45min); Florence (1 daily; 2hr); Gubbio (Mon–Sat 10 daily, 4 on Sun; 1hr 10min); Norcia (1 daily; 2hr 50min); Orvieto (1 daily; 2hr 25min); Passignano (Mon–Sat 7 daily; 1hr 10min); Rome (5–6 daily; 2hr 30min–3hr); Rome Fiumicino airport (4–5 daily; 3–4hr); Siena (3–7 daily; 1hr

30min); Spello (Mon–Sat 4 daily; 55min); Spoleto (Mon–Sat 1 daily; 1hr 20min); Todi (4 daily; 30min–1hr 10min).

BY CAR

The *centro storico* is usually closed to traffic, and is almost impossible to navigate, much less park, when it is open. Your best bet is to follow the signs for Piazza dei Partigiani in the south, where there's a large covered car park. From here you can jump on a *scala mobile* (escalator) through the subterranean Via Baglioni Sotteranea to Piazza Italia.

Another good option in the west is the car park in Viale Pompeo Pellini, connected by escalators to Via dei Priori. If you're driving in from the north, try the car park in Viale Sant'Antonio.

Car rental Avis: airport ☎ 075 692 9346 or 075 692 9796; Piazza Vittorio Veneto 7 (train station) ☎ 075 500 0395; Hertz, Piazza Vittorio Veneto 4 (train station) ☎ 075 500 2439.

Taxis Radio Taxi ☎ 075 500 4888; Piazza Italia ☎ 075 573 6092; Corso Vannucci ☎ 075 572 1979; train station ☎ 075 501 0800.

10

INFORMATION AND TOURS

Tourist office Piazza Matteotti 18 (daily 8.30am–6.30pm; ☎ 075 577 2686 or 075 573 6458, ⊛ www.regioneumbria.eu).

Local information The monthly *Viva Perugia* is a good source of information, including events and transport

schedules; it's sold at kiosks for €1.

Guided tours Guide in Umbria, Via della Luna 19, just west of Piazza della Repubblica (Mon–Fri 9.30am–1pm & 3–6.30pm, Sat 9.30am–1pm; tours start at €60 for 90min; ☎ 075 573 2933, ⊛ guideinumbria.com).

ACCOMMODATION

Perugia has plenty of **accommodation**, though you should book ahead as some of the best-value places may be taken up by long-stay students; book, too, during the July jazz festival and other major events, when rates will certainly be at their highest.

Anna Via dei Priori 48 ☎ 075 573 6304, ⊛ albergoanna.it. This central, atmospheric hotel on the fourth floor of a medieval town house has fourteen rooms, all with bathrooms, some with parquet floors or original coffered ceilings. Free pass for vehicle access to the historic centre, as well as (limited) free parking. Continental breakfast included. **€80**

★ **Brufani Palace** Piazza Italia 7 ☎ 075 573 2541, ⊛ brufanipalace.com. Luxury property in a perfect (and panoramic) position, with over a century of tradition to call on – the obvious choice if money is no object. Frescoed public spaces lead to immaculate rooms with regal decor and marble bathrooms. A subterranean fitness centre has a swimming pool framed by medieval vaulting, and transparent panels allow you to admire the remains of the city's Etruscan-era walls. Buffet breakfast included. **€200**

Eden Via Cesare Caporali 9 ☎ 075 572 8102, ⊛ www.hoteleden.perugia.it. An eighteen-room hotel in a thirteenth-century building, down an alley just a few paces west of the Corso. Rooms are plain but bright, modern and comfortable, and all have wi-fi and a/c. Buffet breakfast included; parking garage €25 extra per night. **€90**

Fortuna Via Bonazzi 19 ☎ 075 572 2845, ⊛ umbriahotels.com. This spick-and-span choice in a very elegant thirteenth-century *palazzo* benefits from its central but peaceful location and roof garden with good views of the old city. Most rooms have a/c and some have balcony views or frescoed ceilings. Free wi-fi. Substantial buffet breakfast included; parking €20 extra. **€130**

Locanda della Posta Corso Vannucci 97 ☎ 075 572 8925, ⊛ locandadellaposta.com. This is a central

39-room establishment, the town's first hotel; Goethe and Hans Christian Andersen are just two luminaries to have stayed here. Recently renovated, it's a simple place with elegant touches; rooms have a/c and views. Buffet breakfast included. **€130**

Priori Via Vermiglioli 3 ☎ 075 572 3378, ⊛ hotelpriori.it. Tastefully fitted out and well located in a sixteenth-century building, with a great terrace overlooking the rooftops. The rather spartan rooms vary considerably, so ask to see a selection. Substantial buffet breakfast included; parking garage €15–25/day extra. **€95**

Rosalba Piazza del Circo 7 ☎ 075 572 0626, ⊛ hotelrosalba.com. A clean, old-fashioned and simple facility in a pink detached eighteenth-century villa with eleven spacious, light rooms (though ceilings are low in some). All rooms have a/c and there's a terrace with panoramic views. Parking and breakfast included. **€70**

HOSTELS AND CAMPSITES

Il Rocolo Strada Fontana 1n ☎ 075 517 8550, ⊛ ilrocolo.it. Campsite set amid meadows and mature forest. Facilities include a snack bar serving breakfast, lunch and dinner, internet point, barbecue/picnic area and laundry service. April to mid-Oct. Adults **€8**, plus pitch **€6.50**

Ostello di Perugia Via Bontempi 13 ☎ 075 572 2880, ⊛ ostello.perugia.it. The town's oldest hostel, 2min from the Duomo, has 134 beds in four-, six- and eight-bed dorms; sheets cost €2 per day. Free wi-fi. Midnight curfew; and closed daily 11am–3.30pm. Open Jan 15–Dec 15. Dorm beds **€15**

Ostello Spagnoli Via Coronese 4, Località Pian di Massiano ☎ 075 501 1366, ⓦ umbriahostels.org. Located in a converted historic building 1km from the main train station, this place has its own restaurant and space for 186 people in four- and six-bed dorms, and some single rooms. Open 7am–midnight, all year. Dorm bed plus breakfast €16, single room €22

Paradis d'Été Via del Mercato 29a, Strada Fontana ☎ 075 517 3121, ⓦ www.wel.it/cparadis/index .uk.html. Set amidst forests, this campsite has space for 150 pitches; facilities include a swimming pool, a bar and a playground. Open April to mid-Oct. Adults €8.50, plus pitch €6.50

10 EATING, DRINKING AND ENTERTAINMENT

Perugia's cuisine is rewarding. While a plethora of **fast-food and snack bars** cater for the student market, there are several good mid-range **restaurants** and a couple of top-notch ones. There are also plenty of places to go for a **drink**, some of which lay on **live music** at times. The city's most popular **clubs** are in the suburbs, and vary from year to year; ask at the tourist office or check *Viva Perugia* for the latest hotspots. Perugia is strong on events, with films, theatre and concerts packing a page or so each day in the **listings** of the local *Corriere dell'Umbria* newspaper. Posters and flyers around the city, in particular near the university on Piazza Fortebraccio, give details of **concerts** and English-language **films**.

RESTAURANTS

Da Cesarino Piazza IV Novembre 4–5 ☎ 075 572 8974. A very central trattoria-pizzeria that's been around for over thirty years, focused on Umbrian meat and game dishes and other traditional fare. Booking is advised, as the place attracts students, visitors, locals, Perugia's first-team footballers and politicians alike. Around €25; less for pizzas. Mon, Tues & Thurs–Sun 1–3.30pm & 7–10.30pm.

Dal Mi' Cucco Corso Garibaldi 12 ☎ 075 573 2511. The set menu here (€13) always features rustic Perugian dishes, which vary according to season, such as organic pasta with chickpeas, then salad, a side dish and a home-made dessert. Portions are large and quality reliably good. House wine extra. Book ahead. Closed Mon and for a period in July & Aug.

Del Sole Via Oberdan 28 ☎ 075 573 5031. Two large dining rooms under ancient vaults and a terrace with a fine view offer elegant, romantic dining. Food is classic Umbrian: great antipasti, and their speciality is *scaloppa del sole*, thinly sliced veal in their secret sauce. A full meal should come to no more than €30. Tues–Sun 1–3pm & 7.30–10pm; closed part of July & Aug.

★ **Osteria del Gambero** Via Baldeschi 9 ☎ 075 57 5461, ⓦ osteriadelgambero.it. A great restaurant that's been in business since 1989 and has picked up a clutch of awards for its traditional cooking – everything is absolutely home-made. The interior is elegant and original; *degustazione* set menu averages €30 with wine. Ordering a la carte, a full meal will come to about €34. Mon

1.30–3.45pm, Tues–Fri 1.30–3.45pm & 7.30–10.30pm, Sat & Sun 7.30–11pm.

Osteria Il Gufo Via della Viola 18 ☎ 075 573 4126, ⓦ osteriailgufo.it. The best sort of osteria: a relaxed atmosphere, old marble tables, an open kitchen and traditional regional cooking (wild boar with wild fennel for example) with the odd dash of innovation. Some 100 carefully selected wines to choose from. Just 35 covers, with a few tables on the tiny piazza outside in summer. €18–20 per person. Book ahead. Tues–Sat 7.30–10.30pm; closed part of Aug & Sept.

Osteria Turreno Piazza Danti 16 ☎ 075 572 1976. This *tavola calda* has been in business for several generations and it shows: the handful of hot dishes each lunchtime are simple but well prepared, and very fairly priced. You can buy food to take away, or sit outside at one of a handful of tables by the counter or in the larger (and rather hidden) seating area to the rear. For as little as €10 you can get meat, veg, salad, a hunk of bread and a soft drink. Mon–Fri & Sun noon–4pm.

★ **Pizzeria Mediterranea** Piazza Piccinino 11–12 ☎ 075 572 1322. A very popular, traditional wood-fired pizzeria with simple medieval stone walls and pretty brick vaults. The range of some twenty pizzas includes everything from the simplest Neapolitan-style *margherita* to the fully-loaded version. Pizzas €4–8; drinks and dessert a few euros more. Daily 1–3.45pm & 7.30–10.45pm.

★ **Wine Bartolo Hosteria** Via Bartolo 30 ☎ 075 571 6027. Wonderful, traditional food served in a cosy, bottle-lined dining room that accommodates just forty diners;

FOOD MARKETS

A good place to stock up on picnic fare is the covered **food market**, **Mercato Coperto** (Mon–Sat 7.30am–1pm), off Piazza Matteotti, and the open-air **general market** (Tues & Sat 8am–1pm) on the Scala di Sant'Ercolano, near the church of the same name. You can buy other picnic supplies from Giuliano (Mon–Sat 8am–1pm & 4–8pm) at Via Danzetta 1, a small alley off the east side of the Corso just north of Piazza della Repubblica.

book ahead. Menus change according to season, but you can always be assured of excellent Umbrian meat dishes (and first-class Umbrian wines) that aren't afraid of the odd exotic touch, and prices that shouldn't top €25–40 for a full meal, excluding wine. Mon, Tues & Thurs–Sun 1.30–3.30pm & 7.30–10pm.

CAFÉS AND GELATERIE

Bar Pasticceria dell'Accademia Via dei Priori 52 ☎ 075 573 4384. A good, old-fashioned place on a street with several other cafés and restaurants. Look for the medieval stone building with the archway entrance; inside there's a great spread of pastries, and plenty of seating room. Tues–Sun 7am–9pm.

★ **Caffè di Perugia** Via Mazzini 10 ☎ 075 573 1863, ⓦ caffediperugia.it. A pleasantly smart setting with a superb thirteenth-century vaulted ceiling, this is a good early-evening retreat. All the café staples are on offer, and there's also a wine bar and a pizzeria-grill, where dishes start at about €8. Daily 8am–midnight; closed Tues in Nov & Feb.

Gelateria Gambrinus Via Bonazzi 3 ☎ 075 573 5620. Queues from this ice-cream parlour off the Corso often stretch onto the nearby Piazza della Repubblica, especially at the height of the Sunday passeggiata. A great choice of remarkable flavours – *torrone* (nougat), cheese and pear, profiterole, pine nut and more – as well as very generous scoops. Daily 11am–9pm.

★ **Pasticceria Sandri** Corso Vannucci 32 ☎ 075 572 4112. The most atmospheric café in Perugia: belle époque style with lots of brass, wood panels and frescoed ceilings. Worth a cake and a cappuccino just to gaze at the crystal chandeliers and posh decoration. Tues–Sun 8am–9pm.

BARS

★ **Bottega del Vino** Via del Sole 1 ☎ 075 571 6181. A wine bar and shop that offers wine by the glass or bottle, along with cheeses, sausages and the like for snacks, and full meals (try the luscious home-made Umbrian pastas) that run about €20 per person including a glass of wine. Live jazz several nights a week and an arty, welcoming atmosphere. Mon–Sat 7.30pm–midnight.

Enoteca Provinciale Via Ulisse Rocchi 16–18 ☎ 075 572 4824. This wine shop-cum-bar is the best place in Perugia to taste local wines, with a vast selection of vintages and excellent snacks, too. Mon–Sat, 9.30am–10pm, Sun 9.30am–1pm.

LIVE MUSIC AND CLUBS

Contrappunto Jazz Club Via Scortici 4a. One of the longest-established jazz clubs in town, this place attracts an international clientele, drawn to its views and its beers as well as the live music, no longer limited to only jazz. Good antipasti, too. Tues–Sun 8pm–2am.

Velvet Fashion Café Viale Roma 20 ☎ 075 572 1321, ⓦ velvetfashioncafe.com. The only real club in town, this is a sleek, multi-levelled affair, which offers smart dining (menu €20–25, including club entrance), drinking, dancing and occasional live music. You pay for a drink as you enter. Thurs is the nostalgically chic *La Dolce Vita* night. Wed–Sun 9pm–2am.

DIRECTORY

Banks and exchange The are several banks on Corso Vannucci offering foreign exchange.

Emergencies For first aid, call ☎ 118; for an ambulance, call ☎ 113. The hospital is at Via Bonacci Brunamonti (☎ 800 118 020).

Pharmacies Farmacia San Martino, Piazza Matteotti 26 (☎ 075 572 2335) is a late-night pharmacy.

Police (Questura) ☎ 075 50 621 or 112.

Post office Piazza Matteotti 1 (Mon–Wed 8am–6:30pm, Sat 8am–1.15pm; ☎ 075 575 4812).

Lago Trasimeno

The most tempting getaway option near Perugia – whose surroundings are generally pretty low-key – is the reed-fringed **Lago Trasimeno**. An ideal spot to hole up for a few days and swim (if you don't mind murky water), it's the fourth largest lake in Italy (after Garda, Maggiore and Como). People have lived on or close to Trasimeno's shores since Paleolithic times, though its greatest historical fame dates from 217 BC, when the Romans suffered one of the worst defeats in their history at the hands of **Hannibal**. Its strategic position meant that numerous castles and fortified villages grew up on its shores and in the hills around, predecessors of present-day towns such as **Passignano** or **Castiglione del Lago**.

These days, the main drawback to Trasimeno is its popularity: in high season the surface is buzzed by endless speedboats, yachts and windsurfers, and the lakeside resorts are packed out. If you're after relative seclusion, steer clear of the northern shore

10

> ## MARSHES, MOSQUITOES AND MALARIA
>
> Throughout history, broad and shallow Lago Trasimeno has at times been at risk of drying up completely; even now its marshy zones constantly threaten to become peat bogs. Today, with amplified demands on its water from local agriculture, as well as increased silting, the lake's greatest **depth** is no more than 7m – and the average is 4.9m, which makes for a bath-water warm swim in summer. Attempts to regulate the fluctuating water level – and to do something about the **mosquito** problem – date back to Roman times; a number of serious proposals were put forward even then to drain the lake altogether. Such notions remained largely in abeyance for much of the Middle Ages, but the idea came up again in the nineteenth century, when the lake's swampy surrounds provided a thriving breeding ground for malaria, which was finally put to rest just after World War II by selective drainage and powerful doses of DDT; nonetheless, mosquitoes can still be a nuisance in the summertime.

– recently opened up by Perugia's autostrada spur – and head instead for the stretches south of **Magione** and **Castiglione**, though even here, visitors are in ever greater evidence. Be warned, too, that **unofficial camping** is not as easy as it looks: commercial sites have grabbed the best spots and much of the remaining shoreline is marshy. If you're just passing through, the best option is to settle down for a long fish lunch at one of the lakefront restaurants in Castiglione, or take a **boat trip** from Passignano or Castiglione to the **Isola Maggiore**, one of the three islands on the lake.

Passignano

The lake's most accessible point is **PASSIGNANO**, a newish and reasonably attractive resort strung out along the northern shore. Popular with Italians, the town in summer is often one big traffic jam, Sundays being especially bad. In the evenings, though, it's enjoyable enough as people come flooding in from the surrounding campsites, livening up the bars, discos and fish restaurants. The waterfront strip is the chief focus, and there's plenty of bustle in the web of streets behind as well. Bar two dull Renaissance churches and a bit of a castle, there's nothing much to see: you can skip the town in the daytime unless it's to catch a boat.

ARRIVAL AND DEPARTURE   PASSIGNANO

By train The train station is at Via 2 Giugno, right on the lakeshore, and is served by hourly trains from Perugia and Teróntola (near Cortona).

ACCOMMODATION

Cavalieri Via delle Ginestre ☎075 829 292, ⓦhotelcavalieri.it. Pompeiian-red property, 1km north of town in a quiet spot among olives and oaks. Some of the 35 spacious, immaculate rooms have lovely lake views, as does the outdoor pool and terrace and the restaurant. Breakfast included. €̶80̶

Kursaal Viale Europa 24 ☎075 828 085, ⓦkursaalhotel .net. Set amidst the quiet of a forest of umbrella pines about 1km east of town, this charming villa has light, spacious rooms with balconies and a/c. Facilities include a pool, a solarium, a private beach and a good restaurant with terrace views of the lake, as well as an adjacent campsite. Breakfast included for hotel guests. Camping €̶8̶ per person, plus pitches €̶10̶, double rooms €̶90̶

Castiglione del Lago

CASTIGLIONE DEL LAGO cuts a fine silhouette from other points on the lake, jutting into the water on a fortified promontory. It's a friendly, unpretentious place that can hold your attention for a couple of days – longer if all you want to do is crash out on one of the modest but pleasant **beaches** dotted around the promontory; the best swimming is on the south side, but they get extremely busy in summer. Despite its Etruscan and Roman origins, Castiglione has few specific sights. As well as the castle

HANNIBAL AND THE BATTLE OF LAGO TRASIMENO

On the shore west of Passignano is the spot where the Romans suffered the most traumatic defeat in their history, on 24 June, 217 BC, at the hands of **Hannibal**. The Carthaginian leader was headed for Rome, having already crossed the Alps, and had won a sweeping victory at Placentia – though by this stage only one of his famous elephants was still alive. He was accompanied by a battle-hardened army of around 40,000, and was met by a Roman force of some 25,000 men under the consul **Flaminius** (responsible for the Via Flaminia), close to an amphitheatre of hills above the lake – a location, said the historian Livy, that was "formed by Nature for an ambush".

Things might have gone better for Flaminius if he'd heeded the omens that piled up on the morning of battle. First he fell off his horse, then the legionary standards had to be dug from the mud, then – and this should have been the clincher – the sacred chickens refused their breakfast. (Poultry accompanied all Roman armies in the field, their behaviour or the look of their innards at moments of crisis being interpreted as communications of the will of the gods.)

Hannibal lured Flaminius into a masterful ambush, ranging his men in the hills above the amphitheatre under the cover of early-morning mist. Meanwhile he sent a small detachment over the hills to the rear of the amphitheatre, allowing Flaminius to see them, thus tricking the Roman commander into thinking he had seen the tail end of Hannibal's army vacating the basin. Thus duped, Flaminius abandoned his marshy position on the lakeshore in favour of the amphitheatre's drier ground. As he marched into the trap Hannibal's men poured down the surrounding slopes, wreaking havoc among the Roman soldiers, who were marching in a non-battle formation – many barely had time to draw their swords. The only escape lay in a muddy retreat back to the lakeshore, where they were mercilessly pursued and hacked down by Hannibal's men. Two entire legions (16,000 men) were killed, including the hapless commander, run through with a lance. The slaughter lasted for three hours. Hannibal, for his part, is thought to have lost just 1500 men.

Hannibal's sappers had orders to bury the dead where they fell, and, in fact, 113 mass graves, or *ustrina* – deep stone-lined pits with lids – have been discovered. Scientific dating of the remains tallies exactly with the date of the battle. Permanent memorials to the carnage exist in the form of the names of two local hamlets: **Sanguineto** (Place of Blood), near the battlefield, and **Ossaia** (Place of Bones), to the northwest, just below Cortona.

10

and Palazzo della Corgna, you might want hunt down the church of **Santa Maria Maddalena** at the western end of Via Vittorio Emanuele, where the main left altar has a fine *Madonna and Child* by Eusebio di San Giorgio, a follower of Perugino.

It's easy to reach Castiglione by road and rail, though most of the latter involve slow connections. The town's lively **market** is on Wednesdays.

The castle

April, May & Sept 9.30am–1pm & 3.30–7pm; June–Aug 10am–1.30pm & 4–7.30pm; Oct 9.30am–1pm & 4.30–6pm; Nov–March Sat, Sun & public holidays 9.30am–4.30pm • €4

The largely sixteenth-century **castle**, or Rocca del Leone, is well preserved, its strange fortified passageway part of a defensive scheme that, in the thirteenth century, made it one of Europe's impregnable fortresses. Its design has been attributed to Frate Elias, a controversial Franciscan monk who may also have been responsible for the Basilica di San Francesco in Assisi. The castle ramparts offer good views of the lake, and there's a stage for outdoor summer events.

Palazzo della Corgna

Piazza Gramsci • April, May & Sept 9.30am–1pm & 3.30–7pm; June–Aug 10am–1.30pm & 4–7.30pm; Oct 9.30am–1pm & 4.30–6pm; Nov–March Sat, Sun & public holidays 9.30am–4.30pm • €4

Connected to the castle by a long passageway along the fortified walls, the ducal **Palazzo della Corgna** is full of large rooms with ceilings covered in frescoes of Classical subjects. Machiavelli once stayed here, as did Leonardo da Vinci (in 1503), who made a drawing of the town's fortifications.

10

BOATS ON LAGO TRASIMENO

Boats run throughout the year from **Passignano**'s landing-stage in front of Piazza Garibaldi to the **Isola Maggiore** (around 12 daily; 15min). There's also a shuttle between Passignano and **Castiglione del Lago** (summer Sat & Sun 2 daily; 40min). Boats run to the Isola Maggiore from Castiglione del Lago, but with reduced services outside summer (May–Sept 6–8 daily; Oct–April Sat & Sun 6–8 daily; 30min).

Typical **ticket prices** are €6 return for the trip from Passignano to Isola Maggiore and €6.60 return from Castiglione del Lago to Isola Maggiore. Contact APM-Navigazione (☎075 506 781, ⓦapmperugia.it – click on "orari" and then "Navigazione del Trasimeno") for more information.

INFORMATION

Tourist office Piazza Mazzini 10 (Mon–Fri 8.30am–1pm & 3.30–7pm, Sat 9am–1pm & 3.30–7pm, Sun 9am–1pm & 4–7pm; winter hours: Mon–Fri 8.30am–1pm & 3.30–7pm,

CASTIGLIONE DEL LAGO

Sat 9am–1pm; ☎075 965 2484, ⓦwww.comune .castiglione-del-lago.pg.it).

ACCOMMODATION AND EATING

Badiaccia Camping Via Trasimeno I 91, Località Badiaccia ☎075 965 9097, ⓦbadiaccia.com. This lakeside spot is not just a campsite, with various accommodation options such as bungalows, chalets, mobile homes, apartments and a villa. There's also a pool, tennis courts, beach, restaurant, bar, and more – an entire village. Linens extra. Adult campers **€7.50** per person, plus pitches **€5.50**

Duca della Corgna Via Bruno Buozzi 143 ☎075 953 238, ⓦhotelcorgna.com. Set in a park area about 2km inland from the lake, this pleasant, family-run property is of fairly new construction, light and airy, with a pool and spacious, stylish rooms with balcony. Buffet breakfast included. **€90**

L'Acquario Via Vittorio Emanuele II 69 ☎075 965 2432 This is the best place in town to eat game, fish fresh from the lake (usually carp or eel) and other dishes featuring Umbrian

truffles. About €30 per person. Mon, Tues & Thurs– Sun 1.30–4pm & 7.30–10.30pm; closed Tues in winter.

Miralago Piazza Mazzini 6 ☎075 951 157, ⓦhotelmiralago.com. This traditional and atmospheric hotel is up in the historic centre, with views of the lake behind. Decor is elegant – even rather posh – in both the public spaces and rooms, and there's a restaurant. Breakfast is included. **€85**

Vinolento Via del Forte 75 ☎075 952 5262, ⓦvinolento.it. This osteria-enoteca is a lovely place for a snack or a full meal. The cook is a serious master of local Umbrian-Trasimeno culinary traditions, and the wine list is more than equal to the task. Specialities of home-made pasta and local game are served in a medieval setting with a beautifully frescoed ceiling. About €25 for a full meal, not including wine. Tues–Sun 1.30–4pm & 7.30–11pm.

Isola Maggiore

Regular boats from Passignano and Castiglione make the trip out to **Isola Maggiore**, the second largest of Trasimeno's three islands – a fun ride if you don't mind the crowds. The island boasts a single village of about one hundred people and is traditionally known for its lacemaking and for pretty **walks** – simply follow the paths, both up to the church at the top and around the 2km perimeter. Isola Maggiore is also famous for a protracted visit by St Francis in 1211. During his forty-day sojourn he refused to eat a freshly caught fish offered him – he threw it back, after which the fish reportedly followed him around, requesting his blessing – and consumed just half a loaf of bread; a chapel marks the point of his disembarkation. On the southeast shore, there's a large neo-Gothic castle (under restoration) that was built in the late nineteenth century on the ruins of a fourteenth-century Franciscan monastery.

ACCOMMODATION AND EATING

Da Sauro Via Guglielmi 1 ☎075 826 168, ⓦdasauro.it. Set in a stone building at the village's northern limit, this is Isola Maggiore's only place to eat and sleep; both rooms and tables at the excellent restaurant are very popular in high season, so

ISOLA MAGGIORE

be sure to book ahead. Rooms are comfortable if a bit austere, while the restaurant specializes, of course, in fish creations grills, risotto and stews (full meals €20–30). Restaurant daily 1.30–4pm & 7.30–10.30pm; closed Nov–Feb. **€70**

Northern Umbria

Moving north from Perugia you have two principal options. The most immediately tempting is the 30km journey to **Gubbio**, which is among the best-preserved medieval towns in central Italy. This is easily accomplished as a day-trip by car or bus from Perugia, but there's enough in the town and the countryside beyond to warrant an overnight stay, especially if you want to explore the wild upland countryside further east, the best of which is protected by the **Parco Naturale del Monte Cucco**, a mountain park with some excellent hiking trails.

The second option from Perugia is to follow the course of the River Tiber (Tevere) towards **Sansepolcro** (covered in Chapter 9), an obvious option if you're heading into Tuscany anyway, or, in particular, if you're on the trail of the great painter **Piero della Francesca** (see p.378). The Tiber valley terrain north of Perugia is pretty and pastoral, and mostly lacks the light industry that blights the Valle di Spoleto and stretches of the Tiber further south. The highlight of the area is **Città di Castello**, an unheralded and relatively little-visited town that may not be in quite the same league as Gubbio, but is definitely worth a stop for its pristine medieval centre, outstanding art and trio of fascinating museums.

10

GETTING AROUND | NORTHERN UMBRIA

By train and car If you're without transport, Città di Castello is best reached by rail on the FCU from Perugia (hourly; 1hr 10min). By car, you could combine the northern region's major towns by visiting Gubbio and then heading west on the SS219 road to pick up the SS3bis road north to Città di Castello.

Città di Castello

Umbria's northernmost town, **CITTÀ DI CASTELLO**, is a relatively little-visited spot whose more than passable *centro storico* is a touch spoilt by the industry on its outskirts – mainly tobacco-processing plants, the town being one of Italy's leading producers. On either side of the valley floor, green wooded hills provide a pleasant backdrop, concealing one of Umbria's larger concentrations of rented villas and farmhouses. At the town's southern edge lies the **Pinacoteca Comunale**, the main artistic reason – along with an excellent **diocesan museum** – for visiting the town. The historic centre is also a pleasant enough place to spend a night, particularly if you devote an evening to sampling the local Colli Altotiberini wines, or happen to catch one of the town's two festivals.

The Pinacoteca Comunale

Via della Cannoniera 22 • Tues–Sun: April–Oct 10am–1pm & 2.30–6.30pm; Nov–March 10am–12.30pm & 3–6pm • €6 • ⓦ cdcnet.net

The **Pinacoteca Comunale** is set in the Palazzo Vitelli alla Cannoniera, one of four surviving palaces here formerly owned by the Vitelli, the town's erstwhile overlords. One of the region's more prepossessing buildings, the *palazzo* was built for Alessandro Vitelli between 1521 and 1532 by **Sangallo** the Younger and Pier Francesco da Viterbo, and decorated with some beautiful sgraffito by **Vasari** on the garden facade. Inside, the painted stairwells and period furniture complement the paintings, with recently restored sixteenth-century frescoes by Cola dell'Amatrice on the stairs and in the first-floor *salone* being some of the most striking. Not all the *palazzo*'s former guests, however, had time to appreciate the high-class fittings: Laura, one of the Vitelli women, was wont to throw her rejected lovers to their deaths from the windows.

The collection was being extensively restructured and the displays updated at the time of writing. We've picked out the highlights below, but you'll need to determine where each piece is located upon arrival.

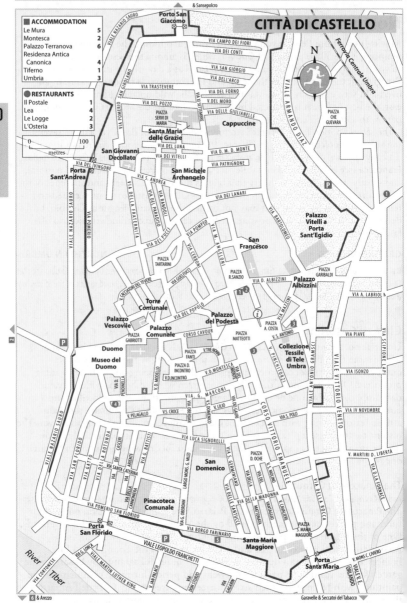

CITTÀ DI CASTELLO

ACCOMMODATION

Le Mura	5
Montesca	2
Palazzo Terranova	6
Residenza Antica Canonica	4
Tiferno	1
Umbria	3

RESTAURANTS

Il Postale	1
Lea	4
Le Logge	2
L'Osteria	3

The paintings

Among the many extraordinary paintings, one of the best is *The Martyrdom of St Sebastian* (1497–8) by **Luca Signorelli** (active in and around the town between 1474 and 1500), the painter of Orvieto's extraordinary fresco cycle and another in Morra, near Città di Castello. More compelling still is the damaged but still ravishing processional standard by **Raphael**, the *Creation of Eve* and *Sts Roch and Sebastian*. It was painted in about 1503 as a votive offering following an epidemic, both Roch and Sebastian being saints traditionally invoked against the plague. Raphael spent about five years in Umbria and the region once had many works by him. Today the only pieces in Umbria painted entirely by him are the standard here and the panel in the church of San Severo in Perugia: many of the others were removed to France by Napoleon.

There are five more exceptional paintings in the gallery: a *Madonna and Child with St John* by Pinturicchio, two paintings of angels by **Giulio Romano** and *Christ in Glory* (1528–30) by Mannerist superstar **Rosso Fiorentino**, with the figures of the Virgin Mary and her mother, St Anna, on the right, and Mary of Egypt and Mary Magdalene on the left. This would be a special painting even if it were in the Uffizi or a gallery of similar stature, so it's a remarkable treat to find it here. It even warranted comment from Vasari, who thought the figures and items pictured were some of the "strangest things in the world", though in every other respect he considered the work outstanding.

10

The rest of the collection

The sculptural high point is provided by the *Reliquary of St Andrew* (1420), which is graced with two gilded bronze statuettes by the workshop of **Lorenzo Ghiberti**. There are also lovely ceramics by the **della Robbias**.

Also not to be missed is a precious and visually striking *paliotto*, or **gilded altar-relief**, reputedly presented to Città di Castello by Pope Celestine II in 1142. Of quite exquisite detail, the work shows Christ surrounded by symbols and scenes from his life. Also here, dated 1324, is a superb **Sienese crozier**, worked in mind-boggling delicacy: note the tiny statuettes of the Virgin and Child and a kneeling bishop in the curl of the crook at the top of the octagonal shaft. Other items include religious ephemera such as reliquaries – most notably a processional cross containing a bone belonging to St Catherine of Siena – and other objects spanning some six centuries.

The Duomo

Piazza Gabriotti • Mon–Sat 7.30am–12.30pm & 3.30–7.30pm • ⓦ cdcnet.net

Many of Città di Castello's buildings have lost their medieval aspect to later facades, most notably the rather odd-looking **Duomo**, whose half-finished Baroque frontage was begun in 1632 and abandoned some fifteen years later. By 580, the church had already been rebuilt at least once, and further versions followed in the eleventh and fourteenth centuries, and again in 1458, when the building had to be reconstructed virtually from the ground up after an earthquake. Something of its chequered construction history can be seen in the wonderful round **campanile**, which combines an eleventh-century base with a newer Gothic upper level, and in the Gothic lines of the **north portal**, with carvings that include two fine panels, *Mercy* and *Justice* (1339–59). The heavily reworked interior promises little, though if you're lucky enough to find the **sacristy** open (door on the right), take a look at its small annexe containing a handful of paintings.

The Museo del Duomo

Piazza Gabriotti 3a • Tues–Sun 10am–1pm & 3–6.30pm • €6

The excellent **Museo del Duomo** is entered to the right of the cathedral's facade. It's arranged over two main floors: pride of place on the ground floor goes to the **Tesoro di Canoscio**, a hoard of paleo-Christian silverware comprising nine plates, eleven spoons and five miscellaneous pieces – some of them beautifully engraved – turned up in the nearby hamlet of Canoscio in 1935 by a farmer ploughing his fields. They were probably made in Constantinople around the sixth century and might have been used to celebrate the Eucharist.

Collezione Tessile di Tele Umbra

Via Sant'Antonio 3 • **Museum** Tues–Sat 10am–noon & 3.30–5.30pm, Sun 10.30am–1pm & 3–6pm, Nov–March Sun closes 5.30pm • €3.50 • **Workshop** Wed–Sat 10am–noon & 3.30–6pm; Oct–March closes 5.30pm • €1 in addition to museum ticket • ⓦ cdcnet.net

The fascinating **Collezione Tessile di Tele Umbra**, just off the main Piazza Matteotti, is annexed to a not-to-be-missed small textile **workshop** set up in 1908 by the Franchetti a local aristocratic family determined to provide employment and keep alive the centuries-old traditions of linen-making in the region; it's still in operation and looks much as it must have done almost a century ago.

The museum traces the history of textiles in the Upper Tiber valley, though in many ways it is less interesting than the workshop, which still employs local women and still – almost uniquely in Italy – uses traditional hand-worked looms. A small shop sells products made here.

10

The Burri collections

Palazzo Albizzini Tues–Sat: 9am–12.30pm & 2.30–6pm; Sun 10.30am–12.30pm & 3–6pm • **Seccatoi del Tabacco** March to mid-Nov same hours • Joint ticket €6 • ⓦ fondazioneburri.org

The fifteenth-century **Palazzo Albizzini** on Piazza Garibaldi houses a collection of paintings donated to the town by the local-born **Alberto Burri** (1915–95), a modern artist of international standing, whose work was at the forefront of postwar avant-gardism. Larger paintings and sculptures by Burri are displayed in the **Seccatoi del Tabacco**, colossal buildings on Via Pierucci on the southern edge of town once used to dry tobacco. They're worth visiting for their own sake and provide a breathtaking display space for Burri's work.

ARRIVAL AND DEPARTURE   CITTÀ DI CASTELLO

By train Services on the private FCU line arrive and depart from the train station at Piazzale della Repubblica 1, just outside the walls to the southeast and a 5min walk from the centre. The closest station served by mainline FS trains is Arezzo, from where ACT buses run to Città di Castello.
Destinations Perugia (hourly; 1hr 10min); Sansepolcro (hourly; 20min).

By bus The bus station is in Piazza Garibaldi, on th' eastern edge of the *centro storico*.
Destinations Arezzo (hourly; 1hr 30min); Rome Tiburtir (1 daily; 3hr 15min); Rome Fiumicino airport (Mon–Sat daily; 4hr); Sansepolcro (1 daily; 20min).
By car Of the car parks around the city walls, one of th' most convenient is on Viale Nazario Sauro in the wes' linked by a path to the piazza in front of the Duomo.

INFORMATION

Tourist office Logge Bufalini, just off Piazza Matteotti (Mon–Sat 9am–1pm & 3.30–6.30pm, Sun 10am–1pm; ☎ 075 855 4922, ⓦ cdcnet.net).

ACCOMMODATION

Le Mura Via Borgo Farinario 24 ☎ 075 852 1070, ⓦ hotellemura.it. This large, renovated rural house has an appealing garden with a fountain and well-appointed rooms with a/c, though bathrooms are rather on the small side. There's also a full-service restaurant, a bar and reserved parking. Breakfast included. €80

★ **Palazzo Terranova** Località Ronti Morra ☎ 075 857 0083, ⓦ palazzoterranova.com. This country palace 7km southwest of town is a sublime retreat. It has just ten individually designed rooms, arranged in a seventeenth-century villa at the end of a wonderful long drive. The chic

restaurant is first-rate, and there's also a pool, and a sp offering luxury treatments. Breakfast included. €400
Residenza Antica Canonica Via San Florido 2 ☎ 075 852 3298, ⓦ umbriaholidays.net. If you' looking for self-catering options, this refurbishe' fifteenth-century *palazzo* offers good-value apartmen' in a very picturesque setting. The functional, comfortab' apartments come in a variety of configurations, some f' two persons, some for families, some with multip' bedrooms for groups. All have full kitchen facilities ar wi-fi. Double apartment €70

> ### CITTÀ DI CASTELLO'S FESTIVALS
>
> Primarily a festival of chamber music, the **Festival delle Nazioni** (ⓦ festivalnazioni.com) takes place over a week or so in late August and early September. The equally alluring **Mostra del Tartufo** (ⓦ iltartufobianco.it), with exhibitions and tastings of white truffles, is held over three days, usually around the first week of November.

★ **Tiferno** Piazza Raffaello Sanzio 13 ☎075 855 0331, ⓦwww.hoteltiferno.it. The town's best hotel is housed in a completely restructured and refurbished seventeenth-century monastery. The public spaces are elegant, full of antiques and period and contemporary art, with coffered wooden ceilings and a large fireplace in the salon; and the rooms are crisply contemporary, very spacious and functional. Reserved parking spots, restaurant, a fitness room, a/c and wi-fi are pluses. Buffet breakfast included. €150

Umbria Via dei Galanti 4 ☎075 855 4925, ⓦhotelumbria.net. Rooms in this unpretentious,

family-run hotel are bright and clean, generally spacious and with little in the way of adornment. Free parking nearby for guests. Breakfast is included. €55

CAMPING
Montesca La Montesca ☎075 855 8566, ⓦlamontesca.it. Located 1km west of town on a hill with views, this comfortable, multi-levelled spot has a pool, recreational facilities, a restaurant, a mini-market and a bar. Besides tent sites, the friendly owners also offer advice on a range of outdoor activities. May–Sept. Adults €8, pitches €6.50

EATING AND DRINKING

Il Postale Via Raffaele de Cesare 8 ☎075 852 1356. Boasting one Michelin star, and offering grander cuisine than you'll find at the other options in town. You'll need to spend at least €65 per person to savour the best of the creative cooking – most certainly something that will involve perfect truffles. With only five tables, booking in advance is a must. Tues–Fri 1.30–3.45pm 7.30–10.30pm; closed Oct–May.

Le Logge Piazza Raffaello Sanzio 13 ☎075 855 0331, ⓦhoteltiferno.it. An elegant dining space with food to match: marvellous regional dishes featuring game and truffles. Full menus go for about €45, antipasti and pasta dishes average €10, main courses €15. Daily 1.30–4pm & 7.30–10.30pm.

★ **Lea** Via San Florido 28 ☎075 852 1678. A locals'

favourite, this is a good old-fashioned sort of trattoria, with regional cooking and fair prices – expect about €20 per person for a full meal. Home-made pasta dishes to go for include *agnolotti* with porcini and tagliatelli with truffles; you can also ask for a *bis*, half portions of each in the same dish. Good house wines to wash it all down. Best to book, or expect a wait. Tues–Sun 1–3.30pm & 7.30–10pm; closed mid-July to mid-Aug.

L'Osteria Via Borgo di Sotto 1 ☎075 855 6995. A good variety of pizzas (starting at just €5), full meals for about €20 per person, and a convivial, arty atmosphere all combine to make this one of the top choices in town. Killer desserts, too, so leave room as portions are large. Mon–Sat 1–3.30pm & 7.30–10pm.

Gubbio

High, remote **GUBBIO** has the most beautiful medieval appearance of the northern Umbrian towns – indeed it's so well preserved that some Italian guides and the local tourist blurb describe it as the Umbrian Siena. It's not quite that, but the streets are all attractive pale pink stone, the monuments impressive, and the medieval nooks and crannies as endearing as any in Italy. In many ways it has become the region's loveliest town to explore, since sheer visitor numbers and tacky commercialism have increasingly compromised Assisi's charms. Better still, the countryside around is gorgeous, with the forest-covered mountains of the Apennines rearing up behind and the waters of the Camignano gorge running through the town itself (in winter at least). A broad and largely unspoilt plain – bar a cement works to the north – stretches out in front of the town.

Piazza Quaranta Martiri makes an obvious place to start exploring Gubbio; it was named after forty innocent citizens murdered by the Nazis in 1944 as a reprisal for partisan attacks in the surrounding hills; the fighting around Gubbio as the Allies advanced north was especially tough, the battle for the town taking three weeks. After taking in **San Francesco** and its fresco cycles you should head into the medieval town proper, where the vast **Palazzo dei Consoli** houses the town's **museum** (home to the famed Eugubine Tablets) and picture gallery, and then wander the short distance to the adjoining **Duomo, Museo Diocesano** and **Palazzo Ducale**, the last based on the Montefeltros' famous palace in Urbino. A lane behind the Duomo – the route taken by competitors during the famous Corsa dei Ceri (see p.427) – leads up to **Monte Ingino**, a hilltop eyrie which offers lovely views and plenty of picnic and strolling opportunities. Alternatively, you could head to **Porta Romana**, where a **funicular** also runs up Monte Ingino.

Brief history

Local folklore insists that Gubbio was one of the first five towns built after the Great Flood. It was actually founded by the **Umbrians** around the third or fourth century BC

10

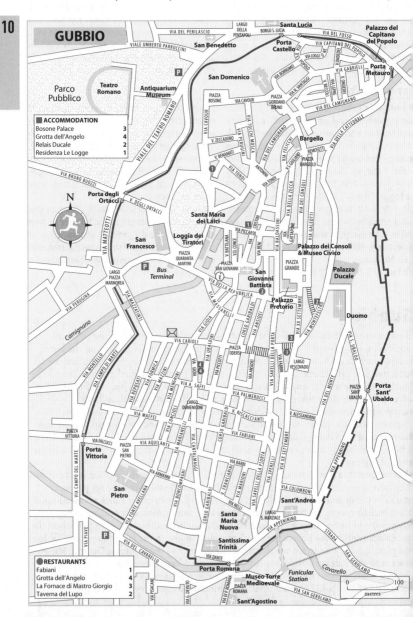

and may even have been their political and religious capital, later passing to the **Etruscans**, for whom it marked the easternmost limit of their territorial ambitions. Several bronze slabs, the **Eugubine Tablets** – now in the Museo Civico – survive as memorials to both cultures, some of the most important archeological finds of their type. The **Romans** followed, building the colony of Iguvium at the edge of the plain, where a sprinkling of monuments and the gridiron plan of their streets survive to this day. Barbarian raids subsequently saw Gubbio's focus move up the hillside, where steep, terraced slopes form the town's present-day heart.

In the medieval period, Gubbio maintained a strategic importance as the pivotal town between Rome and Ravenna, its *comune* achieving a status that rivalled Perugia. According to contemporary chroniclers, the population grew to 50,000 – twice its present number – the town's wealth and size providing not only the wherewithal to build its vast civic palaces, but also the impulse towards artistic and cultural innovation. Umbria's first school of **painting** developed here, as did a **ceramic** tradition that continues today. Gubbio remained in the Duchy of Urbino until 1624, then became part of the **Papal States**, perhaps one reason why it still feels a town apart, not properly a part of Tuscany, Umbria or the Marche.

San Francesco

Piazza Quaranta Martiri

Slightly stranded from the medieval heart of town, the town's finest church is the Gothic **San Francesco**, possibly designed by Fra' Bevignate, the brains behind Perugia's Fontana Maggiore. The restored interior holds an engaging if faded cycle of **frescoes** painted around 1410 by Ottaviano Nelli (c.1375–c.1444), leading light of the Gubbian school. Ranged around the chapel to the left of the apse, the seventeen panels comprise *Scenes from the Life of the Virgin*. High up in the apse you can just make out early thirteenth-century frescoes showing *Christ Enthroned with Saints*, while the chapel to the right of the apse has still more frescoes, this time fourteenth-century *Scenes from the Life of St Francis*. A small chapel in the sacristy is reputedly the room in which St Francis slept when he visited Gubbio, a sojourn that included his famous taming of a wolf that had been terrorizing the town. The simple cloisters beyond still cling to a few fourteenth-century frescoes.

Loggia dei Tiratori

Piazza Quaranta Martiri

Opposite San Francesco is the distinctive fourteenth-century **Loggia dei Tiratori** (Weavers), Italy's best surviving example of this now rare type of building. Wool was stretched out in the shade of its arches to dry and shrink evenly away from the heat of the sun.

The Palazzo dei Consoli

Via dei Consoli 59

Bearing east into the medieval town, along Via della Repubblica, centre-stage is taken by the austere **Palazzo dei Consoli**, a superb building whose crenellated outline and campanile dominate the countryside for miles around. Its western face is particularly impressive, vast buttressing supporting a building that rises almost 100m from the base of the foundations to the tip of the campanile. The plain **facade** is disturbed only by a triple-paired window motif that's unique to Gubbio and repeated elsewhere in the town, by a lovely doorway, and by a hole at the top right-hand corner – made to hold the cage, or *gogna* (from *vergogna*, meaning "shame"), in which criminals were incarcerated. The little lunette above the door features the *Madonna and Child with John the Baptist and Ubaldo*. It stands on the huge **Piazza Grande** (or Piazza della

10

Signoria), a windswept belvedere with excellent views, a suitable setting for this colossal building and for the lesser, unfinished **Palazzo Pretorio** opposite, built to the same Gattapone design.

An overbearing gesture of civic pride, the Palazzo dei Consoli replaced the previous civic headquarters in Via Ducale, which had been embarrassingly overshadowed by a symbol of religious power, the Duomo. Work began on the *palazzo* in 1321, probably to the plans of the eminent Gubbian architect Matteo Gattapone. Angelo da Orvieto (active 1334–52), fresh from civic palaces in Città di Castello, may have designed the doorway and its flanking Gothic windows. Construction took a couple of hundred years, during which time vast tracts of the medieval town were levelled.

The Museo Civico
Daily: April–Sept 10am–1pm & 3–6pm; Oct–March 10am–1pm & 2–5pm; closed May 13–15 • €5

The *palazzo*'s cavernous barrel-vaulted Salone dell'Arengo, where the council officers discussed their business, now accommodates a **Museo Civico**. Much of this consists of coins and sculptures, scattered like a medieval jumble sale in the main hall, but one of its adjoining rooms off to the left also contains Umbria's most important archeological find, the **Eugubine Tablets**.

The Eugubine Tablets
Discovered in 1444 by an illiterate shepherd – who twelve years later was conned by the *comune* into swapping the priceless treasure for a worthless piece of land – the tablets consist of seven bronze slabs, four of which probably date from about 200 BC, and three from around 100 BC. They are the most significant extant record of the **Umbrian language**, believed to have been a vernacular tongue without standard written characters. The bastardized Latin and Etruscan of the tablets' texts aimed at producing a phonetic transliteration of the dialect, using the main languages of the day. Gubbio was close to the shrine of the so-called Apennine Jove, a major pagan deity visited by pilgrims from all over Italy, and it's thought the tablets were the work of Roman and Etruscan priests taking advantage of the established order to impose new religious cults in a region where their languages weren't understood. The ritual text – the most important to have survived from antiquity – comprises a prayer divided into stanzas, a list of Gubbio's enemies, and a series of instructions for conducting services and the art of **divination** from sacrificed animals and the flight of birds. Most importantly, they suggest Romans, Etruscans and Umbrians achieved some sort of coexistence, refuting a long-held belief that succeeding civilizations wiped out their predecessors.

The ceramic collections
Also worth hunting out in the museum are several key examples of Gubbio's **ceramic tradition**, which began at least as early as the fourteenth century. Its greatest exponent, Maestro Giorgio Andreoli, was born in 1498, and distinguished himself by discovering gold and ruby lustre glazes, the latter – *riverbero* – a colour you rarely see in ceramics as it's extremely difficult to achieve. Two works by Giorgio – *Circe* and the *Fall of Phaeton* – are on show in the Sala della Loggetta, from which a corridor leads to the Pinacoteca section.

The Pinacoteca
The **Pinacoteca** is housed in five wonderful medieval rooms at the top of a steep flight of steps on the *palazzo*'s second floor. Though the paintings aren't anything special, they do trace the development of the Gubbian School, one of central Italy's earliest; names to look out for are Guido Palmerucci and Mello. Sienese artists are also represented, notably by Rutilio Manetti, the city's leading follower of Caravaggio, and there's a lovely *Crucifix* by the Maestro di San Francesco (best known for his work in the Basilica di San Francesco in Assisi). Don't miss the tremendous **views** over the Piazza Grande and the lower town from the palace's **loggia**, entered from the gallery.

THE CORSA DEI CERI

The vigil of the feast day of Ubaldo, Gubbio's patron saint, the **Corsa dei Ceri** (May 15) is little known outside Italy, but in Tuscany and Umbria ranks second only to Siena's Palio in its exuberance and bizarre pageantry. The rules and rigmarole of the nine-hundred-year-old ceremony are mind-boggling, but in essence begin with an early-morning Mass and a **procession** through the packed streets with the gigantic wooden **ceri** (candles), removed from Ubaldo's Monte Ingino basilica. Each is dedicated to a particular saint – **Ubaldo**, **Anthony** and **George**. At 10.30am another procession makes its way to the Piazza Grande, where an hour later the four-metre-high *ceri* are raised by members of the town's three traditional confraternities: the builders (represented by St Ubaldo), the artisans (St George) and the peasants (St Anthony). A statue of the relevant saint tops each column. There follows yet another procession through the streets to show the *ceri* to the townspeople (and TV crews from across Italy). The pillars are then dumped until 4.30pm while all concerned adjoin for a gut-busting fish lunch in the Palazzo dei Consoli. Yet another procession ensues, during which the clergy are finally allowed to participate, a journey that takes the *ceri* through just about every last corner of the town.

Back in the Piazza Grande, at 6pm the mayor brandishes a white banner to signal the beginning of a **race**, the climax of the day, which involves lugging the *ceri* all the way back up to the hilltop Basilica di Sant'Ubaldo. No sooner has the race begun than there's a stop at the Porta del Monte. It then resumes up the steep path to the basilica, each confraternity being allowed ten official carriers who have to be replaced every ten minutes – but without stopping. "Race" is something of a misnomer, however, for the *cero* of Ubaldo always wins, the other teams having to ensure they're in the basilica before the leaders shut the doors. The *ceri* are then left in the basilica, and the saints brought down in a candlelit procession. Thereafter there's more celebration and a good deal of drinking.

A scholarly debate rages over the **origins** of the event, generally cited as either a secular feast commemorating the day in 1155 when Ubaldo talked Barbarossa out of flattening Gubbio, or a hangover from some pagan fertility rite. These days the Church claims it as its own, though judging by the very phallic *ceri* and the roar that goes up when they're raised to the vertical in Piazza Grande, there's something more than Christian jubilation going on.

10

The Duomo

Via Federico da Montefeltro • Usually daily 9am–6pm, except during services

A couple of streets east of the Palazzo dei Consoli, the rather plain thirteenth-century Gothic **Duomo** is redeemed by a fine interior. Immediately noticeable is the strange arched ceiling, a Gubbian speciality known as "wagon vaulting", in which the ten arches are gracefully curved, apparently to emulate the meeting of hands in prayer. There are some fine twelfth-century stained-glass windows and a wealth of **frescoes** and **panel paintings**. One key work is the *Adoration of the Shepherds* by Eusebio di San Giorgio (sixth niche on the north wall), a student of Pinturicchio. In the last niche on the north wall is a beautifully restored picture of St Ubaldo with a lovely green background by the Gubbian painter Benedetto Nucci (1515–87). The **presbytery** contains a superb choir dating from 1549, while the altar is a recycled Roman sarcophagus. Back down the south wall towards the church entrance, the outstanding painting is a *Deposition* by Dono Doni, to the left of which is a good fragment of a fresco of *St Sebastian*.

The Palazzo Ducale

Via Ducale • Tues–Sun 8.30am–7pm • €5

Opposite the Duomo – and overshadowing it – is the **Palazzo Ducale**, built in 1470 over an earlier Lombard palace and the twelfth-century Palazzo Comunale by Federigo da Montefeltro, the renowned duke of Urbino, and designed as a scaled-down copy of his palace in that town. The architect of the two buildings was probably the same man, Dalmatian-born Luciano **Laurana**, selected by Federigo after he'd failed to find a suitably bold Florentine designer. The calm Renaissance **courtyard** sets the tone, close to which a stone staircase leads down to a series of vaulted storerooms and excavations that have revealed the remains of four earlier buildings on the site. Among them are fragments from the tenth century and remnants of the former Palazzo Comunale.

As in Urbino, many of the rooms of the main palace appeal as much for their measured architectural calm as for any paintings or furniture. Most are virtually empty, however, and the result is frankly dull, though the views make some amends. The **duke's study** (off room 2) was left bare after its intarsia wood panelling was stripped in the nineteenth century (and found its way to the Metropolitan Museum in New York). The stone-carved windows and doorways are superb, however, as are the fireplaces and terracotta floors. The central **salone** offers lovely views of the Palazzo dei Consoli and contains a fireplace that must have worked wonders during Gubbio's mountain-cold winters.

The northern and western quarters

Wandering the streets around town you'll soon come across examples of **Porte della Morte** ("Doors of Death") – narrow, bricked-up doorways wedged into the facades of medieval town houses, a conundrum found only in Gubbio, Assisi and southern France. The party line has it they were cut to carry a coffin out of the house and then, having been tainted by death, sealed up – a nice theory, and very Italian, but to judge by the constricted stairways behind the doors, their purpose was probably defensive: the main door could be barricaded, leaving the more easily defended passageway as the only entrance. Gubbio's best examples are in Via dei Consoli, but all the lanes and sloping byways around here are worth a slow, thoughtful wander.

Teatro Romano and the Antiquarium Museum

Viale Teatro Romano • Daily: April–Sept 10am–7pm; Oct–March 8.30am–5.30pm • €3

Following the walls anticlockwise back toward Piazza Quaranta Martiri, you could detour west to have a look at the **Teatro Romano**. Built in the first century AD, the theatre was the second largest of the Roman world after the Teatro Marcello in Rome, at 112m in diameter and with the capacity to hold 15,000 spectators. Despite centuries of being used as a rock quarry, it still retains rows of seating and some of its lower arcades.

The green space surrounding the theatre is now a park, and the adjacent **Antiquarium Museum**, ingeniously constructed over the remains of a Roman house, displays some of the ancient finds unearthed hereabouts, including sculpture, pottery, bronze pieces and some very fine and large mosaics.

The southern quarters and Monte Ingino

A path near the Duomo zigzags up Monte Ingino, but the best way up is to take the highly recommended **funicular**. En route to the base station at Porta Romana – walk part of the way on **Corso Garibaldi** for a good view of the large eighteenth-century statue of St Ubaldo at the street's end – you can take in Ottaviano Nelli's masterpiece, the winsome *Madonna del Belvedere* (1413) in the deconsecrated **Santa Maria Nuova**, together with patches of fresco left by his pupils (if the church is shut, try the custodian at Via Dante 66). Little **Sant'Andrea** nearby, probably of eleventh-century foundation and recently restored, is also worth a passing look.

Sant'Agostino

Via di Porta Romana

Just outside Porta Romana, the thirteenth-century **Sant'Agostino** is notable for its apse, which is smothered in 26 Nelli frescoes of *Scenes from the Life of St Augustine* (1420); there's a light on the right (south) side alongside a glass casket containing the waxy image of Beato Pietro of Gubbio. The entire church was once frescoed, and tantalizing fragments remain dotted around the walls: the sixth arch-cum-chapel on the right has a particularly

MONTE INGINO FUNICULAR (P.430) >

good fresco by a follower of Nelli; the third arch has a painting by Nelli and his workshop showing the Madonna with saints, angels and purged souls; and on the north wall the fifth altar features an anonymous *Madonna del Soccorso* (1485) with various Augustinian saints.

Monte Ingino

You can walk up **Monte Ingino** (827m) along the path from the Duomo, or drive there from Porta Metauro in the north, but the **funicular** is by far the best option, offering panormic views as you ascend; you'll find the base station just 100m east of Porta Romana.

Once you're atop Monte Ingino, the views and a bar are the main attractions. Even better vistas are at hand if you climb up to the **Rocca**. The **Basilica di Sant'Ubaldo**, five minutes from the top station, is not of great interest, though it's revered for the body of the town's patron saint, whose missing three fingers were hacked off by his manservant as a religious keepsake. Inside, you can't miss the big wooden pillars, or *ceri* (candles), featured in Gubbio's annual **Corsa dei Ceri**.

The funicular

March Mon–Sat 10am–5.30pm, Sun 9.30am–6pm; April & May Mon–Sat 10am–6.30pm, Sun 9.30am–7pm; July & Aug daily 9am–8pm; June & Sept Mon–Fri 9.30am–1.15pm & 2.30–7pm, Sat & Sun 9am–7.30pm; Oct daily 10am–6pm; Nov & Dec Thurs–Tues 10am–5pm • €5 return

The six-minute **funicular** is the most entertaining way up to the top of Monte Ingino. It has open ski-lift type cages holding two people, and affords ample time to admire the view – and to study your cage's welding and bolts, which are all that lie between you and oblivion. Beware the off-season break for lunch.

ARRIVAL AND DEPARTURE
GUBBIO

By train The nearest train station is at Fossato di Vico, 19km south on the Rome–Foligno–Ancona line, from where buses shuttle to Gubbio (Mon–Sat 10 daily, Sun 6 daily).
Destinations Foligno (9–13 daily; 45min); Rome (10 daily; 2hr 40min); Spoleto (10 daily; 1hr 15min).
By bus Buses serve Gubbio either directly from Perugia, or, usually involving connections, from all major Italian cities. Gubbio's bus terminal is near the medieval heart of the old town in Piazza Quaranta Martiri.
Destinations Florence (Mon–Sat 1 daily; 2hr 30min); Fossato di Vico train station (Mon–Sat 10 daily, Sun 6

daily); Perugia (Mon–Sat 10 daily, 4 on Sun; 1hr 10min); Rome (1 daily; 3hr).
By car By car, you'll most likely approach on the meandering cross-country SS298 from Perugia. You can pay to park at Piazza Quaranta Martiri, except on Tues, when it's the site of the town's weekly market; you pay at the "Easy Gubbio–Cassa Parcheggio" office, a short way up Via della Repubblica on the left (€0.80 per hr, €12 per day or €8 per day if staying in a hotel). Free parking is findable off Viale del Teatro Romano, close to San Domenico, or in Via del Cavarello near Porta Romana.

INFORMATION

Tourist office Via della Repubblica 15 (April–Sept Mon–Fri 8.30am–1.45pm & 3.30–6.30pm, Sat 9am–1pm & 3–6.30pm, Sun 9.30am–1pm & 3–6pm; Oct–March Mon–Fri 8.30am–1.45pm & 3–6pm, Sat 9am–1pm &

3–6pm, Sun 9.30am–1pm & 3–6pm; Jan 6 to end of Feb Mon–Fri 8.30am–1.45pm & 3–6pm, Sat 9am–1pm & 3–6pm, Sun 9.30am–1pm; ☎075 075 922 0693, ⊛www .comune.gubbio.pg.it).

ACCOMMODATION

You shouldn't have any problem finding a place to **stay** in Gubbio, though it does get busy, so it's wise to book if you want to be sure of securing your top choice. There are some very likeable – even opulent – **hotels** both in town and just outside, and the tourist office has details about **rooms** and more than fifty **agriturismi** dotted around the nearby countryside.

★ **Bosone Palace** Via XX Settembre 22 ☎075 922 0668, ⊛hotelbosone.com. This beautifully preserved fourteenth-century palace once hosted the likes of Dante and Petrarch, and the frescoes, medieval vaults and antiques in its common areas offer a touch of grand style. Rooms are comfortable, too, some with frescoes and

wonderful views, and there's a restaurant. Breakfast included, as is wi-fi; parking is extra. **€80**
Grotta dell'Angelo Via Gioia 47 ☎075 927 3438, ⊛www.grottadellangelo.it. Reliable choice in a quiet side street, with simple, clean and light rooms with wood-beam ceilings. Some have great town views, so check first.

There's also a garden, as well as a good restaurant (see below). Breakfast is €5. **€60**

★ **Relais Ducale** Via Galeotti 19 ☏ 075 922 0157, ⓦ relaisducale.com. Three converted medieval *palazzi*, originally built for receiving the guests of the Duke of Urbino, with a garden and gloriously varied accommodations; all have a/c and are decorated with traditional simplicity and elegance. Breakfast on the garden terrace included. **€90**

Residenza Le Logge Via Piccardi 7–9 ☏ 075 927 7574, ⓦ residenzalelogge.com. Fine, well-appointed rooms (some sleeping four, and one with jacuzzi) in a quiet medieval street, well away from urban bustle. Clean, comfortable and nicely presented in a particularly well-maintained building with wood-beam ceilings and a sense of history: there's also a garden. Breakfast included. **€80**

EATING

Fabiani Piazza Quaranta Martiri 26 ☏ 075 927 4639, ⓦ ristorantefabiani.it. Friendly, atmospheric place, with several dining rooms set in part of elegant Palazzo Fabiani, and an attractive terrace for summer dining. The home-made pastas with mushrooms, truffles and more, plus grilled meat and fish, are excellent value (set menu €16; weekend fish menus €20–30). There's a small but select wine list, too. Mon & Wed–Sun 1.30–3.30pm & 7.30–10pm.

Grotta dell'Angelo Via Gioia 47 ☏ 075 927 3438, ⓦ grottadellangelo.it. Part of the eponymous hotel, this rather rustic spot offers very tasty, abundant and reasonably priced regional meals in a wonderful grotto dining room or a delightful garden in the summer. Set menu €17; a la carte about twice as much. Mon & Wed–Sun 1–3.45pm & 7.30–10.45pm.

La Fornace di Mastro Giorgio Via Mastro Giorgio 2 ☏ 075 922 1836. Attractive period dining rooms in the converted workshop/kiln room of Gubbio's most renowned master ceramicist (see p.426). Full meals come in at €40–50, with truffles a speciality, and the wine list offers some 500 choices, several at equally sizeable prices. Mon & Wed–Sun 1.30–4pm & 7.30–10.30pm; closed part of Feb.

★ **Taverna del Lupo** Via Ansidei 21 ☏ 075 927 4368, ⓦ tavernadellupo.it. A smart and long-established place in an attractive medieval setting, well worth a slight splurge (set menus €22–30; mains around €18) for its classic Umbrian dishes; try the excellent pheasant with ginger, the to-die-for truffle risotto or the *strangozzi* pasta with white truffles. Their wine list is astounding. Tues–Sun 1.30–4pm & 7.30–10.30pm; closed part of Aug & Sept.

Parco Regionale del Monte Cucco

Some of Umbria's best upland scenery is to be found in the mountains to the east and north of Gubbio, on the border with the Marche, much of it protected as the **Parco Regionale del Monte Cucco**. Where this area really scores is in its organized trails, some three dozen in all, and backup for outdoor activities of every kind; if you want to don walking boots without too much fuss, this is the area to do it – and the chances are you won't meet another soul all day, maybe only a porcupine or deer, and, if you're very lucky, a wolf or a wild boar.

To get to the heart of the mountains by car, head north past **FOSSATO DI VICO**, a hill-town beyond which the road passes through **SIGILLO** and then, 3km further on, **COSTACCIARO**, a town that looks rather as if it has tried to attract tourists and failed, though it is a centre of sorts for the park's outdoor pursuits and access point for the **Grotta di Monte Cucco**, at 922m the fifth-deepest cave system in the world. The cave was explored as early as 1889, but has only recently been opened up by the hundreds of cavers that flock here from all over Europe; over 40km of galleries have now been charted. Above, the huge, bare-sloped **Monte Cucco** (1566m) is the main playground for walkers.

INFORMATION
PARCO REGIONALE DEL MONTE CUCCO

Park office Comunità Montana Alta Umbria, at Via Matteotti 52 in Sigillo (Mon–Fri 9.30am–1.30pm, plus Mon & Thurs 3–6pm; ☏ 075 917 7326, ⓦ parks.it/parco.monte .cucco), provide a good free 1/16,000 map, and a brochure detailing a dozen or so walks and/or recommended drives that take in the park's magnificent views.

ACCOMMODATION

Monte Cucco di Tobia Val di Ranco ☏ 075 917 7194, ⓦ albergomontecucco.it. A longtime favourite of mountaineers and spelunkers, east of Sigillo in the centre of the park. Comfortable rooms nestled in mountain greenery, and a rustic restaurant. Substantial breakfast included. Open Easter–Oct. **€52**

10

Assisi and the Vale of Spoleto

ASSISI

Assisi and the Vale of Spoleto

The Vale of Spoleto, the broad plain between Perugia and Spoleto, is Umbria's historic and spiritual heartland: a sweep of countryside that's beautiful in parts and has a majestic focus in ASSISI. Birthplace of St Francis, Italy's premier saint, the town has been a magnet of pilgrimage for over seven hundred years, and now attracts a staggering five million or more visitors annually.

Quieter hill-towns are just around the corner: Spello, the most accessible, features art treasures in the shape of Pinturicchio's frescoes in the church of Santa Maria Maggiore. Nearby Bevagna is a tiny, wall-enclosed former outpost on the Roman Via Flaminia, locked around a central square that's almost without equal in Umbria; sitting in the middle of it all, the modern transport hub of Foligno qualifies as the vale's only ungainly spot. Lording it over all is Montefalco, a windblown eyrie of medieval streets that's home to yet another superb fresco cycle – this one by the Tuscan Benozzo Gozzoli – and one of the province's strangest attractions, a quartet of mummified holy corpses. Across the valley is Trevi, relatively little visited, but perhaps the most perfectly situated of all Italian hill-towns.

11

Assisi

ASSISI would be an irresistible target even without its great Basilica and Franciscan sideshow. Visible for miles around, it sits enticingly beneath the whaleback slopes of Monte Subasio, the prominent castle and pink-stoned medieval houses lording it over the Vale of Spoleto. Millions come as an act of faith, but a substantial number visit simply to see the sublime paintings in the **Basilica di San Francesco**, where frescoes by **Giotto** and **Pietro Lorenzetti** comprise one of the greatest monuments of Italian art. Yet for all the coach parties of pilgrims, both religious and secular, Assisi just about remains a town with an uncompromised identity – as an overnight stay, after the car parks have cleared, will reveal. At close quarters, the tacky tourist paraphernalia and religious kitsch are offset by tranquil backstreets, geranium-filled windowboxes and buildings in the muted, rosy stone that distinguishes all the vale's towns. With sufficient enthusiasm you can see almost all the sights in a day, but be warned: this is the third most visited pilgrimage site in Italy (after St Peter's in Rome and Padre Pio's shrine in Puglia).

Brief history

Founded by the **Umbrians** – in contrast to Perugia's Etruscan heritage – Assisi later achieved prominence as Asisium, a **Roman** *municipium*. Thereafter invaders passed it over, attracted by the richer pickings of Perugia, but in the end it fell under the control of that city's monstrous **Baglioni** family. These were characters, said one Franciscan historian, "who did not shudder to murder men, cook their flesh, and give it to the

Highlights

❶ Basilica di San Francesco, Assisi One of Italy's architectural and artistic masterpieces, and the burial place of St Francis. **See p.436**

❷ Tempio di Minerva, Assisi A superbly preserved first-century temple front. **See p.445**

❸ Spello A charming hill-town, where the church of Santa Maria Maggiore hosts a fresco cycle by Pinturicchio. **See p.453**

❹ Monte Subasio Great walks and drives on the mountain above Assisi, with spectacular views and fields of spring wildflowers. **See p.456**

❺ Bevagna Captivating village known for its fine main square and Romanesque churches. **See p.459**

❻ Montefalco Home of the outstanding Sagrantino wines, plus a major fresco cycle by Benozzo Gozzoli. **See p.462**

❼ Trevi The most spectacularly sited of the Umbrian hill-towns. **See p.467**

❽ Fonti and Tempietto del Clitunno Set in a pretty park, these ancient springs and classical-style temple offer plenty of pastoral charm. **See p.469**

HIGHLIGHTS ARE MARKED ON THE MAP ON P.436

relations of the slain to eat in their prison dungeons". Plague, famine and eventually Church control turned the town into a moribund backwater. However, Francis's elevation to the status of national saint in 1939 managed to reverse its economic decline, and today religious and other tourism has made this a very prosperous town indeed.

The Basilica di San Francesco

Via San Francesco 2 • ☎ 075 819 0084, ⊛ sanfrancescoassisi.org

The **Basilica di San Francesco** is a major site of worldwide Catholic pilgrimage, and its cycle of paintings by Giotto has long been considered one of the turning points in Western art, moving from the Byzantine world of iconic saints and Madonnas to one of humanist narrative.

The construction of the Basilica is in two tiers, with the **Upper Church** above the **Lower Church**. This posed enormous engineering problems, which were solved by the

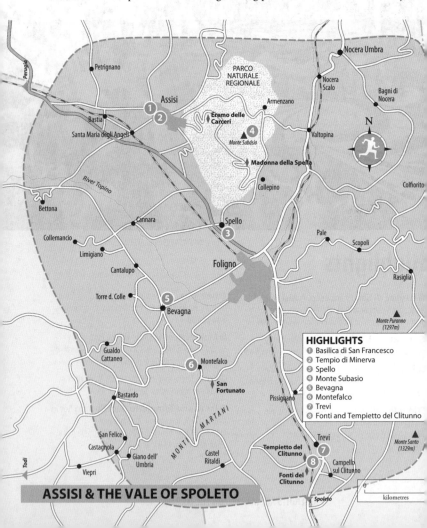

HIGHLIGHTS
1. Basilica di San Francesco
2. Tempio di Minerva
3. Spello
4. Monte Subasio
5. Bevagna
6. Montefalco
7. Trevi
8. Fonti and Tempietto del Clitunno

ASSISI & THE VALE OF SPOLETO

ASSISI'S FESTIVALS

Easter Processions and festivities throughout Easter week.
Calendimaggio Week following the first Tuesday in May. Procession to celebrate St Francis's vision of Lady Poverty.
Festa del Voto June 22. Procession in medieval costume to celebrate the town's salvation.
Perdono August 1–2. Pilgrimage to the church of Santa Maria degli Angeli.
Palio della Balestra August 11. Medieval tournament.
Festa di San Francesco October 3–4. Assisi's big event: a major pilgrimage that draws crowds of pilgrims and ecclesiastics from all over Italy and beyond.
Festa del Corpus Domini November. Another major procession, through flower-strewn streets.

---

use of massive arched buttressing that effectively propped up the western end of the town. One of the wonders of early medieval architecture, its creator remains unknown, as all the original drawings were burnt in a raid by the Perugians. It's usually presumed to have been the work of Lombard masons, who would have drawn their inspiration from the Gothic churches of southern France. As one of the earliest examples of Italian Gothic, the Basilica exerted great architectural influence, its single-naved Upper Church becoming a model for countless Franciscan churches around the country.

11

The history of the Basilica

The Basilica was conceived, shortly after Francis's death, by **Elias of Cortona**, one of the saint's earliest disciples, who served as vicar-general of the Franciscans until 1239. In the early years of the post-Francis order, Elias ran things very much his way, capitalizing on the saint's popularity to build the order into a powerful force, and raising the money to make the founder's Basilica one of the great Christian shrines. To the horror of the more ascetic and zealous followers of the saint – to whom Francis himself was allied in his final years – Elias hawked religious indulgences across Europe, a fundraising project that detractors argued was inexcusable corruption. Furthermore, they held, the Basilica's proposed magnificence was at odds with Francis's preference for humbler churches. Francis's choice of **burial site** was clearly intended as a gesture of humility: he had picked one of the most despised spots of medieval Assisi, known as the Colle del Inferno, where criminals were taken for execution. It was to no avail. The burial site was rechristened Colle del Paradiso and a building more ambitious than any in Italy was begun.

The burial of St Francis

While construction of the Basilica proceeded, the **political background** became increasingly murky, the strangest twist coming on the very day of Francis's canonization. Elias by this time had had a complete falling out with the papacy, who were organizing the ceremony, and just as the saint's hearse was proceeding through the streets of Assisi, he and some cohorts burst onto the scene and seized the coffin, spiriting it into the Lower Church and bolting the doors behind them. Prompted perhaps by the fear that his master's remains would be stolen or desecrated (relics had enormous financial and spiritual value), Elias had plotted to bury Francis in a **secret tomb** deep within the Basilica. The episode gave rise to a myth, recycled by Vasari, that a vast hidden church had been built below the Basilica, far greater in beauty and grandeur than the churches above. Inside this sealed chamber, it was believed, the body of the "almost alive saint" hovered above the altar awaiting his call to heaven. The tomb remained undiscovered, or at least unreached, until a two-month search in 1818.

ASSISI

Cemetery & Car Park

Basilica di
San Francesco

Porta San
Giacomo

PIAZZA
SUPERIORE DI
S.FRANCESCO

VIA MERRY DEL VAL

VIA SANTA CROCE

VIA DEL COLLE

PIAZZA INFERIORE
DI S.FRANCESCO

Santa
Margherita

Santa Croce

VIA SERMETTAI

VIA METASTASIO

Casa dei
Maestri
Comacini

VIA FRATE ELIA

VIA SAN FRANCESCO

Pinacoteca Comunale

VIA S. PAOLO

STRADA PIAGGIA S. FRANCESCO

VIA SEMINARIO

VIA ALDINO

SS. Stefano
e Fortunato

Porta San
Francesco

Oratorio dei Pellegrini

VIA FONTEBELLA

PUNTA
D'ITALIA

PIAZZETTAGA
RIBALDI

VIA DEL FOSSO CUPO

VIA A. CRISTOFANI

Penugia

SS 147

Bus Stop

Porta San Pietro

PIAZZA
S. PIETRO

Bus
Stop

VIA ANCAIANI

VIA BORGO S. PIETRO

San Pietro

VIA S. APOLLINARE

VIALE MARCONI

VIALE VITTORIO EMANUELE II

Porta
Sermentone

11

■ ACCOMMODATION	
Alexander	9
Del Viaggiatore	11
Fontebella	7
Hermitage	8
Ideale	10
La Fortezza	4
Le Silve	2
Ostello della Pace	12
Ostello di Fontemaggio	1
Pallotta	5
Subasio	3
Umbra	6

● EATING & DRINKING	
Il Frantoio	4
La Fortezza	1
Pallotta	2
Sensi	5
Umbra	3

Train Station & Santa Maria degli Angeli

The Lower Church

The sombre **Lower Church** is the place to begin if you want to follow the architectural and artistic chronology of the shrine. Its convoluted floor plan and low-lit vaults are intended to create a mood of calm and meditative introspection; the natural light has been augmented by fairly discreet spotlighting – a concession that has altered the atmosphere, but which makes it possible to study the frescoes and intricate decoration that cover every surface.

The main nave

The highlights span a century of continuous artistic development. Important but somewhat stilted early works by Byzantine-influenced artists line the walls of the main nave, many credited to the mysterious **Maestro di San Francesco**, the anonymous hand that crops up elsewhere in Umbria. These are the oldest frescoes in the Basilica (1253), the *Scenes from the Passion* (right wall) and *Episodes from the Life of St Francis* (left wall). Faded in places, they have also been partly obliterated by the subsequent opening up of the side chapels, a necessity forced on the Franciscans by the need to accommodate the growing number of pilgrims visiting Assisi.

VISITING THE BASILICA

Admission to both parts of the Basilica is free. Both are usually open daily (8.30am–6.50pm), but from November to March the Basilica closes at lunch (noon–2pm) and at 5.50pm. The Upper Church may close or have restricted opening on Sundays; both close on holy days. The Lower Church is usually open earlier than the listed time in the mornings (that is, from around 6/6.30am), making this a good time to visit. Indeed, you'd do best to always visit early or late in the day, to avoid the crowds. The custodians of the Basilica enforce their **dress code** extremely vigorously: you should always cover your arms and legs. However, their repeated exhortations for everybody to remain **silent** seem to fall on deaf ears.

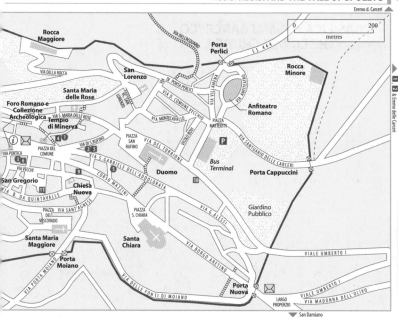

Don't overlook the church's minor works, notably the little *Madonna Enthroned* (1422) by the Gubbian artist Ottaviano Nelli (on the left as you enter, just right of the Cappella di San Sebastiano), or the **Tomb of Cardinal Albornoz** (marked 5 on our plan), built as a temporary resting place for the Spanish firebrand responsible for reinforcing papal power in Umbria. He rebuilt and regarrisoned the castles of Assisi, Narni and Spoleto, among others, and was rewarded for his pains with a tomb in the Basilica. The tomb is the work of **Matteo di Gattapone**, the architect responsible for Spoleto's Ponte delle Torri and Gubbio's Palazzo dei Consoli, projects conceived on a far greater scale.

The Cappella di San Martino

Simone Martini's frescoes in the **Cappella di San Martino** (21), the first chapel on the left as you enter the nave, are among the Lower Church's highlights. He worked here in the mid-1310s, shortly after painting the great *Maestà* in Siena, and was given completely free rein: every detail, even the floor and stained glass, came under his control. The panels on the underside of the arch as you enter the chapel were probably painted in 1317. They show eight saints, and were painted to honour St Louis of Toulouse, who had just been sanctified; he is the red-robed figure in the upper left panel, flanked by saints Francis, Anthony and Clare.

The right transept

Cenno di Pepo, popularly known as **Cimabue** (c.1240–1302), was the first great named artist to work on the Basilica. Vasari's *Lives of the Artists* opens with an account of him, in which he is described as the father of Italian painting, and an obsessive perfectionist, often destroying work with which he was not completely happy. He probably painted in the transepts of the Upper Church between 1270 and 1280, and was active in the Lower Church some time later. His major painting in the Lower Church – where much of his work was later overpainted – is in the **right transept** (right wall), the over-restored *Madonna, Child and Angels with St Francis*, a work that survives from the church's

BASILICA DI SAN FRANCESCO THE LOWER CHURCH

1   Cappella di San Sebastiano
2   Pulpit (1459)
3   Tomb of Filippo di Courtenay
4   Tomb of Blascio Fernandez
5   Tomb of Cardinal Albornoz (by Gattapone)
    Frescoes (1368) by Andrea da Bologna
6   Life of St Stephen by Dono Doni (1575)
7   Cappella di San Antonio di Padova
    Frescoes (1610) by Cesare Sermei da Orvieto
8   Stairway to the crypt and the Tomb of St Francis
9   Frescoes by Giotto or school of Giotto
10 Right transept: frescoes by Giotto, Cimabue and
    followers
11 Portrait of St Francis (Cimabue?)
12 Five Saints (Martini?) incl. Portrait of St Clare
    (fourth left)
13 Cappella di San Nicola: scenes from the Life of St
    Nicola by Giotto and followers of Giotto

14 Entrance to cloisters, Tesoro and the Upper Church
15 Choir (1471)
16 Vaults of the High Altar by Giotto and/or followers of Giotto:
    a St Francis Enthroned
    b Allegory of Obedience
    c Allegory of Poverty
    d Allegory of Chastity
17 Left transept: frescoes by Pietro Lorenzetti
    (assisted by Ambrogio Lorenzetti?)
18 Cappella di S.G. Battista (1288). Madonna and
    Child with SS. Francis and John by Pietro Lorenzetti
19 Sacristy. Relics of St Francis and Madonna
    and Child (Umbrian anon.)
20 Coronation of the Virgin by Puccio Capanna d'Assisi
21 Cappella di San Martino. Scenes from the Life of
    St Martin (1322) by Simone Martini

earlier decorative scheme (1280), and which Ruskin described as "the noblest depiction of the Virgin in Christendom". It includes the famous portrait of St Francis, which you'll already have seen plastered all over the town. Next to it, the *Crucifixion* has been attributed to **Giotto**, as have – though with less certainty – the scenes on the end wall and vaults depicting the *Childhood of Christ*. To the left are a half-length *Madonna and Child* and pair of saints, while on the side wall is a set of five saints, all the work of **Simone Martini**. One of the figures – another image much duplicated around town – is believed to be **St Clare**, founder of the women's chapter of the Franciscans. The painting shows a clear attempt at the depiction of emotion, the use of light and shade to add verisimilitude to figures, and the creation of a coherent three-dimensional sense of space – all steps on the path trodden with equal certainty by Giotto and Martini's Sienese contemporary, Pietro Lorenzetti.

The left transept and the Cappella di San Giovanni Battista
Pietro Lorenzetti is represented by a beautiful series of works in the **left transept** (17). These *Scenes of the Passion* are thought to include his earliest surviving frescoes, portraying events leading up to and including Christ's crucifixion. Of particular note is

THE CAPPELLA DI SAN MARTINO FRESCOES

The **interior chapel** holds Simone Martini's complete fresco cycle of the life of **St Martin of Tours**. The father of monasticism in France, Martin was venerated as far afield as Ireland and Africa; here, however, he is featured partly as a sop to the Franciscan friar who commissioned the chapel (the friar had been made cardinal with the title of San Martino ai Monti).

The **ten-panel cycle** starts on the left-hand wall and moves **clockwise** around the chapel, the lowest four panels representing scenes from the secular part of Martin's life up to and including his conversion, the remaining four wall frescoes and two painted ceiling vaults treating the period after his conversion. Martin was born in 315 in what is now Hungary and brought up in Italy at Pavia. The key event of his conversion – and the first depicted in the cycle – came as a young officer at Amiens, when he gave half his cloak to a beggar, a figure he was later led to recognize as Christ. To the right is the *Dream of St Martin*, in which Christ and angels appear to the saint, a panel that mingles secular and sacred iconography amid a panoply of courtly emblems.

This trait is continued in the next panel on the right-hand wall, *St Martin is Knighted*, an out-and-out evocation of life at court without religious iconography of any kind. To its right is *St Martin Renounces his Weapons*: "I am Christ's soldier; I am not allowed to fight." Notably, Martini seems to reserve his finest painting for the background – the tents, spears, lances and costumes of the Roman camp and Emperor Julian.

The narrative moves to the second tier back on the left-hand wall, starting with the *Miracle of the Resurrected Child*, another episode never before depicted in Italian art, in which Martin, transported presumably by artistic licence to Siena (the city's Palazzo Pubblico is in the background), raises a child from the dead before its mother and an expectant crowd. Alongside is the *Meditation*, with the saint moved to distraction by contemplation of the Divine, and unmoved by the acolytes trying to direct his attention to the Mass. Round to its right is the *Miraculous Mass*, an unusual subject portrayed here for the first time. Martin has again given a cloak to a beggar, and is about to celebrate Mass when angels appear to present him with a beautifully embroidered piece of material. The next fresco, the *Miracle of Fire*, is damaged, though the sense of the scene is clear: a tongue of flame is forced down the throat of Emperor Valentinian for refusing to give Martin an audience.

The uppermost level depicts two self-explanatory scenes, the saint's death and burial, both distinguished by the exquisite detail of the saint's robes, and by the architectural details that correspond to the moods of the episodes – severe, bare-walled and geometrical around the scene of death, and more ornate in the Gothic chapel that hosts the funeral.

the *Last Supper*, in which Christ and the apostles are crowded into a curious hexagonal *loggi*, and which reveals a treatment of light and shadow hardly matched during the fourteenth century. The moon and stars light the sky, while to the left is a kitchen illuminated by light from a fire, in which servants unconcernedly scrape food into a dog's bowl – a fine incidental detail paralleled by the two chattering servants to the left of Christ, who are quite oblivious to events before them. The only illumination at the table is from the haloes of Christ and the apostles, a deliberate juxtaposition of material and spiritual light.

Three other panels stand out in the cycle: the *Entombment*, *Crucifixion* and *Deposition*. Dominating almost an entire wall, the *Crucifixion* shows an amazing sense of drama, with Christ raised high above a crowd of onlookers; closer study reveals carefully observed nuances of character in the crowd. These natural touches recur in the faces of the *Deposition*, less immediately striking but still amongst Lorenzetti's masterpieces for its bold and simple composition. The upper portion of the Cross is completely missing, leaving just the broad horizontal and huge amounts of vacant space, all focusing on the figure of Christ, his limbs bent in rigor mortis.

Lorenzetti also painted in the chapel beyond, the **Cappella di San Giovanni Battista** (18), where he left the frescoed triptych of the *Madonna and Child with Sts Francis and John the Baptist*.

GIOTTO AND THE ALTAR VAULTS

The question of **Giotto**'s involvement in the Basilica remains at the centre of one of Italy's greatest art history controversies. Certain twentieth-century historians have opined that Giotto had never painted in Assisi at all. Some still hold this view, though the modern consensus is that Giotto was indeed responsible for the bulk of the paintings in the Upper Church, executed from about 1295. Authorship in the Lower Church is more dubious, and credit for the allegorical frescoes in the **vaults over the altar** – some of the church's most beautiful and complex – has been taken from Giotto and given to nameless assistants. The same goes for the *Life of Mary Magdalene* cycle (c.1309) in the **Cappella della Maddalena**, the third chapel on the right, as well as the right transept's *Childhood of Christ*. In the hothouse atmosphere of the Basilica during its decoration, however, cooperative efforts must have been commonplace: definitive attributions are all but impossible.

The tomb of St Francis

11

Before leaving the Lower Church, drop down to the crypt (8) and the **tomb of St Francis**, a spot that remained hidden until 1818. The present tomb, rebuilt in the 1920s, honours Francis's desire for a humble burial, replacing a more elaborate tabernacle raised in the excitement of discovery. Above the main altar is the simple stone coffin that contains the body; at the four corners of the central canopy are the bodies of Francis's earliest key companions, the beatific Leone, Rufino, Masseo and Angelo.

There's a short English-language account of the tomb's fascinating history and discovery tacked on to the stone walls.

The Museo del Tesoro

Easter–Oct Mon–Sat 9.30am–5pm, closed Sun & religious holidays • Donation expected

The well-presented **Museo del Tesoro e Collezioni F.M. Perkins** is entered from doors in the transept behind the main altar (14). It contains a rich collection of paintings, including 55 masterpieces from the Frederick Mason Perkins Collection, a bequest from an American philanthropist which includes work by Fra' Angelico, Pier Francesco Fiorentino, Luca Signorelli and Masolino. It's also particularly strong on the Sienese masters, and Umbrians in evidence include Benozzo Gozzoli and others. The remainder of the gallery is crammed with liturgical paraphernalia bestowed on the Franciscans over the centuries. Pride of place goes to a tapestry of St Francis (1479) and an altar front (1478), both presented by Pope Sixtus IV, the latter with figures by Antonio del Pollaiuolo.

The Upper Church

The **Upper Church** is a completely different architectural, aesthetic and emotional experience, its airy Gothic plan intended to inspire celebration rather than contemplation. It feels less a church than a gallery for **Giotto's dazzling Life of St Francis frescoes**, rightly regarded – recurring doubt as to its attribution notwithstanding – as one of the greatest of all Italian fresco cycles.

Giotto's Life of St Francis

Giotto's *Life of St Francis* cycle starts from the far right-hand side of the nave. Although critics haven't reached a consensus on the date of the frescoes, most believe they are early works, painted with assistants some time around 1296, when Giotto was 29. The style and peripheral narrative content of the last four has led to their being attributed to the so-called Maestro di Santa Cecilia, who may also have overpainted parts of the first panel.

Giotto was by far the most important artist to work in the Basilica. Dante immediately recognized his supremacy, and in a famous passage (intended to illustrate the hollowness of earthly glory) wrote: "Cimabue thought to lord it over painting's field. And now his fame is obscured and the cry is Giotto." It seems that Giotto got the commission on the prompting of Cimabue, and that some test pieces in the Lower Church persuaded the friars that Giotto was up to the task of decorating the upper part of the Basilica. Like many writers and artists of the age, Giotto was a member of the lay **Franciscan Tertiaries**. His frescoes reveal a profound sympathy for the spirit of St Francis and show an almost total rejection of the artistic language of the Byzantines, whose remote icons were highly inappropriate for Francis's very human message. The cycles are full of the natural beauty that moved the saint to profound joy, and the figures are mobile and expressive – aspects of Giotto's art typified by the famous panel

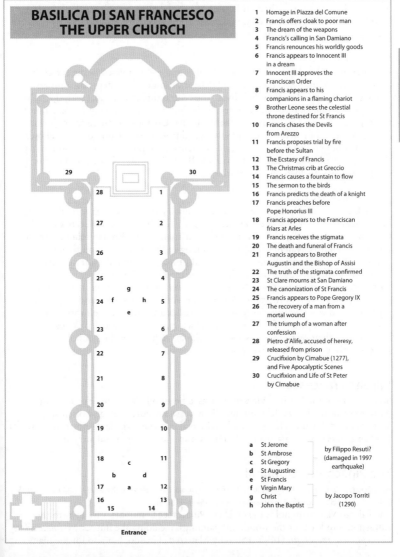

BASILICA DI SAN FRANCESCO
THE UPPER CHURCH

1   Homage in Piazza del Comune
2   Francis offers cloak to poor man
3   The dream of the weapons
4   Francis's calling in San Damiano
5   Francis renounces his worldly goods
6   Francis appears to Innocent III
    in a dream
7   Innocent III approves the
    Franciscan Order
8   Francis appears to his
    companions in a flaming chariot
9   Brother Leone sees the celestial
    throne destined for St Francis
10 Francis chases the Devils
    from Arezzo
11 Francis proposes trial by fire
    before the Sultan
12 The Ecstasy of Francis
13 The Christmas crib at Greccio
14 Francis causes a fountain to flow
15 The sermon to the birds
16 Francis predicts the death of a knight
17 Francis preaches before
    Pope Honorius III
18 Francis appears to the Franciscan
    friars at Arles
19 Francis receives the stigmata
20 The death and funeral of Francis
21 Francis appears to Brother
    Augustin and the Bishop of Assisi
22 The truth of the stigmata confirmed
23 St Clare mourns at San Damiano
24 The canonization of St Francis
25 Francis appears to Pope Gregory IX
26 The recovery of a man from a
    mortal wound
27 The triumph of a woman after
    confession
28 Pietro d'Alife, accused of heresy,
    released from prison
29 Crucifixion by Cimabue (1277),
    and Five Apocalyptic Scenes
30 Crucifixion and Life of St Peter
    by Cimabue

11

a   St Jerome
b   St Ambrose   by Filippo Resuti?
c   St Gregory   (damaged in 1997
d   St Augustine   earthquake)
e   St Francis
f   Virgin Mary
g   Christ   by Jacopo Torriti
h   John the Baptist   (1290)

Entrance

The Sermon to the Birds (marked 15 on our plan). More than any other, this fresco crystallizes the essence of Franciscan humility, with the flock addressed as an indivisible part of God's creation and attending to the saint as distinct from them solely by virtue of the power of speech.

Giotto's narrative genius cuts straight to the heart of the matter, as seen in the very first panel, **The Homage in Piazza del Comune** (1), in which the universality of Francis's appeal is evoked in a single act of tribute. Moreover, the frescoes display a wealth of everyday detail that made them accessible to the ordinary people of his age. The first people to look at **Francis Offering his Cloak to a Poor Man** (2) would have recognized the world in which it is set as the one they themselves inhabited: the backdrop includes a detailed view of Assisi from the Porta Nuova, along with the Benedictine abbey on Monte Subasio, now vanished. This attention to the tone and substance of the real world, to its textures and solidity, makes the art of Giotto as revolutionary as Francis's message to the medieval Church.

11

Cimabue and the choir

The **choir** is a second focal point. Its 105 inlaid stalls – completed in the fifteenth century – are of immense intricacy and delicacy, most of them depicting famous Franciscans or episodes from their lives. The central throne is a papal seat, the only one in the country outside St Peter's in Rome. Behind the throne, and in the **left** (**north**) **transept**, are frescoes by Giotto's probable master, **Cimabue**. These suffered during the ceiling collapse, but were already almost ruined from the oxidation of badly chosen pigments, though this transept's *Crucifixion* remains an impressive composition, its dynamism an obvious departure from static Byzantine order. Giotto and Duccio, as pupils, may have helped on the painting.

The other frescoes

Above Giotto's Franciscan panels is another much damaged though virtually complete cycle, *Scenes from the Old and New Testaments*. Vasari believed these scenes were by Cimabue, though today they are attributed to artists of the Roman school – **Torriti**, **Rusuti** and **Pietro Cavallini** – who were working in the church around the same time. Before coming to Assisi all three had worked primarily in mosaic, a traditional Byzantine medium, but in the Basilica they turned to fresco, moving, like Cimabue, with cautious innovation towards a freer interpretation of old themes. The *Four Doctors of the Church* in the vaults (Sts Jerome, Ambrose, Gregory and Augustine), especially, shows a narrative sense absent in earlier art: cloaks are left thrown over chairs, books lie open as if half-read. The Doctors, moreover, are depicted as characters in their own right, distinct individuals rather than the symbolic representatives of artistic convention.

Via San Francesco

Southeast from the Basilica, **Via San Francesco** heads off along the ridge of medieval Assisi towards the Piazza del Comune. From its south side, steep and often stepped alleyways lead down to city gates and peripheral churches. The lanes north and east of Via San Francesco – in particular **Via Metastasio** – are peaceful and attractive.

The Pinacoteca Comunale

Via San Francesco 10 • Daily: mid-March to Oct 10am–1pm & 2.30–6pm, until 7pm in July & Aug; Nov to mid-March 10.30am–1pm & 2–5pm • €3, or combined ticket with Foro Romano and the Rocca €8 • ☎ 075 812 033

The Palazzo Vallemani holds the excellent **Pinacoteca Comunale** – well worth the admission, not least for the wonderful paintings, including the impressive *Immaculate Conception of the Virgin* (1495–1505) by Matteo da Gualdo, but also for the many detached frescoes rescued from churches and other buildings around Assisi, among them important works by the Gubbian artist Ottaviano Nelli. Look out for the wonderfully strange fresco, by an unknown fourteenth-century Umbrian painter, of San Giuliano mistakenly killing his parents, having returned home and mistaken them for his wife and her lover – the artist clearly enjoyed painting the quite unnecessarily graphic and gaping wounds.

The Oratorio dei Pellegrini

Via San Francesco 11 • Mon–Sat 10am–noon & 4–6pm • Free

The **Oratorio dei Pellegrini** is an exquisite fifteenth-century building that served as part of a hospice for visiting pilgrims. The interior is covered in fetching frescoes, one illustrating *Scenes from the Life of St James*, including the comical *Miracle of the Two Hens*, an episode in which the saint restored two dead chickens to life so they could testify to the innocence of a falsely accused pilgrim. Another shows the *Miracle of the Hanged Man*, in which the saint supports an apparently dead man until his parents find him alive.

11

Piazza del Comune

Piazza del Comune was built over either the site of the Roman forum or an important sacred area – theories differ. It's a stunning medieval square, lined with plenty of pricey bars from which to people-watch. Part of the impressive Neo-Gothic former post office, a frescoed mock medieval hall complete with vaulted ceilings, holds the tourist office, and the square is also overlooked by some important **palazzi**, but pride of space goes to the stunning facade of the **Tempio di Minerva**.

Tempio di Minerva

Piazza del Comune • Mon–Sat 7.15am-7.30pm, Sun 8am–7.30pm • Free

The piazza is dominated by the **Tempio di Minerva**, six Corinthian columns and a pediment from a first-century Roman temple – perfectly preserved and dazzlingly restored. It's as good as any classical monument in Italy, and was the only thing Goethe wanted to see in Assisi – "the first complete classical monument I have seen…so perfect in design…I cannot describe the sensations which this work aroused in me, but I know they are going to bear fruit for ever." He didn't bother with the Basilica, calling it a "Babylonian pile".

Outside, the temple frieze contains reference to two brothers, Gneo Cesio Tirone and Tito Cesio Prisco, who helped finance the building. It had a chequered history, not least in the early Middle Ages, when it was in such a parlous state that is was described in records as a *casolino* – a little house – and in the thirteenth century, when it passed to the *comune*, who made the lower area a prison and the upper one a council chamber. The church behind is a seventeenth-century conversion whose lack of interest has been redeemed by a fine restoration of its Baroque interior, which uncovered parts of the original pavement and a massive wall and terracing to the rear.

The piazza's palaces

Piazza del Comune

To the left of the temple stands the **Palazzo del Capitano del Popolo**, completed in 1282 – though various cod medieval adornments were added in 1927 – and the Torre del Popolo, built in 1305. Note the measures at the base of the tower, which record standard sizes for stones and other building materials as they were in 1348.

On the opposite side of the piazza, the much-restored **Palazzo Comunale** once contained the Pinacoteca Comunale, the sign for which remains, since it forms part of a historic building and as such apparently cannot be removed.

Foro Romano e Collezione Archeologica

Via Portica 2 • Daily: mid-March to Oct 10am–1pm & 2.30–6pm, till 7pm in July & Aug • Nov to mid-March 10.30am–1pm & 2–5pm • €4, or combined ticket with Pinacoteca and Rocca €8 • ☎ 075 813 053

The **Foro Romano e Collezione Archeologica**, entered just off Piazza del Comune, is unlikely to divert unless you're interested in archeology and Assisi's Roman heritage. It's housed in the crypt of the defunct church of San Niccolò, documented as early as 1097 but demolished in 1926 to make way for the ersatz-medieval post office building. A passage from the museum runs under Piazza del Comune, where excavations are perpetually in progress to uncover the Roman remains here without disrupting the piazza above; at present it's rather hard to make any sense of the underground maze, which scholars now believe is not the old Roman forum (as was long believed), but a religious sanctuary linked to the surviving Tempio di Minerva; the forum, it's now thought, may have occupied the present-day site of the Duomo. Dotted around the area are parts of statues and pillars, busts, urns and other Roman and Etruscan fragments, all given added lustre by their strange subterranean setting.

The Duomo

Piazza San Rufino • April–Oct Mon–Fri 7am–12.30pm & 2.30–7pm, Sat & Sun & Aug 7am–7pm; Nov–March daily 7am–1pm & 2.30–6pm • Free

As you emerge from the narrow streets east of Piazza del Comune, you're met by the captivating sight of the **Duomo**, or San Rufino, with its typically three-tiered Umbrian facade. According to tradition the first church on the site was built around 412, ostensibly to house the bones of St Rufinus, Assisi's first bishop, martyred some 170 years earlier. Another, better-documented building was raised around 1029 by Bishop Ugone, from which the crypt and present campanile survive. Yet another church – more or less the one that survives today – was begun in 1140 and consecrated in 1253.

Its Romanesque **portal** is a superb piece of carving, guarded by two red marble lions and framed by lilies, leaves, faces, birds, winged crocodiles and a pair of griffons. Look in the lunette for the child being suckled, and its two dour parents. Alongside is a huge, stolid **campanile**, managing somehow to fit into the overall scheme of the church.

The interior

Inside, the main point of interest is the **font** used to baptize St Francis, St Clare and (possibly) the future emperor Frederick II, apparently born prematurely in a nearby village. It's at the near end of the church on the right, fronted by Romanesque statues of a lion and winged ox. Opposite, the beginning of the left aisle contains a little door, which leads to an impressive **Roman cistern**, recent research having led scholars to believe that the cathedral square – rather than Piazza del Comune – was the site of the town's original Roman forum. St Rufinus's remains still lie beneath the altar.

Museo Diocesano

Mid-March to mid-Oct Mon–Fri 10am–1pm & 3–6pm, Sat & Sun 10am–6pm (Aug daily 10am–6pm); Mid-Oct to mid-March Thurs–Tues 10am–1pm & 2.30–5.30pm • €3 • ☎ 075 812 712

Off the right (south) nave, there's the small **Museo Diocesano**, or Museo della Cattedrale, with a handful of good paintings, including a 1470 work by Niccolò Alunno, and an atmospheric crypt, the **Cripta di San Rufino**, or Basilica Ugoniana, entered outside down steps to the right of the facade, which contains fragments from these earlier churches. The crypt was not discovered until 1895, and features remnants of very early frescoes, parts of a Roman wall and conduit and a third-century Roman sarcophagus used as Rufinus's original tomb. Local tradition has it that Bishop Ugone had wanted to bury Rufinus in Santa Maria Maggiore, then the town's cathedral, but the townspeople had argued for the new church. There apparently ensued a literal

PIAZZA DEL COMUNE (P.445) >

tug-of-war with the saint's coffin, the bishop and his cohorts pulling one way, the locals the other. The latter clearly triumphed, though the tale is probably more a parable of the ascendancy of the lay city councils of the time than anything else.

The Basilica di Santa Chiara

Piazza Santa Chiara • Daily: April–Oct 6.30am–noon & 2–7pm; Nov–March 6.30am–noon & 2–6pm • Free

The burial place of St Clare, St Francis's devoted follower, the **Basilica di Santa Chiara** was begun in 1257 and consecrated in 1265, twelve years after her death. It stands on the site formerly occupied by the church of San Giorgio, where St Francis went to school, where his canonization took place, and where his body lay during construction of the Basilica. Clare, too, was buried in the church until her own resting place was completed.

With its simple facade and opulent rose window Santa Chiara is a virtual facsimile of the Upper Church of the Basilica di San Francesco. Its engineering, however, wasn't up to the same standards, and the strange buttresses were added in 1351 to prevent its collapse.

The interior

The **interior** is dark and almost bare, the result of some zealous early censorship: a seventeenth-century German bishop called Spader, afraid that the nuns might be corrupted, had its cycle of frescoes obliterated. Only a few patches of earlier Sienese frescoes from the original San Giorgio have survived, mostly in the transepts and cross vaults above the high altar; high in the south transept are *Scenes from the Apocalypse and Life of Christ*, and under them *The Death and Funeral of St Clare*, all the work of a close collaborator of Giotto. The scenes above the high altar, above which hangs a large thirteenth-century Crucifix, show *Scenes from the Life of St Clare*, while the two registers way up in the north transept depict *Episodes from Genesis*. The altar's *Madonna and Child* (c.1265) is probably the work of the Giottesque artist of the south transept. One of the two chapels off the right aisle, the **Oratorio del Crocifisso**, contains the Byzantine Crucifix that bowed its head and spoke to Francis in San Damiano. Alongside are various clothes and oddments that belonged to Clare and Francis, while the body of Clare herself rests in the Baroque horror of the **crypt**.

ST CLARE

St Clare (Santa Chiara) was a close early companion of St Francis and the founder of the **Poor Clares**, the Franciscan nuns. Born in 1182 into a noble family, her mother provided a deeply religious upbringing – an education which backfired when, enraptured at the age of 17 by the preaching of Francis, she rejected her family and two offers of marriage to live with the saint. In an act of symbolic removal from the world he cut off her blonde hair, the locks of which are still on view in her basilica, and replaced her finery with a rough cassock. A year after her conversion she took her leave of Francis, and – but for the occasional vision – never saw him again until his death.

After initial opposition from the family, Clare's sister, **St Agnes**, joined her in spiritual retreat, and was later joined by her widowed mother. Other young girls from Assisi, similarly inspired by Francis's example, added to the growing community of women, which was soon installed by Francis in the church of San Damiano. In 1215 Clare obtained the "privilege of poverty" from Pope Innocent III – permission for the creation of an order of nuns to live solely on alms and without property of any kind. Over the years the Poor Clares' right to exist was frequently challenged, yet Clare (like Francis) managed to disseminate the movement throughout Europe.

She died on August 12, 1253, outliving Francis by 27 years. She was canonized two years later, and by undignified quirk is now the **patron saint of television**, awarded the honour in 1958 by Pope Pius XII in recognition of her powers: although bedridden, she was able to see and hear the rites of a Christmas service performed by Francis a kilometre away.

THE EREMO DELLE CARCERI

All over Assisi you'll see pictures of the **Eremo delle Carceri** (daily: Easter–Oct 6.30am–7pm; Nov–Easter 6.30am–6pm; closed for religious festivals; donation expected), an active **monastery** situated in oak woods about 6km east. The hermitage was an early place of retreat for Francis and his followers: the saint caused the well in the courtyard to flow (as depicted by Giotto) and a cell known as the **Oratorio Primitivo** has been identified as that occupied by Francis.

A **chapel** in the monastery contains various unlikely relics: Francis's pillow and a piece of the Golden Gate through which Jesus passed into Jerusalem. The hermitage once owned a lock of the Virgin's hair, too, and some earth from the mound that God used to create Adam, though these treasures have sadly disappeared.

Tales associated with Francis also abound here: on the other side of the church is a dry riverbed, once a torrent until Francis told it to hush because it was spoiling his prayers. It reputedly fills up today only when some public calamity is at hand. One of the walls here was built over the so-called *buco del diavolo*, a crevice into which Francis cast a devil by the power of prayer. An old holm oak, kept upright by iron stakes, is said to have shaded the saint, and to have been a spot where birds collected to hear his sermons.

The Eremo delle Carceri can be easily reached by road but the best approach is to follow the **footpath** – climbing very steeply for the first kilometre or so – from the Porta Cappuccini: outside the gate, turn left along the track of cypresses and then follow the marked path up and to the right behind the Rocca Minore. At the major fork a little way beyond, turn right (sometimes the sign's missing), then at the top, keep going level and straight until you hit the road just above the monastery. Allow at least an hour, less coming back.

11

The Rocca Maggiore

Piazzale delle Libertà Comunali • Daily 10am–dusk, July & Aug opens 9am • €5, or combined ticket with Foro Romano and Pinacoteca €8 • ☏ 075 815 292

Rising above the town, the **Rocca Maggiore** dates back to Charlemagne, who is supposed to have raised the first defensive walls here after sacking the town. The structure that survives today, with its looming towers, turrets and parapets, owes most to Cardinal Albornoz, who arrived to assert papal authority in 1367, repairing an earlier castle that had been ravaged by repeated skirmishes with Perugia. Church governors reputedly dispensed justice by hanging criminals from the battlements or by throwing them out of a castle window into the ravine. The seductive **medieval streets** leading up to the Rocca from the Duomo are the quietest in Assisi, partly because of their fierce gradients and their distance from tourist targets. The fortress is well worth the climb: the green surrounds provide ideal picnic territory, and you'll be rewarded with all-embracing **views** taking in Assisi, Perugia and the Vale of Spoleto across to Montefalco and the Monti Martani.

Outside the walls

The Franciscan trail leads south from Santa Chiara to **San Damiano** and, for the energetic, to a couple of sites further outside town – the **Eremo delle Carceri** (4km east) and **Santa Maria degli Angeli** in the new town around the station (5km southwest of the old town). San Damiano is well worth the short detour: in a town increasingly undermined by tacky commercialism, it retains an air of calm and dignity.

San Damiano

Via San Damiano • Daily: April–Sept 10am–noon & 2–6pm; Nov–March 10am–noon & 2–4.30pm • Free

It was in **San Damiano**, in 1205, that Francis received his calling to make repairs, and where he brought St Clare and her followers, "pouring the sweetness of Christ into her ears". Clare remained here till her death, though the nuns left seven years afterwards. After installing the Poor Clares, Francis came to San Damiano just once, towards the end of his life, when – sick and half-blind – he composed the *Canticle of the Sun*. His body rested here briefly after death, fulfilling a promise to Clare that she might see him once more. Owned by Lord Lothian until 1983, the church now belongs to the Friars Minor, who have kept it in much the same state as it was centuries ago – a condition laid down by Lothian when he made his bequest. Lothian had inherited it in turn from descendants of Lord Ripon, a Catholic convert, who bought it in 1870 when Italy's monastic and most other religious institutions passed to the state.

To get to San Damiano, walk down the Borgo Aretino from Santa Chiara and then follow the signs through the car park and olive grove – a very steep downhill walk of about fifteen minutes.

The gardens and exterior

Alone among the places in Assisi with Franciscan associations, San Damiano preserves something of an ideal that is recognizably Franciscan – rural and peaceful in its groves of olives, cypresses and wild flowers, with the pastoral Vale of Spoleto stretching away below, over which a life-sized bronze **statue** of Saint Francis gazes, seated in meditation posture and sublimely absorbed in ecstatic contemplation of the Divine in all things. Signs point the way round the complex, starting outside with a fresco depicting St Roch – the saint invoked against infectious diseases – proudly displaying a plague sore. The little **balcony** above the main entrance is the point from which Clare, holding aloft the Sacrament, turned back an entire Saracen army that was pursuing Assisi's Guelphs.

The interior

Inside, the nave of the church – which was a Benedictine foundation at least as early as 1030 – is simple and smoke-darkened, with a beautifully decrepit wooden choir and lectern. On the right-hand side is the small window where San Damiano's priest threw the money that Francis offered him to repair the church. Nearby you can see the tiny hole where the saint hid "for a month" from the wrath of his father. Beyond some stairs leading to a terrace and small garden is a vestibule with the woodwormed choir and two frescoes, one a lovely *Madonna and Child* by an unknown Giottesque artist. Up the stairs you reach the **oratory**, and then a small **dormitory**, with a cross and flowers marking the spot where Clare died. A door to the right leads to the **cloisters**, where you may catch a glimpse of the refectory, still equipped with its original table and oak benches.

Santa Maria degli Angeli

Via Protomartiri Francescani • Daily 6.15am–12.30pm & 2.30–7.30pm, plus July, Aug & Sept 9–11pm • Free

Difficult to miss from almost any point in the Vale of Spoleto, the huge domed basilica of **Santa Maria degli Angeli** rises from the new town clustered around Assisi train station. A majestically uninspiring pile, it was built between 1569 and 1684, then rebuilt after an earthquake in 1832. Its function is to shelter the **Porzuincola** (Little Portion), the hut-cum-chapel that Francis made the centre of the earliest Franciscan movement. Stranded like a doll's house in the church's austere Baroque bowels, it has been embellished with dreadful nineteenth-century frescoes on the outside, but inside there are features claimed to be those of Francis's rough-stone hovel, as well as good

THE PARDON OF ST FRANCIS

Pilgrims flock to Santa Maria degli Angeli on August 1–2 for the **Pardon of St Francis**, a visit that guarantees automatic absolution. The pardon recalls a vision of Christ that Francis experienced, when he was asked what might be best for the human soul. Francis replied: forgiveness for all who crossed the threshold of his chapel. The already vast numbers of pilgrims were swelled in the 1920s by the supposed movement of the 8m bronze Madonna on the facade.

fourteenth-century frescoes on the life of the saint. Bits of the old monastery have been excavated under the **main altar**, site of the saint's death and of Clare's abrupt conversion.

In the garden are descendants of the **rose bushes** into which Francis threw himself while grappling with some immense nocturnal temptation; their thorns obligingly dropped off after contact with his saintly flesh. They now bloom, thornless, every May, their leaves stained with the blood shed that night.

ARRIVAL AND DEPARTURE

ASSISI

By train Assisi's station is located 5km southwest of town. Half-hourly buses (€1 tickets from the station kiosk) take 20min to reach Piazza Matteotti or Piazza Unità d'Italia, below the Basilica.

Destinations Foligno (18–24 daily; 17min); Passignano sul Trasimeno (18–24 daily; 50min); Perugia (18–24 daily; 30min); Spello (18–24 daily; 9min); Terontola (18–24 daily; connections to Chiusi, Orvieto, Arezzo and Florence; 1hr).

By bus The main bus terminal is in Piazza Matteotti. Long-distance Sulga buses (☎075 500 9641, ⓦ sulga.it) use Piazza San Pietro, at the other end of town.

Destinations Foligno (2 daily Mon–Sat; 50min); Norcia (1 daily Mon–Sat, from Santa Maria degli Angeli; 2hr 10min); Perugia (7–10 daily; 40min); Rome (1 daily; 3hr 30min); Santa Maria degli Angeli (every 30min; 7min); Spello (2 daily Mon–Sat; 25min); Todi (1 weekly on Fri; 90min).

By car Parking legally in central Assisi is virtually impossible. It's best to leave cars at the underground car park in Piazza Matteotti or in Piazza Unità d'Italia. There are hundreds of free spaces up by the Rocca, a long walk to the Basilica, and by the cemetery off Viale Albornoz on the road from Porta San Giacomo. Other fringe car parks are located outside Porta Nuova and Porta Moiano.

INFORMATION

Tourist office Piazza del Comune 22 (April–Oct Mon–Sat 8am–2pm & 3–6pm, Sun 10am–1pm & 2–5pm; Nov–March Mon–Sat 8am–2pm & 3–6pm, Sun 9am–1pm. ☎075 813 8680, ⓦ www.comune.assisi.pg.it). There are also seasonal

information offices in Largo Properzio near Porta Nuova (☎075 816 766), at Santa Maria degli Angeli (☎075 812 479) and at the train station (☎075 813 499), both open April–Oct Mon–Sat 8am–2pm & 3–6pm, Sun 10am–1pm & 2–5pm.

GETTING AROUND

Bike rental Andrea Angelucci, Via Becchetti 31 (☎075 804 2550).

Car rental Costantini, Viale Umberto I 40 (☎075 816 356, ⓦ autonoleggiocostantini.it).

ACCOMMODATION

⭐ **Alexander** Piazza Chiesa Nuova 6 ☎075 816 190, ⓦ hotelalexanderassisi.it. Completely refurbished in 2009, this handy and comfortable spot is a very pleasant option. The nine en-suite rooms, some with great views, all have a/c and wi-fi and are fresh and well appointed. Breakfast included. €98

Del Viaggiatore Via Sant'Antonio 14 ☎075 816 297, ⓦ albergodelviaggiatore.com. This small, very friendly hotel-restaurant has eleven rooms; all are on the small side, but some have views. The place is a bit of a challenge to find; parking nearby goes for €10 per day. Breakfast included. €90

⭐ **Fontebella** Via Fontebella 25 ☎075 812 883, ⓦ fontebella.com. By far the most elegant and intimate of Assisi's smarter hotel-restaurants. The plush rooms have marble bathrooms, and those on one of the top two floors

have views over Assisi's rooftops and the Vale of Spoleto. Excellent breakfast included, and a good restaurant (see p.452). Parking extra. €250

Hermitage Via degli Aromatari 1 ☎075 812 080, ⓦ hotels-hermitage.it. Small and arty, with each room themed according to an artist or musician, this popular hotel offers a/c and internet, as well as terraces with views. Substantial breakfast included; parking extra. €94

Ideale Piazza Matteotti 1 ☎075 813 570, ⓦ hotelideale.it. Follow the signs south from Piazza Matteotti to reach this eleven-room hotel with a garden, a short way outside the walls. The welcome is very genuine, and all rooms have private bathroom. Hotel parking is a bonus; excellent breakfast included. €80

La Fortezza Vicolo della Fortezza 2b ☎075 812 418, ⓦ lafortezzahotel.com. This friendly hotel-restaurant has

THE ASSISICARD

The Assisicard (provided free by most hotels, otherwise €2) offers discounts on parking, museum entry and tours, plus other advantages. It's also available from the tourist offices.

seven rooms in a fourteenth-century building, and excellent cuisine in its restaurant (see below). Rooms have ceiling fans, heating and wi-fi. A substantial breakfast and afternoon tea, served on the rooftop, are included. **€80**

Le Silve Località Armenzano 89 **☎**075 801 9000, ⓦlesilve.it. In lovely countryside 10km east of Assisi on the slopes of Monte Subasio, this resort makes an excellent alternative to staying in town. Set in a converted rural house (parts of which date back to the tenth century), it offers a swimming pool, tennis and riding. Buffet breakfast included, in their own otherwise very expensive restaurant, *Armentum*. **€180**

Pallotta Via San Rufino 6 **☎**075 812 307, ⓦpallottaassisi. it. This hotel-restaurant is one of Assisi's better options. All rooms have wi-fi and private bathroom, and some have balconies with panoramic views, the very welcoming hosts provide a free audioguide of the town's sights, and there's an excellent restaurant (see below). Private parking nearby, at €5 per day; breakfast included. **€80**

Subasio Via Frate Elia 2 **☎**075 812 206, ⓦhotelsubasioassisi.com. This grande-dame is Assisi's traditional hotel of choice, though it has seen better days: past guests include Marlene Dietrich, Charlie Chaplin and Elizabeth Taylor. The 61 rooms vary considerably; some have stunning views of the valley, which is really the only reason to stay here. Breakfast included. **€165**

★ Umbra Vicolo degli Archi 6 **☎**075 812 240, ⓦhotelumbra.it. This excellent and very popular family-run hotel-restaurant has 25 elegantly appointed rooms with a/c, and some with wonderful views, plus very friendly and helpful staff and a nice garden terrace with views, too. Internet available; parking can be a problem. Breakfast included in their own fine restaurant. **€115**

HOSTELS AND CAMPSITES

Ostello della Pace Via di Valecchie 177 **☎**075 816 767, ⓦassisihostel.com. In peaceful countryside, a 10min walk downhill from Piazza Unità d'Italia, this hostel is set in a you'll find a restored seventeenth-century stone farmhouse, set amidst a garden and with very welcoming staff. It's signed off the big right-hand bend shortly after the roundabout junction with Viale Vittorio Emanuele II; coming from the station by bus, ask to be dropped at "Villa Guardi": the hostel is signposted from here, too. Breakfast included, dinner €10.50. Dorm bed **€17**

Ostello di Fontemaggio Strada Eremo delle Carceri 8 **☎**075 813 636, ⓦfontemaggio.it. Set in at hamlet of Fontemaggio, 2km east of town, with clean, ten-bed single-sex dorms or a choice of one-star private rooms. Breakfast is €7 per person. There's also a two-star campsite attached to the hostel, open all year. Camping: adults **€6**, tent pitch **€5**, dorm beds **€20**, double rooms **€52**

EATING AND DRINKING

Il Frantoio Via Fontebella 25 **☎**075 812 883, ⓦfontebella.com. This gourmet in-hotel restaurant has panoramic views and specializes in succulent truffle omelettes and *stringozzi* pasta with porcini and truffle. Full meals run to about €50, depending on wine; the owner is one of the region's top sommeliers, and has crafted a distinguished wine list. Mon, Tues & Thurs–Sun 1–4pm & 7–10.30pm.

La Fortezza Vicolo della Fortezza 2b **☎**075 812 418, ⓦlafortezzahotel.com. The set menus at this excellent restaurant are recommended: one goes for about €30, and there's a tasting menu at around €45. The setting is part ancient Roman, part medieval, with a terrace affording great views, and specialities include truffle-laced pheasant en croute. Good wine list, too. Mon–Wed & Fri–Sun 1–3.30pm & 7–10pm; closed fifteen days in July.

★ Pallotta Via San Rufino 6 **☎**075 812 307, ⓦpallottaassisi.it. This very welcoming hotel trattoria is

really excellent. Specialities include ravioli with fresh sage butter, as well as roasted pigeon, all washed down with Sagrantino wine. The portions are large, so order accordingly. Full meals go for about €35 per person. Mon & Wed–Sun 1.30–3.30pm & 7.30–10.30pm.

Sensi Corso Mazzini 14 **☎**075 812 529. This elegant and traditional café and bar, offering wines by the glass along with local cold meats and cheeses, is also a popular purveyor of home-made pastries and *gelato*, as well as pizzas and sandwiches. Mon–Sat 7.30am–11.30pm, Sun 7.30am–1pm.

★ Umbra Vicolo degli Archi 6 **☎**075 812 240, ⓦhotelumbra.it. The best seating here is under the wonderful arbour on the terrace; menu highlights include asparagus risotto or the mixed Umbrian grill, featuring wild boar. A full meal will cost about €30, excluding wine. Mon–Sat 1–4pm & 7.30–10.45pm, Sun 1–4pm.

DIRECTORY

Banks and exchange ATMs outside banks in Piazza del Comune and Piazza Unità d'Italia; Banca Popolare, Piazza Santa Chiara 19; and Banca Toscana, Piazza San Pietro 6. Numerous exchange kiosks around town.

Hospital Ospedale di Assisi, 1km southeast of Porta Nuova on Via Fuori Porta Nuova (**☎**075 812 824 or 075 813 9227).

Markets Assisi's main market is in Piazza Matteotti (Sat

8am–1.30pm). Piazza Chiesa Nuova hosts an antiques market on the second weekend of each month (Sat & Sun 8am–6.30pm).

Police Piazza Matteotti 3b (**☎**075 812 239), and Piazza del Comune (**☎**075 812 215).

Post office Largo Properzio 4 (**☎**075 81 314), and Piazza San Pietro 4 (**☎**075 815 178).

Spello

Ranged impressively on broad walled terraces above the Vale of Spoleto, with the lofty slopes of Monte Subasio beyond, pink-stoned **SPELLO** offers an easily accessible taste of medieval small-town Umbria – and a major art attraction by way of **Pinturicchio**'s superlative frescoes in the church of **Santa Maria Maggiore**. Spello is easily explored, most of its main sights being on or just off the main street, **Via Consolare** and its continuation, **Via Cavour**, which winds through the town from the southern Porta Consolare, one of several minor monuments to the town's Roman heyday. In addition to the Santa Maria Maggiore frescoes, more paintings and works of art await in the **Pinacoteca** and the churches of **Sant'Andrea** and **San Lorenzo**. Much of Spello's appeal – as so often in small Umbrian towns – resides in the charm of its small streets and alleys. Once you're off the main street, the main core of the medieval town is magical.

Some history

As Roman Hispellum, the town served as a retirement home for pensioned-off legionaries and an important staging post on the Via Flaminia. Later it fell to the Lombards – who destroyed it – then became part of the Duchy of Spoleto. In 1238 it fell to Frederick II (who also destroyed it) and then passed under the yoke of Perugia. Today, it's tourism that makes it tick, though despite its proximity to Assisi and Spoleto, it remains relatively quiet.

Porta Consolare

The **Porta Consolare** is one of five Roman gates in the Augustan-era walls that still more or less enclose Spello. The gate is in a slightly sorry state, with an ancient olive tree growing from its crumbling upper reaches – a sixteenth-century fresco in the Palazzo Comunale shows the tower with its tree even then – but it still gives some idea of its former glory, and retains three original **statues**, figures removed from the town's amphitheatre that local folklore claims depict a family killed by eating poisonous mushrooms. Parts of the old Roman road are also exposed here, while to the left along Via Roma range some well-preserved stretches of the original Augustan-era walls (some of the best-preserved in Italy).

Capella Tega

Inside the Porta Consolare begins the main street, **Via Consolare** (later **Via Cavour**), which bends and climbs steeply:

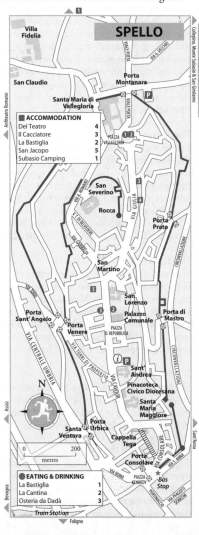

SPELLO

Villa Fidelia

San Claudio

Santa Maria di Vallegloria

Porta Montanara

San Severino

Rocca

Porta Prato

San Martino

San Lorenzo

Porta di Mastro

Porta Sant' Angelo

Porta Venere

Palazzo Comunale

PIAZZA D. REPUBBLICA

Sant' Andrea

Pinacoteca Civico Diocesana

Santa Maria Maggiore

Santa Ventura

Porta Urbica

Cappella Tega

Porta Consolare

PIAZZA KENNEDY

Bus Stop

Train Station

■ ACCOMMODATION	
Del Teatro	4
Il Cacciatore	3
La Bastiglia	2
San Jacopo	5
Subasio Camping	1

● EATING & DRINKING	
La Bastiglia	1
La Cantina	2
Osteria da Dadà	3

0   200
metres

it has no pavements, so beware – you're forever dodging cars. A couple of minutes' wall (you might take the rubber-surfaced alley on the left as a short cut) brings you to the odd little **Cappella Tega** (open to view behind glass), half-covered in frescoes from 146 by Niccolò Alunno.

Santa Maria Maggiore

Piazza Giacomo Matteotti 18 • Daily: April–Sept 8.30am–12.30pm & 3–7pm; Nov–March 8.30am–12.30pm & 3–6pm • ⓦ smariamaggiore.com

In 1600 Spello had some two thousand inhabitants – compared with around eight thousand today – and a staggering one hundred churches, of which 22 were dedicated to the Virgin. One of the most important of these was **Santa Maria Maggiore**, which celebrated both the Virgin's Birth (Sept 8) and the Assumption (Aug 15).

Begun in the twelfth century, the church was remodelled five centuries later to dull effect, the most obvious alterations being the **facade**, which was shifted forward a full nine metres, and the mundane Baroque botch job visited on the interior. The facade did keep parts of the original Romanesque portal, however, some of whose fine carving has been attributed to Binello and Ridolfo, the mysterious craftsmen responsible for the strange sculptures on the churches of nearby Bevagna. The two columns at the base of the campanile are from an earlier Roman building; Spello's main street follows exactly the course of the old Roman road, and a Roman aqueduct runs beneath it to this day.

The stoup

Inside is another outstanding Roman piece, now a **stoup** for holy water, fashioned from the altar tomb (AD 60) of Gaius Titienus Flaccus, a leading light of Hispellum's most important family. The dead man is shown on horseback above an inscription, while in the lower part of the stoup you can still make out a little hollow once used to store his ashes. Another similar tomb – that of a young woman – was moved from the church in the eighteenth century and now supports the cross on top of the campanile.

The vast eye-catching **Crucifix** here, formerly in the church of Sant'Andrea, is by an unknown fourteenth-century Umbrian follower of Giotto.

The frescoes

The interior's real draw are the **frescoes** (1501) by **Pinturicchio** that cover the Cappella Baglioni on the left as you enter: monumental achievements which rank with the artist's masterpieces in Siena's Libreria Piccolomini and Rome's Sistine Chapel and Borgia apartments. Sadly, they are behind glass, and you need coins to illuminate them. The barrier also means you can't get a proper look at the chapel's **ceramic pavement** (1566), a faded testimony to the skill of Deruta's craftsmen (see p.521). The three panels are read **from left to right**; the ceiling vaults showing the *Four Sibyls*.

The Annunciation

The **first fresco** features the *Annunciation*, with the Virgin having just read the prophetic text from the Bible open in front of her. Below and to the right, the obvious hanging painting is a **self-portrait of Pinturicchio**, and under it a plaque with his name from which dangle brushes, styluses and other tools of the painter's trade.

The Adoration of the Child

The **central fresco** on the rear wall depicts the *Adoration of the Child*, with the shepherds shown left of Christ and the Magi behind them to the left. Behind the Magi one of the group of armed men amidst the rocks bears an anachronistic detail: a shield with the **Baglioni coat of arms** (the chapel was commissioned by a prelate belonging to the infamous family in 1500). The painting is also remarkable for its preponderance of symbols, in particular the cross (a prefiguration of Christ's Crucifixion), the peacock (symbolizing eternal life and the incorruptibility of the flesh) and the flask of wine and bread in the bottom right-hand corner (an allusion to the Eucharist).

The Disputation in the Temple

The **final fresco**, the *Disputation in the Temple*, includes a portrait of Troilo Baglioni (the man who commissioned the paintings), shown in his black prior's habit. Alongside him stands his treasurer, with his bag of money, a reminder of who paid for the frescoes. Over on the extreme right the grisly-featured old woman is an allusion to the 'Old Woman of the Cross", the central character in one of Spello's seminal **medieval legends**. In 1346, the harridan reputedly tried to fan the mutual hatred of the inhabitants of the upper and lower town, but before any bloody encounter could take place she was vaporized by the miraculous apparition of a cross.

Pinturicchio also makes another appearance, in a sense, his **name** being picked out on the note held by the character in the prominent white headgear in the group to the right of Christ. The artist's hand can also be seen in the disturbing details in the background: the disabled beggars in front of the temple and, more macabre, the tiny figure dangling from a gibbet on the hill-top to the right of the large palm tree.

The rest of the church

Elsewhere in the church are two more Pinturicchio paintings: the **Cappella del Sacramento**, the chapel to the left of the apse, has a faintly etched angel holding a plaque above a little lavabo; the inscription – *Lavamini et mundi, estote* – means "Wash yourself and be pure." Beyond that, in the **canon's room**, is an overpainted but beautifully lyrical *Madonna and Child*. Two good late paintings by **Perugino** adorn the two pillars flanking the apse, one a *Pietà*, the other a *Madonna and Child with Sts Blaise and Catherine*.

The Pinacoteca Civica Diocesana

Piazza Giacomo Matteotti 10 • Tues–Sun: April–Sept 10.30am–1pm & 3–6.30pm; Oct–March 10.30am–12.30pm & 3.30–5.30pm • €2.60
• ☎ 0742 301 497, 🖩 smariamaggiore.com

Spello's **Pinacoteca Civica Diocesana** has a vaguely open-plan arrangement, which makes it hard to figure out which room is which, but everything is well labelled. The best pieces include the wonderful polychrome wooden statue, *Madonna and Child*, an Umbrian work dating from the end of the twelfth century. Also outstanding is an extraordinary statue of the crucified Christ, its arms hinged to resemble a crude marionette. Religious confraternities used such statues, now extremely rare, during Holy Week celebrations: the arms would be opened or folded according to the particular religious celebration.

The paintings

Note the little diptych (1391) by **Cola Petruccioli**, designed as a portable preaching aid for itinerant monks, which shows the *Crucifixion* on one panel and the *Coronation of the Virgin* on the other. Also a pair of early fifteenth-century panels of a triptych by the anonymous Maestro dell'Assunta di Amelia: *St John and the Prophet Isaiah*, and *John the Baptist and Nicholas of Bari*. The original triptych was stolen in 1970, and the main central panel – a *Madonna and Child* – has never been recovered. A similar fate befell another *Madonna*, the central part of a triptych, attributed to Pinturicchio, stolen in the same year from Santa Maria Maggiore, but here the work was recovered in 2004 and is now exhibited in the gallery.

Other paintings include the superbly restored *Crucifixion, Virgin and Saints* by **Niccolò Alunno**. Elsewhere, look out for the five canvases by **Marcantonio Grecchi**, especially the *Madonna and Child with St Felix and Andrea Caccioli*; St Felix, an early bishop of Spello, is one of the town's patron saints. The painting's charm lies in the perfectly realized little portrait of Spello held by the two protagonists, the town looking much the same as it does today.

The gonfaloni

Note the double-sided **gonfaloni** (banners): one (1576) by Lorenzo Doni and one depicting a particularly graphic *Martyrdom of St Barbara* on one side and the members of Spello's Confraternity of St Barbara on the other. Another one, probably painted by one of Alunno's assistants, shows the *Madonna della Misericordia* shielding Spello's citizens beneath her cloak on one side and, on its other side, the *Miracle of the Cross of Spello*, the event alluded to in Pinturicchio's fresco of the *Disputation in the Temple* in Santa Maria Maggiorre.

Porta Venere

Via Torri di Properzio

The best remnant of Roman Spello, perfectly preserved **Porta Venere** is thought to have been named after a long-vanished temple to Venus: Constantine is said to have built one of Umbria's largest shrines to the goddess in the vicinity. Flanking the gate, the imposing dodecagonal twin columns of the so-called Towers of Propertius are thought to be partly Roman, as evidenced by the excellent, tight-fitting masonry on their lower sections.

Piazza della Repubblica to San Lorenzo

The main **Piazza della Repubblica** is part grotesque twentieth-century, part medieval, with its arched **Palazzo Comunale** boasting a couple of fourteenth-century frescoes by local painters. Just to the north, **San Lorenzo** rates as one of Umbria's more successful Baroque conversions. A mongrel of a church, it had a succession of architects who left a variety of decorative effects, some laughable, like the obviously fake marbles, others more persuasive – as with the *baldacchino*, a bronze canopy copied from Bernini's piece for St Peter's in Rome. The most arresting sight is the minutely realistic statue of St Peter the Martyr, midway down the west wall, complete with trickle of blood from the cleaver delicately planted in his head.

Up to the Rocca

At the top of Spello's main street (first Via Cavour, then later Via Garibaldi) you can explore alleys and backstreets redolent with typical Umbrian charm. Views from the

---

EXPLORING MONTE SUBASIO

Just beyond the Rocca, the Porta Montarana is the starting point for a tough but wonderful **walking trail**. After just twenty minutes, you can take in superb views of Spello and the Vale of Spoleto in its early reaches, but if you want to follow the trail to its end, you can reach Assisi (allow a full day for this) via the summit of **Monte Subasio** and/or the Eremo delle Carceri. The path is marked by the Club Alpino Italiano: look for trail no.50 on a sign at the start and the red-spot markings which run all the way to Assisi. It's a good idea to have a detailed walking **map** to hand – you should be able to get one at the newsagents to the right of San Lorenzo in Spello. To find the start of the route, take the second right turn after the Porta Montanara (signposted for Collepino), walk past the olive-oil works on the right, and after 100m take the (initially surfaced) track left at the fountain.

You can also **drive** on the part-gravel road from the northern end of Spello over Monte Subasio to Assisi (signed "Monte Subasio" and for the *La Baita* bar-restaurant): be certain not to miss the left turn after a couple of kilometres, or you'll end up in Collepino and Armenzano. The **views** are superlative and there are sensational spreads of orchids and narcissi in late May and early June.

east side of town are especially good, with lovely panoramas over the bucolic countryside below Monte Subasio. The arch almost opposite San Lorenzo leads to the highest point of the town, occupied by the **belvedere** and **Rocca** – the latter giving the only view you need of the overgrown remains of the first-century Roman amphitheatre to the west.

Villa Fidelia

Via Flaminia 70 • April–June & Sept Thurs–Sun 10.30am–1pm & 3.30–6pm; July & Aug daily 10.30am–1pm & 4–7pm; Oct–March Sat & Sun 10.30am–1pm & 3–6pm • €3 • ☎ 0742 651 726

A ten-minute walk north of the walls – also accessible via a country lane which drops down from Piazza Vallegloria – is the little-known, early nineteenth-century **Villa Fidelia**, with beautiful and extensive formal gardens, fantastic views and the fascinatingly eclectic Straka-Coppa private collection of paintings, sculptures, old furniture and costumes, together with displays on the Italian Futurist painters, who glorified modernism in largely abstract works reminiscent in style of analytical Cubism.

11

ARRIVAL AND DEPARTURE

SPELLO

By train Spello's station, 600m southwest of Porta Consolare, is unstaffed, but there's a ticket machine in the waiting room.

Destinations Assisi (hourly; 7–16min); Foligno (hourly; 6–12min); Perugia (hourly; 30–50min); Teróntola (hourly; 1hr 9min–1hr 40min); Trevi (6 daily; 13–28min).

By bus Buses drop you off at the foot of the town just outside the Porta Consolare.

Destinations Assisi (4 daily; 15min); Foligno (11 daily; 25min).

By car The tortuous main street is entirely one-way, with the most central car park on the right immediately after Sant'Andrea. Alternatively you can walk down from the big car park off Via Cimitero by Porta Montanara.

INFORMATION

Tourist office Piazza Matteotti 3 (daily: April–Oct 9.30am–12.30pm & 3.30–5.30pm; Nov–March 9.30am–12.30pm & 3.30–5pm; ☎ 0742 301 009, ⓦ www .comune.spello.pg.it).

ACCOMMODATION

Del Teatro Via Giulia 24 ☎ 075 301 140, ⓦ hoteldelteatro.it. This small hotel in a completely refurbished medieval building has every comfort and luxury, with marble and wood touches throughout, plus wonderful views from the terrace of the town and countryside. Breakfast included. €110

Il Cacciatore Via Giulia 42 ☎ 0742 651 141, ⓦ ilcacciatorehotel.com. Very friendly family-run hotel, with fine views from some rooms, all of which are homely and spacious with good bathrooms. The restaurant boasts a great terrace, though food and service are patchy. Free garage parking. €100

La Bastiglia Via Salnitraria 15 ☎ 0742 651 277, ⓦ labastiglia.com. This beautifully restored hotel-restaurant at the top of the town offers smart rooms, suites and apartments, many with great views; there's also a swimming pool and a terrace. Breakfast included in their own fine restaurant (see p.458). Doubles €100

San Jacopo Via Borgo di via Giulia 1 ☎ 0742 301 260, ⓦ residencesanjacopo.com. This *residenze* is an excellent option if you want to self-cater or are travelling in a group. The seven light-filled one-bedroom mini-apartments have linen, TV, private bathroom and kitchen; decor features wrought iron, terracotta flooring and natural wood accents. €75

Subasio Camping Via del Campeggio, Località Sportella ☎ 0742 801 0655, ⓦ campeggiosubasio.com. Spello's nearest campsite is about 3km to the northeast, at a height of 840m on the slopes of Subasio. It's set amidst dense forest and very rustic, with barbecuing facilities and

---

SPELLO'S FESTIVALS

Spello's main **festival** is the **Infiorita** on Corpus Domini (late May or early June), when the streets are laid with carpets of minutely detailed pictorial scenes created entirely by hand from millions of flower petals. In the weeks leading up to the event you will see people everywhere patiently removing petals from stalks.

There's also a *sagra* celebrating the area's **olive oil** in the week before Shrove Tuesday.

a communal table. Besides camping, they also rent out trailer accommodations for up to four persons. Open April to early Oct. Adults €8, tents €9, double trailers €40

EATING AND DRINKING

La Bastiglia Via Salnitraria 15 ☎ 0742 651 277, ⓦ labastiglia.com. Boasting one Michelin star, this in-hotel restaurant offers excellent local cuisine and perfectly combined wine selections. A meal can run about €100 and up; the adjoining osteria offers simpler meals for about €35 per person. Mon, Tues & Thurs–Sun 1.30–4pm & 7.30–10.30pm.

★ **La Cantina** Via Cavour 2 ☎ 0742 651 775, ⓦ lacantinadispello.com. A very friendly country kitchen in a beautiful vaulted medieval setting, serving plenty of regional dishes – wild boar goulash is a speciality. There are wonderful fresh pastas such as *gnocchi* with truffles, and a good wine list, too. They also do memorable things with caramel and chocolate for dessert. About €30 per person, depending on wine. Mon, Tues & Thurs–Sun 1–3.30pm & 7.30–10pm.

Osteria da Dadà Via Cavour 47 ☎ 0742 301 327. This little osteria with a few shared tables is a great find. The *bruschette* are very generous, and don't miss the *stringozzi* pasta and other local favourites such as the onion and chickpea soup. The dishes of the day are usually the best choice, however. About €45 for a full meal for two. Tues–Sun 1–3.45pm & 7.30–10pm.

Foligno

On public transport, sooner or later you're likely to find yourself passing through **FOLIGNO**, a hub for trains and buses. Although this was the place where, in 1472, the first book was printed in Italian – three hundred copies of Dante's *Divine Comedy* – today Foligno is a largely modern place, its historic structures having been bombed during World War II. What remains is a not unpleasant provincial town, though with nothing that would merit a special visit.

The Duomo

Largo Giosuè Carducci

The **Duomo** is the main eye-catcher, the twelfth-century Palazzo Comunale opposite having been ruined by the addition of a Neoclassical facade at the beginning of the nineteenth century. Unusually, the church boasts two facades, the south frontage containing one of the most impressive portals in the region: a riot of carving full of zodiac signs, intricate patterning and bizarre animals, as well as a likeness of Frederick II on the left (one of only two in Italy) and a Muslim star and crescent near the apex of the arch. The mosaics of the other facade are a nineteenth-century afterthought. Inside, a panel by Niccolò Alunno in the sacristy is the only feature worth seeking out.

Palazzo Trinci

Piazza della Repubblica • April–Oct Tues–Sun 9am–1pm & 3–7pm • €6

At the western end of the piazza is the **Palazzo Trinci** (1389–1407), the much-altered home of the Trinci, Foligno's medieval big shots. The *palazzo* is by far the best reason to visit the town; highlights include a fine courtyard, palace frescoes and painted staircase, and a small **archeological museum** and linked **Pinacoteca Comunale**. The key sight in the latter is a fine fresco cycle by **Gentile da Fabriano** depicting the story of the founding of Rome, the Seven Liberal Arts, the Seven Ages of Man, the hours of the day, the cycle of the planets and more. Other high points include a frescoed chapel by Ottaviano Nelli and an *Annunciation* attributed to Benozzo Gozzoli.

Santa Maria Infraportas

The only other monument which hints at Foligno's former glory is **Santa Maria Infraportas**, a church of pagan origins in which St Peter is said to have celebrated Mass. The oldest part of the current eighth-century church is the Cappella dell'Assunta off the left nave; behind its altar the Byzantine mural with lions is the town's most precious piece of art.

ARRIVAL AND DEPARTURE   FOLIGNO

By train The train station is at Piazzale Unità d'Italia, some way east of the main square, Piazza della Repubblica.

Destinations Assisi (hourly; 17min); Fossato di Vico (for Gubbio; hourly; 28min–1hr 5min); Narni (hourly; 52min–1hr 8min); Passignano sul Trasimeno (hourly; 1hr 4min–1hr 27min); Perugia (hourly; 32–56min); Rome (hourly; 1hr 22min–2hr 17min); Spello (hourly; 6–12min); Spoleto (hourly; 13–22min); Terni (hourly; 32–58min); Teróntola (hourly; connections to Chiusi, Orvieto, Arezzo and

Florence; 1hr 8min–1hr 44min); Trevi (hourly; 5–7min).

By bus Buses arrive and depart in Piazzale Unità d'Italia, close to the train station.

Destinations Assisi (4 daily Mon–Sat; 50min); Bevagna (5–8 daily Mon–Fri; 20min); Montefalco (5–8 daily Mon–Sat; 30min); Norcia (1 daily Mon–Sat; 1hr 35min); Perugia (7–10 daily; 1hr 20min); Rome (2–3 daily; 3hr); Spello (11 daily Mon–Sat; 25min); Spoleto (4–8 daily; 50min); Trevi (4 daily Mon–Sat; 23min).

INFORMATION

Tourist office Corso Cavour 126 (April–Oct Mon–Sat 10am–1pm & 4–7pm, Sun 10am–1pm; Nov–March

Mon–Sat 10am–1pm & 3–6pm, Sun 10am–1pm; ☎0742 354 459 , ⓦ profoligno.it).

EATING AND DRINKING

Il Cavaliere Via XX Settembre 39 ☎0742 350 608, ⓦristoranteilcavaliere.eu. Set in pleasant medieval-era rooms, this is a fine gourmet restaurant, with everything home-made and a good wine list. Try the *gnocchi* with a Sagrantino sauce for a local speciality; there's a wonderful selection of cheeses, too. About €50 per person for a full meal. Tues–Sun 1–3.45pm & 7–10pm.

★ **Premiata Officina del Gusto** Piazza Don Minzoni 1–3 ☎0742 620 452, ⓦpremiataofficinadelgusto.it. This recently-opened restaurant is notable for its innovative takes on traditional Italian cuisine, such as salmon with black rice and smoked tea, or tagliatelle with king crab and raspberries. Great wine suggestions, too, and a chic yet warmly welcoming setting. About €40 per person. Mon & Wed–Sun 1.30–4pm & 7.30–10.30pm.

11

Bevagna and around

BEVAGNA, shadowed by the Martani hills 8km southwest of Foligno, is even more serene and handsome a backwater than Spello, with a windswept central piazza of austere perfection and two of Umbria's finest Romanesque **churches**. An Umbrian and then an Etruscan settlement, the town became Mevania under the Romans, and a staging post on the Via Flaminia (built in 220 BC) – now the Corso Matteotti, which bisects the town. Its decline dates from the building of a new spur to the Flaminia five centuries later, a road that was routed through Terni and Spoleto rather than Bevagna. After the Roman era it was sacked by Barbarossa, Frederick II, Foligno's Trinci family and, inevitably, Perugia's Baglioni. Today it has scarcely spread beyond its medieval walls, remaining miraculously unscarred by the urban blight of most nearby hill-towns.

Piazza Silvestri

Bevagna's backstreets sooner or later converge on the pedestrianized main square, **Piazza Silvestri**, broad and open after its shadowed surroundings. Nearly every element of this consummate arrangement is thoroughly medieval, the sole exception being the nineteenth-century fountain, and even that blends in perfectly. The churches of **San Silvestro** and **San Michele** face each other across the square, both untouched and creaking with age, while the third major component is the notable **Palazzo dei Consoli**.

San Silvestro

Piazza Silvestri

The deconsecrated **San Silvestro** is a magnificent if squat example of early Umbrian-Romanesque; its exterior bears a plaque with the date of construction – 1195 – and the name of the builder, Binello, who was also responsible for San Michele opposite, but of whom nothing else is known except for his work on Spello's Santa Maria Maggiore. Pieces of Roman remains are woven into the **facade**, whose upper half is faced in pink Subasio stone and boasts the stump of an unfinished tower. The **interior** – which tends to be open when the rest of the town is shut – is superbly ancient in look and feel, with a raised presbytery and sunken crypt. Look out for the capitals of the blunt columns in the nave, which are of an Egyptian order (rather than Doric, Ionic or Corinthian) and were perhaps copied from a Roman temple to distant deities.

San Michele

Piazza Silvestri

San Michele appears more recent, perhaps owing to its rose window, punched through in the eighteenth century. It is in fact San Silvestro's contemporary and is built to a similar interior plan; its capitals are similarly eccentric, as are the magnificently surreal gargoyles over the main doorway.

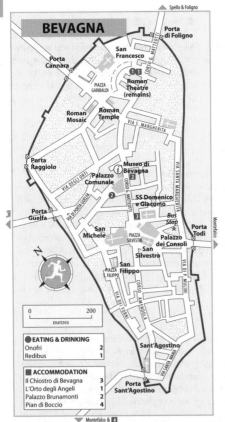

Palazzo dei Consoli

Piazza Silvestri

The twelfth-century **Palazzo dei Consoli** is distinguished by a broad stone staircase. Infiltrated into it is the delightful nineteenth-century **Teatro F. Torti**, full of minuscule boxes and balconies, one of only a few surviving examples of the tiny provincial theatres that once flourished across Italy. Enquire at the Museo di Bevagna (see box, opposite) for admittance.

Sts Domenico e Giacomo

Piazza Silvestri

The church of **Sts Domenico e Giacomo** is rectangular and workaday, its Baroque interior relieved only by fragments of fresco and two early wooden sculptures. Its prime position was a gift from the *comune* to the Dominicans for help in rebuilding the town after one of its sackings. Be sure to have a look at the small cloister, reached through the church.

San Francesco

Piazza Garibaldi

At the town's highest point, the church of **San Francesco** claims to have the stone from which St Francis

ROMAN AND MEDIEVAL BEVAGNA

Since the town failed to progress much after it was bypassed by the Via Flaminia in about the fourth century AD, Bevagna's Roman and medieval periods are well represented by a wealth of remains. The **Museo di Bevagna**, Corso Matteotti 70 (April, May & Sept daily 10.30am–1pm & 2.30–6pm; July & Aug daily 10.30am–1pm & 3–6.30pm; Oct–March Tues–Sun 10.30am–1pm & 2.30–5pm; €4, or €5 including guided tour of the ruins) is devoted to the history of the village, with three modest sections covering archeological displays, art and history by way of maps, letters and other documents. **Guided tours** of the town's Roman and medieval sights depart roughly every twenty minutes.

Just to the north of the town centre, **Porta Cannara**, the best preserved of the town's gates, offers access to a nice stretch of the medieval walls. On the north side of Via Porta Guelfa, the impressive black-and-white **Roman mosaic** was laid down in the second century, and formed part of a bath complex – hence the depiction of dolphins, lobsters and other sea creatures. To the south, the pillars and half-columns of the **Roman temple** date from roughly the same period. Farther east on Corso G. Matteotti, be sure to explore Via dell'Anfiteatro, where diminutive houses follow the line of the ancient **Roman theatre**, and which gives access to a series of little tunnels that burrow mysteriously into the old under-stage area.

11

preached his famous sermon to the birds, a discourse that supposedly occurred on the road between Bevagna and Cannara (the spot is also commemorated at Assisi's Eremo delle Carceri).

ARRIVAL AND INFORMATION

BEVAGNA

By bus Buses arrive and depart from Largo Gramsci.
Destinations Foligno (5 daily Mon–Sat; 30min); Montefalco (4–5 daily Mon–Sat; 40min).

Tourist office Santa Maria Laurentia 1 (daily: Easter to Sept 9.30am–12.30pm & 3–7pm; Oct to Easter 9.30am–12.30pm & 3–5.30pm; ☎0742 361 667, ⓦwww.comune.bevagna.pg.it).

ACCOMMODATION

Il Chiostro di Bevagna Corso Matteotti 107 ☎0742 361 987, ⓦilchiostrodibevagna.com. This atmospheric Dominican convent dates from the thirteenth century, with an original cloister where you can take breakfast (included) in good weather. All fourteen homely rooms are non-smoking, and there's free wi-fi and parking. **€80**

★ **L'Orto degli Angeli** Via Dante Alighieri 1 ☎0742 360 130, ⓦortoangeli.it. This magnificent pair of luxurious historic mansions has been in the same family since 1788, with porticoes and beautiful gardens. Each of the fourteen luxurious rooms and apartments is uniquely decorated with period antiques original to the mansion, and the first-rate *Redibus* restaurant is on site. Breakfast included. **€350**

Palazzo Brunamonti Corso G. Matteotti 79 ☎0742 361 932, ⓦbrunamonti.com. A sumptuous, central aristocratic palace from the seventeenth century, with period fittings, beamed ceilings and *trompe l'oeil* decorations. The palatial rooms have a/c and wi-fi. Usually closed Jan & Feb. **€80**

Pian di Boccio Località Pian di Boccio 10 ☎0742 360 164, ⓦpiandiboccio.com. Some 3km southwest of the village, this pleasant agriturismo has a pool, nine rustic apartments with kitchens, a pizzeria and plenty to keep kids entertained, as well as campsites. Camping **€7.50** per person, __€6__ per tent, double rooms **€40**, two-person apartments **€90**

EATING

★ **Onofri** Piazza Onofri 1 ☎0742 361 926, ⓦenotecaonofri.it. This restaurant-cum-*enoteca* offers delicious meals based on traditional dishes executed with a slight twist; desserts are usually excellent (try the chocolate soufflé). A full meal will cost about €60 for two, depending on which of the four hundred wines you choose. Tues–Sun 1–4.30pm & 7–10.45pm.

★ **Redibus** Via Dante Alighieri 1 ☎0742 360 130, ⓦredibis.it. This wonderful in-hotel restaurant boasts an extraordinary setting, partly built into the remains of the Roman theatre. The tasting menu goes for €45, and there's a vegetarian menu for €38; a full meal à la carte may run about €65 per person, not including wine. All pastas are handmade, and there's a full range of meat dishes including chicken Marengo, pork and veal. Mon & Wed–Sun 1–4pm & 7.30–10pm; closed Jan–mid-Feb.

Around Bevagna

With your own transport, you can explore the rich agricultural plain surrounding Bevagna. The most rewarding trip follows the minor road northwest towards **Cannara**. Some 2km out is the pretty, restored **Convento dell'Annunziata**, followed by the one-horse hamlet of **Cantalupo** and the tiny stone chapel of Madonna della Pia. Take a minor left turn 1km beyond and you hit **Limigiano**, a classic fortified hamlet centred on a thirteenth-century church, San Michele. At the crossroads for Cannara, a left turn leads to **Collemancio**, where 500m north of the village's public gardens are the unexcavated ruins of **Urbinum Hortense**, a Roman or possibly Etruscan settlement destroyed by Totila in 545. The odds and ends – traces of a temple, pavement and mosaics – merit a wander, while the views over the Vale of Spoleto are superb.

Cannara

CANNARA, stranded mid-plain but sheltered by trees, has three churches, each with significant paintings by major Umbrian artists: **San Giovanni** sports frescoes by Lo Spagna, while **San Matteo** and **San Francesco** have works by Niccolò Alunno. The Palazzo Comunale in Piazza Umberto I houses a small **gallery** with frescoes detached from local churches and archeological finds from Urbinium.

Montefalco

MONTEFALCO – "the Falcon's Mount" – commands the Vale of Spoleto. The local tag of *la ringhiera dell'Umbria* ("the balcony of Umbria") may be a touch hyperbolic, but the views are nonetheless majestic and within the modern suburbs lies one of the finest hill-towns in the area, a maze of tiny, cobbled streets, with an artistic heritage – including pictures by Perugino and a stunning Gozzoli fresco cycle – out of all proportion to its size. Montefalco's chief attraction, the ex-church of **San Francesco**, now the civic museum, is a stone's throw from **Piazza del Comune**, the main square, while the rest of the town is little more than five-minutes' walk from end to end. The only outlying site, **San Fortunato**, is about fifteen-minutes' walk away, the stroll relieved by the comprehensively frescoed church of **Sant'Illuminata** en route.

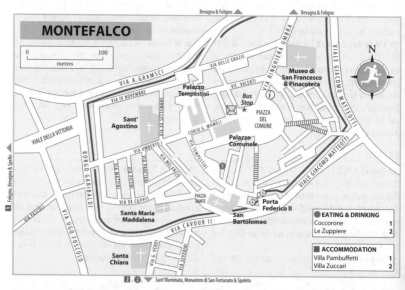

Brief history

The town was the birthplace of eight saints, good going even by Italian standards, and began life as a small independent medieval *comune* known as Coccorone. It was destroyed by **Frederick II** in 1249, his only legacy a gate named in his honour, after which Montefalco took its new name, supposedly inspired by the imperial eagle of Frederick's crest. Its chief historical interest lies in a brief interlude in the fourteenth century, when the town became a refuge to Spoleto's papal governors, left vulnerable by the defection of the popes to Avignon. Their munificent presence resulted in the rich decoration of local churches and the commissioning of **Lorenzo Maitani**, who was later to work on the Duomo in Orvieto, to strengthen the town walls (still impressively intact) and to build a fortress for the exiled rulers. Power thereafter devolved to Foligno's Trinci family, to the rapacious Baglioni and eventually to the Church – a cue for several centuries of quiet decline.

Museo Civico di San Francesco and the Pinacoteca

11

Via Ringhiera Umbra 6 • March–May & Sept–Oct daily 10.30am–1pm & 2–6pm; June–Aug daily 10.30am–1pm & 3–7pm, until 7.30pm in Aug; Nov–Feb Tues–Sun 10.30am–1pm & 2.30–5pm • €5 • ☎ 0742 379 598, ⓦ montefalcodoc.it

Set in the cavernous fourteenth-century church of San Francesco, the **Museo Civico** hosts one of the great Renaissance fresco cycles, a series of panels on the *Life of St Francis* (1452) by **Benozzo Gozzoli**, a pupil of Fra' Angelico. His delightful cycle – which duplicates in its subjects many of Giotto's panels in Assisi – is bold in its colouring and utterly assured of its narrative, and is also of interest for its closely observed townscapes: Arezzo is depicted, as is Montefalco (visited by St Francis after his sermon to the birds). The panels completely fill the apse, with twenty medallions around them depicting famous Franciscans; underneath the main window appear Petrarch, Dante and Giotto, members of the lay tertiary order. Further work by Gozzoli fills the walls and vaults to the right, as well as the first chapel on the left (south) side of the church. The striking but cruder frescoes in the fourth, fifth and sixth chapels on this side are the work of the fifteenth-century Foligno artist Giovanni di Corraduccio.

The Pinacoteca

Elsewhere are paintings by many of the leading lights of the Umbrian Renaissance, such as **Perugino**, **Niccolò Alunno** and Tiberio d'Assisi. Perugino's *Nativity* (1503) on the west wall, in particular, is worth looking out for, as Lago Trasimeno is featured in the background. Works originally commissioned for San Francesco remain *in situ*, with others housed in the excellent **Pinacoteca** up the stairs. Look out for Francesco Melanzio's *Madonna Enthroned with Six Saints*, the work of a local Renaissance painter, and for the two panels – one by Melanzio – showing the *Madonna del Soccorso*. The story, common in Umbria though rarely painted elsewhere, concerns a young mother who, tired of her whingeing child, cries, "Would that the Devil might take you away!", whereupon the Devil appears, prompting the mother to invoke the Virgin to save her infant.

Sant'Agostino

Via Verdi 23 • Daily 8.30am–1pm & 3–6pm • Free

The Augustinians' monastery and church of **Sant'Agostino** is a simple Gothic hall, begun in 1275, and is typical of the order, designed with a view to minimizing the fripperies and maximizing the preaching space. It has a few excellent frescoes that have survived the damp – including a *Coronation of the Virgin* by Caporali (1522) – but its main interest, lending a distinctly spooky air, lies in its collection of **mummies**. Midway down

11

SAGRANTINO WINES AND VINEYARDS

Montefalco's **wines** have always been prized within Umbria, but now enjoy wider fame, too. Their reputation rests not on the serviceable Rosso di Montefalco but on two powerful reds of mysterious origin, the extraordinary **Sagrantino** and **Sagrantino Passito**, both made from the Sagrantino grape, a variety found nowhere else in Europe. Why it should be unique to a tiny area of central Italy is a mystery: it appears in records in the nineteenth century, but experts claim a far more ancient pedigree, some saying it was imported by the Saracens, others that it was introduced by Syrian monks in the seventh century, or perhaps came from Piedmont or Catalonia. Its name may derive from its sacramental use by Franciscan communities who used to cultivate this grape.

Sagrantino is a dry red, usually made with up to five percent of the common Trebbiano Toscano. Sagrantino Passito is similar, with the important difference that it uses semi-dried or passito grapes to produce that rarest of drinks – a sweet red dessert wine. According to Italian wine guru Burton Anderson, both varieties have a remarkable "dark purple-garnet colour; rich, berry-like scent; and warm, rich full flavour". The *alimentari* and bar-*enoteche* in Montefalco's Piazza del Comune carry a superb selection of both.

SAGRANTINO VINEYARDS

There are numerous small producers, with **Adanti** being reliable leading exponents of both Sagrantino varieties. Any of the many producers in the tiny DOC area, however, should come up trumps, especially **Caprai** at Torre di Montefalco (☎0742 378 802, ⓦarnaldocaprai.it) and **Paolo Bea** at Cerrette (☎0742 378 128, ⓦpaolobea.com). **Antonelli**, **Benincasa** and **Rocca di Fabbri** are also first-rate. Most vineyards are open to the public (Caprai usually daily in summer, Paolo Bea and others more restricted opening).

---

the right nave are the first of these – the tiny bodies of **Beata Illuminata** and **Beata Chiarella**, clad in dusty muslin which only half hides their bones, skin and yellow faces.

At the top of the left-hand side of the church is another dusty cadaver, propped on one elbow and looking very comfortable in a glass-fronted wardrobe. Known as the **Beato Pellegrino** (Holy Pilgrim), he apparently came to venerate Illuminata and Chiarella, fell asleep in the church in the position he's in now, and was found dead next morning against a confessional. Immediately placed in a sepulchre, he was found outside it the next day, and refused to stay put on several subsequent occasions. His body and clothes didn't decay for a hundred years. Despite this impressive behaviour, nothing was known of his character, so there was no sainthood, and he was plonked for posterity in his wardrobe.

Santa Chiara

Via Verdi 23 • Daily 8.30am–1pm & 3–6pm • Free

In the church of **Santa Chiara**, the wizened body of St Clare of Montefalco languishes in a transparent casket high up on the altar. The saint – not to be confused with her more famous namesake at Assisi – was born in Montefalco in 1290, became a nun at the age of 6 and embarked on a series of miracles connected with the Passion of Christ. There's a small fresco cycle on her life in a chapel inside the convent (ring the bell on the door to the right of the casket and ask one of the nuns to unlock it). The nuns might also show you around the rest of the adjoining **convent**. On show is a small Crucifix enshrining three of the saint's gallstones (representing the Trinity) as well as the remains of her heart and the scissors with which the relic was hacked out of her, all of which are kept in a cupboard under her body – shared by the main church and this private chapel. The story relates that Christ appeared to Clare, saying the burden of the Cross was becoming too heavy; the saint replied she would help by carrying it within, and when she was opened up a cross-shaped piece of tissue was duly found on her heart.

VINEYARDS AROUND MONTEFALCO >

Other sights here include a miraculous tree that grew from a staff planted by Christ, who appeared again to Clare in the shrubbery. The nuns believe it to be the sole wild specimen of its species in all of Europe; the berries are used to make rosaries, and are said to have powerful medicinal properties.

Sant'Illuminata

Via Verdi 23 • Daily 8.30am–1pm & 3–6pm • Free

Down Via Verdi from Santa Chiara is the tiny church of **Sant'Illuminata**, worth a visit for its triple-arched Renaissance portico and comprehensively frescoed interior. The standard of painting isn't always high – most works are by the obscure local man Melanzio – but the overall effect is captivating.

Monastero di San Fortunato

Daily 8.30am–noon & 4–6pm • Free

Head 2km south out of town past Sant'Illuminata, down the avenue of horse chestnuts, then turn left at the T-junction, and a ten-minute trudge brings you out at the **Monastero di San Fortunato** set among ilex woods, the site home to a church since the fifth century. It has noted frescoes on the *Life of St Francis* (1512) by Tiberio d'Assisi – one of Perugino's leading disciples – in its Cappella delle Rose, to the left of the main courtyard. Gozzoli painted the very faded *Madonna and Child with Angels* over the door of the main church (the *St Sebastian* is by Tiberio), the dark fresco of St Fortunatus inside on the left altar and the three worn *tondi* on the sarcophagus of St Severus in the little chapel off the right aisle.

ARRIVAL AND INFORMATION   MONTEFALCO

By bus The bus stop is in the main square, Piazza del Comune. Destinations Bevagna (4–5 daily Mon–Sat; 20–40min); Foligno (3–5 daily Mon–Sat; 30min); Perugia (1–3 daily Mon–Sat; 1hr).

Tourist office Via Ringhiera Umbra (Mon–Fri 11am–1pm & 2–6pm; ☎0742 847 570, ⓦ promontefalco.com).

ACCOMMODATION

Villa Pambuffetti Via Vittoria 3 ☎0742 379 417, ⓦ villapambuffetti.com. This centuries-old villa hotel is a marvellous period piece, set in an oak park and with a swimming pool. Make sure you're in the main villa, not the gatehouse, which can feel cramped; the best (and most expensive) room is the one in the old tower, with a 360-degree view of the valley. The restaurant and wine cellar are also good, the dining room a lovely glass-enclosed space with views onto the garden. Breakfast and wi-fi included. **€180**

★ **Villa Zuccari** Località San Luca ☎0742 399 402, ⓦ villazuccari.com. A divine rural hotel, 8km southeast of town at the fringe of the hills adjoining the valley floor. The Zuccari family has lived here for some four hundred years, though most of the present villa, now superbly restored, dates from the eighteenth and nineteenth centuries. Rooms have balconies and delightful period furniture, and there's a fine Italianate garden with a pool, as well as an excellent restaurant (see below). Buffet breakfast included. **€150**

EATING AND DRINKING

★ **Coccorone** Largo Tempestivi ☎0742 379 535, ⓦ coccorone.com. An elegant setting in a medieval building with a garden terrace, and great pasta and *crespelli* (rolled pancakes), gigantic steaks (for two) and superlative tiramisù. To find it, follow the off-putting yellow signs for the "Tipical Ristorant". Full meals start at about €40 per person, excluding wine. Daily 1.30–4pm & 7.30–10pm; Oct to Easter closed Wed.

★ **Le Zuppiere** Località San Luca ☎0742 399 402, ⓦ villazuccari.com. The restaurant of the *Villa Zuccari* hotel is as outstanding as the resort, with tables in the elegant interior or in a flower-filled outdoor setting. They do a wonderful black truffle omelette (€10) or lamb chops grilled with rosemary (€13), while home-made *gnocchi* with truffle, their speciality, goes for €17; add truffle shavings to any dish for €6 extra. Daily 1–4.30pm & 7–10.30pm.

Trevi and around

From afar, **TREVI** looks merely enticing, but at closer range it has the most stupendous appearance of any town in Umbria, its medieval houses perched on a pyramidal hill and encircled by miles of olive groves renowned for producing central Italy's finest oil. Its daunting inaccessibility is one of the reasons for its easygoing, old-fashioned charm. As with most Umbrian hill-towns, Trevi's chief pleasure lies in tramping the medieval streets, which are obsessively well kept and characterized by complicated patterns of cobblestones. Ancient Roman fragments are embedded in the inner of two sets of medieval **walls**, raised when Trevi paraded as a minor independent *comune*.

The town's name, incidentally, has no relation to Rome's celebrated Trevi Fountain, other than the fact that it derives, like that of the fountain, from the fact that three roads, or *tre vie*, met here.

Pinacoteca Comunale

Largo Don Bosco • June–Aug Tues–Sun 10.30am–1pm & 3.30–7pm, until 7.30pm in Aug; April, May & Sept Tues–Sun 10.30am–1pm & 2.30–6pm; Oct–March Fri, Sat & Sun 10.30am–1pm & 2.30–5pm • €4 • ☎ 0742 332 222

Trevi's key sight is the modern **Pinacoteca Comunale**, or **Raccolta d'Arte di San Francisco**, in the former Convento di San Francesco, where St Francis's preaching was once interrupted by the braying of an "indomitable ass". It houses a well-presented display of coins, ceramics and Roman fragments, several paintings by Umbrian masters and one outstanding work, a *Coronation of the Virgin* (1522) by Lo Spagna, removed from the church of San Martino; it was commissioned by Trevi's medieval governors as a copy of a more famous work by the Florentine Ghirlandaio, mainly because they couldn't afford the real thing. Also look out for *Scenes from the Life of Christ* by Giovanni di Corraduccio, a fifteenth-century painter from Foligno whose frescoes are on display in Montefalco's San Francesco.

Sant'Emiliano

Via Placido Riccardi • Daily 8.30am–1pm & 4–6pm • Free

The highest point of the town is **Sant'Emiliano**, comely twelfth-century Romanesque on the outside, Baroque horror-show within. Emilianus was an Armenian missionary

11

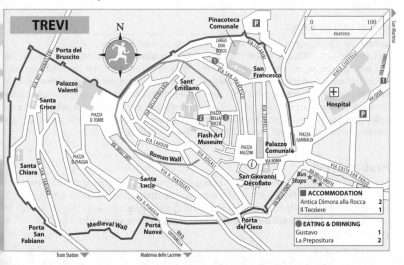

and bishop of the town cut off in his prime in 302: his feast day (Jan 27) is celebrated by a procession. The only early survivors of the butchery of the building are a captivating *Altar of the Sacrament* (1522) in the second chapel on the left and frescoes by Melanzio, who was active in many villages hereabouts (notably Montefalco) at the start of the sixteenth century.

San Martino

Viale Augusto Ciuffelli • 8.30am–1pm & 4–6pm • Free

A stroll from the central Piazza Garibaldi, following the tree-lined Viale Ciuffelli, offers a superb view of the valley and after ten minutes brings you to the church of **San Martino**, site of Trevi's original parish church. It has a lunette above the door by Tiberio d'Assisi plus two pictures in the tabernacles on either side of the presbytery, *St Martin Dividing his Cloak with Beggar* by Tiberio, and a fifteenth-century *Madonna and Child with St Francis and St Antony of Padua* by Mezzastris, a local painter. In the Cappella di San Girolamo, to the left of the church, is an *Assumption and Saints* (1512) by Lo Spagna, another Spoletan artist, and *St Emilianus* by Tiberio d'Assisi.

ARRIVAL AND INFORMATION

TREVI

By train The train station is 4km southwest of town. Buses make the steep uphill run, but there are only 2–5 per day. Destinations Perugia (hourly; 1hr); Spello (6 daily; 13–28min); Spoleto (hourly; 10–15min).

By bus Buses arrive and depart from Via Delle Grotte, 200m southeast of the centre.

Destination Foligno (4 daily Mon–Sat; 23min).

Tourist office The Pro Loco office at Piazza Mazzini 6 (daily 9am–1pm & 3.30–6/7pm; ☎0742 781 150, ⓦwww.protrevi.com) is volunteer-run, and hours can be erratic.

ACCOMMODATION

Antica Dimora alla Rocca Piazza della Rocca 1 ☎0742 38 541, ⓦhotelallarocca.it. Set in a sixteenth-century *palazzo*, with rooms that vary wildly, so choose wisely: some refurbishing is needed. Still, it's smart in a shabby-chic way, and there's internet, a/c, a pool and an excellent restaurant. Buffet breakfast included. **€75**

Il Terziere Via Coste 1 ☎0742 78 359, ⓦilterziere

.com. Just northeast of the town walls, this modern hotel-restaurant sits on a hill with panoramic views and features a pleasant garden and pool. Country-elegant in style, the a/c rooms are spacious and well appointed; some have balconies with views over the Umbrian landscape. Breakfast included. **€100**

EATING AND DRINKING

Gustavo Via San Francesco 22a ☎0742 78 545, ⓦgustavogustavino.it. With a chic, romantic atmosphere, this restaurant-cum-*enoteca* offers an extraordinary selection of Umbria's (and Italy's) top wines as well as wonderful local dishes. The tasting menu, which varies according to season and the day's market, goes for €25 and might include *gnocchi* with *radicchio*, walnuts and crispy *guanciale* (bacon made with pigs' cheeks) Tues–Sun

1.30–3.30pm & 7.30–10pm.

La Prepositura Vicolo Oscura 2 ☎0742 38 541, ⓦristorantelaprepositura.com. This in-hotel restaurant has tables in medieval vaulted rooms and terrace dining in the evenings. The cuisine is generally excellent, specializing in truffles, and you start with complimentary prosecco and great bread. Full meals are €25–40 per person. Daily 1–4pm & 7–10pm; hours can vary.

Around Trevi

South of Trevi, the Vale of Spoleto becomes increasingly pockmarked with new houses and small factories. It's all the more unexpected, then, to come across the sacred **Fonti del Clitunno**, a series of beautiful springs revered since Roman times, and the nearby **Tempietto del Clitunno**, looking for all the world like a perfect ancient temple.

Fonti del Clitunno

Via Flaminia 7 • Daily: early March 9am–1pm & 2–6pm; late March 9am–1pm & 2–6.30pm; early April 9am–7.30pm; late April 9am–8pm; May–Aug 8.30am–8pm; early Sept 8.30am–7.30pm; late Sept 9am–7.30pm; Oct 9am–1pm & 2–6pm; Nov–Feb 10am–1pm & 2–4.30pm • €3 • ☎ 0743 521 141, ⓦ fontidelclitunno.it

Some 5km southwest of Trevi, the **Fonti del Clitunno**, originally dedicated to the oracular god Clitunnus, have inspired poets since ancient times. The springs were also used as a party venue by the likes of Caligula and Claudius, even though the major curative effect of these waters is allegedly that of removing any appetite for alcohol. Earthquakes over the ensuing years have upset many of the underground sources, so the waters aren't as plentiful as they once were, but they still flow as limpid as they did when Byron extolled "the sweetest wave of the most living crystal...the purest god of gentle waters".

There's some commercial fuss around the entrance, including a good restaurant (see below), but the springs, streams and willow-shaded lake beyond are languidly romantic, though the occasional coach party can be an intrusion, especially on weekends, as is the proximity of the road, with its roaring trucks and buses.

11

Tempietto del Clitunno

Opening days change weekly, but always open Thurs, Fri & Sat,10.15am–7.15pm • €2

A few hundred metres north of the Fonti, and easily missed, is the so-called **Tempietto del Clitunno**, accessible only from the road (not directly from the springs). It looks like a miniature classical temple, but is actually an eighth-century Christian church cobbled together with columns from the ruins of Roman temples and villas, all long vanished. Until recently, scholars were fooled into thinking it a genuine piece of Roman antiquity, though Goethe was one notable dissenter from the party line. The track that runs below the facade is the remains of the original Via Flaminia. The entrance is to the side (if it's shut, try ringing the bell on the gate); inside are some faded Byzantine frescoes, dated to the eighth century and said to be the oldest in Umbria, representing Christ, St Peter and St Paul.

EATING AND DRINKING   **FONTI DEL CLITUNNO**

Fonti del Clitunno Via Flaminia 7 ☎ 0743 275 057, ⓦ fontidelclitunno.it. Along with a bar, the Fonti also has a restaurant with views over the gardens. Antipasti include spelt and shrimp salad (€7), while the menu is dominated by seafood: pasta dishes feature *tagliolini* with scampi and courgettes (€12), and mains such as grilled swordfish average about €12. There's a good wine list, too. Daily 1–3.30pm & 7–10pm; closed for ten days in Jan.

Spoleto and the Valnerina

PRECI

Spoleto and the Valnerina

Eastern Umbria is the most enjoyable part of the region in terms of its landscapes, offering superb walking and car or cycle touring amid some of the wildest scenery in central Italy. Its main city and transport hub, Spoleto, is one of Umbria's more stimulating bases, its many Romanesque churches and other monuments and cultural events making it an essential feature of any itinerary.

The walking and scenery are at their best in the east of the region, where the spectacular **Monti Sibillini** look down over the **Piano Grande**, a breathtaking highland plain which in spring becomes an expanse of wild flowers. There is sporadic public transport access to these areas from Spoleto and **Norcia**, a friendly town and the earthquake-prone birthplace of St Benedict, founder of Western monasticism. Equally beautiful, and a little easier to reach, are the villages of the **Valnerina**, an upland valley enclosed by mountains that arc through the region east of Spoleto. Much of the Sibillini and the upper reaches of the Valnerina are best seen using Norcia as a base.

GETTING AROUND

12

Spoleto Access to Spoleto is straightforward, as the town lies on the Rome–Ancona train line, with links to Terni and Narni to the south, and Foligno, Assisi and Perugia to the north.

The Valnerina Buses provide links for the main villages of the Valnerina, but not for the trailheads of the Mont Sibillini and Piano Grande; to get the most from the countryside you really need your own transport.

Spoleto

"The most romantic city I ever saw," said Percy Bysshe Shelley of **SPOLETO**, a place that would demand a visit with or without its famous summer **Spoleto Festival dei Due Mondi**, a cultural jamboree with considerable international kudos. One of the most graceful of all Italian hill-towns, Spoleto maintains a bustling life of its own, a seductively medieval appearance and a superb assembly of museums and Romanesque monuments. Its major architectural attractions are in the medieval **Upper Town**, though the largely modern **Lower Town** also boasts three major Romanesque churches. The whole is relatively compact and getting around is easy enough on foot – though you don't want to be trudging between the Upper and Lower towns too often in the summer heat. Road and transport links make Spoleto a natural base for exploring: even Assisi is an easy day-trip. The one drawback to the place is its popularity; hotels are relatively thin on the ground and, during the festival, accommodation is tight and prices are inflated.

Brief history

Of Bronze Age origin, the city was an important Umbrian centre, the vast gorge-surrounded crag at its heart an obvious point of strategic importance. Its ancient grandeur is attested to by a series of well-preserved **Roman walls**. Cicero described

PIAZZA DEL DUOMO, SPOLETO

Highlights

❶ San Salvatore, Spoleto The best of Spoleto's many fine Romanesque churches. See p.475

❷ Duomo, Spoleto The region's prettiest cathedral, celebrated for its facade and Fra' Lippo Lippi frescoes. **See p.478**

❸ Ponte delle Torri, Spoleto An awe-inspiring medieval aqueduct and bridge with spectacular views. **See p.482**

❹ The Valnerina A verdant, mountain-edged valley dotted with hill–villages and spectacular views. **See p.485**

❺ Abbazia San Pietro in Valle Umbria's loveliest abbey, in a beautiful location, with works of art dating from the eighth century. See p.488

❻ Norcia Mountain town renowned for its ham, cheese, truffles and other gastronomic treats. See p.491

❼ Piano Grande Glorious upland plain, centrepiece of the magnificent Monti Sibillini national park. **See p.496**

❽ Mountain drives The journey between Sant'Anatolia, Monteleone and Cascia is one of Umbria's most exhilarating and picturesque drives. **See p.486**

HIGHLIGHTS ARE MARKED ON THE MAP ON P.474

Spoletium, founded in 241 BC, as Rome's most renowned colony, and it was strong enough to distract and turn away **Hannibal** in 217 BC after his victory at Trasimeno (see p.417) – had it not, history might have been very different, as the Carthaginian general was forced into the Marche when a defenceless Rome lay at his mercy. Strategically sited between Rome and Ravenna, Spoleto prospered while the focus of the Western Empire shifted from one to the other, though its real prominence came after 576 when it was established first as a **Lombard** and later as a **Frankish** dukedom. The autonomous **Duchy of Spoleto** eventually stretched to Benevento near Naples, dominating most of central Italy.

During the emergence of the city states it became "the magnificent city, defended by a hundred towers". Its fall from grace came in the shape of **Barbarossa**, who flattened the city in 1155 during an Italian sojourn to restore his imperial authority. This cleared the way for rebuilding, rapid growth and the powerful re-emergence of a quasi-democratic regime (already in existence before 1155) that saw Spoleto at the height of its powers during much of the thirteenth century. Decline and deliverance into the hands of the Church followed a century later, and thereafter, Spoleto fell into obscurity until the arrival of Giancarlo Menotti's performing arts festival some sixty years ago (see box, opposite).

The Lower Town

Spoleto's cultural credentials are immediately established by a rather grotesque monumental **sculpture** by Alexander Calder outside the train station. A relic of the 1962 festival, it serves as a gateway to the **Lower Town**, a quarter much rebuilt after

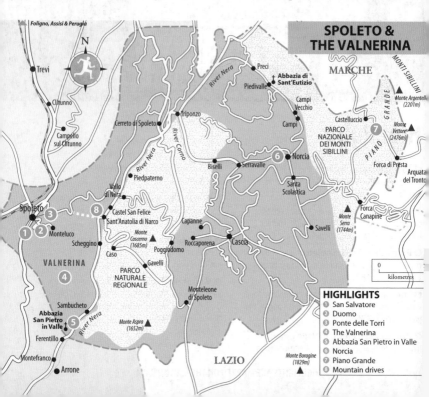

HIGHLIGHTS
1. San Salvatore
2. Duomo
3. Ponte delle Torri
4. The Valnerina
5. Abbazia San Pietro in Valle
6. Norcia
7. Piano Grande
8. Mountain drives

THE SPOLETO FESTIVAL

Long established as Italy's leading international arts festival, the Festival dei Due Mondi (Festival of the Two Worlds), now renamed as the **Spoleto Festival** (Ⓦfestivaldispoleto.com) was first staged here in 1958, when composer **Gian Carlo Menotti** and his advisers chose the town over thirty other contenders on account of its small venues, outstanding scenery and an artistic, historical and cultural heritage almost without equal. Menotti's original dream was to combine the best of young Italian and American talent (hence the "Two Worlds" tag), an idea which eventually saw the birth of a sister event in Charleston, South Carolina. Melbourne, Australia, also came on board, albeit in a half-hearted way, to make it an unofficial Festival of the Three Worlds. After Menotti's death in 2007, disputes between his successors and the town resulted in the new name, but the festival's high standards have been maintained.

Performances take place in June and July, and **tickets** range from €13 to €120. The **box office** is at Piazza della Libertà 10 (Mon–Fri 9am–1pm & 4–8pm; ☎0743 776 444, ☎0743 212 889 or ☎0743 47 967).

Allies inflicted bomb damage in the last war. The area does offer a trio of outstanding **Romanesque churches**, however, as well as a handful of **Roman remains**. If these don't appeal, catch the city bus from the station to Piazza della Libertà, up into the old town, tempting from this vantage with its skyline of spires and tiled roofs and splashes of craggy countryside; the fifteen-minute walk is reasonably enjoyable too, once you're beyond the concrete of Viale Trento e Trieste. Head up Corso Garibaldi from Piazza Garibaldi for the most direct approach on foot.

San Salvatore

Piazza Salmi 1 • Daily: March, April, Sept & Oct 7am–6pm; May–Aug 7am–7pm; Nov–Feb closes 7am–5pm • Free

One of Italy's oldest churches, **San Salvatore** lies on the edge of the Lower Town, half-hidden in the cemetery, a faintly bizarre attraction in its own right. Little has changed in the church since it was built by monks from the eastern Mediterranean in the fourth or fifth century, on a site probably chosen for its proximity to Christian and Neolithic catacombs. Most of the decoration and building materials are Roman and it was conceived when the only models for religious buildings were Roman temples. Not surprisingly, the end result has a distinctly pagan feel, the church's **interior** evoking an almost eerie antiquity. The walls are bare, the floors covered in fallen stone, the crumbling Corinthian columns are wedged awkwardly alongside one another and the arches in the nave have been filled in to prevent total collapse. The apse, ringed round with Roman friezes and capitals, is a later addition that gives the church's upper half a crowded and lopsided appearance.

San Ponziano

Via della Basilica San Salvatore 2• Usually open daily 8.30am–5.30pm; otherwise ask to be let in at the adjacent monastery • Free

Just a couple of minutes' away is twelfth-century **San Ponziano**, dedicated to Spoleto's patron saint. Its Romanesque frontage promises much but delivers little inside. An admiring glance is all the place merits, though the **tenth-century crypt** inside is a fascinating structure of odd, triangular columns believed to be *metae* (turning posts) from a Roman *circo* (race-track), backed by well-preserved patches of Byzantine fresco.

San Gregorio Maggiore

Piazza Garibaldi 34 • Daily 8am–noon & 4–6pm • Free

San Gregorio Maggiore dates from 1069, its narrow, porticoed **facade** a patchwork of fragments filched from Roman remains. The pragmatic mix of materials is most obvious in the tower, its lower half built of massive Roman blocks, the upper of more refined fifteenth-century workmanship. The similarly patchworked portico was a sixteenth-century afterthought, added when the church was heightened to

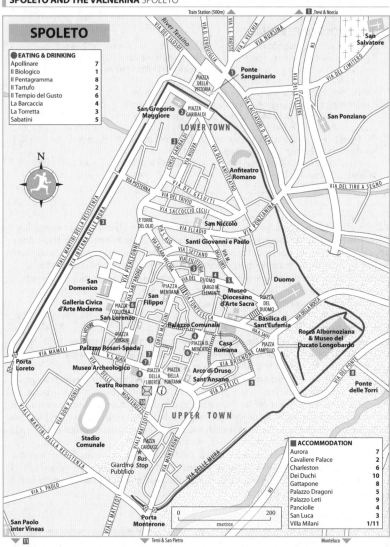

SPOLETO

EATING & DRINKING

Apollinare	7
Il Biologico	1
Il Pentagramma	8
Il Tartufo	2
Il Tempio del Gusto	6
La Barcaccia	4
La Torretta	3
Sabatini	5

ACCOMMODATION

Aurora	7
Cavaliere Palace	2
Charleston	6
Dei Duchi	10
Gattapone	8
Palazzo Dragoni	5
Palazzo Leti	9
Panciolle	4
San Luca	3
Villa Milani	1/11

imitate the Duomo in the Upper Town. The **interior** commands most interest,
its walls stripped back to their Romanesque state, with substantial frescoes
interrupted by a series of intimidating stone confessionals. The frescoes are local
fourteenth-century efforts, the best of them in the presbytery, which is raised several
metres above the nave, allowing for a **crypt** supported by dozens of tiny,
mismatched pillars.

Anfiteatro Romano

Via dell'Anfiteatro • Daily 8.30am–7.30pm • €4, includes Archeological Museum • ☎ 0743 223 277

The rudimentary remains of the **Anfiteatro Romano** lie in the barracks on Via
dell'Anfiteatro. When the Romans passed on, the huge arena was almost completely
cannibalized for its stone, first by Totila and then by Cardinal Albornoz for the castle in

the Upper Town. What remained was adapted as a medieval shopping arcade, and later bricked up in the courtyard you see today.

The ever-ingenious Romans constructed special gutters to drain blood from the arena into the Tessino River, which ran crimson as a result. The liberal flow of Christian blood is said to have inspired the name for the Roman **Ponte Sanguinario**, now under nearby Piazza Garibaldi. It formed part of the improvements to the Via Flaminia ordered by the Emperor Augustus, remaining in use until the fourteenth century, and rediscovered in 1817.

The Upper Town

The first place to head in the **Upper Town** is **Piazza della Libertà**, the terminus for local and inter-town buses and home to the tourist office. Orientation is difficult in the jumble of levels and twisting, narrow streets around, though everything worthwhile is a short walk from here. Shops, banks and services are mostly concentrated in **Corso Mazzini**, which runs north from the square, and in **Corso Garibaldi**, which drops down to Piazza Garibaldi. Corso Mazzini is the scene of a rumbustious passeggiata, Sunday's walk being a particularly fine spectacle, but for the day-to-day social heart of the town you need to make for **Piazza del Mercato**, site of the ancient Roman forum. Continuing on, there's the magnificent **Duomo**, renowned **Sant'Eufemia** and its adjacent **Museo Diocesano**.

Piazza della Libertà

For an introduction to Spoleto's Roman heritage, you only have to cross **Piazza della Libertà** from the tourist office. Here you can look through the railings at the much-restored first-century **Roman theatre**, excavated in 1891 and now used for summer performances. Its past includes a grisly episode in 1319 when four hundred Guelph supporters were rounded up by the Spoletans and dumped on the stage with their throats cut; the corpses were then pushed into a pile and burnt. Today it's overshadowed by the buildings on all sides, notably the deconstructed church and convent of **Sant'Agata**, which in the Middle Ages absorbed much of the ancient stage area, the theatre having been damaged and half-buried over the centuries by landslips. Part of the conventual buildings now house the **archeological museum**.

Museo Archeologico

Via Sant'Agata • Daily 8.30am–7.30pm • €4, includes Roman Theatre • ☎ 0743 223 277

Entered through the extraordinary vaulted tunnel beneath the tiered seats of the Roman theatre, the **Museo Archeologico**'s two first rooms display a superb shield, rings and other fragments from a Bronze Age tomb discovered in Piazza d'Armi. Next door to the right is a longer room, graced with a fine fresco, the *Last Supper*, and a well-presented gallery of Roman portrait busts and miscellaneous statuary. A small annex at the end is devoted to the remarkable Lex Spoletina, a pair of tawny-brown Roman stone inscriptions that forbade the felling of trees in the sacred woods of Monteluco.

Piazza del Mercato

Nowhere do you get a better sense of Spoleto's market-town roots than in the cosy **Piazza del Mercato**, home to the town's bustling market (Mon–Sat 8.30am–1pm). Women wash fruit and vegetables in the striking 1746 fountain (its crown embellished with an attractive clock), men drink in the bars and swap gossip, while visitors browse the food shops. The left-hand crest of the coat of arms atop the fountain monument, built by Carlo Maderno in 1626 for Pope Urban VIII, features three bees, symbols of the Barberini, the Roman family from which Urban hailed.

Straddling the entrance to the square – which was the ancient forum – is the **Arco di Druso**, raised in 23 AD by the Spoletan senate to commemorate victories in Germany by Drusus, son of Tiberius and heir to the empire until his early death, courtesy of Caligula. The **walls** hereabouts, and in Via dei Felici, are the city's oldest, built in the sixth century BC by the mysterious Umbrians. Beside the arch is what's described as a **Roman temple and shop**, though you'll need a vivid imagination to see it as anything other than a ditch.

Sant'Ansano and Cripta di Sant'Isacco

Via Brignone • Daily: April–Oct 8am–12.30pm & 3–7pm; Nov–March 8am–12.30pm & 3–6pm • Free

Pop into the church of **Sant'Ansano** for the **Cripta di Sant'Isacco**, the latter entered down the stairs to the left of the high altar (where fragments of the Roman temple have been uncovered). As well as containing more persuasive chunks of the temple than lie outside, the crude stone walls are decorated with frescoes that may date from the sixth century, a time when it was home to refugee Christian monks. The main structure dates from the twelfth century.

The Duomo

Piazza del Duomo • Daily April–Oct 8.30am–12.30pm & 3.30–7pm; Nov–March 8.30am–12.30pm & 3.30–6pm • Free

It's a short walk from Piazza del Mercato to the **Duomo**, or Cattedrale di Santa Maria Assunta, whose restrained and elegant facade is one of the loveliest in Umbria. The careful balance of Romanesque and Renaissance elements is framed by a gently sloping piazza and hanging gardens, with the broad background of sky and open countryside setting the seal on the beautifully unified whole. The lovely, carving-swathed **portico**, an obvious addition, dates from 1491 and is flanked by two little external pulpits, one of which was used by the wandering St Bernardino of Siena to preach to the notoriously wayward Spoletans.

Brief history

The building was consecrated in 1198, having been commissioned by Pope Innocent III to replace a seventh-century church flattened by Barbarossa. The twelfth-century **campanile** (with fifteenth- and sixteenth-century additions) borrowed much of its stone from Roman ruins, a hotchpotch technique continued in the rest of the building. Architectural details unusual in Italy add interest for the technically minded, most notably the **flying buttresses** tucked out of sight on the side walls; climb to Piazza F. Campello to the right for the best view. Strange, too, are the eight rose windows, clustered around a restored thirteenth-century mosaic of *Christ, the Virgin and St John*.

Less successful transformations were commissioned for the interior, where Pope Urban VIII's architect, Luigi Arrigucci, applied great dollops of Baroque midway through the seventeenth century. Urban – named Maffeo Barberini – had been bishop of Spoleto before becoming pope: his impetus and the money of a nephew, another of the town's bishops, financed the works.

Cappella Eroli

On the first altar on the left, behind glass, stands a brightly restored Crucifix (1187) by Alberto Sotio, the earliest documented Umbrian painter. Walking across to the right-hand side of the church, look in on the **Cappella Eroli** (1497), named after the Spoletan bishop Costantino Eroli: it features Pinturicchio's faded but beautifully lyrical *Madonna and Child with the Baptist and St Stephen*, with a depiction of Lago Trasimeno in the background.

Cappella dell'Assunta

In the larger **Cappella dell'Assunta** adjoining to its right are cruder but nonetheless striking frescoes by the Sicilian Jacopo Santori: that on the left wall shows another Eroli bishop, Francesco, who commissioned the chapel at the beginning of the sixteenth century, kneeling before a separate inset painting of the *Madonna*. The wall to its right has frescoes of saints – *Michael the Archangel* (with sword) and *Lucy*, a popular Spoletan saint: further right, the wall is adorned with the Eroli family shields.

Cappella delle Reliquie

Back across the church is the **Cappella delle Reliquie**, entered at the top of the left aisle. Restored in 1993, it features impressive intarsia work, vivid painted panels that depict characters from the Old Testament, and some beautifully frescoed ceiling vaults. The vaults and panels are the work of Francesco Nardini, an otherwise little-known sixteenth-century painter. On the right is an outstanding fourteenth-century polychrome wooden statue, the *Madonna and Child*. To its right, behind glass in a gaudy blue-columned frame, is a fragmentary **letter** in Latin, written by St Francis to Fra' Leone, one of the saint's earliest and most besotted followers (he hoarded virtually every scrap and relic associated with Francis). It is one of only two letters written by the saint to have survived and was written after Francis received the stigmata at La Verna (see p.382), by which time he was virtually blind – hence the shaky handwriting. It salutes Leone and wishes him peace (the word *pacem* is clearly visible near the beginning), urging him to follow his own conscience in matters of faith rather than constantly coming to Francis for advice.

The rest of the cathedral

All other works of art in the cathedral are eclipsed by the building's original **marble floor**, and by magnificent **frescoes** on the *Life of the Virgin*, painted in 1467 by **Filippo Lippi** and his assistants Fra' Diamanti and Pier Matteo. The cycle fills the domed apse, starting from the left wall with *The Annunciation* and *The Assumption of the Virgin*, the latter with portraits of the three painters to the right: Lippi is the figure with the white monk's habit over a black tunic. It concludes with the *Nativity* (mostly by Matteo and Diamanti), while above spreads the most glittering scene of all, the *Coronation of the Virgin*. Note the columns and classical motifs separating the panels, many of which Lippi copied directly from old buildings around Spoleto, notably the church of San Salvatore in the Lower Town.

12

Basilica di Sant'Eufemia

Via Aurelio Saffi 13 • Mid-March to July & Sept–Oct Mon–Fri 10am–1pm & 3–6pm, Sat & Sun 10am–6pm; Aug daily 10am–6pm; Nov to mid-March Tues–Fri 10.30am–1pm & 3–5.30pm, Sat & Sun 11am–5pm • €3, includes Museo Diocesano • ⓦ arcidiocesidispoletonorcia.it

Spoleto's most celebrated church is the twelfth-century **Basilica di Sant'Eufemia**, above Piazza del Duomo; the entrance is easily missed, as the church lies inside a courtyard complex off the street. It was probably built in honour of a local bishop, **San Giovanni**, who was martyred by the Goths and reputedly buried here in 980, on a site within both the precincts of the old **Benedictine** monastery and the archbishop's palace. Excavations have revealed that it also lies over the **Lombards**' eighth-century ducal

---

THE LIPPI TOMB

The renowned Florentine painter **Filippo Lippi** died shortly after he completed the fresco cycle in Spoleto's Duomo, the rumour being that he was poisoned for seducing the daughter of a local noble family. The Spoletan cathedral authorities, not too bothered by such moral laxity, were delighted to have someone famous to put in their cathedral, being, as Vasari put it, "poorly provided with ... distinguished men". Thus they refused to send the dead artist back to Lorenzo de' Medici, his patron, who had loaned Filippo to Spoleto, reputedly to stop his Florentine philandering. Interred in a **tomb** designed by his son **Filippino Lippi**, the corpse disappeared during restoration two centuries later, spirited away, according to local legend, by descendants of the compromised girl. The empty tomb is on the left wall of the Duomo's right (south) transept.

palace, and Roman remains have been found, too. Good use was obviously made of materials from these previous buildings: one of the mismatched columns – that separating the first and second arches on the right – is carved with distinctive Lombard motifs. Many of the mismatched capitals, too, are clearly from an earlier building.

The interior

The church is unique in Umbria for its **matroneum**, a high-arched gallery above the aisles (reached from a tiny door at the beginning of the left aisle) that served the purpose of segregating the women of the congregation from the men. Rebuilding took place in the early part of the twelfth century, when northern Italian models were used as inspiration.

Today, Sant'Eufemia is redolent with age and dank solemnity, its walls bare but for the odd patch of **fresco**, notably a *St Lucy* (1455), complete with eyes in a bowl, on the second column on the right (the church was known as Santa Lucia for several centuries). The only other frills are a stone chair and simple but stunning **altar**, both brought from the Duomo in the thirteenth century.

Museo Diocesano d'Arte Sacra

Mid-March to July & Sept–Oct Mon–Fri 10am–1pm & 3–6pm, Sat & Sun 10am–6pm; Aug daily 10am–6pm; Nov to mid-March Tues–Fri 10.30am–1pm & 3–5.30pm, Sat & Sun 11am–5pm • €3, includes Basilica di Sant'Eufemia

The excellent **Museo Diocesano d'Arte Sacra** occupies the same courtyard as Sant'Eufemia, and displays a wealth of fascinating paintings and other artefacts culled from churches across the diocese. The displays were undergoing reorganization at the time of writing, but all the works by major artists should be displayed, though you will have to determine the location of each piece upon arrival. During your visit, don't miss the upper gallery, or matroneum, of Sant'Eufemia, offering a wonderful view of the church

The Filippino Lippi altarpiece

The gallery's single greatest pictorial work is a sublime freestanding *Madonna and Child with Sts Montano and Bartholomew* (1485) by **Filippino Lippi**. It's strange enough that Lippi, a Florentine, should have painted in Umbria, and stranger still that the painting should have been commissioned for Todiano, a now almost deserted village lost in the depths of the Valnerina (see p.491). The theory is that it was commissioned by a merchant who left the village and grew wealthy as a result of trade. Bartholomew and Montano are Todiano's patron saints, the latter best known for having tamed a bear and commanded it to take the place of an ox it had devoured. The little scene in the predella shows the bear alongside an ox pulling a plough. The parallel predella scene to the right shows St Bartholomew with his skin slung over his shoulder (the saint was flayed alive).

Beccafumi and di Bicci paintings

Also of great interest and importance is another premier painting, the *Adoration of the Child* by the Sienese Mannerist **Domenico Beccafumi**. **Neri di Bicci**'s *Madonna della Neve* (1464), meanwhile, is an excellent example of a relatively common theme, the *neve* (snow) referring to the miraculous fall of snow in Rome in August which is traditionally said to have marked out the site of the city's ancient Basilica di Santa Maria Maggiore. The painting's presence here is explained by the strong medieval trading links between Spoleto and Rome.

Other altar paintings

An interesting triptych of *Saints Sebastian and Catherine of Alexandria* is attributed to **Bartolomeo da Miranda**, active locally in the mid-fifteenth century. Sebastian was often invoked against plague, and this painting was probably a votive offering during an epidemic, a theory reinforced by the green of the Virgin's cloak (as opposed to the more usual blue), a colour symbolizing rebirth as well as being associated with Hope, one of the three Theological Virtues.

12

Seek out, too, a *Madonna and Child with Sts Sebastian and Leonardo*. **Sebastian**, unusually, is shown holding a clutch of arrows rather than being shot through with them, an allusion to the fact that he recovered from his ordeal by archery (he was martyred by being pummelled to death). St Leonard is rarely portrayed in central Italian art. Little is known of this sixth-century figure, other than that his faith persuaded King Clovis to grant him the right to release any prisoner he met. As a result he is the patron saint of prisoners, who would traditionally have made a votive offering of a shackle to the saint on their release – which is why he is shown in this painting holding a vast leg-iron.

More saintly mayhem is found in two triptychs featuring the tribulations of **St Lucy**. In one, she's depicted to the right of the work's central *Crucifixion*. The saint, a fourth-century martyr from Sicily, was much venerated in Spoleto and the Valnerina. She was killed for refusing to marry a high-ranking pagan Roman magistrate, the spurned official having her dragged behind two oxen and then boiled alive; on hearing that the magistrate had been captivated by the beauty of her eyes, Lucy is reputed to have torn them out and sent them to her tormentor (hence her usual depiction holding a dish containing a pair of eyes). In the other triptych, three episodes from Lucy's life make up the predella: giving to the poor; her denunciation in front of the governor of Syracuse; and her ordeal by oxen.

Ex-votos and related works

Also of interest are an exquisite little *Madonna and Child*, an anonymous Florentine work; and various detached frescoes, notably a *St Michael with the Devil*, with Satan just visible at the bottom trying to tilt the scales in which Michael is weighing the souls of sinners and the saved. Most entertaining of these works in limbo are numerous decorated **wooden tiles**, a series of ex-votos painted with often amusing cartoon-like depictions of sick-bed scenes and escapes from perilous (and not so perilous) episodes for which the tiles give thanks. These show events such as women being gored by bulls and a man hanging upside down from a tree and losing his hat, or a precipitous fall from a hayrick (the Virgin, as in other tiles, looks down from a cloud in the top left) and a cart falling from a bridge and hurling its inhabitants into a river.

Sculptural works

There are two important sculptural pieces by masters of the Baroque: the large bust of **Pope Urban VIII** by **Gianlorenzo Bernini**, which once adorned the cathedral, and a sculpture of St Filippo Neri attributed to **Algardi**.

Also worth a look is a series of wooden statues of the Madonna and Child, as well as an unusual and fascinating statue of Christ with movable arms: the arms were extended during processions on Good Friday to mark the Crucifixion, and lowered on Easter Sunday to celebrate the Resurrection.

Casa Romana

Via di Visiale • Daily: mid-March to mid-Oct 10am–8pm; mid-Oct to mid-March 10am–6pm, but may close 1–3pm • €2.50 • ☎ 0743 234 250

Entered from Via Aurelio Saffi, the **Casa Romana** (Roman House) sits in a side street below the Palazzo del Municipio. This dark and atmospheric little corner contains the remains of a house fancifully believed to have belonged to Vespasia Polla, the mother of the emperor Vespasian. Bedrooms, bath and other remnants survive, including swathes of patterned black-and-white mosaic floor.

Galleria Civica d'Arte Moderna

Piazza Collicola • Mon & Thurs–Sun: mid-March to mid-Oct 10.30am–1pm & 3.30–7pm; mid-Oct to mid-March 10.30am–1pm & 3.30–5.30pm • €4 • ☎ 0743 46 434

Over the years, Spoleto's festival has attracted some high-profile contemporary artists, and many of their works are now on view in the **Galleria Civica d'Arte Moderna**. The collection has works by leading Italian artists, alive and dead, including Guttoso, Burri, Dorazio and Accardi, plus pieces by non-Italians, including the likes of Calder (he of the railway station sculpture), and a section devoted to the glazed terracotta and other sculptures of Spoleto's own Leoncillo Leonardi (1915–68).

The Rocca Albornoziana and Museo del Ducato Longobardo

Piazza Campello • **Rocca** Daily 10am–noon & 3–8pm, last entry 7.15pm • Guided tours hourly included in the entry • €6.50 • **Museo** Thurs–Sun 10am–7pm, last entry 6.15pm • €6 • Combined Rocca and Museo ticket €7.50 • 🕿 0743 46 434

The **Rocca Albornoziana** is a perfectly endowed castle, built as one of a chain of fortresses with which the tireless Cardinal Albornoz tried to re-establish Church authority in central Italy. Not long after its completion, the Rocca became part-fortress, part-holiday home, with several popes staying over, most notably Julius II, sometimes accompanied by Michelangelo, Nicholas V, who fled here from the plague in 1449, and the Sienese Pius II. The fort's main latter-day function (until 1982) was as a high-security prison; as many as five hundred prisoners were kept here by the papal authorities between 1817 and 1860; Slavic and Italian political prisoners were held here during the war, while more recent inmates included members of the Red Brigades and Pope John Paul II's would-be assassin, Mohammed Ali Agca. If you pay to enter the Rocca only, you get access to just the courtyards; better to get a combined ticket covering the **museum** in the ducal apartments on the upper storey.

The Rocca's entrance is the castle drive on Piazza Campello at the top of Via Aurelio Saffi, just to the left of the large fountain, whose massive stone face marks the end of a Roman and medieval aqueduct.

The first courtyard

Highlights of the interior start with the **first courtyard**, the Cortile d'Onore, an upper storey supported on vast arches and dotted with patches of fresco. The arches are slightly different: one set belongs to Gattapone, the original designer, the other to Bernardo Rossellino, Pius II's architect in Pienza, who worked here. An arched passage leads to a plainer courtyard beyond, the arch frescoed with six towns in the papal domain, with Spoleto obvious on the right thanks to the depiction of the Ponte delle Torri, along with Perugia (middle left) and Orvieto (far left), obvious from its cathedral. The missing patches of fresco (two of the four Cardinal Virtues also illustrated are missing) were damaged by fires lit by guards, who sheltered on duty in the passage.

The second courtyard

The **second courtyard** was once the prison exercise yard: turn round to see the coats of arms above the entrance arch, which belong to Albornoz, Urban V, Eugenius IV – also represented is the monogram of Christ and the crossed keys, symbols of the Church's temporal power, a motif repeated throughout the fortress. Some idea of the castle's past importance, and its illustrious visitors and inhabitants, can be gained from the wealth of other leading family and papal arms around the place – the Barberini bees, Medici, Borgia, Colonna, Della Rovere, Piccolomini, Visconti, Aldobrandini, Lambertini and many more.

The Museo del Ducato Longobardo

Set in the upper storey of the Cortile d'Onore, the rooms of the **Museo del Ducato Longobardo** are impressive more for their size and views than for any surviving frescoes or other artefacts. The exceptions are the bedroom and studio-bathroom, which have well-preserved and pretty courtly scenes from the early fifteenth century appropriate to a bedroom, and riding and hunting vignettes in the studio.

The Ponte delle Torri

If you do nothing else in Spoleto, take the short walk to the **Ponte delle Torri**, best taken in as part of a circular walk around the base of the Rocca, or on the longer trek o San Pietro. Within minutes of leaving the shady gardens of Piazza F. Campello, ou'll find yourself in open countryside, with a dramatic view across the Tessino orge, bridged by the Ponte delle Torri itself, an astonishing piece of medieval ngineering with a 240-metre span supported by ten vast arches, the most central nes some 76m high. Probably designed by the Gubbian architect **Gattapone** – the nan responsible for Gubbio's Palazzo dei Consoli – it was initially planned as an queduct to bring water from Monteluco, replacing a Roman causeway whose design Gattapone borrowed and enlarged upon. In time it became part of the town's lefences, providing an escape from the castle when Spoleto was under siege. The emains of what used to be a covered passageway connecting the two are still visible traggling down the hillside. It's possible to walk across the bridge, with obvious aths on the other side (head up the stone steps to the right) leading left into lovely lex woods with superb belvederes overlooking the bridge and gorge. Follow the level ath for 1km or so and you bend round an arm of the gorge to emerge in peaceful live groves.

San Pietro

trada Statale Flaminia 3 • Daily summer 9am–6.30pm, winter closes at 4.30pm • If closed, ring the bell of the custodian in the house djacent • Free

To get to the church of **San Pietro**, in the Monteluco district about 1km southwest of the Duomo, take the sceneic Via Giro del Ponte from the Ponte delle Torri. The hurch's facade is its main draw, visible from the bridge; as you draw close, it reveals series of twelfth-century **sculptures** that – with Maitani's bas-reliefs in Orvieto – constitute the finest Romanesque carving in Umbria. Partly Lombard in their nspiration, they draw on the Gospels and medieval legend for their complicated narrative and symbolic purpose. Much of the allegory is elusive, but reasonably elf-explanatory panels include *A Wolf Disguised as a Friar* before a fleeing ram – a dig at dodgy monastic morals – and, particularly juicy, the *Death of a Sinner* (left eries, second from the top). Here the Archangel Michael abandons the sinner to a ouple of demons who bind and torture the unfortunate before bringing in the urning oil to finish him off. Compare this with the panel above, the *Death of a Just Man*, where St Peter frees the man of his chains while Michael holds his soul in his cales; the Devil, lashed by the keys of St Peter, tries to tip the scales in his favour nd holds a scroll that laments *doleo quia ante erat meus* ("I mourn because he was nine before").

12

ARRIVAL AND DEPARTURE

SPOLETO

By train From the station at Piazzale Giovanni Polvani 1 in he Lower Town, orange shuttle buses A, B and C ("Centro") un every 20min until around 8pm to Piazza della Libertà in he Upper Town; buy tickets (€0.90) from the station bar nd newspaper stall.

Destinations Assisi (hourly; 40min); Florence (8 daily; 1hr 0min–2hr 30min); Foligno via Trevi (12–18 daily; 20min; onnections for Spello, Assisi, Perugia & Teróntola); ossato di Vico (for Gubbio; 9–13 daily; 1hr); Narni (10–17 aily; 45min); Orte (10–17 daily; 1hr; additional onnections to Rome and Florence); Perugia direct (15–20 aily; 45min); Rome (hourly; 1hr 15min–1hr 45min); Terni 10–17 daily; 30min).

By bus Most inter-town buses, notably from Montefalco nd Perugia, are run by Spoletina (☎ 0743 212 209, ⊕ spoletina.com); most terminate in the Upper Town at iazza Carducci, just south of Piazza della Libertà, a few in

the Lower Town at Piazza Garibaldi. Buses from Norcia and the Valnerina arrive at the train station. Note that all buses between Spoleto, Norcia and Cascia run via Sant'Anatolia di Narco; Cascia services to and from Norcia, Spoleto or Rome require a connection at Serravalle.

Destinations Cascia (Mon–Sat 5–7 daily, 3 on Sun; 1hr 5min); Foligno (Mon–Sat 4 daily; 50min); Montefalco (Mon–Sat 3–4 daily; 1hr); Monteleone (Mon–Sat 1 daily, via Caso and Gavelli); Norcia (Mon–Sat 6 daily, 3 on Sun; 1hr); Perugia (Mon–Sat 1 daily, via Spello and Santa Maria degli Angeli; 1hr 45min; additional connections at Foligno); Scheggino (Mon–Sat 4 daily with change at Sant'Anatolia di Narco; 45min); Terni (Mon–Sat 5 daily; 45min).

By car It's difficult to park in the Upper Town (the likeliest slots are on Via della Rocca), but there are large car parks on Via Don P. Bonilli by the stadium and Viale Cappuccini south of the Giardino Pubblico.

INFORMATION

Tourist office Piazza della Libertà 7 (Mon–Thurs 9am–1.30pm & 3–5pm, Fri 9am–1.30pm; ☎0743 218 615, ⓦ www.comunespoleto.gov.it or ⓦ prospoleto.it).

ACCOMMODATION

Spoleto's **hotels** charge vastly different prices for different rooms within a single establishment: if the one you're offered seems too expensive, it's worth asking if there's anything cheaper. Several new hotels have opened in recent years, most of them superb historic properties and all in the upper price brackets. Accommodation is very hard to come by during the summer festival.

Aurora Via dell'Apollinare 3 ☎0743 220 315, ⓦ hotel auroraspoleto.it. This excellent and very popular hotel has its own courtyard, and many of the public areas retain their medieval stone walls. Rooms are comfortably appointed with a/c and wood-beam ceilings, and there's free parking. Breakfast included. **€75**

Cavaliere Palace Corso Garibaldi 49 ☎0743 220 350, ⓦ hotelcavaliere.eu. This sumptuous seventeenth-century palace has 29 mostly large, plush rooms, the two best with frescoed ceilings and all with full amenities, such as a/c and wi-fi. There's also a garden, and a good restaurant in a frescoed dining room. Buffet breakfast included; free parking nearby. **€100**

Charleston Piazza Collicola 10 ☎0743 220 052, ⓦ www.hotelcharleston.it. This cosy hotel occupies a seventeenth-century building that has been recently refurbished and offers all modern amenities, including a sauna and a massage room. Rooms have parquet floors, each is uniquely decorated and some have views, and there's free wi-fi and private garage. Buffet breakfast in their terrace garden included. **€90**

Dei Duchi Viale G. Matteotti 4 ☎0473 44 541, ⓦ hoteldeiduchi.com. Built in the late 1950s, this large hotel is strictly modern, even a touch spartan, but it's been renovated recently enough and the staff are very helpful and professional. The best rooms are on the upper floors, with views south to the hills, and there's a solarium with views of the Roman Theatre. Check online for steep reductions on rates. **€180**

Gattapone Via del Ponte ☎0743 223 447, ⓦ hotelgattapone.it. Just outside town, with a peaceful setting looking over to Monteluco (faint road noise apart); it's worth paying a little more for a room with views over the gorge and Ponte delle Torri. Note that there are older and newer parts of this converted country residence, so

check to make sure you have one of the refurbished rooms in the newer section. Breakfast included. **€140**

Palazzo Dragoni Via del Duomo 13 ☎0743 222 220, ⓦ palazzodragoni.it. Relatively unknown *residenza d'epoca* set in a glorious sixteenth-century converted town house, with a handful of elegant rooms full of frescoes, antique furniture and other period details. A definite first choice for luxury in town. Breakfast included in the dining room with the panoramic views. **€125**

★ **Palazzo Leti** Via degli Eremiti 10 ☎0743 223 340, ⓦ palazzoleti.com. A superb *residenza d'epoca* combining romantic period splendour with bucolic charm, in a peaceful position and with great views. Sumptuous attention to detail, from the quality bed linens and thick towels to the antique china service at breakfast (included in the rates). **€140**

Panciolle Via Duomo 3 ☎0743 45 677, ⓦ ilpanciolle .it. This hotel-restaurant is on the simple side, but the staff are so welcoming that it feels very homely, with regulars coming back year after year. The rooms are plain but clean, with a/c, and there's a garden and a gourmet restaurant. Free parking. **€85**

San Luca Via Interna delle Mura 21 ☎0743 223 399, ⓦ hotelsanluca.com. With wonderful service and all the amenities, this comfortable hotel has it all. The carefully maintained rooms have soundproofing, a/c, wi-fi and marble bathrooms, and the formal garden is another plus. Great buffet breakfast (included) with fresh juices, too. **€115**

Villa Milani Attivoli 4, Località Colle ☎0473 225 056, ⓦ villamilani.com. This exclusive resort is just 2.5km from the centre in a delightful and eclectic villa with perfect views. There are eleven rooms, with elegant decor and antique furnishings, plus a pool and a beautiful garden. Breakfast on the flowery terrace is included; carefully prepared lunch and dinner in their own restaurant also offered (May–Sept only). Open April–Oct. **€240**

EATING AND DRINKING

Food is taken pretty seriously in Spoleto. The town lies at the heart of renowned olive oil country, and the oils of its top producer, Monini, used in kitchens across Italy. These can be bought just about anywhere, but for a **picnic**, stock up at the morning market and regular food shops in the Piazza del Mercato.

★ **Apollinare** Via Sant'Agata 14 ☎0743 223 256,

ⓦ ristoranteapollinare.it. The blue and gold upholstery is initially off-putting, but the medieval-era setting and the friendly welcome combine to make this one of the town's best restaurants. The set *menù sorpresa* is excellent value at €25–35. Don't miss the sublime *caramello* starter – cheese and truffle delight. Mon & Wed–Sun 1.30–3.30pm & 7.30–10pm.

★ **Il Biologico** Via Cacciatori delle Alpi 1 ☎0743 40 164, ⊕ilbiologico-spoleto.com. Shop-cum-restaurant that specialises in natural, organic local produce, preparing vegetarian dishes with tofu, seitan or tempeh, and transforming traditional recipes such as *strangozzi con porcini* by using pasta made of kamut or quinoa instead of wheat – the local *farro* (spelt) also figures prominently. The set menu changes daily; you pay €10–20 for a full meal. Mon–Wed & Fri–Sat 8am–8pm, Thurs 8am–3.30pm; Oct–March closes 7.30pm Fri & Sat.

Il Pentagramma Via Tommaso Martani 6 ☎0743 223 131, ⊕ristorantepentagramma.com. A warmly inviting medieval setting sets the tone for the traditional welcome you receive. The menu varies with the season and the day's market, but one speciality that always turns up is their soup of creamed veggies with cheese and seasonings. Antipasti run about €12, while a full meal can go from €30 to as much as €80, depending in part on wine. Tues–Sun 1.30–4pm & 7.30–10.30pm.

Il Tartufo Piazza Garibaldi 24 ☎0743 40 236, ⊕ristoranteiltartufo.it. This restaurant is particularly renowned for its superlative white and black truffle dishes (about €20 each). The medieval interior is wonderful and you can eat outdoors in summer. Full meals start at about €35, so be prepared to spend. Tues–Sat 1.30–3.45pm & 7.30–10.45pm, Sun 1–4pm; closed part of Feb & July.

Il Tempio del Gusto Via Arco del Druso 11 ☎0743 47 121, ⊕iltempiodelgusto.com. "The Temple of Taste" was founded by Eros Patrizi, a former pupil of the legendary Vissani, patron of the eponymous top-rated restaurant near Baschi in southern Umbria. You can expect Michelin-star-style standards at this spot, too – as well as often recherché cooking – and you'll pay around €75 for the full tasting menu, with wines specially selected for each course. Mon–Wed & Fri–Sun 1.30–4pm & 7.30–10.30pm.

La Barcaccia Piazza Fratelli Bandiera 5 ☎0743 225 082, ⊕ristorantelabarcaccia.it. A friendly, family-run atmosphere, a summertime pergola and fair prices have made this spacious place one of the town's most popular trattorie. The *strangozzi al tartufo nero* is their speciality pasta, and the house red is a Sagrantino. Full meals go for about €25. Mon & Wed–Sun 1–3.30pm & 7.30–10pm.

★ **La Torretta** Via Filitteria 43 ☎0743 44 954, ⊕trattorialatorretta.com. Welcoming and rustic osteria, where a full meal will come to about €30. Antipasti such as vegetable and sausage pie start at €8; pasta dishes, including *pappardelle* with lamb ragù and artichokes, go for about €10, as does their great truffle omelette. Don't miss the meringue with berries for dessert. Mon & Wed–Sun 1–3.30pm & 7.30–10pm.

Sabatini Corso Mazzini 54 ☎0743 221 831, ⊕ristorantesabatinispoleto.it. This well-known restaurant has a simple, elegant interior and small garden for summer eating, and serves imaginative – if occasionally over-elaborate – variations of local dishes; the ravioli with ricotta and pistachio are memorable and cost just €10, while the wild boar with porcini is only €14. Good wines, too. Tues–Sun 1.30–4pm & 7.30–10.30pm.

The Valnerina

The **Valnerina** is a valley that curves in a broad arc through the east of Umbria, rising in the mountains of the Sibillini and then following a southwesterly course through scenery with a stark, wild beauty which is all the more dramatic after the pastoral hill country to the west. Desolate and sparsely populated these days, the "little valley of the Nera" was once the hub of communications between the kingdom of Naples and the dukedom of Spoleto, and later a bone of contention between the Church and the Holy Roman Empire – which explains its liberal sprinkling of fortified villages. Today, it constitutes a self-contained area of high mountains, steep wooded valleys, lonely hamlets and vast stretches of upland wilderness.

There is no easy way of visiting the valley's highlights. The best approach is from Spoleto, either on the winding scenic road over the mountains, which meets the valley just below Vallo di Nera, or via the fast tunnel that emerges close to Sant'Anatolia di Narco. You should first head south from either point to visit the region's main highlight, the abbey of **San Pietro in Valle**. Beyond this the valley loses most of its appeal, becoming more scrappy and built-up in the run past Ferentillo and Arrone towards Terni. A route following the Nera all the way to Terni only makes sense if you are making for Narni, Orte and the road to Rome or the north.

From San Pietro in Valle you should double back and head north – no hardship, as the scenery is delightful – picking one of three options: the slow but scenic mountain road from Sant'Anatolia di Narco to Monteleone (and then on to Norcia via Cascia and the SS320); the direct but still striking SS396 road to Norcia from just south of Triponzo; or exploring the **Upper Valnerina**, following the SS209 valley road before diverting south towards Norcia via Preci and another fine abbey, **Sant'Eutizio**, and the pretty Val Castoriana (also easily explored using Norcia as a base).

GETTING AROUND

By bus Access to the heart of the region can be very tricky without your own transport, but there are several bus services daily from Spoleto east to Norcia, stopping at most villages along the way. In many cases you'll find a bus waiting at key junctions such as the one below Sant'Anatolia di Narco, to connect with more remote villages to the south and east.

The Lower Valnerina

East of Spoleto, the beautiful and tortuous SS395 road towards Norcia climbs and then – amidst tremendous views – drops to meet the main SS209 running along the floor of the Valnerina at the junction at the hamlet of **Piedipaterno**. This twenty-kilometre route is slow, however, so if you want to have more time to explore the valley, take the tunnel between Spoleto and Sant'Anatolia di Narco.

To Sant'Anatolia di Narco

About 1km south of Piedipaterno lies a turnoff left to the village of **VALLO DI NERA**, a self-contained medieval ensemble perched on a hill, the type of fortified village you'll see all the way up and down the valley. In the church of **Santa Maria** in the lower part of the village (the house at no. 4 has the key if the building is shut) are minor but beautiful fourteenth-century apse frescoes. Later, but no less arresting frescoes (1536) adorn the church of **San Giovanni Battista** at the top of the village (try the priest's house next door for access if the church is shut). They're the work of the Sicilian artist Jacopo Santori (or Siculo), who also frescoed one of the Eroli chapels in Spoleto's Duomo.

Around 2km south on the main road you pass **Castel San Felice**, another picture-perfect fortified village, and a couple of kilometres further arrive at a turnoff to the less alluring **SANT'ANATOLIA DI NARCO**. Take the turn left just before the village (visible on the hill above), cross the river and look for the small yellow sign 100m or so beyond on the left directing you to the little twelfth-century church of **San Felice**. Its facade bears only the bare essentials – arched doorway, rose window and two pairs of narrow windows. Lumpen red and white marble slabs floor the lovely interior, which is distinguished by a raised sanctuary, an ancient sarcophagus in the crypt, fifteenth-century frescoes of Christ (in the apse) and the *Adoration of the Magi* (on the left wall of the nave).

From Sant'Anatolia to Monteleone di Spoleto

From Sant'Anatolia a sensational minor road strikes southeast to Monteleone di Spoleto, offering great **views** and cutting across the main mountain ridge. You pass the somnolent little hamlets of **CASO** and **GAVELLI** (1127m), both looking across an immense tree-covered gorge. Around 1km past Caso look out on the left for the little bell tower of **Santa Cristina** (signed), a Romanesque church with a scattering of frescoes. The church of **San Michele** in Gavelli is even better, and one of the extraordinary and unexpected artistic gems so common in Umbria. The entire interior is covered in sixteenth-century frescoes by Lo Spagna, restored with the aid of UK-based walking company, ATG-Oxford.

Scheggino

About 3km south of Sant'Anatolia, and again laid out below a castle, **SCHEGGINO** is one of the more appealing spots in the region. Much of its charm derives from a couple of canals below the tiny and much-tidied medieval streets. A further fine incentive for stopping, especially at lunch, is the town's excellent hotel-restaurant.

CASTELLUCCIO (P.496) ›

★ **Del Ponte Scatolini** Via di Borgo 15 ☎ 075 61 253, ⓦ albergoristorantedelponte.com. There are twelve cool, quiet and attractive modern rooms at this hotel-restaurant, and a four-room annexe at Via Roma 6. The restaurant serves the local speciality, trout and truffles, the former plucked from the ice-clear river, the latter harvested by the local Urbani family, top operators in the Italian truffle world; there's outside dining in season. A full meal averages €30. Restaurant Tues–Sun 1–4pm & 7–10.30pm; closed early Sept. **€80**

Abbazia di San Pietro in Valle

Via Case Sparse 4, Ferentillo Terni • April–Sept daily 10am–1pm & 3–6pm; Oct–March Sat & Sun 10am–12.30pm & 2.30–4pm • Free • ⓦ sanpietroinvalle.com

From Scheggino, the SS209 continues south 8km to an easily missed turning on the right immediately before the hamlet of Colleponte, signed to the **Abbazia di San Pietro in Valle**. Set high on the hillside near a thickly wooded cleft, this is one of central Italy's finest abbeys and one of Umbria's few memorials to the Lombards' dukedom of Spoleto. The abbey buildings, which have been in private hands since 1860 (the church is a state-owned national monument), have been part-converted into a **hotel**, a lovely place but a development that has slightly compromised the peace of this perfect medieval ensemble.

The highlight of the complex is the **church**, much of which survives from two separate periods of building – the eighth and twelfth centuries, the earlier date probably having yielded the transept, the three apses and parts of the rough mosaic pavement behind the main altar. However, don't miss the faultless two-tiered **cloister**, with two exquisite ninth-century statues of saints Peter and Paul, flanking the portal. Highlights inside, covering most of the side walls, are two breathtaking, if faded, **fresco cycles**. Painted in 1190, they are some of the most important paintings of their period in Italy, being amongst the first attempts to move away from the stylized influence of Byzantine painting; the artist is unknown. Most of these precocious pictures are biblical scenes, showing a startling sense of invention and composition, full of narrative detail and attempts at light and shade unique for their time. Those on the left-hand wall are from the **Old Testament**, those on the right from the **New Testament**.

The Old Testament frescoes

The **Old Testament** scenes are better preserved, and are worth studying. They are arranged in three tiers, and progress left to right from the top tier down. The **first tier**

THE HISTORY OF SAN PIETRO IN VALLE

In **Roman** times there was probably a pagan temple on the abbey's site, later replaced by a series of small hermitic communities. Meanwhile, in Spoleto, the sixth Lombard Duke of Spoleto, **Faroaldo II**, who reigned between 703 and 720, experienced a vision in which St Peter told him to found a monastery in his honour at a place in which he would discover a lone and disconsolate monk. While hunting some time later he came across a recently bereaved monk, and so duly founded an abbey, but also abdicated his throne in favour of the monastic life. At his death eight years later he was buried in the abbey, his tomb a magnificent Roman **sarcophagus** that survives to this day to the right of the high altar.

The abbey was sacked by **Saracens** in 881 and restored in 991, when a series of fortresses were built to lend it added protection. One of these, **Umbriano**, can still be seen on the opposite side of the valley. Thereafter the abbey became one of the most powerful religious houses in the region, controlling vast tracts of land and dominating the lives of thousands of people. In 1234 it passed from the Benedictines to the **Cistercians**, but by 1300 had become so corrupt that Boniface VIII was forced to transfer responsibility for its operation to Rome. In 1484 Innocent VIII sold its land and feudal rights to Franceschetto Cybo and his descendants, who took the title of Count of Ferentillo: it remained in their domain until 1730, then passed through several aristocratic hands until 1860, when the church was appropriated by the newly formed Italian state and the buildings sold to the local Costanzi family, still the owners today.

comprises the *Creation of the World, Creation of Adam, Creation of Eve* (who is shown emerging from Adam's rib, with the four Rivers of Paradise – looking like fish – at Adam's side), *Adam Naming the Animals, Original Sin, God's Warning* and *The Expulsion from Paradise*. The **second tier** comprises the *Sacrifice of Cain and Abel, Cain Slaying Abel, God's Warning to Noah, The Construction of the Ark, Noah Giving Thanks to God, Abraham and the Three Angels, The Sacrifice of Isaac* and *Isaac and Jacob*. Only one fresco survives of the **lowest tier**, its theme unclear.

The New Testament frescoes

The **New Testament** scenes on the opposite wall depict, in the badly faded **upper tier**, angels and Old Testament characters. The **second tier** has seven better-preserved panels, from left to right: *The Shepherds being told of Christ's Birth, Journey of the Magi, Epiphany, Departure of the Magi, Massacre of the Innocents, Baptism of Christ* and the *Wedding at Cana*. The **lowest tier** has four panels that can be clearly made out: *Christ's Entry into Jerusalem, The Last Supper, The Washing of the Feet* and *Calvary*.

The altar

Moving down the church you cross a **stone division** set into the floor, flanked by two small pillars: this marked the point beyond which those who had not been baptized were forbidden to progress. Ahead, the magnificently preserved **altar** is one of only a tiny handful of dated works of art anywhere in Italy of Lombard vintage – its age is obvious even from a cursory glance at the almost Celtic figures and motifs that decorate its two main faces. It was carved by Ursus, the left of the two crude figures depicted in the lower front section (his signature is still clearly visible): the other figure is Ilderico, Duke of Spoleto between 739 and 742, who commissioned the piece. To each side are well-preserved Roman **sarcophagi**, the right-hand specimen – Faroaldo's tomb – especially appealing, backed by some of the gloriously coloured Giottesque frescoes (c.1320) that dot much of the apse and shallow transepts.

The rest of the church

In the **left transept**, look for the tiny fresco on the side wall depicting Faroaldo's vision of St Peter: the duke is shown lying in a canopied bed while his companions play dice to the right. The capitals in the apse are probably from the original Roman building on the site, likely crowning fluted columns that are now concealed under the plasterwork of subsequent centuries. Three other carved sarcophagi lie elsewhere in the church, along with odd stone fragments around the walls, including a bas-relief of a monk, brought from Syria by refugee Christians in the seventh century.

ACCOMMODATION	ABBAZIA DI SAN PIETRO IN VALLE
★ **Abbazia di San Pietro Hotel** ☏ 0744 780 129, ⓦ sanpietroinvalle.it. The abbey is a lovely place to stay, with gardens and a spa offering sauna, hydromassage and more. Most of the very varied rooms are former monks'	cells, but now evoke a sense of quiet, timeless luxury. Breakfast is included in the old refectory, and there's a restaurant on site. **€129**

The Upper Valnerina

The **Upper Valnerina** is the most beautiful part of the valley, the mountains higher and closer to the road, the villages more remote and less visited. If short of time, you can head directly to **Norcia**, the region's obvious base, but it's well worth following the river simply for the scenery, perhaps branching off to explore some of the empty upland roads above the valley's succession of small villages, such as **Preci** and **Piedvalle**. Just above the latter is the area's highlight, the Benedictine **Abbazia di Sant'Eutizio**; a visit here leaves you well placed for the short drive south to Norcia.

THE SURGEONS OF PRECI

Preci was once famous for its thirty families of **surgeons**, who from the twelfth to the mid-eighteenth centuries handed down their medical knowledge and hearsay from generation to generation. Over the years their patients included such luminaries as Pope Sixtus V, Sultan Mehmed the Conqueror and Elizabeth I of England. Their most notorious sideline, however, was the castration of young boys foolish enough to show operatic potential, a spin-off that developed from the technique of using castration to prevent death from hernia – an area of expertise that the Preci surgeons picked up from their work on pigs.

Preci and around

Just before **Triponzo**, an ancient hamlet whose prominent marking on the map belies its size (it's just a shop and a couple of houses), the SS396 heads off through a tunnel into the deep **Corno valley** on the way to Norcia, the scenery becoming increasingly impressive. In the Nera valley, 12km north of Triponzo, lies the fortified village of **PRECI**, a likeable place, despite some terrible damage in the 1997 earthquake.

From Preci, the most direct route to Norcia continues up the valley past Piedivalle to the Forca d'Ancarano pass (see opposite). A longer alternative runs north through Visso (in the Marche), then onwards by the desolate and stunning road over the Passo di Gualdo (1496m) and through Castelluccio (see p.496).

INFORMATION   PRECI

Park information The Sibillini Park information centre is at Via del Mulino, Borgo Garibaldi (May & June Sat & Sun 9.30am–12.30pm & 3.30–6.30pm; July & Aug daily 9.30am–12.30pm & 3.30–6.30pm; ☏329 781 8113, ⓦsibillini.net).

ACCOMMODATION AND EATING

Dei Cacciatori Biselli ☏0743 822 237, ⓦhoteldei cacciatori.com. This modern hotel-restaurant, set in greenery 13km southwest of Preci, has a pool and a river-rafting centre. Rooms are simple and clean, with views from their balconies, and there's a restaurant that specializes in grills and truffles. Breakfast included. **€100**

★ **Il Castoro** Via Roma ☏0743 939 248, ⓦwww .ristoranteilcastoro.com. Very rustic trattoria, where the truffle omelette and the wild boar are not to be missed. Can get a bit too busy at weekends, but it's always welcoming. About €30 per person for a full meal. Easter to Sept daily 1.30–3.30pm & 7.30–10pm; Oct to Easter Mon–Wed & Fri–Sun 1.30–3.30pm & 7.30–10pm; closed part of Nov.

★ **Il Collaccio** Località Castelvecchio ☏0743 665 108, ⓦilcollaccio.com. This beautifully situated complex in a hamlet 2km northwest of Preci has friendly, English-speaking owners, and good facilities that include a pool, riding, cycling, tennis and hang-gliding. There are nice camping pitches, plus chalets and bungalows that sleep four to twelve, as well as spotless, pleasantly old-fashioned hotel rooms with balconies. The restaurant offers wood-fired pizzas and home-made pasta dishes. Breakfast included for hotel guests. Camping: adults **€9.50**, pitches **€9.50**, chalets and bungalows **€55**, double hotel rooms **€100**

Abbazia di Sant'Eutizio

Irregular opening hours, but generally daily 10am–noon & 3–5pm • Free

Some 2km south of Preci, signposted off the Norcia road at Piedivalle, is the monastic complex of **Abbazia di Sant'Eutizio**, one of the cradles of the **Benedictine** movement. Initially the site of a Roman building, then a cemetery for hermits who had lived in the hills here, it became a community that eventually controlled over a hundred churches and local castles, its domain extending as far as the Adriatic. Restoration has left it a little too tidy, but there's no denying the beauty and tranquillity of the place, nor its seminal role in the history of the Benedictines.

The church and the caves

The abbey's Romanesque **church**, built in 1190, has a fourteenth-century apse and gallery and, inside, a *Crucifixion* by Nicola da Siena (1461) above the high altar.

The altar houses the sepulchre of St Eutizio, one of the early hermits, known for his missionary zeal and for his ability to induce rain; when there's a drought, locals still parade his tunic round the fields. In addition, crawling through the specially constructed tunnel below his altar is supposed to guarantee relief from all manner of back ailments. Down in the **crypt** are a couple of vast sandstone columns, perhaps remnants of the original Roman building on the site. Steps behind the abbey church, to the right of the fountain, lead to the **caves** of the earliest monks; according to Gregory the Great, it was in these grottoes that Benedict – in conversation with Eutizio and a fellow hermit, Spes – discovered his religious vocation.

Campi and Campi Vecchio

The road south from the Abbazia di Sant'Eutizio runs for 15km through delightful and pastoral country, the Castoriana and Nida valleys, which once made up one of the most important north-to-south trading routes in this part of the Apennines. It passes little medieval hamlets such as Piedivalle and **CAMPI**. Just before the latter is the church of **San Salvatore**, a double-fronted Romanesque beauty. The interior is smothered with frescoes by Giovanni and Antonio Sparapane, part of a fifteenth-century dynasty of painters active around Spoleto and the Valnerina.

Campi Vecchio

Above Campi is the village of **CAMPI VECCHIO**, across the wooded hillside to the north, and worth a detour for **Sant'Andrea**, the church clearly visible at the side of the village, its portico framing one of the loveliest views in the area. For the key, walk down the steps from the portico and take the lane right in the little piazza: the house is about four down on the right. The custodian also holds the key to the chapel of **Santa Maria di Piazza**, in the same little street as her house, about 50m down on the right. The vaults are covered in several superbly well-preserved and accomplished frescoes on the *Life of the Virgin*, the work of the Sparapane.

Onwards to Norcia

Across the valley, the villages of **Abeto** and **Todiano** appear invitingly over the woods and hilly ridges – but, though they were once stuffed with paintings and other works of art (now in Spoleto's Museo Diocesano), they're now very sleepy. Continuing on the road to Norcia, 4km south of Piedivalle beyond Sant'Angelo, you climb to 1008m at **Forca d'Ancarano**, a pass that affords spectacular views over surrounding mountains before the precipitous drop to Norcia.

Norcia

Noted on the one hand as the birthplace of St Benedict – founder of Western monasticism – and on the other as one of Italy's great culinary capitals, **NORCIA** is small, walled and stolid, the only place of substance in eastern Umbria. Its low, sturdy houses are a world away from the bucolic towns to the west, a contrast explained by the constant threat of earthquakes. Thick-walled and heavily buttressed, Norcia's buildings have been compulsorily stunted since 1859, when a law forbade the raising of houses over 12.5m high. (The last tremor, a particularly violent one, was in 1979.) At the same time Norcia is a prosperous and likeable place, the sort of town where everything works and everybody knows everyone else. Its streets are relieved by glimpses of the mountains, views of which unfold unexpectedly at many corners. The town can serve as the base for some good trips into the **Monti Sibillini** and **Piano Grande** (see p.496) and north to the Castoriana valley and abbey of **Sant'Eutizio** (see p.490).

Brief history

Norcia has been inhabited since prehistoric times, thanks to its abundant springs, fine agricultural land and a vital position commanding one of the lowest east-to-west routes across the Apennines. Ancient Norcia was the northernmost town of the **Sabines**, contemporaries of the Umbrians, before becoming Nursia, a minor Roman *municipio* (290 BC). After the attentions of sixth-century barbarians, recovery took a long time to come – and when it did, **earthquakes** periodically discouraged long-term development. For five centuries before Italian Unification, though, the town was effectively a frontier post between the Papal States and the kingdom of Naples, making it a safe haven for bandits and refugees from opposing sides. Papal reaction was to build the **Castellina** in 1554, a huge, blunt fortress that dominates the town centre. Thereafter Norcia and the surrounding countryside was drained by emigration, a trend whose effects have been tempered by the success of tourism and small food-processing concerns.

Piazza San Benedetto

The main **Piazza San Benedetto** is a large, open area with something of a *High Noon* atmosphere in mid-afternoon, but at other times is the lively focus of the town's comings and goings. It's presided over by a statue of a suitably severe and disapproving Benedict, erected in 1880 on the 1400th anniversary of his birth. In earlier centuries the square was the site of a bullring and a place of execution for witches, traitors, adulterers and necromancers. The only one of the Piazza's grand buildings not open to the public, is the oddly but beautifully multicoloured **Palazzo Comunale**, based around a 1492 portico and with later additions which blend delightfully to create the town's most distinctive building.

San Benedetto

Piazza San Benedetto • Mon & Wed–Sun 8.20am–8.15pm, Tues 8.20am–3 pm & 6–8.15pm • Free

The piazza's key sight is the basilica of **San Benedetto**, built, according to legend, over the house where Benedict and his sister, St Scholastica, were born; it's more likely to have been the site of a Roman temple, as the square itself was the site of the forum. Despite repeated post-earthquake reconstructions, the facade – sole survivor from the 1389 original – features a lovely Gothic portal, rose window, niche statues of Benedict and Scholastica and a fourteenth-century campanile to the rear. During Norcia's blast-furnace summers the newer arched gallery (1570) to the right provides welcome shade, and it has a drinking fountain too. The unusual old stone measures were used for selling or distributing wine and olive oil when the gallery was used as a market.

The interior

On the left as you enter the church is a good niche **fresco** – possibly the work of Francesco Sparapane, one of a dynasty of local fifteenth-century painters – of *Sts Barbara and Michael*, with a *Madonna and Child* above. The only other worthwhile painting is Filippo Napoletano's *St Benedict and Totila* (1621), located in the left arm of the left transept. Down in the **crypt**, excavated as recently as 1910, the little apse at the head of the left aisle is traditionally held to be the place where Benedict and Scholastica were born. It's half-covered in faded frescoes depicting the *Annunciation*, *Nativity* and other scenes. Nearby, stone fragments of a late Roman edifice are visible, though closed off, making this by far the most evocative part of the church.

The Castellina and Museo Civico

Piazza San Benedetto • **Museo** May–Sept Tues–Sun 10am–1pm & 4–7.30pm; Oct–April Thurs–Sun 10am–1pm & 3–5pm • €4 • ☎ 0743 817 030

Across the square from San Benedetto is the **Castellina**, an extraordinarily gaunt fortress with no concessions to architectural subtlety. The superb granite lions outside came

THE PIANO GRANDE (P.496) >

12

originally from the crypt of San Benedetto. It was built on the site of a Benedictine priory and Norcia's old parish church for Pope Julius III by the usually sophisticated Vignola and now houses the town's **Museo Civico**.

The building and the museum's handful of top-quality exhibits are well worth the admission. Most of the rooms are taken up with **sculptures**, the highlights being a rare thirteenth-century *Deposition* (five figures in all) a *St Sebastian* (minus arrows) and a poignant life-size glazed terracotta *Madonna* by **Giovanni della Robbia**. Among the **paintings** look for a bizarre *Risen Christ* (1460) by **Nicola da Siena**, in which a near-naked but beardless and curiously androgynous Christ is shown stepping coolly from his marble sepulchre. There is also a lovely picture attached to a casket lid of Benedict and Scholastica, the former shown holding a painted church, as well as a beautifully restored *Madonna and Child with Saints* by Giacomo di Giovannofrio, the Virgin sitting atop a gloriously decorated throne beneath a coffered Renaissance vault.

The Duomo

Piazza San Benedetto • Daily 8am–12.15pm & 3.30–7pm • Free

Almost beside the Castellina is the largely uninteresting sixteenth-century **Duomo**, its less-than-dominating position a result of comparative modernity, its forlorn interior the legacy of countless earthquakes. It does have one outstanding work, however: the **Cappella della Madonna della Misericordia**, located at the end of the north aisle and consisting of an ornate altar (1640–41) of inlaid marble whose appearance, so at odds with central Italian work of the period, has led experts to attribute it to Francesco Duquesnoy, a noted sculptor in the employ of the Neapolitan court. At the heart of the altar is an early sixteenth-century painting, probably by Francesco Sparapane, the *Madonna and Child with Sts Benedict and Scholastica*. Benedict is shown pointing to a painted miniature of Norcia, whose prominent Gothic campanile no longer exists, having collapsed in the eighteenth century.

The Tempietto

Cnr Via del Tempietto and Via Umberto

Just north of Piazza San Benedetto is the **Tempietto**, or Edicola (literally "Kiosk"), one of the town's more unusual buildings. Built in 1354 by Vanni Tuzi, it's a small arched structure, decorated with bas-reliefs and open to the street on all sides. Its purpose is unknown, but it may have been commissioned in honour of San Felicianus, who evangelized Norcia, as a shrine to be used in Holy Week processions – hence the signs of the Passion which figure among its decoration; possibly it was used as a *contra pestum*, a votive offering against the plague (an epidemic ravaged much of Italy at the time that the work was built).

Sant'Antonio Abate and around

Beyond the Tempietto is an area that fell into disrepair during the Middle Ages and was taken over by shepherds from Castelluccio. Adopting it as their own, they built small houses – complete with stalls for their sheep – amidst a jumble of streets that contrasts with the central grid. Look out for the church of **Sant'Antonio Abate** – the shepherds' saint, invoked to protect their flocks – and the nearby **San Giovanni**, known for its wooden ceiling and magnificent Renaissance altar of the *Madonna della Palla*, located on the right wall; the arched and gilt marble surround frames a painting of the Madonna (1469), so-called because someone is supposed to have kicked a ball (*palla*) against the painting, causing the Virgin's expression to change miraculously at an act of such wanton sacrilege.

The church of **Sant'Agostino**, in Via Anicia, is half-filled with surprisingly accomplished and well-preserved frescoes, those on the entrance wall depicting, among other things, the grisly martyrdoms of several saints. Also make time for the tremendous wooden ceiling of the **Oratorio di Sant'Agostinuccio** just behind Piazza Palatina.

12

ARRIVAL AND INFORMATION

NORCIA

By bus Norcia is well served by buses from Spoleto, Terni, Perugia, Foligno and Assisi; they drop off at the Porta Romana, from where it's a straight walk on Corso Sertorio to the central Piazza San Benedetto.
Note that all buses between Spoleto and Norcia and Cascia run via Sant'Anatolia di Narco; Cascia services to and from Norcia, Spoleto or Rome require a connection at Serravalle.
Destinations Borgo Cerreto via Campi, Preci and Triponzo

(Mon–Sat 1 daily; 1hr); Cascia (Mon–Sat 5–8 daily, 1 on Sun; 45min); Castelluccio via Forca Canapine (1 on Thurs; 1hr); Perugia (Mon–Sat 1 direct daily; 2hr); Rome (Stazione Tibertina; Mon–Sat 2 daily, 1 on Sun; 3hr); Spoleto (Mon–Sat 5 daily; 3 on Sun; 1hr).
Tourist office Sibillini National Park information office, Piazza San Benedetto (daily 9.30am–12.30pm & 3.30–6.30pm; ☎ 0743 828 173, ⓦ sibillini.net), has information on both the town and the mountains.

ACCOMMODATION

Casa Religiosa San Benedetto Via delle Vergini 13 ☎ 0743 828 208. This active monastery has 35 spartan guest rooms with private bathrooms, and there are good half- and full-board deals available, with communal dining in the old refectory. Open April to Oct. €60
Da Benito Via Marconi 5 ☎ 0743 816 670,

ⓦ norcia.hotelbenito.it. The eight rooms of this hotel-restaurant are adequate, if plain and not very spacious, but it's clean, the staff is professional and the restaurant pretty decent. Breakfast included. €80
★ **Grotta Azzurra** Via Alfieri 6 ☎ 0743 816 513, ⓦ hotelgrottaazzurra.com. The best, busiest and

friendliest hotel in town, run by the same family for generations. It's set in a listed sixteenth-century building, part of an old papal granary, so rooms are very varied; decor is rather posh, and there's a/c and free wi-fi. Breakfast included in the fine *Granaro del Monte* restaurant (see below). **€90**

Ostello Norcia Via Manzoni 2 ☎0743 817 487, ⓦmontepatino.com. Set in a pleasant period building, Norcia's hostel sleeps 52 people in two-, four-, five- and ten-bed rooms, and there's a garden for guests to use.

Dorm bed with breakfast €15

Palazzo Seneca Via Cesare Battisti 12 ☎0743 817 434, ⓦpalazzoseneca.com. This fabulous, meticulously converted sixteenth-century palace and stables is the Norcia showcase of the Relais & Chateaux hotel chain. The colour scheme of the rooms is beige and golden, and every comfort and luxury has been seen to. Facilities include sports options, a pool, a spa and a superb gourmet restaurant. Buffet breakfast included. **€165**

EATING AND DRINKING

Norcia is a justly renowned gastronomic centre, noted mostly for its **wild boar**, **hams**, **salamis**, **truffles** and **porcini** mushrooms, plus the famous **Castelluccio lentils** and the celebrated mountain sheep's cheese, **pecorino** – this last unforgettably delicious when served with honey, walnuts and truffle. Local specialities can be savoured in one of the town's many good **restaurants**, while shops on every street and square sell a wide range of local products.

Dal Francese Via Riguardati 16 ☎0743 816 290. The most lauded place in town in most Italian foodie guides, this is a very large, very traditional and very popular trattoria (so booking advised). The food is good-to-excellent, almost all truffle-based, with full meals, including tasting menus, in the €25–50 range. Mon–Thurs & Sat–Sun 1–4pm & 7–10pm.

★ **Il Granaro del Monte** Via Alfieri 12 ☎0743 816 513, ⓦbianconi.com. The frankly theatrical medieval dining halls of this in-hotel restaurant are resplendent with suits of armour, tapestries and a huge fire. Treat yourself to risotto with truffles or *tagliolini al tartufo*, the

classic way to tackle a truffle (€10); if finances allow, indulge in their award-winning marriage of truffle and steak, *Filetto del Cavatore* (€13). You can choose a three-course set menu, with wine and water, for only €18. Mon & Wed–Sun 1–4pm & 7–11pm.

Taverna de' Massari Via Roma 13 ☎0743 816 218, ⓦtavernademassari.com. Truffles and cured meats are the name of the game here, as just about everywhere in Norcia. Two antipasti, such as a plate of local cold meats, and two pasta dishes such as tagliatelli or ricotta with porcini, plus drinks, will come to about €60, with truffles €10 or so extra. Mon & Wed–Sun 1.30–3.30pm & 7.30–10pm.

The Piano Grande and the Monti Sibillini

The mountainous landscape east of Norcia is one of the most distinctive in Italy, with its centrepiece the eerie **Piano Grande**, a vast, desolate upland prairie devoid of any feature outside the summer months save sheep, hang-gliders and the odd bedraggled haystack. Surrounded on all sides by the steep and barren mountains of the **Monti Sibillini**, the Piano Grande forms a colossal amphitheatre that's often swathed in a dense, early morning mist. Gazing down on this wilderness from the remote frontier hamlet of **Castelluccio**, it's easy to imagine the hazards for the unsuspecting traveller in past centuries. Papal rulers forbade crossing the plain during winter, and even today the bells of Castelluccio toll on gloomy days to guide shepherds across its desolation.

Castelluccio

An isolated farming village at 1452m, **CASTELLUCCIO** is one of Italy's highest continually inhabited settlements, and the only habitation for many kilometres around. As well as its appeal as a belvedere onto the grasslands and a trailhead for **mountain walks**, the village attracts **hang-gliders**, drawn by the Sibillini's treeless slopes.

A couple of the bars have tried to smarten themselves up, as has the long-established hang-gliding school, but the place has made few other concessions to tourism and the feel is of an uncompromising and bleak frontier village. The exception is summer, when the presence of tour buses and the like underline the fact that even this remote little outpost has finally (and sadly) succumbed to the

TRUFFLES

Though disconcertingly turd-like in appearance, weight for weight **truffles** are one of the world's costliest foodstuffs – only saffron costs more. Norcia is one of Italy's truffle capitals, home to the fabled black truffle – *Tuber melanosporum*.

Truffles have been known, if not understood, since ancient times. They were enjoyed by the Babylonians, the Greeks and the Romans, who consumed them as much for their reputed aphrodisiac qualities as their gastronomic allure. Plutarch believed they were mud cooked by lightning; Juvenal that they were the product of thunder and rain. Pliny, bewildered by their origins, considered them Nature's greatest miracle. In the Middle Ages they were considered a manifestation of the Devil. And no wonder, for here was a plant apparently without root, branch, or stem; without leaf, fruit or flower; lacking, in fact, all visible means of growth.

Truffles' underground existence precludes photosynthesis, meaning they rely for nutrients on a symbiotic relationship with the roots of certain trees, most commonly the oak, hazel, beech and lime. Unlike a normal mushroom, their spores are spread not by the wind, but by truffle-eating animals such as rodents, deer, slugs and wild boar – and to ensure they're snuffled up, they need to advertise their presence.

And this is where the truffle's famous perfume – and dogs and pigs – come in. The fungi mature slowly, often over the course of several months, attaining their final dimensions – anything from the size of a pea to the size of a football – over a few days during the spring. Only when ripe – from about November onwards – do they give off their distinctive perfume, and only then for about ten days, thus ensuring they're snaffled up only when laden with viable spores. Thereafter they become poisonous and rot.

Pigs and truffles once went together, pigs being foremost among the sleuths inclined to nose them out (goats, foxes, ferrets and – in Russia – even bear cubs are used). Pigs love truffles – at least female ones do – for among the volatile compounds exuded by the truffle is one that resembles the musky pheromones of the wild boar. This is all well and good, but not only are sows huge and difficult to manage, they're also prone to attacks of sexual frenzy when close to a truffle. Dogs are therefore now preferred, and can be worth anything up to £2500 when trained.

There are countless **types of truffle**. Nine are edible, though only six are well known and commercialized. Four are considered a delicacy, and of these two are found in quantity around Norcia and Spoleto. Varieties mature at different depths and at different times of the year, so that April and May are the only times of the year when fresh truffles are not available. Umbria's most common type is the **tartufo nero**, gathered from a few centimetres below the ground between mid-November and mid-March. More prized is the **tartufo pregiato**, available over the same period. Rarer are the two summer and autumn **scorzone** varieties.

Many a *cavatore*, or truffle-hunter, sells either directly to a restaurant, or, more likely than not, to an agent working for Signor Urbani, king of the truffle world, whose small company, based just outside Scheggino (see p.486), a village a few kilometres from Norcia, controls 65 percent of the world's truffle trade. Truffles, after all, are big business: a kilo of white Alban truffles could be yours for anything between £2000 and £3000. Black truffles, of the type found in France and Umbria, retail at around £850 a kilo.

But why all the fuss? The fungi's perfume has been compared to leaf mould, over-ripe cheese, garlic, methane and armpits. But for enthusiasts, the appeal lies in the truffle's unique and subtle flavour. Elizabeth David, in her classic cookbook *Italian Food*, called them the "most delicious of all foods anywhere".

12

curse of mass tourism. This said, the almost incestuously interrelated population has nevertheless dropped from 700 in 1951 to around 150 today, most of whom are migrant shepherds, many of them Sardinians or former Yugoslavs, who spend the glacial winter months down in Norcia.

The most immediately noticeable thing in the village is its **graffiti**, daubed in thick white paint on huge walls; this forms a kind of social document for the community, the pieces – often malicious and some going back generations – recording stories and myths about local people. Wander up to the **parish church**, which has a marvellous fresco cycle on the left wall describing the life of St Anthony Abbot, patron saint of

THE PIANO GRANDE IN BLOOM

The best period to visit the Piano Grande is late spring to early summer, when it blazes with an extraordinary profusion of **wild flowers**. In about mid-May crocuses and narcissi bloom, giving way in early June to buttercups, wild tulips and fritillaries, followed by poppies and cornflowers in late June/early July. These are only approximate timings though, and can vary by up to two weeks. Woven into the floral carpet are rare **Alpine flora**, including the *Carex buxbaumi*, an Ice-Age relic discovered in 1971 and believed to be unique. On the mountains around can be found further rarities such as Apennine edelweiss (found elsewhere only in parts of Abruzzo), the martagon lily, bear's grape, Apennine potentilla and the Alpine buckthorn – but you don't need to be an expert to enjoy the startling spectacle, well documented by postcards on sale here.

shepherds and their flocks. On the arch outside the church to the right as you look down to the Piano Grande is a Fascist plaque, of a type long ago removed from other, less remote towns and villages in Italy, which salutes Il Duce, "refounder of the Italian Empire".

The Monti Sibillini

The **Monti Sibillini** are the only really wild mountains of Tuscany and Umbria, and the most precious natural environment for many hundreds of miles. The northernmost of the big Apennine massifs, they run north–south for about 40km, their summit ridge marking both the Umbrian border and the watershed between the Adriatic and Tyrrhenian seas. In **Monte Vettore** (2476m) they have the third-highest point on the peninsula, a massive, barren mountain that rises above the Piano Grande with majestic grandeur. The Sibillini have been designated a **national park**, a status that sadly exists more on paper than on the ground.

The hikes

Hiking in the Sibillini is superb, whether it's day hikes or more demanding backpack ventures. Unlike the Alps or Abruzzo, there are few marked paths and you're unlikely to meet many people other than shepherds. The 1:50,000 *Kompass: Sibillini* **map** is adequate and widely available, though locally you should be able to pick up better 1:25,000 maps. **Paths** marked on maps do generally exist but in good weather the hills are so open (bar a few glorious beech woods) that you can wander pretty much at will, at least on the western, Umbrian side of the mountains. This is not true on the eastern flanks (in the Marche), which are dotted with dangerous crags and screes. However, around Castelluccio and the western ramparts the worst you'll have to contend with are some of the steepest grass slopes you'll ever come across.

From Forca di Presta

Castelluccio is the best base for **day hikes**, with trails leaving from the village in all directions. **Monte Vettore** via Forca di Presta (8km east of Castelluccio on the road to the Marche) is the obvious target, returning along the ridge via Quarto San Lorenzo and Forca Viola. This is a pretty tough full day's outing, which you could take at a more leisurely pace by starting at the summer-only **refuge** at Forca di Presta.

Another good walk from Forca di Presta or Castelluccio, mainly downhill through woods, takes you to **ARQUATA DEL TRONTO** in the Marche, a smallish place with two **hotels**.

From Castelluccio to Norcia

A third rewarding hike is to strike across country **from Castelluccio to Norcia**, a route comfortably accomplished in a day, though the route-finding here requires a little more diligence: paths to the ridge (around 1800m) are straightforward, but the drop from the ridge can be a bit of a scramble if you miss the path. Trails lower down, which you'll easily pick up, are much better.

North of Castelluccio

For a quick and easy glimpse of the scenery **north of Castelluccio** follow the *strada bianca* (gravel road), for about twenty minutes, past the *Scuola di Volo*, round the corner into the Valle Canatra and on to the **Fonte Valle Canatra**. It's an all-but-level stroll which you could prolong by following the obvious cart track to the head of the lovely valley and the open plains under Monte delle Rose (1881m).

Another excellent, straightforward and not overly demanding walk is to leave Castelluccio on the upper *strada bianca* west and then follow the rough road and clear path along the ridges of the Piano Grande's western rim (Colle Tosto, Monte Vetica and others).

To the Lago di Pilato

A more ambitious and longer hiking route is to cross over the ridge **east of Castelluccio** into the Marche, where the best-known walk runs to a lake, the **Lago di Pilato**, an idyllic spot under Monte Vettore, which can be easily tackled from here. This is supposedly the burial place of **Pontius Pilate**, the story being that Pilate's body was dispatched from Rome on a cart pulled by two oxen, which traipsed through wild country and then plunged into the lake, disappearing without trace. The legend has made the lake the heart of the mountains' supposed necromantic goings-on; Norcians used to practice animal sacrifice here, as well as human, so it is said, to placate the demons and protect themselves from storms and bad weather. In many recent summers the lake has all but dried up, putting in danger an endemic crustacean (*Chirocephalus marchesonii*), which used to stain the water **red**, a colouring anciently attributed to the blood of Pilate.

ARRIVAL AND INFORMATION

MONTI SIBILLINI

By bus Castelluccio is served by one bus a week (on Thurs) from Norcia.

Information There are no visitor centres in the park itself or in Castelluccio, but there are two in surrounding towns (see p.490 & p.495).

ACCOMMODATION AND EATING

Camartina Ascoli Piceno, Le Marche ☎ 0736 809 261, ⓦ hotelcamartina.it. This large hotel-restaurant sits on a side road just north of Arquata Del Tronto, and is well placed for the paths on and off the hills. The place is modern, simple and spacious, and many of the rooms take in the stupendous views all around. The restaurant specializes in fresh trout and truffles; a full meal will cost about €25, exclusive of wine. Breakfast included. **€70**

Rifugio ANA Forca di Presta ☎ 0736 809 278 or ☎ 347 087 5331, ⓦ rifugiomontisibillini.it. Sited at 1500m, the *rifugio* is a source of basic food, maps and information, plus accommodation by way of beds in rooms and dorms available. It's essential to call in advance if you want to stay. Full meals, with grills a speciality, run about €20, and home-made pastries and other desserts are also on offer. Open daily mid-June to mid-Sept; weekends only rest of the year. Dorm bed with breakfast **€16.50**

THE SIBYLS

According to local tradition, the **Monti Sibillini** are home to one of the dozen or so ancient **sibyls** – crones with oracular powers, some of whom were supposed to have foretold the coming of Christ. Later versions of the sibyl myth transformed them into temptresses possessed by the Devil – those lured to the sibyls' caves were doomed to remain trapped there until the Day of Judgement – which perhaps explains why these mountains have a reputation for necromancy and Satanism. By happy coincidence the code for the *Kompass* map to the area is 666, the Devil's number.

Sibilla Via del Piano Grande, Castelluccio ☎ 0743 870 113, ⓦ sibillacastelluccio.com. This Alpine-style building in the village centre is Castelluccio's only real hotel. Half of the rooms look onto the scrappy car park piazza, so ask for one of those with views over the Piano Grande. There's also a restaurant which, though less appealingly rustic, serves up remarkably good food. Breakfast is included. Open April–Oct. €70

Cascia and around

CASCIA, 18km south of Norcia, figures large on the map but is very disappointing in actuality, a deathly mix of programmed piety and chintzy kitsch, recommendable only to pilgrims in search of **St Rita**. Her presence – and the stupendously ugly twentieth-century Basilica – dominates both the new and the earthquake-damaged hill-town, which was abandoned for a time in the eighteenth century. Little known elsewhere, St Rita has a massive cult following in Italy, especially amongst women, for whom she is a semi-official patron saint. Every year on May 21 and 22, thousands flock here for the torchlight **Celebrazioni Ritiane**, when the saint's shrine is venerated.

Rita's **Basilica**, which contains her wizened mummy, is a monument to religious bad taste probably without equal – a piece of Fascist architectural brutalism that attempts to place Byzantine and Romanesque elements in a modern context, and in doing so produces a delirium of white marble that might sit more fittingly in some nightmare Disneyworld.

12 Chiesa-Museo di Sant'Antonio Abate

Via Porta Leonina • Mid-March to April & Sept 19 to Oct Sat & Sun 10.30am–1pm & 3–6pm; May–July & Sept 1–18 Fri–Sun 10.30am–1pm & 3–6pm; Aug & Dec 24–Jan 6 daily 10.30am–1pm & 3–6pm; Nov–March Sat & Sun 10.30am–1pm & 3–5pm, plus other days during special exhibitions • €3 • ☎ 0743 753 055

Just outside the walls, the excellent **Chiesa-Museo di Sant'Antonio Abate** contains two marvellously preserved fresco cycles: the fifteenth-century, sixteen-panel cycle on the *Life of St Anthony* by the Maestro della Dormito di Terni, and *Stories of the Passion and the Life of Christ* (1461) by **Nicola da Siena**. The presbytery holds a precious sixteenth-century group of wooden statues depicting Tobias and the Angel.

ARRIVAL AND INFORMATION CASCIA

By bus All buses between Spoleto and Norcia and Cascia run via Sant'Anatolia di Narco; Cascia services to and from Norcia, Spoleto or Rome require a connection at Serravalle. Destinations Foligno (Mon–Sat 1 direct daily; 2hr); Norcia (Mon–Sat 5–8 daily, 1 on Sun; 45min); Roccaporena (1–3 daily; 15min); Rome (Mon–Sat 2 daily, 1 on Sun; 3hr); Spoleto (Mon–Sat 5–7 daily, 3 on Sun; 1hr 5min).

Tourist office Piazza Garibaldi 1 (Mon–Sat 9am–1pm & 3.30–6pm, plus Sun 8.30am–12.30pm in summer; ☎ 0743 71 147, ⓦ www.comune.cascia.pg.it).

Roccaporena

Cascia's bucolic countryside is considerably more rewarding than the town. If you want a quick taste – and to stay on the St Rita trail – the trip to **ROCCAPORENA**, the saint's birthplace, fits the bill. The best way to get here is to take the marked and well-worn **Sentiero-Passeggiata di Santa Rita**, a perfectly level path that contours above the Corno gorge for 6km between Cascia and the village. The track can be picked up in the centre of town through the forecourt of the *Delle Rose* hotel: drop down into the underground car park, walk through it and take the gate 100m beyond, slightly to the left when you emerge. The last kilometre, after crossing the river, is on the road.

The surreal little village sits at the bend of a deep-sided, heavily wooded valley, dominated by a soaring crag, the **Scoglio di Santa Rita**. Perched on the needle-point summit is a tiny chapel, tiring to reach but with magnificent views. In the village, a small but often pilgrim-thronged place devoted almost entirely to Rita, the parish

ST RITA

St Rita, patron saint of Cascia, experienced – and survived – the kinds of hardships borne by women throughout history, which is the main reason for her appeal, and also why she's sometimes known as the "saint of the impossible". Born in 1381, a poor child of aged parents, she was forced to marry at 15 and endured eighteen years of mistreatment from an alcoholic husband. Having weaned himself from the bottle and repented his past, the husband died in a brawl a few weeks later. Rita's children, for the most part wretched wasters, both died attempting to avenge their father.

Beaten, widowed and childless, Rita sensibly thought it about time she became a nun. Her knowledge of the marital bed, however, made this impossible; only a relaxation of convent rules allowed her to become an Augustinian, a development held up as one of her "impossible" miracles. No sooner had she joined than she developed a sore in the middle of her forehead, an excrescence so foul-smelling that none of the nuns would come near her. This supposedly developed when a thorn fell from a crown of thorns as she was praying to a statue of Christ, and so was regarded by her companions as a kind of stigmata. The smell abated only once – to allow her to join her companions on a week's visit to Rome to meet the pope; on their return the odour returned as virulent as ever.

church of **San Montano,** has the graves of Rita's family, and is the spot where she concluded her unfortunate marriage. More people make the pilgrimage to the **Orto di Santa Rita**, site of the saint's now rather tatty garden.

ACCOMMODATION AND EATING   ROCCAPORENA   12

Hotel Roccaporena Via Roccaporena ☎0743 7549, ⓦhotelroccaporena.com. This institutional but spotless pilgrims' hotel-restaurant is fairly comfortable, though it can get noisy, but makes a good base if you're here to hike. The restaurant serves up typical local dishes. Breakfast included, and free wi-fi in the lobby. **€90**

Monteleone di Spoleto

MONTELEONE DI SPOLETO, on the only road south into Lazio, is a fine (if in parts earthquake-battered) medieval village, surrounded by grand hill country and noted for its woodcarving and delicacies such as olives, wine and truffles. The main sight is the church of **San Francesco**, graced with an exceptional Gothic door, and scattered with artistic and archeological fragments excavated from a massive Neolithic necropolis nearby. Monteleone is best known, however, for **farro**, a wheat-like grain (a softer version of the trendy **spelt** in English) that finds its way into soups – *zuppa di farro* – across the Valnerina. The Romans and Etruscans used *farro* as a staple grain, and allegedly fed it to their soldiers before they went into battle.

Orvieto and southern Umbria

ORVIETO

13

Orvieto and southern Umbria

Southern Umbria features two of the region's most illustrious hill-towns – Orvieto and Todi. The latter, especially, has become a little too popular for its own good, but both are essential visits, the former for Italy's richest Gothic cathedral, the latter for the atmosphere, museum, main square and stunning high-altitude location. Often sidestepped in the rush to these star attractions are a number of smaller but still enjoyable centres to the south along the River Nera, notably Narni – occupying a promontory above the valley, and Amelia, whose encircling walls are among the most redoubtable in the country.

Terni, a transport hub and the region's largest centre after Perugia, is the area's low spot, a grim industrial city that serves only as the southern gateway to the **Valnerina**. Roads up the valley pass the most celebrated landscape attraction in this part of Umbria, the **Cascate delle Marmore** – a partly artificial waterfall that nonetheless provides an impressive spectacle – and continue towards Norcia and the rest of the Valnerina.

ARRIVAL AND GETTING AROUND

By train Mainline trains from Terni head north to Spoleto and south to Narni, connecting with the Rome–Florence route (and Orvieto trains) at Orte; Orvieto is a major stop for all but the fastest Rome-Florence trains. The private single-track Ferrovia Centrale Umbra (FCU) provides the most enjoyable ride, running through lovely countryside from Terni to Perugia (for access to Todi and Deruta), and on to Città di Castello and Sansepolcro.

By car Good road links follow almost identical routes: if you're driving, the big junction with the A1 at Orte – an obvious gateway in and out of the region – offers options in all directions.

Terni

TERNI, the southernmost major town in Umbria, was the unlikely birthplace of **St Valentine**, patron saint of lovers and bishop of the town until his martyrdom in 273 – but a less romantic city would be hard to imagine. Prewar Terni formed the cradle of Italy's industrial revolution, claiming the country's first steel mill and producing the world's first viable plastic; its armaments and steel industries made it a target for Allied bombing in 1944. During over a hundred air raids, most of the town – including the best part of its Roman and medieval heritage – was reduced to rubble. These days Terni remains an unattractive industrial town, if no longer quite the manufacturing powerhouse it was in the past, with arms and chemicals still well to the fore: the gun that allegedly shot Kennedy was made here.

To give the town credit, it does its best: the piazzas are often filled with sculpture; cultural life is rich and varied; and the arrival of **film-makers** and production companies, increasingly put off by high costs in Rome, has seen the growth of Terni as

PIAZZA DEL POPOLO, TODI

reated by the
ears ago, this
Europe's highest

with an
al streets and
509

partly enclosed
ightiest walls.

azza plus imposing
a fascinating

❺ Duomo, Orvieto Umbria's most spectacular
cathedral, with the finest facade in Italy and an
outstanding and influential fresco cycle by
Signorelli. **See p.523**

❻ Underground Orvieto Guided tours
explore the labyrinth below the town.
See p.531

❼ Pozzo di San Patrizio, Orvieto This colossal
well is a dazzling example of medieval
engineering. **See p.530**

❽ Necropoli Etruschi, Orvieto An Etruscan
city of the dead, with the name of the
indwelling family chiselled above the door of
each "house". **See p.531**

HLIGHTS ARE MARKED ON THE MAP ON P.506

13

a movie production centre. Much of Roberto Benigni's *Life is Beautiful*, for example, was shot in a local suburb.

Pinacoteca Comunale

Via Campofregoso 98 • Tues–Sun 10am–1pm & 4–7pm • €5 • ☎ 0744 285 946, ⓦ caosmuseum.si2.it

The best reason for visiting Terni is the **Pinacoteca Comunale**, in the Centro Arti Opificio Siri (CAOS). Its star turns are *The Marriage of St Catherine* by **Benozzo Gozzoli**, the *Pala dei Francescani* by Piermatteo d'Amelia, and a *Crucifixion* by the Folignese artist **Nicolò Alunno**, along with works by several key **moderns** – Chagall, Braque, Picasso, Ernst, Kandinsky and Miró. Contemporary works are arranged in a separate section of the gallery. There's also a generous helping of canvases by Orneore Metelli (1872–1938), an impoverished shoemaker from Terni who chronicled his daily life in colourful and appealing naive paintings.

ARRIVAL AND DEPARTURE   TERNI

By train Terni is a major rail junction, with trains running on the state network from Rome, Orte (connection point from Orvieto and Florence), Spoleto, Foligno (connection point from Assisi, Spello and Perugia) and Rieti. There's also the private FCU train line, which shares the main railway station, with hourly trains from Todi, Perugia, Città di Castello, Sansepolcro and stations en route. The train station is on Piazza Dante Alighieri, 1km northeast of the Duomo.

Destinations Foligno (hourly; 40min; connections for Assisi); Fossato di Vico (5 daily; 1hr 30min; additional

connections at Foligno); Narni (12 daily; 15min); Orte (hourly; 30min; connections to Rome, Orvieto, Chiusi, Arezzo & Florence); Perugia Ponte San Giovanni/Sant'Anna (hourly; 1hr 30min; connections at Sant'Anna for FCU services to Città di Castello and Sansepolcro; connections at Ponte San Giovanni for Trenitalia services to Teróntola and Foligno); Rome (hourly; 50min–1hr 20min); Spoleto (12 daily; 20min); Todi (hourly; 40min).

By bus ATC buses leave from the forecourt near the train station to numerous local villages, and to Narni, Todi, the

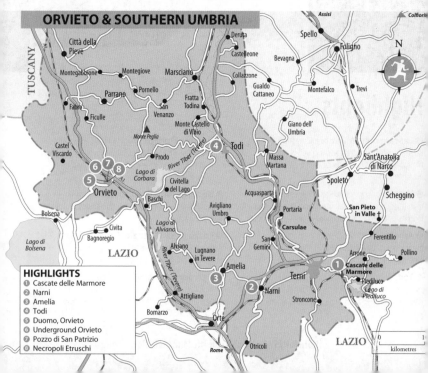

ORVIETO & SOUTHERN UMBRIA

HIGHLIGHTS
❶ Cascate delle Marmore
❷ Narni
❸ Amelia
❹ Todi
❺ Duomo, Orvieto
❻ Underground Orvieto
❼ Pozzo di San Patrizio
❽ Necropoli Etruschi

13

ST VALENTINE

According to the "delicate tradition" about this saint, **Valentine** was elected first bishop of Terni in 197 AD and attempted to bring converts to Christianity – then still outlawed – by encouraging the religious marriage of young people. It's also said that star-crossed lovers would turn to him for advice, drawn by his open-mindedness and his custom of giving them flowers from his garden. His most famous success was the union of Sabinus and Serapia, two lovers – he pagan, she Christian – barred from marriage by their lack of a shared faith. Valentine comforted them with the assurance that their souls would never be separated; when the young Serapia died, he converted Sabinus and thus achieved the reunion of the lovers when Sabinus died soon after. Another theory suggests the saint's feast day was the same day on which birds in Umbria were traditionally thought to mate. Evidence of Valentine's other qualifications for sainthood is scarce, though after his martyrdom in Rome, his head is said to have rolled 93km from its place of execution. Interestingly enough, his following in Italy is considerably less than in the "unromantic" Anglo-Saxon countries.

Terni itself marks St Valentine's Day (Feb 14) with a festival, market and evening disco.

Cascate delle Marmore, Piediluco, Arrone, Ferentillo, Triponzo, Spoleto, Orvieto, Viterbo and Scheggino.
Destinations Amelia (10 or more daily Mon–Sat, 1 on Sun; 50min–1hr); Cascata delle Marmore (hourly Mon–Sat, 11 on Sun; 15min); Ferentillo (hourly Mon–Sat, 12 on Sun; 40min); Narni (10 or more daily Mon–Sat, 1 on Sun; 20min); Orvieto (via Baschi, Guardea, Montecchio and Amelia; 12 daily Mon–Sat; 2hr); Piediluco (9–11 daily Mon–Sat, 6 on Sun; 30min); Scheggino (8 daily Mon–Sat, 5 on Sun; 55min); Todi (via Sangemini, Acquasparta or Avigliano; 3–6 daily Mon–Sat; 1hr 15min–2hr).

INFORMATION

Tourist office The office is close to the station at Viale Cesare Battisti 7a (Mon–Sat 9am–1pm, plus Tues & Fri 3–6pm; ☎ 0744 423 047, ⊛ www.comune.terni.it); head 300m along Viale della Stazione to the seventh turning on the right.

EATING AND DRINKING

★ **Lillero** Via de Filis 8 ☎ 339 591 4140, ⊛ lillero.it. A simple brick-arched medieval setting and some very authentic cooking by one of Umbria's friendliest chefs, who delights in explaining each dish and the many types of local cheeses, pastas and cured meats. About €30 per person. Mon–Sat 12.30–3.30pm & 7.30–11pm; closed Mon lunch.
Pazzaglia Corso Tacito 10 ☎ 0744 407 102, ⊛ pazzagliaristocafe.eu. The city's oldest café-bar is an especially great source of cakes and pastries, including *l'amour polenta*, the house speciality, a delicate rum-flavoured cake made with maize flour and almond. They also serve full meals, with pastas for €5, mains averaging €10 and pizzas starting at €4. Casual and always bustling, with live music some evenings. Daily 7am–11pm.

The Lower Valnerina

Terni is a southern point of entry for the **Lower Valnerina** and on to Norcia and the Sibillini: drive or take a bus along the SS209, which follows the valley into its upper reaches (covered in Chapter 12). Buses from Terni go as far as Triponzo, via Piedipaterno, where you could link with bus connections on to Norcia or Spoleto, passing a number of fine natural diversions, such as the **Marmore waterfalls**. Scenery is generally scrappy until **Ferentillo**, however – when the hills start to rise in impressive fashion – so there's an argument for ignoring the valley's lower reaches until you hit the abbey of San Pietro (see p.488).

Cascate delle Marmore

Unrestricted access • Free

The first stop of interest in the valley comes just 6km southeast of Terni at the **Cascate delle Marmore** (access by train or buses from Terni's Piazza Dante), which at 165m are

13

among the highest waterfalls in Europe. They were created by the **Romans** in 271 BC, when they diverted the River Velino into the Nera during drainage of marshlands to the south. Further channels were cut in 1400 and 1785, both with the intention of draining Rieti's plain without flooding Terni, though the falls' major boost came with the damming of nearby Lago di Piediluco in the 1930s to satisfy industrial demand for hydroelectric power. Terni's power-station complex is the largest hydroelectric plant in Italy.

Pictures of the falls in full spate adorn most Umbrian tourist offices, but what they don't tell you is that the water can be diverted through turbines at the flick of a switch, leaving a none-too-spectacular trickle. **Flow times** are notoriously variable, though in general, afternoons, summer evenings and Sunday mornings are likeliest, especially during July and August when there's an impressive *son et lumière*.

Observation points

There are two **observation points**: the belvedere in Marmore village, and the SS209 road down below. A steep and frequently muddy path connects the two, starting 100m downstream of the falls, and there are swimming pools at the bottom of the cascade when the water's turned off. The green and luxuriant setting, tumbling water and acres of gleaming marble add up to a spectacular show – shame about the factories around the corner.

ACCOMMODATION	CASCATE DELLE MARMORE
Camping Le Marmore Località Campacci ☎0744 67 198 ⓦcampinglemarmore.com. This campsite is just 50m from the falls, immersed in greenery and handy for the regional park, and has a market, bar and restaurant	on site, plus caravans as well as tent pitches. Activities include visits to the Marmore caves, rafting and bungee jumping. Open April–Sept. Adults €6, pitches €4, caravans €34

Ferentillo

FERENTILLO is rapidly becoming the **free-climbing** capital of Italy, its crags swarming at weekends as new and more difficult routes are pioneered. The village itself sprawls across two rocky hillsides, guarded by twin fourteenth-century towers, and merits a stop for one of Umbria's more grotesque ménages – a collection of **mummies**.

Museo delle Mummie

Via della Rocca • Daily: March & Oct 9am–12.30pm & 2.30–6pm; April–Sept 9am–12.30pm & 2.30–7.30pm; Nov–Feb 10am–12.30pm & 2.30–5pm • €3 • ☎ 335 654 3008

The **Museo delle Mummie** is in the crypt of the church of San Stefano, signposted off the main road on the east side of the Nera, in the Precetto quarter. Now behind glass and viewed on guided tours – a precaution taken after a head was stolen – the corpses were simply dumped in the crypt and preserved by accident, apparently dried by their bed of sandy soil and a desiccating wind from the south-facing windows. The characters are a curious mix: two French soldiers hanged during the Napoleonic wars; a bearded dwarf; a mother who died in childbirth (the child displayed alongside her); a papal soldier, bolt upright with his gun, housed in the case of a grandfather clock; a lawyer shot in a local feud over a farm; a farmer whose gun backfired in the same feud and blasted a hole in his stomach; and a hapless Chinese couple who came to Italy in 1880 for their honeymoon and died of cholera. To round things off, there's a pile of leering skulls with a mummified owl perched in their midst.

ACCOMMODATION AND EATING	FERENTILLO
Il Tiglio Via Abruzzo 4 ☎0744 389 104, ⓔatreks @yahoo.it. This 25-bed hostel is in the middle of the Valnerina park, convenient to all activities and sights, and has dorms as	well as en-suite private rooms. Dorm bed €20, doubles €35 **Monterivoso** Via dell'Arrampicata ☎0744 780 772, ⓦmonterivoso.it. The eleven-room hotel-restaurant is set

in a very picturesque converted mill in the nearby hamlet of Monteriviso. Accommodation is pretty rustic, but the staff is helpful, and it's a good jumping off point for park activities. Breakfast included. **€74**

Piermarini Via F. Ancaiano 23 ☎0744 780 714, 🌐 saporipiermarini.it. This popular restaurant ventures beyond the more usual Umbrian standards: their speciality is *coccorè*, a delicious egg dish enhanced with truffle pesto. Expect to pay about €40 per person for a full meal, depending on wine. Booking is a must. Tues–Sat 12.30–2.30pm & 7.30–9.30pm, Sun 12.30–2.30pm; closed three weeks in Aug & Sept.

13

Narni

NARNI is an intimate, unspoilt hill-town that juts into the Nera valley on a majestic spur crowned by another of Cardinal Albornoz's formidable citadels. From train or road, the fortress draws an admiring glance before you see the welter of chemical works around Narni Scalo, the new town around the station – thankfully almost invisible from the medieval centre. Old Narni's stage-set medievalism is even more complete than Perugia's or Assisi's, its quiet piazzas, Romanesque churches – notably the **Duomo** and **Santa Maria in Pensole** – and labyrinth of ancient streets and stepped passageways forming one of Italy's most congenial townscapes.

Brief history

As the Roman colony of Narnia, established in 299 BC, Narni was one of the first such settlements in Umbria – and a linchpin in Rome's defences, standing close to the Tiber valley and the undefended road to the capital. It was the birthplace, in 32 AD, of the Roman emperor Nerva, and of Erasmo da Narni, better known as Gattamelata (1370–1443), one of the greatest of all medieval mercenaries.

Ponte di Augusto

The circuitous route from Narni Scalo to the medieval town allows a brief view of the Roman **Ponte di Augusto**, a solitary arch built in 27 BC in the middle of the river (a second collapsed in 1855), remnant of a bridge that in its day was 30m high and spanned 160m, a product of Augustan-era renovations to the Via Flaminia. In the eighteenth century this was one of the key sights on the Grand Tour – Corot, among others, painted the scene (the picture is in the Louvre) – but now is so lost among the lower town's development that you could easily miss it completely: the best viewpoint is provided by the train from Orte, just before you pull into Narni.

Piazza Garibaldi

Piazza Garibaldi is the town's rather oddly shaped and disjointed social hub; its ancient name, Piazza del Lago, hints at one reason for the strangeness, for the square was once a medieval cistern (or *lacus*), built over a Roman cistern fed by an aqueduct from the surrounding hills. Note the piazza's restored fountain (1527), decorated by imaginary animals. From the square, the main street, Via Garibaldi (and its continuation, Via Mazzini), leads north to the heart of the old town – still built on the old Roman grid – through an arch in the city walls, following the course of the Via Flaminia, whose construction in 220 BC set the seal on Narni's importance.

The Duomo

Piazza Cavour • Daily 8.30am–12.30pm & 3.30–7pm • Free

The **Duomo** was built around 1047 and named after Narni's first bishop, who was buried in accordance with Roman custom outside what were then the town walls in 376; other religious worthies buried on the site include San Cassio, a former Bishop of

13

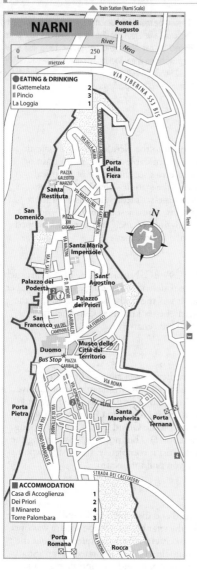

Narni, interred here in 558. By the ninth century (perhaps earlier), a chapel had been built which provided the basis for the 1047 church – by then within the town's medieval borders. It was consecrated in 1145 by Pope Eugenius III and amended over the years so that it is now an intriguing mix of accretions from most centuries since. Its **facade** is small and unassuming, cramped by surrounding buildings and by the Lombard-influenced portico, which dates from 1492 (with later additions). The portal, laced with carvings, dates from the twelfth century.

The interior

Inside, the church has a slightly lopsided feel, owing to the addition of an outer south aisle in the fifteenth century. The extravagant Baroque altar is overshadowed by gold-leafed **pulpits** on either side of the nave and an intricate **screen** – all mainly late fifteenth-century works, but incorporating fragments of Romanesque and paleo-Christian reliefs. The **Cosmati pavement** is also attractive, while elsewhere parts of the original church show through, chiefly in the patches of fresco – notably a little niche *Madonna and Child* on the west (rear) wall and in the apse behind the choir. The little wooden summer **statue** (1474) representing St Anthony Abbot, near the rear wall at the start of the left aisle, is by the Sienese master Vecchietta, who may also have been responsible for *San Giovenale*, a painting of Narni's patron saint on the last pillar of the right aisle.

The Sacello di San Giovenale e San Cassio
Giovenale's tomb lies in the cellar-like chapel midway down the south aisle, the extraordinary **Sacello di San Giovenale e San Cassio** (also known as the Oratorio di San Cassio). It's shielded by a Cosmatesque marble screen and pillars, possibly from the presbytery of the Romanesque church here rebuilt in 1322, and a relief of *Two Lambs Adoring the Cross*, together with two thirteenth-century niche statues of the *Pietà* and *San Giovenale*. An important piece of early Christian architecture, the chapel dates from 558; its crude, age-blackened walls contain a ninth-century **mosaic** of Christ high up on an inner wall, the oldest in the region. Inside are more Cosmati fragments and reliefs, together with the eighth- or ninth-century sarcophagus used as Giovenale's tomb: the stones beyond the tomb represent part of the original Roman wall.

THE SAN GIOVENALE FESTIVAL

San Giovenale is the focus of Narni's main **festival**, during which a fortnight of festivities lead up to the Corsa dell'Anello, held on the second Sunday in May. On the Saturday evening of that weekend a torchlit procession takes place. The next day, contestants from the town's three medieval quarters compete to thrust a lance through a ring (*anello*) suspended in Via Maggiore.

Museo della Città e del Territorio

Via Aurelio Saffi 1 • April–June & Sept Tues–Sun 10.30am–1pm & 3.30–6pm; July & Aug Tues–Sun 10.30am–1pm & 4.30–7.30pm; Oct–March Fri–Sun 10.30am–1pm & 3–5.30pm • €5 • ☎ 0744 717 117, ⓦ sistemamuseo.it

The bulk of the town's paintings and other works of art are housed in the **Museo della Città e del Territorio** in Palazzo Eroli. The influence of **Tuscan artists** in the region is acknowledged in Benozzo Gozzoli's *Annunciation* (1451–2) and a tabernacle attributed to the school of Agostino di Duccio. One section is devoted to San Girolamo, an important former Franciscan convent 13km southeast of Narni that was once home to the town's best painting, **Domenico Ghirlandaio**'s *Coronation of the Virgin*, commissioned for the convent in 1486 by Cardinal Eroli, a cleric who was also busy in Spoleto's cathedral (see p.478). Collections here include a section devoted to the gold and silverware from the cathedral treasury.

Piazza dei Priori

North of the Duomo, Via Garibaldi continues through a vibrant residential centre, following the line of the old Roman Cardo Maximus past Via del Campanile on the left, which provides a glimpse of the cathedral's fifteenth-century campanile (built on a Roman base). It soon emerges into the **Piazza dei Priori**, a perfect little civic square where pride of place goes to the fourteenth-century **Palazzo dei Priori** and its *loggia*, designed by the Gubbian Matteo Gattapone, the architect responsible for Gubbio's Palazzo dei Consoli and Spoleto's vast Ponte delle Torri. Next to its high arches and Roman inscription is a little exterior pulpit, built for the peripatetic St Bernardino. The striking Palazzo Sacripante alongside is covered in medieval reliefs.

Opposite the Palazzo dei Priori is the **Palazzo del Podestà**, or Palazzo Comunale, cobbled together by amalgamating three town houses and adding some token decoration. The thirteenth-century Romanesque sculptures above the main door are worth a glance, as are the numerous Roman fragments of the courtyard.

Sant'Agostino

Via Gattamelata • Daily 8.30am–noon & 4–7pm • Free

The large, bare portal of the tatty, water-stained church of **Sant'Agostino** conceals an interior with a redoubtable fourteenth-century stone altar and a few medieval faded frescoes amidst half-hearted Baroque. The best fresco, to the right of the main door, is a *Madonna Enthroned with Sts Lucy and Apollonia* (1482) by the accomplished local artist Pier Matteo d'Amelia, best known as one of Fra' Filippo Lippi's two assistants on the apse frescoes in Spoleto cathedral. Also spare a moment for the fresco fragments in the apse, which depict a variety of saints.

Santa Maria Impensole

Via Mazzini • Daily 8.30am–12.30pm & 3.30–7.30pm • Free

The inconspicuous but lovely church of **Santa Maria Impensole** is a simple basilica, unchanged since it was built in 1175 over a pagan place of worship that in turn was the site of a cemetery, and then a Roman-era house with two still extant cisterns. It has an enchanting triple-arched Romanesque portico and a beautiful carved frieze around the square doorways. The **interior** is plain save for a few simple carvings and capitals, though interesting rooms below the nave with Roman remains are occasionally open, including one with a sixth-century tomb.

San Domenico and around

The ex-church of **San Domenico** (Mon–Thurs 9am–1pm & 3.15–6pm, Fri 9am–1pm; free) is a slightly forlorn building, now home to Narni's archives and public library. It's worth dropping by for the wealth of medieval fresco fragments around the walls and the funerary wall monument (1494) to Gabriele Massei, crafted by followers of Agostino di Duccio. You could also try asking in the library to view the Roman **aqueduct** that lies below the building. Behind the church to the left, at the beginning of Via Aurelio Saffi, a small **garden** with fragments of an old tower offers great views down into the Nera gorge: the distinctive building way down below is the recently restored twelfth-century Benedictine **Abbazia di San Cassiano** (usually open Sun 7.30am–1pm).

The Rocca

Fri–Sun 11am–1pm & 4.30–7.30pm • €3

Returning to Piazza Garibaldi and heading south takes you into a warren of little streets, worth wandering for their own sake. At the top of this quarter lies the **Rocca**, a massive affair, lording it over the town and surrounding country and reached by Via del Monte, a street that threads through the *terziere di Mezule*, one of the three areas into which the medieval town was divided. The castle was commissioned by Cardinal Albornoz in the 1370s and is attributed to Gattapone, responsible for the town's Loggia dei Priori; it formed a link in the chain of fortresses by which Albornoz sought to reassert papal authority across Umbria. The park around the castle is a perfect spot for a picnic and siesta.

ARRIVAL AND DEPARTURE

NARNI

By train Frequent trains from both Terni and Orte (where you can pick up connections to Orvieto on the Rome–Florence line) arrive at Narni Scalo station. From the station forecourt buses run into town, stopping at Piazza Garibaldi; buy tickets on board or from the station news kiosk. You may have to wait, but don't be tempted into the long and tedious walk.
Destinations Foligno (9–13 daily; 55min; connections for Assisi, Nocera Umbra, Gualdo Tadino, Fossato di Vico – for Gubbio – and Perugia); Fossato di Vico (5 daily; 1hr 45min); Orte (hourly; 15min; connections for Rome, Orvieto, Chiusi,

Arezzo and Florence); Rome direct (10 daily; 1hr); Terni (12 daily; 15min).

By bus Buses from nearby towns as well as the station arrive at Piazza Garibaldi, where there's an ATC office for bus information and tickets.
Destinations Amelia (10 daily Mon–Sat, 1 on Sun; 25min); Orvieto (5 daily Mon–Sat; 1hr 40min); Terni (10 daily Mon–Sat, 1 on Sun; 20min).

By car There is limited parking in Piazza Garibaldi, and more spaces on the approach to the square in Via Roma.

UNDERGROUND NARNI

Narni Sotterranea, Via San Bernardo 12 (📞 0744 722 292, 🌐 narnisotterranea.it), offers 1.5hr **guided tours** (April to mid-June & mid-Sept to Oct Sat 3pm, 4.30pm & 6pm, Sun 10am, 11.15am, 12.30pm, 3pm, 4.15pm & 5.30; mid-June to mid-Sept Mon–Fri noon & 5pm, Sat 3pm, 4.30pm & 6pm, Sun 10am, 11.15am, 12.30pm, 3pm, 4.15pm & 5.30pm; Nov–March Sun 11am, 12.15pm, 3pm & 4.15pm; €5) of some of the town's ancient **subterranean chambers** and **tunnels**, notably those around San Domenico, Santa Maria Impensole and the Roman "Formina" aqueduct that brought water to Piazza Garibaldi.

13

INFORMATION

Tourist office Piazza dei Priori 3 (Mon & Tues 9.30am–12.30pm & 4.30–7.30pm, Wed–Sun 9.30am–12.30pm & 3.30–7pm; 0744 715 362, www .comune.narni.tr.it).

ACCOMMODATION

Casa di Accoglienza Via Gattemelata 74 0744 715 217, ostellidellagioventu.org. This spartan place run by the nuns of Santa Anna has beds in quadruple, double or single rooms (for men and women). Breakfast included; other meals available. Doubles **€38**

Dei Priori Vicolo del Comune 4 0744 726 843, www.loggiadeipriori.it. All old-world from the outside, this hotel is right in the centre of the old quarter and dates to the fifteenth century. Rooms are spacious, modern and rather plain, but some have views. There's a restaurant, and breakfast is included. **€75**

Il Minareto Via dei Cappuccini Nuovi 32 0744 726 343, ilchiostroeventi.com. Part of the Il Chiostro monastery complex, this hotel has rooms looking onto the old cloister and well and beyond. Though hardly luxurious the accommodations are handsome and very clean. No breakfast. **€90**

★ **Torre Palombara** Strada della Cantinetta 3 0744 744 617, torrepalombara.com. This luxury fifteenth-century property offers views of Narni and the castle, gardens and vineyards, a pool and elegant accommodations filled with antique touches, including a thirteenth-century fireplace in the lounge. Rooms have a/c and wi-fi, and breakfast is included. **€160**

EATING AND DRINKING

Il Gattemelata Via Pozza della Comunità 4 0744 717 245, bellaumbria.net/ristorante-Gattamelata. A pleasantly understated trattoria just off Piazza Garibaldi, with ambitious Umbrian cooking: try the wild boar *raviolini* in spicy tomato sauce (€12). The tasting menu (€40, not including drinks) serves up hearty medieval recipes, and €30 should buy you a good meal. Tues–Sun 12.30–3.30pm & 7.30–10pm; closed Sat eve.

Il Pincio Via XX Settembre 117 0744 722 241, ristoranteilpincio.it. Occupying part of an ancient grotto, and run by the charming Cesare and Rita. The cooking is classic Umbrian, with virtually all produce sourced locally; the *tagliata di filetto con rucola e aceto*

balsamico (tender strip steak pan-fried with rocket and balsamic) is superb. Without wine, expect to pay around €25 a head. Daily 12.30–3pm & 7.30–9.45pm; closed Wed Oct to mid-April.

La Loggia Vicolo del Comune 4 0744 722 744, ristorantinarni.it. This long-established restaurant in the heart of Narni's old town is a classic and cosy place, part of the *Dei Priori* hotel, with vaulted stone ceilings and a nice terrace garden. A full meal runs about €35, unless you go for such pricey specialities as trout with truffles and potatoes (€20). Tues–Sun 12.30am–3pm & 7.30–9.30pm; closed late July.

Amelia and around

Perched atop a sugarloaf hill 11km west of Narni Scalo, **AMELIA** is as delightful as its setting, enclosed by some of the oldest and mightiest **walls** in Italy. Access to the town is through one of the four original gates: the main entry is the **Porta Romana**; the walls can be seen from a small park to the left of the gate, and from the pleasant 2km path that starts here and encircles Amelia. The surrounding countryside is equally appealing, and the church at nearby **Lugnano in Teverina** is one of southern Umbria's Romanesque highlights.

Some history

Formed from vast polygonal blocks joined without mortar, Amelia's walls are up to 4m wide and 8m high. Parts are known to have belonged to an Umbrian acropolis of the fifth century BC, though the Roman historian Pliny claimed the town was formed in the eleventh century BC, three centuries before Rome. The Romans took advantage of the fortifications in 90 BC when they used the town, then named Amerina, as a staging post on the Via Amerina, one of nine military roads linking Etruria to the Via Flaminia. Thereafter the town within the walls was all but destroyed by Totila, and later history followed a predictable course through rule by the nobility and slow decline.

San Francesco

Via Nocicchia

13

Immediately inside the gate stands the church of **San Francesco**, also known as Sts Filippo e Giacomo, its typically plain-faced facade relieved by a rose window of 1401. Inside, the Cappella di Sant'Antonio contains six tombs belonging to members of the Geraldini family, the clan that held sway over Amelia for long periods during the Middle Ages. The monuments (1477) on the top right, to Matteo and Elisabetta Geraldini, are the work of **Agostino di Duccio**.

Museo Archeologico di Amelia

Piazza Augusto Vera 10 • April–June & Sept Tues–Sun 10.30am–1pm & 4–7pm; July & Aug Tues–Sun 10.30am–1pm & 4.30–7.30pm; Oct–March Fri–Sun 10.30am–1pm & 3.30–6pm • €5 • ☎ 0744 978 120, ⓦ sistemamuseo.it

The ex-Collegio Boccarini, with its beautiful courtyard and double *loggia*, is home to the **Museo Archeologico di Amelia**, where the star exhibit is a bronze statue discovered locally in 1963 of the Roman general Nerone Claudio Druso, better known as Germanico, a nephew of Tiberius who died in mysterious circumstances in AD 17. There's also a picture gallery of paintings removed from local churches and palaces.

The Duomo

Piazza del Duomo • Mon–Sat 7.30am–1pm & 4–7pm, Sun 6.30am–1pm & 5–7.30pm • Free

From San Francesco, the spiralling Via della Repubblica draws you to **Piazza Marconi**, a lovely old square from where the stepped Via del Duomo leads steeply to the town's summit, site of a cathedral square with panoramic views. A small park here offers the best views. The most striking feature of the **Duomo**, a Romanesque church ruined by Baroque superfluities and nineteenth-century frescoes, is a twelve-sided **tower**, dated 1050 and claimed by some to symbolize the Apostles, by others to represent the signs of the zodiac. It's studded with Roman fragments and originally served as the town's principal civic tower.

Inside, flanking the second chapel on the right are two standards reputedly won from the Turks at the Battle of Lepanto. The first chapel in the north aisle holds the *Tomb of Giovanni Geraldini* (1476) by Agostino di Duccio, and the first column on the right was the one against which St Fermina, the local patron saint, is said to have been martyred. A distinctive **octagonal chapel** is attributed to Antonio da Sangallo, its two funerary monuments to Ippolito Scalza, who played a key role during the construction of Orvieto's Duomo.

Lugnano in Teverina

The run along the back roads between Orvieto and Amelia (possible by bus) is a treat, offering plenty of oak forests and the chance to visit the twelfth-century **Santa Maria Assunta** in **LUGNANO IN TEVERINA**, some 9km northwest of Amelia. Fronted by an exotic, restored portico (1230), the church has finely carved twin pulpits and has somehow hung onto a triptych by **Nicolò Alunno** in the apse. The interior also has plenty of lovely carved capitals, a reconstructed *cantoria* and a **Cosmatesque** floor, while the beautifully pillared crypt features a fine sculpted screen and further Cosmati marble work.

ARRIVAL AND INFORMATION

AMELIA

By bus Buses run to Amelia from Terni and Orvieto, and there are also shuttle buses from the two nearest train stations, Narni Scalo and Orte. The bus stop is on Via Nocicchia at the southeast edge of town, 500m down from the main square; a

lift from the lower car park, near the bus stop goes to the upper town, letting you out near the post office.

Destinations Avigliano (3 daily Mon–Sat, 1 connecting to Todi via Dunarobba; 25min); Lugnano in

13

Teverina (Mon–Sat 10 daily, 1 on Sun; 20min); Narni (10 daily Mon–Sat, 1 on Sun; 25min); Orvieto (5–7 daily Mon–Sat; 1hr 15min); Terni (10 or more daily Mon–Sat, 1 on Sun; 50min–1hr).

Tourist office Via Roma 4, beside the Porta Romana (Mon & Sun 9.30am–12.30pm; Tues–Sat 9am–1pm & 3.30–6.30pm; closed Sat morning Oct–March; ☎ 0744 981 453, ⊕ amelia.it).

ACCOMMODATION AND EATING

Giustiniani Piazza Mazzini 9 ☎ 0744 978 673, ⊕ ostellogiustiniani.it. The local youth hostel has dorms and private en-suite rooms sleeping two to six people. Accommodations are extremely spartan but clean, and some of the rooms have the original wood-beam ceilings. Open March–Sept daily 8–10am & 4pm to midnight. Dorm beds **€16**, doubles **€40**

La Gabelletta Strada Tuderte 20 ☎ 0744 981 775, ⊕ lagabelletta.it. Some 3.5km northeast of town, this is a large and popular restaurant with courteous staff and good local cooking. They do a great *cacio e pepe*, and the sausage

sautéed with grapes is delectable. Full meals go for as little as €25 per person, depending on wine. Daily 12.30–3.30pm & 7.30–9.30pm; closed Mon & late July.

★ **Palazzo Farattini** Via Farattini 52 ☎ 0744 983 399, ⊕ palazzofarrattini.it. This sixteenth-centry *palazzo* boasts original period furnishings, but has been upgraded with all usual mod cons. The rooms are on the very elegantly decorated, high-ceilinged first floor where the nobles lived, and are grandly appointed with antiques, paintings and beautiful original ceilings. In addition, there are extensive gardens, a pool and wi-fi. Breakfast included. **€120**

Todi

TODI, some 25km east of Orvieto, provides a graphic illustration of what has happened in much of Umbria over the last few decades. Once a sleepy, simple agricultural centre, it became a favoured retreat for expats and Rome's arts and media types, attracted as much by the town's considerable rustic charms as its relative proximity to the Italian capital. These days the transformation is all but complete: Todi is firmly on the tourist trail and has been smartened up to within a whisker of its life. Gentrification is manifest in a scattering of estate agents, shuttered holiday homes and the revamped and decidedly high-profile **Todi Festival** (⊕ todiartefestival.com), ten days of music, ballet and other arts at the beginning of September. Don't be put off, for the town is still has charm and many sights, notably an impressive **Piazza del Popolo** and the churches of **San Fortunato** and **Santa Maria della Consolazione**, though perhaps what lingers most in the memory is its position 410m up, a stunning and daunting prospect from below.

Brief history

Iron Age remains suggest Todi has seen some three thousand years of continual habitation. Tradition purports that the town was built where an eagle dropped a tablecloth snatched from a local family – hence the eagle and cloth in the town's insignia. More certain is the **Etruscan** heritage: coins bearing the name Tutare ("border") suggest a town of some independence, probably one of several outposts used by the Etruscans to defend their frontier along the Tiber. Local necropolises have yielded some of the finest Etruscan treasures, most of them – including a famous bronze statue of Mars – shipped off to Rome. Ancient Roman rule came (in 42 BC) and went, leaving little except a second set of walls.

The town's heyday was the thirteenth century, when as a free *comune* – one of Umbria's first – it managed to annex Amelia and Terni, hold its own in skirmishes with

> ### TODI ORIENTATION
> All Todi's main sights are within a few minutes' walk of each other, though the southeast part of the town around Porta Romana involves a long downhill hike, as does the walk to Santa Maria della Consolazione. From the bus terminal, the minibus drops you at the central **Piazza del Popolo**, home to the cathedral and an outstanding museum; walking up via the footpath leaves you in the municipal gardens, near the church of San Fortunato.

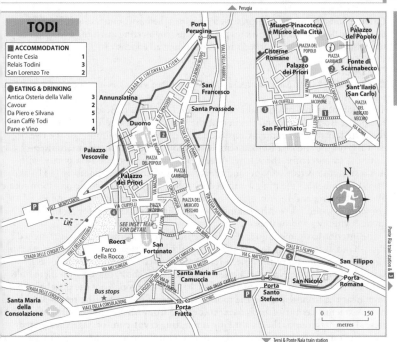

Spoleto, Narni and Orvieto, and build a third set of walls and crop of civic palaces. The two small eaglets under the wings of the Todi eagle on some of the town's coats of arms represent the towns of Amelia and Terni. The **Atti** were the leading noble family, overseeing – in tandem with the Church's representatives – a period of decline interrupted only by a flicker of sixteenth-century prosperity that produced more palaces and Todi's great Renaissance church of Santa Maria della Consolazione.

Piazza del Popolo and around

The **Piazza del Popolo** is often described as the most perfect medieval piazza in Italy – and with justice, flanked by a range of *palazzi* housing the excellent **Museo-Pinacoteca e Museo della Città** and a superb **Duomo**. The **Palazzo dei Priori** here, built between 1293 and 1337, was the seat of Todi's various rulers and is now the town hall – note the eagle coat of arms, complete with tablecloth.

The best place to enjoy the piazza's street life is from the **bar** down on its southwest corner, a locals' local, though the smarter place midway down the piazza's western side enjoys more sunshine. For some wonderful **views** of the surrounding countryside, wander to **Piazza Garibaldi** just alongside the square. The statue here (1890) is of Giuseppe Garibaldi, while the scenically perfect cypress is supposed to have been planted to celebrate Garibaldi's visit to Todi with his wife in 1849.

The Cisterne Romane

Piazza del Popolo • April–Oct Tues–Sun 10.30am–1pm & 2.30–6.30pm; Nov–March Sat & Sun 10.30am–1pm & 2–4.30pm • €2, or joint 3-day ticket with Museo-Pinacoteca and San Fortunato campanile €7.50 • ☎ 075 894 4148

Originally the site of the Roman forum, the Piazza del Popolo is built above a surviving complex of Roman cisterns (signed off the square down a small alley), of which the

13

Cisterne Romane are the well-preserved remains. There isn't much to see, but the cisterns' scale graphically illustrates the Romans' engineering acumen: some 5km of tunnels, 30 cisterns and 500 wells in all, including all epochs.

The Duomo

Via del Duomo ☎ 075 894 3041 • Daily: summer 8.30am–12.30pm & 2.30–6.30pm; winter 8.30am–12.30pm & 2.30–5.30pm • €2 for the treasury & crypt

The **Duomo**, atop a broad flight of steps added in 1740, represents a merging of the last of the Romanesque and the first of the Gothic forms filtering in from France in the early fourteenth century. Construction started at the beginning of the twelfth century, on the site of a Roman temple to Apollo, and continued intermittently until the seventeenth. The square, three-tiered **facade** is inspired simplicity, with just a sumptuous rose window and ornately carved composite doorway (1513 and 1639) to embellish the pink weathered marble – the classic example of a form found all over Umbria and the Abruzzo. The exterior sides of the church are more complicated, and it's worth walking down adjoining side streets for glimpses of arches, windows and buttresses.

The **interior** has some impressive nineteenth-century stained glass in the arched right-hand aisle, a lovely font (1507), an exquisite fourteenth-century *Madonna and Child* and, at the end of the aisle, a fetching altarpiece by Perugino's follower Giannicolo di Paolo. Nothing, however, matches the **choir**, carved with incredible delicacy and precision between 1521 and 1530; a nice touch are the panels at floor level near the front depicting the tools used to carve the piece. The rear west wall has a sixteenth-century *Last Judgement* (derived from Michelangelo's Sistine Chapel fresco). Underground, there's a mildly interesting **crypt**-cum-passageway entered from the top of the north aisle and scattered with Roman and possibly Etruscan fragments. The little cells in the corridor were used as tombs until the nineteenth century.

The piazza's palazzi

The Piazza del Popolo's other key buildings are a trio of thirteenth-century public palaces, squared off near the Duomo in provocative fashion – the *comune*'s aim being to put one over on the Church. The **Palazzo del Capitano**, built around 1290, and the adjoining **Palazzo del Popolo**, dating from 1213 (one of Italy's earliest civic palaces), are the most prominent, thanks mainly to their external staircase, which looks like the set for a thousand B-movie swordfights.

Museo-Pinacoteca e Museo della Città

Piazza del Popolo 29–30 • Tues–Sun: April–Oct 10.30am–1pm & 2.30–6.30pm; Nov–March 10.30am–1pm & 2.30–5pm • €5, or joint 3-day ticket with Cisterne Romane and San Fortunato campanile €7.50 • ☎ 075 894 6216

The upper floor of the Palazzo del Capitano houses the town's superb museum, the **Museo-Pinacoteca e Museo della Città**. Before entering the gallery proper, take a look at the poignant painting by the ticket desk, of Todi near the Porta Romana as it appeared in the early twentieth century: the walls are unsullied by modern building, the only incongruous detail a single early car.

The first area of the museum delves into Todi's earlier history, related through further fascinating paintings and artefacts. Look out in particular, in **Section IV**, for the large painting (1592) of Todi's patron saints and protectors (including Fortunato defending the town from the Goths) by Pietro Paolo Sensini. Todi's *Book of Martyrs* lists no fewer than 853 saints and martyrs who had some sort of connection with the town (plus 53 Servants of God): only five were elevated to the position of patron saints – Fortunato, Callisto, Cassiano, Degna and Romana. Along the wall to the left are several extremely old statues and carvings, some going back to the eighth century, though this section's greatest oddity is the saddle of Anita Garibaldi, left behind when

13

he passed through the town in an advanced state of pregnancy and could no longer bear the discomfort it caused her.

The sections that follow are devoted to archeology, coins and medals (including an important collection of Republican and Imperial-era **Roman coins**), medallions and fabrics. In many cases the rooms are more alluring than their exhibits, particularly the lovely **salon** devoted to ceramics, which was frescoed in 1367 on the orders of the town's priors when it became their home: most of the surviving pictures date from the seventeenth to the twentieth centuries, and include portraits of illustrious Todians and a map by Sensin (1612) of the territory once controlled by the town. The museum's star painting is the sumptuous **Coronation of the Virgin** (1507) by **Lo Spagna**, which greets you as you walk into the picture gallery. Its predella was appropriated by Napoleon in 1811 and now resides, sadly, in the Louvre.

Piazza del Mercato Vecchio

For a further reminder of ancient Todi, take a look at the so-called *nicchioni* (niches) in **Piazza del Mercato Vecchio**, just below Piazza del Popolo; cisterns and walls aside, they constitute more or less all that's left of the Roman colony: four slightly overgrown arches, which perhaps formed the wall of an Augustan basilica. The piazza also holds another work by Lo Spagna, in the ancient Lombard chapel of **San Ilario** (also known as San Carlo), all too often locked to protect his fresco of the Madonna della Misericordia. While there, note just beyond the church, adjoining a flower-strewn arbour, the **Fonte Scarnabecco** (1241), an unusual arched fountain that was Todi's lifeblood and social meeting place before piped water.

San Fortunato

Piazza Umberto 1 • Summer daily 8.30am–12.30pm & 3–7pm; winter Tues–Sun 9.30am–12.30pm & 3–5pm • Free

The enormous **San Fortunato** is set above some half-hearted gardens a stroll south of the piazza. Its disproportionate size is testimony to Todi's medieval wealth, and the messy-looking and squat facade – an amalgam of Romanesque and Gothic – reflects the time it took to build the church (1292–1462). **Lorenzo Maitani** was commissioned to decorate the facade as he did Orvieto's Duomo, and the story goes that the burghers of that town, unable to stomach the prospect of a rival church, took out a contract on his life. If true, it was money spent too late, because his florid **doorway** stands good comparison with that in Orvieto. The Annunciate angel in the niche to the left of the portico is outstanding, and has been attributed to the Sienese sculptor **Iacopo della Quercia.** Look out for some of the smaller details, especially the tiny figures – small jokes, you suspect, on the part of the sculptor – which are hidden in the twists of the portal's spiral columns.

The interior

The light, airy **interior** marks the pinnacle of the Umbrian Gothic tradition of large vaulted churches. The style was based on the smaller, German-influenced "barn" churches common in Tuscany, distinguished – as here – by a single, low-pitched roof with naves and aisles of equal height. Note the grey stone brackets, added to correct the increasingly alarming lean of the supporting pilasters. The two scruffy stoups may date from an earlier church on the site. At the rear sits an excellent **choir** (1590), with more hints of the Baroque than the one in the Duomo, as well as a few scant patches of fresco – the *Madonna* by **Masolino di Panicale** (1432) in the fourth chapel on the right is a good if somewhat battered example of this painter's rare work. The sixth chapel on this side contains further good fresco fragments of the Crucifixion and scenes from the life of St Francis from around 1340 by an unknown Umbrian follower of Giotto.

13

The campanile

Tues–Sun: April–Oct 10am–1pm & 3–6.30pm; Nov–March 10.30am–1pm & 2.30–5pm • €2, or joint 3-day ticket with Museo-Pinacoteca di Todi and Cisterne Romane €7.50

Climbing the 153 steps of the church **campanile** affords some fine views; the entrance is on the north aisle. Be sure to pay homage to the tomb of renowned local poet **Jacopone da Todi** in the crypt, which was built in 1596 on the orders of Bishop Angelo Cesi to house this tomb and those of the town's five patron saints. Cesi was one of a family who managed to retain control of the town's clergy for decades, holding the bishopric continually from 1523 to 1606 – probably not unconnected with the fact that one of the Cesi, Paolo Emilio, managed to become Pope Paul III.

Up to the Rocca

A quiet lane leads from the right of San Fortunato into **public gardens**, full of shady nooks and narrow pathways, and an enjoyable spot for a siesta or picnic on the route to Santa Maria della Consolazione. On this western edge of town, there's also a kids' playground and a small **Rocca** of Albornoz vintage, both far less noteworthy than the views. At the gardens' western end a zigzag path cuts down to Viale della Consolazione for the church.

Santa Maria della Consolazione

Mon & Wed–Sun: April–Oct 9am–12.30pm & 3–6.30pm; Nov–March 9.30am–12.30pm & 2.30–5pm • Free

One of the finest Renaissance churches in Italy, **Santa Maria della Consolazione** was inspired by an apparition of the Virgin on the site and completed in 1607. It was initiated a century earlier, probably by the virtually unknown Cola da Caprarola, possibly using one of Bramante's drafts from St Peter's in Rome. The church's use of alternating types of window in the cupola – known as rhythmic bays – is a Bramante trademark. Over the years, virtually every leading architect of the day had his say in the building's design, including Sangallo, Peruzzi and Vignola. Tantalizingly, a picture from 1489 of the church was also found among the architectural drawings of Leonardo da Vinci, pre-dating Caprarola's involvement.

Whatever the convoluted and mysterious origins of the so-called **Tempio**, it eventually came to conform to most of the precepts articulated by Alberti, the great theoretician of Renaissance architecture: a Greek-cross floor plan (purity of form and proportion), isolation in an open piazza, a white or near-white finish (purity again), high windows (cutting off from impure earthly contact) and a preference for statuary (again of greater "purity" than painting).

ARRIVAL AND DEPARTURE   TODI

By train The town has two train stations on the FCU line between Terni (33km) and Perugia (41km), but both are in the middle of nowhere and connecting buses can involve a longish wait. The Ponte Rio station, 6km east, is marginally closer, and has a more reliable shuttle minibus to the old town (Linea C; around 12 daily Mon–Sat; tickets from the station ticket office); the other station is Ponte Naia, southeast of the town. Buses back to Ponte Rio station leave from Piazza Jacopone – between Piazza del Popolo and San Fortunato – fifteen minutes before each train departure. Local taxi companies can be contacted on ☎ 075 894 2375 and ☎ 075 894 2525.

Destinations Perugia Ponte San Giovanni/Sant'Anna (hourly; 1hr); Terni (hourly; 40min; with connections for Orvieto, via Orte, 1hr 30min).

By bus From Perugia, buses are more convenient. Most stop in Piazzale della Consolazione (on Vioale della Consolazione) next to Santa Maria della Consolazione. From here to the centre, you can take an orange minibus (Linea A), or follow the marked footpath that strikes off Viale della Consolazione, 20m beyond the corner on the right. Buy tickets for the minibuses and long-haul buses from the unlikely looking stall that sells nuts and snacks. Some inter-town buses – plus a once-daily service to Rome – continue to (and leave from) Piazza Jacopone. Get tickets and information from the fruit shop in the piazza.

Destinations Orvieto (1 daily Mon–Sat; 2hr); Perugia (3–6 daily Mon–Sat; 1hr); Terni (via Sangemini, Acquasparta or vigliano; 3–6 daily Mon–Sat; 1hr 15min–2hr).

By car By car, you'll be hard pressed to navigate Todi's narrow streets and one-way system, never mind find a central parking place. The best plan is to leave your car

outside the walls at Porta Perugina, Piazzale della Consolazione or Porta Romana. There are limited paid places in Piazza del Mercato Vecchio.

INFORMATION

Tourist office Piazza del Popolo 37 (April–Oct Mon–Sat 9.30am–1pm & 3.30–6.30pm, Sun 10am–1.30pm;

Nov–March Mon–Sat 10am–1pm & 3–6pm, Sun 10am–1pm; ☎075 894 5418, ⓦ www.comune.todi.pg.it).

ACCOMMODATION

Fonte Cesia Via Lorenzo Leoni 3 ☎075 894 3737, ⓦfontecesia.it. This central four-star is the only hotel within Todi's walls, and is definitely the first choice in town if finances allow. Set in a beautiful converted *palazzo* on several levels, it has very comfortable rooms, an excellent restaurant and good service. **€219**

Relais Todini Frazione Collevalenza ☎075 887 182, ⓦrelaistodini.com. A glorious thirteenth-century hilltop castle 9km south of Todi. Beautifully appointed, its twelve pastel-coloured rooms have period fittings,

antiques, oil paintings, wood and stone floors and the original medieval stone walls. Facilities include tennis courts and a swimming pool. Breakfast included. **€260**

★ **San Lorenzo Tre** Via San Lorenzo 3 ☎075 894 4555, ⓦsanlorenzo3.it. This very pleasant and elegantly furnished nineteenth-century town house has a garden, a sun roof, wi-fi and stupendous views, while rooms feel like they're in someone's immaculately maintained home. Breakfast included. **€110**

EATING AND DRINKING

★ **Antica Osteria della Valle** Via Ciufelli 19 ☎075 894 4848. An excellent restaurant, with a cosy brick-vaulted interior and a terrace. The cooking is creative, the house speciality is *taglioni* with fresh tomato and truffle (in season), and the house wines are very good. Full meals about €30. Tues–Sun 12.30–3pm & 7.30–10pm.

Cavour Corso Cavour 21 ☎075 894 3730, ⓦristorantecavour-todi.com. A friendly option, with good, basic food (including pizzas) and outside dining on a fine multi-level garden terrace with views. Pizzas start at €5, set menus from €15, and a full meal à la carte about €25, excluding wine. Daily noon–3pm & 7.30–11pm; closed Thurs in winter.

★ **Da Piero e Silvana** Via Matteotti 91 ☎075 894 4633, ⓦtodi.net/silvanaepiero. Small and charming, with a medieval interior, this trattoria-pizzeria is run by

a very welcoming couple. The deeply authentic cooking is based on local traditions employing truffles, mushrooms and game, and all bread and pasta is home-made. Pizzas (evenings only) start at €4; there are set menus for €18 and €20, and mains average €10. Daily 12.30–3pm & 7.30–10pm.

Gran Caffè Todi Piazza del Popolo 47 ☎075 894 4611. Good for drinks or snacks as you watch the world go by, with a great view of the Duomo as a backdrop. Mon–Wed & Fri–Sun 8am–1am.

Pane e Vino Via Augusto Ciufelli 33 ☎075 894 5448, ⓦpanevinotodi.com. Very welcoming family-run restaurant, with cosy, rustic dining rooms and a terrace. Specialities are braised meats and a chickpea and porcini soup. Set menu €25, a la carte about €30 for a full meal. The attached wine bar has a good *cava*. Mon, Tues & Thurs–Sun 12.30–4pm & 7.30–10.30pm.

North of Todi

North of Todi, the Tiber valley broadens out to a plain, edged with low hills and dotted with light industry. It's not an area where you'll want to spend a lot of time – and most people tear through (or crawl along on the FCU train). A few of the castles, villages and Romanesque churches, however, are well worthwhile if you're in no hurry to get to Perugia.

Deruta

DERUTA, 18km west of Assisi, is best known for its handmade, hand-painted **ceramics** – by general consent among Italy's best. The Romans worked the local clay, but it was the discovery of distinctive blue and yellow glazes in the fifteenth century, allied with

13

the Moorish-influenced designs of southern Spain, that put the town firmly on the map. Some fifty workshops traded as far afield as Britain, and pieces from Deruta's sixteenth-century heyday have found their way into the world's major museums. Designs these days are mainly copies of the original works; if you want to acquire pieces, avoid the roadside stalls in the (new) lower town and explore the shops around the museum up in the old town.

The Museo Regionale della Ceramica

Largo San Francesco 1 • April–June daily 10.30am–1pm & 3–6pm; July–Sept daily 10am–1pm & 3.30–7pm; Oct–March Mon & Wed–Sun 10.30am–1pm & 2.30–5pm • €3 • ☎ 075 971 1000, ⓦ museoceramicaderuta.it

The **Museo Regionale della Ceramica** stands atop the hill in the old town, alongside the church of San Francesco. The best pieces are on the second floor, with ceramics from the Renaissance period; elsewhere you'll find exhibits from the Roman period to the present day.

Torgiano

Torgiano, 7km north of Deruta, is home to some of Umbria's finest **wines**, all of them produced by **Giorgio Lungarotti**, first of the postwar new breed of Italian producers. A self-made man and now something of a national celebrity, he's put together an excellent and extensive **Museo del Vino** (daily: April–June 10am–1pm & 3–6pm; July–Sept 10am–6pm; Oct–March 10am–1pm & 3–5pm; €4; ☎ 075 988 0200, ⓦ lungarotti.it) in the suitably atmospheric cellars of the Palazzo Graziani-Baglioni, Corso Vittorio Emanuele 31. Early sections look at the origins of viticulture, followed by documentation and artefacts relating to wine-making in the Middle Ages. Subsequent rooms are devoted to Vin Santo, commerce, the legal niceties of wine-making, cultivation, wine mythology and memorabilia, everything well labelled in English.

Orvieto

ORVIETO sits on a spectacular tabletop of volcanic tufa whose sheer sides fall 325m to the vine-covered valley floor – a cliff-edged remnant of the four volcanoes whose eruptions also bequeathed the soils that produce Orvieto's well-known wines. Out on a limb from the rest of Umbria, the town is perfectly placed between Rome and Florence to serve as a historical picnic for tour operators, and visitors flood here in their millions during high season, drawn mainly by the **Duomo** – one of the greatest Gothic buildings in Italy and home of some sublime frescoes by Luca Signorelli. Other highlights include the **Etruscan necropolis**, two intriguing **wells** and some very fine **museums**.

Brief history

The city is one of the most ancient in Italy, thanks to its irresistible **site**. Bronze and Iron Age tribes were present before it became an **Etruscan** settlement, later named Volsinii Veteres, or Velzna, in around the ninth century BC. Eventually it became a leading member of the twelve-strong Etruscan federation, and possibly the site of the Etruscans' principal religious shrine, the Fanum Voltumnae. In 264 BC (possibly earlier), the **Romans** ravaged the town and displaced the Etruscans to present-day Bolsena, or Volsinii Novi – the place they abandoned becoming known as Urbs Vetus (the Old City), thus Orvieto.

Its medieval influence was considerable, the independent *comune* challenging Florence and eventually claiming land as far as Monte Amiata in the north and to the coast at Orbetello in the west. Power and prestige remained high until the usual internecine squabbling, the **Black Death** of 1348 sounding the town's effective death knell. It passed definitively to the Church a hundred years later and became something

LA CARTA UNICA

If you plan to take in all of Orvieto's major sights, it's well worth buying the **La Carta Unica** (🕸 cartaunica.it), which offers savings of at least fifty percent on entry to the Duomo, Museo Claudio Faina, Orvieto Underground, Torre del Moro, Museo dell'Opera del Duomo, Pozzo della Cava, Museo Archeologico Nazionale, Pozzo di San Patrizio and Necropoli del Crocifisso del Tufo, as well as some public transport and parking in the Parcheggio ex-Campo dell Fiera, and discounts at participating hotels, restaurants and shops. It costs €18, and is available from the tourist office and all museums and monuments.

of a papal home-from-home: 32 popes in all stayed in the city. One of them, Gregory I, even met **Edward I** of England here on Edward's return from the Crusades.

The Duomo

Piazza del Duomo • Daily: March & Oct 7.30am–12.45pm & 2.30–6.15pm; April–Sept 7.30am–12.45pm & 2.30–7.15pm; Nov–Feb 7.30am–12.45pm & 2.30–6.15.15pm • €2 or combined ticket with Cappella di San Brizio €5, available from the tourist office across the square • ☎ 0763 341 167, 🕸 www.comune.orvieto.tr.it

The Swiss art historian Jacob Burckhardt proclaimed Orvieto's **Duomo** "the greatest and richest polychrome monument in the world"; Pope Leo XIII called it the "Golden Lily of Italian cathedrals", adding that on the Day of Judgement it would float to heaven carried by its own beauty. Though the structure's overall effect might be a bit rich for some tastes, it rates – with Assisi's Basilica di San Francesco – as one of Umbria's two essential sights.

The monumental **facade** of the Duomo is just the right side of overkill: a delicate riot of columns, spires, bas-reliefs, sculptures, dazzling colour, colossal doorways and hundreds of capricious details held together by four enormous fluted pillars. Many have compared it to a painted triptych in an elaborate frame. Some 52m high, it is a stunning spectacle from the piazza, particularly at sunset or under floodlights. Most of the basic work was accomplished by **Lorenzo Maitani** (see box, p.525), but such illustrious names as **Andrea Pisano** and **Andrea Orcagna** – responsible for much of the rose window – also had a hand in design and construction.

The facade

The four pillars at the base are among the highlights of fourteenth-century Italian **sculpture**. The work of Maitani and his pupils, they depict episodes from the Old and New Testaments in staggering detail: lashings of plague, famine, martyrdom, mutilation and murder. The panels read from left to right, starting with the Creation on the left-most pillar. The stories in stone here are wonderfully graphic and self-explanatory, but the delicacy of the carving, especially of the trees, which have the intricacy of coral, is extraordinary. Look in particular at the scene of Eve emerging from Adam's rib (second tier), the casting out of Adam and Eve (fourth tier) and Cain slaying Abel (fifth tier, right-hand panel), the last especially powerful. The second pillar has the stories of Abraham and David, and the third, scenes from the lives of Christ and the Virgin. The extraordinary fourth and final pillar makes clear, with its depictions of the Last Judgement, hell and paradise, and the damned packed off to eternal fire, brimstone and the company of an awful lot of snakes.

Maitani was also responsible for the four large bronzes of the symbols of the Evangelists across the first tier, and for the angels over the beautiful central **doorway**. The **mosaics**, the facade's showiest aspect, are mostly eighteenth- and nineteenth-century additions, replacements for originals nabbed by Rome. Only the four examples in the corners of Orcagna's huge **rose window** (1359) have any vintage, completed around 1388. The central bronze doors, by Emilio Greco, were made as recently as 1965.

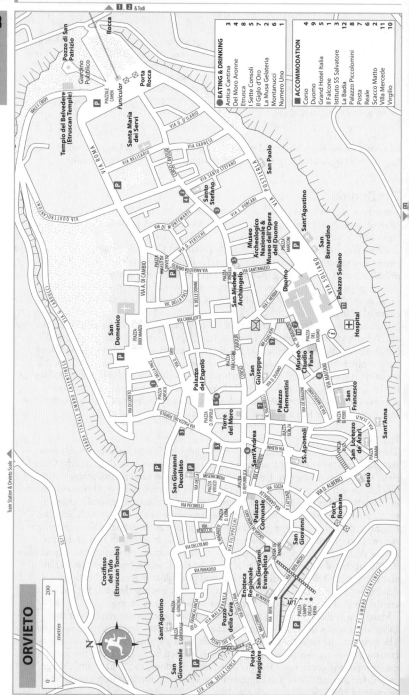

ORVIETO

0 ——— 200
metres

N

Pozzo di San Patrizio
Rocca
Giardino Pubblico
Porta Rocca
PIAZZALE CAHEN
Funicular

Tempio del Belvedere (Etruscan Temple)
Santa Maria dei Servi

VIA ROMA
VIA U. D'ILARIO
VIA FARNESE
VIA BELISARIO
CORSO CAVOUR
VIA SANTO STEFANO

Santo Stefano
VIA DI MONTEMARTE
VIA DI PERTICHE
VIA S. PORCARI
San Paolo
Sant'Agostino

San Bernardino
Palazzo Soliano

Museo Archeologico Nazionale & Museo dell'Opera del Duomo
PIAZZA MARCONI
San Michele Arcangelo
Duomo

San Domenico
VIA CAVALLOTTI
PIAZZA XXIX MARZO

VIA SOLIANA
Hospital
Sant'Anna

VIA POSTIERLA

VIA A. DI CAMBIO
PIAZZA ANGELO DA ORVIETO
VIA ANGELO DA ORVIETO
VIA SANT'ANGELO
PIAZZA SAN ANGELO
V. DELLE DONNE
VIC. DELLA PACE
VIA FRACASSINI
CORSO CAVOUR

Palazzo del Popolo
PIAZZA DEL POPOLO

San Giuseppe
VIA DEL DUOMO
PIAZZA DEL DUOMO

Museo Claudio Faina
VIA MAITANI

Torre del Moro
Palazzo Clementini
San Francesco

VIA LORETO
VIA FELICE CAVALLOTTI
PIAZZA CORSICA
VIA DI PIAZZA DEL POPOLO

Sant'Andrea
SS. Apostoli
VIA DEI MAGONI
VIA MAGALOTTI
San Lorenzo de' Arari
Gesù

San Giovanni Decollato
VIA DELLA MISERICORDIA
PIAZZA VITOZZI
VIA DELLA REPUBBLICA
PIAZZA L. VERNA

Palazzo Comunale
VIA GARIBALDI
VIA COZZA
VIA D. ALBERICI
Porta Romana

VIA PECORELLI
VIA BENEDUCCI
VIA FILIPPESCHI
San Giovanni
VIA DELL'OLMO
VIA PARADISO

Enoteca Regionale
San Giovanni Evangelista
Pozzo della Cava
Sant'Agostino

San Giovanni
PIAZZA G. GIORDANO
VIA MALABRANCA
VIA DEI CACCIA

Porta Maggiore
PIAZZA DELLA PACE
STR. COM. DELLA CONCA

VIA QUATTROCANTONI
VIA S. CADUSCI

Crocifisso del Tufo (Etruscan Tombs)

STRADA STATALE UMBRO CASENTINESE
SS71

VIA SS 71 UMBRO CASENTINESE

Train Station & Orvieto Scalo

Viterbo & Bolsena

Rocca
1, 2, & Todi

13

CONSTRUCTION OF ORVIETO'S DUOMO

Church tradition holds that the Duomo was built to celebrate the **Miracle of Bolsena**, which occurred in 1263. The protagonist, a young Bavarian priest, was on a pilgrimage to Rome to shake off his disbelief in transubstantiation (the idea that the body and blood of Christ are physically present in the Eucharist). While he celebrated Mass in a church near Lago di Bolsena, blood started to drip from the Host onto the *corporale*, the white linen cloth that covers the altar. The linen was whisked off to Pope Urban IV, who was holed up in Orvieto to escape the literal and political heat in Rome. He proclaimed a miracle and a year later Thomas Aquinas, then teaching in Orvieto's San Domenico, drew up a papal bull instigating the feast of Corpus Domini.

The cornerstone of the Duomo was not put in place for another 25 years (laid by Pope Nicholas IV on Nov 13, 1290) and Aquinas's bull makes no specific mention of Bolsena, so it's likely that the raising of the Duomo was as much a shrewd piece of political pragmatism as a celebration of a miracle. The papacy at the time was in retreat and the Umbrian towns – not least Orvieto – at the height of their civic expansion. Thus it seems likely that the building of this awe-inspiring cathedral, in one of the region's most powerful towns, was a piece of political muscle-flexing to remind errant citizens of the papacy's power.

The site posed no problems: the city's highest point was previously home to an Etruscan temple and Orvieto's first cathedral, Santa Maria Prisca; and although the architect is unknown, **Arnolfo di Cambio**, designer of Florence's Duomo, is a probable candidate. The plan initially was for a simple and orthodox Romanesque church, but in the early years of work a local architect's extravagant departures into the Gothic brought the structure close to collapse, leading to the call-up in 1310 of the Sienese master, **Lorenzo Maitani**. In the course of three decades he guided the construction at its most crucial stage and produced the magnificent carvings on the facade. Though building dragged on for over three hundred years, exhausting 33 architects, 152 sculptors, 68 painters and 90 mosaicists, the final product is a surprisingly unified example of the transitional Romanesque-Gothic style.

The Cappella di San Brizio

Jan & Feb Mon–Sat 10am–12.45pm & 2.30–5.15pm, Sun 2.30–5.45pm; March & Oct 10am–12.45pm & 2.30–6.15pm, Sun 2.30–5.45pm; April–May 10am–12.45pm & 2.30–7.15pm, Sun 2.30–5.45pm; June–Sept 10am–12.45pm & 2.30–7.15pm, Sun 2.30–6.45pm • €5, includes entrance to the Duomo; tickets only available from the tourist office across the square

At first, little save the colossal scale grabs your attention in the Duomo's **interior**, but in the right transept – the **Cappella di San Brizio** – are **Luca Signorelli**'s superlative paintings of the Last Judgement (1499–1504), one of Italy's great fresco cycles and one that had a profound influence on Michelangelo's version in the Sistine Chapel, painted forty years later.

Several painters tackled the chapel before Signorelli. **Fra' Angelico** made a start in 1447, completing two of the ceiling's eight vaults, *Christ in Glory with Angels* (marked as 1 on our plan) and *The Prophets* (3), with the assistance of **Benozzo Gozzoli**, whose hand can be seen in the angels of the latter panel. Angelico, it appears, suggested the frescoes' central theme, the Last Judgement, but was then called to Rome to work in the Vatican, never to return. The murder of a local grandee involved in financing the project, Arigo Monaldeschi, then brought work on the Duomo to one of its periodic halts. **Perugino** popped up forty years later and disappeared for reasons unknown – never to return – after working for just five days. Signorelli saved the day, graciously restoring Fra' Angelico's work and completing the vaults according to the original plan.

Work then started in earnest on the walls, all but the lowest of which are crowded with passionate and beautifully observed muscular figures, creating an effect that's both realistic and almost grotesquely fantastic at the same time. Seven main episodes are painted in the eight panels of the vaults and the twelve floor-level groups of frescoes.

The End of the World

The first fresco is the **End of the World** (9) on the entrance wall, actually the last of the major episodes painted (1503–4). In the lower right foreground are depicted Eritrea, a

13 sibyl, shown holding a book of prophecies, while alongside is the Prophet David, who is shown asserting the veracity of the prophecies. Behind them an earthquake brings down a temple and three youths fall prey to brigands; in the background, ships are tossed on a sea convulsed by a tidal wave brought on by the earthquake. High up on the left you see the fall of the rebel angels, many of whom unleash thunderbolts of fire which fall on a terrified crowd below. A putto in the panel's centre holds a sign with the mark of the Opera del Duomo (OPSM), a reminder of the cathedral works committee responsible for commissioning and overseeing the project.

CAPPELLA DI SAN BRIZIO, ORVIETO

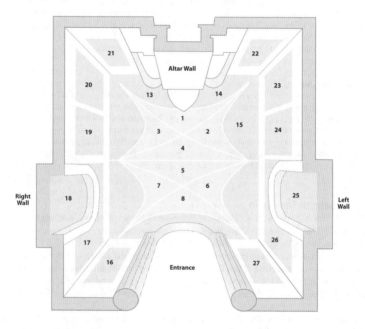

1. Christ in Glory with Angels
2. The Apostles
3. The Prophets
4. Portents of the Last Judgement
5. The Martyrs
6. The Patriarchs
7. The Doctor of the Church
8. The Virgins
9. The End of the World
10. The Preaching of the Antichrist
11. The Resurrection of the Dead
12. Inferno
13. Purgatory
14. The Calling of the Saved
15. Paradiso

16. Monument to Cardinal Ferdinando Nuzzi (d. 1717)
17. Portrait of Tibullus
18. Pietà, SS. Faustino and Pietro Parenzo, and Martyrdom of the Saints by Luca Signorelli
19. Ovid and four tondo scenes from Metamorphoses
20. Portrait of Claudian
21. Scenes from Ovid's Metamorphoses
22. Scenes from Dante's Purgatorio
23. Portrait of Statius
24. Portrait of Dante: Medallions here and around and joining panels show scenes from Cantos 1–11 of Purgatorio
25. Cappella Gualtieri (1736); painting of Saints (1724) by Ludovico Muratori
26. Portrait of Sallust: Medallions – Classical scenes and grape harvest
27. Empedocles (?) and The End of The World

The Preaching of the Antichrist

The first lunette panel on the wall left of the entrance depicts one of the cycle's most powerful works, the **Preaching of the Antichrist** (10), the iconography of which is unique (the subject itself is very rare in Italian painting). It derives from a text whose precise authorship is unknown, but which unites elements from St Augustine's *City of God*, ancient millennial texts – the world was widely expected to end in the year 1000 – and the *Golden Legend* of Jacopo de Voragine, (also the inspiration for Piero della Francesca's Arezzo cycle: see p.374).

The Antichrist is shown preaching and bears the image of Christ, albeit one that displays a demonic demeanour, with a devil whispering in his ear. Various historical figures stand amidst the crowd to the left and right of the Antichrist, designed to represent all colours, creeds and conditions of the human family: Signorelli has portrayed himself with Fra' Angelico behind (in the black of a Dominican monk) in the left foreground, both apparently unperturbed by the garrotting taking place in front of them. Also present in the left-hand group are Dante (rear right, in profile with red hat), Cesare Borgia (with beard, blond hair and red hat, on the extreme left of the group) and Pius II, the corpulent fellow in yellow behind the figure with hands on hips alongside the Antichrist. Also here is the figure of Signorelli's mistress, who jilted him during the time the frescoes were being painted, and as punishment is prominently portrayed in the foreground of the group as a prostitute taking money. Groups of Franciscan and Dominican monks can be seen to the rear and right of the Antichrist trying to calculate the precise date of the end of the world – one counts off three and a half years with his fingers, the 1290 days that the reign of the Antichrist was expected to endure. The two other group vignettes behind the monks to right and left show a false miracle and the execution of two penitents. In the background is the Temple of Solomon, while in the heavens, the Archangel Michael is seen preventing the ascension of the Antichrist and unleashing a storm of fire onto the corrupt below.

The Resurrection of the Dead and Inferno

The sequence then moves to the first lunette on the right wall with the **Resurrection of the Dead** (11) summoned by the trumpets of the angels depicted on high. Signorelli here departs from convention, painting the figures emerging dramatically from the bare earth rather than from tombs, the traditional iconography employed in depictions of this scene. Note the small scratched figures at the centre of the panel, probably drawn by Signorelli to illustrate some point to the cathedral committee. The adjoining lunette on the right wall depicts **Inferno** (12), probably Signorelli's first completed fresco in the chapel.

The Punishment of the Damned

On the altar wall right of the window is the **Punishment of the Damned**, or **Purgatory** (13), which in its portrayal of the damned inevitably draws on Dante's *Divine Comedy*, but also utilizes the iconography of pagan works such as the battle scenes carved on the reliefs on Trajan's Column in Rome. Signorelli's mistress is again prominently painted, this time as the figure at the centre of the picture being carried by a flying winged devil.

The Calling of the Saved and Paradiso

The panel left of the window shows the **Calling of the Saved** (14), a portrayal that includes two of Orvieto's saintly protectors, Costanzo and Brizio, at its centre; St Michael weighing the souls; and angels serenading and guiding the elected to **Paradiso** (15), the scene portrayed in the adjoining lunette on the left wall. In this last mural, paradise's peace and harmony are symbolized by a heavenly choir of nine angel musicians and – in the centre – by two angels who scatter roses and camellias. These flowers were painted onto dry plaster, a less durable technique than the more usual

13

practice of adding paint to wet plaster, hence their faded appearance. The altarpiece, incidentally, is the *Madonna di San Brizio*, an anonymous work held by tradition to have been painted by St Luke, but in truth probably executed towards the end of the fourteenth century.

The lower walls

The outstanding **frescoes and medallions** (numbered 16 to 27) on the lower parts of the walls are also by Signorelli and include depictions of Homer, Dante, Ovid, Virgil, Horace, Lucan, Empedocles and others, together with episodes from classical myth, notably Ovid's *Metamorphoses* and Dante's *Divine Comedy*. Of particular note is the *Pietà with Sts Faustino and Pietro Parenzo* (18) in the recess on the right. Vasari claimed that the figure of the dead Christ was a close portrait of Signorelli's own son, Antonio, who died from the plague in 1502 while the artist was employed on the frescoes.

Everything here has a didactic purpose, further illustrating or drawing allusions to the main theme of the frescoes above. Dante's *Divine Comedy* – which is frequently evoked – forms an obvious corollary, with its themes of salvation and damnation. Elsewhere, however, Signorelli uses Classical myth and literary figures to his own ends; *Empedocles* (27), for example, is shown in shocked contemplation of the end of the world, though he in fact never prophesied such an event. Some critics believe this is actually a figure of a common man who has not converted to Christianity, and looks on at the horrors that await him as one of the damned. The separate portrait of *Stazio* (23) is used in a similar way. The figure looks towards the chapel's high altar as if receiving spiritual illumination, but Dante writes that while the poet converted to Christianity, he kept his conversion and subsequent faith a secret. Throughout the Middle Ages the figure was therefore a symbol of salvation and also of only partial redemption – just the sort of character who would have been compromised, to say the least, come the Day of Judgement.

The Cappella del Corporale and the apse

The artistic pyrotechnics of the Cappella di San Brizio rather overshadow the opposite transept's **Cappella del Corporale**, which contains the sacred *corporale* of the Miracle of Bolsena, usually locked away in a massive, jewel-encrusted casket on the left designed in 1358 as a copy of the facade. On the chapel walls are extensive **frescoes** (1357–64) by a local artist, Ugolino di Prete Ilario, depicting episodes from the *Miracle of Bolsena* (right-hand wall) and various *Miracles of the Sacrament* (opposite). The chapel also houses (on the right) the glorious freestanding *Madonna dei Raccomandati* (1339) by the Sienese painter Lippo Memmi.

Ugolino covered the entire **apse** in frescoes (1370–84) of scenes from the *Life of the Virgin*, many of which were touched up by Pinturicchio, who was eventually kicked off the job for "consuming too much gold, too much azure, and too much wine".

The Palazzi Papali museums

Piazza del Duomo

Adjoined at the back of the Duomo in their own niche, the **Palazzi Papali** house the **Museo Archeologico Nazionale**, with Etruscan and Greek finds, and the **Museo dell'Opera del Duomo**, displaying a carefully selected portion of the painting and sculpture from centuries of the cathedral's history.

Museo Archeologico Nazionale

Daily 8.30am–7.30pm • €3, combined ticket with Necropoli Etrusca €5

The **Museo Archeologico Nazionale** contains fourth-century BC Greek vases, Etruscan *buccheri*, two reconstructed painted Etruscan tombs from Porano with their original murals, as well as other Etruscan artefacts such as bronze armour, excavated during digs at Orvieto's own Cannicella and Crocifisso del Tufo tombs.

Museo dell'Opera del Duomo

Mon & Wed–Sun: March & Oct 9.30am–1pm & 3–6pm; April–Sept 9.30am–7pm; Nov–Jan 9.30am–1pm & 3–5pm • €5 • ☎ 0763 342 477

To the rear of the Duomo and up a stairway to the left, the **Museo dell'Opera del Duomo** displays some top-notch paintings, notably a self-portrait by **Signorelli**, a *Madonna and Child* (1268) by the influential early Tuscan painter Coppo di Marcovaldo and five parts of a polyptych from San Domenico by the Sienese master **Simone Martini**. Among the sculptures are wooden and marble Madonnas by **Nino**, **Giovanni** and **Andrea Pisano**, a lovely font filled with Escher-like fishes and unfinished but important pieces by **Arnolfo di Cambio**.

Museo Claudio Faina

Piazza del Duomo 29 • April–Sept daily 9.30am–6pm; Oct & March daily 10am–5pm; Nov–Feb Tues–Sun 10am–5pm • €4.50 • ☎ 0763 341 511, Ⓦ museofaina.it

Opposite the Duomo, the **Museo Claudio Faina** is a wonderful showcase for one of Italy's leading private archeological collections, though it's worth the admission price simply for a view of the Duomo from the upper floor. The core of the collection is 34 **ancient vases** given in the nineteenth century to Mauro Faina, a Perugian count, by Princess Maria Bonaparte, Napoleon's grandniece (the count had been a regular "visitor" to the princess's home). Over the years, Faina, together with his nephew, added obsessively to the collection, which was left to the city in 1954. The exhibits spread over 22 rooms on two upper floors of the Palazzo Faina (plus a small ground-floor civic collection), arranged in a modern museum setting that would be the envy of far grander galleries.

Highlights include three vast, sixth-century BC Attic **amphorae** (room 6) attributed to Exekias, one of antiquity's finest vase painters – their presence in Orvieto testimony to the town's prosperity at the time. Also famous is the so-called **Vanth group** (rooms 11, 18 and 22), the name given to a collection of pots made locally in the last two decades of the fourth century BC. Vanth was an important female divinity associated with the Etruscan underworld, often portrayed with two serpents around each arm and, in the manner of medieval saints, with symbols such as keys, taper, mantle and scroll, the last partially unrolled to reveal the name of the goddess. As here, she was often portrayed greeting the recently deceased on their arrival in the underworld.

The museum also has a large collection of coins, bronzes and miscellaneous funerary objects.

The Etruscan and Greek vases

The Etruscans were renowned for their black **bucchero vases**, of which the museum has many (rooms 10, 11 and 14). These pots are so-called because at the time of their discovery they were thought to resemble vases from South America known to the Spanish as *bucaro*. The black colour was imparted in the kiln, where the firing process oxidized iron compounds in specially chosen clay. Quality declined around the fifth century BC, the result of insufficiently pure clays, a shortfall that resulted in *bucchero grigio*, or grey ware (gradually replaced by simple black-glazed pottery).

A similar falling-off of quality occurred with the familiar **black-figure Attic vases** (rooms 11, 13 and 16), invented in Corinth around 700 BC, and made by painting a figure in black silhouette before incising detail so that the lighter-coloured clay beneath showed through. Such pottery was wildly popular throughout the Mediterranean, but no market was as large as Tyrrhenian Etruria. It was eventually replaced by Attic **red-figure pottery** (rooms 11, 14, 17 and 18), invented in Athens around 530 BC, in which figures and decorative details were composed in the clay and the rest of the pot painted black.

13

Torre del Moro

Corso Cavour 87 • Daily: March, April, Sept & Oct 10am–7pm; May–Aug 10am–8pm; Nov–Feb 10.30am–1pm & 2.30–5pm • €2.80

For an orienting and breathtaking overview of the town and the countryside, make a beeline for the medieval **Torre del Moro**, just northwest of Piazza del Duomo. Of the two bells atop the 47m tower, the smaller comes from an earlier Torre di Sant'Andrea and the larger from Palazzo del Popolo, dating to 1313. From the beginning, the latter was proclaimed a symbol of the city's artisans, and it, along with the mechanical clock, was installed here as part of restoration works in 1866.

San Lorenzo de' Arari

Piazza Santa Chiara • Daily 9.30am–1pm & 3–7pm • Free

The tiny Romanesque **San Lorenzo de' Arari** (or dell'Ara), just west of Piazza del Duomo, was built in 1291 on the site of a church destroyed by monks from nearby San Francesco because the sound of its bells got on their nerves. Four restored frescoes (1330) on the left of the nave depict traumatic scenes from the Life of St Lawrence, including execution by roasting, and there's a Byzantine-influenced Christ Enthroned with Four Saints in the apse. An Etruscan sacrificial slab rather oddly serves as the altar (*arari*) from which the church derives its name.

San Giovenale

Piazza San Giovenale • Daily 8.30am–noon & 4–6.30pm • Free

At the extreme western edge of town – requiring a big drop to the Porta Maggiore and a climb up again – is the ancient **San Giovenale**, set amid rustic surroundings on the western tip of Orvieto's plateau. It's not much to look at from outside, but the musty interior is a distinctive hybrid of a church, the thirteenth-century Gothic transept, with its two pointed arches, standing rather oddly a metre above the rounded Romanesque nave. Beautiful thirteenth- and fifteenth-century frescoes cover all available surfaces; they include a Tree of Life to the right of the main door and the macabre Calendar of Funeral Anniversaries partly covered by the side entrance.

Make the walk worthwhile by taking in the glorious view from the town wall just to the west, or by following the wall-top lane (Via Volsinia II) down towards the Porta Maggiore. Otherwise, from San Giovenale back to the centre of town, Via Malabranca and Via Filippeschi are the best preserved of the medieval streets.

San Domenico

Piazza XXIX Marzo • Daily 10am–12.30pm & 3–6.30pm • Free

At the northern edge of town, **San Domenico** stands next to a Fascist-era barracks – the latter far and away the ugliest building in town. Half of the church, built between 1233 and 1264 (and thus Italy's first church to be dedicated to St Dominic) was sliced off during the construction of the barracks. The principal artwork inside is the Tomb of Cardinal de Braye (died 1281), a pioneering work by Arnolfo di Cambio in the Cappella Petrucci, entered via a door on the south (right) wall. This defined the format of wall tombs for the next century, showing the deceased lying on a coffin below the Madonna and Child, within an elaborate architectural framework.

The Pozzo di San Patrizio

Viale Sangallo • Daily: May–Aug 9am–8pm • March, April, Sept & Oct 9am–5pm • Nov–Feb 10am–5pm • €5 • ☎ 0763 343 768

Orvieto's novelty act is the huge cylindrical well known as the **Pozzo di San Patrizio**, signposted beside the funicular terminus in Piazza Cahen east of the centre. Pope

UNDERGROUND ORVIETO

Cut into the tufa plateau that supports Orvieto are the fascinating **Grotte della Rupe**, an extraordinary honeycomb of caves, wine cellars, aqueducts, quarries and tunnels used – and added to – since Etruscan times. A staggering 1200 separate caves have been found beneath Orvieto, around a third of the entire area under the town having been excavated at one time or another. **Guided tours** in English are run by Orvieto Underground, Piazza del Duomo 23 (daily 11am, 12.15pm, 4pm & 5.15pm; €5.50; ☏0763 344 891, ☏339 733 2764 or ☏347 383 1472, ☻orvietounderground.it); tours leave from the tourist office.

If you haven't time for the full underground tour, you could visit the **Pozzo della Cava**, Via della Cava 28 (Tues–Sun 9am–8pm; €3; ☻pozzodellacava.it), a large smooth-sided Etruscan-era well (one of about forty found around the town) which incorporates nine caves in all.

Clement VII commissioned it from Antonio da Sangallo the Younger two years after the Sack of Rome, which he'd been forced to flee disguised as a greengrocer. An attack on Orvieto was expected from the imperial troops, and the well was designed to guarantee the town's water supply during a siege. The attack never materialized – which was fortunate, as it took ten years of digging to hit water. It was while in Orvieto that Clement took the fateful decision not to annul Henry VIII's marriage to Catherine of Aragon.

The well is a virtuoso piece of engineering, 13m wide and 62m deep, and takes its name from a supposed resemblance to the Irish cave where St Patrick died at the ripe old age of 133. Water was brought to the surface by donkeys on two broad 248-step staircases, cannily designed in a double helix so that they never intersect. Half the well is carved from solid tufa, half is brick-lined, and the whole thing is lit by 72 strange windows cut from the spirals into the central shaft.

The Rocca and around

The direct recipient of the water from the Pozzo di San Patrizio was the nearby **Rocca**, built in 1364 by Cardinal Albornoz, the papal firebrand recruited to restore Church authority across central Italy. Views from the ruins are wonderful; nearby are the small but pleasant **public gardens**, one of Orvieto's few patches of green and home to the prominent remains of an Etruscan temple, the **Tempio del Belvedere**. The castle itself was built over the only stratum of travertine in the town, a robust piece of rock that escapes the landslips that strike the tufa underpinnings with increasing regularity. Miles of tunnels and caves dating back to the Etruscans still honeycomb the rock, a labyrinth once used for quarrying, burials and the fermenting of wine.

The Necropoli Etrusca

Daily April–Sept 8.30am–7pm; Oct–March 8.30am–5pm • €3, combined ticket with Museo Archeologico €5 • ☏0763 343 611

Down below a cliff, the **Necropoli Etrusca**, or **Crocifisso del Tufo** – a set of sixth-century BC Etruscan tombs – are well worth a look: to get there, walk or drive down the town's approach road from Piazza Cahen (or from Porta Maggiore on the town's west side) to the small car park on the south side of the road and follow the signs. There are rows of massive and sombre stone graves (more are being excavated), though none has the grandeur or the paintings of the more famous necropolises in Tarquinia or Cerveteri. Still visible, however, are Etruscan carvings above the tomb entrances, thought to be the family names of the erstwhile occupants.

ARRIVAL AND DEPARTURE   ORVIETO

By train The fastest trains on the Rome–Florence run now bypass Orvieto, but there are still plenty that stop here. The train station is in the new town of Orvieto Scalo, a twisting 3km down from the old centre. From the station forecourt, a wonderful restored nineteenth-century Bracci funicular (Mon–Sat every 10min

13

7.20am–8.30pm, Sun every 15min 8am–8.30pm; €1, including bus) runs up to Piazza Cahen in the old town, from where it's a pleasant five- or ten-minute walk along Corso Cavour to the centre. Minibuses shuttle every few minutes from the top station to Piazza del Duomo – either direct (bus A) or via Piazza della Repubblica (bus B). After 8.30pm, buses replace the funicular.

Destinations Arezzo (hourly; 50min–1hr 50min); Castiglione del Lago (hourly; 40min–1hr 10min); Chiusi (hourly; 20–30min; connections to Siena, 1hr 10min–1hr 35min); Florence (hourly; 1hr 30min–2hr 45min); Orte (hourly; 30–40min; connections to Narni 10–15min, Terni 15–25min, Spoleto 40min–1hr 5min & Foligno 1hr–1hr 30min); Rome (hourly; 50min–1hr 30min); Teróntola (7–10 daily; 50min–1hr 15min; connections to Perugia, 30–50min).

By bus Inter-town buses take you to Piazza Cahen, Piazza XXIX Marzo or Piazza della Repubblica, depending on the service; some terminate at the train station.

Destinations Amelia (5–7 daily Mon–Sat; 1hr 15min); Perugia (1 daily; 2hr); Terni (12 daily Mon–Sat; 2hr); Todi (1 daily Mon–Sat; 2hr).

By car Cars are prohibited in the old town, but even when they're not, finding a (legal) parking space is a tall order. There are car parks in Piazzale Cahen and off Via Roma just to the west, or you could use the huge free car park on the east side of the station and take the funicular. Better still, aim to park at Campo della Fiera, below the southwest corner of the old town, where you can pick up local buses (Linea B or C) on their run from the station to Piazza della Repubblica; pedestrian lifts and escalators up to the centre (exiting near Via Garibaldi and Via Ripa Medici) also run from this point.

INFORMATION

Tourist office Piazza del Duomo 24 (Mon–Fri 8.10am–1.50pm & 4–7pm, Sat & Sun 10am–1pm & 3–6pm; variable and reduced hours in winter; ☎0763 341 772, ⓦwww.comune.orvieto.tr.it).

ACCOMMODATION

Corso Corso Cavour 343 ☎0763 342 020, ⓦhotelcorso .net. Occupying part of a renovated medieval town house in a convenient position, with nine spotless, spacious, rather plush rooms (some with terraces and views). Buffet breakfast included on a garden terrace with panoramic views. There's a pub opposite, so be prepared for noise. €108

Duomo Vicolo di Maurizio 7 ☎0763 341 887, ⓦorvietohotelduomo.com. An excellent sixteen-room three-star hotel in a peaceful and perfect location, with large, light-filled rooms with marble bathrooms. Free wi-fi in the lobby; €5 extra in room. Garage parking €10/night. Good buffet breakfast included. €100

Grand Hotel Italia Piazza del Popolo 13 ☎0763 342 065, ⓦgrandhotelitalia.it. This "grand hotel" is at least large, but it's by no means luxurious, merely adequate in most ways. Rooms have been recently refurbished and offer a/c and wi-fi; many have balconies. Breakfast included, but coffee is from a machine. €160

Istituto SS Salvatore Via Piazza del Popolo 1 ☎0763 342 910, ⓦdomenicanedisansisto.org. This lovely Dominican convent is an inexpensive place to stay, with a garden and terrace with views, but there's a 10.30pm curfew (9pm autumn & winter). Free parking; no breakfast. Closed July. €60

★ **La Badia** Località La Badia ☎0763 301 959, ⓦlabadiahotel.it. Luxurious out-of-town option, in a converted abbey 5km south on the Bagnoregio road. It's not as grand as some newer conversions and could do with a revamp of the relatively austere rooms, which are former monks' cells, but the grounds are really lovely, with good views of Orvieto, and there are all the usual smart facilities, including tennis courts, a pool and a rather fabulous medieval-style restaurant. Breakfast included; free parking. €160

★ **Palazzo Piccolomini** Piazza Ranieri 36 ☎0763 341 743, ⓦhotelpiccolomini.it. Stylish, tasteful and refined historic hotel with 32 rooms, including singles and suites, set in a converted sixteenth-century palace. Rooms are a comfortable blend of contemporary design and antique eclectic, with all amenities. Valet parking €15 per night. Buffet breakfast included. €154

Posta Via Luca Signorelli 18 ☎0763 341 909, ⓦwww .orvietohotels.it. Recently refurbished hotel in a charmingly old-fashioned medieval house, with a garden and twenty basic but pleasant rooms, with and without private bathrooms. The bells of the Torre del Moro will keep you constant company. No breakfast. €56

Reale Piazza del Popolo 25 ☎0763 341 247, ⓦorvietohotels.it. Despite the frescoed ceilings in the giant old *palazzo*, this hotel is past its glory days. It's pleasantly shabby, with rooms in need of a refurbish, but its charm is still apparent, despite the sometimes modular bathrooms. Breakfast €8 extra. €68

Scacco Matto Autostrada 448, Todi–Baschi ☎0744 950 163, ⓦscaccomatto.net. This restaurant and campsite overlooks the Lago di Corbara, about 10km east of Orvieto on the road to Todi. Hotel rooms have a/c and balconies with lake views, and there's a restaurant serving local country dishes. Breakfast included. €70

Villa Mercede Via Soliana 2 ☎0763 341 766, ⓦwww .villamercede.it. It's harder to imagine a cheaper bed close to the cathedral than in this simple but perfectly situated twelve-room religious house, with doubles (all en suite) open to men, women and couples. Ample breakfast

13

ORVIETO'S WINES

The subterranean conditions of Orvieto's many caves were once said to be responsible for the excellence of the local **wines**; modern methods now make a drier product, better selling but less exalted than the traditional semi-sweet *abboccato*. The local vintages are sold at the excellent **Enoteca Regionale**, on the southern edge of town at Via Ripa Serancia 16 (Mon–Sat 9am–1pm & 3–7pm; ☎0763 393 529), which also offers **wine-tasting tours** (mid-April to mid-Sept daily 11am & 5pm, rest of year daily 4pm; €5–10, more if food included). If you're interested in visiting local **vineyards**, contact the Consorzio Tutela Vino, Corso Cavour 36 (☎0763 343 790).

included. **€70**

Virgilio Piazza del Duomo 5–6 ☎0763 342 325, ⊛orvietohotelvirgilio.com. Justly celebrated for its perfect position – make sure you have your view of the Duomo, though do expect street noise on summer evenings. Rooms are very fresh and handsomely appointed, rather unexpectedly so considering the dilapidated exterior. Breakfast €10; parking extra. **€160**

CAMPSITES

Il Falcone Località Vallonganino 2a, Civitella del Lago ☎0744 950 249 or 348 327 2851, ⊛campingilfalcone .com. A well-run two-star campsite with a friendly owner, overlooking Lago di Corbara, some 10km east of Orvieto on the way to Todi. Pluses include a pool and a minimarket, and there are bungalows sleeping up to four as well as tent pitches. Open April–Sept. Adult campers **€7.30**, plus pitch **€6.20**, bungalows **€70**

EATING AND DRINKING

Orvieto's tourist traffic once inflated prices in the town's many **restaurants**, and for years it has had fewer genuine culinary high spots than neighbouring towns. In recent years, however, a crop of good small **trattorie** has opened, together with a selection of excellent more upmarket places. Cheaper **pizzerias** are mostly clustered together at the very eastern end of Corso Cavour. There are plenty of **bars**, with those in front of the Duomo and in Piazza della Repubblica being the key sites for watching the world go by.

Antica Cantina Piazza Monaldeschi 18 ☎347 828 684. One of the best places on the Corso, with an old-fashioned trattoria atmosphere, very authentic food and seating inside and out. Try the cheese plate, the *ombrichelli* pasta with truffles, or the veal marinated with porcini. A full meal starts at €30 per person; occasional tasting menu with selected wines €40. Mon, Tues & Thurs–Sun 12.30–2.45pm & 7.30–9.30pm.

★ **Del Moro Aronne** Via San Leonardo 7 ☎0763 342 763, ⊛trattoriadelmoro.info. This long-established family-run trattoria is a local favourite, noted for its perfectly prepared and authentic food. Truffles and porcini play a big part, of course, and you'll find none better. Don't miss their signature dish, *nidi*, a heavenly creation of pasta, pecorino cheese and honey. Meals cost about €30 per person. Mon & Wed–Sun 12.30–3pm & 7.30–9.45pm.

Etrusca Via Lorenzo Maitani 10 ☎0763 344 016, ⊛argoweb.it/trattoria_etrusca. A traditional-looking restaurant with a medieval vaulted dining room, serving wonderful Umbrian specialities with white and black truffles and mushrooms – reckon on about €30 for three courses, and heed your waiter's advice on wines. Be sure to go downstairs to see the wine cellars, carved out of solid tufa. Tues–Sun 12.30–3pm & 7.30–9.45pm; closed mid-Jan to mid-Feb.

★ **I Sette Consoli** Piazza Sant'Angelo 1a ☎0763 343 911, ⊛www.isetteconsoli.it. The amazing garden

setting is not to be missed, so come in fine weather and be sure to book. Inside is more ordinary, but the food is always delectable: white truffle pasta and artichoke-stuffed lamb are highlights. Set menus are €30 and €45. Mon, Tues & Thurs–Sun 12.30–2.30pm & 7.30–10pm; closed Sun dinner Nov–March & part of Feb or March.

Il Giglio d'Oro Piazza del Duomo 8 ☎0763 341 903, ⊛ilgigliodoro.it. The cooking here is inventive and the quality is always high: the cod with chickpea sauce is memorable, as is the pumpkin risotto with crayfish. Three-course meals start at about €40, served in elegant surroundings in the shadow of the Duomo. Mon, Tues & Thurs–Sun 12.30–2.30pm & 7.30–9.30pm.

★ **La Musa Gelateria** Corso Cavour 351 ☎0763 393 861. The *gelato* here is prepared with seasonal ingredients, and has absolutely no additives, hence the limited choice. The result, however, is the town's very best ice cream, and prices are lower than at most *gelaterie*, probably because it's a bit out of the way. Definitely worth seeking out. Tues–Sun 11am–10pm.

Montanucci Corso Cavour 21 ☎0763 341 261, ⊛barmontanucci.it. This smart and traditional café-bar was founded in 1917, and specializes in semolina *torta* and chocolates. You can check your email in the basement café, and there's also a self-service restaurant with a daily menu (mains €7–12) that features lots of

13

organic produce. The risotto with artichokes is wonderful, as is the wild salmon, steamed with pink peppercorns. Daily 7am–midnight.

★ **Numero Uno** Via Ripa Corsica 2a ☎ 0763 341 845, ⓦ osterianumerouno.eu. This osteria turns out deeply authentic Umbrian dishes: cured meats, truffles, wild boar and home-made pastas and breads, all washed down with an excellent house red. Full meals about €50 per person. Tues–Sun 12.30–3pm & 7.30–10pm; closed Tues in winter.

Città della Pieve

The Umbrian environs of Orvieto are not the most compelling. However, if you have transport and time to spare (perhaps en route to Montepulciano), you should definitely make for little-visited but interesting **CITTÀ DELLA PIEVE**, some 41km north of Orvieto (or 47km via the prettier, winding SS47). Straggling impressively along its 500m-high ridge, and best known as the birthplace of painter **Perugino**, born in 1446, this homely town was founded by the **Etruscans**, and consists of tiny, red-brick houses (there being no local building stone) and famously narrow streets, one of which, **Via della Baciadonna**, claims to be the narrowest in Italy – the width of a woman's kiss, the name proclaims (or so narrow that you have no option but to kiss anyone you pass).

Via Garibaldi and Via Vittorio Veneto make up the main east–west axis, meeting in the linked central squares of **Piazza Gramsci** and **Piazza del Plebiscito**, where you'll find the seventeenth-century **Duomo**. This has a couple of late works that show **Perugino** in his worst light, the *Baptism of Christ* (1510) on the first altar of the north (left) aisle, and the *Madonna Enthroned with Sts Peter, Paul, Gervasio and Protasio* (1514) in the apse: the original ninth-century parish church, or *pieve* (which gave the town its name), on the site of the Duomo, was dedicated to the last two saints. The same square contains the **Torre del Pubblico**, thirteenth-century Romanesque at the base (built in travertine) and fifteenth-century Gothic higher up.

Museo Aperto

Daily: May–Sept 9.30am–1pm & 4–7.30pm; Oct–April 10am–12.30pm & 3.30–6pm • €4

Opposite the Duomo, the Palazzo della Corgna – with the church of Sant'Agostino and the Oratorio di Santa Maria dei Bianchi – has been united in a self-contained circuit known as the **Museo Aperto**, with a single-ticket admission available from any of the three sites. The ground floor of the characteristically Renaissance **Palazzo della Corgna** holds a rare memento of the town's Etruscan heritage, a sixth-century BC stone obelisk, while the ceilings of its state rooms are elaborately frescoed. Along with the Duomo, **Sant'Agostino** contains some decent sixteenth-century works by the Mannerist painters Salvio Savini and Pomarancio.

Oratorio di Santa Maria dei Bianchi

Via Pietro Vannucci

The **Oratorio di Santa Maria dei Bianchi** is reached by returning to the main Piazza del Plebiscito and continuing north on Via Pietro Vannucci. The **Perugino** here, *The Adoration of the Magi*, is one of his masterpieces; note Lago Trasimeno in the background. It was painted in just 29 days in 1504, perhaps, claim some critics, with the assistance of Perugino's pupil, the young Raphael. Perugino initially asked for 200 florins for the work, then said he'd be happy with half that as he was a native of the town; in the end the confraternity that owned the Oratorio (it exists to this day as a charitable institution) paid him just 75. Two letters from the artist displayed with the painting document the financial wrangling.

Santa Maria dei Servi

Via Pieve

Santa Maria dei Servi (rarely open) contains Perugino's *Deposition* (1517), an important late fresco damaged when monks erected a choir screen nearby. Greater damage was done to Città's artistic patrimony by foreigners, not least by Napoleon, who removed cartloads of the town's other Peruginos to the Louvre.

ARRIVAL AND INFORMATION

By bus Buses stop along the east side of the town centre on Viale Marconi.

Destinations: Castiglione del Lago (1 daily Mon–Sat; 35min); Perugia (2 daily; 1hr 20min).

CITTÀ DELLA PIEVE

Tourist office Piazza Matteotti 1 (Mon–Sat 10.30am–12.30pm & 4–6/7pm; ☎ 0578 299 375, ⟨w⟩ www .comune.cittadella.pd.it).

ACCOMMODATION AND EATING

Relais dei Magi Località le Selve Nuove ☎ 0578 298 133, ⟨w⟩ relaismagi.it. Four kilometres northeast of town, this stylish thirteen-room rural retreat is beautifully set in broad swathes of woodland and olive groves. It has indoor and outdoor pools, sauna, Turkish bath, spa, free wi-fi, its own restaurant and wine-tastings. Breakfast included. Three-night minimum in high season. Open April–Oct. **€185**

★ **Taverna del Perugino** Via Pietro Vannucci 37 ☎ 0578 298 848, ⟨w⟩ tavernadelperugino.com. As *simpatico* and traditional as it gets, down to the red-checked tablecloths, with cheerful service and wonderful

home-made pastas – the local *pici al tartufo e funghi* (hand-rolled pasta with truffles and mushrooms) is a winner, and there's great *bruschette* and pizza, too. €20–25 per person for a full meal. Tues–Sun 12.30–2.30pm & 7.30–9.30pm.

Vannucci Via Icilio Vanni 1 ☎ 0578 298 063, ⟨w⟩ hotel -vannucci.com. This fine hotel has a small spa and pool with sundeck, a garden and two restaurants, one gourmet, one casual. The rooms are large and comfortably appointed, all with a/c and high-speed internet, and some have balconies with panoramic views. Buffet breakfast included. **€125**

13

SALA DI SATU[R]

PALAZZO PITTI, FLORENCE

Contexts

History: Tuscany

A comprehensive history of Tuscany in its medieval and Renaissance heyday would consist in large part of a mosaic of more or less independent histories, as each of the region's cities has a complex story to tell. In an overview such as this, fidelity to the entanglements of central Italy's past is impossible. Instead, within a broad account of the main trends in the evolution of Tuscany, we have concentrated on the city that emerged as the dominant force – Florence.

Etruscans and Romans

The name of the province of Tuscany derives from the **Etruscans**, the most powerful civilization of pre-Roman Italy. There's no scholarly consensus on the origins of this people, with some experts insisting that they migrated into Italy from Anatolia at the start of the ninth century BC, and others maintaining that they were an indigenous tribe. All that's known for certain is that the Etruscans were spread throughout central Italy from the eighth century BC, and that the centre of gravity of their domain was in the southern part of the modern province, roughly along a line drawn from Orbetello to Lago Trasimeno. Their principal settlements in Tuscany were Roselle, Vetulonia, Populonia, Volterra, Chiusi, Cortona, Arezzo and – most northerly of all – Fiesole.

The substantial development of Tuscany's chief city began with the **Roman** colony of Florentia, established by Julius Caesar in 59 BC as a settlement for army veterans – by which time Romans had either subsumed or exterminated most Etruscan towns, including nearby Fiesole. Expansion of Florentia itself was rapid, with a steady traffic of trading vessels along the Arno providing the basis of accelerated growth in the second and third centuries AD.

This rise under the empire was paralleled by the growth of **Siena**, **Pisa** and **Lucca**, establishing an economic primacy in the north of Tuscany that has endured to the present. According to legend Siena was founded by the sons of Remus, supposedly fleeing their uncle Romulus, while the port at Pisa was developed by the Romans in the second century BC. Lucca was even more important, and it was there that Julius Caesar, Crassus and Pompey established their triumvirate in 56 BC.

Goths, Lombards and Franks

Under the comparative tranquillity of the Roman colonial regime, **Christianity** began to spread through the region. Lucca claims to have been the first Christian city in Tuscany – evangelized by a disciple of St Peter – though Pisa's church of San Pietro a Grado is said to have been founded by Peter himself. In Florence, the church of San Lorenzo and the martyr's shrine at San Miniato were both established in the fourth century.

This period of calm was shattered in the fifth century by the invasions of the **Goths** from the north, though the scale of the destruction in this first barbarian wave was

Eighth century BC	59 BC	552 AD
The Etruscans establish settlements in Tuscany; Fiesole is their northernmost town	The Roman colony of Florentia, forerunner of Florence, is established by Julius Caesar	Florence is stormed by the Goths, under their king Totila

nothing compared to the havoc of the following century. After the fall of Rome, the empire had split in two, with the western half ruled from Ravenna and the eastern from Constantinople (Byzantium). By the 490s Ravenna was occupied by the Ostrogoths, and forty years later the Byzantine emperor Justinian launched a campaign to repossess the Italian peninsula.

The ensuing mayhem between the Byzantine armies of Belisarius and Narsus and the fast-moving Goths was probably the most destructive phase of central Italian history, with virtually all major settlements ravaged by one side or the other – and sometimes both. In 552 Florence fell to the hordes of the Gothic king **Totila**, whose depredations so weakened the province that less than twenty years later the **Lombards** were able to storm in, subjugating Florence to the duchy whose capital was in Pavia, though its dukes preferred to rule from Lucca.

By the end of the eighth century Charlemagne's **Franks** had taken control of much of Italy, with the administration being overseen by imperial **margraves**, again based in Lucca. These proxy rulers developed into some of the most powerful figures in the Holy Roman Empire and were instrumental in spreading Christianity even further. Willa, widow of the margrave Uberto, established the Badìa in Florence in 978, the first monastic foundation in the centre of the city; her son Ugo, margrave in turn, is buried in the Badìa's church.

Matilda of Canossa

The central authority of the Holy Roman Empire was often tenuous, with feudal grievances making the region all but ungovernable, and it was under the imperial margraves that an autonomous Tuscany began to emerge. In 1027 the position of margrave was passed to the **Canossa** family, who took the title of the Counts of Tuscia, as Tuscany was then called. The most influential figure produced by this dynasty was **Matilda**, daughter of the first Canossa margrave. When her father died she was abducted by the German emperor Henry III, and on her release and return to her home territory she began to take the side of the papacy in its protracted disputes with the empire. The culmination of her anti-imperialist policy came in 1077, when she obliged the emperor Henry IV to wait in the snow outside the gates of Canossa before making obeisance to Pope Gregory VII. Later friction between the papacy, empire and Tuscan cities was assured when Matilda bequeathed all her lands to the pope, with the crucial exceptions of Florence, Siena and Lucca.

Though Lucca had been the titular base of the imperial margraves, Ugo and his successors had shown a degree of favouritism towards **Florence**, and over the next three hundred years Florence gained pre-eminence among the cities of Tuscany, becoming especially important as a religious centre. In 1078 Countess Matilda supervised the construction of new fortifications for Florence, and in the year of her death – 1115 – granted it the status of an independent city.

Guelphs and Ghibellines

The new *comune* of Florence was essentially governed by a council of one hundred men, the great majority drawn from the rising merchant class. In 1125 the city's increasing dominance of the region was confirmed when it crushed the rival town of

Late sixth century	Late eighth century	978
Florence comes under the control of the Lombards	Charlemagne's Franks take control of much of Italy	Willa, widow of the margrave Uberto, establishes the Badìa, Florence's first monastic foundation

Fiesole. Fifty years later, as the population boomed with the rise of the textile industry, new walls were built around what was then one of the largest cities in Europe.

Not that the other mercantile centres of Tuscany were completely eclipsed. **Pisa** in the tenth and eleventh centuries had become one of the peninsula's wealthiest ports, and its traders played a vital part in bringing the cultural influences of France, Byzantium and the Muslim world into Italy. Twelfth-century **Siena**, though racked by conflicts between the bishops and the secular authorities and between the nobility and the merchant class, was booming thanks to its cloth industries and its exploitation of a local silver mine – foundation of a banking empire that was to see the city rivalling the bankers of Venice and Florence on the international markets.

Throughout and beyond the thirteenth century Tuscany was torn by conflict between the **Ghibelline** faction and the **Guelphs**. The names of these two political alignments derive from Welf, the family name of Emperor Otto IV, and Waiblingen, the name of a castle owned by their implacable rivals, the Hohenstaufen. Though there's no clear documentation, it seems that the terms Guelph and Ghibelline entered the Italian vocabulary at the end of the twelfth century, when supporters of Otto IV battled for control of the central peninsula with the future Frederick II, nephew of Otto and grandson of the Hohenstaufen emperor Barbarossa (1152–90). Within the first few years of Frederick II's reign (1212–50), the labels Guelph and Ghibelline had changed their meaning – the latter still referred to the allies of the Hohenstaufen, but the Guelph party was defined chiefly by its loyalty to the papacy, thus reviving the battle lines drawn up during the reign of Matilda.

To muddy the waters yet further, when Charles of Anjou conquered Naples in 1266, alliance with the anti-imperial French became another component of Guelphism, and a loose Guelph alliance soon stretched from Paris to Naples, substantially funded by the bankers of Tuscany.

Ghibelline/Guelph divisions broadly corresponded to a split between the feudal **nobility** and the rising **business classes**. By the beginning of the thirteenth century the major cities of Tuscany were becoming increasingly self-sufficient and inter-city strife was soon a commonplace of medieval life. In this climate, affiliations with the empire and the papacy were often struck on the basis that "my enemy's enemy is my friend", and allegiances changed at baffling speed. Nonetheless, certain patterns did emerge from the confusion: Florence and Lucca were generally Guelph strongholds, while Pisa, Arezzo, Prato, Pistoia and Siena tended to side with the empire.

As a final complicating factor, this was also the great age of **mercenary** armies, whose loyalties changed even quicker than those of the towns that paid for their services. Thus **Sir John Hawkwood** – whose White Company was the most fearsome band of hoodlums on the peninsula – was employed early in his career by Ghibelline Pisa to fight the Florentines. He was then taken on by Pope Gregory XI, whom he deserted on the grounds of underpayment, and in the end was granted a pension of 1200 florins a year by Florence, basically as a form of protection money.

The ascendancy of Florence

In this period of superpower manoeuvring and shifting economic structures, city governments in Tuscany were volatile. The administration of Siena, for example, was

1115	Twelfth century	Thirteenth century
Countess Matilda grants Florence the status of an independent city	Siena, enriched by its cloth factories, silver mines and banks, becomes a major city	Tuscany riven by clashes between the Ghibellines and the Guelphs

carried out by various combinations of councils and governors and in 1368 its constitution was redrawn no fewer than four times. However, Florence provides perhaps the best illustration of the turbulence of Tuscan politics in the late Middle Ages.

In 1207 the city's governing council was replaced by the **podestà**, an executive official who was traditionally a non-Florentine, in a semi-autocratic form of government that was common throughout the region. It was around this time, too, that the first **arti** (guilds) were formed to promote the interests of the traders and bankers, a constituency of ever-increasing power. Then in 1215 Florence was riven by a feud that was typical of the internecine violence of central Italy at this period. On Easter Sunday one **Buondelmonte de' Buondelmonti**, on his way to his wedding, was stabbed to death at the foot of the Ponte Vecchio by a member of the Amidei clan, in revenge for breaking his engagement to a young woman of that family. The prosecution of the murderers and their allies polarized the city into those who supported the *comune* – which regarded itself as the protector of the commercial city against imperial ambitions – and the followers of the Amidei, who seem to have politicized their personal grievances by aligning themselves against the *comune* and with the emperor.

These Ghibellines eventually enlisted the help of Emperor Frederick II to oust the Guelphs in 1248, but within two years they had been displaced by the Guelph-backed regime of the **Primo Popolo**, a quasi-democratic government drawn from the mercantile class. The Primo Popolo was in turn displaced in 1260, when the Florentine army marched on Siena to demand the surrender of some exiles who were hiding out in the city. Though greatly outnumbered, the Sienese army and its Ghibelline allies overwhelmed the aggressors at **Montaperti**, after which the Sienese were prevented from razing Florence only by the intervention of Farinata degli Uberti, head of the Ghibelline exiles.

By the 1280s the balance had again moved back in favour of Florence, where the Guelphs were back in control – after the intervention of Charles of Anjou – through the **Secondo Popolo**, a regime run by the Arti Maggiori (Great Guilds). It was this second bourgeois administration that definitively shifted the fulcrum of power in Florence towards its bankers, merchants and manufacturers: in 1293 the Secondo Popolo passed a programme of political reforms known as the Ordinamenti della Giustizia, excluding the nobility from government and investing power in the **Signoria**, a council drawn from the Arti Maggiori.

Strife between the virulently anti-imperial "Black" and more conciliatory "White" factions within the Guelph camp marked the start of the fourteenth century in Florence, with many of the Whites – Dante among them – being exiled in 1302. Worse disarray was to come. In 1325 the army of Lucca under **Castruccio Castracani** defeated the Florentines and was about to overwhelm the city when the death of their leader took the momentum out of the campaign. Then in 1339 the Bardi and Peruzzi banks – Florence's largest – both collapsed, mainly owing to the bad debts of Edward III of England. The ultimate catastrophe came in 1348, when the **Black Death** killed as many as half the city's population.

However, even though the epidemic hit Florence so badly that it was generally referred to as the Florentine Plague, its effects were equally devastating throughout the region, and did nothing to reverse the economic – and thus political – supremacy of the city. Florence had subsumed Pistoia in 1329 and gained Prato in the 1350s. In

1260	1348	1406
The Florentine army is routed by the Sienese at Montaperti, but Siena's ascendancy is short-lived	The Black Death kills half the population of Florence and devastates much of Italy	Florence takes control of Pisa, and becomes the strongest city in Tuscany by far

DESCENDANTS OF COSIMO IL VECCHIO

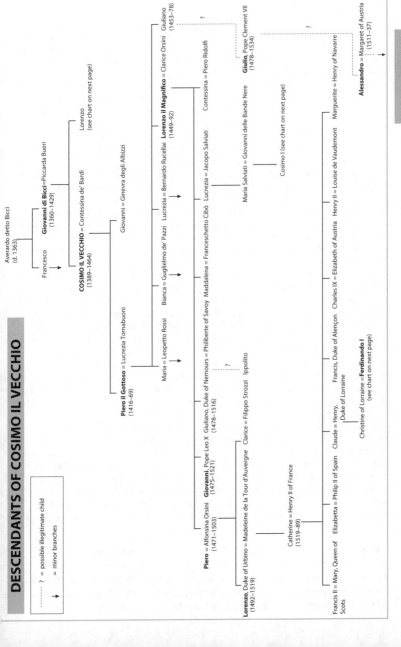

------ = possible illegitimate child

= minor branches

1406 it took control of Pisa and thus gained a long-coveted sea port. From this time on, despite the survival of Sienese independence into the sixteenth century, the history of Tuscany increasingly becomes the history of Florence.

The early Medici

A crucial episode in the liberation of Florence from the influence of the papacy was the so-called **War of the Eight Saints** in 1375–78, which brought Florence into direct territorial conflict with Pope Gregory XI. This not only signalled the dissolution of the old Guelph alliance, but had immense repercussions for the internal politics of Florence. The increased taxation and other economic hardships of the war provoked an uprising of the industrial day-labourers, the **Ciompi**, on whom the wool and cloth factories depended. Their short-lived revolt resulted in the formation of three new guilds and direct representation for the workers for the first time. However, the prospect of increased proletarian presence in the machinery of state provoked a consolidation of the city's oligarchs and in 1382 an alliance of the city's Guelph party and the **Popolo Grasso** (the wealthiest merchants) took control of the Signoria away from the guilds, a situation that lasted for four decades.

Not all of Florence's most prosperous citizens aligned themselves with the Popolo Grasso, and the foremost of the well-off mavericks were the **Medici**, a family from the Mugello region whose fortune had been made by the banking prowess of Giovanni Bicci de' Medici. The political rise of his son, **Cosimo de' Medici**, was to some extent due to his family's sympathies with the Popolo Minuto, as the members of the disenfranchised lesser guilds were known. With the increase in public discontent at the autocratic rule of the Signoria – where the Albizzi clan were the dominant force – Cosimo came to be seen as the figurehead of the more democratically inclined sector of the upper class. In 1431 the authorities imprisoned him in the tower of the Palazzo Vecchio and two years later, as Florence became embroiled in a futile war against Lucca, they sent him into exile. He was away for only a year. In 1434, after a session of the Parlamento – a general council called in times of emergency – it was decided to invite him to return. Having secured the military support of the Sforza family of Milan, Cosimo became the pre-eminent figure in the city's political life, a position he maintained for more than three decades. Cosimo il Vecchio – as he came to be known – rarely held office himself, preferring to exercise power through backstage manipulation and adroit investment. His generosity to charities and religious foundations in Florence was no doubt motivated in part by genuine piety, but clearly did no harm as a public relations exercise.

In the first half of the fourteenth century, Dante, Boccaccio and Giotto had established the literary and artistic ascendancy of Florence, laying the foundations of Italian humanism with their emphasis on the importance of the vernacular and the dignity of humanity. Florence's reputation as the most innovative **cultural centre** in Europe was strengthened during the fifteenth century, to a large extent through Medici patronage. Cosimo commissioned work from Donatello, Michelozzo and a host of other Florentine artists, and took advantage of the 1439 Council of Florence – a conference of the Catholic and Eastern churches – to foster scholars who were familiar

1434	**1478**	**1494–98**
Cosimo de' Medici becomes the most powerful figure in the political life of Florence	The Pazzi conspiracy sees Lorenzo de' Medici badly injured and his brother Giuliano murdered	The Medici flee, and the monk Girolamo Savonarola is effectively the ruler of Florence

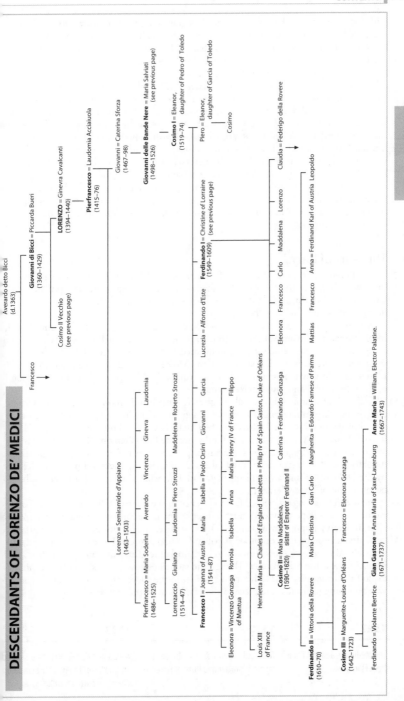

DESCENDANTS OF LORENZO DE' MEDICI

with the literatures of the ancient world. His grandson **Lorenzo il Magnifico** (who succeeded Piero il Gottoso, the Gouty) continued this literary patronage, promoting the study of the classics in the academy that used to meet at the Medici villas. Other Medici were to fund projects by Botticelli, Michelangelo, Pontormo – in fact, most of the seminal figures of the Florentine Renaissance.

Lorenzo il Magnifico's status as the *de facto* ruler of Florence was even more secure than that of Cosimo il Vecchio, but it did meet one stiff challenge. While many of Florence's financial dynasties were content to advise and support the Medici, others were resentful of the power now wielded by their fellow businessmen. In 1478 one of these disgruntled families, the **Pazzi**, conspired with Pope Sixtus IV in a plot to murder Lorenzo and his brother Giuliano (see p.52); Lorenzo was badly injured and Giuliano killed, an outcome that only increased the esteem in which Lorenzo was held. Now that the plot had failed, Sixtus joined forces with the ferocious King Ferrante of Naples to launch a war on Florence, and excommunicated Lorenzo into the bargain. Taking his life in his hands, Lorenzo left Florence to persuade Ferrante to leave the alliance, a mission he somehow accomplished successfully, to the jubilation of the city.

The wars of Italy

Before Lorenzo's death in 1492 the Medici bank failed, and in 1494 Lorenzo's son Piero was obliged to flee following his surrender to the invading French army of Charles VIII. This invasion was the commencement of a bloody half-century dominated by the so-called **Wars of Italy**.

After the departure of Charles's troops, Florence was virtually under the control of the inspirational monk **Girolamo Savonarola**, but his career was brief. He was executed as a heretic in 1498, after which the city continued to function as a republic that was somewhat more democratic than that of the Medici. In 1512, however, following Florence's defeat by the Spanish and papal armies, the Medici returned, in the person of the vicious **Giuliano, Duke of Nemours**.

Giuliano's successors – his equally unattractive nephew Lorenzo, the Duke of Urbino, and Giulio, illegitimate son of Lorenzo il Magnifico's brother – were in effect just the mouthpieces of Giovanni de' Medici (the Duke of Nemours' brother), who in 1519 became **Pope Leo X**. Similarly, when Giulio became **Pope Clement VII**, he was really the absentee ruler of Florence, where the family presence was maintained by the ghastly **Ippolito** (the illegitimate son of the Duke of Nemours) and **Alessandro** (acknowledged by the Duke of Urbino as his illegitimate son, but believed by most historians to have been the son of Pope Clement).

The Medici were again evicted from Florence in the wake of Charles V's pillage of Rome in 1527, Pope Clement's humiliation by the imperial army providing the spur to eject his deeply unpopular relatives. Three years later the pendulum swung the other way: after a siege by the combined papal and imperial forces, Florence capitulated and was obliged to receive Alessandro, who was proclaimed **Duke of Florence**, the first Medici to bear the title of ruler. Though the sadistic Alessandro lost no opportunity to exploit the immunity that came from his title, in the wider scheme of things Tuscany was becoming just one more piece in the vast jigsaw of the Habsburg empire, a

1527	1530	1537
The Medici are again evicted from Florence	The Medici return: Alessandro de' Medici is proclaimed Duke of Florence	Alessandro de' Medici is assassinated Cosimo I, son-in-law of the emperor Charles V, becomes Duke

superpower far more interventionist than the medieval empire of Frederick II could ever have been.

The later Medici

After the assassination of Alessandro in 1537, power passed to another **Cosimo**, a descendant of Cosimo il Vecchio's brother. The emperor Charles V, now related to the Medici through the marriage of his daughter to Alessandro, gave his assent to the succession of this seemingly pliable young man – indeed, without Habsburg consent it would not have happened. Yet it turned out that Cosimo had the clear intention of maintaining Florence's role as the regional power-broker, and he proved immensely skilful at judging just how far he could push the city's autonomy without provoking the imperial policy-makers.

Having finally extinguished the subversive threat of the rival Strozzi faction at the battle of **Montemurlo**, Cosimo went on to buy the territory of Siena from the Habsburgs in 1557, giving Florence control of all of Tuscany with the solitary exception of Lucca. Two years later Florentine hegemony in Tuscany was confirmed in the Treaty of Cateau-Cambrésis, the final act in the Wars of Italy.

Imperial and papal approval of Cosimo's rule was sealed in 1570, when he was allowed to take the title **Cosimo I, Grand Duke of Tuscany**. In European terms Tuscany was a second-rank power, but by comparison with other states on the peninsula it was in a very comfortable position, and during Cosimo's reign there would have been little perception that Florence was drifting towards the margins of European politics. It was Cosimo who built the Uffizi, extended and overhauled the Palazzo Vecchio, installed the Medici in the Palazzo Pitti, and commissioned much of the public sculpture around the Piazza della Signoria.

Cosimo's descendants were to remain in power until 1737, and aspects of their rule continued the city's intellectual tradition: the Medici were among Galileo's strongest supporters, for example. Yet it was a story of almost continual economic decline, as bad harvests and recurrent epidemics worsened the gloom created by the shift of European trading patterns in favour of northern Europe. The half-century reign of **Ferdinando II** had scarcely begun when the market for Florence's woollen goods collapsed in the 1630s, and the city's banks simultaneously went into a terminal slump. The last two male Medici, the insanely pious **Cosimo III** and the drunken **Gian Gastone** – who was seen in public only once, vomiting from the window of the state coach – were fitting symbols of the moribund Florentine state.

The world wars

Under the terms of a treaty signed by Gian Gastone's sister, Anna Maria de' Medici, Florence passed in 1737 to the **House of Lorraine**, cousins of the Austrian Habsburgs. The first Lorraine prince, the future Francis I of Austria, was a more enlightened ruler than the last Medici had been and his successors presided over a placid and generally untroubled region, doing much to improve Tuscany's agricultural land and rationalize its production methods. Austrian rule lasted until the coming of the French in 1799,

1559	1737	1799–1815
The Treaty of Cateau-Cambrésis formalizes Florence's hegemony over all of Tuscany	Death of Gian Gastone, the last male Medici; Tuscany passes to the House of Lorraine, relatives of the Austrian Habsburgs	Tuscany under French rule, until the fall of Napoleon

an interlude that ended with the fall of **Napoleon**, who had made his sister Elisa Baciocchi Grand Duchess of Tuscany.

After this, the Lorraine dynasty was brought back, remaining in residence until the last of the line, Leopold II, consented to his own deposition in 1859. Absorbed into the new **Kingdom of Italy** in the following year, Florence became the **capital** in 1865, a position it held until the beginning of 1871, when Rome – having at last become part of the otherwise united country – took over the role.

The economic disruption that followed World War I was exploited by the regime of Benito **Mussolini**. The corporate Fascist state of the 1920s did make various improvements in the infrastructure of the region, but Mussolini's alliance with Hitler's Germany was to prove a calamity. In 1943, as the Allied landing at Monte Cassino was followed by a campaign to sweep the occupying German forces out of the peninsula, Tuscany became a battlefield between the Nazis and the **partisans**. The districts around Monte Amiata and the Val d'Órcia sheltered particularly strong partisan groups, and many of the province's hill-towns had their resistance cells, as numerous well-tended war memorials testify.

Yet, as elsewhere in Italy, the loyalties of Tuscany were split, as is well illustrated by the case of Florence, an ideological centre for the resistance but also home to some of Italy's most ardent Nazi collaborators. Wartime Florence in fact produced one of the strangest paradoxes of the time: a Fascist sympathizer in charge of the British Institute and a German consul who did so much to protect suspected partisans that he was granted the freedom of the city after the war.

Although most of the major monuments of Tuscany survived the war, there was inevitably widespread destruction. Grosseto, Pisa and Livorno were badly damaged by Allied bombing raids, while Florence was wrecked by the retreating German army, who bombed all the bridges except the Ponte Vecchio and blew up much of the medieval city near the banks of the Arno.

Postwar Tuscany

Tuscany is a prosperous and conservative region that has tended to return right-of-centre members of parliament. On a local level, however, left-wing support is high, partly as a consequence of the Italian communist party's record in the war and subsequent work on land reform. Since the 1970s the town halls of the region have been governed predominantly by leftist coalitions, forming the heartland of the so-called "red belt" of central Italy. Maintaining the image of Tuscany as a state within the state, the region's politicians often present themselves as the representatives of grassroots opposition to the centralization and corruption of Roman politics.

Despite migration from the land in the 1950s and 1960s, the **economy** of Tuscany has been adroitly managed. The labour-intensive vineyards, olive groves and farms continue to provide a dependable source of income, boosted by industrial development in the Arno valley and around Livorno and Piombino. Production of textiles, leather goods and jewellery have brought money into Prato, Florence and Arezzo, while wine has brought untold prosperity to previously moribund towns such as Montalcino and Montepulciano. But, as with much of Europe, the rise of Asian manufacturing has taken a toll on the factories of Tuscany, and **tourism** plays an ever-increasing part in balancing the books.

1815–59	1865–71	1939–45	1966
Return of the Lorraine dynasty	Florence is capital of the new Kingdom of Italy	Grosseto, Pisa, Livorno and Florence are badly damaged during World War II	The River Arno breaks its banks, causing massive destruction in Florence

History: Umbria

Although the history of Umbria overlaps with that of Tuscany in the eras of the Etruscans and the Romans, the emergence of self-governing cities marks a divergence between the economically dynamic Tuscan region and landlocked, more inward-looking Umbria. As with the summary of Tuscan history, what follows is but a sketch of what is an immensely complex story, more details of which are to be found in the accounts of the various Umbrian towns.

Pre-Roman Umbria

Over 1500 years before the birth of Christ, a large-scale migration of primitive tribes from central Europe and the east brought permanent settlers to the marshy lowlands around Terni and Perugia. As time went by, these tribes started to move away from the plains in favour of the uplands around Norcia, giving rise to the first of the **hill-towns** that eventually dominated the entire region.

By the eighth century BC these peoples were absorbed by the larger and more sophisticated tribes that followed them from the north. These gradually formed themselves into three distinct groups: the Samnites, the Latins (who later became the Romans), and the **Umbrians**. All three had common cultural roots, spoke dialects of a shared language and between them occupied all but the southernmost tip of the Italian peninsula. The Umbrians' own territory extended far beyond the region's present boundaries, including the best part of what is now Tuscany and the Marche – a vast area for a people of whom almost nothing is known. Only the Eugubine Marbles found near Gubbio yield any clues as to the religion or language of what was clearly a cogent civilization. Other than these, the Umbrians' only memorials are the walls still standing, more or less intact, in a dozen-odd cities in the region.

When the **Etruscans** began to encroach on these cities, their predominantly agricultural inhabitants retreated quietly into the mountains and carried on life much as they had done before. In time they started to trade and intermarry with their new neighbours and the two cultures became more or less indistinguishable. By 700 BC Etruscan influence in Umbria extended as far east as the Tiber, and in some isolated cases – Gubbio for example – some way beyond it. All aspects of their life point to a sophisticated and ordered social set-up, with a political system formed around a confederation of cities, of which two – Perugia and Orvieto – were situated in what is now Umbria.

Roman Umbria

The first time Umbria appears in **Roman** records is in 309 BC, the occasion being Perugia's defeat at the hands of the Roman consul Fabius. The battle marked the beginning of the end for the Etruscan cities, and though some continued to cling to

Eighth century BC	309 BC	40 BC
The rise of the Etruscans	Perugia is taken by the Roman consul Fabius	Octavius, the future Emperor Augustus, destroys Perugia; Umbria becomes a Roman province

independence, by the second century BC most had become reluctant allies of the Romans. Any vestiges of autonomy were stripped away when Perugia was defeated a second time, a consequence of the power struggle that followed the murder of Julius Caesar in 44 BC. This effectively amounted to a confrontation between the consul Mark Antony, his brother Lucius, and **Octavius**, Caesar's great-nephew. In 40 BC the dispute reached crisis point, and while Antony was preoccupied with Cleopatra in Egypt, Octavius succeeded in harrying Lucius from Rome. Lucius, unhappily for the citizens of Perugia, decided to take refuge within their walls – an action that resulted in the city's destruction at the hands of Octavius.

Octavius went on to proclaim himself **Emperor Augustus**, and with this proclamation the Imperial Age began. Under his rule, Umbria continued to enjoy a period of prosperity that had begun with the opening of the **Via Flaminia** in 220 BC. The new road linked Rome to the Adriatic coast and to the cities of the north, and gave Umbria immense strategic importance. It superseded the Tiber as the focal point of the region and brought in its wake a massive increase in trade and prosperity: colonies were built from scratch or on the sites of Umbrian and Etruscan settlements, land was drained and roads constructed. Umbria – named as such for the first time – became a unified and thriving province.

Early Christianity and the barbarian invasions

Christianity spread quickly in Umbria, thanks mainly to Roman lines of communication. By the first century AD towns such as Spoleto and Foligno had become bishoprics, and within two hundred years most towns had Christian communities. As religious practice increasingly adhered to the monastic pattern established in the eastern Mediterranean, it was in Umbria's remote countryside, rather than its cities, that Christianity found its most enduring home. The first recorded **monastery** was founded at Monteluco, near Spoleto, by Julian, a Syrian from Antioch. From such beginnings was born Umbria's extraordinary religious and monastic tradition, which culminated with St Francis, nearly a millennium later.

St Benedict, the most significant of Umbria's early saints, was born in Norcia in 480 AD, within a few years of the deposition of the last Roman Emperor, and at the very moment that the first barbarian invaders from the north were turning towards Italy. The order he founded and the rule he drew up to guide its members were of incalculable importance in ensuring the survival of Western culture in the tumult that followed the fall of Rome. The rule aimed to move men to a perfect love of God through a combination of prayer, study and work, thus ensuring that countless monks were quietly working, studying and preserving aspects of learning that might otherwise have vanished for good.

As the **Goths** and **Huns** plundered the country, Umbria succumbed to the consequences of plague and famine. The only order in these desperate times came from the clergy, who began to take over the civic functions formerly carried out by the Roman state. Bishops took it upon themselves to become generals, frequently instigating resistance to the invaders. While on the face of things their achievements seemed negligible, in that virtually every Umbrian city was razed to the ground, they won increasing respect for themselves and the Church they represented.

217 BC	480 AD	571
Hannibal crushes the Romans at Trasimeno, one of the worst defeats in Rome's history	St Benedict is born in Norcia	The Lombards establish the Dukedom of Spoleto, which contains most of Umbria

After the death of their leader, Totila, at Gualdo Tadino, the Goths were replaced by the **Lombards**, who by 571 had established three principalities in Italy, the central one of which contained most of Umbria and had Spoleto as its capital. This Dukedom of Spoleto was to achieve great importance throughout central Italy, despite being cut off from the Lombard kingdom centred on Pavia to the north by a narrow corridor of territory controlled by the Byzantines – a ribbon of land running from the Adriatic to Rome, including Narni, Amelia, Terni and Perugia. This buffer-state remained a thorn in the Lombards' side for three hundred years, though in Umbria it had the effect of guaranteeing the Dukedom of Spoleto considerable independence of action, a habit that in the coming years would be a hard one to break. The Lombards generally adopted the manners and customs of the local people, establishing an order which brought a short-lived increase in artistic and commercial initiative. Acknowledging the increasing growth of Christianity, they built monasteries alongside those of the Benedictines.

In 754 the growing power of the papacy as a force in Italian politics was illustrated by Pope Stephen III's appeal to the **Franks** to rid Italy of the Lombards. The Franks took up the invitation, first under Pepin the Short, and then under his more famous son, **Charlemagne**. By 800 the Lombards and Byzantines had both been driven out of the country.

Between the empire and the papacy

The papacy received great tracts of land from Charlemagne, who in return demanded that Pope Leo III crown him emperor of the new **Holy Roman Empire**. Peace reigned while Charlemagne lived, but the harmony between papacy and empire disappeared within a few years of his death. The divisions amongst his successors and their preoccupations in northern Europe again left much of Italy prey to invasion and conflict. The papacy was no healthier, weakened by the rival claims of powerful families; with no central authority, it wasn't long before the whole country reverted once more to chaos.

The anarchy of the next few years set the tone for centuries to come. Many towns and old Roman centres, such as Carsulae (near Todi), unsuited to the rigours of constant invasion and siege, were either abandoned or destroyed, to be replaced by **fortified villas** and **castles**, for which the region's hilly terrain was ideal. Around these fortresses developed independent and self-sufficient communities, creating a pattern of isolated, ambitious hill-towns, each with an eye on the territory of its neighbour.

Throughout this period Italy was the scene of a complicated, confused and constantly shifting conflict between the parties of the empire and the papacy, the **Guelphs** and **Ghibellines** (see p.539). As elsewhere, Umbrian towns frequently switched their allegiances, exacting new measures of independence from whomever ruled them at the time, in exchange for promises of loyalty. Yet of all its cities, only Perugia ever really came to merit attention on a national scale. It had become a free *comune* in 1139, owing its wealth to trade links with Rome and the burgeoning economic power of Florence, and was soon the prime mover in any machinations that affected the region as a whole.

Occasionally, however, the Umbrians were distracted from their squabbles by events taking place in the world at large. In 1152, for example, the truce between the empire

---

754

The pope appeals to the Franks to rid Italy of the Lombards; by 800 Charlemagne's Franks are in control

814

Death of Charlemagne; in the following centuries, Umbria is embroiled in conflicts between empire and papacy, and between Guelphs and Ghibellines

and the papacy produced by the Concordat of Worms was shattered by the election of a new and ambitious emperor: Frederick Hohenstaufen. His determination to reassert the power of the empire in Italy spelt doom for the Umbrian cities, who soon had cause to fear the man better known by his Italian nickname of **Barbarossa**. As he marched south, some towns, such as Assisi, took his side while others, such as Perugia, tried to stand up to him; the majority – of which Spoleto was the most notable example – were partly or completely destroyed.

Like Charlemagne before him, Barbarossa was unable to ensure the survival of the authority he had imposed on the empire. After his death **Pope Innocent III** set about exploiting the anti-imperialist feeling aroused in Italy by the ferocity of his campaigns, and to ally it with the collective guilt at the capture of Jerusalem by the infidel Saladin in 1187, hoping thereby to resurrect papal fortunes. When he came to Umbria, however, he met with little success, cities such as Perugia and Spoleto being quite happy to accept new powers of autonomy, but turning obstructive when papal governors were sent to oversee them.

Medieval comunes and war lords

In 1308 the papacy moved to Avignon, and the outlook for the Church grew even more bleak from 1387 until 1417, when Europe was divided in its support for rival popes in Rome and France. The power vacuum that resulted from this **Great Schism** was the single most important factor in allowing the development of democratic *comunes* in central Italy. At the same time, the influence of the older noble families was eclipsed by the emergence of a mercantile class, brought to prominence by the increase and diversification of trade. With the influx of new money and new men, secular building took place on an unprecedented scale, giving the rapidly expanding cities the appearances that they have largely retained to the present day.

Liberal and sophisticated constitutions were drawn up to administer the new towns, of which **Spoleto**'s, instituted at the end of the thirteenth century, serves as a typical example. Originally civic issues were decided by a show of hands in the *arringo*, a general assembly of all adult males convoked in the central piazza. By 1296, when a new constitution was drawn up, the size of the population made such an arrangement impracticable, and the role of the *arringo* was reduced to a body that could express opinions, but no longer take decisions. The legislative function was taken over by a General Council elected from the twelve parishes that made up Spoleto's administrative districts. Final executive and judicial power lay with the **podestà**, a kind of troubleshooter elected for a year and often brought in from outside the city – as in Tuscany. He was answerable to the **capitano del popolo**, a police chief and appeals judge who was also responsible for the day-to-day running of the administration. Below him were a host of elected minor officials, all of whom were, in the manner of contemporary Italian bureaucracy, constrained by rigid job specifications.

The theory was reasonable, but the practice was often rather different. First, the cities spent so much time arguing with their neighbours that their administrations were obliged to be almost constantly prepared for war. Second, towns were plagued by continual dissent from within as Guelphs and Ghibellines fought each other, most of them citing their allegiances to distant authority merely as an excuse to wipe out local rivals and seize

1226	1354	1439
Death of St Francis of Assisi	Spoleto is seized for the papacy by Cardinal Albornoz, as Rome begins to assert its power in the region	The papacy takes control of Foligno

power. Citizens soon came to realize that a strong executive was the only means to combat such disorder, and began to accept the domination of forceful individuals, usually the heads of the strongest **noble families** of the moment, or the person who could muster the largest private army – in most cases one and the same man.

At about the same time, other powerful individuals began to figure in Umbria's affairs: the **condottieri**, or itinerant private soldiers hired to fight battles on behalf of their citizens. Most of them were English or French refugees from the Hundred Years' War, or German and Swiss stragglers from the imperial armies. Some were astute enough to form themselves into efficient bands and soon found in Umbria a healthy market for their services. The cities were losers in every way in these contracts, wasting money on unreliable allies while property was destroyed and land plundered. Added to this, there was the everyday chaos produced by warring noble families, whose disputes were often settled in bloodshed worthy of Jacobean tragedy. Taking into account the normal range of calamities, such as plague and famine, which could strike the medieval world at any time, life in Umbria should have been intolerable.

But against this background of violence and suffering, the artistic and intellectual life of the region went from strength to strength. The same subtle changes being wrought throughout northern Italy that were to culminate in the **Renaissance** were also taking place in Umbria. In religion, St Francis had almost single-handedly revitalized man's relations to the divine. In painting, Cimabue, Giotto and their followers had introduced a naturalism that left behind the stilted beauty of the Byzantines. A university was founded in Perugia as early as 1308, and the first edition of Dante's *Divine Comedy* was printed not in Florence, but in Foligno.

Papal consolidation and the Risorgimento

Gradually the infighting exhausted the cities, and the **papacy** – which out of choice or necessity had largely stood back from the centuries of bloody disorder – seized the opportunity to exert its power. One by one the cities fell: Spoleto in 1354 to the crusading Cardinal Albornoz; Foligno in 1439, when the ruling Trinci family surrendered to soldiers of Pope Euginius V; Spello in 1535, after 150 years of despotic rule; and Gubbio in 1624, handed over to Urban VIII by the last of the ruling Montefeltro.

The old civic administrations were replaced by papal governors and for the two centuries before Unification Umbria slumbered under the rule of the Church. Although order was restored, peace and papal rule were no guarantee of prosperity. The isolation that had once served the region so well now began to tell against it. Absentee landlords – amongst whom the papacy figured large – collected rents but took little interest in land management, so that the soil deteriorated and with it the agriculture on which Umbria depended. Such industry as existed was agriculture-based and so shared in its stagnation, and in any case it was cut off from the prosperous markets to the north by poor communications. To anyone surveying the Umbrian scene at the end of the eighteenth century it would have seemed as if very little had changed in almost five hundred years.

Matters improved somewhat in the upheaval that followed the French Revolution and the rule of **Napoleon**, when the French organized the region into two districts and

1535	1624	1860
Spello becomes part of the Papal States	Gubbio is handed over to Pope Urban VIII	Garibaldi is welcomed as a hero in Perugia

tried to encourage economic growth. In the more liberal atmosphere of the times, a free-thinking class of merchants emerged, which the return of papal rule after Napoleon's death could do little to repress. By the time of the battle for the Unification of Italy, this spirit had found broader and more popular support, and Umbria welcomed **Garibaldi**'s troops into Perugia on September 11, 1860.

Unfortunately, when trade barriers between the regions were abolished the Umbrian economy was subjected to the rigours of free competition, with which it was ill-equipped to deal. Traditional craft and agricultural industries crumbled in the face of industrialization in the north. Private wealth remained idle, or was invested in the north, while the state failed to make the improvements to the region's infrastructure that might have halted the agricultural decline.

Umbria in the twentieth century

In the first years of the twentieth century the Italian economy as a whole was on an upswing, and for a while things began to look up for Umbria as well, with light industry appearing in the region for the first time. But this flicker of prosperity came to an abrupt end when the small **Banca di Perugia**, which had been largely responsible for funding the new investments, was swallowed by the Banca Commerciale, which preferred to invest in the more profitable and less risky ventures in the north.

Where the capital went, the people went too. Although in 1911 half the region's population was illiterate, they did not need education to know that their future lay outside Umbria. Thousands **emigrated** to America or to the new factories of Turin and Germany, leaving a population at home who increasingly saw socialism as the answer to the region's ills. By 1919, Umbria's scattered left-wing parties commanded 48 percent of the vote and had established control of many local and regional councils. Hopes of reform, however, were quickly dashed by the rise of Mussolini, even if the preparations for war did put some energy into the regional economy.

World War II left Umbria relatively unscathed until the German retreat up the peninsula, when the key strategic corridors – between Lago Trasimeno, Perugia and Orvieto – made it the seat of bitter fighting. Resistance groups were active in the hills above the main valleys, with the area around Gubbio seeing particularly intense partisan activity.

Postwar emigration rates were higher than ever. Only when central government devolved more power to the regions did Umbria begin to prosper. Political control by now was in the hands of the Communist Party, which carefully directed funds at cooperative ventures and projects appropriate to the region's special needs, with transport, agriculture and latterly tourism as the main priorities. Road and rail links at last provided an economic lifeline to Rome and the north.

Finally, and perhaps most importantly, the last few decades have seen the birth of what can only be described as a new pride and enthusiasm in Umbria. There is still poverty and there are still problems, but there is also a powerful sense of vigour and community which seems determined to overcome them. It is a spirit that even the most casual visitor cannot fail to notice, manifestly obvious in the region's extraordinary range of cultural events, the diversity and skill of its craftspeople, the Umbrians' own obvious pride in their countryside and their heritage, and a host of more minor signs that at last point to progress.

1927	1944
Umbria's modern borders are fixed, with the separation of the province of Rieti, which is incorporated into Lazio	Intense fighting between partisans and the retreating German army

A directory of artists and architects

Agostino di Duccio (1418–81). Born in Florence, Agostino served as a mercenary before turning to sculpture. Having possibly studied with Jacopo della Quercia, he carved the altarpiece for Modena cathedral then returned to Florence in 1442. His masterpiece is the Tempio Malatestiano in Rimini, on which Alberti and Piero della Francesca also worked; the best example of his marble relief work in Tuscany and Umbria is the Oratorio di San Bernardino in Perugia. He returned to Florence briefly in the 1460s, a period during which he spoiled the marble block that was to become Michelangelo's *David*.

Alberti, Leon Battista (1404–72). Born illegitimately to a Florentine exile, probably in Genoa, Alberti was educated in Padua and Bologna. One of the most complete personifications of the Renaissance ideal of universal genius, he was above all a writer and theorist: his *De Re Aedificatoria* (1452) was the first architectural treatise of the Renaissance, and he also wrote a tract on the art of painting, *Della Pittura*, dedicated to his friend Brunelleschi. His theory of harmonic proportions in musical and visual forms was first put into practice in the facade of Santa Maria Novella in Florence, while his archeological interest in classical architecture found expression in the same city's Palazzo Rucellai. His other buildings are in Mantua and Rimini.

Alunno, Nicolò (1430–1502). The greatest of the purely Umbrian painters before Perugino, Alunno was probably the pupil of the Venetian Carlo Crivelli, whose bright colouring and precise contours are a feature of his work. Emotionally more intense than Perugino, he usually rejects the conventional dulcet pastoralism of Umbrian art for a bleaker landscape such as that around Gubbio and Foligno.

Ammannati, Bartolomeo (1511–92). A Florentine sculptor-architect, much indebted to Michelangelo, Ammannati is best known for his additions to Palazzo Pitti and for the Ponte San Trìnita (though in all likelihood this was largely designed by Michelangelo). He created the fountain in the Piazza della Signoria, with some assistance from his pupil Giambologna, and the Bargello contains some other pieces.

Arnolfo di Cambio (c.1245–1302). Pupil of Nicola Pisano, with whom he worked on sculptural projects in Bologna, Siena and Perugia before going to Rome in 1277. The most important of his independent sculptures are the pieces in Florence's Museo dell'Opera del Duomo and the *Tomb of Cardinal de Braye* in San Domenico in Orvieto: the latter defined the format of wall tombs for the next century. However, Arnolfo is best known as the architect of Florence's Duomo and Palazzo Vecchio, and various fortifications in central Tuscany, including the fortress at Poppi.

Bandinelli, Baccio (1493–1560). Born in Florence, Bandinelli trained as a goldsmith, sculptor and painter. He perceived himself as an equal to Michelangelo and to Cellini, his most vocal critic. Despite manifest shortcomings as a sculptor, he was given prestigious commissions by Cosimo I, the most conspicuous of which is the *Hercules and Cacus* outside the Palazzo Vecchio. Other pieces by him are in the Bargello.

Beccafumi, Domenico (1484/6–1551). The last great Sienese painter, Beccafumi was in Rome during the painting of the Sistine Chapel ceiling and Raphael's *Stanze*. He returned to Siena in 1513, when his work showed tendencies that were to become prevalent in Mannerist art: contorted poses, strong lighting, vivid artificial coloration. His decorative skill is especially evident in his frescoes in the Palazzo Pubblico and the pavement of the Duomo.

Benedetto da Maiano (1442–97). Florentine sculptor, best known for his portrait busts in the Bargello and the pulpit in Santa Croce.

Botticelli, Sandro (c.1445–1510). Possibly a pupil of Filippo Lippi, Botticelli was certainly influenced by the Pollaiuolo brothers, whose paintings of the *Virtues* he completed. The mythological paintings for which he is celebrated – including the *Birth of Venus* and *Primavera* – are distinguished by their emphasis on line rather than mass, and by their complicated symbolic meaning, a reflection on his involvement with the Neo-Platonist philosophers whom the Medici gathered about them. In the last decade of his life his devotional pictures became rather didactic – a result, perhaps, of his involvement with Savonarola and his followers.

Bronzino, Agnolo (1503–72). The adopted son of Pontormo, Bronzino became the court painter to Cosimo I. He frescoed parts of the Palazzo Vecchio, but his reputation rests on his glacially elegant portraits.

Brunelleschi, Filippo (1377–1446). Trained as a sculptor and goldsmith, Brunelleschi abandoned this career after his failure in the competition for the Florence Baptistery doors. He then devoted himself to the study of the buildings of ancient Rome, a city he visited with Donatello in 1402. In 1417 he submitted his design for the dome of Florence's Duomo, and all his subsequent work was in that city – San Lorenzo, the Spedale degli Innocenti, Cappella Pazzi (Santa Croce) and Santa Spirito. Unlike the other great architect of this period, Alberti, his work is based on no theoretical premise, but rather on an empiricist's admiration for the buildings of Rome.

Buonarroti, Michelangelo (1475–1564). See box, p.554.

Buontalenti, Bernardo (c.1536–1608). Florentine architect, who began as a military architect to the papacy.

MICHELANGELO

Michelangelo spent much of his life in Rome, and some of his greatest masterpieces are to be seen there, but in Florence you can fully appreciate the extraordinary scope of his achievement, because the city possesses creations from every phase of his life, in the genres of painting, sculpture and architecture.

THE EARLY YEARS

Michelangelo Buonarroti was born on March 16, 1475 in Caprese, in eastern Tuscany, the second son of Francesca di Neri (who was to die six years later) and Lodovico di Leonardo Buonarroti Simoni, the town's chief magistrate. One month later the family moved to Florence, where, in 1488, Michelangelo was apprenticed to the painters Davide and Domenico Ghirlandaio. Little is known about how Michelangelo learned to carve: Vasari says he trained with Bertaldo di Giovanni (a pupil of Donatello), but Michelangelo always insisted that he was self-taught. What's certain is that his first stone reliefs were made for Lorenzo de' Medici, in whose household he lived from 1490 to 1492. In the Casa Buonarroti you can see two pieces from this period: the *Battle of the Lapiths and Centaurs* and the *Madonna of the Stairs*. In the church of Santo Spirito hangs a delicate *Crucifix* that was also (almost certainly) made by Michelangelo at this time, and is his only carving in wood.

THE FLIGHT TO ROME – AND RETURN TO FLORENCE

In October 1494, as the French invaded Italy, Michelangelo fled Florence – a month before the expulsion of the Medici. His journey eventually took him, in 1496, to Rome. There he carved the *Bacchus* that's now in the Bargello, and by the spring of 1499 he had completed the *Pietà* for St Peter's, a work that secured his reputation as the pre-eminent sculptor of his day.

Meanwhile, Florence had become more peaceable after the overthrow of Savonarola, and in 1501 Michelangelo went back to his home city, where he was promptly commissioned to create the *David*, and then a sequence of *Apostles* for the Duomo, of which only the *St Matthew* (now in the Accademia, with *David*) was started. The *Doni Tondo* – one of his very few forays into what he regarded as the menial art of easel painting – was also created during this period, as was the *Pitti Tondo*, now in the Bargello. Although his fresco of the *Battle of Cáscina*, for the Palazzo Vecchio, never advanced beyond the cartoon stage, it became the single most influential work of art in the city, with its unprecedented emphasis on the nude male form and its use of twisting figures, a recurrent motif in later Mannerist art.

Much of his later output was for the court of the Medici – the grotto of the Bóboli gardens, the gardens of the villa at Pratolino and tableaux for court spectaculars. Less frivolous work included the Fortezza del Belvedere, the facade of Santa Trìnita, the Villa Artimino and the fortifications at Livorno.

Castagno, Andrea (c.1421–57). The early years of Castagno's life are mysterious, but around 1440 he painted the portraits of some executed rebels in the Bargello, a job that earned him the nickname "Andrea of the Hanged Men". In 1442 he was working in Venice, but a couple of years later he was back in Florence, creating stained glass for the Duomo and frescoes for Sant'Apollonia. His taut sinewy style is to a large extent derived from the sculpture of his contemporary Donatello, an affinity that is especially clear in his frescoes for Santissima Annunziata. His last painting was the fresco of *Niccolò da Tolentino* in Florence's Duomo.

Cellini, Benvenuto (1500–71). Cellini began his career in Rome, where he fought in defence of the city against the imperial army in 1527. His sculpture is greatly influenced by Michelangelo, as is evident in his most famous large-scale piece, the *Perseus* in the Loggia della Signoria. His other masterpiece in Florence is the *Bust of Cosimo I* in the Bargello. Cellini was an even more accomplished goldsmith and jeweller, creating some exquisite pieces for Francis I, by whom he was employed in the 1530s and 1540s. He also wrote a racy *Autobiography*, a fascinating insight into the artistic world of sixteenth-century Italy and France.

Cimabue (c.1240–1302). Though celebrated by Dante as the foremost painter of the generation before Giotto, very little is known about Cimabue – in fact, the only work that is definitely by him is the mosaic in Pisa's Duomo. Some works can be attributed to him with more confidence than others; the shortlist would include *The Madonna of St Francis* in the lower church at Assisi, the *Passion* cycle in the upper church, the *Maestà* in the Uffizi and the crucifixes in Santa Croce (Florence) and San Domenico (Arezzo).

Civitali, Matteo (1436–1501). Probably self-taught sculptor from Lucca, where all his important work is to be found.

1505–16: ROME

In 1505 Michelangelo was called to Rome, to create a tomb for Pope Julius II. When completed in 1545, the tomb had seven instead of the planned forty statues, only three of them by Michelangelo: *Moses*, *Leah* and *Rachel*. The latter two (both 1542) were the last sculptures that Michelangelo finished; the unfinished *Slaves* in the Accademia was made for another version of the tomb. His relationship with the fiery Julius was always fractious, and in 1506 he returned to Florence. In 1508, however, he was summoned back to the Vatican to commence the most superhuman of all his undertakings – the Sistine Chapel ceiling.

FINAL RETURN TO FLORENCE

In 1516, with the Sistine ceiling finished, Michelangelo returned to Florence, where in 1521 Pope Leo X contracted him to design a new sacristy for San Lorenzo church, as a Medici mausoleum. Work on this, Michelangelo's first architectural project, was interrupted frequently, and building really only began in 1523, when he was also asked to build a library – the Biblioteca Laurenziana – alongside the church. In the San Lorenzo project Michelangelo created an architectural vocabulary that was to provide the basis of Mannerist design, and he carved a remarkable group of sculptures for the sacristy.

The Medici were expelled from Florence in 1527, and Michelangelo stayed on to supervise the defences when it was besieged in 1530 by Emperor Charles V, who then installed the despotic Alessandro de' Medici as his puppet ruler. Once Alessandro was in place, Michelangelo's life in the city was far from easy. In 1534 he left Florence for the last time.

1534–64: BACK TO ROME

Michelangelo was to spend his last thirty years in Rome, where he was soon appointed architect to St Peter's, which Bramante had begun to rebuild in 1506. The colossal dome was his most spectacular addition to the architecture of the Vatican; he made a similarly profound alteration to the civic fabric of the city when he remodelled the Campidoglio in the 1540s. In 1536–41 he produced the tumultuous *Last Judgement* in the Sistine Chapel, and some time around 1540 he carved his last secular work, the *Brutus* (now in the Bargello), but the greatest sculptures of his last years are versions of the *Pietà*. One of these – an ensemble that exemplifies the quality that contemporaries termed *terribilità* ("awesome powerfulness" is an approximation) – was intended for his own tomb, and is now in Florence's Museo dell'Opera del Duomo. Michelangelo died in Rome on February 18, 1564; his body was transported to Florence, where it was borne in torchlit procession to Santa Croce.

Daddi, Bernardo (c.1290–1349). A pupil of Giotto, Daddi combined the solidity of his master's style with the more decorative aspects of the Sienese style. His work can be seen in the Uffizi and Santa Croce in Florence.

Desiderio da Settignano (c.1428–64). Desiderio continued the low relief technique pioneered by Donatello in the panel for the Orsanmichele *St George*, and carved the tomb of Carlo Marsuppini in Santa Croce, Florence. Better known for his exquisite busts of women and children, a good selection of which are on show in the Bargello.

Donatello (c.1386–1466). See box, p.556.

Duccio di Buoninsegna (c.1255–1318). Though occupying much the same pivotal position in the history of Sienese art as Giotto does in Florentine art, Duccio was a less revolutionary figure, refining the stately Byzantine tradition rather than subverting its conventions. One of his earliest works was ordered by Florence's church of Santa Maria Novella – the *Maestà* now in the Uffizi – but the bulk of his output is in his home city. In 1308 he received his most prestigious assignment, the painting of a *Maestà* for Siena's Duomo. The polyptych no longer exists in its original form, but most of the panels are now in Siena's Museo dell'Opera del Duomo. This iconic image of the Madonna, with its rich use of gold and decorative colour, was to profoundly influence such painters as the Lorenzettis and Simone Martini.

Fra' Angelico (c.1395–1455). Born in Vicchio, Fra' Angelico joined the Dominican order in Fiesole, near his home town, and later entered their monasteries in Cortona and Foligno. His first authenticated painting dates from the mid-1420s, but the first that can be definitively dated is a *Madonna* he produced for the linen guild of Florence in 1433. Three years later the Dominicans took over the San Marco monastery in Florence, and soon after he embarked on the series of frescoes and altarpieces now displayed in the museum there. In the mid-1440s he was called to Rome to work on the Vatican, after which he worked at Orvieto, served for three years as prior of the monastery in Fiesole, and returned to Rome around 1452, where he died.

Fra' Bartolommeo (c.1474–1517). Fra' Bartolommeo's

DONATELLO

A pupil of Ghiberti, **Donatello** assisted in the casting of the first set of Florence Baptistery doors in 1403, then worked for Nanni di Banco on the Duomo. His early marble *David* (Bargello) is still Gothic in its form, but a new departure is evident in his heroic *St Mark* for Orsanmichele (1411) – possibly produced after studying the sculpture of ancient Rome. Four years later he began the series of prophets for the Campanile, and at the same time produced the *St George* for Orsanmichele, the epitome of early Renaissance humanism, featuring a relief that is the very first application of rigorous perspective in Western art. In the mid-1420s Donatello started a partnership with Michelozzo, with whom he created the tomb of Pope John XXIII in the Florence Baptistery, a refinement of the genre initiated by Arnolfo di Cambio. He went to Rome in 1431, possibly with Brunelleschi, and it was probably on his return that he made the classical bronze *David* (Bargello), one of the first nude statues of the Renaissance period. Also at this time he made the *cantoria* to be placed opposite the one already made by Luca della Robbia, the pulpit for Prato cathedral (with Michelozzo) and the decorations for the old sacristy in Florence's church of San Lorenzo – the parish church of his great patrons, the Medici. After a period in Padua – where he created the first bronze equestrian statue since Roman times – he returned to Florence, where his last works show an extraordinary harshness and angularity. The main sculptures from this period are the *Judith and Holofernes* (Palazzo Vecchio), the *Magdalene* (Museo dell'Opera del Duomo) and the two bronze pulpits for San Lorenzo.

earliest known work is the Raphael-influenced *Last Judgement* painted for the San Marco monastery in Florence in 1499. The following year he became a monk there, then in 1504 became head of the workshop, a post previously occupied by Fra' Angelico. The works he produced in Florence had an influence on High Renaissance art, with their suppression of elaborate backgrounds and anecdotal detail, concentrating instead on expression and gesture.

Francesco di Giorgio Martini (1439–1501/2). Sienese painter, sculptor and architect, whose treatise on architectural theory was circulated widely in manuscript form; Leonardo had a copy. He was employed for a long period by the ruler of Urbino, Federico da Montefeltro. The church of Santa Maria degli Angeli in Siena and the Palazzo Ducale in Gubbio might be by him; the one Tuscan building that is certainly by him is Santa Maria del Calcinaio in Cortona.

Gaddi, Taddeo (d.1366). According to tradition, Taddeo Gaddi worked with Giotto for 24 years, and throughout his life barely wavered from the precepts of his master's style. His first major independent work is the cycle for the Cappella Baroncelli in Santa Croce, Florence. Other works by him are in Florence's Uffizi, Accademia, Bargello and Museo Horne.

Agnolo Gaddi (d.1396), Taddeo's son, continued his father's Giottesque style; his major projects were for Santa Croce in Florence and the Duomo of Prato.

Gentile da Fabriano (c.1370–1427). Chief exponent of the International Gothic style in Italy, Gentile da Fabriano came to Florence in 1422, when he painted the gorgeous *Adoration of the Magi* now in the Uffizi. In 1425 he went on to Siena and Orvieto, where the intellectual climate was perhaps more conducive than that in the Florence of Masaccio; he finished his career in Rome.

Ghiberti, Lorenzo (1378–1455). Trained as a goldsmith, painter and sculptor, Ghiberti concentrated on the last discipline almost exclusively after winning the competition to design the doors for Florence's Baptistery. His workshop was a virtual academy for the seminal figures of the early Florentine Renaissance, Donatello and Uccello among them. The commission took around twenty years to complete, during which time he also worked on the Siena Baptistery and the church of Orsanmichele in Florence, where his *Baptist and St Matthew* show the influence of classical statuary. This classicism reached its peak in the second set of doors for Florence's Baptistery (the Gates of Paradise); these panels occupied much of the rest of his life, but in his final years he wrote his *Commentarii*, the main source of information on fourteenth-century art in Florence and Siena, and the first autobiography by an artist.

Ghirlandaio, Domenico (1449–94). The most accomplished fresco artist of his generation, Ghirlandaio was the teacher of Michelangelo. After a short period working on the Sistine Chapel with Botticelli, he came back to Florence, where he painted the great cycles in Santa Trinita and Santa Maria Novella.

Giambologna (1529–1608). Born in northern France, Giambologna – Jean de Boulogne – arrived in Italy in the mid-1550s, becoming the most influential Florentine sculptor after Michelangelo's death. Having helped Ammannati on the fountain for the Piazza della Signoria he went on to produce a succession of pieces that typify the Mannerist predilection for sculptures with multiple viewpoints, such as the *Rape of the Sabines* (Loggia della Signoria) and the *Mercury* (Bargello).

Giotto di Bondone (1267–1337). It was with Giotto's fresco cycles that the dramatic presentation of incident became central to religious art: his eye for the significant gesture, his ability to encapsulate moments of extreme emotion and his technical command of figure modelling and spatial depth brought him early recognition as the greatest artist of his generation. Yet, as with Cimabue, the precise attribution of work is problematic. In all probability his first major cycle was the *Life of St Francis* in the upper church at Assisi, though the extent to which his assistants carried out his designs is still disputed. The Arena chapel in Padua is certainly by him, as are large parts of the Bardi and Peruzzi chapels in Santa Croce in Florence. Of his attributed panel paintings, the Uffizi *Maestà* is the only one universally accepted, but most authorities agree that he created the Crucifixes in Florence's Santa Maria Novella and Ognissanti.

Gozzoli, Benozzo (1421–97). Though a pupil of Fra' Angelico, Gozzoli was one of the more worldly artists of the fifteenth century, with a fondness for pageantry that is seen to most impressive effect in the frescoes in Florence's Palazzo Medici-Ricardi. His celebrated cycle in Pisa's Camposanto was all but destroyed in World War II; his other surviving fresco cycles include the *Life of St Francis* in Montefalco and the *Life of St Augustine* in San Gimignano.

Guido da Siena (active mid-thirteenth century). Guido was the founder of the Sienese school of painters, but his life is one of the most problematic areas of Siena's art history. A signed painting by him in the Palazzo Pubblico is dated 1221, but some experts think that the date may have been altered, and that the work is from the 1260s or 1270s – a period when other pictures associated with him are known to have been painted.

Leonardo da Vinci (1452–1519). See box, below.

Lippi, Filippo (c.1406–69). In 1421 Filippo Lippi entered the monastery of the Carmine in Florence, just as Masaccio was beginning work on the Cappella Brancacci there. His early works all bear the stamp of Masaccio, but by the 1430s he was becoming interested in the representation of movement and a more luxuriant surface detail. The frescoes in the cathedral at Prato, executed in the 1450s, show his highly personal vision, as do his panel paintings of wistful Madonnas – many of them executed for the Medici. His last work, the *Life of the Virgin* fresco cycle in Spoleto, was probably largely executed by assistants.

Lippi, Filippino (1457/8–1504). The son of Filippo completed his father's work in Spoleto then travelled to Florence, where his first major commission was the completion of Masaccio's frescoes in Santa Maria del Carmine (c.1484). At around this time he also painted the *Vision of St Bernard* for the Badìa, which shows an affinity with Botticelli, with whom he is known to have worked. His later researches in Rome led him to develop a self-consciously antique style – seen at its most ambitious in Santa Maria Novella.

Lorenzetti, Ambrogio (active 1319–47). Though Sienese, Ambrogio spent part of the 1320s and 1330s in Florence, where he would have witnessed the decoration of Santa Croce by Giotto and his pupils. He's best known for the *Allegory of Good and Bad Government* in the Palazzo Pubblico, which shows painting being used for a secular, didactic purpose for the first time. The Uffizi *Presentation of the Virgin* highlights the difference between Ambrogio's inventive complexity and the comparative simplicity of his brother Pietro's style. There's also a fine altarpiece by him in Massa Maríttima.

LEONARDO DA VINCI

Leonardo trained as a painter under Verrocchio, and it is said that his precocious talent caused his master to abandon painting in favour of sculpture. Drawings of landscapes and drapery have survived from the 1470s, but the first completed picture is the *Annunciation* in the Uffizi. The sketch of the *Adoration of the Magi*, also in the Uffizi, dates from 1481, at which time there was no precedent for its fusion of geometric form and dynamic action. Two years later he was in the employment of Lodovico Sforza of Milan, remaining there for sixteen years. During this second phase of his career he produced the *Lady with the Ermine* (Kraków), the fresco of the *Last Supper* and – probably – the two versions of *The Virgin of the Rocks*, the fullest demonstrations to date of his so-called sfumato, a blurring of tones from light to dark. Innumerable scientific studies and military projects engaged him at this time, and he also made a massive clay model for an equestrian statue of Francesco Sforza – never completed, like so many of his schemes.

When the French took Milan in 1499 Leonardo returned to **Florence**, where he devoted much of his time to anatomical researches. It was during this period that he was commissioned to paint a fresco of the *Battle of Anghiari* in the main hall of the Palazzo Ducale, where his detested rival Michelangelo was also set to work. Only a fragment was completed, and the innovative technique that Leonardo had employed resulted in its speedy disintegration. His cartoons for the *Madonna and Child with St Anne* (Louvre and National Gallery, London) also date from this time, as does the most famous of all his paintings, the Louvre's *Mona Lisa*. In 1506 he went back to Milan, thence to Rome and finally, in 1517, to France. Again, military and scientific work occupied much of this last period – the only painting to have survived is the *St John*, also in the Louvre.

Lorenzetti, Pietro (active 1306–48). Brother of Ambrogio, Pietro Lorenzetti was possibly a pupil of Duccio's in Siena. His first authenticated work is the altarpiece in Arezzo's Pieve di Santa Maria (1320); others include frescoes in Assisi's lower church, in which the impact of Giotto is particularly noticeable, and the *Birth of the Virgin* in Siena's Museo dell'Opera del Duomo. It's probable that both the Lorenzettis died during the Black Death.

Lorenzo Monaco (1372–1425). A Sienese artist, Lorenzo Monaco joined the Camaldolese monastery in Florence, for which he painted the *Coronation of the Virgin*, now in the Uffizi. This and his other earlier works are fairly conventional Sienese-style altarpieces, but his late *Adoration of the Magi* (Uffizi), with its fastidious detailing, anticipates the arrival of Gentile da Fabriano and fully fledged International Gothic.

Maitini, Lorenzo (c.1270–1330). Sienese architect and sculptor Maitini was the only local artist to challenge the supremacy of the Pisani. In 1310 he was made supervisor of Orvieto's Duomo, for which he designed the panels of the facade – though it's not certain how much of the carving was actually by him. Virtually nothing else about him is known.

Martini, Simone (c.1284–1344). The most important Sienese painter, Simone Martini was a pupil of Duccio but equally influenced by Giovanni Pisano's sculpture and the carvings of French Gothic artists. He began his career by painting a fresco counterpart of Duccio's *Maestà* in the city's Palazzo Pubblico (1315). Soon after he was employed by Robert of Anjou, King of Naples, and there developed a sinuous, graceful and courtly style. In the late 1320s he was back in Siena, where he probably produced the portrait of Guidoriccio da Fogliano – though some experts doubt its authenticity. At some point he went to Assisi, where he painted a cycle of *The Life of St Martin* in the lower church. In 1333 he produced a sumptuous *Annunciation* for the Siena Duomo; now in the Uffizi, this is the quintessential fourteenth-century Sienese painting, with its immaculately

WHAT IS THE RENAISSANCE?

In the middle of the sixteenth century **Giorgio Vasari** coined the term *Rinascenza* (rebirth) to designate the period that stretched from around 1300 (when Giotto was active) to the time of Michelangelo. In the late nineteenth century the term **"Renaissance"** entered general usage, largely thanks to the writings of Jacob Burckhardt, whose book *The Civilization of the Renaissance in Italy* (published in German in 1860, and in English translation in 1878) is perhaps the single most influential study of the subject. To historians of this period, the Renaissance was often seen as a singular and all-pervasive phenomenon, in which the rediscovery of ancient classical culture gave impetus to a regeneration of European civilization after the intellectual impoverishment of the Middle Ages. It was characterized by its focus on humanity, and the epicentre of this explosion of humanist art and scholarship was Florence.

While nobody doubts that many of the artists, writers and patrons of Renaissance Italy believed themselves to be participants in the creation of a new society, it's debatable that "Renaissance values" reached deeply into the lives of most ordinary people. For the general populace, life continued to be "medieval" long after their masters had taken to reading Plato. Not only was a peasant's existence as harsh as ever, but there can have been few more dangerous periods in Italian history than the so-called "High Renaissance" – from 1494 to 1559 the peninsula was an almost continuous battleground for the major powers of Europe.

THE PROBLEM OF BEGINNINGS

Locating the beginnings of the Italian Renaissance is a problematic business. **Giotto** (1267–1337) is often taken as a starting point, and when his paintings are compared to the art of the "Gothic" era, it does indeed seem as if he introduced a new realism and drama to European art. His great contemporary **Dante** (1265–1321), who presents Giotto as an innovator in the *Divine Comedy*, appears modern in his use of vernacular Tuscan rather than Latin. On the other hand, the stern theology of Dante's masterpiece strikes us as belonging to a distinctly pre-modern world.

Dante's immediate successors, Petrarch (1304–1374) and Boccaccio (1313–75) – both of them Tuscans – certainly feel more modern than he does. **Petrarch**'s love poetry, his collecting of classical manuscripts and his appreciation of landscape for itself might be described as manifestations of a Renaissance spirit. Similarly, **Boccaccio**'s *Decameron* has a claim to be the first example of modern prose fiction. And yet in the visual arts it can seem that in the century after Giotto, painting didn't change enough to support the idea that his work initiated an unstoppable process. It wasn't until Masaccio's frescoes in the Brancacci chapel, painted a hundred years after Giotto's in Santa Croce, that Italian art could be said to have taken its next big leap.

crafted gold surfaces and emphasis on fluid outline and bright coloration. In 1340 Martini travelled to the papal court of Avignon, where he spent the rest of his life.

Masaccio (1401–28). Born near Florence, Tomasso di ser Giovanni di Mone Cassai – universally known as Masaccio – entered the city's painters' guild in 1422. His first large commission was an altarpiece for the Carmelites of Pisa (the central panel is now in the National Gallery in London), which shows a massive grandeur at odds with the International Gothic style then being promulgated by Gentile da Fabriano. His masterpieces – the *Trinity* fresco in Santa Maria Novella and the fresco cycle in Santa Maria del Carmine – were produced in the last three years of his life, the latter being painted in collaboration with Masolino. With the architecture of Brunelleschi and the sculpture of Donatello, the Carmine frescoes are the most important achievements of the early Renaissance.

Maso di Banco (active 1340s). Maso was perhaps the most inventive of Giotto's acolytes, and his reputation depends chiefly on the cycle of the *Life of St Sylvester* in Santa Croce, Florence.

Masolino da Panicale (1383–1447). Masolino was employed in Ghiberti's workshop for the production of the first set of Florence's Baptistery doors, and the style of Ghiberti conditioned much of his subsequent work. His other great influence was Masaccio, with whom he worked on the Brancacci chapel.

Memmi Lippo (d.1357). Brother-in-law of Simone Martini, Lippo Memmi was his assistant on the Uffizi *Annunciation*. His major work is the *Maestà* in the Palazzo Pubblico in San Gimignano, and he may also have been responsible for the dramatic New Testament frescoes in the Collegiata of the same town.

Michelangelo (1475–1564). See box, p.554.

Michelozzo di Bartolommeo (1396–1472). Born in Florence, Michelozzo worked in Ghiberti's studio and

---

THE CASE OF FLORENCE

If it's impossible to say exactly where and when the Renaissance begins, there's no doubt that the high culture of **Florence** (and most of Italy) in 1500 was radically different from that of 1300. Furthermore, Florence in the fifteenth century nurtured more of these "avant garde" figures than any other city in Italy. But what were the circumstances that made Florence the pre-eminent centre of creativity?

A primary factor was the city's **wealth**. Buoyed by revenues from banking and manufacture, the Florentine upper classes had plenty of surplus cash with which to fund the accumulation of libraries and art collections. Competing against each other in displays of educated taste, clans such as the Strozzi, the Medici, the Rucellai and the Tornabuoni were furthering a Florentine self-image that can be traced back at least as far as Giovanni Villani (1275–1348), author of a twelve-volume history of the city (written in Tuscan), in which he wrote that Florence, "the daughter and offspring of Rome, is on the increase and destined to do great things."

Even before Villani, Florence had something of a **humanist tradition**. Dante's teacher, Brunetto Latini (c.1210–94), for instance, studied Aristotle and Cicero, wrote in the vernacular (both Italian and French) and with his *Livre du trésor* produced what might be called the first encyclopedia. A century later, Florence's university invited Manuel Chrysoloras (c.1350–1415) to travel from Constantinople to teach Greek – the first time for seven hundred years that the language had been taught in Italy. Chrysoloras translated Plato and Homer, wrote about the monuments of Rome and Byzantium, and numbered among his pupils Leonardo Bruni – chancellor of the Florentine Republic, author of the *History of the Florentine People* and books on Dante, Petrarch and Boccaccio, translator of Plato and Aristotle, and the first scholar to define his work as *studia humanitatis*.

In 1439 the Council of Florence – convened to forge a reconciliation between the Roman and Eastern churches – brought a host of classical scholars to the city, some of whom remained in Florence, to be joined after 1453 by others who fled from Constantinople following its conquest by the Turks. These refugees further enriched an environment in which developed so many great artists and such prodigious philosopher scholars as Marsilio Ficino, Poliziano and Pico della Mirandola, all of whom were members of the Medici court.

But while Botticelli's *Birth of Venus* or Michelangelo's *David* unarguably embody something new, Renaissance philosophy was essentially an elaboration of the work of ancient thinkers – of Plato in particular. For all their learning, Ficino and the rest produced nothing to equal the originality of medieval philosophers such as Thomas Aquinas or Duns Scotus.

collaborated with Donatello before turning exclusively to architecture. His main patrons were the Medici, for whom he altered the villa at Careggi and built the Palazzo Medici, which set a prototype for patrician mansions in the city. He later designed the Villa Medici at Fiesole for the family, and for Cosimo de' Medici he added the light and airy library to the monastery of San Marco. In the Alberti-influenced tribune for the church of Santissima Annunziata, Michelozzo produced the first centrally planned church design to be built in the Renaissance period.

Mino da Fiesole (1429–84). Florentine sculptor, perhaps a pupil of Desiderio da Settignano, Mino is known chiefly for his tombs and portrait busts; there are examples of the former in Fiesole's Duomo and the Badìa in Florence, and of the latter in the Bargello.

Nanni di Banco (c.1384–1421). A Florentine sculptor who began his career as an assistant to his father, Maso, Nanni was an exact contemporary of Donatello: Donatello's first *David* was ordered at the same time as an *Isaiah* from Nanni. The finest works produced in his short life are his niche sculptures at Orsanmichele (especially the *Four Saints*) and the relief above the Duomo's Porta della Mandorla.

Nelli, Ottaviano (active 1400–44). The artist who brought the International Gothic style to Umbria; his intricate and glittering paintings can be seen in Foligno, Assisi and Gubbio.

Odersi, or Oderigi (1240–99). The founder of the Umbrian school, little is known of Odersi except that he was a friend of Giotto and worked mainly in Gubbio. Only a handful of his miniatures survive, but Dante called him *l'onor d'Agobbio* ("the pride of Gubbio") and stuck him in Purgatory as punishment for an obsession with art that left him no time for anything else.

Orcagna, Andrea (c.1308–68). Architect-sculptor-painter Orcagna was a dominant figure in the period following the death of Giotto, whose emphasis on spatial depth he rejected – as shown in his only authenticated panel painting, the Strozzi altarpiece in Santa Maria Novella. Damaged frescoes can be seen in Santa Croce and Santo Spirito, but Florence's principal work by Orcagna is the massive tabernacle in Orsanmichele. Orcagna's brothers Nardo and Jacopo di Cione were the most influential painters in Florence at the close of the fourteenth century: the frescoes in the Strozzi chapel are by Nardo.

Perugino (1445/50–1523). Born Pietro di Cristoforo Vannucci in Città della Pieve, Perugino was the greatest Umbrian artist. Possibly a pupil of Piero della Francesca, he later trained in Florence in the workshop of Andrea Verrocchio, studying alongside Leonardo da Vinci. By 1480 his reputation was such that he was invited to paint in the Sistine Chapel; today only one of Perugino's original three panels remains. In 1500 he executed his greatest work in Umbria, a fresco cycle for the Collegio di Cambio. This was probably the first occasion on which he was assisted by his

pupil Raphael – and the moment his own career began to wane: the production-line altarpieces that his workshop later turned out were often lacking in genuine passion. In Tuscany he is best seen in the Uffizi and in the church of Santa Maria Maddalena dei Pazzi.

Piero della Francesca (1410/20–1492). Piero was born in Borgo Sansepolcro, on the border of Tuscany and Umbria. In the late 1430s he was in Florence, working with Domenico Veneziano, and his later work shows the influence of such Florentine contemporaries as Castagno and Uccello, as well as the impact of Masaccio's frescoes. The chronology of his career is contentious, but much of his working life was spent in his native town, for which he produced the *Madonna della Misericordia* and the *Resurrection*, both now in the Museo Civico. Other patrons included Sigismondo Malatesta of Rimini and Federico da Montefeltro of Urbino, of whom there's a portrait by Piero in the Uffizi. In the 1450s he was in Arezzo, working on the fresco cycle in the church of San Francesco, the only frescoes in Tuscany that can bear comparison with the Masaccio cycle in Florence. He seems to have stopped painting in the early 1470s, perhaps to concentrate on his vastly influential treatises on perspective and geometry, but more likely because of failing eyesight.

Piero di Cosimo (c.1462–1521). One of the more enigmatic figures of the High Renaissance, Piero di Cosimo shared Leonardo's scholarly interest in the natural world but turned his knowledge to the production of allusive mythological paintings. There are pictures by him in the Uffizi, Palazzo Pitti, Museo degli Innocenti and Museo Horne.

Pietro da Cortona (1596–1669). Painter-architect, born Pietro Berrettini, who with Bernini was the guiding force of Roman Baroque. The style was introduced to Florence by Pietro's ceiling frescoes in the Palazzo Pitti. His last painting is in his home town of Cortona.

Pinturicchio (1454–1513). Born Bernardino di Betto in Perugia, Pinturicchio was taught by Perugino, with whom he collaborated on the painting of the Sistine Chapel. Most of his work is in Rome but his last commission, one of his most ambitious projects, was his *Life of Pius II* for the Libreria Piccolomini in Siena.

Pisano, Andrea (c.1290–1348). Nothing is known of Andrea Pisano's life until 1330, when he was given the commission to make a new set of doors for the Florence Baptistery. He then succeeded Giotto as master mason of the Campanile; the set of reliefs he produced for it are the only other works definitely by him (now in the Museo dell'Opera del Duomo). In 1347 he became the supervisor of Orvieto's Duomo, a job later held by his sculptor son, Nino.

Pisano, Nicola (c.1220–84). Born somewhere in the southern Italian kingdom of the emperor Frederick II, Nicola Pisano was the first great classicizing sculptor in pre-Renaissance Italy; the pulpit in Pisa's Baptistery (1260), his first masterpiece, shows clearly the influence of Roman figures. Five years later he produced the pulpit for the Duomo in Siena, with the assistance of his son Giovanni (c.1248–1314) and Arnolfo di Cambio. Father and son again worked together on the Fonte Gaia in Perugia, which was Nicola's last major project. Giovanni's more turbulent style is seen in two other pulpits, for San Andrea in Pistoia and for the Pisa Duomo. The Museo dell'Opera del Duomo in Siena has some fine large-scale figures by Giovanni, while its counterpart in Pisa contains a large collection of work by both the Pisani.

Pollaiuolo, Antonio del (c.1432–98) and **Piero del** (c.1441–96). Though their Florence workshop turned out engravings, jewellery and embroideries, the Pollaiuolo brothers were known mainly for their advances in oil-painting technique and for their anatomical researches, which bore fruit in paintings and small-scale bronze sculptures. The influences of Donatello and Castagno (Piero's teacher) are evident in their dramatic, often violent work, which is especially well represented in the Bargello. The Uffizi's collection of paintings suggests that Antonio was the more skilled artist.

Pontormo, Jacopo (1494–1556). Born near Empoli, Jacopo Carrucci – better known as Pontormo after his native village – was successively a pupil of Leonardo da Vinci, Piero di Cosimo and Andrea del Sarto, and became a crucial figure in the evolution of the hyper-refined Mannerist style. It was through del Sarto that he received one of his earliest commissions, for *The Visitation* in the atrium of Santissima Annunziata in Florence, where del Sarto had already completed several frescoes. In the early 1520s he was hired by the Medici to decorate part of their villa at Poggio a Caiano, then executed a *Passion* cycle for the Certosa, to the south of the city, after which he painted what is generally regarded as his masterpiece: the *Deposition* in Santa Felicita. The major project of his later years, a fresco cycle of the *Last Judgement*, painted in the chancel of San Lorenzo, has been destroyed, but other paintings by him can be seen in the Uffizi, at Carmignano and at Sansepolcro.

Quercia, Jacopo della (1374–1438). A Sienese contemporary of Donatello and Ghiberti, della Quercia entered the competition for the Florence Baptistery doors which Ghiberti won in 1401. The first known work by him is the tomb of Ilaria del Carretto in Lucca's Duomo. His next major commission was a fountain for Siena's main square, a piece now reassembled in the *loggia* of the Palazzo Pubblico; before that was finished (1419) he had begun work on a set of reliefs for Siena's Baptistery, a project to which Ghiberti and Donatello also contributed. From 1425 he expended much of his energy on reliefs for San Petronio in Bologna – so much so that the Sienese authorities ordered him to return some of the money he had been paid for the baptistery job.

Raffaello Sanzio (Raphael) (1483–1520). With Leonardo and Michelangelo, Raphael completes the triumvirate whose works define the essence of the High Renaissance. Born in Urbino, he joined Perugino's workshop some time around 1494 and within five years was receiving commissions independently of his master. From 1505 to 1508 he was in Florence, where he absorbed the compositional and tonal innovations of Leonardo; many of the pictures he produced at that time are now in the Palazzo Pitti. From Florence he went to Rome, where Pope Julius II set him to work on the papal apartments (the Stanze). Michelangelo's Sistine ceiling was largely instrumental in modulating Raphael's style from its earlier lyrical grace into something more monumental, but all the works from this more rugged later period are in Rome.

Robbia, Luca della (1400–82). Luca began as a sculptor in conventional materials, his earliest achievement being the marble *cantoria* (choir gallery) now in the Museo dell'Opera del Duomo in Florence. Thirty years later he made the sacristy doors for this city's Duomo, but by then he had devised a technique for applying durable potter's glaze to clay sculpture and most of his energies were given to the art of glazed terracotta. His distinctive blue, white and yellow compositions are seen at their best in the Pazzi chapel in Santa Croce, the Bargello, and at Impruneta, just outside Florence. The best work of his nephew, **Andrea della Robbia** (1435–1525), who continued the lucrative terracotta business, is at the Spedale degli Innocenti in Florence and the monastery of La Verna. **Giovanni della Robbia** (1469–1529), son of Andrea, is best known for the frieze of the Ceppo in Pistoia.

Rossellino, Bernardo (1409–64). An architect-sculptor, Rossellino worked with Alberti and carried out his plans for the Palazzo Rucellai in Florence. His major architectural commission was Pius II's new town of Pienza. As a sculptor he's best known for the monument to Leonardo Bruni in Santa Croce. His brother and pupil **Antonio** (1427–79) produced the tomb of the Cardinal of Portugal in Florence's San Miniato al Monte, and a number of excellent portrait busts (Bargello).

Rosso Fiorentino (1494–1540). Like Pontormo, Rosso Fiorentino was a pupil of Andrea del Sarto, but went on to develop a far more aggressive, acidic style than his colleague and friend. His early *Deposition* in Volterra (1521) and the roughly contemporaneous *Moses Defending the Daughters of Jethro* (Uffizi) are typical of his work. After a period in Rome and Venice, he eventually went to France, where with Primaticcio he developed the distinctive Mannerist art of the Fontainebleau school.

Sangallo, Antonio da, the Elder (1455–1534). A Florence-born architect, Antonio da Sangallo the Elder produced just one major building, but one of the most influential of his period – San Biagio in Montepulciano, based on Bramante's plan for St Peter's in Rome. His brother, **Giuliano da Sangallo** (1445–1516), sculptor, architect and military engineer, produced a number of buildings in and around Florence – the Villa Medici at

Poggio a Caiano, Santa Maria delle Carceri in Prato (the first Renaissance church to have a Greek-cross plan) and the Palazzo Strozzi, the most ambitious palace of the century. Antonio's nephew, **Antonio the Younger** (1485–1546), did most of his work in Rome, where he went on to design the Palazzo Farnese, the most spectacular Roman palace of its time; in Tuscany his most important building is the Fortezza da Basso in Florence.

Sarto, Andrea del (1486–1530). The dominant artist in Florence at the time of Michelangelo and Raphael's ascendancy in Rome, del Sarto made his name with frescoes for two Florentine churches in the San Marco district – the Scalzo and Santissima Annunziata. For a period in the 1510s he was in France, and the received wisdom is that his talent did not develop after that. However, two of his other major works in Florence date from after his return – the *Last Supper* in San Salvi and the *Madonna del Sacco* in the cloister of the Annunziata. His major easel painting is the *Madonna of the Harpies* in the Uffizi.

Signorelli, Luca (1450–1523). Though a pupil of Piero della Francesca, Signorelli is more indebted to the muscular drama of the Pollaiuolo brothers and the gestural vocabulary developed by Donatello. In the early 1480s he was probably working on the Sistine Chapel with Perugino and Botticelli, but his most important commission came in 1499, when he was hired to complete the cycle begun by Fra' Angelico in Orvieto's Duomo. The emphasis on the nude figure in his *Last Judgement* was to greatly affect Michelangelo. Shortly after finishing this cycle he went to Rome but the competition from Raphael and Michelangelo drove him back to his native Cortona. Works are to be seen in Cortona, Arezzo, Monte Oliveto, Perugia, Sansepolcro and in the Uffizi and Museo Horne in Florence.

Sodoma, Il (1477–1549). After training in Milan (where he became familiar with the work of Leonardo da Vinci) and Siena, Giovanni Antonio Bazzi was taken to Rome by the Sienese banker Agostino Chigi in 1508. Having failed to make much of an impact there, he returned to Siena, which was his base for the rest of his life. His major creation in Tuscany is his fresco cycle at the monastery of Monte Oliveto Maggiore, begun immediately before his sojourn in Rome. Vasari states that the nickname by which he's always known came about because he "loved small boys more than was decent", but it's possible that it was a joke of Bazzi's own devising.

Spinello Aretino (active 1370s–1410). Probably born in Arezzo, Spinello studied in Florence, possibly under Agnolo Gaddi. He harks back to the monumental aspects of Giotto's style – thus paradoxically paving the way for the most radical painter of the next generation, Masaccio. His main works are in Florence's church of San Miniato al Monte and Santa Caterina d'Antella, just to the south of the city.

Uccello, Paolo (1396–1475). After training in Ghiberti's workshop, Uccello went to Venice, where he worked on mosaics for the Basilica di San Marco. He returned to Florence in 1431 and five years later was contracted to paint the commemorative portrait of Sir John Hawkwood in the Duomo. This *trompe l'oeil* painting is the first evidence of his interest in the problems of perspective and foreshortening, a subject that was later to obsess him. After an interlude in Padua, he painted the frescoes for the cloister of Santa Maria Novella (c.1445), and in the following decade he painted the three-scene sequence *Battle of San Romano* (Louvre, London National Gallery and Uffizi) for the Medici – his most ambitious non-fresco paintings, and similarly notable for their strange use of foreshortening.

Vasari, Giorgio (1511–74). Born in Arezzo, Vasari trained with Luca Signorelli and Andrea del Sarto. He became the leading artistic impresario of his day, working for the papacy in Rome and for the Medici in Florence, where he supervised (and partly executed) the redecoration of the Palazzo Vecchio. His own house in Arezzo is perhaps the most impressive display of his limited pictorial talents. He also designed the Uffizi gallery and oversaw a number of other architectural projects, but is now chiefly famous for his Tuscan-biased *Lives of the Most Excellent Painters, Sculptors and Architects*.

Veneziano, Domenico (1404–61). Despite the name, Domenico Veneziano was probably born in Florence, where from 1439 to 1445 he worked on a fresco cycle with Piero della Francesca, a work that has now perished. Only a dozen surviving works can be attributed to him with any degree of certainty and only two signed pieces by him are left – one of them is the central panel of the so-called *St Lucy Altar* in the Uffizi.

Verrocchio, Andrea del (c.1435–88). A Florentine painter, sculptor and goldsmith, Verrocchio was possibly a pupil of Donatello and certainly his successor as the city's leading sculptor. He ran one of Florence's busiest workshops, whose employees included the young Leonardo da Vinci. In Florence his work can be seen in the Uffizi, Bargello, San Lorenzo, Santo Spirito, Orsanmichele and Museo dell'Opera del Duomo.

Books

Most of the books recommended below are currently in print, and those that aren't shouldn't be too difficult to track down on websites such as ⦿abebooks.com or ⦿alibris.com. Titles that are currently out of print in both the US and UK are marked o/p. ★ symbol indicates titles that are especially recommended.

TRAVEL BOOKS AND JOURNALS

D.H. Lawrence *Sketches of Etruscan Places*. Published posthumously, these are Lawrence's provocative musings on Etruscan art and civilization – which he considered more or less ideal ("ripe with the phallic knowledge", etc).

Mary McCarthy *The Stones of Florence*. Written in the mid-1960s, *Stones* is a mix of high-class reporting on the contemporary city and anecdotal detail on its history – one of the few accounts that doesn't read as if it's been written in a library.

H.V. Morton *A Traveller in Italy*. Morton's leisurely and amiable books were written in the 1930s, and their nostalgic charm has a lot to do with their enduring popularity; this one is packed with learned details and marvellously evocative descriptions.

Iris Origo *War in the Val d'Orcia*. A stirring account of Origo's activities in the last war, hiding partisans and Allied troops on her estate near Montepulciano.

MEDIEVAL HISTORY AND SOCIETY

Adrian House *Francis of Assisi*. A much-needed modern biography that brings to life a saint who is respected by Christians and non-believers alike. House doesn't dodge difficult issues, such as Francis's relationship with St Clare or the possible causes of his stigmata, and provides an entertaining account of his early – apparently dissolute – life.

Iris Origo *The Merchant of Prato*. Based on the massive documentation of Francesco di Marco Datini's business

empire, this is a wonderfully lively re-creation of domestic life in fourteenth-century Tuscany.

★ **Frances Stonor Saunders** *Hawkwood: Diabolical Englishman*. Fascinating study of the rapacious mercenary captain whose private army terrorized vast tracts of Italy in the late fourteenth century, in the wake of the miseries of the Black Death. More than an excellent biography, this book is a vivid reconstruction of a hellish period of Italian history.

FLORENCE AND THE RENAISSANCE

Jacob Burckhardt *The Civilization of the Renaissance in Italy*. A pioneering nineteenth-century classic of Renaissance scholarship – the book that did more than any other to form our image of the period.

J.R. Hale *Florence and the Medici*. Scholarly yet lively, this covers the full span of the Medici story from the foundation of the family fortune to the calamitous eighteenth century. Vivid in its re-creation of the various personalities involved, it also presents a fascinating picture of the evolution of the mechanics of power in the Florentine state.

Christopher Hibbert *The House of Medici: its Rise and Fall*. A gripping read, chock-full of heroic successes and squalid failures. His *Florence: The Biography of a City* is yet another excellent production, packed with illuminating anecdotes and fascinating illustrations – unlike most books on the city, it's as interesting on the political history as on the artistic achievements, and doesn't grind to a standstill with the fall of the Medici.

Luaro Martines *April Blood: Florence and the Plot Against the Medici*. A thorough and engrossing account of the most notorious conspiracy in Florentine history.

ART AND ARCHITECTURE

★ **Michael Baxandall** *Painting and Experience in Fifteenth-Century Italy*. Invaluable analysis, concentrating on the way in which the art of the period would have been perceived at the time.

Rona Goffen *Renaissance Rivals*. It's a truism that the cultural history of Renaissance Italy is to a large extent a history of competition – between artists, between individual patrons and between the various city states.

However, Rona Goffen's masterly book is revelatory in its analysis of the depth and the complexity of the antagonisms involved in the production of high art in this period. She illuminates a world in which painters, sculptors and architects were ceaselessly endeavouring to supersede their contemporary rivals and the exemplars of the ancient world.

★ **Richard Goy** *Florence: the City and its Architecture*. Goy's superb book uses multiple perspectives to illuminate the architecture of Florence: the first section summarizes the city's development up to the unification of Italy; part two looks at the influence of the two chief "nuclei of power" – the Church and the State; part three analyses the fabric of the city according to building type (*palazzi*, churches, fortifications, etc); and the final section looks at the changes that Florence has undergone in the last century and a half. Encompassing everything from the Baptistery to the football stadium, and magnificently illustrated, this is a clear first choice.

J.R. Hale (ed.) *Concise Encyclopaedia of the Italian Renaissance* (o/p). Exemplary reference book, many of whose summaries are as informative as essays twice their length; covers individual artists, movements, cities, philosophical concepts, the lot.

★ **Frederick Hartt & David Wilkins** *History of Italian Renaissance Art*. If one book on this vast subject can be said to be indispensable, this is it. In view of its comprehensiveness and the range of its illustrations, it's a bargain.

Michael Levey *Early Renaissance* (o/p). Precise and fluently written account from former director of the National Gallery, and well illustrated; probably the best introduction to the subject. Levey's *High Renaissance* (Penguin, o/p) continues the story in the same style.

Peter Murray *The Architecture of the Italian Renaissance*. Begins with Romanesque buildings and finishes with Palladio – useful both as a gazetteer of the main monuments and as a synopsis of the underlying concepts.

Giorgio Vasari *Lives of the Artists*. Penguin's two-volume abridgement is the fullest available translation of Vasari's classic (and highly tendentious) work on his predecessors and contemporaries. Includes essays on Giotto, Brunelleschi, Leonardo and Michelangelo. The first real work of art history, and still among the most revealing books on Italian Renaissance art. Oxford University Press publishes a newer and briefer one-volume selection.

CONTEMPORARY ITALY

David Gilmour *The Pursuit of Italy*. Published in 2011, this history of the Italian peninsula culminates with an incisive analysis of the nation at the start of the twenty-first century, emphasising the centrifugal forces at work in a country in which regional identities are still extremely powerful.

★ **Paul Ginsborg** *Italy and its Discontents*. If you want to understand contemporary Italy's baffling mixture of dynamism and ideological sterility, this is an essential read, lucidly argued and formidably well-informed. There is no better book on the subject.

Tobias Jones *The Dark Heart of Italy*. Written during a three-year period in Parma, and comprising essays

dealing with aspects of modern Italian society, from the legal and political systems to the media and football. An affectionate but clear-eyed corrective to the sentimentalizing claptrap perpetrated by so many English and American expats.

Charles Richards *The New Italians*. An affectionate and very well-informed survey of modern Italy, with plenty of vivid anecdotes that illustrate the tensions within a culture that is at once deeply traditional yet at the same time enthralled by the trappings of modernity. Somewhat outdated, in that it was published before the rise of Berlusconi, but nonetheless pertinent.

LITERATURE

Dante Alighieri *The Divine Comedy*. No work in any other language bears comparison with Dante's poetic exegesis of the moral scheme of God's creation: in late medieval Italy it was venerated both as a book of almost scriptural authority and as the ultimate refinement of the vernacular Tuscan language. There are numerous translations; John D. Sinclair's prose version (published in three volumes by Oxford University Press) has the huge advantage of presenting the original text opposite the English, and has exemplary notes.

Giovanni Boccaccio *The Decameron*. Set in the plague-racked Florence of 1348, Boccaccio's assembly of one hundred short stories is a fascinating social record as well as a constantly diverting and often smutty comedy.

Benvenuto Cellini *Autobiography*. Shamelessly egocentric record of the travails and triumphs of the

sculptor and goldsmith's career; one of the freshest literary productions of its time. There are two good translations – one from Penguin and one from Oxford University (under the title *My Life*).

Niccolo Machiavelli *The Prince*. A treatise on statecraft which actually did less to form the political thought of Italy than it did to form foreigners' perceptions of the country; yet there was far more to Machiavelli than the *Realpolitik* of *The Prince*, as is shown by the selection of writings included in Viking's superb anthology *The Portable Machiavelli*.

Petrarch (Francesco Petrarca) *Selections from the Canzoniere*. Often described as the first modern poet, by virtue of his preoccupation with worldly fame and secular love, Petrarch wrote some of the Italian language's greatest lyrics. This slim selection from Oxford University Press at least hints at what is lost in translation.

Language

The ability to speak English confers prestige in Italy, and there's often no shortage of people willing to show off their knowledge, particularly in the main cities and resorts. However, in more remote areas you may find that no one speaks English at all.

Wherever you are, it's a good idea to master at least a little Italian, a task made easier by the fact that your halting efforts will often be rewarded by smiles and genuine surprise. In any case, it's one of the easiest European languages to learn, especially if you already have a smattering of French or Spanish, which are extremely similar to Italian grammatically.

Pronunciation

Easiest of all is the **pronunciation**, since most words are spoken exactly as they're written, and usually enunciated with exaggerated, open-mouthed clarity. The only difficulties you're likely to encounter are the few consonants that are different from English.

c before e or i is pronounced as in **ch**urch.

ch before e or i is hard, as in **c**at.

sci pronounced as in **sh**eet.

sce pronounced as in **sh**elter.

g is soft before e or i, as in **g**eranium; hard before h, as in **g**arlic.

gn as in o**ni**on.

gl is softened (the g is silent), as in stallion.

h is not aspirated, as in honour.

When **speaking to strangers**, the third person is the polite form (ie *Lei* instead of *Tu* for "you"); using the second person is a mark of disrespect. It's also worth remembering that Italians don't use "please" and "thank you" half as much as we do: it's all implied in the tone, though if you're in any doubt, err on the polite side.

All Italian words are **stressed** on the penultimate syllable unless a stress mark – ′ or ` – denotes otherwise. Note that the ending *-ia* or *-ie* comprises two syllables, hence *trattoria* is stressed on the i. Generally, we've added stress marks whenever it isn't immediately obvious how a word should be pronounced, though these are omitted in Italian. **Accents** look similar to stress marks – generally ` – but they have the function of altering a word's final vowel sound, as in *città* or *caffè*, and can never be dropped. Only "e" can take both an acute and a grave accent: è is an open sound, as in "hell", whereas é is more closed, as in "gourmet".

ITALIAN WORDS AND PHRASES

BASICS

good morning	buongiorno	alright/that's OK	va bene
good afternoon/evening	buonasera	excuse me (apology)	mi scusi
good night	buonanotte	excuse me (in a crowd)	permesso
hello/goodbye (informal)	ciao	sorry	mi dispiace
goodbye (formal)	arrivederci	How are you? (informal)	Come stai?
yes	sì	How are you? (formal)	Come sta?
no	no	I'm fine	bene
please	per favore	Do you speak English?	Parla inglese?
thank you(very much)	(molte/mille) grazie	I don't understand	Non ho capito
you're welcome	prego	I don't know	Non lo so
		I'm here on holiday	Sono qui in vacanza

I live in …	Abito a …
I'm …	Sono …
English/Scottish	inglese/scozzese
Welsh/Irish	gallese/irlandese
American (m/f)	americano/a
Canadian/	canadese/nuova
New Zealand	zelandese
Australian (m/f)	australiano/a
Mr …	Signor …
Mrs …	Signora …
Miss …	Signorina …
good/bad	buono/cattivo
big/small	grande/píccolo
cheap/expensive	económico/caro
early/late	presto/tardi
hot/cold	caldo/freddo
near/far	vicino/lontano
quickly/slowly	velocemente/lentamente
slowly or quietly	piano
with/without	con/senza
more/less	più/meno
enough, no more	basta
wait a minute!	aspetta!
here/there	qui/là
today	oggi
tomorrow	domani
day after tomorrow	dopodomani
yesterday	ieri
now	adesso
later	più tardi
in the morning	di mattina
in the afternoon	nel pomeriggio
in the evening	di sera

QUESTIONS

Where?	Dove?
Where is/are …?	Dov'è ?/Dove sono ?
When?	Quando?
What?	Cosa?
Why?	Perchè?
What is it?	Cos'è?
How much/many?	Quanto/Quanti?
How much does it cost?	Quant'è?
Is it …?/Is there …?	È ?/C'è ?
What time does it open/close?	A che ora apre/chiude?
What's it called in Italian?	Come si chiama in italiano?
What time is it?	Che ore sono?

ACCOMMODATION

I'd like to book a room	Vorrei prenotare una cámera
I have a booking	Ho una prenotazione

Is there a hotel nearby?	C'è un albergo qui vicino?
Do you have rooms free?	Avete cámere libere?
a single/ double room	una cámera singola/ doppia
Do you have a room …	Ha una cámera
for one person	per una persona
for two/three people	per due/tre persone
for one night	per una notte
for two/three nights	per due/tre notti
for one week	per una settimana
for two weeks	per due settimane
with a double bed	con un letto matrimoniale
with twin beds	a due letti
with a shower/bath	con doccia/bagno
with a balcony	con balcone
hot/cold water	acqua calda/fredda
Could I see the room?	Potrei vedere la cámera?
Could I see another room?	Potrei vedere un'altra cámera?
How much is it?	Quanto costa?
Is breakfast included?	È compresa la prima colazione?
half/full board	mezza pensione/pensione completa
Do you have anything cheaper?	Ha niente che costa di meno?
I'll take it	La prendo
Can we camp here?	Possiamo fare il campeggio qui?
Is there a campsite nearby?	C'è un campeggio qui vicino?
tent	tenda
cabin	cabina
youth hostel	ostello per la gioventù
porter	facchino
lift	ascensore
key	chiave

TRAVEL AND DIRECTIONS

bus	autobus/pullman
bus station	autostazione
train	treno
train station	stazione ferroviaria
ferry	traghetto
hydrofoil	aliscafo
ship	nave
ferry terminal	stazione maríttima
port	porto
A ticket to…	Un biglietto a…
one-way	solo andata
return	andata e ritorno
Can I book a seat?	Posso prenotare un posto?

What time does it leave?	A che ora parte?	**stop**	alt
When is the next train to…?	Quando parte il prossimo treno per…?	**out of order**	guasto
		no smoking	vietato fumare
Do I have to change?	Devo cambiare?	**ring the bell**	suonare il campanello
Where does it leave from?	Da dove parte?	**drinking water**	acqua potabile
What platform does it leave from?	Da quale binario parte?	**gents/ladies toilet**	signori/signore
		WC	bagno
How many kilometres is it?	Quanti chilometri sono?	**vacant/engaged**	líbero/occupato
		arrivals/departures	arrivi/partenze
How long does it take?	Quanto ci vuole?	**customs**	dogana
What number bus is it to …?	Che número di autobus per ?	**platform**	binario
		cash desk	cassa
How do I get to …?	Per andare a …?	**to let**	affítasi
How far is it to …?	Quant'è lontano a ?	**first aid**	pronto soccorso
Can you give me a lift to …?	Mi può dare un passaggio a ?		

NUMBERS

left/right	sinistra/destra
go straight ahead	sempre diritto
turn left/right	gira a sinistra/destra
Can you tell me when to get off?	Mi può dire quando devo scendere?
Next stop please	La prossima fermata, per favore
bicycle	bicicletta
hitchhiking	autostop
on foot	a piedi

1	uno
2	due
3	tre
4	quattro
5	cinque
6	sei
7	sette
8	otto
9	nove
10	dieci
11	undici
12	dodici

DRIVING

car	macchina
Where's the road to …?	Dov'è la strada a ?
parking	parcheggio
no parking	divieto di sosta/sosta vietata
one-way street	senso único
no entry	senso vietato
slow down	rallentare
road closed	strada chiusa/guasta
no through road	vietato il transito
no overtaking	vietato il sorpasso
crossroads	incrocio
speed limit	limite di velocità

13	tredici
14	quattordici
15	quindici
16	sedici
17	diciassette
18	diciotto
19	diciannove
20	venti
21	ventuno
22	ventidue
30	trenta
40	quaranta
50	cinquanta
60	sessanta
70	settanta
80	ottanta
90	novanta

SIGNS

entrance/exit	entrata/uscita
free admission	ingresso líbero
open/closed	aperto/chiuso
closed for restoration	chiuso per restauro
closed for holidays	chiuso per férie
pull/push	tirare/spingere
do not touch	non toccare
danger	perícolo
beware	attenzione
go or walk	avanti

100	cento
101	centuno
110	centodieci
200	duecento
500	cinquecento
1000	mille
5000	cinquemila

RESTAURANTS

I'd like to reserve a table	Vorrei riservare una távola
Have you a table for two?	Avete una távola per due?
I'd like to order	Vorrei ordinare
I'm a vegetarian (m/f)	Sono vegetariano/a
Is there meat in it?	C'è carne dentro?
I'd like …	Vorrei …
It's good/delicious	È buono/buonissimo
The bill, please	Il conto, per favore
Is service included?	Il servizio è incluso?

ITALIAN MENU READER

MEALS AND COURSES

colazione	breakfast
pranzo	lunch
cena	dinner
antipasti	starters
primi	first courses
zuppe/minestre	soups
secondi	main courses
contorni	vegetables
dolci	desserts
menù degustazione	tasting menu

GENERAL TERMS

cameriere	waiter
menù/lista	menu
lista dei vini	wine list
coltello	knife
forchetta	fork
cucchiaio	spoon
senza carne	without meat
coperto	cover charge
servizio	service charge
aceto	vinegar
aglio	garlic
biscotti	biscuits
burro	butter
caramelle	sweets
cioccolato	chocolate
frittata	omelette
grissini	breadsticks
maionese	mayonnaise
marmellata	jam (jelly)
olio	oil
olive	olives
pane	bread
pane integrale	wholemeal bread
panna	cream
patatine	crisps (potato chips)
patatine fritte	chips (french fries)
pepe	pepper
pizzetta	small cheese and tomato pizza
riso	rice
sale	salt
uova	eggs
zucchero	sugar

COOKING TERMS

affumicato	smoked
arrosto	roast
ben cotto	well done
bollito/lesso	boiled
brasato	braised
cotto	cooked
crudo	raw
al dente	firm (not overcooked)
aí ferri	grilled without oil
fritto	fried
grattuggiato	grated
alla griglia	grilled
al Marsala	cooked with Marsala wine
Milanese	fried in egg and breadcrumbs
pizzaiola	cooked with tomato sauce
al puntino	medium (steak)
ripieno	stuffed
al sangue	rare (steak)
allo spiedo	on the spit
surgelato	frozen
in úmido	steamed/stewed

PIZZAS

calzone	folded pizza
capricciosa	literally "capricious"; topped with whatever they've got in the kitchen, usually including baby artichoke, ham and egg
cardinale	ham and olives
frutta di mare	seafood; usually mussels, prawns and clams
funghi	mushrooms; the tinned sliced variety, unless it specifies fresh (funghi freschi)
margherita	cheese and tomato
marinara	tomato, anchovy and olive oil
napo/napoletana	tomato
quattro formaggi	"four cheeses", usually including mozzarella, fontina and gruyère

LANGUAGE **CONTEXTS** | 569

quattro stagioni	"four seasons"; the toppings split into four separate sections, usually including ham, green pepper, onion and egg.

ANTIPASTI

antipasto misto	mixed cold meats and cheeses
caponata	mixed aubergine, olives, tomatoes
caprese	tomato and mozzarella salad
crostini	mixed chicken liver canapes
insalata di mare	seafood salad
insalata di riso	rice salad
insalata russa	Russian salad (diced vegetables in mayonnaise)
melanzane alla parmigiana	aubergine (eggplant) baked with tomato and Parmesan cheese
peperonata	green and red peppers stewed in olive oil
pomodori ripieni	stuffed tomatoes
prosciutto	ham

TUSCAN ANTIPASTI

crostini di milza	minced spleen on pieces of toast
donzelle/donzelline	fried dough balls
fettuna/bruschetta	garlic toast with olive oil
finocchiona	pork sausage flavoured with fennel
pinzimonio	raw seasonal vegetable in olive oil, with salt and pepper
prosciutto di cinghiale	cured wild boar ham
salame toscano	pork sausage with pepper and cubes of fat
salsicce	pork or wild boar sausages

UMBRIAN ANTIPASTI

prosciutto di Norcia	cured ham from Norcia
salame mezzafegato	sausage spiced with a mixture of pine nuts, pork liver, candied orange, sugar and raisins
schiacciata	flat bread baked with olive oil, or flavoured with onions or cooked greens

torta al testo	unleavened bread baked on a stone slab

PRIMI

SOUPS

brodo	clear broth
minestrina	any light soup
minestrone	thick vegetable soup
pasta fagioli	pasta soup with beans
pastini in brodo	pasta pieces in clear broth
stracciatella	broth with egg

PASTA

cannelloni	large tubes of pasta, stuffed
farfalle	literally "butterfly"-shaped pasta
fettucine	narrow pasta ribbons
gnocchi	small potato and dough dumplings
maccheroni	tubular spaghetti
pasta al forno	pasta baked with minced meat, eggs, tomato and cheese
penne	smaller pieces of rigatoni
rigatoni	large, grooved tubular pasta
risotto	cooked rice dish, with sauce
spaghettini	thin spaghetti
tagliatelle	pasta ribbons (another word for fettucine)
tortellini	small rings of pasta stuffed with meat or cheese
vermicelli	"little worms" (very thin spaghetti)

PASTA SAUCE (SALSA)

amatriciana	tomato and cubed pork
arrabbiata	spicy tomato sauce with chillies
bolognese	tomato and meat
burro	butter
carbonara	cream, ham and beaten egg
funghi	mushrooms
panna	cream
parmigiano	Parmesan cheese
peperoncino	olive oil, garlic and fresh chillies
pesto	basil and garlic sauce
pomodoro	tomato sauce

ragù	meat sauce
vóngole	clam and tomato sauce

TUSCAN PRIMI

acquacotta	onion soup served with toast and poached egg
cacciucco	fish stew with tomatoes, bread and red wine
carabaccia	onion soup
garmugia	soup made with fava beans, peas, artichokes, asparagus and bacon
gnocchi di ricotta	dumplings filled with ricotta and spinach
minestra di farro	wheat and bean soup
minestrone alla fiorentina	haricot bean soup with red cabbage, tomatoes, onions and herbs
panzanella	summer salad of tomatoes basil, cucumber, onion and bread
pappa al pomodoro	tomato soup thickened with bread
pappardelle	wide, short noodles, often served with hare sauce (*con lepre*)
pasta alla carrettiera	pasta with tomato, garlic, pepper, parsley and chilli
penne strasciate	pasta in meat sauce
ribollita	winter vegetable soup, based on beans and thickened with bread
risotto nero	rice cooked with cuttlefish (in its own ink)
zuppa di fagioli	bean soup

UMBRIAN PRIMI

manfrigoli	rustic pasta made from emmer, a coarse type of wheat introduced into the region by the Romans
minestra di farro	tomato, wheat and vegetable soup
pici/stringozzi/ ceriole	thread-like spaghetti, usually served with garlicky tomato sauce
spaghetti alla norcina	spaghetti with an oily sauce of black truffles, garlic and anchovies
umbrici	large, heavy noodles

SECONDI

MEAT (CARNE)

agnello	lamb
bistecca	steak
cervello	brain
cinghiale	wild boar
coniglio	rabbit
costolette	chops
cotolette	cutlets
fagiano	pheasant
faraona	guinea fowl
fegatini	chicken livers
fégato	liver
involtini	meat slices, rolled and stuffed
lepre	hare
lingua	tongue
maiale	pork
manzo	beef
ossobuco	shin of veal
pernice	partridge
pancetta	bacon
pollo	chicken
polpette	meatballs
rognoni	kidneys
salsiccia	sausage
saltimbocca	veal with ham
spezzatino	stew
tacchino	turkey
trippa	tripe
vitello	veal

FISH (PESCE) AND SHELLFISH (CROSTACEI)

acciughe	anchovies
anguilla	eel
aragosta	lobster
baccalà	dried salted cod
calamari	squid
céfalo	mullet
cozze	mussels
dentice	dentex
gamberetti	shrimps
gámberi	prawns
granchio	crab
merluzzo	cod
óstriche	oysters
pesce spada	swordfish
polpo	octopus
sardine	sardines
sgombro	mackerel
sogliola	sole
tonno	tuna

triglie	red mullet
trota	trout
vóngole	clams

TUSCAN SECONDI

árista	roast pork loin with garlic and rosemary
asparagi alla fiorentina	asparagus with butter, fried egg and cheese
baccalà alla livornese	salt cod with garlic, tomatoes and parsley
bistecca alla fiorentina	thick grilled T-bone steak
cibreo	chicken liver and egg stew
cieche alla pisana	small eels cooked with sage and tomatoes, served with Parmesan
lombatina	veal chop
peposo	peppered beef stew
pollo alla diavola/ al mattone	chicken flattened with a brick, grilled with herbs
scottiglia	stew of veal, game and poultry, cooked with white wine and tomatoes
spiedini di maiale	skewered spiced cubes of pork loin and liver, with bread and bay leaves
tonno con fagioli	tuna with white beans and raw onion
trigile alla livornese	red mullet cooked with tomatoes, garlic and parsley
trippa alla fiorentina	tripe in tomato sauce, served with Parmesan

UMBRIAN SECONDI

anguilla alla brace	grilled eel
anguilla in úmido	eel cooked with tomatoes, onions, garlic and white wine
frittata di tartufi	black truffle omelette
gobbi alla perugina	deep-fried cardoons (like artichokes) with meat sauce
lepre alle olive	hare cooked with herbs, white wine and olives
palombe/palombacci	woodpigeon, usually spit-roasted
pollo in porchetta	chicken cooked in the same way as suckling pig
porchetta	suckling pig cooked in a wood oven with fennel, garlic, mint and rosemary

regina in porchetta	Lago Trasimeno carp, cooked in a wood oven with fennel, garlic, mint and rosemary
salsiccia all'uva	pork sausage cooked with grapes
tegamaccio	freshwater-fish stew with white wine and herbs

VEGETABLES (CONTORNI) AND SALAD (INSALATA)

asparagi	asparagus
basílico	basil
capperi	capers
carciofi	artichokes
carciofini	artichoke hearts
carote	carrots
cavolfiore	cauliflower
cávolo	cabbage
cetriolo	cucumber
cipolla	onion
fagiolini	green beans
finocchio	fennel
funghi	mushrooms
insalata mista	mixed salad
insalata verde	green salad
melanzane	aubergine (eggplant)
orígano	oregano
patate	potatoes
peperoni	peppers
piselli	peas
pomodori	tomatoes
radicchio	chicory
spinaci	spinach
zucchini	courgettes

TUSCAN CONTORNI

fagioli all'olio	white beans served with olive oil
fagioli all'uccelletto	white beans cooked with tomatoes, garlic and sage
frittata di carciofi	fried artichoke flan

SWEETS (DOLCI), FRUIT (FRUTTA), CHEESE (FORMAGGI) AND NUTS (NOCE)

amaretti	macaroons
ananas	pineapple
anguria/coccómero	watermelon
arance	oranges
banane	bananas
cacchi	persimmons
ciliégie	cherries
fichi	figs

fichi d'India	prickly pears
fontina	northern Italian cooking cheese
frágole	strawberries
gelato	ice cream
gorgonzola	a soft blue cheese
limone	lemon
macedónia	fruit salad
mándorle	almonds
mele	apples
melone	melon
mozzarella	soft white cheese
nespole	medlars
parmigiano	Parmesan cheese
pecorino	strong hard sheep's cheese
pere	pears
pesche	peaches
pinoli	pine nuts
provolone	strong hard cheese
ricotta	soft white sheep's cheese
torta	cake, tart
uva	grapes
zabaglione	dessert made with eggs, sugar and Marsala wine
zuppa inglese	trifle

Tuscan dolci

brigidini	anise wafer biscuits
buccellato	anise raisin cake
cantucci/cantuccini	small almond biscuits, served with Vinsanto wine
castagnaccio	unleavened chestnut-flour cake containing raisins, walnuts and rosemary
cenci	fried dough dusted with powdered sugar
frittelle di riso	rice fritters
meringa	frozen meringue with whipped cream and chocolate
necci	chestnut-flour crêpes
panforte	hard fruit, nut and spice cake
ricciarelli	marzipan almond biscuits
schiacciata alla fiorentina	orange-flavoured cake covered with powdered sugar, eaten at carnival time

schiacciata con l'uva	grape- and sugar-covered bread dessert
zuccotto	sponge cake filled with chocolate and whipped cream

UMBRIAN DOLCI

cialde	paper-thin sweet biscuits
fave di morte	almond biscuits
pinoccate	pine nut biscuits
serpentone/torcolato	almond and dried fruit dessert in the shape of a coiled snake (*torcolo*)

DRINKING ESSENTIALS

aperitivo	pre-dinner drink
digestivo	after-dinner drink
vino rosso	red wine
vino bianco	white wine
vino rosato	rosé wine
spumante	sparkling wine
secco	dry
dolce	sweet
birra	beer
litro	litre
mezzo	half-litre
quarto	quarter-litre
Salute!	Cheers! (toast)
acqua minerale	mineral water
naturale/liscia	still
frizzante/con gas	sparkling
bicchiere	glass
bottiglia	bottle
tazza	cup
caffè	coffee
tè	tea
cioccolato caldo	hot chocolate
latte	milk
frappé	milkshake made with ice cream
frullato	milkshake
ghiáccio	ice
granita	iced drink with coffee or fruit
limonata	lemonade
aranciata	orangeade
spremuta	fresh fruit juice
succo di frutta	concentrated fruit juice with sugar
soda	soda water
tónico	tonic water

Small print and index

Rough Guide credits

Editor: Polly Thomas
Layout: Ajay Verma
Cartography: Animesh Pathak
Picture editor: Emily Taylor
Proofreader: Anita Sachs
Managing editor: Keith Drew
Assistant editor: Prema Dutta
Production: Rebecca Short
Cover design: Nicole Newman, Ajay Verma, Emily Taylor
Photographers: Chris Hutty, Roger d'Olivere Mapp, Michelle Grant, James McConnachie, Dylan Reisenberger

Editorial assistant: Eleanor Aldridge
Senior pre-press designer: Dan May
Design director: Scott Stickland
Travel publisher: Joanna Kirby
Digital travel publisher: Peter Buckley
Reference director: Andrew Lockett
Operations coordinator: Becky Doyle
Publishing director (Travel): Clare Currie
Commercial manager: Gino Magnotta
Managing director: John Duhigg

Publishing information

This 8th edition published May 2012 by
Rough Guides Ltd,
80 Strand, London WC2R 0RL
11, Community Centre, Panchsheel Park,
New Delhi 110017, India
Distributed by the Penguin Group
Penguin Books Ltd,
80 Strand, London WC2R 0RL
Penguin Group (USA)
375 Hudson Street, NY 10014, USA
Penguin Group (Australia)
250 Camberwell Road, Camberwell,
Victoria 3124, Australia
Penguin Group (NZ)
67 Apollo Drive, Mairangi Bay, Auckland 1310,
New Zealand
Penguin Group (South Africa)
Block D, Rosebank Office Park, 181 Jan Smuts Avenue,
Parktown North, Gauteng, South Africa 2193
Rough Guides is represented in Canada by Tourmaline
Editions Inc. 662 King Street West, Suite 304, Toronto,
Ontario M5V 1M7
Printed in Singapore by Toppan Security Printing Pte. Ltd.

MIX
Paper from
responsible sources
FSC
www.fsc.org
FSC™ C018179

Help us update

We've gone to a lot of effort to ensure that the eighth edition of **The Rough Guide to Tuscany & Umbria** is accurate and up-to-date. However, things change – places get "discovered", opening hours are notoriously fickle, restaurants and rooms raise prices or lower standards. If you feel we've got it wrong or left something out, we'd like to know, and if you can remember the address, the price, the hours, the phone number, so much the better.

Please send your comments with the subject line "Rough Guide Tuscany & Umbria Update" to ✉ mail@uk.roughguides.com. We'll credit all contributions and send a copy of the next edition (or any other Rough Guide if you prefer) for the very best emails.

Find more travel information, connect with fellow travellers and book your trip on ⓦ roughguides.com

Acknowledgements

Jonathan Buckley and **Tim Jepson**: thanks to Polly Thomas for an excellent and very steady editing process.
Jeffrey Kennedy: thanks to the following for help with my research: Principe Gianluca Borghese; Susanna Carpenter; Russell & Virginia Case; Principessa Francesca Chigi; Principessa Isabel Chigi; Helen Craddick; Mirella D'Angelo; Massimiliano Delgado; Andrew Dowling; Prinz Cyril Ester-

hàzy; Silvia Ferrer; Principe Giovanni Fieschi Ravaschieri del Drago; Bella Freud; Diane Tantum Green; Linda Goubeaux Grunow; Suzanne Hartley; Terri Howell; Conte Ulisse Igliori; Professor Carolyn Johnston; Conte Adriano Matarazzo; Dr Patricia Pèrez-Arce; Elena Piccioni; Giuseppe & Barbara Potente; Dennis Sweet; Jim & Roseanne Ullman; Professor Lila Yawn; Nancy Yeilding.

Readers' letters

Thanks to all the readers who have taken the time to write in with comments and suggestions (and apologies if we've inadvertently omitted or misspelt anyone's name):

Linda Baker, Ms I.A. Batchelor, Mrs L Beardsley, Janet Brennan & Michael Rowe, Stan Fletcher, Jenny Howard

ABOUT THE AUTHORS

Mark Ellingham wrote the first Rough Guide – to Greece – and was Rough Guides' publisher for 25 years. He continues to work as a co-editor on the encyclopedic Rough Guide to World Music, is a contributing editor at Songlines World Music magazine and runs a green and ethical publishing list for Profile Books.

Tim Jepson has worked in Rome as a journalist and is co-author of Rough Guides on Canada, Florence & Siena, the Pacific Northwest and Vancouver. He is also author of some twenty books on Italy and works on the travel desk of a UK broadsheet.

Jonathan Buckley has written and contributed to several Rough Guides and has published seven novels. He is a fellow of the Royal Literary Fund.

Photo credits

All photos © Rough Guides except the following:
(Key: t-top; c-centre; b-bottom; l-left; r-right)

p.2 Corbis, Richard Cummins
p.5 Fotolia, Pitrs (b)
p.12 Corbis, Ocean (b)
p.14 Corbis, National Geographic (b); Superstock (t)
p.15 Corbis, Sandro Vannini (tr); Superstock, Paolo Barbanera (c)
p.16 Getty Images, The Bridgeman Art Gallery (tr); Superstock, Giulio Andreini (c)
p.17 Alamy, NDP (br); TipsImages, Andrea Pistolesi (bl)
p.40–41 Axiom Photographic Agency, Tips Images
p.43 4Corners, Colin Dutton/SIME (t)
p.65 AWL Images, Christian Kober
p.113 Superstock (t)
p.138–139 4Corners, Stefano Amantini
p.141 Superstock
p.147 Superstock, Claudio Ciabochi
p.178–179 Alamy, LOOK Die Bildagentur der Fotografen
p.181 Getty Images, Tancredi J. Bavosi
p.189 Getty Images, Roger d'Olivere Mapp
p.208–209 4Corners, Maurizio Rellini/SIME
p.211 Getty Images, Vincenzo Lombardo
p.235 TipsImages, Francesco Tomasinelli
p.236–237 TipsImages, Wojtek Buss
p.247 Getty Images, Otto Stadler (b); TipsImages, Santini Marco (t)
p.256–257 Getty Images, Jean-Pierre Lescourret

p.259 4Corners, Maurizio Rellini/SIME
p.264 Getty Images, Franco Origlia
p.265 Getty Images, Franco Origlia (tr)
p.294–295 Getty Images, Simeone Huber
p.366–367 Axiom Photographic Agency, Tips Images
p.369 Corbis, Chris Hendrickson
p.385 4Corners, Stefano Amantini (b); Tips Images, Andrea Pistolesi (t)
p.394–395 Tips Images, Angelo Cavalli/Tips Images
p.397 Tips Images, Danielela Monaca
p.429 Getty Images, Gallo Images
p.432–433 Travel Pictures Ltd
p.435 Corbis, Atlantide Phototravel
p.447 Fotolia, Davide_69
p.465 Getty Images, Slow Images
p.470–471 Alamy, Brian Jannsen
p.473 4Corners, Sandra Raccanello/SIME
p.487 Fotolia, Maurosessanta
p.493 Getty Images, Danin Tulic
p.502–503 AWL Images, Amar Grover
p.505 TipsImages
p.511 TipsImages, Hermes Images

Front cover Val D'Orcia © Masterfile, Frank Krahmer
Back cover Collegiata, San Gimignano © Rough Guides; Piazza Grande, Montepulciano © Rough Guides

Index

Maps are marked in grey

Map symbols

The symbols below are used on maps throughout the book

✈ Airport	⌂ Mountains	⊞ Hospital	⬭ Stadium
★ Bus/taxi	▲ Mountain peak	✡ Synagogue	⊞ Christian cemetery
✉ Post office	⌣ Bridge	⚑ Church (regional maps)	▢ Park
ⓘ Information office	◠ Cave	⌖ Church (town maps)	▢ Beach
@ Internet access	✗ Battlefield	▓ Building	⋯ Funicular
◆ Point of interest	♙ Castle	▢ Market	•--• Cable car
P Car park	⊠ Gate		

Listings key

- ▪ Accommodation
- ● Restaurant/café
- ▪ Bar/club
- ● Shop

ROUGH GUIDES

SO NOW WE'VE TOLD YOU HOW TO MAKE THE MOST OF YOUR TIME, WE WANT YOU TO STAY SAFE AND COVERED WITH OUR FAVOURITE TRAVEL INSURER

WorldNomads.com
keep travelling safely

GET AN ONLINE QUOTE
roughguides.com/insurance

RECOMMENDED BY
ROUGH GUIDES

MAKE THE MOST OF YOUR TIME ON EARTH™

ROUGH GUIDES

WE GET AROUND

ONLINE start your journey at roughguides.com

EBOOKS & MOBILE APPS

GUIDEBOOKS from Amsterdam to Zanzibar

PHRASEBOOKS learn the lingo

MAPS so you don't get lost

GIFTBOOKS inspiration is our middle name

LIFESTYLE from iPads to climate change

...SO YOU CAN TOO

BOOKS | EBOOKS | APPS

Start your journey at **roughguides.com**
MAKE THE MOST OF YOUR TIME ON EARTH[TM]